European Historical Statistics 1750–1975

SECOND REVISED EDITION

B. R. Mitchell

Facts on File
119 West 57th Street, New York, N.Y. 10019

First published in the United Kingdom 1975, abridged edition 1978, Second Revised Edition 1980
THE MACMILLAN PRESS LTD
London and Basingstoke

Second revised edition published in the United States in 1981
FACTS ON FILE, INC.
New York

Library of Congress Catalog Card Number 80-67014
ISBN 0-87196-329-9

Typeset by
LITHOSET
Chichester

Printed in Great Britain by
BUTLER & TANNER LTD
Frome & London

CONTENTS

PREFACE TO THE SECOND EDITION

In preparing this second edition no change has been made to the basic format of the original edition. The main difference is the addition of statistics up to the year 1975, and there is one new table in Section A. The opportunity has been taken to correct a number of errors which appeared earlier, most of these relating to single figures. Revisions of the more recent statistics made by the authorities of various countries have also been incorporated, most conspicuously in Section K, where many of the national accounts aggregates since 1950 have been altered, and some additional earlier estimates have been added.

INTRODUCTION

Statistics are used nowadays not just as illustrations or to give a rough sense of proportions or magnitudes involved, but as a major raw material of much economic history, especially of that concerned with economic growth. Since the subject is by its very nature concerned with quantities, this is an inevitable and welcome development. In response to it there has appeared over the past two decades or so a number of collections of the historical statistics of individual countries – the U.S.A.[1], Canada[2], Italy, Netherlands, Norway, Sweden, the U.S.S.R. and the United Kingdom[3] – and the French have long designated occasional volumes of their *Annuaire Statistique* as Volumes Retrospectifs. However, these collections are for single countries, and many such countries remain for which no convenient source of their historical statistics exist. And increasingly in recent years, notably under the influence of Professor Simon Kuznets, there has been a strong focus of economic historical interest on the comparative development of different countries. The time would therefore seem to be ripe for the gathering together into one place of the major statistical series for a number of different countries, and the most obvious group of countries for which much material is available for periods before the First (or even the Second) World War is that of the European continent. The objective of this volume has been to do just this, so as to provide economists and historians with a wide range of statistical data without the difficulty of identifying sources, and the often considerable labour of extracting data from many different places and of transforming sometimes variously defined annual figures into long comparable time-series.

There is a variety of statistical data going back into the Middle Ages for some countries, but it is usually of a rather haphazard and incomplete nature the output of precious metals, or the trade of a particular port or in a particular commodity, for example. In view of this, and in view also of the fact that modern economic growth is generally held to have begun with the British industrial revolution, and that that is dated at the earliest from the middle of the eighteenth century, it was decided to fix the starting date for this volume at 1750. This is not to imply that there are no useful statistics for earlier periods; and it will be obvious to even the casual user of this work that there was no sudden beginning to the collection of large numbers of statistical series in the second half of the eighteenth century. However, there is this to be said for 1750 – with the single exception of price data for Spain and north-western Europe, few series of much overall economic significance began before that date.

That there are pitfalls for the unwary user of statistics need no saying these days, and this is scarcely the place to attempt to summarise those traps of which any introductory textbook will warn. However, there are certain problems which are of particular prominence in historical statistics, to which attention may be properly drawn. That the biggest single problem is lack of availability of the data we should like to have, at any rate until the last three or four decades, is glaringly obvious. But there is a comparable but less apparent problem in the existence of data which *seem* to relate to the same things in different countries or at different times, but which do not in fact do so. Some sort of data are available in these cases, but not the precise sort which we want. Basically these problems are ones of definition. In some times and places exports include bullion, in others they do not, pig iron can include, or exclude, ferro-alloys, bank deposits may include those of other banks, or they may not, corn output can be measured by volume, or by weight; and so on. Often there is nothing one can do about this lack of uniformity except indicate its existence and warn against glib comparisons. (One can find little comfort, however, in the fact that failure to observe such warning is one of the main reasons why statistics have sometimes been held to be worse than "damned lies"!) Kindred definitional difficulties are provided by the numerous changes which have taken place in the boundaries of European countries during the 220 years covered here. These are plentifully referred to in the footnotes to the tables, but to help the user a complete list of boundary changes for each country is given below (p. ix).

[1] *Historical Statistics of the United States* (U.S. Bureau of the Census, Washington, 1947 and 1960).

[2] M.C. Urquhart and K.A. Buckley, *Historical Statistics of Canada* (Cambridge, 1965).

[3] Except for the United Kingdom, these volumes have been official publications of the countries concerned, and are cited below (p.xv). The U.K. works are B.R. Mitchell and Phyllis Deane, *Abstract of British Historical Statistics* (Cambridge, 1962), and B.R. Mitchell and H.G. Jones, *Second Abstract of British Historical Statistics* (Cambridge, 1971).

Two other problems are peculiar to historical statistics. The first is, in a sense, a mechanical one. That is the variable and unknown efficiency of past collectors and compilers of statistics, and of their printers, and the impossibility of ever being able to check on these qualities. This is something one simply has to live with, keeping a vigilant eye on one's credulity, and endeavouring to estimate margins of error so far as possible. Too often, users of historical statistics – and we are nearly all guilty of this – simply take best-estimate figures for their calculations, without working out the effects on their analysis of compounding margins of error.

The second peculiar problem concerns the purposes for which statistics were usually collected up to around the end of the nineteenth century, and, indeed, for which they often are still. Professor William Robson has rightly said that "the most important methodological development of the present century" is "the introduction of measurement in varying degrees in virtually every one of the social sciences"[1], and it is only with this development that there has come much collection and publication of statistical material for its own sake, as it were. Actually, it began to develop a little before the end of the nineteenth century in some countries; but still, it is generally true to say that most statistics prior to 1900 were by-products of taxation or military preparedness; though some of these – and notably population censuses – had outgrown their origins some time before then. Many early series, therefore, have to be viewed with a measure of scepticism, because there was clearly a premium on evading inclusion in the data; registration of one's true age if one was a young man liable to military service, and the smuggling of dutiable imports, are only two of the most obvious examples. But understatement is not the only error to which early statistics were liable. Some countries found it convenient to inflate their population or wealth in order to impress potential enemies. To all these difficulties there is no ready solution. All one can do is be careful and keep a firm rein on credulity, without going to the other extreme of a stultifying total scepticism.

Anyone who looks carefully at the volumes of British historical statistics, which I was involved in compiling some years ago (cited above), and then at this present work, will be aware of a difference between them, related principally to the sources used. The two volumes on Britian provided more detail than is given here, and in order to do so more specialised sources were used. These were readily available to me, working in Britain, in a way in which similar sources for most other countries rather seldom have been. In this case, therefore, the main reliance has been on the official collections of statistics which most governments were publishing well before the end of the nineteenth century. For the depth of coverage which could be included in the space available here, this sort of source-material is generally quite satisfactory. But two problems do arise when one is confined to it alone. The first is the omission from statistical annuals of some statistics for some years, either through accidents of publication or because a series had ceased to be, or had not yet become, of clear general interest and significance. The second is the universal habit of government statistical services of changing the detail of coverage and of concepts from one yearbook to the next. Such changes, of course, often occur in the collection of the statistics, and there is nothing that could be done about it other than indicating the break in continuity. But frequently the changes are no more than ones of presentation in the yearbook, and access to the more detailed sources can enable one to reconstruct the original format. With a few exceptions it has not been possible for me to do this in the tables which follow, and as a result they undoubtedly contain more breaks in continuity than are strictly necessary. However, both this latter problem, and the one caused by non-publication in statistical annuals, have been mitigated to some extent by the co-operation which I have had from colleagues in various European universities and from officials of several national statistical offices. These are acknowledged below. When all is said, though, it must be admitted that this is not to any great extent a work of original research, in the sense that comparable statistical time-series have been compiled where only the raw materials for such a compilation existed in the sources. It is, rather, almost entirely a collection of already-published statistics, with many of their inconsistences not eliminated. I shall, of course, be grateful for any help which users of this work can give me in improving the series for a future edition.

These few generalities are not intended as a critique of the usefulness of statistics in historical studies, but simply as a warning against their careless and casual use in comparisons over time and between different countries. It has been rightly said that "numbers are useful when they attain a level of subtlety and precision beyond that of words"[2]. Let the user of this volume be in no doubt of the need to seek for subtelty and of the difficulties in the way of precision.

Some of the problems peculiar to each topic are mentioned briefly in the introductions to each of the separate sections, but it must be pointed out that these are not intended to be comprehensive critiques of the statistics presented. To do this properly would require at least another volume, and it is the intention here only to draw the user's attention to the main types of difficulty in using the statistics. The problems for each individual country are not generally dealt with, unless they are outstandingly important. However, most of them are readily apparent from a careful use of the notes and footnotes to the tables.

[1] W.A. Robson (ed.), *Man and the Social Sciences* (London, 1972).

[2] W. Paul Strassman, *Risk and Technological Innovation* (Ithaca, N.Y., 1959). p.5.

Boundary Changes

One of the main difficulties in using the historical statistics of Europe is caused by the numerous changes which have taken place in national boundaries. These are frequently referred to in the footnotes to the tables, but to help the user a consolidated list of the changes follows here:

Albania: Part of the Turkish Empire until established as a separate state in 1913. It was occupied by Italy (and later by the Germans) from 1939 to 1944.

Austria. Up to 1918 this name was given to the Cisleithanian part of the Habsburg monarchy, consisting of the provinces listed in table B3. The Italian provinces of the monarchy were sometimes included until their cession in 1859 (Lombardy) and 1866 (Venetia). In the period to 1815, and especially during the Napoleonic Wars, there were various changes in Austrian territory, which are not worth listing here, since the only statistics given for that period relate to central government finances. From 1815 to 1918 there were few changes, apart from the loss of Lombardy and Venetia. Krakow was incorporated in 1846, and Bosnia-Hercegovina was occupied in 1878 and formally annexed in 1908. Its statistics were not included with those of either Austria or Hungary, however.

The Republic of Austria established in 1919 consisted of the old German-speaking provinces of Cisleithania, excluding parts of Carinthia, Styria, and Tirol. From 1922 it also included parts of what had previously been territories of the Hungarian Crown, combined into the new province of Burgenland. The republic was absorbed in Greater Germany from 1938 to 1945.

Belgium: Apart from the independent Principality of Liège, the territory later forming Belgium was ruled by the Austrians in the eighteenth century. In 1795 it was incorporated in revolutionary France, and in 1815 sovereignty was transferred to The Netherlands. Belgium's independence was established in 1830 by secession from The Netherlands, though in 1839 the Grand Duchy of Luxembourg was separated from the Belgian province of the same name and receded to The Netherlands and the province of Limburg was also divided. Since 1839 the only territorial change has been the acquisition of Eupen, Malmedy, and surrounding districts from Germany in 1920. These were temporarily returned in 1940-1944.

Bulgaria: Formerly part of the Turkish Empire, it was established as an independent country in 1878, covering approximately the northern two-thirds of the present territory. Much of the remainder became semi-independent, though under Turkish suzerainty, as Eastern Roumelia. This was united with Bulgaria in 1885. As a result of the two Balkan Wars in 1912-13, Southern Dobrudja was ceded to Romania, and a larger area in the south and west was acquired from Turkey, including part of eastern Thrace. This was enlarged in 1915, when Bulgaria entered the First World War on the side of the Central Powers, and a large part of Serbia was also seized. In 1916 Southern Dobrudja was also re-taken. In 1918 these wartime gains were all lost, together with the Aegean coastal strip won in 1913. Southern Dobrudja was permanently re-acquired in September 1940.

Czechoslovakia. Established in 1918/9 from the three Czech provinces of Cisleithania (Bohemia, Moravia, and Silesia) and the Slovak and Ruthene territories of the Hungarian Crown. These last (known as Sub-Carpathian Russia) were ceded to the U.S.S.R., along with a few Slovak villages, in 1945. A small area on the south bank of the Danube – the so-called Bratislava Bridgehead – was acquired from Hungary in 1947. From 1938 to 1945 Czechoslovakia was dismembered. The so-called Sudetenlands, along the frontier, were incorporated in Greater Germany; Teschen was seized by Poland; the remaining Czech lands were made a protectorate of Germany; and Slovakia was given nominal independence as a separate state.

Denmark: Denmark proper, and the Duchies of Schleswig, Holstein, and Lauenburg, were usually kept separate in the official statistics, though there are breaks in some series when the Duchies were ceded to Prussia in 1864. In 1920 the northern part of the old Duchy of Schleswig was returned to Denmark, and is known as South Jutland.

Finland: Part of the Swedish Kingdom until 1809, though separately administered. It was then ceded to Russia, though as a Grand Duchy with an autonomous administration. This continued until 1917, the boundaries of the Grand Duchy being enlarged in 1809, 1811, and 1820 by the addition respectively of part of the Tornie River basin, of Viipuri province, and of Petsamo. Independence was declared in 1917 and established the following year. Petsamo, Viipuri, and certain other areas along the frontier were ceded to the U.S.S.R. in 1940, and though temporarily re-acquired in 1941-42, their cession was confirmed in 1945.

France: The boundaries of France were enlarged substantially during the Revolutionary and Napoleonic period, though most of the available statistics can be, and have been, given for the territory established in 1815. The main differences between this and the pre-Revolution territory were the inclusion of Gex and the exclusion of Philippeville and part of Wissembourg. In 1860 Savoy and Nice were acquired from Piedmont. From 1871 to 1918 Alsace (excluding the territory of Belfort) and Lorraine (excluding the areas organised as the department of Meurthe-et-Moselle) were ceded to Germany, and from 1940 to 1944 these districts were temporarily lost again. In 1947 Tende and Brigue were acquired from Italy.

Germany: The German Empire was established in 1870, but many statistics for the area then covered have been synthesised for earlier years, though none prior to 1815. The boundaries then established for the state of Germany were only marginally changed to 1871, in which year most of Alsace and Lorraine were acquired. This was lost again in 1918, and various other territories were also ceded after the First World War. The mainly Polish provinces were taken from Germany in 1919; Danzig, Memel, northern Schleswig, and Eupen etc. were formally ceded in 1920, and eastern Upper Silesia was taken by Poland in 1922, following a plebiscite. In addition, Saarland was separately administered by France from 1920 to February 1935 (an arrangement which was followed again after the Second World War to the middle of 1959). During the period 1938-1941 various territories were incorporated in Greater Germany, but these were generally kept separate in the statistics. Four-power occupation was instituted following Germany's defeat in 1945, and during the next three or four years two *de facto* territories were established, which were formalised in 1949 as the Federal Republic of (West) Germany and the Democratic Republic of (East) Germany. East Berlin was included with the latter, and West Berlin, though not wholly incorporated in the former, is generally included in its statistics. Large parts of the pre-1939 eastern territories of Germany were ceded to Poland and the U.S.S.R. in 1945, but there have been only very minor boundary changes in the west and south.

Greece: Formerly part of the Turkish Empire, Greece was established as an independent country in 1829, comprising the Morea, Euboea, the Cyclades Islands, and the mainland south of Arta and Thessaly. The Ionian Islands were ceded by Britain in 1864. In 1881 Thessaly and Arta were acquired from Turkey, though a small strip of the former was returned in 1897. In 1913 the present territories in Epiros, Macedonia, and western Thrace were acquired, along with Crete and most of the remaining Aegean islands except the Dodecanese. Eastern Thrace was added in 1919, though this was not confirmed until the treaty of Lausanne in 1923, when the loss (in 1921) of postwar acquisitions on the mainland of Asia Minor was also confirmed. The Dodecanese Islands were formally acquired from Italy in 1947.

Hungary: Up to 1918 this name could be given either to all the lands of the Hungarian Crown (i.e. Transleithania) or to the more restricted Ancient Kingdom. The former included Transylvania, the Banat and Backa, and the semi-autonomous Croatia-Slavonia, though from 1849 to 1868 the Banat and Backa (along with its associated military frontier regions) constituted the autonomous Voivodina, and Croatia-Slavonia was attached to Austria rather than Hungary. In 1868 the Voividina was incorporated in Hungary, and Croatia-Slavonia returned to Hungarian domination, whilst in 1870 the latter's port of Fiume (Rijeka) was directly attached to Hungary. The remaining military frontier regions, which so long as they existed were always under Austria, were incorporated in Croatia-Slavonia in 1881.

The territory of Hungary established in 1919 by the treaty of Trianon was greatly reduced compared with Transleithania, or even the Ancient Kingdom. The Slovak and Ruthene counties were lost to Czechoslovakia; Transylvania and several counties of Hungary proper, together with part of the Banat, were lost to Romania; the rest of the Banat, Backa, and parts of Hungary proper went to Yugoslavia. Finally, in 1922, the German-speaking western fringe was ceded to Austria. During 1939-1945 there were various enlargements of Hungarian territory, all of which were lost in 1945. In 1947 the Bratislava Bridgehead was ceded to Czechoslovakia.

Ireland: The twenty-six counties of southern Ireland became independent in 1921.

Italy: The Italian nation-state was established in 1860, though some statistics for the area covered by it have been synthesised for earlier years. Venetia was added to the original territory in 1866, and the Papal States in 1870. In 1919 South Tirol, the old Austrian Küstenland provinces, and the port of Zara (Zadar) in Dalmatia were acquired, and Fiume was added in 1922. In 1945 the last two, together with Istria and part of Venezia-Giulia were ceded to Yugoslavia. Trieste and its neighbourhood were disputed, and were in international occupation. This was ended in 1954, when the city and a strip of coast went to Italy, and the hinterland to Yugoslavia. In 1947 Tenda and Briga were ceded to France.

Montenegro: Though formally under Turkey, it had much *de facto* independence even before 1878/80, when it was formally recognised. It was enlarged in 1878/80 and again in 1913.

Netherlands: Dutch independence was temporarily lost in the Napoleonic period, but re-established in 1814/5, when the old Austrian Netherlands and Liège were added to its territories. These revolted and became the independent kingdom of Belgium in 1830, though the Grand Duchy of Luxembourg and part of Limburg were formally re-acquired in 1839. The Grand Duchy was administered separately, and became independent in 1890 as a result of a difference in inheritance laws. Since 1839 the only boundary change has been the acquisition of the villages of Elten and Tuddern from Germany in 1949.

Norway: Part of the lands of the Danish Crown to 1814 and of the Swedish Crown from then to 1905, when it became independent. It was always administered as a separate unit.

Poland: There are no useful statistics for that part of the eighteenth century before Poland lost its independence in the partitions (the last one being 1795). It was re-established as an independent country in 1919, consisting of the former German territories of Posen, West Prussia, and part of Pomerania; the former Austrian territory of Galicia; and the former Polish provinces of Russia together with parts of Russia proper. To these were added eastern Upper Silesia in July 1922, and Teschen (taken from Czechoslovakia) in October 1938 (and returned in 1945). From October 1939 to March 1945 Poland was, in effect, dismembered, and when reconstituted its territory was shifted westwards by the cession to the U.S.S.R. of the eastern one-third of the pre-war lands, and the acquisition from Germany of most of East Prussia and of the territory east of the Oder and Neisse Rivers, including the post of Stettin (Szczecin). There was a minor exchange of territory with the U.S.S.R. in the Przemysl area in 1951.

Portugal: No territorial changes.

Romania: The separate principalities of Wallachia and Moldavia, under Turkish suzerainty, were united *de facto* in 1859. This was regularised in 1866, when Romania in practice acquired independence, though this was not formally recognised until 1878. At that date, Southern Bessarabia was ceded to Russia, and all except the southern part of Dobrudja was acquired from Turkey. In 1913 this southern part was acquired from Bulgaria. Romania entered the First World War in 1916, and in the treaty of Bucharest in 1918 lost Southern Dobrudja and many areas along the frontier with Hungary, but acquired Bessarabia from Russia. The losses were temporary, being reversed in 1919, and in 1920 Bukovina, part of the Banat, and Transylvania (including some counties of Hungary proper) were acquired in the break-up of the Habsburg Empire. In 1940 Southern Dobrudja was again ceded to Bulgaria (this time permanently), and Bessarabia and Northern Bukovina to the U.S.S.R. (also permanently, apart from the wartime seizure in 1941-43). Northern Transylvania was also lost to Hungary from 1940 to 1944.

Russia: Russian territorial acquisitions since 1750 have been very large, interrupted only in the period immediately following the 1917 Revolution. Russia received Polish territory in each of the three partitions (1772, 1793, and 1795), and acquired Turkish territory in the southern Ukraine, the Crimea, and the Kuban and Caucasia in 1774 and 1791. Georgia proper was acquired in 1801, Imeretia in 1810, Guria in 1829, Mingelia in 1857, Svanetia in 1858, and Abkhazia in 1864. Most of Azerbaijan was acquired in 1813. Yerevan and Nakhichevan were acquired in 1828, and the Kars region in 1878, which completed Russian territory in that area. Bessarabia was also acquired from Turkey, in 1812. The southern part was lost to Moldavia from 1856 to 1878, when it was re-acquired. The whole of it was lost to Romania from 1918 to 1940. In central Asia there were acquisitions pushing the frontier southwards and eastwards in 1864, 1865 (Tashkent), 1868 (Samarkand and Bukhara), 1871, 1873 (Khiva), 1876 (the Ferghana), 1881 (Askahabad), 1884 (Merw), and 1885. Finland, though always separately administered, was acquired in 1809. After the 1917 Revolution there were substantial territorial losses in Europe. Finland became independent, as did Estonia, Latvia, and Lithuania; Bessarabia was ceded to Romania, and the Polish provinces became part of independent Poland, taking with them parts of Russia proper. All these were re-acquired in 1939-40, except for central Poland and Finland (though Viipuri and Petsamo were recovered). These reacquisitions were confirmed in 1945, with minor adjustments on the Polish and Finnish frontiers. In addition northern Bukovina, taken in 1940 from Romania, was confirmed, and Sub-Carpathian Russia (Ruthenia) and the north-eastern part of East Prussia were added to the U.S.S.R.

Serbia. Established as an autonomous principality under Turkish suzerainty in 1817 and enlarged in 1833, Serbia became formally independent in 1878, when the Nis area was incorporated. In 1913 it was greatly enlarged by the addition of part of the Sanjak of Novi Pazar and much of Macedonia. In 1919 it formed the main nucleus of Yugoslavia.

Spain. No territorial changes.

Sweden Apart from the acquisition of separately-administered Norway by the Swedish Crown from 1814 to 1905, and the loss of separately-administered Finland in 1809, there have been no territorial changes.

Switzerland. After various vicissitudes in the Napoleonic period (including incorporation in France), the federal system of the pre-Revolutionary cantons, as modified by the Act of Mediation of 1803, which ended the tributary status of certain areas, was restored. Moreover, the previously independent cantons of Geneva and Valais were added in 1815, and so was Neuchâtel, which had been (and anomalously continued to be until 1857) a fief of the Prussian Crown.

United Kingdom: Ireland was a separate kingdom until 1801, when it was incorporated. In 1921 the twenty-six counties of southern Ireland became independent. The term Great Britain as used in the tables refers to the United Kingdom excluding any Irish territory.

Yugoslavia. Constituted in 1919 by adding to the previously independent Montenegro and Serbia, Croatia-Slavonia; part of the Banat, Backa, and parts of Hungary proper; and the former Austrian provinces of Carniola and Dalmatia (except Zara), together with parts of Carinthia and Styria. In 1945 Zara (Zadar), and other territories in the north-west were added, disputed parts near Trieste being finally acquired in 1954.

Currency Changes

In addition to difficulties in comparing statistics over time which result from boundary changes, there are others caused by changes in currency units. It has not been possible to identify all of these prior to 1914, but the most important are listed below. Most of the others do not, in any case, matter so far as this volume is concerned, since in these cases statistics have been standardised in terms of later currency units.

Austria 1893; the florin (or gulden) was divided into two of a new currency unit, the krone.
June 1925; a new unit, the schilling, was established, worth 10,000 kronen.
1947/8, a new schilling was issued, worth three old ones.[1]

Bulgaria: March 1947, the value of the lev was doubled, the circulation being halved by decree.
May 1952; a new lev was issued, worth 100 old leva.[1]
January 1962; a new lev was issued, worth 10 old leva.

Czechoslovakia: June 1953, a new korun was issued, worth 5 old koruna.[1]

Denmark: 1873; the rigsdaler was divided into two of a new currency unit, the krone.

Finland: Swedish and Russian currency were both legal tender from 1809 to 1840, when the former was withdrawn. In 1864 Finnish marks were introduced alongside Russian currency, 4 marks equalling one rubel.
January 1963; a new mark was issued, worth 100 old marks.

France: January 1960; a new franc was issued, worth 100 old francs.

Germany. November 1923; a new mark (the rentenmark) was issued, worth one million million old marks.[1]

West Germany. June 1948, a new unit, the Deutschmark, was established, worth 10 Reichsmarks.[2]

Greece: November 1944; a new drachma was issued, worth 50,000 million old drachmae.
May 1954; a new drachma was issued, worth 1,000 old drachmae.

Hungary: 1893, the florin (or gulden) was divided into two of a new currency unit, the krone.
Dec. 1926; a new unit, the pengo, was established, worth 12,500 paper kronen.
July 1946; a new unit, the forint, was established, worth 400,000 quadrillion pengos.

[1] Privileged rates of exchange existed, usually for small sums, but the rate given here applied to most currency.

Poland	May 1924; a new unit, the zloty, was established, worth 1,800,000 marks. October 1950; a new zloty was issued, worth 100 old zlotys.[2]
Romania:	1866; a new currency unit, the leu, was established, worth, one-quarter of a piastre. August 1947; a new leu was issued, worth 20,000 old lei.
Russia:	1837; the silver rubel replaced the paper rubel as the basis of official statistics. It was worth approximately four times as much. October 1922; a new currency unit, the chernovetz, was established, worth 10 old gold rubels, but paper rubels continued to circulate and depreciate. By March 1924, 1 chernovetz (later renamed rubel) equalled 50,000 million paper rubels.
Yugoslavia:	January 1966; a new dinar was issued, worth 100 old dinars.

[1] This was a *de facto* change. It became *de jure* in October 1924 with the issue of the Reichsmark.

[2] Privileged rates of exchange existed, usually for small sums, but the rate given here applied to most currency.

OFFICIAL SOURCES

The main sources used have been the official publications of the various European governments. In order to avoid excessive repetition of these in the notes to the tables, there follows a list of those used in more than one of the tables in this book:

Austria	*Nachrichten über Industrie, Handel und Verkehr* (1873–1908) *Österreichisches Statistisches Handbuch* (1880–1917) *Statistisches Handbuch für die Republik Österreich* (1920–1937, 1950–77) *Statistisches Handbüchlein für die Österreichische Monarchie* (1861 and 1867) *Statistisches Jahrbuch der Österreichischen Monarchie* (1861–1881) *Statistisches Jahrbuch für Österreich* (1938) *Statistik des auswärtigen Handels* (1891–1917) *Tafeln zur Statistik der Österreichischen Monarchie* (1842–1859) *Übersichtstafeln zur Statistik der Österreishischen Monarchie für 1861 and 1862*
Belgium	*Annuaire Statistique de la Belgique* (1870–1977) *Bulletin de la Commission Centrale de Statistique* (1843–1928) *Documents Statistiques Recueillis et Publiés par le Ministre de l'Intérieur* (1836–41; 1857–59) *Statistique Generale de la Belgique: Exposé de la Situation du Royaume* (1841–50; 1851–60; 1861–75; 1876–1900)
Bulgaria	*Annuaire Statistique du Royaume de Bulgarie* (1910–1942) *Statistickeski Godishnik* (1956–1977)
Czechoslovakia	*Manuel Statistique de la Republique Tchécoslovaque* (1920–1932) *Statistical Digest of the Czechoslovak Republic* (1948) *Statistical Handbook of the Czechoslovak Republic* (London, 1942) *Statistická Príručka Slovenska* (1947–1948) *Statistická Ročenka* (1934–1938, 1953–1977) *Statisticky Zpravodaj* (1938–1947) *Zahranični Obchod ČSR* (1925–1939, 1947–1977) *Zahranični Obchod Čech, Moravya, Slezeka* (1940–1945) *Zprávy Státního Úradu Statistického Republiky Československé* (1934–1947)
Denmark	*Meddelelser fra det Statistiske Bureau* (1852–1861) *Sammendrag af Statistiske Oplysninger* (1869–1893) *Statistisk Ärbog* (1896–1977) *Statistisk Fjerde Raekke* (1867–1959) *Statistisk Meddelelser* (1862–1958) *Statistisk Ny Raekke* (1845–1858) *Statistisk Tabelvaerk* (1801–1849) *Statistisk Tredje Raekke* (1860–1897)
Finland	*Bidrag till Finlands Officiela Statistik* (1886–1914) *Suomen Tilastollinen Vuosikinja* (1883–1976)

France	*Annuaire Statistique de la France* (1878–1977)
Germany	*Statistisches Jahrbuch für das Deutsches Reich* (1880–1941) *Statistisches Jahrbuch der Deutschen Demokratischen Republik* (1953–1977) *Statistisches Jahrbuch für die Bundesrepublik Deutschland* (1952–1977) *Statistik des Deutsches Reich* (1873–1939) *Statistik der Bundesrepublik Deutschland* (1950–1977) *Die Wirtschaft des Auslendes, 1900–1927*
Greece	*Annuaire Economique de la Grèce* (1938) *Annuaire Statistique de la Grèce/Statistical Yearbook of Greece* (1930–1937, 1954–1975)
Hungary	*Magyar Statistikai Évkönyv* (1881–1977)
Iceland	*Tolfraedihandbok* (1930–1977)
Ireland	*Agricultural Statistics 1934–1956* *Statistical Abstract of Ireland* (1931–1975)
Italy	*Annali di Statistica* (1871–1977) *Annuario Statistico Italiano* (1878–1977) *Cento Anno di Sviluppo Economico e Sociale dell' Italia* *Sommario di Statistiche Storiche Italiane, 1861–1955*
Netherlands	*Bijdragen to de Statistiek van Nederland* (1894–) *Jaarcijfers voor Nederland* (1881–1977) *Statistisch Jaarboekje* (1851–1882) *1899–1969: Zeventig Jaren Statistiek in Tijdreeksen*
Norway	*Historisk Statistikk 1968* *Statistisk Ärbok* (1879–1977) *Statistisk Oversikter 1948*
Poland	*Petit Annuaire Statistique de la Pologne* (1939) *Rocznik Statystyczny* (1920–1938, 1947–1977)
Portugal	*Anuario Estatistico* (1875–1975)
Romania	*Anuarul Statistic al României* (1904–1941, 1957–1973) *Buletin Statistic General* (1892–1939) *Comertul Exterior al României* (1871–)
Russia	*Annuaire de la Russie* (1904–1911) *Celskoe Khozyistvo S.S.S.R.* (1960) *Narodnoe Khozyistvo S.S.S.R.* (1932, 1956–1977) *Promishlenost S.S.S.R.* *Statistika Rossieskoie Imperie* (1887–1904) *Statistieski Sbornik 1918–1966* *Strana Sovetov za 50 Let* *Vneshnaya Torgovilya S.S.S.R. 1918–1966*

Spain	*Anuario Estadistico de España* (1858–1867, 1915–1935, 1946–1977)
	Cuadro (later *Estadistica*) *General del Comercio Exterior de España* (1849–1977) with gaps)
	Estadistica Minera (1861– with gaps)
	Memoria sobre el Movimento de la Poblacion de España (1858–1861, 1861–1870, 1900–1905)
Sweden	*Historisk Statistisk för Sverige* (3 parts in 4 volumes, 1955–1972)
	Statistisk Årsbok (1914–1977)
	Statistisk Tidskrift (1860–1913)
Switzerland	*Statistisches Jahrbuch der Schweiz* (1891–1977)
United Kingdom	*Annual Abstract of Statistics* (1946–1977)
	Annual Statement of the Trade of the U.K. (1854–1974)
	Statistical Abstract for the Principal and Other Foreign Countries (1872–1912)[1]
	Statistical Abstract of the United Kingdom (1854–1938)
	Tables of Revenue, Population, Commerce, etc. (1833–1854)
Yugoslavia	*Annuaire Statistique du Royaume de Serbie* (1895–1908)
	Matériaux pour la Statistique du Serbie (1888–1896)
	Statistički Godišnjek (1929–1940, 1954–1975)
	Jugoslavija 1945–1964: Statistički Pregled

[1] Occasional collections of tables relating to foreign countries were published in Parliamentary Papers from 1844 to 1870, and have been used.

ACKNOWLEDGEMENTS

In compiling a volume of this kind I have, inevitably, contracted a large number of debts for the help which I have been given by a great variety of people. It is impossible to mention every single one of these here, and I hope that those who are not named below will accept this general expression of my gratitude.

My principal acknowledgement must be to my friend and former pupil, Hywel Jones, who collected much of the data for Russia in the original section and much also of that for other east European countries. In addition, for a time, he lived with the worksheets almost as intimately as I did myself, and I sought his advice on numerous occasions.

Other former pupils who have helped me with the collection of data and to whom I am extremely grateful are Mrs Penelope Francks (*nee* Gant), Willem Buiter, and Petr Krŏslak.

In the nature of our work we have been particularly demanding users of a number of libraries, and the very willing response of their staffs cannot go unacknowledged. Particular mention must be made of Mr. Finkell of the Marshall Library, Cambridge, of Mr. Vickery and his staff in the Official Publications department of the Cambridge University Library, and of Mr. Spinney and his staff in the State Paper Room of the British Museum (including Mr Griscome and Mr Hopgood at the Woolwich Repository).

In the later stages of compilation I appealed for help in filling gaps to a number of individual scholars and to the government statistical services of almost every European country. For their assistance at this stage I would particularly like to thank Professor Lennart Jorberg of the University of Lund, Mrs Riitta Hjerppe of the University of Helsinki, Mr G. Radulescu, editor-in-chief of the *Enciclopedica Romana,* and the directors and staffs of the central government statistical services of Austria, Belgium, Czechoslovakia, Finland, France, the German Federal Republic, Greece, Hungary, Ireland, Italy, Luxembourg, the Netherlands, Norway, Poland, Portugal, and Sweden. Most of the data supplied by these services is acknowledged specifically in the tables, but some was transcribed from published sources unavailable to me, and in this connection I would like to make special mention of the help given by the central statistical services of Finland, the Netherlands, and Sweden. In addition some data, for which I am very grateful, has been supplied by the Mission des Archives of the French Ministry of National Education, by the statistical service of the French Ministry of Industrial and Scientific Development, by the statistical information centre of the French Ministry of the Economy and of Finances, and by the director of the Groupement des Industries Siderurgiques Luxembourgeoises.

I have received financial assistance during the compilation of this volume which I am happy to acknowledge. The principal source has been the Social Science Research Council, which enabled me to employ Mr Jones and Mr Buiter, and which contributed to travelling expenses. In addition I have received help with travelling expenses from Trinity College, Cambridge. I am also grateful for the facilities which were made available to Mr Jones and myself by the Cambridge University Department of Applied Economics, and especially for the help of its librarian, Mrs Olga Peppercorn, and of Miss Marion Clarke and the computing staff.

In addition to these personal acknowledgements, the author and publishers wish to thank the following, who have kindly given permission for the use of copyright material:
Almqvist & Wiksell Forlag AB and Professor Jorberg for statistics from *Growth and Fluctuations of Swedish Industry 1869–1922,* and Professor Johansson for use of *The Gross Domestic Product of Sweden and its Composition 1861–1955; Annales, Economies, Societes, Civilisations* for use of an index from The Industrial Production in France in the 19th Century from *Annales E.S.C. No. 1/1970* by Francois

Crouzet; Paul Bairoch and Universite Libre de Bruxelles for statistics from *The Working Population and Its Structure* by P. Bairoch; Cambridge University Press for extracts from *National Income, Expenditure and Output of the United Kingdom 1855–1965* by C.H. Feinstein; Economic Commission for Europe for an extract from *Growth and Stagnation in the European Economy* by Ingvar Svennilson; Harvard University Press for extracts from *Economic Elements in the Pax Britannica* by A. H. Imlah, *The Real National Income of Soviet Russia Since 1928* by A. Bergson; I.A.R.I.W. for extracts from *Review of Income & Wealth (1971)* by Frederic L. Pryor, *Review of Income and Wealth (1968)* by Phyllis Deane, *Income and Wealth (Series V)* by Alexander Eckstein, *Income and Wealth (Series IX)* 1953 by I. Vinski; National Bureau of Economic Research for use of *The Growth of Industrial Production in the Soviet Union* by G.W. Nutter; Springer-Verlag New York Inc. for use of extracts from *Das Wachstum der Deutschen Wirtschaft seit der Mitte Das 19 Jahrhunderts* by W. G. Hoffman; W. Woodruff for extracts from *Impact of Western Man.*

The publishers have made every effort to trace the copyright-holders but if they have inadvertently overlooked any, they will be pleased to make the necessary arrangement at the first opportunity.

WEIGHTS AND MEASURES: CONVERSION RATIOS

The following is not a complete guide to all weights and measures used in Europe during the period covered by this volume. It is simply a list of those conversion ratios used in compiling the tables given here.

1 Imperial ton = 1.016047 metric tons
1 Zugthierlast (Switzerland) = 0.75 metric tons
1 Wiener centner = 0.056 metric tons
1 cantar = 0.056 metric tons
1 Zoll centner (Austria-Hungary) = 0.05 metric tons
1 pund (Denmark) or 1 pond (Netherlands) = 0.05 metric tons
1 Swedish centner (or 100 skalpund) = 0.0425 metric tons
1 skeppund (ores) = 0.253 metric tons
1 skeppund (pig iron) = 0.176 metric tons
1 skeppund (bar iron) = 0.1506 metric tons
1 pood = 0.016388 metric tons
1 tonde (coal) = 0.12 metric tons
1 tonde (butter = 0.112 metric tons
1 ocque (or oke) = 0.001288 metric tons

1 dessiatine = 1.09 hectares
1 katastraljoch (Austria-Hungary) = 0.575464 hectares
1 tonde (land) = 0.551625 hectares
1 acre = 0.404686 hectares
1 stremma = 0.127 hectares

1 Danish mile = 7.532 kilometres
1 English mile = 1.609344 kilometres
1 verst = 1.067593 kilometres

1 last (Sweden and Netherlands) = 2 register tons
1 last (Finland) = 1.7985 register tons

1 eimer = 1,767 hectolitres
1 bulk barrel (oil) = 1.636547 hectolitres
1 tunna = 1.45468 hectolitres
1 tonde (corn) = 1.391212 hectolitres
1 tonde (beer) = 1.3139 hectolitres
1 Lower Austrian metze = 0.618048 hectolitres
1 fanega = 0.546 hectolitres
1 Imperial bushel = 0.363677 hectolitres
1 chetvert = 0.2625 hectolitres
1 arroba (wine) = 0.1614 hectolitres
1 arroba (oil) = 0.1256 hectolitres
1 Imperial gallon = 0.0454596 hectolitres

SYMBOLS

... = not available
- - = less than half the smallest digit used in the table
– = nil

A. CLIMATE

There is a great amount and variety of meteorological data available, and only a small selection on two topics is given here. This restriction is dictated by considerations of space, and the rather remote nature of the subject from the interests of most economists and historians. In the first edition of this book, only table 1, showing annual figures of precipitation, was given, since there seemed to be an obvious link between rainfall and the success of harvests, thus making these series seem of rather less remote interest than most meterological series. Critics have since pointed out that data on average temperatures are equally relevant, and a selection on this topic has been added, therefore, as table 2. The precipitation series cover thirty-nine different places, selected to give as wide a geographical spread as possible, yet including at least one locality in almost all countries. The mean temperature series cover a smaller number of places, partly because local variations are less pronounced than is the case with precipitation, but partly also because there are available fewer long runs of comparable statistics. As noted in the sources to table 1, the main place where historical data about the weather can be found is *World Weather Records*, pioneered by H. Helm Clayton and initially published by the Smithsonian Institution. A vast amount of additional information can be found in that source.

A1 ANNUAL PRECIPITATION (in millimetres)

1750–1799

	Brussells	Edinburgh	London	Lund	Manchester	Marseilles	Milan	Paris	Rome	Stockholm
1750	...	...	(612)	462	...	482	...	...	...	...
1751	...	...	(752)	...	...	560	...	626	...	...
1752	...	...	(492)	...	...	455	...	498	...	...
1753	...	...	(521)	489	...	489	...	481	...	...
1754	...	...	(602)	456	...	634	...	372	...	...
1755	...	...	(734)	364	...	782	...	...	...	...
1756	...	...	(682)	383	...	496	...	...	...	...
1757	...	...	(553)	471	...	325	...	...	...	...
1758	...	...	(630)	411	...	564	...	...	...	...
1759	...	...	(507)	391	...	472	...	...	...	...
1760	...	...	(595)	609	...	403	...	...	...	...
1761	...	...	(576)	545	...	588	...	...	...	...
1762	...	...	(548)	548	...	332	...	...	...	...
1763	...	...	(656)	526	...	468	...	...	...	...
1764	...	...	(635)	408	...	538	937	...	...	...
1765	...	...	[1] 569	476	...	810	1,286	...	...	...
1766	...	...	597	420	...	618	...	...	...	...
1767	...	...	651	590	...	505	...	...	...	...
1768	...	...	808	537	...	466	908	...	...	...
1769	...	...	622	511	...	475	906	...	...	...
1770	...	...	677	559	...	306	833	...	...	...
1771	...	564	549	532	...	518	730	...	...	...
1772		817	598	598	...	1,216	1,117	...	...	...
1773	...	730	681	506	...	633	974	593	...	...
1774	...	767	667	564	...	415	778	703	...	...
1775	...	865	678	580	...	433	726	534	...	...
1776	...	663	573	452	...	491	908	631	...	...
1777	...	...	605	493	...	699	1,044	443	...	...
1778	...	...	584	513	...	602	733	507	...	...
1779	794	...	740	527	...	494	787	560	...	...
1780	...	...	486	523	...	428	877	448	...	...
1781	...	...	452[1]	551	...	443	928	361	...	...
1782	...	...	783	671	...	350	758	602	773	...
1783	...	...	591	431	...	452	1,030	597	812	...
1784	...	...	691	493	...	382	910	526	1,097	...
1785	...	778	498	608	...	661	916	443	693	313
1786	606	...	570	636	...	476	1,075	629	645	470
1787	611	811	518	511	...	525	859	596	661	653
1788	504	493	439	475	...	823	1,099	462	851	356
1789	621	745	706	562	...	442	754	500	911	548
1790	599	699	567	574	...	655	755	352	728	568
1791	...	685	520[1]	476	...	597	1,082	401	854	569
1792	...	948	(626)	665	...	386	862	...	602	748
1793	...	526	(550)	432	...	684	1,082	331	923	602
1794	...	730	(593)	464	950	575	915	394	599	828
1795	...	908	(542)	515	832	318	1,098	404	783	676
1796	...	493	(475)	500	778	661	1,033	350	991	599
1797	...	659	(730)	648	986	689	1,064	524	1,087	625
1798	...	606	(625)	626	794	435	959	...	694	392
1799	...	652	(632)	592	981	371	935	...	779	681

See p. 15 for footnotes

A1 Annual Precipitation (in millimetres)

1800–1849

	Brussells (Uccle)	Budapest[2]	Copenhagen	Edinburgh	Frankfurt-on-Main	Geneva	Helsinki	Kaliningrad (Königsburg)	London	Lund
1800	...	...	...	548	...	...	...	...	(609)	686
1801	...	...	...	518	...	...	...	...	(617)	750
1802	...	...	...	541	...	...	...	...	(449)	621
1803	...	...	...	402	...	...	...	...	(576)	592
1804	...	...	...	624	...	...	...	...	(675)	548
1805	...	...	...	...	...	...	...	...	(655)	491
1806	...	...	...	...	...	...	...	...	(657)	...
1807	...	...	...	...	...	...	...	...	(456)	618
1808	...	...	...	...	...	...	...	...	(594)	579
1809	...	...	...	...	...	...	...	...	(665)[1]	645
1810	...	...	...	...	...	...	...	...	678	398
1811	...	...	...	829	...	...	...	...	576	491
1812	...	...	...	689	...	...	...	...	655	396
1813	...	...	...	512	...	...	...	...	520[1]	482
1814	...	...	...	...	...	...	...	...	(709)[1]	311
1815	...	...	...	554	...	...	...	...	572	551
1816	...	...	...	...	...	...	...	...	765	556
1817	...	...	...	...	...	...	...	...	737	510
1818	...	...	...	535	...	...	...	494	653	526
1819	...	...	...	688	...	...	...	526	790	500
1820	...	...	...	568	...	...	...	724	704	528
1821	...	...	499	...	...	...	...	733	876	533
1822	...	...	512	664	...	...	...	672	704	443
1823	...	...	620	769	...	...	...	627	688	473
1824	...	...	688	630	...	...	...	786	922	541
1825	...	...	750	562	...	...	...	720	625	499
1826	...	...	447	388	...	583	...	...	584	329
1827	...	...	645	828	...	890	...	...	632	423
1828	...	...	693	641	...	777	...	...	800	516
1829	...	...	701	761	...	958	...	...	640	562
1830	...	...	705	845	...	875	...	...	691	574
1831	...	...	557	623	...	926	...	...	782	478
1832	...	...	435	590	...	524	...	...	490	387
1833	762	...	740	530	...	756	...	...	584	588
1834	511	...	503	534	...	619	...	...	498	501
1835	618	...	470	641	...	730	...	...	632	428
1836	828	...	651	839	...	688	...	...	688	473
1837	740	...	451	680	707	528	...	...	533	441
1838	598	...	533	788	550	901	...	...	605	427
1839	778	...	469	596	715	884	...	...	752	390
1840	655	...	517	648	538	969	...	...	417	465
1841	780	633	769	655	801	1,258	...	...	845	716
1842	629	538	399	428	545	850	...	...	573	371
1843	803	467	691	605	775	939	...	...	622	486
1844	804	698	664	532	743	876	...	...	589	388
1845	809	737	734	676	727	907	498	...	567	578
1846	634	640	487	801	745	1,013	449	...	642	414
1847	612	646	469	578	522	693	410	...	447	373
1848	795	571	635	586	742	850	694	627	765	600
1849	685	(550)	631	372	...	853	597	694	599	504

See p. 15 for footnotes

A1 Annual Precipitation (in millimetres)

1800–1849

	Manchester	Marseilles	Milan	Oslo	Paris	Prague	Rome	Stockholm	Trier	Utrecht	Vienna
1800	821	451	907	...	...	...	898	702	...	...	...
1801	890	620	1,194	...	...	...	751	540	...	...	...
1802	908	527	790	...	...	...	761	557	...	...	...
1803	698	425	823	...	...	...	528	498	...	...	...
1804	744	494	1,128	...	703	...	893	486	...	...	...
1805	700	337	835	...	530	330	796	446	...	...	...
1806	851	366	1,132	...	489	358	914	691	798	...	...
1807	829	348	988	...	473	370	802	622	700	...	...
1808	791	253	733	...	435	363	896	733	651	...	...
1809	(825)	355	1,017	...	490	287	979	489	998	...	...
1810	890	517	1,345	...	437	329	998	542	656	...	...
1811	933	...	908	...	598	377	507	458	668	...	...
1812	903	328	1,075	...	497	439	929	336	619	...	...
1813	859	...	1,194	...	502	327	854	488	627	...	...
1814	796	456	1,578	...	382	375	1,016	406	419	...	...
1815	953	...	1,030	...	451	414	955	517	644	...	...
1816	1,006	...	869	...	546	364	780	273	640	...	...
1817	925	230	670	...	565	420	848	323	708	...	...
1818	903	303	969	...	432	320	949	274	567	...	...
1819	895	...	1,102	...	615	373	888	333	623	...	...
1820	952	...	970	...	379	305	687	533	588	...	...
1821	993	...	1,143	...	584	379	672	426	654	...	...
1822	1,001	311	879	...	424	306	1,104	414	496	...	...
1823	1,137	404	1,079	...	457	334	1,105	504	649	...	...
1824	1,091	443	936	...	572	386	1,040	532	788	...	...
1825	951	434	828	...	469	256	945	445	571	...	...
1826	633	536	1,287	...	410	275	935	261	450	...	...
1827	985	617	1,014	...	501	386	685	340	565	...	...
1828	1,150	484	696	...	585	490	473	381	683	...	...
1829	863	643	954	...	560	477	906	208	732	...	...
1830	1,038	305	884	...	573	384	680	339	661	...	...
1831	900	349	931	...	529	470	739	332	...	...	...
1832	931	341	1,033	...	456	275	616	320	...	...	...
1833	1,059	400	1,100	...	503	490	663	425	...	...	...
1834	881	562	804	...	421	256	319	459	...	...	...
1835	928	498	921	...	438	265	588	303	...	...	...
1836	1,152	722	1,142	...	611	421	735	391	...	...	...
1837	842	267	1,160	...	547	472	665	409	...	...	...
1838	798	490	1,274	...	492	405	805	377	...	...	...
1839	847	906	1,348	565	580	473	789	424	...	...	...
1840	871	650	899	565	523	370	519	585	...	...	...
1841	1,047	729	969	647	606	477	714	453	...	...	...
1842	801	895	1,260	331	393	238	819	359	...	...	...
1843	1,019	817	1,179	431	623	444	555	300	...	...	...
1844	677	747	1,147	516	655	600	815	592	...	...	...
1845	1,051	544	1,355	602	668	444	979	414	...	...	578
1846	846	640	1,338	563	649	470	966	419	...	...	706
1847	1,108	484	915	413	495	592	799	330	...	...	669
1848	1,126	763	1,238	676	661	430	638	416	...	...	589
1849	916	451	984	416	686	400	532	325	679	734	610

A1 Annual Precipitation (in millimetres)

1850–1899

	Athens	Belgrade	Bergen	Berlin	Brussells (Uccle)	Bucharest	Budapest	Copenhagen	Edinburgh	Frankfurt-on-Main
1850	...	...	...	...	837	...	(690)	600	541	437
1851	...	...	...	623	772	...	(759)	572	579	(429)
1852	...	...	...	673	889	...	(589)	680	800	695
1853	...	...	...	602	662	...	750	487	(718)	(589)
1854	...	...	...	629	728	...	414	582	531	(808)
1855	...	...	...	625	664	...	607	527	517	(725)
1856	...	...	...	473	796	...	590	574	723	869
1857	...	...	...	362	459	...	326	359	633	449
1858	...	...	...	746	506	...	597	403	618	479
1859	...	...	...	571	754	...	611	604[1]	659	604
1860	...	...	...	731	805	...	696	597[1]	(663)	(816)
1861	...	...	2,134	681	781	...	437	596	(676)	(691)
1862	...	...	1,905	652	676	...	549	597	862	717
1863	...	...	2,831	567	591	...	357	590	651	532
1864	...	...	1,811	546	449	...	528	644	713	366
1865	...	...	1,730	513	666	463	405	356	601	485
1866	...	...	2,135	677	797	561	519	729	679	750
1867	...	...	2,089	647	817	508	792	701	788	798
1868	...	...	2,225	596	712	549	538	518	726	610
1869	...	...	1,798	610	819	491	526	441	565	525
1870	...	...	1,358	710	674	710[1]	684	431	562	621
1871	...	...	1,971	571	637	726	520	411	682	648
1872	...	...	1,891	512	908	508	625	682	990	756
1873	...	...	2,358	496	651	403	455	667	716	526
1874	...	...	2,479	430	626	476	597	521	654	447
1875	...	...	1,654	630	677	575	771	487	619	661
1876	...	...	1,423	638	821	784	634	515	906	655
1877	...	...	1,911	631	954	578	628	673	914	647
1878	...	...	1,594	557	1,046	604	824	528	632	783
1879	...	...	1,645	573	705	466	766	522	725	740
1880	...	...	1,791	589	875	522	855	588	631	667
1881	...	...	1,729	515	784	772	864	501	717	531
1882	...	...	1,996	763	906	663	896	553	768	936
1883	...	...	1,878	491	688	560	701	506	588	553
1884	...	...	2,033	606	706	638	611	599	626	540
1885	...	...	2,345	573	718	647	565	552	456	660
1886	...	...	2,286	429	753[1]	745	572	451	662	577
					714					
1887	...	...	2,833	501	526	490	673	459	495	484
1888	...	581	2,117	611	793	632[1]	584	553	631	609
1889	...	823	1,743	567	724	556	796	530	567	515
1890	...	700	2,277	521	799	649	483	499	680	597
1891	...	596	1,999	677	671	584	679	731	615	629
1892	...	701	2,268	473	591	583	638	559	569	419
1893	...	637	2,077	523	587	760	670	598	532	612
1894	...	473	1,772	630	761	342	509	671	718	582
1895	338	715	1,576	504	748	648	708	564	679	522
1896	[372[3]]	720	2,400	593	711	471	633	590	599	527
1897	381	755	2,201	587	696	861	605	633	(582)	496
1898	116	472	2,613	542	536	496	580	685	618	547
1899	416	611	2,528	554	677	480	551	517	759	565

See p. 15 for footnotes

A1 Annual Precipitation (in millimetres)

1850–1899

	Geneva	Helsinki	Kaliningrad (Königsburg)	Kiev	Leningrad (St. Petersburg)	Lisbon	Ljubljana (Laibach)	London	Lund	Lvov (Lemberg)
1850	738	601	743	...	...	...	...	496	433	...
1851	719	529	815	...	...	...	1,815	598	469	...
1852	1,032	588	602	...	...	...	1,438	864	741	...
1853	827	440	670	...	...	...	1,800	762	381	...
1854	652	561	718	...	...	...	1,398	483	460	518
1855	1,024	371	658	...	...	...	1,558	599	491	780
1856	1,041	585	641	...	...	...	1,360	591	412	702
1857	537	374	375	...	...	...	767	537	357	...
1858	728	464	328	...	...	...	1,237	450	346	...
1859	683	719	453	...	...	...	1,454	656	574	...
1860	1,042	706	565	...	...	...	1,490	810	545	...
1861	781	450	646	...	...	...	1,109	519	558	...
1862	759	543	481	...	...	...	1,117	669	492	...
1863	856	554	578	...	...	...	1,239	499	590	...
1864	625	561	699	...	...	891	1,305	416	517	936
1865	715	366	487	...	...	923	819	729	344	611
1866	1,002	746	611	...	...	607	1,637	780	674	678
1867	914	632	838	...	...	631	1,557	675	664	974
1868	818	470	615	...	...	623	1,224	553	514	665
1869	629	555	606	...	...	495	1,741	610	536	737
1870	727	629	432	...	...	681	1,617	471[1]	488	789
1871	641	574	638	...	...	956	1,353	550	486	759
1872	1,137	685	644	...	...	907	1,695	704	757	...
1873	714	712	553	...	...	721	1,494	545	842	378
1874	652	553	559	...	...	440	1,327	500	501	715
1875	880	364	545	...	...	468	1,132	656	577	745
1876	925	528	734	...	...	1,107	1,788	631	522	766
1877	954	813	626	...	...	807	974	726	705	682
1878	1,083	682	723	...	...	744	1,863	757	578	719
1879	806	611	628	...	...	760	1,414	841	576	889
1880	877	644	831	...	...	681	1,345	730	677	516
1881	884	538	416	440	521	960	1,305	648	581	636
1882	1,077	708	749	546	400	538	1,738	650	634	941
1883	817	861	735	505	634	684	1,081	570	678	647
1884	536	541	732	651	437	759	1,414	481	632	817
1885	851	739	827	655	556	884	1,664	667	523	739
1886	981	529	517	639	567	857	1,315	647	465	478
1887	770	498	680	626	541	787	1,472	483	504	723
1888	1,000	550	711	542	451	855	1,493	659	597	641
1889	1,049	603	740	713	399	550	1,411	599	567	587
1890	912	689	783	448	545	592	810	539	595	494
1891	1,007	646	720	527	428	736	1,202	683	720	643
1892	831	755	648	665	614	989	1,267	616	617	681
1893	692	635	699	653	601	821	1,355	495	627	939
1894	850	660	517	615	639	711	1,252	713	724	722
1895	938	728	762	723	489	1,421	1,666	568	674	818
1896	1,193	702	565	543	499	482	1,433	533	703	807
1897	735	621	696	568	523	750	1,439	555	649	862
1898	862	797	745	427	544	544	1,552	463	730	716
1899	793	670	767	454	574	788	1,446	530	509	695

See p. 15 for footnotes

A1 **Annual Precipitation** (in millimetres)

1850–1899

	Madrid	Manchester	Marseilles	Milan	Moscow	Odessa	Oslo	Palermo	Paris	Prague
1850	...	847	432	1,205	...	...	531	...	646	520
1851	...	826	601	1,362	...	...	566	...	539	468
1852	...	1,162	493	1,100	...	...	497	...	685	367
1853	...	823	955	957	...	...	408	...	522	481
1854	...	831	355	753	...	...	451	...	742	354
1855	...	614	582	1,327	...	...	469	...	465	449
1856	...	868	623	1,068	...	...	572	...	652	379
1857	...	741	827	769	...	...	488	...	557	...
1858	...	700	579	916	...	...	502	...	536	...
1859	...	870	501	899	...	...	522	...	627	...
1860	301	902	561	964	...	...	745	...	753	...
1861	373	718	365	672	...	...	590	...	528	...
1862	400	932	932	1,315	...	...	676	...	593	...
1863	317	910	779	1,164	...	...	586	...	489	...
1864	505	689	795	976	...	...	501	...	423	239
1865	517	718	524	807	...	...	440	...	623	307
1866	490	1,028	541	862	...	...	718	323	742	445
1867	371	866	373	985	...	...	605	444	652	394
1868	338	768	743	974	...	...	603	799	591	388
1969	258	844	396	835	...	...	499	516	550	409
1870	335	713	495	721	...	...	443	454	482	392
1871	418	741	532	640	...	...	397	609	601	352
1872	384	1,224	1,095	1,569	...	...	814	591	762	394
1873	339	693	486	1,054	...	...	577	782	667	415
1874	328	774	606	681	...	...	522	801	482	345
1875	285	798	438	1,044	...	...	398	596	595	522
1876	393	897	454	1,170	...	...	441[1]	...	557	417
1877	431	1,108	312	884	...	...	770	724	671	432
1878	331	829	469	984	...	...	500	459	752	380
1879	392	801	727	1,008	...	...	620	507	642	485
1880	458	935	506	1,007	...	...	428	613	488	584
1881	460	926	395	1,098	443	562	476	674	564	498
1882	359	1,103	476	1,268	437	449	806	530	660	579
1883	421	908	433	868	531	288	681	885	570	476
1884	516	689	477	799	574	485	430	647	442	459
1885	698	711	624	1,169	572	403	554	686	590	351
1886	603	925	821	1,219	479	484	546	936	681	522
1887	456	472	650	995	517	480	573	821	496	491
1888	622	755	652	1,158	520	459	448	630	542	546
1889	373	758	451	1,179	576	528	455	638	532	532
1890	384	726	624	1,031	473	415	681	912	510	636
1891	375	902	459	1,108	526	321	571	808	588	505
1892	461	876	814	1,193	497	363	537	765	587	388
1893	515	682	487	862	649	365	567	676	524	362
1894	481	771	351	838	751	380	630	641	493	477
1895	615	731	412	863	561	367	626	903	508	504
1896	319	764	636	1,310	581	279	529	1,010	654	538
1897	559	776	535	935	405	420	778	838	620	511
1898	287	729	761	1,361	634	323	675	716	553	391
1899	386	731	512	881	675	240	474	650	418	573

See p. 15 for footnotes

A1 Annual Precipitation (in millimetres)

1850–1899

	Rome	Stockholm	Tiflis	Trier	Utrecht (or de Bilt)	Valentia	Vienna	Warsaw	Wroclaw (Breslau)
1850	742	457	...	737	818	...	558	...	...
1851	801	468	...	603	636	...	665[4]	...	...
1852	554	408	...	833	1,045	...	426[4][1]	...	...
1853	962	318	...	675	735	...	691	...	...
1854	754	258	...	848	823	...	577	...	...
1855	848	369	...	699	631	...	574	...	...
1856	805	431	...	838	771	...	488	...	...
1857	781	514	...	483	449	...	472	...	...
1858	882	307	...	549	638	...	420	...	...
1859	718	356	...	794	667	...	671	...	626
1860	967	459	...	842	692	...	561	...	626
1861	676	420	...	619	663	...	559	...	597
1862	948	337	...	648	590	...	621	...	522
1863	943	359	...	634	525	...	443	...	535
1864	931	355	...	461	459	...	655	...	457
1865	681	377	...	639	706	...	516	...	529
1866	526	543	...	859	817	...	572	...	552
1867	739	367	...	859	686	...	667	...	637
1868	915	444	...	745	563	...	623	...	585
1869	723	441	...	642	796	...	513	...	(550)
1870	816	357	...	623	733	...	725	...	474
1871	662	316	...	685	640	1,403	593	...	577
1872	1,050	438	...	847	877	1,746	640[4]	...	548
1873	855	477	...	558	575	1,554	506	...	455
1874	864	406	...	548	695	1,410	625	...	506
1875	1,233	299	...	703	778	1,525	694	...	623
1876	746	380	...	673	704	1,563	673	...	625
1877	720	500	...	880	819	1,738	587	...	535
1878	1,010	529	...	699	740	1,358	802	...	458
1879	782	437	...	673	682	1,350	861	...	537
1880	540	335	...	744	790	1,358	759	...	691
1881	969	467	467	644	776	1,473	620	...	419
1882	746	538	427	887	952	1,638	669	...	555
1883	785	530	401	558	618	1,541	527	...	567
1884	939	466	399	601	634	1,620	637	...	550
1885	954	576	430	792	636	1,438	653	492	615
1886	794	407	554	658	702	1,595	730	401	607
1887	1,021	413	495	608	473	1,111	615	574	468
1888	787	464	566	790	668	1,215	732	654	654
1889	1,137	466	568	661	874	1,442	689	670	672
1890	862	641	574	694	778	1,471	601	482	712
1891	825	412	414	684	788	1,511	571	579	548
1892	971	340	389	492	751	1,381	705	420	516
1893	677	445	544	623	712	1,100	533	475	461
1894	652	555	422	666	949	1,432	535	511	536
1895	932	556	684	689	741	1,273	730	424	507
1896	1,025	577	556	632	695	1,238	650	473	640
1897	853	604	465	664	758	1,610	725	578	602
1898	865	634	492	563	724	1,282	647	594	757
1899	904	564	513	651	691	1,532	602	783	630

See p. 15 for footnotes

A1 Annual Precipitation (in millimetres)

1900–1949

	Athens	Belgrade	Bergen	Berlin	Brussells	Bucharest	Budapest	Copenhagen	Edinburgh	Frankfurt-on-Main
1900	[359[3]]	854	2,113	520	675	733	752	680	795	645
1901	426	728	2,028	514	604	682	605	615	577	657
1902	[297[5]]	573	1,868	638	716	473	622	514	418	518
1903	[319[3]]	596	2,352	543	779	425	542	676	814	488
1904	404	494	2,128[1] / 1,714	484	602	414	460	530	611	(560)
1905	...	677	1,848	685	866	567	655	649	494	563
1906	487	573	1,901	598	753	602	788	550	793	597
1907	...	326	1,776	724	577	421	488	537	767	539
1908	404	494	1,851	474	678	613	482	541	540	551
1909	[344[5]]	642	1,913	624	817	532	550	544	751	664
1910	[589[5]]	796	1,697	663	967	641	708[2]	660	699	634
1911	375	436	1,991	397	735	507	540	617	537	428
1912	[493[5]]	859	1,962	494	913	706	692	660	683	640
1913	387	755	1,888	447	801	649	588	523	519	573
1914	451	...	1,897	632	...	687	786	582	578	710
1915	277	...	1,380	595	...	805	941	524	685	525
1916	[314[5]]	582	1,891	623	...	599	675	757	990	731
1917	[538[3]]	456	2,444	484	...	588	446	564	536	523
1918	469	...	2,080	589	...	595	648	531	614	579
1919	[370[5]]	...	1,760	582	980	632	662	525	646	658
1920	...	474	2,334	525	760	510	648	623	699	600
1921	524	653	2,727	640	418	548	478	584	628	360
1922	287	645	1,805	717	929	659	658	546	540	890
1923	351	423	2,199	573	812	621	628	630	615	767
1924	368	778	2,048	479	850	619	660	398	726	788
1925	414	758	1,952	629	1,073	608	657	563	808	614
1926	292	701	1,738	805	899	430	632	568	785	600
1927	329	683	1,734	693	840	572	587	826	875	687
1928	445	424	1,980	518	884	567	434	652	840	715
1929	371	625	2,391	500	710	475	695	582	611	506
1930	491	516	2,064	766	955	549	721	642	805	884
1931	521	...	1,785	708	859	633	615	626	810	842
1932	260	...	2,200	467	858	405	548	608	727	792
1933	415	...	1,488	518	739	785	673	478	556	519
1934	407	...	2,582	537	688	536	605	583	687	622
1935	324	...	2,147	670	914	673	623	619	702	720
1936	574	...	1,814	486	766	478	772	554	639	739
1937	511	...	1,425	622	901	659	989	570	736	586
1938	474	...	2,853	654	737	517	582	444	724	664
1939	521	...	1,858	755	928	747	743	513	564	818
1940	351	...	1,428	578	837	612	778	541	706	848
1941	290	857	1,416	722	707	663	609	498	638	758
1942	427	723	2,022	481	771	614	553	603	567	564
1943	253	544	2,216	389	724	571	465	584	582	514
1944	434	728	1,904	573	823	658	722	530	749	702
1945	422	603	1,657	630	747	277	581	664	716	(709)
1946	368	639	2,176	571	862	509	556	607	624	669
1947	303	568	1,592	627	630	591	440	464	658	648
1948	290	681	2,184	695	794	594	532	549	924	643
1949	486	801	2,826	594	521	570	558	599	711	515

See p. 15 for footnotes

A1 Annual Precipitation (in millimetres)

1900–1949

	Geneva	Helsinki	Kaliningrad (Konigsberg)	Kiev	Leningrad (St. Petersburg)	Lisbon	Ljubljana (Laibach)	London	Lund	Lvov (Lemberg)
1900	930	727	689	668	522	743	1,663	555	662	614
1901	967	487	677	598	403	726	1,740	476	597	602
1902	1,012	760	623	562	571	925	1,427	544	542	585
1903	902	811	762	524	625	793	1,566	970	664	579
1904	684	697	614	523	551	623	1,325	538	565	390
1905	840	669	847	818	500	588	1,536	574	607	551
1906	588	747	633	851	609	462	1,369	601	579	712
1907	942	620	748	464	437	867	1,347	606	532	811
1908	773	507	718	527	528	698	1,064	566	720	769
1909	855	679	552	405	451	725	1,376	603	566	653
1910	1,148	767	642	524	452	798	1,617	649	728	591
1911	798	631	619	631	559	878	1,302	586	575	648
1912	848	775	802	628	545	746	1,386	711	708	754
1913	929	526	753	(788)	484	804	1,259	555	555	821
1914	1,058	555	763	528	466	867	1,446	688	603	653
1915	1,002	723	797	704	504	822	1,751	606	559	703
1916	1,209	778	796	828	677	770	1,632	759	710	669
1917	1,029	568	657	563	479	601	1,379	719	644	590
1918	956	704	498	618	583	722	1,098	711	510	743
1919	1,020	628	786	705	460	584	1,614	617	612	811
1920	841	621	511	456	397	540	850	617	615	522
1921	457	706	713	424	662	543	931	309	621	620
1922	1,271	659	627	790	692	436	1,760	568	608	808
1923	1,188	799	743	748	589	448	1,685	638	625	519
1924	779	731	750	597	615	718	1,315	785	499	528
1925	758	804	852	664	679	605	1,789	649	639	684
1926	937	563	841	610	540	532	1,835	604	602	590
1927	1,050	794	932	597	638	554	1,594	816	707	525
1928	1,027	783	769	675	688	609	1,389	638	682	451
1929	678	705	618	552	531	474	1,329	543	609	540
1930	1,207	644	917	685	554	514	1,666	644	672	555
1931	873	702	882	669	605	459	1,534	605	561	610
1932	874	687	732	862	499	646	1,300	559	599	516
1933	823	490	686	925	606	568	2,003	463	489	790
1934	705	629	625	525	555	500	1,790	501	594	617
1935	1,013	832	674	558	781	431	1,527	653	675	650
1936	835	641	685	624	497	766	1,571	603	563	616
1937	1,042	626	728	753	555	997	2,379	754	611	490
1938	705	538	649	...	529	512	1,175	465	581	699
1939	1,050	401	696	557	462	843	1,483	687	556	...
1940	955	592	751	677	552	784	1,520	658	523	...
1941	732	496	674	...	401	791	1,531	718	578	...
1942	652	550	681	464	464	866	864	574	628	455
1943	795	821	615	...	562	631	1,251	525	684	433
1944	844	941	577	578	404	420	1,282	483	525	519
1945	629	707	...	418	639	531	1,060	504	776	610
1946	855	578	...	493	495	706	873	776	634	462
1947	827	543	...	891	656	949	1,235	505	421	542
1948	882	570	...	527	609	705	1,458	550	551	754
1949	663	636	...	557	474	516	956	478	549	450

A1 Annual Precipitation (in millimetres)

1900–1949

	Madrid	Manchester	Marseilles	Milan	Moscow	Odessa	Oslo	Palermo	Paris	Prague
1900	311	795	500	1,152	612	403	562	1,008	444	504
1901	452	678	730	1,274	559	461	601	656	465	464
1902	549	593	455	908	698	349	488	786	540	360
1903	269	888	467	1,238	570	280	686	508	536	459
1904	505	641	353	881	666	228	428	730	518	384
1905	394	701	654	1,304	685	281	562	657	638	413
1906	474	849	693	888	742	365	492	814	595	507
1907	338	801	883	997	555	250	734	895	546	415
1908	416	722	344	797	834	447	640	397	568	...
1909	449	837	620	820	678	370	774	864	666	...[1]
1910	396	820	754	970	699	412	758	635	751	595
1911	512	724	437	1,244	496	262	603	678	481	326
1912	422	890	626	1,063	658	632	680	887	609	534
1913	380	668	662	918	729	242	557	437	645	460
1914	415	809	740	1,081	640	577	556	797	626	550
1915	431	730	651	1,139	665	544	665	990	655	563
1916	389	753	531	1,327	700	357	781	497	705	587
1917	374	711	654	864	442	481	534	653	573	346
1918	282	1,006	573	1,044	582	411	671	597	578	448
1919	483	745	451	870	648	479	510	746	648	571
1920	450	898	864	1,192	338	281	776	797	547	546
1921	426	630	282	427	408	204	414	590	279	334
1922	417	773	419	534	618	383	596	717	757	605
1923	349	993	608	633	597	288	715	604	714	533
1924	392	879	685	830	448	272	852	901	681	492
1925	431	829	456	703	636	314	661	821	715	569
1926	404	857	674	1,208	513	420	758	449	688	617
1927	448	875	565	930	698	319	919	697	772	487
1928	425	978	454	[753[6]]	546	274	674	779	738	462
1929	354	862	374	739	360	288	791	1,150	494	437
1930	458	938	682	1,048	593	382	786	740	831	458
1931	312	1,047	565	875	553	275	362	992	801	593
1932	400	762	1,018	853	526	394	746	1,303	551	459
1933	386	549	689	1,005	696	471	557	863	553	330
1934	328	780	534	1,127	577	275	865	881	596	484
1935	406	945	769	1,061	760	362	822	663	630	416
1936	607	859	661	1,175	487	...	646[1]	630	748	512
1937	469	782	613	1,355	578	...	647	571	714	479
1938	252	1,022	793	860	373	349	788	885	551	598
1939	...	1,008	616	1,022	481	345	674	1,435	808	746
1940	512	904	634	887	519	396	697	1,322	604	593
1941	508	750	879	1,197	597	...	528	865	732	611
1942	542	909	581	737	556	...	785	502	813	340
1943	419	960	664	772	455	448	676	453	549	269
1944	405	1,103	437	708	491	340	853	403	694	571
1945	309	944	361	806	678	307	564	488	475	565
1946	323	1,091	392	795	511	290	812	444	583	638
1947	691	826	528	1,013	681	413	398	493	513	399
1948	356	969	656	937	464	246	845	525	610	480
1949	401	850	501	1,080	576	431	787	555	392	477

See p. 15 for footnotes

A1 Annual Precipitation (in millimetres)

1900–1949

	Rome	Stockholm	Tiflis	Trier	Utrecht (or de Bilt)	Valentia	Vienna	Warsaw	Wroclaw (Breslau)
1900	1,470	574	546	607	724	1,565	791	529	556
1901	1,055	358	584	772	705	1,321	506	634	558
1902	851	527	402	662	625	1,272	692	522	497
1903	990	644	461	691	926	1,709	867	653	642
1904	837	503	574	676	596	1,675	652	400	404
1905	1,045	554	661	730	776	1,352	643	677	590
1906	1,087	457	612	741	724	1,272	728	492	561
1907	1,101	525	468	622	660	1,302	703	565	643
1908	758	489	533	676	644	1,279	486	566	562
1909	962	551	446	704	831	1,148	660	472	675
1910	837	718	596	863	818	1,340	903	536	617
1911	979	505	365	562	641	1,412	646	490	473
1912	638	693	456	675	1,027	1,441	759	627	660
1913	784	495	384	753	719	1,601	683	686	562
1914	921	394	596	830	785	1,738	603	475	526
1915	1,341	580	738	674	891	1,603	862	578	827
1916	945	631	495	837	895	1,537	871	687	624
1917	930	434	394	745	782	1,289	574	529	547
1918	775	604	428	736	884	1,511	787	570	561
1919	693	607	589	735	742	1,162	791	598	669
1920	633	500	742	628	640	1,649	792	458	563
1921	913	512	556	382	398	1,172	659	402	540
1922	876	625	543	995	649	1,358	753	438	734
1923	870	720	531	866	841	1,522	671	523	521
1924	741	664	418	852	778	1,575	536	516	568
1925	703	653	354	809	899	1,332	705	611	684
1926	611	528	522	804	712	1,305	706	610	724
1927	934	625	463	881	875	1,345	588	592	769
1928	905	630	514	754	815	1,782	597	538	503
1929	730	623	444	688	626	1,529	537	510	538
1930	843	719	542	969	911	1,664	777	633	770
1931	813[1]	598	714	915	772	1,423	660	550	741
	785								
1932	739	545	512	806	744	1,245	404	448	556
1933	897	429	423	503	511	1,147	611	468	482
1934	880	686	430	591	710	1,576	501	597	490
1935	758	684	435	775	917	1,304	605	582	595
1936	916	592	753	783	750	1,253	721	640	506
1937	856	695	497	...	727	1,625	829	527	...
1938	870	508	496	639	782	1,556	751	545	726
1939	962	464	581	831	839	1,311	723	...	...
1940	875	492	599	811	821	1,328	666	...	498
1941	955	449	367	640	744	1,289	988	...	892
1942	500	437	568	630	781	1,247	576	...	530
1943	665	601	563	699	670	1,408	566	...	391
1944	504	707	468	(726)	808	1,262	907	...	722
1945	306	635	436	(717)	799	1,444	630	...	...
1946	446	551	546	(736)	817	1,547	622	...	...
1947	665	373	365	622	752	1,506	568	597	641
1948	548	526	613	694	736	1,475	643	749	555
1949	534	518	487	576	668	1,323	686	647	548

See p. 15 for footnotes

A1 Annual Precipitation (in millimetres)

1950–1975

	Athens	Belgrade	Bergen	Berlin	Brussells (Uccle)	Bucharest	Budapest	Copenhagen	Edinburgh	Frankfurt-on-Main
1950	354	494	2,254	666	950	520	619	695	734	798
1951	346	705	1,723	574	880	417	647	689	787	606
1952	433	755	1,819	569	925	673	789	618	620	823
1953	560	698	2,536	541	557	498	527	499	600	466
1954	414	927	2,111	811	...	759	642	839	893	651
1955	548	878	1,813	578	617	727	899	646	459	632
1956	281	719	1,920	735	796	576	569	614	716	741
1957	305	605	2,378	568	803	698	567	622	652	686
1958	349	585	1,702	724	834	516	558	833	750	830
1959	216	599	1,536	556	560	542	537	513	458	415
1960	356	595	1,419	594	962	591	565	857	619	783
1961	357	465	1,917	713	902	610	400	593	642	857[7]
1962	478	507	2,044	527	862	510	534	602	656	661[7]
1963	459	538	1,699	386	713	528	657	582	768	642[7]
1964	273	714	2,350	611	786	634	621	488	503	420[7]
1965	379	666	1,493	627	1,073	469	817	616	827	885[7]
1966	383	685	2,037	773	1,056	803	745	687	731	887[7]
1967	407	575	3,069	629	707	532	505	699	637	762[7]
1968	546	673	1,584	601	777	552	498	615	809	838[7]
1969	301	801	1,944	607	777	854	684	482	559	525[7]
1970	240	810	2,002	628	727	709	665	665	614	680[7]
1971	363	695	2,344	489	692	786	461	534	530	439[7]
1972	457	721	1,918	575	710	698	612	554	438	539[7]
1973	398	546	1,958	547	690	...	400	614	461	474[7]
1974	373	900	2,073	784	1,040	541	659	666	623	649[7]
1975	407[11]	722	2,642	463	734	...	521	452	532	661[7]

	Geneva	Helsinki	Kaliningrad (Königsburg)	Kiev	Leningrad	Lisbon	Ljubljana	London	Lund	Lvov
1950	888	735	...	479	502	521	1,235	637	709	...
1951	936	557	507	517	551	808	...	763	657	527
1952	1,036	847	720	718	661	730	...	654	736	725
1953	609	657	538	487	611	719	...	499	433	569
1954	968	720	753	499	632	477	...	645	317	642
1955	930	583	663	607	519	960	...	463	568	930
1956	804	711	746	730	487	754	...	617	570	596
1957	635	797	779	545	683	588	...	591	547	632
1958	927	570	885	535	659	762	...	754	704	807
1959	831	493	618	445	595	1,013	...	435	473	671
1960	1,271	777	771	784	561	984	...	709	664	735
1961	...	581	...	500	570	664	1,372	563	918	410
1962	694	758	...	600	640	782	1,604	567	709	670
1963	1,010	530	...	420	510	1,335	1,430	538	522	530
1964	742	464	...	540	460	600	1,437	542	539	...
1965	1,121	605	...	480[3]	530	938	1,849	625	612	...
1966	912	557	...	880	780	817	...	700	733	970
1967	898	699	...	690	680	586	...	652	783	720
1968	1,156	582	...	...	...	909	...	710	608	...
1969	826	519	...	...	618	1,003	...	552	577	...
1970	1,039	710	...	898	671	777	1,396	636	723	855
1971	703	482	...	691	488	613	1,107	621	591	...
1972	761	654	...	...	432	837	1,608	424	558	744
1973	799	549	...	595	610	597	1,270	476	643	694
1974	1,021	880	...	670	543[3]	443	1,412	725	699	853
1975	1,119	435	...	387	619	533	1,435	641	496	...

See p. 15 for footnotes

A1 Annual Precipitation (in millimetres)

1950–1975

	Madrid	Manchester	Marseilles	Milan	Moscow	Odessa	Oslo	Palermo	Paris	Prague
1950	293	1,093	355	876	626	270	1,062	455	696	492
1951	571	1,062	803	1,306	490	287	964	491	705	446
1952	382	966	388	660	810	598	717	400	707	450
1953	394	867	480	816	665	312	728	638	378	290
1954	241	1,370	459	964	496	435	892	700	423	565
1955	554	689	442	712	592	420	537	558	603	557
1956	472	948	574	815	886	459	530	460	507	509
1957	394	920	515	1,025	580	386	766	534	597	407
1958	467	1,022	401	860	658	543	708	524	787	633
1959	577	678	707	1,347	660	365	799	375	549	331
1960	587	1,008	706	1,234	686	517	921	469	760	506
1961	446	974	576	940	560	420	784	395	562	447
1962	513	840	447	840	590[5]	540	811	490	504	377
1963	747	747	682	1,310	...	...	746	648	614	403
1964	356	815	489	979	440	...	727	549	541	418
1965	582	1,015	472	901	730	330	917	583	880	590
1966	530	1,045	548	1,084	780	610	894	488	835	694
1967	530	937	222	731	570	420	908	369	591	513
1968	389	976	646	885	...	...	677	421	633	497
1969	589	898	624	792	600	...	604	490	618	392
1970	307	817	498	777	864[8]	693	808	275	631	527
1971	510	666	544	709	593[9]	521	635	487	508	443
1972	739	834	905	1,204	497	...	627	378	740	406
1973	355	864	730	762	852	...	589	560	579	360
1974	300	820	624	766	685	428	838	366	668	553
1975	436	562	536	1,307	624	...	684	400	659	459

	Rome	Stockholm	Tiflis	Trier	Utrecht (or de Bilt)	Valentia	Vienna	Warsaw	Wroclaw (Breslau)
1950	563	591	483	987	950	1,632	805	546	511
1951	922	473	544	815	810	1,604	709	331	454
1952	482	576	581	937	792	1,069	538	600	529
1953	933	436	346	474	607	1,282	498	372	318
1954	483	637	375	771	818	1,551	693	429	533
1955	577	442	767	644	660	1,124	626	490	555
1956	754	499	468	780	752	1,240	618	499	617
1957	548	618	307	664	928	1,441	559	520	509
1958	913	623	538	875	828	1,582	693	493	650
1959	926	456	570	594	536	1,474	796	379	375
1960	1,017	806	468	832[7]	929	1,691	571	592	629
1961	836	620	370	835[7]	925	1,370	611	556	620
1962	828	606	240	660[7]	750	1,250	543	770	520
1963	796	860	700	616[7]	777	1,400	472	530	512
1964	607	376	...	614[7]	760	1.489	594	489	591
1965	945	580	...	879[7]	1,152	1,358	873	696	533
1966	715	553	...	1,060[7]	1,148	1,408	781	608	650
1967	510	625	490	1,001[7]	853	1,347	569	518	570
1968	610	579	...	924[7]	858	1,460	504	432	588
1969	671	431	...	605[7]	748	902	644	410	405
1970	531	472	438	987[7]	909	1,389	706	767	765
1971	566	491	302[3]	570[7]	562	990	530	501	659
1972	834	440	815	676[7]	656	1,510	535	648	670
1973	508	440	487[10]	592[7]	780	1,230	619	520	501
1974	717	685	457[3]	731[7]	993	1,591	588	691	774
1975	674	386	...	786[7]	628	1,200	658	431	669

See p.15 for footnotes

A1 **Annual Precipitation** (in millimetres)

NOTES

1. SOURCES:— The main source used has been *World Weather Records.* The first three volumes, edited by H. Helm Clayton, were published by the Smithsonian Institution, Washington, in 1927, 1934, and 1947. Subsequent volumes have been published by the United States Weather Bureau in 1959 and 1966. The following additional sources have been used:— Bergen, Brussells (from 1893), Lund, Marseilles, Oslo, Palermo, Rome (from 1931), Paris, and Stockholm, and most statistics since 1960 — official publications listed on p. xv. Statistics since 1960 for Berlin, Geneva, Kiev, Leningrad, Lvov, Milan, Moscow, Odessa, Tiflis and Valentia, for Belgrade in 1966-69 and 1974-5, for Lisbon in 1963 and 1969-75, for Budapest, Edinburgh, London, Manchester and Vienna in 1970-75, and for Marseilles in 1972-75 — *Monthly Climatic Data of the World.* Brussells and Uccle to 1893 — *La Pluie en Belgique* (Brussells, 1894). Edinburgh, Manchester, and London to 1969 — data supplied by the Meteorological Office, Bracknell, the figures in round brackets being previously unpublished estimates made by Mr B. Wales-Smith; Ljubljana to 1950 — V. Manshin, "Kratek Pregled Temperatur in Padavin in Ljubljana v 100-letni opazovalni dobi 1851—1950", *Geog. Vestnik* 24 (1952); Lvov (early figures), Prague (to 1916), and Vienna (early figures) — *Jahrbuch der k.k. Central Anstalt für Meteorologie und Erdmagnetismus* (1848—1918); Warsaw (1938—50) — data supplied by the Polish Central Statistical Office.

2. Figures in square brackets are incomplete, the reason being given in footnotes. Figures in round brackets include estimates for some months.

FOOTNOTES

[1] Continuity of the series is broken by a change in the location of the rain gauge. Two figures are given wherever possible, but the difference between them should not be taken as an indicator of any regularity in this difference over a number of years.

[2] Figures prior to 1911 are based on scattered records from several gauges in the Budapest area, standardised to accord with records from the location used since that date, by Z Berkes, "A légnyomas valtozáscu Magyoszágon....", Magyország Éghajlata (1944).

[3] Excluding August.

[4] The observations for 1851 and 1852 are standardised to accord with records from the 1853—72 location, whilst these are said to be "strictly comparable" with later figures.

[5] Excluding July.

[6] Excluding February.

[7] These figures are for years ended 31 October.

[8] Excluding September.

[9] Excluding November.

[10] Excluding October.

[11] Excluding January and April.

A2 MEAN TEMPERATURE IN JANUARY AND JULY (in degrees centigrade)

1750–1799

	Berlin		Copenhagen		Edinburgh		Geneva		Stockholm		Vienna	
	Jan	July	Jan	July	Jan	July	Jan	July	Jan	July	Jan	July
1750	...	...	...	...	...	...	...	...	...	...	...	...
1751	...	...	...	...	...	...	...	...	...	...	...	...
1752	...	...	...	...	...	...	...	...	...	...	...	...
1753	...	...	...	...	...	...	...	...	...	...	...	...
1754	...	...	...	...	...	...	...	...	...	...	...	...
1755	...	...	...	...	...	...	...	...	...	...	...	...
1756	...	...	...	...	...	...	...	...	–2.6	17.8	...	...
1757	...	...	...	...	...	...	...	...	–6.8	19.9	...	...
1758	...	...	...	...	...	...	...	...	–5.8	16.6	...	...
1759	...	...	...	...	...	...	...	...	–0.9	17.9	...	...
1760	...	...	...	...	...	...	...	...	–10.5	17.2	...	...
1761	...	...	...	...	...	...	...	...	–2.4	16.4	...	...
1762	...	...	...	...	...	...	...	...	–0.6	15.9	...	...
1763	...	...	...	...	...	...	...	...	–5.9	18.1	...	...
1764	...	...	...	...	2.4	15.5	...	...	–2.4	20.6	...	...
1765	...	...	...	...	4.3	14.7	...	...	–3.6	15.9	...	...
1766	...	...	...	...	1.5	14.9	...	...	–5.4	18.7	...	...
1767	...	...	...	...	–0.2	13.6	...	...	–11.2	15.7	...	...
1768	...	...	–2.1	17.4	0.7	14.6	–1.9	19.6	–5.1	16.7	...	...
1769	1.2	18.1	1.0	17.2	1.8	15.6	1.2	19.5	–1.5	16.3	...	...
1770	–1.8	19.0	–0.9	17.9	4.4	13.9	–1.6	16.9	–4.9	16.8	...	...
1771	–3.6	17.6	–2.7	17.3	1.0	14.1	1.1	20.8	–7.5	16.8	...	...
1772	–1.1	17.4	–2.3	16.9	0.3	14.4	0.7	19.6	–4.1	17.5	...	...
1773	1.9	19.1	1.0	18.3	3.6	13.4	2.1	18.6	–2.9	18.8	...	...
1774	–2.6	17.9	–4.2	17.8	–1.1	13.8	2.0	18.7	–11.7	18.7	...	...
1775	–0.5	20.6	–1.9	19.4	3.5	15.4	1.4	18.9	–4.5	19.8	–2.9	20.1
1776	–9.8	20.1	–7.8	20.5	–1.6	15.3	–2.2	20.3	–8.9	19.5	–7.3	20.3
1777	–3.2	18.0	...	...	1.9	14.2	–0.3	18.5	–5.5	15.5	–3.7	19.2
1778	–2.6	21.8	...	...	3.2	16.2	0.1	21.8	–5.1	18.4	0.7	22.3
1779	–1.5	19.8	...	...	3.1	18.4	–4.3	19.3	–2.0	17.0	–3.7	19.1
1780	–2.2	18.8	...	...	–2.0	15.9	–1.8	20.9	–6.0	18.7	–3.8	19.9
1781	–1.8	20.2	...	...	2.4	15.8	1.4	21.1	–5.6	17.6	–2.6	20.8
1782	1.8	20.6	1.7	17.7	4.1	15.6	2.6	22.3	–2.1	15.7	1.9	24.0
1783	1.6	21.6	–0.3	21.4	2.8	17.3	2.8	22.0	–6.6	21.1	2.6	22.7
1784	–6.6	18.5	–3.8	17.2	0.1	14.7	–1.2	20.7	–7.4	16.4	–6.0	21.3
1785	–0.8	17.8	–0.6	17.1	3.4	14.6	0.5	19.0	–4.6	17.3	–2.4	19.8
1786	–0.1	17.1	–1.1	16.6	2.2	13.6	0.3	18.3	–6.2	16.8	–0.9	18.8
1787	–2.0	18.3	–0.2	17.6	4.4	15.6	–2.3	19.2	–2.8	15.8	–2.2	20.3
1788	1.1	20.9	1.2	20.4	3.8	15.7	1.2	21.3	–3.9	19.7	1.1	23.8
1789	–4.5	19.0	...	...	1.4	16.1	–1.3	18.6	–8.2	20.0	–2.5	21.4
1790	1.4	17.3	...	...	4.1	15.0	0.7	18.5	0.0	14.5	–0.6	19.7
1791	2.5	19.5	...	...	3.8	14.8	3.0	19.9	1.9	18.8	3.7	20.7
1792	–1.3	20.8	...	...	1.6	14.7	0.9	19.9	–5.0	19.4	–0.9	21.4
1793	–2.9	21.0	...	...	3.0	16.0	–1.1	22.6	–2.4	18.6	–3.0	22.5
1794	–0.7	22.2	...	...	3.4	15.9	0.3	23.2	–0.1	18.7	1.2	24.6
1795	–8.3	18.3	...	...	–1.2	14.2	–5.9	17.8	–7.3	16.7	–7.9	18.9
1796	6.5	19.8	...	...	6.6	14.2	2.1	18.9	2.4	17.2	–5.0	21.2
1797	0.3	20.9	...	...	4.8	16.1	0.0	21.5	–2.4	18.0	0.3	23.5
1798	0.4	19.5	0.1	20.0	3.6	15.9	0.4	19.2	–4.1	19.4	0.8	21.2
1799	–5.6	17.7	–2.2	17.3	2.9	14.4	–2.0	18.3	–2.5	16.4	–7.0	20.4

A2 Mean Temperature in January and July (in degrees Centigrade)

1800–1849

	Berlin		Copenhagen		Edinburgh		Geneva		London	
	Jan	July	Jan	July	Jan	July	Jan	July	Jan	July
1800	–3.2	16.5	–2.5	16.4	1.8	16.4	2.3	20.7	...	...
1801	0.3	18.2	0.3	19.2	3.9	14.9	1.9	19.1	...	...
1802	–3.3	16.7	–2.1	13.5	2.7	13.5	–5.5	18.4	...	...
1803	–8.7	21.3	–5.1	17.2	2.0	17.1	–0.8	21.3	...	...
1804	2.5	19.2	1.2	17.3	4.6	15.1	5.3	18.6	...	...
1805	–6.9	17.3	–3.5	15.9	2.9	15.2	–1.0	18.3	...	...
1806	1.7	17.0	1.1	15.3	1.7	14.2	3.6	18.5	...	...
1807	0.0	19.4	1.1	17.4	2.4	16.1	–1.8	22.0	...	...
1808	–1.1	20.5	0.2	19.2	1.8	16.9	–1.0	19.6	...	...
1809	–6.1	18.3	–4.4	16.5	–0.9	14.1	2.4	18.0	...	...
1810	–3.3	18.9	–0.5	17.6	2.7	14.0	–4.4	17.4	...	...
1811	–5.4	20.1	–1.9	19.0	0.9	15.2	–3.2	20.6	...	...
1812	–3.4	16.2	–0.7	14.7	2.4	13.9	–5.4	18.1	...	...
1813	–3.6	17.6	–0.9	18.1	2.0	15.2	–2.4	15.8	...	...
1814	–4.7	20.2	–5.9	17.8	–3.1	15.2	–2.2	19.0	...	...
1815	–5.5	15.5	–2.1	15.1	0.8	14.6	–3.2	18.8	...	...
1816	–0.8	17.3	–0.2	17.0	1.9	13.2	0.4	15.6	...	...
1817	1.2	17.0	2.3	15.7	3.7	14.0	2.7	18.2	...	...
1818	1.0	19.5	0.8	18.2	2.9	15.6	0.2	20.3	...	...
1819	1.1	20.7	2.7	18.5	3.2	15.3	1.8	18.7	...	...
1820	–6.3	16.4	–3.8	16.1	–0.9	15.0	–0.4	17.8	...	...
1821	0.1	17.1	–1.3	14.3	3.9	14.2	2.0	17.0	...	...
1822	1.8	19.7	1.6	16.9	3.9	14.4	0.2	19.6	...	...
1823	–11.9	16.5	–3.8	15.4	–0.5	13.6	–1.9	17.8	...	...
1824	2.1	18.0	2.9	15.8	4.3	15.5	–0.9	20.4	...	...
1825	2.4	18.1	2.5	17.3	3.9	16.3	–0.4	18.9	...	...
1826	–6.8	22.5	–3.1	20.7	–0.2	16.7	–5.2	20.4	...	...
1827	–2.1	19.7	–1.7	16.7	1.9	14.7	–0.9	22.0	...	...
1828	–2.8	20.2	–1.7	18.3	4.1	14.2	2.6	19.5	...	...
1829	–6.1	19.2	–2.9	16.4	0.1	13.6	–1.8	18.9	...	...
1830	–7.4	19.1	–4.6	17.1	1.3	14.3	–6.2	19.4	...	...
1831	–5.0	19.3	–3.3	19.7	1.5	15.2	–2.2	19.1	...	...
1832	–1.4	15.7	0.3	15.4	3.9	14.3	–0.8	20.4	...	...
1833	–3.5	17.5	–1.6	17.3	1.5	14.9	–1.0	17.2	...	...
1834	3.5	23.6	1.2	20.4	5.2	15.2	5.4	21.6	...	...
1835	0.8	19.3	0.7	17.8	3.3	14.2	0.8	21.8	...	...
1836	–1.1	17.6	–1.3	15.4	3.4	13.3	–0.4	20.4	...	...
1837	0.0	17.6	–1.4	16.1	1.7	15.3	0.0	18.8	...	...
1838	–10.2	18.2	–5.1	16.5	–0.8	15.1	–5.4	18.6	...	...
1839	–0.4	19.7	–1.9	16.7	1.9	14.8	–0.2	19.6	...	...
1840	–1.3	17.2	–2.7	12.6	4.0	13.3	2.2	16.8	...	...
1841	–2.2	17.3	–3.2	13.0	0.8	13.4	–1.0	16.7	1.1	14.3
1842	–3.7	17.5	–1.9	15.3	1.7	13.6	–2.3	18.6	0.4	15.6
1843	1.0	18.3	0.6	15.7	4.1	14.9	1.4	16.9	4.3	16.0
1844	–0.8	15.9	–1.7	13.9	5.1	13.8	–0.1	18.2	4.1	16.5
1845	0.0	19.9	–0.1	16.8	2.6	12.7	1.4	18.8	3.8	15.5
1846	0.3	20.2	–0.4	17.4	5.6	15.2	0.6	20.0	6.4	18.2
1847	–3.3	19.7	–1.2	17.4	2.3	16.4	–0.4	19.3	1.9	18.5
1848	–9.5	18.0	–4.3	15.8	0.9	15.1	–4.2	18.9	1.6	16.8
1849	–1.9	16.8	–1.9	15.1	2.7	13.8	–2.0	19.4	4.9	16.8

A2 Mean Temperature in January and July (in degrees Centigrade)

1800–1849

	Oslo		Rome		Stockholm		Utrecht/de Bilt		Vienna	
	Jan	July	Jan	July	Jan	July	Jan	July	Jan	July
1800	...	...	...	...	–6.0	15.4	...	...	–0.7	20.4
1801	...	...	...	...	–4.2	18.4	...	...	0.6	20.9
1802	...	...	...	...	–7.6	15.0	...	...	2.2	22.2
1803	...	...	...	...	–9.8	18.0	...	...	–5.0	21.4
1804	...	...	...	...	–4.5	19.5	...	...	2.6	21.3
1805	...	...	...	...	–5.9	17.7	...	...	–2.3	19.4
1806	...	...	...	...	–2.6	15.4	...	...	3.3	20.7
1807	...	...	...	...	–4.2	18.6	...	...	–0.3	22.6
1808	...	...	...	...	–2.1	17.8	...	...	–0.2	22.6
1809	...	...	...	...	–12.1	17.6	...	...	–1.7	21.4
1810	...	...	...	...	–2.1	18.1	...	...	–2.5	21.2
1811	...	...	7.4	25.6	–4.1	19.9	...	...	–6.2	24.3
1812	...	...	5.9	23.5	–4.2	14.5	...	...	–4.3	19.9
1813	...	...	6.7	22.9	–3.8	17.1	...	...	–4.0	19.3
1814	...	...	9.4	23.9	–14.3	19.2	...	...	–2.1	21.8
1815	...	...	6.1	22.5	–3.5	15.7	...	...	–3.0	19.1
1816	–5.2	16.4	7.5	22.7	–3.3	18.5	...	...	0.7	19.0
1817	–2.0	14.1	8.2	25.1	0.7	17.3	...	...	2.3	20.8
1818	–5.5	17.1	8.4	24.7	–3.0	20.8	...	...	1.8	21.3
1819	–0.9	18.1	7.0	24.2	1.2	20.2	...	...	–0.1	21.8
1820	–10.0	17.0	8.5	26.0	–8.6	16.7	...	...	–4.6	19.8
1821	–8.5	13.1	9.6	23.7	–4.1	14.9	...	...	1.1	18.8
1822	–2.6	15.9	6.5	26.9	–1.5	17.0	...	...	1.9	22.5
1823	–8.3	14.8	7.0	24.7	–5.7	16.8	...	...	–7.3	19.3
1824	–0.1	15.0	...	...	1.6	17.3	...	...	0.5	20.7
1825	0.4	15.6	6.5	23.0	–0.3	16.1	...	...	2.3	20.1
1826	–6.1	17.9	5.4	23.2	–5.6	21.1	...	...	–6.2	22.7
1827	–5.8	14.3	6.9	25.0	–5.2	15.8	...	...	–0.8	23.0
1828	–5.4	18.0	7.6	26.5	–4.7	18.5	...	...	–1.4	21.8
1829	–3.7	15.8	7.4	24.4	–5.0	17.4	...	...	–3.7	20.6
1830	–5.1	17.0	5.1	25.6	–5.6	17.8	...	...	–8.3	21.0
1831	–7.0	18.0	7.6	24.5	–8.4	18.6	...	...	–3.4	21.4
1832	–3.7	14.0	7.6	24.5	–2.1	12.9	...	...	–1.0	19.4
1833	–6.2	17.5	6.4	22.5	–2.6	15.9	...	...	–5.8	18.2
1834	–4.4	19.9	9.4	25.2	–3.7,	19.8	...	...	4.2	24.2
1835	–1.3	15.7	8.4	23.9	–1.8	16.1	...	...	0.5	22.1
1836	–5.6	15.1	6.0	24.5	–4.1	15.1	...	...	–1.8	20.4
1837	–7.8	16.3	7.6	23.6	–5.2	14.5	...	...	–1.4	17.4
1838	–8.7	17.2	9.4	23.5	–7.8	16.4	...	...	–8.1	19.3
1839	–5.4	17.0	6.9	24.2	–4.1	18.0	...	...	–0.3	21.5
1840	–5.0	14.3	8.5	23.5	–3.6	15.2	...	...	–0.4	19.1
1841	–8.8	14.3	8.1	25.1	–6.4	14.5	...	...	–1.3	19.6
1842	–4.8	15.5	6.6	25.4	–2.2	14.8	...	...	–5.2	20.2
1843	–2.5	16.9	7.7	22.2	–0.5	17.1	...	...	0.8	19.4
1844	–5.9	16.0	6.6	24.4	–5.0	14.0	...	...	–1.9	18.3
1845	–3.4	16.6	10.4	25.1	–0.4	17.6	...	...	0.6	20.9
1846	–3.6	17.3	7.6	25.7	–3.5	18.2	...	...	1.2	23.3
1847	–7.0	17.8	8.1	23.5	–4.0	15.9	...	...	–3.7	20.2
1848	–7.3	14.5	5.1	23.5	–6.6	16.9	...	...	–7.8	20.1
1849	–8.3	–15.5	5.6	23.7	–5.9	15.8	1.7	18.5	–2.7	19.5

A2 Mean Temperature in January and July (in degrees Centigrade)

1850–1899

	Athens		Belgrade		Berlin		Bucharest		Copenhagen		Edinburgh		Geneva		Leningrad	
	Jan	July	Jan	July	Jan	July	Jan	July	Jan	July	Jan	July	Jan	July	Jan	July
1850	...	...	...	...	–6.6	18.4	...	...	–4.4	16.6	–0.3	15.1	–2.4	18.4	...	...
1851	...	...	...	...	1.1	17.6	...	...	0.4	15.4	4.8	13.4	0.8	17.2	...	...
1852	...	...	...	...	3.3	20.8	...	...	1.8	19.3	3.9	17.8	2.4	19.8	...	...
1853	...	...	...	...	3.1	19.3	...	...	2.0	16.9	3.8	15.1	3.2	19.0	...	...
1854	...	...	...	...	–0.2	19.9	...	...	–1.8	17.1	2.7	15.3	0.0	18.6	...	...
1855	...	...	...	...	–1.9	18.3	...	...	–2.3	17.9	3.1	16.4	–1.5	18.2	...	...
1856	...	...	...	...	0.3	16.8	...	...	–0.9	14.1	2.7	15.2	2.4	18.4	...	...
1857	...	...	...	...	–1.5	19.5	–2.9	22.0	–2.6	16.6	3.3	16.1	–0.2	21.2	...	...
1858	...	...	...	...	–1.4	18.6	–7.6	23.9	0.0	17.7	4.8	13.1	–2.4	17.4	...	...
1859	...	...	...	...	1.9	21.3	–0.6	23.4	1.5	17.5	4.4	14.8	0.1	23.0	...	...
1860	...	...	...	...	2.0	17.6	–0.3	21.5	0.6	17.0	1.4	14.2	3.2	17.2	...	...
1861	...	...	...	...	–5.6	19.9	–5.4	24.8	–3.9	17.6	2.4	13.7	–2.5	17.9	...	...
1862	...	...	...	...	–1.9	17.2	–3.1	23.7	–2.0	14.2	3.4	12.5	1.0	20.6	...	...
1863	...	...	...	...	3.0	16.9	1.7	23.6	2.9	14.2	3.7	14.4	2.5	20.0	...	...
1864	...	...	...	...	–4.6	17.2	–5.8	22.6	–1.9	16.0	2.2	13.9	–3.2	20.2	...	...
1865	...	...	...	...	–0.1	21.8	–1.1	22.0	–0.4	17.9	1.7	14.9	2.7	20.6	...	...
1866	...	...	...	...	4.3	17.3	–2.2	24.4	3.2	15.6	4.4	14.4	3.7	19.1	...	...
1867	...	...	...	...	–0.3	17.1	0.6	23.2	–3.0	14.6	0.4	13.4	1.0	18.5	...	...
1868	...	...	...	...	–0.6	20.5	–4.1	21.7	–1.3	18.7	3.3	16.8	–0.5	20.0	...	...
1869	...	...	...	...	0.1	20.6	–5.7	22.0	1.2	16.5	4.6	15.6	1.0	21.5	...	...
1870	...	...	...	...	1.0	19.5	–1.3	24.3	0.4	17.0	2.5	16.0	0.3	22.2	...	...
1871	10.9	28.4	...	...	–5.0	18.9	–2.8	25.1	–3.5	16.6	1.9	14.4	–2.7	19.9	–10.5	19.4
1872	9.5	27.1	...	...	0.8	20.5	0.1	22.5	0.9	18.3	3.6	15.1	1.1	20.3	–4.7	16.5
1873	11.0	27.6	...	...	4.1	20.2	1.9	25.0	3.4	17.5	4.8	15.6	2.2	21.4	–5.7	18.3
1874	7.7	27.7	...	...	3.1	21.4	–4.2	25.1	2.9	17.4	4.8	15.6	0.3	21.4	–2.5	16.5
1875	7.3	27.7	...	...	1.8	19.6	–2.5	21.7	–0.7	16.8	4.9	13.9	2.6	17.9	–14.7	18.2
1876	7.6	26.4	...	...	–2.1	19.6	–6.9	21.6	–1.1	17.5	4.7	15.1	–1.3	20.7	–9.9	17.8
1877	9.5	27.1	...	...	3.1	19.5	–1.8	23.0	0.6	16.4	4.0	14.3	4.0	19.3	–10.3	17.0
1878	7.0	27.6	...	...	1.9	17.4	–5.7	21.6	–0.1	16.0	3.6	16.1	–0.5	19.1	–9.2	14.1
1879	9.4	27.6	...	...	–2.3	17.2	–4.0	22.7	–3.3	15.0	–0.4	12.4	0.0	16.8	–10.2	15.0
1880	5.2	28.3	...	...	–0.8	19.9	–6.9	23.3	–1.8	17.3	2.8	14.2	–3.7	20.7	–8.4	16.9
1881	11.4	26.5	...	...	–4.6	20.2	–5.3	21.7	–4.4	16.3	–1.6	14.7	–1.4	22.7	–11.7	17.1
1882	7.0	27.1	...	...	1.9	19.4	–2.6	23.1	2.1	17.5	5.6	14.3	0.1	17.5	–1.4	18.8
1883	8.8	27.5	...	...	0.3	18.7	–6.4	23.6	–0.6	17.6	3.9	13.4	2.0	18.0	–12.8	17.3
1884	6.8	26.3	...	...	3.9	19.8	–4.2	19.9	2.6	17.5	5.2	13.9	3.0	20.3	–6.5	17.0
1885	8.2	26.1	...	...	–1.7	18.9	–4.4	21.9	–0.4	17.3	2.8	15.6	–1.8	20.8	–6.6	20.8
1886	11.5	26.7	...	...	–0.6	17.9	0.0	20.3	–0.4	15.9	1.6	14.7	–0.6	20.1	–9.4	18.0
1887	8.6	27.5	...	...	–2.5	20.2	–0.3	23.5	–0.7	17.7	4.0	16.3	–2.2	21.6	–4.2	17.7
1888	6.3	29.5	–6.5	21.2	–0.5	16.7	–10.0	22.8	–0.9	14.9	4.1	12.9	–1.2	17.3	–11.4	15.7
1889	7.8	28.4	–4.0	21.4	–2.4	18.3	–7.9	23.8	–0.5	16.5	4.3	14.7	–0.3	18.9	–7.8	17.2
1890	8.6	28.8	1.3	22.1	2.7	17.8	–3.7	23.7	1.9	15.3	5.3	13.7	1.5	18.1	–5.7	17.5
1891	7.7	27.6	–6.4	22.4	–3.0	18.5	–6.4	23.0	–3.5	17.6	2.7	14.9	–4.4	18.6	–9.0	18.3
1892	10.8	26.4	0.4	21.0	–1.5	18.1	–3.4	21.3	–1.1	15.7	2.6	13.3	0.2	18.7	–10.6	16.2
1893	7.3	27.4	–9.4	21.5	–7.4	19.3	–10.6	21.4	–6.7	17.9	3.1	14.3	–3.7	19.7	–15.3	16.1
1894	7.9	28.0	–2.3	24.7	–0.9	20.5	–7.5	24.8	–0.2	18.0	3.3	15.0	–0.4	19.7	–3.9	16.7
1895	11.9	27.8	1.3	23.1	–2.6	19.4	1.8	24.3	–1.7	16.1	–0.1	14.0	–3.3	20.1	–7.8	16.5
1896	5.7	27.0	–6.5	21.9	0.1	19.3	–4.4	23.1	0.4	18.6	5.1	14.7	–0.8	19.3	–6.4	19.1
1897	10.5	27.4	0.6	22.2	–2.8	18.2	–1.8	22.7	–2.1	16.6	1.7	15.1	–0.5	20.1	–10.0	18.3
1898	8.5	26.6	0.8	20.4	3.2	15.6	–1.1	21.4	3.3	14.2	7.0	14.7	1.4	18.5	–3.7	16.8
1899	10.7	26.7	4.8	20.9	2.9	19.7	–0.8	22.6	1.6	19.0	3.4	15.5	4.1	19.1	–6.9	19.6

A2 Mean Temperature in January and July (in degrees Centigrade)

1850–1899

	Lisbon		London		Madrid		Marseilles		Milan		Moscow		Oslo	
	Jan	July	Jan	July	Jan	July	Jan	July	Jan	July	Jan	July	Jan	July
1850	...	...	1.2	16.8	...	...	...	...	...	...	...	...	–10.1	17.1
1851	...	...	6.1	15.7	...	...	...	...	...	...	...	...	–2.5	14.1
1852	...	...	5.5	19.4	...	...	...	...	...	...	...	...	–2.4	19.1
1853	...	...	5.9	16.1	...	...	...	...	...	...	...	...	–1.5	16.9
1854	...	...	4.1	16.1	...	...	...	...	...	...	...	...	–5.8	18.6
1855	...	...	1.6	17.0	...	...	...	...	...	...	...	...	–6.3	20.8
1856	...	...	4.0	16.4	...	...	...	...	...	...	...	...	–5.1	14.9
1857	...	...	2.7	18.4	...	...	...	...	...	...	...	...	–7.1	16.1
1858	...	...	3.1	16.3	...	...	...	...	...	...	...	...	–1.1	17.8
1859	...	...	4.7	20.5	...	...	...	...	...	...	...	...	–1.0	18.1
1860	...	...	4.4	14.6	6.9	24.5	...	...	...	...	...	...	–5.0	16.3
1861	...	...	1.1	16.4	5.0	24.1	...	...	...	...	...	...	–8.6	16.6
1862	...	...	4.1	15.3	4.8	26.4	...	...	...	...	...	...	–5.6	14.0
1863	...	...	5.7	16.3	4.4	26.3	...	...	...	...	...	...	–0.3	15.1
1864	9.3	21.1	2.6	16.8	4.2	25.8	...	...	...	...	...	...	–5.4	17.1
1865	11.6	21.7	2.5	18.1	5.9	25.1	...	...	...	...	...	...	–3.4	16.9
1866	10.2	20.5	6.2	16.6	4.8	24.4	...	...	2.9	24.7	...	...	0.0	16.9
1867	12.3	20.1	1.4	15.6	6.0	25.6	...	...	0.7	23.9	...	...	–10.3	16.3
1868	9.8	20.8	3.1	20.1	4.1	25.3	...	...	–1.8	23.3	...	...	–5.8	19.4
1869	11.3	21.2	5.2	18.2	5.7	27.0	...	...	0.0	26.0	...	...	–3.5	17.3
1870	8.6	22.3	3.6	18.9	3.1	27.1	...	...	–0.5	25.1	...	...	–4.3	18.0
1871	9.1	21.4	0.8	16.7	1.6	27.1	3.0	21.6	–1.4	25.4	...	...	–7.4	16.3
1872	11.4	20.7	5.3	18.6	5.6	26.5	7.7	22.7	1.1	24.6	...	...	–0.5	19.0
1873	11.2	20.8	5.7	17.8	5.6	27.2	9.2	23.3	3.8	26.3	...	...	–0.1	18.0
1874	11.0	21.0	5.5	18.3	5.9	27.2	7.4	22.4	–0.3	26.0	...	...	0.9	17.4
1875	10.9	19.1	6.4	15.5	5.9	23.7	8.8	20.9	1.2	22.6	...	...	–8.6	17.9
1876	8.4	23.7	2.9	19.3	3.1	28.8	7.5	23.0	–0.3	25.3	...	...	–3.7	17.7
1877	12.4	22.3	6.1	16.4	6.5	25.7	8.8	23.1	4.2	24.1	...	...	–6.3	15.9
1878	9.7	21.7	4.7	17.3	4.0	26.7	5.9	22.6	0.9	24.2	...	...	–5.6	17.0
1879	11.6	20.0	–0.1	14.6	6.4	26.8	7.5	20.2	1.4	23.8	...	...	–6.2	16.7
1880	9.2	19.1	0.7	16.4	3.1	26.6	6.0	23.1	–3.4	25.9	...	...	–5.0	16.3
1881	11.4	21.8	–0.2	18.6	5.4	26.5	6.2	23.0	–0.7	26.6	–13.2	18.2	–8.7	15.9
1882	10.1	20.3	4.7	15.7	5.6	24.0	9.1	21.1	1.9	23.5	–3.0	20.1	0.2	16.6
1883	10.9	19.5	5.2	15.4	5.3	24.5	7.7	21.2	1.9	23.0	–16.6	18.7	–5.3	17.4
1884	11.2	21.4	6.6	17.3	6.1	24.6	8.3	22.4	2.6	24.3	–10.0	17.0	–3.2	17.2
1885	9.4	19.5	2.6	17.6	2.3	23.5	5.9	23.7	0.2	25.2	–11.0	22.1	–6.0	17.3
1886	9.7	21.6	2.4	17.3	3.9	24.9	6.1	21.8	0.2	24.2	–9.0	17.9	–3.0	16.9
1887	10.1	22.2	2.1	19.2	4.8	26.2	5.4	23.1	–1.4	25.1	–7.8	17.9	–1.5	16.7
1888	9.8	19.7	3.3	14.4	4.8	22.8	5.8	20.0	–1.0	21.7	–14.2	17.2	–3.8	16.2
1889	9.3	20.0	2.9	16.1	4.2	24.6	6.9	21.6	2.1	23.1	–15.0	18.1	–1.6	16.7
1890	10.9	20.5	6.4	15.3	5.5	24.6	9.3	20.0	2.6	22.2	–7.8	20.2	0.4	14.8
1891	8.4	21.1	1.2	15.6	2.5	25.9	3.6	21.8	–1.5	23.7	–17.6	19.9	–5.9	17.6
1892	10.1	20.9	2.6	15.3	4.9	25.3	7.8	22.2	0.8	23.5	–13.0	17.5	–7.2	16.9
1893	9.9	22.7	1.9	17.2	4.1	25.2	3.0	22.7	2.6	23.5	–21.6	19.1	–8.2	18.1
1894	10.0	20.8	3.6	16.6	3.2	25.1	6.2	22.9	–0.4	25.3	–9.2	16.8	–1.7	19.0
1895	9.7	21.0	0.9	17.1	3.2	24.2	3.6	23.0	–0.5	24.6	–8.6	18.9	–6.9	15.5
1896	9.9	21.5	4.7	18.4	4.9	25.0	6.1	22.9	0.3	23.7	–13.5	18.7	–4.8	19.2
1897	9.3	22.3	1.9	18.1	3.8	25.6	7.3	23.9	3.5	25.2	–10.8	20.5	–5.5	19.6
1898	10.7	22.5	6.5	16.6	6.2	26.0	9.4	21.9	3.3	23.1	–7.8	19.0	0.6	15.5
1899	11.0	23.1	6.0	18.8	4.6	25.1	9.2	22.1	5.5	24.6	–4.4	18.5	–5.6	19.9

A2 Mean Temperature in January and July (in degrees Centigrade)

1850–1899

	Paris		Rome		Stockholm		Tiflis		Utrecht/de Bilt		Valentia		Vienna	
	Jan	July	Jan	July	Jan	July	Jan	July	Jan	July	Jan	July	Jan	July
1850	...	...	4.2	23.1	–8.6	17.8	...	...	–3.3	18.5	...	...	–5.3	19.3
1851	0.2	16.8	7.7	23.2	–1.8	16.6	...	...	3.9	17.5	...	...	–1.4	17.9
1852	4.1	21.5	7.6	23.7	–1.6	19.8	...	...	4.3	22.3	...	...	0.7	20.8
1853	5.4	17.5	8.4	24.4	–0.3	18.9	...	...	5.2	18.7	...	...	0.7	19.9
1854	2.4	18.3	9.2	23.7	–4.4	19.6	...	...	2.0	18.8	...	...	–1.3	19.4
1855	–0.4	17.8	5.2	24.4	–5.6	21.4	...	...	–0.4	18.3	...	...	–2.9	19.2
1856	4.6	17.5	10.4	24.6	–4.1	16.4	...	...	3.0	17.4	...	...	–0.1	17.1
1857	1.8	19.5	6.3	23.9	–5.9	16.9	...	...	0.9	19.8	...	...	–1.8	21.1
1858	–0.1	16.5	4.0	24.5	–1.5	19.9	...	...	0.8	17.5	...	...	–3.6	19.0
1859	3.1	22.0	4.4	25.4	0.1	17.0	...	...	3.6	21.7	...	...	–0.8	23.1
1860	4.3	15.8	7.9	23.2	–1.8	16.4	...	...	3.5	17.0	...	...	1.1	16.8
1861	–1.7	17.5	7.4	24.3	–8.6	18.1	...	...	–2.4	19.3	...	...	–4.5	19.4
1862	2.4	17.6	6.6	24.8	–7.3	14.0	...	...	1.8	17.4	...	...	–3.0	19.8
1863	4.5	17.7	8.9	25.1	0.8	14.3	...	...	5.0	17.8	...	...	3.0	19.0
1864	0.6	18.2	3.7	25.1	–4.1	16.0	...	...	–1.1	17.7	...	...	–6.9	17.5
1865	2.4	19.0	8.5	25.7	–2.8	18.5	...	...	1.6	19.7	...	...	–0.3	21.8
1866	5.1	17.9	7.0	25.3	1.4	14.3	...	...	5.8	17.6	...	...	0.9	18.6
1867	1.5	16.7	9.3	24.6	–9.4	14.6	...	...	0.9	16.5	...	...	–0.6	18.3
1868	0.4	20.6	6.6	23.6	–5.5	18.5	...	...	0.9	22.0	...	...	–1.6	19.9
1869	2.8	19.5	4.8	25.5	–2.1	16.0	...	...	2.2	19.3	8.7	16.3	–2.4	21.0
1870	3.0	20.4	5.2	25.3	–1.0	17.0	...	...	2.6	20.0	6.8	16.1	–1.3	20.0
1871	–1.6	18.2	6.7	24.9	–5.2	16.5	...	...	–2.0	18.6	6.2	14.7	–4.4	19.6
1872	3.7	19.7	7.6	24.7	0.0	18.7	...	...	3.5	21.4	7.6	15.4	–1.5	20.1
1873	4.7	19.1	7.6	26.1	1.9	18.3	...	...	4.7	20.7	7.5	14.7	1.2	21.3
1874	4.2	20.5	5.8	25.8	1.3	16.9	...	...	4.5	20.7	7.9	15.6	–0.8	22.1
1875	5.2	16.8	7.8	24.2	–9.1	17.1	...	...	4.2	19.0	9.6	14.5	–0.3	19.6
1876	–0.3	20.0	6.7	24.1	–3.4	17.7	...	...	–0.4	19.8	7.6	15.4	–4.9	19.7
1877	6.2	17.5	8.0	25.3	–4.4	16.4	...	...	4.8	18.5	8.1	14.2	1.3	19.2
1878	2.3	18.0	5.8	23.9	–2.6	14.7	...	...	3.2	18.5	8.3	16.7	–1.6	18.4
1879	0.0	15.6	8.2	23.0	–5.2	16.0	...	...	–1.2	16.5	5.3	13.1	–2.1	17.1
1880	–1.2	18.4	3.7	26.1	–3.0	17.1	...	...	0.1	18.6	6.8	14.9	–2.3	20.9
1881	–1.3	20.1	8.4	26.3	–7.5	15.8	1.4	23.3	–2.3	20.3	3.7	14.4	–4.9	20.9
1882	2.0	16.9	6.9	24.6	1.2	17.0	0.2	26.0	2.8	18.0	8.7	13.9	0.5	19.5
1883	4.0	16.6	7.7	23.9	–3.1	16.9	–3.3	26.2	2.7	17.8	7.9	13.5	–1.8	19.1
1884	5.6	19.3	6.9	24.7	–1.3	16.8	–0.4	23.5	5.8	20.4	8.8	14.9	2.3	20.1
1885	–0.2	18.5	6.0	25.2	–4.1	16.9	–2.1	25.1	0.1	19.2	6.9	15.2	–4.0	19.9
1886	2.2	18.3	7.4	24.6	–3.1	16.7	1.4	22.0	1.1	18.6	5.5	15.0	–1.8	19.3
1887	–0.2	19.4	5.7	26.1	–0.7	17.2	–1.1	22.3	0.1	19.9	7.5	16.4	–3.9	21.9
1888	0.9	15.7	5.1	23.6	–3.4	15.2	0.5	23.5	0.8	16.2	7.2	13.9	–2.7	17.7
1889	1.1	17.8	5.8	24.5	–1.3	15.7	–4.1	25.2	1.2	17.6	7.5	14.6	–2.6	19.2
1890	5.8	16.3	8.0	23.3	0.8	15.2	–1.1	24.2	4.6	17.1	7.9	13.7	1.2	18.6
1891	–0.8	16.8	4.7	24.7	–4.6	18.2	0.2	24.0	–1.3	17.5	5.9	14.3	–6.3	18.4
1892	2.0	17.8	8.1	24.8	–5.5	15.3	1.6	25.0	1.0	17.4	5.6	14.7	–1.2	18.4
1893	–1.3	18.8	4.2	25.0	–7.4	17.0	–2.1	23.9	–1.4	19.2	6.5	15.8	–7.9	19.3
1894	2.5	18.4	6.4	25.5	–0.8	17.5	–2.0	23.0	1.8	19.0	5.8	14.3	–4.2	20.3
1895	–0.2	17.8	6.9	24.9	–5.3	16.1	0.3	23.2	–0.3	18.3	4.2	14.3	–2.7	20.3
1896	2.5	18.9	4.8	25.1	–2.0	19.4	2.1	22.4	2.7	19.7	7.6	15.2	–4.6	19.5
1897	2.2	18.5	7.5	26.3	–4.7	17.7	1.3	24.6	–1.3	18.4	4.7	16.0	–1.2	19.1
1898	3.6	17.1	6.7	23.7	1.4	15.3	–2.0	26.3	4.9	16.3	9.1	15.9	0.4	17.9
1899	6.0	19.6	9.1	23.6	–3.6	19.7	0.9	26.2	4.3	20.0	6.7	15.8	2.4	19.2

A2 Mean Temperature in January and July (in degrees Centigrade)

1900–1949

	Athens		Belgrade		Berlin		Bucharest		Copenhagen		Edinburgh		Geneva		Leningrad	
	Jan	July	Jan	July	Jan	July	Jan	July	Jan	July	Jan	July	Jan	July	Jan	July
1900	11.4	26.9	2.1	...	0.9	20.7	–2.5	22.9	–0.4	17.7	4.0	16.1	2.8	21.0	–8.6	16.3
1901	7.4	27.4	–4.7	...	–3.1	21.1	–6.9	22.0	–1.5	19.9	3.6	16.6	0.0	19.6	–3.2	19.3
1902	9.9	26.7	3.1	21.0	4.1	17.0	1.1	21.8	2.8	14.7	3.7	13.1	1.1	19.9	–9.2	14.9
1903	8.9	26.1	0.8	...	1.1	18.7	–3.8	22.0	0.3	16.4	3.1	14.1	1.1	18.3	–6.6	16.5
1904	9.0	27.1	–1.1	...	–0.3	20.3	–3.8	24.3	0.2	17.1	4.3	14.4	0.0	21.9	–3.1	14.3
1905	7.0	27.5	–4.4	...	–0.5	19.8	–6.9	24.2	–0.2	17.6	4.3	16.0	–1.8	22.0	–8.5	16.9
1906	9.3	27.2	0.1	...	1.8	19.4	–5.3	23.1	0.9	17.1	4.5	14.1	1.9	19.7	–4.9	18.6
1907	6.5	27.0	–1.8	21.7	0.2	16.2	–7.3	22.6	–0.3	15.6	3.9	13.1	0.2	17.8	–12.5	17.7
1908	8.8	26.6	–2.4	21.3	–0.1	19.8	–4.3	22.2	0.0	18.4	3.3	14.7	–1.6	19.0	–8.0	16.6
1909	7.4	27.6	–3.1	21.2	–0.5	17.4	–6.2	24.0	–0.1	15.4	4.2	13.8	–1.2	17.2	–4.4	16.3
1910	8.8	26.6	2.6	20.3	2.5	17.7	–0.1	22.3	1.0	17.1	2.8	13.4	2.1	17.2	–5.4	17.5
1911	8.1	25.8	0.5	22.8	1.0	20.5	–0.4	23.1	1.2	17.1	4.6	15.9	–1.7	21.9	–6.3	15.9
1912	7.6	26.3	–1.6	21.4	–2.3	20.8	–5.9	21.2	–2.5	18.9	3.1	14.1	2.4	18.2	–11.8	17.2
1913	9.1	25.3	–0.6	18.2	–0.1	17.3	–3.0	20.1	0.0	16.3	3.2	14.1	3.3	16.4	–6.0	19.0
1914	9.1	26.3	–5.5	...	–1.7	20.6	–5.6	22.0	–0.8	20.3	3.7	14.9	–2.8	17.5	–8.7	21.1
1915	12.0	27.2	...	...	0.9	18.2	2.2	22.5	–0.4	16.0	3.4	14.2	1.9	18.5	–7.9	19.1
1916	9.1	28.6	3.1	21.6	4.1	17.7	1.4	22.7	2.9	16.8	6.8	14.3	3.0	18.1	–4.9	19.4
1917	11.2	27.4	1.4	21.8	–1.9	19.3	–0.2	22.2	–1.6	18.0	2.1	15.3	–0.9	19.1	–11.0	15.9
1918	10.0	27.4	2.7	21.7	1.0	18.5	1.4	22.5	–0.7	16.5	2.7	14.7	1.0	18.9	–10.7	17.9
1919	11.5	26.7	...	...	1.7	16.8	0.9	21.3	1.3	16.0	3.2	13.6	1.6	16.3	–5.3	19.5
1920	10.2	27.3	3.6	22.3	2.4	20.0	0.0	23.3	0.6	17.4	4.0	13.4	3.9	19.1	–9.6	19.7
1921	10.8	28.0	4.9	22.9	5.0	20.5	2.9	22.7	3.2	17.3	6.0	16.1	4.1	22.0	–7.6	15.7
1922	9.7	28.3	–1.5	22.7	–3.2	17.5	–4.6	23.9	–1.5	15.4	2.9	12.9	0.8	17.9	–9.9	17.7
1923	9.6	26.8	1.4	23.1	2.8	20.1	–1.7	21.7	2.4	17.2	5.9	15.5	1.1	21.8	–3.8	17.1
1924	6.8	28.1	–3.5	20.7	–2.3	18.7	–7.1	22.5	–2.6	15.6	4.4	14.3	0.6	19.2	–10.0	17.2
1925	8.4	27.3	0.6	21.3	3.9	20.5	–2.1	22.9	3.7	19.2	5.0	15.6	2.5	18.7	–0.4	20.3
1926	11.3	26.6	0.8	19.6	0.5	19.9	–2.6	22.6	0.9	18.6	4.9	15.7	1.2	18.7	–12.8	17.9
1927	10.7	28.9	2.4	23.9	3.0	20.0	–0.9	23.7	2.7	18.1	4.3	15.0	1.9	19.2	–9.6	21.9
1928	10.5	28.7	0.5	26.0	2.2	20.1	–2.9	24.5	0.9	15.9	4.8	14.3	2.7	23.2	–5.8	15.1
1929	8.3	27.4	–4.0	21.7	–3.7	19.5	–4.5	21.9	–2.2	16.0	2.4	15.0	–2.6	20.4	–10.2	17.9
1930	10.2	27.9	1.7	23.1	3.2	18.5	–1.1	23.5	3.3	17.4	4.2	14.6	2.9	18.4	0.8	18.5
1931	11.3	29.0	1.5	24.2	0.2	18.5	–0.2	24.2	0.7	16.5	3.1	14.3	2.3	18.6	–7.7	19.2
1932	8.5	28.2	–1.1	23.4	1.7	19.9	–2.6	23.9	3.1	18.9	6.5	14.8	1.5	18.2	–2.3	20.2
1933	8.9	26.3	–3.1	21.1	–3.0	19.2	–6.4	21.0	0.0	18.2	3.1	16.6	–1.3	20.6	–8.8	18.8
1934	9.6	27.9	–1.2	21.7	1.2	19.6	–5.4	22.3	1.7	18.8	5.2	16.6	1.1	20.9	–3.0	20.0
1935	9.0	27.6	–4.0	22.2	–0.5	18.8	–4.4	21.7	0.3	17.6	4.5	15.3	–0.3	21.1	–8.0	15.7
1936	13.5	28.6	6.7	24.9	3.3	18.4	4.2	25.7	2.8	17.8	2.7	14.6	5.3	18.1	–4.3	20.6
1937	8.8	29.0	–1.1	21.9	–3.0	18.3	–4.3	25.0	–0.3	18.0	4.5	14.4	2.9	20.6	–7.5	18.2
1938	9.7	29.2	–0.2	22.7	1.8	18.8	–4.0	24.2	2.1	17.4	4.8	14.2	2.6	18.7	–6.7	21.6
1939	11.6	29.2	...	...	3.0	18.6	0.4	23.7	1.9	17.8	3.1	14.4	3.4	18.4	–7.4	19.0
1940	8.1	28.1	...	...	–9.6	17.8	–6.9	22.5	–4.1	17.3	0.2	13.6	–2.8	18.2	–14.6	19.2
1941	11.2	28.6	0.3	20.6	–6.3	20.2	–4.0	21.8	–5.8	19.9	0.1	15.1	–0.1	20.7	–14.0	21.1
1942	7.0	27.2	–7.8	23.7	–7.2	17.2	–10.3	22.3	–0.4	16.0	1.7	14.4	–2.2	20.1	–18.7	16.6
1943	7.8	27.9	–1.6	22.9	–0.6	19.1	–6.2	22.2	–0.6	17.9	3.8	14.3	1.8	20.0	–11.8	17.5
1944	8.7	27.4	2.4	21.7	4.0	19.4	–2.8	21.9	3.0	18.6	5.4	14.6	1.8	19.7	3.4	18.5
1945	8.6	28.6	–1.8	23.5	–2.9	...	–4.0	24.2	–1.0	18.2	0.9	15.6	–2.9	21.8	–6.6	19.1
1946	9.3	28.8	–2.4	25.4	–0.8	20.7	–4.3	25.7	0.2	18.8	3.2	15.1	–0.2	20.9	–5.7	18.7
1947	7.1	28.0	–6.3	23.3	–5.3	19.8	–8.9	23.8	–2.4	18.2	2.3	14.8	–1.1	21.5	–8.4	17.1
1948	12.6	26.7	7.0	20.9	2.7	18.0	4.0	21.9	1.1	17.5	3.4	14.3	4.1	17.2	–7.7	16.7
1949	9.0	26.2	2.4	20.7	1.6	18.4	0.9	22.0	2.2	18.7	5.1	15.7	1.6	21.6	–2.2	17.1

A2 Mean Temperature in January and July (in degrees Centigrade)

1900–1949

	Lisbon		London		Madrid		Marseilles		Milan		Moscow		Oslo	
	Jan	July	Jan	July	Jan	July	Jan	July	Jan	July	Jan	July	Jan	July
1900	10.4	22.5	4.6	19.2	4.8	25.5	7.8	22.2	3.4	25.5	–13.8	17.1	–3.6	17.1
1901	10.5	21.9	3.8	18.2	4.8	24.2	6.9	22.5	1.1	23.6	–6.6	17.4	–5.7	22.7
1902	10.4	20.6	5.6	16.1	4.2	24.7	7.3	22.3	2.3	25.2	–7.7	16.2	–1.2	14.9
1903	10.1	21.5	5.1	16.4	4.3	23.8	7.5	21.6	1.7	23.7	–8.0	18.6	–5.8	16.2
1904	10.5	20.7	4.2	18.6	4.5	25.5	7.3	24.6	3.3	26.4	–7.6	14.6	–1.5	18.0
1905	9.7	21.7	3.6	18.9	3.8	24.5	5.1	24.9	0.0	25.9	–12.1	16.4	–2.5	18.1
1906	11.1	21.7	5.8	17.4	5.6	24.1	6.9	22.1	1.5	24.2	–6.9	18.6	–2.3	17.1
1907	9.3	20.2	3.8	14.8	3.9	23.4	5.4	21.0	–0.4	23.7	–15.9	17.8	–4.9	15.6
1908	10.9	21.3	2.7	16.8	6.1	24.2	6.8	22.1	1.9	23.5	–11.6	16.7	–3.7	17.6
1909	9.9	22.1	3.8	15.6	3.4	23.7	5.7	20.4	1.4	23.5	–10.5	16.1	–1.7	16.1
1910	10.3	20.5	4.4	14.5	4.1	23.2	7.0	20.4	2.8	22.7	–7.8	18.2	–4.5	16.7
1911	8.3	22.7	3.4	19.6	2.6	25.0	5.3	24.4	0.5	25.9	–11.5	15.5	–2.5	18.2
1912	10.8	18.4	4.6	17.4	4.4	21.8	8.8	21.6	3.1	23.4	–15.9	14.7	–7.3	18.6
1913	12.3	21.4	5.1	14.7	5.9	24.6	9.7	20.3	1.8	22.0	–9.9	17.4	–4.3	18.3
1914	9.6	20.2	3.0	16.9	2.0	23.1	3.5	21.0	–0.1	23.1	–10.3	19.5	–5.9	21.8
1915	10.3	21.6	4.3	15.9	4.4	25.0	5.8	21.5	1.5	23.7	–6.5	18.3	–5.0	15.9
1916	10.8	20.5	7.7	15.4	5.1	23.9	8.6	22.0	2.2	23.3	–6.0	17.1	–0.9	17.6
1917	10.0	22.2	1.9	16.8	3.7	25.8	4.9	22.6	0.7	23.9	–11.9	17.6	–10.9	17.1
1918	11.5	21.9	4.2	17.0	5.4	24.4	7.6	22.3	0.7	24.2	–7.4	17.5	–6.4	17.2
1919	10.9	20.7	3.2	14.2	4.1	23.0	6.4	20.1	4.0	21.7	–9.5	18.6	–1.7	19.2
1920	11.0	20.5	5.2	15.2	...	...	8.3	22.1	5.4	24.2	–9.7	20.8	–5.0	16.3
1921	11.2	22.8	7.8	19.8	5.2	24.4	8.0	23.8	5.2	24.9	–9.7	15.9	–1.7	17.8
1922	11.1	20.8	4.6	14.8	5.1	23.7	6.8	21.0	1.0	23.6	–10.5	18.6	–5.4	16.0
1923	9.4	22.2	5.3	19.1	4.0	24.5	4.7	25.1	2.8	25.8	–7.5	16.1	0.5	17.3
1924	11.1	21.6	4.9	16.4	5.5	24.3	6.7	24.0	0.7	24.5	–13.9	16.4	–3.7	15.8
1925	11.0	20.8	5.4	17.8	5.1	21.1	8.0	22.3	3.4	23.0	–3.7	19.5	–0.1	20.0
1926	11.9	22.6	4.7	17.3	4.2	23.3	6.3	22.6	0.1	23.5	–12.4	17.2	–3.1	18.7
1927	11.3	20.0	5.0	16.1	5.1	21.8	6.4	23.0	3.5	24.5	–14.8	19.0	–0.8	18.4
1928	10.4	24.2	5.1	18.7	4.1	25.3	7.0	24.6	3.5	27.8	–7.4	16.8	–2.9	14.7
1929	9.9	21.6	1.6	17.4	3.1	23.7	3.4	23.3	–0.7	25.0	–11.5	18.7	–5.6	16.6
1930	11.1	21.1	6.7	16.4	6.1	22.8	9.2	22.3	2.3	23.4	–4.8	17.3	1.4	17.5
1931	10.7	20.5	3.9	16.3	5.6	24.1	5.7	22.5	2.6	24.5	–11.2	20.4	–5.3	16.6
1932	10.1	20.7	6.7	16.9	4.7	22.4	7.4	19.8	3.4	22.3	–4.0	19.3	1.1	17.6
1933	9.7	22.3	3.0	19.1	4.1	26.4	4.9	22.9	1.8	25.4	–13.1	19.8	–2.2	19.2
1934	9.3	21.3	4.2	19.1	3.6	25.8	5.2	23.6	1.6	25.1	–7.4	19.6	0.1	18.4
1935	8.6	21.3	4.8	18.9	3.5	25.9	3.8	23.8	0.1	25.6	–11.1	15.2	–3.0	18.6
1936	12.7	19.9	4.9	16.0	7.7	22.9	9.4	22.4	5.1	24.4	–4.9	22.9	–2.6	17.6
1937	10.8	22.0	5.5	17.3	...	26.1	9.0	24.0	...	...	–11.6	17.8	–2.6	18.6
1938	10.4	20.6	6.4	16.3	4.5	24.3	5.1	22.7	...	...	–8.9	23.5	–3.0	16.6
1939	12.4	20.8	5.4	16.2	7.2	23.9	8.0	21.8	...	...	–8.6	20.4	–3.9	16.1
1940	11.5	20.4	–0.7	15.9	3.8	23.9	3.0	21.5	...	...	–19.4	19.2	–8.0	16.2
1941	9.4	22.1	1.2	18.9	3.5	23.2	3.8	23.5	0.5	24.8	–14.2	21.0	–13.0	19.2
1942	10.5	22.2	0.8	16.5	4.8	23.8	2.4	22.8	0.6	25.1	–20.2	18.0	–12.1	16.3
1943	12.6	21.6	5.5	17.5	6.2	22.2	8.0	...	0.8	25.3	–15.3	17.6	–5.5	16.9
1944	10.0	22.0	6.7	17.2	5.2	23.2	...	...	2.4	24.6	–3.7	18.2	–2.2	17.8
1945	8.3	21.2	0.8	17.8	2.0	24.6	...	...	1.8	27.9	–10.6	18.1	–5.3	18.6
1946	10.0	23.4	3.4	17.6	3.3	24.2	6.0	23.2	1.1	26.3	–8.0	18.6	–4.4	17.5
1947	10.0	21.5	1.9	18.4	3.9	25.4	3.4	24.4	2.6	26.9	–10.3	18.2	–3.7	18.5
1948	12.4	21.7	6.4	16.5	6.3	23.6	8.0	21.1	3.7	22.7	–7.8	16.4	–7.0	17.5
1949	11.2	23.4	5.9	18.9	6.4	25.9	6.8	23.8	2.9	25.2	–3.8	17.3	–0.3	18.3

A2 Mean Temperature in January and July (in degrees Centigrade)

1900–1949

	Paris		Rome		Stockholm		Tiflis		Utrecht/de Bilt		Valentia		Vienna	
	Jan	July	Jan	July	Jan	July	Jan	July	Jan	July	Jan	July	Jan	July
1900	4.8	21.6	8.4	24.0	–2.8	17.0	1.5	23.5	3.3	20.5	7.3	16.0	0.4	20.4
1901	2.7	19.8	5.1	24.7	–3.1	21.2	1.0	24.8	0.0	20.8	7.0	15.6	–4.5	20.5
1902	4.2	18.2	7.4	25.2	–1.1	13.7	1.9	23.7	4.8	17.3	7.6	14.8	3.3	17.6
1903	3.5	17.7	6.7	25.5	–3.1	16.5	0.4	23.6	3.2	17.3	6.9	15.0	–2.4	18.4
1904	1.9	21.1	8.2	26.2	–0.1	15.8	–3.0	23.6	1.1	20.3	6.9	15.2	–2.0	21.2
1905	1.4	19.9	4.1	26.2	–3.1	16.9	–0.2	24.2	1.5	19.9	8.1	15.9	–2.8	20.9
1906	4.7	18.7	6.4	24.2	–0.7	17.5	0.0	23.1	3.8	18.9	7.7	14.8	0.4	19.0
1907	2.5	16.3	5.7	23.0	–3.7	14.9	0.2	24.4	2.0	15.4	6.8	14.9	–0.7	17.3
1908	–0.1	18.1	5.9	24.3	–2.0	16.1	0.6	22.9	–0.7	18.3	6.4	15.1	–2.2	19.1
1909	1.4	15.7	5.9	22.1	–1.2	15.4	–1.1	26.1	1.2	16.0	7.7	14.3	–2.1	17.5
1910	3.8	16.3	7.9	22.4	–1.5	15.1	2.8	25.6	3.8	16.6	6.9	14.7	1.0	17.6
1911	0.8	21.1	5.5	24.9	–1.1	16.2	–2.5	24.9	1.4	20.7	7.1	16.5	–0.8	20.8
1912	4.5	18.6	8.5	24.6	–5.1	18.4	1.6	22.9	2.2	20.4	7.2	14.3	–2.8	18.6
1913	5.8	16.3	8.0	22.2	–2.9	16.4	0.8	24.6	2.6	16.1	6.8	14.8	–1.8	16.1
1914	–0.3	17.5	5.1	23.5	–3.3	21.1	2.5	24.8	0.3	19.7	7.2	14.4	–4.6	18.1
1915	4.0	17.2	7.7	24.0	–4.4	16.1	5.7	23.1	3.3	17.1	6.7	14.5	1.6	18.2
1916	7.0	16.9	7.3	24.2	–1.5	16.8	2.3	24.9	6.2	16.9	9.1	15.0	4.8	18.6
1917	0.4	18.2	7.3	24.8	–7.7	16.2	3.2	25.5	–0.2	18.5	4.7	15.7	–1.6	20.4
1918	2.7	18.2	6.7	24.3	–5.3	17.2	2.7	24.4	3.1	17.8	6.6	14.9	–0.2	18.3
1919	2.8	15.2	8.3	22.8	–1.1	17.8	3.1	23.0	2.3	15.0	6.3	14.1	1.4	16.8
1920	5.2	17.3	8.6	26.0	–2.9	17.0	2.0	23.0	4.5	17.8	7.5	13.5	2.9	19.2
1921	7.0	21.7	8.9	24.9	–1.4	15.1	2.0	24.1	6.5	20.4	9.2	17.6	4.8	20.4
1922	4.2	16.7	6.8	24.8	–5.3	15.7	2.4	24.0	0.8	16.6	7.7	13.0	–2.2	18.7
1923	4.4	20.4	6.4	25.8	–0.3	17.1	3.0	24.5	4.3	20.7	8.3	15.7	1.8	20.3
1924	4.2	17.8	6.4	26.0	–3.6	16.6	3.8	24.9	0.4	18.0	7.9	14.1	–2.6	18.8
1925	4.6	18.3	7.4	23.6	0.9	19.3	–2.0	24.0	4.2	20.4	8.4	14.3	1.5	18.9
1926	4.0	18.7	7.5	23.1	–3.4	18.7	2.5	23.3	2.4	19.3	7.9	16.9	–0.8	18.4
1927	4.5	17.9	7.9	25.4	–1.3	19.2	0.0	24.4	4.0	18.3	7.3	14.9	1.8	19.7
1928	5.4	20.3	8.3	27.6	–2.6	14.9	0.0	24.2	3.9	19.4	8.3	14.8	0.8	21.6
1929	–0.1	19.9	4.6	25.8	–4.1	15.7	0.1	23.7	–1.0	19.2	5.8	14.8	–4.7	19.9
1930	6.6	17.5	8.1	25.7	2.1	18.2	1.2	25.6	5.2	17.6	6.6	14.2	0.3	19.3
1931	4.1	17.9	...	...	–3.1	16.2	–1.5	24.7	2.7	18.1	7.2	14.7	0.5	20.2
1932	5.0	18.1	...	...	1.4	18.9	0.4	22.4	4.5	19.0	9.3	15.1	0.6	20.8
1933	1.7	20.4	...	...	–1.9	18.6	–1.2	24.0	0.6	20.0	6.2	16.6	–3.7	19.7
1934	3.5	21.1	...	...	0.4	16.6	–1.5	24.3	2.7	19.7	8.2	17.0	–0.6	21.3
1935	3.3	20.1	...	...	–2.0	17.5	–2.9	24.4	3.1	19.6	7.4	15.6	–2.4	19.9
1936	6.5	17.2	...	...	–1.0	19.1	1.5	24.4	5.0	17.9	6.4	14.9	2.7	19.9
1937	5.7	18.8	...	...	–1.2	19.0	–1.0	25.8	2.9	18.1	7.7	15.0	–2.9	19.4
1938	5.3	17.9	...	...	–1.0	18.0	3.1	26.0	4.3	17.8	8.0	14.1	0.8	19.5
1939	6.0	17.5	...	...	–0.9	18.2	2.6	24.4	4.5	18.6	6.6	14.4	1.2	19.4
1940	–2.4	17.3	...	...	–6.9	18.3	–0.1	24.8	–5.1	17.3	6.2	14.4	–8.4	18.2
1941	–0.0	20.2	7.9	26.0	–10.4	20.5	2.2	26.2	–2.3	21.3	5.2	15.1	–4.4	18.4
1942	–1.1	18.0	3.7	26.4	–10.6	16.4	0.6	24.7	–4.7	17.3	7.4	14.9	–9.3	18.2
1943	5.6	20.2	5.0	25.5	–3.2	17.1	0.9	23.8	3.0	19.1	8.4	15.8	–3.8	19.0
1944	5.3	19.0	5.9	24.7	–1.3	19.4	1.8	23.8	5.5	18.3	9.5	15.7	–3.5	18.8
1945	–1.9	20.6	4.7	26.6	–2.2	19.1	1.7	24.7	–1.2	19.6	4.8	15.6	–4.7	20.9
1946	0.8	19.8	6.5	25.7	–1.9	18.9	1.3	22.9	0.6	19.3	7.7	14.7	–3.5	21.0
1947	0.6	21.4	5.0	27.0	–3.7	19.1	1.9	25.8	–1.0	20.9	5.9	14.6	–5.9	21.2
1948	6.8	18.0	7.7	22.4	–4.7	18.3	5.3	25.1	5.4	18.1	7.8	14.7	3.0	17.7
1949	4.6	21.6	8.8	25.4	0.5	18.0	–0.9	26.4	4.2	19.5	9.1	16.5	1.5	19.5

A2 Mean Temperature in January and July (in degrees Centigrade)

1950–1975

	Athens		Belgrade		Berlin		Bucharest		Copenhagen		Edinburgh		Geneva		Leningrad	
	Jan	July	Jan	July	Jan	July	Jan	July	Jan	July	Jan	July	Jan	July	Jan	July
1950	7.6	29.0	−2.2	25.5	−1.6	18.5	−6.4	25.3	−0.7	17.3	4.4	14.6	0.7	22.3	−13.9	15.9
1951	10.9	27.4	3.7	22.0	0.9	18.4	−0.2	22.4	0.8	16.7	3.1	14.8	2.7	20.0	−8.3	16.0
1952	10.0	27.0	2.0	24.4	1.0	18.4	1.2	22.8	1.4	16.4	1.1	15.0	0.6	23.4	−2.4	17.3
1953	9.1	27.9	1.5	23.6	0.5	19.0	−1.4	23.7	0.6	17.8	4.7	14.2	−0.8	20.5	−7.2	18.1
1954	8.1	28.1	−5.1	21.5	−3.3	15.4	−7.9	22.1	−0.5	15.4	3.3	13.2	0.0	18.3	−8.7	18.6
1955	12.2	27.5	2.5	21.2	−1.7	19.3	−0.7	21.3	−0.4	19.7	1.9	16.2	2.9	20.0	−6.0	17.5
1956	10.3	27.7	3.3	22.4	0.3	18.6	−0.4	22.1	0.4	17.5	2.9	14.1	3.8	19.5	−9.2	15.3
1957	8.3	27.4	−1.2	22.8	1.2	19.1	−2.4	22.9	2.4	17.9	5.1	14.8	−0.2	19.5	−3.3	19.5
1958	9.1	27.6	−0.1	23.6	−0.2	18.4	−1.1	22.9	−0.2	17.3	3.1	14.3	1.5	19.6	−7.5	16.6
1959	9.1	26.8	1.8	22.3	0.4	20.6	−1.5	23.4	1.1	19.4	1.2	15.6	2.4	21.8	−4.1	19.1
1960	10.4	27.2	0.1	20.4	0.3	16.8	0.4	21.6	−0.2	16.1	3.5	14.3	1.6	18.0	−10.0	20.2
1961	9.6	27.0	1.0	21.2	−1.0	16.7	−2.9	22.1	1.1	15.6	2.9	13.8	2.6	19.2	−3.4	17.8
1962	10.5	27.6	2.0	21.0	2.4	16.1	−2.3	23.4	2.1	15.5	3.5	13.2	3.8	19.4	−5.2	16.2
1963	9.5	28.0	−5.2	23.8	−7.2	20.5	−7.8	24.0	−4.1	17.5	0.1	13.3	−3.1	20.8	−12.9	18.4
1964	6.8	26.4	−5.5	21.2	−1.8	19.6	−5.2	22.7	0.9	16.1	4.1	14.6	−1.0	22.1	−4.0	18.0
1965	9.6	27.7	2.0	22.8	1.8	16.4	0.3	23.8	1.7	14.5	2.4	12.1	1.5	18.4	−5.3	15.6
1966	9.4	27.5	−2.5	21.4	−2.7	17.9	−1.5	23.6	−1.7	...	2.9	14.0	0.5	18.5	−14.9	18.3
1967	9.0	26.6	−1.5	23.1	0.7	20.8	−4.0	23.2	0.2	17.7	4.3	14.7	1.5	21.5	−12.2	17.5
1968	8.2	27.4	−0.8	21.7	−0.8	18.2	−2.2	23.3	−0.4	16.3	3.9	13.7	0.3	19.5	...	14.2
1969	8.1	25.9	−1.8	20.6	−0.8	20.8	−5.7	20.8	−0.1	17.0	4.5	15.4	2.1	20.6	−12.2	16.8
1970	11.3	27.5	1.2	20.8	−4.1	18.1	−1.0	23.4	−1.7	16.2	2.8	13.5	0.4	18.8	−9.6	18.4
1971	11.2	26.0	1.7	21.5	−0.7	20.2	−0.1	21.2	1.1	18.1	4.4	15.0	−1.4	20.2	−2.4	17.6
1972	9.3	26.5	0.5	21.4	−3.4	20.2	−2.5	23.0	−0.8	18.8	4.1	14.3	1.2	18.2	−11.2	22.1
1973	8.9	27.9	0.4	22.0	0.5	19.6	−2.6	21.9	1.8	19.0	4.7	15.0	0.3	18.2	−5.3	20.3
1974	8.0	27.0	2.0	20.9	3.7	16.7	−3.0	21.5	3.1	15.7	6.0	14.1	3.4	18.2	−7.1	18.2
1975	8.9	27.1	3.7	21.4	5.4	20.6	1.1	22.3	5.0	18.9	5.7	15.7	3.5	18.9	−2.0	17.0

	Lisbon		London		Madrid		Marseilles		Milan		Moscow		Oslo	
	Jan	July	Jan	July	Jan	July	Jan	July	Jan	July	Jan	July	Jan	July
1950	10.4	22.4	4.7	17.9	5.5	26.0	5.5	25.6	1.7	28.3	−18.0	15.7	−5.4	15.9
1951	11.4	21.9	4.8	18.3	5.3	24.6	7.1	23.0	3.9	21.3	−12.1	18.6	−5.3	15.4
1952	9.9	22.2	4.1	18.6	2.6	24.6	4.4	25.4	0.6	22.5	−4.2	17.9	−4.0	16.3
1953	10.4	22.4	3.5	16.9	4.0	25.2	2.3	23.3	−0.3	18.9	−10.4	19.0	−4.7	16.5
1954	9.6	22.0	3.8	15.8	3.5	25.2	4.0	21.9	−0.6	21.0	−14.2	21.0	−5.7	15.5
1955	14.0	21.6	3.5	18.5	8.8	25.7	9.2	23.8	3.8	20.4	−6.3	17.9	−4.4	21.3
1956	11.8	21.9	4.8	17.1	6.0	22.8	7.4	22.4	2.0	19.1	−10.9	15.2	−6.9	16.8
1957	9.2	23.4	6.2	18.5	3.0	24.9	4.9	23.3	0.3	20.7	−6.0	18.6	−2.0	17.1
1958	11.7	22.2	4.5	17.5	5.4	24.3	6.2	22.4	1.0	20.0	−7.0	18.4	−4.6	16.9
1959	12.7	22.6	2.8	19.3	6.9	26.3	6.3	25.0	1.8	21.3	−4.4	20.6	−6.7	18.5
1960	11.4	22.3	4.7	16.3	5.6	24.7	5.1	22.6	0.5	21.5	−9.4	21.0	−4.0	15.0
1961	16.0	22.5	4.7	17.1	4.6	24.5	6.4	23.3	0.2	22.6	−6.2	19.4	−4.8	16.2
1962	11.1	22.2	5.3	16.3	6.9	24.2	8.6	23.4	2.5	22.6	−4.2	...	−2.5	14.7
1963	11.4	22.5	−1.1	16.5	5.7	23.8	3.5	24.7	−2.0	23.2	−15.9	19.1	−8.6	16.1
1964	11.1	21.9	4.1	18.3	5.8	24.7	5.1	24.5	−1.5	23.3	−8.1	20.0	−2.6	14.3
1965	11.1	20.8	4.6	15.8	5.4	23.2	6.5	22.3	1.5	22.5	−9.6	16.7	−2.9	14.3
1966	13.6	22.1	3.9	16.5	8.0	24.1	6.2	21.7	−1.3	21.4	−9.7	19.2	−8.2	16.8
1967	10.5	21.6	5.3	18.9	4.9	25.9	6.1	25.1	−0.2	24.3	−13.9	17.7	−7.6	16.3
1968	11.4	22.8	5.0	16.7	6.4	24.3	5.0	23.3	0.3	23.7	−15.6	15.7	−6.9	16.0
1969	12.0	23.9	6.4	17.9	6.8	25.0	6.8	23.1	−1.0	23.0	−16.2	17.8	−3.1	16.9
1970	12.3	22.4	4.3	16.3	7.1	24.6	8.0	23.3	1.9	22.9	−10.4	19.3	−7.5	14.4
1971	10.7	22.2	5.3	17.5	4.7	23.4	5.6	24.3	0.4	23.8	−3.5	17.5	−2.4	16.8
1972	10.6	21.4	4.3	16.7	4.5	23.5	7.3	22.9	2.6	22.2	−14.9	22.4	−6.1	18.1
1973	10.5	21.2	4.7	16.1	5.7	23.6	6.3	24.1	2.2	22.9	−10.2	18.0	−0.2	18.3
1974	12.7	24.2	6.9	16.1	8.3	24.2	8.8	23.1	7.3	23.8	−10.2	18.2	0.1	15.1
1975	11.7	22.4	7.6	17.9	7.3	25.1	8.5	24.0	3.6	23.8	−3.7	18.5	0.1	18.0

A2 Mean Temperature in January and July (in degrees Centigrade)

1950–1975

	Paris		Rome		Stockholm		Tiflis		Utrecht/de Bilt		Valentia		Vienna	
	Jan	July	Jan	July	Jan	July	Jan	July	Jan	July	Jan	July	Jan	July
1950	2.5	20.3	6.9	27.4	–4.4	16.0	–2.9	23.7	1.5	18.8	8.2	15.7	–2.9	21.4
1951	5.5	19.0	9.0	24.1	–2.8	16.5	1.5	25.7	4.0	16.7	6.3	15.4	1.5	20.0
1952	3.5	20.7	6.6	26.4	–1.1	16.3	2.4	25.0	2.5	17.1	5.9	15.9	1.0	21.2
1953	0.7	18.5	4.7	21.2	–2.6	17.3	3.8	24.5	1.3	16.8	7.3	14.8	–0.2	21.0
1954	1.5	17.2	5.5	23.0	–4.2	16.5	0.0	26.0	0.2	14.3	6.7	13.6	–4.2	17.7
1955	4.0	19.9	10.8	24.9	–2.7	19.6	3.6	24.8	0.1	17.6	6.1	16.4	–1.6	19.6
1956	4.1	18.5	9.1	24.3	–3.9	16.1	3.6	23.2	2.2	16.4	6.8	14.6	0.8	20.2
1957	3.2	19.6	6.8	24.2	0.2	17.7	0.4	24.9	3.7	17.6	7.3	15.4	–0.9	20.5
1958	4.3	18.5	7.4	23.9	–3.4	16.5	4.2	23.5	2.1	16.6	7.1	14.6	0.2	20.2
1959	3.2	21.7	7.3	25.1	–3.7	19.3	3.8	25.0	1.7	18.5	6.1	15.3	0.5	20.4
1960	4.0	17.3	8.1	23.7	–3.9	16.2	4.4	23.5	2.8	15.4	6.8	14.4	–0.9	18.1
1961	3.9	18.5	6.2	20.5	–2.0	15.7	1.8	23.9	2.0	15.6	6.9	14.4	–2.1	18.5
1962	5.4	18.3	8.9	23.7	–1.3	14.7	3.6	26.6	3.5	14.7	7.1	14.4	1.1	18.3
1963	–2.1	19.8	5.6	24.4	–6.9	17.2	4.9	23.8	–5.2	16.3	2.6	14.4	–6.0	21.4
1964	1.4	20.8	5.0	24.1	–1.3	16.8	–0.4	23.4	0.6	16.8	7.7	14.6	–4.7	20.9
1965	4.1	16.9	...	23.1	–1.3	14.9	–5.3	21.2	2.7	14.9	5.7	14.6	0.8	18.5
1966	1.2	16.9	9.4	21.9	–6.5	18.4	0.9	26.7	0.4	15.4	6.5	14.5	–3.3	18.7
1967	3.6	19.9	6.7	24.3	–4.5	18.2	2.5	22.7	3.1	18.2	7.0	14.6	–0.2	21.6
1968	3.8	17.4	5.0	23.5	–6.2	16.5	...	24.3	2.0	16.3	8.1	14.3	–1.1	19.5
1969	5.5	19.2	7.9	22.8	–2.1	18.8	–1.6	22.6	4.4	18.1	6.6	15.0	–1.6	20.3
1970	4.9	18.6	9.8	23.2	–6.8	16.8	3.5	25.3	0.6	15.7	6.7	14.2	–2.0	19.5
1971	4.2	20.8	9.4	24.2	–0.4	17.6	1.9	29.1	2.3	17.2	7.7	15.3	–2.2	20.1
1972	3.7	19.2	9.2	23.0	–3.0	20.1	–3.4	24.5	0.5	17.2	5.9	14.9	–2.2	20.0
1973	3.9	18.9	8.9	24.6	1.5	20.1	–1.4	23.4	2.9	17.0	7.8	14.2	–0.2	20.0
1974	7.2	17.2	9.6	23.1	1.0	15.5	–0.3	22.8	5.2	15.4	8.0	14.3	2.2	14.3
1975	7.5	19.1	8.4	23.7	1.9	19.3	2.5	...	6.2	17.8	8.0	15.7	3.6	20.1

NOTES

1. SOURCES:— The main source used has been *World Weather Records* (for details of which see Note 1 to Table A1). In addition, statistics for Oslo, Paris, and Stockholm, and many statistics since 1960 are taken from official publications listed on p. xv. Statistics since 1960 for Berlin, Edinburgh, Geneva, Leningrad, Lisbon, London, Marseilles, Milan, Moscow, Rome, Tiflis, and Valentia are taken from *Monthly Climatic Data of the World.*

2. Break lines indicate a change of location of the temperature gauge within the same town.

B. POPULATION AND VITAL STATISTICS

The principal sources of population data are official censuses and registration records. In Europe, the earliest regular enumeration of national population dates from around the beginning of the period covered in this work. But, outside Scandinavia (and some, though by no means all, Italian states), systematic census-taking and registration of births, deaths, and marriages have been nineteenth, or even twentieth century phenomena. Historical coverage of the different countries, therefore, varies widely in scope. There is also good reason to believe, unfortunately, that it varies in accuracy. The almost universal tendency of censuses is to under-enumerate, though published results may sometimes have been deliberately inflated for political purposes. A proportion of vital events similarly escapes the registrar's net. But in most countries these tendencies have probably declined over time, as officials became more sophisticated, and the population became more accustomed to procedures and less suspicious of their purpose. However, the increase in the number of town-dwellers living alone in recent decades may have reversed this process in some countries. Until quite recently[1] there was no means of knowing either the extent of understatement or its variation over time, so that for the most part it is impossible to do more than guess at margins of error in the past. By and large, it seems safe to take all regular censuses after the first two or three in a series as accurate to within five per cent overall.[2] Isolated, sporadic censuses are probably rather less reliable, in general.

Some kinds of information elicited in censuses are likely to be less accurate than others. Data about occupations present special difficulties, and these are considered in the next section. But the table in this section showing age-group data probably contains some of the largest margins of error of all. For in addition to accidental errors, this information is peculiarly liable to deliberate falsification by respondents. When censuses were taken wholly or partly, or even only in popular belief, in connection with military service obligations, the male age-groups at risk might be seriously understated if the census officials were not particularly skilled. And at all times, vanity may have had some influence on the statistics. A further source of error, especially amongst illiterate people and in times of disturbance, has been ignorance, at any rate, incomplete knowledge. In many censuses, in the Balkan countries especially, right up to the interwar period the number of people enumerated in single years of age was far higher for the ages of 60, 70, 80, etc. or even for 65, 75, 85, than for 61, 72, 83, or other "unrounded" ages. In the absence of birth certificates or other literary evidence, it seems that knowledge of one's exact age had become, by the later stages of life, often only approximate.

Boundary changes often affect the comparability of national population data over time. But these are an obvious pitfall, which few are likely to fall into unawares, and a list of changes is given on p. ix above. Almost equally obvious are the changes which take place in the boundaries of districts within the various countries, which are shown in table B3. These are adequately indicated in the footnotes. Less obvious, however, are the changes in the limits of the major cities, whose populations are given in table B4. As cities grow in population they generally grow, too, in space, taking in areas which, whilst not previously uninhabited, were clearly not part of a city. This presents no conceptual problem, and the general rule adopted here has been to show the statistics which apply to the city limits of the year to which they refer. A problem does, however, arise when suburban areas which become functionally part of a central city remain administratively separate from it. So far as possible, wherever such separate areas are of significant size, this has been dealt with by including these areas with the centre as "Greater London", "Greater Paris", and so on.

Demographers may find the vital statistics here to be among the least sophisticated that are nowadays available; but they have the merit, from the historical point of view, of being extant for much longer periods than the more refined series. Even so, there is a serious question mark over their accuracy in many countries for some time after the start of their collection. Drake reckons that there was between five and ten per cent under-registration in Norway in the eighteenth century, and that clerical errors may account for part of some of the very sharp fluctuations.[3] Presumably the same applies to Finland and Sweden, which exhibit similar characteristics and where a similar system of registration by the clergy of the state church was in operation. In England and Wales there were serious defects in the first two decades or so of civil registration;[4] and it would seem to be wise to assume similar unreliability in the early days of registration in every country. This applies to the U.S.S.R. in the interwar period, quite possibly to Poland and Greece, and perhaps to other east European countries as well.

A variety of statistics on overseas migration is available for different countries, though much that is desirable is lacking altogether. Two tables on this subject have been included here. The first, B8, is essentially a work of synthesis, the result of extensive research into intractable material by Professor Woodruff. It is impossible to summarise this here, and though the statistics are broadly accurate, anyone who intends to use them for further calculations should consult the source for details of definitions and methods of estimation. The second table, B9, presents some of the raw data on the subject, and a glance at note 2, showing the composition of the series for different countries, will indicate how difficult it is to make comparisons between them.

[1] The first occasion when this was possible was in 1950, when the U.S. Bureau of the Census undertook a post-census 1sample survey which indicated a net under enumeration of about 1.4 per cent.

[2] Note, however, that in the case of Norway, the 1801 census is reckoned better than any other until 1865, though the other two early censuses (in 1769 and 1815) *were* the least good. (K. Ofstad, "Population Statistics and Population Registration in Norway", *Population Studies* (1949).)

[3] M. Drake, "The Growth of Population in Norway, 1735–1855", *Scandinavian Economic History Review* (1965).

[4] See D.V. Glass, "A Note on Under-Registration in Britain in the Nineteenth Century", *Population Studies* (1951).

B1 POPULATION OF COUNTRIES AT CENSUSES (in thousands)

Albania[6 7]

Date	Total	M	F
1930	1,003	...	...
1945	1,122	571	552
1950	1,219	626	593
1955	1,391	713	678
1960	1,626	835	791

Austria: Cisleithania[1]

Date	Total	M	F
1818	13,381[2]	...	...
1821	13,964[2]	...	...
1824	14,519[2]	...	...
1827	15,131[2]	7,278[2]	7,854
1830	15,588[2]	7,502[2]	8,086
1834	15,714[2]	7,509[2]	8,205
1837	16,083[2]	7,710[2]	8,373
1840	16,575[2]	7,970[2]	8,606
1843	17,073[2]	8,219[2]	8,854
1846	17,613[2]	8,510[2]	9,104
1851	17,535[2]	8,399[2]	9,136
1857	18,225[2]	8,802[2]	9,422
1869	20,218[2]	9,814[2]	10,403
1880	22,144	10,820	11,325
1890	23,708	11,502	12,206
1900	25,922	12,624	13,298
1910	28,572	14,034	14,538

Austria: Bosnia & Hercegovina

Date	Total	M	F
1879	1,158	608	551
1885	1,360	729	631
1895	1,568	828	740
1910	1,898	995	903

Austria: Republic

Date	Total	M	F
1910	6,648	3,285	3,364
1923[3]	6,535	3,148	3,387
1934[4]	6,760	3,248	3,512
1951[4]	6,934	3,217	3,717
1961[4]	7,009	3,296	3,713
1971[4]	7,456	3,502	3,955

Belgium

Date	Total	M	F
1816	4,166	...	...
1831	4,090	...	...
1846	4,337[5]	2,164	2,174
1856	4,530	2,272	2,258
1866	4,828	2,420	2,408
1880	5,520	2,758	2,762
1890	6,069	3,027	3,042
1900	6,694	3,325	3,369
1910	7,424	3,681	3,743
1920	7,406[6]	3,644[6]	3,761[6]
1930	8,092	4,007	4,085
1947	8,512	4,200	4,312
1961	9,190	4,497	4,693
1970	9,651	4,722	4,929

Bulgaria

Date	Total	M	F
1881	2,008[7]	1,028[7]	980[7]
1888	3,154	1,605	1,549
1893	3,311	1,691	1,620
1900	3,744	1,910	1,835
1905	4,036	2,057	1,978
1910	4,338[8]	2,207[8]	2,131[8]
1920	4,847	2,421	2,426
1926	5,479	2,743	2,736
1934	6,078	3,054	3,024
1946	7,029	3,517	3,513
1956	7,614	3,799	3,814
1965	8,228	4,114	4,114
1975	8,728	4,358	4,370

Czechoslovakia

Date	Total	M	F
1910	13,599	6,613	6,983
1921	13,612	6,559	7,063
1930	14,730[9]	7,143[9]	7,586[9]
1946/7[10]	12,162	5,908	6,254
1950	12,338	5,997	6,342
1961	13,746	6,705	7,041
1970	14,345	6,989	7,356

Denmark[11]

Date	Total	M	F
1769	798	398	400
1787	842	417	425
1801	929	460	469
1834	1,231	609	622
1840	1,289	636	653
1845	1,357	671	686
1850	1,415	696	719
1855	1,507	746	762
1860	1,608	797	811
1870	1,785	881	904
1880	1,969	967	1,002
1890	2,172	1,059	1,113
1901	2,450	1,193	1,256
1906	2,589	1,258	1,331
1911	2,757	1,338	1,419
1916	2,921	1,416	1,506
1921	3,104	1,511	1,593
	3,268[12]	1,592[12]	1,676[12]
1925	3,435	1,676	1,758
1930	3,551	1,736	1,814
1935	3,706	1,824	1,882
1940	3,844	1,900	1,944
1945	4,045	2,002	2,043
1950	4,281	2,123	2,158
1960	4,585	2,273	2,312
1970	4,938	2,451	2,486

Estonia

Date	Total	M	F
1922	1,107	520	587
1934	1,126	529	597

See p.35 for footnotes

B1 Population of Countries at Censuses (in thousands)

Finland

Date	Total	M	F
1750	422	201	221
1760	491	236	255
1770	561	273	288
1775	610	298	312
1780	664	325	338
1785	679	333	346
1790	706	341	365
1795	771	375	396
1800	833	405	428
1805	896 [13]	435 [13]	460 [13]
1810	863 [14]	414 [14]	449 [14]
1815	1,096	527	569
1820	1,178	567	610
1825	1,259 [15]	607 [15]	652 [15]
1830	1,372	664	708
1835	1,394	675	719
1840	1,446	700	745
1845	1,548	751	796
1850	1,637	796	841
1855	1,689	819	870
1860	1,747	849	898
1865	1,843	899	944
1870	1,769	860	908
1875	1,913	935	978
1880	2,061	1,008	1,053
1890	2,380	1,172	1,209
1900	2,656	1,311	1,345
1910	2,943 [16]	1,445 [16]	1,499 [16]
1920	3,148	1,533	1,617
1930	3,463	1,689	1,774
1940	3,696 [17]	1,793 [17]	1,903 [17]
1950	4,030	1,926	2,104
1960	4,446	2,142	2,304
1970	4,598	2,220	2,378

France[18]

Date	Total	M	F
1801	27,349	13,312	14,037
1806	29,107 [19]	14,313 [19]	14,795 [19]
1821	30,462	14,797	15,665
1831	32,569	15,950	16,619
1836	33,541	16,461	17,080
1841	34,230	16,898	17,319
1846	35,402	17,542	17,858
1851	35,783	17,795	17,988
1856	36,013 [20]	17,857 [20]	18,155 [20]
1861	37,386	18,645	18,741
1866	38,067 [21]	19,014 [21]	19,053 [21]
1872	36,103	17,983	18,120
1876	36,906	18,374	18,532
1881	37,406	18,657	18,749
1886	37,930	18,900	19,030
1891	38,133	18,932	19,201
1896	38,269	18,923	19,346
1901	38,451	18,917	19,534
1906	38,845	19,100	19,745
1911	39,192 [21]	19,254 [21]	19,938 [21]
1921	38,798	18,445	20,353
1926	40,228	19,310	20,919
1931	41,228	19,912	21,317
1936	41,183	19,797	21,386
1946	39,848 [22]	18,878 [22]	20,970 [22]
1954	42,781 [23]	20,507 [23]	22,274
1962	46,500	22,595	23,905
1968	49,655	24,197	25,458
1975	52,599	25,744	26,855

Germany[24]

Date	Total	M	F
1816	22,377	...	...
1828	26,646	...	...
1834	28,237	...	...
1840	30,382	...	...
1852	33,413	...	...
1861	35,567	...	...
1864	37,804 [24]	...	...
	39,392		
1871	41,059	20,157	20,907
1880	45,234	22,185	23,049
1890	49,428	24,231	25,198
1900	56,367	27,737	28,630
1910	64,926 [25]	32,040 [25]	32,886 [25]
	58,451	28,824	29,627
1925[26]	63,181	30,583	32,598
1933[26]	66,030 [27]	32,086 [27]	33,944 [27]
1939	69,460	33,912	35,405

East Germany (including East Berlin)

Date	Total	M	F
1939	16,745	8,191	8,555
1946	18,488	7,860	10,629
1950	18,388	8,161	10,277
1964	17,004	7,748	9,255
1971	17,068	7,865	9,203

West Germany (including West Berlin)

Date	Total	M	F
1939	42,998	21,033	21,965
1946	46,560	20,804	25,756
1950[28]	50,787	23,711	27,076
1961	56,115	26,413	29,761
1970	60,651	28,867	31,784

See p.35 for footnotes

B1 Population of Countries at Censuses (in thousands)

Greece

Date	Total	M	F
1821	939	...	...
1828	753	...	...
1838	752	...	...
1843	915	...	...
1848	987	...	...
1853	1,036	...	...
1856	1,063	550	513
1861	1,097[29]	567[29]	529[29]
1870	1,458	754	704
1879	1,679[30]	881[30]	799[30]
1889	2,187	1,134	1,054
1896	2,434[31]	1,267[31]	1,167[31]
1907	2,632[32]	1,325[32]	1,307[32]
1920	5,017	2,495	2,522
1928	6,205	3,076	3,128.
1940	7,345[33]	3,658[33]	3,686[33]
1951	7,633	3,722	3,911
1961	8,389	4,091	4,297
1971	8,769	4,287	4,482

Hungary: Transleithania[34]

Date	Total	M	F
1850	13,192[2]	6,520[2]	6,672
1857	14,349	7,379	6,970
1869	15,512	7,848	7,764
1880	15,739	7,800	7,939
1890	17,578	8,783	8,796
1900	19,255	9,582	9,672
1910	20,886	10,345	10,541

Hungary: Trianon Territory

Date	Total	M	F
1910	7,615	3,794	3,821
1920	7,990	3,876	4,114
1930	8,688	4,250	4,438
1941	9,317[35,36]	4,561[35,36]	4,756[35,36]
1949	9,205	4,423	4,781
1960	9,961	4,804	5,157
1970	10,322	5,004	5,318

Iceland

Date	Total	M	F
1769	46	21	25
1801	47	22	26
1840	57	27	30
1850	59	28	31
1860	67	32	35
1870	70	33	37
1880	72	34	38
1890	71	34	37
1901	78	38	41
1910	85	41	44
1920	95	46	49
1930	109	54	55
1940	121	60	61
1950	144	72	72
1960	177	90	88
1970	205	104	101

Ireland[37]

Date	Total	M	F
1821	6,802[2]	3,342[2]	3,460
1831	7,767[2]	3,795[2]	3,973
1841	8,175[2]	4,020[2]	4,156
1851	6,552[2]	3,191[2]	3,362
1861	5,799	2,837	2,962
1871	5,412	2,640	2,773
1881	5,175	2,533	2,642
1891	4,705	2,319	2,386
1901	4,459	2,200	2,259
1911	4,390	2,192	2,198

Northern Ireland

Date	Total	M	F
1926	1,257	608	648
1937	1,280	623	657
1951	1,371	668	703
1961	1,425	694	731
1966	1,485	724	761
1971	1,536	755	781

Republic of Ireland

Date	Total	M	F
1926	2,972	1,507	1,465
1936	2,968	1,520	1,448
1946	2,955	1,494	1,459
1951	2,961	1,507	1,454
1956	2,898	1,463	1,435
1961	2,818	1,417	1,402
1966	2,884	1,449	1,435
1971	2,978	1,496	1,482

Italy[38]

Date	Total	M	F
circa 1770	14,689	...	...
circa 1795	16,257	...	...
circa 1800	17,237	...	...
circa 1816	18,381	...	...
circa 1825	19,727	...	...
1833	21,212	...	...
1838	21,975	...	...
1844	22,936	...	...
1848	23,617	...	...
1852	24,351	...	...
1858	24,857	...	...
1861	25,017[39]	...	...
1871	26,801	13,472	13,329
1881	28,460	14,265	14,194
1901	32,475	16,155	16,320
1911	34,671	17,022	17,650
1921	36,406[40]	17,940[40]	18,466[40]
	37,974	18,726	19,248
1931	41,177	20,134	21,043
1936	42,919[41]	21,068[41]	21,851[41]
1951	47,159[42]	22,961[42]	24,198[42]
	47,516	23,259	24,257
1961	50,624	24,784	25,840
1971	54,137	26,476	27,661

Latvia

Date	Total	M	F
1925	1,845	860	985
1930	1,900	886	1,014
1935	1,950	912	1,038

Lithuania[43]

Date	Total	M	F
1923	2,029	968	1,061

See p.35 for footnotes

B1 Population of Countries at Censuses (in thousands)

Luxembourg

Date	Total	M	F
1839	170	...	...
1843	180	...	...
1846	186	...	...
1849	190	...	...
1852	193	...	...
1855	189	...	...
1861	198	...	...
1864	203	...	...
1867	200	100	100
1871	198	98	99
1875	205	103	102
1880	210	105	104
1885	213	107	106
1890	211	105	106
1895	218	109	108
1900	236	122	114
1905	246	126	120
1910	260	134	126
1922	261	132	129
1930	300	154	146
1935	297	149	147
1947	291	145	146
1960	315	155	159
1966	335	165	170
1970	340	167	173

Netherlands

Date	Total	M	F
1816[44]	2,047	...	...
1829[45]	2,613	1,278	1,335
1839	2,861	1,401	1,460
1849	3,057	1,499	1,558
1859	3,309	1,629	1,680
1869	3,580	1,764	1,815
1879	4,013	1,983	2,030
1889	4,511	2,228	2,283
1899	5,104	2,521	2,584
1909	5,858	2,899	2,959
1920	6,865	3,410	3,455
1930	7,936	3,943	3,993
1940	8,923	4,454	4,469
1947	9,625	4,791	4,834
1960	11,556	5,754	5,802
1970[66]	13,119	6,550	6,570

Norway

Date	Total	M	F
1769	724	343	380
1801	883	423	461
1815	885	...	...
1825	1,051	511	540
1835	1,195	585	609
1845	1,328	652	676
1855	1,490	730	760
1865	1,702	836	866
1875	1,819	889	930
1890	2,001	966	1,035
1900	2,240	1,088	1,152
1910	2,392	1,156	1,236
1920	2,650	1,290	1,359
1930	2,814	1,372	1,442
1946	3,157	1,557	1,600
1950	3,278	1,625	1,653
1960	3,591	1,789	1,802
1970	3,874	1,926	1,948

Poland[46]

Date	Total	M	F
1897/1900[47]	25,106	12,482	12,624
1921	27,177	13,133	14,044
1931	32,107[48]	15,619[48]	16,488[48]
1946	23,930	10,954	12,976
1950	25,008	11,928	13,080
1960	29,776	14,404	15,372
1970	32,642	15,854	16,789

Portugal[49]

Date	Total	M	F
1768	2,410	...	...
1801	2,932	...	...
1821	3,026	...	...
1835	3,062	...	...
1838	3,224	...	...
1841	3,397[50]	...	...
	3,737		
1854	3,844	...	...
1858	3,923	...	...
1861	4,035[49]	...	...
1864	4,188	2,006	2,183
1878	4,551	2,176	2,375
1890	5,060	2,430	2,629
1900	5,423	2,592	2,832
1911	5,958	2,829	3,129
1920	6,087	2,910	3,177
1930	6,826	3,256	3,570
1940	7,722	3,712	4,010
1950	8,381	4,060	4,301
1960	8,889	4,254	4,635
1970	8,663	4,109	4,554

See p.35 for footnotes

B1 Population of Countries at Censuses (in thousands)

Romania[51]

Date	Total	M	F
1899	5,957	3,027	2,930
1912	7,235[52]	3,656[52]	3,759[52]
1930	18,057[53]	8,887[53]	9,170[53]
1941	16,126	7,989	8,138
1948	15,873	7,672	8,201
1956	17,489	8,503	8,986
1966	19,103	9,351	9,752

Russia[54]

Date	Total	M	F
1897[55]	126,367[56]	63,208[56]	63,159[56]
1926	147,028	71,053	75,985
1939	170,467[57]	81,665[57]	88,802[57]
1959	208,827	94,050	114,776
1970	241,720	111,399	130,321

Serbia[58]

Date	Total	M	F
1834	678	...	...
1840	830	...	...
1843	861	...	...
1846	915	...	...
1850	957	...	...
1854	999	...	...
1859	1,078	557	521
1863	1,109	572	537
1866	1,216	627	584
1874	1,354[59]	696[59]	658[59]
1884	1,902[58]	973[58]	929[58]
1890	2,162	1,110	1,052
1895	2,312	1,187	1,126
1900	2,494	1,281	1,212
1905	2,689	1,382	1,306
1910	2,912	1,504	1,408

Spain[60]

Date	Total	M	F
1768/9	9,160	4,534	4,626
1787	10,268	5,109	5,159
1797	10,541	5,220	5,321
1857	15,455	7,664	7,791
1860	15,645	7,741	7,904
1877	16,622	8,126	8,496
1887	17,550	8,601	8,948
1897	18,109	8,779	9,329
1900	18,594	9,072	9,522
1910	19,927	9,674	10,253
1920	21,303	10,316	10,988
1930	23,564	11,498	12,066
1940	25,878	12,414	13,464
1950	27,977	13,470	14,507
1960	30,431	14,763	15,667
1970	33,824	16,505	17,319

Sweden

Date	Total	M	F
1750	1,781	837	944
1760	1,924	912	1,012
1770	2,043	974	1,068
1775	2,021	967	1,054
1780	2,118	1,018	1,101
1785	2,150	1,037	1,113
1790	2,188	1,043	1,145
1795	2,281	1,093	1,188
1800	2,347	1,121	1,227
1805	2,427	1,167	1,261
1810	2,396	1,141	1,255
1815	2,465	1,177	1,288
1820	2,585	1,240	1,345
1825	2,771	1,333	1,438
1830	2,888	1,391	1,497
1835	3,025	1,462	1,564
1840	3,139	1,516	1,622
1845	3,317	1,604	1,713
1850	3,471	1,687	1,784
1855	3,641	1,765	1,876
1860	3,860	1,875	1,985
1870	4,169	2,017	2,152
1890	4,566	2,215	2,351
1890	4,785	2,317	2,468
1900	5,137	2,506	2,630
1910	5,522	2,699	2,824
1915	5,713	2,795	2,918
1920	5,905	2,898	3,006
1925	6,054	2,973	3,081
1930	6,142	3,021	3,121
1935	6,251	2,091	3,160
1940	6,372	3,160	3,211
1945	6,674	3,320	3,354
1950	7,041	3,505	3,535
1955	7,235	3,605	3,630
1960	7,495	3,739	3,757
1965	7,767	3,881	3,887
1970	8,077	4,034	4,043

See p.35 for footnotes

B1 Population of Countries at Censuses (in thousands)

Switzerland

Date	Total	M	F
1837	2,190	1,085	1,105
1850	2,393	1,182	1,211
1860	2,507	1,235	1,272
1870	2,669	1,305	1,364
1880	2,846	1,395	1,451
1888	2,933[61]	1,426[61]	1,507[61]
	2,918	1,418	1,500
1900	2,315	1,627	1,688
1910	3,753	1,846	1,908
1920	3,880	1,871	2,009
1930	4,006	1,958	2,108
1940	4,266	2,060	2,205
1950	4,715	2,272	2,443
1960	5,429	2,663	2,766
1970	6,270	3,089	3,180

United Kingdom
Great Britain: England & Wales

Date	Total	M	F
1801	8,893	4,255	4,638
1811	10,164	4,874	5,291
1821	12,000	5,850	6,150
1831	13,897	6,771	7,126
1841	15,914	7,778	8,137
1851	17,928	8,781	9,146
1861	20,066	9,776	10,290
1871	22,712	11,059	11,653
1881	25,974	12,640	13,335
1891	29,003	14,060	14,942
1901	32,528	15,729	16,799
1911	36,070	17,446	18,625
1921	37,887	18,075	19,811
1931	39,952	19,133	20,819
1951	43,758	21,016	22,742
1961	46,105	22,304	23,801
1971	48,750	23,683	25,067

Great Britain: Scotland

Date	Total	M	F
1755[63]	1,265	...	...
1801	1,608	739	869
1811	1,806	826	980
1821	2,092	983	1,109
1831	2,364	1,114	1,250
1841	2,620	1,242	1,378
1851	2,889	1,375	1,513
1861	3,062	1,450	1,612
1871	3,360	1,603	1,757
1881	3,736	1,799	1,936
1891	4,026	1,943	2,083
1901	4,472	2,174	2,298
1911	4,761	2,309	2,452
1921	4,882	2,348	2,535
1931	4,843	2,326	2,517
1951	5,096	2,434	2,662
1961	5,179	2,483	2,697
1971	5,229	2,515	2,714

Yugoslavia

Date	Total	M	F
1921	11,985	5,880	6,105
1931	13,934[64]	6,892[64]	7,042[64]
1948	15,772	7,582	8,190
1953	16,937[65]	8,205[65]	8,732[65]
1961	18,549	9,043	9,506
1971	20,523	10,077	10,446

See p.35 for footnotes

B1 Population of Countries at Censuses (in thousands)

NOTES

1. SOURCES:– With the following exceptions all figures are taken from the official publications noted on p. xv:– Albania (1930), Estonia, Latvia, and Lithania – League of Nations, *Statistical Yearbook;* Finland (1775–1875) and Sweden (years ending in 5 to 1855)–J. Bertillon, *Statistique Internationale des Rencensements de la Population....* (Paris, 1899); Luxembourg (to 1852), Serbia (to 1859), and Switzerland (1837)–*Annuaire Internationale de Statistique* (The Hague, 1916); Scotland (1755)–J.G. Kyd, *Scottish Population Statistics* (Edinburgh, 1952).

2. A few of the figures given are official estimates rather than the results of complete censuses, but all were published as being comparable to the latter. The sole exception to this is Germany, for which estimates have been made for the period up to 1864 for the dates of the Prussian censuses. These are made on the basis of censuses in the various component states in years which were not always the same as that of the Prussian censuses, especially before 1834. This has been done because official published estimates include areas which were not incorporated in German states up to 1864.

3. No census was ever taken for Montenegro. Bertillon, *op cit.* above, and the *Annuaire Internationale de Statistique* (1916) give the following estimates of total population (in thousands):–

1857:120 1864:146 1897: 228 1910:250.

The country was enlarged in 1878 by the acquisition of territory from Turkey.

4. Unless otherwise stated in footnotes, statistics are of population actually present.

FOOTNOTES

[1] The Italian provinces are not included.
[2] Civil population only.
[3] The census in Burgenland was on a different date from the other provinces.
[4] Resident population.
[5] In 1839 areas with a population of 326 thousand were ceded to the Netherlands.
[6] Between 1920 and 1930 three cantons were acquired from Germany.
[7] Between 1881 and 1888 Eastern Roumelia was added.
[8] Between 1910 and 1920 there were several boundary changes, involving the loss of Southern Dobrudja to Romania, and the gain of rather larger territories from Turkey.
[9] Between 1930 and 1946/7 Sub-Carpathian Russia (Ruthenia) and a few villages in Slovakia were ceded to the U.S.S.R.
[10] The censuses were on 4 October 1946 in Slovakia and 22 May 1947 in the Czech lands.
[11] The Duchies of Schleswig, Holstein, and Lauenburg are not included. Their total combined populations were as follows:– 1840: 849 1945: 889 1855: 969 1860: 1,004 1864: 1,010.
[12] From 1921 (2nd line) the part of Schleswig acquired from Germany in that year is included.
[13] In 1809 certain parishes in the Tornie River basin, with a population of 12 thousand, were added.
[14] In 1811 Viipuri province, with a population of 185 thousand, was added.
[15] The Greek Orthodox population was included for the first time in 1830, when it numbered 25 thousand.
[16] In 1820 Petsamo, with a population of 1.5 thousand, was added.
[17] Between 1940 and 1950 Viipuri and Petsamo were ceded to the U.S.S.R, but the population was moved to the remaining territory.
[18] Resident population. Estimates in the eighteenth century are as follows:–
1700: 19,669 1762: 21,769 1784: 24,800.
[19] In 1814/5 Philippeville and part of Wissembourg was excluded, and Gex was included. The total population in 1806 of the 1815 territory was 29,053 thousand.
[20] In 1860 Savoy and Nice were acquired from Italy. Their population in 1848 was 702 thousand.
[21] From 1871 to 1918 most of Alsace and Lorraine was incorporated in Germany and is not included here.
[22] In 1947 the villages of Tende and Brigue were acquired from Italy.
[23] Military personnel stationed overseas are subsequently included.
[24] The figures to 1864 (1st line) relate to the territories composing the German Empire in 1870, exclusive of areas ceded by Austria, Denmark, and France in 1864–1871. These latter are included from 1864 (2nd line).
[25] From 1910 (2nd line) the territories ceded after the First World War are excluded.
[26] The censuses in Saarland were in July 1927 and June 1935 respectively.

[27] It has been impossible to exclude a small part of Austria, incorporated in 1938, from the 1939 statistics; but all other territorial acquisitions in 1937–39 have been excluded.

[28] The census in Saarland was on a different date from the rest of Germany.

[29] In 1864 the Ionian Islands were acquired frôm Britain.

[30] In 1881 Thessaly and Arta were acquired from Turkey. Their population was 294 thousand.

[31] Between 1896 and 1907 a small strip of Thessaly was ceded to Turkey.

[32] Between 1907 and 1920 Epiros, Thrace, and part of Macedonia were acquired from Turkey.

[33] In 1949 the Dodecanese Islands were acquired from Italy. Their population in 1951 was 121 thousand.

[34] Including Croatia-Slavonia. Earlier figures are given by J. Kovacsis, "Situation Demographique de la Hongrie à la Fin du XVIII Siècle, 1787–1815", *Annales de Dêmographie Historique* (1965) as follows (in thousands):—

1787: 7,117 1793: 7,141 1804: 7,961 1817: 8,314.

Official estimates for 1843 and 1846 were 13,854 thousand and 14,542 thousand respectively. These appear to be too high. A. Fényes, *Statistik der Königreichs Ungarn* (Pesth, 1843) gives 12,880 for 1840

[35] The population of Greater Hungary in 1941 was 13,644 thousand.

[36] In 1947 the Bratislava Bridgehead was ceded to Czechoslovakia.

[37] Earlier estimates are given by K.H. Connell, *The Population of Ireland, 1750–1845* (Oxford, 1950) as follows (in thousands):—

1754: 3,191 1772: 3,584 1781: 4,048 1788: 4,389
1767: 3,480 1,777: 3,740 1785: 4,019 1790: 4,591 1791: 4,753.

[38] Statistics to 1861 are estimates made on the basis of censuses at different dates (but in the same year from 1833) in the various states which constitued the Kingdom of Italy in 1871.

[39] The census of 1861 gave the population in the area ruled by Italy at that time as follows (in thousands):—

Total 21,777; Males 10,897; Females 10,880.

[40] From 1921 (2nd line) the territories acquired after the First World War are included.

[41] In 1945–7 territories in Istria and Piedmont were ceded to Yuogoslavia and France.

[42] Subsequent statistics are of resident population.

[43] Excluding Memel.

[44] Excluding the Belgian provinces.

[45] Excluding the Belgian provinces, but including the part of Limburg ceded by Belgium in 1839.

[46] Earlier estimates for Russian Poland are given in J. Bertillon, *op.cit.* above, as follows (in thousands):—

	Total	Males	Females		Total	Males	Females
1815	2,600	...	...	1863	4,840	...	...
1823	3,702	...	...	1867	5,706	2,760	2,946
1835	4,060	...	...	1870	6,026	2,931	3,096
1854	4,852	...	...	1885	7,960	...	...
1858	4,764	2,298	2,466				

[47] Based on Austrian, German, and Russian data. The 1897 figures for Russian Poland are as follows (in thousands):— Total 9,456; Males 4,764; Females 4,692.

[48] In 1945 Poland ceded large areas to the U.S.S.R. and acquired other large areas from Germany. In both cases much of the population was moved to the remaining territory of the ceding country.

[49] Statistics to 1861 are of resident population.

[50] To 1841 (1st line) the Azores and Maderia are not included.

[51] Earlier estimates, based on partial censuses, are available as follows (in thousands):—

	Total	Males	Females		Total	Males	Females
1844	3,578	...	...	1889	5,038	2,565	2,473
1859	3,865	...	...	1894	5,406	2,739	2,667

Part of Bessarabia was acquired from Russia in 1856, but returned in 1878, when Northern Dobrudja was acquired from Turkey.

[52] As a result of the Balkan Wars and the first World War, Romania acquired Southern Dobrudja, Bessarabia, Bukovina, Transylvania, part of the Banat, and parts of Hungary proper. The population of these areas in 1915 was estimated at 4,772 thousand.

[53] Between 1939 and 1941 there were several boundary changes. The statistics for 1941 given here relate to the territory established after the Second World War, the main changes from 1930 being the cession of Bessarabia and much of Bukovina to the U.S.S.R., and of Southern Dobrudja to Bulgaria.

[54] The statistics for 1897 are for the Russian Empire excluding Finland. Later statistics are for the U.S.S.R.. Other official estimates are available as follows (in thousands):—

	Total	Males	Females
1851	65,077	32,212	32,865
1858	67,299	32,839	34,459
1885	106,611	52,996	52,779

(164 thousand not distinguished by sex).

P.A. Khromov, *Economic Development of Russia in the 19th and 20th Centuries, 1800–1917* (Moscow, 1950) gives the following estimates at decennial intervals (in thousands):—

1800: 35,500 1830: 56,100 1860: 74,100 1890: 117,800
1810: 40,700 1840: 62,400 1870: 84,500 1900: 132,900
1820: 48,600 1850: 68,500 1880: 97,700 1910: 160,700.

[55] Statistics for the 50 Provinces of European Russia (i.e. excluding Finland, Poland, and the Caucasus) are as follows (in thousands):—

Total 94,215: Males 46,448: Females 47,767.

[56] The population of the areas of the former Empire excluded from the U.S.S.R. was 21,734 thousand in 1897 (excluding Finland).

[57] The population of areas incorporated in the U.S.S.R. between 1939 and 1945 was approximately 22,200 thousand in 1939.

[58] Resident population to 1884.

[59] In 1878 Vranje, Niš, Pirot, and Toplica were acquired from Turkey. Their population was 303 thousand.

[60] Including the Canary Islands. A. Moreau de Jonnès, *Statistique de l'Espagne* (Paris, 1834) gives the following estimates (in thousands):—

1803: 10,351 1826: 13,953 1834:14,660.

[61] From 1888 (2nd line) the statistics are of resident population.

[62] The Channel Islands and the Isle of Man are not included.

[63] Alexander Webster's census.

[64] Territories in Slovenia and Croatia, and the town of Zara (Zadar) were acquired from Italy in 1945.

[65] In 1954 the final boundary settlement with Italy added certain territories in the Trieste area.

[66] These are not census figures but estimates at 31 December.

[67] Estimated population in 1970: Males 1,097, Females 1,039, Total 2,136 thousand.

B2 POPULATION OF COUNTRIES BY SEX AND AGE GROUPS (in thousands)

ALBANIA

	1945		1950		1955		1960	
	M	F	M	F	M	F	M	F
0—4	88	75	91	84	115	107	148	138
5—9	84	71	81	72	88	81	...	...
10—14	69	58	76	66	80	70	...	...
15—19	47	50	64	54	76	65	...	71
20—24	30	40	56	48	63	54	...	65
25—29	35	36	41	41	55	48	...	54
30—34	30	33	38	36	40	40	...	48
35—39	34	34	35	33	37	36	...	40
40—44	26	27	30	31	34	33	...	35
45—49	28	27	24	23	29	30	...	32
50—54	...	...	23	24	22	22	...	29
55—59	...	...	15	18	20	23	...	22
60—64	....	...	16	19	14	18	...	...
65—69	...	...	13	15	14	16	...	...
70—74	99	101	9	11	10	13	...	...
75—79	...	...	6	7	7	9	...	...
80 and over	...	...	7	9	7	10	...	...
Unknown	- -	- -	1	1	3	4	...	2

Abbreviations used throughout this table : M = males, F = females.

B2 Population of Countries by Sex and Age Groups (in thousands)

AUSTRIA

1. Austrian Provinces of the Hapsburg Empire[1]

	1869[2]		1880		1890		1900		1910	
	M	F	M	F	M	F	M	F	M	F
0–4	1,323	1,335	1,449	1,466	1,528	1,544	1,708	1,706	2,106	2,094
5–9	1,096	1,116	1,209	1,213	1,321	1,312	1,464	1,445	1,660	1,663
10–14	1,019	1,009	1,090	1,102	1,222	1,234	1,328	1,347	1,521	1,536
15–19	916	974	1,021	1,065	1,110	1,159	1,219	1,274	1,287	1,359
20–24	719	887	951	994	1,004	1,047	1,133	1,152	1,150	1,181
25–29	783	870	801	843	892	936	975	1,003	998	1,067
30–34	707	762	742	791	826	872	870	912	928	976
35–39	642	698	699	737	705	733	791	809	848	880
40–44	557	616	642	693	656	698	740	767	755	776
45–49	545	590	538	577	602	637	609	634	691	729
50–54	463	477	465	533	527	584	556	606	594	624
55–59	375	391	399	441	412	451	474	507	494	541
60–64	269	276	342	371	332	389	387	436	380	418
65–69	207	211	228	237	248	278	266	300	296	337
70–74	108	103	138	147	174	191	178	210	180	207
75–79	57	58	71	73	85	91	97	116	99	118
80 and over	28	29	36	40	45	51	61	75	47	62
unknown	—	—	—	—	—	—	—	—	—	—

2. Republic of Austria

	1923[3]		1934		1951		1961		1971	
	M	F	M	F	M	F	M	F	M	F
0–4	281	275	237	231	271	259	298	285	304	289
5–9	226	225	273	266	261	252	249	239	329	314
10–14	315	312	299	292	276	267	263	251	300	286
15–19	318	316	196	196	224	216	263	254	260	252
20–24	302	311	293	296	244	243	265	252	268	260
25–29	249	289	294	300	224	294	207	202	246	241
30–34	222	263	288	298	159	213	229	232	254	249
35–39	216	251	237	278	203	260	211	282	205	202
40–44	207	233	203	247	242	295	147	200	225	230
45–49	195	215	196	238	254	287	194	254	204	277
50–54	169	180	184	214	227	267	224	281	142	198
55–59	145	156	168	197	177	233	226	267	175	239
60–64	117	131	136	156	149	201	186	241	189	258
65–69	86	100	104	122	124	168	132	199	169	233
70–74			72	88	92	128	96	153	117	188
75–79	101	129	30	52	56	80	63	104	66	129
80 and over			23	33	34	51	46	81	49	109
Unknown			5	7	2	2	- -	- -	—	—

See p.65 for footnotes

B2 Population of Countries by Sex and Age Groups (in thousands)

BELGIUM

	1846		1856		1866		1880		1890		1900	
	M	F	M	F	M	F	M	F	M	F	M	F
0–4	254	251	245	244	291	289	344	339	353	351	394	389
5–9	240	234	224	221	254	251	309	305	330	327	347	345
10–14	217	207	222	216	223	221	279	274	316	313	325	323
15–19	197	193	217	210	214	210	256	252	301	296	324	321
20–24	198	196	201	192	204	203	232	231	279	264	305	301
25–29	165	162	179	173	190	186	196	194	231	230	276	275
30–34	151	150	170	166	169	166	175	176	205	207	242	240
35–39	144	141	151	147	158	149	175	173	175	175	211	211
40–44	134	127	138	136	147	142	159	159	156	158	186	189
45–49	128	123	126	124	127	124	138	137	154	156	166	173
50–54	91	100	116	111	116	116	127	126	136	139	135	142
55–59	65	83	101	99	100	101	112	114	113	116	128	136
60–64	61	72	68	75	88	87	90	94	97	102	106	114
65–69	49	56	46	59	71	72	69	75	78	86	80	88
70–74	34	38	33	41	38	45	50	56	53	60	57	65
75–79	21	24	21	25	20	28	31	34	31	37	35	42
80 and over	15	18	13	17	13	19	18	23	20	26	20	27
Unknown	—	—	—	—	—	—	—	—	—	—	—	—

	1910		1920		1930[4]		1947		1961		1970	
	M	F	M	F	M	F	M	F	M	F	M	F
0–4	382	378	257	254	336	332	327	314	392	373	364	347
5–9	384	381	320	318	349	343	268	262	371	355	403	386
10–14	372	370	349	347	252	248	294	288	357	343	395	378
15–19	344	343	364	363	326	323	328	323	308	297	371	357
20–24	317	315	342	345	357	346	348	332	277	275	369	354
25–29	305	302	292	308	366	354	308	296	301	301	294	283
30–34	282	281	271	282	336	336	266	260	327	326	299	293
35–39	258	257	267	271	286	301	325	322	334	334	316	314
40–44	225	226	250	254	263	273	330	331	260	263	324	325
45–49	193	196	228	232	255	261	313	322	274	279	324	331
50–54	156	160	195	201	234	241	265	291	295	309	221	290
55–59	132	143	160	170	204	213	221	249	284	307	261	282
60–64	107	120	128	143	165	176	198	223	243	282	249	286
65–69	92	105	90	107	123	138	166	191	182	234	214	278
70–74	64	75	62	77	83	100	126	150	132	179	153	217
75–79	36	45	39	51	44	58	73	93	91	127	92	148
80 and over	23	32	22	32	27	41	44	58	70	108	74	133
Unknown	—	—	4	3	—	—	—	—	—	—	—	—

See p.65 for footnotes

B2 Population of Countries by Sex and Age Groups (in thousands)

BULGARIA

	1881[5]		1888		1892		1900		1905		1910		1920[16]	
	M	F	M	F	M	F	M	F	M	F	M	F	M	F
0–4	147	141	274	263	246	239	276	270	295	290	314	307	253	243
5–9	184	172	217	209	259	251	247	245	269	264	294	288	315	303
10–14	109	104	178	164	198	186	238	229	239	232	267	255	330	312
15–19	64	87	130	135	146	142	208	202	209	207	211	212	271	268
20–24	68	66	83	94	109	111	137	132	182	176	182	185	213	221
25–29	83	90	89	99	100	105	121	123	134	133	177	173	165	178
30–34	65	61	81	96	85	97	109	110	114	114	128	122	138	163
35–39	80	69	108	101	104	94	108	94	118	101	119	106	151	160
40–44	54	37	95	86	85	83	82	85	85	86	94	92	108	117
45–49	48	39	91	67	85	68	82	71	81	75	85	78	95	96
50–54	24	20	61	56	68	63	66	73	65	77	66	79	87	92
55–59	30	32	48	39	54	42	68	53	84	62	80	64	83	91
60–64	19	16	45	43	53	48	64	58	67	63	68	64	67	70
65–69	22	20	29	25	30	24	38	28	45	33	46	37	51	45
70–74	10	8	28	29	28	27	31	29	34	31	37	33	41	41
75–79	11	11	15	13	13	11	12	10	15	13	17	13	21	18
80 & over	10	8	28	29	27	26	22	22	22	22	23	22	28	28
Unknown	--	--	3	2	2	2	--	--	--	—	--	--	1	1

	1926		1934		1946		1956		1965		1975	
	M	F	M	F	M	F	M	F	M	F	M	F
0–4	397	385	364	350	338	324	350	336	322	306	343	326
5–9	290	278	367	353	307	295	362	348	336	321	321	304
10–14	290	274	370	355	355	341	319	308	346	331	315	291
15–19	307	297	225	218	354	342	288	282	358	346	328	314
20–24	263	266	290	283	367	363	327	326	294	290	333	329
25–29	221	225	272	265	249	249	327	321	288	285	329	326
30–34	169	175	236	232	258	256	339	338	328	322	285	285
35–39	143	162	190	192	271	261	232	231	331	325	289	290
40–44	144	154	144	154	244	237	243	239	325	325	323	326
45–49	113	118	137	154	196	192	253	243	197	198	323	319
50–54	84	97	129	135	146	150	224	218	250	243	313	323
55–59	97	85	94	197	114	147	171	177	234	237	182	183
60–64	76	73	76	80	125	139	123	139	188	193	224	234
65–69	56	54	63	59	82	91	90	116	137	152	189	207
70–74	41	42	46	46	49	57	79	97	81	100	133	152
75–79	25	23	25	24	33	35	43	53	53	76	73	92
80 and over	28	28	27	27	30	33	32	40	47	63	54	74
Unknown	--	--	1	1	--	--	--	--	—	—	--	--

See p.65 for footnotes

B2 Population of Countries by Sex and Age Groups (in thousands)

CZECHOSLOVAKIA

	1921		1930		1946/7[7]		1950		1961		1970	
	M	F	M	F	M	F	M	F	M	F	M	F
0–4	526	511	713	697	582	562	640	616	587	560	548	522
5–9	698	693	769	753	471	458	522	506	665	636	566	539
10–14	784	777	476	465	446	436	429	420	661	635	584	556
15–19	733	746	684	684	512	504	471	464	538	523	659	630
20–24	645	681	737	731	525	544	489	499	442	432	639	616
25–29	494	568	669	683	410	422	507	533	448	445	508	502
30–34	422	494	574	624	393	413	289	301	481	491	417	418
35–39	394	453	454	525	505	519	485	502	501	527	433	439
40–44	367	414	391	460	466	484	480	494	309	327	459	479
45–49	348	384	360	416	414	446	439	460	427	450	474	512
50–54	315	345	327	378	316	373	352	401	457	482	278	303
55–59	261	286	297	336	249	303	261	319	394	432	393	434
60–64	220	258	241	277	209	261	213	271	305	374	382	438
65–69	158	189	179	211	165	207	168	218	204	285	289	369
70–74	103	132	127	160	120	155	122	161	136	203	189	287
75–79	55	71	70	93	73	94	77	102	86	134	99	177
80 and over	31	45	39	60	44	64	48	69	59	98	66	132
unknown	6	7	7	9	8	9	4	5	—	—	4	4

DENMARK[8]

	1801		1834		1840		1850		1860	
	M	F	M	F	M	F	M	F	M	F
0–4	107	107	143	141	80	79	87	86	106	104
5–9					67	66	78	76	89	87
10–14	80	81	130	127	65	64	71	69	77	76
15–19					67	66	64	63	73	72
20–24	73	77	99	100	59	61	55	63	66	69
25–29					49	50	58	63	60	61
30–34	62	61	82	82	42	43	52	53	55	56
35–39					44	43	45	45	56	56
40–44	54	53	58	62	35	35	39	39	48	48
45–49					31	33	38	39	39	40
50–54	42	42	47	51	24	26	30	31	33	35
55–59					22	24	24	26	31	32
60–64	27	30	29	34	18	21	18	21	22	24
65–69					13	16	15	18	16	20
70–74	11	13	13	16	9	11	10	12	10	13
75–79					5	7	6	7	6	8
80 and over	2	4	3	5	3	5	4	5	4	6
unknown	...	...	...	...	...	...	...	...	...	...

See p.65 for footnotes

B2 Population of Countries by Sex and Age Groups (in thousands)

DENMARK (cont'd.)

	1870		1880		1890		1901		1911	
	M	F	M	F	M	F	M	F	M	F
0–4	112	110	128	125	140	138	154	152	168	165
5–9	97	94	108	106	127	124	136	134	153	150
10–14	92	91	100	98	115	112	128	126	145	143
15–19	83	82	89	88	98	97	119	118	127	127
20–24	70	74	81	87	80	90	100	106	108	119
25–29	65	68	71	76	71	81	85	92	99	110
30–34	58	62	61	66	70	78	75	83	92	100
35–39	56	57	57	61	64	68	67	74	80	86
40–44	51	52	52	55	54	59	66	73	70	77
45–49	50	51	48	49	52	54	57	62	61	69
50–54	42	43	43	45	46	49	50	55	59	66
55–59	33	34	41	43	39	42	43	48	50	55
60–64	25	29	33	36	34	37	37	41	41	47
65–69	21	24	23	27	30	34	29	34	33	38
70–74	13	16	15	19	20	24	21	24	24	29
75–79	8	10	10	13	11	14	14	18	15	19
80 and over	4	7	6	8	7	10	9	13	10	15
unknown	- -	- -	1	1	1	1	3	3	5	5

	1921[9]		1930		1940		1950		1960		1970	
	M	F	M	F	M	F	M	F	M	F	M	F
0–4	173	169	157	154	162	157	214	204	202	193	200	190
5–9	169	167	169	165	150	146	201	193	189	180	200	191
10–14	170	168	166	162	155	151	160	155	190	181	188	179
15–19	156	156	164	164	167	164	148	144	211	201	191	181
20–24	137	148	156	162	160	161	148	148	194	187	215	203
25–29	119	130	140	150	161	162	157	160	153	150	190	180
30–34	109	119	129	141	157	160	155	157	139	140	153	148
35–39	102	110	115	124	142	147	156	158	141	144	140	140
40–44	93	99	104	113	129	137	152	155	151	156	142	143
45–49	80	84	96	103	112	119	136	142	148	151	151	155
50–54	68	75	87	92	99	106	121	130	147	151	142	146
55–59	57	64	72	76	88	94	103	111	137	145	141	147
60–64	52	60	59	65	76	80	87	95	115	128	126	138
65–69	40	47	45	52	58	62	72	79	93	109	100	118
70–74	29	35	36	42	40	46	55	59	69	84	74	95
75–79	19	22	22	26	43	52	34	38	46	57	49	66
80 and over	13	18	15	20			24	29	38	49	41	59
unknown	5	4	4	4	- -	- -	—	—	—	—	—	—

See p.65 for footnotes

B2 Population of Countries by Sex and Age Groups (in thousands)

FINLAND

	1751		1775		1800		1825	
	M	F	M	F	M	F	M	F
0–9	57	59	82	83	110	110	159	161
10–19	42	43	64	63	78	81	113	116
20–29	35	38	49	52	68	72	107	113
30–39	22	23	37	39	55	60	85	90
40–49	18	21	30	33	42	46	65	73
50–59	15	18	18	20	27	31	44	52
60–69	9	13	11	13	16	19	24	32
70–79	5	7	5	7	7	8	8	12
80 and over	2	3	1	2	1	2	1	2
unknown	—	—	—	—	—	—	—	—

	1850		1865		1870		1880		1890		1900	
	M	F	M	F	M	F	M	F	M	F	M	F
0–4	114	114	133	131	112	111	146	143	163	161	178	174
5–9	90	91	99	98	98	98	120	120	139	138	150	148
10–14	77	79	92	92	90	89	92	92	126	124	144	142
15–19	71	73	85	86	85	87	96	96	115	113	133	130
20–24	72	74	79	82	78	81	87	87	88	88	120	118
25–29	68	69	68	70	73	76	82	83	90	91	108	107
30–34	60	62	60	64	62	65	72	75	79	80	82	82
35–39	50	52	59	63	53	57	67	71	75	76	83	84
40–44	40	43	54	58	52	56	56	59	65	69	72	74
45–49	40	44	46	50	45	49	46	50	60	64	67	70
50–54	36	40	37	40	37	42	44	49	48	53	57	62
55–59	29	33	27	32	27	32	37	43	38	44	50	56
60–64	19	24	25	30	19	23	27	34	33	40	37	43
65–69	14	19	18	23	15	19	18	23	25	31	27	33
70–74	9	13	11	15	9	13	9	13	15	20	19	25
75–79	4	7	4	7	4	7	5	8	7	10	11	15
80 and over	2	4	2	4	2	3	3	5	3	5	5	8
unknown	—	—	—	—	—	—	—	—	—	—	—	—

	1910		1920		1930		1940		1950		1960		1970	
	M	F	M	F	M	F	M	F	M	F	M	F	M	F
0–4	202	197	177	171	171	165	172	166	257	246	208	199	173	166
5–9	176	172	181	175	183	177	161	156	193	184	224	215	194	187
10–14	161	158	165	159	188	183	173	168	167	162	251	241	203	195
15–19	143	140	179	172	167	164	176	171	158	154	189	183	216	205
20–24	137	135	179	175	144	148	153	154	165	162	159	153	228	217
25–29	125	123	155	155	127	130	158	162	148	161	148	141	169	162
30–34	112	111	134	139	122	124	158	162	124	144	155	153	146	142
35–39	100	99	117	122	112	114	134	141	135	152	140	146	139	136
40–44	76	76	112	117	99	102	113	125	137	152	117	139	146	148
45–49	75	77	101	105	88	91	94	106	115	131	126	147	130	149
50–54	63	67	87	93	64	68	82	96	94	114	125	146	106	132
55–59	56	61	72	81	61	68	69	84	74	93	100	122	109	138
60–64	44	52	50	58	48	56	56	72	59	82	75	103	101	133
65–69	35	43	42	53	38	47	42	58	43	66	53	78	72	105
70–74	22	29	28	39	25	33	25	37	29	49	36	60	46	79
75–79	12	17	18	26	15	21	16	26	17	31	20	39	25	48
80 and over	8	12	13	19	9	14	12	20	10	21	13	28	16	36
unknown	—	—	--	--	--	--	--	--	1	1		4	--	--

B2 Population of Countries by Sex and Age Groups (in thousands)

FRANCE

	1851		1856		1861[10]		1866		1872[11]	
	M	F	M	F	M	F	M	F	M	F
0–4	1,684	1,640	1,749	1,700	1,830	1,790	1884	1,836	1,698	1,656
5–9	1,678	1,620	1,666	1,621	1,654	1,626	1,700	1,659	1,660	1,610
10–14	1,604	1,545	1,621	1,559	1,644	1,598	1,614	1,567	1,599	1,544
15–19	1,595	1,555	1,543	1,532	1,637	1,618	1,627	1,608	1,531	1,518
20–24	1,455	1,524	1,358	1,552	1,503	1,577	1,547	1,598	1,511	1,664
25–29	1,436	1,434	1,419	1,489	1,463	1,474	1,495	1,498	1,292	1,314
30–34	1,354	1,353	1,370	1,357	1,401	1,372	1,398	1,389	1,278	1,266
35–39	1,296	1,277	1,320	1,291	1,340	1,312	1,356	1,333	1,249	1,238
40–44	1,186	1,175	1,214	1,181	1,250	1,225	1,253	1,237	1,170	1,161
45–49	1,055	1,045	1,091	1,083	1,155	1,145	1,176	1,177	1,098	1,099
50–54	1,041	1,029	958	955	1,009	1,002	1,041	1,044	984	992
55–59	739	832	860	880	844	859	881	889	890	897
60–64	592	722	630	714	771	784	754	754	748	756
65–69	470	526	452	540	510	589	613	638	534	568
70–74	334	364	323	361	326	399	371	433	407	431
75–79	171	209	183	208	194	226	190	245	218	251
80 and over	104	139	100	132	114	144	115	150	113	155
unknown	—	—	—	—	—	—	—	—	—	—

	1876		1881		1886		1891		1896	
	M	F	M	F	M	F	M	F	M	F
0–4	1,819	1,781	1,742	1,712	1,759	1,731	1,668	1,656	1,652	1,648
5–9	1,618	1,584	1,716	1,687	1,702	1,696	1,678	1,677	1,652	1,651
10–14	1,629	1,580	1,590	1,553	1,683	1,658	1,671	1,656	1,673	1,667
15–19	1,591	1,575	1,631	1,614	1,603	1,611	1,670	1,671	1,675	1,680
20–24	1,557	1,672	1,632	1,748	1,743	1,842	1,587	1,694	1,624	1,721
25–29	1,305	1,312	1,296	1,256	1,383	1,325	1,479	1,443	1,434	1,438
30–34	1,310	1,299	1,316	1,293	1,304	1,284	1,373	1,344	1,398	1,391
35–39	1,270	1,249	1,282	1,254	1,276	1,267	1,281	1,265	1,324	1,316
40–44	1,192	1,173	1,205	1,189	1,193	1,176	1,191	1,212	1,193	1,192
45–49	1,106	1,121	1,107	1,122	1,117	1,119	1,147	1,150	1,120	1,154
50–54	999	1,018	1,009	1,036	1,004	1,031	1,018	1,031	1,017	1,052
55–59	871	913	892	917	895	909	882	917	890	923
60–64	756	777	782	793	768	803	789	823	767	818
65–69	577	599	605	636	605	637	613	656	614	671
70–74	394	425	428	451	435	457	450	486	442	490
75–79	245	273	250	276	264	282	270	308	271	310
80 and over	144	182	174	211	168	201	165	212	175	225
unknown	—	—	—	—	—	—	—	—	—	—

See p.65 for footnotes

B2 Population of Countries by Sex and Age Groups (in thousands)

FRANCE (cont'd.)

	1901[12]		1906		1911		1921[11]		1926	
	M	F	M	F	M	F	M	F	M	F
0–4	1,714	1,713	1,735	1,721	1,693	1,670	1,148	1,121	1,781	1,752
5–9	1,610	1,614	1,660	1,652	1,671	1,656	1,507	1,501	1,156	1,129
10–14	1,623	1,614	1,617	1,601	1,661	1,639	1,714	1,699	1,559	1,538
15–19	1,636	1,643	1,590	1,604	1,593	1,596	1,734	1,721	1,730	1,703
20–24	1,568	1,620	1,560	1,600	1,535	1,570	1,410	1,643	1,662	1,708
25–29	1,503	1,515	1,527	1,559	1,523	1,553	1,235	1,556	1,630	1,657
30–34	1,383	1,410	1,436	1,437	1,482	1,499	1,256	1,516	1,272	1,543
35–39	1,340	1,350	1,336	1,372	1,401	1,406	1,277	1,501	1,277	1,513
40–44	1,231	1,243	1,264	1,273	1,270	1,302	1,320	1,444	1,251	1,453
45–49	1,115	1,132	1,158	1,194	1,194	1,226	1,275	1,335	1,267	1,396
50–54	1,007	1,093	1,922	2,061	1,060	1,113	1,137	1,209	1,139	1,262
55–59	927	976			916	979	1,021	1,107	1,030	1,132
60–64	791	861	799	862	770	891	852	966	886	1,000
65–69	612	687	631	725	640	734	651	774	690	830
70–74	459	535	707	853	451	551	736	984	753	1,011
75–79	263	318			259	333				
80 and over	156	214	155	225	158	241	160	265	172	286
unknown	—	—	—	—	—	—	—	—	—	—

	1931		1936		1946		1954		1962	
	M	F	M	F	M	F	M	F	M	F
0–4	1,756	1,715	1,604	1,584	1,397	1,351	2,028	1,953	2,061	1,985
5–9	1,790	1,746	1,697	1,678	1,384	1,364	1,832	1,765	2,047	1,974
10–14	1,185	1,147	1,768	1,735	1,560	1,536	1,358	1,315	2,125	2,046
15–19	1,560	1,518	1,147	1,123	1,631	1,615	1,471	1,443	1,603	1,541
20–24	1,721	1,667	1,485	1,474	1,634	1,643	1,621	1,561	1,417	1,338
25–29	1,798	1,699	1,674	1,643	1,046	1,070	1,629	1,573	1,601	1,514
30–34	1,624	1,648	1,715	1,659	1,384	1,419	1,537	1,526	1,674	1,616
35–39	1,259	1,534	1,556	1,606	1,558	1,569	991	998	1,641	1,629
40–44	1,227	1,460	1,182	1,467	1,566	1,565	1,497	1,504	1,243	1,250
45–49	1,184	1,404	1,143	1,398	1,363	1,481	1,499	1,520	1,220	1,262
50–54	1,175	1,324	1,089	1,326	1,009	1,350	1,421	1,469	1,418	1,482
55–59	1,078	1,187	1,058	1,240	940	1,250	1,348	1,348	1,351	1,453
60–64	895	1,031	933	1,080	845	1,153	835	1,199	1,130	1,332
65–69	722	872	727	892	739	997	721	1,068	754	1,154
70–74	506	659	530	699	552	772	549	860	571	940
75–79	291	414	311	453	317	497	389	618	389	704
80 and over	174	308	183	334	192	374	247	478	308	650
unknown	—	—	—	—	—	—	—	—	—	—

1968						1975					
	M	F		M	F		M	F		M	F
0–4	1,772	1,699	50–54	953	1,006	0–4	1,753	1,672	50–54	1,567	1,636
5–9	2,136	2,055	55–59	1,354	1,469	5–9	2,138	2,047	55–59	972	1,040
10–14	2,104	2,025	60–64	1,249	1,423	10–14	2,197	2,103	60–64	1,148	1,318
15–19	2,147	2,070	65–69	1,062	1,308	15–19	2,162	2,080	65–69	1,093	1,349
20–24	1,935	1,851	70–74	686	1,090	20–24	2,127	2,084	70–74	882	1,214
25–29	1,481	1,382	75–79	428	819	25–29	2,264	2,126	75–79	556	937
30–34	1,594	1,514	80 and over	387	883	30–34	1,595	1,466	80 and over	414	1,053
35–39	1,708	1,646	unknown	—	—	35–39	1,554	1,468	unknown	—	—
40–44	1,671	1,656				40–44	1,658	1,613			
45–49	1,530	1,561				45–49	1,663	1,649			

See p.65 for footnotes

B2 Population of Countries by Sex and Age Group (in thousands)

GERMANY

	1871		1880		1890		1900	
	M	F	M	F	M	F	M	F
0–4	2,602	2,590	3,092	3,077	3,225	3,204	3,698	3,672
5–9	2,313	2,313	2,583	2,588	2,769	2,762	3,207	3,199
10–14	2,144	2,126	2,343	2,333	2,712	2,700	2,926	2,912
15–19	1,852	1,893	2,101	2,126	2,392	2,410	2,666	2,653
20–24	1,722	1,825	1,902	1,973	2,105	2,152	2,540	2,560
25–29	1,546	1,670	1,620	1,696	1,842	1,903	2,225	2,243
30–34	2,672	2,800	1,501	1,583	1,662	1,725	1,962	1,990
35–39			1,365	1,432	1,429	1,491	1,708	1,741
40–44	2,130	2,245	1,239	1,317	1,297	1,392	1,510	1,578
45–49			1,039	1,099	1,175	1,267	1,260	1,345
50–54	1,663	1,770	906	1,002	1,012	1,126	1,105	1,239
55–59			805	895	814	915	948	1,081
60–64	1,017	1,122	670	754	654	770	756	891
65–69			461	524	524	621	545	655
70–74	408	453	290	334	352	420	357	446
75–79			160	187	178	218	211	268
80 and over	66	83	79	97	90	119	114	154
Unknown	–	–	–	–	–	–	–	–

	1910		1925[13]		1933[13]		1939[14]	
	M	F	M	F	M	F	M	F
0–4	3,923	3,867	2,984	2,887	2,418	2,331	3,056	2,926
5–9	3,714	3,684	2,023	1,963	2,705	2,627	2,441	2,353
10–14	3,471	3,449	3,134	3,079	2,904	2,808	2,729	2,650
15–19	3,149	3,138	3,285	3,258	2,067	2,019	3,077	2,968
20–24	2,807	2,802	3,065	3,086	3,077	3,064	1,985	1,918
25–29	2,509	2,517	2,468	2,839	3,077	3,089	3,131	3,075
30–34	2,406	2,416	2,027	2,553	2,856	2,915	3,156	3,118
35–39	2,096	2,105	1,965	2,319	2,197	2,681	2,905	2,922
40–44	1,813	1,853	1,853	2,054	1,915	2,380	2,221	2,673
45–49	1,537	1,606	1,860	1,986	1,836	2,141	1,874	2,357
50–54	1,312	1,433	1,588	1,645	1,704	1,892	1,772	2,093
55–59	1,033	1,173	1,327	1,401	1,630	1,753	1,597	1,806
60–64	838	1,009	1,029	1,137	1,274	1,366	1,486	1,635
65–69	642	793	740	876	953	1,069	1,094	1,208
70–74	430	549	467	591	630	752	737	853
75–79	232	305	246	338	334	434	417	519
80 and over	130	187	135	200	186	278	230	329
Unknown	–	–	–	–	–	–	–	–

See p.65 for footnotes

B2 Population of Countries by Sex and Age Groups (in thousands)

WEST GERMANY
(including West Berlin)

	1946[15]		1950[13]		1961		1970	
	M	F	M	F	M	F	M	F
0–4			1,764	1,676	2,294	2,181	2,416	2,300
5–9	7,101	6,953	1,897	1,821	2,004	1,909	2,556	2,434
10–14			2,271	2,190	1,946	1,851	2,234	2,118
15–19			1,823	1,754	1,883	1,800	2,044	1,952
20–24	1,107	1,927	1,824	1,862	2,437	2,321	1,905	1,820
25–29	908	1,575	1,563	2,095	2,002	1,892	2,227	2,066
30–34	2,477	3,838	1,090	1,466	1,956	1,926	2,588	2,367
35–39			1,624	2,145	1,647	2,156	2,047	1,882
40–44	3,000	3,618	1,825	2,233	1,225	1,692	1,947	1,978
45–49			1,850	2,042	1,563	2,105	1,623	2,192
50–54	2,129	2,763	1,495	1,823	1,795	2,294	1,056	1,468
55–59			1,142	1,552	1,772	2,077	1,574	2,180
60–64	896	1,074	1,000	1,303	1,390	1,803	1,563	2,124
65–69			839	1,041	949	1,455	1,350	1,814
70–74	1,789	2,064	662	802	711	1,078	858	1,410
75–79			385	466	473	692	488	942
80 and over			209	286	350	512	391	738
Unknown	- -	1	—	—	16	19	—	—

EAST GERMANY
(including East Berlin)

	1946[16]		1950		1964		1971	
	M	F	M	F	M	F	M	F
0–4	613	588	578	552	736	701	621	592
5–9	868	835	755	725	671	638	732	696
10–14	715	694	918	987	666	633	681	648
15–19	609	681	702	704	445	429	676	641
20–24	309	707	551	686	624	616	495	475
25–29	263	589	441	722	656	646	556	549
30–34	335	698	315	520	529	523	675	664
35–39	457	834	429	838	442	541	544	535
40–44	567	811	660	937	361	584	470	537
45–49	575	761	725	901	230	377	348	551
50–54	482	677	625	842	425	673	245	403
55–59	445	599	508	742	506	715	367	602
60–64	381	493	465	648	509	663	439	665
65–69	324	404	372	495	375	569	424	589
70–74	244	299	287	377	260	438	291	477
75–79	127	165	160	213	180	296	168	324
80 and over	65	100	77	121	133	216	133	254
Unknown	—	—	—	—	—	—	—	—

BERLIN

	1946			1946	
	M	F		M	F
0–4	90	88	50–54	104	164
5–9	115	90	55–59	105	148
10–14	89	69	60–64	93	117
15–19	70	80	65–69	72	94
20–24	40	92	70–74	44	59
25–29	43	80	75–79	19	33
30–34	63	134	80 and over	7	18
35–39	96	168	Unknown	—	—
40–44	122	169			
45–49	119	170			

See p.65 for footnotes

B2 Population of Countries by Sex and Age Groups (in thousands)

GREECE

	1861		1870		1879		1889		1907	
	M	F	M	F	M	F	M	F	M	F
0–4			105	102	129	121	173	160	193	181
5–9	257	244	97	91	111	102	148	133	179	165
10–14			81	71	101	86	132	113	150	140
15–19			63	74	77	86	102	114	121	152
20–24	63	70	56	61	59	63	79	83	103	107
25–29	56	49	74	69	70	72	93	95	104	115
30–34	66	61	54	47	56	60	75	71	65	56
35–39			52	46	64	35	85	78	108	112
40–44	51	47	33	29	54	36	71	45	64	56
45–49			31	32	42	19	55	47	66	63
50–54	34	31	22	20	22	25	30	26	43	34
55–59			23	23	25	13	32	33	46	46
60–64	19	17	15	13	15	14	20	18	29	25
65–69			13	12	14	6	19	19	28	28
70–74	9	9	7	6	7	5	9	8	13	11
75–79			4	4	5	5	7	6	9	9
80 and over			3	3	3	3	4	4	5	6
unknown	--	--	--	--	--	--	--	--	--	--

	1920		1928		1940		1950		1961	
	M	F	M	F	M	F	M	F	M	F
0–4	253	231	390	374	388	371	382	361	407	385
5–9	322	297	320	305	424	397	335	315	371	349
10–14	321	293	313	286	428	415	391	375	375	358
15–19	261	276	343	351	344	339	393	397	313	310
20–24	197	216	260	288	274	279	357	375	355	370
25–29	158	190	253	265	299	304	291	315	348	373
30–34	134	164	184	198	278	273	239	264	342	366
35–39	152	170	174	201	247	248	244	265	253	272
40–44	141	145	152	174	202	218	240	254	213	240
45–49	137	123	160	153	160	164	211	221	244	258
50–54	115	109	139	136	145	166	168	186	229	238
55–59	89	79	108	101	134	137	131	155	194	201
60–64	74	81	92	99	118	127	108	136	151	185
65–69	54	52	71	71	86	87	89	110	103	127
70–74	40	45	49	55	63	75	67	83	83	116
75–79	21	21	30	29	35	42	41	50	57	71
80 and over	22	26	26	33	47	44	34	29	52	78
unknown	---	---	---	---	—	—	—	—	—	—

	1971			1971	
	M	F		M	F
0–4	390	380	50–54	204	238
5–9	359	339	55–59	241	255
10–14	368	346	60–64	218	231
15–19	336	323	65–69	173	193
20–24	327	305	70–74	119	161
25–29	244	258	75–79	66	86
30–34	286	319	80 and over	69	110
35–39	314	337	unknown	—	—
40–44	321	342			
45–49	244	268			

B2 Population of Countries by Sex and Age Groups (in thousands)

HUNGARY

1. Ancient Kingdom of Hungary

	1869		1880		1890		1900		1910	
	M	F	M	F	M	F	M	F	M	F
0–4	1,131	1,144	1,237	1,236	1,225	1,225	1,292	1,286	1,373	1,358
5–9	891	901	950	952	1,068	1,064	1,117	1,116	1,204	1,194
10–14	834	838	901	908	909	911	1,021	1,023	1,154	1,143
15–19	689	782	805	893	762	783	950	989	1,010	1,049
20–24	621	646	764	789	664	710	762	793	803	871
25–29	663	670	700	695	664	678	654	672	772	800
30–34	571	549	628	653	638	652	626	654	654	692
35–39	537	526	593	565	560	535	603	593	570	595
40–44	418	399	568	567	506	519	583	574	556	575
45–49	422	404	430	406	438	414	480	459	515	513
50–54	304	284	359	393	402	415	430	448	491	502
55–59	256	247	272	270	280	273	341	324	399	382
60–64	172	156	255	267	235	261	299	310	319	336
65–69	130	120	138	131	154	152	190	185	230	222
70–74	56	48	86	90	112	117	123	134	161	168
75–79	34	29	38	37	49	48	64	64	82	83
80 and over	17	15	25	27	29	33	43	49	49	59
Unknown	—	—	8	10	4	6	1	1	1	2

2. Hungary as established by the Treaty of Trianon

	1910		1920		1930		1941		1949		1960		1970	
	M	F	M	F	M	F	M	F	M	F	M	F	M	F
0–4	488	483	336	327	444	438	396	386	408	392	424	406	363	341
5–9	425	421	433	433	454	444	399	390	383	372	467	448	334	316
10–14	415	412	458	456	311	303	428	422	371	364	400	387	423	401
15–19	372	381	419	426	413	421	448	442	389	387	378	375	470	448
20–24	307	321	350	405	416	423	283	298	383	400	330	349	396	383
25–29	297	299	285	341	373	377	387	395	366	407	355	368	372	369
30–34	255	257	250	298	339	364	408	404	228	259	367	386	326	346
35–39	224	224	243	276	267	311	363	360	357	393	358	396	349	363
40–44	207	207	217	240	235	275	325	347	324	351	212	239	358	379
45–49	184	180	194	200	225	253	251	293	308	326	338	377	346	386
50–54	173	175	182	185	196	217	214	256	246	296	309	340	202	229
55–59	148	145	156	153	167	176	197	229	188	233	276	305	309	356
60–64			134	140	146	153	160	186	167	213	217	265	264	311
65–69			101	103	113	116	124	139	131	164	148	201	213	262
70–74	296	311	61	68	80	87	92	102	90	113	110	154	145	204
75–79			33	35	46	51	54	61	53	65	70	99	78	127
80 and over			18	23	24	31	34	44	32	44	44	64	56	99
Unknown			2	2	1	1	1	1	- -	- -	- -	- -	—	—

B2 Population of Countries by Sex and Age Groups (in thousands)

IRELAND 1. The whole country

	1861		1871		1881		1891		1901		1911	
	M	F	M	F	M	F	M	F	M	F	M	F
0–4	352	342	331	322	292	284	239	232	225	218	221	215
5–9	310	302	320	312	315	307	258	250	228	223	222	216
10–14	306	291	322	307	315	301	280	270	234	225	217	210
15–19	329	344	259	273	274	285	276	274	235	238	215	208
20–24	298	317	214	244	232	246	224	221	217	227	191	185
25–34	367	391	343	390	296	338	286	312	321	336	312	324
35–44	277	319	260	284	263	296	227	261	234	249	273	264
45–54	262	286	225	252	214	229	218	241	195	219	198	196
55–64	205	224	205	220	172	192	163	171	169	182	138	145
65–74	87	97	112	113	106	108	93	99	96	95	144	170
75–79	35[17]	41[17]	39[17]	44[17]	47[17]	47[17]	44[17]	46[17]	38[17]	40[17]	53[17]	58[17]
80 and over	6[18]	8[18]	8[18]	9[18]	7[18]	8[18]	9[18]	10[18]	8[18]	8[18]	8[18]	8[18]
Unknown	3	1	2	2	2	1	1	1	–	–	–	–

2. NORTHERN IRELAND

	1926		1937		1951		1961		1966		1971	
	M	F	M	F	M	F	M	F	M	F	M	F
0–4	65	63	57	55	71	67	75	71	83	78	82	77
5–9	59	58	58	56	66	63	68	64	75	71	82	76
10–14	60	59	62	59	57	55	68	65	68	64	74	70
15–19	59	61	57	57	55	53	60	60	64	62	67	62
20–24	53	57	51	54	49	52	47	47	52	54	60	56
25–29	46	54	48	53	48	52	42	44	43	44	48	48
29–34	38	44	44	47	45	47	42	45	41	43	42	42
35–39	35	41	42	47	46	49	44	47	41	44	41	41
40–44	33	37	36	40	43	46	42	43	43	46	40	43
45–49	34	37	32	36	39	42	42	45	41	43	42	44
50–54	32	33	29	33	36	40	40	43	40	43	39	41
54–59	27	28	28	30	29	33	34	38	37	41	38	41
60–64	21	22	27	28	24	30	29	36	31	37	33	38
65–69	19	20	23	24	22	26	23	29	25	33	26	34
70–74	14	18	16	19	18	22	17	23	18	25	19	28
75–79	8	10	9	11	12	15	11	16	12	17	12	19
80 and over	6	8	6	8	8	11	10	15	10	16	10	17
Unknown	–	–	–	–	–	–	–	–	–	–	–	–

3. SOUTHERN IRELAND (Irish Republic)

	1926		1936		1951		1961		1966		1971	
	M	F	M	F	M	F	M	F	M	F	M	F
0–4	146	142	136	132	160	153	153	147	161	155	162	154
5–9	149	140	136	133	144	138	147	141	152	147	162	155
10–14	151	145	144	139	133	128	148	141	146	140	152	146
15–19	146	140	138	130	126	115	120	114	133	126	137	131
20–24	125	116	135	120	105	97	80	78	95	91	110	105
25–29	107	109	113	104	100	99	72	73	75	74	88	85
30–34	93	91	94	89	96	95	75	78	74	73	77	75
35–39	87	88	97	96	102	99	82	85	77	78	75	74
40–44	86	83	84	79	94	86	85	86	81	82	76	76
45–49	87	82	81	76	82	79	89	86	84	83	80	81
50–54	86	77	79	74	83	80	82	75	84	81	80	79
55–59	67	59	75	68	65	64	69	68	76	71	78	76
60–64	54	52	68	62	61	61	65	67	62	62	68	66
56–69	52	50	60	53	54	53	51	52	55	59	54	57
70–74	38	45	41	45	49	51	44	49	42	48	45	54
75–79	21	25	25	28	32	33	30	34	29	34	28	34
80 and over	19	24	15	19	20	24	24	31	24	32	24	34
Unknown	–	–	–	–	–	–	–	–	–	–	–	–

See p.65 for footnotes

B2 Population of Countries by Sex and Age Groups (in thousands)

ITALY

	1861		1871[19]		1881		1901		1911	
	M	F	M	F	M	F	M	F	M	F
0–4	1,495	1,465	1,571	1,526	1,751	1,688	2,147	2,061	2,197	2,116
5–9	1,189	1,157	1,483	1,434	1,530	1,479	1,812	1,750	1,911	1,840
10–14	1,084	1,056	1,369	1,320	1,383	1,327	1,714	1,674	1,862	1,808
15–19	959	1,079	1,176	1,241	1,301	1,334	1,495	1,526	1,560	1,673
20–24	915	934	1,169	1,176	1,213	1,233	1,305	1,335	1,393	1,521
25–29	912	945	1,027	1,046	1,050	1,078	1,071	1,134	1,131	1,309
30–34	720	705	957	967	1,015	1,042	995	1,054	1,023	1,146
35–39	850	842	835	829	886	891	952	983	931	1.018
40–44	571	541	848	845	893	902	894	926	884	947
45–49	602	611	700	683	692	689	810	827	846	881
50–54	438	403	700	682	723	738	760	797	805	838
55–59	434	444	449	430	539	532	664	674	690	703
60–64	270	247	487	485	542	548	560	587	624	652
65–69	220	225	288	268	301	284	414	422	477	479
70–74	118	107	225	217	248	244	297	302	334	347
75–79	80	79	102	91	117	103	172	168	184	185
80 and over	43	40	87	90	81	82	95	100	115	124
unknown	—	—	..	..	2	2	1	1	57	63

	1921[20]		1931		1936		1951[21]		1961	
	M	F	M	F	M	F	M	F	M	F
0–4	1,813	1,736	2,328	2,246	2,218	2,140	2,219	2,113	2,152	2,044
5–9	2,062	1,989	2,278	2,205	2,210	2,148	1,981	1,893	2,031	1,948
10–14	2,131	2,058	1,619	1,567	2,233	2,180	2,141	2,074	2,159	2,070
15–19	1,879	1,862	2,032	2,014	1,562	1,529	2,037	2,004	1,917	1,860
20–24	1,627	1,703	1,910	1,914	1,979	1,955	2,062	2,039	2,060	2,013
25–29	1,307	1,500	1,565	1,650	1,833	1,841	1,960	2,024	1,900	1,894
30–34	1,206	1,374	1,350	1,520	1,536	1,584	1,382	1,477	1,919	1,944
35–39	1,093	1,214	1,139	1,370	1,323	1,470	1,675	1,757	1,859	1,949
40–44	1,023	1,079	1,071	1,273	1,113	1,322	1,665	1,714	1,314	1,415
45–49	947	966	992	1,131	1,031	1,217	1,409	1,477	1,597	1,690
50–54	841	860	904	980	948	1,079	1,183	1,327	1557	1,643
55–59	775	781	809	856	842	915	950	1,179	1,268	1,382
60–64	687	713	694	743	730	783	837	1,042	1,010	1,209
65–69	518	527	597	635	588	641	689	844	751	1,014
70–74	385	401	430	468	463	504	516	605	590	808
75–79	220	220	256	282	282	321	334	398	399	542
80 and over	129	148	153	185	176	220	220	290	301	424
unknown	84	116	6	6	2	2	—	—	—	—

	1971			1971	
	M	F		M	F
0–4	2,272	2,156	50–54	1,228	1,357
5–9	2,366	2,252	55–59	1,430	1,574
10–14	2,142	2,041	60–64	1,371	1,539
15–19	1,961	1,889	65–69	1,043	1,263
20–24	2,081	2,013	70–74	715	988
25–29	1,755	1,752	75–79 80 and over	793	1,300
30–34	1,917	1,939			
35–39	1,805	1,845	unknown	—	—
40–44	1,840	1,882			
45–49	1,757	1,871			

See p.65 for footnotes

B2 Population of Countries by Sex and Age Group (in thousands)

NETHERLANDS

	1840		1849		1859		1869		1879		1889	
	M	F	M	F	M	F	M	F	M	F	M	F
0–4	190	188	173	171	202	199	234	232	276	273	299	294
5–9	158	154	175	171	181	177	197	193	225	225	256	255
10–19	293	290	308	305	320	315	335	331	390	387	456	455
20–29	229	241	262	271	274	283	276	288	300	306	347	359
30–39	184	193	201	210	230	237	238	247	249	257	270	277
40–49	145	157	157	167	176	183	201	205	214	219	225	230
50–54			117	132	127	138	145	155	169	177	182	191
55–59	135	155										
60–64			40	50	48	55	49	55	61	67	69	76
65–69			27	34	33	41	40	47	44	52	56	63
70–74	66	82	18	23	21	27	27	32	28	33	36	43
75–79			11	15	11	14	14	19	17	21	20	25
80 and over			7	10	6	9	8	11	10	13	12	16
Unknown	1	--	--	--	1	1	1	1	--	--	--	--

	1899		1909		1920		1930		1940		1947		1960	
	M	F	M	F	M	F	M	F	M	F	M	F	M	F
0–4	334	328	373	365	396	381	427	409	434	415	599	568	594	565
5–9	290	287	338	331	377	367	427	412	419	399	432	414	567	539
10–14	271	267	311	306	363	354	384	372	418	402	412	394	614	585
15–19	244	243	279	277	341	334	374	370	422	408	415	401	472	451
20–24	220	227	246	251	298	301	351	359	376	366	400	401	414	400
25–29	186	197	217	226	263	271	320	331	362	363	363	370	388	378
30–34	167	175	201	211	233	242	283	295	340	351	345	355	379	381
35–39	150	154	175	184	213	220	252	263	311	323	325	339	374	387
40–44	127	129	156	163	196	204	224	232	274	285	303	318	336	347
45–49	119	121	138	142	171	178	203	209	242	253	265	281	324	339
50–54	99	104	114	118	146	153	184	190	212	219	236	248	305	324
55–59	94	99	103	107	127	133	155	161	186	192	200	210	273	295
60–64	79	86	80	87	97	102	126	132	160	167	170	178	227	252
65–69	58	65	70	76	77	84	100	106	124	131	136	144	185	208
70–74	41	48	50	57	54	60	66	71	87	94	98	106	139	157
75–79	26	32	28	35	35	40	41	46	54	60	56	63	93	106
80 and over	15	20	19	25	23	30	28	34	34	41	36	43	73	88
Unknown	--	--	--	--	--	--	--	--	—	—	—	—	—	—

	1970			1970	
	M	F		M	F
0–4	607	579	50–54	323	339
5–9	624	595	55–59	301	326
10–14	594	567	60–64	267	304
15–19	569	543	65–69	220	265
20–24	618	585	70–74	161	209
25–29	483	444	75–79	110	147
30–34	431	394	80 and over	97	182
35–39	397	377	Unknown	—	—
40–44	380	379			
45–49	368	383			

B2 Population of Countries by Sex and Age Groups (in thousands)

NORWAY

	1801		1855		1865		1875		1890		1900	
	M	F	M	F	M	F	M	F	M	F	M	F
0–4	110	109	103	99	117	113	115	111	133	128	144	139
5–9			86	84	103	100	102	99	120	115	134	128
10–14	81	80	76	73	91	88	100	97	110	106	123	118
15–19			64	64	81	80	92	91	90	93	110	108
20–24	64	73	63	70	67	71	76	83	67	82	90	98
25–29			60	66	56	62	61	69	59	76	73	83
30–34	54	60	100	102	54	57	53	59	55	68	61	72
35–39					55	57	46	51	52	63	57	68
40–44	47	54	64	67	47	48	46	49	46	54	53	61
45–49					43	45	46	49	42	49	49	57
50–54	34	39	29	33	29	32	42	45	37	42	43	50
55–59			26	28	25	27	34	37	36	39	37	42
60–64	21	27	22	26	22	25	24	27	34	38	30	35
65–69			17	20	19	23	18	20	29	32	29	33
70–74	10	14	16	21	14	16	14	17	20	24	24	27
75–79					8	11	10	13	12	14	17	20
80 and over	3	4	5	7	5	8	8	11	8	12	12	16
Unknown	..	..	—	—	—	—	—	—	1	1	—	—

	1910		1920		1930		1946		1950		1960		1970	
	M	F	M	F	M	F	M	F	M	F	M	F	M	F
0–4	144	138	150	144	121	116	151	144	164	155	158	150	169	160
5–9	143	138	143	138	142	137	111	107	137	130	155	147	161	152
10–14	137	132	140	135	145	140	103	99	109	105	163	154	157	150
15–19	120	118	135	133	137	133	116	113	104	100	135	129	155	148
20–24	90	100	118	123	122	124	134	130	117	112	107	103	162	152
25–29	73	87	100	105	110	118	137	136	133	129	101	98	134	126
30–34	70	81	82	90	104	110	128	127	132	131	114	110	105	102
35–39	62	70	70	80	91	96	120	121	126	124	130	127	99	97
40–44	54	63	67	75	76	84	109	114	116	118	129	129	111	108
45–49	51	61	58	65	64	74	101	107	105	111	122	121	126	124
50–54	48	56	50	58	62	69	88	93	96	103	111	114	123	126
55–59	43	50	46	55	52	59	70	78	81	87	98	106	113	117
60–64	36	41	40	48	43	51	57	67	64	73	86	96	98	108
65–69	29	35	34	41	36	45	48	56	50	60	68	77	81	96
70–74	21	26	25	31	29	36	38	45	41	49	49	59	104	136
75–79	17	20	17	21	20	26	23	31	27	34	32	42		
80 and over	15	20	14	20	17	23	22	32	23	33	30	41	34	53
Unknown	—	—	—	—	1	1	2	2	..	..	—	—	—	—

B2 Population of Countries by Sex and Age Groups (in thousands)

POLAND

	1921		1931		1950		1960		1970	
	M	F	M	F	M	F	M	F	M	F
0–4	1,315	1,283	2,020	1,962	1,538	1,485	1,729	1,652	1,281	1,225
5–9	1,476	1,464	2,005	1,962	1,006	983	1,793	1,722	1,399	1,334
10–14	1,790	1,754	1,405	1,372	1,156	1,136	1,547	1,493	1,730	1,659
15–19	1,478	1,662	1,474	1,562	1,196	1,191	968	956	1,772	1,706
20–24	1,113	1,328	1,514	1,707	894	1,208	863	1,088	1,499	1,459
25–29	887	970	1,417	1,506	928	1,129	1,134	1,149	949	939
30–34	695	843	1,119	1,265	641	751	1,123	1,188	1,076	1,079
35–39	651	732	880	991	756	921	949	1,105	1,127	1,130
40–44	582	662	742	859	858	952	625	725	1,097	1,158
45–49	590	584	650	737	728	821	744	878	915	1,071
50–54	518	574	558	652	563	700	797	900	587	694
55–59	433	436	494	549	399	513	648	766	674	827
60–64			420	496	314	441	466	627	676	824
65–69			333	379	220	314	295	435	498	665
70–74	893	953	212	257	148	225	194	320	307	490
75–79			173	217	90	144	105	187	155	286
80 and over					62	118	69	144	102	232
Unknown	- -	- -	204[23]	15	28[24]	34[24]	35	36	10	10

See p.65 for footnotes

B2 Population of Countries by Sex and Age Groups (in thousands)

PORTUGAL

	1864		1875		1890		1900		1911	
	M	F	M	F	M	F	M	F	M	F
0–4	246	237	321[29]	314[29]	298	291	324	313	358	348
5–9	219	210	239[28]	231[28]	283	272	310	300	357	346
10–14	259[27]	247[27]	220[28]	211[28]	271	254	295	285	324	312
15–19	161[28]	203[28]	189[28]	220[28]	225	237	251	265	278	292
20–24	156[28]	187[28]	170	195[28]	191	214	217	248	233	278
25–29	166[28]	194[28]	173[28]	206[28]	169	197	184	208	195	237
30–34	115[28]	129[28]	126[28]	145[28]	155	180	162	189	177	214
35–39	166[28]	182[28]	161[28]	183[28]	139	159	142	164	156	183
40–44	107[28]	113[28]	101[28]	114[28]	145	164	145	169	151	176
45–49	124[28]	139[28]	132[28]	153[28]	117	135	119	139	124	147
50–54	61[28]	71[28]	85[28]	98[28]	120	139	124	150	127	157
55–59	85[28]	106[28]	106[28]	122[28]	78	94	86	104	92	111
60–64	48[28]	55[28]	55[28]	59[28]	93	109	92	115	96	122
65–69	45[28]	55[28]	46[28]	58[28]	57	76	52	64	59	74
70–74	19[28]	22[28]	21[28]	26[28]	44	52	42	56	48	64
75–79	16[28]	20[28]	18[28]	23[28]	20	23	22	28	24	30
80 and over	9[28]	11[28]	10[28]	13[28]	16	22	19	27	21	32
unknown	3	3	3	3	9	10	6	6	7	7

	1920		1930		1940		1950		1960	
	M	F	M	F	M	F	M	F	M	F
0–4	306	298	389	381	425	404	454	435	424	403
5–9	347	335	388	374	427	409	406	392	400	385
10–14	348	335	330	316	408	395	406	394	393	385
15–19	307	320	338	344	373	375	404	407	341	354
20–24	240	276	303	322	315	316	380	382	316	343
25–29	204	242	247	288	297	311	335	347	304	326
30–34	175	217	203	239	267	290	263	278	288	302
35–39	162	196	190	220	230	266	273	294	268	287
40–44	153	187	172	205	194	228	248	277	225	243
45–49	139	161	151	181	171	204	211	249	229	250
50–54	124	154	144	174	154	192	176	215	210	241
55–59	96	118	117	142	126	160	146	186	173	211
60–64	91	117	102	128	114	148	126	169	136	177
65–69	61	78	72	94	82	112	95	135	105	144
70–74	45	63	51	73	57	83	99	100	79	116
75–79	24	33	30	43	34	53	41	66	50	81
80 and over	20	32	22	39	26	50	27	57	35	72
unknown	13	15	6	7	11	13	—	—	—	—

	1970	
	M	F
0–4	402	387
5–9	432	417
10–14	411	402
15–19	355	375
20–24	298	330
25–29	241	277
30–34	250	284
35–39	263	292
40–44	261	290
45–49	243	270
50–54	209	235
55–59	206	234
60–64	184	226
65–69	140	186
70–74		
75–79		
80 and over	192	314
unknown	—	—

See p.65 for footnotes

B2 Population of Countries by Sex and Age Groups (in thousands)

ROMANIA

	1899		1912		1930[30]		1930[31]		1956		1966	
	M	F	M	F	M	F	M	F	M	F	M	F
0–4	475	474	493	490	1,316	1,288	1,027	1,007	944	904	712	676
5–9	369	369	457	453	1,090	1,077	840	829	832	803	892	853
10–14	355	344	407	399	719	702	551	526	675	655	938	898
15–19	293	316	369	374	1,007	1,096	786	852	782	800	811	779
20–24	244	206	312	315	850	796	673	637	805	790	640	628
25–29	220	241	293	297	767	812	614	649	786	775	779	778
30–34	161	155	239	226	533	559	429	449	660	715	786	777
35–39	233	229	203	192	536	645	428	518	390	467	762	760
40–44	143	118	177	169	437	469	352	377	525	606	652	711
45–49	161	151	160	146	428	491	342	396	543	568	363	445
50–54	78	68	147	154	291	292	231	236	459	470	498	580
55–59	114	123	104	102	267	316	213	257	374	426	489	538
60–64	125	100	124	115	214	204	175	168	269	352	402	446
65–69			62	54	185	192	152	159	202	278	279	348
70–74	43	29	55	52	103	92	85	77	145	202	172	250
75–79			24	16	65	62	54	47	71	110	104	162
80 and over	11	7	29	23	34	35	29	29	40	66	64	112
Unknown	1	1	2	1	44	44	36	36	1	1	7	10

RUSSIA

	1897		1926		1939[33]		1959		1970	
	M	F	M	F	M	F	M	F	M	F
0–4	7,031	7,099	11,238	11,085	11,027	10,779	23,608	22,734	10,435	10,075
5–9	10,875	11,007	7,650	7,620	8,737	8,764			12,475	12,001
10–14			8,643	8,448	10,455	10,521	16,066	15,742	12,730	12,258
15–19	8,304	8,952	8,133	8,844	8,110	8,320			11,225	10,774
20–24			6,712	7,101	7,164	7,207	10,056	10,287	8,627	8,478
25–29	6,270	6,691	5,490	6,547	7,937	8,512	8,917	9,273	6,813	6,957
30–34			4,297	4,768	6,541	7,194	8,611	10,388	10,408	10,736
35–39	5,117	5,287	3,994	4,458	5,330	6,418	4,528	7,062	8,140	8,454
40–44			3,393	3,562	3,748	4,772	3,998	6,410	8,758	10,244
45–49	3,658	3,906	2,893	3,015	2,986	3,821	4,706	7,558	4,744	7,512
50–54			2,343	2,698	2,690	3,287	4,010	6,437	3,430	5,648
55–59	2,566	2,710	1,887	2,318	2,235	2,720	2,905	5,793	4,273	7,740
60–64			1,709	2,126	1,765	2,276	2,348	4,349	5,922	11,673
65–69	1,340	1,447	1,157	1,407	1,321	1,777	1,751	3,289		
70–74			722	981	865	1,236	2,021	4,148	2,506	5,519
75–79	573	579	369	463	507	775				
80 and over			363	506	248	424	520	1,283	783	2,112
Unknown	16	15	50	38	–	–	4	4	130	138

SERBIA

	1890 M	1890 F		1890 M	1890 F
0–4	198	195	50–54	27	20
5–9	159	155	55–59	33	36
10–14	121	111	60–64	19	11
15–19	114	112	65–69	18	16
20–24	90	79	70–74	5	4
25–29	85	89	75–79	8	8
30–34	55	50	80 and over	7	6
35–39	75	73	Unknown	1	..
40–44	40	34			
45–49	55	53			

See p.65 for footnotes

B2 Population of Countries by Sex and Age Groups (in thousands)

SPAIN

	1857 M	1857 F		1860 M	1860 F
0–1	222	213	0–1	209	200
1–7	1,284	1,258	1–5	927	896
8–15	1,286	1,237	6–10	844	823
16–20	666	740	11–15	795	765
21–25	607	660	16–20	683	786
26–30	728	751	21–25	620	663
31–40	1,156	1,136	26–30	672	720
41–50	761	784	31–40	1,185	1,174
51–60	544	577	41–50	832	841
61–70	308	318	51–60	545	583
71–80	92	97	61–70	328	331
81 and over	19	23	71–80	94	101
			81 and over	19	23

	1877 M	1877 F	1887 M	1887 F	1900 M	1900 F	1910 M	1910 F
0–4	1,028	992	1,063	1,035	1,091	1,070	1,196	1,170
5–9	840	818	937	912	1,055	1,047	1,174	1,054
10–14	816	787	909	885	987	971	1,047	1,043
15–19	711	777	676	734	754	804	855	914
20–24	599	734	696	747	734	820	776	857
25–29	591	664	808[34]	883[34]	678	736	694	760
30–34	580	636	516	554	622	665	652	718
35–39	496	509	591	651	553	583	569	621
40–44	503	537	459	467	552	601	566	609
45–49	416	424	472	518	440	491	489	515
50–54	448	467	700	749	455	499	466	512
55–59	330	323			337	358	357	390
60–64	303	316	478	473	329	364	356	407
65–69	149	150			192	205	229	248
70–74	100	107	142	146	147	160	159	178
75–79	49	49			73	77	76	84
80 and over	34	45	22	30	69	66	55	77
Unknown	3	3	2	3	11	10	9	10

	1920 M	1920 F	1930 M	1930 F	1940 M	1940 F	1950 M	1950 F	1960 M	1960 F	1970 M	1970 F
0–4	1,130	1,120	1,324	1,283	1,137	1,111	1,318	1,255	1,514	1,456	1,658	1,560
5–9	1,175	1,153	1,313	1,272	1,390	1,370	1,251	1,184	1,377	1,323	1,652	1,591
10–14	1,157	1,148	1,153	1,308	1,376	1,365	1,180	1,147	1,369	1,309	1,543	1,474
15–19	1,003	1,081	1,080	1,108	1,248	1,297	2,649	2,710	2,389	2,312	1,363	1,337
20–24	859	955	1,053	1,097	1,015	1,167					1,279	1,262
25–29	750	833	933	988	952	1,107	2,066	2,255	2,365	2,450	1,117	1,119
30–34	704	771	803	851	929	994					1,022	1,049
35–39	594	646	686	745	826	908	1,737	1,951	1,920	2,076	1,200	1,208
40–44	617	679	656	697	734	808					1,150	1,180
45–49	506	550	558	602	628	702	1,443	1,618	1,599	1,803	1,054	1,083
50–54	490	532	530	583	572	622					805	907
55–59	396	421	424	479	466	530	992	1,187	1,235	1,463	752	880
60–64	475	430	385	443	423	513					683	811
65–69	237	270	281	321	309	392	828	1,194	1,027	1,478	571	712
70–74	173	207	192	234	208	269					380	534
75–79	86	100	102	132	124	167					413	689
80 and over	57	86	66	110	79	144						
Unknown	34	34	25	23	—	—	7	7	16	48	—	—

See p.65 for footnotes

B2 Population of Countries by Sex and Age Groups (in thousands)

SWEDEN

	1751		1760		1770		1780		1790		1800	
	M	F	M	F	M	F	M	F	M	F	M	F
0–4	123	124	128	130	131	132	140	140	136	136	149	149
5–9	88	89	102	95	102	103	95	96	106	104	122	121
10–14	88	88	95	95	101	102	100	102	105	104	114	112
15–19	79	84	77	82	95	95	93	97	89	92	100	103
20–24	70	82	70	83	81	89	90	98	86	96	94	104
25–29	68	76	67	80	70	77	84	91	82	92	82	92
30–34	58	65	65	75	67	75	75	81	78	84	80	89
35–39	50	55	58	65	65	70	64	69	71	77	74	83
40–44	44	51	50	57	59	65	59	64	64	69	71	77
45–49	38	44	42	49	49	57	52	59	53	58	62	70
50–54	34	43	36	43	41	49	47	54	46	53	53	60
55–59	25	34	30	38	33	41	38	45	40	48	41	48
60–64	26	40	26	35	28	36	31	38	33	40	33	41
65–69	20	28	18	26	19	28	20	26	24	30	25	33
70–74	13	20	13	21	13	18	12	17	14	20	16	23
75–79	6	9	7	12	7	10	7	10	7	11	9	12
80 and over	6	9	5	9	6	9	4	7	4	7	4	7
Unknown	—	—	—	—	—	—	—	—	—	—	—	—

	1810		1820		1830		1840		1850		1860	
	M	F	M	F	M	F	M	F	M	F	M	F
0–4	141	141	168	167	193	192	194	193	219	216	259	255
5–9	120	120	129	130	168	168	173	171	184	184	205	203
10–14	119	118	116	116	144	144	163	164	168	168	177	186
15–19	111	114	115	117	129	131	165	166	169	170	177	177
20–24	93	106	110	115	107	111	133	137	154	158	154	159
25–29	86	97	104	110	106	110	115	119	148	153	150	156
30–34	82	91	88	97	102	106	97	102	123	128	138	146
35–39	69	77	78	87	93	100	94	100	104	110	138	145
40–44	66	76	72	82	76	87	87	95	86	93	111	119
45–49	61	70	58	67	65	77	77	88	80	89	90	101
50–54	54	63	54	64	58	70	61	74	72	83	69	80
55–59	47	55	46	58	44	55	49	62	60	73	62	74
60–64	35	44	38	48	37	49	42	56	45	60	52	64
65–69	24	30	28	38	28	39	26	36	30	43	40	53
70–74	15	21	17	24	19	27	18	27	20	31	23	34
75–79	9	12	8	12	10	16	10	16	10	16	12	19
80 and over	4	8	4	7	5	9	5	10	6	11	7	13
Unknown	—	—	—	—	—	—	—	—	—	—	—	—

B2 Population of Countries by Sex and Age Groups (in thousands)

SWEDEN (cont'd.)

	1870		1880		1890		1900		1910	
	M	F	M	F	M	F	M	F	M	F
0–4	248	243	285	278	295	288	300	289	316	303
5–9	243	241	246	240	265	258	278	269	296	286
10–14	273	221	222	218	247	241	268	262	280	270
15–19	189	188	227	225	219	213	248	238	260	252
20–24	160	168	193	200	170	179	216	210	227	230
25–29	145	159	157	167	166	181	175	180	198	205
30–34	131	144	137	151	149	168	144	158	180	188
35–39	130	141	129	144	131	146	146	164	156	165
40–44	119	131	117	130	119	134	135	154	131	146
45–49	118	129	115	127	113	129	118	133	134	152
50–54	92	104	103	117	101	116	106	122	122	140
55–59	72	86	98	112	97	111	98	114	104	119
60–64	52	64	73	86	83	98	83	99	89	105
65–69	41	54	52	65	73	87	74	89	76	92
70–74	28	39	31	42	47	58	56	69	57	72
75–79	16	25	20	28	26	36	39	49	41	53
80 and over	8	15	11	20	15	24	22	32	31	44
unknown	. .	. .	. .	. .	—	—	—	—	—	—

	1920		1930		1940		1950		1960	
	M	F	M	F	M	F	M	F	M	F
0–4	288	276	231	223	227	218	312	297	260	245
5–9	292	281	267	257	209	200	302	288	274	259
10–14	302	289	278	268	227	220	230	222	313	298
15–19	283	274	284	274	264	255	211	205	303	291
20–24	257	252	280	275	273	264	230	229	236	230
25–29	223	230	250	256	276	269	269	264	220	216
30–34	200	213	228	236	275	270	274	268	236	234
35–39	180	191	204	217	248	251	275	269	269	265
40–44	166	176	187	202	223	230	272	268	271	265
45–49	144	154	169	180	197	208	242	247	269	265
50–54	120	134	154	163	177	190	213	222	261	261
55–59	119	137	130	140	155	166	183	197	226	235
60–64	103	122	104	118	134	145	156	173	191	206
65–69	82	100	95	113	105	116	129	143	152	173
70–74	62	76	74	90	74	87	100	112	116	138
75–79	42	55	47	59	54	67	64	72	78	94
80 and over	34	47	37	51	42	55	47	60	64	81
unknown	—	—	—	—	—	—	—	—	—	—

	1970			1970	
	M	F		M	F
0–4	297	281	50–54	260	259
5–9	293	279	55–59	253	256
10–14	273	258	60–64	234	245
15–19	282	270	65–69	187	211
20–24	339	323	70–74	140	169
25–29	326	301	75–79	91	122
30–34	252	237	80 & over	77	112
35–39	226	219	Unknown	—	—
40–44	238	235			
45–49	266	264			

B2 Population of Countries by Sex and Age Groups (in thousands)

SWITZERLAND

	1860		1870		1880		1888		1900		1910	
	M	F	M	F	M	F	M	F	M	F	M	F
0–4	137	138	148	148	167	167	162	161	189	189	203	201
5–9	115	116	141	141	150	149	155	155	169	168	197	197
10–14	117	117	128	129	137	138	153	154	157	157	188	187
15–19	121	122	110	112	134	135	135	136	159	156	180	177
20–24	111	117	102	114	114	122	117	127	148	153	155	161
25–29	97	103	103	112	98	101	108	117	137	136	153	151
30–34	94	99	95	103	95	99	91	98	118	120	145	145
35–39	84	88	87	91	94	98	85	91	107	111	129	128
40–44	73	77	82	87	86	91	81	88	93	98	109	113
45–49	67	69	73	77	75	79	79	86	76	81	97	103
50–54	60	64	61	66	68	74	68	76	69	78	80	89
55–59	53	55	54	57	58	64	57	64	65	73	62	71
60–64	41	43	45	48	44	50	49	56	52	62	52	63
65–69	27	28	35	37	34	37	38	43	39	46	43	53
70–74	20	21	22	22	23	25	22	25	27	32	29	36
75–79	10	10	10	10	13	14	12	14	15	18	16	20
80 and over	6	6	6	6	6	6	7	8	8	9	9	12
Unknown	2	2	8	7	—	—	—	—	—	—	—	—

	1920		1930		1941		1950		1960		1970	
	M	F	M	F	M	F	M	F	M	F	M	F
0–4	166	162	165	160	155	150	211	201	228	216	251	239
5–9	183	181	176	172	160	154	200	192	207	196	261	250
10–14	196	195	164	161	164	160	156	151	214	210	237	228
15–19	191	196	180	183	172	169	164	164	224	204	230	220
20–24	165	184	182	194	163	163	168	182	206	196	259	253
25–29	143	162	170	185	166	169	173	185	209	199	269	251
30–34	131	146	152	170	175	185	157	162	193	194	234	217
35–39	129	138	134	150	166	179	169	177	188	191	216	205
40–44	126	133	122	136	150	168	174	185	158	159	197	198
45–49	112	118	118	127	129	147	160	176	172	179	186	192
50–54	93	102	110	121	112	129	138	159	173	179	156	162
55–59	79	90	93	104	103	117	114	136	145	165	157	170
60–64	60	73	72	85	89	106	94	115	119	143	145	170
65–69	41	52	55	69	70	86	79	98	92	120	117	150
70–74	28	39	35	48	45	59	59	78	65	89	82	120
75–79	17	24	18	26	27	39	35	49	45	66	51	82
80 and over	10	15	11	18	15	24	21	35	33	54	39	72
Unknown	—	—	—	—	—	—	—	—	—	—	—	—

B2 Population of Countries by Sex and Age Groups (in thousands)

UNITED KINGDOM
England and Wales

	1841[35]		1851		1861		1871		1881		1891	
	M	F	M	F	M	F	M	F	M	F	M	F
0–4	1,048	1,058	1,177	1,171	1,355	1,346	1,536	1,535	1,758	1,763	1,775	1,778
5–9	953	952	1,050	1,042	1,173	1,172	1,351	1,356	1,569	1,579	1,693	1,702
10–14	880	852	964	949	1,060	1,045	1,221	1,204	1,402	1,398	1,611	1,613
15–19	782	805	873	884	958	975	1,085	1,096	1,268	1,279	1,465	1,486
20–24	723	827	796	871	860	969	952	1,053	1,112	1,216	1,247	1,399
25–29	611	672	699	771	734	835	843	937	981	1,067	1,111	1,239
30–34	565	602	618	658	662	725	746	814	840	905	978	1,050
35–39	435	450	533	556	590	634	641	700	745	797	866	916
40–44	436	452	474	494	551	583	590	640	673	726	746	802
45–49	314	325	394	406	453	478	507	546	548	604	642	695
50–54	307	327	346	363	392	414	456	489	486	536	550	611
55–59	190	202	255	271	299	315	346	372	382	425	413	471
60–64	209	231	227	254	266	291	295	328	341	387	357	416
65–69	121	139	152	176	176	201	205	236	232	271	260	312
70–74	104	120	115	135	128	153	150	174	158	192	185	233
75–79	56	64	65	81	72	89	82	100	90	113	102	132
80 and over	44	58	45	62	47	66	53	74	56	78	60	89
Unknown	—	—	—	—	—	—	—	—	—	—	—	—

	1901		1911		1921		1931		1951		1961	
	M	F	M	F	M	F	M	F	M	F	M	F
0–4	1,855	1,861	1,936	1,918	1,682	1,640	1,510	1,480	1,904	1,814	1,846	1,751
5–9	1,739	1,748	1,847	1,850	1,767	1,752	1,678	1,645	1,616	1,546	1,671	1,592
10–14	1,671	1,671	1,748	1,752	1,837	1,823	1,620	1,587	1,429	1,383	1,907	1,818
15–19	1,608	1,639	1,655	1,682	1,728	1,775	1,710	1,725	1,335	1,369	1,622	1,579
20–24	1,473	1,648	1,503	1,673	1,448	1,703	1,699	1,795	1,427	1,500	1,434	1,443
25–29	1,328	1,496	1,456	1,623	1,340	1,620	1,629	1,728	1,625	1,654	1,446	1,400
30–34	1,158	1,274	1,376	1,501	1,281	1,520	1,433	1,622	1,514	1,565	1,502	1,483
35–39	1,035	1,111	1,261	1,352	1,273	1,472	1,283	1,520	1,633	1,691	1,616	1,626
40–44	898	953	1,075	1,158	1,223	1,378	1,229	1,434	1,658	1,707	1,494	1,543
45–49	760	813	926	1,000	1,162	1,244	1,187	1,367	1,556	1,616	1,584	1,645
50–54	636	693	768	834	971	1,043	1,116	1,265	1,318	1,507	1,575	1,646
55–59	498	555	608	670	782	849	987	1,081	1,089	1,334	1,408	1,520
60–64	410	480	477	543	601	681	778	879	939	1,204	1,096	1,362
65–69	282	347	366	441	449	537	578	693	781	1,049	819	1,160
70–74	196	251	237	317	281	376	377	494	591	837	600	942
75–79	113	151	128	183	159	234	204	296	375	549	389	680
80 and over	70	107	79	129	92	164	114	208	226	418	295	612
Unknown	—	—	—	—	—	—	—	—	—	—	—	—

	1971			1971	
	M	F		M	F
0–4	2,003	1,902	50–54	1,412	1,485
5–9	2,074	1,970	55–59	1,434	1,542
10–14	1,865	1,762	60–64	1,330	1,511
15–19	1,696	1,618	65–69	1,063	1,336
20–24	1,876	1,855	70–74	692	1,085
25–29	1,612	1,579	75–79	410	776
30–34	1,460	1,411	80 and over	327	805
35–39	1,410	1,376	Unknown	—	—
40–44	1,467	1,468			
45–49	1,552	1,584			

See p.65 for footnotes

B2 Population of Countries by Sex and Age Groups (in thousands)

UNITED KINGDOM
Scotland

	1841[35]		1841		1861		1871		1881		1891	
	M	F	M	F	M	F	M	F	M	F	M	F
0–4	174	169	189	183	212	205	231	225	258	252	255	248
5–9	159	155	172	168	184	179	205	200	228	222	242	236
10–14	151	146	163	155	165	158	190	182	206	199	229	223
15–19	128	142	146	154	150	157	167	168	190	189	211	207
20–24	113	141	129	152	127	153	138	154	167	177	174	190
25–29	93	113	104	126	101	132	116	139	137	152	145	168
30–34	86	102	89	105	91	111	100	120	112	125	129	141
35–39	65	77	76	89	79	96	85	105	98	114	114	124
40–44	67	79	71	83	74	89	80	96	91	106	97	108
45–49	46	53	57	66	62	73	67	80	74	89	85	98
50–54	45	56	54	65	56	68	61	74	67	81	74	89
55–59	29	34	37	44	43	51	48	58	51	62	56	68
60–64	34	43	33	45	41	53	43	55	46	60	50	64
65–69	17	22	22	29	24	33	29	38	31	42	34	46
70–74	16	21	18	24	18	26	23	32	23	33	25	36
75–79	9	11	10	14	11	15	12	17	13	19	14	22
80 and over	8	12	8	13	8	13	9	14	10	16	10	17
Unknown	3	2	—	—	3	..	—	—	—	—	—	—

	1901		1911		1921		1931		1951		1961	
	M	F	M	F	M	F	M	F	M	F	M	F
0–4	268	265	268	265	239	234	214	210	241	230	240	229
5–9	249	243	258	256	240	237	229	226	203	195	215	206
10–14	238	231	247	243	247	243	215	211	196	191	230	219
15–19	230	226	233	229	239	239	219	220	173	189	187	187
20–24	210	223	202	218	203	226	206	216	172	192	159	174
25–29	181	198	182	204	173	204	187	203	187	194	161	166
30–34	151	164	170	185	155	183	162	187	166	179	163	170
34–39	133	145	158	167	150	174	144	172	178	191	171	177
40–44	119	127	133	143	146	163	135	158	180	190	153	167
45–49	101	108	115	126	142	148	130	151	169	181	164	179
50–54	84	93	98	108	119	125	127	140	141	167	164	178
55–59	86	77	79	87	97	104	116	123	116	145	147	165
60–64	56	70	60	70	76	85	92	100	98	127	113	146
65–69	37	50	46	58	57	67	68	81	83	109	83	121
70–74	26	38	32	48	35	49	46	60	66	86	60	94
75–79	15	23	17	26	19	30	25	36	42	56	40	65
80 and over	10	18	10	19	12	23	13	25	24	41	31	54
Unknown	—	—	..	..	..	..	..	..	1	1	—	—

	1971			1971	
	M	F		M	F
0–4	228	216	50–54	140	156
5–9	240	228	55–59	143	163
10–14	227	216	60–64	134	159
15–19	199	193	65–69	107	141
20–24	197	194	70–74	68	111
25–29	158	158	75–79	39	76
30–34	148	152	80 and over	31	72
34–39	147	153	Unknown	—	—
40–44	151	157			
45–49	157	166			

See p.65 for footnotes

B2 Population of Countries by Sex and Age Group (in thousands)

YUGOSLAVIA

	1921		1931		1948		1953	
	M	F	M	F	M	F	M	F
0–4	612	585	1,000	971	840	808	1,046	1,002
5–9	705	671	898	858	858	828	769	738
10–14	768	727	563	535	915	883	818	787
15–19	624	628	643	642	866	857	891	866
20–24	495	546	701	670	668	782	873	850
25–29	363	413	588	587	478	585	664	771
30–34	337	430	485	516	360	426	483	583
35–39	327	381	360	399	543	594	341	412
40–44	300	354	326	399	499	501	521	566
45–49	245	257	300	339	425	468	481	497
50–54	245	263	260	311	297	357	402	439
55–59	204	199	210	225	244	326	280	349
60–64	195	202	193	215	210	274	211	285
65–69	122	112	150	151	164	222	178	243
70–74	92	94	108	116	103	131	123	169
75–79	48	44	56	56	64	85	70	98
80 and over	49	52	49	53	48	64	53	77
unknown	1	1	1	1	--	--	--	1

	1961		1971	
	M	F	M	F
0–4	990	947	918	877
5–9	1,023	978	938	893
10–14	936	897	959	914
15–19	694	684	1,013	971
20–24	797	784	900	854
25–29	825	823	649	642
30–34	767	792	762	761
35–39	563	682	803	799
40–44	343	414	738	767
45–49	423	492	540	663
50–54	483	515	323	399
55–59	409	442	383	465
60–64	311	373	414	467
65–69	184	246	315	369
70–74	136	202	206	276
75–79	86	125	94	145
80 and over	64	102	76	134
unknown	9	9	46	47

B2 Population of Countries by Sex and Age Groups (in thousands)

NOTES

1. SOURCES:— With the following exceptions, all figures are taken from the official publications listed on p. xv. Czechoslovakia 1930 (ages over 60) — data supplied by the Federal Statistical Office of Czechoslovakia; Finland 1865 and Greece 1870, 1879, and 1889 — J. Bertillon, *Statistique Internationale des Rencensements de la Population....* (Paris, 1899); Greece 1861 — U.N., *The Aging of Populations and its Economic and Social Implications* (1956); Russia 1897 — A.D. Webb, *New Dictionary of Statistics,* London, 1911); Russia 1926 and 1939 — F. Lorimer, *The Population of the Soviet Union* (Geneva, 1946); Sweden 1751–1850 — G. Sundbarg, *Statistisk Tidskrift, 1908.*

2. For fuller footnotes on territorial changes and on the nature of these statistics see table B.1.

FOOTNOTES

[1] Excluding Lombardy and Venetia.

[2] The statistics in 1869 relate to civil population only. The following classification of the civil population is available for 1857:-

	M	F		M	F
0–6	1,288	1,290	25–40	1,964	2,297
7–14	1,506	1,543	41–60	1,661	1,710
15–24	1,768	1,945	over 60	503	521

[3] 1st January in all provinces except Burgenland, for which the census was on 7th March.

[4] In 1930 and subsequently the eastern cantons ceded by Germany after the First World War are included.

[5] This does not include Eastern Roumelia. The figures given for the age group 5-9 are actually for 5-10, and older age groups are for 11-15, 16-20 etc. to 81 and over.

[6] The territory was enlarged between 1910 and 1920.

[7] Sub-Carpathian Russia (Ruthenia) and a few Slovak villages were ceded to Russia in 1945. The censuses were on 4th October 1946 in Slovakia and 22 May 1947 in the Czech lands.

[8] Denmark proper, excluding the Faroe Islands, Greenland, Iceland, and the Duchies of Schleswig, Holstein, and Lauenburg.

[9] Figures from 1921 onwards include the nortern part of Schleswig, returned to Denmark by Germany after the First World War.

[10] Subsequently includes Savoy and Nice, acquired in 1860.

[11] Figures from 1872 to 1911 exclude most of Alasace and Lorraine, ceded to Germany in 1871 and reacquired in 1918.

[12] Subsequent figures are not census results but estimates at 1 January in each census year.

[13] Excluding Saarland.

[14] 1937 territory.

[15] Excluding West Berlin and Saarland.

[16] Excluding East Berlin.

[17] The figures are for the age-group 75–84.

[18] These figures are for the age-group 85 and over.

[19] Subsequent figures include Venetia.

[20] Subsequent figures include South Tirol and, up to 1936 (inclusive) Istria.

[21] Istria and certain other areas ceded to Yugoslavia and France after the Second World War are not subsequently included.

[22] The figures relate to the territory of the year in question. There were considerable boundary changes after the Second World War.

[23] Including 191 thousand soldiers in barracks.

[24] Excluding 394 thousand not tabulated by age or sex.

[25] Excluding civilian aliens, and including civilian nationals temporarily abroad. The classification in this year was based on year of birth rather than completed years of age.

[26] Including Maderia and the Azores.

[27] Age-group 10–15, comprising six years.

[28] These figures are for age-groups one year older than shown in the stub (i.e. 16–20 instead of 15–19, etc.)

[29] Age-group 1–5, comprising six years.

[30] The territory of Romania was much enlarged between 1912 and 1930.

[31] These figures are for the territory established after the Second World War.
[32] European Russia (excluding Finland and the Caucasus).
[33] These are estimates by F. Lorimer (see note 1 above).
[34] These figures are for the age group 25–30, comprising six years. Subsequent figures are for age-groups 31–35, 36–40, etc.
[35] These figures are only approximate.

B3 POPULATION OF MAJOR DISTRICTS (in thousands)

AUSTRIA (a)
Habsburg Austria [3]

	1843	1846	1851	1857	1869	1880	1890	1900	1910
Lower Austria	1,453	1,531	1,538[1]	1,682[1]	1,991	2,331	2,662	3,100	3,532
Upper Austria	865	871	706[1]	707[1]	737	760	786	810	853
Salzburg			146[1]	147[1]	153	164	174	193	215
Styria	997	1,023	1,006[1]	1,057[1]	1,138	1,214	1,301	1,356	1,444
Tirol & Voralberg	848	866	858[1]	851[1]	886	913	929	982	1,092
Carinthia	777	796	319[1]	332[1]	338	349	361	367	396
Carniola			464[1]	452[1]	466	481	499	508	526
Küstenland	493	508	553[1]	521[1]	601	648	695	757	894
Dalmatia	406	418	394[1]	404[1]	457	476	527	594	646
Bohemia	4,319	4,410	4,386[1]	4,706[1]	5,141	5,561	5,843	6,319	6,770
Moravia	2,242	2,290	1,800[1]	1,867[1]	2,017	2,153	2,277	2,438	2,622
Silesia			439[1]	444[1]	513	565	606	680	757
Galicia	4,980	5,189	4,555[1]	4,597[1]	5,445	5,959	6,608	7,316	8,026
Bukowina			380[1]	457[1]	513	572	647	730	800

AUSTRIA (b)
Republic of Austria

	1910	1923	1934	1951	1961	1971
Lower Austria	1,425	1,427	1,447	1,400	1,374	1,414
Upper Austria	854	877	903	1,109	1,132	1,223
Salzburg	215	223	246	327	347	402
Styria	958	979	1.015	1,109	1,138	1,192
Tirol	305	314	349	427	446	541
Vorarlberg	145	140	155	194	226	271
Carinthia	371	371	405	475	495	526
Burgenland	292	286	299	275	271	272
Vienna	2,083	1,919	1,936	1,616	1,628	1,615

BELGIUM

	1801	1806	1811	1816	1831	1846	1856	1866	1976	1880	1890	1900	1910	1920	1930	1947	1961	1970
Antwerp	246	285	282	295	350	406	434	466	538	577	700	819	969	1,017	1,173	1,281	1,444	1,533
Brabant	246	303	...	445	562	691	749	814	936	985	1,106	1,264	1,470	1,522	1,680	1,798	1,992	2,176
East Flanders	560	602	601	622	743	793	777	806	863	882	950	1,030	1,120	1,107	1,149	1,217	1,277	1,310
West Flanders	460	492	...	521	608	643	625	642	684	692	738	805	874	804	902	997	1,073	1,054
Hainaut	415	474	...	494	613	715	769	845	956	978	1,049	1,143	1,233	1,220	1,270	1,225	1,260	1,317
Liége	...	311	...	361	375	453	504	557	632	664	757	826	888	863	973[5]	964	1,011	1,009
Limbourg	...	...	...	330	319	186[3]	192	195	205	211	223	241	276	300	368	460	579	653
Luxembourg	...	...	...	320	306	186[4]	194	200	204	209	212	219	231	224	221	213	219	217
Namur	...	...	...	223	214	264	286	303	316	323	335	347	363	348	356	356	373	381

CZECHOSLAVAKIA

	1910	1921	1930	1946/7[7]	1950	1961	1970
Bohemia, Moravia & Silesia	10,079	10,010	10,674	8,762	8,896	9,572	9,808
Slovakia	2,925	2,998	3,330	3,328[8]	3,442	4,174	4,537
Sub-Carpathian Russia (Ruthenia)	596	605	725				

See p.84 for footnotes

B3 Population of Major Districts (in thousands)

FRANCE

	1801	1831	1841	1851	1861	1872	1881	1891	1901	1911	1921	1931	1946	1954	1962	1968	1975
Ain	297	346[9]	356	373	370	363	363	357	350	342	316	323	307	312	328	339	376
Aisne	426	513	542	559	565	552	557	545	536	530	422	489	453	487	510	526	534
Allier	249	298	311	337	356	391	417	424	422	406	371	374	373	373	379	387	378
Alpes, Basses	134	156	156	152	146	139	132	124	115	107	92	88	83	84	92	105	112
Alpes, Hautes	113	129	133	132	125	119	122	116	110	105	89	88	85	85	89	92	97
Alpes Maritimes					195	199	227	259	293	356	358	493	453	515	614	722	817
Ardèche	267	341	364	387	389	380	377	371	354	332	294	283	255	249	246	257	257
Ardènnes	260[19]	291	319	331	329	320	334	325	316	319	278	294	245	280	297	309	309
Ariège	196	254	266	267	252	246	241	227	211	199	173	161	146	140	135	138	138
Aveyron	318[11]	359	375	394	396	402	415	400	382	369	333	324	308	293	287	282	278
Aube	231	246	258	265	263	256	255	256	246	241	228	243	235	241	252	270	285
Aude	225	270	284	290	284	286	328	317	314	301	287	297	269	268	268	278	272
Bouches-du-Rhône	285	359	375	429	507	555	589	631	734	806	842	1,012[12]	972	1,049	1,241	1,470	1,633
Calvados	452	495	496	491	481	454	440	429	410	396	385	401	400	443	477	520	561
Cantal	220	259	257	253	241	232	236	240	231	223	199	194	187	177	171	169	167
Charente	299	363	368	383	379	368	371	360	350	347	316	310	311	314	325	331	337
Charente-Maritime	399	445	460	470	481	466	466	456	452	451	418	415	416	448	471	484	498
Cher	218	256	274	306	323	335	351	359	346	338	305	294	286	284	291	305	316
Corrèze	244	295	306	321	310	303	317	328	318	310	274	264	255	243	239	238	240
Corsica[13]	164	198	221	236	253	259	273	289	296	291	282	297	268	247	276	274	290
Côte-d'Or	341	375	393	400	384	375	383	377	362	350	321	334	336	357	386	421	450
Côtes-du-Nord	504	599	608	633	629	622	628	619	609	606	558	540	527	503	498	506	526
Creuse	218	265	278	287	270	275	279	285	278	266	228	208	189	173	163	157	146
Dordogne	409	483	490	506	502	480	495	478	453	437	397	384	388	378	370	374	373
Doubs	216	266	286	297	296	291	311	303	299	300	285	306	298	327	383	426	471
Drôme	235	300	312	327	327	320	314	306	297	291	264	267	268	275	304	343	362
Eure	403	424	426	416	399	378	364	349	335	324	303	306	316	333	360	383	423
Eure-et-Loir	258	279	286	295	290	283	280	285	275	272	251	255	258	261	277	302	335
Finistère	439	524	576	618	627	643	682	727	773	810	763	744	725	728	739	769	804
Gard	300	357	376	408	422	420	416	419	421	413	396	407	381	397	433	479	495
Garonne, Haute	340[11]	428	468	482	484	479	478	472	448	432	425	442	512	526	592	691	777
Gers	258[11]	312	311	307	299	285	282	261	238	222	194	193	190	185	180	182	175
Gironde	503	554	568	614	667	705	749	794	821	829	819	853	858	897	936	1,009	1,061
Hérault	275	346	367	389	409	430	442	461	489	480	488	515	461	471	513	591	648
Ille-et-Vilaine	489	547	549	575	585	590	615	627	614	608	559	563	578	587	610	653	702
Indre	206	245	253	272	270	278	288	293	289	288	260	248	252	247	249	247	249
Indre-et-Loire	269	297	306	316	324	317	329	337	336	341	328	335	350	365	393	438	479
Isère	436	550	589	603	578	576	580	572	569	556	526	584	574	626	726	768	860
Jura	288	313	317	313	298	288	285	273	261	253	229	229	216	220	224	233	239
Landes	224	282	288	302	301[14]	301	301	298	292	289	264	257	248	249	260	277	288

See p.84 for footnotes

B3 **Population of Major Districts** (in thousands)

FRANCE (Cond.)

	1801	1831	1841	1851	1861	1872	1881	1891	1901	1911	1921	1931	1946	1954	1962	1968	1975
Loire	291	391	434	473	518	551	600	616	648	641	637	665	632	654	687	722	742
Loire Atlantique	369	470	487	536	580	602	626	645	665	670	650	652	665	734	794	861	934
Loire, Haute	230	292	298	305	306	309	316	317	314	304	269	252	228	216	210	208	205
Loir-et-Cher	210	236	249	262	269	269	276	280	276	271	252	242	242	240	248	268	284
Loiret	286	305	318	341	353	353	369	378	367	364	337	343	347	361	390	431	490
Lot	261[11]	285	288	296	296	281	280	254	227	206	177	167	155	148	149	151	151
Lot-et-Garonne	299[11]	347	347	341	332	319	312	295	279	268	240	248	265	266	272	291	293
Lozère	127	140	141	145	137	135	144	136	129	123	109	102	91	82	81	77	75
Maine-et-Loire	376	468	488	515	526	518	523	519	515	508	475	476	496	518	554	586	630
Manche	531	591	597	601	591	545	526	514	491	476	426	433	435	447	443	452	452
Marne	305	337	357	373	385	386	422	435	433	436	367	412	387	415	444	485	530
Marne, Haute	227	250	258	268	259	251	255	244	227	215	199	190	182	197	207	214	212
Mayenne	306	353	361	375	375	351	345	332	313	298	262	254	256	252	247	253	262
Meurthe[15]	338	416	445	450	429												
Meurthe-et-Moselle[15]						365	419	444	485	565	504	593	529	607	678	705	723
Meuse	270	315	326	329	306	385	290	292	283	278	207	216	189	207	218	210	204
Morbihan	401	434	448	478	487	490	522	544	563	578	546	538	507	521	527	540	564
Moselle[15]	348	417	440	460	446	(490)	(493)	(510)	(565)	(655)	589	693	622	769	923	971	1,006
Nièvre	233	282	305	327	333	340	348	344	324	299	270	255	249	240	243	248	245
Nord	765	990	1,085	1,158	1,303	1,448	1,603	1,736	1,867	1,962	1,788	2,029	1,917	2,099	2,274	2,418	2,511
Oise	351	398	399	404	401	397	405	402	408	411	388	407	397	435	482	541	606
Orne	396	442	442	440	423	398	376	354	327	307	275	274	273	275	278	289	294
Pas-de-Calais	506	655	685	693	724	761	819	874	955	1,068	990	1,205	1,169	1,277	1,348	1,396	1,403
Puy-de-Dôme	507	573	591	597	576	566	566	564	544	526	491	501	479	481	509	548	580
Pyrenées, Basses	356	428	452	447	436[14]	427	434	425	426	433	403	423	416	420	469	509	535
Pyrenées, Hautes	175	233	244	251	240	235	236	226	216	206	186	190	202	204	212	226	227
Pyrenées Orientales	111	157	174	182	182	192	209	210	212	213	218	239	229	230	252	282	300
Rhin, Bas	450	540	560	587	578	(600)[16]	(612)	(622)	(659)	(701)	652	688	673	708	764	827	882
Rhin, Hautes	304	424	465	494	516	(459)[17]	(462)	(472)	(495)	(518)	469	517	472	510	544	585	635
Rhône	299	434	501	575	662	670	741	807	843	916[18]	957[18]	1,046[18]	919	967	1,110	1,326	1,430
Sâone, Haute	292	339	347	347	317	303	296	281	267	258	228	219	203	209	208	214	222
Sâone-et-Loire	453	524	552	575	582	598	626	620	620	604	555	539	507	511	530	550	570
Sarthe	388	457	471	473	466	447	439	430	423	419	389	385	412	420	441	462	490
Savoie					275	268	266	263	255	248	225	236	236	252	266	289	305
Savoie, Haute					267	273	274	268	264	255	236	253	271	294	333	379	448

See p.84 for footnotes

B3 **Population of Major Districts** (in thousands)

FRANCE (Contd.)

	1801	1831	1841	1851	1861	1872	1881	1891	1901	1911	1921	1931	1946	1954	1962	1968	1975
Seine	632	935	1,195	1,422	1,954	2,220	2,799	3,142	3,670	4,154	4,412	4,934	4,776	5,155	5,575	...	...
Seine-et-Marne	299	324	333	345	352	341	349	357	358	364	349	406	407	453	526	604	756
Seine-et-Oise	422	448	471	484	513	580	578	629	707	818	922	1,366	1,415	1,709	2,302	...	...
Seine Maritime	610	694	737	762	790	790	814	840	854	877	881	905	846	942	1,025	1,114	1,173
Sèvres, Deux	242	295	310	324	329	331	350	354	342	338	310	308	313	313	317	326	336
Somme	459	544	560	571	573	557	551	546	538	520	453	467	441	464	482	511	538
Tarn	271	336	352	363	354	353	359	347	332	324	296	303	298	308	318	332	338
Tarn-et-Garonne	228[11]	242	239	238	233	222	217	207	196	183	160	164	168	172	175	184	183
Var	272	322	328	358	316[19]	294	289	288	326	331	323	377	371	413	485	556	626
Vaucluse	191	239	251	265	268	263	244	235	237	239	220	242	250	268	302	354	390
Vendée	243	330	356	384	396	401	422	442	441	439	397	390	394	396	403	421	451
Vienne	241	283	294	317	322	321	340	344	336	332	306	303	314	319	329	340	357
Vienne, Haute	245	285	293	319	320	322	349	373	382	385	350	336	336	324	329	342	352
Vosges	309	398	420	427	415	393[16]	407	410	421	434	384	378	342	373	380	388	398
Yonne	321	352	363	381	370	364	357	345	321	304	273	276	266	266	269	283	300
Territory of Belfort[17]	...	...	...	...	...	57	74	84	92	101	94	99	87	99	110	118	128
Ville de Paris	...	...	...	...	...	...	...	...	...	...	...	...	...	...	...	2,591	2,300
Yvelines	...	...	...	...	...	...	...	...	...	...	...	...	...	...	...	854	1,082
Essonne	...	...	...	...	...	...	...	...	...	...	...	...	...	...	...	673	923
Hauts-de-Seine	...	...	...	...	...	...	...	...	...	...	...	...	...	...	...	1,462	1,439
Seine-St. Denis	...	...	...	...	...	...	...	...	...	...	...	...	...	...	...	1,250	1,322
Val-de-Marne	...	...	...	...	...	...	...	...	...	...	...	...	...	...	...	1,121	1,216
Val-d'Oise	...	...	...	...	...	...	...	...	...	...	...	...	...	...	...	693	841

See p.84 for footnotes

B3 Population of Major Districts (in thousands)

GERMANY
(a) Constituents of United Germany

	1816	1828	1834	1840	1852	1861	1864
Prussia	10,349	12,726	13,510	14,929	16,935	18,491	19,255
States later incorporated in Prussia[20]	2,154	2,617	2,793	2,960	3,104	3,193	3,257
Bavaria	3,655	4,088	4,247	4,371	4,559	4,690	4,807
Kingdom of Saxony	1,190	1,373	1,596	1,706	1,988	2,225	2,337
Württemburg	1,411	1,549	1,570	1,646	1,733	1,721	1,748
Baden	1,006	1,176	1,231	1,296	1,362	1,373	1,432
Hesse	607	718	761	812	854	857	853
Thuringian states[21]	709	802	855	896	960	1,004	1,035
Other states[22]	1,491	1,596	1,676	1,766	1,918	2,013	2,068

(b) United Germany

	1864	1871	1880	1890	1900	1910	1910[23]	1925	1933	1939[24]
Prussia[25]	23,582	24,689[26]	27,279	29,957	34,473	40,165	35,053	38,176	39,934	41,334
of which										
East Prussia	1,761	1,823	1,934	1,959	1,997	2,064	2,147	2,256	2,333	2,186
West Prussia	1,253	1,315	1,406	1,434	1,564	1,703	310	332	338	. . .
Posen	1,524	1,584	1,703	1,752	1,887	2,100				
Pomerania	1,438	1,432	1,540	1,521	1,635	1,717	1,719	1,879	1,921	2,394
Berlin	633	826	1,122	1,579	1,889	2,071	3,734	4,024	4,243	4,339
Brandenburg	1,984	2,037	2,267	2,542	3,109	4,093	2,429	2,592	2,726	3,008
Silesia	3,511	3,707	4,008	4,224	4,669	5,226	4,259	4,512	4,687	4,869
Saxony	2,045	2,103	2,312	2,580	2,833	3,089	3,105	3,293	3,401	3,618
Schleswig-Holstein	999	1,045	1,127	1,220	1,388	1,621	1,455	1,519	1,590	1,589
Hanover	1,926	1,961	2,120	2,278	2,591	2,942	2,985	3,223	3,368	3,458
Westphalia	1,667	1,775	2,043	2,429	3,188	4,125	4,089	4,784	5,040	5,209
Hesse-Nassau	1,388	1,400	1,554	1,664	1,898	2,221	2,287	2,475	2,585	2,675
Rhineland	3,372	3,579	4,074	4,710	5,760	7,121	6,463	7,214	7,632	7,906
Hohenzollern	65	66	68	66	67	71	71	72	73	74
Bavaria	4,775	4,863	5,285	5,595	6,176	6,887	6,882	7,380	7,682	8,223
Kingdom of Saxony	2,337	2,556	2,973	3,503	4,202	4,807	4,809	4,994	5,197	5,232
Württemburg	1,748	1,819	1,971	2,037	2,169	2,438	2,438	2,580	2,696	2,897
Baden	1,432	1,462	1,570	1,658	1,868	2,143	2,143	2,312	2,413	2,502
Hesse	817	853	936	993	1,120	1,282	1,282	1,347	1,429	1,469

See p.84 for footnotes

B3 Population of Major Districts (in thousands)

GERMANY
(b) United Germany (Contd.)

	1864	1871	1880	1890	1900	1910	1910[23]	1925	1933	1939[24]
Mecklenburg[26]	652	655	677	676	711	746	746	784	805	900
Oldenburg[27]	314	317	337	355	399	483	483	545	574	578
Brunswick	293	312	349	404	465	494	494	502	513	603
Bremen	104	122	157	180	225	300	300	339	372	450
Hamburg	279	339	454	623	768	1,015	1,015	1,153	1,218	1,712
Thuringian states[21]	1,035	1,067	1,170	1,272	1,420	1,586	1,509	1,607	1,660	1,744
Alsace-Lorraine	(1,584)	1,550	1,567	1,604	1,719	1,874				
Saarland[28]							652	770[29]	812[30]	842
Other states[31]	440	454	509	574	653	708	646	691	726	671

(c) West Germany

	1939	1946	1950	1961	1970
Schleswig-Holstein	1,589	2,573	2,595	2,317	2,494
Hamburg	1,712	1,403	1,606	1,832	1,794
Lower Saxony	4,540	6,228	6,797	6,641	7,082
Bremen	563	485	559	706	723
North Rhine-Westphalia	11,934	11,683	13,196	15,902	16,914
Hesse	3,479	3,974	4,324	4,814	5,382
Rhineland-Palatinate	2,960	2,741	3,005	3,417	3,645
Baden-Württemburg	5,476	5,817	6,430	7,759	8,895
Bavaria	7,084	8,791	9,185	9,515	10,479
Saarland	910	853	945	1,073	1,120
West Berlin	2,751	2,013	2,147	2,197	2,122

(d) East Germany

	1939	1946	1950	1964	1971
Saxony-Anhalt	3,090	3,682	3,637	3,254	3,245
Brandenburg	2,518	2,638	2,669	2,674	2,677
Mecklenburg	1,572	2,313	2,253	2,062	2,096
Saxony	5,668	5,792	5,945	5,486	5,292
Thuringia	2,309	2,756	2,694	2,530	2,538
East Berlin	1,588	1,175	1,189	1,071	1,086

See p.84 for footnotes

B3 Population of Major Districts (in thousands)

ITALY

(a) Constituents of United Italy

	circa 1770	circa 1800	circa 1816	circa 1825	1833	1838	1844/5	1848	1852	1857/8	1861
Mainland Sardinia[32]	2,481	2,661	3,243	3,494	3,791	3,449	3,992	3,773	...	3,800	3,812
Island of Sardinia						525		547	...	573	588
Lombardy	1,751	1,754	2,179	2,310	2,429	2,498	2,640	2,724	2,774	2,881	2,986
Veneto	1,698	1,845	1,953	1,941	1,963	2,094	2,236	...	2,315	2,294	2,339
Parma	400	415	427	433	466	474	494	495	503	502	504
Modena	300	388	373	404	438	485	507	576	598	610	602
Tuscany[33]	1,063	1,224	1,288	1,396	1,549	1,632	1,703	1,722	1,778	1,794	1,826
Papal States	1,609	2,310	2,355	2,435	2,732	...	2,930	3,019	...	3,125	3,180
Mainland Naples	4,094	4,985	4,914	5,600	5,933	6,149	6,383	6,610	6,830	6,963	6,787
Sicily	1,294	1,656	1,649	1,714	1,912	1,937	2,051	2,104	2,208	2,316	2,392

(b) United Italy

	1861	1871	1881	1901	1911	1921	1931	1936	1951	1961	1971
Piedmont	3,041[32]	2,900	3,070	3,317	3,424	3,384	3,498	3,506	3,612[35]	4,015	4,544[34]
Liguria	771	844	892	1,077	1,197	1,336	1,437	1,467	1,567	1,735	1,849
Lombardy	3,305	3,461	3,681	4,283	4,790	5,050	5,547	5,836	6,560	7,406	8,527
Venetia	(2,339)	2,643	2,814	3,134	3,527	4,200	4,123	4,288	3,918[35]	3,847	4,110
Emilia	2,047	2,114	2,183	2,445	2,681	3,033	3,218	3,339	3,544	3,667	3,841
Tuscany	2,006	2,152	2,209	2,549	2,695	2,766	2,892	2,974	3,293	3,286	3,471
Marches	883	915	939	1,061	1,093	1,148	1,218	1,278	1,364	1,347	1,359
Umbria	513	550	572	667	687	636	694	726	822	795	773
Latium	...	837	903	1,197	1,302	1,619	2,393	2,647	3,806	3,959	4,702
Abruzzi & Molise	1,213	1,283	1,317	1,442	1,431	1,433	1,499	1,601	1,685	1,564	1,483
Campania	3,110	2,755	2,897	3,160	3,312	3,547	3,487	3,699	4,795	4,761	5,055
Apulia	1,755	1,421	1,589	1,960	2,130	2,297	2,487	2,637	3,478	3,421	3,562
Basilicata	493	502	525	491	474	469	508	543	666	644	602
Calabria	1,140	1,206	1,258	1,370	1,402	1,512	1,669	1,772	2,167	2,045	1,963
Sicily	2,392	2,584	2,928	3,530	3,672	4,061	3,897	4,000	4,833	4,721	4,667
Sardinia	588	637	682	792	852	864	973	1,034	1,438	1,419	1,469
Trentino-Aldo Adige						642	659	669	729	786	839
Friuli-Venezia Giulia						729	979	977	1,226[35]	1,166	1,210

See p.84 for footnotes

B3 **Population of Major Districts** (in thousands)

NETHERLANDS

	1830	1840	1849	1859	1869	1879	1889	1899	1909	1920	1930	1940	1950	1960
Groningen	158	176	188	208	225	253	273	300	328	366	392	427	462	478
Friesland	205	228	247	274	292	330	336	340	360	383	400	428	468	480
Drenthe	64	72	83	95	106	119	131	149	173	210	222	250	285	314
Overyssel	179	198	216	235	254	274	295	333	383	439	521	585	682	783
Gelderland	310	346	371	404	433	467	512	567	640	730	829	938	1,101	1,288
Utrecht	132	145	149	160	174	192	221	251	289	342	407	490	584	687
North Holland	414	443	477	524	577	680	829	968	1,108	1,298	1,510	1,701	1,875	2,073
South Holland	480	526	563	619	688	804	950	1,144	1,391	1,679	1,958	2,174	2,425	2,726
Zeeland	137	151	160	166	178	189	199	216	233	245	248	254	272	284
North Brabant	349	378	396	408	429	466	510	554	623	734	898	1,052	1,267	1,513
Limburg	186	197	205	216	224	239	256	282	332	440	551	620	745	894

PORTUGAL

	1838	1858	1864	1878	1890	1900	1911	1920	1930	1940	1950	1960	1970
Viana de Castello				201	207	215	227	226	240	259	275	275	250
Braga	872	860	952	319	338	357	382	376	415	483	541	594	617
Porto				462	546	598	680	702	810	938	1,053	1,192	1,315
Vila Real	331	324	386	225	237	242	246	235	254	289	317	323	265
Braganca				169	180	185	192	170	185	213	227	230	177
Aveiro				257	287	303	336	344	382	430	477	522	546
Viseu				372	391	402	417	405	431	466	487	477	410
Coimbra	1,106	1,187	1,287	292	317	332	360	353	388	412	432	434	396
Guarda				228	250	261	272	256	268	294	304	276	212
Castelo Branca				174	205	217	242	239	266	300	320	311	252
Leiria				193	217	239	263	279	315	354	389	400	383
Santarem	791	755	836	221	255	283	323	332	379	422	453	462	435
Lisbon				498	611	710	853	934	907[36]	1,070	1,227	1,403	1,612
Portalegre				101	113	124	142	147	166	186	197	184	145
Evora	314	305	348	107	118	128	144	153	181	208	220	215	176
Beja				142	158	164	192	201	240	275	287	269	202
Algarve (Fara)	135	153	180	199	229	255	274	268	301	318	326	313	267
Azores	...	240	252	260	256	256	243	232	254	287	317	328	277
Maderia	...	99	112	131	134	151	170	179	212	250	267	268	253
Setubal[36]	...	...	...	...	...	...	...	...	234	269	324	376	464

See p.84 for footnotes

B3 Population of Major Districts (in thousands)

RUSSIA

(a) Fifty Provinces of European Russia

	1811	1838	1851	1863	1885	1897	1914
Archangel	210	230	234	284	316	347	484
Astrakhan	76	259	387	377	803	1,004	1,316
Bessarabia	300	790	874	1,026	1,527	1,935	2,657
Chernigov	1,260	1,300	1,375	1,487	2,076	2,298	3,132
Don Region	250	640	794	950	1,591	2,564	3,876
Ekaterinoslav	666	790	902	1,205	1,793	2,114	3,456
Estland	263	282	290	313	387	413	507
Grodno				894	1,321	1,603	2,048
Kovno				1,052	1,504	1,545	1,857
Mogilev	5,087	4,957	4,974	924	1,234	1,687	2,466
Minsk				1,001	1,647	2,148	3,036
Vilna				900	1,273	1,591	2,076
Vitebsk				777	1,235	1,489	1,953
Kaluga	987	915	941	965	1,174	1,133	1,477
Kavan	1,049	1,221	1,347	1,607	2,066	2,171	2,867
Kharkov	1,030	1,334	1,366	1,591	2,254	2,492	3,417
Kherson	370	766	889	1,330	2,027	2,734	3,745
Kiev	1,066	1,460	1,636	2,012	2,848	3,559	4,793
Kostromo	1,014	959	1,021	1,074	1,316	1,387	1,823
Kurland	510	503	539	574	668	674	798
Kursk	1,424	1,527	1,665	1,827	2,267	2,371	3,257
Livonia	715	740	822	925	1,208	1,299	1,744
Moscow	947	1,250	1,348	1,564	2,184	2,431	3,591
Nishegorod	1,043	1,071	1,127	1,285	1,469	1,585	2,067
Novgorod	766	825	891	1,006	1,194	1,367	1,672
Olonetz	245	239	263	297	333	364	466
Orel	1,228	1,366	1,407	1,534	1,964	2,034	2,782
Orenburg	788	1,771	1,713	1,843	3,118	3,797	5.270
Ufa							
Penza	869	988	1,056	1,179	1,471	1,471	1,912
Perm	1,113	1,489	1,742	2,139	2,650	2,994	4,008
Podolia	1,298	1,548	1,578	1,869	2,365	3,018	4,057
Poltava	1,625	1,622	1,689	1,911	2,653	2,778	3,792
Pskov	782	705	657	719	948	1,122	1,425
Ryazan	1,088	1,242	1,309	1,418	1,784	1,802	2,774
St. Petersburg	600	585	566	1,174	1,646	2,112	3,137
Samara				1,691	2,413	2,751	3,801
Saratov	1,901	2,761	3,777	1,687	2,222	2,406	3,269
Simbirsk				1,183	1,528	1,528	2,068
Smolensk	1,190	1,064	1,070	1,137	1,278	1,525	2,164
Tambov	1,267	1,592	1,667	1,975	2,608	2,684	3,530
Taurida	255	520	609	606	1,060	1,448	2,059
Tver	1,201	1,298	1,360	1,518	1,682	1,770	2,394
Tula	1,115	1,116	1,093	1,153	1,409	1,420	1,886
Vladimir	1,005	1,133	1,168	1,217	1,376	1,516	2,027
Volhynia	1,213	1,314	1,469	1,603	2,196	2,990	4,189
Vologda	703	748	864	975	1,199	1,342	1,752
Voronezh	1,180	1,507	1,630	1,938	2,569	2,531	3.631
Vyatka	1,120	1,512	1,819	2,221	2,859	3,031	3,927
Yaroslav	993	917	943	970	1,050	1,071	1,297
Other Districts							
Caucasus			2,709	4,158	7,285	9,289	12,717
Siberia			2,887	3,141	4,314	5,759	9,895
Steppe districts[38]	...	...	...	1,485	1,589	2,466	3,930
Central Asia	...	...	...	...	3,739	5,281	7,106

(b) U.S.S.R.

	1926	1939	1959	1970
Armenia S.S.R.	881	1,282	1,763	2,492
Azerbaizhan S.S.R.	2,314	3,210	3,698	5,117
Belorussia S.S.R.	4,983	5,568	8,055[39]	9,002
Estonia S.S.R.			1,197	1,356
Georgia S.S.R.	2,677	3,542	4,044	4,686
Kazakh S.S.R.	6,074	6,146	9,310	12,849
Kirghiz S.S.R.	1,002	1,459	2,065	2,933
Latvia S.S.R.			2,093	2,364
Lithuania S.S.R.			2,711	3,128
Moldavia S.S.R.			2,884	3,569
R.S.F.S.R.	93,459	109,277	117,534[39]	130,079
Tadzhik S.S.R.	1,032	1,485	1,980	2,900
Turkmen S.S.R.	998	1,254	1,516	2,159
Ukraine S.S.R.	29,043	30,960	41,869[39]	47,127
Uzbek S.S.R.	4,565	6,282	8,106	11,960

See p.84 for footnotes

B3 Population of Major Districts (in thousands)

SPAIN

	1833[41]	1850[41]	1857	1860	1877	1887	1897	1900	1910	1920	1930	1940	1950	1960	1970
Almeria	235	292	316	315	349	339	345	359	380	358	342	360	357	361	378
Cadiz	325	358	383	391	429	430	434	439	446	513	508	600	700	819	878
Cordoba	315	349	352	359	385	421	444	456	499	565	669	761	782	798	731
Granada	371	427	442	441	479	485	478	492	523	574	644	738	783	769	742
Huelva	133	153	174	177	210	255	254	261	310	330	355	367	368	400	403
Jaen	267	307	346	362	423	438	464	474	527	592	674	753	766	736	668
Malaga	391	438	451	447	500	519	485	512	523	554	613	677	750	775	854
Sevilla	367	420	463	474	507	545	547	555	597	704	805	963	1,099	1,234	1,337
Andalusia	*2,404*	*2,744*	*2,927*	*2,966*	*3,283*	*3,432*	*3,450*	*3,549*	*3,805*	*4,190*	*4,610*	*5,219*	*5,606*	*5,893*	*5,991*
Huesca	215	247	258	263	252	255	239	245	248	251	243	232	236	234	222
Teruel	218	250	239	237	242	242	240	246	255	252	253	232	236	215	174
Zaragoza	301	350	384	393	401	415	413	422	449	495	536	595	622	657	757
Aragon	*734*	*847*	*880*	*891*	*895*	*912*	*892*	*912*	*953*	*997*	*1,032*	*1,059*	*1,094*	*1,105*	*1,153*
Asturias (Oviedo)	*435*	*510*	*525*	*541*	*576*	*595*	*613*	*627*	*685*	*744*	*792*	*837*	*888*	*989*	*1,052*
Alava	68	81	96	98	94	93	95	96	97	99	104	113	118	139	200
Guipuzcoa	109	142	156	163	167	182	192	196	227	259	302	332	374	478	626
Viscaya	111	150	161	169	190	236	290	311	350	410	485	511	569	754	1,041
Basque Provinces	*288*	*373*	*413*	*429*	*451*	*510*	*577*	*604*	*674*	*767*	*892*	*956*	*1,061*	*1,371*	*1,867*
Barcelona	442	534	714	726	837	903	1,035	1,055	1,141	1,349	1,801	1,932	2,232	2,878	3,915
Gerona	214	263	311	311	300	307	298	299	320	326	326	322	327	351	412
Lerida	151	197	307	315	285	285	275	275	285	315	314	297	324	334	347
Tarragona	233	290	321	322	330	349	334	338	338	355	351	339	357	363	433
Catalonia	*1,040*	*1,284*	*1,652*	*1,674*	*1,752*	*1,844*	*1,942*	*1,966*	*2,084*	*2,345*	*2,791*	*2,891*	*3,240*	*3,926*	*5,107*
Badajoz	306	336	405	404	433	482	491	520	593	645	702	743	816	834	702
Caceres	241	265	302	294	307	340	354	362	398	410	450	511	549	544	468
Extremedura	*547*	*601*	*707*	*697*	*739*	*821*	*845*	*882*	*991*	*1,055*	*1,152*	*1,154*	*1,365*	*1,379*	*1,169*
Corunna	436	511	552	557	596	614	631	654	677	709	768	883	956	992	1,031
Lugo	357	419	424	433	411	432	459	465	480	470	469	513	509	480	423
Orense	319	380	372	369	389	405	403	404	412	412	426	458	468	451	441
Pontevedra	360	420	483	446	452	443	448	457	495	533	568	642	672	680	781
Galicia	*1,472*	*1,730*	*1,777*	*1,805*	*1,848*	*1,895*	*1,941*	*1,981*	*2,062*	*2,124*	*2,230*	*2,496*	*2,604*	*2,603*	*2,676*
Leon	267	289	349	340	350	381	384	386	395	412	442	493	546	585	563

See p.89 for footnotes

B3 Population of Major Districts (in thousands)

SPAIN ((Contd.)

	1833[41]	1850[41]	1857	1860	1877	1887	1897	1900	1910	1920	1930	1940	1950	1960	1970
Salamanca	210	240	264	262	286	314	317	321	334	322	339	390	412	406	380
Zamora	159	180	249	249	250	270	275	276	273	266	280	299	316	301	259
Leon	*636*	*709*	*861*	*851*	*885*	*965*	*977*	*982*	*1,003*	*1,000*	*1,061*	*1,182*	*1,273*	*1,291*	*1,201*
Albacete	191	196	201	206	219	229	233	238	265	292	333	374	397	371	341
Murcia	284	400	381	383	452	491	518	578	615	639	645	720	757	800	832
Murcia	*475*	*596*	*582*	*589*	*671*	*721*	*751*	*816*	*880*	*930*	*978*	*1,094*	*1,154*	*1,171*	*1,173*
Navarre	*230*	*280*	*297*	*300*	*304*	*304*	*303*	*308*	*312*	*330*	*346*	*370*	*383*	*402*	*467*
Cuidad Real	278	303	244	248	260	292	305	322	380	427	492	530	567	584	513
Cuenca	234	253	230	230	236	242	242	250	270	282	310	333	326	315	252
Guadalajara	159	200	199	205	201	202	199	200	209	201	204	206	203	184	150
Madrid	320	406	476	489	594	683	737	775	879	1,068	1,384	1,580	1,926	2,606	3,761
Toledo	282	330	329	334	335	360	370	377	413	443	489	480	527	522	478
New Castile	*1,273*	*1,492*	*1,478*	*1,505*	*1,627*	*1,778*	*1,853*	*1,923*	*2,151*	*1,421*	*2,879*	*3,129*	*3,560*	*4,211*	*5,154*
Avila	138	133	164	169	180	193	198	200	209	209	221	235	251	238	212
Burgos	224	234	333	337	333	339	340	339	347	336	355	379	397	381	361
Logrono	148	186	174	175	174	181	186	189	188	193	204	221	230	230	235
Palencia	148	180	186	186	181	189	193	192	196	192	208	217	233	232	202
Santander	169	190	214	220	235	244	264	276	303	328	364	394	405	432	469
Segovia	135	155	147	146	150	154	156	159	168	167	174	189	201	196	162
Soria	116	140	148	150	154	152	148	150	156	152	156	160	161	147	117
Valladolid	185	210	244	247	247	267	276	279	284	281	302	333	348	363	413
Old Castile	*1,263*	*1,418*	*1,610*	*1,630*	*1,655*	*1,719*	*1,761*	*1,785*	*1,852*	*1,858*	*1,984*	*2,127*	*2,226*	*2,219*	*2,171*
Alicante	369	363	379	391	412	433	451	470	498	513	546	608	634	712	922
Castellon de la Plana	199	248	261	267	284	292	304	311	322	307	309	312	325	339	387
Valencia	389	500	607	618	679	734	776	807	884	926	1,042	1,257	1,348	1,430	1,770
Valencia	*957*	*1,111*	*1,240*	*1,275*	*1,374*	*1,459*	*1,532*	*1,588*	*1,704*	*1,745*	*1,897*	*2,177*	*2,307*	*2,481*	*3,078*
Balearic Islands	*229*	*253*	*263*	*270*	*289*	*313*	*302*	*312*	*326*	*339*	*366*	*407*	*422*	*443*	*533*
Las Palmas	...	...	...	...	...	...	...	157	193	206	251	321	375	454	549
Santa Cruz de Tenerife	...	...	...	...	...	...	...	202	251	251	304	360	418	491	576
Canary Islands	*200*	*258*	*234*	*237*	*281*	*292*	*335*	*359*	*444*	*458*	*555*	*680*	*793*	*944*	*1,125*

See p.84 for footnotes

B 3 Population of Major Districts (in thousands)

SWEDEN

	1750	1760	1772	1795	1800	1810	1820	1830	1840	1850
Alveborg	126	120	127	148	153	152	170	198	219	246
Blekinge	35	40	54	60	62	69	79	86	96	108
Gävleborg	110[40]	120[40]	68	81	83	84	92	103	110	120
Göteborg & Bohus	80	81	88	111	117	117	135	154	165	188
Gotland	24	25	28	30	31	33	36	39	42	45
Halland	58	62	66	70	72	74	80	89	95	106
Jämtland	...[40]	...[40]	67[41]	79[41]	85[41]	61	37	42	46	52
Jönköping	104	113	116	113	114	116	122	137	150	163
Kalmar	89	105	116	130	130	138	150	166	185	202
Kopparberg	97	105	110	119	123	119	122	135	138	151
Kristianstad	91	94	100	113	117	121	135	150	166	190
Kronoberg	66	71	74	86	88	90	96	109	121	137
Malmöhus	106	108	116	137	142	154	177	200	222	253
Norrbotten	36[42]	41[42]	44[42]	68[42]	71[42]	32	37	44	49	59
Orebro	...[43]	...[43]	...[43]	95	95	95	100	116	125	138
Ostergötland	128	133	141	155	158	163	173	188	207	222
Skaraborg	109	106	110	135	136	135	149	167	181	200
Södermanland	79	82	87	94	97	99	101	108	115	120
Stockholm City	54	69	72	75	76	65	76	81	84	93
Stockholm County	90	94	99	93	96	97	98	104	110	115
Uppsala	63	66	70	78	81	81	80	82	85	89
Värmland	172[43]	184[43]	194[43]	130	135	135	148	173	196	222
Västerbotten	...[41]	...[41]	...[41]	...[41]	...[41]	34	40	50	55	68
Västernorrland	...[40]	...[40]	...[41]	...[41]	...[41]	33	67	78	86	100
Västmanland	71	73	77	81	87	82	86	89	92	97

See p.84 for footnotes

B3 Population of Major Districts (in thousands)

SWEDEN (Contd.)

	1860	1870	1880	1890	1900	1910	1920	1930	1940	1950	1960	1970
Alveborg	269	279	289	276	280	288	300	313	329	359	375	403
Blekinge	118	126	137	143	146	149	147	145	145	146	144	154
Gävleborg	136	147	179	207	238	254	268	280	274	285	293	293
Göteborg & Bohus	214	232	262	298	337	381	425	457	486	557	625	715
Gotland	50	54	55	51	53	55	56	57	59	59	54	54
Halland	120	127	135	136	142	147	149	150	152	163	170	193
Jämtland	61	70	84	100	111	118	134	135	139	144	140	125
Jönköping	171	180	196	194	203	214	228	232	242	271	285	307
Kalmar	221	233	245	233	228	228	231	231	228	237	236	241
Kopparberg	167	176	190	197	218	234	254	250	249	267	286	277
Kristianstad	210	222	231	222	219	228	241	246	248	259	256	264
Kronoberg	152	159	170	161	159	158	159	156	151	158	159	167
Malmöhus	284	316	349	369	409	457	487	511	530	582	626	719
Norrbotten	69	76	91	105	135	161	183	200	216	241	262	255
Orebro	152	168	182	183	195	207	219	219	226	247	262	277
Ostergötland	141	254	267	267	279	294	306	307	317	348	358	382
Skaraborg	222	244	258	247	241	241	244	242	239	248	250	257
Södermanland	127	136	147	155	167	179	190	189	192	214	228	248
Stockholm City	112	136	169	246	301	342	419	502	591	744	809	747
Stockholm County	122	131	147	153	173	229	243	265	288	357	461	730
Uppsala	93	101	111	121	124	128	137	138	138	155	168	217
Värmland	247	260	268	253	254	260	269	270	268	281	291	284
Västerbotten	81	92	106	123	144	161	182	204	220	232	240	233
Västernorland	117	135	169	209	232	251	265	279	275	284	286	274
Västmanland	103	114	128	137	148	156	169	162	169	204	233	260

B3 **Population of Major Districts** (in thousands)

SWITZERLAND

	1850	1870	1880	1888	1900	1910	1920	1930	1941	1950	1960	1970
Appenzell A.R.	44	49	52	54	55	58	55	49	45	48	49	49
Appenzell I.R.	11	12	13	13	13	15	15	14	13	13	13	13
Aargau	200	199	198	194	206	231	241	260	270	301	361	433
Basel Land	48	54	59	62	68	76	82	93	94	108	148	205
Basel City	30	47	64	74	112	136	141	155	170	196	226	235
Bern	458	502	530	537	589	646	674	689	729	802	890	983
Fribourg	100	110	115	119	128	140	143	143	152	159	159	180
Geneva	64	89	100	106	133	155	171	171	175	203	259	332
Glarus	30	35	34	34	32	33	34	36	35	38	40	38
Grisons	90	92	94	95	105	117	120	126	128	137	147	162
Lucerne	133	132	135	135	147	167	177	189	207	223	253	290
Neuchâtel	71	95	103	108	126	133	131	124	118	128	148	169
Nidwalden	11	12	12	13	13	14	14	15	17	19	17	26
Obwalden	14	14	15	15	15	17	18	19	20	22	23	25
St. Gallen	170	191	210	228	250	303	296	286	286	309	339	384
Schaffhausen	35	38	38	38	42	46	50	51	54	58	66	73
Schwyz	44	48	51	50	55	58	60	62	67	71	78	92
Solothurn	70	75	80	86	101	117	131	144	155	171	201	224
Ticino	118	122	130	127	139	156	152	159	162	175	196	245
Thurgau	89	93	99	105	113	135	136	136	138	150	166	183
Uri	15	16	24	17	20	22	24	23	27	29	32	34
Valais	82	97	100	102	114	128	128	136	148	159	178	207
Vaud	200	230	235	248	281	317	317	332	343	378	430	512
Zug	17	21	23	23	25	28	32	34	37	42	52	68
Zürich	251	284	316	337	431	504	539	618	675	777	952	1,108

B3 **Population of Major Districts** (in thousands)

UNITED KINGDOM
(a) England and Wales

	1801	1811	1821	1831	1841	1851	1861	1871	1881	1891[44]	1901	1911	192	1931	1951	1961	1971
Bedfordshire	63	70	84	95	108	124	135	146	149	161	172	195	206	221	312	381	464
Berkshire	111	120	133	147	162	170	176	196	218	241	259	281	295	311	403	504	637
Buckinghamshire	108	118	135	147	156	164	168	176	176	187	197	219	236	271	386	488	588
Cambridgeshire	89	101	122	144	164	185	176	187	186	185	186	199	207	221	256	279[48]	303
Cheshire	192	227	270	334	396	456	505	561	644	755	842	962	1,020	1,088	1,259	1,369	1,546
Cornwall	192	221	261	301	342	356	369	362	331	323	322	328	321	318	345	342[48]	382
Cumberland	117	134	156	169	178	195	205	220	251	267	267	266	273	263	285	294	292
Derbyshire	162	186	214	237	272	296	339	379	462	511	596	679	709	750	826	878[48]	885
Devonshire	340	383	438	494	533	567	584	601	604	633	662	700	710	733	798	824	898
Dorsetshire	114	125	145	159	175	184	189	196	191	192	200	221	225	239	291	313	362
Durham	149	165	194	239	308	391	509	685	867	1,017	1,187	1,370	1,479	1,486	1,464	1,516	1,410
Essex[45]	200	218	249	272	295	310	319	337	338	377	405	488	554	643	847	1,104	1,358
Gloucestershire	251	286	336	387	431	459	486	535	572	656	710	738	760	791	939	1,002	1,077
Hampshire[49]	219	246	283	314	355	405	482	544	593	694	801	953	1,008	1,103	1,293	1,433	1,675
Herefordshire	88	94	103	111	113	115	124	125	121	116	114	114	113	112	127	131	139
Hertfordshire[45]	97	110	128	140	155	165	171	188	194	214	242	290	311	373	562	788	925
Huntingdonshire	38	42	49	53	59	64	64	64	59	55	54	56	55	56	69	80[48]	203
Kent[45]	245	290	336	377	422	457	513	565	618	710	806	869	938	959	1,090	1,199	1,399
Lancashire	673	828	1,053	1,337	1,667	2,031	2,429	2,819	3,454	3,897	4,373	4,762	4,934	5,040	5,118	5,129	5,118
Leicestershire	130	150	174	197	216	230	237	269	321	376	438	477	494	542	631	683	772
Lincolnshire	209	238	283	317	363	407	412	437	470	474	500	564	602	624	706	743[48]	809
London[45]	1,097	1,304	1,523	1,878	2,208	2,652	3,188	3,841	4,713	5,572	6,507	7,160	7,387	8,110	8,194	7,992	7,452
Monmouthshire	46	62	76	98	134	157	175	195	211	258	297	395	450	432	425	445	462
Norfolk	273	292	344	390	413	443	435	439	445	468	476	498	501	502	548	561	618
Northamptonshire	132	141	163	179	199	212	228	244	273	300	336	349	349	361	423	473[48]	469
Northumberland	168	183	213	237	266	304	343	387	434	506	603	697	746	757	798	821	796
Nottinghamshire	140	163	187	225	250	270	294	320	392	446	514	604	641	713	841	903	976
Oxfordshire	112	120	138	154	163	170	171	178	180	185	180	190	190	210	276	309	382
Rutland	16	16	18	19	21	23	22	22	21	21	20	20	18	17	21	24	27
Shropshire	170	185	198	214	226	229	241	248	248	237	240	246	243	244	290	297	337
Somerset	274	303	356	404	436	444	445	463	469	428	433	455	462	470	551	599	683
Staffordshire	243	295	346	409	509	609	747	858	981	1,053	1,184	1,286	1,356	1,434	1,621	1,734	1,858
Suffolk	214	234	272	296	315	337	337	349	357	362	373	394	400	401	443	472	546
Surrey[45]	85	96	109	120	136	142	165	208	247	271	325	393	423	507	747	906	1,003

See p.84 for footnotes

B3 Population of Major Districts (in thousands)

UNITED KINGDOM
(a) England and Wales (Contd.)

	1801	1811	1821	1831	1841	1851	1861	1871	1881	1891[44]	1901	1911	1912	1931	1951	1961	1971
Sussex	159	190	233	273	300	337	364	417	491	548	602	663	728	770	937	1,078	1,240
Warwickshire	207	229	274	337	402	475	562	634	737	921	1,087	1,250	1,393	1,533	1,862	2,025	2,082
Westmorland	41	46	51	55	56	58	61	65	64	66	64	64	66	65	67	67	73
Wiltshire	184	192	219	237	256	254	249	257	259	262	271	286	292	303	387	423	487
Worcestershire	146	169	194	223	248	277	307	339	380	337	360	380	398	420	523	570	693
Yorkshire																	
East Riding	111	133	154	168	194	219	238	265	309	342	385	433	461	483	511	527	543
North Riding	158	169	187	191	203	213	242	290	341	359	377	419	456	467	525	554	726
West Riding	591	684	833	1,013	1,195	1,366	1,553	1,882	2,237	2,521	2,843	3,131	3,270	3,446	3,586	3,645	3,785

(b) Wales

	1801	1811	1821	1831	1841	1851	1861	1871	1881	1891[44]	1901	1911	1912	1931	1951	1961	1971
Anglesey	34	37	45	48	51	57	55	51	51	50	51	51	52	49	51	52	60
Brecknockshire	32	38	44	48	56	61	62	60	58	51	54	59	61	58	57	55	53
Caernarvonshire	42	50	58	67	81	88	96	106	119	116	123	123	128	121	124	122	123
Cardiganshire	43	50	58	65	69	71	72	73	70	63	61	60	61	55	53	54	55
Carmarthenshire	67	77	90	101	106	111	112	116	125	131	135	160	175	179	172	168	163
Denbighshire	60	64	76	83	88	93	101	105	112	121	134	147	158	158	171	174	185
Flintshire	39	46	54	60	67	68	70	76	81	77	81	93	107	113	145	150	176
Glamorganshire	71	85	102	127	171	232	318	398	511	688	861	1,122	1,254	1,229	1,203	1,230	1,257
Merionethshire	30	31	34	35	39	39	47	52	52	49	49	46	45	43	41	38	35
Montgomeryshire	48	52	60	67	70	67	67	68	66	58	55	53	51	48	46	44	43
Pembrokeshire	56	61	74	81	88	94	96	92	92	88	88	90	92	87	91	94	99
Radnorshire	19	20	23	25	25	25	25	25	24	22	23	23	24	21	20	18	18

See p.84 for footnotes

B3 **Population of Major Districts** (in thousands)

UNITED KINGDOM (Contd.)
(c) Scotland[46]

	1801	1811	1821	1831	1841	1851	1861	1871	1881	1891[44]	1901	1911	1921	1931	1951	1961	1971
Aberdeenshire	121	134	155	178	192	212	222	245	268	283	304	312	301	300	308	321[46]	320
Angusshire	99	107	113	140	170	191	204	238	266	278	284	281	271	270	275	278	280
Argyllshire	81	87	97	101	97	89	80	76	76	74	74	71	77	63	63	59	60
Ayrshire	84	104	127	145	164	190	199	201	218	226	254	268	299	285	321	343	361
Banffshire	37	38	44	48	50	54	59	62	63	61	60	61	57	55	50	46	44
Berwickshire	30	31	33	34	34	36	37	36	35	32	31	30	28	27	25	22	21
Buteshire	12	12	14	14	16	17	16	17	18	18	19	18	34[47]	19	19	15	13
Caithness-shire	23	23	29	35	36	39	41	40	39	37	34	32	28	26	23	27	28
Clackmannanshire	11	12	13	15	19	23	21	24	26	32	32	31	33	32	38	41	46
Dumfriesshire	55	63	71	74	73	78	76	75	76	74	73	73	75	75	86[46]	88	88
Dunbartonshire	21	24	27	33	44	45	52	59	75	98[46]	114	140	151[46]	148	164	185	238
East Lothianshire	30	31	35	36	36	36	38	38	39	37	39	43	47	47	52	53	56
Fifeshire	94	101	115	129	140	154	155	161	172	190[46]	219	268	293	276	307	321	327
Inverness-shire	73	78	90	95	98	97	89	88	90	90	90	87	82	82	85	83	90
Kincardinshire	26	27	29	31	33	35	34	35	34	36	41	41	42	41	47	26[46]	26
Kinross-shire	7	7	8	9	9	9	8	7	7	7	7	8	8	7	7	7	6
Kirkcudbrightshire	29	34	39	41	41	43	43	42	42	40	39	38	37	37	31[46]	29	28
Lanarkshire	148	191	244	317	427	530	632	765	904	1,136[46]	1,339	1.447	1,539[46]	·1,586[46]	1,614	1,626	1,524
Midlothianshire	123	149	192	219	225	259	274	328	389	434	489	508	506	526	566	580	596
Morayshire	28	28	31	34	35	39	43	44	44	43	45	43	42	41	48	49	52
Nairnshire	8	8	9	9	9	10	10	10	10	9	9	9	9	8	9	8	11
Orkney	24	23	27	29	31	31	32	31	32	30	29	26	24	22	21	19	17
Peebleshire	9	10	10	11	10	11	11	12	14	15	15	15	15	15	15	14	14
Perthshire	126	134	138	142	137	139	134	128	129	122[46]	123	124	126	121	128	127	127
Renfrewshire	79	93	112	133	155	161	178	217	263	225[46]	269	315	299[46]	289[46]	325	339	362
Ross & Cromarty	56	61	69	75	79	83	81	81	78	79	76	77	71	63	61	58	58
Roxburghshire	34	37	41	44	46	52	54	54	53[46]	53	49	47	45	46	46	43	42
Selkirkshire	5	6	7	7	8	10	10	14	26[46]	28	23	25	23	23	22	21	21
Shetland	22	23	26	29	31	31	32	32	30	29	28	28	26	21	19	18	17
Stirlingshire	51	58	65	73	82	86	92	98	112	119[46]	142	161	162	168	188	195	209
Sutherlandshire	23	24	24	26	25	26	25	24	23	22	21	20	18	16	14	14	13
West Lothianshire	18	19	22	23	27	30	39	41	44	53	66	80	84	81	89	93	108
Wigtownshire	23	27	33	36	39	43	42	39	39	36	33	32	31	29	32	29	27

See p.84 for footnotes

B3 Population of Major Districts (in thousands)

NOTES

1. SOURCES:— As for table B.1, except that Russian statistics to 1914 are taken from A.F. Rashin, *Russian Population for 100 Years* (Moscow, 1956).

2. For fuller footnotes on territorial changes and on the nature of these statistics see table B.1.

FOOTNOTES

[1] Civil population only.
[2] The Italian provinces are included under Italy.
[3] Part of the province, with a population of 168 thousand, was ceded to the Netherlands in 1839.
[4] Part of the province (the Grand Duchy), with a population of 158 thousand, was ceded to the Netherlands in 1839.
[5] Eupen and Malmédy, with a population of 60 thousand in 1920, were acquired from Germany in 1921.
[6] Ceded to the U.S.S.R. in 1945.
[7] The census was in October 1946 in Slovakia and May 1947 in the Czech lands.
[8] Part of the district, with a population of 6 thousand in 1930, was ceded to the U.S.S.R. in 1945.
[9] The commune of Gex was acquired in 1815.
[10] Part of Rocroi canton was ceded to the United Netherlands in 1815.
[11] Tarn-et-Garonne is estimated in 1801. It was formed out of Aveyron, Haute Garonne, Gers, and Lot-et-Garonne, and their populations are also consequently estimated in 1801.
[12] The population of Marseille (and hence of Bouches-du-Rhône) was overestimated by 191 thousand in 1931.
[13] The population of Corsica is overestimated, for a large number of people not normally resident were wrongly included. The overestimation was about 100 thousand in 1954 and 1962.
[14] A small part of Landes was transferred to Basses-Pyrenées in 1857.
[15] The parts of Meurthe and of Moselle annexed by Germany have constituted Moselle since 1872. The parts left to France have constituted Meurthe-et-Moselle.
[16] A small part of Vosges was tranferred to Bas-Rhin in 1871.
[17] The Belfort Territory was part of Haut-Rhin until 1871.
[18] The population of Lyon (and hence of Rhône) was overestimated by 64 thousand in 1911, 102 thousand in 1921, and 120 thousand in 1931.
[19] Part of Var, with a population of 68 thousand, was transferred to Alpes-Maritimes in 1861.
[20] Hanover, Kurhessen, Nassau, Hesse-Homburg, and Frankfurt.
[21] Saxe-Weimer, Saxe-Meningen, Saxe-Altenburg, Saxe-Coburg-Gotha, Schwarzburg-Rudolstadt, Schwarzburg-Sondershausen, Reuss (elder line), and Reuss (younger line).
[22] Mecklenburg-Schwerin, Mecklenburg-Strelitz, Oldenburg, Brunswick, Anhalt, Waldeck, Schaumburg-Lippe, Lippe, and the cities of Bremen, Hamburg, and Lübeck.
[23] Post-First World War boundaries
[24] The 1933 boundaries have been used so far as possible, but there are some unavoidable changes. The 1933 populations within the 1939 boundaries in these cases were as follows (in thousands):—

Prussia	39,692
Brandenburg	*2,692*
Pomerania	*2,268*
Silesia	*4,710*
Schleswig-Holstein	*1.420*
Hanover	*3,237*
Rhineland	*7,960*
Hamburg	1,676
Oldenburg	495
Other states	590.

[25] The principal change from part (a) of this table is the inclusion here of Schleswig-Holstein and Lauenburg, ceded by Denmark in 1864.
[26] i.e. both Mecklenburg-Schwerin and Mecklenburg-Strelitz.
[27] Including Birkenfeld and the Principality of Lübeck.
[28] Constituted out of part of Prussian Rhineland and part of Birkenfeld.
[29] The census was in July 1927.

[30]The census was in June 1935.

[31]Anhalt, Waldeck, Schaumburg-Lippe, Lippe, and (except in 1939) the city of Lübeck.

[32]Excluding Nice.

[33]Including Lucca.

[34]Including Valle d'Aosta province, which was formerly part of Piedmont, and had a population in 1951 of 94 thousand, in 1961 of 101 thousand, and in 1971 of 109 thousand.

[35]Territory from this province was ceded to France and to Yuogoslavia after the Second World War.

[36]Setubal was part of Lisbon province prior to 1930.

[37]These are estimates on which too much reliance should not be placed.

[38]Urals, Turgai, Akmolinsk, and Semipalatinsk.

[39]Enlarged by territory incorporated in 1940–45.

[40]Västernorrland and Jamtland were included with Gävleborg in 1750 and 1760.

[41]Västernorrland was included with Jamtland in 1772, 1795, and 1800.

[42]Västerbotten was included with Norrbotten in these years.

[43]Orebro was included with Värmland in these years.

[44]The great majority of counties in England and Wales experienced some boundary change in 1891, on the establishment of Administrative Counties instead of the Ancient Counties. The most important of these, with the change effected (in thousands), were as follows:—

Cheshire	+25	Staffordshire	–30
Derbyshire	–17	Suffolk	–9
Gloucestershire	+56	Surrey	–20
Kent	+23	Sussex	–12
Lancashire	–30	Warwickshire	+116
Middlesex	–21	Worcestershire	–77
Norfolk	+13	Yorkshire:	
Somerset	–56	West Riding	+14.

[45]The population of the County of London is for the 1961 area throughout. It has been deducted from the counties of which its was previously a part.

[46]All figures for Scotland relate to the counties as constituted at the time of the census concerned. The main transfers of population resulting from boundary changes were as follows (showing the population in thousands at the previous census of the area affected):—

1881 Roxburgh –5; Selkirk +5

1891 (these figures are at the 1891 census) Dunbarton +4; Fife +3; Lanark +90; Perth –4; Renfrew –66; Stirling –7;

1921 Dunbarton –4; Lanark +35; Renfrew –32

1931 Lanark +15; Renfrew –15

1951 Dumfries +6; Kirkcudbright –6

1961 Aberdeen +20; Kincardine –20.

[47]This figure was inflated because the 1921 census was taken during the holiday season.

[48]1961 population for the 1971 area differed in these cases and was as follows:—

Cambridgeshire	277	Huntingdon & Peterborough	159	Worcestershire	623
Cornwall	343	Lincolnshire	744	Yorkshire: North Riding	665
Derbyshire	845	Northamptonshire	398	Yorkshire: West Riding	3,681
Devon	823	Shropshire	298		
Dorset	314	Staffordshire	1,689		
Durham	1,402	Warwickshire	2,017		

[49]Including the Isle of Wight.

[50]Between the 1962 and 1968 censuses the old departments of Seine and Seine-et-Oise were divided into the seven new departments listed at the end of the table.

B4 POPULATION OF MAJOR CITIES (in thousands)

	1800/1	1850/1	1860/1	1870/1	1880/1	1890/1	1900/1	1910/1	1920/1	1930/1	1940/1[1]	1950/1	1960/1	1970/1
Amsterdam	201	224	244	264	326	408	511	574	642	752	794	804	865	820
Antwerp[2]	62	88	117	127	169	224	273	302,*'07*	334	576,*'28*	595	584	643	671
Athens	12	31	41,*'63*	45	63,*'85*	108,*'88*	111	167	301	453,*'26*	481	565[3]	628[3]	867[3]
Baku	. . .	. . .	14,*'57*	16	46	87	112	218	256	453	809*	. . .	971* *'59*	1,266*
Barcelona	115,*'21*	175	180	. . .	346	397	533	587	710	783,*'26*	1,081,*'37*	1,280	1,558	1,745
Belfast	37	103	122	174	208	273	349	387	. . .	415	438	444	416[4]	360
Belgrade	. . .	. . .	. . .	26 *'66*	30	54	69	91	112,*'19*	267,*'33*	. . .	368 *'48*	585	746
Berlin	172	419	548	826	1,122	1,579	1,889	2,071	3,801	4,243	4,332	3.337[5]	3,261[5]	3,208[5]
Birmingham	74,*'91*	233	296	344	437	478	523	840	922	1,003	1,053,*'36*	1,113	1,107	1,015
Bologna	71	73	75	116,*'72*	104	. . .	152	173	211	246	270,*'36*	316,*'54*[6]	445,*'62*[6]	490,*'68*[6]
Bordeaux	91	131	163	194	221	252	257	262	267	263	258	258	250	267
Bradford	13	104	106	147	194	266	280	288	291	299	288	292	296	294
Bremen	40	53	67	83	112	126	163	247	258 *'19*	323 *'33*	342	445	565	582
Bristol	64	137	154	183	207	289	339	357	377	404	419,*'38*	443	436	427
Brussels[7]	66	251	281	314	421	500	599,*'99*	720,*'12*	685,*'17*	840	913	956	1,020	1,075
Bucharest	. . .	120	122,*'57*	142	. . .	220	276	341	309	631	648	886	1,226	1,475
Budapest	54	178	187	202	371	506	732	880	1,185,*'19*	1,006,*'33*	1,163	1,571*	1,805*	1,945*
Cologne	50	97	121	129	145	282	373	517	634	757	768	595	809	848
Copenhagen	101	129	155	181	235	313	401,*'97*	559	561	771*,*'26*	890*	1,168*	1,262*,*'59*	1,380*
Donetsk (Stalino, Yuzovka)	—,*'11*	—	—	—	. . .,*'85*	. . .,*'88*	32	48	38	174,*'26*	462	. . .	699,*'59*	879
Dniepropetrovsk (Ekaterinoslav)	9	12	19	24	47	47	121	196	163,*'19*	237,*'33*	501	. . .	660 *'59*	862
Dortmund	4	11	23	44	67	90	142	214	295,*'19*	541,*'33*	537	507	648	640
Dresden	60	97	128	177	221	277	396	548	529	642,*'26*	625,*'37*	494	492	502
Dublin	165	272	250	246	250	245	373	305	399,*'19*	419,*'33*	489	522	537[8]	566
Duisburg	4	9	13	31	41	59	93	229	244	440	431	411	504	455
Düsseldorf	10	27	41	69	95	145	214	359	407 *'19*	499 *'33*	540	501	705	664
Edinburgh	83	202	203	244	295	342	394,*'97*	401	420	439,*'26*	476	467	468,*'59*	454
Erevan	. . .	12	. . .	12	12	. . .	29	33	. . .,*'19*	65,*'33*	200	. . .	509	767
Essen	4	9	21	52	57	79	119	295	439,*'19*	654,*'33*	660	605	730	698
Frankfurt-on-Main	48,*'16*	65	76	91	137	180	289	415	433	556,*'33*	547	532	692	670
Gdansk (Danzig)	53	60	83	89	109	120	134	162	195	263	266	170	286	364

Superior figures in italics show census dates.

See p.89 for footnotes

B4 Population of Major Cities (in thousands)

	1800/1	1850/1	1860/1	1870/1	1880/1	1890/1	1900/1	1910/1	1920/1	1930/1	1940/1[1]	1950/1	1960/1	1970/1
Geneva	22	31	41	44	49	52	59	58	56	124	124	145	176[9]	175[9]
Genoa	91 *'99*	120	129	130	180	. . .	235	272	316	608	635 *'36*	648	784	812
Glasgow	77	357	420	522	587	658	776	1,000	1,052	1,093	1,132	1,090	1,055	897
Gorky (Nizhne Novgorod)	14 *'11*	31	42 *'63*	41 *'67*	67 *'85*	73 *'88*	90 *'97*	109	106	222 *'26*	644	. . .	942 *'59* [10]	1,170
Gothenburg	13	26	37	56	76	105	131	168	202	243	281	354[10]	404[10]	451
The Hague	38	72	79	90	118	166	212	281	353	437	496	533[11]	605[11]	538[11]
Hamburg	130	132	134	240	290	324	706	931	986 *'19*	1,129 *'33*	1,682	1,606	1,832	1,794
Hanover	18	29	71	88	123	164	236	302	310 *'19*	444 *'33*	473	444	573	524
Helsinki	9	21	19	26	43	62	91	147	189 *'19*	241	317	369[12]	453[12]	510
Kaliningrad (Königsberg)	61 *'16*	73	95	112	141	162	188	246	261 *'19*	316 *'33*	368	. . .	204 *'59*	297
Kazan	54 *'11*	45	63 *'63*	79 *'67*	94	134	132 *'97*	188	148	179 *'26*	402	. . .	647 *'59*	869
Kharkov	10 *'11*	25	52 *'63*	60 *'67*	101 *'79*	188 *'88*	175 *'97*	236	220	417 *'26*	833	. . .	934 *'59*	1,223
Kiev	23 *'11*	50	68 *'63*	71 *'67*	166 *'85*	184	247 *'97*	505	366	514 *'26*	846	. . .	1,104 *'59*	1,632
Krakow	24	50	42	50	66	75	91	150	184	221	255	347	479	583
Kuibyshev (Samara)	4 *'11*	24	34 *'63*	34 *'67*	52	95 *'88*	92 *'97*	96	176	176 *'26*	390	. . .	806	1,045
Leeds	53	72	207	259	309	368	429	453	463	483	497	505	511	496
Leipzig	30	63	78	107	149	295	456	590	604 *'19*	713 *'33*	702	618	585	584
Leningrad (Petrograd/St. Petersburg)	220	485	539 *'63*	667 *'69*	877	1,003 *'89*	1,267 *'97*	1,962	722	1,690 *'26*	3,191	. . .	3,321* *'59*	3,950*
Lisbon	180	240	224 *'64*	. . .	242 *'78*	301	356	435	486	594	702	790	817	760
Liverpool	80	376	444	493	553	630	704	753	805	856	822	789	747	610
Lodz	0.2	16	30	34	57	113	315 *'97*	408	452	605	665	593	708	762
London[13]	1,117	2,685	3,227	3,890	4,770	5,638	6,586	7,256	7,488	8,216	8,700 *'38*	8,348	8,172	7,452
Lvov (Lemberg)	39	68	70 *'57*	87	110	128	160	206	219	316	318	. . .	411 *'59*	553
Lyon	110	177	319	323 *'72*	377	416	459	460	460	460	470 *'36*	471[14]	529[14]	528[14]
Madrid	160	281	271 *'57*	332	398	470 *'87*	540	600	751	834	1,089	1,618	2,260	3,146
Manchester	90	303	339	351	462	505	645	714	736	766	728	703	661	543
Marseille	111	194	261	313 *'72*	360	404	491	551	586	610	620 *'36*	661 *'54*	778 *'62*	889 *'68*
Milan	135	242	242	262	322	. . .	493	579	836	992	1,116 *'36*	1,260	1,583	1,724
Minsk	11 *'11*	24	30 *'63*	36 *'67*	58 *'85*	71 *'88*	91 *'97*	101	104	132 *'26*	239	. . .	509 *'59*	907
Moscow	250	365	352 *'63*	612	748 *'82*	799 *'88*	989 *'97*	1,533	1,050	2,029 *'26*	4,137	. . .	5,046 *'59*	7,061*
Munich	40	110	148	169	230	349	500	596	631 *'19*	735 *'33*	828	832	1,085	1,294

Superior figures in italics show census dates.

See p.89 for footnotes

B4 Population of Major Cities (in thousands)

	1800/1	1850/1	1860/1	1870/1	1880/1	1890/1	1900/1	1910/1	1920/1	1930/1	1940/1[1]	1950/1	1960/1	1970/1
Naples	427['96]	449	417	449	494	...	564	723*	722*	839*	866*['36]	1,011*	1,183	1,233
Nuremberg	30	54	63	83	100	143	261	333	353['191]	410['33]	431	362	455	474
Odessa	6	90	119['63]	121['67]	194['77]	314	405['97]	506	428	421['26]	604	...	667['59]	892
Oslo (Christiania)	10	28	40	67	119	151	228	243	258	253	275['38]	434[15]	476[15]	487
Palermo	139['15]	180	186	219	245	...	310	342	394	390	412['36]	491*	588	651
Paris	547	1,053	1,696	1,852['72]	2,269	2,448	2,714	2,888	2,907	2,891	2,830['36]	2,850[16]	2,790[16]	2,489
Perm (Molotov)	...	13	13	23['67]	32	39	45['97]	50	68	120['26]	255	...	629['59]	850
Prague	75	118	143['57]	157	162	184	202	224[17]	677*	849*	928*['35]	922*['47]	1,005	1,080
Riga	30	70	77['63]	102['67]	160	196['88]	256['97]	331	285['23]	378	393	...	580['59]	732
Rome[18]	163['90]	175	184	244	300	...	463	542	692	1,008	1,156['36]	1,652	2,188	2,800
Rostov-on-Don	4['11]	13	29['63]	39['67]	61['85]	67['88]	120['97]	121	233	308['26]	510	...	600['59]	789
Rotterdam	53	90	106	116	153	202	319	427	511	582	612	646[19]	729[19]	679[19]
Saratov	27['11]	62	84['63]	93['67]	80	123	137['97]	206	189	220['26]	376	...	581['59]	757
Sheffield	31	135	185	240	285	324	409	465	512	518	522	513	494	520
Sofia	...	...	...	19	21	42	68	103	154	287['34]	401	435['46]	687*	877*
Stockholm	76	93	112	136	169	246	301	342	419	502	591	744[20]	809[20]	787
Strasbourg	49	76	82	86	105	124	151	179	167	181	193['36]	201['54][21]	229['62][21]	249['68][21]
Stuttgart	18	47['52]	56	92	117	140	177	286	309['19]	415['33]	460	498	638	633
Szczecin (Stettin)	...	48['52]	64	76	92	116	211	232	233['19]	271['33]	269	159	269	337
Toulouse	50	94	113	125['72]	140	150	150	150	175	195	213['36]	269['54]	324['62]	370['68]
Tiflis	30['25]	35['54]	61['63]	61['67]	90['85]	101['85]	161['97]	188	327	294['26]	519	...	695['59]	889
Turin	78	135	178	208	254	...	336	427	502	597	629['36]	711	1,026	1,178
Ufa	...	13	17	20['67]	26['84]	30['88]	50['97]	103	93	99['26]	246	...	547['59]	771
Valencia	100	90	87['57]	...	138['77]	171['87]	214	233	244	275	451	509	505	654
Venice	134['02]	106	118['57]	129	129	...	152	161	192	260*	264*['36]	317*	347*	364*
Vienna	247	444	476['57]	834	1,104	1,365	1,675	2,031	1,866['23]	1,874['34]	1,918	1,766	1,628	1,615
Volgograd (Stalingrad/Tsaritsyn)	...	...	7	...	31	38['88]	56['97]	78	90	151['26]	445	...	592['59]	818
Warsaw	100	160	163['63]	252	339	454	638['97]	872	931	1,179	1,266	601	1,136	1,308
Wroclaw (Breslau)	60	114	146	208	273	335	423	512	528['19]	625['33]	615	279	429	523
Wuppertal	16	80['52]	106	146	189	242	299	339	314['19]	409['33]	398	363	421	419
Zagreb (Agram)	...	14	17['57]	20	28	38	61	79	108	186	...	280['48]	431	566
Zürich	12	17	20	57*	79*	94*	151*	191*	207	250	336	390	440[22]	427[22]

Superior figures in italics show census dates.

See p.89 for footnotes

B4 Population of Major Cities (in thousands)

NOTES

1. SOURCES:— The official publications noted on p. xv; early editions of the *Encyclopaedia Britannica* for some Russian cities in 1850, 1860, and 1870; and data supplied by various national statistical offices. Official estimates as well as census figures have been used. Where none is available for the 0/1 years, the nearest available date has been used and indicated.

2. The cities included in this table all had a population of 500,000 or more in 1960/1, or a population of 250,000 or more in 1900/1, with the exception of a few leading cities in countries which had few or none meeting these criteria.

3. The cities are in alphabetical order of their current name (or its English version where one exists). Older names by which they were known are given in brackets.

4. The statistics do not generally include the population of distinct suburbs, except where this seems most appropriate. Such cases are indicated in footnotes or by an asterisk. Normally the statistics apply to the boundaries of the day.

FOOTNOTES

* = suburbs included

[1] So many of the figures in this column are for 1939 that no special indication is given of this.
[2] Greater Antwerp throughout.
[3] The figures for Greater Athens in 1950/1, 1960/1 and 1970/1 were 1,379, 1,853 and 2,540 respectively.
[4] Greater Belfast 529.
[5] East and West Berlin combined.
[6] The figures for Greater Bordeaux in 1954, 1962 and 1968 were 416, 462 and 555 respectively.
[7] Greater Brussells throughout, except in 1800/1.
[8] Greater Dublin 593.
[9] The figures for Greater Geneva in 1960 and 1970 were 251 and 321 respectively.
[10] The figures for Greater Gothenburg in 1950 and 1960 were 380 and 487 respectively.
[11] The figures for Greater Hague in 1950, 1960 and 1970 were 592, 737 and 711 respectively.
[12] The figures for Greater Helsinki in 1950, 1960 and 1970 were 414, 566 and 803 respectively.
[13] Greater London throughout.
[14] The figures for Greater Lyon in 1954, 1962 and 1968 were 650, 886 and 1,075 respectively.
[15] The figures for Greater Oslo in 1950 and 1960 were 506 and 579 respectively.
[16] The figures for Greater Paris in 1954, 1962 and 1968 were 4,823, 7,369 and 8,197 respectively.
[17] Greater Prague 586
[18] Greater Rome throughout.
[19] The figures for Greater Rotterdam in 1950, 1960 and 1970 were 716, 993 and 1,066 respectively.
[20] The figures for Greater Stockholm in 1950, 1960 and 1970 were 928, 1,149 and 1,345 respectively.
[21] The figures for Greater Strasbourg in 1954, 1962 and 1968 were 239, 302 and 335 respectively.
[22] The figures for Greater Zürich in 1960 and 1970 were 630 and 719 respectively.

B5 VITAL STATISTICS: NUMBERS (in thousands)

1749–1799

	Finland			France[8]			Norway[1]			Sweden[1]		
	B	D	M	B	D	M	B	D	M	B	D	M
1749	...	...	...	971	831	212	20	17	...	59	50	15.0
1750	...	...	...	957	781	218	19	17	...	65	48	16.4
1751	19	10	4.6	980	677	235	22	17	...	69	47	16.6
1752	19	11	4.4	968	739	201	21	16	...	65	49	16.8
1753	19	12	4.2	1,006	825	235	22	15	...	66	44	16.0
1754	21	16	4.4	1,018	817	228	23	16	...	69	49	17.5
1755	21	14	4.3	1,018	738	236	22	16	...	70	51	17.1
1756	21	17	3.9	1,091	723	236	24	18	...	68	52	16.0
1757	20	12	3.7	1,031	705	200	23	15	...	62	57	15.1
1758	20	14	4.2	1,038	812	226	22	16	...	63	61	15.3
1759	21	14	4.7	1,026	897	213	22	13	...	64	50	18.5
1760	23	14	4.8	1,010	809	209	24	16	...	68	47	18.7
1761	23	14	4.2	1,053	872	193	25	17	...	67	50	18.3
1762	21	15	4.0	989	874	197	25	18	...	68	61	17.4
1763	22	21	4.1	1,004	851	202	24	27	...	68	64	16.9
1764	24	17	4.3	1,004	806	230	25	20	...	68	53	17.2
1765	22	15	4.2	1,041	868	228	24	21	...	66	55	16.1
1766	22	16	4.1	1,022	875	240	24	22	...	67	50	16.4
1767	22	16	4.2	1,037	921	235	25	18	...	71	51	16.5
1768	23	14	4.8	983	839	203	24	18	...	68	55	17.0
1769	23	16	4.6	1,051	705	232	25	17	...	67	55	16.5
1770	23	17	4.1	1,008	732	191	24	18	5.4	67	53	16.5
1771	21	15	4.3	979	819	176	23	17	5.0	66	57	15.9
1772	22	14	4.4	988	922	204	21	19	4.4	59	76	13.9
1773	22	13	5.0	988	885	212	18	35	4.4	51	105	15.6
1774	24	13	5.5	1,018	855	221	21	19	6.2	69	44	17.4
1775	24	15	5.2	1,022	883	220	25	17	6.8	72	50	19.0
1776	24	19	5.2	1,014	774	250	21	15	6.2	67	46	18.3
1777	25	20	5.5	1,081	796	241	23	16	6.2	68	51	18.6
1778	27	16	6.2	1,000	798	211	23	15	6.0	72	55	18.6
1779	28	14	5.8	1,028	1,077	238	24	21	6.1	76	59	18.0
1780	27	14	5.4	1,054	945	258	25	20	5.9	75	46	17.9
1781	25	18	5.0	1,052	948	251	24	16	6.2	71	54	16.6
1782	28	17	5.6	1,044	1,006	227	24	18	5.5	68	58	16.4
1783	27	21	5.4	1,026	988	227	22	19	6.3	65	60	17.1
1784	29	17	3.4	1,039	927	246	24	19	...	68	64	16.0
1785	27	21	5.3	1,077	976	255	23	26	...	67	61	16.8
1786	27	18	4.8	1,103	952	256	24	19	...	71	56	17.3
1787	28	16	5.3	1,091	912	241	23	18	...	68	52	17.3
1788	25	23	4.7	1,081	913	233	24	21	...	74	58	17.2
1789	24	27	5.3	1,053	876	216	24	24	...	70	73	17.4
1790	26	27	6.6	1,054	871	220	26	18	...	67	67	18.1
1791	25	29	8.3	1,014	939	246	26	19	...	72	56	23.8
1792	30	18	8.0	1,038	966	253	28	20	...	81	53	22.2
1793	32	19	7.1	1,023	885	327	28	18	...	77	54	19.9
1794	31	24	6.9	1,079	1,097	325	28	17	...	76	53	18.5
1795	32	18	6.0	1,031	829	239	27	19	6.5	73	64	17.3
1796	31	18	6.5	1,010	754	246	27	18	6.7	79	56	19.7
1797	33	16	6.5	1,072	734	271	28	19	7.0	80	55	19.5
1798	31	18	6.1	1,070	706	...	28	20	7.2	79	54	19.3
1799	32	23	6.3	1,053	713	...	29	18	6.9	75	59	17.3

Abbreviations used throughout this table: B=births; D=deaths; M=marriages.

See p.111 for footnotes

B5 Vital Statistics: Numbers (in thousands)

1800–1849

	Austria[2]			Belgium			Denmark[4]			Finland		
	B	D	M	B	D	M	B	D	M	B	D	M
1800	...	...	...	...	...	...	28	26	8.7	31	21	6.8
1801	...	...	...	...	...	...	29	26	7.3	33	18	6.6
1802	...	...	...	...	...	...	30	22	8.7	34	19	6.3
1803	...	...	...	...	...	...	31	21	8.2	31	29	6.3
1804	...	...	...	...	...	...	31	23	8.4	34	22	6.9
1805	...	...	...	...	...	...	32	22	7.6	34	19	7.1
1806	...	...	...	...	...	...	29	22	7.7	32	20	6.9
1807	...	...	...	...	...	...	30	22	7.2	33	26	5.9
1808	...	...	...	...	...	...	30	25	7.2	27[5]	54[5]	4.5[5]
1809	...	...	...	...	...	...	29	25	7.7	25	52	7.6
1810	...	...	...	...	...	...	30	23	8.9	35[6]	21[6]	10.1[6]
1811	...	...	...	...	...	...	31	24	9.5	32	27	7.9
1812	...	...	...	...	...	...	30	27	8.2	41	26	8.6
1813	...	...	...	...	...	...	29	23	8.4	38	29	8.1
1814	...	...	...	...	...	...	31	25	9.7	40	35	8.9
1815	...	...	...	...	...	...	35	22	10.9	41	28	9.5
1816	...	...	...	...	...	...	34	22	10.0	43	26	9.8
1817	...	...	...	...	...	...	35	20	8.4	44	27	9.7
1818	...	...	...	...	...	...	34	20	9.3	43	28	9.8
1819	...	...	...	...	...	...	35	21	9.2	42	31	8.8
	Years ending 31 October									----[7]	----[7]	----[7]
1820	595	369	120	...	...	...	35	23	9.0	43	30	10.9
1821	583	362	111	...	...	...	36	27	9.3	49	27	11.2
1822	550	388	108	...	...	...	38	23	9.7	43	34	9.8
1823	572	416	104	...	...	...	37	20	9.0	49	30	10.8
1824	586	387	115	...	...	...	36	21	9.3	47	34	10.7
1825	598	398	116	...	...	...	36	22	9.7	48	33	10.2
1826	596	416	120	...	...	...	37	25	9.8	48	32	10.5
1827	588	441	131	...	...	...	35	24	9.1	47	28	11.7
1828	579	504	131	...	...	...	36	28	9.5	51	29	11.8
1829	560	488	135	...	...	...	36	35	9.9	51	35	10.9
1830	594	474	126	132	104	26	35	31	10.2	49	34	10.2
1831	556	660	113	135	98	31	36	36	9.7	49	39	11.9
1832	571	555	151	129	115	28	33	32	10.6	48	47	8.9
1833	632	497	136	138	111	27	39	28	10.6	41	64	9.3
1834	620	488	132	140	117	30	41	29	10.6	50	33	10.4
1835	613	493	128	143	101	24	39	28	10.1	48	34	9.7
1836	606	530	140	144	103	25	38	28	9.5	43	44	9.0
1837	641	537	142	143	118	26	38	27	9.6	44	40	10.1
1838	618	460	128	152[3]	110[3]	29[3]	38	25	8.9	45	32	10.0
1839	626	494	130	136	105	25	37	26	8.8	48	29	10.9
1840	642	506	132	138	104	31	39	27	9.4	50	32	11.1
1841	644	496	142	138	97	30	39	26	9.9	49	33	11.6
1842	699	522	138	135	103	29	40	27	10.2	55	32	12.2
1843	674	539	146	133	97	28	40	26	10.3	54	33	12.0
1844	687	496	142	134	95	29	41	26	10.9	53	33	12.3
1845	692	521	133	137	98	29	42	26	11.1	55	35	11.7
1846	654	526	142	120	108	26	41	29	11.0	52	39	11.4
1847	635	782	128	118	120	24	42	30	11.0	53	37	12.7
1848	572	722	152	120	108	29	43	29	10.4	58	38	14.7
1849	695	610	161	133	121	32	44	32	11.3	60	39	13.9

See p. 111 for footnotes

B5 Vital Statistics: Numbers (in thousands)

1800–1849

	France[8]			Germany[9]			Hungary[10]			Netherlands[12]		
	B	D	M	B	D	M	B	D	M	B	D	M
1800	1,003	811	...	...	...	...	...	...	...	...	...	...
1801	965	788	211	...	...	...	...	...	...	...	...	...
1802	970	840	235	...	...	...	...	...	...	...	...	...
1803	952	975	208	...	...	...	...	...	...	...	...	...
1804	934	1,018	220	...	...	...	...	...	...	...	...	...
1805	974	820	229	...	...	...	...	...	...	...	...	...
1806	944	808	214	...	...	...	...	...	...	...	...	...
1807	950	840	228	...	...	...	...	...	...	...	...	...
1808	964	813	239	...	...	...	...	...	...	...	...	...
1809	980	770	270	...	...	...	...	...	...	...	...	...
1810	962	753	248	...	...	...	...	...	...	...	...	...
1811	970	784	211	...	...	...	...	...	...	...	...	...
1812	930	800	236	...	...	...	...	...	...	...	...	...
1813	989	860	414	...	...	...	...	...	...	...	...	...
1814	1,061	960	196	...	...	...	...	...	...	...	...	...
1815	1,015	808	278									
	953[8]	763[8]	246[8]	...	...	...	...	...	...	...	...	...
1816	969	724	249	...	...	...	...	...	...	...	...	...
1817	944	751	206	...	...	...	...	...	...	...	...	...
1818	915	756	213	...	...	...	...	...	...	...	...	...
1819	988	786	215	...	...	...	...	...	...	...	...	...
1820	960	769	209	...	...	...	...	...	...	...	...	...
1821	965	741	223	...	...	...	...	...	...	...	...	...
1822	973	777	236	...	...	...	...	...	...	...	...	...
1823	963	743	262	...	...	...	...	...	...	...	...	...
1824	984	764	238	...	...	...	...	...	...	...	...	...
1825	973	800	243	...	...	...	...	...	...	...	...	...
1826	992	838	247	...	...	...	...	...	...	...	...	...
1827	980	792	256	...	...	...	...	...	...	...	...	...
1828	977	837	246	...	...	...	...	...	...	...	...	...
1829	965	803	251	...	...	...	...	...	...	...	...	...
1830	968	808	270	...	...	...	...	...	...	...	...	...
1831	987	801	246	...	...	...	...	...	...	...	...	...
1832	937	934	242	...	...	...	...	...	...	...	...	...
1833	970	812	264	...	...	...	...	...	...	...	...	...
1834	987	918	271	...	...	...	...	...	...	...	...	...
1835	994	817	276	...	...	...	...	...	...	...	...	...
1836	980	748	274	...	...	...	...	...	...	...	...	...
1837	944	853	267	...	...	...	...	...	...	...	...	...
1838	963	818	273	...	...	...	...	...	...	...	...	...
1839	958	772	267	...	...	...	...	...	...	...	...	...
1840	952	809	283	...	...	...	...	...	...	101	68	22
1841	977	795	282	1,152	829	259	Years ended 31 October			103	68	22
1842	983	826	281	1,201	865	267	550	438	117	101	76	21
1843	978	799	285	1,161	870	264	534	424	124	100	69	21
1844	959	768	280	1,167	797	267	549	393[11]	119	103	72	22
1845	983	742	283	1,269	835	268	551	397	115	104	70	23
1846	966	821	268	1,197	905	263	542	512	125	96	87	21
1847	902	849	250	1,115	946	242	519	543	114	87	95	19
1848	940	837	294	1,116	976	257	...	...	...	92	89	22
1849	986	973	279	1,287	910	276	...	...	...	104	95	25

See p.111 for footnotes

B5 Vital Statistics: Numbers (in thousands) **1800–1849**

	Norway			Sweden			United Kingdom: England and Wales		
	B	D	M	B	D	M	B	D	M
1800	...	...	...	68	74	17.5	...	...	...
1801	24	24	6.1	71	61	17.1	...	...	...
1802	24	22	6.7	75	56	18.5	...	...	...
1803	26	22	6.8	75	57	19.5	...	...	...
1804	25	21	7.1	76	60	19.3	...	...	...
1805	26	18	7.2	77	57	20.2	...	...	...
1806	27	19	7.3	75	67	19.5	...	...	...
1807	26	20	6.3	76	64	20.0	...	...	...
1808	24	24	5.3	74	85	19.8	...	...	...
1809	20	32	5.4	64	97	18.8	...	...	...
1810	24	24	7.1	79	76	25.8	...	...	...
1811	24	22	7.9	85	69	25.6	...	...	...
1812	26	19	7.9	81	73	22.1	...	...	...
1813	23	26	6.5	72	66	18.7	...	...	...
1814	22	20	5.8	76	61	18.3	...	...	...
1815	27	18	9.2	85	58	24	...	...	...
1816	32	18	9.4	88	56	23	...	...	...
1817	30	16	8.0	84	61	21	...	...	...
1818	29	18	7.7	86	62	21	...	...	...
1819	31	19	7.7	84	70	21	...	...	...
1820	32	18	8.7	85	63	22	...	...	...
1821	34	20	8.9	92	66	23	...	...	...
1822	33	19	8.9	94	59	24	...	...	...
1823	34	18	8.8	98	56	24	...	...	...
1824	33	19	8.4	94	56	24	...	...	...
1825	36	18	9.0	100	56	24	...	...	...
1826	37	20	8.8	97	63	23	...	...	...
1827	35	19	8.1	88	65	20	...	...	...
1828	35	21	8.4	95	76	22	...	...	...
1829	37	21	8.6	99	83	23	...	...	...
1830	36	22	8.7	95	69	22	...	...	...
1831	35	23	8.2	88	75	20	...	...	...
1832	34	21	7.8	90	68	21	...	...	...
1833	36	24	8.5	100	64	23	...	...	...
1834	37	26	8.9	100	76	24	...	...	...
1835	39	23	8.8	98	56	23	...	...	...
1836	35	23	8.4	97	61	22	...	...	...
1837	35	25	8.1	95	76	21	...	...	...
1838	34	24	7.6	90	74	19	464[13]	343[13]	118[13]
1839	33	27	7.9	91	73	21	493	339	123
1840	35	25	8.6	98	64	22	502	360	123
1841	37	22	9.6	96	61	23	512	344	122
1842	39	23	10.0	101	67	23	518	350	119
1843	39	23	10.2	99	69	23	527	346	124
1844	39	22	10.3	105	66	24	541	357	132
1845	41	22	10.6	104	62	24	544	349	144
1846	42	24	11.2	100	73	23	573	390	146
1847	42	27	9.9	99	79	23	540	423	136
1848	41	28	10.2	103	67	25	563	399	138
1849	44	25	10.6	112	68	27	578	441	142

See p. 111 for footnotes

B5 Vital Statistics: Numbers (in thousands)

1850–1899

	Austria			Belgium			Bulgaria			Denmark		
	B	D	M	B	D	M	B	D	M	B	D	M
1850	692	575	169	131	93	34	...	...	...	45	27	10.8
1851	691	526	154	134	97	33	...	...	...	43	27	14.2
1852	668	524	140	134	96	31	...	...	...	48	29	14.2
1853	679	561	138	128	100	31	...	...	...	47	37	13.5
1854	654	612	124	132	103	29	...	...	...	49	27	13.0
1855	577	774	115	126	113	30	...	...	...	48	30	12.8
	Years ending 31 December[15]											
1856	653	542	147	134	97	33	...	...	...	50	29	13.2
1857	725	504	148	143	103	37	...	...	...	51	34	13.8
1858	730	533	155	145	108	38	...	...	...	52	36	13.6
1859	754	540	131	150	112	37	...	...	...	53	32	13.3
1860	716	503	158	145	93	35	...	...	...	53	33	12.8
1861	710	563	151	147	106	34	...	...	...	52	30	12.1
1862	726	563	169	146	100	34	...	...	...	51	30	12.0
1863	781	576	163	156	108	36	...	...	...	52	30	12.5
1864	790	585	161	156	116	37	...	...	...	51	39	9.5
1865	746	599	153	156	122	38	...	...	...	53	39	15.1
1866	747	804	128	158	151	38	...	...	...	55	36	14.4
1867	727	580	192	157	106	38	...	...	...	53	35	13.2
1868	759	572	183	156	108	36	...	...	...	54	34	12.8
1869	795	584	209	159	110	37	...	...	...	52	34	13.0
1870	808	599	199	165	118	35	...	...	...	54	34	13.1
1871	802[16]	617[16]	195[16]	159	146	38	...	...	...	54	35	13.2
1872	810	677	192	167	120	40	...	...	...	55	33	13.6
1873	828	811	195	171	113	41	...	...	...	57	34	14.9
1874	830	663	189	174	110	40	...	...	...	57	37	15.3
1875	842	634	180	176	122	39	...	...	...	60	39	15.9
1876	853	634	176	177	117	38	...	...	...	62	37	16.2
1877	831	678	161	175	114	37	...	...	...	62	36	15.4
1878	833	684	164	173	118	37	...	...	...	61	36	14.3
1879	856	652	169	175	121	37	...	...	...	62	39	14.3
1880	828	654	167	172	123	39	...	...	...	63	40	15.0
1881	833	677	177	175	117	39	68	33	20	64	36	15.5
1882	874	687	183	176	114	39	75	39	20	65	39	15.5
1883	859	677	176	174	119	39	79	41	20	66	37	15.6
1884	878	667	179	177	121	39	80	36	18	70	38	16.0
1885	861	689	175	175	118	40	79	34	14	67	37	15.6
1886	877	680	181	175	125	40	70	41	20	68	38	14.8
1887	890	674	182	175	115	42	83[18]	39[18]	20[18]	67	39	14.7
1888	891	688	186	176	121	42	119	58	26	67	42	15.1
1889	899	648	178	178	120	44	117	59	25	67	40	15.2
1890	870	698	179	177	127	45	113	68	29	66	41	15.0
1891	920	675	187	182	129	45	127	87	30	68	44	14.9
1892	872	695	188	177	134	47	118	104	28	65	43	15.0
1893	924	662	194	183	126	47	116	92	22	69	42	15.7
1894	902	684	194	181	118	48	128	92	27	68	40	15.7
1895	941	683	200	183	125	50	138	90	31	69	39	16.1
1896	948	657	198	189	114	53	143	84	29	70	36	16.8
1897	945	646	204	191[17]	114[17]	54[17]	150	90	28	70	39	17.5
1898	923	635	200	190	115	55	141	83	32	72	37	17.9
1899	960	658	214	193	124	56	148	90	31	71	41	17.9

See p.111 for footnotes

B5 Vital Statistics: Numbers (in thousands)

1850–1899

	Finland			France			Germany			Greece[21]		
	B	D	M	B	D	M	B	D	M	B	D	M
1850	58	43	13.1	954	762	298	1,263	870	288	...	...	...
1851	63	39	13.7	971	799	287	1,258	853	286	...	...	...
1852	58	50	12.0	965	811	281	1,226	980	264	...	...	...
1853	58	49	12.3	937	796	281	1,200	941	264	...	...	...
1854	63	43	13.0	923	993	271	1,184	929	246	...	...	...
1855	60	54	13.3	902	938	283	1,123	971	243	...	...	...
1856	61	57	13.4	952	837	284	1,169	880	261	...	...	...
1857	56	55	12.0	941	859	296	1,270	960	293	...	...	...
1858	62	50	13.1	969	874	307	1,307	948	301	...	...	...
1859	61	43	13.8	1,018	979	298	1,343	919	287	...	...	...
1860	63	43	15.5	957[19]	782[19]	289[19]	1,319	840	291	31	22	6.1
1861	67	42	15.1	1,005	867	305	1,308	936	283	32	23	7.2
1862	66	50	14.1	995	813	304	1,310	910	300	...	...	...
1863	65	53	13.2	1,013	847	301	1,402	957	318	...	...	...
1864	71	41	14.1	1,006	860	300	1,431	989	323	39	28	8.4
1865	63	46	12.8	1,006	922	299	1,438	1,052	343	40	29	9.2
1866	59	62	11.1	1,006	885	304	1,457	1,175	307	39	27	8.6
1867	59	70	11.7	1,004	867	300	1,420	1,006	351	42	28	8.6
1868	44	138	10.1	984	922	301	1,432	1,068	346	41	32	8.7
1869	58	44	17.2	1,000	906	317	1,478	1,048	371	42	33	9.5
1870	64	32	17.9	996[20]	1,091[20]	234[20]	1,517[20]	1,074[20]	304[20]	41	32	9.0
1871	67	32	17.3	826	1,271	262	1,414	1,213	337	42	30	9.5
1872	66	36	15.8	966	793	353	1,626	1,195	424	43	31	8.9
1873	68	44	15.6	946	845	321	1,648	1,174	416	42	37	9.0
1874	71	45	16.9	955	782	303	1,683	1,122	400	45	30	9.5
1875	70	43	15.9	951	845	300	1,724	1,172	387	44	31	10.3
1876	71	42	15.8	967	834	291	1,761	1,134	367	47	31	9.8
1877	75	47	16.1	947	802	278	1,745	1,152	348	46	31	9.5
1878	70	48	15.3	937	839	280	1,714	1,158	340	45	31	9.6
1879	76	39	15.0	937	840	283	1,736	1,144	335	42	30	9.3
1880	75	49	15.8	920	858	279	1,696	1,173	337	41	30	8.5
1881	72	52	14.3	937	829	282	1,682	1,156	339	42[22]	32[22]	7.8[22]
1882	76	47	15.9	936	839	281	1,702	1,177	350	43	32	11.2
1883	76	44	16.5	938	841	285	1,687	1,190	353	43	35	11.6
1884	78	45	16.6	938	859	290	1,726	1,204	363	58	36	13.7
1885	75	48	16.0	925	837	283	1,730	1,200	369	58	40	13.1
1886	79	50	16.2	913	860	283	1,746	1,234	372	...	...	...
1887	82	43	17.2	900	843	277	1,757	1,152	371	...	...	...
1888	80	45	16.7	883	838	277	1,761	1,143	377	...	...	...
1889	78	46	16.1	880	795	273	1,773	1,153	389	75	54	19
1890	78	46	16.9	838	877	269	1,759[9]	1,199[9]	395[9]	78	56	20
1891	82	51	16.6	866	877	285	1,840	1,164	399	...	...	...
1892	76	57	14.8	856	876	290	1,796	1,211	399	...	...	...
1893	73	51	14.1	875	868	287	1,866	1,248	401	...	...	...
1894	76	47	16.1	855	816	287	1,841	1,144	408	...	...	...
1895	82	44	18.3	834	852	283	1,877	1,151	414	...	...	...
1896	82	47	19.2	866	772	290	1,915	1,099	432	...	...	...
1897	82	45	19.9	859	751	291	1,927	1,142	448	...	...	...
1898	89	46	20.6	844	810	287	1,965	1,118	459	...	...	...
1899	88	53	19.5	848	816	296	1,980	1,185	472	...	...	...

See p. 111 for footnotes

B5 **Vital Statistics: Numbers** (in thousands)

1850–1899

	Hungary[10]			Ireland			Italy			Netherlands		
	B	D	M	B	D	M	B	D	M	B	D	M
1850	...[23]	...[23]	...[23]	...	...	...	...	...	...	105	68	27
1851	...	...	154	...	...	...	...	...	...	107	69	27
1852	577	404	145	...	...	...	...	...	...	110	75	26
1853	560	483	117	...	...	...	...	...	...	104	77	24
1854	508	515	110	...	...	...	...	...	...	104	76	24
1855	524[24]	607[24]	105[24]	...	...	...	...	...	...	103	90	23
	Years ending 31 December											
1856	538	405	134	...	...	...	...	...	...	106	76	25
1857	587	416	123	...	...	...	...	...	...	113	88	26
1858	571	470	114	...	...	...	...	...	...	107	92	26
1859	595	431	100	...	...	...	...	...	...	116	103	27
1860	...	...	...	...	...	...	...	...	...	106	83	27
1861	...	...	...	...	...	...	...	...	...	119	85	27
1862	...	...	...	...	...	...	923	752	199	113	81	27
1863	...	...	...	...	...	...	964	760	201	125	82	28
1864	568	481	116	136	93	27	939	737	199	124	88	29
1865	586	423	132	145	93	31	961	747	226	127	91	30
1866	546	504	106	146	93	30	980[27]	733[27]	142[27]	125	102	30
1867	506	436	136	144	94	30	927	867	170	127	85	30
1868	558	444	180	146	86	28	900	777	183	126	90	28
1869	566	424	146	146	90	27	952	714	205	124	83	28
1870	571	446	134	150	90	29	951	773	189	130	93	29
1871	591	535	143	151	88	29	960[27]	779[27]	193[27]	128	107	29
1872	563	580	148	149	97	27	1,021	827	202	132	95	30
1873	567	874	153	144	98	26	985	814	215	134	90	32
1874	572	572	150	141	92	24	952	827	208	136	85	31
1875	608	501	170	138	98	24	1,035	843	230	138	97	32
1876	617	479	135	140	92	26	1,084	796	225	142	90	32
1877	589	500	125	140	94	25	1,029	788	215	143	86	31
1878	585	521	130	134	99	25	1,012	814	200	143	91	31
1879	627	502	140	135	105	23	1,064	837	213	147	90	31
1880	589	529	125	128	103	20	958	870	197	144	95	30
1881	595	484	137	126	90	22	1,081	784	230	143	88	30
1882	613	501	142	123	89	22	1,061	787	224	146	86	30
1883	630	451	145	118	96	21	1,071	794	232	144	92	30
1884	650	439	145	119	87	23	1,131	780	240	148	94	31
1885	644	463	143	116	91	21	1,126	787	234	148	90	30
1886	662	469	140	114	87	21	1,087	845	233	151	95	30
1887	649	506	133	112	89	21	1,153	829	236	149	87	31
1888	651	479	139	110	86	20	1,120	820	237	151	91	31
1889	656	447	122	108	83	22	1,149	768	230	151	91	31
1890	615[25]	491[25]	124[25]	105	86	21	1,083	796	222	149	93	32
1891	648	509	131	108	86	21	1,132	795	228	155	95	33
1892	622	532	141	104	90	22	1,111	802	229	149	98	33
1893	664	480	144	106	83	22	1,126	777	228	159	90	34
1894	649	474	143	105	84	22	1,103	776	232	155	88	34
1895	659[26]	469[26]	135[26]	106	84	23	1,092	784	228	158	90	36
1896	648	456	127	108	76	23	1,096	758	223	160	84	36
1897	652	454	131	107	84	23	1,102	696	229	161	84	37
1898	614	457	135	105	82	23	1,070	732	220	161	86	37
1899	645	449	148	104	80	22	1,089	703	236	163	87	38

See p. 111 for footnotes

B5 Vital Statistics: Numbers (in thousands)

1850–1899

	Norway			Portugal[66]			Romania[28]			Russia[30]		
	B	D	M	B	D	M	B	D	M	B	D	M
1850	43	24	10.6	...	...	...	...	...	...	...	...	...
1851	45	24	10.6	...	...	...	...	...	...	...	...	...
1852	44	26	10.2	...	...	...	...	...	...	...	...	...
1853	46	26	11.3	...	...	...	...	...	...	...	...	...
1854	50	23	12.5	...	...	...	...	...	...	...	...	...
1855	49	25	12.0	...	...	...	...	...	...	...	...	...
1856	48	25	11.6	...	...	...	...	...	...	...	...	...
1857	50	26	11.4	...	...	...	...	...	...	...	...	...
1858	52	25	11.7	...	...	...	...	...	...	...	2,039	...
1859	55	27	12.1	...	...	...	114	65	...	...	...	...
1860	53	27	11.4	...	...	...	124	80	...	...	...	...
1861	50	37	10.9	...	...	...	129	86	...	2,993	2,140	...
1862	52	33	11.2	...	...	...	129	88	...	3,106	2,082	...
1863	54	31	11.8	...	...	...	123	106	...	3,045	2,341	...
1864	53	30	11.4	...	...	...	147	106	...	3,234	2,365	...
1865	54	28	11.6	...	...	...	143	112	...	3,069	2,291	...
1866	54	29	11.4	...	...	...	129	156	24	...	...	...
1867	52	32	11.1	...	...	...	132	104	29	3,201	2,299	640
1868	51	32	10.7	...	...	...	140	105	31	3,093	2,517	607
1869	50	30	10.6	...	...	...	145	103	34	3,179	2,450	647
1870	51	28	11.2	...	...	...	148	112	31	3,180	2,263	671
1871	51	29	11.6	...	...	...	145	115	28	3,344	2,484[31]	679
1872	53	29	12.3	...	...	...	139	133	36	3,313	2,731	691
1873	53	30	12.8	...	...	...	142	142	29	3,495	2,441	648
1874	55	33	13.7	...	...	...	149	152	31	3,488	2,387	665
1875	57	34	14.2	...	...	...	171	141	33	3,548	2,384	670
1876	58	34	14.0	...	...	...	165	126	32	3,549	2,443	590
1877	59	31	14.0	...	...	...	159	133	29	3,531	2,451	527
1878	59	30	13.7	...	...	...	141[29]	149[29]	36[29]	3,418	2,760	665
1879	61	29	12.9	...	...	...	168	132	46	3,662	2,541	743
1880	59	31	12.8	...	...	...	171	163	40	3,681	2,670	709
1881	58	33	12.3	...	...	...	192	123	42	3,680	2,561	731
1882	59	36	12.9	...	...	...	189	132	44	3,927	3,076	719
1883	59	33	12.7	...	...	...	204	124	47	3,885	2,881	735
1884	61	32	13.2	...	...	...	201	124	41	4,008	2,674	693
1885	61	32	13.0	...	...	...	214	124	40	3,958	2,833	683
1886	60	32	12.8	156	99	34	213	135	39	3,973	2,662	682
1887	62	32	12.5	166	108	33	210	156	39	4,063	2,758	734
1888	60	34	12.2	164	107	34	220	159	38	4,269	2,761	808
1889	59	35	12.4	168	112	35	213	143	41	4,233	2,992	743
1890	61	36	12.9	165	127	36	205	151	39	4,228	3,131	718
1891	62	36	13.2	162	116	35	228	162	44	4,372	3,096	747
1892	60	36	12.7	159	104	35	212	188	42	4,033	3,597	784
1893	62	34	13.0	164	110	34	222	169	41	4,298	3,028	788
1894	61	35	13.0	154	107	33	227	176	50	4,392	3,062	848
1895	63	33	13.3	156	108	33	238	156	41	4,539	3,214	843
1896	63	32	14.0	158	120	33	232	166	47	4,635	3,063	810
1897	64	33	14.2	161	116	36	249	172	42	4,693	2,976	857
1898	66	33	15.0	161	114	35	215	155	44	4,626	3,156	826
1899	66	37	15.5	161	108	37	250	165	50	4,764	3,013	898

See p.111 for footnotes

B5 Vital Statistics: Numbers (in thousands)

1850–1899

	Serbia			Spain[33]			Sweden		
	B	D	M	B	D	M	B	D	M
1850	...	...	...	...	...	...	110	69	26
1851	...	...	...	...	...	...	111	73	26
1852	...	...	...	...	...	...	108	80	24
1853	...	...	...	...	...	...	111	84	26
1854	...	...	...	...	...	...	120	71	28
1855	...	...	...	...	...	...	115	78	27
1856	...	...	...	...	...	...	115	80	27
1857	...	...	...	...	...	...	119	101	29
1858	...	...	...	546	434	113	129	80	30
1859	...	...	...	559	449	113	132	76	31
1860	...	...	...	573	429	126	133	68	30
1861	...	...	...	612	418	131	127	72	28
1862	45	43	13.4	607	431	129	132	84	28
1863	49	40	17.0	598	462	124	134	77	29
1864	52	36	13.1	621	499	126	136	82	28
1865	55	30	14.3	615	539	129	134	79	29
1866	56	29	13.6	612	464	132	137	83	28
1867	55	32	12.9	618	487	118	129	82	25
1868	57	41	13.5	574	549	112	115	88	23
1869	58	38	15.3	597	551	137	118	93	24
1870	58	43	14.4	594	512	104	120	82	25
1871	57	43	13.5	...	...	...	127	72	27
1872	52	42	17.5	...	...	...	127	69	29
1873	56	43	14.6	...	...	...	132	74	31
1874	56	49	15.5	...	...	...	133	88	31
1875	63	43	15.1	...	...	...	136	88	31
1876	57	66	10.6	...	...	...	136	86	31
1877	46	46	17.4	...	...	...	138	83	31
1878	53[32]	46[32]	13.8[32]	601	508	118	134	81	29
1879	67	53	25	601	511	111	139	77	29
1880	70	54	20	598	507	104	134	83	29
1881	81	44	21	630	512	108	133	81	28
1882	80	42	22	617	535	103	134	79	29
1883	87	42	22	611	560	106	133	79	29
1884	90	48	20	632	526	114	139	81	30
1885	91	52	17	629	658	110	137	83	31
1886	83	59	23	639	509	111	140	78	30
1887	94	50	23	632	573	96	140	76	30
1888	95	51	23	641	529	99	136	76	28
1889	94	54	22	643	538	138	132	76	28
1890	87	55	22	610	570	141	134	82	29
1891	99	58	23	630	558	156	136	81	28
1892	93	74	21	642	548	151	130	86	27
1893	95	67	24	640	535	141	132	81	27
1894	96	64	25	628	549	141	131	79	28
1895	102	62	21	636	527	140	135	74	29
1896	97	63	21	655	539	133	134	77	29
1897	102	63	21	625	520	129	133	77	30
1898	85	55	23	612	519	125	137	76	31
1899	96	60	24	633	533	156	134	90	32

See p.111 for footnotes

B5 Vital Statistics: Numbers (in thousands)

1850–1899

	Switzerland			United Kingdom: England and Wales			United Kingdom: Scotland		
	B	D	M	B	D	M	B	D	M
1850	...	...	...	593	369	153	...	...	...
1851	...	...	...	616	395	154	...	...	...
1852	...	...	...	624	407	159	...	...	...
1853	...	...	...	612	421	165	...	...	...
1854	...	...	...	634	438	160	...	...	...
1855	...	...	...	635	426	152	93[10]	62[10]	20[10]
1856	...	...	...	657	391	159	102	59	21
1857	...	...	...	663	420	159	103	62	21
1858	...	...	...	655	450	156	104	64	20
1859	...	...	...	690	441	168	107	62	21
1860	...	...	...	684	423	170	106	68	21
1861	...	...	...	696	435	164	107	62	21
1862	...	...	...	713	437	164	107	67	21
1863	...	...	...	727	474	174	109	71	22
1864	...	...	...	740	496	180	112	74	23
1865	...	...	...	748	491	185	113	71	24
1866	...	...	...	754	501	188	114	71	24
1867	...	...	...	768	471	179	114	69	23
1868	...	...	18	787	481	177	116	69	22
1869	...	...	19	773	495	177	113	76	22
1870	79	69	19	793	515	182	115	74	24
1871	78	74	20	797	515	190	116	75	24
1872	80	60	21	826	492	201	119	76	26
1873	81	62	21	830	493	206	120	77	27
1874	83	61	23	855	527	202	124	81	26
1875	88	66	25	851	546	201	124	82	26
1876	91	67	22	888	510	202	127	74	27
1877	89	65	22	888	500	194	127	74	26
1878	88	65	21	892	540	190	127	77	24
1879	86	64	19	880	526	182	126	73	24
1880	84	62	19	882	529	192	125	76	25
1881	85	64	19	884	492	197	126	72	26
1882	83	63	19	889	517	204	126	73	27
1883	82	59	20	891	523	206	124	77	27
1884	82	58	20	907	531	204	129	75	26
1885	80	62	20	894	523	198	126	75	25
1886	81	60	20	904	537	196	128	74	25
1887	81	59	21	886	531	201	124	75	25
1888	81	58	21	880	511	204	123	71	25
1889	81	60	21	886	518	214	123	73	26
1890	79	62	21	870	562	223	122	79	27
1891	84	61	21	914	588	227	126	84	28
1892	83	57	22	898	560	227	125	76	29
1893	85	61	22	915	570	219	127	80	27
1894	84	62	22	890	499	226	124	71	28
1895	85	60	23	922	569	228	126	82	28
1896	88	56	24	915	527	243	129	71	30
1897	90	56	25	922	541	249	129	79	31
1898	92	59	25	923	552	255	131	78	32
1899	94	58	25	929	582	262	131	80	33

See p.111 for footnotes

B5 Vital Statistics: Numbers (in thousands)

1900–1949

	Albania			Austria			Belgium			Bulgaria		
	B	D	M	B	D	M	B	D	M	B	D	M
1900	...	...	...	968	659	214	193	127	58	157	84	33
1901	...	...	...	962	631	214	199	113	57	141	87	36
1902	...	...	...	984	656	207	195	116	56	149	91	37
1903	...	...	...	944	638	209	192	116	55	159	88	45
1904	...	...	...	961	642	210	191	117	57	167	84	43
1905	...	...	...	922	685	213	187	115	57	174	87	43
1906	...	...	...	961	619	217	186	116	58	179	91	39
1907	...	...	...	942	630	210	184	113	59	180	92	41
1908	...	...	...	941	628	214	183	119	58	169	102	37
1909	...	...	...	941	646	213	176	115	57	173	113	39
1910	...	...	...	924	602	215	176	110	59	180	100	39
1911	...	...	...	899	628	217	171	120	59	176	94	41
1912	...	...	...	903	592	212	170	109	61	185	91	25
1913	...	...	...	865[2]	590[2]	196[2]	170	108	61	108	122	24
1914	...	...	...	152	118	47	156	109	41	191	88	53
1915	...	...	...	119	137	29	124	101	25	172	85	27
1916	...	...	...	94	133	29	99	101	30	99	97	10
1917	...	...	...	87	144	30	87	125	33	81	99	21
1918	...	...	...	93	173	42	85	157	44	100	152	45
1919	...	...	...	119	131	80	128	113	97	157	97	75
1920	...	...	...	147	123	86	164	103	107	193	104	68
1921	...	...	...	151	110	81	162	100	88	197	106	60
1922	...	...	...	151	113	74	153	104	83	203	106	59
1923	...	...	...	147	100	57	155	98	80	192	108	53
1924	...	...	...	142	98	53	152	98	80	207	108	55
1925	...	...	...	136	95	51	153[34]	100[34]	75[34]	196	102	53
1926	...	...	...	127	99	48	149	101	73	203	93	54
1927	...	...	...	119	99	48	144	103	72	183	112	51
1928	...	...	...	117	96	49	146	102	71	185	99	56
1929	...	...	...	112	97	51	146	116	72	173	103	56
1930	...	...	...	112	90	52	150	103	72	180	93	54
1931	...	...	...	106	94	50	147	104	66	171	98	56
1932	25	18	4.8	102	94	45	144	104	62	186	96	57
1933	...	...	...	96	89	44	135	105	65	174	93	56
1934	...	...	...	92	86	44	132	97	63	182	85	56
1935	...	...	...	89	93	46	126	102	63	161	89	48
1936	...	...	...	88	89	46	126	102	65	159	88	49
1937	...	...	...	86	90	46	125	104	63	151	85	51
1938	36	19	7.0	94	95	89	130	105	62	142	85	53
1939	30	16	5.4	138	102	117	126	110	55	135	84	57
1940	34	18	6.7	146	99	78	110[35]	125[35]	36[35]	141[36]	85[36]	57[36]
1941	31	18	6.9	135	94	56	98[35]	119[35]	53[35]	147	85	61
1942	...	16	7.9	116	91	53	106[35]	117[35]	62[35]	153	88	71
1943	...	...	...	122	94	49	121[35]	108[35]	52[35]	149	88	69
1944	...	...	...	127	110	41	124	125	45	151	94[37]	63
1945	...	...	...	101	174	31	127	121	83	167	104[37]	83
1946	...	...	...	111	94	63	147	110	91	179	96	77
1947	...	22	...	129	90	75	145	108	84	170	95	78
1948	...	19	...	123	84	72	148	104	80	176	90	80
1949	...	15	11.6	113	89	69	145	107	73	178	85	78

See p.111 for footnotes

B5 Vital Statistics: Numbers (in thousands)

1900–1949

	Czechoslavakia			Denmark			Finland			France		
	B	D	M	B	D	M	B	D	M	B	D	M
1900	...	...	...	72	41	18.5	86	58	18.3	827	853	299
1901	...	...	...	73	39	17.6	89	56	18.5	857	785	303
1902	...	...	...	73	36	17.6	87	51	17.5	845	761	295
1903	...	...	...	72	37	17.9	85	50	17.7	827	754	296
1904	...	...	...	74	36	18.2	90	50	18.6	818	761	299
1905	...	...	...	73	39	18.5	87	53	18.6	807	770	303
1906	...	...	...	74	35	19.4	91	51	19.9	807	780	306
1907	...	...	...	74	37	20.1	92	53	20.3	773	792	314
1908	...	...	...	76	39	20.0	92	55	20.1	792	744	316
1909	...	...	...	76	36	19.9	95	51	19.4	770	755	308
1910	...	...	...	75	35	20.0	93	51	18.8	774	703	308
1911	...	...	...	74	37	19.9	91	52	18.7	742	775	308
1912	...	...	...	75	36	20.5	92	52	18.7	750	692	312
1913	...	...	...	72	35	20.5	87	52	18.9	746[20]	702[20]	299[20]
1914	...	...	...	73	36	19.8	88	51	18.4	753[41]	770[41]	205[41]
1915	...	...	...	70	37	19.0	83	52	17.8	480[41]	745[41]	86[41]
1916	...	...	...	72	39	21	80	55	19.3	382[41]	695[41]	125[41]
1917	...	...	...	70	39	21	81	59	20.0	410[41]	710[41]	180[41]
1918	...	...	...	73	39	23	79	95	15.0	470[41]	865[41]	202[41]
1919	303	248	92	69	40	25	64	63	18.8	504	737	553
1920	363	258	89	78	40	27	85	53	24	834	671	623
1921	399	242	82	79	36	27	82	47	24	812	693	456
1922	388	240	71	74	39	26	80	49	24	760	688	385
1923	380	209	65	75	38	27	82	48	24	761	666	355
1924	363	216	63	74	38	26	78	53	22	753	679	355
1925	356	216	65	72	37	26	78	47	22	770	708	353
1926	352	223	65	71	38	26	77	48	23	768	713	345
1927	336	231	65	68	40	26	76	52	24	744	676	336
1928	337	219	69	69	38	27	78	49	26	749	674	339
1929	326	226	70	65	39	28	76	54	25	730	739	334
1930	333	208	68	66	38	29	75	48	25	750	649	342
1931	318	212	65	64	41	29	72	49	24	734	679	327
1932	312	210	64	65	40	28	69	47	23	722	660	315
1933	288	205	62	63	38	32	65	48	24	679	660	316
1934	281	199	59	65	38	35	68	46	28	678	634	299
1935	271	204	58	65	41	34	70	45	29	640	658	285
1936	265	202	61	66	41	35	69	49	30	631	642	280
1937	263	202	63	67	40	34	72	46	32	618	629	274
1938	258[38]	196[38]	56[38]	68	39	34	77	47	34	612	647	274
1939	274	196	80	68	39	36	78	53	31	612	643[42]	258
1940	303	206	73	70	40	35	66	72	31	559[41]	738[41]	177[41]
1941	295	206	63	71	40	34	90	73	38	520[41]	673[41]	226[41]
1942	287	209	66	80	38	36	62	56	27	573[41]	654[41]	267[41]
1943	313	204	58	84	38	37	76	50	32	613[41]	624[41]	219[41]
1944	321[38]	220[38]	50[38]	91	41	38	79	71	32	627[41]	664[41]	205[41]
1945	276	252	53	95	42	36	96[40]	49[40]	44[40]	643[41]	641[41]	393[41]
1946	293	182	65	96	42	40	106	45	50	840[42]	542[42]	517[42]
1947	294[39]	147[39]	68[39]	92	40	40	108	46	44	867	534	427
1948	289	142	66	85	36	39	108	44	39	867	510	371
1949	277	146	65	80	38	37	104	45	35	869	570	341

See p.111 for footnotes

B5 Vital Statistics: Numbers (in thousands)

1900–1949

	Germany			East Germany			Greece[21]			Hungary[10]		
	B	D	M	B	D	M	B	D	M	B	D	M
1900	1,996	1,236	476	...	...	...	...	...	...	656	450	149
1901	2,032	1,174	468	...	...	...	...	...	...	637	425	148
1902	2,025	1,122	457	...	...	...	...	...	...	658	461	147
1903	1,953	1,171	463	...	...	...	...	...	...	629	450	138
1904	2,026	1,163	478	...	...	...	...	...	...	642	431	157
1905	1,987	1,194	486	...	...	...	...	...	...	620	486	148
1906	2,022	1,112	499	...	...	...	...	...	...	634	438	154
1907	2,000	1,117	504	...	...	...	...	...	...	641	454	178
1908	2,015	1,135	501	...	...	...	...	...	...	655	447	165
1909	1,978	1,094	494	...	...	...	...	...	...	668	458	158
1910	1,925	1,046	496	...	...	...	...	...	...	644	426	158
1911	1,871	1,131	513	...	...	...	...	...	...	638	455	171
1912	1,870	1,030	523	...	...	...	...	...	...	665	425	161
1913	1,839	1,005	513	...	...	...	...	...	...	641	433	172
1914	1,819[43]	1,291[43]	461[43]	...	...	...	...	...	...	649	440	136
1915	1,383[43]	1,450[43]	278[43]	...	...	...	...	...	...	445	475	61
1916	1,029[9][43]	1,298[9][43]	279[9][43]	...	...	...	...	...	...	314	392	63
1917	912	1,345	308	...	...	...	...	...	...	297	385	75
1918	927[44]	1,606[44]	353[44]	...	...	...	...	...	...	281[10]	473[10]	127[10]
										128	207	59
1919	1,261	978	844	...	...	...	...	...	...	217	157	161
1920	1,599	933	895	...	...	...	...	...	...	249	170	104
1921	1,581[45]	870[45]	740[45]	...	...	...	107	69	28	255	170	93
1922	1,425	890	691	...	...	...	110	82	30	249	173	88
1923	1,318	867	588	...	...	...	114	102	44	239	159	79
1924	1,291[46]	767[46]	446[46]	...	...	...	117	93	44	221	168	75
1925	1,311	753	489	...	...	...	156	89	48	235	142	74
1926	1,245	743	490	...	...	...	181	84	44	229	140	77
1927	1,179	765	545	...	...	...	177	100	44	219	151	77
1928	1,200	747	595	...	...	...	189	106	41	225	146	80
1929	1,164	815	597	...	...	...	182	116	44	215	153	79
1930	1,144	719	570	...	...	...	200	104	45	220	134	78
1931	1,048	734	523	...	...	...	199	114	46	207	145	76
1932	993	708	517	...	...	...	186	118	39	206	157	71
1933	971	738	639	...	...	...	190	111	46	194	130	73
1934	1,198	725	740	...	...	...	209	101	47	194	129	79
1935	1,264	792	651	...	...	...	193	101	46	189	137	76
1936	1,279	796	610	...	...	...	193	105	39	183	128	77
1937	1,277	794	620	...	...	...	184	106	46	182	128	80
1938	1,349	799	645	...	...	...	185	94	46	182	131	74
1939	1,413	854	774	...	...	...	179	100	48	179	125	80
1940	1,402	889	613	...	...	...	179	94	43	186	133	72
1941	1,308	846	505	...	...	...	135[48]	126[48]	37[48]	177	123	79
1942	1,056	848	525	...	...	...	133[48]	191[48]	45[48]	187	137	73
1943	1,125	853	514	...	...	...	122[48]	111[48]	44[48]	173	127	76
1944	...	...	...	...	...	...	146[48]	111[48]	35[48]	...	...	68
1945	...	...	...	...	...	...	183[48]	86[48]	47[48]	169	211	73
	West Germany (including West Berlin)											
1946	733	588	400	189	413	125	209[48]	74[48]	52[48]	169	135	99
1947	781	575	482	247	358	164	206[48]	70[48]	50[48]	187[50]	118[50]	98[50]
1948	806	515	525	243	290	183	210[48][49]	96[48][49]	44[48][49]	192	106	98
1949	833	517	506	274	254	191	139	59	42	190	106	108

See p.111 for footnotes

B5 Vital Statistics: Numbers (in thousands)

1900–1949

	Ireland			Northern Ireland			Italy			Netherlands		
	B	D	M	B	D	M	B	D	M	B	D	M
1900	101	88	21				1,067	769	233	163	92	39
1901	101	79	23				1,058	715	235	168	90	40
1902	102	78	23				1,093	727	238	169	86	40
1903	102	77	23				1,042	736	237	170	84	40
1904	104	80	23				1,085	699	248	171	87	41
1905	103	75	23				1,085	730	256	171	85	41
1906	104	74	23				1,071	697	261	171	83	42
1907	102	77	23				1,062	700	260	172	83	43
1908	102	77	23				1,139	770	283	172	87	42
1909	103	75	23				1,116	738	266	171	80	42
1910	102	75	22				1,144	682	269	169	80	43
1911	102	72	23				1,094	743	260	167	87	43
1912	101	72	23				1,134	636	265	170	75	46
1913	100	75	22				1,122	664	264	174	76	48
1914	99	71	24				1,114	643	252	177	78	43
1915	96	76	24				1,109	810	186	167	80	43
1916	91	71	22				882	855	106	173	84	47
1917	86	73	21				714[51]	949[51]	99[51]	173 [55]	87 [55]	49
1918	87	79	23				655[51]	1,268[51]	107[51]	169	117	50
1919	89	79	27				771 [52]	676 [52]	333 [52]	166	91	58
1920	100	67	27				1,158	682	509	195	84	65
1921	91	64	23	...	...	...	1,163	670	439	191	79	64
	Southern Ireland											
1922	59	45	15	30	20	8	1,176	690	365	184	82	61
1923	62	42	16	30	19	8	1,155	655	334	188	73	57
1924	63	45	15	28	20	8	1,124	663	307	182	71	56
1925	62	44	14	28	20	8	1,110	670	296	179	72	55
1926	61	42	14	28	19	7	1,095	680	296	177	73	55
1927	60	44	13	27	18	7	1,094	640	303	175	78	57
1928	59	42	14	26	18	7	1,072	646	285	179	74	59
1929	58	43	14	25	20	7	1,038	667	288	177	83	61
1930	58	42	14	26	17	8	1,093	577	303	182	72	63
1931	57	43	13	26	18	7	1,026	609	276	177	77	59
1932	56	43	13	25	18	7	991	611	268	179	73	56
1933	57	41	14	25	18	8	996	574	290	171	72	59
1934	58	39	14	25	18	8	993	563	313	172	70	61
1935	58	42	14	25	19	9	997	595	288	170	74	61
1936	58	43	15	26	18	9	963	593	317	172	74	63
1937	56	45	15	25	19	9	992	618	377	170	76	66
1938	57	40	15	26	18	9	1,037	615	325	178	74	67
1939	56	42	15	25	18	9	1,040	591	323	181	76	81
1940	57	42	15	25	19	10	1,046	607[54]	314	185	88	67
1941	57	44	15	27	20	12	938	622[54]	274	182	90	66
1942	66	42	17	30	18	12	926 [53]	644[54] [53]	287 [53]	190	86[57]	88
1943	64	43	17	32	18	10	882	676[54]	215	209	91[57]	65
1944	65	45	17	31	17	10	815	680[54]	215	220	108[57]	50
1945	67	43	17	29	16	10	816	610[54]	309	210	141[57]	72
1946	68	41	18	30	17	10	1,036	545	416	284	80	107
1947	69	44	16	31	17	10	1,011	521	438	267	78	99
1948	66	36	16	30	15	9	1,006	486	385	247 [56]	72 [56]	88 [56]
1949	64	38	16	29	16	9	937	482	360	236	81	82

See p.111 for footnotes

B5 Vital Statistics: Numbers (in thousands)

1900–1949

	Norway			Poland[58]			Portugal[66]			Romania[28]		
	B	D	M	B	D	M	B	D	M	B	D	M
1900	66	35	15.2	...	...	...	165	110	37	235	146	40
1901	67	34	14.8	...	...	...	171	114	38	241	160	44
1902	66	32	14.4	...	...	...	176	108	39	242	172	55
1903	65	34	13.6	...	...	...	183	112	39	252	156	55
1904	64	33	13.5	...	...	...	177	106	37	256	156	52
1905	63	34	13.3	...	...	...	180	113	38	248	160	51
1906	62	32	13.6	...	...	...	183	125	35	262	157	67
1907	61	33	14.0	...	...	...	176	113	35	274	176	70
1908	62	33	14.2	...	...	...	175	116	36	273	185	61
1909	63	32	14.1	...	...	...	175	112	36	282	188	63
1910	61	32	14.6	...	...	...	187	113	39	274	173	64
1911	62	32	14.8	...	...	...	230	131	41	300	179	75
1912	61	33	14.8	...	...	...	208	120	44	314	166	62
1913	61	32	15.3	...	...	...	194	123	35	310	192	67
1914	62	33	15.8	...	...	...	188	116	37	327	183	65
1915	59	33	15.9	...	...	...	195	123	36	320	194	56
1916	61	35	17.3	...	...	...	193	129	36	...	...	...
1917	64	35	18.1	...	...	...	188	134	33	...	...	...
1918	63	44	20.0	...	...	...	179	249	30	...[59]	...[59]	...[59]
1919	59	36	15.4	...	...	...	166	153	47	366	328	107
1920	69	34	18.5	...	...	...	203	143	53	539	415	206
1921	65	31	18.1	890	568	317	197	126	51	620	372	198
1922	63	32	17.2	983	555	319	204	126	50	614	376	170
1923	62	32	17.0	1,015	494	287	207	142	49	609	372	165
1924	58	31	16.6	1,000	519	269	207	126	46	623	383	154
1925	54	30	16.2	1,037	492	239	208	117	46	606	362	154
1926	54	30	15.9	989	533	257	217	128	48	608	373	160
1927	50	31	15.8	958	525	259	203	123	42	603	393	172
1928	50	30	16.7	984	505	295	211	124	45	624	352	159
1929	48	32	17.8	988	520	301	201	119	45	601	378	159
1930	48	30	18.1	1,016	490	300	203	116	48	625	347	167
1931	46	31	17.7	966	495	273	204	115	45	605	379	167
1932	45	30	17.6	932	487	270	208	119	45	662	399	175
1933	42	29	18.0	869	466	274	204	121	46	598	348	155
1934	42	28	19.2	882	480	277	203	119	47	612	391	175
1935	41	30	21	877	471	280	204	123	49	586	403	166
1936	42	30	22	892	483	284	206	119	47	609	382	177
1937	44	30	24	856	482	276	198	117	47	601	378	185
1938	45	29	24	850	480	279	199	115	49	585	379	174
1939	47	30	26	...	...	...	199	116	49	564[59]	370[59]	157[59]
1940	48	32	28	...	...	...	188	120	47	352[30]	254[30]	121[30]
1941	46	32	26	...	...	...	184	135	55	311[30]	261[30]	103[30]
1942	53	32	...	...	...	...	188	127	59	291[30]	265[30]	105[30]
1943	57	32	24	...	...	...	198	122	58	396[30]	306[30]	117[30]
1944	62	33	22	...	...	...	201	119	60	297[30]	269[30]	71[30]
1945	62	30	24	...	...	...	209	116	61	268[30]	273[30]	145[30]
1946	71	29	30	...	...	...	206	121	62	391	296	186
1947	68	29	30	630	271	...	200	110	67	371	349	155
1948	66	28	30	702	268	...	221	108	65	380	248	179
1949	63	29	27	719	284	274	212	117	65	444	220	186

See p. 111 for footnotes

B5 Vital Statistics: Numbers (in thousands)

1900–1949

	Russia[31]			Serbia			Spain			Sweden		
	B	D	M	B	D	M	B	D	M	B	D	M
1900	4,854	3,055	873	105	58	31	628	537	161	138	86	31
1901	4,801	3,219	862	96	53	21	651	518	158	139	83	31
1902	4,993	3,204	878	98	57	27	667	488	164	137	80	31
1903	4,978	3,103	919	106	60	25	685	470	154	134	79	30
1904	5,125	3,153	803	106	56	31	650	487	145	135	80	31
1905	4,819	3,411	840	100	65	27	671	491	137	135	82	31
1906	5,117	3,254	1,048	113	66	28	650	499	138	137	76	33
1907	5,221	3,152	986	111	62	30	646	472	136	137	78	33
1908	5,043	3,189	902	104	67	26	658	461	141	139	81	33
1909	5,124	3,375	917	110	83	27	650	467	129	140	75	33
1910	...	...	...	112	64	30	647	456	139	136	77	33
1911	...	...	...	107	64	30	628	467	143	133	76	33
1912	...	...	...	114	63	26	638	426	144	133	79	33
1913	...	...	...	...	...	...	618	449	138	130	77	33
1914	...	...	...	...	...	...	608	450	134	129	78	33
1915	...	...	...	...	...	...	631	452	128	123	84	33
1916	...	...	...	...	...	...	599	442	137	122	78	35
1917	...	...	...	...	...	...	602	466	142	121	77	36
1918	...	...	...	...	...	...	613	696	141	118	106	39
1919	...	...	...	...	...	...	586	483	167	115	84	40
1920	...	...	...	...	...	...	623	495	176	139	78	43
1921	...	...	...	...	...	...	649	455	165	128	74	40
1922	...	...	...	...	...	...	656	441	163	117	76	37
1923	...	...	...	...	...	...	663	450	158	113	68	38
1924	...	...	...	...	...	...	653	431	158	109	72	37
1925	...	...	...	...	...	...	645	432	159	106	71	37
1926	...	...	...	...	...	...	663	421	162	102	71	38
1927	...	...	...	...	...	...	636	420	159	98	77	39
1928	...	...	...	...	...	...	666	413	171	98	73	41
1929	...	...	...	...	...	...	654	407	169	93	75	42
1930	...	...	...	...	...	...	661	394	174	94	72	44
1931	...	...	...	...	...	...	649	409	175	91	77	43
1932	...	...	...	...	...	...	671	389	159	90	71	42
1933	...	...	...	...	...	...	668	395	148	85	70	43
1934	...	...	...	...	...	...	638	389	146	85	70	48
1935	...	...	...	...	...	...	633	385	151	86	73	51
1936	...	...	...	...	...	...	614	414	139	89	75	53
1937	...	...	...	...	...	...	566	472	143	90	75	56
1938	...	....	...	...	...	...	506	485	113	94	73	58
1939	...	...	...	...	...	...	420	470	144	97	73	61
1940	...	...	...	...	...	...	628	425	216	96	73	59
1941	...	...	...	...	...	...	508	484	190	100	72	58
1942	...	...	...	...	...	...	528	385	188	114	64	64
1943	...	...	...	...	...	...	603	349	174	125	66	63
1944	...	...	...	...	...	...	599	346	188	135	72	65
1945	...	...	...	...	...	...	618	327	192	135	72	64
1946	...	...	...	...	...	...	579	348	202	133	71	64
1947	...	...	...	...	...	...	582	325	225	129	74	60
1948	...	...	...	...	...	...	635	300	214	127	68	58
1949	...	...	...	...	...	...	595	316	197	121	70	55

See p.111 for footnotes

B5 Vital Statistics: Numbers (in thousands)

1900–1949

	Switzerland			United Kingdom: England and Wales			United Kingdom: Scotland			Yugoslavia[60]		
	B	D	M	B	D	M	B	D	M	B	D	M
1900	94	64	26	927	588	257	131	82	32	...	...	...
1901	97	60	25	930	552	259	132	80	31	...	...	...
1902	96	58	25	941	536	262	132	78	32	...	...	...
1903	94	60	25	945	515	261	134	76	32	...	...	...
1904	95	61	26	945	550	258	133	78	32	...	...	...
1905	95	62	26	929	520	261	131	75	31	...	...	...
1906	96	59	27	935	531	271	132	76	33	...	...	...
1907	95	59	28	918	524	276	129	77	33	...	...	...
1908	96	58	28	940	520	265	131	78	32	...	...	...
1909	94	59	27	914	518	261	129	75	30	...	...	...
1910	94	56	27	897	483	268	124	72	31	...	...	...
1911	91	60	28	881	528	275	122	72	32	...	...	...
1912	92	54	28	873	487	284	123	72	33	...	...	...
1913	90	55	26	882	505	287	121	73	34	...	...	...
1914	87	54	22	879	517	294	124	74	35	...	...	...
1915	75	52	20	815	562	361	114	82	36	...	...	...
1916	74	51	22	786	508	280	110	71	31	...	...	...
1917	72	53	23	668	499	259	97	69	30	...	...	...
1918	73	75	26	663	612	287	99	78	35	...	...	...
1919	72	55	31	692	504	369	106	75	44	...	...	...
1920	81	56	35	958	466	380	137	68	47	...	...	...
1921	81	50	33	849	459	321	123	66	39	423	252	157
1922	76	50	30	780	487	300	115	73	34	421	254	132
1923	76	46	30	758	445	292	112	63	35	433	253	130
1924	74	49	29	730	473	296	107	70	32	443	255	115
1925	73	48	28	711	473	296	104	66	32	437	239	123
1926	72	46	28	695	454	280	102	64	31	459	245	124
1927	70	49	29	654	485	308	97	66	33	452	276	124
1928	70	48	30	660	460	303	97	65	33	438	273	121
1929	69	50	31	644	532	313	93	71	33	453	286	128
1930	70	47	32	649	455	315	95	64	33	489	261	138
1931	68	49	32	632	492	312	92	64	33	470	277	126
1932	69	50	32	614	484	307	91	66	33	466	272	111
1933	68	47	32	580	496	318	87	65	34	452	244	112
1934	67	47	32	598	477	342	89	64	37	461	249	100
1935	66	50	30	599	477	350	88	65	38	442	249	110
1936	65	48	30	605	496	355	89	67	38	436	241	110
1937	62	47	30	611	510	359	88	69	38	424	242	118
1938	64	49	31	621	479	362	89	63	39	411	240	122
1939	64	49	32	614	500	440	87	64	46	404	233	124
1940	64	51	32	590	582	471	86	73	54	...	...	...
1941	72	47	36	579	535	389	90	73	48	...	...	...
1942	79	47	37	652	480	370	91	65	47	...	...	...
1943	83	47	36	684	501	296	95	67	38	...	...	...
1944	86	52	35	751	492	303	96	65	37	...	...	...
1945	89	51	36	680	488	398	87	63	49	...	...	...
1946	89	50	39	821	492	386	104	65	46	...[61]	...[61]	...[61]
1947	88	51	39	881	518	401	113	66	44	417	200	206
1948	88	50	39	775	470	397	100	61	44	447	214	204
1949	85	49	37	731	511	375	96	63	42	484	217	184

See p.111 for footnotes

B5 Vital Statistics: Numbers (in thousands)

1950–1975

	Albania			Austria			Belgium			Bulgaria		
	B	D	M	B	D	M	B	D	M	B	D	M
1950	47	17	12.3	108	86	65	143	104	72	183	74	78
1951	48	19	12.6	103	88	63	143	108	71	153	77	64
1952	45	20	13.1	103	83	58	146	104	67	154	84	70
1953	53	18	12.6	103	83	54	147	106	68	153	68	68
1954	55	18	10.8	104	85	54	148	105	68	150	68	64
1955	61	21	11.3	109	85	57	149	108	69	151	68	63
1956	60	16	10.4	116	87	57	150	108	69	148	71	67
1957	57	17	11.8	119	89	57	152	107	68	141	66	67
1958	63	14	11.9	120	86	55	156	106	67	138	61	71
1959	65	15	11.5	124	88	56	161	104	65	137	74	67
1960	70	17	12.6	126	90	59	156	113	65	140	64	69
1961	68	15	18.7	132	86	60	158	106	62	138	63	67
1962	67	18	12.8	133	91	60	154	112	62	134	70	65
1963	69	18	13.2	135	92	58	158	116	62	132	66	66
1964	69	16	13.0	134	89	58	160	109	65	131	64	66
1965	66	17	13.9	130	94	57	155	115	67	126	67	66
1966	65	16	13.0	129	91	56	151	115	68	123	68	67
1967	69	17	16.9	127	95	56	146	115	68	125	75	72
1968	72	16	15.8	126	96	56	142	122	70	142	72	74
1969	73	16	15.3	121	99	55	142	120	72	143	80	74
1970	70	20	14.4	112	99	53	142	119	73	139	77	73
1971	73	18	15.3	109	97	48	142	119	74	135	83	70
1972	...	...	...	104	95	57	136	117	74	131	84	70
1973	...	...	...	98	93	49	129	118	74	140	81	74
1974	...	...	...	97	94	49	124	116	74	149	85	74
1975	...	...	...	94	96	46	120	119	73	145	90	75

	Czechoslavakia			Denmark			Finland			France		
	B	D	M	B	D	M	B	D	M	B	D	M
1950	288	143	67	80	39	39	98	41	34	858	530	331
1951	286	143	64	77	38	37	93	40	32	823	562	320
1952	281[62]	135[62]	56	77	39	36	94	39	32	819	521	314
1953	272	134	49	78	39	35	91	40	32	801	553	308
1954	267	135	51	76	40	35	90	38	33	807	515	314
1955	265	126	52	77	39	35	90	40	33	802	523	313
1956	262	126	58	77	40	34	89	39	33	803	542	294
1957	253	134	46	75	42	34	87	41	31	813	528	310
1958	235	126	50	75	42	34	81	39	31	809	497	312
1959	217	131	51	74	42	34	83	39	32	826	506	321
1960	217	125	53	76	44	36	82	40	33	816	517	320
1961	218	126	53	76	43	36	82	41	34	835	497	315
1962	217	139	54	78	45	38	81	43	34	829	538	317
1963	236	133	55	82	46	39	82	42	33	865	554	339
1964	241	135	55	83	47	40	80	43	35	874	517	347
1965	232	141	56	86	48	42	78	44	36	862	540	346
1966	223	142	58	88	49	41	78	44	38	860	526	340
1967	216	144	60	81	48	41	77	44	41	838	540	346
1968	214	153	61	75	47	39	74	45	40	833	551	357
1969	223	161	63	71	48	39	68	46	41	840	571	381
1970	229	166	63	71	48	36	65	44	41	848	540	394
1971	237	165	65	75	49	33	62	46	38	879	552	406
1972	251	161	68	76	50	31	59	44	35	875	548	417
1973	275	168	71	72	51	31	57	43	35	855	557	401
1974	291	171	70	71	52	33	63	45	35	799	551	395
1975	289	170	71	72	51	32	66	44	32	743	559	387

See p.111 for footnotes

B5 **Vital Statistics: Numbers** (in thousands)

1950–1975

	Germany			East Germany			Greece			Hungary		
	B	D	M	B	D	M	B	D	M	B	D	M
1950	813	529	536	304	220	215	151	54	58	196	107	106
1951	796	544	522	311	209	195	155	58	63	191	110	93
1952	799	546	483	306	222	176	150	53	50	186	107	105
1953	796	578	462	299	213	158	144	57	61	207	112	92
1954	816	555	453	294	220	152	152	56	64	223	107	107
1955	820	582	462	293	214	155	154[63]	55[63]	66[63]	210	98	103
1956	856	599	478	281	213	153	158	59	55	193	104	96
1957	892	615	483	273	225	150	156	62	69	167	104	98
1958	904	597	494	271	221	154	155	58	69	158	98	91
1959	952	606	504	292	230	162	160	61	74	151	104	90
1960	969	643	521	293	234	168	157	61	58	146	102	89
1961	1,013	628	530	301	223	169	151	64	71	140	96	83
1962	1,019	645	531	298	234	166	152	67	71	130	108	81
1963	1,054	673	508	301	222	148	148	67	78	132	100	84
1964	1,065	644	506	292	226	136	153	69	76	132	101	88
1965	1,044	678	492	281	230	129	151	67	81	133	108	90
1966	1,050	686	485	268	226	122	155	68	72	138	102	93
1967	1,019	687	483	253	227	117	163	72	82	149	110	96
1968	970	734	444	245	242	120	160	73	65	154	115	96
1969	903	744	447	239	244	125	154	72	73	154	117	96
1970	811	735	445	237	241	131	145	74	67	152	120	97
1971	779	731	432	235	235	130	141	74	73	151	123	94
1972	701	731	415	200	234	134	141	77	60	153	119	98
1973	636	731	395	180	232	137	138	78	74	156	123	102
1974	626	728	377	179	229	139	144	76	68	186	126	100
1975	601	749	387	182	240	142	142	80	76	194	131	104

	Ireland			Northern Ireland			Italy			Netherlands		
	B	D	M	B	D	M	B	D	M	B	D	M
1950	64	38	16	29	16	9	909[53]	452[53]	356[53]	230	76	83
1951	63	42	16	28	18	9	864	485	331	228	78	90
1952	65	35	16	29	15	9	847	478	337	232	76	87[64]
1953	63	35	16	29	15	9	842	476	343	228	81	86
1954	63	36	16	29	15	9	871	442	360	228	80	88
1955	62	37	16	29	15	10	869	447	367	229	82	89
1956	61	34	17	29	15	9	874	498	364	231	85	92
1957	61	34	15	30	15	9	879	484	365	234	83	94
1958	60	34	15	30	15	9	870	458	374	237	84[65]	92
1959	60	34	15	31	15	10	901	455	381	243	86	88
1960	61	33	15	32	15	10	910	481	388	239	88	89
1961	60	35	15	32	16	10	930	468	397	247	88	93
1962	62	34	16	33	15	10	937	509	406	246	94	93
1963	63	34	16	33	16	10	960	516	420	250	96	95
1964	64	33	16	34	15	11	1,016	490	417	251	93	103
1965	64	33	17	34	16	10	990	518	399	245	98	109
1966	62	35	17	33	16	11	980	496	385	240	101	112
1967	61	32	18	33	15	11	949	510	380	239	100	115
1968	61	33	19	33	16	11	930	533	374	237	105	118
1969	63	34	20	32	16	12	932	539	385	248	108	117
1970	64	34	21	32	17	12	901	521	396	239	110	124
1971	68	32	22	32	16	12	906	523	404	227	110	122
1972	69	34	22	30	17	12	888	524	419	214	114	118
1973	69	34	23	29	18	11	875	547	418	195	111	108
1974	69	34	23	27	17	11	869	532	403	186	109	110
1975	68	34	22	26	17	11	828	551	374	178	114	100

See p.111 for footnotes

B5 Vital Statistics: Numbers (in thousands)

1950–1975

	Norway			Poland			Portugal			Romania		
	B	D	M	B	D	M	B	D	M	B	D	M
1950	62	30	27	763	289	267	205	103	65	427	202	190
1951	61	28	27	784	312	270	208	105	67	413	210	170
1952	63	28	27	779	287	268	211	100	67	413	195	169
1953	63	28	27	779	267	262	202	97	67	402	195	175
1954	63	27	27	778	276	263	198	95	69	422	195	206
1955	64	29	26	794	277	259	210	99	73	443	168	197
1956	64	30	25	780	250	260	203	107	66	426	175	205
1957	63	31	24	782	269	257	211	102	72	408	182	204
1958	63	32	24	756	241	264	212	92	73	391	157	211
1959	63	32	23	723	252	277	213	98	76	368	187	195
1960	62	33	24	661	224	244	214	95	69	352	161	198
1961	63	33	24	628	228	236	218	100	78	325	162	180
1962	62	34	24	600	239	228	220	97	71	302	172	185
1963	63	37	24	588	230	220	212	98	71	295	156	175
1964	66	35	25	563	236	231	217	97	73	287	152	170
1965	66	35	24	546	232	200	210	95	75	278	163	164
1966	67	36	28	530	233	226	207	100	77	274	157	171
1967	67	36	29	520	248	238	202	96	79	528	179	154
1968	67	39	29	524	244	258	195	95	77	526	189	147
1969	68	39	30	531	263	270	190	101	79	466	201	140
1970	65	39	29	546	267	280	173	93	81	427	193	146
1971	66	39	30	562	284	292	189	99	83	400	194	150
1972	64	39	29	576	265	308	175	90	77	389	190	157
1973	61	40	28	599	277	315	172	95	84	379	204	170
1974	60	39	27	621	277	320	172	96	82	428	191	175
1975	56	39	26	644	297	331	180	98	103	418	198	188

	Russia[31]			Spain			Sweden		
	B	D	M	B	D	M	B	D	M
1950	4,805	1,745		559	301	209	115	70	54
1951				561	322	210	110	70	54
1952	4,948	1,749		586	272	219	110	68	53
1953				583	274	217	110	70	53
1954				572	260	229	105	69	53
1955	5,047	1,613		592	269	236	107	69	52
1956	5,023			601	285	256	108	70	52
1957	5,164			639	290	251	107	73	53
1958	5,240	1,491		646	256	252	106	71	51
1959	5,265	1,604	2,558	647	264	243	105	71	50
1960	5,341	1,529		655	262	236	102	75	50
1961	5,192	1,563	2,404	646	256	237	105	74	52
1962	4,959	1,667	2,222	650	271	236	107	77	54
1963	4,758	1,627	2,051	663	275	237	113	76	53
1964	4,457	1,581	1,940	689	267	233	123	77	58
1965	4,253	1,690	2,009	668	267	227	123	78	60
1966	4,242	1,711	2,088	662	270	230	123	78	61
1967	4,093	1,799	2,132	672	274	233	121	80	57
1968	4,088	1,833	2,121	660	277	232	113	82	53
1969	4,087	1,957	2,251	659	297	239	108	83	48
1970	4,226	1,996	2,365	656	280	247	110	80	43
1971	4,372	2,015	2,460	665	303	253	114	83	40
1972	4,404	2,105	2,333	666	280	262	112	84	40
1973	4,386	2,164	2,516	666	297	269	110	86	38
1974	4,546	2,191	2,607	682	295	267	110	86	45
1975	4,611	2,363	2,723	669	298	271	104	88	44

See p.111 for footnotes

B5 Vital Statistics: Numbers (in thousands)

1950–1975

	Switzerland			United Kingdom: England and Wales			United Kingdom: Scotland			Yugoslavia[60]		
	B	D	M	B	D	M	B	D	M	B	D	M
1950	85	47	37	697	510	358	93	64	40	494	212	186
1951	82	50	38	678	549	361	91	66	41	447	235	170
1952	84	48	37	674	497	349	90	62	41	499	198	176
1953	83	50	37	684	504	345	91	59	41	484	212	168
1954	84	49	38	674	502	342	92	61	42	494	188	172
1955	85	50	40	668	519	358	93	62	43	471	200	163
1956	88	52	40	700	521	353	95	62	44	460	198	156
1957	91	51	42	723	514	347	98	61	43	427	190	155
1958	91	49	40	741	527	340	99	62	41	432	167	170
1959	93	50	40	749	528	340	99	63	40	424	181	164
1960	94	52	42	785	526	344	101	62	40	433	183	168
1961	99	51	42	811	552	347	101	64	41	422	167	169
1962	104	55	44	839	557	348	104	63	40	413	187	163
1963	110	57	44	854	572	351	103	66	40	407	170	158
1964	113	54	44	876	535	359	104	61	40	401	181	167
1965	112	56	45	863	549	371	101	63	40	408	171	174
1966	110	56	44	850	564	384	97	64	42	400	160	169
1967	107	55	45	832	546	386	96	60	42	390	174	169
1968	105	57	46	819	573	408	95	63	44	383	175	170
1969	103	58	47	798	581	397	90	64	43	383	189	175
1970	99	57	47	784	573	415	87	64	43	363	182	183
1971	96	58	45	783	566	405	87	62	42	376	179	184
1972	91	56	43	725	592	423	79	65	42	381	191	186
1973	88	57	41	676	587	400	74	65	42	379	181	184
1974	85	56	38	640	585	384	70	65	41	383	178	181
1975	78	56	35	603	583	379	68	63	39	387	185	181

See p.111 for footnotes

B5 **Numbers of Births, Deaths, and Marriages** (in thousands)

NOTES

1. SOURCES:— All figures are taken from the official publications notes on p. xv except for the following:— Albania—League of Nations *Statistical Yearbook* and United Nations, *Demographic Yearbook;* France to 1815 (1st line) — estimates made by the Institut National des Etudes Démographiques, and taken from the appendix to Jacques Dupâquier, "les caractères originaux de l'histoire démographique francaise an XVIIIe siècle", *Revue d'histoire moderne et contemporaine* (xxiii, 1976), and Serbia 1911–12 — *Annuaire Internationale de Statistique* (The Hague, 1916).

2. In principle birth statistics are of live births in all cases, and death statistics do not include stillbirths.

FOOTNOTES

[1] Earlier, slightly less reliable data are as follows (in thousands):—

	Norway		Sweden			Norway		Sweden	
	Births	Deaths	Births	Deaths		Births	Deaths	Births	Deaths
1735	18	12	... .	. . .	1742	16	42	54	66
1736	19	13	51	46	1743	17	17	51	74
1737	19	15	52	57	1744	18	13	59	43
1738	17	14	57	52	1745	20	11	63	40
1739	19	14	62	53	1746	17	13	60	46
1740	19	16	55	61	1747	20	15	60	48
1741	17	23	55	55	1748	20	20	59	46

[2] Cisleithania (excluding Lombardy and Venetia) to 1913, and the present Republic subsequently.

[3] Parts of Limburg and Luxembourg were ceded to the Netherlands.

[4] Excluding the Duchies of Schleswig, Holstein, and Lauenburg.

[5] Figures from 1809 include the area in the Tornie River basin transferred from Russia.

[6] Figures from 1811 include Viipuri province.

[7] Figures from 1820 include Petsamo.

[8] **Statistics to 1815 (1st line) are estimates for the 1861 territory, made by the I.N.E.D. (see note 1 above).**

Earlier figures are as follows (in thousands):—

	Births	Deaths	Marriages		Births	Deaths	Marriages
1740	973	852	212	1745	1,013	701	218
1741	992	963	199	1746	1,006	811	208
1742	928	879	228	1747	955	1,062	202
1743	993	961	264	1748	918	924	192
1744	1,017	754	243				

According to J. Dupâquier, *loc cit.* in sources, the estimates of deaths are "certainly incomplete", and births for the period 1793–1800 are underestimated by about half-a-million.

Earlier statistics for the 1815 territory are as follows (in thousands):—

	Births	Deaths	Marriages		Births	Deaths	Marriages
1801	904	762	199	1806	916	782	210
1802	919	772	203	1807	925	803	213
1803	919	882	206	1808	913	774	221
1804	907	898	207	1809	933	749	268
1805	913	833	215	1810	932	730	233
				1811	927	766	204
				1812	824	770	223
				1813	896	775	387
				1814	994	873	193

(Figures for 1801–5 are for years ended 22 September)

[9] Figures up to 1916 apply to the German Empire as constituted before the First World War, except that Alsace-Lorraine is not included before 1871, and Heligoland is not included before 1891. Later boundary changes are indicated in other footnotes. Statistics are available for years prior to 1841 for several German states, and though these are not shown here, they have been used to calculate the rates shown in table B.6.

[10] The Ancient Kingdom up to 1918 (excluding Croatia-Slavonia). Subsequently the territory established by the treaty of Trianon and later adjusted. For statistics for Croatia-Slavonia see footnote 60.

[11] The component applicable to the military frontier region has been estimated.

[12] The Grand Duchy of Luxembourg is excluded throughout.

[13] These figures are known to be underestimates. It is also known that registration was incomplete until the 1860's.

[14] Figures for November and December 1855 are as follows (in thousands):—

births 94; deaths 91; marriages 31.

[15] Figures to 1871 relate to the civil population only.

[16] Figures from 1898 apply to the resident population only. This makes a reduction of approximately 1 thousand.
[17] Figures from 1888 include Eastern Roumelia.
[18] Figures from 1861 include Savoy and Nice.
[19] Between 1871 and 1913 the parts of Alsace-Lorraine ceded by France to Germany are included with the latter country and not the former. The statistics for the period for this area are as follows (in thousands):—

	Births	Deaths	Marriages		Births	Deaths	Marriages
1871	45	49	11	1891	49	36	11
1872	54	38	16	1892	47	36	11
1873	53	41	13	1893	49	37	12
1874	54	41	12	1894	48	37	12
1875	55	44	11	1895	49	35	12
1876	55	40	11	1896	50	33	12
1877	53	40	10	1897	51	33	12
1878	53	38	10	1898	50	37	13
1879	52	40	10	1899	52	34	13
1880	50	40	10	1900	52	37	13
1881	50	40	10	1901	52	34	13
1882	50	39	10	1902	53	34	13
1883	49	37	10	1903	52	35	13
1884	50	37	10	1904	53	35	13
1885	48	39	10	1905	62	36	14
1886	48	38	10	1906	52	34	14
1887	48	35	10	1907	51	33	13
1888	47	38	10	1908	51	35	13
1889	47	36	10	1909	49	32	13
1890	46	38	11	1910	48	29	13
				1911	46	33	13
				1912	46	29	13
				1913	44	29	13

[20] The statistics for the period up to 1890 are known to be incomplete.
[21] Figures from 1882 include Thessaly and Arta, acquired from Turkey.
[22] There appears to be a break in the series at this point, probably due to subsequent inclusion of Voivodina and the Banat.
[23] Statistics for November and December 1855 are as follows (in thousands):—
Births: 83; Deaths: 84: Marriages: 40.
[24] Figures from 1891 include Fiume.
[25] Figures to 1895 relate to the civil population only.
[26] Venetia and the Papal States are not included prior to their incorporation.
[27] The statistics up to 1878 are known to be incomplete.
[28] Figures from 1879 include Dobrudja but exclude southern Bessarabia.
[29] Excluding northern Transylvania, and Bessarabia and northern Bukovina (except when reconquered in 1943). Statistics from 1946 are for the present territory.
[30] Statistics prior to the First World War relate to the 50 provinces of European Russia (excluding Finland, Poland, and the Caucasus). Later statistics are for the U.S.S.R.
[31] Excluding Bessarabia.
[32] Figures from 1879 include Vranje, Niš, Pirot, and Toplica, acquired from Turkey.
[33] Including the Canary Islands.
[34] Figures from 1925 include Eupen, Malmédy, etc.
[35] 41 communes were excluded in these years. In addition, in 1940 the statistics for Tournai and Wavre are missing.
[36] Figures from 1941 include Southern Dobrudja. The marriage statistics subsequently exclude aliens and include those of Bulgarians abroad.
[37] Includes deaths in the armed forces stationed abroad.
[38] Figures from 1939 exclude Sub-Carpathian Russia (Ruthenia), and those from 1945 also exclude 12 villages in Slovakia which were ceded to the U.S.S.R.
[39] Figures from 1949 include the Bratislava Bridgehead.
[40] Whilst Petsamo and Viipuri were ceded to the U.S.S.R., their populations were transferred to the remaining territory.
[41] Estimates were made for the departments affected by the war. The deaths do not include military losses, which were approximately as follows (in thousands):—
1914: 360; 1915: 320; 1916: 270; 1917: 145; 1918: 250; 1939–45: 600.
[42] Figures from 1947 include Tende and Brigue, acquired from Italy.
[43] Alsace-Lorraine statistics are included here as well as in France.
[44] Figures from 1919 exclude territory ceded to Denmark, Czechoslavakia, and Poland (except in Silesia).
[45] Figures from 1922 exclude part of Upper Silesia ceded to Poland.

[46] Figures from 1925 exclude Eupen, Malmédy, etc.

[47] Statistics for the equivalent area in 1938 are as follows (in thousands):—

Births: 838; Deaths: 486; Marriages: 495.

[48] These statistics are less reliable than the others for the period since 1920.

[49] Figures from 1949 include the Dodecanese Islands.

[50] Figures from 1948 exclude the Bratislava Bridgehead.

[51] Includes estimated for the areas affected by the war.

[52] Figures from 1920 include areas acquired from Austria-Hungary.

[53] Figures from 1943 are for the Post-Second World War territory, except that Trieste is not included until 1951.

[54] Deaths in the war zone and of military personnel abroad are not included.

[55] Up to 1917 children born alive but dying before registration were included in neither births nor deaths. Subsequently they are included in both. The increases resulting in 1918 were about 1 thousand.

[56] Figures from 1949 include Elten and Tuddern, acquired from Germany.

[57] Deaths outside the country are normally included if registered within one year, but in these years deaths of deportees were excluded. Deaths among alien armed forces were also excluded.

[58] Statistics are for the boundaries of the day.

[59] From 1919 to 1939 statistics apply to the territory established by the treaty of Trianon. In the following six years there were several boundary changes, but only two of those, made in 1940, were permanent, namely the cession of southern Dobrudja to Bulgaria and of Bessarabia and northern Bukovina to the U.S.S.R. The statistics for 1919 appear to be defective.

[60] Pre-First World War statistics for Croatia-Slavonia are as follows (in thousands):—

	Births	Deaths	Marriages		Births	Deaths	Marriages
1881	82	59	21	1898	93	68	22
1882	84	60	22	1899	99	66	23
1883	89	65	22	1900	97	65	21
1884	91	65	23	1901	95	67	22
1885	93	61	23	1902	101	67	22
1886	97	58	21	1903	97	66	22
1887	95	63	19	1904	99	65	25
1888	95	65	20	1905	100	75	23
1889	97	66	18	1906	100	66	23
1890	86	72	19	1907	100	65	23
1891	94	72	19	1908	100	70	23
1892	91	87	21	1909	108	69	21
1893	94	75	22	1910	99	65	21
1894	96	73	23	1911	95	69	22
1895	99	70	19	1912	101	67	21
1896	95	74	21	1913	95	68	23
1897	96	75	20	1914	98	66	17

[61] Figures from 1947 include territory acquired from Italy.

[62] Figures from 1953 exclude unviable infants who died within 24 hours of birth.

[63] Statistics to 1955 apply to the year of registration. Subsequently they apply to the year of birth, or marriage.

[64] The previous practice of including marriages abroad if registered within one year was subsequently discontinued.

[65] Figures to 1958 exclude deaths in refugee camps for Amboynese.

[66] Including the Azores and Maderia.

B6 VITAL STATISTICS: RATES PER 1,000 POPULATION

1749–1799

	Finland			Norway[1]			Sweden[1]		
	B	D	M	B	D	M	B	D	M
1749				33.0	27.9	...	33.8	28.1	17.1
1750				30.6	27.2	...	36.4	26.9	18.5
1751	44.3	24.6	21.8	35.0	27.0	...	38.7	26.2	18.5
1752	44.7	26.3	20.2	33.5	25.4	...	35.9	27.3	18.5
1753	44.1	26.1	19.0	34.8	23.4	...	36.1	24.0	17.4
1754	46.4	35.1	19.8	35.3	24.1	...	37.2	26.3	18.9
1755	46.9	30.7	18.8	33.5	25.1	...	37.5	27.4	18.3
1756	45.8	36.3	17.0	36.1	27.2	...	36.1	27.7	17.0
1757	43.3	36.2	16.0	34.5	22.1	...	32.6	29.9	15.9
1758	42.3	29.5	17.8	33.6	24.6	...	33.4	32.4	16.1
1759	44.5	28.1	19.6	32.3	19.5	...	33.6	26.3	19.5
1760	46.6	27.9	19.6	35.0	23.1	...	35.7	24.8	19.5
1761	45.8	28.3	16.8	35.9	24.4	...	34.8	25.8	18.9
1762	41.3	29.6	16.0	35.8	25.9	...	35.1	31.2	17.9
1763	43.0	41.0	16.0	34.5	38.8	...	35.0	32.9	17.3
1764	45.7	33.1	16.6	35.8	29.1	...	34.7	27.2	17.6
1765	42.9	29.7	16.2	34.5	30.2	...	33.4	27.7	16.3
1766	41.5	28.6	15.6	34.0	30.4	...	33.8	25.1	16.5
1767	40.7	29.1	15.6	35.1	25.1	...	35.4	25.6	16.5
1768	42.9	25.8	17.8	32.8	24.4	...	33.6	27.2	16.9
1769	42.4	28.3	16.8	33.7	23.7	...	33.1	27.2	16.3
1770	40.9	30.2	14.6	32.1	24.0	14.7	33.0	26.1	16.2
1771	38.0	26.1	15.2	31.6	23.2	13.5	32.2	27.8	15.5
1772	37.6	23.9	15.4	28.2	26.2	11.9	28.9	37.4	13.6
1773	37.9	21.5	17.0	25.0	48.1	12.0	25.5	52.5	15.5
1774	40.3	21.5	18.6	28.3	25.8	17.1	34.5	22.4	17.5
1775	40.4	25.6	17.2	33.8	23.6	18.6	35.6	24.8	18.9
1776	39.0	30.5	17.0	28.8	20.7	16.9	32.9	22.5	18.0
1777	40.1	32.0	17.6	31.3	21.0	16.8	33.0	24.9	18.1
1778	42.7	25.0	19.6	31.2	20.2	16.0	34.8	26.7	18.1
1779	43.2	21.9	18.2	31.5	27.4	18.2	36.7	28.5	17.3
1780	41.2	21.1	16.4	32.4	25.6	15.4	35.7	21.7	17.1
1781	37.7	26.5	15.2	31.4	20.9	16.1	33.5	25.6	15.7
1782	41.7	25.1	16.8	30.9	22.6	14.1	32.1	27.3	15.4
1783	40.0	31.2	16.2	27.6	24.8	16.2	30.3	28.1	16.0
1784	42.7	25.3	16.2	30.5	24.0	...	31.5	29.8	15.0
1785	39.8	30.3	15.6	28.9	33.3	...	31.4	28.3	15.6
1786	39.9	26.3	14.0	30.6	24.4	...	32.9	25.9	16.0
1787	40.4	23.7	15.4	29.2	22.8	...	31.5	24.0	15.9
1788	36.1	33.3	13.4	30.7	26.1	...	33.9	26.7	15.8
1789	34.2	37.7	15.2	30.6	30.6	...	32.0	33.1	15.9
1790	37.0	38.1	18.8	32.0	23.0	...	30.5	30.5	16.5
1791	36.0	40.9	23.4	32.7	23.0	...	32.6	25.5	21.7
1792	42.2	25.0	22.4	34.7	24.0	...	36.6	23.9	20.0
1793	43.8	25.6	19.4	34.1	22.1	...	34.4	24.3	17.8
1794	41.4	32.0	18.6	33.7	20.8	...	33.8	23.6	16.4
1795	42.1	23.6	15.8	32.3	22.6	15.5	32.0	27.9	15.2
1796	39.7	23.4	16.8	31.5	21.5	15.7	34.7	24.7	17.2
1797	41.2	20.2	16.4	32.7	22.4	16.2	34.8	23.8	16.9
1798	38.6	22.0	15.2	32.3	22.6	16.6	33.7	23.1	16.6
1799	38.7	27.6	15.4	32.5	20.9	15.7	32.0	25.2	14.7

See p.135 for footnotes

B6 Vital Statistics: Rates per 1,000 Population

1800–1849

	Austria[2]			Belgium			Denmark[4]			Finland		
	B	D	M	B	D	M	B	D	M	B	D	M
1800	...	...	...	...	...	...	29.9	28.5	18.8	37.6	25.5	16.4
1801	...	...	...	...	...	...	31.1	27.7	15.7	39.6	21.8	15.8
1802	...	...	...	...	...	...	32.2	23.2	18.4	39.2	22.3	14.6
1803	...	...	...	...	...	...	33.1	22.5	17.3	35.6	33.1	15.4
1804	...	...	...	...	...	...	32.2	23.7	17.6	39.1	25.0	15.8
1805	...	...	...	...	...	...	32.8	23.2	15.9	38.4	21.2	16.0
1806	...	...	...	...	...	...	30.2	22.3	14.8	35.7	21.9	15.2
1807	...	...	...	...	...	...	31.0	22.9	14.7	36.2	29.2	13.2
1808	...	...	...	...	...	...	30.6	25.2	14.5	30.4	60.5	10.0
1809	...	...	...	...	...	...	29.3	25.1	15.3	28.6	59.2	17.4
1810	...	...	...	...	...	...	30.3	22.7	17.6	40.5[5]	24.6[5]	23.6[5]
1811	...	...	...	...	...	...	30.5	24.4	17.5	36.4	30.8	18.2
1812	...	...	...	...	...	...	29.8	27.0	15.9	38.9	24.1	16.2
1813	...	...	...	...	...	...	29.1	22.8	16.1	35.6	27.3	15.0
1814	...	...	...	...	...	...	30.4	24.7	18.3	36.7	32.4	16.6
1815	...	...	...	...	...	...	34.1	21.6	20.4	37.5	26.0	17.4
1816	...	...	...	...	...	...	32.9	20.7	18.6	38.8	23.4	17.8
1817	...	...	...	...	...	...	32.8	19.0	15.4	39.0	24.0	17.2
1818	...	...	...	...	...	...	32.1	18.9	16.9	38.4	24.8	17.2
1819	...	...	...	...	...	...	32.5	19.5	16.7	36.1	27.2	15.2
	Years ending 31 October											
1820	43.0	26.6	17.3	...	...	...	31.5	20.9	16.2	36.6	25.3	18.6
1821	41.4	25.7	15.8	...	...	...	32.1	24.0	16.1	41.4	22.9	19.0
1822	38.5	27.2	15.1	...	...	...	33.7	20.3	17.1	35.6	27.8	16.2
1823	39.6	28.8	14.5	...	...	...	32.6	17.7	15.7	40.3	24.2	17.8
1824	40.1	26.4	15.7	...	...	...	31.3	18.6	16.2	37.8	27.3	17.2
1825	40.3	26.9	15.6	...	...	...	31.3	19.2	16.7	38.5	26.1	16.4
1826	39.6	27.7	16.0	...	...	...	31.4	21.1	16.7	37.6	25.2	16.6
1827	38.6	28.9	17.2	...	...	...	29.2	20.0	15.4	36.7	21.5	18.2
1828	37.6	32.7	17.0	...	...	...	30.3	23.6	16.0	39.3	22.6	18.0
1829	36.1	31.4	17.4	...	...	...	29.6	28.8	16.6	38.7	26.3	16.6
1830	38.0	30.3	16.2	32.3	25.6	13.0	28.9	25.3	16.8	36.6	25.4	15.2
1831	35.6	42.2	14.5	33.0	24.0	15.1	29.7	30.1	16.0	35.2	28.5	17.2
1832	36.6	35.6	19.4	31.5	28.0	13.4	27.0	26.3	17.3	34.5	33.8	13.0
1833	40.4	31.8	17.3	33.2	26.8	12.9	32.2	23.3	17.2	30.2	46.4	13.6
1834	39.3	30.9	16.7	33.3	27.8	14.5	33.0	23.5	17.1	36.6	23.9	15.2
1835	38.5	30.2	16.2	34.0	24.0	16.1	31.7	22.9	16.2	34.3	24.7	14.0
1836	37.8	33.1	17.4	34.0	23.9	13.9	30.5	22.3	15.1	31.1	31.9	13.0
1837	39.7	33.2	17.5	33.4	27.6	15.1	30.0	21.7	15.2	31.6	28.4	14.6
1838	37.9	28.3	15.7	35.2[3]	25.5[3]	14.6[3]	29.8	20.0	13.1	31.8	22.5	14.2
1839	38.0	30.0	15.8	33.7	26.1	14.7	29.0	20.5	13.7	33.7	20.6	15.4
1840	38.6	30.4	15.9	34.2	25.0	15.1	30.4	21.0	14.6	34.7	22.1	15.6
1841	38.3	29.5	16.9	34.0	23.8	14.7	29.7	19.8	15.2	34.0	22.4	16.0
1842	41.2	30.8	16.3	32.6	24.9	14.0	30.1	20.2	15.4	37.2	21.9	16.6
1843	39.3	31.4	17.0	31.9	23.3	13.5	29.8	19.3	15.6	35.8	22.2	16.2
1844	39.7	28.9	16.4	31.8	22.5	13.9	30.3	19.3	16.3	35.0	21.8	16.2
1845	39.5	29.7	15.2	32.2	23.0	12.2	30.6	19.4	16.4	35.7	22.9	15.2
1846	37.0	28.9	16.0	27.8	25.1	11.9	30.1	21.5	16.1	33.2	25.1	14.8
1847	36.0	44.4	14.6	27.2	27.7	11.1	30.6	21.7	15.9	33.9	23.3	16.2
1848	32.7	41.3	17.8	27.7	24.0	13.3	30.6	21.1	15.0	36.5	23.8	18.6
1849	40.0	35.0	18.5	31.0	27.7	14.5	31.0	22.4	16.1	37.5	24.5	17.2

See p. 135 for footnotes

B6 Vital Statistics: Rates per 1,000 Population

1800–1849

	France			Germany[6]			Netherlands[7]		
	B	D	M	B	D	M	B	D	M
1800	Years ending 22 September			...	...	...	...	...	...
1801	32.9	27.7	14.5	...	...	...	...	...	...
1802	33.0	27.7	14.6	...	...	...	...	...	...
1803	32.5	31.2	14.6	...	...	...	...	...	...
1804	31.3	31.0	14.3	...	...	...	...	...	...
1805	31.6	28.8	14.9	...	...	...	...	...	...
	Years ending 31 December								
1806	31.4	26.8	14.4	...	...	...	...	...	...
1807	31.8	27.6	14.6	...	...	...	...	...	...
1808	31.3	26.5	15.2	...	...	...	...	...	...
1809	32.0	25.0	18.4	...	...	...	...	...	...
1810	31.8	24.9	15.9	...	...	...	...	...	...
1811	31.6	26.1	13.1	...	...	...	...	...	...
1812	30.1	26.2	15.1	...	...	...	...	...	...
1813	30.5	26.4	26.4	...	...	...	...	...	...
1814	33.9	29.8	13.2	...	...	...	...	...	...
1815	32.5	26.0	16.7	...	...	...	...	...	...
1816	32.9	24.5	16.9	...	...	...	...	...	...
1817	31.8	25.3	13.9	39.5	26.7	19.5	...	...	...
1818	30.6	25.3	14.3	39.5	27.1	18.9	...	...	...
1819	32.9	26.1	14.3	41.5	27.9	18.5	...	...	...
1820	31.7	25.4	13.8	39.9	24.4	17.9	...	...	...
1821	31.7	24.3	14.6	40.8	22.9	17.0	...	...	...
1822	31.7	25.3	15.4	39.8	24.6	16.8	...	...	...
1823	31.2	24.0	16.9	38.8	24.5	15.9	...	...	...
1824	31.6	24.5	15.3	38.6	24.2	16.3	...	...	...
1825	31.0	25.9	15.5	39.1	24.5	16.9	...	...	...
1826	31.4	26.5	15.7	38.9	26.1	16.6	...	...	...
1827	30.8	24.9	16.1	36.1	26.4	15.8	...	...	...
1828	30.5	26.2	15.4	36.1	26.6	15.4	...	...	...
1829	30.0	25.0	15.6	35.3	27.8	15.5	...	...	...
1830	29.9	25.0	16.7	35.5	27.4	15.5	...	...	...
1831	30.3	24.6	15.1	35.0	30.4	14.4	...	...	...
1832	28.6	28.5	14.8	34.1	28.9	17.2	...	...	...
1833	29.5	24.7	16.0	36.7	28.5	17.4	...	...	...
1834	29.8	27.8	16.4	37.6	29.4	17.3	...	...	...
1835	29.9	24.5	16.6	36.4	26.2	16.5	...	...	...
1836	29.2	22.3	16.3	36.7	25.9	16.3	...	...	...
1837	28.0	25.3	15.8	36.3	29.1	16.4	...	...	...
1838	28.5	24.2	16.2	36.3	26.0	15.9	...	...	...
1839	28.2	22.7	15.8	36.4	27.2	16.1	...	...	...
1840	27.9	23.7	16.6	36.4	26.5	16.2	35.0	23.5	15.6
1841	28.5	23.2	16.5	36.4	26.2	16.4	35.5	23.3	15.0
1842	28.5	24.0	16.3	37.6	27.1	16.7	34.2	25.8	14.4
1843	28.2	23.1	16.5	36.0	26.9	16.4	33.8	23.1	14.2
1844	27.5	22.0	16.0	35.9	24.5	16.4	34.4	24.1	15.0
1845	27.9	21.1	16.1	37.3	25.3	16.3	34.2	23.2	15.0
1846	27.3	23.2	15.2	36.0	27.1	15.8	31.4	28.5	13.6
1847	25.4	23.9	14.1	33.3	28.3	14.4	28.6	31.1	12.6
1848	26.5	23.6	16.5	33.3	29.0	15.2	30.1	29.2	14.4
1849	27.7	27.4	15.7	38.1	27.1	16.4	34.2	31.2	16.4

See p.135 for footnotes

B6 Vital Statistics: Rates per 1,000 Population

1800–1849

	Norway			Sweden			United Kingdom: England and Wales		
	B	D	M	B	D	M	B	D	M
1800	...	...	...	28.7	31.4	14.9	...	...	...
1801	22.7	27.6	13.8	30.0	26.1	14.5	...	...	...
1802	27.6	24.9	15.3	31.7	23.7	15.7	...	...	...
1803	28.9	24.6	15.3	31.4	23.8	16.4	...	...	...
1804	27.7	23.2	15.9	31.9	24.9	16.1	...	...	...
1805	29.2	20.4	16.2	31.7	23.5	16.7	...	...	...
1806	29.6	20.7	16.2	30.8	27.5	16.1	...	...	...
1807	29.0	22.1	13.9	31.2	26.2	16.4	...	...	...
1808	26.9	26.4	11.6	30.4	34.9	16.2	...	...	...
1809	22.2	35.3	11.9	26.7	40.0	15.6	...	...	...
1810	26.3	26.8	15.8	33.0	31.6	21.5	...	...	...
1811	26.7	24.7	17.5	35.3	28.8	21.3	...	...	...
1812	29.1	21.3	17.4	33.6	30.3	18.3	...	...	...
1813	25.6	28.9	14.2	29.7	27.4	15.5	...	...	...
1814	24.2	22.2	12.9	31.2	25.1	15.0	...	...	...
1815	29.9	19.7	20.2	34.8	23.6	19.2	...	...	...
1816	35.1	19.3	20.5	35.3	22.7	18.6	...	...	...
1817	32.5	17.7	17.2	33.4	24.3	16.7	...	...	...
1818	30.8	19.1	16.3	33.8	24.4	16.9	...	...	...
1819	31.9	19.7	16.1	33.0	27.4	18.3	...	...	...
1820	33.3	18.9	18.0	33.0	24.5	16.9	...	...	...
1821	34.7	20.5	18.1	35.4	25.6	17.6	...	...	...
1822	32.9	19.5	17.9	35.9	22.6	18.6	...	...	...
1823	33.9	17.7	17.5	36.8	21.0	18.0	...	...	...
1824	32.5	18.5	16.3	34.6	20.8	17.7	...	...	...
1825	34.3	17.4	17.3	36.5	20.5	17.2	...	...	...
1826	34.8	18.5	16.5	34.8	22.6	16.2	...	...	...
1827	32.0	18.0	15.0	31.3	23.1	14.4	...	...	...
1828	31.8	19.4	15.3	33.6	26.7	15.8	...	...	...
1829	33.6	19.4	15.6	34.9	29.0	15.8	...	...	...
1830	32.3	19.7	15.4	32.9	24.1	15.5	...	...	...
1831	31.0	19.8	14.4	30.5	26.0	13.8	...	...	...
1832	29.9	18.5	13.6	30.9	23.4	14.4	...	...	...
1833	30.7	20.3	14.6	34.1	21.7	15.7	...	...	...
1834	31.7	22.4	15.1	33.7	25.7	16.0	...	...	...
1835	32.6	19.5	14.8	32.7	18.6	15.0	...	...	...
1836	29.4	19.2	14.0	31.8	20.0	14.3	...	...	...
1837	28.7	20.8	13.4	30.8	24.7	13.8	...	...	...
1838	27.7	19.9	12.4	29.4	24.1	12.2	30.3[8]	22.4[8]	15.4[8]
1839	26.7	21.6	12.9	29.5	23.6	13.5	31.8	21.8	15.9
1840	27.8	19.8	13.8	31.4	20.4	14.1	32.0	22.9	15.6
1841	29.8	17.3	15.3	30.3	19.4	14.3	32.2	21.6	15.4
1842	30.7	18.0	15.7	31.7	21.1	14.2	32.1	21.7	14.7
1843	30.2	17.9	15.8	30.8	21.5	14.4	32.3	21.2	15.2
1844	29.9	17.1	15.8	32.2	20.3	14.9	32.7	21.6	16.0
1845	31.2	16.9	16.0	31.5	18.8	14.6	32.5	20.9	17.2
1846	31.1	17.9	16.7	29.9	21.8	13.8	33.8	23.0	17.2
1847	30.8	20.3	14.6	29.6	23.7	13.6	31.5	24.7	15.9
1848	29.8	20.5	14.9	30.3	19.7	14.6	32.5	23.0	15.9
1849	32.0	18.3	15.4	32.8	19.8	15.7	32.9	25.1	16.2

See p.135 for footnotes

B6 Vital Statistics: Rates per 1,000 Population

1850–1899

	Austria			Belgium			Bulgaria			Denmark		
	B	D	M	B	D	M	B	D	M	B	D	M
1850	39.6	32.9	19.3	30.0	21.2	15.4	...	...	...	31.4	19.1	15.2
1851	39.2	29.8	17.5	30.3	21.4	15.0	...	...	...	30.1	18.4	19.7
1852	37.5	30.9	15.8	30.0	21.5	13.9	...	...	...	33.2	19.6	19.4
1853	37.2	31.9	15.4	28.3	22.2	13.5	...	...	...	31.6	25.0	18.3
1854	36.3	34.5	13.8	28.8	20.5	12.9	...	...	...	32.7	18.4	17.4
1855	32.2	43.9	12.8	27.7	24.7	13.0	...	...	...	31.9	20.0	17.0
	Years ending 31 December											
1856	35.6	30.2	16.3	29.1	24.1	14.3	...	...	...	32.4	18.7	17.2
1857	39.4	28.2	16.7	31.6	22.8	16.5	...	...	...	32.9	21.8	17.8
1858	39.8	29.1	16.9	31.7	23.6	16.7	...	...	...	33.2	23.2	17.4
1859	40.7	29.2	14.1	32.4	24.2	16.0	...	...	...	33.6	20.3	16.7
1860	38.2	26.8	16.9	31.0	19.9	15.1	...	...	...	32.6	20.2	16.0
1861	37.4	29.8	16.0	31.1	22.5	14.3	...	...	...	31.6	18.4	14.9
1862	38.1	29.5	17.7	30.4	20.9	14.3	...	...	...	30.8	18.3	14.7
1863	40.6	29.9	16.9	32.2	22.3	14.8	...	...	...	30.9	18.1	15.0
1864	40.6	30.1	16.5	32.1	23.7	15.1	...	...	...	30.1	23.2	11.3
1865	38.0	30.5	15.6	31.6	24.7	15.2	...	...	...	31.1	23.0	17.8
1866	37.9	40.8	13.0	31.7	30.3	15.2	...	...	...	32.0	20.2	16.8
1867	36.8	29.4	19.4	32.6	21.9	15.8	...	...	...	30.3	19.8	15.3
1868	38.1	28.7	18.4	31.9	22.0	14.8	...	...	...	31.0	19.2	14.6
1869	39.6	29.0	20.8	32.0	22.1	15.0	...	...	...	29.3	19.0	14.7
1870	39.8	29.4	19.6	32.7	23.6	14.0	...	...	...	30.3	19.0	14.7
1871	38.7[9]	29.8[9]	18.8[9]	31.2	28.1	14.7	...	...	...	30.1	19.4	14.6
1872	38.9	32.6	18.6	32.7	23.5	15.7	...	...	...	30.3	18.4	15.0
1873	39.6	38.9	18.8	33.0	21.8	15.7	...	...	...	30.8	18.6	16.2
1874	39.6	31.7	18.0	33.1	20.9	15.4	...	...	...	30.9	20.0	16.4
1875	39.8	30.0	17.0	32.9	22.9	14.6	...	...	...	31.9	21.0	17.0
1876	40.0	29.8	16.6	32.7	21.6	14.1	...	...	...	32.6	19.7	17.1
1877	38.5	31.5	15.0	32.8	21.4	13.7	...	...	...	32.3	18.7	16.1
1878	38.4	31.6	15.2	31.9	21.7	13.5	...	...	...	31.6	18.4	14.8
1879	39.1	29.9	15.4	31.9	22.1	12.2	...	...	...	31.9	19.7	14.7
1880	37.5	29.7	15.2	31.0	22.3	14.1	...	...	...	31.7	20.4	15.2
1881	37.5	30.5	16.0	31.8	21.2	14.3	33.7	16.4	20.2	32.2	18.3	15.6
1882	39.0	30.8	16.4	31.6	20.5	14.0	36.7	19.1	19.4	32.3	19.2	15.4
1883	38.1	30.1	15.6	30.9	21.1	13.7	38.5	19.8	19.8	31.8	18.4	15.4
1884	38.6	29.3	15.8	30.9	21.2	13.6	38.5	17.2	17.6	33.3	18.3	15.6
1885	37.5	30.1	15.2	30.3	21.4	13.8	37.6	16.7	13.2	32.5	17.8	15.1
1886	37.9	29.4	15.6	29.9	21.3	13.5	32.6	19.2	18.4	32.4	18.1	14.2
1887	38.2	28.9	15.6	29.7	19.3	14.4	38.4[10]	18.2[10]	18.6[10]	31.7	18.2	14.0
1888	37.8	29.2	15.8	29.4	20.3	14.2	37.7	18.2	16.6	31.5	19.5	14.2
1889	37.8	27.3	15.0	29.4	19.8	14.5	36.7	18.5	16.0	31.2	18.5	14.2
1890	36.2	29.1	15.0	29.0	20.8	14.6	35.1	21.1	18.2	30.5	19.0	13.8
1891	38.2	28.0	15.4	30.0	21.2	15.0	39.1	26.7	18.2	31.0	20.0	13.6
1892	36.0	28.8	15.6	28.9	21.8	15.4	36.0	31.6	16.8	29.6	19.5	13.5
1893	37.9	27.1	15.8	29.5	20.3	15.2	35.0	27.6	13.2	30.8	19.0	14.0
1894	36.6	27.8	15.8	29.0	18.6	15.0	38.0	27.4	15.8	30.4	17.6	13.8
1895	37.9	27.5	16.0	28.5	19.5	15.5	40.7	26.5	18.4	30.3	16.9	14.1
1896	37.8	26.2	15.8	29.0	17.5	16.2	41.4	24.3	16.8	30.5	15.7	14.5
1897	37.2	25.5	16.0	29.0	17.2	16.5	42.5	25.6	16.6	29.8	16.6	14.9
1898	36.0	24.8	15.8	28.6	17.6	16.6	39.4	23.1	15.8	30.2	15.5	15.1
1899	36.8	25.2	16.4	28.8	18.8	16.5	40.7	24.8	17.6	29.7	17.3	15.0

See p.135 for footnotes

B6 Vital Statistics: Rates per 1,000 Population

1850–1899

	Finland			France			Germany			Greece[13]		
	B	D	M	B	D	M	B	D	M	B	D	M
1850	35.7	26.3	16.2	26.8	21.4	16.7	37.2	25.6	17.0	...	...	...
1851	38.2	23.7	16.6	27.1	22.3	16.0	36.7	25.0	16.7	...	...	...
1852	35.0	30.0	14.4	26.8	22.6	15.7	35.5	28.4	15.3	...	...	...
1853	35.1	29.3	14.8	26.0	22.0	15.6	34.6	27.2	15.3	...	...	...
1854	37.5	25.9	15.6	25.5	27.4	15.0	34.0	27.0	14.1	...	...	...
1855	35.8	32.0	15.8	25.0	26.0	15.7	32.2	28.1	14.0	...	...	...
1856	36.3	34.0	15.8	26.3	23.1	15.7	33.5	25.2	15.0	...	...	...
1857	32.8	32.5	14.2	25.9	23.7	16.3	36.0	27.2	16.7	...	...	...
1858	36.5	29.7	15.4	26.7	24.1	16.9	36.5	26.8	17.0	...	...	...
1859	35.8	25.0	16.0	27.9	26.8	16.3	37.5	25.7	16.1	...	...	...
1860	36.4	24.8	17.8	26.2[11]	21.4[11]	15.8[11]	36.4	23.2	16.1	28.4	20.4	11.2
1861	37.8	23.8	17.2	26.9	23.2	16.3	35.7	25.6	15.5	29.5	20.9	11.0
1862	37.3	28.1	15.8	26.5	21.7	16.2	35.4	24.7	16.3	...	...	...
1863	36.2	29.6	14.8	26.9	22.5	16.0	37.5	25.7	17.0	...	...	...
1864	39.3	22.6	15.6	26.6	22.7	15.8	37.8	26.2	17.1	28.2	20.6	12.2
1865	34.2	24.9	14.0	26.5	24.7	15.7	37.6	27.6	17.9	29.4	21.4	13.2
1866	32.0	33.6	12.2	26.4	23.2	16.0	37.8	30.6	16.0	27.8	19.7	12.1
1867	32.3	38.1	12.8	26.2	22.7	15.7	36.8	26.1	18.2	30.1	20.0	12.0
1868	24.6	77.6	11.4	25.7	24.1	15.7	36.8	27.6	17.8	28.6	22.7	12.1
1869	33.7	25.2	19.8	26.0	23.6	16.5	37.8	26.9	19.0	28.8	22.6	13.1
1870	36.3	18.2	20.4	25.9[12]	28.4[12]	12.2[12]	38.5	27.4	15.4	28.1	21.9	12.3
1871	37.3	17.9	19.4	22.9	35.1	14.5	34.5	29.6	16.4	28.4	20.0	12.8
1872	36.4	19.7	17.4	26.7	22.0	19.5	39.4	29.0	20.6	28.6	20.6	11.8
1873	37.0	23.6	17.0	26.0	23.3	17.7	39.7	28.3	20.0	27.6	24.1	11.8
1874	37.9	24.1	18.0	26.2	21.4	16.6	40.1	26.7	19.1	29.2	19.3	12.4
1875	36.6	22.9	16.8	25.9	23.0	16.4	40.6	27.6	18.2	28.2	19.7	13.0
1876	36.7	21.9	16.4	26.2	22.6	15.8	40.9	26.4	17.0	29.6	19.4	13.2
1877	38.2	24.2	16.4	25.5	21.6	15.0	40.6	26.4	16.0	28.5	19.2	11.6
1878	35.4	24.1	15.4	25.2	22.5	15.0	38.9	26.2	15.4	27.2	18.5	11.4
1879	37.8	19.6	14.8	25.1	22.5	15.1	38.9	25.6	15.0	24.8	18.2	11.2
1880	36.5	23.9	15.4	24.6	22.9	14.9	37.6	26.0	15.0	24.4	17.9	11.0
1881	35.0	25.0	13.8	24.9	22.0	15.0	37.0	25.5	14.9	24.5[14]	18.9[14]	9.1[14]
1882	36.3	22.3	15.2	24.8	22.2	14.9	37.2	25.7	15.3	25.2	18.8	12.8
1883	35.9	20.8	15.6	24.8	22.2	15.0	36.6	25.9	15.3	25.0	20.1	13.2
1884	36.1	20.9	15.4	24.7	22.6	15.2	37.2	26.0	15.7	28.6	17.7	13.4
1885	34.2	22.0	14.6	24.3	22.0	14.9	37.0	25.7	15.8	28.5	19.9	13.0
1886	35.3	22.2	14.6	23.9	22.5	14.8	37.1	26.2	15.8	...	...	...
1887	36.2	19.0	15.2	23.5	22.0	14.5	36.9	24.2	15.6	...	...	...
1888	34.9	19.8	14.6	23.1	21.9	14.4	36.6	23.7	15.6	...	...	...
1889	33.4	19.6	13.8	23.0	20.7	14.2	36.4	23.7	16.0	34.1	24.5	12.4
1890	32.9	19.6	14.2	21.8	22.8	14.0	35.7	24.4	16.1	35.3	23.2	11.7
1891	34.3	21.2	13.8	22.6	22.9	14.9	37.0	23.4	16.1	...	...	...
1892	31.6	23.8	12.2	22.3	22.8	15.1	35.7	24.1	15.9	...	...	...
1893	30.1	21.0	11.6	22.8	22.5	14.9	36.8	24.4	15.8	...	...	...
1894	31.1	19.4	13.2	22.3	21.2	14.9	35.9	22.3	15.9	...	...	...
1895	32.9	17.9	14.8	21.7	22.2	14.7	36.1	22.1	15.9	...	...	...
1896	32.5	18.7	15.2	22.5	20.0	15.1	36.3	20.8	16.4	...	...	...
1897	32.3	17.7	15.6	22.2	19.4	15.1	36.0	21.3	16.7	...	...	...
1898	34.4	17.7	16.0	21.7	20.9	14.8	36.1	20.6	16.9	...	...	...
1899	33.7	20.2	14.8	21.8	21.0	15.2	35.8	21.5	17.1	...	...	...

See p.135 for footnotes

B6 **Vital Statistics: Rates per 1,000 Population**

1850–1899

	Hungary[15]			Ireland			Italy[17]			Netherlands		
	B	D	M	B	D	M	B	D	M	B	D	M
1850	...	...	...	...	...	...	...	...	...	34.6	22.2	17.8
1851	...	...	...	...	...	...	...	...	...	35.1	22.5	17.4
1852	...	...	...	...	...	...	...	...	...	35.5	24.0	16.2
1853	...	...	...	...	...	...	...	...	...	33.2	24.6	15.4
1854	...	...	...	...	...	...	...	...	...	32.8	24.1	14.8
1855	...	...	...	...	...	...	...	...	...	32.1	28.1	14.4
1856	...	...	...	...	...	...	...	...	...	32.8	23.5	15.0
1857	...	...	...	...	...	...	...	...	...	34.7	26.8	15.6
1858	...	...	...	...	...	...	...	...	...	32.4	27.9	15.8
1859	...	...	...	...	...	...	...	...	...	34.9	31.0	16.2
1860	...	...	...	...	...	...	...	...	...	31.6	24.8	16.4
1861	39.7	32.2	18.8	...	...	...	...	...	...	35.1	25.3	16.2
1862	41.8	32.3	21.4	...	...	...	38.0	30.9	16.4	33.0	23.9	15.6
1863	44.3	33.9	19.9	...	...	...	39.4	31.0	16.4	36.1	23.9	16.6
1864	41.2	30.9	16.8	24.2	16.8	9.7	38.0	29.8	16.0	35.4	25.3	16.8
1865	41.8	30.3	19.0	25.9	16.9	11.0	38.5	29.9	18.2	35.9	25.9	17.0
1866	41.1	38.0	16.0	26.5	17.1	10.9	38.9	29.1	11.2	35.1	28.7	16.8
1867	38.0	32.8	20.4	26.3	17.6	10.8	36.6	34.2	13.4	35.2	23.7	16.8
1868	41.7	33.1	26.9	26.7	16.3	10.1	35.4	30.6	14.4	34.7	24.8	15.4
1869	41.9	31.3	21.7	26.7	16.9	10.0	37.2	27.9	16.0	34.4	23.1	15.4
1870	42.1	33.5	19.8	27.7	17.2	10.6	36.8	29.9	14.6	35.9	25.9	16.0
1871	42.8	40.1	20.4	28.1	16.8	10.7	37.0	30.0	14.8	35.2	29.4	16.0
1872	40.6	42.9	21.4	27.8	18.8	10.0	38.0	30.8	15.0	35.8	25.9	16.6
1873	42.4	62.9	22.4	27.1	18.9	9.6	36.4	30.1	15.8	36.1	24.1	17.2
1874	42.8	43.3	21.4	26.6	18.1	9.2	35.0	30.4	15.2	36.2	22.7	16.8
1875	45.4	37.7	22.2	26.1	19.0	9.1	37.8	30.8	16.8	36.4	25.5	16.6
1876	45.9	36.0	20.1	26.4	17.9	9.9	39.3	28.9	16.4	37.1	23.5	16.6
1877	43.3	36.9	18.5	26.2	18.2	9.3	37.1	28.4	15.6	36.6	22.2	16.2
1878	42.8	37.7	18.9	25.1	19.3	9.5	36.3	29.2	14.4	36.1	23.0	15.6
1879	45.7	36.3	20.8	25.2	20.1	8.7	37.9	29.8	15.2	36.6	22.4	15.2
1880	42.8	37.8	18.3	24.7	20.4	7.8	33.9	30.8	14.0	35.6	23.6	15.0
1881	43.2	35.1	20.0	24.5	17.9	8.5	38.1	27.6	16.2	35.0	21.5	14.6
1882	44.2	36.1	20.4	24.0	17.4	8.6	37.2	27.6	15.6	35.3	20.7	14.2
1883	45.0	32.2	20.8	23.5	19.4	8.5	37.2	27.6	16.2	34.3	21.8	14.2
1884	45.8	31.0	20.4	23.9	17.9	9.1	39.0	26.9	16.6	34.9	22.2	14.4
1885	44.9	32.3	19.8	23.5	18.7	8.6	38.6	27.0	16.0	34.4	21.0	13.8
1886	45.6	32.3	19.2	23.2	18.0	8.4	37.0	28.7	15.8	34.6	21.8	13.9
1887	44.3	34.5	18.0	23.1	18.4	8.6	38.9	28.0	16.0	33.7	19.7	14.0
1888	43.9	32.3	18.8	22.8	17.9	8.4	37.5	27.5	15.8	33.7	20.4	13.8
1889	43.8	29.9	16.4	22.7	17.4	9.0	38.3	25.6	15.4	33.4	20.2	13.9
1890	40.7[16]	32.5[16]	16.4[16]	22.3	18.2	8.9	35.8	26.3	14.6	32.9	20.5	14.2
1891	42.6	33.4	17.2	23.1	18.4	9.2	37.2	26.1	15.0	33.7	20.6	14.2
1892	40.6	34.7	18.4	22.5	19.4	9.3	36.2	26.2	15.0	32.0	21.0	14.4
1893	43.0	31.1	18.6	23.0	18.0	9.4	36.5	25.2	14.8	33.8	19.2	14.6
1894	41.6	30.4	18.4	22.9	18.2	9.4	35.5	25.0	14.8	32.5	18.5	14.4
1895	41.8[8]	29.7[8]	17.0[8]	23.3	18.5	10.1	34.9	25.0	14.6	32.8	18.6	14.7
1896	40.7	28.6	16.0	23.7	16.7	10.2	34.8	24.1	14.2	32.7	17.2	14.9
1897	40.5	28.1	16.2	23.5	18.5	10.1	34.7	21.9	14.4	32.5	16.9	14.8
1898	37.8	28.0	16.6	23.3	18.2	10.0	33.5	22.9	13.8	31.9	17.0	14.6
1899	39.2	27.3	18.0	23.1	17.7	9.9	33.9	21.9	14.6	32.0	17.1	14.9

See p. 135 for footnotes

B6 Vital Statistics: Rates per 1,000 Population

1850–1899

	Norway			Portugal[18]			Romania[19]			Russia[21]		
	B	D	M	B	D	M	B	D	M	B	D	M
1850	31.0	17.2	15.3	...	...	...	...	...	...	...	...	...
1851	31.9	17.1	15.0	...	...	...	...	...	...	...	...	...
1852	31.0	17.9	14.3	...	...	...	...	...	...	...	...	...
1853	32.0	18.3	15.6	...	...	...	...	...	...	...	...	...
1854	34.3	16.0	17.1	...	...	...	...	...	...	...	...	...
1855	33.4	17.2	16.2	...	...	...	...	...	...	...	...	...
1856	32.2	16.9	15.5	...	...	...	...	...	...	...	...	...
1857	33.0	17.1	15.1	...	...	...	...	...	...	...	...	...
1858	33.5	16.1	15.2	...	...	...	...	...	...	...	...	...
1859	34.8	17.0	15.4	...	...	...	29.6	16.9	...	...	...	...
1860	33.3	17.2	14.3	...	...	...	31.6	20.3	...	...	...	...
1861	30.7	19.5	13.6	...	...	...	32.0	21.6	...	49.7	35.4	23.2
1862	32.1	20.0	13.8	...	...	...	32.0	21.8	...	51.1	34.0	21.8
1863	32.7	18.9	14.3	...	...	...	30.4	26.2	...	50.0	37.7	18.8
1864	31.9	17.8	13.6	...	...	...	36.0	26.0	...	52.9	38.7	...
1865	31.9	16.6	13.7	...	...	...	34.6	27.1	...	50.0	36.9	...
1866	31.7	17.1	13.4	...	...	...	31.3	38.0	11.6	...	...	...
1867	30.1	18.5	12.9	...	...	...	31.7	25.1	13.9	51.2	36.8	20.4
1868	29.5	18.3	12.4	...	...	...	33.4	25.1	14.6	48.8	39.7	19.2
1869	28.9	17.2	12.3	...	...	...	34.0	24.3	16.1	49.7	38.3	20.2
1870	29.2	16.2	12.9	...	...	...	34.4	26.1	14.4	49.2	35.0	20.8
1871	29.3	16.9	13.3	...	...	...	33.5	26.4	12.9	51.0	37.9	20.8
1872	30.0	16.7	14.0	...	...	...	32.0	30.5	16.5	50.0	41.2	20.8
1873	29.9	17.0	14.5	...	...	...	32.5	32.6	13.4	52.3	36.5	19.4
1874	31.0	18.3	15.4	...	...	...	34.3	34.9	14.2	51.4	35.2	19.6
1875	31.5	18.8	15.7	...	...	...	38.8	32.0	15.0	51.5	34.6	19.4
1876	31.6	18.9	15.4	...	...	...	37.0	28.3	14.2	50.6	34.9	16.8
1877	31.7	16.9	15.1	...	...	...	35.4	29.8	13.1	49.6	34.4	14.8
1878	31.5	16.0	14.6	...	...	...	31.5[20]	33.2[20]	15.9[20]	47.3	38.2	18.4
1879	32.1	15.1	13.5	...	...	...	37.1	29.2	20.5	50.2	34.8	20.4
1880	30.9	16.2	13.3	...	...	...	37.7	35.9	17.5	49.7	36.1	19.2
1881	30.0	17.0	12.8	...	...	...	41.5	26.7	18.2	49.1	34.1	19.6
1882	30.6	18.6	13.4	...	...	...	40.4	28.2	18.8	51.6	40.4	19.0
1883	31.0	17.0	13.2	...	...	...	42.8	26.0	19.8	50.6	37.5	19.2
1884	31.6	16.6	13.7	...	...	...	41.4	25.5	16.6	51.5	34.4	17.8
1885	31.5	16.5	13.4	...	...	...	43.1	25.0	16.0	50.0	35.8	17.2
1886	30.9	16.3	13.1	31.9	20.4	13.8	42.2	26.7	15.4	49.0	33.2	17.0
1887	31.4	16.2	12.7	33.7	22.1	14.0	41.0	30.5	15.2	49.5	33.8	18.0
1888	30.4	17.3	12.3	33.1	21.7	13.7	42.4	30.6	14.8	49.9	33.4	19.6
1889	29.6	17.8	12.5	33.7	22.5	14.0	40.6	27.2	15.6	51.6	35.5	17.6
1890	30.4	18.0	12.9	32.6	25.2	14.2	38.5	28.4	14.6	50.3	36.7	16.8
1891	30.8	17.7	13.1	32.0	22.8	13.7	42.3	30.1	16.6	50.6	35.8	17.2
1892	29.6	17.9	12.6	31.2	20.3	13.6	39.0	34.7	15.4	46.0	41.0	17.8
1893	30.3	16.5	12.7	31.9	21.4	13.2	40.5	30.8	14.8	48.8	34.4	17.8
1894	29.6	16.9	12.6	29.7	20.7	12.8	40.9	31.7	17.8	49.2	34.3	19.0
1895	30.4	15.6	12.8	30.0	20.8	12.7	42.3	27.6	14.8	50.1	35.5	18.6
1896	30.0	15.2	13.2	30.0	22.7	12.6	40.7	29.1	16.6	50.4	33.3	17.6
1897	30.0	15.4	13.3	30.4	21.9	13.7	42.9	29.6	14.4	50.0	31.7	18.2
1898	30.3	15.3	13.8	30.2	21.4	13.1	36.7	26.5	15.0	48.6	33.2	17.4
1899	29.9	16.8	14.1	29.9	20.2	13.6	42.0	27.5	16.8	49.3	31.2	18.6

See p.135 for footnotes

B6 Vital Statistics: Rates per 1,000 Population

1850–1899

	Serbia			Spain[23]			Sweden		
	B	D	M	B	D	M	B	D	M
1850	...	...	...	...	...	...	31.9	19.8	15.2
1851	...	...	...	...	...	...	31.7	20.7	14.7
1852	...	...	...	...	...	...	30.7	22.7	13.7
1853	...	...	...	...	...	...	31.4	23.7	14.4
1854	...	...	...	...	...	...	33.5	19.8	15.4
1855	...	...	...	...	...	...	31.8	21.5	15.0
1856	...	...	...	...	...	...	31.5	21.8	14.9
1857	...	...	...	...	...	...	32.4	27.6	15.5
1858	...	...	...	35.2	28.0	14.6	34.8	21.7	16.2
1859	...	...	...	38.4	28.8	14.6	35.0	20.1	16.6
1860	...	...	...	36.7	27.4	16.2	34.8	17.7	15.6
1861	...	...	...	39.0	26.6	16.6	32.6	18.5	14.5
1862	40.5	38.6	24.2	38.5	27.3	16.4	33.4	21.4	14.1
1863	43.0	35.1	30.2	37.8	29.2	15.8	33.6	19.3	14.5
1864	45.1	31.3	22.6	39.2	31.5	16.0	33.6	20.3	14.0
1865	46.7	25.5	24.2	38.6	33.8	16.2	32.8	19.4	14.1
1866	45.7	24.3	22.4	38.3	29.0	16.6	33.1	20.0	13.4
1867	44.8	25.7	20.9	38.5	30.4	14.8	30.8	19.6	12.2
1868	45.7	32.7	21.5	35.7	34.1	14.0	27.5	21.0	10.9
1869	45.2	29.7	23.8	37.0	34.1	17.0	28.3	22.3	11.3
1870	44.8	33.2	22.0	36.6	31.6	12.8	28.8	19.8	12.0
1871	43.2	32.4	20.6	...	...	...	30.4	17.2	13.0
1872	39.1	32.1	26.6	...	...	...	30.0	16.3	13.9
1873	42.4	32.6	22.0	...	...	...	30.8	17.2	14.6
1874	41.7	36.4	22.9	...	...	...	30.9	20.3	14.5
1875	45.8	31.3	21.9	...	...	...	31.2	20.3	14.1
1876	41.6	48.3	15.3	...	...	...	30.8	19.6	14.2
1877	33.3	33.6	25.3	...	...	...	31.1	18.7	13.7
1878	38.1[22]	33.4[22]	19.9[22]	36.1	30.5	14.2	29.8	18.1	12.9
1879	39.4	31.3	28.7	35.8	30.5	13.2	30.5	16.9	12.6
1880	40.7	31.5	23.5	35.5	30.1	12.4	29.4	18.1	12.6
1881	45.7	24.7	23.4	37.1	30.2	12.7	29.1	17.7	12.4
1882	44.4	23.1	24.2	36.2	31.4	12.1	29.4	17.4	12.7
1883	47.0	22.8	23.6	35.6	32.7	12.4	28.9	17.3	12.9
1884	47.6	25.0	21.4	36.7	30.6	13.2	30.0	17.5	13.1
1885	46.6	26.9	17.6	36.3	38.0	12.7	29.4	17.8	13.3
1886	42.0	29.6	23.6	36.7	29.2	12.7	29.8	16.6	12.8
1887	46.3	24.9	22.2	36.1	32.8	11.0	29.7	16.1	12.5
1888	45.7	24.4	21.8	36.4	30.1	11.2	28.8	16.0	11.8
1889	44.1	25.5	20.4	36.4	30.4	15.6	27.7	16.0	12.0
1890	40.3	25.3	19.9	34.4	32.1	15.8	28.0	17.1	12.0
1891	45.0	26.5	21.1	35.3	31.8	17.5	28.3	16.8	11.7
1892	42.4	33.5	19.0	35.8	30.6	16.9	27.0	17.9	11.4
1893	42.5	29.7	21.1	35.6	29.7	15.6	27.4	16.8	11.3
1894	42.5	28.1	21.9	34.8	30.3	15.6	27.1	16.4	11.5
1895	44.0	26.9	17.8	35.0	29.0	15.4	27.5	15.2	11.7
1896	41.2	27.0	17.7	35.9	29.6	14.5	27.2	15.6	11.9
1897	42.6	26.5	17.7	34.1	28.4	14.0	26.7	15.4	12.1
1898	35.1	22.9	18.3	33.3	28.2	13.6	27.1	15.1	12.3
1899	39.3	24.3	19.9	34.2	28.8	16.9	26.4	17.7	12.5

See p. 135 for footnotes

B6 Vital Statistics: Rates per 1,000 Population

1850–1899

	Switzerland			United Kingdom: England and Wales			United Kingdom: Scotland		
	B	D	M	B	D	M	B	D	M
1850	...	...	...	33.4	20.8	17.2	...	...	...
1851	...	...	...	34.3	22.0	17.2	...	...	...
1852	...	...	...	34.3	22.4	17.4	...	...	...
1853	...	...	...	33.3	22.9	17.9	...	...	...
1854	...	...	...	34.1	23.5	17.2	...	...	...
1855	...	...	...	33.8	22.6	16.2	31.3[8]	20.8[8]	13.2[8]
1856	...	...	...	34.5	20.5	16.7	34.0	19.5	13.8
1857	...	...	...	34.4	21.8	16.5	34.3	20.6	14.2
1858	...	...	...	33.7	23.1	16.0	34.4	21.0	13.0
1859	...	...	...	35.0	22.4	17.0	35.0	20.3	13.9
1860	...	...	...	34.3	21.2	17.1	35.6	22.3	13.9
1861	...	...	...	34.6	21.6	16.3	34.9	20.3	13.6
1862	...	...	...	35.0	21.4	16.1	34.6	21.7	13.3
1863	...	...	...	35.3	23.0	16.8	35.0	22.9	14.3
1864	...	...	...	35.4	23.7	17.6	35.6	23.6	14.4
1865	...	...	...	35.4	23.2	17.5	35.5	22.3	14.8
1866	...	...	...	35.2	23.4	17.5	35.4	22.2	14.7
1867	...	...	...	35.4	21.7	16.5	35.1	21.3	13.9
1868	...	...	13.4	35.8	21.8	16.1	35.3	21.2	13.3
1869	...	...	14.4	34.8	22.3	15.9	34.3	23.0	13.4
1870	29.8	25.8	14.0	35.2	22.9	16.1	34.6	22.2	14.3
1871	29.0	27.6	14.6	35.0	22.6	16.7	34.5	22.2	14.3
1872	29.8	22.2	15.8	35.6	21.3	17.4	34.9	22.3	15.1
1873	29.7	22.7	15.4	35.4	21.0	17.6	34.8	22.4	15.5
1874	30.4	22.3	16.6	36.0	22.2	17.0	35.6	23.2	15.2
1875	31.8	24.0	18.0	35.4	22.7	16.7	35.2	23.3	14.8
1876	32.8	24.1	16.2	36.3	20.9	16.5	35.6	20.9	15.0
1877	32.0	23.5	15.8	36.0	20.3	15.7	35.3	20.6	14.4
1878	31.3	23.3	14.6	35.6	21.6	15.2	34.9	21.2	13.4
1879	30.5	22.6	13.8	34.7	20.7	14.4	34.3	20.0	12.8
1880	29.6	21.9	13.6	34.2	20.5	14.9	33.6	20.5	13.2
1881	29.8	22.4	13.6	33.9	18.9	15.1	33.7	19.3	13.9
1882	28.9	21.9	13.6	33.8	19.6	15.5	33.5	19.4	14.1
1883	28.5	20.4	13.8	33.5	19.6	15.5	32.8	20.2	14.1
1884	28.3	20.2	13.8	33.6	19.7	15.1	33.7	19.6	13.6
1885	27.7	21.3	13.8	32.9	19.2	14.5	32.7	19.3	13.1
1886	27.8	20.7	13.8	32.8	19.5	14.2	32.9	19.0	12.6
1887	27.9	20.2	14.2	31.9	19.1	14.4	31.8	19.0	12.7
1888	27.7	19.9	14.2	31.2	18.1	14.4	31.3	18.0	12.8
1889	27.7	20.3	14.0	31.1	18.2	15.0	30.9	18.4	13.3
1890	26.6	20.9	14.2	30.2	19.5	15.5	30.4	19.7	13.7
1891	28.2	20.6	14.4	31.4	20.2	15.6	31.2	20.7	13.9
1892	27.7	19.0	14.6	30.4	19.0	15.4	30.7	18.5	14.1
1893	27.9	20.1	14.4	30.7	19.2	14.7	30.8	19.3	13.2
1894	27.3	20.1	14.4	29.6	16.6	15.0	29.9	17.1	13.3
1895	27.3	19.2	14.6	30.3	18.7	15.0	30.0	19.4	13.5
1896	28.1	17.8	15.0	29.6	17.1	15.7	30.4	16.6	14.2
1897	28.3	17.7	15.6	29.6	17.4	16.0	30.0	18.4	14.4
1898	28.5	18.3	15.6	29.3	17.5	16.2	30.1	18.0	14.8
1899	29.0	17.7	15.6	29.1	18.2	16.5	29.8	18.1	15.0

See p.135 for footnotes

B6 Vital Statistics: Rate per 1,000 Population

1900–1949

	Albania			Austria[2]			Belgium			Bulgaria		
	B	D	M	B	D	M	B	D	M	B	D	M
1900	...	...	...	35.0	25.2	16.4	28.9	19.3	17.2	42.3	22.6	16.6
1901	...	...	...	36.6	24.0	16.3	29.4	17.2	17.4	37.7	23.3	17.6
1902	...	...	...	37.0	24.7	15.5	28.4	17.3	16.2	39.1	24.0	19.0
1903	...	...	...	35.2	23.8	15.6	27.5	17.0	15.7	41.3	22.9	19.0
1904	...	...	...	35.6	23.8	15.6	27.1	16.9	16.0	42.8	21.4	22.8
1905	...	...	...	33.8	25.1	15.6	26.2	17.5	15.8	43.5	21.7	21.5
1906	...	...	...	35.0	22.6	15.8	25.6	16.0	16.1	43.7	22.2	18.9
1907	...	...	...	34.0	22.7	15.1	25.2	15.4	16.0	43.3	22.2	19.7
1908	...	...	...	33.7	22.5	15.3	24.8	16.1	15.6	40.3	24.2	17.6
1909	...	...	...	33.4	22.9	15.1	23.5	15.4	15.3	40.4	26.5	18.2
1910	...	...	...	32.5	21.2	15.1	23.7	14.9	15.8	41.4	23.0	18.9
1911	...	...	...	31.3	21.9	15.2	22.8	16.0	15.9	39.9	21.4	18.7
1912	...	...	...	31.3	20.5	14.7	22.5	14.5	16.2	41.7	20.6	5.6
1913	...	...	...	29.7[2]	20.3[2]	13.5[2]	22.3	14.2	16.0	25.7	29.0	5.7
1914	...	...	...	...	...	...	20.4	14.2	10.7	45.1	20.7	12.6
1915	...	...	...	...	...	...	16.1	13.1	6.4	40.2	19.9	6.4
1916	...	...	...	...	...	...	12.9	13.1	7.9	21.3	20.8	2.2
1917	...	...	...	...	...	...	11.3	16.3	8.6	17.2	21.2	4.4
1918	...	...	...	14.1	26.4	13.1	11.3	20.8	11.5	21.2	32.0	9.6
1919	...	...	...	18.5	20.4	25.0	16.9	14.9	25.6	32.8	20.2	15.8
1920	...	...	...	22.7	19.0	26.6	22.2	13.9	28.8	39.9	21.4	14.1
1921	...	...	...	23.2	17.0	25.0	21.7	13.4	23.7	40.2	21.7	21.7
1922	...	...	...	23.1	17.4	22.8	20.4	13.9	22.0	40.5	23.6	21.2
1923	...	...	...	22.5	15.3	17.2	20.3	12.9	21.0	37.7	21.2	20.8
1924	...	...	...	21.7	15.0	16.2	19.8	12.7	20.8	39.8	20.7	21.3
1925	...	...	...	20.6	14.4	15.4	19.6[24]	12.8[24]	19.1[24]	36.9	19.2	19.8
1926	...	...	...	19.3	15.0	14.6	18.9	12.8	18.4	37.4	17.2	20.0
1927	...	...	...	17.9	15.0	14.6	18.2	13.0	18.1	33.2	20.3	18.6
1928	...	...	...	17.6	14.5	14.8	18.2	12.8	17.9	33.1	17.7	20.0
1929	...	...	...	16.8	14.6	15.4	18.1	14.4	17.8	30.6	18.1	19.7
1930	...	16.3	11.6	16.8	13.5	15.4	18.6	12.8	17.7	31.4	16.2	19.0
1931	...	...	...	15.9	14.0	14.8	18.1	12.7	16.2	29.5	16.9	19.2
1932	25.1	17.9	9.4	15.2	13.9	13.4	17.5	12.7	15.1	31.5	16.3	19.2
1933	...	...	...	14.3	13.2	13.0	16.3	12.7	15.8	29.2	15.6	18.8
1934	...	...	...	13.6	12.7	13.0	15.9	11.7	15.2	30.1	14.1	18.7
1935	...	...	...	13.1	13.7	13.6	15.2	12.3	15.2	26.4	14.6	15.8
1936	...	16.6	11.4	13.1	13.2	13.6	15.1	12.2	15.5	25.9	14.3	16.0
1937	...	19.5	11.2	12.8	13.3	13.8	15.0	12.5	15.2	24.3	13.6	16.6
1938	34.3	17.7	13.4	13.9	14.0	26.6	15.5	12.5	14.7	22.8	13.7	17.0
1939	27.9	15.0	10.0	20.7	15.3	35.2	15.0	13.2	13.1	21.4	13.4	18.2
1940	31.3	16.4	12.2	...	...	...	13.3[25]	15.1[25]	8.6[25]	22.2[26]	13.4[26]	18.0[26]
1941	28.0	16.6	12.6	...	...	...	11.9[25]	14.4[25]	12.8[25]	21.9	12.7	18.2
1942	...	14.2	14.0	...	...	...	12.8[25]	14.2[25]	15.0[25]	22.7	13.0	21.0
1943	...	...	...	...	...	...	14.6[25]	13.1[25]	12.6[25]	21.8	18.8	20.2
1944	...	...	...	...	...	...	15.0	15.1	10.9	22.0	18.4[27]	18.4
1945	...	...	...	...	...	...	15.3	14.5	19.9	24.1	16.2[27]	23.8
1946	...	...	...	15.9	13.4	18.0	17.5	13.2	21.7	25.6	12.2	22.0
1947	...	18.9	...	18.5	12.9	21.6	17.0	12.7	19.7	24.0	11.6	22.0
1948	...	16.1	...	17.7	12.1	20.6	17.2	12.0	18.5	24.6	11.4	22.2
1949	...	12.5	19.4	16.3	12.8	19.8	16.8	12.4	17.0	24.7	12.2	21.8

See p.135 for footnotes

B6 Vital Statistics: Rates per 1,000 Population

1900–1949

	Czechoslovakia			Denmark			Finland			France		
	B	D	M	B	D	M	B	D	M	B	D	M
1900	...	...	...	29.7	16.8	15.3	32.6	21.9	13.8	21.3	21.9	15.5
1901	...	...	...	29.7	15.7	14.2	33.2	21.1	13.8	22.0	20.1	15.6
1902	...	...	...	29.2	14.6	14.2	32.4	19.0	13.0	21.6	19.5	15.1
1903	...	...	...	28.7	14.6	14.2	31.5	18.5	13.0	21.1	19.3	15.1
1904	...	...	...	28.9	14.1	14.4	33.0	18.4	13.6	20.9	19.4	15.2
1905	...	...	...	28.4	15.0	14.4	31.8	19.1	13.4	20.6	19.6	15.4
1906	...	...	...	28.5	13.5	14.8	32.8	18.2	14.4	20.5	19.9	15.6
1907	...	...	...	28.2	14.1	15.2	32.8	18.8	14.4	19.7	20.2	16.0
1908	...	...	...	28.6	14.6	15.0	32.2	19.3	14.0	20.1	18.9	16.0
1909	...	...	...	28.2	13.3	14.8	32.8	17.4	13.4	19.5	19.1	15.6
1910	...	...	...	27.5	12.9	14.6	31.7	17.4	12.8	19.6	17.8	15.6
1911	...	...	...	26.7	13.4	14.4	30.8	17.4	12.6	18.7	19.6	15.6
1912	...	...	...	26.6	13.0	14.6	30.8	17.2	12.4	18.9	17.5	15.8
1913	...	...	...	25.6	12.5	14.4	28.8	17.1	12.6	18.8[12]	17.7[12]	15.0[12]
1914	...	...	...	25.6	12.5	13.8	28.7	16.6	12.0	18.1[30]	18.5[30]	9.8[30]
1915	...	...	...	24.2	12.8	13.0	27.0	16.9	11.6	11.8[30]	18.3[30]	4.2[30]
1916	...	...	...	24.4	13.4	14.4	25.7	17.6	12.4	9.5[30]	17.3[30]	6.2[30]
1917	...	...	...	23.7	13.2	14.0	25.9	18.8	12.8	10.4[30]	18.0[30]	9.1[30]
1918	...	...	...	24.1	13.0	15.2	25.4	30.4	9.6	12.1[30]	22.3[30]	10.4[30]
1919	22.4	18.3	27.4	22.6	13.0	16.4	20.5	20.2	12.0	13.0	19.0	28.6
1920	26.7	19.0	26.4	25.4	12.9	17.6	27.0	17.0	15.0	21.4	17.2	31.9
1921	29.2	17.7	24.2	24.0	11.0	16.2	25.9	14.9	15.0	20.7	17.7	23.2
1922	28.2	17.4	20.6	22.2	11.9	15.8	25.0	15.3	14.6	19.3	17.5	19.5
1923	27.3	15.0	18.8	22.3	11.3	16.0	25.3	14.7	14.6	19.1	16.7	17.8
1924	25.8	15.3	18.0	21.8	11.2	15.6	23.8	16.3	13.4	18.7	16.9	17.6
1925	25.1	15.2	18.4	21.0	10.8	15.0	23.7	14.4	13.4	19.0	17.4	17.4
1926	24.6	15.6	18.2	20.5	11.0	15.0	23.0	14.2	13.6	18.8	17.4	16.9
1927	23.3	16.0	18.0	19.6	11.6	15.0	22.5	15.4	14.4	18.2	16.5	16.4
1928	23.3	15.1	19.0	19.6	11.0	15.6	22.8	14.3	15.0	18.3	16.4	16.5
1929	22.4	15.5	19.0	18.6	11.2	15.8	22.2	15.9	14.6	17.7	17.9	16.2
1930	22.7	14.2	18.6	18.7	10.8	16.4	21.8	14.0	14.4	18.0	15.6	16.4
1931	21.5	14.4	17.6	18.0	11.4	16.2	20.7	14.1	13.8	17.5	16.2	15.6
1932	21.0	14.1	17.2	18.0	11.0	15.6	19.8	13.3	13.2	17.3	15.8	15.1
1933	19.2	13.7	16.6	17.3	10.6	17.6	18.4	13.6	13.8	16.2	15.8	15.1
1934	18.7	13.2	15.8	17.8	10.4	19.0	19.1	13.1	15.4	16.2	15.1	14.2
1935	17.9	13.5	15.2	17.7	11.1	18.6	19.6	12.7	16.0	15.3	15.7	13.6
1936	17.4	13.3	16.0	17.8	11.0	18.6	19.1	13.6	16.6	15.0	15.3	13.4
1937	17.2	13.3	16.6	18.0	10.8	18.2	19.9	12.8	18.0	14.7	15.0	13.1
1938	16.8[28]	12.8[28]	14.4[28]	18.1	10.3	17.8	21.0	12.8	18.4	14.6	15.4	13.1
1939	18.6	13.3	18.2	17.8	10.1	18.8	21.2	14.3	16.6	14.6	15.3[30]	12.3
1940	20.6	14.0	19.8	18.3	10.4	18.4	17.8	19.4	16.6	13.6[30]	18.0[30]	8.6[30]
1941	20.1	14.0	17.2	18.5	10.3	17.4	24.2	19.8	20.4	13.1[30]	17.0[30]	11.4[30]
1942	19.7	14.3	18.2	20.4	9.6	18.4	16.6	15.1	14.6	14.5[30]	16.6[30]	13.6[30]
1943	21.5	14.1	15.8	21.4	9.6	18.6	20.4	13.3	17.2	15.7[30]	16.0[30]	11.2[30]
1944	22.1[28]	15.0[28]	13.6[28]	22.7	10.2	18.6	21.3	18.9	16.8	16.1[30]	17.1[30]	10.5[30]
1945	19.5	17.8	15.0	23.5	10.5	18.0	25.5	13.1	23.6	16.2[30]	16.1[30]	19.8[30]
1946	22.7	14.1	20.2	23.4	10.2	19.6	27.9	11.8	26.2	20.9	13.5	25.7
1947	24.2[29]	12.1[29]	22.2[29]	22.1	9.7	19.2	28.0	11.9	22.6	21.3	13.1	21.0
1948	23.4	11.5	21.4	20.3	8.6	18.8	27.6	11.2	20.0	21.1	12.4	18.0
1949	22.4	11.9	21.2	18.9	8.9	17.8	26.1	11.2	17.6	20.9	13.7	16.4

See p.135 for footnotes

B6 Vital Statistics: Rate per 1,000 Population

1900–1949

	Germany			East Germany			Greece			Hungary		
	B	D	M	B	D	M	B	D	M	B	D	M
1900	35.6	22.1	17.0	...	...	...	...	...	...	39.4	27.0	17.8
1901	35.7	20.7	16.5	...	...	...	...	...	...	37.6	25.0	17.4
1902	35.1	19.4	15.8	...	...	...	...	...	...	38.6	26.9	17.2
1903	33.8	20.0	15.8	...	...	...	...	...	...	36.5	26.1	16.0
1904	34.1	19.6	16.1	...	...	...	...	...	...	37.0	24.8	18.0
1905	33.0	19.8	16.1	...	...	...	...	...	...	35.5	27.8	17.0
1906	33.1	18.2	16.3	...	...	...	...	...	...	36.1	24.9	17.6
1907	32.3	18.0	16.3	...	...	...	...	...	...	36.2	25.6	20.0
1908	32.1	18.1	15.9	...	...	...	...	...	...	36.7	25.0	18.6
1909	31.1	17.2	15.5	...	...	...	...	...	...	37.1	25.4	17.4
1910	29.8	16.2	15.4	...	...	...	...	...	...	35.4	23.4	17.4
1911	28.6	17.3	15.7	...	...	...	...	...	...	34.8	24.8	18.6
1912	28.3	15.6	15.8	...	...	...	...	...	...	36.0	23.0	17.4
1913	27.5	15.0	15.3	...	...	...	...	...	...	34.3	23.2	18.4
1914	26.8	19.0[18]	13.6	...	...	...	...	...	...	34.5	23.4	14.4
1915	20.4	21.4[31]	8.2	...	...	...	...	...	...	23.7	25.3	13.0
1916	15.2[6]	19.2[31] [6]	8.2[6]	...	...	...	...	...	...	16.8	20.9	6.8
1917	13.9	20.6[31]	9.4	...	...	...	...	...	...	16.0	20.7	8.2
1918	14.3[32]	24.8[31] [32]	10.8[32]	...	...	...	...	...	...	15.3[15]	25.7[15]	13.8[15]
							...	...	...	16.3	26.4	15.2
1919	20.0	15.6	26.8	...	...	...	...	...	...	27.6	20.0	40.8
1920	25.9	15.1	29.0	...	...	...	...	...	...	31.4	21.4	26.2
1921	25.3[33]	13.9[33]	23.8[33]	...	...	...	21.2	13.6	11.2	31.8	21.2	23.2
1922	23.0	14.4	22.3	...	...	...	21.5	16.0	12.0	30.8	21.4	21.6
1923	21.2	13.9	18.9	...	...	...	19.0	17.0	14.8	29.2	19.5	19.2
1924	20.6	12.2	14.2	...	...	...	19.5	15.6	14.8	26.9	20.4	18.2
1925	20.8	11.9	15.5	...	...	...	26.3	14.9	16.2	28.3	17.1	17.8
1926	19.6	11.7	15.4	...	...	...	30.0	13.9	14.6	27.4	16.7	18.4
1927	18.4	12.0	17.0	...	...	...	28.8	16.3	14.4	25.8	17.8	18.2
1928	18.6	11.6	18.5	...	...	...	30.5	17.0	13.2	26.4	17.2	18.6
1929	18.0	12.6	18.4	...	...	...	28.9	18.4	14.2	25.1	17.8	18.2
1930	17.6	11.0	17.5	...	...	...	31.3	16.3	14.0	25.4	15.5	18.0
1931	16.0	11.2	16.0	...	...	...	30.8	17.7	14.0	23.7	16.6	17.6
1932	15.1	10.8	15.7	...	...	...	28.5	18.0	12.0	23.4	17.9	16.2
1933	14.7	11.2	19.3	...	...	...	28.6	16.8	14.0	21.9	14.7	16.6
1934	18.0	10.9	22.3	...	...	...	31.1	15.0	14.0	21.8	14.5	17.8
1935	18.9	11.8	19.5	...	...	...	28.2	14.8	13.4	21.1	15.3	17.0
1936	19.0	11.8	18.1	...	...	...	27.9	15.1	11.2	20.3	14.3	17.2
1937	18.8	11.7	18.3	...	...	...	26.2	15.0	13.0	20.0	14.2	17.8
1938	19.7	11.7	18.8	...	...	...	25.9	13.2	13.0	19.9	14.3	16.4
1939	20.4	12.3[31]	22.4	...	...	...	24.8	13.9	13.2	19.4	13.5[37]	17.4
1940	20.1	12.7[31]	17.6	...	...	...	24.5	12.8	9.0	20.0	14.3[37]	15.6
1941	18.1	12.1[31]	14.4	...	...	...	18.3[35]	17.1[35]	10.0[35]	19.0	13.2[37]	17.0
1942	14.9	12.0[31]	14.8	...	...	...	18.1[35]	26.0[35]	12.2[35]	19.9	14.6[37]	15.6
1943	16.0	12.1[31]	14.6	...	...	...	16.7[35]	15.3[35]	12.0[35]	18.4	13.5[37]	16.0[38]
1944	...	...	...	...	...	...	20.0[35]	15.2[35]	9.6[35]	...	...	...
1945	...	...	...	...	...	...	25.1[35]	11.7[35]	12.8[35]	18.7	23.4[37]	16.2
	West Germany[34]											
1946	16.1	13.0	17.6	10.4	22.9	13.8	28.2[35]	9.9[35]	14.0[35]	18.7	15.0	21.8
1947	16.4	12.1	20.2	13.1	19.0	17.4	27.4[35]	9.3[35]	13.2[35]	20.6[38]	12.9[38]	21.6
1948	16.5	10.5	21.4	12.8	15.2	19.2	27.0[35] [36]	12.4[15] [16]	11.2[35] [36]	20.9	11.6	21.4
1949	16.8	10.4	20.4	14.5	13.4	20.2	18.6	7.9	11.2	20.6	11.4	23.4

See p.135 for footnotes

B6 Vital Statistics: Rates per 1,000 Population

1900–1949

	Ireland			Northern Ireland			Italy			Netherlands		
	B	D	M	B	D	M	B	D	M	B	D	M
1900	22.7	19.6	9.5				33.0	23.8	14.4	31.6	17.9	15.2
1901	22.7	17.8	10.1				32.5	22.0	14.4	32.2	17.2	15.4
1902	23.0	17.5	10.4				33.4	22.2	14.6	31.8	16.3	15.1
1903	23.1	17.5	10.4				31.7	22.4	14.4	31.6	15.6	14.7
1904	23.6	18.0	10.4				32.9	21.2	15.0	31.4	15.9	14.7
1905	23.4	17.1	10.5				32.7	22.0	15.4	30.8	15.3	14.6
1906	23.5	16.9	10.3				32.1	20.9	15.6	30.4	14.8	15.0
1907	23.2	17.6	10.3				31.7	20.9	15.6	30.0	14.6	15.2
1908	23.3	17.5	10.4				33.7	22.8	16.8	29.7	15.0	14.6
1909	23.4	17.1	10.3				32.8	21.7	15.6	29.2	13.7	14.2
1910	23.3	17.1	10.1				33.3	19.9	15.6	28.6	13.6	14.6
1911	23.2	16.5	10.7				31.5	21.4	15.0	27.8	14.5	14.4
1912	23.0	16.5	10.6				32.4	18.2	15.2	28.1	12.3	15.2
1913	22.8	17.1	10.2				31.7	18.7	15.0	28.2	12.3	15.8
1914	22.6	16.3	10.8				31.0	17.9	14.0	28.2	12.4	13.6
1915	22.0	17.6	11.1				30.5	22.3	10.2	26.2	12.5	13.4
1916	20.9	16.3	10.2				24.1	23.3	5.8	26.5	12.9	14.6
1917	19.7	16.6	9.6				19.5[39]	26.0[39]	5.4[39]	26.0[43]	13.1[43]	15.0
1918	19.8	17.9	10.3				18.2[39]	35.1[39]	6.0[39]	25.1	17.4	14.8
1919	20.0	17.6	12.2				21.5	18.9	18.6	24.4	13.4	17.2
1920	22.8	14.8	12.0				[40] 32.2	[40] 19.0	[40] 28.2	28.6	12.3	19.2
1921	20.8	14.2	10.4	...	...	...	30.7	17.7	23.2	27.7	11.4	18.4
	Southern Ireland											
1922	19.5	14.7	10.0	23.3	15.4	12.6	30.8	18.1	19.2	26.1	11.7	17.4
1923	20.5	14.0	10.4	23.9	14.7	12.5	30.0	17.0	17.4	26.2	10.2	16.0
1924	21.1	15.0	9.8	22.7	15.9	11.9	29.0	17.1	15.8	25.1	9.8	15.6
1925	20.8	14.6	9.2	22.0	15.7	12.2	28.4	17.1	15.2	24.2	9.8	14.8
1926	20.6	14.1	9.2	22.5	15.0	11.5	27.7	17.2	15.0	23.8	9.8	14.8
1927	20.3	14.8	9.0	21.3	14.6	11.5	27.5	16.1	15.2	23.1	10.2	15.0
1928	20.1	14.2	9.4	20.8	14.4	11.7	26.7	16.1	14.2	23.3	9.6	15.4
1929	19.8	14.6	9.2	20.4	15.9	12.0	25.6	16.5	14.2	22.8	10.7	15.8
1930	19.9	14.3	9.4	20.8	13.8	12.2	26.7	14.1	14.8	23.1	9.1	16.0
1931	19.5	14.6	9.0	20.5	14.4	11.9	24.9	14.8	13.4	22.2	9.6	14.8
1932	19.1	14.6	8.8	19.9	14.1	11.1	23.8	14.7	12.8	22.0	9.0	13.8
1933	19.4	13.7	9.4	19.6	14.3	12.1	23.8	13.7	13.8	20.8	8.8	14.4
1934	19.5	13.2	9.6	20.1	13.9	13.0	23.5	13.3	14.8	20.6	8.4	14.6
1935	19.6	14.0	9.6	19.5	14.6	13.9	23.4	14.0	13.4	20.2	8.7	14.4
1936	19.6	14.4	10.0	20.3	14.4	14.3	22.4	13.8	14.8	20.2	8.7	15.0
1937	19.2	15.3	10.0	19.8	15.1	13.5	22.9	14.3	17.4	19.8	8.8	15.4
1938	19.4	13.6	10.2	20.0	13.7	13.4	23.8	14.1	15.0	20.5	8.5	15.4
1939	19.1	14.2	10.4	19.5	13.5	14.2	23.6	13.4	14.6	20.6	8.6	18.4
1940	19.1	14.2	10.2	19.5	14.6	15.1	23.5	13.6[41]	14.2	20.8	9.9	15.2
1941	19.0	14.6	10.0	20.5	15.2	18.3	20.9	13.9[41]	12.2	20.3	10.0	14.6
1942	22.3	14.1	11.8	22.3	13.3	17.6	20.5[42]	14.3[41] [42]	12.8[42]	21.0[44]	9.5[44]	19.4
1943	21.9	14.8	11.8	23.5	13.4	15.1	19.9	15.2[41]	9.6	23.0	10.0[44]	14.4
1944	22.2	15.3	11.4	22.8	12.8	14.0	18.3	15.3[41]	9.6	24.0	11.8[44]	11.0
1945	22.7	14.5	11.8	21.3	12.3	15.4	18.3	13.6[41]	13.8	22.6	15.3[44]	15.6
1946	22.9	14.0	11.8	22.3	12.5	14.5	23.0	12.1	18.4	30.2	8.5	22.8
1947	23.2	14.8	11.0	23.2	12.6	14.1	22.3	11.5	19.4	27.8	8.1	20.4
1948	22.0	12.1	10.8	21.7	11.2	13.8	22.0	10.6	16.8	25.3	7.4	18.0
1949	21.5	12.7	10.8	21.2	11.5	13.4	20.4	10.5	15.6	23.7	8.1	16.6

See p.135 for footnotes

B6 Vital Statistics: Rates per 1,000 Population

1900–1949

	Norway			Poland[45]			Portugal			Romania		
	B	D	M	B	D	M	B	D	M	B	D	M
1900	29.7	15.8	13.6	...	...	...	30.5	20.3	13.6	38.8	24.2	13.4
1901	29.9	15.0	13.1	...	...	...	31.3	20.9	13.9	39.3	26.2	14.2
1902	29.2	13.9	12.6	...	...	...	32.0	19.7	14.1	39.0	27.7	18.0
1903	28.6	14.8	11.9	...	...	...	33.0	20.1	13.9	40.1	24.8	17.4
1904	27.9	14.3	11.7	...	...	...	31.6	18.9	13.1	40.1	24.4	16.2
1905	27.1	14.8	11.5	...	...	...	31.8	20.0	13.3	38.3	24.7	15.8
1906	26.8	13.7	11.7	...	...	...	32.1	22.0	12.5	39.9	23.9	20.3
1907	26.3	14.3	12.0	...	...	...	30.7	19.7	12.3	41.1	26.3	21.0
1908	26.3	14.2	12.1	...	...	...	30.3	20.0	12.3	40.3	27.4	18.2
1909	26.8	13.6	11.9	...	...	...	29.9	19.2	12.3	41.1	27.4	18.4
1910	25.8	13.5	12.2	...	...	...	31.7	19.2	13.2	39.3	24.8	18.5
1911	25.7	13.2	12.4	...	...	...	38.6	22.0	13.8	42.3	25.3	21.0
1912	25.4	13.5	12.2	...	...	...	34.9	20.1	14.8	43.4	22.9	17.3
1913	25.1	13.3	12.5	...	...	...	32.5	20.6	11.7	42.1	26.1	18.3
1914	25.1	13.5	12.8	...	...	...	31.5	19.3	12.2	42.1	23.5	16.8
1915	23.6	13.4	12.8	...	...	...	32.6	20.5	12.0	40.5	24.5	14.3
1916	24.2	13.8	13.7	...	...	...	32.1	21.6	12.0	...	...	...
1917	25.1	13.6	14.2	...	...	...	31.4	22.3	11.1	...	...	...
1918	24.6	17.2	15.5	...	...	...	29.7	41.4	10.1	...[46]	...[46]	...[46]
1919	22.7	13.8	11.8	...	...	...	27.6	25.4	15.6	23.0	20.6	13.5
1920	26.1	12.8	14.0	...	...	...	33.6	23.7	17.6	33.7	25.9	25.8
1921	24.2	11.5	13.5	32.8	20.9	23.4	32.4	20.8	16.8	38.2	22.9	24.4
1922	23.3	12.1	12.8	35.3	19.9	22.9	33.1	20.4	16.3	37.2	22.8	20.6
1923	22.8	11.6	12.5	36.0	17.5	20.4	33.2	22.7	15.7	36.4	22.1	19.7
1924	21.3	11.3	12.2	35.0	18.2	18.8	32.8	20.0	14.6	36.7	22.5	18.2
1925	19.7	11.1	11.8	35.4	16.8	16.3	32.6	18.4	14.2	35.2	21.1	17.9
1926	19.6	10.8	11.5	33.1	17.8	17.2	33.5	19.8	14.8	34.8	21.4	18.3
1927	18.1	11.2	11.4	31.6	17.3	17.1	31.0	18.8	12.7	34.1	22.2	19.4
1928	17.9	10.9	12.0	32.0	16.4	19.2	31.9	18.7	13.7	34.7	19.6	17.7
1929	17.3	11.5	12.7	31.8	16.7	19.3	29.9	17.7	13.3	34.1	21.4	17.5
1930	17.0	10.6	12.9	32.3	15.6	19.1	29.7	17.1	14.0	35.0	19.4	18.6
1931	16.3	10.9	12.5	30.2	15.5	17.1	29.7	16.8	13.1	33.3	20.8	18.4
1932	16.0	10.6	12.4	28.9	15.0	16.7	29.9	17.1	13.0	35.9	21.7	19.0
1933	14.7	10.1	12.6	26.5	14.2	16.7	28.9	17.2	13.0	32.1	18.7	16.6
1934	14.6	9.9	13.4	26.6	14.4	16.7	28.4	16.6	13.3	32.4	20.7	18.4
1935	14.3	10.3	14.2	26.1	14.0	16.7	28.2	17.0	13.5	30.7	21.1	17.4
1936	14.6	10.4	15.4	26.2	14.2	16.7	28.1	16.3	12.7	31.5	19.8	18.4
1937	15.0	10.4	16.4	24.9	14.0	16.0	26.7	15.8	12.6	30.8	19.3	19.0
1938	15.4	10.0	16.6	24.3	13.7	16.1	26.6	15.4	13.0	29.6	19.2	17.6
1939	15.8	10.1	17.7	...	...	...	26.2	15.3	12.8	28.3[46]	18.6[46]	15.8[46]
1940	16.1	10.8	18.8	...	...	...	24.3	15.6	12.1	26.5[47]	19.1[47]	18.2[47]
1941	15.3	10.8	17.7	...	...	...	23.8	17.4	14.2	23.0[47]	19.3[47]	15.2[47]
1942	17.7	10.7	...	...	...	...	24.0	16.1	15.0	21.4[47]	19.5[47]	15.4[47]
1943	18.9	10.4	15.8	...	...	...	25.1	15.3	14.8	23.4[47]	18.1[47]	13.8[47]
1944	20.3	10.7	14.4	...	...	...	25.3	14.8	15.0	21.7[47]	19.6[47]	10.4[47]
1945	20.0	9.7	15.2	...	...	...	26.0	14.2	15.3	19.6[47]	20.0[47]	21.2[47]
1946	22.6	9.4	19.0	22.8	13.4	...	25.4	14.7	15.4	24.8	18.8	23.6
1947	21.4	9.5	18.9	26.2	11.3	...	24.5	13.3	16.5	23.4	22.0	19.6
1948	20.5	8.9	18.5	29.3	11.2	...	26.8	13.0	15.6	23.9	15.6	22.4
1949	19.5	9.0	17.0	29.4	11.6	22.4	25.5	14.1	15.7	27.6	13.7	23.2

See p.135 for footnotes

B6 Vital Statistics: Rates per 1,000 Population

1900–1949

	Russia[21]			Serbia			Spain			Sweden		
	B	D	M	B	D	M	B	D	M	B	D	M
1900	49.3	31.1	17.8	42.4	23.5	25.2	33.9	29.0	17.7	27.0	16.8	12.3
1901	47.9	32.1	17.2	38.0	21.0	16.6	35.0	27.8	16.9	27.0	16.1	12.1
1902	49.1	31.5	17.2	38.0	22.3	20.6	35.6	26.1	17.5	26.5	15.4	11.9
1903	48.1	30.0	17.8	40.9	23.5	19.0	36.4	25.0	16.4	25.7	15.1	11.6
1904	48.6	29.9	15.2	39.8	21.1	22.9	34.2	25.7	15.3	25.8	15.3	11.7
1905	45.0	31.7	15.2	37.3	24.8	19.8	35.1	25.7	14.3	25.7	15.6	11.7
1906	47.1	29.9	19.2	42.0	24.5	20.8	33.8	25.9	14.4	25.7	14.4	12.3
1907	47.5	28.4	18.0	40.0	22.4	21.2	33.3	24.4	14.1	25.5	14.6	12.4
1908	44.8	28.3	16.0	36.8	23.7	18.0	33.7	23.6	14.5	25.7	14.9	12.2
1909	44.7	29.5	16.0	38.7	29.3	18.8	33.1	23.7	13.2	25.6	13.7	11.9
1910	45.1	31.5	16.8	39.0	22.4	20.8	32.7	23.1	14.1	24.7	14.0	12.1
1911	45.0	27.4	16.0	36.3	21.8	20.6	31.5	23.4	14.3	24.0	13.8	11.8
1912	43.7	26.5	...	...	...	20.8	31.8	21.3	14.3	23.8	14.2	11.9
1913	43.1[21]	27.4[21]	...[21]	...	...	...	30.6	22.3	13.6	23.2	13.7	11.9
	47.0	30.2										
1914	...	...	...	...	...	...	29.9	22.2	13.2	22.9	13.8	11.6
1915	...	...	...	...	...	...	30.9	22.1	12.5	21.6	14.7	11.7
1916	...	...	...	...	...	...	29.1	21.4	13.3	21.2	13.6	12.2
1917	...	...	...	...	...	...	29.0	22.5	13.7	20.9	13.4	12.3
1918	...	...	...	...	...	...	29.3	33.3	13.5	20.3	18.0	13.3
1919	...	...	...	...	...	...	27.9	23.0	15.9	19.8	14.5	13.8
1920	30.9	...	...	...	...	...	29.5	23.4	16.6	23.6	13.3	14.6
1921	32.6	...	...	...	...	...	30.5	21.4	15.5	21.5	12.4	13.3
1922	33.4[21]	...	...	...	...	...	30.5	20.5	15.2	19.6	12.8	12.3
1923	38.8	...	...	...	...	...	30.5	20.7	14.5	18.9	11.4	12.6
1924	43.1	...	...	...	...	...	29.7	19.6	14.4	18.1	12.0	12.4
1925	44.7	...	...	...	...	...	29.1	19.2	14.3	17.6	11.7	12.4
1926	43.6	19.9	...	...	...	...	29.6	18.8	14.5	16.8	11.8	12.6
1927	43.2[21]	20.8[21]	...	...	...	...	28.1	18.6	14.1	16.1	12.7	12.8
1928	44.3	23.3	...	...	...	...	29.1	18.1	14.9	16.1	12.0	13.3
1929	...	...	...	...	...	...	28.3	17.6	14.6	15.2	12.2	13.7
1930	...	...	...	...	...	...	28.3	16.9	14.9	15.4	11.7	14.3
1931	...	...	...	...	...	...	27.6	17.4	14.9	14.8	12.5	13.9
1932	...	...	...	...	...	...	28.2	16.4	13.3	14.5	11.6	13.5
1933	...	...	...	...	...	...	27.7	16.4	12.3	13.7	11.2	14.0
1934	...	...	...	...	...	...	26.2	16.0	12.0	13.7	11.2	15.5
1935	30.1[21]	...	...	...	...	...	25.7	15.7	12.3	13.8	11.7	16.4
1936	33.6[21]	...	...	...	...	...	24.7	16.7	11.2	14.2	12.0	17.0
1937	38.7	18.9	...	...	...	...	22.6	18.9	11.4	14.4	12.0	17.7
1938	37.5	17.5	...	...	...	...	20.0	19.2	8.9	14.9	11.5	18.5
1939	36.5	17.3	...	...	...	...	16.5	18.4	11.3	15.4	11.5	19.4
1940	31.2	18.3	...	...	...	...	24.4	16.5	16.8	15.1	11.4	18.6
1941	...	...	...	...	...	...	19.6	18.6	14.6	15.6	11.3	18.2
1942	...	...	...	...	...	...	20.2	14.7	14.3	17.7	9.9	19.8
1943	...	...	...	...	...	...	22.9	13.2	13.2	19.3	10.2	19.4
1944	...	...	...	...	...	...	22.5	13.0	14.1	20.6	11.0	19.7
1945	...	...	...	...	...	...	23.1	12.2	14.4	20.4	10.8	19.4
1946	23.8	10.8	...	...	...	...	21.4	12.9	15.0	19.7	10.5	19.0
1947	...	...	...	...	...	...	21.4	12.0	16.5	18.9	10.8	17.5
1948	...	...	...	...	...	...	23.1	10.9	15.6	18.4	9.8	16.9
1949	...	...	...	...	...	...	21.5	11.4	14.2	17.4	10.0	15.9

See p.135 for footnotes

B6 Vital Statistics: Rates per 1,000 Population

1900–1949

	Switzerland			United Kingdom: England and Wales			United Kingdom: Scotland			Yugoslavia[48]		
	B	D	M	B	D	M	B	D	M	B	D	M
1900	28.6	19.3	15.4	28.7	18.2	16.0	29.6	18.5	14.6	...	...	...
1901	29.0	18.0	15.2	28.5	16.9	15.9	29.5	17.9	14.0	...	...	...
1902	28.5	17.0	14.8	28.5	16.3	15.9	29.3	17.3	14.2	...	...	...
1903	27.4	17.4	14.8	28.5	15.5	15.7	29.4	16.8	14.3	...	...	...
1904	27.3	17.5	14.6	28.0	16.3	15.3	29.1	17.1	14.1	...	...	...
1905	26.9	17.6	15.0	27.3	15.3	15.3	28.6	16.2	13.6	...	...	...
1906	26.9	16.6	15.4	27.2	15.5	15.7	28.6	16.4	14.3	...	...	...
1907	26.2	16.4	15.4	26.5	15.1	15.9	27.7	16.6	14.3	...	...	...
1908	26.4	15.8	15.2	26.7	14.8	15.1	28.1	16.6	13.5	...	...	...
1909	25.5	16.1	14.8	25.8	14.6	14.7	27.3	15.8	12.8	...	...	...
1910	25.0	15.1	14.6	25.1	13.5	15.0	26.2	15.3	13.0	...	...	...
1911	24.2	15.8	14.8	24.3	14.6	15.2	25.6	15.1	13.4	...	...	...
1912	24.2	14.2	14.6	23.9	13.3	15.6	25.9	15.3	13.7	...	...	...
1913	23.2	14.3	13.8	24.1	13.8	15.7	25.5	15.5	14.2	...	...	...
1914	22.4	13.8	11.4	23.8	14.0	15.9	26.1	15.5	14.8	...	...	...
1915	19.5	13.3	10.0	21.9	15.7[31]	19.4	23.9	17.1	15.2	...	...	...
1916	18.9	13.0	11.4	20.9	14.3[31]	14.9	22.8	14.7	13.1	...	...	...
1917	18.5	13.7	12.0	17.8	14.2[31]	13.8	20.1	14.4	12.6	...	...	...
1918	18.7	19.3	13.4	17.7	17.3[31]	15.3	20.2	16.3	14.3	...	...	...
1919	18.6	14.2	15.8	18.5	14.0[31]	19.7	21.7	15.6	18.3	...	...	...
1920	20.9	14.4	18.0	25.5	12.4	20.2	28.1	14.0	19.2	...	...	...
1921	20.8	12.8	16.8	22.4	12.1	16.9	25.2	13.6	16.1	36.7	20.9	26.0
1922	19.7	13.0	15.6	20.4	12.7	15.7	23.5	14.9	14.0	34.4	20.8	21.6
1923	19.4	11.8	15.2	19.7	11.6	15.2	22.9	12.9	14.4	34.8	20.3	20.8
1924	18.9	12.6	14.6	18.8	12.2	15.3	22.0	14.5	13.3	35.1	20.2	18.2
1925	18.5	12.2	14.4	18.3	12.1	15.2	21.4	13.5	13.3	34.2	18.7	19.2
1926	18.3	11.8	14.2	17.8	11.6	14.3	21.1	13.1	12.8	35.3	18.8	19.2
1927	17.5	12.4	14.4	16.6	12.3	15.7	19.9	13.6	13.4	34.3	21.0	18.8
1928	17.4	12.0	15.0	16.7	11.7	15.4	20.0	13.5	13.6	32.7	20.4	18.2
1929	17.1	12.5	15.6	16.3	13.4	15.8	19.2	14.7	13.6	33.3	21.1	18.8
1930	17.2	11.6	15.8	16.3	11.4	15.8	19.6	13.3	13.8	35.5	19.0	20.0
1931	16.7	12.1	15.8	15.8	12.3	15.6	19.0	13.3	13.5	33.6	19.8	18.0
1932	16.7	12.2	15.6	15.3	12.0	15.3	18.6	13.5	13.6	32.9	19.2	15.6
1933	16.4	11.4	15.6	14.4	12.3	15.8	17.6	13.2	13.9	31.5	17.0	15.4
1934	16.3	11.3	15.6	14.8	11.8	16.9	18.0	12.9	15.0	31.6	17.1	13.6
1935	16.0	12.1	14.6	14.7	11.7	17.2	17.8	13.2	15.3	29.9	16.9	15.0
1936	15.6	11.4	14.2	14.8	12.1	17.4	17.9	13.4	15.3	29.1	16.1	14.6
1937	14.9	11.3	14.6	14.9	12.4	17.5	17.6	13.9	15.4	28.0	16.0	15.6
1938	15.2	11.6	14.8	15.1	11.6	17.6	17.7	12.6	15.5	26.7	15.6	15.8
1939	15.2	11.8	15.0	14.8	12.1[31]	21.2	17.4	12.9	18.5	25.9	15.0	15.8
1940	15.2	12.0	15.4	14.1	14.4[31]	22.5	17.1	14.9	21.2	...	...	...
1941	16.9	11.1	17.0	13.9	13.5[31]	18.6	17.5	14.7	18.6	...	...	...
1942	18.4	10.9	17.2	15.6	12.3[31]	17.7	17.6	13.3	18.4	...	...	...
1943	19.2	11.0	16.6	16.2	13.0[31]	14.0	18.4	14.0	14.8	...	...	...
1944	19.6	12.0	16.0	17.7	12.7[31]	14.3	18.5	13.6	14.3	...	...	...
1945	20.1	11.6	16.2	15.9	12.6[31]	18.7	16.9	13.2	18.9	...	...	...
1946	20.0	11.3	17.4	19.2	12.0[31]	18.1	20.3	13.1	17.8	...[49]	...[49]	...[49]
1947	19.4	11.4	17.4	20.5	12.3	18.6	22.3	13.1	17.5	26.6	12.8	26.2
1948	19.2	10.8	17.2	17.8	11.0	18.2	19.7	12.0	17.2	28.1	13.5	25.6
1949	18.4	10.7	16.0	16.7	11.8	17.1	18.8	12.5	16.4	30.0	13.5	22.8

See p.135 for footnotes

B6 Vital Statistics: Rates per 1,000 Population

1950–1975

	Albania			Austria			Belgium			Bulgaria		
	B	D	M	B	D	M	B	D	M	B	D	M
1950	38.8	14.1	20.2	15.6	12.4	18.6	16.5	12.0	16.6	25.2	11.5	21.4
1951	38.5	15.2	20.2	14.8	12.7	18.2	16.4	12.4	16.2	21.1	10.7	17.6
1952	35.2	15.6	20.6	14.9	12.0	16.6	16.7	11.8	15.4	21.2	11.6	19.2
1953	40.9	13.7	19.4	14.8	12.0	15.6	16.7	12.1	15.4	20.9	9.3	18.6
1954	40.8	13.1	16.0	15.0	12.2	15.6	16.8	11.9	15.4	20.2	9.2	17.2
1955	44.5	15.1	16.4	15.6	12.2	16.4	16.7	12.2	15.5	20.1	9.1	17.0
1956	41.9	11.5	14.6	16.7	12.5	16.6	16.8	12.1	15.3	19.5	9.4	17.6
1957	39.1	11.8	16.2	17.0	12.8	16.2	17.0	11.9	15.1	18.4	8.6	17.4
1958	41.8	9.3	15.8	17.1	12.3	15.8	17.1	11.7	14.8	17.9	7.9	18.2
1959	41.9	9.8	14.8	17.7	12.5	15.8	17.4	11.4	14.3	17.6	9.5	17.2
1960	43.4	10.4	15.6	17.9	12.7	16.6	16.9	12.4	14.2	17.8	8.1	17.6
1961	41.2	9.3	22.6	18.6	12.1	17.0	17.2	11.6	13.6	17.4	7.9	16.8
1962	39.3	10.7	15.0	18.7	12.7	16.8	16.8	12.2	13.4	16.7	8.7	16.2
1963	39.1	10.0	15.0	18.8	12.8	16.2	17.1	12.5	13.4	16.4	8.2	16.4
1964	37.8	8.7	14.4	18.5	12.3	16.0	17.1	11.7	13.8	16.1	7.9	16.2
1965	35.2	9.0	15.0	17.9	13.0	15.6	16.4	12.1	14.0	15.3	8.2	16.0
1966	34.0	8.6	13.6	17.6	12.5	15.4	15.9	12.1	14.3	14.9	8.3	16.4
1967	35.3	8.4	17.2	17.4	13.0	15.4	15.3	12.0	14.2	15.0	9.0	17.4
1968	35.6	8.0	15.6	17.2	13.1	15.2	14.8	12.6	14.4	16.9	8.6	17.8
1969	35.3	7.5	14.8	16.5	13.4	15.8	14.7	12.5	15.0	17.0	9.5	17.4
1970	32.5	9.3	13.6	15.2	13.4	14.2	14.7	12.3	15.2	16.3	9.1	17.2
1971	33.3	8.1	14.0	14.6	13.1	13.0	14.6	12.3	15.2	15.9	9.7	16.3
1972	...	...	...	13.9	12.7	15.4	14.0	12.1	15.4	15.3	9.8	16.4
1973	...	...	...	13.0	12.3	13.2	13.3	12.1	15.2	16.2	9.5	17.2
1974	...	...	...	12.9	12.5	13.0	12.7	11.9	15.4	17.2	9.8	17.0
1975	...	...	...	12.5	12.8	12.4	12.2	12.2	14.8	16.6	10.3	17.2

	Czechoslovakia			Denmark			Finland			France		
	B	D	M	B	D	M	B	D	M	B	D	M
1950	23.3	11.5	21.6	18.7	9.2	18.2	24.5	10.2	17.0	20.5	12.7	15.8
1951	22.8	11.4	20.2	17.8	8.8	17.0	23.0	10.0	16.0	19.5	13.3	15.2
1952	22.2[50]	10.6[50]	17.6	17.8	9.0	16.4	23.1	9.5	15.8	19.3	12.3	14.8
1953	21.2	10.5	15.4	17.9	9.0	16.2	22.0	9.6	15.4	18.7	12.9	14.4
1954	20.6	10.4	15.8	17.3	9.1	15.8	21.5	9.1	15.6	18.7	12.0	14.6
1955	20.3	9.6	15.8	17.3	8.7	15.8	21.2	9.3	15.4	18.5	12.0	14.4
1956	19.8	9.6	17.6	17.2	8.9	15.4	20.8	9.0	15.4	18.4	12.4	13.5
1957	18.9	10.1	13.6	16.8	9.3	15.2	20.1	9.4	14.4	18.4	11.9	14.0
1958	17.4	9.3	14.8	16.5	9.2	15.0	18.6	8.9	14.4	18.1	11.1	13.9
1959	16.0	9.7	15.2	16.3	9.3	15.2	18.9	8.8	14.4	18.3	11.2	14.2
1960	15.9	9.2	15.6	16.6	9.5	15.6	18.5	9.0	14.8	17.9	11.3	14.0
1961	15.8	9.2	15.4	16.6	9.4	15.8	18.4	9.1	15.4	18.2	10.8	13.6
1962	15.7	10.0	15.6	16.7	9.7	16.2	18.1	9.6	15.2	17.7	11.4	13.5
1963	16.9	9.5	15.8	17.6	9.8	16.4	18.2	9.3	14.8	18.2	11.6	14.2
1964	17.2	9.6	15.8	17.7	9.9	16.8	17.7	9.4	15.2	18.2	10.7	14.4
1965	16.4	10.0	15.8	18.0	10.1	17.6	17.1	9.7	15.8	17.8	11.1	14.1
1966	15.6	10.0	16.2	18.4	10.3	17.2	17.0	9.5	16.8	17.6	10.7	13.8
1967	15.1	10.1	16.8	16.8	9.9	17.0	16.8	9.5	18.0	17.0	10.9	14.0
1968	14.9	10.7	17.2	15.3	9.7	16.2	15.9	9.7	17.4	16.7	11.0	14.2
1969	15.5	11.2	17.4	14.6	9.8	16.0	14.6	9.9	17.8	16.7	11.5	15.2
1970	15.9	11.6	17.6	14.4	9.8	14.8	14.0	9.6	17.8	16.7	10.6	15.6
1971	16.5	11.5	18.0	15.2	9.8	13.2	13.2	9.9	16.4	17.1	10.7	15.8
1972	17.4	11.1	18.6	15.1	10.1	12.4	12.7	9.5	15.4	16.9	10.6	16.2
1973	18.9	11.6	19.4	14.3	10.1	12.2	12.2	9.3	15.0	16.4	10.7	15.4
1974	19.8	11.7	19.2	14.1	10.2	13.2	13.3	9.5	14.8	15.3	10.5	15.0
1975	19.5	11.5	19.0	14.2	10.0	12.6	14.1	9.3	14.4	14.1	10.6	14.6

See p.135 for footnotes

B6 Vital Statistics: Rates per 1,000 Population

1950–1975

	West Germany			East Germany			Greece			Hungary		
	B	D	M	B	D	M	B	D	M	B	D	M
1950	16.2	10.5	21.4	16.5	11.9	23.4	20.0	7.1	15.4	20.9	11.5	22.8
1951	15.7	10.8	20.6	16.9	11.4	21.2	20.3	7.5	16.6	20.2	11.7	19.8
1952	15.7	10.7	19.0	16.7	12.1	19.2	19.3	6.9	12.8	19.6	11.3	22.0
1953	15.5	11.3	18.0	16.4	11.7	17.4	18.4	7.3	15.6	21.6	11.7	19.0
1954	15.7	10.7	17.4	16.3	12.2	16.8	19.2	7.0	16.0	23.0	11.0	22.2
1955	15.7	11.1	17.6	16.3	11.9	17.4	19.4[51]	6.9[51]	16.6[51]	21.4	10.0	21.0
1956	16.1	11.3	18.0	15.9	12.0	17.2	19.7	7.4	13.8	19.5	10.5	19.4
1957	16.6	11.5	18.0	15.6	12.9	17.2	19.3	7.6	17.0	17.0	10.5	20.0
1958	16.7	11.0	18.2	15.6	12.7	17.8	19.0	7.1	16.9	16.0	9.9	18.6
1959	17.3	11.0	18.4	16.9	13.3	18.8	19.4	7.4	18.0	15.2	10.5	18.2
1960	17.4	11.6	18.8	17.0	13.6	19.4	18.9	7.3	14.0	14.7	10.2	17.8
1961	18.0	11.2	18.8	17.6	13.0	19.8	17.9	7.6	16.9	14.0	9.6	16.6
1962	17.9	11.3	18.6	17.4	13.7	19.4	18.0	7.9	16.7	12.9	10.8	16.2
1963	18.3	11.7	17.6	17.6	12.9	17.2	17.5	7.9	18.4	13.1	9.9	16.8
1964	18.2	11.0	17.4	17.2	13.3	16.0	18.0	8.2	17.9	13.1	10.0	17.4
1965	17.7	11.5	16.6	16.5	13.5	15.2	17.7	7.9	18.9	13.1	10.7	17.6
1966	17.6	11.5	16.2	15.7	13.2	14.2	17.9	7.9	16.6	13.6	10.0	18.4
1967	17.0	11.5	16.2	14.8	13.3	13.8	18.7	8.3	18.7	14.6	10.7	18.8
1968	16.1	12.2	14.8	14.3	14.2	14.0	18.3	8.4	15.0	15.0	11.2	18.6
1969	14.8	12.2	14.6	14.0	14.3	14.6	17.6	8.2	16.6	15.0	11.3	18.6
1970	13.4	12.1	14.6	13.9	14.1	15.4	16.5	8.4	15.4	14.7	11.6	18.8
1971	12.7	11.9	14.0	13.8	13.8	15.2	16.0	8.4	16.6	14.5	11.9	18.2
1972	11.3	11.8	13.4	11.8	13.8	15.6	15.9	8.6	13.6	14.7	11.4	18.8
1973	10.3	11.8	12.8	10.6	13.7	16.2	15.4	8.7	16.6	15.0	11.8	19.4
1974	10.1	11.7	12.2	10.6	13.5	16.2	16.1	8.5	15.2	17.8	12.0	19.0
1975	9.7	12.1	12.6	10.8	14.3	16.8	15.7	8.9	17.0	18.4	12.4	19.8

	Ireland			Northern Ireland			Italy			Netherlands		
	B	D	M	B	D	M	B	D	M	B	D	M
1950	21.4	12.7	10.8	21.0	11.6	13.3	19.6[42]	9.8[42]	15.4[42]	22.7	7.5	16.4
1951	21.2	14.3	10.8	20.7	12.8	13.7	18.4	10.3	14.0	22.3	7.6	17.6
1952	21.9	11.9	10.8	20.9	10.8	13.5	17.8	10.0	14.2	22.3	7.4	16.8[52]
1953	21.2	11.8	10.8	20.9	10.7	13.6	17.5	9.9	14.2	21.7	7.7	16.4
1954	21.3	12.1	10.8	20.8	10.9	13.2	18.0	9.1	14.8	21.5	7.5	16.6
1955	21.0	12.6	11.2	20.8	11.1	13.7	17.7	9.1	15.0	21.3	7.6	16.6
1956	21.0	11.7	11.6	21.1	10.6	13.4	17.7	10.1	14.8	21.3	7.8	17.0
1957	21.2	11.9	10.2	21.5	10.9	13.4	17.7	9.7	14.6	21.2	7.5	17.0
1958	20.9	12.0	10.6	21.6	10.8	13.2	17.6	9.3	15.2	21.2	7.6[53]	16.4
1959	21.1	12.0	10.8	21.9	10.9	13.7	18.1	9.1	15.4	21.4	7.6	15.6
1960	21.5	11.5	11.0	22.5	10.8	13.9	18.1	9.6	15.4	20.8	7.7	15.6
1961	21.2	12.3	10.8	22.4	11.3	13.8	18.4	9.3	15.8	21.3	7.6	17.0
1962	21.8	12.0	11.0	22.7	10.6	13.8	18.4	10.0	16.0	20.9	8.0	15.8
1963	22.2	11.9	11.0	23.1	11.0	14.0	18.6	10.0	16.4	20.9	8.0	16.0
1964	22.4	11.4	11.2	23.6	10.5	14.6	19.5	9.4	16.0	20.7	7.7	17.0
1965	22.1	11.5	11.8	23.1	10.6	14.2	18.8	9.8	15.2	19.9	8.0	17.6
1966	21.6	12.2	11.6	22.5	11.1	14.5	18.4	9.3	14.4	19.2	8.1	18.0
1967	21.1	10.8	12.2	22.4	9.8	14.7	17.7	9.5	14.2	18.9	7.9	18.2
1968	20.9	11.4	13.0	22.1	10.6	15.0	17.3	9.9	14.0	18.6	8.2	18.4
1969	21.5	11.5	14.0	21.4	10.8	15.3	17.5	10.0	14.2	19.2	8.4	18.2
1970	21.8	11.4	14.2	21.0	10.8	16.2	16.8	9.6	14.6	18.3	8.4	19.0
1971	22.7	10.7	14.6	20.7	10.5	15.8	16.8	9.7	15.0	17.2	8.4	18.6
1972	22.7	11.4	14.8	19.4	11.0	15.4	16.3	9.6	15.4	16.1	8.5	17.6
1973	22.5	11.3	15.0	18.9	11.4	14.6	15.9	10.0	15.2	14.5	8.2	16.0
1974	22.3	11.2	14.6	17.6	11.2	14.0	15.7	9.6	14.6	13.7	8.1	16.2
1975	21.6	10.7	13.8	17.0	10.7	14.2	14.8	9.9	13.4	13.0	8.3	14.6

See p. 135 for footnotes

B6 Vital Statistics: Rates per 1,000 Population

1950–1975

	Norway			Poland			Portugal			Romania		
	B	D	M	B	D	M	B	D	M	B	D	M
1950	19.1	9.1	16.7	30.7	11.6	21.6	24.3	12.2	15.5	26.2	12.4	23.4
1951	18.4	8.4	16.5	31.0	12.4	21.4	24.6	12.5	15.8	25.1	12.8	20.6
1952	18.8	8.5	16.5	30.2	11.1	20.8	24.9	11.8	15.8	24.8	11.7	20.4
1953	18.8	8.5	16.1	29.7	10.2	20.0	23.7	11.4	15.8	23.8	11.6	20.8
1954	18.5	8.6	15.9	29.1	10.3	19.6	23.1	11.1	16.2	24.8	11.5	24.2
1955	18.5	8.5	15.3	29.1	9.6	19.0	24.4	11.6	17.0	25.6	9.7	22.8
1956	18.5	8.7	14.5	28.1	9.0	18.8	23.4	12.4	15.2	24.2	9.9	23.4
1957	18.1	8.8	14.0	27.6	9.5	18.2	24.4	11.7	16.5	22.9	10.2	22.8
1958	17.9	9.0	13.6	26.3	8.4	18.4	24.4	10.5	16.8	21.6	8.7	23.4
1959	17.7	8.9	13.1	24.7	8.6	19.0	24.3	11.1	17.3	20.2	10.2	21.4
1960	17.3	9.1	13.2	22.6	7.6	16.4	24.2	10.8	15.7	19.1	8.7	21.4
1961	17.3	9.2	13.4	20.9	7.6	15.8	24.5	11.2	17.5	17.5	8.7	19.4
1962	17.1	9.4	13.2	19.8	7.9	15.0	24.5	10.8	15.7	16.2	9.2	19.8
1963	17.3	10.1	13.1	19.2	7.5	14.4	23.5	10.8	15.7	15.7	8.3	18.6
1964	17.8	9.5	13.5	18.1	7.6	14.8	23.8	10.6	16.0	15.2	8.1	18.0
1965	17.8	9.5	13.0	17.4	7.4	12.6	22.9	10.3	16.3	14.6	8.6	17.2
1966	17.9	9.6	14.8	16.7	7.3	14.2	22.2	10.8	16.5	14.3	8.2	17.8
1967	17.6	9.6	15.4	16.3	7.8	15.0	21.5	10.2	16.8	27.4	9.3	16.0
1968	17.6	9.9	15.4	16.2	7.6	16.0	20.6	10.0	16.1	26.7	9.6	15.0
1969	17.6	10.1	15.4	16.3	8.1	16.6	21.7	10.6	18.2	23.3	10.1	14.0
1970	16.6	10.0	15.2	16.8	8.2	17.2	20.0	10.7	18.3	21.1	9.5	14.4
1971	16.8	10.0	15.2	17.1	8.6	17.8	21.9	11.4	18.8	19.5	9.5	14.6
1972	16.3	10.0	14.6	17.4	8.0	18.6	20.3	10.5	18.0	18.8	9.2	15.2
1973	15.5	10.1	14.2	17.9	8.3	18.8	20.1	11.1	19.7	18.2	9.8	16.4
1974	15.0	9.9	13.8	18.4	8.2	19.0	19.6	11.0	18.6	20.3	9.1	16.8
1975	14.1	9.9	13.2	18.9	8.7	19.4	19.0	10.4	21.8	19.7	9.3	17.8

	Russia			Spain			Sweden		
	B	D	M	B	D	M	B	D	M
1950	26.7	9.7	...	20.1	10.8	15.0	16.5	10.0	15.5
1951	27.0	9.7	...	20.0	11.5	14.9	15.6	9.9	15.3
1952	26.5	9.4	...	20.7	9.6	15.5	15.5	9.6	15.0
1953	25.1	9.1	...	20.4	9.6	15.2	15.4	9.7	14.8
1954	26.6	8.9	...	19.8	9.0	15.9	14.6	9.6	14.7
1955	25.7	8.2	...	20.4	9.3	16.2	14.8	9.5	14.4
1956	25.7	7.6	...	20.5	9.7	17.5	14.8	9.6	14.1
1957	25.4	7.8	...	21.6	9.8	17.0	14.6	9.9	14.3
1958	25.3	7.2	...	21.7	8.6	16.9	14.2	9.6	13.7
1959	25.0	7.6	24.4	21.5	8.8	16.2	14.1	9.5	13.5
1960	24.9	7.1	...	21.6	8.7	15.6	13.7	10.0	13.4
1961	23.8	7.2	22.0	21.1	8.4	15.5	13.9	9.8	13.9
1962	22.4	7.5	20.0	21.1	8.8	15.3	14.2	10.2	14.3
1963	21.2	7.2	18.2	21.3	8.9	15.2	14.9	10.1	14.1
1964	19.6	6.9	17.0	21.8	8.5	14.7	16.0	10.0	15.3
1965	18.4	7.3	17.4	20.9	8.4	14.3	15.9	10.1	15.5
1966	18.2	7.3	17.8	20.5	8.4	14.2	15.8	10.1	15.7
1967	17.3	7.6	18.0	20.6	8.4	14.3	15.4	10.1	14.4
1968	17.2	7.7	17.8	20.0	8.4	14.1	14.3	10.4	13.3
1969	17.0	8.1	18.8	19.8	8.9	14.4	13.5	10.5	12.2
1970	17.4	8.2	19.6	19.5	11.2	14.7	13.7	9.9	10.8
1971	17.8	8.2	20.0	19.6	10.6	14.9	14.1	10.2	9.8
1972	17.8	8.5	18.8	19.4	11.2	15.3	13.8	10.3	9.8
1973	17.6	8.7	20.2	19.2	10.7	15.5	13.5	10.5	9.4
1974	18.0	8.7	20.8	19.4	11.0	15.2	13.5	10.6	11.0
1975	18.1	9.3	21.4	18.9	11.5	15.3	12.6	10.8	10.8

B6 Vital Statistics: Rates per 1,000 Population

1950–1975

	Switzerland			United Kingdom: England and Wales			United Kingdom: Scotland			Yugoslavia		
	B	D	M	B	D	M	B	D	M	B	D	M
1950	18.1	10.1	15.8	15.8	11.6	16.3	18.1	12.5	15.8	30.2	13.0	22.8
1951	17.2	10.5	15.8	15.5	12.5	16.5	17.8	12.9	16.2	27.0	14.1	20.6
1952	17.4	9.9	15.6	15.3	11.3	15.9	17.7	12.1	16.1	29.7	11.8	21.0
1953	17.0	10.2	15.4	15.5	11.4	15.6	17.8	11.5	16.0	28.4	12.4	19.6
1954	17.0	10.0	15.6	15.2	11.3	15.4	18.1	12.0	16.4	28.6	10.9	19.8
1955	17.1	10.1	16.0	15.0	11.7	16.1	18.1	12.1	16.9	26.9	11.4	18.6
1956	17.4	10.2	16.0	15.7	11.7	15.8	18.6	12.1	17.2	26.0	11.2	17.6
1957	17.7	10.0	16.2	16.1	11.5	15.4	19.1	11.9	16.7	23.9	10.7	17.4
1958	17.6	9.5	15.4	16.4	11.7	15.1	19.4	12.1	16.0	24.0	9.3	18.8
1959	17.7	9.5	15.2	16.5	11.6	15.0	19.2	12.2	15.7	23.4	9.9	18.0
1960	17.6	9.7	15.6	17.1	11.5	15.0	19.6	11.9	15.5	23.5	9.9	18.2
1961	18.3	9.5	15.6	17.6	11.9	15.0	19.5	12.3	15.7	22.7	9.0	18.2
1962	18.7	9.9	16.0	18.0	11.9	14.9	20.1	12.2	15.5	21.9	9.9	17.2
1963	19.3	10.1	15.4	18.2	12.2	14.9	19.7	12.6	15.2	21.4	8.9	16.6
1964	19.5	9.3	15.2	18.5	11.3	15.2	20.0	11.7	15.5	20.8	9.4	17.4
1965	19.1	9.5	15.4	18.1	11.6	15.6	19.3	12.1	15.5	21.0	8.8	18.0
1966	18.5	9.4	15.0	17.8	11.8	16.1	18.6	12.2	16.1	20.4	8.1	17.2
1967	17.9	9.2	15.2	17.3	11.4	16.0	18.5	11.4	16.2	19.6	8.8	17.0
1968	17.3	9.5	15.0	16.9	11.8	16.9	18.2	12.2	16.8	19.1	8.7	17.0
1969	16.7	9.5	15.2	16.4	12.0	16.3	17.3	12.3	16.6	18.9	9.3	17.2
1970	16.0	9.2	15.2	16.1	11.8	17.1	16.8	12.2	16.6	17.8	8.9	18.0
1971	15.5	9.3	14.4	16.0	11.6	16.6	16.6	11.8	16.3	18.3	8.7	17.8
1972	14.3	8.8	13.6	14.8	12.1	17.4	15.1	12.5	16.2	18.3	9.2	18.0
1973	13.6	8.9	12.6	13.8	12.0	16.3	14.3	12.4	16.1	18.0	8.6	17.6
1974	13.1	8.8	12.0	13.0	11.9	15.6	13.4	12.4	15.8	18.1	8.4	17.2
1975	12.3	8.7	11.0	12.2	11.1	15.4	13.1	12.1	15.1	18.1	8.7	17.0

B6 Vital Statistics: Rates per 1,000 Population

NOTES

1. SOURCES:— As for table B.5, except that Russian statistics to 1913 are taken from A.F. Rashin, *Naselenie Rossii za 100 let* (Moscow, 1956), and the U.S.S.R. statistics for the interwar period are taken from F. Lorimer, *The Population of the Soviet Union* (Geneva, 1946).

2. In principle birth rates refer to live births and death rates do not include stillbirths.

FOOTNOTES

[1] Earlier, slightly less reliable data, are as follows:—

	Norway		Sweden	
	Births	Deaths	Births	Deaths
1735	29.4	19.3	...	...
1736	30.7	20.9	29.8	27.0
1737	30.5	24.8	30.5	33.7
1738	28.1	23.2	33.6	30.5
1739	30.9	23.2	36.4	30.6
1740	29.6	26.1	32.0	35.5
1741	27.1	36.9	31.9	32.2
1742	26.3	69.3	31.5	39.0
1743	28.5	29.2	30.1	43.7
1744	30.1	22.1	35.1	25.3
1745	32.8	18.8	36.9	23.3
1746	28.2	21.2	34.8	26.4
1747	33.0	23.9	34.6	27.5
1748	32.9	33.1	33.5	26.0

[2] Cisleithania (excluding Lombardy and Venetia) to 1913. The present territory of the Republic subsequently.
[3] Parts of Limburg and Luxembourg were ceded to the Netherlands.
[4] Excluding the Duchies of Schleswig, Holstein, and Lauenburg.
[5] Of the territorial changes affecting Finland in 1809, 1811, and 1820 (referred to on p.viii) only the inclusion of Viipuri province in 1811 can have affected vital rates at all.
[6] Figures to 1916 apply to the German Empire as it was in 1913. This means that Alsace-Lorraine and Schleswig-Holstein are included throughout. Alsace-Lorraine is excluded from 1917. Other territorial changes are referred to in subsequent footnotes.
[7] The Grand Duchy of Luxembourg is excluded throughout.
[8] These figures are known to be underestimates. It is also known that registration was incomplete until the 1860's.
[9] Previously the figures apply to the civil population only.
[10] Figures from 1888 include Eastern Roumelia.
[11] Figures from 1861 include Savoy and Nice.
[12] Figures from 1871 to 1913 exclude the parts of Alsace and Lorraine ceded to Germany.
[13] The statistics for the period up to 1890 are known to be incomplete.
[14] Figures from 1882 include Thessaly and Arta.
[15] The Ancient Kingdom (excluding Croatia-Slavonia) up to 1918 (1st line). Subsequently the territory established by the treaty of Trianon and later adjusted. For statistics for Croatia-Slavonia see footnote 48.
[16] Figures from 1891 include Fiume.
[17] Venetia and the Papal States are included prior to their incorporation.
[18] Including the Azores and Maderia.
[19] The statistics for the period to 1878 are known to be incomplete.
[20] Figures from 1879 include northern Dobrudja but exclude southern Bessarabia.
[21] Figures to 1913 (1st line) apply to the 50 provinces of European Russia (excluding Finland, Poland and the Caucasus). The 2nd line for 1913 relates to the U.S.S.R. as constitued in 1924. The figures for 1920–22 relate to 20 European provinces, and those for 1923–27 to the European part of the U.S.S.R. Figures from 1928 apply to the U.S.S.R. as cinstituted at the time. The statistics for 1935–36 are estimates (see source).
[22] Figures from 1879 include Vranje, Niš, Pirot, and Toplica, acquired from Turkey.
[23] Including the Canary Islands.
[24] Figures from 1925 include Eupen, Malmédy, etc., acquired from Germany.
[25] 41 communes were excluded in these years. In addition, in 1940 the statistics for Tournai and Wavre are missing.
[26] Figures from 1941 include southern Dobrudja.
[27] Includes deaths in the armed forces stationed abroad.
[28] Figures from 1939 exclude Sub-Carpathian Russia (Ruthenia), and those from 1945 exclude 12 villages in Slovakia ceded to the U.S.S.R.
[29] Figures from 1948 include the Bratislava Bridgehead.
[30] Estimates were made for the departments affected by war. Military losses are excluded.

[31] Military losses are excluded.
[32] Figures from 1919 exclude territory ceded to Czechoslovakia, Denmark, and Poland (except in Silesia).
[33] Figures from 1922 exclude Eupen, Malmédy, etc., and part of Upper Silesia ceded to Poland.
[34] Rates for the same area in 1938 are as follows:–
births: 19.5; deaths: 11.4; marriages 19.0.
[35] These statistics are less reliable than the remainder since 1920.
[36] Figures from 1949 include the Dodecanese Islands.
[37] Excludes deaths among the armed forces, but the rates were calculated on the basis of the population including the armed forces.
[38] Subsequently excludes the Bratislava Bridgehead, ceded to Czechoslovakia in 1947.
[39] Includes estimates for areas affected by the war.
[40] Figures from 1920 include territory acquired from Austria-Hungary.
[41] Deaths in the war zone and of military personnel abroad are not included.
[42] Figures from 1943 are for the territory established after the Second World War, except that Trieste is not included until 1951.
[43] Up to 1917 children born alive but dying before registration were included in neither births nor deaths. Subsequently they were included in both.
[44] Deaths outside the country are normally included if registered within 1 year, but in these years deaths of deportees were excluded. Deaths among alien armed forces were also excluded.
[45] Boundaries of the day.
[46] From 1919 to 1939 the statistics apply to the territory established by the treaty of Trianon. In the following six years there were several boundary changes, but only two of them, made in 1940, were permanent, namely the cession of southern Dobrudja to Bulgaria, and of Bessarabia and northern Bukovina to the U.S.S.R. The figures for 1919 appear to be defective.
[47] Excluding northern Transylvania, temporarily ceded to Hungary, and Bessarabia and northern Bukovina (except when reconquered in 1943), ceded to the U.S.S.R. Statistics from 1946 are for present boundaries.
[48] Pre-First World War statistics for Croatia-Slavonia are as follows:–

	Births	Deaths	Marriages		Births	Deaths	Marriages
1881	42.9	31.1	21.6	1898	39.8	29.1	18.6
1882	43.4	31.2	22.4	1899	42.0	27.9	19.4
1883	45.3	33.3	22.8	1900	40.7	27.5	17.6
1884	46.0	32.7	23.0	1901	39.2	27.4	18.0
1885	46.1	30.1	22.4	1902	41.5	27.6	18.2
1886	47.4	28.5	20.2	1903	39.3	26.9	17.6
1887	45.5	30.1	18.0	1904	40.0	26.2	20.4
1888	44.8	30.8	18.6	1905	40.1	30.1	18.4
1889	46.0	30.5	16.8	1906	39.7	26.3	18.2
1890	39.6	33.0	17.2	1907	39.3	25.4	18.2
1891	43.0	32.9	17.6	1908	39.2	27.2	18.0
1892	41.2	39.5	19.2	1909	41.7	26.7	16.4
1893	42.6	33.7	19.8	1910	37.9	24.8	16.2
1894	43.0	32.6	20.2	1911	36.0	26.4	16.8
1895	43.8	30.9	17.0	1912	38.1	25.2	16.0
1896	41.6	32.5	18.0	1913	35.7	25.5	17.2
1897	41.8	32.6	17.4	1914	36.6	24.7	13.0

[49] Figures from 1947 include territory acquired from Italy.
[50] Figures from 1953 exclude unviable infants who die within 24 hours of birth.
[51] Statistics up to 1955 apply to the year of registration. Subsequently they apply to the year of birth, death, or marriage.
[52] The previous practice of including marriages abroad, if registered within 1 year, was subsequently discontinued.
[53] Up to 1958 deaths in refugee camps for Amboynese are excluded.

B7 DEATHS OF INFANTS UNDER ONE YEAR OLD PER 1,000 LIVE BIRTHS

1751–1799

	Sweden
1751	186
1752	222
1753	190
1754	206
1755	225
1756	220
1757	221
1758	209
1759	190
1760	179
1761	209
1762	239
1763	240
1764	207
1765	212
1766	209
1767	199
1768	220
1769	217
1770	209
1771	211
1772	239
1773	286
1774	167
1775	185
1776	174
1777	195
1778	211
1779	215
1780	164
1781	192
1782	188
1783	202
1784	195
1785	193
1786	202
1787	187
1788	207
1789	224
1790	209
1791	187
1792	193
1793	200
1794	181
1795	202
1796	193
1797	196
1798	184
1799	191

1800–1849

	Austria[1]	Belgium	Denmark	France	Germany[3]	N'lands	Norway	Sweden	UK E & W
1800	...	...	...	...	...	...	...	240	...
1801	...	...	...	...	...	...	...	204	...
1802	...	...	...	...	...	...	...	182	...
1803	...	...	...	...	...	...	...	184	...
1804	...	...	...	...	...	...	...	185	...
1805	...	...	...	...	...	...	...	176	...
1806	190	...	...	...	...	...	...	230	...
1807	200	...	...	...	...	...	...	188	...
1808	194	...	...	...	...	...	...	220	...
1809	184	...	...	...	...	...	...	232	...
1810	186	...	...	...	...	...	...	193	...
1811	189	...	...	...	...	...	...	194	...
1812	182	...	...	...	...	...	...	204	...
1813	186	...	...	...	...	...	...	198	...
1814	201	...	...	...	...	...	...	195	...
1815	188	...	...	...	...	...	...	170	...
1816	178	...	...	...	...	...	...	184	...
1817	180	...	...	...	...	...	...	179	...
1818	181	...	...	...	...	...	...	169	...
1819	189	...	...	...	...	...	...	183	...
1820	184	...	...	...	...	...	...	163	...
1821	185	...	...	...	...	...	...	176	...
1822	198	...	...	...	...	...	...	162	...
1823	183	...	...	...	...	...	...	148	...
1824	192	...	...	...	...	...	...	156	...
1825	197	...	...	...	...	...	...	154	...
1826	195	...	...	...	...	...	...	172	...
1827	181	...	...	...	...	...	...	161	...
1828	188	...	...	...	...	...	...	170	...
1829	175	...	...	...	...	...	...	194	...
1830	237	...	...	182	...	...	...	181	...
1831	269	...	...	175	...	...	...	198	...
1832	243	...	...	182	...	...	...	166	...
1833	260	...	...	175	...	...	...	159	...
1834	271	192	...	209	...	...	...	174	...
1835	248	167	152	175	...	...	...	143	...
1836	236	173	162	168	292	...	134	153	...
1837	253	185	142	169	302	...	135	195	...
1838	240	190[2]	127	170	297	...	135	176	...
1839	255	185	147	160	285	...	158	164	151
1840	244	182	141	162	299	164	139	146	154
1841	251	152	142	158	300	171	115	159	145
1842	245	160	142	167	318	198	123	162	152
1843	259	149	129	157	287	169	118	159	150
1844	230	138	131	154	287	164	117	141	148
1845	247	145	139	144	289	168	118	149	142
1846	251	184	171	171	318	230	118	163	164
1847	...	156	153	159	286	208	120	173	164
1848	...	141	145	160	312	182	121	141	153
1849	243	147	145	173	285	169	99	142	160

N'lands: Netherlands: UK, E & W: United Kingdom, England and Wales

See p.143 for footnotes

Abbreviations used where space demands:— Czech' Czechoslovakia; Den: Denmark; Gr: Greece; N'lands: Netherlands; Pol: Poland; Port: Portugal; Switz: Switzerland; UK:E & W: United Kingdom:England and Wales; UK :Scotland: United Kingdom:Scotland; Yug: Yugoslavia

B7 Deaths of Infants Under One Year Old per 1,000 Live Births

1850–1899

	Austria	Belgium	Bulgaria	Denmark	Finland	France	Germany	Hungary[10]	Ireland	Italy
1850	251	141	...	127	...	146	297[3]	...	...	...
1851	242	148	...	135	...	163	287[7]	...	...	...
1852	242	147	...	137	...	162	298	229	...	...
1853	227	145	...	153	...	149	285	263	...	...
1854	273	149	...	121	...	179	291	264	...	...
1855	278[1]	161	...	126	...	175	285	268[11]	...	...
1856	241	148	...	122	...	170	253	245	...	...
1857	239	168	...	148	...	185	307	255	...	...
1858	250	164	...	142	...	177	289	246	...	...
1859	254	165	...	133	...	215	324	249	...	...
1860	237	139	...	136	...	150[5]	260	...	...	...
1861	264	164	...	126	...	190	...[8]	...	...	...
1862	250	150	...	131	...	163	...[8]	...	...	...
1863	259	157	...	125	...	180	298	...	...	232
1864	250	165	...	155	...	173	297	256	98	233
1865	270	189	...	145	...	191	332	224	98	229
1866	278	164	...	126	218	162	301	...	94	214
1867	253	128	...	134	223	171	312	...	97	223
1868	248	142	...	145	392	191	307	...	95	238
1869	242	130	...	125	141	177	293	...	93	215
1870	253	145	...	131	137	201[6]	298[3]	...	95	230
1871	255	173	...	129	141	228	330	...	91	227
1872	270	145	...	131	173	159	301	...	97	223
1873	290	142	...	126	184	178	307	...	96	214
1874	260	137	...	145	181	159	297[3]	...	94	224
1875	243	158	...	154	171	170	242[9]	...	95	215
1876	247	139	...	144	163	166	228	...	94	203
1877	258	131	...	130	161	157	225	...	92	208
1878	252	161	...	138	190	169	226	...	97	205
1879	240	159	...	131	138	158	218	...	101	207
1880	250	187	...	151	167	179	240	...	112	225
1881	250	155	...	121	186	166	224	...	91	192
1882	256	151	...	151	164	165	228	...	95	206
1883	253	154	...	138	149	165	232	...	98	198
1884	247	168	...	137	148	177	235	...	92	186
1885	255	150	...	128	162	161	226	...	95	194
1886	250	178	...	136	157	173	235	...	94	200
1887	244	137	...	131	132	160	217	...	95	193
1888	249	165	...	139	144	164	218	...	97	200
1889	236	160	...	141	142	155	226	...	94	184
1890	259	166	...	133	142	174	226	...	95	198
1891	243	162	...[4]	134	145	162	219	259	95	184
1892	259	169	144	140	169	181	230	275	105	186
1893	232	165	147	149	143	174	224	240	102	179
1894	251	152	142	134	140	157	219	247	102	186
1895	241	172	144	137	129	177	230	242	104	188
1896	230	142	134	126	143	149	208	226	95	177
1897	228	149	147	129	133	152	222	223	109	164
1898	224	160	143	123	128	168	210	226	110	171
1899	219	167	158	154	137	163	216	209	108	155

See p.143 for footnotes

B7 Deaths of Infants Under One Year Old per 1,000 Live Births

1850–1899

	Netherlands	Norway	Romania	Russia[12]	Serbia	Spain	Sweden	Switzerland	UK E & W	UK Scotland
1850	169	102	...	...	...	...	146	...	162	...
1851	179	108	...	...	...	...	152	...	153	...
1852	201	119	...	...	...	...	163	...	158	...
1853	187	103	...	...	...	...	161	...	159	...
1854	183	97	...	...	...	...	126	...	157	...
1855	199	103	...	...	...	...	145	...	153	125
1856	179	97	...	...	...	...	145	...	143	118
1857	212	100	...	...	...	...	165	...	156	118
1858	212	102	...	...	...	175	143	...	151	121
1859	227	104	...	...	...	191	143	...	153	108
1860	192	102	...	...	...	174	124	...	148	127
1861	196	113	...	...	...	168	137	...	153	111
1862	193	110	...	...	...	175	139	...	142	117
1863	184	106	...	...	...	190	133	...	149	120
1864	191	101	245	...	...	200	137	...	153	126
1865	220	103	219	...	...	201	135	...	160	125
1866	190	108	239	...	...	185	127	...	160	122
1867	197	122	194	243	...	188	140	...	153	119
1868	223	126	203	299	...	212	168	...	155	118
1869	192	111	193	275	...	196	146	...	156	129
1870	211	101	159	248	...	203	132	...	160	123
1871	227	99	144	274	...	...	114	222	158	130
1872	213	103	198	295	...	...	128	183	150	124
1873	206	106	191	262	...	...	129	200	149	125
1874	191	113	214	262	...	...	147	189	151	125
1875	220	115	203	266	...	...	149	197	158	132
1876	201	108	196	278	...	...	140	197	146	121
1877	188	107	190	260	...	...	126	191	136	115
1878	197	103	224	300	...	196	134	191	152	123
1879	182	92	185	252	...	191	111	181	135	108
1880	218	95	230	286	...	190	121	180	153	125
1881	182	97	177	252	...	189	113	187	130	113
1882	174	111	199	301	...	192	125	172	141	118
1883	187	97	175	284	...	204	116	164	137	119
1884	194	96	178	254	...	186	113	161	147	118
1885	169	93	170	270	...	192	114	173	138	121
1886	192	91	183	248	...	175	111	164	149	116
1887	163	88	193	256	...	199	103	162	145	122
1888	173	97	199	250	140	184	100	153	136	113
1889	176	110	191	275	155	...	107	159	144	121
1890	171	97	211	292	145	...	103	157	151	131
1891	169	97	209	272	167	...	108	163	149	128
1892	174	104	243	307	196	...	109	150	148	117
1893	164	89	217	252	175	...	101	152	159	136
1894	152	104	227	265	163	...	101	153	137	117
1895	167	96	201	279	158	...	95	159	161	133
1896	148	97	230	274	167	...	103	132	148	115
1897	148	96	215	260	167	...	99	141	156	138
1898	156	89	222	279	161	...	91	155	160	134
1899	149	107	198	240	152	...	112	136	163	131

See p. 143 for footnotes

B7 Deaths of Infants Under One Year Old per 1,000 Liver Births

1900–1949

	Austria	Belgium	Bulgaria	Czech	Den	Finland	France	Germany	East Germany	Gr	Hungary	Ireland	Northern Ireland
1900	231	172	132		128	153	160	229[19]		...	223	109	
1901	209	143	143		136	145	143	207		...	207	101	
1902	216	144	143		114	129	135	183		...	219	100	
1903	215	155	154		114	127	136	204		...	204	96	
1904	210	152	142		113	120	144	196		...	197	100	
1905	231	147	160		120	135	135	205		...	232	95	
1906	202	154	154		111	119	144	185		...	207	93	
1907	209	133	154		108	112	130	176		...	212	92	
1908	199	148	169		124	125	128	178		...	201	97	
1909	209	138	171		99	111	117	170		...	214	92	
1910	189	135	159		101	118	111	162		...	195	95	
1911	207	167	156		105	114	155	192		...	208	94	
1912	181	120	133		94	109	105	147		...	186	86	
1913	190[1]	130	...		92	113	112[6]	151		...	201	97	
1914	172	130[13]	...		99	104	111[17]	164		...	197	87	
1915	218	125	...		93	115	123[17]	148		...	264	92	
1916	192	116	...		101	110	117[17]	140[20]		...	219	83	
1917	186	140	...		99	118	129[17]	149		...	216	88	
1918	193	134[13]	146	...	76	116	146[17]	158[21]		...	217[10]	86	
1919	156	99	110	142	91	134	125[18]	145		...	164	88	
1920	...	110	146	178	91	96	123	131		...	196	83	
1921	...	122	183	173	77	95	121	134[22]		68	193	...	...
1922	156	114	155	166	82	99	90	130		82	198	69	77
1923	142	100	165	145	85	92	102	131		92	184	66	77
1924	128	95	150	148	84	107	90	108[23]		98	193	72	85
1925	119	100[14]	152	145	80	85	95	105		90	168	68	86
1926	123	104	127	154	84	86	102	102		75	167	74	85
1927	125	98	168	157	84	97	88	97		100	185	71	78
1928	120	94	149	146	81	84	97	89		94	177	68	78
1929	113	110	156	142	83	98	100	97		111	179	70	86
1930	104	100	138	137	82	75	84	85		99	153	68	68
1931	103	89	156	134	81	75	80	83		134	162	69	73
1932	106	94	150	137	72	71	82	79		123	184	72	83
1933	94	92	146	127	68	76	78	77		123	136	65	80
1934	92	82	131	128	64	73	74	66		112	148	63	70
1935	99	85	154	123	71	67	72	99		113	152	68	86
1936	93	86	144	124	67	66	72	66		114	139	74	77
1937	92	83	150	122	66	69	70	64		122	133	73	78
1938	80	81	144	121[15]	59	68	70	60		99	131	67	75
1939	73	82	139	98	58	70	68	72		118	121	66	71
1940	74	93[13]	136	99	50	88	91[17]	64		98	130	66	86
1941	70	92[13]	125	100	55	59	75[17]	...		...	116	74	77
1942	74	84[13]	131	111	47	67	77[17]	...		...	133	69	76
1943	79	75[13]	130	109	45	50	81[17]	...		...	116	83	78
1944	88	83	121	109	48	69	82[17]	...		...	...	79	67
1945	162	100	145	137[15]	48	63	114[17]	...[3]	...	...	169	71	68
1946	81	75	125	109	46	56	78	97	131	...	117	65	54
1947	78	69	130	89[16]	40	59	71	86	114	...	103[25]	68	53
1948	76	59	118	84	35	52	56	69	89	...[24]	94	50	46
1949	75	57	116	83	34	48	60	60	78	42	91	53	45

Czech: Czechoslovakia; Den: Denmark; Gr: Greece

See p.143 for footnotes

B7 Deaths of Infants Under One Year Old per 1,000 Live births

1900–1949

	Italy	N'lands	Norway	Pol[29]	Port[30]	Romania	Russia[12]	Serbia	Spain[32]	Sweden	Switz	UK E & W	UK Scotland	Yug[30 33]
1900	174	155	91	...	...	197	252	150	204	99	150	154	128	...
1901	166	149	91	...	...	202	272	145	185	103	137	151	129	...
1902	172	130	74	...	...	212	258	151	180	86	132	133	113	...
1903	172	135	78	...	...	294	250	151	162	93	133	132	118	...
1904	161	137	75	...	...	...	232	135	173	84	140	145	123	...
1905	166	131	82	...	...	...	272	163	161	88	129	128	116	...
1906	161	127	69	...	...	...	248	143	174	81	127	132	115	...
1907	150	112	66	...	...	...	225	147	158	77	121	118	110	...
1908	150[27]	125	75	...	...	...	244	158	160	85	108	120	121	...
1909	157	99	70	...	...	...	248	181	154	72	115	109	108	...
1910	140	108	67	...	134	...	271	139	149	75	105	105	108	...
1911	157	137	65	...	...	...	237	...	162	72	123	130	112	...
1912	128	87	67	...	...	216	...	...	138	71	94	95	105	...
1913	138	91	64	...	160	233	...	...	155	70	96	108	110	...
1914	130	95	68	...	148	217	...	...	152	73	93	105	111	...
1915	148[26]	87	67	...	148	199	...		152	76	90	110	126	...
1916	166	85	64	...	154	...	...		147	70	78	91	97	...
1917	159	87	64	...	148	...	...		155	65	79	96	107	...
1918	196	103	63	...	209	...	...		183	65	88	97	100	...
1919	129	93	62	...	182	...	...		156	70	82	89	102	...
1920	127[27]	83	58	...	164	221[31]	...		114	63	84	80	92	...
1921	131	85	54	187	148	200	...		147	64	74	83	90	...
1922	128	77	55	167	144	207	...		142	63	70	77	101	...
1923	129	66	50	...	164	207	...		148	56	61	69	80	...
1924	126	61	50	...	144	201	...		140	60	62	75	98	...
1925	119	58	50	...	132	192	198		137	56	58	75	91	143
1926	127	61	48	...	144	194	172		128	56	57	70	83	143
1927	120	59	51	151	142	209	190		127	60	57	70	89	163
1928	120	52	49	145	...	184	155		126	59	54	65	86	150
1929	125	59	54	149	151	197	...		123	59	52	74	87	147
1930	106	51	46	143	144	176	...		117	55	51	60	83	153
1931	113	49	46	142	141	180	...		117	57	49	66	82	165
1932	110	46	47	144	147	185	...		112	51	51	64	86	167
1933	100	43	48	128	149	174	...		112	50	48	63	81	140
1934	99	43	39	141	144	182	...		113	47	46	59	78	150
1935	101	40	44	127	149	192	...		109	46	48	57	77	149
1936	100	39	42	141	140	175	...		109	43	47	59	82	137
1937	109	38	42	136	151	178	...		130	45	47	58	80	141
1938	106	37	37	140	137	183	...		120	43	43	53	70	140
1939	97	34	37	...	120	176[31]	...		135	40	43	51	69	132
1940	103	39	39	...	126	188	...		109	39	46	57	78	...
1941	115	44	43	...	151	166	...		143	37	41	60	83	...
1942	112[28]	40	36	...	131	178[31]	...		103	29	38	51	69	...
1943	115	40	35	...	133	184	...		99	29	40	49	65	...
1944	103	46	37	...	122	162	...		93	31	42	45	65	...
1945	103	80	36	...	115	188[31]	...		85	30	41	46	56	...
1946	87	39	35	...	119	164	...		87	27	39	43	54	...
1947	84	34	35	...	107	200	...		71	25	39	41	56	...
1948	72	29	30	111	100	143	...		64	23	36	34	45	...
1949	74	27	28	107	115	136	...		69	23	34	32	41	102

N'lands: Netherlands: Pol: Poland; Port: Portugal; Switz: Switzerland; UK E & W: United Kingdom England and Wales; UK Scotland: United Kingdom Scotland; Yug: Yugoslavia

See p.143 for footnotes

B7 Deaths of Infants Under One Year Old per 1,000 Live Births

1950–1975

	Albania	Austria	Belgium	Bulgaria	Czech	Denmark	Finland	France	West Ger	East Ger	Greece	Hungary	Ireland	Northern Ireland
1950	...	66	53	95	78	31	44	52	55	72	35	86	46	41
1951	124	61	50	108	73	29	35	50	53	64	44	84	46	41
1952	100	52	45	98	56[34]	29	32	45	48	59	48	70	41	39
1953	100	50	42	81	45	27	34	42	47	54	45	71	39	38
1954	98	48	41	86	38	27	31	41	44	50	50	61	38	33
1955	104	46	41	82	34	25	30	39	42	49	44[35]	60	37	32
1956	82	43	39	72	31	25	26	36	39	47	39	59	36	29
1957	87	44	36	66	34	23	28	34	37	46	44	63	33	29
1958	68	41	31	52	30	22	25	32	36	44	39	58	35	28
1959	77	40	30	56	26	22	24	30	34	41	41	52	32	28
1960	83	38	31	45	24	22	21	27	34	39	40	48	29	27
1961	80	33	28	38	23	22	21	26	32	34	40	44	31	27
1962	92	33	28	37	23	20	21	26	29	32	40	48	29	27
1963	91	31	27	36	22	19	18	26	27	31	39	43	27	27
1964	82	29	25	33	21	19	17	23	25	29	36	40	27	26
1965	87	28	24	31	26	19	18	22	24	25	34	39	25	25
1966	...	28	25	32	24	17	15	22	24	23	34	38	25	26
1967	...	26	23	33	23	16	15	21	23	21	34	37	24	23
1968	...	26	22	28	22	16	14	20	23	20	34	36	21	24
1969	...	25	21	31	23	15	14	20	23	20	32	36	21	24
1970	...	26	21	27	22	14	14	18	23	19	30	36	20	23
1971	...	26	20	25	22	14	14	17	23	18	27	35	18	23
1972	...	25	19	26	22	12	12	16	22	18	27	33	18	21
1973	...	24	18	26	21	12	11	15	23	16	24	34	18	21
1974	...	24	17	26	20	11	11	14	21	16	24	34	18	21
1975	...	21	16	23	21	10	10	14	20	16	24	33	18	20

Czech: Czechoslovakia; Ger: Germany; East Ger: East Germany

	Italy	N'lands	Norway	Poland	Port	Romania	Russia	Spain	Sweden	Switz	UK E & W	UK Scotland	Yugoslavia
1950	64[28]	25	28	108	94	117	81	64	21	31	30	39	119
1951	67	25	26	115	89	118	84	63	22	30	30	37	140
1952	63	23	24	95	94	105	75	55	20	29	28	35	105
1953	58	22[36]	22	88	96	96	68	53	19	30	27	31	116
1954	53	23	21	83	86	89	68	49	19	27	25	31	102
1955	51	22	21	81	90	78	60	51	17	26	25	30	113
1956	51	20	21	71	88	82	47	46	17	26	24	29	98
1957	50	18	21	77	88	81	45	47	18	23	23	29	102
1958	48	19	20	72	84	69	41	43	16	22	23	28	86
1959	45	18	19	72	89	76	41	42	17	22	22	28	92
1960	44	18	19	57	78	75	35	36	17	21	22	26	88
1961	41	17	18	54	89	69	32	37	16	21	21	26	82
1962	42	17	18	55	79	59	32	33	15	21	22	27	84
1963	40	16	17	49	73	55	31	32	15	20	21	26	78
1964	36	15	16	48	69	49	29	31	14	19	20	24	76
1965	36	14	17	42	65	44	27	30	13	18	19	23	72
1966	35	15	15	39	65	47	26	28	13	17	19	23	62
1967	33	13	15	38	59	47	26	32	13	17	18	21	61
1968	32	14	14	33	61	60	26	31	13	16	18	21	59
1969	30	13	14	34	55	55	26	29	12	15	18	21	57
1970	29	13	13	33	58	49	25	27	11	15	18	20	56
1971	28	12	13	30	50	42	23	24	11	14	18	20	50
1972	27	12	12	23	41	40	25	22	11	13	17	19	44
1973	26	12	12	28	45	38	26	20	10	13	17	19	44
1974	23	11	10	24	38	35	28	19	10	13	16	19	41
1975	21	11	11	25	39	35	...	19	9	11	16	17	40

N'lands: Netherlands; Port: Portugal; Switz: Switzerland; UK, E & W: United Kingdom, England and Wales; UK Scotland: United Kingdom, Scotland

See p.143 for footnotes

B7 Deaths of Infants under One Year Old per 1,000 Live Births

NOTE

SOURCES:— As for table B.6

FOOTNOTES

[1] Cisleithania (excluding Lombardy and Venetia) to 1913, but excluding Dalmatia to 1855. From 1914 the statistics apply to the present Republic, except that Burgenland is not included until 1922. The figures to 1855 are for years ended 31 October.

[2] Figures from 1839 exclude parts of Limburg and Luxembourg ceded to the Netherlands.

[3] Bavaria only for 1836–50; Bavaria and the Kingdom of Saxony for 1851–70; Bavaria, Saxony, Baden, and Württemberg for 1871–74; Bavaria, Saxony, Baden, Württemberg, and Prussia for 1875–1900; German Empire and Republic for 1901–40; West Germany (including West Berlin and Saarland) since 1946. The Bavarian statistics up to 1869 were for years ended 30 September.

[4] The sources contain statistics back to 1881, but they appear to be extremely defective before 1892.

[5] Figures from 1861 include Savoy and Nice.

[6] Figures from 1871 to 1913 exclude the parts of Alsace and Lorraine ceded to Germany.

[7] The Bavarian figure for 1851 is 304.

[8] Statistics for Saxony only are as follows:—

1860: 228; 1861: 294; 1862: 243: 1863: 230.

[9] The figure without Prussia for 1875 is 308.

[10] The Ancient Kingdom (excluding Croatia-Slavonia) to 1918, and subsequently the territory established by the treaty of Trianon. For statistics for Croatia-Slavonia see footnote 33.

[11] Statistics to 1855 are for years ended 31 October.

[12] Statistics to 1911 apply to the 50 provinces of European Russia (excluding Finland, Poland, and the Caucasus). Later statistics apply to the U.S.S.R.

[13] Figures for some communes were missing.

[14] Figures from 1925 include Eupen, Malmédy, etc.

[15] Figures from 1939 exclude Sub-Carpathian Russia (Ruthenia), and from 1945 they exclude 12 villages in Slovakia which were ceded to the U.S.S.R.

[16] Figures from 1948 include the Bratislava Bridgehead.

[17] Estimates were made for departments affected by war.

[18] Figures from 1920 are based on the numbers actually born alive, whereas previously they did not include those who died before registration. The figure for 1920 on the old basis is 118.

[19] The figure for 1901 for the five states previously covered is 211.

[20] The figures from 1917 exclude Alsace-Lorraine.

[21] Figures from 1919 exclude territory ceded to Czechoslovakia, Denmark, and Poland (except in Silesia).

[22] Figures from 1922 exclude part of Upper Silesia ceded to Poland.

[23] Figures from 1925 exclude Eupen, Malmédy, etc.

[24] Figures from 1949 include the Dodecanese Islands.

[25] Figures from 1948 exclude the Bratislava Bridgehead.

[26] Estimates were made for earthquake victims.

[27] Figures from 1920 include territory acquired from Austria-Hungary.

[28] Figures from 1943 are for the post-Second World War territory, except that Trieste is not included until 1951.

[29] Boundaries of the day.

[30] Including the Azores and Madeira.

[31] Figures from 1919 to 1939 apply to the territory established by the treaty of Trianon. In 1940 this was reduced by the cession of Southern Dobrudja to Bulgaria (which proved permanent), of Bessarabia and northern Bukovina to the U.S.S.R. (which, apart from the reconquest in 1943, also proved permanent), and of northern Transylvania (which was recovered in 1945) to Hungary.

[32] Including the Canary Islands.

[33] Pre-First World War statistics for Croatia-Slavonia are as follows:—

1891	226	1897	213	1903	211	1909	195
1892	266	1898	201	1904	182	1910	191
1893	225	1899	187	1905	220	1911	201
1894	220	1900	198	1906	194	1912	184
1895	225	1901	195	1907	183	1913	203
1896	224	1902	200	1908	189	1914	181.

[34] From 1953 unviable infants who died within 24 hours of birth are excluded from both births and deaths.
[35] Statistics to 1955 apply to the year of registration not year of death.
[36] Up to 1953 infants of less than 28 weeks gestation born alive are excluded.

B8 EMIGRATION FROM EUROPE BY DECADES (in thousands)

	1851-60	1861-70	1871-80	1881-90	1891-1900	1901-10	1911-20	1921-30	1931-40	1941-50	1951-60
Austria-Hungary[1]	31	40	46	248	440	1,111	418	61	11[2]	...	53[3]
Belgium	1	2	2	21	16	30	21[4]	33	20[5]	29[6]	109
Denmark	...	8	39	82	51	73	52	64	100	38	68
Finland	...	...	...	26	59	159	67	73	3	7	32
France	27	36	66	119	51	53	32	4	5		155
Germany[7]	671	779	626	1,342	527	274	91	564	121[8]	618	872
Italy	5	27	168	992	1,580	3,615	2,194	1,370	235	467	858
Netherlands	16	20	17	52	24	28	22	32	4[8]	75[9]	341[10]
Norway	36	98	85	187	95	191	62	87	6	10[9]	25
Poland	...	...	...	...	...	...	...	634[11]	164[12]	...	...
Portugal	45	79	131	185	266	324	402	995	108	69[13]	346
Russia	...	...	58	288	481	911	420	...	...	...	...
Spain	3	7	13	572	791	1,091	1,306	560	132	166	543
Sweden	17	122	103	327	205	324	86	107	8	23	43
Switzerland	6	15	36	85	35	37	31	50	47	18[14]	23
United Kingdom and Ireland	1,313[15][16]	1,572[16]	1,849[16]	3,259	2,149	3,150	2,587	2,151	262	755[9]	1,454

NOTES

1. SOURCE:— W. Woodruff, *Impact of Western Man* (London, 1966)
2. Except as indicated in footnotes, this table refers to emigration outside Europe.

FOOTNOTES

[1] Republic of Austria from 1921 onwards.
[2] 1931–37.
[3] 1954–60.
[4] Excluding 1913–18.
[5] 1931–39.
[6] 1948–50.
[7] West Germany in 1941–50 and 1951–60.
[8] 1932–36.
[9] 1946–50.
[10] Excluding emigration to Dutch colonies.
[11] Incomplete figures.
[12] 1931–38.
[13] For the years 1941–49 emigration to European countries is included.
[14] For the years 1941–44 emigration to European countries is included.
[15] 1853–60.
[16] Excluding emigration direct from Irish ports.

B9 ANNUAL MIGRATION STATISTICS (in thousands)

1815–1849

	Austria		Belgium		Germany	Netherlands		Norway	Russia		United Kingdom	
	E	I	E	I	E	E	I	E	E	I	E	I
1815	...	...	...	...	...	...	...	...	...	...	2.1	...
1816	...	...	...	...	...	...	...	...	...	...	12.5	...
1817	...	...	...	...	...	...	...	...	...	...	20.6	...
1818	...	...	...	...	...	...	...	...	...	...	27.8	...
1819	1.3	4.9	...	...	...	...	...	...	...	...	34.8	...
1820	1.6	5.8	...	...	...	...	...	...	...	...	25.7	...
1821	2.7	6.0	...	...	...	...	...	—	...	...	18.3	...
1822	2.5	5.4	...	...	...	...	...	...	...	...	20.4	...
1823	2.3	3.0	...	...	...	...	...	...	...	...	16.6	...
1824	1.3	1.3	...	...	...	...	...	...	...	...	14.0	...
1825	0.9	0.8	...	...	...	...	...	0.1	...	...	14.9	...
1826	0.8	0.9	...	...	...	...	...	...	...	...	20.9	...
1827	0.8	1.0	...	...	...	...	...	...	...	...	28.0	...
1828	1.1	1.0	...	...	...	...	...	...	−0.5	0.4	26.1	...
1829	2.4	1.0	...	...	...	...	...	...	−1.6	1.3	31.2	...
1830	1.3	0.8	...	...	...	...	...	...	−0.6	2.2	56.9	...
	2.0											
1831	1.7	0.5	...	...	...	—	...	...	−23.7	7.7	83.2	...
1832	1.4	1.1	...	...	10.3	—	...	...	−3.1	0.6	103.1	...
1833	1.5	1.4	...	...	8.9	...	...	...	−0.6	1.7	62.5	...
1834	1.8	0.7	...	...	13.1	...	...	...	0.1	0.9	76.2	...
1835	1.5	0.9	...	...	6.2	—	...	...	−2.4	2.3	44.5	...
1836	1.5	0.9	...	...	14.1	—	...	0.2	−1.2	1.9	75.4	...
					17.0							
1837	2.4	0.9	...	...	17.5	—	...	0.2	0.3	3.9	72.0	...
1838	1.8	0.9	...	...	10.3	...	...	0.1	−1.1	4.2	33.2	...
1839	1.5	1.0	...	...	14.0	—	...	0.4	−6.5	−0.1	62.2	...
1840	1.3	0.9	...	...	14.5	—	...	0.3	−3.4	0.5	90.7	...
1841	1.5	...	3.8	2.9	11.0	...	...	0.4	−2.5	2.0	118.6	...
1842	...	...	4.2	2.8	14.2	—	...	0.7	1.5	2.4	128.3	...
1843	1.5	1.1	3.9	4.1	11.7	0.1	...	1.6	−1.4	3.0	57.2	...
1844	...	...	4.2	2.7	21.6	0.2	...	1.2	−1.5	4.7	70.0	...
1845	...	...	6.5	3.0	34.2	0.7	...	1.1	−1.5	4.1	93.5	...
1846	1.5	1.1			37.2	1.8	...	1.3	0.4	6.9	129.9	...
1847	...	...	6.3	4.4	41.3	5.3	...	1.6	0.6	1.6	258.3	...
1848	...	...	5.0	5.4	36.5	2.2	...	1.4	−0.1	−0.8	248.1	...
1849	0.9	0.7	5.1	3.9	34.2	2.1	...	4.0	−13.1	−1.7	299.5	...

E: Emigrants; I: Immigrants

Abbreviations used throughout this table: E: Emigrants; I: Immigrants

Other abbreviations used where space demands: Czech: Czechoslovakia

B9 Annual Migration Statistics (in thousands)

1850–1899

	Austria		Belgium		Bulgaria	Denmark		France		Germany	
	E	I	E	I	E	E	I	E	I	E	I
1850	1.3	0.9	6.4	4.2		...	...	...	...	33.2	...
1851	4.7	1.0	6.1	4.1		...	...	...	...	49.8	...
1852	2.5	1.1	7.8	5.0		...	...	...	...	82.5	...
1853	9.5	3.3	9.5	4.9		...	...	...	...	81.5	...
1854	14.3	1.9	8.0	5.0		...	...	...	...	116.2	...
	7.1										
1855	4.0	...	9.5	5.2		...	...	...	...	45.2	...
1856	2.8	...	13.3	5.6		...	...	...	...	58.7	...
1857	2.8	...	8.6	6.7		...	...	5.7	...	75.9	...
1858	2.1	...	8.1	7.8		...	...	3.7	...	38.4	...
1859	1.4	...	8.4	7.7		...	...	2.6	...	31.7	...
1860	2.0	...	9.3	8.3		...	...	3.5	...	42.1	...
1861	2.5	...	10.2	8.9		...	...	2.7	...	27.4	...
1862	1.6	...	9.5	9.2		...	...	2.3	...	28.8	...
1863	1.5	...	9.1	8.8		...	...	2.4	...	36.1	...
1864	2.3	...	10.7	9.2		...	...	3.1	...	47.8	...
1865	3.0	...	12.0	9.6		...	...	4.7	...	77.6	...
1866	3.8	...	14.3	10.6		...	...	5.6	...	84.4	...
1867	9.3	...	9.7	11.8		...	...	6.0	...	88.7	...
1868	4.1	...	9.9	11.2		...	...	6.4	...	96.0	...
1869	5.5	...	11.6	10.7		4.4	...	7.9	...	88.5	...
1870	5.9	...	7.3	16.6		3.5	...	4.6	...	59.1	...
1871	6.2	...	13.2	16.7		3.9	...	5.9	...	76.2	...
	9.2										
1872	9.0	...	11.0	15.8		6.9	...	15.8	...	128.2	...
1873	10.3	...	8.0	15.8		7.2	...	8.4	...	110.4	...
1874	9.0	...	8.2	16.8		3.3	...	7.2	...	47.7	...
1875	11.1[1]	...	10.2	15.4		2.1	...	4.3	...	32.3	...
1876	10.8	...	13.1	14.4		1.6	...	2.2	...	29.6	...
1877	6.7	...	11.8	15.1		1.9	...	2.1	...	22.9	...
1878	5.1	...	11.6	14.3		3.0	...	2.3	...	25.6	...
1879	7.4	...	12.5	14.2		3.1	...	3.6	...	35.9	...
1880	21.0	...	15.1	16.5		5.7	...	4.6	...	117.1	...
1881	24.7	...	15.8	17.7		8.0	...	4.5	...	220.9	...
1882	18.1	...	16.3	18.1		11.6	...	4.9	...	203.6	...
1883	19.6	...	15.2	17.5		8.4	...	4.0	...	173.6	...
1884	21.0	...	14.0	16.6		6.3	...	6.1	...	149.1	...
1885	16.4[2]	...	13.2	18.3		4.3	...	6.1	...	110.1	...
1886	19.4[2]	...	17.0	19.8		6.3	...	7.3	...	83.2	...
1887	20.2[2]	...	17.5	19.3		8.8	...	11.2	...	104.8	...
1888	24.8[2,3]	...	23.0	21.2		8.7	...	23.3	...	104.0	...
1889	30.1[2]	...	23.2	22.2		9.0	...	31.4	...	96.1	...
1890	38.7[2]	...	21.7	21.5	...	10.3	...	20.6	...	97.1	...
1891	53.8[2]	...	19.0	20.7	...	10.4	...	6.2	...	120.1	...
1892	50.3[2]	...	22.5	21.8	...	10.4	...	...	...	116.3	...
1893	48.8[2]	...	22.1	21.7	11.6	9.2	...	...	...	87.7	...
1894	18.8[2]	...	18.3	24.6	8.9	4.1	...	...	...	41.0	...
1895	46.0[2]	...	18.6	23.5	5.2	3.6	...	...	...	37.5	...
1896	51.5[2]	...	19.8	24.5	2.0	2.9	...	...	...	33.8	...
1897	25.1[2]	...	21.8	26.9	2.9	2.3	...	...	...	24.6	...
1898	32.3[2]	...	22.9	27.4	7.0	2.3	...	...	...	22.2	...
1899	55.9[2,4]	...	23.0	29.4	7.7	2.8	...	...	...	24.3	...

See p.158 for footnotes

B9 Annual Migration Statistics (in thousands)

1850–1899

	Hungary		Ireland		Italy		Netherlands		Norway	Poland	Portugal
	E	I	E	I	E	I	E	I	E	E	E
1850	...	...	...	...	...	...	0.8	...	3.7	...	...
1851	...	...	152.1[6]	...	...	...	1.2	...	2.6	...	...
1852	...	...	190.3	...	...	...	1.2	...	4.0	...	...
1853	...	...	173.1	...	...	...	1.6	...	6.1	...	...
1854	...	...	140.6	...	...	...	3.6	...	6.0	...	...
1855	...	...	90.9	...	...	...	2.1	...	1.6		
1856	...	...	90.8	...	...	...	1.9	...	3.2		
1857	...	...	95.1	...	...	...	1.7	...	6.4		
1858	...	...	64.3	...	...	...	1.2	...	2.5		
1859	...	...	80.6	...	...	...	0.5	...	1.8		
1860	...	...	84.6	...	...	...	0.9	...	1.9		80.8
1861	...	...	64.3	...	...	...	0.8	...	8.9		
1862	...	...	70.1	...	...	...	0.8	...	5.3		
1863	...	...	117.2	...	...	...	1.1	...	1.1		
1864	...	...	114.2	...	...	...	0.7	...	4.3		
1865	...	...	101.5	...	...	...	8.4	6.9	4.0		
1866	...	...	99.5	...	...	...	10.4	6.3	15.5		6.0[7]
1867	...	...	80.6	...	...	...	11.0	6.8	12.8		7.2[7]
1868	...	...	61.0	...	...	...	9.8	7.4	13.2		6.7[7]
1869	...	...	66.6	...	134.9	...	14.8	7.5	18.1		8.4[7]
1870	...	...	74.9	...	107.2	...	8.5	7.8	14.8		10.4[7]
1871	0.3	...	71.2	...	122.5	...	11.7	7.0	11.4		12.7[7]
1872	0.6	...	78.1	...	146.3	86.5	12.7	8.1	13.3		17.3
1873	1.0	...	90.1	...	151.8	86.8	14.7	8.3	9.9		13.0
1874	0.9	...	73.2	...	108.2	79.0	9.8	8.4	4.4		14.8
1875	1.1	...	51.5	...	103.2	83.2	9.0	9.2	4.0		15.4
1876	0.6	...	37.6	...	108.8	73.6	8.6	9.9	4.4		11.0
1877	0.7	...	38.5	...	99.2	...	7.6	12.0	3.2		11.1
1878	0.8	...	41.1	...	96.3	...	8.1	13.6	4.9		9.9
1879	1.8	...	47.1	...	119.8	...	10.4	14.0	7.6		13.2
1880	8.8	...	95.5	...	119.9	...	12.7	11.9	20.2		12.6
1881	11.3	...	78.4	...	135.8	...	18.8	13.9	26.0		14.6
1882	17.5	...	89.1	...	161.6	...	19.8	15.3	28.8		18.3
1883	14.8	...	108.7	...	169.1	...	16.8	14.4	22.2		19.3
1884	13.2	...	75.9	...	147.0	...	16.2	14.1	14.8		17.5
1885	12.3	...	62.0	...	157.2	...	15.0	13.7	14.0		15.0
1886	25.1	...	63.1	...	167.8	...	15.5	13.9	15.2		14.0
1887	18.3	...	82.9	...	215.7	...	17.5	13.5	20.7		16.9
1888	17.6[5]	...	78.7	...	290.7	...	19.0	13.4	21.5		24.0
1889	25.1	...	70.5	...	218.4	...	23.0	15.3	12.6		20.6
1890	31.5	...	61.3	...	217.2	...	19.0	13.1	11.0	19.3	29.4
1891	33.0	...	59.6	...	293.6	...	19.9	15.2	13.3	17.5	33.6
1892	35.1	...	50.9	...	223.7	...	21.4	15.9	17.0	13.1	21.1
1893	23.0	...	48.1	...	246.8	...	22.9	16.0	18.8	8.8	30.4
1894	8.0	...	35.9	...	225.3	...	21.1	15.7	5.6	5.6	26.9
1895	25.9	...	48.7	...	293.2	...	18.4	14.8	6.2	7.1	44.7
1896	24.6	...	39.0	...	307.5	...	23.2	16.6	6.7	6.2	28.0
1897	14.1	...	32.5	...	299.9	...	23.6	19.2	4.7	5.7	21.6
1898	22.8	...	32.2	...	283.7	...	25.4	19.3	4.9	7.8	23.5
1899	43.4	4.7	41.2	...	308.3	...	28.9	22.0	6.7	8.7	17.8

See p.158 for footnotes

B9 **Annual Migration Statistics** (in thousands)

1850–1899

	Russia		Serbia		Spain		Sweden		Switzerland		United Kingdom	
	E	I	E	I	E	I	E	I	E	I	E	I
1850	0.4	0.2	...	...	....	...	...	...	...	...	280.8	...
1851	1.7	2.1	...	...	...	...	1.1	...	...	...	336.0	...
1852	1.4	−3.8	...	...	...	...	3.3	...	...	...	368.8	...
1853	1.7	23.6	...	...	...	...	3.0	...	...	...	329.9	...
1854	−2.3	10.6	...	...	...	...	4.2	...	...	...	323.4	...
1855	3.0	−16.2	...	...	...	...	1.1	...	...	...	176.8	22.8
1856	−1.0	29.9	...	...	...	...	1.1	...	...	...	176.6	...
1857	−2.1	−5.2	...	...	...	...	1.8	...	...	...	212.9	...
1858	2.9	26.0	...	...	...	...	0.6	...	...	...	114.0	23.7
1859	37.9	31.3	...	...	...	...	0.3	...	...	...	120.4	19.9
1860	190.7	32.5	...	...	...	...	0.3	...	...	...	128.5	24.4
1861	20.7	46.8	...	...	...	...	2.3	...	...	...	91.8	32.0
1862	4.6	43.2	...	...	...	...	2.5	...	...	...	121.2	...
1863	1.5	38.9	...	...	...	...	3.1	...	...	...	223.8	17.6
1864	0.8	46.3	...	...	...	...	5.2	...	...	...	208.9	25.8
1865	3.4	72.6	...	...	...	...	6.7	...	...	...	209.8	33.5
1866	5.5	55.4	...	...	...	...	7.2	...	...	...	204.9	31.1
1867	4.5	58.7	...	...	...	...	9.3	...	...	...	196.0	36.6
1868	3.8	63.3	...	...	...	...	27.0	...	5.0	...	196.3	...
1869	−19.5	1.3	...	...	...	...	39.1	...	5.2	...	258.0	36.0
1870	20.7	34.9	...	...	...	...	20.0	...	3.5	...	256.9	41.5
1871	25.3	46.0	...	...	...	...	17.5	...	3.9	...	252.4	45.0
1872	10.3	66.9	...	...	...	...	15.9	...	4.9	...	295.2	41.7
1873	32.0	44.8	...	...	...	...	13.6	...	5.0	...	310.6	74.9
1874	33.5	72.8	...	...	...	...	7.8	...	2.7	...	241.0	118.1
1875	9.9	28.6	...	...	...	...	9.7	2.8	1.8	...	173.8	94.2
1876	1.3	35.3	...	...	...	...	9.4	3.2	1.7	...	109.5	71.4
1877	9.4	28.1	...	...	...	...	7.6	3.3	1.7	...	95.2	63.9
1878	0.2	76.9	...	...	...	...	9.0	2.8	2.6	...	112.9	54.9
1879	8.4	47.8	...	...	...	...	17.6	2.6	4.3	...	164.3	37.9
1880	−1.2	62.7	...	...	...	...	42.1	3.0	7.3	...	227.5	47.0
1881	24.8	46.9	...	...	...	...	46.0	3.0	10.9	...	243.0	52.7
1882	14.1	59.0	...	...	13.3	...	50.2	3.6	12.0	...	279.4	54.7
1883	23.6	47.7	...	...	3.9	...	31.6	4.2	13.5	...	320.1	73.8
1884	17.3	37.7	...	...	4.8	...	23.6	4.9	9.6	...	242.2	91.4
1885	9.7	51.0	...	...	0.6	...	23.5	5.5	7.6	...	207.6	85.5
1886	15.0	42.8	...	...	4.6	...	32.9	5.2	6.3	...	232.9	80.0
1887	18.9	11.3	...	...	14.2	...	50.8	4.6	7.6	...	281.5	85.5
1888	12.8	10.0	...	...	23.6	...	50.3	4.8	8.3	...	279.9	94.1
1889	36.5	7.5	4.9	22.9	72.4	...	33.4	5.5	8.4	...	254.0	103.1
1890	40.9	4.7	2.9	15.4	11.1	...	34.2	6.0	7.7	...	218.1	109.5
1891	41.2	−6.7	4.5	7.3	5.2	...	42.8	6.1	7.5	...	218.5	103.0
1892	36.0	0.5	1.0	5.0	8.3	...	45.5	6.5	7.8	...	210.0	97.8
1893	48.5	2.0	2.2	0.5	19.8	...	40.9	7.4	6.2	...	208.8	102.1
1894	25.6	7.9	7.2	8.0	14.7	...	13.4	10.4	3.8	...	156.0	118.3
1895	27.6	17.1	3.2	4.7	64.5	...	19.0	8.5	4.3	...	185.2	109.4
1896	27.1	6.9	0.4	8.5	98.9	...	20.0	7.8	3.3	...	161.9	101.7
1897	24.3	18.1	1.7	13.8	−9.2	...	14.6	7.9	2.5	...	146.5	95.2
1898	31.6	27.3	8.0	18.2	−77.7	...	13.7	8.0	2.3	...	140.6	91.2
1899	40.7	14.9	7.6	15.7	−62.7	...	16.9	8.2	2.5	...	146.4	100.2

B9 Annual Migration Statistics (in thousands)

1900–1949

	Austria		Belgium		Bulgaria	Czech	Denmark		Finland	France	
	E	I	E	I	E	E	E	I	E	E	I
1900	62.6	...	25.1	29.3	7.8	...	3.6	...	10.4	...	...
1901	65.1	...	19.7	29.1	9.5	...	4.7	...	12.6	...	...
1902	93.7[8]	...	23.1	29.4	9.9	...	6.8	...	23.2	...	...
1903	102.3[9]	...	25.0	34.3	...	...	8.2	...	17.0	...	...
1904	79.0[10]	...	27.3	35.6	...	...	9.0	...	11.0	...	...
1905	123.7	...	28.0	36.9	...	...	8.1	...	17.4	...	...
1906	136.4	...	32.9	37.4	...	...	8.5	...	17.5	...	...
1907	177.4	...	32.4	38.9	...	...	7.9	...	16.3	...	...
1908	58.9	...	32.3	38.2	...	...	4.6	...	5.8	...	...
1909	129.8	...	35.2	39.7	...	...	6.8	...	19.1	...	...
1910	138.9	...	38.9	45.0	...	...	8.9	...	19.0	...	...
1911	91.9	...	33.0	41.1	...	...	8.3	...	9.4	...	...
1912	131.2	...	35.8	43.0	...	...	8.6	...	10.7	...	...
1913	194.5	...	41.3	45.5	...	...	8.8	...	20.1	...	...
1914	...	...	...	...	...	...	6.2	...	6.5	...	...
1915	...	...	...	...	...	...	3.3	...	4.0	...	...
1916	...	...	...	...	...	...	4.3	...	5.3	...	...
1917	...	...	...	...	...	...	1.6	...	2.8	...	...
1918	...	...	...	...	...	...	0.8	...	1.9	...	...
1919	...	...	57.8	50.0	...	...	3.3	...	1.1	...	...
1920	...	...	53.3	44.3	...	...	6.3	...	5.6	...	...
1921	5.2	...	27.4	24.4	...	...	5.3	...	3.6	...	...
1922	10.6	...	32.6	30.6	...	39.4	4.1	...	5.7	...	...
1923	15.5	...	31.1	34.7	...	32.3	7.6	...	13.8	...	...
1924	2.7	...	31.9	51.3	...	54.4	6.3	...	5.4	...	...
1925	4.6	4.4	35.3	46.9	...	19.4	4.6	...	2.5	...	...
1926	3.9	3.9	36.2	44.5	...	26.1	5.8	...	6.0	...	...
1927	5.3	5.1	29.9	41.2	...	23.6	8.0	...	6.1	...	...
1928	4.6	6.1	28.3	42.0	...	24.5	7.7	...	5.1	...	...
1929	4.9	7.4	29.2	55.6	...	30.7	6.3	...	6.4	...	...
1930	4.2	8.2	29.6	54.4	...	25.7	3.3	...	4.0	...	...
1931	2.6	6.3	19.3	32.0	10.7	9.6	1.2	...	0.7	...	...
1932	2.1	6.7	18.3	26.2	6.8	5.2	0.8[12]	...	1.2	...	...
1933	1.4	4.8	16.2	19.3	5.7	4.7	7.5	12.1	0.7	...	...
1934	2.2	10.3	18.5	16.0	11.3	5.1	8.1	12.4	0.4	...	...
1935	...	6.3	16.2	16.4	28.7	5.7	8.9	11.7	0.6	...	...
1936	...	7.1	13.5	17.7	20.9	7.2	9.8	10.9	0.7	...	...
1937	...	6.9	14.2	22.2	20.4	14.8	9.5	10.0	1.5	...	...
1938	...	...	16.1	14.5	21.7	9.0	11.1	10.6	1.3	...	...
1939	...	...	18.0	11.8	29.1	...	11.3	13.9	1.0	...	...
1940	...	...	6.9	13.7	14.4	...	14.4	8.9	0.8	...	...
1941	...	...	3.2	13.8	18.5	...	6.2	7.7	0.7	...	...
1942	...	...	3.9	10.7	...	...	2.7	4.6	0.1	...	...
1943	...	...	3.6	5.2	...	...	3.2	3.7	—	...	...
1944	...	...	4.1	2.9	...	...	1.7	2.6	0.1	...	...
1945	...	...	19.4	12.6	...	...	5.1	6.8	—	...	...
1946	...	...	30.3	20.3	...	...	25.7	20.1	0.3	...	30.2
1947	0.4[11]	25.9[11]	47.5	19.5	...	...	28.6	21.7	0.3	...	73.2
1948	1.4	11.5	45.5	89.9	...	...	33.1	26.4	10.1	...	82.9
1949	0.7	5.0	44.0	31.8	...	...	25.9	24.5	7.7	...	85.4

See p. 158 for footnotes

B9 Annual Migration Statistics (in thousands)

1900–1949

	Germany		Greece		Hungary		Ireland		Italy	
	E	I	E	I	E	I	E	I	E	I
1900	22.3	...	...	...	54.8	6.2	45.3	...	352.8	...
1901	22.1	...	...	...	71.5	8.5	39.6	...	533.2	...
1902	32.1	...	...	...	91.8	11.5	40.2	...	531.5	...
1903	36.3	...	...	...	119.9[17]	20.2	39.8	...	508.0	...
1904	28.0	...	...	...	97.3[18]	16.9	36.9	...	471.2	...
1905	28.1	...	...	...	170.4	17.6	30.7	...	726.3	...
1906	31.1	...	...	...	178.2	27.6	35.3	...	788.0	...
1907	31.7	...	...	...	209.2	51.2	39.1	...	704.7	...
1908	19.9	...	...	...	49.4[19]	53.8	23.3	...	486.7	...
1909	24.9	...	...	...	129.3	17.0	28.7	...	625.6	
1910	25.5	...	...	...	119.9	24.7	32.5	...	651.5	...
1911	22.7	...	...	...	73.7	32.8	30.6	...	533.8	...
1912	18.5	...	...	...	120.5	23.6	29.3	...	711.4	...
1913	25.8	...	38.1	...	119.2	21.8	31.0	...	872.6	...
1914	11.8	...	...	...	...	...	20.3	...	479.2	...
1915	0.5	...	...	...	...	...	10.7	...	146.0	...
1916	0.3	...	...	...	...	...	7.3	...	142.4	...
1917	—	...	...	...	...	...	2.1	...	46.5	...
1918	...	...	...	...	...	...	1.0	...	28.3	...
1919	3.1	...	...	12.0[15]	...	...	3.0	...	253.2	...
1920	8.5	48.6	12.2	7.7	...	...	15.5	...	614.6	...
1921	23.5	64.9	4.1	9.1	6.0[20]	...	13.6	...	201.3	124.0
1922	36.5	82.0	...	7.8	5.5	...	...	...	281.3	110.8
1923	115.4	48.2	15.3	9.5	5.1	...	...	...	390.0	119.7
1924	58.3	61.0	...	10.3	1.7	...	19.1	2.5	364.6	172.8
1925	59.5	78.0	3.6[16]	...	3.5	0.5	30.2	2.2	280.1	189.1
1926	62.7	76.4	6.7[16]	...	5.9	22.5	30.0	1.8	262.4	177.6
1927	59.3	88.8	9.3[16]	...	5.6	...	27.1	1.9	218.9	140.4
1928	56.0	103.3	...	...	5.5	...	24.7	2.2	150.0	98.9
1929	47.8	109.7	...	...	9.7	...	20.8	2.1	149.8	115.9
1930	36.5	129.2	...	...	6.2	...	16.0	2.6	280.1	129.0
1931	13.2	110.2	23.4	19.6	1.5	...	1.5	3.4	165.9	107.7
1932	10.3	106.6	26.6	19.0	0.8	2.2	0.8	4.1	83.3	73.2
1933	12.9	83.6	21.8	18.3	0.8	1.4	0.9	2.6	83.1	65.8
1934	14.2	89.0	26.0	22.2	0.9	1.7	1.0	1.7	68.5	49.8
1935	12.2	...	21.4	17.7	1.1	1.4	1.0	1.6	57.4	39.5
1936	15.2	...	17.2	14.5	1.1	1.0	1.3	1.5	41.7	32.8
1937	14.2	3.0	21.1	15.2	1.5	0.5	1.2	1.2	59.9	35.7
1938	22.7[13]	7.8	19.5	17.9	1.6	0.2	1.8	1.3	61.5	36.9
1939	25.5[13,14]	12.9[14]	15.6	27.7	2.1	0.2	1.1[21]	0.7[21]	29.5	87.3
1940	...	...	8.4	13.3	1.2	0.2	...	...	51.8	61.1
1941	...	...	...	...	0.4	0.1	...	...	8.8	46.1
1942	...	...	...	...	—	—	...	...	8.2	20.5
1943	...	...	...	...	...	...	...	...	...	...
1944	...	...	...	...	...	...	...	...	...	...
1945	...	...	...	...	...	...	...	...	...	...
1946	...	...	1.6	...	...	...	...	...	110.3	4.6
1947	...	...	4.9	...	2.1	0.9	...	...	254.1	65.5
1948	...	...	4.8	...	...	...	...	...	308.5	119.3
1949	...	...	4.3	...	...	...	...	...	254.5	118.6

See p.158 for footnotes

B9 Annual Migration Statistics (in thousands)

1900–1949

	Netherlands		Norway	Poland	Portugal	Romania		Russia		Serbia	
	E	I	E	E	E	E	I	E	I	E	I
1900	25.1	24.1	10.9	9.8	21.3	...	...	32.4	11.6	−1.6	6.9
1901	13.5	24.4	12.7	11.4	20.6	...	...	35.1	13.9	8.9	6.4
1902	14.8	24.5	20.3	9.1	24.2	...	...	30.8	10.7	9.3	17.2
1903	28.3	25.6	26.8	10.9[24]	21.6	...	...	62.0	9.9	7.3	10.9
1904	27.7	23.7	22.3	...	28.3	...	...	66.6	4.4	8.6	28.5
1905	27.5	25.2	21.1	...	33.6	...	...	92.9	2.3	10.5	13.5
1906	30.9	26.2	22.0	...	38.1	...	...	116.7	5.6	17.0	8.3
1907	38.4	27.3	22.1	35.6	41.9	...	...	89.9	13.2	14.2	15.6
1908	34.6	30.0	8.5	17.3	40.1	...	...	37.4	17.4	8.4	−5.1
1909	37.1	32.2	16.2	15.1	38.2	...	...	54.5	17.3		
1910	35.1	31.1	18.9	21.7	39.5	...	...	71.3	22.1		
1911	38.9	33.6	12.5	20.3	59.7	...	...	66.2	18.7		
1912	39.0	36.2	9.1	17.2	88.9	...	...	94.6	15.4		
1913	40.1	40.0	9.9	...	77.6	...	...	223.8	127.2	...	...
1914	29.8	51.7	8.5	...	25.7	...	...	54.0	7.5	...	...
1915	17.1	32.5	4.6	...	19.3	...	...	−8.2	−6.1	...	...
1916	11.1	50.9	5.2	...	24.7	...	...	...	...	...	...
1917	8.8	50.5	2.5	...	15.7	...	...	...	...	...	...
1918	20.6	22.7	1.2	...	11.9	...	...	...	...	...	...
1919	45.4	32.3	2.4	...	37.1	...	...	...	...	...	...
1920	63.1	41.6	5.6	...	64.8	...	...	...	...	...	...
1921	35.4	30.3	4.6	...	24.6	...	...	...	...	...	...
1922	34.4	43.0	6.5	46.8	39.8	...	...	...	...	...	...
1923	40.1	51.2	18.3	...	40.2	...	...	...	...	...	...
1924	50.2	41.3	8.5	26.1	29.7	...	...	...	...	...	...
1925	43.7	38.4	7.0	...	22.9	...	...	...	...	...	...
1926	41.9	48.2	9.3	49.9	47.1	21.7	1.3	...	...	...	...
1927	45.2	47.5	11.9	58.2	27.7	8.9	3.2	...	...	...	...
1928	48.4	48.6	8.8	64.6	34.3	12.0	4.2	...	...	...	...
1929	49.5	57.8	8.0	65.3	40.4	12.8	3.1	...	...	...	...
1930	56.7	66.7	3.7	76.0	23.2	10.9	3.6	...	...	...	...
1931	37.4	65.4	0.8	21.4	6.0	2.7	2.6	...	...	...	...
1932	38.6	55.9	0.4	35.5	5.9	1.4	2.0	...	...	...	...
1933	41.5	49.6	0.3	42.6	8.9	1.2	1.4	...	...	...	...
1934	44.5	43.7	0.5	53.8	7.5	1.4	1.0	...	...	...	...
1935	48.4	34.3	0.5	54.6	9.1	2.4	0.7	...	...	...	...
1936	48.3	32.5	0.5	102.5	12.5	1.6	0.4	...	...	...	...
1937	45.5	33.9	0.6	129.1	14.7	1.3	0.6	...	...	...	...
1938	48.2	33.1	0.8	...	13.6	1.7	0.4	...	...	...	...
1939	50.8	50.1	0.7	...	17.8	1.4	0.2	...	...	...	...
1940	26.4	19.5	0.3[23]	...	13.2	0.5	—	...	...	...	...
1941	17.3	10.7	...	...	6.3	0.5	—	...	...	...	...
1942	42.7[22]	8.3	...	...	2.2	...	...	...	...	...	...
1943	70.7[22]	8.8	...	...	0.9	...	...	...	...	...	...
1944	24.4[22]	5.3	...	...	2.4	...	...	...	...	...	...
1945	15.7[22]	29.1	...	...	5.9	...	...	...	...	...	...
1946	66.8	107.4	1.0	...	8.3	...	...	...	...	...	...
1947	65.9	54.4	1.5	...	12.8	...	...	...	...	...	...
1948	66.5	46.3	2.4	...	12.3	...	...	...	...	...	...
1949	58.2	36.3	2.7	...	17.3	...	...	...	...	...	...

See p. 158 for footnotes

B9 Annual Migration Statistics (in thousands)

1900–1949

	Spain		Sweden		Switzerland		United Kingdom		Yugoslavia	
	E	I	E	I	E	I	E	I	E	I
1900	5.6	...	20.7	8.0	3.8	...	168.8	97.6	...	...
1901	3.8	...	24.6	7.6	3.9	...	171.7	99.7	...	...
1902	−6.6	...	37.1	6.8	4.7	...	205.7	104.1	...	...
1903	2.6	...	39.5	7.6	5.8	...	260.0	112.9	...	...
1904	30.1	...	22.4	9.3	4.8	...	271.4	144.6	...	...
1905	64.0	...	24.0	8.6	5.0	...	262.1	122.7	...	...
1906	52.9	...	24.7	9.6	5.3	...	325.1	130.5	...	...
1907	51.3	...	23.0	8.9	5.7	...	395.7	160.6	...	...
1908	71.4	...	12.5	9.8	3.7	...	263.2	172.0	...	...
1909	111.1	...	22.0	8.1	4.9	...	288.8	149.1	...	...
1910	160.9	...	27.8	8.1	5.2	...	397.8	164.1	...	...
1911	139.7	...	20.0	7.8	5.5	...	454.5	192.7	...	...
1912	194.4	...	18.1	8.3	5.9	...	467.7	199.2	...	...
1913	151.0	...	20.3	8.4	6.2	...	469.6	227.6	...	...
1914	66.6	...	13.0	8.6	3.9	...	293.2	229.9	...	...
1915	50.4	...	7.5	6.4	2.0	...	104.9	129.7	...	...
1916	62.2	46.4	10.6	6.7	1.5	...	76.5	84.7	...	...
1917	43.1	37.7	6.4	5.8	0.7	...	20.6	21.0	...	...
1918	20.2	28.4	4.9	4.9	0.3	...	17.3	15.4	...	...
1919	69.5	47.2	7.3	7.8	3.1	...	180.2	153.2	...	...
1920	150.6	46.5	10.2	10.8	9.3	...	285.1	86.1	...	...
1921	62.5	76.4	9.0	8.6	7.1	...	199.5	71.4	13.0	...
1922	63.5	50.1	11.8	6.3	5.8	...	174.1[25]	68.0[25]	6.1	...
1923	93.2	32.1	29.2	5.8	8.0	...	167.6	58.9	11.5	...
1924	86.9	36.5	10.7	5.9	4.1	...	174.5	66.7	19.6	4.8
1925	55.5	37.9	11.9	5.1	4.3	...	140.6	56.3	17.6	5.7
1926	45.1	39.9	13.0	5.4	4.9	7.1	166.6	51.1	18.2	5.6
1927	43.9	41.5	12.8	5.7	5.3	8.4	153.5	55.7	22.0	5.8
1928	48.6	38.6	13.5	5.6	4.8	9.7	136.8	59.1	21.8	5.8
1929	50.2	36.6	11.0	6.3	4.6	9.3	143.7	56.2	18.2	6.0
1930	41.6	41.6	5.7	7.5	3.6	10.4	92.2	66.2	13.6	7.6
1931	14.4	53.9	3.0	8.4	1.7	10.0	34.3	71.4	4.8	8.1
1932	10.2	47.5	2.1	9.0	1.3	9.3	27.0	75.6	2.5	6.0
1933	6.7	31.7	2.4	7.3	1.2	7.6	26.3	59.3	2.2	3.4
1934	15.7	20.0	2.4	5.7	1.2	2.3	29.2	49.8	2.9	2.3
1935	17.0	15.2	2.5	5.4	1.3	1.9	29.8	46.2	3.3	1.9
1936	...	...	2.4	4.7	2.0	1.9	29.8	47.2	3.9	1.9
1937	...	...	2.3	4.5	2.8	2.5	31.8	42.6	5.4	2.5
1938	...	...	2.1	5.8	2.0	2.0	34.1	40.6	5.7	2.1
1939	1.0	0.7	3.6	7.2	2.2	1.2	...	...	...	...
1940	2.9	2.1	3.1	6.8	1.1	0.9	...	...	...	...
1941	7.9	1.5	1.1	4.3	1.4	0.6	...	...	...	...
1942	3.4	0.8	0.9	3.1	0.3	0.6	...	...	...	...
1943	2.3	1.1	0.7	6.2	—	0.5	...	...	...	...
1944	2.0	1.7	0.5	13.3	—	0.1	...	...	...	...
1945	3.5	2.6	8.3	21.1	0.3	0.1	...	...	...	...
1946	7.5	5.1	6.9	31.4	1.8	2.4	166.6[26]	63.1[26]	...	...
1947	15.2	6.3	6.5	31.4	2.6	3.3	121.6	56.5	...	...
1948	20.9	6.1	9.8	32.9	3.6	4.2	157.3	61.4	...	...
1949	44.8	6.9	14.2	24.0	2.9	4.2	144.5	59.4	...	...

See p.158 for footnotes

B9 Annual Migration Statistics (in thousands)

1950–1975

	Austria		Belgium		Denmark		Finland	France		West Germany	
	E	I	E	I	E	I	E	E	I	E	I
1950	0.7	...	36.5	27.9	25.5	22.4	14.0	...	19.3	172.7	550.7
1951	3.6	...	43.0	60.0	29.0	20.3	19.6	...	26.3	248.6	386.2
1952	1.5	...	38.8	52.2	24.5	20.8	6.0	...	39.4	247.5	312.4
1953	1.8	0.7	38.1	40.1	18.4	19.3	5.1	...	20.2	151.4	500.3
1954	3.6	0.4	34.1	34.6	19.8	18.2	3.0	...	16.4	189.2	410.4
1955	5.1	1.0	32.8	51.1	26.8	18.7	1.8	173.4	225.4	190.9	510.7
1956	5.6	1.7	36.7	52.6	32.3	20.1	2.5	81.9	156.9	222.5	561.9
1957	2.3	1.8	36.6	68.8	33.7	21.9	5.2	57.7	196.5	231.5	648.2
1958	1.5	0.8	40.3	47.1	25.2	23.2	5.6	59.3	143.4	210.7	539.6
1959	2.1	1.0	35.2	32.3	22.6	24.4	3.5	52.4	127.3	224.1	434.8
1960	2.1	1.0	32.2	42.2	23.6	26.6	1.8	58.3	137.9	259.9[27]	623.9[27]
										264.7	659.5
1961	0.2	2.3	35.5	36.1	25.1	27.9	1.9	73.5	234.2	306.2	742.2
1962	0.5	2.7	33.1	52.7	24.2	27.9	3.6	155.0	340.2	355.4	607.4
1963	0.8	2.1	35.4	72.6	26.0	26.6	2.8	211.5	421.2	435.5	646.3
1964	1.1	2.5	38.2	92.3	25.8	27.1	3.6	225.7	470.6	486.1	763.7
1965	1.2	1.9	40.4	80.8	29.4	29.9	7.0	237.4	228.1	496.2	839.9
1966	1.2	2.6	40.8	71.1	28.1	29.8	9.9	220.4	256.0	614.1	745.7
1967	1.2	2.5	40.3	63.7	29.1	30.7	11.0	199.7	210.9	608.7	431.8
1968	1.4	2.7	44.3	57.1	30.1	26.7	12.2	198.2	230.9	407.9	686.1
1969	1.3	3.5	41.5	55.2	29.5	36.3	20.4	230.3	257.6	439.9	1,012.2
1970	1.3	4.7	45.6	62.1	27.0	35.6	44.5	291.6	352.5	498.4	1,072.4
1971	1.5	4.9	37.3	62.7	31.6	35.0	18.5	372.5	409.3	557.0	987.7
1972	0.8	4.6	42.7	62.5	25.8	31.2	12.8	385.4	409.1	572.3	903.1
1973	0.6	4.2	40.4	64.3	29.7	41.9	10.3	434.8	476.0	583.9	967.9
1974	0.5	4.1	40.8	71.9	39.8	33.1	12.0	541.8	549.9	639.1	629.8
1975	0.2	4.1	40.2	69.9	40.7	31.9	12.2	596.0	592.5	655.3	456.1

	Greece		Italy		Netherlands		Norway	Portugal
	E	I	E	I	E	I	E	E
1950	4.6	...	200.3	72.0	50.7	70.6	2.3	21.9
1951	14.2	...	293.1	91.9	58.8	37.6	2.9	33.7
1952	6.6	...	277.5	96.9	71.8	22.7	3.0	47.0
1953	8.8	...	224.7	103.0	57.5	37.6	2.5	39.7
1954	18.7	...	250.9	107.2	52.3	29.8	2.8	41.0
1955	29.8	...	320.1	141.9	43.1	39.0	2.6	29.8
1956	35.3	...	344.8	155.3	51.3	39.0	2.6	27.0
							10.2	
1957	30.4	...	341.7	163.3	50.5	35.5	12.4	35.4
1958	24.5	...	255.5	139.0	44.7	54.4	11.3	34.0
1959	23.7	...	268.5	156.1	44.9	25.7	11.8	33.5
1960	47.8	...	383.9	192.2	48.9	33.1	18.7	32.3
1961	58.8	...	387.1	210.2	38.0	42.5	10.6	33.5
1962	84.1	...	365.6	229.1	37.2	51.1	12.5	33.5
1963	100.1	...	277.6	221.2	32.3	43.5	11.4	39.5
1964	105.6	...	258.5	190.2	38.9	55.5	14.3	55.6
1965	117.2	...	282.6	196.4	43.3	65.1	14.0	89.1
1966	86.7	...	296.5	206.5	46.5	69.3	13.4	120.2
1967	42.7	...	229.3	168.3	52.4	44.5	13.0	92.5
1968	50.9	...	215.7	150.0	47.7	53.7	13.6	80.5
1969	91.6	...	182.2	153.3	45.3	66.6	13.5	...
					56.2[30]	76.4[30]		
1970	92.7	...	151.9	142.5	57.4	90.8	18.4	66.4
1971	61.7	...	167.7	128.6	62.0	95.1	12.7	50.4
1972	43.4	...	141.9	138.2	62.2	81.3	14.0	54.1
1973	27.5	...	123.8	125.2	63.6	84.7	13.9	79.5
1974	24.4	...	112.0	116.7	60.7	93.8	14.3	43.4
1975	20.3	...	92.7	122.8	55.2	127.3	14.8	24.8

See p.158 for footnotes

B9 **Annual Migration Statistics** (in thousands)

1950–1975

	Spain		Sweden		Switzerland		United Kingdom	
	E	I	E	I	E	I	E	I
1950	59.1	9.6	12.9	27.9	2.7	4.5	130.3	66.0
1951	61.3	11.6	16.6	31.6	3.4	4.4	150.8	67.7
1952	63.0	19.5	15.0	26.3	3.6	4.3	165.9	68.7
1953	50.7	19.8	17.5	19.2	2.7	4.8	144.1	69.6
1954	59.3	18.6	13.8	20.8	2.3	4.2	135.7	82.6
					7.5	5.5		
1955	67.6	18.6	12.7	30.1	7.7	5.8	116.4	72.7
1956	57.0	17.4	14.7	28.0	8.2	5.8	129.8	64.1
1957	62.5	22.2	15.1	33.0	8.3	6.3	153.6	56.0
1958	54.5	29.5	14.2	22.1	7.9	6.7	105.1	61.0
1959	34.6	19.1	15.6	19.1	7.9	6.4	95.6	67.2
1960	33.2	23.1	15.1	26.1	8.6	6.4	88.7	80.2
1961	34.3[29]							
1961	36.5	24.2	15.0	29.6	8.6	7.3	91.0	83.7
1962	36.2	22.3	14.9	25.1	8.7	7.6	91.2	68.0
1963	25.9	22.3	15.3	27.0	8.9	7.7	107.2	47.1
1964	24.3	22.4	15.7	38.3	9.4	7.5	271.4	211.0
1965	21.4	21.2	16.0	49.6	10.2	7.7	284.3	206.3
1966	21.4	20.1	19.7	47.0	10.8	7.9	301.6	219.2
1967	19.3	18.6	20.0	30.0	10.9	8.5	309.0	225.0
1968	19.4	16.0	23.2	36.0	10.3	8.4	277.7	221.6
1969	20.0	13.7	20.4	64.5	11.2	8.5	292.7	205.6
1970	16.8	13.2	28.7	77.3	10.4	8.5	290.7	225.6
1971	14.4	11.6	39.6	42.6	10.0	8.8	240.0	199.7
1972	6.0	...	41.6	29.9	9.3	8.5	233.2	221.9
1973	5.1	...	40.3	29.4	10.0	8.0	245.8	195.7
1974	4.6	...	28.4	37.4	9.7	7.6	269.0	183.8
1975	3.9	...	27.2	44.1	9.8	6.8	230.7	188.9

See p. 158 for footnotes

B9 Annual Migration Statistics (in thousands)

NOTES

1. SOURCES:– Four main sources have been used – I. Ferenczi *International Migration,* vol.I (New York, 1929); U.N., *Sex and Age of International Migrants: Statistics for 1918–1947* (1953); U.N., *Economic Characteristics of International Migrants: Statistics for Selected Countries, 1918–1954* (no date); and the annual U.N., *Demographic Yearbook.* In addition use was made of the official publications noted on p. xv and statistics for Greece from 1946 to 1969 were supplied by the National Statistical Service of Greece.

2. The nature of the statistics varies greatly from country to country. Descriptions of the main characteristics (minor changes are indicated in footnotes) are as follows:–

Austria
1819–30 – authorised migrants to and from Cisleithania and the Italian provinces;
1830–54 – the same plus unauthorised migrants against whom proceedings were taken;
1854–71 – authorised emigrants only (apparently) from Cisleithania;
1871–1913 – intercontinental emigrants of Austrian citizenship via Hamburg and Bremen, and subsequently other ports (see footnotes);
1921 onwards – (a) intercontinental emigrants of Austrian citizenship embarking for non-European countries, Turkey, or Russia at Hamburg, Bremen, Cherbourg, le Havre, Antwerp, Amsterdam, and Genoa, and (b) aliens receiving immigrant work-permits, and their dependants. The movements of refugees are excluded.

Belgium
Departures and arrivals to and from foreign countries and Belgian colonies as recorded in local registers of resident population. These appear to have been incomplete before the late 1900's.

Bulgaria
Permanent emigrants who had been resident in the country.

Czechoslovakia
Citizens and resident aliens receiving emigrant passports.

Denmark
1869–1932 – intercontinental emigration of citizens; 1933 onwards – migration to and from all overseas countries by citizens and resident aliens.

Finland
1900–1923 – intercontinental emigration of all residents; 1924 onwards – emigration to all countries of all residents. (Incomplete figures are available in Ferenczi, *op. cit.,* back to 1881.)

France
1857–91 – steerage (or equivalent) passengers of French citizenship at le Havre, Bordeaux, Bayonne, and at various times other French ports;
Immigration statistics from 1946 relate to permanent workers placed by the National Immigration Office, with migrants from Algeria added since 1955.
Emigration statistics since 1955 relate solely to movements to Algeria.

Germany
1832–36 – all emigrants via Bremen;
1836–51 – all emigrants via Bremen and Hamburg;
1852–70 – citizens of German states migrating via Bremen and Hamburg;
1871–1939 – intercontinental migration of citizens through German and the major foreign ports;
1946 onwards – all migrants to and from West Germany, including movements across the frontier with East Germany, and including short-term movements.

Greece
To 1940 – all migrants of Greek citizenship or origin, except for the 1919–24 immigration figures, which are of aliens.
1946–53 – all permanent transoceanic emigrants;
1954 onwards – all permanent emigrants.

Hungary
1871–1913 – intercontinental emigrants of Hungarian citizenship via Bremen and Hamburg and, at various times, other ports (see footnotes).

Ireland
1851–1921 – all natives who left Irish ports, including to Great Britain;
1924–33 – citizens migrating other than to Europe and the Mediterranean area;
1934 onwards – the same plus British citizens.
Statistics are not available after 1940, but see note 4 below.

Italy	1869–1913 – intercontinental migration of citizens "in straitened circumstances"; 1914–17 – intercontinental migration of manual workers, petty traders, and their families; 1928–42 – intercontinental migration of all workers; 1943 onwards – all migration of citizens.
Netherlands	1843–65 – intercontinental emigration of citizens via Dutch ports; 1865 onwards – departures and arrivals to and from overseas recorded in local registers of resident population. These were incomplete before 1920.
Norway	1821–1956 – intercontinental emigration of citizens, though from 1866 to 1876 only emigrants to the U.S.A. are included; 1956 onwards – emigration to all countries of all residents.
Poland	1890–1913 – permanent emigrants, other than to Russia, of all residents of Congress Poland; 1922–37 – permanent emigration to all residents.
Portugal	1855–1917 – intercontinental emigration of citizens; 1918 onwards – emigration to all countries of citizens.
Romania	All movements of citizens.
Russia	Emigration statistics relate to the outward balance of citizens crossing the frontiers, and immigration statistics to the inward balance of aliens. (Negative signs indicate net immigration of citizens and net emigration of aliens);
Serbia	As for Russia.
Spain	1851–1909 – outward balance of passenger movements by sea; 1909 onwards – steerage (or equivalent) passengers, whether citizens or aliens.
Sweden	All residents moving to take up permanent residence.
Switzerland	1868–1954 – emigration statistics relate to intercontinental movement of citizens and resident aliens; immigration statistics are of aliens only. (Statistics to 1889 are known to be incomplete.) 1954 onwards – all emigrants and returned immigrants.
United Kingdom	1815–76 – intercontinental passengers to and from U.K. ports (including Irish ports); 1876–1919 – intercontinental citizen passengers to and from U.K. ports; 1920–63 – intercontinental migration of U.K. and Commonwealth citizens for permanent residence; 1964 onwards – all migration of U.K. and Commonwealth citizens, other than to and from Ireland.
Yugoslavia	Intercontinental migration of citizens, though emigration statistics since 1925 include a small number of resident aliens.

Break lines in the table which are not followed by a footnote number refer to the changes listed above.

3. A few series, deemed to be too short for inclusion in the table proper, are shown here (in thousands):—

Czechoslovakia- Immigrants (citizens and aliens)

1922	12.8
1923	7.2
1924	9.1
1925	7.7
1926	6.9
1927	7.2

Germany—Emigrants (citizens)

1844	24.0	1850	45.3
1845	39.0	1851	56.5
1846	56.5	1852	72.5
1847	67.1	1853	55.7
1848	44.4	1854	124.2
1849	52.9		

4. Annual average net emigration from southern Ireland for intercensal periods is as follows (in thousands):—

1936–46	18.7
1946–51	24.4
1951–56	39.4
1956–61	42.4
1961–66	16.1
1966–71	10.8.

FOOTNOTES

[1] Bordeaux, le Havre, and Marseille were included from 1875.
[2] A small proportion of Hungarians is included in these years.
[3] Amsterdam, Antwerp, Genoa, Rotterdam, and the minor German ports were included from 1889, though the latter were dropped from 1899 without significantly affecting the series.
[4] Bordeaux, le Havre, and Marseille were dropped from 1900.
[5] Amsterdam, Antwerp, Genoa, and Rotterdam were included from 1889.
[6] From 1 May.
[7] Migrants from the Azores and Maderia are included.
[8] Trieste was included from 1903.
[9] Cherbourg and Fiume were included from 1904.
[10] le Havre was included again from 1905.
[11] From 1 March.
[12] The occasion of this break is described in note 2. A comparable figure on the later basis for 1931 is 9.6 thousand;
[13] Including Austria and Sudetenland.
[14] To 31 August only.
[15] From 1 April.
[16] Intercontinental migrants only.
[17] Fiume, Liverpool and Trieste were included from 1904.
[18] le Havre was included from 1905.
[19] Cherbourg was included from 1910.
[20] From 1 October.
[21] Excluding migrants through U.K. ports after June.
[22] Including deportees.
[23] To 30 April only.
[24] Excluding emigrants from the towns, who numbered 2.1 thousand in 1902 and 13.0 thousand in 1904.
[25] Migration via southern Irish ports was subsequently excluded.
[26] These are known to be incomplete.
[27] West Berlin is included from 1960.
[28] Subsequent statistics are from the *Statistical Yearbook of the Netherlands* rather than the U.N. *Demographic Yearbook.*
[29] Previously excluding emigration by air.
[30] This break occurs on a change of source from U.N. to national publications.

C. LABOUR FORCE

The statistics in this section cover a wide range of topics and come from a variety of sources. The occupation data were almost entirely derived by Professor Bairoch and his colleagues from national censuses of population. The problems of accuracy referred to in the last section appear here also, therefore. But a more significant difficulty is the very considerable variations which have occurred in classification, both between countries and over time. When Jacques Bertillon came to put together his volume of nineteenth century European population censuses for the International Institute of Statistics in 1899, he expressed the view that "the nomenclatures adopted by the different countries are so different that international comparisons would have been either very difficult or fallacious".[1] Professor Bairoch's group, having made every possible effort to achieve international and intertemporal comparability, in effect echo Bertillon, when they write that "because of the frequent changes in criteria and methods used in census taking...it is practically impossible to come up with statistics that are perfectly comparable in time and space".[2]

An even greater degree of heterogeneity is to be found in the unemployment statistics, some of which come from trade union records (of varying character and reliability), some from insurance statistics (which can be just as variable), and some from either total registration or sample surveys. In addition to variations in the definition of the unemployed, where percentages are shown there are also likely to be variations in the definition of the total workforce. It will be readily understood, therefore, that comparisons over time must be made with due regard to changes in the nature of the series, and that comparisons between countries must not be made without taking differences of definition into account. Availability of some indicator of the level of unemployment has varied from time to time, though the exceptional levels of the early 1930s led to much greater interest in the details of it at that time. However, French data were always poor, and the Nazi regime in Germany discontinued publication of the relevant information. Much better data are available for western Europe since the Second World War, but there has rarely been any for the centrally-planned economies of eastern Europe.

Data on industrial disputes are likewise lacking for the centrally-planned economies and for many periods and places where there was an authoritarian government in the market economies. However, the statistics which do exist are reasonably homogeneous and reliable for each country individually, though comparisons between countries are difficult because of differences in reporting systems.

Wage data are notoriously intractable, and perhaps it is best to treat the indices shown here in tables C4 and C5 as little more than impressions of the general course of money wages. Apart from the well-known technical problems of index numbers, dealt with in any textbook of statistics, there are problems in each country of availability and selection of data; of weighting different occupations, and of the appropriateness (which often takes the form of assessing obsolescence) of the chosen weights; of the differences between hourly, daily or weekly wage rates, and weekly or longer-period earnings. Moreover, it must be stressed that these tables are concerned with money wages, not real wages, for which a rough detailed comparisons between different countries require a degree of original research which it has not been possible to afford here, and as yet there has been little scholarly effort devoted to this subject, despite—or, perhaps, because of—its intermittent interest for journalists.

[1] J. Bertillon, *Statistique Internationale des Rencensements de la Population.......* (Paris, 1899).

[2] P. Bairoch *et al, La Population active et sa Structure* (Brussells, 1968)

C1 ECONOMICALLY ACTIVE POPULATION BY MAJOR INDUSTRIAL GROUPS (in thousands)[1]

AUSTRIA[4] 1857–1971

	Agriculture Forestry & Fishing	Extractive Industry	Manufacturing[2] Industry	Construction	Commerce Finance etc	Transport & Communications	Services[3]	Others Occupied
All								
1857	3,638[6]		1,225		111		698[9]	1,286[6]
1869	7,506	104[5]	1,859[5]	236	303	95	1,198[9]	215
Males								
1880	3,432[6]	108[5,7]	1,632[5,7]		241[8]	111	633[9]	454[6]
1890	4,165	130[5,7]	1,753[5,7]	273	289[8]	183	495[9]	119
1900	4,083	184[5,7]	1,880[5,7]	357	333	246	582[9]	212
1910	4,212	369[7]	2,361[7]		575[8]	375	654[9]	87
1920	638	778			269[8]		263[9]	21
1934	654	22	792		233[8]	134	205[9]	60
1939	655	26[5]	634[5]	251	131	172	283[9,8]	–
1951	513	48	632	256	157	159	233[9,8]	25
1961	362	47	652	314	181	173	261[8]	21
1971	228	25	681	246	277[8]	167	243	33
Females								
1880	2,729[6]	10[5,7]	525[5,7]		79[8]	5	693[9]	428[6]
1890	4,305	14[5,7]	691[5,7]	20	89[8]	13	562[9]	120
1900	4,123	10[5,7]	692[5,7]	16	126[8]	15	633[9]	246[6]
1910	4,294	53[7]	845[7]		349[8]	22	586[9]	169
1920	346		248		106[8]		89[9]	326
1934	350	1	244		148[8]	11	280[9]	35
1939	768	1[5]	260[5]	10	141	19	299[8,9]	–
1951	567	3	266	11	138	19	279[8,9]	14
1961	407	3	345[5]	19	189	25	354[8]	17
1971	199	2	327	15	328[8]	28	271	28

BELGIUM 1846–1970

	Agriculture Forestry & Fishing	Extractive Industry	Manufacturing[2] Industry	Construction	Commerce Finance etc	Transport & Communications	Services[3]	Others Occupied
Males								
1846	681	44	329	41	45[10]	16[10]	117[10]	–
1856	712	63	400	62	53[10]	26[10]	132[10]	–
1866	705	93	466	68	67[10]	30[10]	145[10,11]	–
1880	674	104	513	84	149[10]	29[29]	206[10]	–
1890	640	130	604	93	217[10]	41[10]	268[10]	–
1900	616	166	738	131	264[10]	72[10]	271[10]	–
1910	585	192	807	185	182	184	256	–
1920	525	212	774	187	186	232	187	–
1930	505	201	987	238	277	242	304	–
1947	364	188	981	178	307	234	352	5
1961	213	109	961	246	306	220	446	5
1970[23]	133	49	902	283	450	211	439	47
Females								
1846	342	4	310	––	23[10]	1[10]	57[10]	–
1856	354	10	317	––	32[10]	1[10]	115[10]	–
1866	372	15	275	1	37[10]	1[10]	151[10]	–
1880	387	10	259	1	88[10]	1[10]	176[10]	–
1890	268	9	256	1	96[10]	1[10]	207[10]	–
1900	249	7	321	1	122[10]	6[10]	225[10]	–
1910	217	8	383	2	111	7	342	–
1920	151	10	306	3	90	12	230	–
1930	141	6	346	3	166	12	310	–
1947	61	3	307	2	171	16	244	1
1961	41	1	285	4	212	19	345	1
1970	29	1	298	9	315	23	345	25

See p.172 for footnotes

C1 Economically Active Population by Major Industrial Groups (in thousands)

BULGARIA 1910–1965

	Agriculture Forestry & Fishing	Extractive Industry	Manufacturing[2] Industry	Construction	Commerce Finance etc	Transport & Communications	Services[3]	Others
Males								
1910	929	2	158		67	28	84	15
1920	1,035	6	176		66	33	100	10
1934	1,348	8	220		75	47	149	58
1946	1,541	20	318		106	64	233	51
1956	1,317		482[12]	108	100	114	259[12]	24
1965	857		728	256	99	156	36	258
Females								
1910	892	–	20		1	—	28	—
1920	1,108	– –	29		4	1	33	—
1934	1,397	–	46		6	1	54	29
1946	1,619	—	92		19	2	68	50
1956	1,346		176[12]	7	42	17	148[12]	9
1965	1,034		414	25	107	33	26	238

CZECHOSLOVAKIA 1921–1970

	Agriculture Forestry & Fishing	Extractive Industry	Manufacturing Industry	Construction	Commerce Finance etc	Transport & Communications	Services	Others
Males								
1921	1,666	150	1,598		255	223	350	55
1930[13]	1,447	129	1,428	362	362	266	421	65
1947	1,123	133	1,506		244	261	518	8
1961	716		1,440	459	180	288	407	–
1970	637	175	1,422	501	211	344	530	40
Females								
1921	759	10	455		107	20	330	38
1930[13]	1,037	4	568	10	197	15	380	33
1947	1,084	10	536		133	25	259	13
1961	736		934	63	324	94	525	–
1970	506	29	1,129	97	478	148	714	12

DENMARK 1850–1970

	Agriculture Forestry & Fishing	Extractive Industry	Manufacturing Industry	Construction	Commerce Finance etc	Transport & Communications	Services	Others
All								
1850[14]	654		291		57		98	225
Males								
1860[14]	366		177		38		48	119
1870[14]	411		192		58		54	138
1880[14]	478		231		75		67	88
1890[14]	463		268		82	35	71	90
1901	381		165	43	110		64	13
1911	403		231		91	48	55	18
1921	405		302		103	71	71	5
1930	438		365		137	84	68	11
1940	435	4	360	115	155	101	106	10
1950	397	4	402	128	176	117	130	15
1960	332	4	455	147	193	127	156	33
1970	189	3	435	198	249	124	216	51
Females								
1860[14]	361		169		40		53	126
1870[14]	405		181		60		61	146
1880[14]	479		220		81		78	99
1890[14]	452		266		91	33	84	104
1901	150		67	—	21		117	8
1911	110		66		37	4	144	24
1921	69		66		44	9	204	11
1930	122		66		59	7	220	11
1940	127	—	123	1	86	14	330	4
1950	121	—	149	4	103	22	287	8
1960	35	—	155	4	120	24	306	3
1970	55	—	177	12	214	29	244	16

See p.172 for footnotes

C1 Economically Active Population by Major Industrial Groups (in thousands)

FINLAND 1754–1970

	Agriculture Forestry & Fishing	Extractive Industry	Manufacturing Industry[2]	Construction	Commerce Finance etc	Transport & Communications	Services[2]	Others Occupied
All								
1754[15]	350		13		2	2	67	11
1769[15]	434		21		3	3	66	14
1805[15]	702		31		6	6	90	20
Males								
1880	260		39		6	17	37	–
1900	326	1	61	13	12	25	30	134
1910	568	- -	103		15	26	19	92
1920	603	1	140		27	35	27	56
1930	634	1	158	28	38[8]	44	35	71
1940	629	3	224	39	48	60	55	93
1950	543	5	259	117	75	85	71	22
1960	466	6	292	166	106	102	89	5
1970	287	6	343	164	147	116	142	21
Females								
1880	98		9		4	1	31	–
1900	103	- -	20	- -	5	1	34	68
1910	329	–	34		12	2	35	60
1920	429	–	51		23	5	47	55
1930	473	–	63	2	39[8]	7	65	55
1940	529	- -	104	5	63	12	100	55
1950	369	1	162	6	85	22	156	7
1960	255	1	165	10	130	27	212	1
1970	142	1	200	12	252	35	242	8

FRANCE 1856–1968

	Agriculture Forestry & Fishing	Extractive Industry	Manufacturing Industry[2]	Construction	Commerce Finance etc	Transport & Communications	Services[2]	Others Occupied
Males								
1856	5,146	177[18]	2,002[18]	486	510	214	1,174[9]	–
1866[16]	5,299	145[18]	2,303[18]	561	525	276	1,372[9]	–
1866[17]	5,248	223[18]	2,019[18]	712	910	274	1,679[9]	–
1896[17]	5,741	224	2,903	543	783	552	1,811[9]	–
1901[17]	5,581	264	3,083	563	873	603	1,905[9]	–
1906[17]	5,525	279	3,169	539	972	631	1,913[9]	–
1911[17]	5,331	240	4,189		1,218	657	1,577[9]	–
1921	5,062	317	3,396	620	1,025	915	1,780[9]	–
1926	4,809	433	3,869	697	1,193	871	1,685[9]	–
1931	4.510	442	3,886	821	1,265	935	1,853[9]	–
1936	4,282	350	3,442	679	1,272	904	2,012[9]	–
1946	4,221	369	3,128	1,022	1,169	1,238	1,767[9]	–
1954	3,369	364	3,598	1,337	1,269	843	1,950[9]	–
1962	2,634	310	3,846	1,553	1,479	862	2,331	–
1968	2,120	234	4,058	1,990	1,890	970	1,816	
Females								
1856	2,159	17[18]	1,095[18]	16	228	10	889	–
1866[16]	2,237	14[18]	1,196[18]	18	260	14	923	–
1886[17]	2,598	30[18]	1,250[18]	61	504	21	1,179	–
1896[17]	2,760	6	1,716	2	510	161	1,219	–
1901[17]	2,664	6	1,926	2	791	213	1,427	–
1906[17]	3,330	6	2,059	1	642	241	1,422	–
1911[17]	3,241	6	2,496		835	60	1,082	–
1921	3,961	11	2,021	6	778	270	1,555	–
1926	3,391	16	2,000	6	780	160	1,487	–
1931	3,194	18	2,019	9	881	135	1,646	–
1936	2,922	8	1,695	8	859	132	1,698	–
1946	3,263	13	1,630	24	922	275	1,753	–
1954	1,826	9	1,642	53	875	177	1,954	–
1962	1,273	10	1,647	60	1,117	201	2,170	–
1968	1,013	7	1,696	102	1,477	252	2,377	–

See p.172 for footnotes

C1 Economically Active Population by Major Industrial Groups (in thousands)

	Agriculture Forestry & Fishing	Extractive Industry	Manufacturing[2] Industry	Construction	Commerce Finance etc.	Transport & Communications	Services[3]	Others Occupied
GERMANY								**1882–1939**
Males								
1882	5,702	569	3,721	940	678	423	1,173	168
1895	5,540	789	4,565	1,340	930	598	1,596	150
1907	5,284	1,197	5,959	1,887	1,251	983	1,907	114
1925[19]	4,793	1,232	7,422	1,676	1,983	1,423	1,834	168
1933[19]	4,694	1,053	7,279	1,963	2,208	1,460	2,161	–
1939[20]	4,065	723	8,053	2,307	2,115	1,760	2,792	–
Females								
1882	2,535	22	995	6	176	14	443	67
1895	2,753	32	1,351	14	300	18	745	51
1907	4,599	48	1,875	19	549	43	1,069	42
1925	4,969	40	2,837	32	1,100	97	2,322	81
1933	4,685	30	2,688	40	1,409	92	2,570	–
1939	4,920	11	3,455	68	1,324	137	2,888	–
EAST GERMANY								**1946–1971**
Males								
1946	1,046	228	1,586	411	313	351	529	–
1950	962	370	1,782	432	333	356	526	7
1960[21]	772		2,061	453	321	356	486	–
1971[21]	529	153	1,829	525	293	357	728	–
Females								
1946	1,332	47	1,095	52	330	67	752	–
1950	1,097	54	920	43	384	78	566	13
1960[21]	630		1,311	40	606	178	834	–
1971[21]	431	46	1,356	89	638	198	1,044	–
WEST GERMANY								**1946–1970**
Males								
1946	2,735	614	4,087	1,125	898	1,035	1,629	–
1950	2,328	685	5,206	1,867	1,312	1,079	1,992	240
1961[22]	1,625	591	6,853	1,957	1,738	1,259	2,620	73
1970[22]	1,025	311	7,083	2,015	2,512	1,183	2,875	71
Females								
1946	2,852	43	1,467	50	617	124	1,878	–
1950	1,806	16	2,067	71	967	143	2,034	265
1961[22]	1,959	14	3,126	84	1,863	221	2,695	45
1970[22]	966	12	3,181	148	2,758	260	2,164	46
GREECE[23]								**1920–1971**
Males								
1920	817	8	235		147	77	117	122
1928	1,008	6	330		202	106	130	191
1951	1,152	13	340	74	199	135	273	144
1961	1,178	20	352	166	226	148	288	21
1971	834	20	426	255	342	199	228	26
Females								
1920	109	1	59		4	1	47	123
1928	468	- -	100		7	1	58	140
1951	215	1	121	1	21	3	115	32
1961	782	2	157	1	40	6	152	6
1971	478	2	153	2	99	13	121	39

See p.172 for footnotes

C1 Economically Active Population by Major Industrial Groups (in thousands)

HUNGARY[24] 1857–1970

	Agriculture Forestry & Fishing	Extractive Industry	Manufacturing[2] Industry	Construction	Commerce Finance etc.	Transport & Communications	Services[3]	Others Occupied
All								
1857	2,275		410		67		540	764[6]
1869	5,015	50	584	63	105	29	1,338	—
Males								
1880	3,547[6 25]	26[7]	714[7]		166		188[26]	443[6 26]
1890	3,954	44[7]	630[7]	93	145	76	321	185
1900	4,234	56[7]	758[7]	122	184	131	398	223
1910	4,332	72	1,204		246	193	386	196
1920	1,494	39	547		135	106	214	45
1930	1,560	35	714		170	104	188	64
1949	1,545	72	604	93	128	148	227	134
1960	**1,171**	**145**	**803**	**273**	**156**	**245**	**237**	**137**
1970	**752**	**141**	**983**	**313**	**162**	**267**	**317**	
Females								
1880	973[6 25]	—[7]	715[7]		20		402	506[6]
1890	1,471	1[7]	95[7]	1	38	3	415	165
1900	1,821	1[7]	149[7]	3	42	6	429	133
1910	1,269	1	256		54	10	422	110
1920	632	1	132		49	12	198	49
1930	471	—	173		56	9	226	59
1949	651	3	189	3	66	17	137	138
1960	**702**	**12**	**443**	**31**	**170**	**52**	**271**	**30**
1970	**471**	**22**	**750**	**57**	**258**	**78**	**419**	

IRELAND 1841–1911

	Agriculture Forestry & Fishing	Extractive Industry	Manufacturing[2] Industry	Construction	Commerce Finance etc.	Transport & Communications	Services[3]	Others Occupied
Males								
1841	1,699	9[27]	303	72[27]	78		101	219[27]
1851	1,293	12[27]	257	58[27]	106		67	319[27]
1861	1,072	10[27]	231	66[27]	117		76	346[27]
1871	943	9[27]	194	58[27]	125		61	345[27]
1881	890	8[27]	164	56[27]	121		67	307[27]
1911	716	5	255		53	22	111	164
Females								
1841	145	...	686	...	33		281	...
1851	167	...	430	...	46		260	...
1861	101	...	335	...	46		334	...
1871	103	...	306	...	46		377	...
1881	96	...	215	...	39		412	...
1911	59	—	156		73	1	182	8

See p. 172 for footnotes

C1 Economically Active Population by Major Industrial Groups (in thousands)

SOUTHERN IRELAND 1926–1971

	Agriculture Forestry & Fishing	Extractive Industry	Manufacturing Industry[2]	Construction	Commerce Finance etc.	Transport & Communications	Services[3]	Others Occupied
Males								
1926	556	3	155		73	67	79	26
1936	542	3	100	62	68	67	98	47
1946	516	3	101	54	62	58	115	55
1951	436	10	140	95	103	54	98	10
1961	348	10	136	73	109	51	90	5
1971	259	11	171	98	139	54	92	7
Females								
1926	122	–	33		35	2	143	8
1936	107	–	37	–	36	2	166	4
1946	81	–	35	–	37	1	172	8
1951	68	—	63	1	53	6	131	4
1961	42	—	62	1	55	7	118	1
1971	26	—	69	2	77	10	103	2

NORTHERN IRELAND 1926–1971

	Agriculture Forestry & Fishing	Extractive Industry	Manufacturing Industry[2]	Construction	Commerce Finance etc.	Transport & Communications	Services[3]	Others Occupied
Males								
1926	133	3	107	22	51	21	50	4
1951	93	2	120	40	51	31	54	30
1961	68	1	112	41	54	28	70	
1971	48	1	113	54	55	31	110	
Females								
1926	16	–	95	—	19	1	50	1
1951	6	–	87	1	25	3	51	10
1961	3	—	73	1	32	3	60	
1971	2	—	49	—	67	2	80	

ITALY 1871–1971

	Agriculture Forestry & Fishing	Extractive Industry	Manufacturing Industry[2]	Construction	Commerce Finance etc.	Transport & Communications	Services[3]	Others Occupied
Males								
1871	5,664	38	1,929		167	263	1,176	19
1881	5,498	59	1,446	836	247	310	904	876
1901	6,466	91	2,528		524	416	998	80
1911	6,112	110	2,877		723	530	844	78
1921	7,147	99	3,146		939	717	987	–
1931	6,545[28]		4,057[28]		1,039	767	951	
1936	6,412	126	2,707	974	1,156	667	865	190
1951	6,228	3,452		1,462	150	731	2,642	–
1961	4,150		6,333			4,135		
1971	2,299	4,688		1,991	1,849	906	2,015	627
Females								
1871	3,036	—	1,358		33	8	567	4
1881	3,101	1	1,835	69	33	3	646	877
1901	3,200	1	1,370		113	8	592	67
1911	2,973	3	1,378		199	14	550	10
1921	3,117	1	1,245		231	22	632	–
1931	1,539[28]		1,252		280	27	805	
1936	2,431	2	1,342	5	449	35	955	29
1951	2,033	1,365		11	26	54	1,423	–
1961	1,507		1,553			1,841		
1971	943	1,635		35	961	86	1,422	348

See p.172 for footnotes

C1 Economically Active Population by Major Industrial Groups (in thousands)

NORWAY 1875–1970

	Agriculture Forestry & Fishing	Extractive Industry	Manufacturing[2] Industry	Construction	Commerce Finance etc.	Transport & Communications	Services[3]	Others Occupied
Males								
1875	202[29]	4	92		25	42[29]	134[29]	24
1891	297		127			76[30]	25[30]	5
1900	288		177			94	28	13
1910	321	8	176		47	74	29	6
1920	336	15	233		66	84	34	4
1930	372	19	178	52	83	102	40	4
1946	367	9[31]	243[31]	121	84	117	81	11
1950	333	9	285	127	90	124	86	7
1960	261	9	302	131	113	147	116	5
1970	140	9	334	126	160	132	154	2
Females								
1875	16[29]	—	33		4	- -	224[29]	14
1891	87		50			15[30]	88[30]	4
1900	72		66			28	108	8
1910	53	- -	61		37	4	125	4
1920	58	1	61		53	8	118	1
1930	41	1	59	- -	62	6	146	- -
1946	41	- -[31]	78[31]	1	55	14	160	3
1950	27	- -	83	2	60	16	139	1
1960	13	- -	69	2	74	20	143	- -
1970	30	- -	73	3	131	25	141	1

NETHERLANDS 1849–1971

	Agriculture Forestry & Fishing	Extractive Industry	Manufacturing[2] Industry	Construction	Commerce Finance etc.	Transport & Communications	Services[3]	Others Occupied
Males								
1849	394	2	191	60	61	55	92	27
1859	389	2	214	67	67	68	107	27
1889	468	13	316	113	123	110	131	25
1899	512	14	389	130	179	103	129	34
1909	528	20	469	154	221	154	151	23
1920	551	42	610	184	272	208	192	29
1930	546	48	710	253	360	230	237	33
1947[11]	578	53	918	287	377	239	418	53
1960	406	60	1,121	374	448	269	469	94
1971	251	19	993	509	732	251	535	218
Females								
1849	158	- -	48	- -	20	2	134	7
1859	79	—	44	- -	18	1	161	5
1889	73	2	54	- -	30	2	186	- -
1899	80	2	72	- -	40	3	234	- -
1909	112	3	94	- -	48	4	277	—
1920	90	3	128	1	76	10	321	1
1930	110	2	145	1	112	10	384	- -
1947[11]	169	1	164	2	173	18	413	3
1960	41	1	208	5	222	22	428	2
1971	37	1	199	14	341	29	476	128

See p.172 for footnotes

C1 Economically Active Population by Major Industrial Groups (in thousands)

POLAND[36] 1897–1970

	Agriculture Forestry & Fishing	Extractive Industry	Manufacturing Industry[2]	Construction	Commerce Finance etc.	Transport & Communications	Services[3]	Others Occupied
Males								
1897[32]	1,082	18	381	44	128	44	528[35]	15
1921[33]	5,148	85	941		375	227	589	161
1931	5,429	169	1,850		517	323	429	303
1950[34]	3,295		1,639[37]	448	365[37]	406[37]	665[37]	40
1960[34]	3,009		2,269[37]	711	341[37]	572[37]	852[37]	
1970	2,958	331	2,699	963	350[37]	851[37]	998[37]	
Females								
1897[32]	219	1	77	. .	21	1	259[35]	14
1921[33]	5,122	8	232		144	17	365	—
1931	4,323	6	513		296	18	614	—
1950[34]	3,795		689[36]	71	279[35]	63[37]	599[37]	51
1960[34]	3,627		967[37]	80	459[37]	101[37]	918[37]	
1970	3,586	44	1,626	163	776[37]	217[37]	1,341[37]	

PORTUGAL 1890–1970

	Agriculture Forestry & Fishing	Extractive Industry	Manufacturing Industry[2]	Construction	Commerce Finance etc.	Transport & Communications	Services[3]	Others Occupied
Males								
1890	1,076	4	297		72	50	81	—
1900	1,147	4	327		96	62	78	—
1911	1,127	9	393		125	73	122	—
1930	1,122	11	376		126	61	232	112
1940[38]	1,263	20	331	139	162	81	230	145
1950	1,348	24	455	165	206	106	242	6
1960	1,341	26	538	228	233	113	258	27
1970	824	12	492	253	298	130	396	71
Females								
1890	487	. .	298		31	2	6	—
1900	382	. .	194		46	4	9	—
1911	335	. .	155		30	3	173	—
1930	775	7	305		92	42	603	86
1940[38]	225	1	137	2	29	8	254	22
1950	242	2	175	1	34	8	273	2
1960	107	1	173	2	40	11	269	2
1970	179	. .	261	3	103	18	233	32

ROMANIA 1913–1966

	Agriculture Forestry & Fishing	Extractive Industry	Manufacturing Industry[2]	Construction	Commerce Finance etc.	Transport & Communications	Services[3]	Others Occupied
Males								
1913	1,584	9	246		100	70	212	9
1930[39]	4,055	49	500	265	241	158	388	233
1956	3,380[40]		1,150[40]	242	227	259	426[40]	43
1966	2,531[55]		1,556[55]	493	240	375	477	4
Females								
1913	1,575	. .	63		7	1	83	11
1930[39]	4,176	4	132	3	117	17	99	221
1956	3,898[40]		328[40]	23	122	38	284[40]	45
1966	3,390[55]		514[55]	44	184	62	491	3

See p. 172 for footnotes

C1 Economically Active Population by Major Industrial Groups (in thousands)

RUSSIA 1897–1970

	Agriculture Forestry & Fishing	Extractive Industry	Manufacturing Industry[2]	Construction	Commerce Finance etc.	Transport & Communications	Services[3]	Others Occupied[54]
Males								
1897[41]	15,077	155	2,920	671	1,051[36,35]	649	3,207[35]	227
1926[38]	36,170		3,487	356	900	1,195[44]	1,270[44]	610
1959	18,577[42]		22,866[43]		1,993[36,45]	–[43]	5,249[45]	133
1970	14,652		31,813[43]		2,086[36,45]	–[43]	8,945[45]	495
Females								
1897[41]	1,867	8	894	2	141[36,35]	21	1,777[35]	242
1926[38]	35,565		1,171	8	257	98[44]	759[44]	866
1959	29,715[42]		14,400[43]		3,178[36,45]	–[43]	9,204[45]	58
1970	16,109		20,959[43]		5,798	–	15,612[45]	560

SPAIN 1860–1970

	Agriculture Forestry & Fishing	Extractive Industry	Manufacturing Industry[2]	Construction	Commerce Finance etc.	Transport & Communications	Services[3]	Others Occupied[54]
Males								
1860	4,333	23		943	138	50	711	–
1877	4,112		755		144	208	511	–
1887[46]	4,033		921		167	115	345	–[46]
1900	4,324	76		775	226	133	437	190
1910	3,861		860		115	153	436	1,058
1920	4,217	130		1,284	349	219	489	283
1940	4,519	99	1,430	372	518	304	850	11
1950	4,853	171	1,543	570	594	402	799	152
1964	3,368	228	2,281	908	896	539	956	73
1970	2,646	124	2,405	1,196	1,347	605	1,126	126
Females								
1860	–	–		224	–	–	110	–
1877	933		143		21	1	359	–
1887[46]	821		195		28	1	370	–[46]
1900	815	1		175	27	2	331	31
1910	359		174		20	2	352	107
1920	321	2		279	58	3	348	111
1940	262	1	309	2	71	6	466	–
1950	418	3	418	4	103	19	724	20
1964	809	1	797	9	451	30	695	21
1970	312	2	702	22	466	54	745	31

See p. 172 for footnotes

C1 Economically Active Population by Major Industrial Groups (in thousands)

SWEDEN 1860–1970

	Agriculture Forestry & Fishing	Extractive Industry	Manufacturing[2] Industry	Construction	Commerce Finance etc.	Transport & Communications	Services[3]	Others Occupied
Males								
1860	510		164		15	21	79	–
1870	707		118			43	79	182[49]
1880	738		157			68	82	207[49]
1890	771		233			90	77	130[49]
1900	772		362			125	81	113[49]
1910	758	13		467	82	106	114	47
1920	808	21		634	126	136	81	21
1930	799	37		704	170	169	98	18
1945	688	15	717	214	205	187[48]	182	34
1950	579	15[5]	802[5]	241	233	208	192	16
1960[47]	408	22	893	285	229	199	233	8
1970	221	18	777	319	341	199	325	6
Females								
1860	154		10		6	–	78	–
1870	307		9			3	74	136[49]
1880	332		17			5	90	104[49]
1890	333		30			13	87	101[49]
1900	336		51			23	103	106[49]
1910	258	–		85	38	6	176	49
1920	251	- -		153	92	18	246	15
1930	242	- -		186	149	22	295	2
1945	45	- -	181	3	147	33[48]	329	8
1950	53	- -[5]	205[5]	4	170	43	337	7
1960[47]	39	1	251	10	209	43	410	3
1970	56	1	245	13	318	48	523	2

SWITZERLAND 1890–1970

	Agriculture Forestry & Fishing	Extractive Industry	Manufacturing Industry	Construction	Commerce Finance etc.	Transport & Communications	Services	Others Occupied
Males								
1890	410		334		59	47	43	–
1900	405			435	69	52	47	–
1910	376	6		539	108	79	65	6
1920	386	6		557	118	83	77	3
1930	362[35]	7		638	123	78	124[35]	–
1941	385	7	520	136	128	70	146	30
1950	325	6	594	172	157	88	160	13
1960[38]	257	6	746	234	197	119	193	–
1970	178	6	826	272	350	139	199	4
Females								
1890	148		217		36	2	22	–
1900	80			225	55	4	32	–
1910	101	–		270	86	6	138	3
1920	97	- -		265	99	8	162	- -
1930	51[35]	- -		229	67	7	256[35]	–
1941	30	- -	203	2	71	6	251	8
1950	30	- -	228	4	96	10	267	6
1960[38]	23	- -	275	5	149	16	286	–
1970	53	–	327	13	334	31	261	3

See p. 172 for footnotes

C1 Economically Active Population by Major Industrial Groups (in thousands)

U.K. (Great Britain) 1841–1971

	Agriculture Forestry & Fishing	Extractive Industry	Manufacturing[2] Industry	Construction	Commerce Finance etc.	Transport & Communications	Services[3]	Others Occupied
Males								
1841[50]	1,458	218	1,816	376	94	196	459	474
1851	1,824	383	2,349	496	91	433	482	438
1861	1,818	457	2,609	593	130	579	564	511
1871	1,681	517	2,815	712	212	654	664	972
1881[51]	1,575	604	3,001	875	352	870	815	862
1891	1,475	751	3,460	899	449	1,104	860	1,009
1901	1,390	931	4,062	1,216	597	1,409	1,056	887
1911	1,489	1,202	4,688	1,140	739	1,571	1,361	741
1921	1,261	1,396	4,813	783	1,702	1,461	1,897	344
1931	1,181	1,272	4,958	1,108	2,314	1,563	2,267	137
1951	1,025	847	6,153	1,390	1,838	1,517	2,806	73
1961	777	728	6,308	1,597	2,066	1,486	3,136	135
1971	643	256	6,121	1,476	2,391	1,811	2,910	276
Females								
1841[50]	81	7	639	1	1	4	1,041	41
1851	230	11	1,263	1	—	13	1,241	75
1861	164	6	1,456	1	2	11	1,537	80
1871	136	11	1,541	4	5	16	1,837	106
1881[51]	119	8	1,685	2	11	15	1,968	78
1891	81	7	1,948	3	26	20	2,317	89
1901	86	6	2,123	3	76	27	2,358	75
1911	117	8	2,430	5	157	38	2,560	98
1921	111	14	2,187	12	863	109	2,331	75
1931	76	9	2,355	14	1,021	110	2,644	44
1951	117	14	2,654	41	1,322	217	2,560	36
1961	97	21	2,666	69	1,773	230	2,861	64
1971	97	5	1,505	182	3,561	453	3,128	375

YUGOSLAVIA 1921–1971

	Agriculture Forestry & Fishing	Extractive Industry	Manufacturing Industry	Construction	Commerce Finance etc.	Transport & Communications	Services	Others Occupied
All								
1921	4,848		651[43]		133	—[43]	264	
Males								
1931	3.234		593		131	94	242	96
1948	3,322[52]		725		29[53]	112	547[53]	129
1953	3,079	106	649	224	161	151	375	16
1961	2,729	136	997	291	159	221	418	252
1971	2,270		1,093	364	287	283	507	23
Females								
1931	1,865		124		39	8	64	38
1948	4,074[52]		183		8[53]	4	196[53]	180
1953	2,161	7	191	17	79	17	174	4
1961	2,019	8	374	26	106	28	310	60
1971	1,695		482	33	236	40	414	10

See p.172 for footnotes

C1 Economically Active Population by Major Industrial Groups (in thousands)

NOTES

1. SOURCES:– The immediate source of all statistics (except the most recent) is P. Bairoch *et al, The Working Population and its Structure* (Institut de Sociologie, Universite Libre de Bruxelles, 1968). The original sources are described in detail there. The 1968/71 data come from I.L.O., *Yearbook of Labour Statistics.*

2. Professor Bairoch and his collaborators "tried to as great an extent as possible to unify the statistics in different countries during different periods", but were unable to achieve anything like perfect comparability. Comparisons between countries must be made with especially great caution owing to differences in classification, including differences in the definition of "economically active".

3. Where the original data were for an occupational rather than an industrial classification, this was usually transposed, with, of course, some degree of estimation involved. One exception is the statistics for Great Britain up to 1911, which are on an occupational basis.

FOOTNOTES

[1] Unless otherwise stated all statistics relate to the boundaries of the year in question.
[2] Unless otherwise stated, gas, water, electricity, and sanitary service workers are included under this heading.
[3] Except as otherwise indicated, armed forces are included under this heading.
[4] Cisleithania (excluding the Italian provinces) up to the First World War.
[5] Quarrying is included with "manufacturing industry".
[6] Many agricultural day-labourers were included in "others occupied".
[7] Metallurgy is included with "extractive industry".
[8] Includes catering services.
[9] Includes sanitary services.
[10] Some transport workers are included with both "Commerce, etc." and "Services".
[11] Military conscripts were assigned to their previous occupation in this year.
[12] Printing and publishing is included with "Services".
[13] 1945 territory.
[14] Statistics are of economically active heads of family and their dependents living in. Living out servants and their dependants and all servants of retired persons and rentiers were included in "Services".
[15] Statistics are of economically active heads of family and their dependants.
[16] Savoy and Nice are subsequently included.
[17] Excludes the parts of Alsace and Lorraine ceded to Germany.
[18] Gas, water, and electricity workers are included with "extractive industry".
[19] Excluding Saarland.
[20] 1937 territory.
[21] Including East Berlin.
[22] Including West Berlin.
[23] Conscripts in the armed forces are excluded.
[24] Transleithania up to the First World War.
[25] Excluding some family workers.
[26] Armed forces are included with "others occupied".
[27] These statistics cover workers of both sexes, but the number of females in extractive industry and in construction was negligible and was probably very small amongst "others occupied".
[28] Fishing is included with "manufacturing industry".
[29] Some agricultural workers were probably included with "services", as were some transport workers.
[30] Hotel workers were included with "commerce, etc.", and some transport workers were included with "services".
[31] Smelting is included with "extractive industry".
[32] Russian Poland only.
[33] Excluding Upper Silesia and part of Wilno.
[34] Excluding 394 thousand persons in 1950 and 370 thousand in 1960 who were not classified.
[35] Day labourers are included with "services".
[36] Catering is included with "commerce, etc.".
[37] Banks, urban transport, water, and sanitary services (and gas and electricity also in 1960) are included with "services".
[38] Excluding unemployed workers.
[39] Including rentiers and the retired.

[40] Forestry and fishing are included with "manufacturing industry", and gas, water, and sanitary services are included with "services".
[41] Excluding Poland.
[42] Including dependants.
[43] "Transport and Communications" are included with "Industry".
[44] "Communications" are included with "services".
[45] "Banking and finance" are included with "services".
[46] Excluding activities inadequately described.
[47] Excluding conscripts to the armed forces, persons unemployed for over four months, and persons seeking work for the first time.
[48] Excluding storage workers, who were distributed over various classes.
[49] Including railway workers, day labourers, servants living out, and probably in 1870 some inactive persons.
[50] Many who would later have been assigned to an occupation group were classed as unoccupied. The Islands in the British Seas are included in this year.
[51] Previously, retired persons who stated their former occupation were classified according to the latter.
[52] Includes all persons in agricultural households aged 14 and over who were capable of working.
[53] Clerical staff included with "services".
[54] In Russia in 1970 this includes persons employed in activities not adequately described.
[55] Fishing is included with "manufacturing industry".

C2 UNEMPLOYMENT (Numbers in thousands and Percentage of Appropriate Workforce)

	Austria[1]		Belgium[3]		Czech[4]	Denmark[5]		Finland[6]		France[7]	
	No	%	No	%	No	No	%	No	%	No	%
1887	...	...	...	...	...	...	...	...	...	...	...
1888	...	...	...	...	...	...	...	...	...	...	...
1889	...	...	...	...	...	...	...	...	...	...	...
1890	...	...	...	...	...	...	...	...	...	...	...
1891	...	...	...	...	...	...	...	...	...	...	...
1892	...	...	...	...	...	...	...	...	...	...	...
1893	...	...	...	...	...	...	...	...	...	...	...
1894	...	...	...	...	...	...	...	...	...	...	...
1895	...	...	...	...	...	...	...	...	...	...	7.0
1896	...	...	...	...	...	...	...	...	...	...	6.7
1897	...	...	...	...	...	...	...	...	...	...	6.9
1898	...	...	...	...	...	...	...	...	...	...	7.3
1899	...	...	...	...	...	...	...	...	...	...	6.6
1900	...	...	...	...	...	...	...	...	...	...	6.8
1901	...	...	...	...	...	...	...	...	...	...	7.8
1902	...	...	...	...	...	...	...	...	...	...	9.9
1903	...	...	...	...	...	9	...	...	...	...	9.4
1904	...	...	...	...	...	10	...	...	...	...	10.2
1905	...	...	...	...	...	11	...	...	...	...	9.0
1906	...	...	...	...	...	5	...	...	...	...	7.6
1907	...	...	...	...	...	6	...	...	...	...	7.0
1908	...	...	...	...	...	10	...	...	...	...	8.6
1909	...	...	...	...	...	12	...	...	...	...	7.3
1910	...	...	...	...	...	11	10.7	...	...	...	5.8
1911	...	...	3.0	...	...	10	9.5	...	...	...	5.7
1912	...	...	3.0	...	...	8	7.6	...	...	...	5.4
1913	...	...	4.0	...	...	8	7.5	...	...	...	4.7
1914	...	...	...	...	...	13	9.9	...	...	...	...
1915	...	...	...	...	...	10	8.1	...	...	...	...
1916	...	...	...	...	...	7	5.1	...	...	...	...
1917	...	...	...	...	...	15	9.7	...	...	...	...
1918	...	...	...	...	...	38	18.1	...	...	...	...
1919	147	...	...	...	...	32	10.9	...	...	...	...
1920	58[2] / 19	...	...	...	...	17	6.1	...	...	13	...
1921	12	...	35.0	11.5	72	57	19.7	...	...	28	...
1922	49	...	12.9	4.2	127	50	19.3	...	...	13	...
1923	110[1]	...	4.0	1.3	207	33	12.7	...	...	10	...
1924	127	...	4.8	1.6	96	28	10.7	...	...	10	...
1925	184	...	7.3	2.4	49	40	14.7	2.5	...	12	...
1926	202	...	6.1	2.0	59	58	20.7	2.0	...	11	...
1927	200	...	7.7	2.5	53	62	22.5	1.9	...	47	
1928	182	...	5.3	1.7	39	50	18.5	1.7	...	16	...
1929	192	...	5.6	1.9	42	43	15.5	3.9	...	10	...

See p.180 for footnotes

Czech: Czechoslovakia

Abbreviations used throughout this table: No: Number

C2 Unemployment (Numbers in thousands and Percentage of Appropriate Workforce)

	Germany[8]		Greece[5]	Hungary[9]	Ireland		Italy[10]		Netherlands[11]	
	No	%	No	No	No	%	No	%	No	%
1887	...	0.2	...	...	...	...	...	...	...	...
1888	...	3.8	...	...	...	...	...	...	...	...
1889	...	0.2	...	...	...	...	...	...	...	...
1890	...	2.3	...	...	...	...	...	...	...	...
1891	...	3.9	...	...	...	...	...	...	...	...
1892	...	6.3	...	...	...	...	...	...	...	...
1893	...	2.8	...	...	...	...	...	...	...	...
1894	...	3.1	...	...	...	...	...	...	...	...
1895	...	2.8	...	...	...	...	...	...	...	...
1896	...	0.6	...	...	...	...	...	...	...	...
1897	...	1.2	...	...	...	...	...	...	...	...
1898	...	0.4	...	...	...	...	...	...	...	...
1899	...	1.2	...	...	...	...	...	...	...	...
1900	...	2.0	...	...	...	...	...	...	...	...
1901	...	6.7	...	...	...	...	...	...	...	...
1902	...	2.9	...	...	...	...	...	...	...	...
1903	...	2.7	...	...	...	...	...	...	...	...
1904	...	2.1	...	...	...	...	...	...	...	...
1905	...	1.6	...	...	...	...	...	...	...	...
1906	...	1.1	...	...	...	...	...	...	...	...
1907	...	1.6	...	...	...	...	...	...	...	...
1908	...	2.9	...	...	...	...	...	...	...	...
1909	...	2.8	...	...	...	...	...	...	...	...
1910	...	1.9	...	...	...	...	...	...	...	...
1911	...	1.9	...	...	...	...	...	...	...	2.5
1912	...	2.0	...	...	...	...	...	...	...	4.0
1913	...	2.9	...	...	...	...	...	...	...	5.0
1914	...	7.2	...	...	...	...	...	...	...	13.8
1915	...	3.3	...	...	...	...	...	...	16	12.0
1916	...	2.2	...	...	...	...	...	...	8	5.1
1917	...	1.0	...	...	...	...	...	...	14	6.5
1918	...	1.2	...	...	...	...	...	...	19	7.5
1919	...	3.7	...	...	...	...	...	...	27	7.7
1920	...	3.8	...	...	...	...	...	...	29	5.8
1921	...	2.8	...	...	...	...	...	...	43	9.0
1922	...	1.5	...	...	...	...	...	...	45	11.0
1923	...	9.6	...	...	36	...	...	...	38	11.2
1924	...	13.5	...	...	36	...	...	...	28	8.8
1925	...	6.7	...	13	34	...	110	...	26	8.1
1926	...	18.0	...	13	25	...	114	...	25	7.3
1927	...	8.8	...	14	21	...	278	...	27	7.5
1928	...	8.4	...	15	22	...	324	...	22	5.6
1929	1,899	13.1[8] 4.3	...	15	21	...	301	...	28	5.9

See p. 180 for footnotes

C2 **Unemployment** (Numbers in thousands and Percentage of Appropriate Workforce)

	Norway[12]		Poland[13]		Romania[14]	Sweden[15]	Switz[17]		UK: GB[18]		Yugoslavia[14]	
	No	%	No	%	No	%	No	%	No	%	No	%
1887	...	...	...	...	...	...	...	...	...		...	...
1888	...	...	...	...	...	...	...	...	...	4.9	...	...
1889	...	...	...	...	...	...	...	...	...	2.1	...	...
1890	...	...	...	...	...	...	...	...	...	2.1	...	...
1891	...	...	...	...	...	...	...	...	...	3.5	...	...
1892	...	...	...	...	...	...	...	...	...	6.3	...	...
1893	...	...	...	...	...	...	...	...	...	7.5	...	...
1894	...	...	...	...	...	...	...	...	...	6.9	...	...
1895	...	...	...	...	...	...	...	...	...	5.8	...	...
1896	...	...	...	...	...	...	...	...	...	3.3	...	...
1897	...	...	...	...	...	...	...	...	...	3.3	...	...
1898	...	...	...	...	...	...	...	...	...	2.8	...	...
1899	...	...	...	...	...	...	...	...	...	2.0	...	...
1900	...	...	...	...	...	...	...	...	...	2.5	...	...
1901	...	...	...	...	...	...	...	...	...	3.3	...	...
1902	...	...	...	...	...	...	...	...	...	4.0	...	...
1903	...	...	...	...	...	...	...	...	...	4.7	...	...
1904	...	3.9	...	...	...	...	...	...	...	6.0	...	...
1905	...	4.4	...	...	...	...	...	...	...	5.0	...	...
1906	...	3.2	...	...	...	...	...	...	...	3.6	...	...
1907	...	2.5	...	...	...	...	...	...	...	3.7	...	...
1908	...	3.7	...	...	...	...	...	...	...	7.8	...	...
1909	...	5.0	...	...	...	...	...	...	...	7.7	...	...
1910	...	2.9	...	...	...	...	...	...	...	4.7	...	...
1911	...	1.9	...	...	...	...	...	...	...	3.0	...	...
1912	...	1.3	...	...	...	...	...	...	...	3.2	...	...
1913	...	1.6	...	...	...	...	...	...	...	2.1	...	...
1914	...	2.4	...	...	...	...	...	...	...	3.3	...	...
1915	...	2.1	...	...	...	...	...	...	...	1.1	...	...
1916	...	0.8	...	...	...	...	...	...	...	0.4	...	...
1917	...	0.9	...	...	...	...	...	...	...	0.7	...	...
1918	...	1.4	...	...	...	...	...	...	...	0.8	...	...
1919	...	1.6	...	...	...	...	...	...	...	2.4	...	...
1920	...	2.3	...	...	...	...	...	...	...	2.4	...	...
1921	...	17.6	...	...	...	...	...	...	...	14.8	...	...
1922	...	17.1	...	...	...	...	...	...	1,543	15.2	...	...
1923	...	10.6	...	...	...	...	...	...	1.275	11.3[18]	...	...
										11.6		
1924	...	8.5	...	...	...	...	...	...	1,130	10.9	...	...
1925	...	13.2	241	...	...	11.0	...	...	1,226	11.2	...	...
1926	...	24.3	217	...	...	12.2	...	3.4	1,385	12.7	...	...
1927	...	25.4	165	7.4	...	12.0	...	2.7	1,088	10.6	...	...
1928	...	19.1	126	5.0	10	10.6[16]	...	2.1	1,217	11.2	6	...
1929	...	15.4	129	4.9	7	11.2	...	1.8[16]	1,216	11.0	8	...

Switz: Switzerland: UK: GB: United Kingdon: Great Britain

See p.180 for footnotes

C2 Unemployment (Numbers in thousands and Percentages of Appropriate Workforce)

	Austria[1]		Belgium[3]		Czech[4]	Denmark[5]		Finland[6]		France[7]	
	No	%	No	%	No	No	%	No	%	No	%
1930	243		16.5	5.4	105	40	13.7	8.0	...	13	...
1931	300		41.1	14.5	291	53	17.9	11.5	...	64	...
1932	378		71.8	23.5	554	100	31.7	17.4	...	301	...
1933	406		62.4	20.4	738	97	28.8	17.1	...	305	...
1934	370		72.3	23.4	677	82	22.1	10.0	...	368	...
1935	349		65.5	22.9	686[4]	76	19.7	7.2	...	464	...
1936	350		49.2	16.8	623	79	19.3	4.8	...	470	...
1937	321		39.9	13.8	409	95	21.9	3.7	...	380	...
1938	245		53.7	18.4	...	98	21.3	3.6	...	402	...
1939	66		57.3[2]	19.3	...	89	18.4	3.3	...	418	...
1940	...	...	...	...	...	120	23.9	4.0	...	961	...
1941	...	...	...	...	...	130[19] / 40	25.1[19] / 7.5	3.4	...	395	...
1942	...	...	...	...	...	49	9.1	1.6	...	124	...
1943	...	...	...	...	...	34	6.3[20] / 10.7	0.9	...	42	...
1944	...	...	...	...	...	25	8.3	2.0[6]	...	23	...
1945	...	...	117	...	...	47	13.4	5	...	68	...
1946	74[1]	...	48	...		28	8.9	1	...	57	...
1947	32	1.7	36	...	...	29[20] / 52	8.9	—	...	46	...
1948	43	2.3	81	4.0	...	52	8.6	4	...	78	...
1949	91	4.6	174	8.6	...	59	9.6	26	...	131	...
1950	125	6.2	185	9.0	...	55	8.7	19	...	153	...
1951	116	5.7	159	7.6	...	63	9.7	6	...	120	...
1952	157	7.7	185	8.8	...	82	12.5	8	...	132	...
1953	184	9.0	192	9.2	...	61	9.2	29	...	180	...
1954	163	7.9	172	8.3	...	54	8.0	19	...	184	...
1955	118	5.4	118	5.8	...	66	9.7	9	...	160	...
1956	115[16]	5.1[16]	95	4.5	...	75	11.1	...	...	112	...
1957	108	4.7	81	3.9	...	71	10.2	...	...	81	...
1958	118	5.1	116	5.5	...	68	9.6	64	3.1	93	...
1959	107	4.6	132	6.3	...	44	6.1	46	2.2	141	...
1960	82	3.5	114	5.4	...	31	4.3	31	1.5	130	...
1961	64	2.7	89	4.2	...	29	3.9	27	1.2	111	...
1962	65	2.7	71	3.3	...	25	3.3	27	1.2	123	...
1963	71	2.9	59	2.7	...	33	4.3	32	1.5	140	...
1964	66	2.7	50	2.3	...	22	2.8	33	1.5	114	...
1965	66	2.7	55	2.4	...	18	2.3	31	1.4	142	...
1966	61	2.5	61	2.7	...	21	2.6	35	1.5	148	...
1967	65	2.7	85	3.7	...	25	3.2	63	2.9	196	...
1968	71	2.9	103	4.5	...	41	5.3	85	3.9	254	...
1969	68	2.8	85	3.7	...	31	3.9	61	2.8	223	...
1970	58	2.4	71	2.9	...	24	2.9	41[6]	1.9[6]	262	...
1971	52	2.1	71	2.9	...	30	3.7	49	2.3	338	...
1972	49	1.9	87	3.4	...	30	3.6	55	2.5	383[7]	...
1973	41	1.6	92	3.6	...	20	2.4	51	2.3	394	...
1974	41	1.5	105	4.0	...	44	5.2	39	1.7	498	...
1975	55	2.0	177	6.7	...	103	11.1	51	2.2	840	...

See p. 180 for footnotes

Czech: Czechoslovakia

C2 Unemployment (Numbers in thousands and Percentage of Appropriate Workforce)

	Germany[8]		Greece[5]	Hungary[9]	Ireland[5]		Italy[10]		Netherlands[11]		Norway[12]	
	No	%	No	No	No	%	No	%	No	%	No	%
1930	3,076	15.3	...	44	22	...	425	...	41[16] / 74	7.8	...	16.6
1931	4,520	23.3	...	52	25[16] / 63	...	734	...	138	14.8	...	22.3
1932	5,575	30.1	...	66	63	...	1,006[10]	...	271	25.3	...	30.8
1933	4,804	26.3	...	61	72	...	1,019	...	323	26.9	...	33.4
1934	2,718	14.9	...	52	104	...	964	...	333	28.0	...	30.7
1935	2,151	11.6	...	52	123	...	...	...	385	31.7	...	25.3
1936	1,593	8.3	...	52	100	...	...	...	414	32.7	...	18.8
1937	912	4.6	...	48	82	...	874	4.6	374	26.9	...	20.0
1938	429	2.1	...	47	87	...	810	4.3	354	25.0	...	22.0
1939	119	...	...	...	92	15.6	706[21]	3.8[21]	296	19.9 / [11]	...	18.3
1940	52	...	...	...	84	15.5	...	...	253	...	...	23.1
1941	...	...	...	...	75	14.6	...	...	175	...	...	11.4
1942	...	...	...	...	78	14.2	...	...	119	...	...	...
1943	...	...	...	...	67	12.5	...	...	...	...	...	...
1944	...	...	...	...	59	11.3	...	...	...	...	...	...
1945	... / [8]	... / [8]	...	...	59	10.6	...	...	137[23]	...	...	...
1946	...	...	...	...	60	10.6	1,324		89	...	...	3.6
1947	...	...	...	...	56	9.3	1,620	8.3	47	...	...	3.1
1948	592[8]	4.2[8]	...	...	61	9.4	1,742[22]	8.9[22]	43	1.0	10	2.7
1949	1,230	8.3	...	...	61	9.0	1,673	8.6	63	1.5	8	2.2
1950	1,580	10.2	...	...	53	7.5	1,615	8.3	80	2.0	9	2.7
1951	1,432	9.0	...	...	50	7.3	1,721	8.8	93	2.3	11	3.6
1952	1,379	8.4	...	...	61[16] / 71	9.1[16] / 9.6	1,850	9.5	139	3.5	12	2.4
1953	1,259	7.5	...	...	71	9.6	1,947	10.0	107	2.7	14[16] / 13	3.3
1954	1,221	7.0	...	...	62	8.1	1,959[10] / 1,699	10.0[10] / 8.8	76	1.9	13	2.2
1955	928	5.1	...	...	55	6.8	1,479	7.6	53	1.3	13	2.5
1956	761	4.0	38[27]	...	61	7.7	1,847	9.4	40	0.9	13	3.1
1957	662	3.4	87	...	70	9.2	1,643	8.2	52	1.2	15	3.2
1958	683[8] / 480	3.5[8] / 2.4	79	...	65	8.6	1,322	6.6	98	2.3	24	...
1959	480	2.4	89	...	62	8.0	1,117	5.6	77	1.8	23	...
1960	237	1.2	87	...	53	6.7	836	4.2	49	1.2	17	2.5
1961	161	0.8	76	...	47	5.7	710	3.5	35	0.9	13	2.0
1962	142	0.7	75	...	47	5.7	611	3.0	33	0.8	15	2.1
1963	174	0.8	70	...	50	6.1	504	2.5	34	0.9	18	2.5
1964	157	0.7	65	...	49	5.7	549	2.7	30	0.8	16	2.0
1965	139	0.6	64	...	49	5.6	714	3.6	35	0.9	13	1.8
1966	154	0.7	65	...	48	6.1	759	3.9	45	1.1	12	1.8
1967	445	2.1	83	...	55	6.7	679	3.5	90	2.2	11	1.2
1968	314	1.5	74	...	58	6.7	684	3.5	84	1.9	17	1.4
1969	173	0.9	66	...	57	6.4	655	3.4	66	1.4	16	...
1970	144	0.7	52 / 49[26]	...	65	7.2	609	3.2	56	1.1	12	...
1971	178	0.8	30	...	62	7.2	609	3.2	69	1.6	12	...
1972	236	1.1	24	...	72	8.1	697	3.7	115	2.7	15	...
1973	263	1.2	21	...	67	7.2	668	3.5	117	2.7	13	...
1974	565	2.6	27	...	71	7.9	560	2.9	143	3.3	11	...
1975	1,043	4.7	35	...	103	12.2	654	3.3	206	4.7	20	...

See p. 180 for footnotes

C2 Unemployment (Numbers in thousands and Percentage of Appropriate Workforce)

	Poland[13]		Port[24]	Rom[14]	Spain[14]	Sweden[15]	Switz[17]		UK: GB[18]		Yugoslavia[14]	
	No	%	No	No	No	%	No	%	No	%	No	%
1930	227	12.7	...	25		12.2	...	3.4	1,917	14.6	8	...
1931	300	14.6	...	36		17.2	...	5.9	2,630	21.5	10	...
1932	256	15.6	33	39	...	22.8	...	9.1	2,745	22.5	15	...
1933	250	16.7	25	29	352[21]	23.7	...	10.8	2,521	21.3	16	...
1934	342	16.3	35	17	407[21]	18.9	...	9.8	2,159	17.7	16	...
1935	382	11.9	42	14	697	16.1	...	11.8	2,036	16.4	18	...
1936	367	11.8	43[24]	14	...	13.6	81	13.2	1,755	14.3	19	...
1937	375	12.8	17	11	...	10.8	58	10.0	1,484	11.3	22	...
1938	348	8.8	17	7	...	10.9[16]	53	8.6	1,791	13.3	23	...
1939	...	...	18	9	...	9.2	37	6.5	1,514[25]	11.7[18]	24	...
1940	...	...	15	7	475	11.8	15	3.1	963	6.0	27	...
1941	...	...	14	6	450	11.3	9	2.0	350	2.2	...	...
1942	...	...	10	6	295	7.5	9	1.9	123	0.8	...	...
1943	...	...	5	6	225	5.7	6	1.4	82	0.6	...	...
1944	...	...	4	...	170	4.9	7	1.6	75	0.5	...	...
1945	...	...	3[24]	...	148	4.5	6	1.6	137	1.3	...	...
1946	79	...	2	...	178	3.2	4	1.0	374	2.5	...	...
1947	69	...	2	...	139	2.8	3	0.8	480	3.1[18]	...	...
1948	79	...	2	...	117	2.8	3	0.6	310	1.5	...	...
1949	...	...	2	...	160	2.7	8	1.6	308	1.5	...	...
1950	...	...	...	...	166	2.2	10	1.8	314	1.5	...	...
1951	...	...	...	...	144	1.8	4	0.8	253	1.2	...	...
1952	...	...	...	...	107	2.3	5		414	2.0	45	2.4
1953	...	...	...	...	107	2.8	5		342	1.6	82	4.0
1954	...	...	...	...	123	2.6	4		285	1.3	76	3.8
1955	...	...	...	...	112	2.5[15]	2.7		232	1.1	67	3.0
1956	...	...	...	...	106	1.7	3.0		258	1.2	99	4.3
1957	...	...	...	...	91	1.9	2.0		327	1.4	116	4.6
1958	...	...	...	...	81	2.5	3.4		451	2.1	132	4.9
1959	...	...	...	...	80	2.0	3.4		480	2.2	162	5.6
1960	...	...	...	...	114	1.4	1.2		377	1.6	159	5.1
1961	41	0.5	...	...	125	1.2	0.6		347	1.5	191	5.6
1962	48	0.6	...	...	98	1.3	0.6		467	2.0	237	6.7
1963	52	0.6	...	...	100	1.4	0.8		558	2.5	230	6.4
1964	75	0.9	...	...	130	1.1	0.3		404	1.6	213	5.6
1965	67	0.7	...	...	147	1.1	0.3		347	1.4	237	6.1
1966	61	0.6	...	...	123	1.4	0.3		361	1.4	258	6.7
1967	56	0.6	...	...	146	1.7	0.3		559	2.3	269	7.0
1968	57	0.6	...	...	182	2.0	0.3		586	2.5	311	8.0
1969	62	0.7	...	...	159	1.7	0.1		581	2.5	331	8.2
1970	79	0.7	...	...	146	1.4	0.1		618	2.6	320	7.7
1971	88	0.8	...	...	190	2.0	0.1		799	3.5	291	6.7
1972	...	...	...	...	191	2.0	0.1		876[18]	3.8[18]	315	7.0
1973	...	...	...	...	150	1.9	0.1		619	2.7	382	8.1
1974	...	...	...	...	150	1.5	0.2		615[28]	2.6	449	9.0
1975	...	...	...	...	257	1.4	10.2		978	4.2	540	10.2

Port: Portugal Rom: Romania Switz: Switzerland UK:GB: United Kingdom: Great Britain

See p.180 for footnotes

C2 Unemployment (Numbers in thousands and percentages of appropriate workforce)

NOTES

1. SOURCES:– I.L.O., *Yearbook of Labour Statistics* (since 1935), and the official publications noted on p. xv.

2. The variety of different indicators of unemployment used is clear from the footnotes. This should serve as a warning against incautious comparisons.

FOOTNOTES

[1] 1919–23 – numbers given public relief; 1924–46 – applicants for work at labour exchanges; 1947–69 – registered unemployed. All figures are averages of monthly observations.
[2] The first figure is for January–April, before the Unemployment Assurance scheme came into force; the second figure is for May–December.
[3] 1911–39 – average number of days' unemployment among insured workers, and percentages of possible days' work; 1945–69 – average of monthly numbers of registered unemployed.
[4] Averages of monthly numbers of applicants for work at labour exchanges and private placement agencies, though excluding the latter from 1936.
[5] Averages of monthly numbers of insured workers unemployed.
[6] 1925–44 – applicants for work at labour exchanges; 1945–69 – numbers given relief works; 1970–5 – excluding persons over 74.
[7] From 1972 excludes certain unemployed people over 60.
[8] 1887–1929 – unemployed in trade unions; 1929–38 and 1960–69 – average of monthly numbers of registered unemployed; 1948–54 – registered unemployed at 30 June; 1954–60 – registered unemployed at 30 September. Figures from 1949 relate to the Federal Republic (excluding West Berlin). The Saar is excluded from 1921 to 1934 and from 1949 to 1958. The 1948 figure relates only to the British and American Occupation Zones.
[9] Averages of monthly numbers of applicants for work at labour exchanges, and, from 1930, at private placement agencies.
[10] 1925–32 – insured workers unemployed; 1933–54 – numbers of registered unemployed; 1954–69 – numbers of unemployed according to sample surveys. All figures are averages of monthly observations.
[11] The numbers, and the percentages since 1948, relate to registered unemployed, excluding married women who were not "breadwinners" prior to 1968. The percentages do not include unemployed persons on relief work. The figures are weekly averages to 1921 and monthly averages subsequently. The percentages to 1939 relate to the proportion of possible days' work lost owing to unemployment.
[12] The numbers are of registered unemployed, the percentages are of trade unionists unemployed. All figures are averages of monthly observations.
[13] 1927–38 – applicants for work; 1961–69 – registered unemployed. All figures are average of monthly observations.
[14] Averages of monthly numbers of registered unemployed.
[15] 1925–55 – members of trade union benefit funds unemployed; 1956–69 – averages of monthly percentages of members of insurance funds unemployed.
[16] The scope of the series was subsequently enlarged.
[17] The numbers are monthly averages of registered unemployed, and the percentages are monthly averages of insured workers unemployed.
[18] 1888–1923 – unemployed in trade unions; 1923–75 – averages of monthly numbers of registered wholly unemployed, (excluding adult students from 1972), though the percentages relate only to insured workers who were unemployed, and, from 1939, include all persons on the register. For 1940–47 the figures include Northern Ireland. Figures of percentages unemployed in certain trade unions, partly computed from benefit expenditure, are available in the source back to 1851.
[19] A different system was adopted on 1 June. The first figure is for January–May and the second for June–December.
[20] Temporarily unemployed workers are subsequently included.
[21] December only.
[22] Excluding the third quarter.
[23] June–December only.
[24] 1937–45 – registered unemployed in December; 1932–36 and 1946–49 – averages of monthly numbers of registered unemployed.
[25] Subsequently excludes men at government Training Centres.
[26] Subsequently excluding seamen.
[27] May–December only.
[28] January–November.

C3 INDUSTRIAL DISPUTES 1888–1929

	Austria[1]			Belgium			Czechoslavakia			Denmark		
	Number	Workers Involved (thou)	Days Lost (thou)	Number	Workers Involved (thou)	Days Lost (thou)	Number	Workers Involved (thou)	Days Lost (thou)	Mumber	Workers Involved (thou)	Days Lost (thou)
1888	...	...	...	...	...	...	...	...	...	...	...	...
1889	...	...	...	...	...	...	...	...	...	...	...	...
1890	...	...	...	...	...	...	...	...	...	...	...	...
1891	...	...	...	...	...	...	...	...	...	...	...	...
1892	...	...	...	...	...	...	...	...	...	...	...	...
1893	...	...	...	...	...	...	...	...	...	...	...	...
1894	159	44	...	...	...	...	...	...	...	...	...	...
1895	205	28	...	...	...	...	...	...	...	...	...	...
1896	294	36	...	139	23	...	...	...	...	...	...	...
1897	221	35	...	130	36	...	...	...	...	111	7	...
1898	255	40	...	91	13	...	...	...	...	147	7	...
1899	311	55	...	104	58	...	...	...	...	98	36	...
1900	303	105	...	146	32	...	...	...	...	82	8	...
1901	270	25	...	117	44	...	...	...	...	57	4	...
1902	264	37	...	73	10	...	...	...	...	68	2	...
1903	324	46	...	70	8	...	...	...	...	61	1	...
1904	414	64	...	81	12	...	...	...	...	86	3	...
1905	686	100	...	133	76	...	...	...	...	75	6	...
1906	1,083	154	...	207	25	...	...	...	...	90	4	...
1907	1,086	177	...	221	45	...	...	...	...	105	8	...
1908	721	79	...	101	14	...	...	...	...	122	8	...
1909	580	62	...	119	11	...	...	...	...	65	2	...
1910	657	55	...	108	26	...	...	...	...	71	2	...
1911	706	122	...	156	55	...	...	...	...	51	28	...
1912	761	121	...	202	61	...	...	...	...	60	4	...
1913	438	40	...	162	16	...	...	...	...	76	10	...
1914	260	33	...	...	...	...	...	...	...	44	3	...
1915	...	...	...	...	...	...	...	...	...	43	2	...
1916	...	...	...	...	...	...	...	...	...	66	13	241
1917	...	...	...	...	...	...	...	...	...	215	10	211
1918	...	...	...	...	...	...	...	...	...	253	9	182
1919	151	70	221	366	158	...	252	...	...	472	36	878
1920	329	199	927	506	289	...	614	...	...	243	22	690
1921	435	302	1,763	252	122	...	454	223	2,250	110	48	1,321
1922	381	307	1,635	169	85	...	290	331	3,975	31	49	2,272
1923	268	133	1,074	164	105	...	248	209	4,714	58	2	20
1924	401	286	2,295	186	83	...	334	98	1,362	71	10	175
1925	287	57	666	108	81	...	267	111	1,683	48	102	4,138
1926	186	25	233	137	70	...	163	49	735	32	1	23
1927	195	37	477	181	36	...	208	172	1,466	17	3	119
1928	242	44	563	191	72	...	280	102	1,728	11	0.5	11
1929	202	38	287	165	46	...	230	64	753	22	1	41

Abbreviations used throughout this table: (thou) (thousands)

See p. 191 for footnotes

C3 Industrial Disputes 1888–1929

	Finland			France[19]			Germany[4 20]			Greece		
	Number	Workers Involved (thos)	Days Lost (thou)	Number	Workers Involved (thou)	Days Lost (thou)	Number	Workers Involved (thou)	Days Lost (thou)	Number	Workers Involved (thou)	Days Lost (thou)
1888	...	...	...	...	...	...	...	...	...	...	...	...
1889	...	...	...	...	...	...	...	...	...	...	...	...
1890	...	...	...	313	119	1,340	...	...	...	...	...	...
1891	...	...	...	267	109	1,717	...	...	...	...	...	...
1892	...	...	...	261	49	918	...	...	...	...	...	...
1893	...	...	...	634	170	3,175	...	...	...	...	...	...
1894	...	...	...	391	55	1,062	...	...	...	...	...	...
1895	...	...	...	405	46	617	...	...	...	...	...	...
1896	...	...	...	476	50	644	...	...	...	...	...	...
1897	...	...	...	356	69	781	...	...	...	...	...	...
1898	...	...	...	368	82	1,216	...	...	...	...	...	...
1899	...	...	...	739	177	3,551	1,311	265	3,381	...	...	...
1900	...	...	...	902	223	3,761	1,468	321	3,712	...	...	...
1901	...	...	...	523	111	1,862	1,091	149	2,427	...	...	...
1902	...	...	...	512	213	4,675	1,106	150	1,951	...	...	...
1903	...	...	...	567	123	2,442	1,444	251	4,158	...	...	...
1904	...	...	...	1,026	271	3,935	1,990	310	5,285	...	...	...
1905	...	...	...	830	178	2,747	2,657	966	18,984	...	...	...
1906	...	...	...	1,309	438	9,439	3,626	839	11,567	...	...	...
1907	176	...	596	1,275	198	3,562	2,512	575	9,017	...	...	...
1908	128	...	436	1,073	99	1,752	1,524	281	3,666	...	...	...
1909	51	...	252	1,025	167	3,560	1,652	291	4,152	...	...	...
1910	54	...	171	1,502	281	4,830	3,228	681	17,848	...	...	...
1911	51	...	291	1,471	231	4,096	2,798	896	11,466	...	...	...
1912	59	...	529	1,116	268	2,318	2,834	1,031	10,724	...	...	...
1913	70	...	74	1,073	220	2,224	2,464	655	11,761	...	...	...
1914	37	...	376	672	162	2,187	1,223	238	2,844	...	...	...
1915	—	—	—	98	9	55	141	48	46	...	...	...
1916	—	—	—	314	41	236	240	423	245	...	...	...
1917	483	...	1,495	696	294	1,482	562	1,468	1,862	...	...	...
1918	6	...	2	499	176	980	532	716	1,453	...	...	...
1919	39	...	160	2,026	1,151	15,478	3,719	2,761	33,083	...	...	...
1920	146	...	456	1,832	1,317	23,112	3,807	2,009	16,755	...	...	...
1921	76	...	120	475	402	7,027	4,455	2,036	25,874	...	...	...
1922	53	...	252	665	290	3,935	4,785	2,566	27,734	...	...	...
1923	50	...	262	1,068	331	4,172	2,046	1,917	12,344	...	...	...
1924	31	...	51	1,083	275	3,863	1,973	2,066	36,198	...	...	...
1925	38	3	113	931	249	2,046	1,708	1,115	2,936	...	...	...
1926	72	10	386	1,660	349	4,072	351	131	1,222	...	...	...
1927	79	13[3]	1,528	396	111	1,046	844	686	6,144	...	...	...
1928	71	21	502	816	204	6,377	739	986	20,339	...	...	...
1929	26	2	75	1,213	240	2,765	429	268	4,251	...	...	...

See p. 191 for footnotes

C3 Industrial Disputes 1888–1929

	Hungary			Ireland			Italy			Netherlands		
	Number	Workers Involved (thou)	Days Lost (thou)	Number	Workers Involved (thou)	Days Lost (thou)	Number	Workers Involved (thou)	Days Lost (thou)	Number	Workers Involved (thou)	Days Lost (thou)
1888	...	...	...	...	...	...	107	30	...	...	...	...
1889	...	...	...	...	...	...	133	25	...	...	...	...
1890	...	...	...	...	...	...	152	45	...	...	...	...
1891	...	...	...	...	...	...	164	44	...	...	...	...
1892	...	...	...	...	...	...	140	34	...	...	...	...
1893	...	...	...	...	...	...	154	25	...	...	...	...
1894	...	...	...	...	...	...	217	98	...	...	...	...
1895	...	...	...	...	...	...	243	104	...	...	...	...
1896	...	...	...	...	...	...	310	47	...	...	...	...
1897	...	...	...	...	...	...	379	46	...	...	...	...
1898	...	...	...	...	...	...	424	85	...	...	...	...
1899	...	...	...	...	...	...	1,701	430	...	...	...	...
1900	...	...	...	...	...	...	1,053	350	...	...	...	...
1901	...	...	...	...	...	...	617	136	...	122	...	...
1902	...	...	...	...	...	...	847	215	...	142	...	...
1903	...	...	...	...	...	...	715	155	...	163	...	...
1904	...	...	...	...	...	...	1,649	382	...	102	...	658
1905	...	...	...	...	...	...	2,268	581	...	132	...	123
1906	...	...	...	...	...	...	1,674	324	...	181	12	295
1907	...	...	...	...	...	...	1,071	189	...	154	12	458
1908	...	...	...	...	...	...	1,109	196	...	135	7	102
1909	...	...	...	...	...	...	1,255	386	...	189	8	297
1910	...	...	...	...	...	...	1,090	241	...	146	15	366
1911	...	...	...	...	...	...	907	465	...	217	21	442
1912	...	...	...	...	...	...	905	217	...	283	26	467
1913	...	...	...	...	...	...	599	174	...	427	55	912
1914	...	...	...	...	...	...	905	217	...	271	17	393
1915	...	...	...	...	...	...	608	180	...	269	17	118
1916	...	...	...	...	...	...	577	138	838	377	20	261
1917	...	...	...	...	...	...	470	175	849	344	32	545
1918	...	...	...	...	...	...	313	159	912	325	44	716
1919	...	...	...	...	...	...	1,871	1,555	22,325	649	62	1,057
1920	...	...	...	...	...	...	2,070	2,314	30,569	481	66	2,355
1921	...	...	...	...	...	...	1,134	724	8,180	299	48	1,282
1922	...	...	...	...	...	...	575	448	6,917	325	44	1,224
1923	...	...	...	131	21	1,209	201	66	296	289	56	1,216
1924	...	...	...	104	16	302	368	187	...	239	27	3,156
1925	...	...	...	86	7	294	618	308	...	262	34	781
1926	56	10	52	57	3	85	...	...	...	212[5]	10[5]	281[5]
1927	84	25	295	53	2	64	169	19	...	230	14	202
1928	31	10	131	52	2	54	77	3	...	105	17	635
1929	63	15	149	53	5	101	83	3	...	226	21	890

See p. 191 for footnotes

C3 Industrial Disputes 1888–1929

	Norway			Poland			Romania			Spain		
	Number	Workers Involved (thou)	Days Lost (thou)	Number	Workers Involved (thou)	Days Lost (thou)	Number	Workers Involved (thou)	Days Lost (thou)	Number[6]	Workers Involved[6] (thou)[6]	Days Lost (thou)[6]
1888	...	...	...	...	...	...	...	...	...	...	...	...
1889	...	...	...	...	...	...	...	...	...	...	...	...
1900	...	...	...	...	...	...	...	...	...	...	...	...
1901	...	...	...	...	...	...	...	...	...	...	...	...
1902	...	...	...	...	...	...	...	...	...	...	...	...
1903	...	...	...	...	...	...	...	...	...	...	...	...
1904	...	...	...	...	...	...	...	...	...	...	...	...
1905	...	...	...	...	...	...	...	...	...	...	...	...
1906	...	...	...	...	...	...	...	...	...	...	...	...
1907	...	...	...	...	...	...	...	...	...	...	...	...
1908	...	...	...	...	...	...	...	...	...	...	...	...
1909	...	...	...	...	...	...	...	...	...	...	...	...
1910	...	...	...	...	...	...	...	...	...	...	...	...
1911	...	...	...	...	...	...	...	...	...	...	...	...
1912	...	...	...	...	...	...	...	...	...	...	...	...
1913	...	...	...	...	...	...	...	...	...	...	...	...
1914	...	...	...	...	...	...	...	...	...	...	...	...
1905	...	...	...	...	...	...	...	...	...	153 (130)	25	...
1906	...	...	...	...	...	...	...	...	...	145 (122)	30	...
1907	...	...	...	...	...	...	...	...	...	152 (118)	20	...
1908	...	...	...	...	...	...	...	...	...	182 (127)	38	...
1909	...	...	...	...	...	...	...	...	...	147 (78)	12	...
1910	...	...	...	...	...	...	...	...	...	246 (151)	41	1.409
1911	...	...	...	...	...	...	...	...	...	311 (118)	29	364
1912	...	...	...	...	...	...	...	...	...	279 (171)	47	1,056
1913	...	...	...	...	...	...	...	...	...	284 (201)	119	2,258
1914	...	...	...	...	...	...	...	...	...	212 (140)	76	1,018
1915	...	...	...	...	...	...	...	...	...	169 (91)	35	383
1916	...	...	...	...	...	...	...	...	...	237 (178)	160	2,415
1917	...	...	...	...	...	...	...	...	...	306 (176)	86	1,785
1918	...	...	...	...	...	...	...	...	...	463 (256)	136	1,819
1919	...	...	...	...	...	...	...	...	...	895 (403)	199	4,001
1920	...	...	...	...	...	...	...	...	...	1,060 (424)	264	7,262
1921	...	...	...	...	...	...	...	...	...	373 (233)	99	2,802
1922	26	2	91	...	...	...	...	...	...	488 (429)	167	2,673
1923	57	25	796	...	...	...	...	...	...	458 (411)	160	3,027
1924	61	63	5,152	929	582	7,137	88	12	212	165 (155)	41	605
1925	84	14	667	538	150	1,322	73	20	210	181 (164)	71	840
1926	113	51	2,205	590	146	1,423	88	20	326	96 (93)	32	247
1927	96	22	1,374	635	237	2,483	51	7	58	107	95	1,312
1928	63	8	364	776	354	2,788	57	11	110	87	143	771
1929	73	5	197	510	222	1,072	127	31	412	96	67	314

See p.191 for footnotes

C3 Industrial Disputes 1888–1929

	Sweden			Switzerland			United Kingdom			Yugoslavia		
	Number	Workers Involved (thou)	Days Lost (thou)	Number	Workers Involved (thou)	Days Lost (thou)	Number	Workers Involved (thou)	Days Lost (thou)	Number	Workers Involved (thou)	Days Lost (thou)
1888	...	...	...	...	...	...	517	119	...	...	...	...
1889	...	...	...	...	...	...	1,211	360	...	...	...	...
1890	...	...	...	...	...	...	1,040	393	...	...	...	...
1891	...	...	...	...	...	...	906	267	6,809	...	...	...
1892	...	...	...	...	...	...	700[8]	358[8]	17,382[8]	...	...	...
1893	...	...	...	...	...	...	615	634	30,468	...	...	...
1894	...	...	...	...	...	...	929	325	9,529	...	...	...
1895	...	...	...	...	...	...	745	263	5,725	...	...	...
1896	...	...	...	...	...	...	926	198	3,746	...	...	...
1897	...	...	...	...	...	...	864	230	10,346	...	...	...
1898	...	...	...	...	...	...	711	254	15,289	...	...	...
1899	...	...	...	...	...	...	719	180	2,516	...	...	...
1900	...	...	...	...	...	...	648	189	3,153	...	...	...
1901	...	...	...	...	...	...	642	180	4,142	...	...	...
1902	...	...	...	...	...	...	442	257	3,479	...	...	...
1903	142	25	642	...	...	...	387	117	2,339	...	...	...
1904	215	12	386	...	...	...	355	87	1,484	...	...	...
1905	189	33	2,390	...	...	...	358	94	2,470	...	...	...
1906	290	19	479	...	...	...	486	218	3,029	...	...	...
1907	312	24	514	...	...	...	601	147	2,162	...	...	...
1908	302	40	1,842	...	...	...	399	296	10,834	...	...	...
1909	138	302	11,800	...	...	...	436	301	2,774	...	...	...
1910	76	4	39	...	...	...	531	515	9,895	...	...	...
1911	98	21	570	85	...	...	903	962	10,320	...	...	...
1912	116	10	292	74	...	...	857	1,463	40,915	...	...	...
1913	119	10	303	64	...	...	1,497[9]	689[9]	11,631[9]	...	...	...
							1,459	664	9,804			
1914	115	14	620	31	...	...	972	447	9,878	...	...	...
1915	80	5	83	15	...	...	672	448	2,953	...	...	...
1916	227	21	475	38	...	...	532	276	2,446	...	...	...
1917	475	47	1,109	140	...	...	730	872	5,647	...	...	...
1918	708	61	1,436	268	...	...	1,165	1,116	5,875	...	...	...
1919	440	81	2,296	237	...	...	1,352	2,591	34,969	...	...	...
1920	486	139	8,943	184	...	...	1,607	1,932	26,568	...	...	...
1921	347	50	2,663	55	...	..	763	1,801	85,872	...	...	...
1922	392	76	2,675	104	...	...	576	552	19,850	...	...	...
1923	206	103	6,907	44	...	...	628	405	10,672	...	...	...
1924	261	24	1,205	70	...	...	710	613	8,424	60	5	76
1925	239	146	1,560	42	...	...	603	441	7,952	44	7	111
1926	206	53	1,711	35[7]	...	...	323	2,734	162,233	46	11	158
1927	189	10	400	26	2	34	308	108	1,174	78	8	239
1928	201	72	4,835	45	5	98	302	124	1,388	...	6	117
1929	180	13	667	39	5	100	431	533	8,287	14	2	13

See p. 191 for footnotes

C3 Industrial Disputes 1930–1975

	Austria			Belgium			Czechoslovakia			Denmark		
	Number	Workers Involved (thou)	Days Lost (thou)	Number	Workers Involved (thou)	Days Lost (thou)	Number	Workers Involved (thou)	Days Lost (thou)	Number	Workers Involved (thou)	Days Lost (thou)
1930	83	10	41	93	54	...	159	31	423	37	5	144
1931	56	12	100	73	20	...	254	50	499	16	4	246
1932	30	7	80	63	161	...	317	103	1,256	18	6	87
1933	23	6	65	86	35	...	209	37	289	26	0.5	18
1934	4	0.3	0.2	79	34	...	213	38	265	38	12	146
1935	2	0.1	0.2	150	99	...	219	40	490	14	0.8	14
1936	5	1.8	1.5	(111)[10]	(39)[10]	...	262	55	637	12	97	2,946
1937	5	1.5	0.4	209	82	...	430	121	1,119	22	1	21
1938	...	...	...	126	33	241	174	36	158	22	4	90
1939	...	...	...	68	43	...	...	...	...	19	0.5	16
1940	...	...	...	...	...	...	...	...	...	9	0.3	5
1941	...	...	...	...	...	...	...	...	...	2	0.1	3
1942	...	...	...	...	...	...	...	...	...	7	3	11
1943	...	...	...	...	...	...	...	...	...	17	6	24
1944	...	...	...	...	...	...	...	...	...	34	8	89
1945	...	...	...	160	140	563	...	...	...	35	9	66
1946	...	...	...	287	170	1,053	...	...	...	59	54	1,389
1947	...	...	...	473	301	2,212	...	...	...	29	8	467
1948	...	...	...	155	334	1,858	...	...	...	24	3	8
1949	...	...	...	99	48	830	...	...	...	17	3	10
1950	...	...	...	122[11]	148[11]	2,769	...	...	...	18	3	4
1951	...	32	84	163	121	593	...	...	...	12	2	4
1952	...	32	75	122	278	863	...	...	...	9	2	4
1953	...	13	38	115	117	412	...	...	...	8	0.4	2
1954	...	21	51	107	61	444	...	...	...	20	8	23
1955	...	26	58	143	119	1,002	...	...	...	13	6	10
1956	...	44	153	148	176	948	...	...	...	98	66	1,087
1957	...	20	46	115	339	3,789	...	...	...	14	3	7
1958	...	29	49	43	63	294	...	...	...	15	9	9
1959	...	47	51	57	123	983	...	...	...	23	6	18
1960	...	31	69	61[11]	19[11]	334	...	...	...	82	20	61
1961	...	39	114	38[11]	13[11]	92	...	...	...	34	153	2,308
1962	...	207	648	40	22	271	...	...	...	26	10	15
1963	...	17	34	48	18	247	...	...	...	19	7	24
1964	...	41	35	41	41	444	...	...	...	40	8	17
1965	...	146	151	63	19	70	...	...	...	37	14	242
1966	...	121	71	74	42	533	...	...	...	22	10	15
1967	...	7	16	58	38	182	...	...	...	22	10	10
1968	...	3	7	71	29	364	...	...	...	17	29	34
1969	...	17	19	88	25	162	...	...	...	48	36	56
1970	...	8	27	151	108	1,432	...	...	...	77	56	102
1971	...	2	4	184	87	1,240	...	...	...	31	6	21
1972	...	7	15	191	67	354	...	...	...	35	8	22
1973	...	78	160	172	62	872	...	...	...	205	337	3,901
1974	...	7	7	235	56	580	...	...	...	134	142	184
1975	...	4	6	243	86	608	...	...	...	147	59	100

See p. 191 for footnotes

C3 Industrial Disputes 1930–1975

	Finland			France			Germany			Greece		
	Number	Workers Involved (thou)	Days Lost (thou)	Number	Workers Involved (thou)	Days Lost (thou)	Number	Workers Involved (thou)	Days Lost (thou)	Number	Workers Involved (thou)	Days Lost (thou)
1930	11	2	12	1,093	582	7,209	353	302	4,029	...	...	...
1931	1	0.1	...	286	48	950	463	297	1,890	...	...	...
1932	3	0.3	2	362	72	1,244	648	172	1,130	...	...	...
1933	4	1	10	343	87	1,199	(69)[12]	(13)[12]	(96)[12]	...	...	...
1934	46	6	90	385	101	2,393	...	...	...	...	...	...
1935	23	2	61	376	109	1,182	...	...	...	...	...	...
1936	29	3	35	16,907	2,423	...	...	...	...	...	...	...
1937	37	6	183	2,616	1,133	...	...	...	...	...	...	...
1938	31	4	111	1,220	324	...	...	...	...	...	...	...
1939	29	6	...	...	...	...	...	...	...	...	...	...
1940	4	0.5	...	...	...	...	...	...	...	...	...	...
1941	12	2	...	...	...	...	...	...	...	...	...	...
1942	...	...	...	...	...	...	...	...	...	...	...	...
1943	...	...	...	...	...	...	...	...	...	...	...	...
1944	...	...	...	...	...	...	...	...	...	...	...	...
							------	------	------			
1945	102	36	358	...	...	...	...	...	...	...	...	...
1946	42	19	116	528	180	386	...	...	...	...	...	...
1947	228	113	480	2,285	2,998	22,673	...	...	...	...	...	...
1948	84	15	244	1,425	6,561	13,133	...	...	...	...	...	...
1949	48	54	1,195	1,426	4,330	7,129	892	58	271	...	...	...
1950	78	108	4,644	2,586	1,527	11,729	1,344[13]	79[13]	380[13]	206	129	434
1951	67	11	324	2,514	1,754	3,495	1,528	174	1,593	184	134	375
1952	43	9	54	1,749	1,155	1,733	2,529	84	443	114	52	110
1953	104	16	64	1,761	1,784	9,722	1,395	51	1,488	196	85	117
1954	36	19	116	1,479	1,319	1,440	538	116	1,587	172	49	39
1955	72	42	344	2,672	1,061	3,079	866	597	847	210	50	69
1956	43	451	6,971	2,440	982	1,423	268	52	1,580	...	...	...
1957	88	59	228	2,623	2,964	4,121	86	45	1,072	169	115	142
1958	50	14	45	954	1,112	1,138	1,484	202	782	113	92	109
1959	49	20	430	1,512	940	1,938	55	22	62	100	42	59
							---------[14]	------[14]	---------[14]			
1960	44	19	96	1,494	1,072	1,070	28	17	38	135	56	81
1961	51	45	41	1,963	2,552	2,601	119	20	61	115	53	188
1962	46	7	33	1,884	1,472	1,901	195	79	451	182	57	129
1963	66	105	1,380	2,382	2,646	5,991	187	316	1,846	227	101	331
1964	76	27	58	2,281	2,603	2,497	34	6	17	399	164	346
1965	29	7	16	1,674	1,237	980	20	6	49	434	256	454
1966	150	66	123	1,711	3,341	2,523	205	196	27	609	349	712
1967	43	27	321	1,675	2,824	4,204	742	60	390	89	91	114
1968	68	27	282	...	...	...	36	25	25	...	...	...
1969	158	83	161	2,207	1,444	2,224	86	90	249	...	...	...
1970	240	202	233	2,942	1,080	1,742	129	184	93	...	...	...
1971	838[18]	403[18]	2,711[18]	4,318	3,234	4,388	624	536	4,484	...	...	...
1972	849	240	473	3,464	2,721	3,755	54	23	66	...	...	...
1973	1,010	678	2,497	3,731	2,246	3,915	732	185	563	...	...	...
1974	1,795	371	435	3,381	1,564	3,380	890	250	1,051	...	...	...
1975	1,530	215	284	3,888	1,827	3,869	201	36	69	...	...	...

See p.191 for footnotes

C3 Industrial Disputes 1930–1975

	Hungary			Ireland			Italy			Netherlands		
	Number	Workers Involved (thou)	Days Lost (thou)	Number	Workers Involved (thou)	Days Lost (thou)	Number	Workers Involved (thou)	Days Lost (thou)	Number	Workers Involved (thou)	Days Lost (thou)
1930	35	6	80	83	3	77	82	3	...	212	11	229
1931	38	11	190	60	5	310	67	4	...	215	28	766
1932	20	5	33	70	4	42	23	0.6	...	216	32	1,636
1933	31	10	125	88	9	200	34	0.8	...	184	15	483
1934	49	13	92	99	9	180	38	0.6	...	152	6	90
1935	50	17	111	99	10	288	43	0.6	...	152	13	244
1936	122	21	233	107	9	186	...	...	...	96	10[17] / 9	77
1937	89	26	161	145	27	1,755	...	...	...	95	5	32
1938	64	9	105	137	14	209	...	...	...	141	8	125
1939	53	26	170	99	7	106	...	...	...	90	6	91
1940	35	33	370	89	8	152	...	...	...	23[15]	3[15]	43[15]
1941	3	0.8	1	71	5	77	...	...	...	...	...	...
1942	7	0.5	2	69	5	115	...	...	...	...	...	...
1943	8	0.5	1	81	6	62	...	...	...	...	...	...
1944	—	—	—	84	4	38	...	...	...	...	...	...
1945	9	6	7	87	9	244	...	...	...	118[16]	39[16]	161[16]
1946	17	26	57	105	11	150	...	...	...	270	75	682
1947	5	5	7	194	22	449	...	...	...	272	63	203
1948	...	...	...	147	17	258	...	...	...	183	19	131
1949	...	...	...	153	10	273	1,159	2,894	16,578	116	15	289
1950	...	...	...	154	19	217	1,272	3,536	7,761	79	21	163
1951	...	...	...	138	25	545	1,190	2,145	4,515	85	15	67
1952	...	...	...	82	15	529	1,363	1,462	3,531	40	4	31
1953	...	...	...	75	7	82	1,415	4,678	5,828	58	11	30
1954	...	...	...	81	8	67	1,990	2,045	5,377	91	21	59
1955	...	...	...	96	12	236	1,981	1,383	5,622	63	24	133
1956	...	...	...	67	4	48	1,904	1,678	4,137	80	38	213
1957	...	...	...	45	4	92	1,731	1,227	4,619	37	2	7
1958	...	...	...	51	12	126	1,937	1,283	4,172	73	5	37
1959	...	...	...	58	9	124	1,925	1,900	9,190	48	8	14
1960	...	...	...	49	6	80	2,471	2,338	5,786	121	85	467
1961	...	...	...	96	27	377	3,502	2,698	9,891	43	10	25
1962	...	...	...	60	9	104	3,652	2,910	22,717	24	2	9
1963	...	...	...	70	16	234	4,145	3,694	11,395	104	30	38
1964	...	...	...	87	25	545	3,841	3,245	13,089	53	9	44
1965	...	...	...	89	40	556	3,191	2,310	6,993	60	23	55
1966	...	...	...	112	52	784	2,387	1,887	14,474	20	11	13
1967	...	...	...	79	21	183	2,658	2,243	8,568	8	2	6
1968	...	...	...	126	39	406	3,377	4,862	9,240	11	6	14
1969	...	...	...	134	62	936	3,788	7,507	37,825	28	12	22
1970	...	...	...	134	29	1,008	4,162	3,722	20,887	99	52	263
1971	...	...	...	133	44	274	5,598	3,891	14,799	15	36	97
1972	...	...	...	131	22	207	4,765	4,405	19,497	31	20	134
1973	...	...	...	182	32	207	3,769	6,133	23,419	7	58	584
1974	...	...	...	219	43	552	5,174	7,824	19,467	14	3	7
1975	...	...	...	151	29	296	3,601	14,110	27,189	5	0.3	0.5

See p. 191 for footnotes

C3 Industrial Disputes 1930–1975

	Norway			Poland			Romania			Spain		
	Number	Workers Involved (thou)	Days Lost (thou)	Number	Workers Involved (thou)	Days Lost (thou)	Number	Workers Involved (thou)	Days Lost (thou)	Number	Workers Involved (thou)	Days Lost (thou)
1930	94	5	240	330	53	427	101	17	180	402 (368)	287	3,745
1931	82	60	7,586	363	109	637	71	17	185	734 (610)	288	3,843
1932	91	6	394	517	315	2,134	102	19	104	68 (435)	444	3,590
1933	93	6	364	649	348	3,844	58	16	57	1,127 (1,046)	937	14,441
1934	85	6	235	957	373	2,414	72	11	156	594	742	11,103
1935	103	4	168	1,187	453	2,026	84	16	361[17]			
1936	175	15	396	2,074	678	4,039	90	15	196	...	...	...
1937	195	29	1,014	2,107	567	3,323	70	7	73	...	...	...
1938	248	24	567	1,457	269	1,289	26	4	52	...	...	...
1939	81	16	860	...	...	...	...	...	...	...	...	...
1940	...	...	...	...	...	...	...	...	...	...	...	...
1941	...	...	...	...	...	...	...	...	...	...	...	...
1942	...	...	...	...	...	...	...	...	...	...	...	...
1943	...	...	...	...	...	...	...	...	...	...	...	...
1944	...	...	...	...	...	...	...	...	...	...	...	...
1945	16	4	65	...	...	...	...	...	...	...	...	...
1946	39	5	79	...	...	...	...	...	...	...	...	...
1947	47	8	41	...	...	...	...	...	...	...	...	...
1948	58	6	92	...	...	...	...	...	...	...	...	...
1949	47	9	105	...	...	...	...	...	...	...	...	...
1950	30	4	42	...	...	...	...	...	...	...	...	...
1951	28	4	36	...	...	...	...	...	...	...	...	...
1952	40	6	124	...	...	...	...	...	...	...	...	...
1953	55	5	41	...	...	...	...	...	...	...	...	...
1954	27	3	105	...	...	...	...	...	...	...	...	...
1955	22	10	108	...	...	...	...	...	...	...	...	...
1956	27	56	964	...	...	...	...	...	...	...	...	...
1957	18	3	27	...	...	...	...	...	...	...	...	...
1958	16	13	60	...	...	...	...	...	...	...	...	...
1959	18	2	48	...	...	...	...	...	...	...	...	...
1960	12	0.7	2	...	...	...	...	...	...	...	...	...
1961	19	23	423	...	...	...	...	..	...	...	...	...
1962	8	1	81	...	...	...	...	..	...	....	...	...
1963	8	11	226	...	...	...	...	...	...	169	39	125
1964	3	0.2	1							209	119	141
1965	7	0.6	9	...	...	...	...	...	...	183	59	190
1966	7	1	5	...	...	...	...	...	...	132	37	185
1967	7	0.4	5	...	...	...	...	...	...	372	199	236
1968	6	0.5	14	...	...	...	...	...	...	309	131	241
1969	4	0.8	22	...	...	...	...	...	...	491	205	560
1970	15	3	47	...	...	...	...	...	...	1,547	440	1,092
1971	10	3	9	...	...	...	...	...	...	549	197	860
1972	9	1	12	...	...	...	...	...	...	710	236	587
1973	12	2	11	...	...	...	...	...	...	731	303	1,081
1974	13	22	318	...	...	...	...	...	...	2,009	557	1,749
1975	22	3	12	...	...	...	...	...	...	2,807	504	1,815

See p.191 for footnotes

C3 Industrial Disputes 1930–1975

	Sweden			Switzerland			United Kingdom			Yugoslavia		
	Number	Workers Involved (thous)	Days Lost (thou)	Number	Workers Involved (thou)	Days Lost (thos)	Number	Workers Involved (thou)	Days Lost (thou)	Number	Workers Involved (thou)	Days Lost (thou)
1930	261	21	1,021	31	6	266	422	307	4,399		5	49
1931	193	41	2,627	25	5	74	420	490	6,983	5	1	14
1932	182	50	3,095	38	5	159	389	379	6,488	7	1	4
1933	140	32	3,434	35	3	69	357	136	1,072	8	3	14
1934	103	14	760	20	3	33	471	134	959	35	7	41
1935	98	17	788	17	0.9	15	553	271	1,955	141	26	221
1936	60	4	438	41	4	39	818	316	1,829	397	88	1,356
1937	67	31	861	37	6	115	1,129	597	3,413	238	53	911
1938	85	29	1,284	17	0.7	16	875	274	1,334	189	32	494
1939	45	2	159	7	0.2	4	940	337	1,356	...	...	...
1940	38	4	78	6	0.6	1	922	299	940	...	...	...
1941	34	2	94	15	0.7	14	1,251	360	1,079	...	...	...
1942	139	1	53	19	0.8	4	1,303	456	1,527	...	...	...
1943	167	7	94	19	1	12	1,785	557	1,810	...	...	...
1944	214	7	228	18	1	18	2,194	821	3,710	...	...	...
1945	163	133	11,321	35	4	37	2,293	531	2,835	...	...	...
1946	137	1	27	55	15	184	2,205	526	2,158	...	...	...
1947	81	57	125	29	7	102	1,721	620	2,433	...	...	...
1948	47	6	151	28	4	61	1,759	424	1,944	...	...	...
1949	31	1	21	12	0.9	41	1,426	433	1,807	...	...	...
1950	23	2	41	6	0.3	5	1,339	302	1,389	...	...	...
1951	28	15	531	8	1	8	1,719	379	1,694	...	...	...
1952	32	2	79	8	1	12	1,714	415	1,792	...	...	...
1953	20	26	582	6	2	61	1,746	1,370	2,184	...	...	...
1954	45	8	24	6	3	26	1,989	448	2,457	...	...	...
1955	18	4	159	4	0.4	1	2,419	659	3,781	...	...	...
1956	12	2	4	5	0.3	1	2,648	507	2,083	...	...	...
1957	20	2	53	2	0.1	1	2,859	1,356	8,412	...	...	...
1958	10	0.1	15	3	0.8	2	2,629	523	3,462	...	...	...
1959	17	1	24	4	0.1	2	2,093	645	5,270	...	...	...
1960	31	1	18	8	0.2	1	2,832	817	3,024	...	...	...
1961	12	0.1	2	—	—	—	2,686	771	3,046	...	...	...
1962	10	4	5	2	0.2	1	2,449	4,420	5,798	...	...	...
1963	24	3	25	4	1	71	2,068	591	1,755	...	...	...
1964	14	2	34	1	0.4	5	2,524	873	2,277	...	...	...
1965	8	0.2	4	2	--	--	2,354	869	2,925	...	...	...
1966	26	29	352	2	--	--	1,937	531	2,398	...	...	...
1967	7	0.1	0.4	1	0.1	2	2,116	732	2,787	...	...	...
1968	7	0.4	1	1	0.1	2	2,378	2,256	4,690	...	...	...
1969	41	9	112	1	--	--	3,116	1,656	6,846	...	...	...
1970	134	27	156	3	0.3	3	3,906	1,793	10,980	...	...	...
1971	60	63	839	11	2	7	2,228	1,175	13,551	...	...	...
1972	44	7	11	5	0.5	2	2,497	1,726	23,909	...	...	...
1973	48	4	12	—	—	—	2,873	1,513	7,197	...	...	...
1974	85	17	58	3	0.3	3	2,922	1,622	14,750	...	...	...
1975	86	24	366	6	0.3	2	2,282	789	6,012	...	...	...

C3 Industrial Disputes

NOTES

1. SOURCES:– I.L.O., *Yearbook of Labour Statistics* (since 1935), and the official publications noted on p.xv. Netherlands data of workers involved for 1906–9 and 1919–24 were supplied by the Dutch Central Office of Statistics, and Italian data for 1914–23 were supplied by the Italian Central Institute of Statistics.

2. Except as indicated in the footnotes, the number of workers involved and the days' work lost by them relate to all those clearly affected by a particular dispute, not just to those directly involved.

3. The reporting systems of countries differ considerably, and comparisons should not be made without taking these differences into account.

FOOTNOTES

[1] Cisleithania to 1913. In this period only workers directly involved are included.
[2] This column refers only to actual strikers.
[3] The figures are unknown for one dispute.
[4] The figures relate to West Germany after 1945.
[5] Previously disputes begun during the year; subsequently all disputes in being during the year.
[6] For the period to 1934 information about workers involved and days lost is not available for the total number of disputes recorded. The number of disputes to which the statistics in the second and third columns relate is shown in brackets in the first column.
[7] Previous statistics are taken from the records of the central employers' association or of the *union syndicale,* whichever shows the higher figure.
[8] Subsequently excludes strike involving less than ten workers or lasting less than one day, except when the number of days lost exceed one hundred.
[9] Southern Ireland is excluded from 1913.
[10] Excluding June–August, when the number of strikes was so great that records were never completely taken.
[11] Excluding general strikes and the political strike of 1950.
[12] First quarter only.
[13] Previously American and British Occupation Zones only.
[14] Subsequently includes West Berlin.
[15] January–May.
[16] May–December.
[17] Subsequently only workers directly involved are included.
[18] Previously excludes workers indirectly affected, though including days lost by these workers. Also previously excludes disputes lasting less than 4 hours, except when a loss of more than 100 days was involved.
[19] Earlier figures of estimated numbers of strikes (to 1864) and of actual numbers of strikes and strikers are given in Edward Shorter and Charles Tilly, *Strikes in France, 1830–1968* (Cambridge, 1974):

	Strikes		Strikes	Strikers (000)		Strikes	Strikers (000)
1830	40	1850	45	...	1870	116	88.2
1831	49	1851	55	...	1871	52	14.1
1832	51	1852	86	...	1872	151	21.1
1833	90	1853	109	...	1873	44	4.9
1834	55	1854	68	...	1874	58	7.8
1835	32	1855	168	...	1875	101	16.6
1836	55	1856	73	...	1876	102	21.2
1837	51	1857	55	...	1877	55	12.9
1838	44	1858	53	...	1878	73	38.5
1839	64	1859	58	...	1879	88	54.4
1840	130	1860	58	...	1880	190	110.4
1841	68	1861	63	...	1881	209	68.0
1842	62	1862	44	...	1882	271	65.5
1843	49	1863	29	...	1883	181	42.0
1844	53	1864	21	...	1884	112	33.9
1845	48	1865	58	27.6	1885	123	20.8
1846	53	1866	52	14.0	1886	195	35.3
1847	55	1867	76	32.1	1887	194	38.1
1848	94	1868	58	20.3	1888	188	51.5
1849	65	1869	72	40.6	1889	199	89.1

Shorter and Tilly's later statistics sometimes differ from those in the *Annuaire Statistique,* but not generally by significant amounts.

[20] Statistics of numbers of strikes for 1892–1913 are given in H. Kaelble and H. Volkmann, "Konjunktur und Streik während des Ubergangs zum Organisierten Kapitalismus in Deutschland", *Zeitschrift für Wirtschafts – und Sozialwissenschaften* (1972). These differ somewhat from those given in the table. They are as follows:–

1892	73	1900	852	1907	2,792
1893	116	1901	727	1908	2,052
1894	131	1902	861	1909	2,045
1895	204	1903	1,282	1910	3,194
1896	483	1904	1,625	1911	2,914
1897	578	1905	2,323	1912	2,825
1898	985	1906	3,480	1913	2,600
1899	976				

C4 MONEY WAGES IN INDUSTRY

1800–1829

	Belgium a	France b[2]	France c[2]	Germany d	Germany e	U.K.[6]
1800	...	...	...	34	26	...
1801	...	...	...	35	26	...
1802	...	...	...	35	26	...
1803	...	...	...	36	27	...
1804	...	...	...	37	27	...
1805	...	...	...	39	30	...
1806	...	44	...	39	30	...
1807	...	...	...	40	28	...
1808	...	...	...	41	28	...
1809	...	...	...	42	28	70
1810	...	...	...	43	28	73
1811	...	...	...	43	29	71
1812	...	...	...	43	29	73
1813	...	...	...	43	31	73
1814	...	...	...	43	31	77
1815	...	...	...	42	33	70
1816	...	...	...	42	35	70
1817	...	...	...	42	33	67
1818	...	...	...	42	32	65
1819	...	...	...	42	33	66
1820	...	...	...	41	33	65
1821	...	...	...	41	35	65
1822	...	...	...	41	35	65
1823	...	...	...	41	35	65
1824	...	...	...	40	36	65
1825	...	...	...	40	36	65
1826	...	...	...	39	36	63
1827	...	...	...	36	36	63
1828	...	44	...	37	36	63
1829	...	...	...	39	36	63

1830–1859

1900=100[1]

	Belgium a	France b[3]	France c[3]	Germany d	Germany e	U.K.[6]
1830	...	...	...	41	37	62
1831	...	...	...	43	38	62
1832	...	...	...	45	37	62
1833	...	...	...	47	39	62
1834	...	...	...	47	38	63
1835	...	...	...	47	38	63
1836	...	...	...	47	38	64
1837	...	...	...	47	39	65
1838	...	...	...	47	40	65
1839	...	...	...	45	41	66
1940	...	...	...	47	44	67
1841	...	...	...	41	43	67
1842	...	52	...	41	45	67
1843	46	...	...	49	43	67
1844	48	...	...	45	45	67
					39[3]	
1845	47	...	...	45	39	67
1846	50	...	...	45	39	67
1847	48	...	...	45	40	67
1848	47	...	...	46	43	67
1849	48	...	...	46	41	67
1850	49	...	...	46	41	66[6]
						67
1851	51	...	...	44	42	66
1852	52	57	...	44	40	66
1853	53	...	51	47	42	72
1854	56	...	...	50	44	74
1855	56	...	...	50	45	75
1856	58	63		54	46	75
1857	59	...	57	53	49	72
1858	59	...	...	55	49	70
1859	59	...	...	...	47	70

a averages wages in 5 industries; b hourly wages in Paris; c hourly wages in the Provinces; d daily wages in coalmining; e gross weekly wages in industry.

See p. 199 for footnotes

C4 Money Wages in Industry 1860–1914

	Belgium	France			Germany	Italy	Sweden	U.K.[6]
	a	b[2]	c[3]	d	e	f	g	
1860	60	...	...	54	48	...	...	72
1861	61	...	...	55	50	...	41	72
1862	62	70	...	54	50	...	45	72
1863	65	...	...	58	50	...	45	74
1864	67	...	...	56	51	...	42	77
1865	70	...	...	58	51	...	45	78
1866	72	...	...	59	54	...	44	81
1867	72	...	...	62	54	...	45	80
1868	72	...	...	63	56	...	49	79
1869	74	...	...	64	58	...	52	79
1870	75	...	...	65	60		49	81
1871	75	...	...	66	63	65	51	84
1872	83	...	...	72	77	69	57	89
1873	91	73	74	74	88	69	61	93
1874	89	...	...	76	85	73	66	94[6] / 92
1875	88	...	...	77	83	73	67	90
1876	85	...	...	...	76	77	64	89
1877	79	...	...	...	71	81	67	88
1878	81	...	...	...	72	81	63	85
1879	79	...	...	...	69	81	59	83
1880	82	93	82	...	70	85	63	83
1881	82	...	...	...	71	85	65	85
1882	80	...	...	80	75	88	67	86
1883	83	...	...	82	74	88	67	86
1884	81	...	...	82	75	88	68	85
1885	79	...	85	80	74	92	68	84
1886	81	...	...	80	74	92	66	83
1887	79	...	...	80	80	92	66	83
1888	82	...	...	80	79	92	68	85
1889	82	...	...	83	80	96	72	88
1890	87	...	...	89	83	96	74	91
1891	86	...	...	89	83	96	75	92
1892	86	...	...	91	83	96	76	90
1893	84	...	...	89	86	96	78	91
1894	86	...	...	89	84	96	79	90
1895	85	...	...	88	85	96	80	89
1896	87	92	96	88	89	96	83	90
1897	88	...	...	89	94	100	87	91
1898	89	...	...	91	97	100	92	93
1899	93	...	...	94	101	100	96	96
1900	100	99	...	100	100	100[5]	100	100
1901	94	100	100	103	103	100	100	99
1902	96	...	...	98	103	103	102	98
1903	97	...	...	98	104	104	103	97
1904	97	...	...	97	106	104	107	97
1905	96	...	...	97	108	102	110	97
1906	99	108	108	102	114	106	116	99
1907	107	...	...	105	119	119	122	102
1908	103	...	...	106	121	119	125	102
1909	104	...	...	107	121	134	129	100
1910	108	...	...	108	125	131	135	101
1911	108	111	112	110	129	133	137	101
1912	114	...	...	111	135	137	142	104
1913	119	...	...	116	138	143	144	107
1914	...	...	...	117	...	142	143	108

a average wages in 5 industries; b hourly wages in Paris; c hourly wages in the Provinces; d daily wages in coal mining; e gross weekly wages in industry; f hourly wages of males in all activities[5]; g hourly wages of males in industry.

See p. 199 for footnotes

C4 Money Wages in Industry 1910–1938

	Austria	Belgium	Bulgaria	Czec	Denmark	Finland	France			Germany	Hungary
		a		b			c	d	e	f	g
1910	...	...	...	...	...	...	...	...	...	...	...
1911	...	...	...	...	...	...	14	12	...	...	...
1912	...	...	...	...	...	...	...	...	...	...	...
1913	...	69	...	11	...		...	...	...	...	...
1914	...	...	...	...	39	7.7	...	...	16	1914=100 100	...
1915	...	...	...	...	...	8.2	...	...	...	110	...
1916	...	...	...	...	...	10.9	17	...	...	130	...
1917	...	...	...	...	...	15.7	...	...	...	160	...
1918	...	...	...	22	...	24.1	...	...	...	200	...
1919	...	...	...	39	109	35.5	...	...	42	340	...
1920	...	127	...	66	147	62	...	...	56	990[9]	...
1921	...	151	...	108	143	68	58	60	57	1,780[9]	...
1922	...	116	...	109	110	73	...	...	50	45,230[9]	...
1923	...	119	...	93	105	81	...	...	58	86,200,000,000,000[9]	
1924	...	106	...	91	110	84	63	68	66	1929=100 54	...
1925	...	94	...	93	117	88	68	73	69	73	...
1926	...	91	...	94	107[7]	93	84	84	83	76	...
1927	98	93	...	95	100	96	84	86	92	85	96
1928	96	97	93	98	99	100	86	90	90	97	98
1929	100	100	100	100	100	100	100	100	100	100	100
1930	104	106	94	100	102	97	109	106	108	92	100
1931	102	99	91	98	102	85	108	106	104	81	96
1932	101	91	79	94	102	82	104	104	96	67	89
1933	97	88	84	89	102	93	104	102	95	68	84
1934	94	84	78	87	102	83	104	102	91	73	81
1935	...	81	78	85	103	84	102	98	90	75	77
1936	...	88	77	86	102	89	116	115	101	78	79
1937	...	97	85	...	105	97	...	146	140	81	79
1938	...	103	90	...	110	103	174	161	160	85	84

Czec: Czechoslovakia

a wages of males in industry and transport; b daily wages of insured workers; c hourly wages in Paris; d hourly wages in the Provinces; e daily wages in coal mining; f weekly wages; g hourly wages.

See p. 199 for footnotes

C4 Money Wages in Industry 1910–1938

	Ireland	Italy	Neth	Norway	Poland	Romania	Russia	Sweden	Switz	U.K.	Yug
	a	b	c	d		e	f	g	h	i	j
1910	...	...	...	31[10]	...	...	...	...	...	...	...
1911	...	...	...	31	...	...	...	...	...	...	...
1912	...	...	...	33	...	...	...	...	...	...	...
1913	...	19	...	35[10]	...	...	...	42	47	...	...
1914	...	19	...	37[10]	...	3.6	...	43	...	53[12]	...
1915	...	19	...	37[10]	...	...	...	46	...	57	...
1916	...	22	...	38[10]	...	...	...	51	...	63	...
1917	...	27	...	59[10]	...	...	...	62	...	76	...
1918	...	33	...	86[10]	...	...	...	90	78	101	...
1919	...	48	...	136[10]	...	...	...	114	91	122	...
1920	...	78	...	171[11]	...	...	...	130	103	151[12]	...
										148	
1921	...	103	...	171	...	...	...	132	103	146	...
1922	...	99	...	130	...	...	...	96	97	107	...
1923	...	93	...	123	...	66	...	90	94	99	...
1924	...	93	...	131	...	76	...	91	97	102	...
1925	...	104	...	141	100	84	56[24]	93	97	103	...
1926	...	112	100	125	72	90	71[24]	94	98	102	...
1927	...	111	100	106	84	98	78[24]	94	98	102	...
1928	...	102	100	101	92	99	88	95	98	100	...
1929	...	100	100	100	100	100	100	100	100	100	1930=100
1930	1931=100	99	100	100	99	96	117	102	101	99	100
1931	100	92	100	97[11]	92	85	141	101	102	98	99
1932	99	87	93	98[11]	85	69	178	99	98	96	91
1933	99	84	93	98	77	63	196	96	96	95	86
1934	99	81	89	96	73	62	232	95	94	95	79
1935	99	78	85	95	71	61	284	98	92	96	78
1936	99	78	85	95	70	1936=100	...	99	90	99	80
						100					
1937	100	81	85	103	73	105	...	103	89	102	83
1938	106	85	89	113	77	107	433	109	93	105	85

Neth: Netherlands; Switz: Switzerland; U.K. United Kingdom; Yug: Yugoslavia

a weekly wages; b daily wages in all activities; c weekly wages of adult males; d hourly wages in engineering;
e wages in all activities; f annual earnings in the Socialist sector; g daily wages in industry, commerce and Communications;
h weekly earnings of insured males involved in accidents; i weekly wages in June in all industries and services;
j monthly earnings.

See p. 199 for footnotes

C4 Money Wages in Industry

1938–1975

1955=100[1]

	Austria	Belgium	Bulgaria[15]	Czech	Denmark	Fin	France			E.Ger	Germany	Hungary
	a	b		c	d	e	f	g	h	i	j	k
	1948=100		1929=100	1938=100			1928=100	1928=100				1929=100
1938	36	...	90	100	33	...	174	161	3.2	...	44	84
1939	...	...	94	96	34	4.6	179	164	3.4	...	45	93
1940		...	107	112	38	...	179	165	3.5	...	47	98
1941	...	...	119	147	40	...	199	197	3.9	...	50	118
1942	...	...	135	178	42	8.2	202	214	4.6	...	50	139
1943	...	...	150	210	45	9.5	209	237	5.3	...	...	198
1944	...	...	269	235	48	11	368	414	6.6	...	...	...
1945	...	...	449	265	52	...	559	715	14	...	...	...
1946	...	...	513	416	57	26	783	968	22	...	West Germany	...
							1955=100[20]					
							22					
1947	63[13]	71	...	504	60	36	30		31	...	...	...
1948	100	78	...	557	65	52	46		47	...	...	1955=100[22]
				1955=100[16]								
				70								52
1949	121	81	...	74	68[18]	55	52		53			52
					70							
1950	136	83	...	81	74	66	57		58	...	70	60
1951	177	93	...	86	81	89	72		76	...	80	64
1952	199	97	...	87	89	93	85		88	...	86	82
	1955=100		1955=100[15]									
	89[14]					[19]						
1953	88	95	89	89	92	93	88		89	...	90	86
1954	93	97	95	94	95	96	93		91	...	93	96
				[16]								
1955	100	100	100	100	100[17]	100	100		100	100	100	100
1956	105	106	101	104	109	111	109		108	103	108	107
1957	110	113	107	106	114	117	118		123	109	114	126
1958	117	115	110	108	119	123	132		138	117	119	127
1959	123	119	116	110	128	130	141		146	127	125	131
1960	134	123	126	114	138	139	150[21]		153	135	137	133
1961	146	127	131	117	155	149	161		164	141	151	135
1962	155	135	134	117	169	157	176		177	143	166	137
1963	165	146	138	117	183	167[21]	192		196	145	178	141
1964	180[19]	161	141	121	199	188	206		213	149	192	145
1965	189	176	145	126	223	205	219		226	155	211	145
1966	212	191	151	129	251	221	232		237	158	223	152
1967	228	203	168	137	272	239	245		252	162	224	156
1968	242	215	179	148	310	266	272		276	169	38	159
1969	257	233	184	159	340	290	301		298	177	263	165
1970	281	260	194	164	279	321	331		322	185	299	175
1971	319[19]	294	199	170	432	370	366		...	192	326	181
1972	356	333	205	177	481	423	407		...	198	351	189
1973	402	391	219	183	564	494	463		...	204	388	206
1974	465	470	223	189	679	603	550		...	210	419	220
1975	527	555	230	195	809	731	644		...	217	438	234

a monthly earnings; b daily wages of males in manufacturing; c daily wages of insured workers; d hourly wages in manufacturing e hourly wages of males in industry; f hourly wages in Paris; g hourly wages in the provinces; h daily wages in coal mining; i monthly earnings in the Socialist Sector; j weekly wages; k hourly wages

See p. 199 for footnotes

C4 Money Wages in Industry 1938–1975

	Ireland	Italy	Netherlands	Norway	Poland	Portugal	Russia	Sweden	Switzerland	U.K.	Yugoslavia
	a	b	c	d	e	f	e	g	h	i	k
											1956=100
1938	47	1.1	38	33	...	...	...	...	...	39	...
1939	48	1.3	38	34	...	...	...	31	43	39	...
			----[19]								
1940	48	1.5	41	36	...	...	46	33	45	45	...
1941	49	1.6	43	...	...	...	...	35	48	48	...
1942	49	1.8	43	...	...	...	...	39	55	52	...
1943	52	2.2	43	...	...	...	...	40	59	54	...
1944	54	3.7	43	40	...	...	...	41	63	57	...
1945	55	7.2	51	46	...	...	61	43	69	59	...
1946	57	19	63	53	...	...	66	46	76	64	...
1947	68	51	65	58	...	...	...	53	82	66[26]	...
			----[19]							59	
1948	74	69	68	61	...	...	...	58	87	62	...
1949	81	73	70	64	...	...	...	59	88	64	...
1950	81	76	76	68	51	...	89	61[25]	88	68	...
								59			
1951	81	84	83	77	56	...	...	71	92	74	...
1952	91	88	84	86	62	...	...	84	95	80	...
1953	100	90	86	90	89	99	...	89	96	85	...
1954	100	94	95	95	95	98	...	92	97	92	...
			----[19]								
1955	100	100[23]	100	100	100	100	100	100	100	100	100
1956	108	105	105	108	111	103	103	109	105	107	109
1957	110	109	117	115	130	104	107	115	109	113	131
1958	112	115	122	120	138	109	109	122	113	115	137
1959	116	117	125	130	149	117	110	128	116	121	156
1960	124	121	135	136	153	124	112	136	123	130	187
1961	126	125	140	146	159	134	116	147	131	138	219
1962	145	135	149	159	164	137	119	159	141	142	229
1963	147	150	159	168	172	143	122	170	152	150	280
1964	166	172	184	177	177	150	124	185	164	162	362
1965	169	186	202	193	183	170	128	204	176	176	501
1966	173	192	222	207	190	184	133	221	188	182	686[21]
1967	189	200	237	222	199	198	140	239	199	192	755
1968	196	207	246	240	209	209	152	255	210	206	830
1969	220	220	270	263	215	...	160	277	222	223	959
1970	252	260	302	295	222	...	167	308	243	252	1,120
1971	297	287	347	331	234	...	172	338	274	277	1,364
								337[25]			
1972	324	311	383	361	248	...	178	377	306	321	1,592
1973	362	375	437	398	276	...	185	409	343	367	1,874
1974	436	470	494	478	315	...	196	458	384	436	2,420
1975	512	593	548	555	352	...	204	466	410	534	2,940

a weekly earnings in production of transportable goods; b daily wages in all activities[23]; c monthly or weekly rates of adult males; d hourly wages of adult males; e monthly earnings in the Socialist sector; f daily wages; g hourly wages of adult males in industry, commerce and communications; h average earnings of all wage-earners in June; i weekly wages of all workers in all industry and services[26]

See p. 199 for footnotes

C4 Money Wages in Industry

NOTES

1. SOURCES:— The main sources were I.L.O., *Year Book* (1931–34); I.L.O., *Yearbook of Labour Statistics* (since 1935); and the official publications noted on p. xv. In addition the following were used:— France, coal miners to 1846 — F. Simiand, *Le salaire des ouvriers des mines de charbon en France* (Paris, 1907); Germany 1871–1913 — based on A.V. Desai, *Real Wages in Germany 1871–1913* (Oxford, 1968). Earlier figures and those from 1914–23 are based on G. Bry, *Wages in Germany, 1871–1945* (Princeton, 1960), and J. Kuczynski, *Die Geschichte der Lage Arbeiter unter dem Kapitalismus* (Berlin, 1961); Sweden to 1930— G. Bagge *et al*, *Wages in Sweden, 1860–1930* (London, 1933); United Kingdom to 1947 — articles by A.L. Bowley and G.H. Wood in the *Journal of the Royal Statistical Society* between 1900 and 1910 and in 1952, and Department of Employment & Productivity, *British Labour Statistics: Historical Abstract 1886–1968* (London, 1971). The Polish figures for 1950–52 are based on data supplied by the Polish Central Statistical Office.

2. Where wages are not specified as being hourly, daily, weekly, etc., there is no indication in the source as to which they were.

3. Both extractive and manufacturing industry are covered by this table, except as otherwise indicated.

FOOTNOTES

[1] Except as otherwise indicated.
[2] 1901=100.
[3] Statistics to 1844 (1st line) relate only to mining.
[4] First half-year only.
[5] From 1901 to 1914 statistics relate to mean daily wages.
[6] Figures to 1850 (1st line) are average wages of compositors, builders, engineers, and cotton workers. From 1850 (2nd line) to 1874 (1st line) they are G.H. Wood's index for workers of unchanged grade in full work (including farmworkers). From 1874 (2nd line) to 1914 they are average wages of all workers in building, engineering, mining, textiles, and agriculture.
[7] Apart from 1914, earlier statistics are based on less than the full four quarterly figures.
[8] Statistics from 1914 to 1923 relate to the weekly earnings of Ruhr coal-miners.
[9] In December of each year.
[10] One month only, in the late summer or autumn.
[11] One quarter-year only.
[12] Statistics for 1914–20 are A.L. Bowley's approximations *(J.R.S.S.*, 1952*)*.
[13] From 1948 allowances supplementary to wages are included.
[14] Second half-year only.
[15] Statistics from 1953 are for monthly earnings in the entire socialist sector.
[16] From 1948 (2nd line) to 1954 the statistics relate to monthly earnings in the entire socialist sector. From 1955 they relate only to the socialist sector of industry.
[17] Previously excluding overtime earnings.
[18] From 1949 (2nd line) vacation pay is included.
[19] The scope of the series was subsequently enlarged.
[20] Statistics from 1946 (2nd line) relate to hourly wages of adult males in all activites.
[21] The introduction of a new currency, one-hundredth the face-value of the old, has been ignored.
[22] Subsequent statistics relate to monthly earnings in the socialist sector of industry.
[23] Statistics from 1956 relate to minimum contract wages (including family allowances) in industry.
[24] These figures are for the economic years ending 30 September.
[25] From 1950 (2nd line) the statistics relate to industry only, and from 1971 (2nd line) to manufacturing industry only.
[26] From 1947 (2nd line) the statistics relate to weekly wages of adult males in manufacturing in October.

C5 MONEY WAGES IN AGRICULTURE

1770–1829

	UK England & Wales	UK Scotland
	a	a
1770-88	47	13[4]
1789	48	...
1790	49	23
1791	50	23
1792	52	23
1793	54	23
1794	56	24
1795	61	26
1796	67	27
1797	70	28
1798	72	28
1799	74	29
1800	76	30
1801	78	31
1802	79	31
1803	80	32
1804	86	36
1805	92	39
1806	96	42
1807	96	42
1808	96	42
1809	96	42
1810	96	42
1811	96	42
1812	96	42
1813	95	40
1814	94	39
1815	94	37
1816	93	37
1817	92	36
1818	90	35
1819	89	34
1820	87	34
1821	81	31
1822	71	28
1823	71	27
1824	66	27
1825	72	27
1826	72	28
1827	72	28
1828	72	28
1829	72	28

1830–1869

1900=100

	Germany[1]	Norway	Sweden[6]	UK England & Wales	UK Scotland
		b	c	a	a
1830	...	...	...	70	28
1831	...	...	...	72	28
1832	...	...	...	73	28
1833	...	...	...	74	28
1834	...	...	...	72	28
1835	...	...	...	70	30
1836	...	...	...	71	31
1837	...	...	...	72	34
1838	...	...	...	73	35
1839	...	...	...	75	38
1840	...	...	...	75	39
1841	...	...	...	75	42
1842	...	...	...	75	43
1843	...	...	...	75	45
1844	...	...	...	71	45
1845	...	...	...	65	44
1846	...	...	...	71	44
1847	...	...	...	71	44
1848	...	...	...	66	44
1849	...	...	...	66	44
1850	48	38	...	66[3]	44
				63	
1851	49	...	...	62	44
1852	50	...	...	62	44
1853	51	...	...	67	50
1854	52	...	...	72	55
1855	53	50	...	74	58
1856	54	...	...	74	58
1857	55	...	...	74	55
1858	56	...	...	73	53
1859	57	...	...	72	53
1860	59	53	49	74	55
1861	59	...	51	75	55
1862	57	...	53	75	55
1863	60	...	52	74	55
1864	61	...	52	74	55
1865	62	60	52	76	55
1866	65	...	51	78	55
1867	64	...	48	80	55
1868	66	...	46	81	56
1869	66	...	46	79	60

a average earnings in a normal week; **b** annual earnings of adult males; **c** daily wages of adult males

See p.205 for footnotes

C5 Money Wages in Agriculture 1870–1914

	Denmark 1915=100	Germany[1]	Norway a[2]	Sweden[6] b	U.K. England & Wales c	U.K. Scotland d
1870	...	68	57	48	80	62
1871	...	71	...	50	81	63
1872	...	79	...	59	86	68
1873	...	86	...	74	90	75
1874	...	88	...	77	94	80
1875	...	92	83	75	94	93
1876	...	93	...	76	95	98
1877	...	90	...	75	95	95
1878	...	84	...	63	95	90
1879	...	79	...	56	92	71
1880	...	79	71	60	92	70
1881	...	80	...	61	92	68
1882	...	80	...	67	92	74
1883	...	79	...	70	92	79
1884	...	79	...	70	92	78
1885	...	79	76	69	91	74
1886	...	79	...	65	90	71
1887	...	79	...	61	89	66
1888	...	80	...	62	89	66
1889	...	80	...	65	90	71
1890	...	82	78	69	91	75
1891	...	82	...	71	93	82
1892	...	83	...	74	93	86
1893	...	83	...	74	93	81
1894	...	86	...	74	92	85
1895	...	87	83	75	93	87
1896	...	88	...	76	93	87
1897	...	90	...	80	94	92
1898	...	94	...	87	95	90
1899	...	97	...	95	97	95
1900	...	100	100	100	100	100
1901	...	100	...	96	101	...
1902	...	102	...	95	101	...
1903	...	103	...	98	101	...
1904	...	105	...	99	101	...
1905	68	108	107	102	102	...
1906	...	111	...	108	...	...
1907	...	114	...	119	...	...
1908	...	116	...	123	...	...
1909	...	119	...	124	...	...
1910	85	121	134	126	103	...
1911	...	124	...	128	...	...
1912	...	128	...	131	...	...
1913	...	133	...	136	...	...
1914	...	...	173[5]	135	113	...

U.K. = United Kingdom

a annual earnings of adult males; b daily wages of adult males; c average wages of labourers; d average earnings in a normal week.

See p.205 for footnotes

C5 Money Wages in Agriculture

1914–1938
1929=100

	Czech[7]	Denmark	Finland	Germany[1]	Hungary	Ireland	Italy
			a		b		c
1914	...	...	...	54[9]	...	...	...
1915	...	73	...	...	...	...	...
1916	...	...	...	...	...	...	...
1917	...	...	...	...	...	...	...
1918	...	103	...	...	...	...	...
1919	...	...	...	...	...	...	...
1920	...	...	...	...	...	...	...
1921	103	189	...	...	...	...	...
1922	...	...[8]	...	...	...	...	...
1923	...	131	...	...	...	...	...
1924	...	125	...	...	...	...	...
1925	92	143	...	74	...	105	...
1926	93	151	...	80	...	102	...
1927	97	127	93	85		102	109
1928	99	109[8] / 106	98	92	105	99	101
1929	100	100	100	100	100	100	100
1930	100	104	100	105	91	98	93
1931	97	107	87	99	72	97	83
1932	96	100	69	82	63	94	75
1933	94	90	65	76	47	89	74
1934		90	72	78	44	84	71
1935		96	74	79	44	85	72
1936		107	80	81	48	87	73
1937		122	86	82	59	88	82
1938		135	110	84		109	86

	Netherlands	Norway[10]	Portugal	Romania	Russia[10]	Sweden	U.K. England & Wales
		a	d	e	f	g	h
1914	...	...	...	...	...	64	53
1915	...	...	...	...	...	66	...
1916	...	74	...	...	...	80	...
1917	...	96	...	...	...	105	...
1918	...	131	...	...	...	151	96[11]
1919	...	181	...	...	...	181	120[11]
1920	...	226	...	...	...	198	136[11]
1921	...	255	...	...	...	142	148[11][12]
1922	...	211	...	...	...	106	107
1923	...	166	...	...	...	100	88
1924	...	153	...	...	...	101	88[12]
1925	...	163	...	...	50	100	95
1926	100	151	...	...	63	100	99
1927	100	125	...	...	67	99	100
1928	100	109	...	...	78	99	100
1929	100	100	100	...	100	100	100
				1930=100			
1930	100	98	98	100	137	99	100
1931	95	92	89	75	200	98	100
1932	80	86	78	60	236	93	99
1933	75	81	80	59	271	93	97
1934	70	78	81	56	323	93	97
1935	70	78	81	57	395	95	99
						1955=100	
1936	70	81	82	62		16	101
1937	70	87	83	73		19	103
1938	70	102	83			21	108

a annual earnings of adult males; b males; c male day labourers; d daily wages of males; e regular day wages; f annual earnings of state employees; g summer day wages of male casual labour; h average county minimum rates.

See p.205 for footnotes

C5 Money Wages in Agriculture 1938–1975

1955=100

	Austria	Belgium	Bulgaria	Czech	Denmark	Finland	France	West Germany	Hungary	Ireland
	a	b	c	d	e	f	g	h	d	i
1938	...	...	...	...	18	2.9	...	...	...	32
1939	...	17	...	...	20	3.3	...	...	...	32
1940	...	...	...	...	21 3.4	3.4	...	...	...	35
1941	...	...	...	...	22	4.0	...	...	...	35
1942	...	...	...	...	25[12]	5.1	...	...	...	39
1943	...	26	...	...	26	7.3	...	...	...	42
1944	...	31	...	...	34	9.7	...	...	...	47
1945	...	45	...	...	44	12[14]	...	...	...	47
1946	...	60	...	...	54	28	...	...	...	53
1947	...	68	...	...	64	37	...	...	...	60
1948	...	71	...	...	63	50	...	...	...	66
1949	...	77	...	...	64	55	...	...	44	72
1950	64	80	...	...	66	81[14]	...	65[16]	45	72
1951	85	83[13] 86	...	...	71	86	63	81	57	80
1952	86	92	...	...	79	91	82	90	71	87
1953	86	95	82	...	87	91[14]	88	92	79	95
1954	94	97	91	93	92	93	92	95	95	100
1955	100[24]	100	100	100	100	100	100	100	100	100
1956	109	101	101	108	104	112	110	110	110	113
1957	116	109	110	112	103	118	123	119	125	113
1958	123	112	114	114	99	119	149	128	132	113
1959	124	116	118	120	102	124	168	136	137	120
1960	130	118	128	123	111	132	176[15]	144	144	125
1961	148	123	128	126	125	136	183	160	147	128
1962	169	129	133	130	148	139	201	181	144	143
1963	180	140	137	130	171	160[15]	223	198	151	143
1964	182	151	137	135	193	179	246	216	158	170
1965	221	169	146	142	218	204	263	239	158	188
1966	232	176	158	151	248	216	275	260	166	203
1967	257	185	171	160	274	234	299	266	173	211
1968	276	194	175	177	279	254	323	276	187	229
1969	295	204	177	192	287	268	369	296	201	270
1970	314	221	188	196	321	298	428	328	216	306
1971	342	245	202	202	349	342	442	366	224	381
1972	377	271	217	212	...	419	464	394	233	416
1973	422	314	237	224	...	517	544	437	245	463
1974	489	372	237	233	...	649	...	500	264	580
1975	560	446	249	240	...	848	...	539	278	712

Czech=Czechoslovakia

a daily wages of permanent workers; b daily wages of adult male hands[13]; c average earnings of agricultural workers on state farms; d monthly earnings on state farms; e yearly earnings of workers on annual engagement; f yearly earnings of adult male labourers[14]; g monthly wages in April of male general hands; h weekly wages; i monthly wages in July of male labourers.

See p.205 for footnotes

C5 Money Wages in Agriculture 1938–1975

	Italy	Netherlands	Norway	Poland	Portugal	Russia	Sweden	U.K.(GB)	Yugoslavia
	a	b	c	d	e	f	g	h	d
1938	1.1	23	...	...	38	...	21[17]	26	...
1939	1.2	25[12]	15	...	37	...	21	26	...
1940	1.3	27	16	...	38	47	23	30[12]	...
1941	1.5	30	18	...	41	...	26	36	...
1942	1.7	32	23	...	53	...	29	44	...
1943	...	33	28	...	62	...	33	45	...
1944	...	33	32	...	70	...	34	48	...
1945	...	43	36	...	75	46	38	51	...
1946	...	58	40	...	93	...	41	54	...
1947	...	60[12]	50	...	107	...	46	61[21]	...
								62	
1948	...	62	59	...	104	...	54	66	...
1949	77	67	66	...	101	...	56	69	...
1950	78	72	70	...	100	82	57[18]	71	...
							61		
1951	79	77	76	...	102	...	70	77	...
1952	83	80	84	...	103	...	88	82	...
1953	92	83	91	82	103	...	89[19]	88	...
1954	97	93[12]	93	93	104	...	91	93	...
1955	100[23]	100	100	100	100	100	100	100	1956=100
1956	105	105	106	110	125	...	106	107	100
1957	108	120	116	117	127	107	113	113	116
1958	113	133	121	131	133	114	120	120	131
1959	115	137	126	152	141	177	125	123	147
1960	116	145	133	159	153	116	139	129	164
1961	121	148	142	166	159	124	154	135	195
1962	133	155	149	171	188	142	170	141	229[22]
1963	156	167	168	178	198	144	187	151	266
1964	178	192	179	185	224	151	201	157	338
1965	195	207	193	192	236	160	219	170	487
1966	206	226	218	204	252	172	241	179	716[15]
1967	225	245	231	215	303	181	265[20]	187	835
1968	237	257	249	226	322	198	286	198	873
1969	262	280	264	234	356	200	310	215	1,004
1970	308	312	299	239	396	217	342	228	1,174
1971	350	355	333	255	448	228	371	257	1,547
1972	414	390	365	281	503	240	407[12]	281	1,837
1973	513	437	423	315	567	252	432	338	2,195
1974	677	499[12]	492	362	754	267	487	378	2,908
1975	898	578	565	405	937	272	590	494	3,477

U.K.(GB)= United Kingdom (Great Britain)

a male day labourers[23]; b weekly or monthly wages of adult males; c summer monthly wages of adult male labourers; d monthly earnings in the Socialist Sector; e daily wages of males; f monthly earnings on state farms; g hourly wages of day labourers; h average county minimum rates in England and Wales.

See p.205 for footnotes

C5 Money Wages in Agriculture

NOTES

1. SOURCES:— The main sources were the same as for table C.4. In addition the following were used as a basis for the indices:— England & Wales to 1850 and Scotland to 1869 — articles by A.L. Bowley and G.H. Wood in the *Journal of the Royal Statistical Society* (1898 and 1899); England & Wales from 1851 and Great Britain in Part III — Department of Employment and Productivity, *British Labour Statistics: Historical Abstract 1886—1968* (London, 1971); Scotland 1870—1900 — R. Mollond & G. Evans, Scottish Farm Wages from 1870 to 1900, *Journal of the Royal Statistical Society* (1950); Germany to 1938 — W.G. Hoffman, *Das Wachstum der Deutschen Wirtschaft seit der Mitte des 19 Jahrhunderts* (Berlin, etc., 1965); and Sweden to 1930 — G. Bagge *et al,* Wages in Sweden, 1860—1930 (London, 1933). The Portugese figure for 1946 is based on data supplied by the National Institute of Statistics.

2. Where wages are not specified as being hourly, daily, weekly, etc., there is no indication in the source as to which they were.

3. Average wages of Belgian male farm workers not provided with food were as follows at the general censuses of agriculture in the nineteenth century (in francs):— 1846 1.18; 1856 1.36; 1874 2.03; 1880 2.04; 1890 1.96; 1895 1.98. (these data were supplied by the Belgian National Institute of Statistics.)

4. Lennart Jorberg, *A History of Prices in Sweden 1732—1914* (2 vols, Lund, 1972), gives the following quinquennial indices of the day wages of male agricultural workers in Sweden:—

1750/4 = 100		1860/4 = 100		1860/4 = 100	
1735/9	102	1805/9	29	1860/4	100
1740/4	92	1810/4	54	1865/9	92
1745/9	88	1815/9	62	1870/4	118
1750/4	100	1820/4	60	1875/9	134
1755/9	112	1825/9	62	1880/4	121
1760/4	163	1830/4	65	1885/9	121
1765/5	188	1835/9	65	1890/4	135
1770/4	172	1840/4	66	1895/9	154
1775/9	209	1845/9	66	1900/4	181
1780/4	218	1850/4	71	1905/9	213
1785/9	209	1855/9	97	1910/4	240
1790/4	227				
1795/9	309				

FOOTNOTES

[1] Statistics to 1938 relate to the average yearly incomes of workers in agriculture, forestry and fishing. The following indices of money wages in agriculture are given in J. Kuczynski, *Die Geschichte der Lage der Arbeiter under dem Kapitalismus* (Berlin, 1961):—

1900=100				1929=100			
1920—9	38	1870—9	80	1924	63	1929	100
1830—9	41	1880—9	88	1925	80	1930	99
1840—9	46	1890—9	97	1926	81	1931	98
1850—9	48	1900—9	106	1927	88	1932	87
1860—9	57	1910—4	121	1928	95		

[2] In rural municipalities only.
[3] This break occurs on a change of source (see note 1 above).
[4] 1770.
[5] 1915.
[6] "Markegang" series.
[7] In Moravia only.
[8] From 1923 to 1928 the statistics relate only to workers aged 17—21 years.
[9] 1913.
[10] Including forestry workers.
[11] These figures are for July 1918—May 1919, May 1919—April 1920, April—August 1920, and August 1920—August 1921.
[12] Slight changes were made in the scope of the series.
[13] Monthly wages from 1951 (2nd line).
[14] From 1946 to 1950 the statistics relate to monthly wages, and from 1951 onwards to hourly wages.

[15] The Introduction of a new currency, one-hundredth the face-value of the old, has been ignored.
[16] Monthly wages.
[17] Daily wages.
[18] Subsequent statistics relate to all grades of farmworker.
[19] Subsequent statistics relate only to 18–64 year olds.
[20] Subsequent statistics relate only to males.
[21] From 1947 (2nd line) the statistics relate to average weekly earnings of regular adult male workers in Great Britain.
[22] March and September only.
[23] Statistics from 1955 relate to hourly rates of all farm workers.
[24] Subsequently monthly wages of adult male permanent workers.

D. AGRICULTURE

As with so many other official statistics, the first half of the nineteenth century saw the beginnings of those relating to agriculture in most of the countries of western Europe, and the second half saw their extension to eastern Europe. In some ways, perhaps, it is surprising that Britain, which was the first country to face difficulties in feeding itself without substantial imports, during the Napoleonic Wars, was not the first to collect agricultural statistics. However, the administrative machinery was lacking there until around the middle of the nineteenth century, and by that time there was a good deal of opposition to the principle of government inquisition; and this was not overcome until the late 1860s, or even, so far as output statistics were concerned, until the 1880s. Meanwhile, official agricultural statistics had begun in almost every other country in Europe, where suspicion of governments was less, or, at any rate, amenability to their enquiries was greater.

There is no reason to believe that, at most times, official agricultural statistics are in any way unreliable. Even in the U.S.S.R. in the 1930s, when there was a deliberate attempt to hide the facts, it was not apparently done by outright falsification so much as by using the disguise of the so-called "biological" yield. In the early days of collection in any country, as with most statistics, there were probably differences in interpretation amongst officials, though these are most likely to arise over grass crops, which are not shown here. Then, there is a fair amount of evidence that in a country like Britain, crop estimates tend to understate year-to-year fluctuations by being somewhat too high in bad harvests and too low in good ones. In countries which are subject to more extreme climatic variations – such as Romania – it seems likely that an opposite tendency prevails; or at any rate, there is a tendency to exaggerate the impact of climatic disasters on total yields. However, neither of these sources of error appears to be of very great significance.

Finally, it is worth pointing out that numbers of livestock at a particular date do not alone give a full picture of the output of animal products. Whether the date of the count is in summer or in winter will make some difference to overall numbers, and in countries and at times when fodder crop production was insufficient to carry all the desired livestock through the winter this difference could be considerable. Then there is a point of more universal signififcane; the average age of flocks and herds has declined greatly since the nineteenth century, especially in western Europe, and, with this, the average annual output per animal has risen. Some indication of this is given by the tables on milk, butter, and meat production, though these series do not go back nearly so far as one would like.

In addition to official agricultural statistics, this section includes a table showing landings of fish in the major countries for which these are significant and available, and two selective tables of the volume of external trade in the products of the land. The first of these, D.10, relates to cereals, and covers those countries where either imports or exports have been of major significance for a substantial period of time. The second is a miscellaneous collection of commodity exports, selected because of their importance to the countries concerned. Since all these commodities are relatively bulky in relation to their total value, there does not seem to be any liklihood of illegal trade throwing any doubts on the accuracy of the statistics.

D1 AREA OF MAIN CEREAL, POTATO, AND SUGAR BEET CROPS (in thousands of hectares)

FRANCE 1815–1844

	Wheat	Rye	Barley	Oats	Maize[1]	Buckwheat	Potatoes	Sugar Beet
1815	4,592	2,574	1,073	2,498	542	655	...	...
1816	4,472	2,541	1,100	2,469	560	658	...	...
1817	4,672	2,585	1,176	2,480	556	715	559	...
1818	4,623	2,575	1,147	2,461	576	668	568	...
1819	4,650	...	...	...	...	...	570	...
1820	4,684	2,697	1,356	2,556	582	645	574	...
1821	4,753	2,792	1,239	2,566	566	652	564	...
1822	4,798	2,789	1,223	2,589	562	645	568	...
1823	4,855	2,790	1,238	2,586	563	647	576	...
1824	4,884	2,751	1,235	2,573	569	648	620	...
1825	4,854	2,727	1,230	2,602	565	626	...	...
1826	4,895	2,722	1,223	2,647	578	633	...	...
1827	4,903	2,735	1,221	2,653	567	640	...	...
1828	4,948	2,739	1,221	2,680	572	659	...	...
1829	5,024	2,765	1,220	2,698	567	679	607	...
1830	5.012	2.696	1,295	2,761	581	659	610	...
1831	5,111	2,701	1,292	2,762	559	685	635	...
1832	5,160	2,669	1,285	2,756	599	681	668	...
1833	5,243	2,663	1,264	2,804	603	687	742	...
1834	5,303	2,599	1,284	2,724	596	691	790	...
1835	5,338	2,639	1,300	2,840	593[1]	701	804	...
1836	5,285	...	...	...	...	...	974	...
1837	5,408	...	...	...	...	...	789	...
1838	5,461	...	...	...	...	...	861	...
1839	5,384	...	...	...	...	...	878	...
1840	5,532	2,725	1,188	2,899	632	651	922	58
1841	5,563	...	...	...	...	...	970	...
1842	5,576	...	...	...	...	...	967	...
1843	5,664	...	...	...	...	...	1,016	...
1844	5,679	...	...	...	...	...	983	...

Abbreviations used where space demands:— B'wheat: Buckwheat; M C: Mixed Corn; M C & B: Mixed Corn and Buckwheat; P's: Potatoes: S B: Sugar Beet

See p.250 for footnotes

D1 Area of Main Cereal, Potato, and Sugar Beet Crops (in thousands of hectares)

AUSTRIA 1845–1889

	Wheat	Rye[2]	Barley	Oats	Maize	Other Cereals	Potatoes	Sugar Beet
1845	...	...	...	...	...	...	...	...
1846	...	...	...	...	..	..	...	...
1847	...	...	...	...	...	...	...	...
1848	...	...	...	...	...	...	...	...
1849	...	...	...	...	...	...	...	...
1850	...	...	...	...	...	...	...	...
1851	...	...	...	...	...	...	...	...
1852	...	...	...	...	...	...	...	...
1853	...	...	...	...	...	...	...	...
1854	...	...	...	...	...	...	...	...
1855	...	...	...	...	...	...	...	...
1856	...	...	...	...	...	...	...	...
1857	...	...	...	...	...	...	...	...
1858	...	...	...	...	...	...	...	...
1859	...	...	...	...	...	....	...	...
1860	...	...	...	...	...	...	...	...
1861	...	...	...	...	...	...	...	...
1862	...	...	...	...	...	...	...	...
1863	...	...	...	...	...	...	...	...
1864	...	...	...	...	...	...	...	...
1865	...	...	...	...	...	...	...	...
1866	...	...	...	...	...	...	...	...
1867	...	...	...	...	...	...	...	...
1868	...	...	...	...	...	...	...	...
1869	...	...	...	...	...	...	...	...
1870	986	2,062	1,119	1,741	303	...	846	122
1871	931	1,986	1,072	1,874	287	...	868	148
1872								
1873								
1874	964	1,956	1,105	1,787	305	233	931	169
1875	973	1,947	1,090	1,761	313	220	951	161
1876	980	1,950	1,115	1,787	312	243	976	238
1877	940	1,943	1,078	1,819	331	277	972	174
1878	1,012	1,933	1,058	1,790	328	279	973	188
1879	982	1,927	1,037	1,798	322	310	983	192
1880	994	1,850	1,079	1,796	335	258	995	209
1881	994	1,881	1,045	1,781	330	257	992	212
1882	1,017	1,924	1,019	1,759	343	224	985	222
1883	1,057	1,904	1,029	1,793	362	344	1,044	227
1884	1,107	1,986	1,075	1,834	362	339	1,084	242
1885	1,194	2,001	1,166	1,829	368	322	1,098	149
1886	1,174	2,018	1,118	1,868	363	300	1,090	180
1887	1,164	2,018	1,133	1,875	361	298	1,116	154
1888	1,186	2,022	1,131	1,874	363	297	1,107	194
1889	1,094	1,980	1,138	1,877	382	313	1,100	225

See p.250 for footnotes

D1 Area of Main Cereal, Potato, and Sugar Beet Crops (in thousands of hectares)

BELGIUM 1845–1889

	Wheat	Rye	Barley	Oats	Mixed Corn[2]	Buckwheat	Potatoes	Sugar Beet
1845	...	...	...	...	...	...	...	...
1846	233	283	40	202	92	28	115	2
1847	...	...	...	...	...	...	...	...
1848	...	...	...	...	...	...	...	...
1849	...	...	...	...	...	...	...	...
1850	...	...	...	...	...	...	...	...
1851	...	...	...	...	...	...	...	...
1852	...	...	...	...	...	...	...	...
1853	...	...	...	...	...	...	...	...
1854	...	...	...	...	...	...	...	...
1855	...	...	...	...	...	...	...	...
1856	367	292	45	219	100	25	150	8
1857	...	...	...	...	...	...	...	...
1858	...	...	...	...	...	...	...	...
1859	...	...	...	...	...	...	...	...
1860	...	...	...	...	...	...	...	...
1861	...	...	...	...	...	...	...	...
1862	...	...	...	...	...	...	...	...
1863	...	...	...	...	...	...	...	...
1864	...	...	...	...	...	...	...	...
1865	...	...	...	...	...	...	...	...
1866	...	...	...	...	...	...	...	...
1867	...	...	...	...	...	...	...	...
1868	...	...	...	...	...	...	...	...
1869	...	...	...	...	...	...	...	...
1870	...	...	...	...	...	...	...	...
1871	...	...	...	...	...	...	...	...
1872	...	...	...	...	...	...	...	...
1873	...	...	...	...	...	...	...	...
1874	...	...	...	...	...	...	...	...
1875	...	...	...	...	...	...	...	...
1876	...	...	...	...	...	...	...	...
1877	...	...	...	...	...	...	...	...
1878	...	...	...	...	...	...	...	...
1879	...	...	...	...	...	...	...	...
1880	276	278	40	249	78	13	199	33
1881	...	...	...	...	...	...	...	...
1882	...	...	...	...	...	...	...	...
1883	...	...	...	...	...	...	...	...
1884	...	...	...	...	...	...	...	...
1885	...	...	...	...	...	...	...	...
1886	...	...	...	...	...	...	...	...
1887	...	...	...	...	...	...	...	...
1888	...	...	...	...	...	...	...	...
1889	...	...	...	...	...	...	...	...

See p.250 for footnotes

D1 **Area of Main Cereal, Potato, and Sugar Beet Crops** (in thousands of hectares)

DENMARK

1845–1889

	Wheat	Rye	Barley	Oats	Mixed Corn	Potatoes	Sugar Beet
1845	...	...	...	...	...	...	...
1846	...	...	...	...	...	...	...
1847	...	...	...	...	...	...	...
1848	...	...	...	...	...	...	...
1849	...	...	...	...	...	...	...
1850	...	...	...	...	...	...	...
1851	...	...	...	...	...	...	...
1852	...	...	...	...	...	...	...
1853	...	...	...	...	...	...	...
1854	...	...	...	...	...	...	...
1855	...	...	...	...	...	...	...
1856	...	...	...	...	...	...	...
1857	...	...	...	...	...	...	...
1858	...	...	...	...	...	...	...
1859	...	...	...	...	...	...	...
1860	...	...	...	...	...	...	...
1861	62[3]	209[3]	303[3]	358[3]	34	31	—
1862	...	...	...	...	...	...	...
1863	...	...	...	...	...	...	...
1864	...	...	...	...	...	...	...
1865	...	...	...	...	...	...	...
1866	53	229	302	365	46	37	—
1867	...	...	...	...	...	...	...
1868	...	...	...	...	...	...	...
1869	...	...	...	...	...	...	...
1870	...	...	...	...	...	...	...
1871	57	248	304	371	55	43	—
1872	...	...	...	...	...	...	...
1873	...	...	...	...	...	...	...
1874	...	...	...	...	...	...	...
1875	61	253	308	379	46	42	0.4
1876	62	254	308	381	49	42	0.3
1877	61	257	310	386	52	43	0.3
1878	60	259	312	390	55	43	0.5
1879	58	262	313	394	58	44	1.0
1880	57	265	315	398	62	44	1.3
1881	56	268	317	402	65	45	1.5
1882	55	270	314	405	69	46	2.5
1883	54	271	312	409	73	47	3.6
1884	53	273	309	412	77	48	6.4
1885	52	275	306	416	81	49	6.6
1886	51	277	303	419	85	50	7.7
1887	50	279	301	423	89	51	6.7
1888	49	281	298	426	93	52	6.9
1889	47	282	296	428	96	52	7.1

See p.250 for footnotes

D1 Area of Main Cereal, Potato, and Sugar Beet Crops (in thousands of hectares)

FRANCE **1845–1889**

	Wheat	Rye	Barley	Oats	Maize	Buckwheat	Potatoes	Sugar Beet
1845	5,743	...	...	...	...	...	1,014	...
1846	5,937	...	...	...	...	...	1,066	...
1847	5,979	...	...	...	...	...	991	...
1848	5,973	...	...	...	...	...	973	...
1849	5,966	...	...	...	...	...	932	...
1850	5,951	...	...	...	...	...	932	...
1851	5,999[4]	...	...	...	...	...	922	...
1852	6,985	2,451	1,041	3,263	602	709	829	111
1853	6,211	...	...	...	...	...	869	...
1854	6,408	...	...	...	...	...	894	...
1855	6,419	...	...	...	...	...	985	...
1856	6,468	...	...	...	...	...	897	...
1857	6,594	...	...	...	...	...	957	...
1858	6,640	...	...	...	...	...	983	...
1859	6,709	...	...	...	...	...	1,006	...
1860	6,711[5]	...[5]	...[5]	...[5]	...[5]	...[5]	1,010[5]	...[5]
1861	6,754	...	...	...	...	...	1,043	...
1862	7,473	1,928	1,087	3,324	586	669	1,234	136
1863	6,919	...	...	...	...	...	1,082	...
1864	6,880	...	...	...	...	...	1,099	...
1865	6,905	...	...	...	...	...	1,210	...
1866	6,916	...	...	...	...	...	1,110	...
1867	6,960	...	...	...	...	...	1,136	...
1868	7,063	...	...	...	...	...	1,129	...
1869	7,034	...	...	...	...	...	1,141	...
1870	6,924[6]	...[6]	...[6]	...[6]	...[6,1]	...[6]	...[6]	...[6]
1871	6,423	1,911	1,283	3,397	698	...	1,127	...
1872	6,938	1,888	1,068	3,145	698	...	1,151	...
1873	6,826	1,913	1,118	3,182	606	...	1,176	253
1874	6,874	1,844	1,083	3,246	650	...	1,169	...
1875	6,947	1,812	1,043	3,182	665	...	1,196	...
1876	6,859	1,820	1,038	3,257	661	...	1,251	...
1877	6,976	1,859	1,150	3,292	662	...	1,243	
1878	6,843	1,810	1,003	3,313	615	...	1,264	...
1879	6,941	1,773	1,010	3,331	613	...	1,266	...
1880	6,880	1,839	1,036	3,472	624[1]	...	1,274	...
1881	6,950	1,777	1,024	3,479	608	...	1,343	220
1882	6,908	1,744	976	3,611	548	645	1,345	237
1883	6,804	1,720	1,066	3,729	630	630	1,389	226
1884	7,052	1,726	1,056	3,697	617	633	1,415	234
1885	6,957	1,673	966	3,689	561	628	1,437	104
1886	6,956	1,634	947	3,736	549	608	1,463	218
1887	6,967	1,624	934	3,720	558	623	1,488	194
1888	6,978	1,629	894	3,734	571	608	1,446	201
1889	7,039	1,599	873	3,759	558	591	1,455	226

See p.250 for footnotes

D1 Area of Main Cereal, Potato, and Sugar Beet Crops (in thousands of hectares)

GERMANY **1845–1889**

	Wheat[2]	Rye	Barley	Oats	Mixed Corn & Buckwheat	Potatoes	Sugar Beet
1845	...	...	...	...	...	...	...
1846	...	...	...	...	...	...	...
1847	...	...	...	...	...	...	...
1848	...	...	...	...	...	...	...
1849	1,766	5,138	1,750	3,384	...	1,602	...
1850	...	...	...	...	...	...	...
1851	...	...	...	...	...	...	...
1852	...	...	...	...	...	...	...
1853	...	...	...	...	...	...	...
1854	...	...	...	...	...	...	...
1855	1,844	5,408	1,737	3,575	...	1,848	...
1856	...	...	...	...	...	...	...
1857	...	...	...	...	...	...	...
1858	...	...	...	...	...	...	...
1859	...	...	...	...	...	...	...
1860	1,902	5,637	1,723	3,734	...	2,056	...
1861	...	...	...	...	...	...	...
1862	...	...	...	...	...	...	...
1863	...	...	...	...	...	...	...
1864	...	...	...	...	...	...	...
1865	...	...	...	...	...	...	...
1866	...	...	...	...	...	...	...
1867	...	...	...	...	...	...	...
1868	...	...	...	...	...	...	...
1869	...	...	...	...	...	...	...
1870	1,964[7]	5,779[7]	1,636[7]	3,689[7]	...[7]	2,396[7]	...[7]
1871	2,170	5,833	1,683	3,777	...	2,517	...
1872	...	...	...	...	...	...	...
1873	...	...	...	...	...	...	...
1874	...	...	...	...	...	...	...
1875	...	...	...	...	...	...	...
1876	...	...	...	...	...	...	...
1877	...	...	...	...	...	...	...
1878	2,217	5,934	1,620	3,746	504	2,753	176
1879	2,306	5,929	1,625	3,746	506	2,758	174
1880	2,201	5,921	1,624	3,743	505	2,763	173
1881	2,195	5,913	1,633	3,745	525	2,768	233
1882	2,204	5,927	1,632	3,744	545	2,766	320
1883	2,294	5,812	1,751	3,763	566	2,906	337
1884	2,297	5,831	1,735	3,768	560	2,908	343
1885	2,294	5,842	1,742	3,767	555	2,921	349
1886	2,290	5,839	1,731	3,807	553	2,916	354
1887	2,291	5,842	1,731	3,810	547	2,918	360
1888	2,299	5,814	1,723	3,832	541	2,920	366
1889	2,322	5,802	1,685	3,887	531	2,918	372

See p.250 for footnotes

D1 Area of Main Cereal, Potato, and Sugar Beet Crops (in thousands of hectares)

1845–1889

	HUNGARY[8]							CROATIA-SLAVONIA						
	Wheat	Rye[9]	Barley	Oats	Maize	P's	SB	Wheat	Rye[9]	Barley	Oats	Maize	P's	SB
1845	...	...	...	...	...	...	...	...	...	...	...	...	...	...
1846	...	...	...	...	...	...	...	...	...	...	...	...	...	...
1847	...	...	...	...	...	...	...	...	...	...	...	...	...	...
1848	...	...	...	...	...	...	...	...	...	...	...	...	...	...
1849	...	...	...	...	...	...	...	...	...	...	...	...	...	...
1850	...	...	...	...	...	...	...	...	...	...	...	...	...	...
1851	...	...	...	...	...	...	...	...	...	...	...	...	...	...
1852	...	...	...	...	...	...	...	...	...	...	...	...	...	...
1853	...	...	...	...	...	...	...	...	...	...	...	...	...	...
1854	...	...	...	...	...	...	...	...	...	...	...	...	...	...
1855	...	...	...	...	...	...	...	...	...	...	...	...	...	...
1856	...	...	...	...	...	...	...	...	...	...	...	...	...	...
1857	...	...	...	...	...	...	...	...	...	...	...	...	...	...
1858	...	...	...	...	...	...	...	...	...	...	...	...	...	...
1859	...	...	...	...	...	...	...	...	...	...	...	...	...	...
1860	...	...	...	...	...	...	...	...	...	...	...	...	...	...
1861	...	...	...	...	...	...	...	...	...	...	...	...	...	...
1862	...	...	...	...	...	...	...	...	...	...	...	...	...	...
1863	...	...	...	...	...	...	...	...	...	...	...	...	...	...
1864	...	...	...	...	...	...	...	...	...	...	...	...	...	...
1865	...	...	...	...	...	...	...	...	...	...	...	...	...	...
1866	...	...	...	...	...	...	...	...	...	...	...	...	...	...
1867	...	...	...	...	...	...	...	...	...	...	...	...	...	...
1868	2,041	1,677	...	...	...	...	...	...	...	...	...	...	...	...
1869	2,158	1,609	788	890	1,404	334	15	...	...	...	...	...	...	...
1870	2,024	1,499	808	940	1,486	359	19	...	...	...	...	...	...	...
1871	1,884	1,510[9]	869	973	1,399	362	19	...	...	...	...	...	...	...
		1,535												
1872	2,020	1,500	882	1,032	1,478	362	19	...	...	...	...	...	...	...
1873	2,142	1,547	902	1,024	1,534	355	17	...	...	...	...	...	...	...
1874	2,246	1,455	947	1,048	1,603	360	21	...	...	...	...	...	...	...
1875	2,291	1,456	908	984	1,765	382	21	...	...	...	...	...	...	...
1876	2,603	1,641	1,078	1,240	2,038	501	26	...	...	...	...	...	...	...
1877	2,448	1,484	937	1,093	1,840	427	24	...	...	...	...	...	...	...
1878	2,503	1,559	1,006	1,155	1,894	466	25	...	...	...	...	...	...	...
1879	2,464	1,727	983	1,089	1,875	411	31							
1880	2,411	1,301	978	1,018	1,866	361	37	...	...	...	...	...	...	...
1881	2,534	1,293	911	956	1,796	371	31	...	...	...	...	...	...	...
1882	2,494	1,293	971	999	1,894	386	33	...	...	...	...	...	...	...
1883	2,605	1,292	972	993	1,824	394	36	...	...	...	...	...	...	...
1884	2,751	1,304	995	995	1,856	412	39	...	...	...	...	...	...	...
1885	2,741	1,316	1,046	1,038	1,875	420	32	162	169	70	112	308	36	1
1886	2,664	1,302	1,044	1,053	1,914	426	38	162	175	69	111	313	43	1
1887	2,777	1,307	1,003	1,046	1,828	413	34	168	171	68	111	313	49	1
1888	2,770	1,282	981	1,045	1,865	439	41	175	168	67	107	320	53	1
1889	2,911	1,253	1,007	1,018	1,938	439	55	180	170	64	98	323	55	1

See p.250 for footnotes

D1 **Area of Main Cereal, Potato, and Sugar Beet Crops** (in thousands of hectares) **1845–1889**

IRELAND

	Wheat	Barley	Oats	Potatoes
1845	...	...	...	...
1846	...	...	...	...
1847	301	135	891	115
1848	...	...	...	...
1849	278	142	834	291
1850	245	130	867	354
1851	204	136	886	352
1852	143	117	924	355
1853	132	122	873	364
1854	166	102	828	401
1855	180	96	858	397
1856	214	76	824	447
1857	227	88	802	464
1858	221	79	802	469
1859	188	74	802	486
1860	189	74	796	474
1861	162	82	809	459
1862	144	79	800	412
1863	105	71	791	414
1864	112	71	735	421
1865	108	73	706	431
1866	121	62	688	425
1867	106	70	672	405
1868	115	76	689	419
1869	113	91	682	422
1870	105	99	668	422
1871	99	90	662	428
1872	91	89	658	401
1873	68	93	611	365
1874	76	86	599	361
1875	64	95	608	365
1876	49	89	602	357
1877	56	92	597	353
1878	62	99	572	343
1879	64	103	538	341
1880	60	89	559	332
1881	62	85	564	346
1882	62	76	565	339
1883	38	74	559	326
1884	28	68	546	323
1885	29	73	538	323
1886	28	74	535	324
1887	27	66	532	323
1888	40	69	518	326
1889	36	75	501	318

ITALY

	Wheat	Rye	Barley	Oats	Maize	Rice	Potatoes	Sugar Beet
1845	...	...	...	...	...	...	...	...
1846	...	...	...	...	...	...	...	...
1847	...	...	...	...	...	...	...	...
1848	...	...	...	...	...	...	...	...
1849	...	...	...	...	...	...	...	...
1850	...	...	...	...	...	...	...	...
1851	...	...	...	...	...	...	...	...
1852	...	...	...	...	...	...	...	...
1853	...	...	...	...	...	...	...	...
1854	...	...	...	...	...	...	...	...
1855	...	...	...	...	...	...	...	...
1856	...	...	...	...	...	...	...	...
1857	...	...	...	...	...	...	...	...
1858	...	...	...	...	...	...	...	...
1859	...	...	...	...	...	...	...	...
1860	...	...	...	...	...	...	...	...
1861	...	...	...	...	...	...	...	...
1862	...	...	...	...	...	...	...	...
1863	...	...	...	...	...	...	...	...
1864	...	...	...	...	...	...	...	...
1865	...	...	...	...	...	...	...	...
1866	...	...	...	...	...	...	...	...
1867	...	...	...	...	...	...	...	...
1868	...	...	...	...	...	...	...	...
1869	...	...	...	...	...	...	...	...
1870	...	...	...	...	...	...	...	...
1871	...	...	...	...	...	...	...	...
1872	4,737	478		380	1,717	232	70	...
1873	...	...	...	...	...	...	...	...
1874	...	...	...	...	...	...	...	...
1875	...	...	...	...	...	...	...	...
1876	...	...	...	...	...	...	...	...
1877	...	...	...	...	...	...	...	...
1878	...	...	...	...	...	...	...	...
1879	...	...	...	...	...	...	...	...
1880	...	...	...	...	...	...	...	...
1881	4,434	161	338	437	1,893	202	151	...
1882	...	...	...	...	...	...	...	...
1883	...	...	...	...	...	...	...	...
1884	...	...	...	...	...	...	...	...
1885	...	...	...	...	...	...	...	...
1886	...	...	...	...	...	...	...	...
1887	...	...	...	...	...	...	...	...
1888	...	...	...	...	...	...	...	...
1889	...	...	...	...	...	...	...	...

D1 Area of Main Cereal, Potato, and Sugar Beet Crops (in thousands of hectares)

1845–1889

	NETHERLANDS							NORWAY[10]					
	Wheat	Rye	Barley	Oats	B'wheat	P's	Sugar Beet	Wheat	Rye	Barley	Oats	Mixed Corn	P's
1845	...	...	...	...	...	...	...	...	...	...	...	...	...
1846	...	...	...	...	...	...	...	...	...	...	...	...	...
1847	...	...	...	...	...	...	...	...	...	...	...	...	...
1848	...	...	...	...	...	...	...	...	...	...	...	...	...
1849	...	...	...	...	...	...	...	...	...	...	...	...	...
1850	...	...	...	...	...	...	...	...	...	...	...	...	...
1851	...	...	...	...	...	...	...	...	...	...	...	...	...
1852	80	182	41	82	63	90	...	...	...	...	...	...	...
1853	71	182	43	86	64	87	...	...	...	...	...	...	...
1854	79	184	42	82	63	90	...	...	...	...	...	...	...
1855	73	183	44	91	64	96	...	...	...	...	...	...	...
1856	81	192	43	89	64	99	...	...	...	...	...	...	...
1857	83	190	43	81	65	100	...	...	...	...	...	...	...
1858	82	193	47	84	62	104	...	...	...	...	...	...	...
1859	85	196	43	84	67	101	...	...	...	...	...	...	...
1860	83	194	44	89	64	105	...	...	...	...	...	...	...
1861	83	189	41	97	68	107	...	...	...	...	...	...	...
1862	84	193	41	92	65	107	...	...	...	...	...	...	...
1863	88	195	42	93	64	110	...	...	...	...	...	...	...
1864	79	193	42	107	66	108	...	...	...	...	...	...	...
1865	82	193	41	97	67	106	...	5.0	12	51	93	20	32
1866	84	203	42	95	68	109	...	...	...	...	...	...	...
1867	79	200	47	105	68	111	...	...	...	...	...	...	...
1868	86	203	43	103	68	117	...	...	...	...	...	...	...
1869	90	206	47	105	68	119	...	...	...	...	...	...	...
1870	84	203	47	105	68	123	9	...	...	...	...	...	...
1871	57	164	58	140	74	127	11	...	...	...	...	...	...
1872	86	200	45	100	67	126	13	...	...	...	...	...	...
1873	87	197	55	104	66	134	15	...	...	...	...	...	...
1874	91	200	44	103	66	131	11	...	...	...	...	...	...
1875	95	202	49	112	66	132	15	4.6	15	57	93	21	36
1876	86	199	47	116	67	132	13	...	...	...	...	...	...
1877	90	200	46	118	65	137	14	...	...	...	...	...	...
1878	94	204	46	111	63	139	15	...	...	...	...	...	...
1879	93	201	48	114	55	142	16	...	...	...	...	...	...
1880	93	197	47	118	59	141	18	...	...	...	...	...	...
1881	89	196	47	119	56	141	16	...	...	...	...	...	...
1882	83	202	46	116	55	141	18	...	...	...	...	...	...
1883	87	199	49	119	54	142	20	...	...	...	...	...	...
1884	89	202	47	113	53	145	21	...	...	...	...	...	...
1885	85	204	50	115	52	142	16	...	...	...	...	...	...
1886	81	204	45	122	51	143	18	...	...	...	...	...	...
1887	85	204	45	115	48	147	19	...	...	...	...	...	...
1888	85	202	45	114	47	149	22	...	...	...	...	...	...
1889	85	203	44	115	46	148	24	...	...	...	...	...	...

See p.250 for footnotes

D1 Area of Main Cereal, Potato, and Sugar Beet Crops (in thousands of hectares)

1845–1889

ROMANIA (in thousands of hectares)

	Wheat	Rye	Barley	Oats	Maize
1845	...	...	...	...	...
1846	...	...	...	...	...
1847	...	...	...	...	...
1848	...	...	...	...	...
1849	...	...	...	...	...
1850	...	...	...	...	...
1851	...	...	...	...	...
1852	...	...	...	...	...
1853	...	...	...	...	...
1854	...	...	...	...	...
1855	...	...	...	...	...
1856	...	...	...	...	...
1857	...	...	...	...	...
1858	...	...	...	...	...
1859	...	...	...	...	...
1860	698	...	...	62	...
1861	...	...	...	...	...
1862	...	...	...	...	...
1863	...	...	...	...	...
1864	...	...	...	...	...
1865	420	44	226	61	892
1866	...	...	...	...	...
1867	874	122	283	66	1,053
1868	894	119	251	59	1,075
1869	897	125	259	61	1,099
1870	865	128	233	59	1,088
1871	855	122	262	72	1,113
1872	731	120	298	92	1,083
1873	992	104	354	99	1,278
1874	1,170	108	458	112	1,366
1875	1,345	132	462	118	1,425
1876	1,065	148	513	110	1,385
1877	...	...	...	...	...
1878	...	...	...	...	...
1879	...	...	...	...	...
1880	...	...	...	...	...
1881	...	...	...	...	...
1882	...	...	...	...	...
1883	...	...	...	...	...
1884	...	...	...	...	...
1885	...	...	...	...	...
1886	1,175	231	555	227	1,714
1887	1,130	237	609	236	1,846
1888	1,256	301	507	214	1,734
1889	1,340	172	512	196	1,795

RUSSIA (in million hectares)[11]

	Wheat	Rye	Barley	Oats	Maize	Potatoes	Sugar Beet
1845	...	...	...	...	...	...	...
1846	...	...	...	...	...	...	...
1847	...	...	...	...	...	...	...
1848	...	...	...	...	...	...	...
1849	...	...	...	...	...	...	...
1850	...	...	...	...	...	...	...
1851	...	...	...	...	...	...	...
1852	...	...	...	...	...	...	...
1853	...	...	...	...	...	...	...
1854	...	...	...	...	...	...	...
1855	...	...	...	...	...	...	...
1856	...	...	...	...	...	...	...
1857	...	...	...	...	...	...	...
1858	...	...	...	...	...	...	...
1859	...	...	...	...	...	...	...
1860	...	...	...	...	...	...	...
1861	...	...	...	...	...	...	...
1862	...	...	...	...	...	...	...
1863	...	...	...	...	...	...	...
1864	...	...	...	...	...	...	...
1865	...	...	...	...	...	...	...
1866	...	...	...	...	...	...	...
1867	...	...	...	...	...	...	...
1868	...	...	...	...	...	...	...
1869	...	...	...	...	...	...	...
1870	...	...	...	...	...	...	...
1871	...	...	...	...	...	...	...
1872	11.6	26.9	6.3	13.3	...	1.2	...
1873	...	...	...	...	...	...	...
1874	...	...	...	...	...	...	...
1875	...	...	...	...	...	...	...
1876	...	...	...	...	...	...	...
1877	...	...	...	...	...	...	...
1878	...	...	...	...	...	...	...
1879	...	...	...	...	...	...	...
1880	...	...	...	...	...	...	...
1881	11.7	26.1	5.0	14.1	...	1.5	...
1882	...	...	...	...	...	...	...
1883	...	...	...	...	...	...	...
1884	...	...	...	...	...	...	...
1885	...	...	...	...	...	...	...
1886	...	...	...	...	...	...	...
1887	...	...	...	...	...	...	...
1888	...	...	...	...	...	...	...
1889	...	...	...	...	...	...	...

See p.250 for footnotes

D1 Area of Main Cereal, Potato, and Sugar Beet Crops (in thousands of hectares)

1845–1889

	SWEDEN							UK: GREAT BRITAIN				
	Wheat	Rye	Barley	Oats	Mixed Corn	Potatoes	Sugar Beet[12]	Wheat	Barley	Oats	Other Corn[13]	Potatoes
1845	...	...	...	...	...	...	...	...	...	...	...	...
1846	...	...	...	...	...	...	...	...	...	...	...	...
1847	...	...	...	...	...	...	...	...	...	...	...	...
1848	...	...	...	...	...	...	...	...	...	...	...	...
1849	...	...	...	...	...	...	...	...	...	...	...	...
1850	...	...	...	...	...	...	...	...	...	...	...	...
1851	...	...	...	...	...	...	...	...	...	...	...	...
1852	...	...	...	...	...	...	...	...	...	...	...	...
1853	...	...	...	...	...	...	...	...	...	...	...	...
1854	...	...	...	...	...	...	...	...	...	...	...	...
1855	...	...	...	...	...	...	...	...	...	...	...	...
1856	...	...	...	...	...	...	...	...	...	...	...	...
1857	...	...	...	...	...	...	...	...	...	...	...	...
1858	...	...	...	...	...	...	...	...	...	...	...	...
1859	...	...	...	...	...	...	...	...	...	...	...	...
1860	...	...	...	...	...	...	...	...	...	...	...	...
1861	...	...	...	...	...	...	...	...	...	...	...	...
1862	...	...	...	...	...	...	...	...	...	...	...	...
1863	...	...	...	...	...	...	...	...	...	...	...	...
1864	...	...	...	...	...	...	...	...	...	...	...	...
1865	48	363	214	428	71	128	7	...	...	...	...	...
1866	48	345	229	485	80	133	10	...	...	...	...	...
1867	48	338	228	504	77	130	8	1,363	914	1,113	367	199
1868	46	344	226	512	78	134	9	1,478	870	1,116	353	219
1869	48	352	226	509	76	137	9	1,492	911	1,126	419	237
1870	51	356	229	523	75	142	11	1,417	960	1,118	369	238
1871	57	356	229	528	76	143	12	1,446	966	1,099	405	254
1872	60	357	231	543	78	144	12	1,456	937	1,095	386	228
1873	63	355	231	557	77	148	11	1,412	945	1,083	387	208
1874	66	353	236	561	80	150	11	1,469	926	1,051	371	210
1875	67	353	239	582	79	151	12	1,352	1,016	1,078	378	212
1876	66	358	233	592	80	151	11	1,212	1,025	1,132	351	204
1877	68	359	232	610	82	154	11	1,282	979	1,115	352	207
1878	67	361	228	619	80	153	11	1,302	1,000	1,092	316	206
1879	68	371	232	630	83	154	12	1,170	1,079	1,075	312	219
1880	71	378	233	659	83	154	12	1,177	998	1,132	284	223
1881	70	380	235	666	84	155	12	1,136	988	1,174	283	234
1882	70	385	237	676	85	155	13	1,216	913	1,147	300	219
1883	71	384	233	683	85	155	13	1,057	928	1,204	299	220
1884	72	385	227	699	91	157	15	1,083	878	1,180	293	229
1885	73	375	220	734	98	153	17	1,003	913	1,190	290	222
1886	73	376	220	751	100	161	19	925	907	1,247	263	224
1887	73	377	224	775	101	156	20	938	844	1,250	265	227
1888	74	380	222	787	101	154	21	1,038	844	1,166	265	239
1889	76	382	220	797	103	155	23	991	859	1,169	249	234

See p.250 for footnotes

D1 Area of Main Cereal, Potato, and Sugar Beet Crops (in thousands of hectares)

1890–1944

	ALBANIA					AUSTRIA							
	Wheat	Rye	Barley	Oats	Maize	Wheat	Rye[2]	Barley	Oats	Maize	Other Cereals	Potatoes	Sugar Beet
1890	...	...	...	...	...	1,147	2,007	1,116	1,874	372	291	1,079	245
1891	...	...	...	...	...	1,112	1,946	1,140	1,894	374	290	1,088	252
1892	...	...	...	...	...	1,125	1,975	1,112	1,873	367	284	1,099	256
1893	...	...	...	...	...	1,120	1,948	1,124	1,842	359	266	1,108	269
1894	...	...	...	...	...	1,098	1,955	1,136	1,879	326	269	1,098	286
1895	...	...	...	...	...	1,064	1,815	1,194	1,950	348	284	1,129	207
1896	...	...	...	...	...	1,059	1,841	1,178	1,917	346	371	1,152	247
1897	...	...	...	...	...	1,058	1,844	1,173	1,912	336	240	1,160	211
1898	...	...	...	...	...	1,056	1,831	1,168	1,901	341	241	1,182	210
1899	...	...	...	...	...	1,072	1,846	1,189	1,867	334	248	1,156	243
1900	...	...	...	...	...	1,065	1,706	1,234	1,899	333	150	1,168	240
1901	...	...	...	...	...	1,070	1,815	1,211	1,871	332	151	1,135	253
1902	...	...	...	...	...	1,058	1,836	1,216	1,832	329	154	1,138	196
1903	...	...	...	...	...	1,052	1,811	1,205	1,833	334	246	1,144	207
1904	...	...	...	...	...	1,115	1,931	1,184	1,822	338	250	1,277	218
1905	...	...	...	...	...	1,126	1,973	1,188	1,808	348	258	1,290	260
1906	...	...	...	...	...	1,161	2,023	1,177	1,834	343	262	1,314	239
1907	...	...	...	...	...	1,179	1,856	1,167	1,936	348	277	1,259	233
1908	...	...	...	...	...	1,198	2,082	1,116	1,819	343	240	1,250	231
1909	...	...	...	...	...	1,191	2,078	1,131	1,851	336	249	1,233	212
1910	...	...	...	...	...	1,214	2,066	1,102	1,833	311	240	1,242	254
1911	...	...	...	...	...	1,215	2,027	1,097	1,878	303	226	1,258	249
1912	...	...	...	...	...	1,260	2,038	1,066	1,867	304	227	1,251	264
1913	...	...	...	...	...	1,213	1,970	1,092	1,905	286	217	1,276	255
1914	...	...	...	...	...	672[14]	1,271[14]	700[14]	1,147[14]	190[14]	124[14]	718[14]	243[14]
1915	...	...	...	...	...	745[14]	1,494[14]	757[14]	1,334[14]	201[14]	114[14]	901[14]	178[14]
1916	...	...	...	...	...	813[14]	1,568[14]	798[14]	1,469[14]	146[14]	127[14]	996[14]	195[14]
1917	...	...	...	...	...	...	...	...	...	...	...	...	...
1918	...	...	...	...	...	...[15]	...[15]	...[15]	...[15]	...[15]	...[15]	...[15]	...[15]
1919	...	...	...	...	...	150	290	94	245	42	23	97	5
1920	...	...	...	...	...	150	288	96	254	41	22	117	7
1921	...	...	...	...	...	153	307	108	269	45	26	133	8
1922	...	...	...	...	...	154[16]	307[16]	106[16]	266[16]	45[16]	26[16]	145[16]	9[16]
						186	338	127	285	60	31	163	11
1923	...	...	...	...	...	192	373	135	325	58	34	151	13
1924	...	...	...	...	...	195	376	138	309	60	34	167	19
1925	...	...	...	...	...	196	384	141	308	60	33	176	20
1926	...	...	...	...	...	202	394	147	315	62	34	178	20
1927	...	...	...	...	...	204	383	148	311	60	30	183	24
1928	...	...	...	...	...	208	379	156	301	58	28	189	30
1929	30	2	5	11	61	208	374	158	297	56	32	190	30
1930	30	2	6	10	65	205	375	174	312	58	35	189	35
1931	29	2	5	10	62	209	378	168	315	62	33	194	43
1932	37	3	5	11	75	216	387	171	307	67	37	202	43
1933	43	3	6	11	77	220	388	171	306	64	40	204	46
1934	39	3	6	9	95	232	382	167	303	65	39	202	50
1935	39	2	4	9	85	243	382	163	298	63	39	202	44
1936	36	3	4	9	88	253	373	163	289	64	41	210	38
1937	40	4	6	12	92	250	358	167	287	70	8	216	40
1938	36	3	5	12	106	250	366	168	287	73	8	215	47
1939	48	4	6	15	104	256	329	161	248	63	10	194	43
1940	...	...	...	...	...	213	276	182	247	65	15	190	41
1941	...	...	...	...	...	226	283	149	221	64	13	187	34
1942	...	...	...	...	...	208	247	152	216	65	17	175	32
1943	...	...	...	...	...	210	249	130	211	53	12	169	32
1944	...	...	...	...	...	208	239	128	204	48	13	174	30

See p.250 for footnotes

D1 **Area of Main Cereal, Potato, and Sugar Beet Crops** (in thousands of hectares)

BELGIUM **1890–1944**

	Wheat	Rye	Barley	Oats	Mixed Corn	Buckwheat	Potatoes	Sugar Beet
1890	...	...	...	...	...	...	...	...
1891	...	...	...	...	...	...	...	...
1892	...	...	...	...	...	...	...	...
1893	...	...	...	...	...	...	...	...
1894	...	...	...	...	...	...	...	...
1895	180	283	40	249	52	5	185	54
1896	...	...	...	...	...	...	...	...
1897	...	...	...	...	...	...	...	...
1898	...	...	...	...	...	...	...	...
1899	...	...	...	...	...	...	...	...
1900	169	245	38	253	37	3	141	64
1901	166	251	38	249	37	3	144	62
1902	168	265	38	262	37	3	142	48
1903	144	254	32	286	33	3	146	54
1904	159	259	40	248	34	3	152	44
1905	163	267	38	237	33	2	146	64
1906	160	253	36	261	31	...	145	56
1907	159	260	37	248	30	...	143	53
1908	153	258	36	255	27	...	141	52
1909	158	258	35	250	26	...	140	58
1910	161	269	25	260	29	...	172	60
1911	161	262	34	259	28	...	157	59
1912	161	263	34	262	24	...	157	62
1913	159	259	34	272	26	...	160	52
1914	...	...	...	...	...	...	...	...
1915	...	...	...	...	...	...	...	...
1916	...	...	...	...	...	...	...	...
1917	...	...	...	...	...	...	...	...
1918	...	...	...	...	...	...	...	...
1919	138	212	32	227	23	...	157	43
1920	124	217	36	237	23	...	148	53
1921	139	226	39	244	22	...	169	58
1922	122	215	33	290	15	...	180	60
1923	140	232	34	265	21	...	152	72
1924	138	227	32	265	21	...	159	81
1925	148	231	32	265	21	...	160	72
1926	143	226	35	270	21	...	161	64
1927	158	232	32	266	20	...	168	71
1928	172	232	31	270	20	...	166	64
1929	144[17]	229[17]	25	301	19	...	171	58
1930	166	232	34	273	19	...	163	57
1931	154	222	33	295	17	...	172	52
1932	156	227	36	288	17	...	176	53
1933	151	224	37	299	18	...	163	52
1934	150	214	38	294	18	...	160	55
1935	172	150	34	209	12	...	163	51
1936	172	156	30	216	12	...	160	48
1937	172	152	35	211	13	...	158	48
1938	174	154	31	213	12	...	147	49
1939	124	135	19	259	9	...	148	54
1940	146[18]	115[18]	23[18]	172[18]	10[18]	...	77[18]	...[18]
1941	178	126	30	167	10	...	105	48
1942	193	137	51	142	13	...	121	59
1943	203	158	77	125	14	...	116	54
1944	198[18]	141[18]	74[18]	128[18]	14[18]	...	103[18]	58[18]

See p.250 for footnotes

D1 Area of Main Cereal, Potato, and Sugar Beet Crops (in thousands of hectares)

1890–1944

	BULGARIA							CZECHOSLOVAKIA						
	Wheat	Rye	Barley	Oats	Maize	P's	SB	Wheat	Rye	Barley	Oats	Maize	P's	SB
1890	...	...	...	...	...	...	...	...	...	...	...	...	...	...
1891	...	...	...	...	...	...	...	...	...	...	...	...	...	...
1892	...	...	...	...	...	...	...	...	...	...	...	...	...	...
1893	...	...	...	...	...	...	...	...	...	...	...	...	...	...
1894	...	...	...	...	...	...	...	...	...	...	...	...	...	...
1895	...	...	...	...	...	...	...	...	...	...	...	...	...	...
1896	...	...	...	...	...	...	...	...	...	...	...	...	...	...
1897	...	...	...	...	...	...	...	...	...	...	...	...	...	...
1898	782	...	...	140	...	2	...	...	...	...	...	...	...	...
1899	826	148	214	137	447	2	1	...	...	...	...	...	...	...
1900	820	152	208	126	447	2	...	...	...	...	...	...	...	...
1901	815	...	...	...	...	...	...	...	...	...	...	...	...	...
1902	810	...	...	...	...	...	...	...	...	...	...	...	...	...
1903	807	169	229	162	488	2		...	...	...	...	...	...	...
1904	915	175	233	185	486	2	...	...	...	...	...	...	...	...
1905	980	176	233	174	473	2	...	...	...	...	...	...	...	...
1906	1,010	187	232	190	508	2	...	...	...	...	...	...	...	...
1907	977	182	232	190	498	2	...	...	...	...	...	...	...	...
1908	980	174	251	228	571	3	...	...	...	...	...	...	...	...
1909	1,040	202	241	197	607	3	2	...	...	...	...	...	...	...
1910	1,089	227	260	198	612	3	2	...	...	...	...	...	...	...
1911	1,118	221	251	181	632	3	3	...	...	...	...	...	...	...
1912	1,168	214	251	176	643	3	3	...	...	...	...	...	...	...
1913	999	194	211	153	579	3	5	...	...	...	...	...	...	...
1914	1,022	207	238	168	625	4	15	...	...	...	...	...	...	...
1915	973	219	249	163	657	5	8	...	...	...	...	...	...	...
1916	964	207	242	152	589	5	14	...	...	...	...	...	...	...
1917	1,004	184	244	141	565	7	15	...	...	...	...	...	...	...
1918	985	191	243	139	591	8	19	...	...	...	...	...	...	...
1919	832	184	196	115	585	6	9	...	...	...	...	...	...	...
1920	883	188	224	140	569	8	9	637	906	695	802	152	607	210
1921	904	189	212	134	575	8	12	630	884	654	796	158	638	221
1922	931	184	222	148	567	9	10	619	881	676	818	160	650	210
1923	932	172	220	150	552	10	12	610	860	687	842	161	637	232
1924	1,008	167	214	152	609	9	26	607	839	679	846	157	635	303
1925	1,030	184	222	144	640	10	- -	618	847	694	838	157	640	307
1926	1,059	187	233	130	613	10	15	628	837	714	847	159	649	278
1927	1,082	188	227	132	681	12	21	642[19]	821[19]	712[19]	855[19]	159[19]	651[19]	294[19]
								751	996	708	840	140	717	288
1928	1,138	197	245	121	648	11	16	757	1,007	720	839	144	728	257
1929	1,077	217	219	157	800	11	19	819	1,089	744	870	135	761	246
1930	1,216	266	280	140	684	12	23	762	1,026	674	800	101	625	224
1931	1,236	243	245	119	680	13	12	797	983	717	797	94	679	186
1932	1,263	220	231	117	744	14	13	812	1,020	709	788	88	690	146
1933	1,253	209	244	132	727	14	12	885	1,023	661	773	87	700	145
1934	1,260	200	229	128	685	14	2	909	976	659	766	97	707	159
1935	1,104[19]	175[19]	203[19]	109[19]	718[19]	15[19]	7[19]	929	990	644	748	96	706	157
1936	1,196	198	217	121	669	16	5	893	987	633	739	104	705	154
1937	1,309	211	218	150	682	22	10	821	951	669	748	114	728	181
1938	1,395	188	225	144	700	20	12	897	1,016	659	763	180	763	136
1939	1,354	172	220	112	685	16	13	850	984	656	706	116	749	169
1940	1,319[20]	169[20]	189[20]	120[20]	674[20]	18[20]	17[20]	746	708	754	799	121	728	200
1941	1,362	182	231	174	806	25	20	800	784	647	655	117	680	205
1942	1,266	165	218	186	867	35	23	871	861	659	636	120	707	190
1943	1,348	169	212	167	789	39	29	910	926	599	602	126	722	196
1944	1,354	171	195	146	753	37	24	912	915	549	572	118	727	203

See p.250 for footnotes

D1 **Area of Main Cereal, Potato, and Sugar Beet Crops** (in thousands of hectares)

1890–1944

	DENMARK							FINLAND						
	Wheat	Rye	Barley	Oats	Mixed Corn	P's	SB	Wheat	Rye	Barley	Oats	Mixed Corn	P's	SB
1890	45	283	293	429	100	52	7.3	...	...	...	...	...	...	...
1891	43	285	291	431	103	52	7.0	...	...	...	...	...	...	...
1892	41	286	289	433	103	52	6.8	...	...	...	...	...	...	...
1893	40	287	287	434	106	52	8.5	...	...	...	...	...	...	...
1894	38	288	284	436	110	52	12	...	...	...	...	...	...	...
1895	36	289	282	438	113	52	11	...	...	...	...	...	...	...
1896	34	291	280	439	120	52	13	...	...	...	...	...	...	...
1897	...	...	...	...	...	...	...	...	...	...	...	...	...	...
1898	...	...	...	...	...	...	...	...	...	...	...	...	...	...
1899	...	...	...	...	...	...	...	...	...	...	...	...	...	...
1900	...	...	...	...	...	...	...	...	...	...	...	...	...	...
1901	13	273	281	433	143	54	15	...	...	...	...	...	...	...
1902	...	...	...	...	...	...	...	...	...	...	...	...	...	...
1903	...	...	...	...	...	...	...	...	...	...	...	...	...	...
1904	...	...	...	...	...	...	...	...	...	...	...	...	...	...
1905	...	...	...	...	...	...	...	...	...	...	...	...	...	...
1906	...	...	...	...	...	...	...	...	...	...	...	...	...	...
1907	41	276	234	403	170	54	16	...	...	...	...	...	...	...
1908	...	...	...	...	...	...	...	...	...	...	...	...	...	...
1909	...	...	...	...	...	...	...	3.2	239	113	376	...	70	–
1910	...	...	...	...	...	...	...	3.2	240	110	399	6.7	73	–
1911	...	...	...	...	...	...	...	3.4	240	113	408	...	74	–
1912	54	246	241	428	180	61	32	3.4	239	113	414	...	74	–
1913	...	...	...	...	...	...	...	3.5	235	112	423	...	75	–
1914	...	...	...	...	...	...	...	4.0	235	110	431	...	77	–
1915	67	211	260	414	180	67	32	5.0	240	111	443	...	80	–
1916	61	195	256	422	185	64	31	6.6	236	113	446	...	81	–
1917	53	177	240	397	195	58	31	7.2	236	116	436	...	82	–
1918	57	220	223	379	194	75	36	7.5	238	115	438	...	81	–
1919	52[21]	236[21]	237[21]	403[21]	202[21]	96[21]	42[21]	7.8	244	118	433	...	83	1
1920	73	227	253	441	201	92	39	8.7	233	116	395	8.5	71	1
1921	89	226	254	450	194	84	35	11	236	110	422	9.2	68	1
1922	96	221	270	453	188	83	24	15	237	112	427	11	67	1
1923	83	233	279	454	207	83	32	15	234	111	431	10	68	1
1924	60	188	302	462	232	72	39	15	238	110	425	10	67	1
1925	80	215	301	445	227	75	38	15	234	110	434	10	68	1
1926	102	208	312	424	237	77	30	16	229	110	441	10	69	2
1927	111	183	333	410	256	72	42	18	229	108	450	11	70	3
1928	102	146	355	404	297	63	46	19	222	110	461	12	70	3
1929	104	152	368	392	305	64	32[23]	14	204	115	434	7.8	70	1
	[22]	[22]	[22]	[22]	[22]	[22]	30[22]							
1930	101	149	376	388	304	68	33	14	208	115	439	10	71	1
1931	105	134	360	379	316	63	30	18	214	118	453	14	75	2
1932	99	120	345	398	318	70	38	24	218	125	455	14	77	2
1933	106	143	350	382	319	77	47	37	233	130	457	14	80	3
1934	114	153	340	382	338	77	48[24]	51	246	132	475	15	83	3
							42							
1935	127	158	345	368	334	75	42	71	242	127	471	16	83	3
1936	120	132	369	378	325	76	38	84	233	130	450	16	87	3
1937	129	139	369	376	309	81	40	113	241	121	455	8.7	87	3
1938	132[22]	145[22]	397[22]	375[22]	302[22]	79[22]	38[22]	131	236	121	463	9.6	85	5
1939	134	137	421	376	304	70	40	136	218	119	472	12	90	6
1940	82	139	390	347	325	65	44	141	186	114	427	9.8	81	3
1941	84	195	383	348	326	74	48	126	179	118	401	6.3	73	3
1942	6	191	421	343	381	101	47	127	159	108	377	4.8	67	2
1943	49	224	398	336	334	105	46	131	177	120	354	5.6	74	3
1944	84	196	396	330	316	98	42	127	162	136	314	6.1	69	4

See p.250 for footnotes

D1 Area of Main Cereal, Potato, and Sugar Beet Crops (in thousands of hectares)

FRANCE

1890–1944

	Wheat	Rye	Barley	Oats	Maize	Buckwheat	Potatoes	Sugar Beet
1890	7,062	1,589	878	3,781	547	606	1,465	239
1891	5,754	1,499	1,223	4,243	558	624	1,493	260
1892	6,987	1,542	916	3,813	559	604	1,512	254
1893	7,073	1,530	875	3,842	567	584	1,529	259
1894	6,991	1,556	890	3,881	578	581	1,541	268
1895	7,002	1,534	891	3,969	585	577	1,542	237
1896	6,870	1,500	854	3,916	584	562	1,543	270
1897	6,584	1,452	858	3,991	585	552	1,548	270
1898	6,964	1,475	814	3,888	562	570	1,543	262
1899	6,940	1,489	806	3,939	561	586	1,565	279
1900	6,864	1,420	757	3,941	541	603	1,510	330
1901	6,794	1,412	744	3,886	547	601	1,546	339
1902	6,564	1,332	694	3,832	503	561	1,458	288
1903	6,479	1,297	697	3,844	502	553	1,436	283
1904	6,529	1,272	705	3,835	496	523	1,479	247
1905	6,510	1,269	707	3,812	502	523	1,487	317
1906	6,517	1,253	709	3,855	467	509	1,513	270
1907	6,577	1,240	713	3,871	500	503	1,522	276
1908	6,564	1,244	730	3,897	496	505	1,545	272
1909	6,596	1,227	734	3,927	495	500	1,547	286
1910	6,554	1,212	748	3,951	482	500	1,547	297
1911	6,433	1,174	772	3,991	425	461	1,559	297
1912	6,572	1,202	760	3,982	476	461	1,564	312
1913	6,542[25]	1,176[25]	760[25]	3,979[25]	458[25]	451[25]	1,548[25]	301[25]
1914	6,060	1,058	720	3,591	456	452	1,488	193
1915	5,489	935	637	3,263	378	433	1,345	104
1916	5,030	870	622	3,147	357	401	1,280	108
1917	4,191	742	687	2,958	343	378	1,370	100
1918	4,449[6] [25]	706[6] [25]	555[6] [25]	2,720[6] [25]	305[6] [25]	311[25]	1,190[25]	85[25]
1919	4,708	813	608	2,953	301	329[6]	1,256[6]	96[6]
1920	5,094	869	664	3,350	336	352	1,441	122
1921	5,382	901	680	3,408	330	342	1,455	141
1922	5,290	888	693	3,436	320	356	1,464	153
1923	5,533	897	681	3,423	342	344	1,451	189
1924	5,512	889	714	3,495	342	363	1,463	229
1925	5,614	869	699	3,480	346	355	1,465	240
1926	5,249	793	691	3,512	337	349	1,461	254
1927	5,287	777	707	3,458	349	365	1,497	266
1928	5,243	769	711	3,503	344	342	1,473	282
1929	5,397	743	787	3,444	340	304	1,401	321
1930	5,374	747	745	3,424	337	321	1,429	324
1931	5,196	712	755	3,465	346	327	1,430	288
1932	5,434	701	720	3,387	340	329	1,413	309
1933	5,464	690	703	3,365	337	312	1,391	318
1934	5,404	685	732	3,322	340	308	1,410	337
1935	5,363	675	723	3,278	345	290	1,412	303
1936	5,206	661	743	3,291	342	286	1,422	311
1937	5,095	663	753	3,253	345	268	1,436	318
1938	5,050[26]	631[26]	759[26]	3,245[26]	340[26]	261[26]	1,425[26]	319[26]
1939	4,584	603	817	3,202	322	262	1,279	348
1940	4,252	515	695	2,681	278	221	1,061	242
1941	4,364	403	664	2,350	237	194	829	239
1942	4,280[26]	389[26]	638[26]	2,315[26]	232[26]	189[26]	777[26]	268[26]
1943	4,227	403	647	2,258	223	169	796	254
1944	4,163[26]	396[26]	622[26]	2,400[26]	217[26]	163[26]	797[26]	246[26]

See p.250 for footnotes

D1 Area of Main Cereal, Potato, and Sugar Beet Crops (in thousands of hectares)

1890–1944

GERMANY

	Wheat[2]	Rye	Barley	Oats	M C & B	P's	SB
1890	2,327	5,820	1,664	3,904	522	2,906	378
1891	2,213	5,480	1,807	4,155	514	2,923	383
1892	2,335	5,679	1,690	3,988	502	2,930	389
1893	2,391	6,012	1,594	3,907	491	3,037	395
1894	2,324	6,045	1,601	3,917	489	3,025	439
1895	2,270	5,894	1,663	4,029	494	3,050	407
1896	2,249	5,982	1,653	3,980	490	3,053	435
1897	2,247	5,967	1,644	3,999	486	3,068	443
1898	2,296	5,945	1,635	3,997	480	3,081	437
1899	2,340	5,871	1,641	4,000	473	3,131	461
1900	2,366	5,955	1,670	4,123	467	3,219	461
1901	1,896	5,812	1,859	4,411	463	3,319	468
1902	2,224	6,155	1,644	4,156	459	3,241	474
1903	2,107	6,013	1,700	4,290	455	3,238	481
1904	2,231	6,099	1,627	4,190	451	3,288	488
1905	2,260	6,146	1,633	4,182	447	3,317	494
1906	2,257	6,102	1,645	4,222	443	3,302	501
1907	2,053	6,043	1,702	4,377	438	3,297	508
1908	2,190	6,120	1,629	4,275	434	3,293	575
1909	2,130	6,131	1,646	4,310	430	3,324	521
1910	2,238	6,187	1,570	4,289	426	3,296	528
1911	2,256	6,136	1,585	4,328	422	3,321	535
1912	2,209	6,268	1,590	4,387	418	3,342	541
1913	2,246	6,414	1,654	4,438	414	3,412	548
1914	2,265	6,299	1,582	4,388	...	3,386	569
1915	2,262	6,411	1,620	4,615	...	3,572	400
1916	1,854	5,999	1,524	3,615	...	2,798	412
1917	1,679[7]	5,550[7]	1,461[7]	3,565[7]	...[7]	2,547[7]	402[7]
1918	1,589	5,747	1,365	3,266	490	2,728	402
1919	1,431	4,403	1,126	2,993	456	2,181	...
1920	1,540	4,325	1,198	3,244	388	2,450	...
1921	1,592	4,265	1,136	3,162	372	2,647	380
1922	1,501	4,142	1,152	3,202	366	2,721	409
1923	1,606	4,366	1,301	3,345	357	2,727	384
1924	1,588	4,259	1,446	3,525	373	2,760	394
1925	1,677	4,708	1,435	3,452	343	2,809	403
1926	1,726	4,732	1,486	3,476	348	2,760	403
1927	1,859	4,721	1,488	3,486	405	2,814	434
1928	1,856	4,634	1,519	3,519	375	2,849	454
1929	1,722	4,727	1,552	3,490	383	2,867	455
1930	1,900	4,711	1,519	3,322	371	2,748	483
1931	2,281	4,366	1,619	3,183	374	2,744	381
1932	2,395	4,450	1,568	3,045	378	2,763	271
1933	2,431	4,524	1,585	2,882	383	2,744	304
1934	2,302[7]	4,491[7]	1,631[7]	2,785[7]	403[7]	2,733[7]	356[7]
1935	2,187	4,555	1,606	2,798	522	2,770	373
1936	2,153	4,514	1,635	2,778	518	2,793	389
1937	2,040	4,156	1,714	2,845	595	2,888	455
1938	2,094	4,263	1,673	2,697	591	2,893	502
1939	2,105	4,223	1,668	2,820	...	2,834	503
1940	1,897	4,975	1,686	2,843	...	2,813	537
1941	1,941	4,096	1,564	2,644	...	2,745	544
1942	1,715	3,381	1,501	2,809	...	2,777	547
1943	1,796	3,977	1,203	2,535	...	2,665	544
1944	1,781	3,851	1,179	2,438	...	2,704	543

GREECE[27]

	Wheat	Rye	Barley	Oats	Maize	M C	P's
1890	...	...	...	...	...	...	...
1891	...	...	...	...	...	...	...
1892	...	...	...	...	...	...	...
1893	...	...	...	...	...	...	...
1894	...	...	...	...	...	...	...
1895	...	...	...	...	...	...	...
1896	...	...	...	...	...	...	...
1897	...	...	...	...	...	...	...
1898	...	...	...	...	...	...	...
1899	...	...	...	...	...	...	...
1900	...	...	...	...	...	...	...
1901	...	...	...	...	...	...	...
1902	...	...	...	...	...	...	...
1903	...	...	...	...	...	...	...
1904	...	...	...	...	...	...	...
1905	...	...	...	...	...	...	...
1906	...	...	...	...	...	...	...
1907	...	...	...	...	...	...	...
1908	...	...	...	...	...	...	...
1909	...	...	...	...	...	...	...
1910	...	...	...	...	...	...	...
1911	351	5.3	79	30	110	...	4.9
1912	...	...	...	...	...	...	...
1913	...[28]	...[28]	...[28]	...[28]	...[28]	...[28]	...[28]
1914	440[28]	32[28]	135[28]	62[28]	196[28]	...[28]	9.2[28]
1915	370	6.9	109	54	143	...	8.3
1916	362[28]	6.6[28]	120[28]	59[28]	155[28]	...	16[28]
1917	423	23	158	67	175	...	10
1918	442	28[28]	167[28]	73[28]	170[28]	...	13[28]
1919	432	33	166	86	183	60	13
1920	436	30	156	65	189	56	10
1921	384[28]	31[28]	137[28]	66[28]	189[28]	52[28]	11[28]
1922	430	36	149	69	166	44	13
1923	430	23	147	76	154	45	12
1924	467	36	166	104	201	42	14
1925	465	43	177	101	201	41	12
1926	528	47	205	111	233	54	14
1927	499	47	188	103	197	48	11
1928	538	55	202	112	183	48	11
1929	501	52	145	102	203	34	7.6
1930	565	64	216	136	221	44	12
1931	605	69	223	139	250	53	14
1932	606	68	226	134	265	56	15
1933	693	74	224	138	261	55	18
1934	792	74	213	136	239	55	18
1935	846	73	206	139	223	52	19
1936	835	64	206	138	258	55	20
1937	857	68	212	145	279	58	25
1938	860	72	195	137	277	60	22
1939	926	54	180	137	258	60	22
1940	...	...	...	...	...	...	...
1941	...	...	...	...	...	...	...
1942	...	...	...	...	...	...	...
1943	...	...	...	...	...	...	...
1944	...	...	...	...	...	...	...

See p.250 for footnotes

D1 Area of Main Cereal, Potato, and Sugar Beet Crops (in thousands of Hectares)

1890–1944

HUNGARY[8]

	Wheat	Rye	Barley	Oats	Maize	P's	SB
1890	2,979	1,239	1,008	993	1,932	433	66
1891	3,012	1,185	1,043	1,007	2,012	432	68
1892	3,064	1,248	1,043	1,004	2,089	458	73
1893	3,278	1,394	1,046	970	2,049	454	82
1894	3,204	1,244	1,056	986	2,022	460	91
1895	3,133	1,132	1,010	962	2,148	461	74
1896	3,126	1,135	1,010	938	2,082	444	75
1897	2,780	1,185	946	897	1,988	440	71
1898	3,057	1,107	975	947	2,114	458	74
1899	3,158	1,143	1,116	964	2,129	456	73
1900	3,295	1,118	1,006	981	2,217	508	90
1901	3,317	1,136	1,013	982	2,199	506	91
1902	3,344	1,139	1,021	985	2,166	506	91
1903	3,445	1,130	1,039	1,023	2,268	537	95
1904	3,400	1,115	1,020	994	1,964	518	90
1905	3,417	1,131	1,033	1,017	2,123	537	94
1906	3,555	1,133	1,053	1,037	2,312	563	110
1907	3,266	1,065	1,103	1,074	2,441	570	110
1908	3,527	1,104	1,071	1,057	2,360	584	102
1909	3,252	1,062	1,157	1,091	2,453	602	112
1910	3,374	1,122	1,099	1,069	2,427	610	115
1911	3,381	1,089	1,107	1,074	2,465	621	139
1912	3,540	1,131	1,053	1,001	2,437	619	172
1913	3,211	1,055	1,193	1,209	2,663	644	182
1914	3,244	1,099	1,095	1,053	2,434	613	178
1915	3,351	1,063	1,145	1,080	2,513	637	107
1916	2,972	989	1,037	1,054	2,255	589	96
1917	3,067	1,003	966	999	2,197	599	110
1918	3,063[8]	974[8]	933[8]	960[8]	2,230[8]	482[8]	114[8]
1919	...	...	...	...	...	...	...
1920	1,077	597	512	325	816	254	31
1921	1,169	543	479	358	877	269	42
1922	1,426	673	463	328	989	257	42
1923	1,333	653	455	325	972	259	52
1924	1,416	663	408	287	995	248	68
1925	1,426	688	412	290	1,074	261	66
1926	1,500	700	425	275	1,065	251	63
1927	1,627	641	406	260	1,062	260	65
1928	1,677	651	413	264	1,062	265	67
1929	1,500	657	477	301	1,123	283	79
1930	1,695	652	458	246	1,054	272	74
1931	1,623	601	472	241	1,101	284	54
1932	1,535	629	469	234	1,176	299	42
1933	1,588	679	485	231	1,140	294	44
1934	1,537	642	478	224	1,124	290	45
1935	1,673	622	428	203	1,151	281	47
1936	1,630	650	470	214	1,137	297	49
1937	1,483	606	467	230	1,196	295	47
1938	1,619	632	454	224	1,174	291	44
1939	1,642	622	444	221	1,174	276	43
1940	1,407	541	410	245	1,146	279	56
1941	1,333	536	419	248	1,127	274	49
1942	1,416	537	415	233	1,085	265	47
1943	1,544	551	437	239	959	266	55
1944	1,539	541	448	240	1,049	266	60

CROATIA-SLAVONIA

	Wheat	Rye	Barley	Oats	Maize	P's	SB
1890	188	169	67	97	330	55	1
1891	196	158	65	95	347	56	1
1892	206	157	68	95	351	58	1
1893	219	160	66	93	355	58	2
1894	227	156	69	93	365	59	1
1895	227	148	66	87	365	78	1
1896	237	149	69	92	366	59	1
1897	233	146	69	95	357	63	1
1898	245	147	71	100	391	85	1
1899	257	144	69	99	368	65	1
1900	269	137	74	100	371	67	1
1901	271	139	72	100	388	68	1
1902	278	128	70	99	379	72	1
1903	289	130	72	101	395	71	1
1904	295	128	70	100	395	72	1
1905	305	122	69	100	400	72	1
1906	298	114	67	102	407	73	2
1907	287	105	65	101	400	74	2
1908	307	97	65	100	406	73	2
1909	309	103	63	100	405	77	2
1910	320	105	64	97	403	78	3
1911	327	104	64	100	414	77	4
1912	335	97	63	96	423	79	4
1913	339	67	64	110	439	79	5
1914	342	90	62	103	428	84	8
1915	325	83	61	109	429	84	4
1916	306	68	59	112	419	82	3
1917	...	...	...	...	...	...	...
1918	...	...	...	...	...	...	...
1919	...	...	...	...	...	...	...
1920	...	...	...	...	...	...	...
1921	...	...	...	...	...	...	...
1922	...	...	...	...	...	...	...
1923	...	...	...	...	...	...	...
1924	...	...	...	...	...	...	...
1925	...	...	...	...	...	...	...
1926	...	...	...	...	...	...	...
1927	...	...	...	...	...	...	...
1928	...	...	...	...	...	...	...
1929	...	...	...	...	...	...	...
1930	...	...	...	...	...	...	...
1931	...	...	...	...	...	...	...
1932	...	...	...	...	...	...	...
1933	...	...	...	...	...	...	...
1934	...	...	...	...	...	...	...
1935	...	...	...	...	...	...	...
1936	...	...	...	...	...	...	...
1937	...	...	...	...	...	...	...
1938	...	...	...	...	...	...	...
1939	...	...	...	...	...	...	...
1940	...	...	...	...	...	...	...
1941	...	...	...	...	...	...	...
1942	...	...	...	...	...	...	...
1943	...	...	...	...	...	...	...
1944	...	...	...	...	...	...	...

See p.250 for footnotes

D1 Area of Main Cereal, Potato, and Sugar Beet Crops (in thousands of hectares)

1890–1944

	IRELAND (Southern Ireland from 1922)					NORTHERN IRELAND			
	Wheat	Barley	Oats	Potatoes	Sugar Beet	Wheat	Barley	Oats	Potatoes
1890	37	74	494	316	–	...	...	...	...
1891	33	72	492	305	–	...	...	...	...
1892	30	71	496	299	–	...	...	...	...
1893	22	68	505	293	–	...	...	...	...
1894	20	67	508	290		...	...	...	...
1895	15	70	492	287	–	...	...	...	...
1896	15	70	483	286	–	...	...	...	...
1897	19	69	476	274	–	...	...	...	...
1898	21	64	471	269	–	...	...	...	...
1899	21	69	460	268	–	...	...	...	...
1900	22	70	447	265	–	...	...	...	...
1901	17	66	445	257	–	...	...	...	...
1902	18	68	430	255	–	...	...	...	...
1903	15	64	444	251	–	...	...	...	...
1904	13	64	437	251	–	...	...	...	...
1905	15	63	432	250	–	...	...	...	...
1906	18	72	435	249	–	...	...	...	...
1907	15	69	435	239	–	...	...	...	...
1908	15	63	429	238	–	...	...	...	...
1909	18	66	419	235	–	...	...	...	...
1910	19	68	435	240	–	...	...	...	...
1911	18	64	421	239	–	...	...	...	...
1912	18	67	423	241	–	...	...	...	...
1913	14	70	424	236	–	...	...	...	...
1914	15	70	416	236	–	...	...	...	...
1915	35	57	441	240	–	...	...	...	...
1916	31	61	434	237	–	...	...	...	...
1917	50	72	592	287	–	...	...	...	...
1918	64	75	639	284	–	...	...	...	...
1919	28	76	584	238	–	...	...	...	...
1920	20	84	539	236	–	...	...	...	...
1921	17	69	491	230	–	...	...	...	...
1922	15	66	311	165	–	2.6	0.8	144	70
1923	15	59	295	161	–	2.8	0.8	142	66
1924	13	63	279	159	–	2.0	1.0	135	64
1925	9	59	272	154	–	1.5	0.9	130	62
1926	12	57	262	152	3.8	2.5	0.7	129	62
1927	14	49	261	148	7.2	2.4	0.6	125	62
1928	13	52	262	147	6.7	2.0	0.8	124	63
1929	12	48	270	147	5.3	1.5	0.8	127	62
1930	11	47	261	140	5.8	1.8	0.9	124	55
1931	8.4	47	252	140	2.0	1.2	0.6	116	54
1932	8.7	42	256	141	5.5	1.3	0.4	116	57
1933	20	47	257	138	6.1	2.5	0.6	117	56
1934	38	58	236	139	18	3.5	1.0	113	55
1935	66	56	248	136	23	3.7	1.3	110	52
1936	103	53	226	135	25	2.8	1.1	107	53
1937	89	53	232	132	25	1.8	1.1	104	51
1938	93	48	231	132	21	2.2	1.4	120	50
1939	103	30	217	128	17	1.2	1.4	118	47
1940	123	53	276	149	25	4.8	7.2	161	55
1941	187	66	316	173	32	7.1	7.1	182	64
1942	233	75	355	172	22	5.0	6.2	192	76
1943	206	85	379	165	34	5.6	5.8	190	80
1944	260	68	382	167	33	2.0	6.5	178	80

D1 Area of Main Cereal, Potato, and Sugar Beet Crops (in thousands of hectares)

1890–1944

ITALY[29]

	Wheat	Rye	Barley	Oats	Maize	Rice	Potatoes	Sugar Beet
1890	4,407	141	332	453	1,912	193	174	...
1891	4,502	142	308	448	1,906	195	181	...
1892	4,530	144	313	450	1,903	198	194	...
1893	4,556	145	323	458	1,920	162	198	...
1894	4,574	142	303	466	1,901	165	200	...
1895	4,593	137	297	474	1,957	163	209	...
1896	4,581				1,956			...
1897	...	...	...	...	...	...	...	...
1898	...	...	...	...	...	...	...	...
1899	...	...	...	...	...	...	...	...
1900	...	...	...	...	...	...	...	...
1901	4,760	...	...	...	1,755	...	...	...
1902	4,750	...	...	...	1,700	...	...	...
1903	5,154	...	...	...	1,688	...	...	...
1904	5,397	...	...	...	1,941	...	...	...
1905	5,315	...	...	...	1,960	...	...	...
1906	5,137	...	...	...	1,896	...	...	...
1907	5,230	...	...	...	1,814	...	...	...
1908	5,108	...	...	...	1,801	...	...	...
1909	4,709	122	250	503	1,636	144	283	45
1910	4,759	122	248	503	1,621	144	284	50
1911	4,752	122	248	514	1,616	145	288	53
1912	4,755	123	244	508	1,594	146	288	54
1913	4,744	124	251	506	1,574	146	292	62
1914	4,769	123	247	491	1,576	146	294	41
1915	5,060	119	246	489	1,573	144	293	50
1916	4,726	116	241	446	1,586	143	295	50
1917	4,272	113	190	448	1,559	138	296	47
1918	4,366[25]	109[25]	193[25]	491[25]	1,440[25]	138[25]	299[25]	43[25]
1919	4,287	111	194	457	1,501	132	309	52
1920	4,569	114	200	469	1,501	112	301	46
1921	4,767[29]	116[29]	219[29]	485[29]	1,504[29]	116[29]	309[29]	64[29]
1922	4,650	129	233	491	1,561	119	349	82
1923	4,676	127	230	495	1,533	123	348	90
1924	4,566	125	232	478	1,540	138	348	124
1925	4,724	126	233	486	1,554	144	346	57
1926	4,915	121	237	498	1,525	148	352	80
1927	4,976	124	236	487	1,520	142	354	88
1928	4,963	126	227	521	1,502	135	354	115
1929	4,773	124	234	523	1,505	137	351	116
1930	4,823	122	236	511	1,516	146	351	116
1931	4,809	123	218	464	1,396	145	349	112
1932	4,931	117	210	446	1,448	135	412	114
1933	5,094	114	207	448	1,431	134	399	82
1934	4,967	112	199	424	1,491	134	400	89
1935	5,005	110	199	428	1,445	138	406	92
1936	5,137	106	195	435	1,489	145	426	120
1937	5,173	105	195	435	1,471	145	422	134
1938	5,031	104	199	442	1,507	148	425	138
1939	5,225	105	201	420	1,459	157	427	147
1940	5,076	105	203	442	1,509	163	429	173
1941	4,970	107	207	445	1.451	167	450	151
1942	5,169	105	254	444	1.428	162	463	148
1943	5,342[29]	102[29]	276[29]	461[29]	1,390[29]	152[29]	474[29]	151[29]
1944	4,763	94	241	425	1.265	127	397	113

See p.250 for footnotes

D1 Area of Main Cereal, Potato, and Sugar Beet Crops (in thousands of hectares)

1890–1944

NETHERLANDS

	Wheat	Rye	Barley	Oats	Buck-wheat	Potatoes	Sugar Beet
1890	85	204	42	115	45	145	28
1891	59	184	45	153	44	150	23
1892	74	201	44	126	39	152	25
1893	71	202	42	126	38	152	28
1894	65	208	38	133	37	150	33
1895	62	210	39	131	36	151	35
1896	62	215	39	128	32	150	46
1897	62	213	36	134	31	151	39
1898	73	215	35	127	30	150	43
1899	72	214	36	128	29	156	46
1900	64	214	38	131	28	156	46
1901	55	216	36	135	27	156	49
1902	62	218	36	137	26	158	33
1903	56	218	32	144	24	151	40
1904	54	216	31	145	22	159	34
1905	61	219	33	132	21	161	47
1906	57	218	29	139	19	161	42
1907	55	220	31	139	18	158	44
1908	57	222	30	140	17	159	48
1909	52	224	28	142	16	161	55
1910	55	222	28	141	14	162	56
1911	58	225	28	138	13	166	56
1912	58	228	27	138	12	172	65
1913	57	228	27	141	10	170	60
1914	60	228	27	141	10	171	63
1915	66	221	26	145	8	177	57
1916	55	200	24	139	7	...[30]	65
1917	49	189	21	155	8	...[30]	46
1918	61	119	24	159	8	...[30]	38
1919	68	201	23	158	8	...[30]	53
1920	62	199	23	160	7	...[30]	67
1921	73	202	25	155	5	179	74
1922	61	202	25	159	4	193	56
1923	62	210	24	154	3	161	67
1924	48	198	25	152	3	168	74
1925	53	201	30	148	2	170	66
1926	53	197	27	154	2	170	62
1927	62	197	27	149	1.2	173	70
1928	60	196	28	152	0.9	179	65
1929	45	197	31	160	0.7	182	55
1930	58	192	31	150	0.5	161	58
1931	78	180	29	149	0.5	164	37
1932	120	166	20	142	0.4	176	40
1933	137	165	18	136	0.5	153	47
1934	148	187	32	131	0.4	143	42
1935	154	210	41	128	0.3	139	41
1936	152	238	43	129	0.3	112	44
1937	119	231	49	153	0.2	123	43
1938	126	243	43	150	...	130	44
1939	124	225	41	163	...	134	46
1940	134	228	43	139	...	137	50
1941	137	241	47	109	...	169	45
1942	144	281	51	104	...	222	41
1943	149	317	46	114	...	226	44
1944	147	299	33	123	...	207	40

NORWAY

	Wheat	Rye	Barley	Oats	Mixed Corn	Potatoes
1890	4.3	14	52	97	14	39
1891	...	...	...	...	...	...
1892	...	...	...	...	...	...
1893	...	...	...	...	...	...
1894	...	...	...	...	...	...
1895	...	...	...	...	...	...
1896	...	...	...	...	...	...
1897	...	...	...	...	...	...
1898	...	...	...	...	...	...
1899	...	...	...	...	...	...
1900	5.0	13	40	97	7.6	37
1901	...	...	...	...	...	...
1902	...	...	...	...	...	...
1903	...	...	...	...	...	...
1904	...	...	...	...	...	...
1905	...	...	...	...	...	...
1906	...	...	...	...	...	...
1907	5.0	15	36	106	6.2	41
1908	...	...	...	...	...	...
1909	...	...	...	...	...	...
1910	5.0	15	36	107	6.1	42
1911	...	...	...	...	...	...
1912	...	...	...	...	...	...
1913	...	...	...	...	...	...
1914	...	...	...	...	...	...
1915	...	...	...	...	...	...
1916	...	...	...	...	...	...
1917	8.6	11	47	103	8.4	46
1918	17	15	63	138	12	53
1919	...	...	...	...	...	...
1920	9.8	12	52	119	8.7	50
1921	...	...	...	...	...	...
1922	...	...	...	...	...	...
1923	10	11	50	103	8.1	46
1924	8.6	10	55	93	7.9	47
1925	8.9	9.0	56	97	7.6	47
1926	8.9	9.5	58	98	7.3	48
1927	9.9	9.3	61	97	6.8	50
1928	12	7.4	60	100	6.8	51
1929	12	7.4	54	97	5.5	46
1930	12	7.7	54	97	5.5	47
1931	12	6.2	56	96	5.5	47
1932	11	6.6	55	95	5.6	50
1933	11	6.3	57	98	5.8	49
1934	19	5.9	60	92	5.0	49
1935	24	6.2	62	87	4.5	50
1936	30	5.9	60	85	4.4	52
1937	32	5.9	60	85	4.5	52
1938	35	5.4	60	85	4.5	54
1939	41	3.2	47	87	4.9	51
1940	41	3.1	48	89	4.9	57
1941	46	3.7	56	93	7.4	63
1942	49	4.3	53	91	7.8	79
1943	48	3.9	51	92	6.8	81
1944	47	3.7	47	89	6.7	73

See p.250 for footnotes

D1 Area of Main Cereal, Potato, and Sugar Beet Crops (in thousands of hectares)

1890–1944

POLAND

	Wheat	Rye	Barley	Oats	Potatoes	SB
1890	...	...	...	...	...	...
1891	...	...	...	...	...	...
1892	...	...	...	...	...	...
1893	...	...	...	...	...	...
1894	...	...	...	...	...	...
1895	...	...	...	...	...	...
1896	...	...	...	...	...	...
1897	...	...	...	...	...	...
1898	...	...	...	...	...	...
1899	...	...	...	...	...	...
1900	...	...	...	...	...	...
1901	...	...	...	...	...	...
1902	...	...	...	...	...	...
1903	...	...	...	...	...	...
1904	...	...	...	...	...	...
1905	...	...	...	...	...	...
1906	...	...	...	...	...	...
1907	...	...	...	...	...	...
1908	...	...	...	...	...	...
1909	...	...	...	...	...	...
1910	...	...	...	...	...	...
1911	...	...	...	...	...	...
1912	...	...	...	...	...	...
1913	...	...	...	...	...	...
1914	...	...	...	...	...	...
1915	...	...	...	...	...	...
1916	...	...	...	...	...	...
1917	...	...	...	...	...	...
1918	...	...	...	...	...	...
1919	430	2,648	532	988	1,152	66
1920	725	2,928	787	1,667	1,644	71
1921	847	3,588	992	1,924	1,941	80
1922	1,042	4,543	1,143	2,379	2,189	109
1923	1,017	4,645	1,199	2,515	2,279	136
1924	1,073	4,417	1,218	2,585	2,331	163
1925	1,094	4,904	1,224	2,577	2,359	172
1926	1,314	5,687	1,113	1,972	2,394	185
1927	1,360	5,764	1,118	1,981	2,440	202
1928	1,290	5,341	1,156	2,038	2,505	234
1929	1,427	5,798	1,259	2,192	2,636	239
1930	1,645	5,895	1,234	2,187	2,672	185
1931	1,819	5,772	1,272	2,172	2,718	149
1932	1,726	5,646	1,207	2,220	2,715	116
1933	1,694	5,775	1,166	2,204	2,740	99
1934	1,746	5,639	1,177	2,190	2,762	112
1935	1,754	5,784	1,219	2,234	2,832	119
1936	1,742	5,831	1,187	2,255	2,893	121
1937	1,693	5,721	1,232	2,294	2,980	147
1938	1,754	5,895	1,178	2,277	3,030	150
1939	1,763	5,967	1,184	2,320	3,060	164
	[31]	[31]	[31]	[31]	[31]	[31]
1940	1,195	4,852	931	1,770	2,781	293
1941	1,193	4,875	959	1,752	2,957	309
1942	1,088	4,345	1,071	1,838	2,651	338
1943	1,055	4,666	944	1,852	2,631	343
1944	1,050	4,418	917	1,798	2,672	329

PORTUGAL

	Wheat	Rye	Barley	Oats	Maize	Rice	Potatoes
1890	...	...	...	...	...	...	..
1891	...	...	...	...	...	...	...
1892	...	...	...	...	...	...	...
1893	...	...	...	...	...	...	...
1894	...	...	...	...	...	...	...
1895	...	...	...	...	...	...	...
1896	...	...	...	...	...	...	...
1897	...	...	...	...	...	...	...
1898	...	...	...	...	...	...	...
1899	...	...	...	...	...	...	...
1900	...	...	...	...	...	...	...
1901	...	...	...	...	...	...	...
1902	...	...	...	...	...	...	...
1903	...	...	...	...	...	...	...
1904	...	...	...	...	...	...	...
1905	...	...	...	...	...	...	...
1906	...	...	...	...	...	...	...
1907	...	...	...	...	...	...	...
1908	...	...	...	...	...	...	...
1909	...	...	...	...	...	...	...
1910	...	...	...	...	...	...	...
1911	490	132	...	...	...	...	...
1912	...	107	...	...	...	...	...
1913	...	91	...	...	...	...	...
1914	376	...	...	...	238	...	11
1915	377	...	...	...	243	7.0	11
1916	376	...	...	...	234	7.3	...
1917	277	...	84	231	...	7.2	...
1918	410	298	78	225	271	15	29
1919	446	314	74	232	287	18	25
1920	444	215	60	183	297	7.3	26
1921	513	232	58	163	289	5.5	18
1922	468	239	76	253	341	5.8	21
1923	427	222	69	213	304	5.0	21
1924	420	270	78	225	266	9.8	28
1925	426	255	77	205	308	9.8	36
1926	430	239	75	202	315	11	36
1927	431	171	73	186	334	13	18
1928	446	163	72	195	351	13	19
1929	435	159	70	175	366	14	19
1930	453	165	69	174	364	14	27
1931	514	173	69	171	380	15	29
1932	591	148	78	186	376	11	31
1933	576	166	85	167	437	15	34
1934	544	141	50	163	430	24	33
1935	557	134	65	209	433	24	32
1936	468	157	78	266	428	18	32
1937	493	140	73	261	368	21	30
1938	459	134	75	250	393	19	31
1939	505	126	64	243	395	20	30
1940	502	116	61	208	394	22	30
1941	555	133	64	170	360	25	32
1942	578	152	81	214	377	26	46
1943	546	169	108	275	467	26	63
1944	605	225	114	252	498	25	61

See p.250 for footnotes

D1 Area of Main Cereal, Potato, and Sugar Beet Crops (in thousands of hectares)

1890–1944

ROMANIA

	Wheat	Rye	Barley	Oats	Maize	Potatoes	Sugar Beet
1890	1,510	167	518	179	1,743	...	...
1891	1,543	122	526	185	1,693	...	...
1892	1,496	133	560	226	1,822	...	...
1893	1,304	143	594	252	1,839	...	...
1894	1,393	160	559	263	1,768	...	...
1895	1,438	218	553	271	1,846	...	...
1896	1,505	243	608	282	1,939	...	...
1897	1,595	226	677	288	1,855	...	...
1898	1,454	193	655	306	2,120	...	...
1899	1,662	189	639	310	2,017	...	...
1900	1,590	164	438	255	2,035	...	...
1901	1,637	211	504	265	2,128	...	...
1902	1,486	173	508	321	2,182	...	...
1903	1,606	158	531	427	2,072	...	...
1904	1,720	134	533	428	2,090	12	8.9
1905	1,958	161	529	373	1,976	11	12
1906	2,023	184	559	382	2,082	11	9.7
1907	1,714	147	510	352	1,929	9.8	6.6
1908	1,802	147	620	490	2,020	3.9	9.0
1909	1,689	137	549	485	2,123	8.7	11
1910	1,948	174	549	447	1,986	10	13
1911	1,931	132	507	401	2,035	12	14
1912	2,069	107	500	382	2,079	12	14
1913	1,623[32]	91[32]	563[32]	522[32]	2,147[32]	10[32]	13[32]
1914	2,112	84	568	428	2,066	11	15
1915	1,904	76	555	431	2,107	11	14
1916	1,960	81	588	432	2,046	14	12
1917	...[32]	...[32]	...[32]	...[32]	...[32]	...[32]	...[32]
1918	2,300	253	858	439	2,318	31	7.3
1919	1,728[32]	303[32]	786[32]	385[32]	2,732[32]	58[32]	3.4[32]
1920	2,023	316	1,400	966	3,295	97	5.6
1921	2,488	327	1,569	1,239	3,444	165	23
1922	2,650	267	1,727	1,334	3,404	143	22
1923	2,690	270	1,878	1,345	3,404	174	37
1924	3,172	271	1,851	1,237	3,621	189	54
1925	3,301	270	1,704	1,185	3,931	186	64
1926	3,327	296	1,552	1,078	4,059	179	82
1927	3,101	281	1,764	1,084	4,219	198	85
1928	3,206	296	1,749	1,116	4,455	206	57
1929	2,737	313	2,054	1,213	4,795	208	49
1930	3,056	392	1,975	1,087	4,427	190	46
1931	3,466	407	1,919	871	4,755	192	20
1932	2,870	348	1,787	792	4,776	191	18
1933	3,116	388	1,815	830	4,827	198	43
1934	3,079	369	1,753	827	5,005	204	37
1935	3,438	389	1,651	797	5,169	207	37
1936	3,432	421	1,611	804	5,260	216	29
1937	3,552	438	1,513	785	5,159	216	30
1938	3,818	482	1,278	651	4,997	193	48
1939	4,079[33]	488[33]	1,096[33]	589[33]	4,932[33]	207[33]	53[33]
1940	2,078	92	588	433	3,567	110	37
1941	2,283	88	522	438	3,251	112	55
1942	1,485	58	588	502	3,099	154	37
1943	2,148	84	587	527	3,012	172	60
1944	2,819[33]	174[33]	610[33]	640[33]	3,225[33]	221[33]	53[33]

See p.250 for footnotes

D1 Area of Main Cereal, Potato, and Sugar Beet Crops (in thousands of hectares)

1890–1944

RUSSIA (in million hectares)[11]

	Wheat	Rye	Barley	Oats	Maize	Potatoes	Sugar Beet
1890	...	...	...	...	...	...	...
1891	...	...	...	...	...	...	...
1892	13.2	27.4	6.3	13.8	0.9	2.2	0.29
1893	13.2	25.3	6.4	13.4	0.9	2.3	0.33
1894	13.3[11]	25.6[11]	6.4[11]	13.3[11]	0.8[11]	2.3[11]	...
	13.8	27.3	6.8	14.3	0.8	3.0	0.34
1895	13.4	27.1	6.8	14.8	0.8	3.1	0.35
1896	14.6	27.9	7.2	15.4	0.9	3.2	0.35
1897	14.9	27.3	7.4	15.7	0.9	3.3	0.40
1898	15.1	27.2	7.5	15.5	1.0	3.4	0.44
1899	15.9	27.6	7.5	15.6	1.0	3.5	0.48
1900	16.7	28.6	7.6	16.2	1.1	3.6	0.53
1901	17.5	28.7	7.8	16.5	1.1	3.8	0.54
1902	17.8	28.7	7.8	16.2	1.2	3.8	0.58
1903	18.2	29.0	8.3	16.4	1.1	3.9	0.54
1904	19.0	28.6	8.6	16.4	1.2	4.0	0.48
1905	20.0	28.2	8.7	16.7	1.2	3.8	0.54
1906	20.4	29.1	8.5	16.6	1.0	3.9	0.58
1907	19.0	28.7	8.8	16.5	1.2	4.0	0.62
1908	19.4	27.6	9.4	16.4	1.2	4.1	0.56
1909	19.7[11]	27.9[11]	9.3[11]	16.4[11]	1.2[11]	4.2[11]	...
	29.0	29.4	11.7	19.0	2.1	4.4	0.56
1910	31.4	29.0	12.3	19.5	2.1	4.5	0.67
1911	32.4	29.9	12.5	19.6	2.0	4.6	0.79
1912	31.6	30.0	12.5	19.0	2.1	4.7	0.76
1913	33.5[11]	30.7[11]	13.6[11]	19.7[11]	2.1[11]	4.9[11]	0.72[11]
	31.6	25.8	10.8	16.9	1.3	3.1	0.65
1914	...	...	...	...	...	...	...
1915	...	...	...	...	...	...	...
1916	...	...	...	...	...	...	...
1917	...	...	...	...	...	...	...
1918	...	...	...	...	...	...	...
1919	...	...	...	...	...	...	0.29
1920	19.2	19.1	6.7	11.3	1.2	2.5	0.16
1921	15.5	19.4	6.4	9.8	1.3	1.4	0.12
1922	10.5	21.5	3.8	7.3	2.2	2.5	0.18
1923	13.2	25.3	6.3	11.7	1.7	3.8	0.26
1924	21.3	27.8	7.3	12.8	2.4	4.7	0.38
1925	24.2	28.4	6.4	12.7	3.4	5.0	0.53
1926	28.7	29.2	7.4	15.2	3.0	5.2	0.54
1927	30.7	28.2	7.1	17.4	2.9	5.5	0.66
1928	27.7	24.6	6.9	17.2	4.4	5.7	0.77
1929	29.7	24.9	8.1	18.9	3.5	5.7	0.77
1930	33.8	28.9	7.4	17.9	3.7	5.7	1.04
1931	36.9	27.6	6.9	17.5	4.0	6.2	1.39
1932	34.5	26.2	6.8	15.4	3.7	6.1	1.54
1933	32.2	25.4	7.3	16.7	4.0	5.6	1.21
1934	35.2	24.0	8.5	18.0	3.7	6.1	1.18
1935	37.1	23.5	9.1	18.3	3.2	7.4	1.23
1936	39.0	21.9	9.2	18.1	3.1	7.6	1.26
1937	41.4	23.1	9.2	17.6	2.8	6.9	1.19
1938	41.5	21.6	9.2	17.9	2.1	7.4	1.18
1939	40.9[11]	17.8[11]	9.3[11]	18.4[11]	2.5[11]	...[11]	1.19[11]
1940	40.3	23.3	10.5	20.2	3.7	7.7	1.23
1941	...	...	...	...	...	...	...
1942	...	...	...	...	...	...	...
1943	...	...	...	...	...	...	...
1944	...	...	...	...	...	...	...

See p.250 for footnotes

D1 Area of Main Cereal, Potato, and Sugar Beet Crops (in thousands of hectares)

1914–1940

ESTONIA

	Wheat	Rye	Barley	Oats	Potatoes
1918	previously included in Russia				
1919	13	132	106	...	56
1920	15	152	120	...	63
1921	13	155	114	146	66
1922	21	159	134	161	76
1923	23	164	126	153	72
1924	18	159	124	166	67
1925	21	155	115	150	69
1926	24	136	121	146	69
1927	27	148	119	146	71
1928	28	144	106	130	65
1929	33	133	114	150	62
1930	37	148	112	149	68
1931	40	144	113	148	68
1932	52	147	108	144	67
1933	63	151	104	139	68
1934	65	147	104	138	72
1935	63	145	105	139	74
1936	66	137	101	138	74
1937	68	149	89	145	76
1938	70	148	88	149	78
1939	75	151	84	144	89
1940	included in Russia				

LATVIA

	Wheat	Rye	Barley	Oats	Potatoes	Sugar Beet
1918	previously included in Russia					
1919	...	...	...	...	...	...
1920	16	197	124	216	49	...
1921	19	227	146	252	59	...
1922	28	236	157	273	69	...
1923	43	267	178	309	79	...
1924	43	266	179	334	75	...
1925	48	267	177	330	79	...
1926	49	251	190	321	82	...
1927	59	256	185	305	86	...
1928	66	258	146	239	78	...
1929	59	238	183	303	80	...
1930	72	267	177	320	94	...
1931	87	231	183	322	100	4
1932	103	240	165	325	102	9
1933	125	258	184	307	104	13
1934	142	268	180	300	108	14
1935	140	271	193	333	124	15
1936	129	258	189	339	120	12
1937	137	288	181	335	127	14
1938	141	287	178	348	138	14
1939	153	298	180	378	145	13
1940	included in Russia					

LITHUANIA

	Wheat	Rye	Barley	Oats	Potatoes	Sugar Beet
1920	previously included in Russia					
1921	73	505	168	310	132	...
1922	79[34]	554[34]	169[34]	311[34]	132[34]	...[34]
1923	82	583	175	331	143	...
1924	85	538	196	325	176	...
1925	112	542	205	345	163	...
1926	122	449	215	382	147	...
1927	120	502	197	310	139	...
1928	159	470	169	288	122	...
1929	198	451	214	350	132	...
1930	213	506	182	368	153	1
1931	194	509	197	368	169	3
1932	206	483	201	373	173	5
1933	202	490	207	343	179	4
1934	208	496	204	329	183	4
1935	217	513	206	340	176	7
1936	199	493	214	357	182	8
1937	211	509	214	349	184	8
1938	203	528	217	355	186	8
1939	202	497	209	348	177	9
1940	included in Russia					

See p.250 for footnotes

D1 **Area of Main Cereal, Potato, and Sugar Beet Crops** (in thousands of hectares)

SPAIN[35] **1890–1944**

	Wheat	Rye	Barley	Oats	Maize	Rice	Potatoes	Sugar Beet
1890	...	...	...	...	...	...	...	...
1891	...	...	...	...	...	...	...	...
1892	...	...	...	...	...	...	...	...
1893	...	...	...	...	...	...	...	...
1894	...	...	...	...	...	...	...	...
1895	...	...	...	...	...	...	...	...
1896	...	...	...	...	...	...	...	...
1897	3,858	...	...	...	...	...	...	...
1898	3,862	...	...	377	...	...	...	...
1899	3,663	...	...	377	...	...	...	...
1900	3,869	...	...	379	...	...	...	...
1901	3,712	797	1,336	382	468	...	...	...
1902	3,693	784	1,457	450	462	...	...	...
1903	3,635	781	1,433	452	373	...	...	...
1904	3,652	765	1,382	447	434	...	...	...
1905	3,593	750	1,350	453	465	...	...	...
1906	3,763	887	1,465	482	446	...	...	...
1907	3,698	902	1,441	480	449	...	241	...
1908	3,757	909	1,403	490	459	...	254	...
1909	3,783	833	1,408	497	465	37	...	24
1910	3,809	821	1,349	508	454	38	264	22
1911	3,928	804	1,444	513	463	38	...	33
1912	3,895	787	1,335	517	465	38	256	43
1913	3,903	776	1,566	547	447	39	...	59
1914	3,918	763	1,378	528	460	39	279	35
1915	4,062	737	1,532	568	466	40	297	40
1916	4,374	747	1,573	566	467	41	301	54
1917	4,185	730	1,621	566	476	43	339	59
1918	4,139	736	1,704	610	473	45	295	66
1919	4,200	732	1,722	646	477	45	326	54
1920	4,150	728	1,748	643	473	48	340	71
1921	4,203	723	1,754	638	477	46	319	54
1922	4,172	711	1,652	613	469	46	328	50
1923	4,245	729	1,837	645	472	46	306	62
1924	4,200	737	1,758	662	470	47	315	179
1925	4,339	747	1,786	728	474	49	...	114
1926	4,361	755	1,810	754	407	50	300	72
1927	4,381	736	1,802	773	462	49	309	62
1928	4,278	621	1,801	792	388	49	336	59
1929	4,299	615	1,817	744	407	48	369	61
1930	4,506	628	1,838	785	447	49	370	80
1931	4,551	613	1,879	804	426	46	415	112
1932	4,552	614	1,957	779	446	50	418	85
1933	4,520	591	1,875	766	432	47	425	83
1934	4,608	577	1,923	782	434	46	413	92
1935	4,554	572	1,841	748	440	47	419	71
1936	...	...	...	...	...	...	...	...
1937	...	...	...	...	...	...	...	...
1938	...	...	...	...	...	...	...	...
1939	3,496	527	1,368	576	446	43	412	36
1940	3,535	551	1,562	646	452	54	430	64
1941	3,762	602	1,652	712	380	47	449	67
1942	3,776	609	1,669	774	354	47	466[36]	48
1943	3,736	630	1,698	792	326	48	400[36]	60
1944	3,710	630	1,669	728	316	49	370	62

See p.250 for footnotes

D1 Area of Main Cereal, Potato, and Sugar Beet Crops (in thousands of hectares)

1890–1944

	SWEDEN							SWITZERLAND					
	Wheat	Rye	Barley	Oats	M C	P's	SB[12]	Wheat	Rye	Barley	Oats	P's	SB
1890	71	391	221	801	105	156	25	...	...	...	...	...	...
1891	71	396	221	806	108	156	27	...	...	...	...	...	...
1892	71	400	223	814	112	159	28	...	...	...	...	...	...
1893	71	403	219	818	116	158	32[12]	...	...	...	...	...	...
1894	71	402	219	818	117	158	22	...	...	...	...	...	...
1895	71	404	220	827	120	159	19	...	...	...	...	...	...
1896	71	407	218	819	122	158	28	...	...	...	...	...	...
1897	72	410	219	823	123	158	23	...	...	...	...	...	...
1898	74	411	221	823	125	158	23	...	...	...	...	...	...
1899	76	410	221	820	126	158	26	...	...	...	...	...	...
1900	78	411	217	825	130	155	29	...	...	...	...	...	...
1901	79	410	218	826	133	155	28	...	...	...	...	...	...
1902	82	412	215	824	135	155	24	...	...	...	...	...	...
1903	81	410	214	824	136	155	27	...	...	...	...	...	...
1904	81	411	213	828	139	154	24	...	...	...	...	...	...
1905	83	410	208	822	141	154	27	...	...	...	...	...	...
1906	85	411	204	813	149	152	31	...	...	...	...	...	...
1907	88	407	197	811	152	151	31	...	...	...	...	...	...
1908	91	404	195	809	155	153	32	43	23	...	...	...	...
1909	96	403	185	797	158	152	33	42	24	5	33	...	...
1910	97	402	182	792	162	152	35	42	25	5	33	...	...
1911	101	400	181[37]	790[37]	163[37]	153	29	42	24	5	33	47	0.5
1912	...	...	...	...	...	...	...	42[38] 66	25	5.0	33	47	—
1913	117	371	182	789	172	152	29	66	24	5.2	33	47	0.8
1914	117	392	170	780	177	152	32	64	25	6.0	34	47	0.8
1915	127	388	170	795	186	152	32	70	27	6.5	37	49	0.8
1916	128	369	167	777	197	148	37	83	18	6.8	26	55	0.5
1917	133	331	176	782	251	158	31	57	29	7.7	29	57	0.4
1918	153	384	185	733	265	164	30	87	29	9.0	35	60	0.4
1919	141	372	168	712	262	163	36	76	22	7.5	23	55	0.3
1920	145	370	161	709	263	147	44	68	20	7.2	23	50	0.7
1921	145	370	160	709	262	147	49	67	23	6.6	21	46	1.2
1922	144	353	173	728	270	162	17	61	22	6.5	21	45	1.2
1923	146	352	155	719	261	159	43	62	22	6.4	21	45	1.2
1924	131	264	173	773	280	158	41	62	22	6.3	20	45	1.3
1925	147	352	167	730	265	159	40	62	22	6.2	20	48	1.4
1926	155	339	179	739	271	160	5	65	20	6.5	20	48	1.5
1927	227	276	124	697	228	140	40	65	20	7	20	48	1.7
1928	227	276	114	693	226	140	43	65	20	7	20	48	1.6
1929	232	256	125	708	232	141	28	65	19	7.3	20	45	1.1
1930	262	241	132	660	268	136	37	67	20	7.2	20	49	1.2
1931	276	207	126	643	269	132	35	67	19	7.1	18	46	1.3
1932	278	212	110	673	234	138	40	68	19	7.0	17	47	1.4
1933	303	226	105	651	236	132	51	74	17	3.6	10	45	1.5
1934	290	236	100	660	239	132	51	79	16	4.2	10	46	1.5
1935	273	228	105	671	251	129	51	85	16	4.2	10	46	1.5
1936	281	215	104	671	258	133	51	88	16	4.3	11	47	1.7
1937	299	197	95	657	252	131	55	85	15	4.4	11	47	2.4
1938	308	189	101	661	253	133	51	86	15	5.0	11	47	2.9
1939	337	175	104	660	252	132	51	94	15	7.9	13	47	3.2
1940	309	171	107	635	284	135	54	88	10	11	21	50	3.1
1941	286	207	99	629	291	137	54	100	14	18	32	60	3.4
1942	279	249	112	597	278	142	53	108	14	22	34	71	3.9
1943	268	220	113	575	277	147	50	119	16	26	38	83	4.8
1944	274	201	96	551	277	138	55	117	14	29	41	85	5.7

See p.250 for footnotes

D1 Area of Main Cereal, Potato, and Sugar Beet Crops (in thousands of hectares)

1890–1944

UK GREAT BRITAIN

	Wheat	Barley	Oats	Other Corn[13]	Potatoes	Sugar Beet
1890	966	854	1,175	256	214	–
1891	934	855	1,173	245	216	–
1892	898	824	1,213	224	212	–
1893	768	840	1,284	223	214	–
1894	780	848	1,316	234	204	–
1895	573	877	1,334	211	219	–
1896	686	852	1,253	212	228	–
1897	764	824	1,229	201	204	–
1898	851	771	1,181	193	212	–
1899	810	802	1,198	188	222	–
1900	747	805	1,225	192	227	–
1901	688	798	1,212	188	234	–
1902	698	773	1,237	199	232	–
1903	640	752	1,271	195	228	–
1904	556	745	1,316	196	231	–
1905	727	694	1,235	199	246	–
1906	711	709	1,231	206	229	–
1907	658	693	1,264	217	222	–
1908	658	675	1,258	207	227	–
1909	738	673	1,207	224	233	–
1910	732	700	1,223	197	219	–
1911	771	647	1,219	213	231	–
1912	779	667	1,226	222[39]	248	–
1913	711	711	1,179	282	239	–
1914	756	688	1,153	214	248	–
1915	909	559	1,243	184	246	–
1916	799	608	1,244	168	226	–
1917	801	655[40]	1,335[40]	166[40]	265	–
1918	1,067	669	1,628	268	325	–
1919	931	681	1,487	288	255	–
1920	781	745	1,337	276	286	—
1921	826	650	1,279	249	288	—
1922	822	616	1,276	275	291	1.2
1923	728	601	1,192	234	244	3.2
1924	645	593	1,211	250	239	3.2
1925	626	595	1,131	205	257	6.9
1926	666	514	1,135	205	259	9.3
1927	689	472	1,072	192	267	23
1928	588	524	1,069	179	256	52
1929	559	494	1,110	191	269	94
1930	567	456	1,068	200	222	72
1931	505	452	1,006	184	233	95
1932	542	416	991	172	264	104
1933	704	328	951	171	272	148
1934	752	387	898	168	254	163
1935	758	351	909	166	240	152
1936	728	361	910	165	239	144
1937	741	366	826	134	239	127
1938	778	398	849	156	247	136
1939	713	409	864	154	238	140
1940	727	535	1,215	210	281	133
1941	909	590	1,417	401	391	142
1942	1,013	612	1,480	426	452	172
1943	1,397	717	1,300	443	483	169
1944	1,301	792	1,301	440	493	174

YUGOSLAVIA (Serbia to 1914)

	Wheat	Rye	Barley	Oats	Maize	Potatoes	Sugar Beet
1890	...	...	...	...	...	...	...
1891	...	...	...	...	...	...	...
1892	...	...	...	...	...	...	...
1893	317	60	92	106	532	8	...
1894	...	...	...	...	...	...	...
1895	...	...	...	...	...	...	...
1896	...	...	...	...	...	...	...
1897	280	37	75	100	448	6	...
1898	282	45	96	95	500	...	...
1899	404	59	114	101	546	...	...
1900	295	36	75	85	463	8	...
1901	305	38	79	91	506	8	...
1902	326	40	88	100	525	10	...
1903	348	43	95	108	534	10	...
1904	366	45	99	105	541	11	...
1905	372	48	108	104	553	11	...
1906	373	49	109	106	548	12	...
1907	368	44	101	96	550	11	...
1908	379	48	104	101	566	11	...
1909	378	50	114	108	584	11	...
1910	386	51	108	108	583	11	...
1911	...	...	...	...	...	...	...
1912	...	...	...	...	...	...	...
1913	...	...	...	...	...	...	...
1914	...	...	...	...	...	...	...
1915	...	...	...	...	...	...	...
1916	...	...	...	...	...	...	...
1917	...	...	...	...	...	...	...
1918	...	...	...	...	...	...	...
1919	...	...	...	...	...	...	...
1920	1,441	198	375	416	1,815	204	16
1921	1,497	187	368	406	1,880	209	17
1922	1,486	197	375	391	1,911	215	19
1923	1,555	187	361	375	1,802	213	27
1924	1,717	195	364	353	1,965	218	48
1925	1,743	198	358	343	2,072	231	33
1926	1,691	202	351	352	1,995	222	35
1927	1,830	209	391	379	2,066	226	41
1928	1,895	201	382	370	2,031	222	55
1929	2,110	238	427	386	2,318	233	59
1930	2,123	247	444	408	2,398	242	52
1931	2,141	244	431	379	2,388	236	44
1932	1,951	243	407	328	2,521	237	43
1933	2,079	256	429	376	2,538	249	30
1934	2,024	248	422	371	2,656	259	26
1935	2,150	252	422	372	2,472	257	29
1936	2,211	254	425	360	2,705	262	30
1937	2,130	254	417	346	2,691	258	21
1938	2,130	254	415	362	2,753	266	29
1939	2,203	254	416	357	2,681	263	46
1940	2,097	258	405	352	2,827[41]	273	42
1941	...	...	...	...	...	...	...
1942	...	...	...	...	...	...	...
1943	...	...	...	...	...	...	...
1944	...	...	...	...	...	...	...

See p.250 for footnotes

D1 Area of Main Cereal, Potato, and Sugar Beet Crops (in thousands of hectares)

1945–1969

AUSTRIA

	Wheat	Rye[2]	Barley	Oats	Maize	Other Cereals	Potatoes	Sugar Beet
1945	187	221	105	195	33	10	149	12
1946	200	229	115	199	52	20	156	16
1947	201	241	114	200	58	21	170	20
1948	203	239	108	200	57	21	175	22
1949	208	241	118	205	58	19	178	26
1950	218	249	134	208	59	17	184	29
1951	188	210	139	203	58	15	168	39
1952	203	213	139	200	60	14	170	40
1953	217	220	149	200	58	14	179	37
1954	238	218	150	191	58	15	177	43
1955	244	214	156	189	56	15	180	45
1956	251	214	168	187	51	15	181	43
1957	258	210	173	184	49	15	180	43
1958	263	206	173	178	49	16	178	51
1959	268	218	179	163	46	19	171	54
1960	277	171	209	161	58	20	180	45
1961	276	212	188	155	51	20	172	39
1962	270	209	193	151	54	21	169	48
1963	275	156	229	152	50	27	161	48
1964	283	166	227	143	50	27	158	53
1965	276	157	220	136	50	28	145	38
1966	314	144	230	126	55	32	137	47
1967	316	139	232	124	60	32	134	42
1968	306	142	238	119	74	32	130	44
1969	286	147	274	102	117	31	113	47

BELGIUM

	Wheat	Rye	Barley	Oats	Mixed Corn[2]	Buckwheat	Potatoes	Sugar Beet
1945	168	116	67	169	10	...	91	38
1946	138	105	62	190	10	...	79	44
1947	78	85	71	230	8	...	84	52
1948	143	86	77	189	6	...	88	45
1949	153	95	72	174	8	...	89	60
1950	174	89	84	178	7	...	98	63
1951	158	82	88	163	8	...	90	65
1952	166	82	90	165	7	...	87	64
1953	170	82	93	161	7	...	89	59
1954	184	82	76	152	8	...	93	57
1955	191	74	82	149	7	...	84	57
1956	188	68	91	158	4	...	86	62
1957	208	66	86	148	7	...	82	62
1958	219	69	95	142	8	...	81	66
1959	200	62	110	141	8	...	79	64
1960	203	63	105	141	7	...	79	63
1961	206	44	121	136	6	...	72	62
1962	209	39	128	125	4	...	68	57
1963	200	41	134	115	5	...	69	57
1964	216	42	128	105	4	...	61	64
1965	227	34	147	99	4	...	57	65
1966	212	30	160	91	4	...	59	67
1967	199	27	154	97	5	...	62	78
1968	203	27	154	87	5	...	55	90
1969	199	22	155	84	6	...	50	90

See p.250 for footnotes

D1 Area of Main Cereal, Potato, and Sugar Beet Crops (in thousands of hectares)

1945–1969

BULGARIA

	Wheat	Rye	Barley	Oats	Maize	P's	SB
1945	1,283	151	169	145	728	30	31
1946	1,332	154	165	127	726	18	34
1947	1,260	162	191	156	760	14	18
1948	1,461	229	212	145	802	19	35
1949	...	...	...	...	...	...	31
1950	1;449	230	245	162	654	30	39
1951	...	...	...	...	...	...	32
1952	1,424	229	259	155	487	36	42
1953	...	...	...	...	...	...	...
1954	1,392	175	257	161	716	36	50
1955	1,368	167	289	159	742	31	48
1956	1,375	143	259	151	791	28	56
1957	1,439	133	253	162	759	31	63
1958	1,435[42] / 1,445	110	259	166	697	34	61
1959	1,402	91	267	181	736	37	65
1960	1,257	78	296	180	634	43	66
1961	1,317	71	305	160	635	41	67
1962	1,249	59	303	152	651	43	66
1963	1,188	57	343	133	660	43	68
1964	1,194	58	358	130	658	41	77
1965	1,145	46	372	119	555	37	66
1966	1,142	41	416	113	574	34	62
1967	1,064	31	387	120	567	33	61
1968	1,060	24	402	96	557	31	55
1969	1,039	24	412	76	578	29	59

CZECHOSLAVAKIA

	Wheat	Rye	Barley	Oats	Maize	P's	SB
1945	852	809	530	576	127	654	158
1946	900	786	546	600	121	640	175
1947	835	709	569	587[38]	128	600	183
1948	869	738	585	678	142	551	182
1949	797	710	572	630	129	569	194
1950	755	626	614	627	129	660	221
1951	740	552	634	569	139	666	244
1952	766	564	624	541	139	669	232
1953	748	534	649	547	149	636	232
1954	712	525	629	506	147	630	215
1955	720	513	642	526	160	621	216
1956	722	515	668	539	183	630	222
1957	742	519	670	536	169	629	227
1958	738	498	669	507	180	607	234
1959	720	476	672	507	187	585	242
1960	652	431	707	504	195	569	242
1961	643	463	696	494	201	515	252
1962	673	441	694	486	237	508	260
1963	720	426	692	453	213	503	259
1964	831	406	686	434	186	491	257
1965	826	411	667	422	161	444	230
1966	892	395	690	434	151	437	230
1967	929	321	712	481	150	408	206
1968	999	339	712	444	138	372	197
1969	1,054	275	780	432	127	325	183

DENMARK

	Wheat	Rye	Barley	Oats	M C	P's	SB
1945	87	161	408	336	304	107	39
1946	90	139	415	346	300	103	43
1947	24	105	466	343	321	106	44
1948	69	167	441	330	284	138	49
1949	83	195	455	308	285	106	63
1950	85	154	494	277	267	105	73
1951	81	119	519	274	262	105	71
1952	74	137	567	268	280	109	72
1953	71	131	622	244	284	107	61
1954	85	112	609	247	286	97	55
1955	67	77	611	266	306	94	40
1956	66	109	648	255	290	96	47
1957	64	116	691	236	288	88	54
1958	77	123	721	203	268	83	91
1959	88	121	752	204	264	87	55
1960	82	157	756	198	252	92	55
1961	105	183	799	195	254	72	39
1962	154	174	830	164	221	62	42
1963	135	116	938	186	195	64	69
1964	128	93	950	211	186	54	84
1965	126	88	1,041	203	138	41	60
1966	94	46	1,112	234	119	40	58
1967	90	37	1,170	243	97	37	53
1968	97	38	1,254	218	78	35	52
1969	98	38	1,305	205	58	34	52

FINLAND

	Wheat	Rye	Barley	Oats	M C	P's	SB
1945	139	149	137	309	5.3	70	3
1946	158	147	140	321	5,5	77	4
1947	161	157	138	371	8.6	91	5
1948	166	144	132	404	15	104	6
1949	159	145	124	424	18	87	7
1950	189	133	115	437	15	96	10
1951	162	122	130	437	19	94	10
1952	137	119	146	473	19	97	11
1953	125	91	169	479	16	93	10
1954	150	93	165	487	17	88	15
1955	124	86	177	467	24	86	16
1956	133	89	193	464	28	93	15
1957	113	85	221	414	26	95	12
1958	127	76	223	442	25	86	13
1959	139	103	233	461	28	85	15
1960	181	111	213	490	24	86	15
1961	237	94	201	473	25	77	18
1962	286	82	205	456	31	74	20
1963	239	76	262	444	35	77	16
1964	268	103	252	470	32	71	20
1965	267	111	252	472	29	73	20
1966	249	93	321	479	30	68	17
1967	252	96	346	455	31	65	18
1968	241	72	359	489	31	65	15
1969	204	70	373	483	28	58	13

See p.250 for footnotes

D1 Area of Main Cereal, Potato, and Sugar Beet Crops (in thousands of hectares)

1945–1969

FRANCE

	Wheat	Rye	Barley	Oats	Maize	B'wheat	P's	SB
1945	3,783	375	689	2,509	221	138	802	197
1946	4,131	442	731	2,509	244	114	852	250
1947	3,393	444	959	2,611	269	120	1,006	292
1948	4,231	565	820	2,439	294	124	1,047	309
1949	4,223	522	896	2,436	304	111	982	400
1950	4,319	504	962	2,353	325	99	988	395
1951	4,250	461	1,019	2,272	349	101	974	407
1952	4,297	431	1,075	2,275	349	93	938	424
1953	4,219	408	1,203	2,270	375	93	950	413
1954	4,491	405	1,231	2,154	411	84	955	380
1955	4,554	387	1,313	2,077	453	75	938	374
1956	2,745	371	2,283	2,277	653	74	962	376
1957	4,668	364	1,643	1,608	544	66	897	347
1958	4,615	347	1,782	1,487	590	60	884	365
1959	4,439	328	1,989	1,504	704	49	887	387
1960	4,358	299	2,089	1,427	824	46	880	428
1961	3,997	261	2,259	1,442	975	45	878	359
1962	4,571	243	2,177	1,356	866	41	852	352
1963	3,850	232	2,539	1,287	952	45	834	371
1964	4,388	220	2,360	1,094	893	35	680	425
1965	4.520	221	2,430	1,070	871	33	564	395
1966	3,992	198	2,642	1,094	964	28	526	295
1967	3,929	175	2,818	1,040	1,016	22	504	314
1968	4,090	163	2,781	949	1,024	18	459	404
1969	4,034	154	2,859	851	1,185	17	409	401

WEST GERMANY[43 44]

	Wheat	Rye	Barley	Oats	M C & B'wheat	P's	Sugar Beet
1945	...	...	...	...	...	...	...
1946	...	...	...	...	...	...	...
1947	...	...	...	...	...	...	...
1948	...	...	...	...	...	...	...
1949	922	1,415	496	1,398		1,124	167
1950	1,013	1,363	613	1,158	249	1,141	193
1951	1,030	1,290	643	1,131	267	1,117	223
1952	1,193	1,356	707	1,112	285	1,147	222
1953	1,155	1,394	788	1,055	340	1,163	224
1954	1,107	1,530	733	943	450	1,190	254
1955	1,171	1,474	779	969	476	1,128	262
1956	1,153[43]	1,483[43]	851[43]	951[43]	495[43]	1,135[43]	269[43]
1957	1,231	1,475	872	905	405	1,133	259
1958	1,315	1,503	881	837	412	1,074	284
1959	1,342	1,426	951	812	431	1,054	287
1960	1,396	1,318	980	748	454	1,042	294
1961	1,397	1,184	1,120	723	475	976	260
1962	1,319	1,092	1,138	805	531	963	290
1963	1,382	1,139	1,144	770	481	925	301
1964	1,447	1,146	1,153	766	467	851	327
1965	1,412	1,128	1,193	727	438	783	299
1966	1,389	1,021	1,288	777	433	732	294
1967	1,414	975	1,308	808	425	707	294
1968	1,464	962	1,330	821	450	659	290
1969	1,494	873	1,387	860	456	589	295

EAST GERMANY

	Wheat	Rye	Barley	Oats	M C & B'wheat	P's	Sugar Beet
1945	...	...	...	...	...	...	...
1946	443	1,092	321	680	206	770	207
1947	335	1,180	298	655	230	732	213
1948	474	1,296	251	563	159	805	212
1949	469	1,304	253	530	139	813	217
1950	479	1,294	261	531	149	812	224
1951	464	1,277	264	553	155	831	224
1952	476	1,291	266	549	152	829	217
1953	420	1,223	317	585	154	833	213
1954	424	1,215	311	517	148	834	216
1955	400	1,074	337	536	132	843	215
1956	380	1,110	322	448	174	783	201
1957	420	1,098	321	455	208	810	219
1958	440	1,094	337	427	207	769	223
1959	435	1,031	354	410	210	771	234
1960	418	946	389	359	205	770	238
1961	377	825	432	351	247	682	218
1962	423	811	374	372	265	742	232
1963	426	820	424	315	252	747	232
1964	433	823	464	295	272	745	230
1965	491	822	497	260	234	725	221
1966	484	771	521	261	230	694	211
1967	533	746	553	270	212	686	209
1968	570	735	595	256	188	672	204
1969	560	690	642	272	182	604	192

See p.250 for footnotes

D1 Area of Main Cereal, Potato, and Sugar Beet Crops (in thousands of hectares)

1945–1969

GREECE

	Wheat	Rye	Barley	Oats	Maize	Mixed Corn	P's
1945	676	43	139	119	206	46	16
1946	751	58	170	122	264	55	26
1947	844	...	...	...	...	52	...
1948	843	57	205	141	246	56	29
1949	763	44	205	135	224	47	36
1950	867	55	206	147	248	42	34
1951	954	64	209	153	253	47	38
1952	965	66	215	153	255	44	39
1953	1,045	68	215	149	269	40	39
1954	1,045	62	211	138	253	36	40
1955	1,040	58	207	146	228	34	41
1956	1,062	53	206	147	228	32	40
1957	1,088	47	199	147	216	31	42
1958	1,111	43	195	143	204	28	39
1959	1,163	33	185	129	206	16	43
1960	1,142	29	181	128	210	18	38
1961	1,173	25	189	149	191	13	56
1962	1,193	22	185	144	166	12	57
1963	1,078	20	175	126	185	7	57
1964	1,263	18	167	119	150	7	58
1965	1,258	16	203	120	144	8	56
1966	1,132	14	284	118	139	6	55
1967	1,051	11	351	111	133	5	56
1969	1,098	8	332	92	147	4	54
1969	1,078	8	282	84	149	4	55

HUNGARY

Wheat	Rye	Barley	Oats	Maize	P's	SB
735	370	519	211	1,221	302	20
1,091	454	464	202	1,159	256	54
1,375	532	444	220	1,329	279	92
1,366	614	434	215	1,325	274	112
1,392	650	466	195	1,124	282	113
1,375	597	479	187	1,151	279	112
1,394	575	447	151	1,153	203	118
1,372	509	437	131	1,054	225	112
1,320	436	407	124	1,161	199	125
1,410	466	415	124	1,210	236	104
1,358	447	404	121	1,291	230	112
1,389	441	407	118	1,162	220	114
1,247	421	482	172	1,346	241	83
1,188	376	538	173	1,304	240	109
1,116	353	541	170	1,358	230	122
1,051	301	508	141	1,401	253	133
1,014	268	522	110	1,340	240	130
1,095	232	548	84	1,288	209	125
1,005	209	486	90	1,289	232	118
1,148	247	522	71	1,209	210	133
1,125	246	501	57	1,218	207	121
1,072	220	489	61	1,237	198	108
1,160	204	447	55	1,237	169	104
1,328	190	385	54	1,259	150	104
1,324	183	381	48	1,255	140	97

IRELAND (Southern Ireland from 1922)

	Wheat	Barley	Oats	P's	Sugar Beet
1945	268	69	338	157	34
1946	260	58	336	158	32
1947	235	59	334	155	25
1948	210	49	356	156	27
1949	147	64	278	142	24
1950	148	50	248	136	24
1951	114	68	251	130	24
1952	103	91	247	125	22
1953	143	76	231	125	26
1954	197	66	216	118	30
1955	145	86	221	116	22
1956	138	96	212	115	24
1957	164	124	187	108	29
1958	170	125	185	106	34
1959	114	135	187	105	28
1960	148	133	172	95	28
1961	140	146	149	86	32
1962	127	164	140	85	32
1963	94	133	134	83	36
1964	87	143	117	74	32
1965	74	188	115	70	27
1966	53	187	98	68	22
1967	77	183	96	65	26
1968	90	184	88	59	26
1969	83	198	77	55	25

NORTHERN IRELAND

Wheat	Barley	Oats	Potatoes
0.7	5.8	181	77
1.0	3.1	167	78
0.7	2.6	154	74
1.8	2.3	158	85
0.8	2.3	151	76
0.8	1.5	140	72
0.5	1.2	128	58
0.8	2.2	122	55
0.9	2.5	117	56
0.8	2.1	108	53
0.5	2.0	102	47
1.1	2.5	104	51
1.6	5.2	96	42
1.6	6.5	88	40
1.0	11	81	39
1.4	24	82	35
2.0	45	74	31
1.7	52	66	31
1.0	60	59	33
1.3	67	51	29
1.5	74	39	25
1.2	70	33	23
1.0	62	33	23
0.8	56	30	20
1.1	55	23	17

D1 Area of Main Cereal, Potato, and Sugar Beet Crops (in thousands of hectares)

1945–1969

ITALY

	Wheat	Rye	Barley	Oats	Maize	Rice	Potatoes	SB
1945	4,481	94	239	434	1,307	97	392	29
1946	4,622	99	238	443	1,259	118	398	101
1947	4,499	98	242	480	1,228	132	419	110
1948	4,665[29]	99[29]	251[29]	476[29]	1,244[29]	143[29]	406[29]	113[29]
1949	4,729	99	250	469	1,239	129	390	131
1950	4,719	98	251	473	1,241	143	383	174
1951	4,728	96	251	462	1,267	156	386	198
1952	4,682	94	253	465	1,273	174	393	222
1953	4,770	93	250	457	1,272	176	393	210
1954	4,770	86	248	452	1,274	179	397	224
1955	4,852	80	244	434	1,237	169	391	258
1956	4,883	74	237	423	1,257	138	387	225
1957	4,911	71	229	420	1,251	126	386	210
1958	4,839	68	224	414	1,217	134	384	247
1959	4,665	68	221	412	1,193	136	386	287
1960	4,556	63	216	409	1,190	129	379	245
1961	4,345	60	220	428	1,197	123	379	227
1962	4,556	56	210	411	1,120	118	377	226
1963	4,394	53	204	400	1,121	115	386	230
1964	4,408	51	197	384	1,072	120	356	231
1965	4,288	48	186	367	1,028	126	348	282
1966	4,274	46	179	359	988	132	347	298
1967	4,012	46	181	358	1,017	144	339	345
1968	4,275	42	175	323	967	156	319	306
1969	4,218	38	175	312	999	169	306	291

NETHERLANDS

	Wheat	Rye	Barley	Oats	B'wheat	Potatoes	SB
1945	119	216	48	148	...	181	18
1946	122	225	62	177	...	203	45
1947	86	181	68	163	...	216	51
1948	99	184	53	142	...	236	47
1949	104[45]	190[45]	49[45]	135[45]	...	197[45]	68[45]
	98	182	47	130		...	...
1950	91	175	69	141	...	175	67
1951	75	161	65	154	...	165	66
1952	82	184	69	153	...	170	63
1953	65	172	103	157	...	158	68
1954	110	167	63	143	...	170	79
1955	89	154	70	171	...	153	67
1956	86	171	74	154	...	146	69
1957	99	157	72	159	...	145	65
1958	111	145	82	137	...	140	81
1959	120	144	72	126	...	145	93
1960	128	153	69	115	...	148	93
1961	123	120	103	123	...	133	85
1962	133	107	100	119	...	130	77
1963	127	106	101	113	...	124	70
1964	151	106	87	103	...	124	79
1965	158	98	99	101	...	125	92
1966	148	74	120	99	...	131	92
1967	154	73	107	88	...	138	100
1968	153	75	107	76	...	147	104
1969	155	62	99	83	...	145	103

NORWAY

	Wheat	Rye	Barley	Oats	MC	P's
1945	48	2.7	42	86	5.4	65
1946	38	2.5	41	84	4.7	62
1947	29	1.3	39	76	3.8	57
1948	33	1.3	37	74	4	65
1949	31	1.0	40	76	4	58
1950	32	1.2	42	78	4	59
1951	24	0.6	55	77	4	59
1952	21	0.5	64	80	3	58
1953	17	0.6	81	72	3	56
1954	20	0.7	93	71	2	55
1955	18	0.6	101	68	3	56
1956	21	0.9	109	66	2	58
1957	14	0.6	135	61	2	55
1958	8.0	0.5	145	57	2	53
1959	9.3	1.1	141	65	2	55
1960	9.2	1.4	145	65	2	57
1961	9.7	0.9	154	62	2	53
1962	9.7	1.8	164	53	1	50
1963	7.0	1.1	179	44	1	52
1964	7.2	0.7	182	52	1	49
1965	4.3	0.6	189	46	1	48
1966	2	...	188	41	1	45
1967	3	1	179	45	1	40
1968	5	1	176	50	1	38
1969	4	1	185	54	1	35

See p.250 for footnotes

D1 Area of Main Cereal, Potato, and Sugar Beet Crops (in thousands of hectares)

1945–1969

POLAND

	Wheat	Rye	Barley	Oats	Potatoes	SB
1945	614	3,564	708	1,294	1,840	201
1946	700	3,083	748	1,100	1,665	170
1947	1,112	4,632	930	1,562	2,303	210
1948	1,384	5,088	863	1,756	2,478	224
1949	1,445	5,166	841	1,775	2,538	261
1950	1,480	5,080	835	1,698	2,616	287
1951	1,524	5,027	814	1,630	2,606	319
1952	1,488	4,954	827	1,691	2,619	349
1953	1,498	4,755	877	1,710	2,563	362
1954	1,559	4,799	839	1,634	2,648	381
1955	1,431	4,952	822	1,641	2,702	392
1956	1,464	4,964	777	1,595	2,714	364
1957	1,441	5,066	777	1,738	2,763	339
1958	1,474	5,213	742	1,709	2,758	358
1959	1,435	5,202	644	1,686	2,788	376
1960	1,361	5,122	717	1,641	2,876	401
1961	1,401	4,880	680	1,602	2,819	420
1962	1,393	4,700	663	1,584	2,910	430
1963	1,542	4,383	749	1,682	2,840	372
1964	1,640	4,417	745	1,574	2,845	444
1965	1,660	4,494	700	1,349	2,803	476
1966	1,679	4,331	683	1,398	2,732	435
1967	1,758	4,299	653	1,428	2,763	434
1968	1,886	4,300	634	1,395	2,747	414
1969	1,965	4,174	759	1,367	2,718	410

PORTUGAL

Wheat	Rye	Barley	Oats	Maize	Rice	Potatoes
618	253	123	270	441	22	63
654	287	128	292	502	26	64
680	285	131	295	504	26	96
698	280	130	312	523	28	87
688	270	140	316	483	28	83
680	265	146	292	494	27	88
673	268	153	290	457	31	93
708	267	157	293	488	34	90
756	266	158	298	475	33	89
779	255	157	293	469	36	89
806	254	151	301	470	38	89
786	254	154	302	487	39	89
814	255	155	309	483	37	90
812	253	152	303	479	35	85
847	272	137	304	481	36	89
738	269	120	302	468	37	92
658	299	127	268	495	38	108
728	309	134	288	503	37	102
740	319	126	296	488	37	107
685	312	110	242	496	38	109
628	316	126	271	484	35	101
523	282	111	218	473	35	101
586	239	107	226	436	32	117
614	239	135	224	438	33	105
568	236	119	218	427	38	107

ROMANIA

	Wheat	Rye	Barley	Oats	Maize	P's	SB
1945	1,890[33]	107[33]	596[33]	627[33]	2,659[33]	191[33]	37[33]
1946	2,739	140	618	638	3,357	206	...
1947	1,660[46]	87[46]	410[46]	510[46]	4,308[46]	230[46]	56[46]
1948	2,545	113	479	566	3,673	172	67
1949	...	...	...	...	...	180[46]	64[46]
1950	2,785	204	534	520	2,853	229	72
1951	2,807	212	510	467	2,871	243	90
1952	2,776	207	502	473	2,960	243	100
1953	2,758	216	518	484	2,887	243	112
1954	2,457	195	438	435	3,302	250	107
1955	2,948	202	390	385	3,265	258	145
1956	2,894	172	300	340	3,571	256	139
1957	2,968	155	303	352	3,722	265	131
1958	2,973	140	292	311	3,645	271	141
1959	2,988	119	280	300	3,555	276	201
1960	2,837	98	266	270	3,572	292	200
1961	2,969	90	284	244	3,428	293	172
1962	3,043	77	251	174	3,107	299	155
1963	2,874	80	224	130	3,379	319	179
1964	2,959	91	196	89	3,319	306	190
1965	2,983	102	233	116	3,306	298	190
1966	3,035	91	246	138	3,288	306	194
1967	2,913	62	257	127	3,221	315	176
1968	2,817	44	292	132	3,344	316	185
1969	2,759	42	307	131	3,293	305	188

RUSSIA (in million hectares)

Wheat	Rye	Barley	Oats	Maize	P's	SB
24.9	20.5	9.6	14.4	4.2	8.3	0.83
...	...	...	...	...	...	...
...	...	...	...	...	...	...
...	...	...	...	...	...	...
...	...	...	...	...	...	...
38.5	23.7	8.2	16.2	4.8	8.6	1.31
...	...	...	...	...	...	...
...	...	...	...	...	...	...
48.3	20.3	9.2	15.3	3.5	8.3	1.57
49.3	20.5	10.3	15.9	4.3	8.7	1.60
60.5	19.1	9.3	14.8	6.2	9.1	1.76
62.0	18.5	11.9	15.1	9.3	9.2	2.01
69.1	18.1	9.2	14.0	5.8	9.8	2.11
66.6	18.0	8.6	14.8	4.4	9.5	2.50
63.0	17.1	8.3	14.3	3.5	9.5	2.75
60.4	16.2	11.0	12.8	5.1	9.1	3.04
63.0	16.8	11.7	11.5	7.2	8.9	3.12
67.4	16.9	14.3	6.9	7.0	8.7	3.17
64.6	15.0	18.4	5.7	7.0	8.5	3.75
67.9	16.8	20.3	5.7	5.1	8.5	4.11
70.2	16.0	18.3	6.6	3.2	8.6	3.88
70.0	13.6	19.4	7.2	3.2	8.4	3.80
67.0	12.4	19.1	8.7	3.5	8.3	3.80
67.2	12.3	19.4	9.0	3.4	8.3	3.56
66.4	9.2	22.5	9.3	4.2	8.1	3.38

See p.250 for footnotes

D1 Area of Main Cereal, Potato, and Sugar Beet Crops (in thousands of hectares)

1949–1969

SPAIN

	Wheat	Rye	Barley	Oats	Maize	Rice	P's	SB
1945	3,766	599	1,594	703	308	48	370	58
1946	3,950	598	1,569	674	325	50	362	71
1947	4,017	607	1,544	640	326	51	359	65
1948	4,041	618	1,504	629	332	52	358	93
1949	4,086	613	1,554	626	332	54	359	93
1950	4,080	617	1,546	624	330	58	363	87
1951	4,214	635	1,567	642	333	63	377	110
1952	4,262	626	1,615	591	345	65	335	179
1953	4,256	598	1,604	602	370	68	342	118
1954	4,260	613	1,604	608	369	71	355	91
1955	4,288	604	1,539	612	357	67	354	98
1956	4,305	607	1,575	617	369	66	364	112
1957	4,378	570	1,533	586	376	67	372	102
1958	4,365	554	1,513	579	389	65	373	133
1959	4,368	540	1,452	572	405	67	400	144
1960	4,234	509	1,428	556	428	66	395	145
1961	3,880	485	1,450	583	447	62	416	158
1962	4,252	486	1,449	549	430	63	409	166
1963	4,239	438	1,447	527	487	63	411	116
1964	4,137	406	1,381	509	514	64	365	144
	[47]	[47]	[47]	[47]	[47]	[47]	[47]	[47]
1965	4,254	393	1,374	502	478	59	368	146
1966	4,185	384	1,338	469	482	59	375	157
1967	4,257	398	1,499	486	478	60	376	171
1968	3,958	366	1,923	508	523	60	382	174
1969	3,770	331	2,110	493	494	65	377	182

SWEDEN

	Wheat	Rye	Barley	Oats	MC	P's	SB
1945	291	168	93	543	277	145	55
1946	303	157	90	531	277	143	55
1947	293	115	100	529	288	142	48
1948	316	160	88	489	281	148	47
1949	307	135	86	502	309	135	49
1950	339	127	94	502	318	130	54
1951	324	97	113	496	319	121	54
1952	328	123	152	496	321	127	54
1953	387	132	189	487	302	127	51
1954	432	149	166	474	299	120	60
1955	353	94	213	509	301	122	53
1956	397	123	240	535	291	122	50
1957	333	115	263	515	272	119	54
1958	282	92	293	532	255	114	51
1959	315[48]	97[48]	317[48]	536[48]	247[48]	119[48]	51[48]
	313	96	315	526	243	108	----
1960	337	103	321	548	227	114	50
1961	273	74	356	558	221	99	49
1962	314	75	369	514	199	92	46
1963	244	40	482	517	191	94	41
1964	270	43	470	510	177	81	44
1965	288	63	498	478	156	73	43
1966	196	40	608	493	125	66	40
1967	256	62	571	488	103	67	39
1968	250	70	600	519	95	69	42
1969	267	73	639	513	84	65	40

SWITZERLAND

	Wheat	Rye	Barley	Oats	P's	SB
1945	112	13	32	44	84	5.6
1946	110	15	30	40	79	5.6
1947	105	13	27	35	67	5.5
1948	98	12	25	33	62	5.4
1949	95	12	24	31	53	5.5
1950	98	16	19	22	56	6.1
1951	98	16	20	24	55	5.9
1952	101	15	24	25	57	5.9
1953	95	15	25	26	57	5.8
1954	104	12	21	22	54	5.8
1955	109	11	22	21	51	5.5
1956	89	13	31	25	56	5.9
1957	105	11	25	19	52	5.9
1958	106	12	24	16	50	5.9
1959	112	13	25	16	50	5.3
1960	110	14	26	14	50	5.2
1961	116	11	29	15	48	5.1
1962	109	16	35	14	47	4.9
1963	108	16	32	12	45	6.9
1964	106	18	30	11	43	7.6
1965	107	15	31	10	37	8.4
1966	108	13	32	10	39	8
1967	100	15	31	9	38	9
1968	108	15	30	8	37	9
1969	107	11	37	10	33	9

See p.250 for footnotes

D1 Area of Main Cereal, Potato, and Sugar Beet Crops (in thousands of hectares)

1945–1969

UK GREAT BRITAIN

	Wheat	Barley	Oats	Other Corn[13]	Potatoes	Sugar Beet
1945	919	891	1,337	405	488	169
1946	834	892	1,276	400	498	176
1947	875	831	1,185	369	465	160
1948	921	841	1,192	432	541	167
1949	794	831	1,165	470	454	170
1950	1,002	718	1,117	531 365[13]	427	174
1951	862	771	1,028	358	367	172
1952	821	921	1,044	359	346	165
1953	896	898	1,033	351	342	168
1954	994	833	939	259	330	177
1955	788	927	943	194	306	172
1956	927	938	934	178	322	172
1957	853	1,056	853	145	287	174
1958	892	1,108	809	121	292	178
1959	780	1,227	742	99	291	176
1960	849	1,341	717	88	300	177
1961	737	1,504	627	66	254	173
1962	911	1,561	549	57	267	172
1963	779	1,847	465	48	278	171
1964	892	1,970	405	40	286	179
1965	1,024	2,109	371	36	275	184
1966	905	2,411	334	32	248	180
1967	932	2,377	377	38	264	185
1968	977	2,345	352	47	259	188
1969	832	2,358	359	62	231	185

YUGOSLAVIA

	Wheat	Rye	Barley	Oats	Maize	Potatoes	Sugar Beet
1945	...	...	...	...	...	...	...
1946	...	...	...	...	...	...	...
1947	... [49]	... [49]	... [49]	... [49]	... [49]	... [49]	... [49]
1948	1,887	249	319	348	2,370	197	79
1949	1,791	258	313	358	2,240	234	90
1950	1,787	256	325	389	2,210	241	98
1951	1,766	287	331	339	2,360	226	100
1952	1,838	295	317	334	2,290	240	76
1953	1,889	298	360	339	2,410	245	84
1954	1,854	276	331	341	2,460	256	79
1955	1,907	278	338	321	2,470	261	70
1956	1,624	252	353	373	2,570	268	70
1957	1,974	256	408	402	2,590	285	83
1958	1,994	248	390	347	2,390	277	71
1959	2,134	236	378	338	2,580	290	82
1960	2,064	213	363	334	2,570	288	79
1961	1,964	180	371	355	2,513	292	83
1962	2,134	177	351	310	2,464	301	78
1963	2,144	157	350	315	2,411	321	98
1964	2,103	157	369	306	2,431	320	89
1965	1,683	146	405	321	2,553	320	82
1966	1,833	141	394	320	2,502	333	106
1967	1,883	138	343	301	2,512	330	102
1968	2,012	132	312	285	2,462	332	79
1969	2,021	124	300	272	2,399	330	95

See p.250 for footnotes

D1 Area of Main Cereal, Potato, and Sugar Beet Crops (in thousands of hectares)

1970–1975

	Wheat	Rye	Barley	Oats	Maize	Other Cereals	Potatoes	Sugar Beet	Rice	Mixed Corn
AUSTRIA										
1970	275	136	290	102	124	34	110	44		
1971	274	145	295	98	125	33	105	39		
1972	274	144	296	96	132	32	101	48		
1973	266	123	318	94	147	34	84	51		
1974	269	123	319	92	149	34	82	54		
1975	270	119	316	101	144	39	69	60		
BELGIUM										
1970	181	20	169	72			46	89		6
1971	193	24	149	71			42	93		8
1972	204	21	149	67			37	101		8
1973	193	16	156	61			43	104		8
1974	190	13	149	60			40	105		8
1975	176	9	122	70			36	120		5
BULGARIA										
1970	1,014	22	403	71	635		31	58		
1971	1,013	19	434	75	655		29	45		
1972	961	17	446	65	689		30	57		
1973	934	15	458	46	623		27	61		
1974	861	15	477	47	523		31	60		
1975	819	17	575	50	652		30	78		
CZECHOSLAVAKIA										
1970	1,081	219	803	399	128		338	183		
1971	1,103	234	851	359	142		332	189		
1972	1,197	232	854	332	148		321	192		
1973	1,235	225	873	280	169		305	199		
1974	1,276	219	867	230	167		280	208		
1975	1,183	191	980	222	158		251	219		
DENMARK										
1970	114	44	1,352	184			37	47		44
1971	121	42	1,370	186			32	49		39
1972	135	43	1,406	163			29	56		31
1973	123	42	1,445	129			32	63		23
1974	111	46	1,437	122			33	67		18
1975	102	50	1,443	111			31	86		15

D1 Area of Main Cereal, Potato, and Sugar Beet Crops (in thousands of hectares)

1970–1975

FINLAND

	Wheat	Rye	Barley	Oats	Maize	Other Cereals	Potatoes	Sugar Beet	Rice	Mixed Corn	Buckwheat
1970	176	66	404	524			60	15		28	
1971	173	59	408	540			50	17		26	
1972	179	59	466	501			48	19		24	
1973	188	52	458	528			46	21		22	
1974	217	73	443	550			48	23		23	
1975	219	38	464	572			49	24		23	

FRANCE

	Wheat	Rye	Barley	Oats	Maize	Other Cereals	Potatoes	Sugar Beet	Rice	Mixed Corn	Buckwheat
1970	3,746	135	2,953	799	1,486		401	403			16
1971	3,978	129	2,671	831	1,642		363	425			15
1972	3,958	128	2,674	762	1,877		301	448			13
1973	3,960	122	2,799	693	1,942		309	512			11
1974	4,140	114	2,714	670	1,907		305	534			11
1975	3,876	110	2,770	655	1,960		279	598			10

WEST GERMANY

	Wheat	Rye	Barley	Oats	Maize	Other Cereals	Potatoes	Sugar Beet	Rice	Mixed Corn	Buckwheat
1970	1,493	865	1,475	825			597	303		426	
1971	1,544	865	1,505	836			554	315		384	
1972	1,626	843	1,549	808			503	331		359	
1973	1,603	739	1,671	821			480	352		345	
1974	1,631	708	1,665	851			467	369		335	
1975	1,569	624	1,756	920			415	426		327	

EAST GERMANY

	Wheat	Rye	Barley	Oats	Maize	Other Cereals	Potatoes	Sugar Beet	Rice	Mixed Corn	Buckwheat
1970	598	680	640	210			667	192		154	
1971	633	668	656	230			658	211		132	
1972	690	646	618	247			647	222		120	
1973	696	646	692	228			650	229		102	
1974	729	637	779	223			635	234		76	
1975	689	593	929	243			574	266		59	

GREECE

	Wheat	Rye	Barley	Oats	Maize	Other Cereals	Potatoes
1970	985	7	342	80	170		59
1971	979	7	381	81	166		51
1972	904	6	411	77	164		52
1973	841	5	412	72	167		56
1974	919	5	407	76	128		56
1975	925	5	395	70	127		57

D1 Area of Main Cereal, Potato, and Sugar Beet Crops (in thousands of hectares)

1970–1975

HUNGARY

	Wheat	Rye	Barley	Oats	Maize	Other Cereals	Potatoes	Sugar Beet	Rice	Mixed Corn
1970	1,274	149	284	44	1,189		137	76		
1971	1,273	127	298	45	1,321		129	73		
1972	1,317	120	291	48	1,392		118	79		
1973	1,294	107	287	37	1,461		106	92		
1974	1,324	106	271	33	1,461		108	98		
1975	1,251	104	257	45	1,413		100	127		

IRELAND (Southern Ireland from 1922)

	Wheat	Rye	Barley	Oats	Maize	Other Cereals	Potatoes	Sugar Beet
1970	95		214	68			57	26
1971	90		235	60			52	30
1972	68		252	52			44	34
1973	58		243	50			48	30
1974	55		246	44			40	26
1975	45		245	45			41	33

NORTHERN IRELAND

	Wheat	Rye	Barley	Oats	Maize	Other Cereals	Potatoes
1970	1.2		50	18			19
1971	1.0		57	15			17
1972	0.9		51	12			15
1973	0.6		48	10			14
1974	0.6		49	9			12
1975	0.6		50	9			11

ITALY

	Wheat	Rye	Barley	Oats	Maize	Other Cereals	Potatoes	Sugar Beet	Rice
1970	4,138	35	179	303	1,026		286	281	173
1971	3,910	29	185	277	934		237	254	175
1972	3,804	18	186	250	891		194	250	183
1973	3,590	18	203	238	890		182	235	190
1974	3,712	17	224	236	890		181	196	188
1975	3,545	17	249	239	897		179	271	174

NETHERLANDS

	Wheat	Rye	Barley	Oats	Maize	Other Cereals	Potatoes	Sugar Beet
1970	142	57	105	55			158	104
1971	142	60	98	45			154	102
1972	156	54	83	33			149	113
1973	138	31	90	30			157	117
1974	130	22	73	33			158	109
1975	107	18	83	34			151	137

D1 Area of Main Cereal, Potato, and Sugar Beet Crops (in thousands of hectares)

1970–1975

NORWAY

	Wheat	Rye	Barley	Oats	Maize	Other Cereals	Potatoes	Sugar Beet	Rice	Mixed Corn
1970	4	2	184	68			34			—
1971	3	1	179	84			31			—
1972	4	1	181	86			29			—
1973	5	2	172	101			29			1
1974	14	3	170	103			30			1
1975	16	1	180	103			25			...

POLAND

	Wheat	Rye	Barley	Oats	Maize	Other Cereals	Potatoes	Sugar Beet	Rice	Mixed Corn
1970	1,985	3,413	924	1,531			2,732	409		
1971	2,061	3,711	899	1,330			2,669	421		
1972	2,048	3,543	1,017	1,359			2,656	438		
1973	1,962	3,416	1,083	1,271			2,678	445		
1974	2,002	3,137	1,230	1,182			2,684	440		
1975	1,842	2,792	1,335	1,291			2,581	496		

PORTUGAL

	Wheat	Rye	Barley	Oats	Maize	Other Cereals	Potatoes	Sugar Beet	Rice	Mixed Corn
1970	602	233	105	193	418		112		42	
1971	509	225	92	168	393		109		42	
1972	480	226	89	168	390		112		43	
1973	442	207	81	157	372		109		39	
1974	462	210	94	171	360		112		33	
1975	462	210	101	207	372		115		30	

ROMANIA

	Wheat	Rye	Barley	Oats	Maize	Other Cereals	Potatoes	Sugar Beet	Rice	Mixed Corn
1970	2,321	45	288	131	3,084		286	170		
1971	2,501	48	330	128	3,131		290	178		
1972	2,523	42	327	121	3,197		296	197		
1973	2,359	34	315	105	2,957		284	235		
1974	2,396	33	403	85	2,963		295	219		
1975	2,351	35	442	70	3,305		289	247		

RUSSIA (in million hectares)

	Wheat	Rye	Barley	Oats	Maize	Other Cereals	Potatoes	Sugar Beet	Rice	Mixed Corn
1970	65.2	10.0	21.3	9.3	3.4		8.1	3.37		
1971	64.0	9.5	21.6	9.6	3.3		7.9	3.32		
1972	58.5	8.2	27.3	11.4	4.0		8.0	3.49		
1973	63.2	7.0	29.4	11.9	4.0		8.0	3.55		
1974	59.7	9.8	31.1	11.6	4.0		8.0	3.61		
1975	62.0	8.0	32.5	12.1	2.7		7.9	3.67		

D1 **Area of Main Cereal, Potato, and Sugar Beet Crops** (in thousands of hectares)

1970–1975

SPAIN

	Wheat	Rye	Barley	Oats	Maize	Other Corn	Potatoes	Sugar Beet	Rice	Mixed Corn
1970	3,754	313	2,220	467	530		398	217	64	
1971	3,655	294	2,371	463	543		394	199	61	
1972	3,587	278	2,519	467	534		401	207	59	
1973	3,151	268	2,773	472	523		409	190	61	
1974	3,163	249	3,027	475	501		407	142	61	
1975	2,661	228	3,262	457	485		376	200	62	

SWEDEN

	Wheat	Rye	Barley	Oats	Maize	Other Corn	Potatoes	Sugar Beet	Rice	Mixed Corn
1970	265	80	610	509			54	40		76
1971	246	83	604	526			50	40		69
1972	270	108	624	539			47	42		71
1973	292	96	642	509			46	42		77
1974	340	110	638	468			48	47		77
1975	303	98	649	497			43	52		71

SWITZERLAND

	Wheat	Rye	Barley	Oats	Maize	Other Corn	Potatoes	Sugar Beet	Rice	Mixed Corn
1970	104	13	41	8			30	9		
1971	97	13	39	10			28	9		
1972	97	13	42	9			27	10		
1973	91	11	44	10			25	10		
1974	88	10	46	11			24	11		
1975	90	6	45	13			25	11		

UK GREAT BRITAIN

	Wheat	Rye	Barley	Oats	Maize	Other Corn	Potatoes	Sugar Beet	Rice	Mixed Corn
1970	1,009		2,193	358		77 78[13]	251	188		
1971	1,096		2,232	347		61	239	191		
1972	1,126		2,237	303		68	222	190		
1973	1,145		2,227	265		64	209	194		
1974	1,232		2,165	244		61	203	195		
1975	1,033		2,295	224		66	193	195		

YUGOSLAVIA

	Wheat	Rye	Barley	Oats	Maize	Other Corn	Potatoes	Sugar Beet	Rice	Mixed Corn
1970	1,833	112	280	283	2,352		346	85		
1971	1,930	110	280	265	2,425		326	85		
1972	1,925	104	290	256	2,383		315	79		
1973	1,657	96	328	251	2,377		317	86		
1974	1,843	91	330	249	2,256		321	104		
1975	1,616	84	360	270	2,363		315	107		

See p.250 for footnotes

D1 Area of Main Cereal, Potato, and Sugar Beet Crops (in thousands of hectares)

NOTES

1. SOURCES:– The official publications noted on p. xv; International Institute of Agriculture, *Yearbook of Agricultural Statistics;* and F.A.O., *Yearbook of Food and Agricultural Statistics.* Belgian data for 1919–21 and for 1940 were taken from a pamphlet, *Statistiques Agricoles 1900–1961,* kindly sent to me by the Belgian National Institute of Statistics. Netherlands data for oats in 1852 and 1865 and for potatoes in 1852 were supplied by the Dutch Central Office of Statistics. Polish data for 1951 and 1952 were supplied by the Polish Central Statistical Office.

2. Most statistics are of areas sown, or, to be more precise, of areas under crops on a particular date during the summer. Some series may be of areas harvested, and where this is known it is indicated in footnotes.

FOOTNOTES

[1] Prior to 1836, and from 1871 to 1880, millet is included.

[2] Including spelt.

[3] The areas in 1837 can be estimated as follows, assuming the same ratios of seed used to areas as in 1861:–

Wheat	Rye	Barley	Oats	Buckwheat
24	206	233	215	25

[4] Subsequent returns were made by cantonal commissions instead of mayors.

[5] Subsequently includes Savoy and Nice.

[6] From 1871 to 1918 the parts of Alsace and Lorraine ceded to Germany are excluded. Areas in these parts in 1919 were as follows:–

Wheat	Rye	Barley	Oats	Maize
104	41	47	98	3

[7] From 1871 to 1917 Alsace-Lorraine is included. From 1918 to 1944 statistics relate to the boundaries of the day, except that Austria and the Sudetenland are never included. Saarland is included from 1935.

[8] Figures to 1918 apply to Transleithania (excluding Croatia-Slavonia). Subsequently they are for the territory established by the treaty of Trianon.

[9] Including mixed corn, but excluding summer rye to 1871 (1st line).

[10] Statistics for 1835 are available as follows:–

Wheat	Rye	Barley	Oats	Mixed Corn	Potatoes
0.7	6.1	33	70	16	15

[11] Figures to 1894 (1st line) apply to the 50 provinces of European Russia (excluding Finland, Poland, and the Caucasus). From 1894 (2nd line) to 1909 (1st line) Poland is also included, though the sugar beet statistics relate to the whole Russian Empire. From 1909 (2nd line) to 1913 (1st line) the figures apply to the whole Empire. From 1913 (2nd line) to 1939 they apply to the U.S.S.R. as constituted in 1924, except that for 1920–23 they exclude central Asia, Transcaucasia, and the Far East. From 1940 the figures apply to the present territory of the U.S.S.R.

[12] Figures to 1893 include fodder beet.

[13] **Rye, mixed corn, beans, and peas to 1950 (1st line). Subsequently only rye and mixed corn for threshing, with maize from 1970**

[14] Excluding part of Kustenland and Galicia, and of Bukovina in 1914 and 1916.

[15] Subsequent figures are for the Republic. Statistics for 1917 and 1918 are available for the provinces later forming the Republic, but including those parts of Carinthia, Styria and Lower Austria which were incorporated in Yugoslavia and Czechoslovakia. They are as follows (in thousands) with the 1913 figures for comparison:–

	Wheat	Rye	Barley	Oats	Maize	Other Cereals	Potatoes	Sugar Beet
1913	197	407	132	347	49	40	161	18
1917	166	332	109	283	49	35	133	9
1918	162	313	103	264	46	33	166	9

[16] Subsequent figures include Burgenland, which was previously part of Hungary.

[17] A different series was given in post-Second World War publications, as follows:–

	Wheat	Rye	Barley	Oats	Potatoes	Sugar Beet
1929	153	186	25	231	153	53

[18] Figures for 1941–44 exclude the Eupen and Malmédy areas, and are reckoned to be underestimates owing to concealment by farmers.

[19] There was a change in the basis of reckoning.

[20] Subsequent statistics include southern Dobrudja, acquired from Romania in 1940.

[21] Subsequent figures include South Jutland, acquired from Germany.

[22] Statistics for 1930–38 are for rural communes only. Statistics which include the towns are available for 1933, as follows:–

Wheat	Rye	Barley	Oats	Mixed Corn	Potatoes
107	145	355	388	324	78

[23] Prior to this a certain amount of fodder beet is included.

[24] Subsequent statistics are of beets sown for sugar production only.

[25] Excluding the invaded departments from 1914–1918 (Italy in 1948 only).

[26] From 1939 to 1944 parts of Alsace and Lorraine annexed by Germany are excluded, and in 1943 and 1944 Corsica is excluded.

[27] Statistics are available for 1860 for the boundaries of the day, as follows:–

Wheat	Rye	Barley	Oats	Maize	Mixed Corn
120	3	46	5	70	46

[28] The following boundary changes affected the area covered between 1911 and 1921:– 1911–4 parts of Thessaly, Epiros, Macedonia, and Thrace and some islands were acquired; 1914–5 Macedonia was temporarily lost; 1916–7 western Macedonia was recovered; 1918–9 present mainland frontiers were achieved, but Thrace was not included in the statistics; 1921–2 Thrace included.

[29] Figures to 1921 apply to the boundaries of 1871; for 1922–43 they apply to the 1924 boundaries; and from 1944 they apply to the boundaries of 1954, except that Trieste is not included until 1949.

[30] The area of potatoes for human consumption is available for these and neighbouring years as follows:–

1915	144	1917	174	1919	180	1921	153
1916	172	1918	178	1920	173		

[31] Figures from 1940 are for postwar boundaries. Those for the war years are only rough estimates.

[32] The following boundary changes affected the area covered between 1913 and 1921:– 1914 Dobrudja acquired; 1918 Bessarabia acquired; 1920 Bukovina, Transylvania, part of the Banat, and parts of Hungary proper acquired.

[33] Southern Dobrudja was ceded to Bulgaria in 1940. Bessarabia and northern Bukovina were ceded to the U.S.S.R. in 1940, but were temporarily reconquered in 1943 and are apparently included in the statistics for 1944. Northern Transylvania was ceded to Hungary in 1940 was reacquired by 1946.

[34] Previously excluding Memel.

[35] Figures are available for 1855 as follows:–

Wheat	Rye	Barley	Potatoes
2,959	1,199	1,288	204

[36] Including potatoes in market gardens.

[37] Small areas previously classified under this heading were subsequently put into a "pasture" category.

[38] Subsequently including mixed corn.

[39] The Scottish component of field beans for fodder was no longer included.

[40] Some fields previously classified as oats or barley are subsequently assigned to the Mixed Corn category.

[41] Area sown rather than area harvested.

[42] Subsequently including spelt.

[43] West Berlin and Saarland are not included until 1957, in which year the areas in these parts were as follows:–

Wheat	Rye	Barley	Oats	Mixed Corn	Potatoes
11	10	4	12	4	13

[44] Only negligible amounts of maize were grown until the 1960's, during which the area of that crop has developed as follows:–

1961	8	1964	18	1967	42
1962	13	1965	27	1968	58
1963	13	1966	31	1969	81

[45] Previously the statistics are of cadastral area, and subsequently of nett area.

[46] These statistics are described by the F.A.O. as "doubtful".

[47] The basis changed from area sown to area harvested.

[48] Subsequently excluding farms of less than 2 hectares.

[49] Territory was acquired from Italy after the Second World War.

D2 OUTPUT OF MAIN CEREAL, POTATO, AND SUGAR BEET CROPS

(in thousands of hectolitres or metric tons)

1802–1834

FRANCE (thousands of metric tons)

	Wheat	Rye[1]	Barley[1]	Oats[1]	Maize[1]	B'wheat[1]	P's[1]
1802	...	...	...	...	...	...	...
1803	...	...	...	...	...	...	...
1804	...	...	...	...	...	...	...
1805	...	...	...	...	...	...	...
1806	...	...	...	...	...	...	...
1807	...	...	...	...	...	...	...
1808	...	...	...	...	...	...	...
1809	...	...	...	...	...	...	...
1810	...	...	...	...	...	...	...
1811	...	...	...	...	...	...	...
1812	...	...	...	...	...	...	...
1813	...	...	...	...	...	...	...
1814	...	...	...	...	...	...	...
1815	2,960	1,400	830	1,710	410	340	1,630
1816	3,250	1,490	890	1,810	290	230	1,960
1817	3,600	1,590	1,070	1,920	410	410	3,610
1818	3,950	1,750	840	1,400	430	210	2,220
1819	4,490	2,190	1,070	1,850	640	...	2,900
1820	3,330	1,800	1,240	1,960	410	500	3,090
1821	4,370	2,150	1,140	2,040	350	510	3,260
1822	3,810	1,920	900	1,660	420	540	3,140
1823	4,400	2,120	1,130	2,040	450	420	3,400
1824	4,630	2,120	1,090	2,120	410	470	3,540
1825	4,580	1,890	920	1,580	460	390	...
1826	4,470	2,110	980	1,780	500	480	...
1827	4,260	1,960	1,000	1,990	350	450	...
1828	4,410	2,120	1,030	1,960	440	630	...
1829	4,820	2,320	1,000	1,960	460	510	4,130
1830	3,960	1,910	1,280	2,460	510	480	4,170
1831	4,230	1,960	1,160	2,500	520	660	5,210
1832	6,010	2,700	1,190	2,190	280	390	3,800
1833	4,960	2,430	1,020	2,010	510	380	5,660
1834	4,650	2,090	1,120	2,130	590	660	5,780

Abbreviations used where space demands:— B'wheat: Buckwheat; M C: Mixed Corn; M C & B: Mixed Corn and Buckwheat; P's: Potatoes; S B: Sugar Beet

See p.296 for footnotes

SWEDEN (thousands of metric tons)

	Wheat	Rye	Barley	Oats	MC	P's
1802	14	140	165	105	50	44
1803	15	167	171	85	49	41
1804	12	155	169	101	53	53
1805	14	158	157	100	51	56
1806	10	135	174	100	50	54
1807	14	160	167	93	47	51
1808	13	157	149	76	42	61
1809	15	206	183	105	58	78
1810	15	193	177	113	62	90
1811	13	156	168	100	51	84
1812	14	179	148	82	39	66
1813	16	181	178	83	49	102
1814	16	176	191	104	57	99
1815	17	172	201	106	59	122
1816	16	186	168	89	46	120
1817	16	159	185	107	55	144
1818	13	153	147	90	47	123
1819	18	196	160	93	45	142
1820	20	213	209	119	64	216
1821	25*	246*	217*	133*	76*	296*
1822	...	...	...	...	...	...
1823	...	...	...	...	...	...
1824	...	...	...	...	...	...
1825	31	286	234	139	82	404
1826	...	...	...	...	...	...
1827	...	...	...	...	...	...
1828	...	...	...	...	...	...
1829	...	...	...	...	...	...
1830	33	307	241	152	83	469
1831	...	...	...	...	...	...
1832	...	...	...	...	...	...
1833	...	...	...	...	...	...
1834	...	...	...	...	...	...

*Averages of 1818–1822

D2 Output of Main Cereal, Potato, and Sugar Beet Crops (in thousands of hectolitres or metric tons)

AUSTRIA **1835–1889**

	Wheat	Rye[3]	Barley	Oats	Maize	Other Corn	Potatoes	Sugar Beet
1835	...	...	...	...	...	...	...	...
1836	...	...	...	...	...	...	...	...
1837	...	...	...	...	...	...	...	...
1838	...	...	...	...	...	...	...	...
1839	...	...	...	...	...	...	...	...
1840	...	...	...	...	...	...	...	...
1841	...	...	...	...	...	...	...	...
			thousands of hectolitres					
1842	9,399	23,521	15,996	28,850	2,156	3,200	41,992	...
1843	9,439	23,523	16,205	28,852	2,211	3,173	40,616	...
1844	9,420	23,493	16,166	28,846	2,111	3,079	41,486	...
1845	9,634	23,534	16,173	30,171	2,677	3,571	40,687	...
1846	9,644	23,367	15,852	29,573	2,475	3,451	31,867	...
1847	9,662	23,373	15,773	29,593	2,572	3,509	32,700	...
1848	...	...	...	...	...	...	...	...
1849	...	...	...	...	...	...	...	...
1850	...	...	...	...	...	...	...	...
1851	9,630	23,519	15,501	29,433	3,110	4,047	40,765	...
1852	...	...	...	...	...	...	...	...
1853	...	...	...	...	...	...	...	...
1854	9,620	24,905	13,107	28,935	3,266	4,392	46,516	...
1855	...	...	...	...	...	...	...	...
1856	...	...	...	...	...	...	...	...
1857	12,587	29,527	16,745	31,148	4,616	4,942	44,245	...
1858	...	...	...	...	...	...	...	...
1859	11,598	29,762	16,030	32,002	4,526	5,132	43,840	...
1860	...	...	...	...	...	...	...	...
1861	...	...	...	...	...	...	...	...
1862	...	...	...	...	...	...	...	...
1863	...	...	...	...	...	...	...	...
1864	...	...	...	...	...	...	...	...
1865	...	...	...	...	...	...	...	...
1866	...	...	...	...	...	...	...	thousands of
1867	...	...	...	...	...	...	...	metric tons
1868	11,819	24,166	16,189	29,987	3,996	5,112	64,405	...
1869	11,377	23,754	14,550	28,086	4,608	3,709	64,843	1,758
1870	12,835	27,401	16,226	28,530	4,250	3,637	83,008	2,215
1871	12,819	26,351	16,431	32,449	3,903	3,295	63,900	2,136
1872	11,285[3]	23,491	17,367	34,935	9,249	3,760	75,227	2,907
1873	10,053[3]	27,976	15,899	26,831	5,367	2,574	69,845	2,403
1874	14,804[3]	28,434	17,460	28,073	5,793	4,373	94,079	2,009[4]
1875	10,885	23,275	13,175	25,564	6,073	3,407	93,460	2,537
1876	12,720	21,240	18,134	33,082	5,918	4,134	91,283	2,678
1877	14,050	28,171	13,817	30,311	5,141	3,389	94,520	3,287
1878	15,927	29,995	17,086	34,570	6,793	4,581	91,856	3,734
1879	12,147	22,360	13,273	30,401	5,455	3,960	57,397	3,402
1880	14,302	22,753	17,809	32,680	6,021	3,110	85,770	4,092
1881	14,507	28,260	16,485	33,609	4,549	2,985	99,555	4,099
1882	15,698	29,062	17,231	32,272	5,514	2,284	85,883	4,618
1883	13,347	24,028	16,354	33,673	7,115	3,882	102,018	4,197
1884	15,441	27,090	18,230	38,009	5,992	3,539	99,292	4,766
1885	17,016	27,984	18,345	33,390	7,008	3,881	129,737	2,537
1886	15,734	27,043	18,768	39,730	6,766	3,280	117,590	3,298
1887	18,450	32,168	20,568	37,034	5,622	2,973	119,085	2,456
							thousands of metric tons	
1888	18,271	28,827	20,210	37,081	5,845	3,543	8,119	4,009
1889	13,525	25,042	16,137	28,524	5,806	2,863	9,033	5,025

See p.296 for footnotes

D2 Output of Main Cereal, Potato, and Sugar Beet Crops (in thousands of hectolitres or metric tons)

1835–1889

	BELGIUM							DENMARK (thousands of hectolitres)					
	Wheat	Rye	Barley	Oats	M Corn	P's	SB	Wheat	Rye	Barley	Oats	M Corn	P's
1835	...	...	...	...	...	...	...	...	...	...	...	...	...
1836	...	...	...	...	...	...	...	...	...	...	...	...	...
1837	...	...	...	...	...	...	...	...	...	...	...	...	...
1838	...	...	...	...	...	...	...	...	...	...	...	...	...
1839	...	...	...	...	...	...	...	...	...	...	...	...	...
1840	...	...	...	...	...	...	...	...	...	...	...	...	...
1841	...	...	...	...	...	...	...	...	...	...	...	...	...
1842	...	...	...	...	...	...	...	...	...	...	...	...	...
1843	...	...	...	...	...	...	...	...	...	...	...	...	...
1844	...	...	...	...	...	...	...	...	...	...	...	...	...
1845	...	...	...	...	...	...	...	...	...	...	...	...	...
		thousands of hectolitres				thousands of metric tons							
1846	3,584	2,055	1,143	4,770	3,317	15,292.	78	...	...	...	...	...	...
1847	...	...	...	...	...	...	...	...	...	...	...	...	...
1848	...	...	...	...	...	...	...	...	...	...	...	...	...
1849	...	...	...	...	...	...	...	...	...	...	...	...	...
1850	...	...	...	...	...	...	...	...	...	...	...	...	...
1851	...	...	...	...	...	...	...	...	...	...	...	...	...
1852	...	...	...	...	...	...	...	...	...	...	...	...	...
1853	...	...	...	...	...	...	...	...	...	...	...	...	...
1854	...	...	...	...	...	...	...	...	...	...	...	...	...
1855	...	...	...	...	...	...	...	...	...	...	...	...	...
1856	3,756	6,066	1,561	7,411	2,719	26,687	304	...	...	...	...	...	...
1857	...	...	...	...	...	...	...	...	...	...	...	...	...
1858	...	...	...	...	...	...	...	...	...	...	...	...	...
1859	...	...	...	...	...	...	...	...	...	...	...	...	...
1860	...	...	...	...	...	...	...	...	...	...	...	...	...
1861	...	...	...	...	...	...	...	...	...	...	...	...	...
1862	...	...	...	...	...	...	...	...	...	...	...	...	...
1863	...	...	...	...	...	...	...	...	...	...	...	...	...
1864	...	...	...	...	...	...	...	...	...	...	...	...	...
1865	...	...	...	...	...	...	...	...	...	...	...	...	...
1866	...	...	...	...	...	...	...	...	...	...	...	...	...
1867	...	...	...	...	...	...	...	...	...	...	...	...	...
1868	...	...	...	...	...	...	...	...	...	...	...	...	...
1869	...	...	...	...	...	...	...	...	...	...	...	...	...
1870	...	...	...	...	...	...	...	...	...	...	...	...	...
		thousands of metric tons											
1871	432[5]	417[5]	78[5]	389[5]	114[5]	2,487[5]	1,123[5]	...	...	...	...	...	...
1872	...	...	...	...	...	...	...	...	...	...	...	...	...
1973	...	...	...	...	...	...	...	...	...	...	...	...	...
1974	...	...	...	...	...	...	...	...	...	...	...	...	...
1875	...	...	...	...	...	...	...	1,759	5,956	8,154	10,798	1,194	4,183
1876	...	...	...	...	...	...	...	1,426	5,049	6,589	8,884	1,190	3,792
1877	...	...	...	...	...	...	...	1,706	5,614	6,968	9,121	1,336	3,030
1878	...	...	...	...	...	...	...	1,824	6,144	8,449	11,747	1,721	3,938
1879	...	...	...	...	...	...	...	1,649	5,237	7,229	10,540	1,626	2,266
1880	...	...	...	...	...	...	...	1,797	6,591	8,857	12,131	1,953	4,798
1881	...	...	...	...	...	...	...	977	6,110	7,688	10,797	1,762	4,403
1882	...	...	...	...	...	...	...	1,575	5,940	8,324	12,257	2,202	2,948
1883	...	...	...	...	...	...	...	1,588	6,230	7,353	10,760	2,004	5,653
1884	...	...	...	...	...	...	...	1,655	5,869	7,304	10,917	2,164	4,853
1885	...	...	...	...	...	...	...	1,806	6,307	7,359	11,996	2,431	5,378
1886	...	...	...	...	...	...	...	1,664	5,834	8,179	12,465	2,604	5,782
1887	...	...	...	...	...	...	...	1,886	6,079	7,712	11,233	2,763	6,039
1888	...	...	...	...	...	...	...	1,158	5,764	7,802	12,501	2,802	4,712
1889	...	...	...	...	...	...	...	1,478	6,390	6,563	9,885	2,554	4,393

M Corn Mixed Corn P's Potatoes SB Sugar Beet

See p.296 for footnotes

D2 Output of Main Cereal, Potato, and Sugar Beet Crops (in thousands of hectolitres or metric tons)

1835–1889

	FINLAND (thousands of hectolitres)						FRANCE (thousands of metric tons)							
	Wheat	Rye	Barley	Oats	Mixed Corn	Potatoes	Wheat	Rye	Barley	Oats	Maize[7]	Buck-wheat	Potatoes	Sugar Beet
1835	...	...	...	...	...	...	5,380	2,340	1,160	2,320	490[7]	330	5,470	...
1836	...	...	...	...	...	...	4,770	...	...	...	...	...	6,160	...
1837	...	...	...	...	...	...	5,090	...	...	...	...	...	5,770	...
1838	...	...	...	...	...	...	5,080	...	...	...	...	...	6,980	...
1839	...	...	...	...	...	...	4,870	...	...	...	...	...	6,460	...
1840	...	...	...	...	...	...	6,070	1,970	1,080	2,290	540	520	6,920	1,570
1841	...	...	...	...	...	...	5,360	...	...	...	...	...	8,930	...
1842	...	...	...	...	...	...	5,350	...	...	...	...	...	7,090	...
1843	...	...	...	...	...	...	5,520	...	...	...	...	...	7,870	...
1844	...	...	...	...	...	...	6,180	...	...	...	...	...	8,950	...
1845	...	...	...	...	...	...	5,400	...	...	...	...	...	5,920	...
1846	...	...	...	...	...	...	4,550	...	...	...	...	...	5,970	...
1847	...	...	...	...	...	...	7,320	...	...	...	...	...	7,600	...
1848	...	...	...	...	...	...	6,600	...	...	...	...	...	6,640	...
1849	...	...	...	...	...	...	6,810	...	...	...	...	...	6,750	...
1850	...	...	...	...	...	...	6,600	...	...	...	...	...	5,620	...
1851	...	...	...	...	...	...	6,450[6]	...	...	...	...	...	5,300	...
1852	...	...	...	...	...	...	7,140	1,790	1,110	2,940	590	650	4,170	3,220
1853	...	...	...	...	...	...	4,780	...	...	...	..	...	4,680	..
1854	...	...	...	...	...	...	7,290	...	...	...	...	...	5,250	...
1855	...	...	...	...	...	...	5,470	...	...	...	...	...	7,210	.
1856	...	...	...	...	...	...	6,400	...	...	...	...	...	6,130	.
1857	...	...	...	...	...	...	8,280	...	...	...	...	...	7,700	...
1858	...	...	...	...	...	...	8,250	...	...	...	...	...	8,310	...
1859	...	...	...	...	...	...	6,570	...	...	...	...	...	7,000	...
1860	...	...	...	...	...	...	7,620	...	...	...	...	...	6,690	...
1861	...	...	...	...	...	...	5,640	...	...	...	...	...	7,050	...
1862	...	...	...	...	...	...	8,240	1,770	1,330	3,330	610	670	10,270	4,430
1863	...	...	...	...	...	...	8,760	...	...	...	...	...	8,910	...
1864	...	...	...	...	...	...	8,340	...	...	...	...	...	8,440	...
1865	...	...	...	...	...	...	7,170	...	...	...	...	...	9,190	...
1866	...	...	...	...	...	...	6,380	...	...	...	...	...	7,360	...
1867	...	...	...	...	...	...	6,220	...	...	...	...	...	8,040	...
1868	...	...	...	...	...	...	8,760	...	...	...	...	...	10,820	...
1859	...	...	...	...	...	...	8,100	...	...	...	...	...	9,430	...
1870	...	...	...	...	...	...	7,420[8]	...[8]	...[8]	...[8]	...[7 8]	...[8]	...[8]	...
1871	...	...	...	...	...	...	5,200	1,940	1,650	4,040	580	620	8,470	
1872	...	...	...	...	...	...	9,060	2,110	1,290	3,570	830	...	8,380	...
1873	...	...	...	...	...	...	6,140	1,470	1,190	3,190	620	...	9,150	7,740
1874	...	...	...	...	...	...	9,980	2,010	1,280	3,360	790	...	11,240	...
1875	...	...	...	...	...	...	7,550	1,960	1,170	3,240	760	590	9,440	...
1876	...	...	...	...	...	...	7,160	1,920	1,130	2,870	510	...	8,650	...
1877	...	...	...	...	...	...	7,510	1,870	1,130	3,080	780	...	9,060	...
1878	36	3,103	1,639	2,683	84	3,307	7,150	1,780	1,030	3,660	770	...	8,410	...
1879	34	3,741	1,901	2,999	91	3,619	5,990	1,360	1,020	3,520	540	...	7,740	...
1880	39	4,036	1,781	2,984	78	3,152	7,550	1,870	1,220	3,990	710[7]	670	10,470	...
1881	32	2,511	1,884	2,948	94	4,686	7,570	2,370	1,120	3,620	610	...	10,130	7,570
1882	42	3,897	2,071	3,289	110	4,615	9,870	2,110	1,250	4,080	740	700	8,550	8,310
1883	43	4,320	2,073	3,619	128	4,902	7,930	1,770	1,290	4,400	690	700	10,340	8,340
1884	43	3,898	1,890	3,610	123	4,126	8,820	1,880	1,230	4,130	710	700	10,680	7,080
1885	42	3,855	1,861	3,699	129	4,975	8,520	1,740	1,110	4,060	640	550	11,250	5,480
1886	47	4,502	2,157	4,345	149	6,974	8,240	1,620	1,140	4,220	640	650	11,290	6,890
1887	55	4,589	2,158	5,015	168	6,712	8,710	1,690	1,090	3,760	750	530	11,710	5,120
1888	52	4,391	1,963	4,659	141	6,111	7,500	1,580	1,000	3,920	710	620	10,350	5,460
1889	53	4,527	2,177	4,784	162	7,115	8,320	1,660	990	3,990	660	580	10,700	7,140

See p.296 for footnotes

D2 Output of Main Cereal, Potato, and Sugar Beet Crops (in thousands of hectolitres or metric tons)

1835–1889

GERMANY (thousands of metric tons)[9]

	Wheat	Rye	Barley	Oats	Mixed Corn & Rye	Potatoes	Sugar Beet
1835	...	...	...	...	...	...	...
1836	...	...	...	...	...	...	...
1837	...	...	...	...	...	...	...
1838	...	...	...	...	...	...	...
1839	...	...	...	...	...	...	...
1840	...	...	...	...	...	...	...
1841	...	...	...	...	...	...	...
1842	...	...	...	...	...	...	...
1843	...	...	...	...	...	...	...
1844	...	...	...	...	...	...	...
1845	...	...	...	...	...	...	...
1846	1,416	2,927	1,533	2,383	...	7,055	233
1857	1,944	6,325	1,945	2,948	...	9,166	316
1858	1,855	5,439	2,150	3,528	...	12,363	464
1949	1,902	5,647	2,065	3,391	...	11,390	556
1850	1,846	4,499	1,872	3,098	596	10,942	627
1851	1,747	4,318	1,912	3,382	593	7,123	853
1852	2,164	4,972	1,741	2,826	572	11,644	1,064
1853	1,836	4,733	1,866	3,372	573	9,060	1,010
1854	2,264	5,567	2,097	3,888	640	9,107	936
1855	1,524	3,894	2,067	3,804	516	10,146	984
1856	2,224	5,949	2,174	4,072	631	13,941	1,121
1857	2,456	6,059	1,585	2,408	528	16,501	1,467
1858	1,822	5,022	1,407	2,470	434	15,973	1,612
1859	2,109	4,694	1,514	3,336	483	14,667	1,861
1860	2,491	6,561	2,261	4,623	640	11,925	1,632
1861	2,326	5,374	2,118	4,118	558	14,212	1,574
1862	2,296	5,705	2,260	4,526	580	17,629	1,610
1863	2,504	6,542	2,052	3,858	569	20,717	1,895
1864	2,497	6,496	2,279	4,474	590	17,974	2,011
1865	2,186	5,645	2,089	4,002	513	21,592	2,205
1866	2,223	5,264	1,989	3,952	494	16,046	2,411
1867	1,981	5,076	1,956	3,946	460	17,664	2,439
1868	2,852	7,499	2,213	3,857	565	22,116	2,300
1869	2,652	6,307	2,201	4,110	530	20,077	2,300
1870	2,409[9]	6,247[9]	2,101[9]	3,973[9]	487[9]	20,366[9]	2,300[9]
1871	2,544	5,821	2,254	4,427	481	14,850	2,300
1872	2,750	6,251	2,264	4,554	497	25,510	2,251
1873	2,720	5,639	2,138	4,326	460	20,163	3,182
1874	4,267	7,051	2,217	4,302	495	26,452	3,529
1875	2,724	6,409	1,979	3,832	432	22,816	2,757
1876	2,562	5,774	1,992	4,202	413	23,914	4,161
1877	2,982	7,374	2,002	4,196	446	20,952	3,550
1878	3,503	8,190	2,770	6,101	552	27,613	4,488
1879	3,161	6,581	2,454	5,169	470	22,092	4,064
1880	3,236	5,862	2,550	5,128	466	22,795	4,738
1881	2,879	6,445	2,466	4,531	466	29,839	6,272
1882	3,441	7,112	2,676	5,429	552	21,132	8,769
1883	3,196	6,568	2,539	4,516	505	29,147	8,897
1884	3,377	6,414	2,672	5,124	525	28,091	10,399
1885	3,513	6,894	2,700	5,264	541	32,774	9,300
1886	3,550	7,182	2,752	5,901	568	29,433	8,370
1887	3,746	7,536	2,614	5,220	550	29,559	8,100
1888	3,270	6,512	2,688	5,595	523	25,608	7,891
1889	3,041	6,324	2,308	5,092	550	31,135	9,200

See p.296 for footnotes

D2 **Output of Main Cereal, Potato, and Sugar Beet Crops** (in thousands of hectolitres or metric tons)

1835–1889

HUNGARY[10]

	Wheat	Mixed Corn & Rye[11]	Barley	Oats	Maize	Potatoes	Sugar Beet	M C & B
1835	...	...	...	...	...	...	...	
1836	...	...	...	...	...	...	...	
1837	...	...	...	...	...	...	...	
1838	...	...	...	...	...	...	...	
1839	...	...	...	...	...	...	...	
1840	...	...	...	...	...	...	...	
1841	...	...	...	...	...	...	...	
1842	...	...	...	...	...	...	...	
1843	...	...	...	...	...	...	...	
1844	...	...	...	...	...	...	...	
1845	...	...	...	...	...	...	...	
1846	...	...	...	...	...	...	...	
1847	...	...	...	...	...	...	...	
1848	...	...	...	...	...	...	...	
1849	...	...	...	...	...	...	...	
		thousands of hectolitres					thousands of metric tons	
1850	...	...	...	...	...	...	...	
1851	20,134	19,520	18,653	29,103	21,287	16,980	...	
1852	...	...	...	...	...	...	...	
1853	...	...	...	...	...	...	...	
1854	21,358	24,072	15,645	31,370	34,057	22,264	...	
1855	...	...	...	...	...	...	...	
1856	...	...	...	...	...	...	...	
1857	29,287	27,540	19,216	36,083	39,142	17,772	...	
1858	...	...	...	...	...	...	...	
1859	27,922[10]	28,927[10]	19,300[10]	35,842[10]	38,338[10]	17,694[10]	...	
1860	...	...	...	...	...	...	...	
1861	...	...	...	...	...	...	...	
1862	...	...	...	...	...	...	...	
1863	...	...	...	...	...	...	...	
1864	...	...	...	...	...	...	...	
1865	...	...	...	...	...	...	...	
1866	...	...	...	...	...	...	...	
1867	...	...	...	...	...	...	...	
1868	...	...	...	...	...	...	...	
1869	17,725	17,223	8,457	10,998	17,683	14,714	94	
1870	22,260	17,728	11,132	12,777	21,821	12,159	138	
1871	15,819	15,852[11] / 16,061	12,256	14,110	12,323	11,327	117	
1872	15,564	13,121	10,738	15,265	17,893	12,560	127	
1873	14,076	7,977	9,900	12,426	12,240	8,418	82	
1874	21,614	14,906	12,449	14,030	7,602	15,514	154	
1875	17,243	12,809	7,609	7,829	28,138	14,447	124	
1876	18,218	10,486	11,117	13,854	22,968	17,418	150	
1877	25,316	15,345	12,043	14,038	20,425	15,681	155	
1878	38,277	21,388	16,709	21,203	36,249	32,422	278	
1879	18,434	10,480	9,200	10,480	23,243	15,851	261	
1880	27,954	14,465	17,943	21,729	34,806	31,024	339	
1881	31,327	16,759	14,065	16,847	28,866	30,395	597	
1882	46,431	21,478	20,286	23,787	37,891	42,713	674	
1883	31,909	16,677	13,849	18,029	30,740	43,285	738	
1884	37,783	18,106	16,498	20,118	31,836	39,978	676	
1885	40,108	17,642	19,141	19,187	38,447	38,607	595	
1886	36,245	15,530	13,344	19,379	29,768	32,839	626	
1887	51,421	21,263	19,636	21,672	25,979	32,602	500	
1888	47,880	17,626	15,899	19,917	33,613	37,549	806	
1889	32,959	14,981	12,164	15,379	36,083	40,101	1,109	

See p.296 for footnotes

D2 Output of Main Cereal, Potato, and Sugar Beet Crops (in thousands of hectolitres or metric tons)

1835–1889

CROATIA-SLAVONIA

	Wheat	Rye	Barley	Oats	Maize	Potatoes	Sugar Beet
1835	...	...	...	...	...	...	...
1836	...	...	...	...	...	...	...
1837	...	...	...	...	...	...	...
1838	...	...	...	...	...	...	...
1839	...	...	...	...	...	...	...
1840	...	...	...	...	...	...	...
1841	...	...	...	...	...	...	...
1842	...	...	...	...	...	...	...
1843	...	...	...	...	...	...	...
1844	...	...	...	...	...	...	...
1845	...	...	...	...	...	...	...
1846	...	...	...	...	...	...	...
1847	...	...	...	...	...	...	...
1848	...	...	...	...	...	...	...
1849	...	...	...	...	...	...	...
1850	...	...	...	...	...	...	...
1851	...	...	...	...	...	...	...
1852	...	...	...	...	...	...	...
1853	...	...	...	...	...	...	...
1854	...	...	...	...	...	...	...
1855	...	...	...	...	...	...	...
1856	...	...	...	...	...	...	...
1857	...	...	...	...	...	...	...
1858	...	...	...	...	...	...	...
1859	...	...	...	...	...	...	...
1860	...	...	...	...	...	...	...
1861	...	...	...	...	...	...	...
1862	...	...	...	...	...	...	...
1863	...	...	...	...	...	...	...
1864	...	...	...	...	...	...	...
1865	...	...	...	...	...	...	...
1866	...	...	...	...	...	...	...
1867	...	...	...	...	...	...	...
1868	...	...	...	...	...	...	...
1869	...	...	...	...	...	...	...
1870	...	...	...	...	...	...	...
1871	...	...	...	...	...	...	...
1872	...	...	...	...	...	...	...
1873	...	...	...	...	...	...	...
1874	...	...	...	...	...	...	...
1875	...	...	...	...	...	...	...
1876	...	...	...	...	...	...	...
1877	...	...	...	...	...	...	...
1878	...	...	...	...	...	...	...
1879	...	...	...	...	...	...	...
1880	...	...	...	...	...	...	...
1881	...	...	...	...	...	...	...
1882	...	...	...	...	...	...	...
1883	...	...	...	...	...	...	...
1884	...	...	...	...	...	...	...
	thousands of hectolitres					thousands of metric tons	
1885	1,884	2,055	920	1,712	3,945	140	4
1886	1,885	2,091	884	1,713	4,594	196	4
1887	1,892	1,957	790	1,500	3,751	244	4
1888	2,099	1,920	769	1,320	4,563	269	7
1889	1,723	1,686	644	859	4,355	300	8

IRELAND (thousands of metric tons)

	Wheat	Barley	Oats	Potatoes
1835	...	...	...	...
1836	...	...	...	...
1837	...	...	...	...
1838	...	...	...	...
1839	...	...	...	...
1840	...	...	...	...
1841	...	...	...	...
1842	...	...	...	...
1843	...	...	...	...
1844	...	...	...	...
1845	...	...	...	...
1846				
1847	624	297	1,639	2,081
1848	...	...	...	...
1849	462	298	1,399	4,079
1850	331	287	1,471	4,009
1851	319	297	1,532	4,512
1852	246	267	1,666	4,324
1853	242	281	1,521	5,834
1854	310	236	1,606	5,143
1855	324	210	1,460	6,335
1856	348	144	1,314	4,479
1857	355	160	1,265	3,566
1858	373	151	1,274	4,971
1859	313	130	1,162	4,399
1860	271	140	1,258	2,785
1861	182	128	1,144	1,888
1862	146	123	1,036	2,183
1863	179	141	1,270	3,501
1864	187	142	1,111	4,382
1865	176	136	1,087	3,928
1866	172	122	1,034	3,118
1867	155	138	1,056	3,197
1868	202	164	1,083	4,127
1869	170	177	990	3,426
1870	161	191	1,073	4,286
1871	150	172	1,052	2,839
1872	130	160	945	1,835
1873	100	187	981	2,726
1874	147	208	1,016	3,609
1875	118	216	1,165	3,569
1876	103	198	1,088	4,222
1877	97	179	907	1,785
1878	117	199	968	2,568
1879	91	166	789	1,132
1880	113	175	994	3,034
1881	117	169	1,001	3,489
1882	105	140	929	2,026
1883	66	144	958	3,507
1884	50	136	920	3,089
1885	56	147	921	3,227
1886	51	141	934	2,711
1887	52	105	770	3,626
1888	69	138	896	2,563
1889	73	165	896	2,894

D2 Output of Main Cereal, Potato, and Sugar Beet Crops (in thousands of hectolitres or metric tons)

1835–1889

ITALY (thousands of metric tons)[1 2]

	Wheat	Rye	Barley	Oats	Maize	Rice	Potatoes	Sugar Beet
1835	...	...	...	...	...	...	...	...
1836	...	...	...	...	...	...	...	...
1837	...	...	...	...	...	...	...	...
1838	...	...	...	...	...	...	...	...
1839	...	...	...	...	...	...	...	...
1840	...	...	...	...	...	...	...	...
1841	...	...	...	...	...	...	...	...
1842	...	...	...	...	...	...	...	...
1843	...	...	...	...	...	...	...	...
1844	...	...	...	...	...	...	...	...
1845	...	...	...	...	...	...	...	...
1846	...	...	...	...	...	...	...	...
1847	...	...	...	...	...	...	...	...
1848	...	...	...	...	...	...	...	...
1849	...	...	...	...	...	...	...	...
1850	...	...	...	...	...	...	...	...
1851	...	...	...	...	...	...	...	...
1852	...	...	...	...	...	...	...	...
1853	...	...	...	...	...	...	...	...
1854	...	...	...	...	...	...	...	...
1855	...	...	...	...	...	...	...	...
1856	...	...	...	...	...	...	...	...
1857	...	...	...	...	...	...	...	...
1858	...	...	...	...	...	...	...	...
1859	...	...	...	...	...	...	...	...
1860	...	...	...	...	...	...	...	...
1861	3,290	168	182	231	1,440	280	864	—
1862	3,300	196	203	239	1,268	167	912	—
1863	3,485	161	238	255	1,620	279	960	—
1864	3,380	148	218	275	1,590	288	1,027	—
1865	3,725	179	190	289	1,830	307	1,088	—
1866	3,943	148	228	285	2,010	329	1,040	—
1867	3,877	144	257	333	1,920	543	946	—
1868	4,307	158	287	313	2,400	525	1,056	—
1869	3,997	149	224	333	2,100	434	1,200	—
1870	4,039	162	197	337	1,860	550	1,248	—
1871	4,010	152	248	340	2,304	529	1,106	—
1872	3,861	137	356	324	2,496	474	1,151	—
1873	4,023	179	302	369	2,010	419	1,195	—
1874	3,917	102	278	365	2,523	433	1,051	—
1875	3,933	130	310	374	2,682	483	1,056	—
1876	3,806	139	317	372	2,971	507	1,109	—
1877	3,836	145	305	366	2,802	408	1,162	—
1878	3,675	133	297	395	2,392	673	1,186	1.0
1879	4,040	117	225	290	2,239	491	1,286	1.6
1880	4,702	176	327	347	2,093	498	1,151	0.3
1881	2,856	113	210	244	1,439	421	1,009	1.0
1882	4,261	144	268	296	1,886	396	1,110	0.6
1883	3,420	130	240	275	1,915	402	1,240	1.8
1884	3,390	121	226	285	2,421	399	1,279	3.2
1885	3,217	112	213	298	2,136	392	1,273	6.2
1886	3,293	116	219	280	2,200	433	1,198	1.1
1887	3,470	118	194	316	2,120	398	1,180	1.5
1888	3,026	100	173	268	1,844	255	1,069	1.6
1889	2,995	104	195	306	2,082	417	966	3.9
								5.5

See p.296 for footnotes

D2 Output of Main Cereal, Potato, and Sugar Beet Crops (in thousands of hectolitres or metric tons)

1835–1889

NETHERLANDS

	Wheat	Rye	Barley	Oats	Buckwheat	Potatoes	Sugar Beet
1835	...	...	...	...	...	...	...
1836	...	...	...	...	...	...	...
1837	...	...	...	...	...	...	...
1838	...	...	...	...	...	...	...
1839	...	...	...	...	...	...	thousands of metric tons
		thousands of hectolitres					
1840	...	...	...	...	...	...	...
1841	...	...	...	...		...	...
1842	1,051	2,642	1,101	2,296	804	...	...
1843	1,455	3,365	1,169	2,612	941	...	...
1844	1,309	3,040	1,252	2,389	991	...	...
1845	1,168	2,927	1,284	2,735	990	...	...
1846	1,200	1,597	1,209	2,057	1,260	5,818	...
1847	1,747	3,776	1,545	2,796	981	9,836	...
1848	1,749	3,410	1,452	2,634	1,446	8,217	...
1849	1,539	3,687	1,373	2,858	1,016	11,492	...
1850	1,531	3,368	1,280	2,504	976	9,651	...
1851	1,583	3,085	1,217	2,285	1,314	10,230	...
1852	1,517	2,887	1,254	2,696	1,036	8,527	...
1853	855	2,577	1,261	2,851	1,394	7,571	...
1854	1,618	3,629	1,530	3,032	1,363	10,629	...
1855	1,190	3,064	1,428	3,356	1,293	9,912	...
1856	1,851	3,899	1,641	3,309	1,154	13,498	...
1857	1,891	3,956	1,431	2,402	870	12,979	...
1858	1,654	3,803	1,737	2,530	1,101	16,979	...
1859	1,610	2,732	1,195	2,496	1,253	11,557	...
1860	1,774	3,758	1,485	3,261	1,232	12,472	...
1861	1,572	3,332	1,823	3,526	1,472	6,737	...
1862	1,646	3,056	1,317	3,971	1,297	16,592	...
1863	1,978	3,766	1,497	3,494	935	17,690	...
1864	1,745	4,088	1,776	4,570	1,104	16,870	...
1865	1,702	3,629	1,514	3,720	1,368	16,857	...
1866	1,561	3,699	1,331	3,382	1,242	13,119	...
1867	1,329	2,309	1,533	4,020	1,482	15,165	...
1868	2,000	3,892	1,645	3,651	611	15,846	...
1869	2,073	3,823	1,750	3,704	953	16,122	...
1870	2,056	3,892	1,849	4,093	967	16,446	277
1871	1,190	2,453	2,037	5,697	1,366	13,291	331
1872	1,951	3,968	1,689	3,824	1,019	18,730	394
1873	1,834	2,860	1,655	3,917	951	17,900	331
1874	2,390	3,755	1,660	4,093	1,007	20,337	333
1875	2,250	3,567	1,938	4,599	1,235	19,811	499
1876	1,920	3,420	1,705	4,511	856	19,027	306
1877	1,753	3,612	1,413	4,136	1,244	17,079	298
1878	1,992	3,507	1,435	4,048	1,170	15,656	401
1879	1,770	3,368	1,449	4,232	867	10,332	314
1880	2,080	3,301	1,751	4,767	881	13,923	449
1881	1,658	2,970	1,541	4,189	780	22,817	382
1882	1,917	3,949	1,645	4,634	893	16,448	419
1883	1,984	3,825	1,800	4,030	911	24,871	579
1884	2,077	3,736	1,722	3,975	992	26,294	595
1885	2,232	4,079	1,929	4,595	464	23,931	402
1886	1,846	3,776	1,660	5,161	744	22,524	392
1887	2,428	4,855	1,846	4,273	427	27,052	443
1888	1,848	3,477	1,501	4,418	812	16,444	348
1889	2,281	3,990	1,708	4,714	840	23,073	773

NORWAY (thousands of metric tons)

	Wheat	Rye	Barley	Oats	Mixed Corn	Potatoes
1835	1.1	7.6	44	86	24	261
1836	...	...	...	...	...	...
1837	...	...	...	...	...	...
1838	...	...	...	...	...	...
1839	...	...	...	...	...	...
1840	...	...	...	...	...	...
1841	...	...	...	...	...	...
1842	...	...	...	...	...	...
1843	...	...	...	...	...	...
1844	...	...	...	...	...	...
1845	1.5	10	62	112	33	394
1846	...	...	...	...	...	...
1847	...	...	...	...	...	...
1848	...	...	...	...	...	...
1849	...	...	...	...	...	...
1850	...	...	...	...	...	...
1851	...	...	...	...	...	...
1852	...	...	...	...	...	...
1853	...	...	...	...	...	...
1854	...	...	...	...	...	....
1855	5.7	18	83	142	40	483
1856	...	...	...	...	...	...
1857	...	...	...	...	...	...
1858	...	...	...	...	...	...
1859	...	...	...	...	...	...
1860	...	...	...	...	...	...
1861	...	...	...	...	...	...
1862	...	...	...	...	...	...
1863	...	...	...	...	...	...
1864	...	...	...	...	...	...
1865	7.6	17	81	133	34	529
1866	...	...	...	...	...	...
1867	...	...	...	...	...	...
1868	...	...	...	...	...	...
1869	...	...	...	...	...	...
1870	...	...	...			
1871						
1872						
1873	7.5	25	104	155	39	587
1874						
1875						
1876	...	...	...	...	...	...
1877	...	...	...	...	...	...
1878	...	...	...	...	...	...
1879	...	...	...	...	...	...
1880	...	...	...	...	...	...
1881	...	...	...	...	...	...
1882	...	...	...	...	...	...
1883	...	...	...	...	...	...
1884	...	...	...	...	...	...
1885	...	...	...	...	...	...
1886						
1887						
1888	7	24	97	166	27	591
1889						

1890 is included in this group of years

D2 Output of Main Cereal, Potato, and Sugar Beet Crops (in thousands of hectolitres or metric tons)

1835–1889

	PORTUGAL (thousands of hectolitres)[13]					ROMANIA (thousands of hectolitres)				
	Wheat	Rye	Barley	Oats	Maize	Wheat	Rye	Barley	Oats	Maize
1835	...	...	...	...	...	...	...	...	...	...
1836	...	...	...	...	...	...	...	...	...	...
1837	...	...	...	...	...	...	...	...	...	...
1838	...	...	...	...	...	...	...	...	...	...
1839	...	...	...	...	...	...	...	...	...	...
1840	...	...	...	...	...	...	...	...	...	...
1841	...	...	...	...	...	...	...	...	...	...
1842	...	...	...	...	...	...	...	...	...	...
1843	...	...	...	...	...	...	...	...	...	...
1844	...	...	...	...	...	...	...	...	...	...
1845	...	...	...	...	...	...	...	...	...	...
1846	...	...	...	...	...	...	...	...	...	...
1847	...	...	...	...	...	...	...	...	...	...
1848	...	...	...	...	...	...	...	...	...	...
1849	...	...	...	...	...	...	...	...	...	...
1850	...	...	...	...	...	...	...	...	...	...
1851	...	...	...	...	...	...	...	...	...	...
1852	...	...	...	...	...	...	...	...	...	...
1853	...	...	...	...	...	...	...	...	...	...
1854	...	...	...	...	...	...	...	...	...	...
1855	...	...	...	...	...	...	...	...	...	...
1856	...	...	...	...	...	...	...	...	...	...
1857	...	...	...	...	...	...	...	...	...	...
1858	...	...	...	...	...	...	...	...	...	...
1859	...	...	...	...	...	...	...	...	...	...
1860	...	...	...	...	...	...	...	...	...	...
1861	...	...	...	...	...	...	...	...	...	...
1862	...	...	...	...	...	...	...	...	...	...
1863	...	...	...	...	...	...	...	...	...	...
1864	...	...	...	...	...	...	...	...	...	...
1865	...	...	...	...	...	...	...	...	...	...
1866	...	...	...	...	...	...	...	...	...	...
1867	...	...	...	...	...	10,230	1,039	2,947	740	12,845
1868	...	...	...	...	...	11,359	1,502	3,559	831	16,013
1869	...	...	...	...	...	8,343	1,326	2,796	823	15,709
1870	...	...	...	...	...	9,864	1,345	2,840	740	14,472
1871	...	...	...	...	...	9,404	1,270	3,306	1,021	15,130
1872	...	...	...	...	...	6,355	864	3,514	1,127	12,458
1873	...	...	...	...	...	10,219	736	4,919	1,586	11,626
1874	...	...	...	...	...	11,929	1,131	7,001	1,715	11,475
1875	...	...	...	...	...	11,836	925	3,375	1,005	22,510
1876	...	...	...	...	...	7,558	1,182	6,364	1,413	22,988
1877	...	...	...	...	...	...	...	...	...	...
1878	...	...	...	...	...	...	...	...	...	...
1879	...	...	...	...	...	...	...	...	...	...
1880	...	...	...	...	...	...	...	...	...	...
1881	...	...	...	...	...	...	...	...	...	...
1882	2,054	1,718	773	294	4,255	...	...	...	...	...
1883	1,963	1,701	749	398	4,644	...	...	...	...	...
1884	1,966	1,694	666	359	4,481	...	...	...	...	...
1885	...	...	...	...	...	...	...	...	...	...
1886	...	...	...	...	...	12,221	2,264	5,105	3,585	25,533
1887	...	...	...	...	...	16,720	2,683	6,576	4,335	17,164
1888	...	...	...	...	...	20,352	5,145	8,104	3,786	22,189
1889	...	...	...	...	...	17,687	2,027	5,575	2,310	24,413

See p.296 for footnotes

D2 Output of Main Cereal, Potato, and Sugar Beet Crops

1835–1889

RUSSIA[14]

	Wheat	Rye	Barley	Oats	Maize	Potatoes	Sugar Beet
			millions of hectolitres				millions of tons
1835	...	...	...	...	...	...	...
1836	...	...	...	...	...	...	...
1837	...	...	...	...	...	...	...
1838	...	...	...	...	...	...	...
1839	...	...	...	...	...	...	...
1840	...	...	...	...	...	...	...
1841	...	...	...	...	...	...	...
1842	...	...	...	...	...	...	...
1843	...	...	...	...	...	...	...
1844	...	...	...	...	...	...	...
1845	...	...	...	...	...	...	...
1846	...	...	...	...	...	...	...
1847	...	...	...	...	...	...	...
1848	...	...	...	...	...	...	...
1849	...	...	...	...	...	...	...
1850	...	...	...	...	...	...	...
1851	...	...	...	...	...	...	...
1852	...	...	...	...	...	...	...
1853	...	...	...	...	...	...	...
1854	...	...	...	...	...	...	...
1855	...	...	...	...	...	...	...
1856	...	...	...	...	...	...	...
1857	...	...	...	...	...	...	...
1858	...	...	...	...	...	...	...
1859	...	...	...	...	...	...	...
1860	...	...	...	...	...	...	...
1861	...	...	...	...	...	...	...
1862	...	...	...	...	...	...	...
1863	...	...	...	...	...	...	...
1864	...	...	...	...	...	...	...
1865	...	...	...	...	...	...	...
1866	...	...	...	...	...	...	...
1867	...	...	...	...	...	...	...
1868	...	...	...	...	...	...	...
1869	...	...	...	...	...	...	...
1870	99	278	58	265	...	146	...
1871	...	...	...	...	...	...	1.4
1872	57	199	43	198	...	135	2.0
1873	...	...	...	...	...	...	2.1
1874	...	...	...	...	...	...	1.7
1875	53	197	32	134	23[14]	124	2.2
1876	...	...	...	...	...	...	3.2
1877	...	...	...	...	...	...	2.4
1878	...	...	...	...	...	...	2.6
1879	60	202	44	179	26[14]	122	2.7
1880	...	...	...	...	...	...	...
1881	...	...	...	...	...	...	3.5
1882	...	...	...	...	...	...	3.8
1883	97	236	57	246	34[14]	112	3.6
1884	118	303	59	221	7	130	4.0
1885	78	309	44	171	8	107	5.5
1886	71	291	59	251	9	123	4.7
1887	123	328	74	273	6	139	4.3
1888	130	311	70	240	9	129	4.6
1889	79	243	51	216	50	134	4.4

See p.296 for footnotes

D2 Output of Main Cereal, Potato, and Sugar Beet Crops (in thousands of hectolitres or metric tons)

1835–1889

	SWEDEN (thousands of metric tons)							UK: GREAT BRITAIN			
	Wheat	Rye	Barley	Oats	Mixed Corn	Potatoes	Sugar Beet	Wheat	Barley	Oats	Potatoes
1835	36	319	230	156	86	517	...	...	...	...	...
1836							...	...	...	...	...
1837							...	...	...	...	...
1838							...	...	...	...	...
1839							...	...	...	...	...
	36	308	244	167	90	596					
1840							...	...	...	...	...
1841							...	...	...	...	...
1842							...	...	...	...	...
1843							...	...	...	...	...
1844							...	...	...	...	...
	44	353	273	199	120	676					
1845							...	...	...	...	...
1846							...	...	...	...	...
1847							...	...	...	...	...
1848							...	...	...	...	...
1849							...	...	...	...	...
	48	366	282	209	111	624					
1850							...	...	...	...	...
1851							...	...	...	...	...
1852							...	...	...	...	...
1853							...	...	...	...	...
1854	52	405	295	273	105	690	...	...	...	...	...
1855							...	...	...	...	...
1856							...	...	...	...	...
1857							...	...	...	...	...
1858	74	515	328	445	125	1,009	...	...	...	...	...
1859							...	...	...	...	...
1860	69	436	286	536	95	...	...	...	...	...	...
1861	58	332	287	493	95	...	...	...	...	...	...
1862	61	439	307	639	115	...	...	...	...	...	...
1863	70	441	280	489	88	...	...	...	...	...	...
1864	71	498	298	592	100	...	...	...	...	...	...
1865	59	420	265	495	86	...	...	...	...	...	...
1866	68	429	250	596	108	953	16	...	...	...	...
1867	41	297	201	564	94	656	13	...	...	...	...
1868	69	403	236	399	72	1,021	12	...	...	...	...
1869	81	515	330	708	125	859	14	...	...	...	...
1870	89	551	365	760	107	1,511	22	...	...	...	...
1871	86	483	377	853	130	1,019	23	...	...	...	...
1872	75	431	344	631	125	1,257	24	...	...	...	...
1873	98	516	311	797	108	927	31	...	...	...	...
1874	102	495	315	488	83	1,289	18	...	...	...	...
1875	95	518	375	816	119	1,301	17	...	...	...	...
1876	90	502	308	685	103	1,271	12	...	...	...	...
1877	74	395	258	740	99	1,000	8	...	...	...	...
1878	100	519	378	907	125	1,232	7	...	...	...	...
1879	85	491	352	896	116	866	11	...	...	...	...
1880	105	568	382	917	128	1,501	19	...	...	...	...
1881	59	405	309	835	107	1,321	16	...	...	...	...
1882	103	522	403	1,035	137	903	19	...	...	...	...
1883	85	477	340	889	122	1,226	38	thousands of hectolitres			thousands of metric tons
1884	110	566	372	985	143	1,178	47	29,169	26,877	39,780	3,803
1885	113	564	274	872	136	1,208	43	28,214	28,819	39,405	3,250
1886	110	529	346	960	153	1,257	54	22,352	26,215	42,399	3,219
1887	123	581	346	1,014	152	1,517	87	27,027	23,746	39,012	3,622
1888	102	509	303	1,036	142	1,003	93	26,160	24,903	39,034	3,108
1889	104	549	311	772	124	1,689	167	26,619	24,519	41,251	3,646

D2 Output of Main Cereal, Potato, and Sugar Beet Crops (in thousands of hectolitres or metric tons)

1890–1944

ALBANIA (thousands of metric tons)

	Wheat[3]	Rye	Barley	Oats	Maize
1890	...	...	...	...	...
1891	...	...	...	...	...
1892	...	...	...	...	...
1893	...	...	...	...	...
1894	...	...	...	...	...
1895	...	...	...	...	...
1896	...	...	...	...	...
1897	...	...	...	...	...
1898	...	...	...	...	...
1899	...	...	...	...	...
1900	...	...	...	...	...
1901	...	...	...	...	...
1902	...	...	...	...	...
1903	...	...	...	...	...
1904	...	...	...	...	...
1905	...	...	...	...	...
1906	...	...	...	...	...
1907	...	...	...	...	...
1908	...	...	...	...	...
1909	...	...	...	...	...
1910	...	...	...	...	...
1911	...	...	...	...	...
1912	...	...	...	...	...
1913	...	...	...	...	...
1914	...	...	...	...	...
1915	...	...	...	...	...
1916	...	...	...	...	...
1917	...	...	...	...	...
1918	...	...	...	...	...
1919	...	...	...	...	...
1920	...	...	...	...	...
1921	...	...	...	...	...
1922	...	...	...	...	...
1923	...	...	...	...	...
1924	...	...	...	...	...
1925	...	...	...	...	...
1926	...	...	...	...	...
1927	...	...	...	...	...
1928	...	...	...	...	...
1929	31	3	5	12	63
1930	29	2	5	11	46
1931	32	2	5	9	70
1932	42	3	7	14	108
1933	65	5	9	12	109
1934	44	4	7	9	148
1935	42	3	4	9	115
1936	30	3	4	8	125
1937	45	4	6	11	137
1938	38	3	4	11	143
1939	50	3	5	13	123
1940	30	...	...	...	...
1941	37	...	...	...	...
1942	...	...	...	...	...
1943	...	...	...	...	...
1944	45	...	...	...	...

AUSTRIA

	Wheat	Rye[3]	Barley	Oats	Maize	Other Cereals	Potatoes	Sugar Beet
	thousands of hectolitres						thousand tons	
1890	15,528	28,538	19,188	36,731	6,774	3,112	8,234	5,523
1891	14,474	24,676	19,478	38,569	6,756	3,005	6,309	5,385
1892	17,681	29,617	21,804	39,683	6,783	2,946	9,532	5,516
1893	15,386	27,854	18,502	31,503	5,468	2,607	8,343	4,923
1894	16,982	30,009	21,321	38,659	4,861	2,919	9,607	6,726
1895	14,720	23,539	20,824	40,013	6,597	3,435	9,845	4,230
	thousands of metric tons							
1896	1,136	1,877	1,227	1,599	448	3,341	8,818	5,935
1897	939	1,604	1,109	1,475	379	3,136	8,001	4,921
1898	1,276	2,026	1,382	1,869	417	4,406	11,614	4,719
1899	1,366	2,168	1,594	2,021	366	3,378	10,790	6,528
1900	1,114	1,394	1,339	1,714	392	3,526	11,702	5,228
1901	1,198	1,920	1,461	1,716	445	3,293	11,896	6,546
1902	1,351	2,096	1,607	1,821	342	2,695	11,654	4,686
1903	1,257	2,062	1,608	1,863	408	2,868	9,719	5,324
1904	1,462	2,330	1,455	1,591	318	2,930	10,840	4,072
1905	1,484	2,495	1,534	1,798	439	3,554	15,835	7,184
1906	1,585	2,523	1,655	2,243	462	3,386	13,997	6,372
1907	1,425	2,199	1,710	2,476	422	3,914	14,663	6,394
						thousand tons		
1908	1,691	2,880	1,513	2,091	385	213	12,951	5,814
1909	1,591	2,909	1,728	2,496	407	260	13,053	5,522
1910	1,567	2,771	1,472	2,063	439	242	13,366	7,062
1911	1,603	2,649	1,620	2,270	304	187	11,605	4,250
1912	1,895	2,981	1,707	2,430	389	185	12,542	7,924
1913	1,623	2,709	1,750	2,677	338	171	11,552	6,962
1914	1,035[15]	1,894[15]	1,273[15]	1,918[15]	274[15]	111[15]	7,758[15]	6,775[15]
1915	882[15]	1,545[15]	759[15]	1,072[15]	287[15]	68[15]	8,672[15]	4,619[15]
1916	757[15]	1,278[15]	850[15]	1,388[15]	145[15]	95[15]	6,234[15]	4,494[15]
1917	163[16]	278[16]	72[16]	158[16]	71	23[16]	895[16]	90[16]
1918	140	270	92	188	58	23	585	170
1919	139	230	83	197	54	14	545	75
1920	148	255	96	232	54	12	669	129
1921	178	335	119	276	64	19	833	94
1922	173[16]	320[16]	103[16]	249[16]	68[16]	17[16]	1,287[16]	126[16]
	202	345	122	266	88	21	1,398	173
1923	242	403	171	375	88	29	1,426	242
1924	231	411	157	332	94	29	1,647	433
1925	290	550	201	388	117	29	2,068	493
1926	257	475	198	435	97	26	1,298	481
1927	325	511	238	439	126	29	2,666	723
1928	352	506	282	462	108	33	2,488	725
1929	315	510	269	451	117	40	2,803	691
1930	327	524	267	401	121	43	2,653	973
1931	300	481	217	332	127	35	2,716	978
1932	322	615	274	390	132	35	2,666	1,020
1933	398	687	333	503	137	46	2,355	1,067
1934	362	575	295	467	155	45	2,749	1,409
1935	422	620	270	391	128	36	2,392	1,500
1936	382	473	278	427	171	43	2,369	912
1937	400	477	288	475	206	13	3,612	1,008
1938	441	591	306	435	200	14	3,257	1,133
1939	447	499	287	360	118	16	2,765	1,235
1940	285	313	280	344	135	19	2,605	875
1941	342	388	234	286	125	18	2,602	832
1942	276	270	222	271	116	21	2,252	744
1943	343	356	215	302	98	18	1,773	666
1944	294	279	181	250	84	15	1,751	576

See p.296 for footnotes

D2 Output of Main Cereal, Potato, and Sugar Beet Crops (in thousands of hectolitres or metric tons)

1890–1944

BELGIUM

	Wheat	Rye	Barley	Oats	Mixed Corn	Potatoes	Sugar Beet
1890	...	...	...	...	...	...	...
1891	...	...	...	...	...	...	...
1892	...	...	...	...	...	...	...
1893	...	...	...	...	...	...	...
1894	...	...	...	...	...	...	...
1895	348	506	87	437	(49)[17]	2,681	1,715
1896	...	...	...	...	...	...	...
1897	...	...	...	...	...	...	...
1898	...	...	...	...	...	...	...
1899	...	...	...	...	...	...	...
1900	375	504	104	569	67	2,393	2,180
1901	385	538	106	589	69	2,751	1,168
1902	395	568	108	662	71	2,264	1,364
1903	336	553	85	702	62	2,356	1,458
1904	376	559	109	544	64	2,494	1,163
1905	338	542	98	490	57	1,556	2,101
1906	353	523	95	657	61	2,413	1,749
1907	431	597	112	667	67	2,400	1,454
1908	365	564	96	625	52	2,255	1,560
1909	397	588	100	628	53	2,459	1,590
1910	381	583	92	631	55	2,912	1,812
1911	429	619	97	628	57	2,747	1,507
1912	418	541	93	509	53	3,306	1,730
1913	402	571	92	696	55	3,201	1,392
1914	...	...	...	...	...	...	...
1915	...	...	...	...	...	...	...
1916	...	...	...	...	...	...	...
1917	...	...	...	...	...	...	...
1918	...	...	...	...	...	...	...
1919	288	368	75	397	44	2,829	1,095
1920	280	462	94	492	46	2,257	1,438
1921	395	540	111	511	57	1,947	1,463
1922	289	467	75	519	22	3,931	1,699
1923	364	528	91	683	45	2,822	2,037
1924	354	525	81	642	41	2,866	2,489
1925	394	551	91	617	48	3,101	2,168
1926	348	511	92	736	43	3,001	1,683
1927	443	555	91	669	42	3,309	1,983
1928	490	588	95	704	46	3,634	1,828
1929	360	563	62	747	32	3,908	1,570
1930	360	473	83	555	31	2,962	1,865
1931	376	520	88	702	31	3,577	1,466
1932	419	601	102	760	36	4,439	1,736
1933	410	567	100	831	37	3,689	1,516
1934	439	565	105	807	39	3,262	1,690
1935	438	382	84	553	24	3,006	1,535
1936	440	357	79	553	24	3,225	1,491
1937	423	345	86	520	27	3,091	1,376
1938	548	385	89	621	27	3,258	1,202
1939	349	349	51	724	20	3,323	1,669
1940	...[18]	...[18]	...[18]	...[18]	...[18]	...[18]	...[18]
1941	374	290	75	331	16	2,152	1,295
1942	402	316	125	281	20	2,175	1,587
1943	534	332	181	315	25	2,270	1,769
1944	505[18]	314[18]	166[18]	305[18]	25[18]	2,121[18]	1,696[18]

BULGARIA (thousands of metric tons)

	Wheat	Rye	Barley	Oats	Maize	Potatoes	Sugar Beet
1890	...	...	...	...	...	...	...
1891	...	...	...	...	...	...	...
1892	...	...	...	...	...	...	...
1893	...	...	...	...	...	...	...
1894	...	...	...	...	...	...	...
1895	...	...	...	...	...	...	...
1896	...	...	...	...	...	...	...
1897	...	...	...	...	...	...	...
1898	...	...	...	...	...	...	...
1899	589	118	145	84	520	21	10
1900	706	171	237	92	495		10
1901	...	...	...	...	...	...	...
1902	...	...	...	...	...	...	...
1903	968	197	278	165	580	9	4
1904	1,150	197	281	162	324	7	23
1905	951	181	249	136	461	8	22
1906	1,064	191	261	172	706	10	44
1907	641	99	147	108	358	8	25
1908	993	142	246	163	526	9	23
1909	873	175	203	136	520	9	21
1910	1,150	230	307	156	720	12	32
1911	1,314	228	270	151	777	14	65
1912	1,218	214	271	126	723	14	61
1913	1,184	205	250	126	736	14	80
1914	632	160	202	113	799	16	190
1915	967	187	267	126	746	19	76
1916	806	152	228	98	490	18	115
1917	791	137	219	87	443	18	97
1918	631	110	148	52	215	15	58
1919	817	156	102	84	647	22	176
1920	810	159	206	102	530	26	82
1921	1 148	155	185	97	416	28	118
1922	886	162	224	112	416	29	150
1923	986	174	241	133	682	33	153
1924	672	109	154	93	629	34	404
1925	1,126	182	263	112	656	37	5
1926	995	181	241	98	694	48	225
1927	1,146	177	280	94	532	38	295
1928	1,338	205	340	89	515	21	176
1929	903	186	204	137	940	44	262
1930	1,560	321	433	111	775	63	402
1931	1,737	271	345	103	889	71	201
1932	1,310	229	296	101	887	72	187
1933	1,509	246	352	130	951	81	296
1934	1,078	164	187	75	790	84	19
1935	1,304[19]	197[19]	282[19]	93[19]	1,009[19]	121[19]	154[19]
1936	1,643	208	322	136	872	109	80
1937	1,767	238	330	147	859	146	209
1938	2,149	188	355	89	532	64	129
1939	1,857	195	362	114	950	127	229
1940	1,306[20]	158[20]	217[20]	105[20]	874[20]	123[20]	277[20]
1941	1,225	138	234	149	923	186	337
1942	782	85	143	115	513	172	219
1943	1,498	148	248	151	526	220	350
1944	1,581	154	169	91	758	182	327

See p.296 for footnotes

D2 Output of Main Cereal, Potato, and Sugar Beet Crops (in thousands of hectolitres or metric tons)

1890–1944

CZECHOSLOVAKIA (thousands of metric tons)

	Wheat	Rye	Barley	Oats	Maize	Potatoes	Sugar Beet
1890	...	...	...	...	...	...	...
1891	...	...	...	...	...	...	...
1892	...	...	...	...	...	...	...
1893	...	...	...	...	...	...	...
1894	...	...	...	...	...	...	...
1895	...	...	...	...	...	...	...
1896	...	...	...	...	...	...	...
1897	...	...	...	...	...	...	...
1898	...	...	...	...	...	...	...
1899	...	...	...	...	...	...	...
1900	...	...	...	...	...	...	...
1901	...	...	...	...	...	...	...
1902	...	...	...	...	...	...	...
1903	...	...	...	...	...	...	...
1904	...	...	...	...	...	...	...
1905	...	...	...	...	...	...	...
1906	...	...	...	...	...	...	...
1907	...	...	...	...	...	...	...
1908	...	...	...	...	...	...	...
1909	...	...	...	...	...	...	...
1910	...	...	...	...	...	...	...
1911	...	...	...	...	...	...	...
1912	...	...	...	...	...	...	...
1913	...	...	...	...	...	...	...
1914	...	...	...	...	...	...	...
1915	...	...	...	...	...	...	...
1916	...	...	...	...	...	...	...
1917	...	...	...	...	...	...	...
1918	...	...	...	...	...	...	...
1919	...	...	...	...	...	...	...
1920	717	837	811	866	245	5,003	4,781
1921	1,053	1,365	1,034	1,075	240	4,329	4,072
1922	915	1,298	1,009	1,039	251	9,069	5,240
1923	986	1,355	1,197	1,331	270	6,224	6,024
1924	877	1,136	971	1,204	260	6,514	8,374
1925	1,070	1,476	1,246	1,304	306	7,499	9,075
1926	929	1,166	1,143	1,380	266	5,047	6,599
1927	1,099[21]	1,252	1,285[21]	1,458[21]	260	9,109[21]	8,124[21]
	1,285	1,523	1,277	1,428		10,074	7,959
1928	1,402	1,779	1,402	1,423	223	8,593	6,226
1929	1,440	1,834	1,395	1,494	231	10,696	6,209
1930	1,335	1,759	1,215	1,279	181	8,642	6,420
1931	1,092	1,368	1,071	1,200	164	9,408	5,238
1932	1,429	2,138	1,499	1,621	212	8,898	3,960
1933	1,937	2,048	1,346	1,546	112	7,894	2,913
1934	1,329	1,501	1,031	1,148	180	9,137	4,240
1935	1,640	1,603	1,058	1,001	150	7,400	3,651
1936	1,457	1,399	1,015	1,189	236	10,243	4,758
1937	1,374	1,471	1,114	1,359	280	11,913	5,986
1938	1,764	1,867	1,326	1,363	279	7,356	3,877
1939	1,572	1,729	1,193	1,265	264	9,971	5,067
1940	1,111	867	1,240	1,277	202	8,236	4,937
1941	1,160	981	910	844	193	6,931	4,775
1942	1,451	1,231	1,143	986	218	7,754	4,237
1943	1,561	1,536	1,021	965	207	5,440	3,981
1944	1,210[22]	1,214[22]	684[22]	744[22]	132[22]	6,815[22]	4,525[22]

DENMARK

	Wheat	Rye	Barley	Oats	Mixed Corn	Potatoes	Sugar Beet
			thousands of hectolitres				
1890	1,330	5,993	8,265	13,148	3,139	4,390	
1891	1,470	6,888	7,980	12,134	3,167	5,076	
1892	1,502	7,181	8,713	14,359	3,659	6,642	
1893	1,359	6,922	6,095	9,813	2,593	7,588	thousand tons
1894	1,150	5,864	7,495	13,506	3,570	5,818	328
1895	1,222	6,483	7,680	14,179	3,816	7,281	349
1896	1,300	7,076	7,488	13,575	3,785	7,647	379
1897	1,224	6,384	6,756	12,411	3,577	7,108	387
1898	1,054	5,685	7,706	14,615	4,037	5,839	277
1899	1,288	6,469	7,645	13,065	3,826	6,643	332
1900	1,270	7,032	8,045	14,212	4,060	8,222	382
1901	332	5,851	7,852	13,183	4,619	7,753	449
1902	1,595	6,618	8,206	14,385	4,723	9,574	292
1903	1,572	6,803	8,225	14,510	4,783	8,900	401
1904	1,509	5,802	7,569	13,097	5,043	8,562	357
1905	1,433	6,783	6,905	11,193	4,851	10,387	512
1906	1,466	6,635	7,039	13,646	5,490	10,120	475
1907	1,530	5,601	7,617	14,986	6,159	8,607	406
1908	1,522	6,756	7,106	14,250	5,967	10,484	434
1909	1,349	6,668	7,611	14,861	6,184	8,573	450
						thousand tons	
1910	1,925	6,352	7,832	14,816	6,252	832	742
		thousands of metric tons					
1911	155	449	514	764	351	823	734
1912	137	418	561	795	369	827	1,052
1913	182	432	596	829	384	1,070	930
1914	158	283	495	685	322	946	967
1915	217	338	618	760	360	1,073	825
1916	165	274	533	750	347	674	736
1917	117	225	389	547	275	888	883
1918	172	323	467	603	325	1,105	944
1919	161	379	534	691	379	1.445	1,017
1920	189[23]	318[23]	513[23]	684[23]	348[23]	1,194[23]	847[23]
	201	337	538	737	366	1,233	868
1921	303	310	600	757	367	1,366	869
1922	252	363	663	848	379	1,340	572
1923	241	385	707	916	443	1,238	765
1924	160	265	745	917	479	742	953
1925	265	349	796	956	508	1,311	1,209
1926	239	317	728	876	488	812	984
1927	256	263	786	883	556	565	1,095
1928	332	246	1,100	1,059	763	1,173	1,282
1929	320[24]	265[24]	1,112[24]	1,035[24]	772[24]	1,072[24]	907[24]
1930	278	255	1,051	998	750	984	1,069
1931	274	214	957	936	740	877	783
1932	299	222	1,009	1,055	794	1,304	1,033
1933	314	251	959	997	796	1,327	1,726
1934	350	274	956	987	809	1,373	1,047
1935	399	284	1,107	1,042	852	1,218	1,886
1936	307	199	898	836	636	1,289	1,817
1937	368	251	1,099	1,025	754	1,324	1,505
1938	461[24]	284[24]	1,359[24]	1,144[24]	795[24]	1,433[24]	1,363[24]
1939	383	262	1,103	1,024	781	1,349	1,572
1940	189	272	1,159	906	712	1,352	1,570
1941	193	306	914	721	573	1,316	1,765
1942	16·	412	1,386	1,011	953	1,667	1,592
1943	179	507	1,288	1,036	861	1,942	1,460
1944	276	412	1,250	979	771	1,409	1,271

See p.296 for footnotes

D2 **Output of Main Cereal, Potato, and Sugar Beet Crops** (in thousands of hectolitres or metric tons)

1890–1944

FINLAND (thousands of hectolitres)

	Wheat	Rye	Barley	Oats	Mixed Corn	Potatoes	Sugar Beet
1890	51.	4,518	2,312	5,518	182	6.068	—
1891	44	4,377	1,788	4,282	119	5,850	—
1892	40	3,243	1,470	4,583	111	3,801	—
1893	45	3.828	1,781	4,858	125	4,181	—
1894	52	4,301	2,030	4,918	151	6,066	—
1895	52	4,667	2,154	6,624	158	6,357	—
1896	43	4.817	2,097	6,174	167	6,508	—
1897	56	4,679	2,114	6,335	171	6,614	—
1898	56	4.578	2,018	6,713	177	5,968	—
1899	51	3,603	1,330	5,280	117	4,524	—
1900	56	4,044	1,634	6,239	148	5,415	—
1901	49	4,459	1,717	6,037	143	5,753	—
1902	28	3,115	1,279	5,353	108	5,391	—
1903	46	3,735	1,844	6,007	152	6,770	—
1904	47	3,652	1,732	5,989	122	5,450	—
1905	46	4,071	1,874	6,364	156	7,296	—
1906	53	4,203	1,895	6,911	151	7,200	—
1907	49	3,888	1,808	7,274	147	6,613	—
1908	39	3,945	1,800	6,456	189	5,707	—
1909	47	4,259	1,722	6,963	189	6,775	—
1910	44	3.632	1,736	7,106	200	6,127	—
1911	50	3,317	1,739	6,683	216	6,497	—
1912	42	3,657	1,795	7,416	261	6,630	—
1913	58	3,618	1,725	7,760	268	6,467	—
1914	69	3,979	1,521	6,897	211	6,603	—
1915	92	3,972	1,769	8,424	204	7,235	—
1916	87	3,488	1,721	7,776	161	6,930	—
1917	80	3,141	1,587	6,625	130	6,737	—
			thousands of metric tons				
1918	6	213	97	325	6	455	—
1919	7	220	99	357	6	492	—
1920	9	250	116	396	9	558	—
1921	16	297	133	506	12	623	—
1922	19	268	141	540	16	525	—
1923	19	239	85	582	10	462	—
1924	22	286	130	492	13	634	—
1925	25	348	141	587	14	723	—
1926	25	303	156	593	14	851	—
1927	29	328	143	633	16	758	—
1928	27	279	126	570	15	689	—
1929	21	265	141	514	11	721	—
1930	24	336	165	627	17	928	—
1931	31	315	166	670	22	978	—
1932	40	329	179	670	23	983	—
1933	67	373	179	636	22	1,282	—
1934	89	395	209	776	28	1,139	—
1935	115	350	116	609	24	1,269	—
1936	143	308	185	693	25	1,433	—
1937	209	431	176	728	15	1,388	—
1938	256	369	207	826	18	1,198	—
1939	231	306	189	768	19	1,234	—
1940	179[25]	210[25]	139[25]	505[25]	13[25]	1,234[25]	—
1941	147	220	118	454	7	745	—
1942	172	204	139	545	6	972	—
1943	177	208	161	475	7	1,081	35
1944	160	167	149	345	6	639	47

See p.296 for footnotes

D2 Output of Main Cereal, Potato, and Sugar Beet Crops (in thousands of hectolitres or metric tons)

1890–1944

FRANCE (thousands of metric tons)

	Wheat	Rye	Barley	Oats	Maize	Buckwheat	Potatoes	Sugar Beet
1890	8,970	1,730	1,080	4,420	590	600	11,040	6,480
1891	5,880	1,540	1,620	4,970	670	640	11,170	6,530
1892	8,460	1,700	1,040	3,890	680	610	13,540	6,220
1893	7,560	1,630	770	2,860	670	550	11,840	6,050
1894	9,370	1,900	1,080	4,270	700	600	12,820	7,640
1895	9,240	1,820	1,080	4,400	670	620	12,920	6,380
1896	9,260	1,770	1,030	4,300	770	530	12,950	8,480
1897	6,590	1,210	900	3,680	770	580	11,320	7,760
1898	9,930	1,700	1,050	4,670	600	470	11,830	6,590
1899	9,950	1,710	1,020	4,470	650	500	12,350	7,230
1900	8,860	1,510	910	4,140	570	510	12,250	8,590
1901	8,460	1,480	870	3,700	680	560	12,020	9,020
1902	8,920	1,160	940	4,640	630	570	11,190	7,440
1903	9,880	1,480	980	5,000	650	630	11,610	7,900
1904	8,150	1,340	850	4,220	500	400	12,280	5,800
1905	9,110	1,490	910	4,440	610	520	14,260	9,550
1906	8,950	1,300	820	4,280	370	280	10,130	7,190
1907	10,380	1,430	970	5,120	610	470	13,940	7,180
1908	8,620	1,310	920	4,750	660	510	17,010	7,790
1909	9,780	1,410	1,040	5,560	660	530	16,680	8,220
1910	6,880	1,110	970	4,820	590	590	8,520	7,740
1911	8,770	1,190	1,090	5,070	430	210	12,770	5,760
1912	9,100	1,240	1,100	5,150	600	500	15,020	9,540
1913	8,690[26]	1,270[26]	1,040[26]	5,180[26]	540[26]	560[26]	13,590[26]	7,990[26]
1914	7,690	1,110	980	4,620	570	530	11,990	6,060
1915	6,060	840	690	3,460	430	460	9,400	1,740
1916	5,580	850	830	4,020	420	270	8,780	2,780
1917	3,660	630	810	3,110	380	380	10,410	2,710
1918	6,140	730	600	2,560	250	220	6,520	1,480
1919	4,970[8]	730[8]	500[8]	2,490[8]	250[8]	270[8]	7,730[8]	1,720[8]
	5,120[26]	780[26]	570[26]	2,620[26]	260[26]	...[26]	...[26]	...[26]
1920	6,450	880	840	4,230	390	360	11,640	2,930
1921	8,800	1,130	830	3,550	260	250	8,310	2,440
1922	6,620	980	890	4,180	320	390	12,650	3,960
1923	7,500	930	980	4,890	320	320	9,920	4,460
1924	7,650	1,020	1,050	4,430	460	420	15,350	6,460
1925	8,990	1,110	1,030	4,760	510	410	15,200	5,980
1926	6,310	760	1,000	5,290	320	370	11,130	5,450
1927	7,520	860	1,100	4,980	530	420	17,530	6,760
1928	7,660	870	1,100	4,940	310	310	11,260	6,560
1929	9,180	930	1,300	5,420	470	340	16,170	7,880
1930	6,210	720	920	4,150	570	360	13,920	10,820
1931	7,190	750	1,040	4,590	630	370	16,300	7,230
1932	9,080	860	1,090	4,820	410	370	16,480	8,850
1933	9,860	900	1,150	5,670	430	300	14,820	8,710
1934	9,210	840	1,030	4,380	510	330	16,650	10,310
1935	7,760	750	1,030	4,460	570	280	14,320	8,280
1936	6,930	710	1,000	4,210	530	340	15,250	8,680
1937	7,020	740	1,020	4,350	510	230	15,880	8,670
1938	9,800[27]	810[27]	1,290[27]	5,460[27]	580[27]	240[27]	17,310[27]	7,980[27]
1939	7,300	750	1,360	5,270	610	290	14,410	11,570
1940	5,060	540	920	3,230	410	220	10,290	5,000
1941	5,580	360	780	2,700	300	180	6,940	5,600
1942	5,480[27]	340[27]	760[27]	3,000[27]	200[27]	85[27]	6,930[27]	7,210[27]
1943	6,380	340	710	2,810	190	95	6,530	6,120
1944	6,360[27]	330[27]	630[27]	2,580[27]	250[27]	84[27]	7,560[27]	5,070[27]

See p.296 for footnotes

D2 Output of Main Cereal, Potato, and Sugar Beet Crops (in thousands of hectolitres or metric tons)

1890–1944

GERMANY (thousands of metric tons)[9]

	Wheat[3]	Rye	Barley	Oats	Maize	Mixed Corn & Buckwheat	Potatoes	Sugar Beet
1890	3,743	6,926	2,712	5,934	...	536	27,316	10,623
1891	3,095	5,644	2,801	6,357	...	486	21,718	9,488
1892	3,987	8,064	2,873	5,743	...	550	32,728	9,790
1893	3,933	8,942	2,360	4,180	...	471	40,724	9,794
1894	3,876	8,343	2,849	6,580	...	548	33,609	12,537
1895	3,643	7,725	2,794	6,244	...	529	37,786	11,196
1896	3,845	8,534	2,727	5,969	...	502	32,329	12,616
1897	3,726	8,171	2,564	5,719	...	515	33,776	12,637
1898	4,122	9,032	2,829	6,754	...	533	36,721	11,569
1899	4,323	8,676	2,984	6,883	...	568	38,486	13,254
1900	4,307	8,551	3,002	7,092	...	546	40,585	16,013
1901	2,931	8,163	3,321	7,050	...	509	48,687	16,030
1902	4,383	9,494	3,100	7,467	...	574	43,462	12,940
1903	4,003	9,904	3,324	7,873	...	587	42,902	15,200
1904	4,259	10,061	2,948	6,936	...	555	36,287	12,340
1905	4,187	9,607	2,922	6,547	...	527	48,323	17,370
1906	4,399	9,626	3,111	8,431	...	571	42,937	16,480
1907	3,937	9,758	3,498	9,149	...	587	45,538	15,900
1908	4,212	10,737	3,060	7,695	...	560	46,393	14,630
1909	4,254	11,348	3,496	9,126	...	606	46,706	15,510
1910	4,249	10,511	2,903	7,900	...	545	43,468	18,150
1911	4,469	10,866	3,160	7,704	...	557	34,374	10,080
1912	4,768	11,548	3,482	8,520	...	594	50,209	17,330
1913	5,094	12,222	3,673	9,714	...	621	54,121	18,540
1914	4,343	10,427	3,138	9,038	...	...	45,570	16,919
1915	4,235	9,152	2,484	5,986	...	...	53,973	10,963
1916	3,288	8,937	2,797	7,025	...	...	25,074	10,145
1917	2,484[9]	7,003[9]	1,865[9]	3,716[9]	...	... [9]	34,882[9]	9,967[9]
1918	2,528[9]	6,676[9]	1,850[9]	4,381[9]	...	... [9]	24,744[9]	9,884[9]
1919	2,315	6,100	1,670	4,494	...	...	21,479	5,819
1920	2,434	4,972	1,800	4,870	...	...	28,249	7,964
1921	3,140[9]	6,798[9]	1,939[9]	5,004[9]	...	... [9]	26,149[9]	7,980[9]
1922	2,071	5,234	1,607	4,015	...	...	40,661	10,792
1923	3,057	6,682	2,361	6,107	...	...	32,580	8,696
1924	3,053	6,876	2,808	6,785	...	558	43,682	10,267
1925	3,878	9,272	2,989	6,423	...	595	47,976	10,326
1926	3,135	7,367	2,832	7,274	...	530	34,536	10,495
1927	3,931	7,859	3,149	7,299	...	650	43,183	10,854
1928	4,424	9,374	3,682	7,696	...	711	45,396	11,011
1929	3,850	8,971	3,499	7,946	...	743	43,660	11,091
1930	4,320	8,447	3,146	5,990	...	622	50,783	14,919
1931	4,804	7,348	3,320	6,478	...	660	46,815	11,039
1932	5,674	9,200	3,537	6,766	...	748	39,632	7,876
1933	6,342	9,600	3,815	6,911	...	788	46,031	8,579
1934	5,144	8,369	3,524	5,300	...	744	48,371	10,394
1935	[9] 5,269	[9] 8,226	[9] 3,727	[9] 5,925	...	[9] 1,040	[9] 45,118	[9] 10,568
1936	4,975	8,125	3,739	6,180	...	1,033	50,956	12,096
1937	5,034	7,609	4,002	6,511	121	1,265	60,841	15,701
1938	6,250	9,467	4,673	7,003	179	1,409[28]	55,983	15,545
1939	4,956	8,404	3,726	6,143	106	1,291	51,867	16,770
1940	4,123	6,537	3,118	5,990	65	1,360	54,794	16,503
1941	4,285	7,320	3,135	5,045	48	1,395	45,238	16,086
1942	3,573	5,654	3,195	6,069	45	2,116	52,993	16,403
1943	4,341	7,745	2,632	5,389	42	1,397	39,127	14,607
1944	3,808	7,508	2,291	4,444	39	1,242	41,240	13,671

See p.296 for footnotes

D2 Output of Main Cereal, Potato, and Sugar Beet Crops (in thousands of hectolitres or metric tons)

1890–1944

GREECE (thousands of metric tons)[29]

	Wheat	Rye	Barley	Oats	Maize	Mixed Corn	Potatoes
1890	...	...	...	...	...	...	...
1891	...	...	...	...	...	...	...
1892	...	...	...	...	...	...	...
1893	...	...	...	...	...	...	...
1894	...	...	...	...	...	...	...
1895	...	...	...	...	...	...	...
1896	...	...	...	...	...	...	...
1897	...	...	...	...	...	...	...
1898	...	...	...	...	...	...	...
1899	...	...	...	...	...	...	...
1900	...	...	...	...	...	...	...
1901	...	...	...	...	...	...	...
1902	...	...	...	...	...	...	...
1903	...	...	...	...	...	...	...
1904	...	...	...	...	...	...	...
1905	...	...	...	...	...	...	...
1906	...	...	...	...	...	...	...
1907	...	...	...	...	...	...	...
1908	...	...	...	...	...	...	...
1909	...	...	...	...	...	...	...
1910	...	...	...	...	...	...	...
1911	344	6	80	32	151	...	28
1912	...[29]	...[29]	..[29]	...[29]	...[29]	...[29]	...[29]
1913	...	...	...	...	...	...	...
1914	357	3	103	54	239	...	44
1915	[29] 246	[29] 4	[29] 87	[29] 45	[29] 147	[29] ...	[29] 46
1916	220[29]	4[29]	86[29]	40[29]	120[29]	...[29]	41[29]
1917	313	18	126	52	155	...	47
1918	374[29]	26[29]	158[29]	66[29]	164[29]	...[29]	47[29]
1919	267	29	118	56	192	34	40
1920	305	26	135	61	204	40	50
1921	281[29]	27[29]	129[29]	54[29]	192[29]	38[29]	42[29]
1922	246	28	129	68	143	27	46
1923	239	16	117	58	162	32	51
1924	210	23	94	45	156	17	48
1925	305	40	151	79	173	24	41
1926	338	41	166	72	207	28	50
1927	353	38	158	68	130	27	33
1928	356	44	158	76	129	23	33
1929	311	34	104	61	178	18	35
1930	264	47	171	86	173	20	54
1931	306	46	156	77	159	29	63
1932	465	53	193	99	214	35	85
1933	773	71	230	134	273	47	113
1934	699	63	196	99	210	32	108
1935	740	55	194	100	192	30	104
1936	532	42	154	94	287	39	129
1937	818	65	219	134	323	44	193
1938	980	58	221	135	217	50	158
1939	923	48	185	127	256	45	187
1940	...	...	...	...	...	...	...
1941	...	...	...	...	...	...	...
1942	...	...	...	...	...	...	...
1943	...	...	...	...	...	...	...
1944	...	...	...	...	...	...	...

See p.296 for footnotes

D2 Output of Main Cereal, Potato, and Sugar Beet Crops (in thousands of hectolitres or metric tons)

1890–1944

HUNGARY[10]

	Wheat	Rye	Barley	Oats	Maize	Potatoes	Sugar Beet
		thousands of hectolitres					thou tons
1890	52,165	20,235	18,647	18,777	31,685	29,755	985
		thousands of metric tons					
1891	3,777	1,096	1,212	986	3,792	2,079	1,312
1892	3,865	1,332	1,161	979	3,026	2,774	1,337
1893	4,371	1,607	1,410	1,055	3,483	3,269	1,543
1894	3,962	1,558	1,311	1,088	1,780	2,838	1,461
1895	4,444	1,251	1,187	1,051	3,709	3,239	1,255
1896	4,127	1,334	1,328	1,084	3,334	3,609	1,512
1897	2,206	926	915	799	2,639	3,041	1,424
1898	3,490	1,180	1,248	1,142	3,236	3,729	1,495
1899	3,845	1,304	1,341	1,179	2,946	3,605	1,618
1900	3,843	1,113	1,173	1,025	3,243	4,497	1,979
1901	3,373	1,127	1,090	988	3,236	4,314	1,918
1902	4,651	1,361	1,358	1,202	2,656	3,852	1,951
1903	4,408	1,291	1,406	1,268	3,448	4,501	2,096
1904	3,731	1,198	1,087	911	1,509	3,005	1,591
1905	4,287	1,374	1,360	1,132	2,389	4,578	1,923
1906	5,373	1,415	1,519	1,273	4,138	4,874	2,649
1907	3,280	1,069	1,373	1,154	3,953	4,849	2,361
1908	4,142	1,219	1,226	1,018	3,712	3,796	2,067
1909	3,085	1,196	1,565	1,339	4,111	4,995	2,593
1910	4,619	1,329	1,168	1,026	4,769	4,816	2,873
1911	4,760	1,279	1,602	1,301	3,491	4,438	2,940
1912	4,717	1,375	1,527	1,114	4,488	5,384	4,796
1913	4,119	1,327	1,738	1,449	4,625	4,875	4,776
1914	2,864	1,077	1,421	1,256	4,377	5,315	4,014
1915	4,048	1,161	1,270	1,174	4,068	5,784	2,532
1916	3,055	950	1,130	1,228	2,370	4,361	2,007
1917	3,354	1,014	804	775	2,632	2,991	1,590
1918	2,588[10]	824[10]	879[10]	667[10]	2,397[10]	3,122[10]	2,154[10]
1919	...	...	...	...	...	...	...
1920	1,032	514	472	324	1,274	2,072	640
1921	1,435	588	466	319	805	1,249	543
1922	1,489	639	483	327	1,238	1,320	711
1923	1,843	794	594	399	1,251	1,334	864
1924	1,403	561	320	228	1,883	1,535	1,274
1925	1,951	826	554	371	2,235	2,310	1,527
1926	2,039	798	555	360	1,944	1,875	1,445
1927	2,094	568	516	327	1,736	2,005	1,455
1928	2,700	828	668	400	1,260	1,471	1,438
1929	2,041	798	683	411	1,794	2,168	1,607
1930	2,295	722	601	261	1,407	1,841	1,461
1931	1,975	550	476	194	1,518	1,447	966
1932	1,754	770	719	316	2,432	1,557	849
1933	2,622	956	841	358	1,809	1,856	944
1934	1,764	619	544	259	2,098	2,119	922
1935	2,292	728	556	246	1,418	1,393	769
1936	2,389	714	658	262	2,593	2,451	1,124
1937	1,964	618	557	270	2,759	2,559	1,013
1938	2,688	805	724	310	2,662	2,141	969
1939	2,689	762	652	321	2,185	2,026	918
1940	1,819	597	551	319	2,379	2,372	1,168
1941	1,886	560	603	339	1,806	2,192	906
1942	1,703	513	511	279	1,444	1,804	738
1943	2,279	669	705	352	1,246	1,821	726
1944	2,319	646	679	318	2,297	2,636	...

CROATIA-SLAVONIA

	Wheat	Rye	Barley	Oats	Maize	Potatoes	Sugar Beet
		thousands of hectolitres					thou tons
1890	2,370	2,031	857	1,258	4,493	232	8
1891	2,325	1,537	738	1,306	5,466	224	8
1892	2,492	1,684	788	1,228	5,461	232	8
		thousands of metric tons					
1893	223	129	53	56	403	301	13
1894	240	141	62	78	320	279	7
1895	234	110	51	65	476	333	8
1896	261	144	65	78	465	263	5
1897	167	95	45	64	371	250	6
1898	310	155	77	102	529	352	6
1899	245	122	60	92	373	260	5
1900	300	113	63	81	475	365	7
1901	291	128	66	84	520	537	16
1902	327	134	71	91	388	355	13
1903	399	151	84	106	604	526	17
1904	268	94	50	71	289	253	9
1905	356	115	62	88	467	343	8
1906	282	94	60	80	520	350	20
1907	277	80	45	61	456	697	24
1908	360	111	56	62	515	575	24
1909	317	93	51	81	553	458	32
1910	311	80	46	58	654	775	49
1911	413	100	57	81	610	609	47
1912	308	69	43	51	611	590	44
1913	435	95	68	95	736	575	89
1914	341	77	51	84	657	537	165
1915	242	53	37	78	393	378	57
1916	223	35	35	91	312	272	46
1917	...	...	...	...	...	...	...
1918	...	...	...	...	...	...	...
1919–		incorporated in Yugoslavia					

See p.296 for footnotes

D2 Output of Main Cereal, Potato, and Sugar Beet Crops (in thousands of hectolitres or metric tons)

1890–1944

	IRELAND (thousands of metric tons)					NORTHERN IRELAND (thousands of metric tons			
	Wheat	Barley	Oats	Potatoes	Sugar Beet	Wheat	Barley	Oats	Potatoes
1890	72	156	904	1,839	...	...	...	...	...
1891	71	168	957	3,086	...	...	...	...	...
1892	60	146	918	2,626	...	...	...	...	...
1893	45	141	985	3,113	...	...	...	...	...
1894	42	143	980	1,903	...	...	...	...	...
1895	30	145	926	3,528	...	...	...	...	...
1896	33	160	864	2,744	...	...	...	...	...
1897	37	132	826	1,522	...	...	...	...	...
1898	51	151	949	2,989	...	...	...	...	...
1899	47	155	909	2,804	...	...	...	...	...
1900	46	141	890	1,872	...	...	...	...	...
1901	40	148	903	3,426	...	...	...	...	...
1902	44	180	952	2,770	...	...	...	...	...
1903	32	132	854	2,401	...	...	...	...	...
1904	28	119	873	2,684	...	...	...	...	...
1905	39	156	882	3,478	...	...	...	...	...
1906	42	157	911	2,704	...	...	...	...	...
1907	36	152	872	2,282	...	...	...	...	...
1908	38	155	927	3,251	...	...	...	...	...
1909	48	182	986	3,254	...	...	...	...	...
1910	47	149	955	2,917	...	...	...	...	...
1911	45	155	859	3,754	...	...	...	...	...
1912	43	158	971	2,588	...	...	...	...	...
1913	35	174	960	3,799	...	...	...	...	...
1914	39	176	919	3,501	...	...	...	...	...
1915	88	128	996	3,770	...	...	...	...	...
1916	77	142	905	2,472	...	...	...	...	...
1917	124	171	1,374	4,220	...	...	...	...	...
1918	154	182	1,472	3,925	...	...	...	...	...
1919	67	177	1,242	2,791	...	...	...	...	...
1920	39	162	906	2,018	...	...	...	...	...
1921	42	126	766	2,597	...	...	...	...	...
1922	42	152	828	3,486	...	...	...	...	...
	SOUTHERN IRELAND								
1923	32	117	474	1,500	...	6.3	1.8	280	931
1924	28	125	490	1,516	...	4.3	2.0	272	842
1925	20	134	595	2,172	...	3.5	2.3	278	1,187
1926	31	146	649	1,963	87	6.2	1.6	297	1,086
1927	39	137	678	2,482	136	5.8	1.5	280	1,074
1928	32	134	648	2,282	143	5.0	2.0	281	1,173
1929	32	130	700	3,055	144	3.9	1.8	291	1,142
1930	30	120	642	2,375	161	4.7	2.1	281	870
1931	21	107	529	1,963	35	2.8	1.3	230	709
1932	23	108	637	3,063	152	3.4	1.1	294	1,144
1933	54	122	634	2,537	205	6.2	1.5	267	964
1934	104	148	570	2,586	492	9.9	2.5	278	938
1935	182	159	626	2,618	572	9.9	3.3	264	901
1936	213	124	525	2,460	600	7.4	2.8	263	798
1937	190	120	582	2,749	564	4.5	2.6	247	882
1938	201	112	568	2,500	401	5.8	3.4	295	722
1939	282	80	548	3,046	396	3.0	3.1	274	878
1940	318	141	736	3,168	648	13	15	384	1,047
1941	442	145	695	3,749	686	18	17	439	1,241
1942	520	175	780	3,170	367	12	14	435	1,251
1943	442	191	809	3,148	710	12	13	400	1,306
1944	555	154	792	3,055	602	4.5	15	385	1,087

D2 Output of Main Cereal, Potato, and Sugar Beet Crops (in thousands of hectolitres or metric tons)

1890–1944

ITALY (thousands of metric tons)[1,2]

	Wheat	Rye	Barley	Oats	Maize	Rice	Potatoes	Sugar Beet
1890	3,613	112	255	335	1,902	315	1,202	6.7
1891	3,889	116	226	351	1,839	347	1,208	13
1892	3,180	108	185	304	1,830	363	970	8.9
1893	3,717	114	184	322	2,100	246	1,373	9.6
1894	3,442	109	194	300	1,512	287	1,073	17
1895	3,237	102	173	338	1,788	300	1,235	22
1896	3,992	125	234	326	2,028	207	1,278	19
1897	2,389	75	170	291	1,672	370	1,429	32
1898	3,775	119	156	317	2,021	371	1,504	49
1899	3,791	121	176	371	2,246	417	1,744	191
1900	3,903	127	204	333	2,359	595	1,521	476
1901	4,808	155	223	505	2,694	558	1,675	589
1902	3,991	132	230	343	1,941	532	1,786	756
1903	5,383	171	171	500	2,387	606	2,056	1,037
1904	4,896	146	165	490	2,428	606	2,138	622
1905	4,682	141	213	575	2,609	539	2,341	745
1906	5,149	162	189	528	2,494	580	2,531	844
1907	5,178	158	223	588	2,374	656	2,497	1,023
1908	4,448	140	234	563	2,573	590	2,689	1,627
1909	5,043	188	238	561	2,666	533	2,841	1,257
1910	4,064	156	212	370	2,729	491	2,545	1,619
1911	5,097	151	243	530	2,513	537	2,796	1,556
1912	4,390	151	187	366	2,647	493	2,534	1,729
1913	5,690	160	241	562	2,908	609	2,958	2,819
1914	4,493	150	154	294	2,816	611	2,749	1,352
1915	4,518	125	246	407	3,269	629	2,554	1,494
1916	4,676	150	225	337	2,188	583	2,442	1,347
1917	3,709	127	165	438	2,221	590	2,165	905
1918	4,856	149	216	587	2,055	587	2,331	1,146
1919	4,497	131	186	449	2,303	546	2,294	1,846
1920	3,744	130	131	313	2,396	506	2,351	1,300
1921	5,108[1,2]	161[1,2]	231[1,2]	489[1,2]	2,477[1,2]	528[1,2]	2,626[1,2]	2,097[1,2]
1922	4,255	137	171	388	2,012	521	2,128	2,507
1923	5,918	160	218	507	2,336	584	2,616	2,859
1924	4,479	151	180	424	2,767	663	2,852	4,433
1925	6,340	165	267	604	2,880	706	3,143	1,409
1926	5,808	160	229	517	3,092	762	3,366	2,517
1927	5,154	147	196	391	2,288	780	2,833	2,190
1928	6,017	161	229	616	1,702	708	2,170	2,965
1929	6,668	175	255	597	2,523	727	2,820	3,362
1930	5,433	155	238	467	2,979	694	2,631	3,433
1931	6,376	165	236	512	1,942	700	2,532	2,560
1932	7,286	160	243	552	3,011	687	3,492	2,435
1933	7,923	171	224	538	2,587	715	2,785	2,153
1934	6,238	142	201	469	3,198	688	3,024	2,719
1935	7,632	158	203	508	2,495	735	2,283	2,436
1936	6,112	132	193	478	3,051	734	2,638	2,613
1937	8,064	145	233	620	3,396	791	3,214	3,524
1938	8,184	138	248	629	2,940	817	2,942	3,281
1939	7,971	151	236	548	2,582	762	2,780	3,671
1940	7,104	152	219	571	3,428	929	3,299	5,246
1941	7,070	147	236	587	2,612	864	3,094	4,171
1942	6,575	140	234	487	2,455	793	2,997	3,689
1943	6,510[1,2]	126[1,2]	228[1,2]	441[1,2]	1,682[1,2]	643[1,2]	2,279[1,2]	3,199[1,2]
1944	6,451	114	221	435	2,183	416	2,303	3,124

See p.296 for footnotes

D2 Output of Main Cereal, Potato, and Sugar Beet Crops (in thousands of hectolitres or metric tons)

1890–1944

NETHERLANDS

	Wheat	Rye	Barley	Oats	Buck-wheat	Potatoes	Sugar Beet
1890	1,912	3,916	1,464	4,666	577	18,941	732
1891	1,235	2,918	1,575	6,531	558	16,001	421
1892	1,896	4,382	1,757	5,288	489	33,166	750
1893	1,752	4,363	1,681	4,345	547	31,585	758
1894	1,468	4,331	1,275	5,322	549	20,858	738
1895	1,509	4,510	1,512	5,471	623	26,306	1,029
1896	1,778	4,782	1,608	5,406	421	29,251	1,742
1897	1,512	4,204	1,317	5,682	557	27,461	1,152
1898	1,905	4,815	1,347	5,856	482	27,538	1,258
1899	1,796	4,570	1,399	5,660	431	33,723	1,603
1900	1,646	4,808	1,615	6,095	425	28,338	1,509
1901	1,491	4,997	1,366	6,514	342	33,446	1,828
1902	1,799	4,923	1,639	6,780	494	33,392	914
1903	1,500	4,924	1,347	7,087	476	25,864	960
1904	1,559	4,763	1,271	6,552	296	33,274	1,018
1905	1,709	4,843	1,414	5,654	411	30,673	1,599
1906	1,742	4,912	1,148	6,629	356	33,655	1,363
1907	1,876	5,104	1,442	7,377	325	33,267	1,306
1908	1,804	5,591	1,393	6,936	322	34,075	1,563
1909	1,465	6,221	1,174	6,823	289	34,279	1,497
1910	1,565	5,412	1,093	6,357	293	31,144	1,627
1911	1,942	5,677	1,204	6,246	133	36,462	2,005
1912	1,975	5,671	1,186	5,750	175	42,949	2,176
1913	1,820	5,954	1,104	6,663	169	38,503	1,665
1914	2,037	4,749	1,064	6,825	151	42,562	1,994
1915	2,498	5,679	1,191	7,292	100	44,663	1,714
1916	1,687	4,104	838	6,317	101	37,051	1,717
1917	1,392	4,673	761	6,293	97	43,690	1,458
1918	1,914	4,589	922	6,561	72	45,913	1,245
1919	2,064	5,185	831	6,520	86	44,896	1,494
1920	2,112	5,214	937	7,204	98	42,821	1,906
1921	3,017	6,339	1,163	7,048	46	37,829	2,708
1922	2,171	6,040	1,108	6,279	66	57,204	1,818
1923	2,189	5,135	1,040	6,569	43	37,650	1,720
1924	1,658	5,567	1,229	6,589	34	41,332	2,426
1925	1,997	5,866	1,230	6,410	26	46,977	2,224
1926	1,965	4,881	1,232	7,109	21	44,211	2,111
1927	2,205	4,826	1,159	6,672	15	37,441	1,826
1928	2,627	6,201	1,557	7,826	12	57,649	2,289
1929	1,958	6,547	1,715	8,134	9	60,961	2,060
1930	2,169	5,328	1,389	6,454	6	45,206	2,138
1931	2,417	5,068	1,131	6,243	6	42,095	1,029
1932	4,597	4,960	864	6,028	6	52,955	1,656
1933	5,488	5,582	803	6,312	7	44,894	1,948
1934	6,461	7,079	1,570	6,249	7	43,575	1,786
1935	5,964	6,595	1,814	6,115	4	39,547	1,526
1936	5,577	6,819	1,927	6,890	5	36,839	1,638
1937	4,556	6,869	2,128	7,730	4	39,229	1,582
		thousands of metric tons					
1938	434	551	140	447	...	2,843	1,520
1939	417	603	146	449	...	3,050	1,716
1940	394	444	144	387	...	2,821	1,894
1941	381	448	141	224	...	3,451	1,653
1942	281	581	140	223	...	4,550	1,322
1943	341	608	113	253	...	4,200	1,574
1944	...	...	...	...	...	...	...

NORWAY (thousands of metric tons)

	Wheat	Rye	Barley	Oats	Mixed Corn	Potatoes
1890	...	...	...	...	...	...
1891	...	...	...	...	...	...
1892	...	...	...	...	...	...
1893	...	...	...	...	...	...
1894	...	...	...	...	...	...
1895	...	...	...	...	...	...
1896	...	...	...	...	...	...
1897	...	...	...	...	...	...
1898	...	...	...	...	...	...
1899	...	...	...	...	...	...
1900	9	23	68	159	14	554
1901	8	23	59	137	11	592
1902	7	21	44	110	8	464
1903	8	23	66	152	12	609
1904	6	20	49	116	9	461
1905	8	28	68	171	12	709
1906	8	28	67	170	12	604
1907	7	25	52	125	8	483
1908	9	22	73	199	13	689
1909	9	26	63	156	10	565
1910	8	23	70	186	13	570
1911	9	23	67	156	10	606
1912	11	25	79	201	14	809
1913	12	22	85	192	15	750
1914	11	22	69	133	10	753
1915	12	17	77	173	13	549
1916	13	15	96	217	17	788
1917	14	15	94	194	16	846
1918	30	27	128	274	24	780
1919	23	23	110	233	20	991
1920	16	21	102	214	17	805
1921	16	22	79	179	14	701
1922	17	22	97	199	16	897
1923	16	20	74	133	11	721
1924	13	17	101	154	14	627
1925	13	16	113	175	16	939
1926	16	16	112	194	15	895
1927	17	15	102	184	12	605
1928	22	12	112	184	13	951
1929	20	14	99	176	11	900
1930	20	14	107	198	12	766
1931	16	10	92	138	8	774
1932	20	13	118	194	12	1,035
1933	21	11	100	180	11	977
1934	33	10	116	176	9	800
1935	51	12	123	182	10	916
1936	57	11	115	171	9	946
1937	68	11	129	188	10	861
1938	72	11	124	197	11	938
1939	78	6	103	201	12	807
1940	69	6	93	159	10	1,308
1941	76	7	106	164	15	1,068
1942	83	8	95	156	15	1,182
1943	79	7	92	171	14	1,378
1944	78	6	77	155	12	938

D2 Output of Main Cereal, Potato, and Sugar Beet Crops (inthousands of hectolitres or metric tons)

1890–1944

POLAND (thousands of metric tons)

	Wheat	Rye	Barley	Oats	Potatoes	Sugar Beet
1890	...	...	...	...	...	...
1891	...	...	...	...	...	...
1892	...	...	...	...	...	...
1893	...	...	...	...	...	...
1894	...	...	...	...	...	...
1895	...	...	...	...	...	...
1896	...	...	...	...	...	...
1897	...	...	...	...	...	...
1898	...	...	...	...	...	...
1899	...	...	...	...	...	...
1900	...	...	...	...	...	...
1901	...	...	...	...	...	...
1902	...	...	...	...	...	...
1903	...	...	...	...	...	...
1904	...	...	...	...	...	...
1905	...	...	...	...	...	...
1906	...	...	...	...	...	...
1907	...	...	...	...	...	...
1908	...	...	...	...	...	...
1909	...	...	...	...	...	...
1910	...	...	...	...	...	...
1911	...	...	...	...	...	...
1912	...	...	...	...	...	...
1913	...	...	...	...	...	...
1914	...	...	...	...	...	...
1915	...	...	...	...	...	...
1916		...	...	...	...	...
1917	...	...	...	...	...	...
1918	...	...	...	...	...	...
1919	429	2,618	606	1,107	10,514	1,241
1920	619	1,871	840	1,873	18,096	1,385
1921	1,018	4,256	1,224	2,181	16,800	1,129
1922	1,153	5,014	1,297	2,506	33,219	2,671
1923	1,354	5,962	1,656	3,522	26,494	2,575
1924	884	3,655	1,208	2,412	26,870	3,211
1925	1,738	6,741	1,301	2,093	24,729	3,687
1926	1,429	5,182	1,214	1,941	21,380	3,725
1927	1,627	5,887	1,276	2,139	26,771	3,620
1928	1,612	6,110	1,527	2,498	27,661	4,921
1929	1,793	7,010	1,660	2,953	31,750	4,970
1930	2,240	6,958	1,464	2,348	30,902	4,717
1931	2,265	5,703	1,476	2,310	30,988	2,761
1932	1,346	6,111	1,401	2,391	29,975	2,379
1933	2,174	7,073	1,436	2,683	28,330	1,852
1934	2,080	6,464	1,453	2,551	33,470	2,567
1935	2,011	6,617	1,468	2,598	32,502	2,501
1936	2,133	6,364	1,401	2,640	34,281	2,555
1937	1,926	5,638	1,363	2,343	40,221	3,246
1938	2,172	7,253	1,371	2,657	34,558	3,162
1939	2,270	7,630	1,480	2,880	...	...
1940	[30] 1,778	[30] 5,984	[30] 1,437	[30] 2,586	[30] 45,207	[30] 7,670
1941	1,790	6,300	1,404	2,413	38,952	7,890
1942	1,332	5,272	1,665	2,758	38,328	8,000
1943	1,559	6,676	1,453	2,767	28,663	7,140
1944	1,349[30]	6,005[30]	1,256[30]	2,404[30]	34,230[30]	6,660[30]

PORTUGAL (thousands of metric tons)

	Wheat	Rye	Barley	Oats	Maize	Rice	Potatoes
1890	...	...	...	...	...	...	...
1891	...	...	...	...	...	...	...
1892	...	...	...	...	...	...	...
1893	...	...	...	...	...	...	...
1894	...	...	...	...	...	...	...
1895	...	...	...	...	...	...	...
1896	...	...	...	...	...	...	...
1897	...	...	...	...	...	...	...
1898	...	...	...	...	...	...	...
1899	...	...	...	...	...	...	...
1900	...	...	...	...	...	...	...
1901	...	...	...	...	...	...	...
1902	...	...	...	...	...	...	...
1903	...	...	...	...	...	...	...
1904	...	...	...	...	...	...	...
1905	...	...	...	...	...	...	...
1906	...	...	...	...	...	...	...
1907	...	...	...	...	...	...	...
1908	...	...	...	...	...	...	...
1909	...	...	...	...	...	...	...
1910	...	...	...	...	...	...	...
1911	322	...	...	...	...	...	...
1912	...	...	...	...	...	...	...
1913	...	...	...	...	...	...	...
1914	191	...	...	...	...	...	...
1915	183	...	...	...	278	17	...
1916	206	81	28	57	263	21	171
1917	202	90	32	66	252	17	165
1918	261	123	32	66	237	23	152
1919	223	98	31	67	248	21	154
1920	282	131	39	89	298	24	169
1921	256	116	35	82	289	11	175
1922	272	138	40	84	296	20	180
1923	359	133	53	118	260	16	180
1924	288	133	45	91	296	18	193
1925	340	129	48	91	364	17	340
1926	233	92	32	69	312	18	259
1927	312	119	43	80	384	22	311
1928	205	101	31	73	363	20	262
1929	294	119	43	81	379	22	345
1930	368	125	52	113	425	25	565
1931	368	129	44	92	446	26	605
1932	151	120	46	92	367	26	672
1933	324	92	31	53	364	47	620
1934	672	125	44	112	304	55	556
1935	601	119	49	97	269	58	513
1936	235	90	35	84	284	64	517
1937	399	96	39	98	320	85	596
1938	430	99	40	92	296	68	596
1939	516	99	39	91	365	72	606
1940	268	75	26	26	397	83	617
1941	449	91	49	82	418	89	625
1942	524	124	66	132	391	79	835
1943	295	99	48	70	481	74	891
1944	368	130	68	77	558	64	896

See p.296 for footnotes

D2 Output of Main Cereal, Potato and Sugar Beet Crops (in thousands of hectolitres or metric tons)

1890–1944

ROMANIA

	Wheat	Rye	Barley	Oats	Maize	Potatoes	Sugar Beet
			thousands of hectolitres			thousands of metric tons	
1890	18,267	1,671	5,699	2,678	21,440	...	...
1891	17,122	1,365	7,836	2,718	21,166	...	...
1892	22,591	1,637	7,227	3,905	32,433	...	...
1893	21,382	2,717	12,591	5,441	25,568	...	...
1894	15,323	2,032	5,985	3,520	10,605	...	...
1895	24,162	3,264	7,902	3,652	25,100	...	...
1896	25,139	4,308	11,182	5,469	23,078	...	...
1897	12,920	2,393	7,449	3,457	28,201	...	...
1898	20,644	2,684	10,478	6,118	35,833	...	...
1899	9,138	700	1,597	2,202	9,682	...	...
1900	19,875	2,119	5,122	3,064	29,920	...	...
1901	25,530	3,383	8,563	5,833	41,284	...	...
1902	26,905	2,454	8,683	10,241	24,219	...	...
1903	26,012	2,513	10,459	11,077	28,387	...	...
1904	18,937	776	4,076	4,443	6,901	93	145
1905	36,413	2,588	9,297	6,686	20,888	102	217
1906	40,127	3,136	11,819	9,220	46,004	126	192
1907	14,884	900	7,070	6,287	20,290	105	109
1908	19,316	930	4,536	6,065	27,801	117	167
			thousands of metric tons				
1909	1,602	79	449	405	1,903	104	208
1910	3,016	201	644	446	2,813	132	308
1911	2,603	157	569	402	3,004	154	263
1912	2,433	92	456	304	2,810	131	292
1913	2,291[31]	95[31]	602[31]	551[31]	3,111[31]	98	282[31]
1914	1,260	50	537	367	2,783	102	225
1915	2,444	74	632	434	2,345	126	185
1916	2,137	...	654	420	...	...	...
1917	...[31]	...[31]	...[31]	...[31]	...[31]	...[31]	...[31]
1918	584	43	109	85	80	72	49
1919	1,797[31]	255[31]	689[31]	331[31]	3,591[31]	[284][31][32]	34[31]
1920	1,669	240	1,472	992	4,624	609	89
1921	2,138	231	1,985	963	2,810	1,388	352
1922	2,504	234	2,042	1,336	3,044	1,116	331
1923	2,779	244	1,325	910	3,846	1,953	643
1924	1,917	151	670	610	3,949	1,669	873
1925	2,851	203	1,019	740	4,159	1,698	988
1926	3.018	286	1,685	1,159	5,840	1,941	1,285
1927	2,633	237	1,262	868	3,533	2,149	1,255
1928	3,145	292	1,511	980	2,756	2,052	1,055
1929	2,715	337	2,740	1,359	6,386	2,484	893
1930	3,559	465	2,371	1,157	4,520	1,958	849
1931	3,682	355	1,414	670	6,063	2,008	310
1932	1,512	267	1,467	643	5,993	1,725	303
1933	3,241	446	1,884	806	4,554	1,502	678
1934	2,084	211	871	563	4,846	2,072	648
1935	2,625	323	924	594	5,379	2,022	627
1936	3,503	453	1,612	847	5,612	2,113	427
1937	3,760	451	917	513	4,752	2,107	498
1938	4,821	517	832	463	5,117	1,804	731
1939	4,453[33]	432[33]	816[33]	487[33]	6,051[33]	1,988[33]	855[33]
1940	1,376	53	496	371	3,743	744	518
1941	1,986	55	391	333	3,347	854	567
1942	855	25	332	337	2,182	1,199	335
1943	2,319	68	587	500	2,884	1,629	739
1944	3,289[33]	166[33]	451[33]	476[33]	4,128[33]	1,905[33]	714[33]

See p.296 for footnotes

D2 Output of Main Cereal, Potato, and Sugar Beet Crops (in thousands of hectolitres or metric tons)

1890–1944

RUSSIA[14]

ESTONIA thousands of metric tons)

	Russia: Wheat	Rye	Barley	Oats	Maize	Potatoes	Sugar Beet	Estonia: Wheat	Rye	Barley	Oats	Potatoes
	(in millions of hectolitres)						(million tons)					
1890	94	197	72	238	107	146	4.9	included in Russia				
1891	74	220	62	159	130	127	4.3					
1892	106	258	74	192	97	203	3.7					
1893	164	321	129	286	170	253	5.6					
1894	161[14]	380[14]	105[14]	286[14]	84[14]	236[14]	5.4					
	169	403	112	306	84	314						
	(in million metric tons)											
1895	8.4	19.6	4.9	10.4	0.6	21.1	5.5[2]					
1896	8.7	19.3	4.9	10.4	0.4	23.2	5.7					
1897	7.0	15.8	4.5	8.5	1.2	21.9	6.0					
1898	9.7	17.9	6.0	8.9	1.0	23.2	6.0					
1899	9.1	22.1	4.3	13.0	0.6	23.8	7.3					
1900	9.2	22.7	4.5	11.5	0.6	25.3	6.4					
1901	9.1	18.5	4.6	8.4	1.5	23.2	8.2					
1902	13.1	22.4	6.4	12.6	1.0	27.5	8.6					
1903	12.9	22.1	6.7	10.3	1.0	23.6	7.7					
1904	11.3	24.6	6.7	15.2	0.5	24.0	6.4					
1905	12.8	17.7	6.4	12.0	0.6	27.6	7.7					
1906	9.9	15.9	5.8	8.8	1.5	25.1	10.1					
1907	9.7	19.4	6.6	11.6	1.1	27.7	8.6					
1908	11.0	19.0	7.0	11.7	1.3	28.4	8.2					
1909	16.5[14]	22.0[14]	8.9[14]	15.0[14]	0.7[14]	31.5[14]	6.9					
	23.0	22.9	10.9	16.9	1.4	32.8						
1910	22.8	22.2	10.6	15.5	2.6	36.6	13.2					
1911	15.3	19.5	9.5	12.7	2.4	32.0	13.6					
1912	21.8	26.7	10.8	15.8	2.4	38.0	10.7					
1913	28.0[14]	25.7[14]	13.1[14]	18.2[14]	2.1[14]	35.9[14]	12.4[14]					
1914	...	...	...	...	...	...	...					
1915	...	...	...	...	...	...	...					
1916	...	...	...	...	...	...	...					
1917	...	...	...	...	...	...	...					
1918	...	...	...	...	...	...	...	...	...	...	...	...
1919	...	...	...	...	...	...	...	12	125	98	...	519
1920	8.7	9.4	4.7	7.0	1.1	20.9	0.7	17	164	130	...	687
1921	5.6[14]	10.2[14]	2.7[14]	5.2[14]	1.2[14]	20.6[14]	0.4[14]	14	185	125	162	782
1922	10.6	18.2	4.3	7.8	3.0	22.2	1.5	21	147	145	146	718
1923	12.3	19.8	5.7	8.4	3.2	34.7	2.6	20	166	89	115	682
1924	13.1	18.8	4.4	8.9	2.3	36.2	3.4	15	139	121	141	675
1925	20.8	22.8	6.0	11.5	4.5	38.6	9.1	22	183	115	127	650
1926	24.4	23.7	5.5	14.8	3.5	43.0	6.4	24	114	132	133	926
1927	21.6	24.2	4.5	13.1	3.1	41.2	10.4	29	171	94	98	742
1928	22.0	19.3	5.7	16.5	3.3	46.4	10.1	28	141	92	99	501
1929	18.9	20.4	7.2	15.7	3.0	45.6	6.3	34	146	124	149	753
1930	26.9	23.6	6.8	16.6	2.7	49.4	14.0	45	226	128	158	863
1931	20.5	22.0	5.2	11.0	4.8	44.8	12.0	47	148	129	164	855
1932	20.3	22.0	5.0	11.2	3.4	43.1	6.6	57	181	100	130	783
1933	27.7	24.2	7.9	15.4	4.8	49.3	9.0	67	222	81	116	949
1934	30.4	20.1	6.8	18.9	3.8	51.0	11.4	85	230	115	160	892
1935	30.8	21.4	8.2	18.3	2.8	69.7	16.2	62	173	92	134	893
1936	30.7	18.0	9.3	13.4	4.1	51.5	16.8	66	154	87	114	1,031
1937	46.9	29.4	10.6	21.9	3.9	65.6	21.9	76	212	81	139	986
1938	40.8	20.9	8.2	17.0	2.7	42.0	16.7	86	188	97	177	998
1939	—[14]	—[14]	—[14]	—[14]	—[14]	—[14]	21.0[14]	85	228	90	149	874
1940	31.8	21.1	12.0	16.8	5.2	76.1	18.0	76	191	83	148	1,047
1941	...	...	...	...	...	26.6	2.0	included in Russia				
1942	...	...	...	...	...	23.5	2.2					
1943	...	...	...	...	...	35.9	1.3					
1944	...	...	...	...	...	54.6	4.1					

See p.296 for footnotes

D2 Output of Main Cereal, Potato, and Sugar Beet Crops (in thousands of hectolitres or metric tons)

1890–1944

LATVIA (thousands of metric tons)

	Wheat	Rye	Barley	Oats	Potatoes	Sugar Beet
1890						
1891						
1892						
1893						
1894						
1895						
1896						
1897						
1898						
1899						
1900						
1901						
1902						
1903						
1904						
1905						
1906						
1907						
1908						
1909						
1910						
1911						
1912						
1913	included in Russia					
1914						
1915						
1916						
1917						
1918						
1919	...	...	...	...	...	...
1920	11	119	67	113	375	...
1921	21	249	141	245	674	...
1922	26	174	147	264	675	...
1923	45	274	131	230	578	...
1924	43	199	162	271	676	...
1925	59	315	178	304	751	...
1926	51	155	189	276	1,014	...
1927	72	259	130	177	717	...
1928	68	215	71	146	314	...
1929	64	241	208	340	1,080	...
1930	111	365	187	342	1,104	...
1931	92	143	192	343	1,167	61
1932	144	300	193	323	1,205	184
1933	183	355	195	331	1,403	186
1934	219	412	218	389	1,446	339
1935	178	364	205	386	1,461	294
1936	144	286	165	284	1,612	244
1937	172	422	218	405	1,782	280
1938	192	379	221	447	1,751	231
1939	212	448	222	485	1,640	218
1940						
1941	included in Russia					
1942						
1943						
1944						

LITHUANIA (thousands of metric tons)

	Wheat	Rye	Barley	Oats	Potatoes	Sugar Beet
1890						
1891						
1892						
1893						
1894						
1895						
1896						
1897						
1898						
1899						
1900						
1901						
1902						
1903						
1904						
1905						
1906						
1907						
1908						
1909						
1910						
1911						
1912						
1913	included in Russia					
1914						
1915						
1916						
1917						
1918						
1919	...	...	...	...	...	...
1920	...	...	...	...	...	...
1921	77	535	145	264	1,386	...
1922	89[34]	616[34]	234[34]	420[34]	1,848[34]	...
1923	81	607	173	331	1,630	
1924	90	465	203	270	1,658	...
1925	144	663	245	285	1,581	...
1926	114	351	249	320	1,665	...
1927	144	538	188	243	1,264	...
1928	172	475	150	267	960	...
1929	254	560	268	439	1,853	...
1930	246	668	202	417	1,760	11
1931	227	412	241	410	1,996	45
1932	257	572	239	356	1,919	120
1933	223	552	232	331	1,824	52
1934	285	669	254	380	2,493	95
1935	275	641	252	400	1,774	136
1936	219	542	233	332	2,118	170
1937	221	607	274	388	2,510	186
1938	251	624	274	420	2,118	144
1939	257	659	257	409	2,354	170
1940						
1941	included in Russia					
1942						
1943						
1944						

See p.296 for footnotes

D2 Output of Main Cereal, Potato, and Sugar Beet Crops (in thousands of hectolitres or metric tons)

1890–1944

SPAIN[35] (thousands of metric tons)

	Wheat	Rye	Barley	Oats	Maize	Rice	Potatoes	Sugar Beet
1890	...	...	...	...	...	...	...	...
1891	...	...	...	...	...	...	...	...
1892	...	...	...	...	...	...	...	...
1893	...	...	...	...	...	...	...	...
1894	...	...	...	...	...	...	...	...
1895	...	...	...	...	...	...	...	...
1896	...	...	...	...	...	...	...	...
1897	...	...	...	...	...	...	...	...
1898	...	...	...	...	...	...	...	...
1899	...	...	...	...	...	...	...	...
1900	...	...	...	...	...	...	...	...
1901	3,726	721	1,738	331	654	174	...	...
1902	3,634	665	1,770	339	642	168	...	...
1903	3,510	572	1,401	333	447	189	...	...
1904	2,596	439	1,172	268	540	179	...	...
1905	2,518	673	1,000	323	810	217	...	...
1906	3,828	785	1,965	408	475	193	...	...
1907	2,731	687	1,167	247	645	216	...	...
1908	3,265	671	1,515	408	511	204	...	...
1909	3,922	886	1,716	498	671	207	...	667
1910	3,741	701	1,661	421	695	211	3,617	483
1911	4,041	734	1,890	492	730	216	...	812
1912	2,988	479	1,306	334	637	244	2,534	1,004
1913	3,059	709	1,493	368	639	223	...	1,341
1914	3,159	608	1,574	453	770	248	2,086	738
1915	3,923	728	1,839	528	643	235	2,750	836
1916	4,147	731	1,891	469	728	242	2,966	1,005
1917	3,883	615	1,697	480	746	236	3,088	1,217
1918	3,693	773	1,970	442	613	208	2,601	1,124
1919	3,518	592	1,782	478	649	303	2,749	705
1920	3,772	707	1,970	548	703	289	2,935	1,627
1921	3,950	714	1,945	517	632	262	2,782	1,816
1922	3,415	667	1,688	453	682	274	2,867	1,399
1923	4,276	713	2,436	587	608	243	2,599	1,220
1924	3,314	668	1,822	438	655	296	2,430	1,660
1925	4,425	760	2,154	631	717	306	...	1,460
1926	3,990	597	2,096	547	437	320	3,165	1,822
1927	3,912	674	2,008	569	663	310	3,610	1,520
1928	3,338	417	1,780	517	535	290	3,807	1,437
1929	4,198	583	2,119	665	630	304	4,623	1,599
1930	3,993	547	2,263	726	733	313	4,203	2,322
1931	3,659	536	1,975	605	670	266	4,677	2,856
1932	5,013	658	2,886	831	693	218	5,026	2,035
1933	3,762	526	2,177	592	660	295	4,782	1,982
1934	5,085	548	2,819	752	788	294	4,418	2,301
1935	4,300	489	2,113	571	736	293	4,337	1,577
1936	...	...	...	...	...	...	...	...
1937	...	...	...	...	...	...	...	...
1938	...	...	...	...	...	...	...	...
1939	2,870	410	1,418	479	843	178	3,494	721
1940	2,161	351	1,396	474	742	269	3,413	1,350
1941	3,078	410	1,698	589	703	208	3,588	1,359
1942	3,662	518	2,381	789	524	207	3,681	931
1943	3,127	460	2,064	659	378	208	2,646	1,129
1944	3,769	515	2,150	598	538	239	3,302	1,183

See p.296 for footnotes

D2 Output of Main Cereal, Potato, and Sugar Beet Crops (in thousands of hectolitres or metric tons)

1890–1944

SWEDEN (thousands of metric tons)

	Wheat	Rye	Barley	Oats	Mixed Corn	Potatoes	Sugar Beet
1890	108	562	356	1,205	184	813	224
1891	122	581	306	964	165	1,180	261
1892	124	614	338	1,221	194	1,340	314
1893	107	636	294	970	154	1,465	411
1894	118	471	323	1,178	190	1,070	564
1895	103	506	326	1,196	186	1,343	565
1896	130	631	321	942	173	1,486	770
1897	129	609	318	972	186	1,292	730
1898	129	541	335	1,217	205	893	514
1899	129	557	264	900	176	787	569
1900	150	669	333	1,193	227	1,587	819
1901	122	565	295	941	176	1,062	838
1902	127	579	280	957	190	1,349	608
1903	151	619	324	1,075	213	1,526	661
1904	143	538	317	866	207	1,204	570
1905	150	650	308	1,055	223	1,763	810
1906	182	686	341	1,192	275	1,605	986
1907	168	534	294	1,136	271	1,258	827
1908	191	665	356	1,273	301	1,792	938
1909	202	651	305	1,182	297	1,471	962
1910	209	622	330	1,290	308	1,604	1,068
1911	220	617	325	1,098	306	1,262	966
1912	212	586	308	1,274	320	1,530	846
1913	259	585	369	1,401	364	1,969	858
1914	242	680	265	806	217	1,704	967
1915	263	601	300	1,253	353	1,953	839
1916	246	642	298	1,239	369	1,497	937
1917	188	354	248	891	312	2,021	834
1918	242	490	252	814	375	1,833	812
1919	254	574	277	1,076	468	2,001	939
1920	281	570	243	1,015	451	1,628	1,039
1921	336	674	261	1,090	498	1,757	1,485
1922	259	562	294	1,120	499	1,929	456
1923	299	594	249	1,052	492	1,631	1,042
1924	185	276	288	1,033	493	1,418	914
1925	364	676	314	1,176	536	2,106	1,364
1926	331	587	326	1,271	531	1,953	142
1927	417	385	201	1,057	403	975	993
1928	499	431	209	1,168	467	1,708	1,096
1929	517	411	248	1,249	511	1,885	767
1930	567	436	240	1,121	529	1,759	1,215
1931	464	283	223	988	500	1,482	876
1932	655	433	223	1,251	518	2,123	1,554
1933	717	462	199	1,099	475	2,031	1,839
1934	757	517	215	1,229	541	1,979	1,862
1935	643	430	222	1,239	564	1,757	1,866
1936	589	351	200	1,203	526	1,806	1,800
1937	689	374	189	1,241	539	1,838	2,077
1938	804	374	240	1,375	628	1,858	1,834
1939	861	354	232	1,271	591	1,809	1,900
1940	421	266	189	937	478	2,294	1,859
1941	331	279	158	776	421	2,071	1,844
1942	472	448	220	926	528	1,840	1,734
1943	524	405	233	850	495	2,171	1,868
1944	543	357	175	730	470	1,435	1,803

SWITZERLAND (thousands of metric tons)

	Wheat	Rye	Barley	Oats	Potatoes	Sugar Beet
1890	...	...	...	...	...	...
1891	...	...	...	...	...	...
1892	...	...	...	...	...	...
1893	...	...	...	...	...	...
1894	...	...	...	...	...	...
1895	...	...	...	...	...	...
1896	...	...	...	...	...	...
1897	...	...	...	...	...	...
1898	...	...	...	...	...	...
1899	...	...	...	...	...	...
1900	...	...	...	...	...	...
1901	...	...	...	...	...	...
1902	...	...	...	...	...	...
1903	...	...	...	...	...	...
1904	...	...	...	...	...	...
1905	...	...	...	...	...	...
1906	...	...	...	...	...	...
1907	...	...	...	...	...	...
1908	...	...	...	...	...	...
1909	37	51	10	80	...	25
1910	75	41	9	63	650	15
1911	96	46	10	70	650	23
1912	87	43	9	58	660	—
1913	97	45	10	75	725	32
1914	89	44	12	75	520	32
1915	108	52	14	81	835	23
1916	111	33	13	60	500	20
1917	122	37	15	61	1,050	12
1918	142[36]	47	15	75	935	13
1919	139	40	14	40	760	8
1920	135	41	14	45	769	28
1921	138	46	12	44	691	42
1922	97	43	11	36	676	34
1923	142	48	12	44	686	32
1924	123	36	11	39	540	45
1925	139	48	12	39	740	43
1926	142	41	12	45	611	49
1927	143	40	12	42	695	50
1928	150	44	12	43	673	52
1929	144	40	14	41	778	37
1930	123	37	11	36	590	40
1931	138	36	12	34	750	38
1932	136	38	13	35	655	50
1933	176	36	7	21	746	61
1934	184	34	8	20	802	64
1935	204	27	8	21	656	59
1936	255	32	7	20	568	63
1937	202	34	8	24	846	86
1938	230	36	11	25	766	92
1939	200	30	13	26	620	108
1940	189	23	23	52	882	129
1941	244	31	40	81	1,084	121
1942	252	30	49	78	1,381	151
1943	293	36	58	94	1,707	154
1944	296	33	63	95	1,719	188

See p.296 for footnotes

D2 Output of Main Cereal, Potato, and Sugar Beet Crops (in thousands of hectolitres or metric tons)

1890–1944

UK: GREAT BRITAIN

	Wheat	Barley	Oats	Potatoes	Sugar Beet
1890	26,674	26,885	43,704	2,857	—
1891	26,228	26,229	40,868	3,102	—
1892	21,295	25,631	42,289	3,098	—
1893	17,908	21,649	41,050	3,532	—
1894	21,517	26,289	49,259	2,834	—
1895	13,519	24,964	44,418	3,651	—
1896	20,747	25,736	41,460	3,619	—
1897	19,979	24,296	42,489	2,650	—
1898	26,556	24,746	43,244	3,336	—
1899	23,829	24,624	41,726	3,126	—
1900	19,142	22,660	41,763	2,779	—
1901	19,076	22,221	40,039	3,730	—
1902	20,610	24,180	47,412	3,245	—
1903	17,325	21,627	45,339	2,961	—
1904	13,411	20,797	46,330	3,646	—
1905	21,419	21,131	42,341	3,823	—
	thousands of metric tons				
1906	1,686	1,495	2,283	3,484	—
1907	1,542	1,458	2,432	3,025	—
1908	1,472	1,328	2,224	3,981	—
1909	1,700	1,466	2,201	3,733	—
1910	1,526	1,360	2,200	3,533	—
1911	1,804	1,279	2,106	3,886	—
1912	1,520	1,214	1,893	3,231	—
1913	1,566	1,437	2,018	3,927	—
1914	1,733	1,389	2,066	4,096	—
1915	1,992	1,002	2,203	3,891	—
1916	1,584	1,128	2,134	3,085	—
1917	1,660	1,208	2,317	4,522	—
1918	2,467	1,320	3,013	5,446	—
1919	1,878	1,221	2,381	3,622	—
1920	1,539	1,413	2,251	4,458	—
1921	2,060	1,190	2,176	4,062	66
1922	1,770	1,114	1,963	5,286	56
1923	1,611	1,117	2,057	3,636	106
1924	1,435	1,161	2,235	3,598	183
1925	1,437	1,172	2,129	4,277	438
1926	1,382	1,041	2,276	3,721	1,135
1927	1,512	971	1,996	3,916	1,527
1928	1,349	1,140	2,181	4,618	1,392
1929	1,350	1,117	2,314	4,819	2,036
1930	1,145	845	2,020	3,661	3,109
1931	1,026	861	1,891	3,205	1,694
1932	1,184	846	2,029	4,521	2,268
1933	1,693	699	1,951	4,628	3,351
1934	1,879	830	1,789	4,536	4,161
1935	1,771	744	1,848	3,825	3,459
1936	1,497	741	1,750	3,865	3,503
1937	1,529	666	1,630	4,113	2,624
1938	1,990	915	1,729	4,475	2,226
1939	1,668	903	1,761	4,424	3,586
1940	1,654	1,106	2,554	5,461	3,227
1941	2,032	1,145	2,860	6,892	3,278
1942	2,597	1,455	3,175	8,293	3,986
1943	3,490	1,658	2,713	8,674	3,820
1944	3,184	1,765	2,615	8,155	3,319

YUGOSLAVIA (Serbia to 1914) (thousands of metric tons)

	Wheat	Rye	Barley	Oats	Maize	Potatoes	Sugar Beet
1890	190	...	...	...	...	...	...
1891	220	...	...	...	...	...	...
1892	300	...	...	...	...	...	...
1893	238	33	55	47	460	22	...
1894	240	...	...	...	...	...	...
1895	240	...	...	...	...	...	...
1896	220	...	...	...	...	...	...
1897	365	48	92	142	865	43	...
1898	264	40	87	93	717	...	...
1899	319	42	85	72	659	...	...
1900	221	17	49	39	469	29	...
1901	220	20	50	50	480	30	...
1902	310	30	80	60	470	40	...
1903	300	30	70	60	490	40	...
1904	320	30	70	50	240	20	...
1905	310	30	80	50	540	30	...
1906	360	40	110	70	710	50	...
1907	230	20	70	40	450	20	...
1908	310	20	70	40	530	20	...
1909	439	45	138	85	873	38	75
1910	348	35	88	63	739	44	63
1911	417	43	100	73	674	59	92
1912	...	...	...	...	...	...	150
1913	...	...	...	...	...	...	...
1914	...						...
	—	—	—	—	—	—	—
1915	...	...	...	...	...	...	...
1916	...	...	...	...	...	...	...
1917	...	...	...	...	...	...	...
1918	...	...	...	...	...	...	...
1919	...	...	...	...	...	...	...
1920	1,171	155	287	323	2,569	1,118	205
1921	1,410	148	291	274	1,874	713	189
1922	1,210	115	241	265	2,281	864	313
1923	1,662	150	306	312	2,154	1,182	373
1924	1,572	141	293	302	3,795	1,039	1,063
1925	2,140	200	395	345	3,791	1,236	511
1926	1,944	189	376	358	3,410	954	592
1927	1,540	150	315	292	2,109	1,021	599
1928	2,811	191	394	366	1,819	863	929
1929	2,585	210	412	351	4,148	1,632	1,098
1930	2,186	199	404	285	3,465	1,471	745
1931	2,689	193	392	265	3,203	1,111	707
1932	1,455	212	392	269	4,793	1,391	733
1933	2,629	245	463	371	3,578	1,468	510
1934	1,860	195	410	333	5,154	1,844	480
1935	1,989	196	376	278	3,028	1,351	484
1936	2,924	203	423	333	5,181	1,628	618
1937	2,347	209	383	295	5,336	1,620	404
1938	3,030	227	421	327	4,756	1,711	557
1939	2,876	244	424	348	4,046	1,384	922
1940	1,887	211	371	288	4,380	1,910	783
1941	...	...	...	...	...	...	...
1942	...	...	...	...	...	...	...
1943	...	...	...	...	...	...	...
1944	...	...	...	...	...	...	...

D2 Output of Main Cereal, Potato, and Sugar Beet Crops (in thousands of hectolitres or metric tons)

1945–1969

ALBANIA (thousands of metric tons)

	Wheat	Rye	Barley	Oats	Maize
1945	41	...	...	...	...
1946	...	...	...	...	...
1947	...	...	...	...	...
1948	...	...	...	...	...
1949	...	...	....	...	...
1950	...	...	...	...	...
1951	...	...	...	...	...
1952	86	8	9	13	97
1953	127	14	16	26	159
1954	116	11	14	22	121
1955	123	15	14	22	177
1956	99	13	11	20	178
1957	125	15	10	17	223
1958	101	9	7	13	167
1959	105	9	9	15	209
1960	64	6	7	11	129
1961	98	7	9	12	164
1962	146	7	7	16	131
1963	62	5	8	11	198
1964	124	6	8	15	188
1965	115	7	7	14	175
1966	154	7	10	16	230
1967	176	7	11	18	263
1968	184	7	6	9	274
1969	210	7	7	11	265

AUSTRIA (thousands of metric tons)

	Wheat[3]	Rye	Barley	Oats	Maize	Other Cereals	Potatoes	Sugar Beet
1945	227	230	120	205	43	...	1,420	128
1946	228	244	112	188	85	20	1,533	225
1947	206	260	110	193	89	21	1,842	245
1948	261	289	125	225	100	23	2,069	360
1949	350	365	199	286	119	30	2,008	480
1950	384	388	230	223	120	25	2,548	821
1951	342	334	246	299	138	25	2,159	1,062
1952	401	340	251	341	122	22	2,567	853
1953	499	421	320	360	151	27	3,293	1,058
1954	452	370	312	334	149	23	2,792	1,345
1955	549	416	346	364	152	28	3,005	1,439
1956	570	434	385	374	144	30	3,229	1,228
1957	574	400	392	340	149	29	4,034	1,655
1958	549	397	335	333	155	30	3,542	2,005
1959	589	417	405	312	146	38	2,946	1,951
1960	702	353	589	343	213	45	3,809	1,906
1961	712	472	512	335	198	45	3,395	1,250
1962	706	467	557	332	193	51	3,214	1,546
1963	690	322	617	342	194	64	3,499	2,090
1964	751	388	605	327	212	67	3,438	2,203
1965	661	315	523	274	187	60	2,539	1,462
1966	897	363	706	325	275	83	3,007	2,308
1967	1,045	377	772	336	316	88	3,049	2,006
1968	1,045	413	770	324	399	96	3,473	1,936
1969	950	440	934	288	698	95	2,941	2,005

BELGIUM (thousands of metric tons)

	Wheat	Rye	Barley	Oats	Mixed Corn[3]	Potatoes	Sugar Beet
1945	310	151	113	367	15	1,222	878
1946	366	222	147	496	18	1,477	1,099
1947	122	162	188	509	11	1,600	1,106
1948	344	184	172	385	10	2,133	1,598
1949	596	258	237	587	19	2,047	2,348
1950	547	240	261	506	15	2,318	2,675
1951	514	204	269	473	19	2,016	1,858
1952	565	221	273	463	17	2,124	2,194
1953	560	213	294	462	16	1,919	2,389
1954	575	245	247	452	17	2,634	2,132
1955	714	220	281	481	18	2,184	2,246
1956	597	196	288	484	10	2,034	2,204
1957	751	190	296	454	17	2,044	2,486
1958	779	200	318	443	20	1,914	2,832
1959	789	176	398	423	22	1,357	1,474
1960	773	183	382	450	19	1,894	3,063
1961	722	114	409	444	18	1,789	2,703
1962	735	117	499	427	12	1,872	2,019
1963	759	119	482	395	15	1,530	2,135
1964	900	133	516	373	13	1,755	3,114
1965	854	98	520	305	12	1,419	2,537
1966	650	76	486	293	12	1,475	2,586
1967	828	90	623	361	17	1,944	3,615
1968	839	87	574	315	18	1,566	4,108
1969	754	70	555	281	21	1,253	4,217

BULGARIA (thousands of metric tons)

	Wheat	Rye	Barley	Oats	Maize	Potatoes	Sugar Beet
1945	992	85	98	50	233	44	126
1946	1,513	145	170	98	424	36	242
1947	912	95	131	77	783	62	176
1948	1,688	225	270	125	713	159	560
1949							
1950	1,757	258	326	121	756	150	331
1951	2,499	313	502	228	1,279	421	400
1952	2,041	262	429	176	703	268	381
1953	2,334	244	505	195	961	325	
1954	1,651[36]	151	340	167	975	268	650
1955	1,930	173	471	161	1,477	364	596
1956	1,726	133	343	135	1,056	212	943
1957	2,408	130	478	205	1,492	313	1,434
1958	2,334	102	444	134	882	251	882
1959	2,437	107	560	244	1,506	421	1,450
1960	2,389	82	622	218	1,505	478	1,650
1961	2,034	70	612	207	1,424	445	1,463
1962	2,086	49	599	114	1,556	361	1,121
1963	1,892	56	618	133	1,732	415	1,122
1964	2,118	64	764	149	2,056	497	2,100
1965	2,921	52	876	104	1,238	285	1,392
1966	3,193	56	1,064	182	2,207	421	2,528
1967	3,254	38	985	169	1,971	381	2,103
1968	2,549	24	807	76	1,768	369	1,447
1969	2,569	29	905	78	2,415	357	1,675

See p.296 for footnotes

D2 **Output of Main Cereal, Potato, and Sugar Beet Crops** (in thousands of hectolitres or metric tons)

1945–1969

CZECHOSLOVAKIA (thousands of metric tons)

	Wheat	Rye	Barley	Oats	Maize	Potatoes	Sugar Beet
1945	1,122	980	665	691	186	6,769	3,241
1946	1,320	1,136	766	825	203	9,159	4,341
1947	853	938	670	714[37]	132	4,678	2,407
1948	1,429	1,143	898	994	297	6,067	4,295
1949	1,556	1,316	1,023	1,062	240	5,772	4,283
1950	1,430	1,147	1,030	895	218	8,156	6,296
1951	1,476	1,015	1,143	929	302	7,356	5,203
1952	1,573	930	1,137	927	212	7,924	4,760
1953	1,556	954	1,247	869	430	9,702	5,588
1954	1,107	803	1,115	866	382	8,314	5,603
1955	1,473	968	1,291	974	391	7,905	6,152
1956	1,541	1,050	1,408	1,034	399	9,635	4,585
1957	1,525	948	1,362	899	445	8,756	6,775
1958	1,346	937	1,199	871	479	6,589	6,946
1959	1,649	967	1,467	929	503	6,334	4,946
1960	1,503	895	1,745	1,020	572	5,093	8,368
1961	1,666	994	1,581	959	461	5,331	6,894
1962	1,644	916	1,752	905	471	5,002	5,811
1963	1,766	880	1,620	797	578	6,506	8,018
1964	1,829	870	1,429	669	465	7,656	7,474
1965	1,992	822	1,399	630	393	3,678	5,662
1966	2,247	790	1,608	746	476	5,846	7,762
1967	2,516	689	1,936	968	421	6,037	7,663
1968	3,153	769	2,113	869	453	6,526	8,098
1969	3,257	687	2,499	969	495	5,180	5,809

DENMARK (thousands of metric tons)

	Wheat	Rye	Barley	Oats	Mixed Corn	Potatoes	Sugar Beet
1945	280	311	1,259	995	737	1,609	1,290
1946	298	287	1,387	1,085	777	1,810	1,533
1947	55	179	1,329	872	702	1,826	1,455
1948	253	400	1,458	937	759	1,500	1,711
1949	300	469	1,571	982	764	1,794	2,130
1950	297	331	1,615	834	682	1,850	2,624
1951	273	270	1,767	847	687	1,950	2,455
1952	301	358	2,130	960	822	2,320	2,045
1953	283	331	2,180	823	813	1,885	2,487
1954	292	276	2,045	800	798	1,938	1,694
1955	254	191	2,200	863	836	1,442	2,022
1956	266	290	2,402	852	853	2,140	2,312
1957	273	313	2,560	786	829	1,781	3,064
1958	274	306	2,485	648	752	1,558	3,240
1959	364	289	2,338	568	602	1,731	1,593
1960	320	454	2,801	681	727	1,963	2,230
1961	434	514	2,808	684	759	1,490	1,397
1962	644	513	3,299	609	719	1,162	1,440
1963	495	319	3,399	671	619	1,334	2,598
1964	541	292	3,900	821	659	1,213	3,154
1965	564	265	4,125	780	479	937	1,883
1966	400	136	4,159	864	401	972	2,159
1967	421	118	4,382	904	328	857	2,139
1968	464	131	5,047	863	280	866	2,148
1969	428	126	5,255	765	200	663	2,008

See p.296 for footnotes

D2 **Output of Main Cereal, Potato, and Sugar Beet Crops** (in thousands of hectolitres or metric tons)

1945–1969

FINLAND (thousands of metric tons)

	Wheat	Rye	Barley	Oats	Mixed Corn	Potatoes	Sugar Beet
1945	265	156	151	331	6	780	37
1946	178	144	151	334	6	891	48
1947	196	186	160	433	10	1,114	80
1948	265	199	214	640	24	1,950	179
1949	323	219	181	723	28	1,157	184
1950	296	215	176	702	26	1,273	231
1951	212	190	211	716	34	1,327	165
1952	227	183	224	809	33	1,504	227
1953	218	130	314	904	32	1,379	299
1954	235	132	262	774	27	1,090	358
1955	190	119	262	644	31	1,067	247
1956	199	124	286	659	35	1,693	259
1957	177	115	348	698	43	1,255	250
1958	215	111	406	799	44	1,381	237
1959	243	162	332	696	32	1,079	257
1960	368	186	440	1,109	52	1,717	411
1961	461	127	365	941	46	1,057	456
1962	422	101	270	616	36	950	367
1963	397	124	492	820	67	1,221	455
1964	463	163	370	742	41	850	431
1965	501	190	502	1,020	59	1,257	408
1966	368	119	597	881	52	1,066	457
1967	507	163	681	940	60	881	432
1968	516	134	718	1,064	51	908	386
1969	481	126	840	1,139	60	780	337

FRANCE (thousands of metric tons)

	Wheat	Rye	Barley	Oats	Maize	Buck-wheat	Potatoes	Sugar Beet
1945	4,210	270	660	2,600	160	85	6,060	4,470
1946	6,760	460	1,060	3,770	210	70	9,880	6,630
1947	3,270	380	1,120	2,810	200	63	10,960	5,890
1948	7,630	640	1,270	3,380	460	86	15,680	9,430
1949	8,080	650	1,430	3,220	190	66	9,650	9,610
1950	7,700	610	1,570	3,310	400	73	12,940	13,580
1951	7,120	490	1,660	3,690	690	88	12,070	11,830
1952	8,420	480	1,730	3,350	480	93	11,070	9,500
1953	8,980	470	2,240	3,660	800	95	13,640	12,540
1954	10,570	510	2,520	3,570	960	75	15,860	11,660
1955	10,360	440	2,670	3,640	1,090	54	13,750	10,980
1956	5,680	470	6,410	4,600	1,740	71	16,850	10,880
1957	11,080	480	3,630	2,580	1,390	64	13,900	11,250
1958	9,600	440	3,890	2,640	1,670	61	12,750	12,890
1959	11,540	470	4,930	2,810	1,820	51	12,210	7,760
1960	11,010	420	5,720	2,740	2,810	45	14,890	19,020
1961	9,570	350	5,410	2,590	2,470	56	14,190	13,240
1962	14,050	360	6,000	2,630	1,860	45	13,260	11,560
1963	10,250	360	7,380	2,880	3,870	46	15,820	13,950
1964	13,840	390	6,790	2,310	2,110	34	11,420	16,240
1965	14,760	387	7,378	2,509	3,420	34	11,068	16,961
1966	11,297	357	7,421	2,578	4,331	30	10,439	12,889
1967	14,288	344	9,874	2,821	4,139	27	10,231	12,769
1968	14,985	327	9,139	2,528	5,379	22	9,836	17,557
1969	14,459	309	9,452	2,309	5,723	22	8,860	17,900

D2 Output of Main Cereal, Potato, and Sugar Beet Crops (in thousands of hectolitres or metric tons)

1945–1969

WEST GERMANY (thousands of metric tons)

	Wheat[3]	Rye	Barley	Oats	Maize	Mixed Corn & B'wheat	Potatoes	Sugar Beet
1945	...	...	...	...	...	...	...	...
1946	...	...	...	...	...	...	...	...
1947	...	...	...	...	...	...	...	...
1948	...	...	...	...	...	...	...	...
1949	2,471	3,310	1,213	2,600	21	607	20,875	4,735
1950	2,614	3,021	1,472	2,545	17	537	27,959	6,975
1951	2,949	3,034	1,688	2,835	21	648	24,103	7,291
1952	3,291	3,119	1,757	2,616	16	686	23,854	6,845
1953	3,179	3,280	2,072	2,554	20	847	24,535	8,422
1954	2,892	4,098	1,920	2,473	20	1,187	26,769	9,013
1955	3,379	3,495	2,079	2,477	20	1,031	22,874	8,936
1956	3,487	3,735	2,310	2,451	20[38]	1,130	26,756	8,346
1957	3,843[38]	3,816[38]	2,504[38]	2,228[38]	16	1,534[38]	26,289[38]	9,690[38]
	3,870	3,838	2,513	2,250		1,537	26,488	9,692
1958	3,721	3,748[39]	2,423	2,172	13	1,089	22,850[39]	11,237
	[39]	3,751	[39]	[39]	[39]	[39]	22,864	[39]
1959	4,522	3,887	2,843	2,039	13	1,105	22,720	8,169
1960	4,965	3,798	3,221	2,179	20	1,349	24,559	12,325
1961	4,038	2,515	2,722	1,913	23	1,203	21,516	9,253
1962	4,592	2,966	3,744	2,333	43	1,554	25,104	9,525
1963	4,856	3,239	3,562	2,321	48	1,409	25,812	12,493
1964	5,203	3,609	3,915	2,308	63	1,453	20,624	12,863
1965	4,348	2,825	3,364	2,052	96	1,201	18,095	10,939
1966	4,533	2,696	3,869	2,340	127	1,259	18,839	12,468
1967	5,819	3,162	4,734	2,718	196	1,396	21,294	13,697
1968	6,198	3,189	4,974	2,893	287	1,527	19,196	13,633
1969	6,000	2,889	5,130	2,976	400	1,535	15,985	12,941

EAST GERMANY (thousands of metric tons)

	Wheat[3]	Rye	Barley	Oats	Mixed Corn	Potatoes	Sugar Beet
1945	...	...	...	...	...	...	...
1946	776	1,403	504	1,111	242	10,404	4,065
1947	504	1,523	446	963	281	8,063	3,122
1948	999	1,950	428	809	204	12,419	4,584
1949	1,065	2,356	517	1,016	226	9,940	3,867
1950	1,214	2,418	587	1,127	282	14,706	5,754
1951	1,494	2,992	746	1,556	387	14,872	6,047
1952	1,442	2,864	685	1,430	369	13,935	6,336
1953	1,152	2,292	806	1,446	352	13,273	6,062
1954	1,081	2,394	749	1,128	305	15,520	6,952
1955	1,211	2,337	924	1,362	326	11,194	5,712
1956	1,086	2,299	834	1,112	411	13,565	4,324
1957	1,259	2,231	897	999	441	14,529	6,465
1958	1,363	2,368	931	1,143	500	11,498	6,976
1959	1,371	2,133	1,039	966	435	12,436	4,659
1960	1,456	2,126	1,269	1,007	516	14,821	6,837
1961	1,038	1,504	947	856	495	8,430	4,657
1962	1,315	1,726	1,164	1,054	675	13,284	4,970
1963	1,280	1,675	1,197	807	574	12,886	6,176
1964	1,348	1,890	1,496	774	675	12,872	6,003
1965	1,802	1,810	1,651	758	610	12,857	5,804
1966	1,521	1,642	1,525	703	525	12,823	6,611
1967	2,012	1,986	1,927	845	583	14,065	6,948
1968	2,377	1,936	2,121	864	530	12,639	6,998
1969	1,987	1,544	2,067	841	480	8,832	4,856

See p.296 for footnotes

D2 Output of Main Cereal, Potato, and Sugar Beet Crops (in thousands of hectolitres or metric tons)

1945–1969

GREECE (thousands of metric tons)

	Wheat	Rye	Barley	Oats	Maize	Mixed Corn	Potatoes
1945	375	24	81	46	141	18	128
1946	729	57	163	89	190	34	230
1947	578	40	130	78	276	30	301
1948	770	43	215	108	229	40	320
1949	839	41	196	113	222	37	394
1950	850	48	200	120	195	32	347
1951	930	46	230	140	250	42	412
1952	1,050	56	213	116	230	34	453
1953	1,400	67	258	167	309	35	445
1954	1,219	51	253	150	254	32	442
1955	1,337	54	224	157	285	31	422
1956	1,245	47	229	148	238	29	456
1957	1,720	45	241	191	257	32	507
1958	1,786	41	266	175	225	23	469
1959	1,767	27	217	139	290	14	490
1960	1,666	28	240	149	288	15	423
1961	1,528	22	221	144	228	8	400
1962	1,722	20	232	152	215	8	403
1963	1,417	18	207	127	253	7	466
1964	2,088	18	242	139	249	6	544
1965	2,072	16	338	150	249	6	517
1966	2,020	15	563	167	275	5	531
1967	1,936	13	774	153	313	5	599
1968	1,568	8	471	98	344	3	603
1969	1,723	9	447	102	413	3	576

HUNGARY (thousands of metric tons)[10]

	Wheat	Rye	Barley	Oats	Maize	Potatoes	Sugar Beet
1945	658	304	442	171	1,871	1,691	178
1946	1,127	424	441	198	1,364	1,143	516
1947	1,152	430	399	167	1,781	1,061	1,159
1948	1,583	786	692	334	2,862	2,117	1,771
1949	1,830	750	690	240	...	1,920	1,240
1950	2,040	790	640	220	...	...	1,240
1951	2,350	790	723	188	2,833	2,050	2,000
1952	1,699	542	567	134	1,172	1,170	1,375
1953	2,182	562	757	164	2,602	1,900	2,850
1954	1,660	480	587	150	2,550	1,991	1,920
1955	2,131	544	794	176	2,912	2,467	2,241
1956	1,845	494	645	176	2,034	2,055	1,948
1957	1,959	487	962	263	3,233	2,707	1,878
1958	1,487	371	735	192	2,833	2,600	2,070
1959	1,909	443	1,093	256	3,558	2,366	2,679
1960	1,768	364	986	219	3,534	3,001	3,370
1961	1,936	310	984	152	2,727	1,830	2,356
1962	1,973	245	1,150	132	3,269	2,149	2,653
1963	1,593	228	875	123	3,582	2,298	3,434
1964	2,143	275	822	60	3,552	1,949	3,554
1965	2,443	288	1,012	63	3,564	1,485	3,452
1966	2,327	242	916	72	3,907	2,433	3,570
1967	3,004	225	934	86	3,522	1,507	3,356
1968	3,352	238	904	68	3,764	1,335	3,471
1969	3,579	235	908	80	4,754	1,590	3,303

IRELAND (thousands of metric tons)

	Wheat	Barley	Oats	Potatoes	Sugar Beet
1945	582	152	737	3,032	714
1946	470	123	700	3,279	502
1947	318	90	663	2,642	458
1948	416	102	805	3,328	603
1949	367	162	568	2,735	639
1950	333	121	537	2,920	538
1951	252	178	586	2,810	568
1952	266	253	587	2,719	555
1953	417	229	576	2,761	822
1954	497	179	482	2,284	681
1955	406	250	576	2,148	598
1956	433	319	544	2,649	636
1957	522	390	438	2,377	808
1958	351	336	456	1,880	797
1959	369	460	482	2,634	942
1960	469	442	426	1,829	950
1961	470	515	381	2,145	891
1962	439	603	396	2,117	930
1963	301	589	368	1,969	952
1964	272	652	313	1,526	893
1965	233	616	324	1,648	758
1966	185	638	283	1,679	704
1967	298	677	293	1,748	956
1968	408	531	286	1,625	1,092
1969	359	578	251	1,453	916

NORTHERN IRELAND (thousands of metric tons)

	Wheat	Barley	Oats	Potatoes
1945	1.5	13	389	1,106
1946	2.2	7.5	382	1,577
1947	1.4	4.6	269	1,040
1948	4.8	6.6	398	1,693
1949	2.1	6.5	360	1,453
1950	2.0	4.1	313	1,365
1951	1.4	3.4	300	1,216
1952	2.2	6.6	294	1,090
1953	2.5	7.2	277	1,143
1954	2.1	6.0	243	927
1955	1.3	5.9	228	769
1956	3.3	7.5	253	888
1957	4.5	15	207	670
1958	4.4	18	185	583
1959	2.9	34	190	734
1960	4.4	74	191	714
1961	5.6	96	143	633
1962	5.9	178	165	651
1963	3.4	171	137	657
1964	4.4	210	121	550
1965	5.8	236	91	511
1966	4.3	197	73	476
1967	4.3	202	79	527
1968	3.6	199	75	469
1969	4.2	183	58	395

See p.296 for footnotes

D2 Output of Main Cereal, Potato, and Sugar Beet Crops (in thousands of hectolitres or metric tons)

1945–1969

ITALY (thousands of metric tons)[1 2]

	Wheat	Rye	Barley	Oats	Maize	Rice	Potatoes	Sugar Beet
1945	4,177	78	129	252	1,438	356	1,467	401
1946	6,126	106	231	461	1,909	489	2,343	2,317
1947	4,702	97	179	447	1,920	636	2,824	2,230
1948	6,166[1 2]	112[1 2]	230[1 2]	486[1 2]	2,250[1 2]	619[1 2]	3,025[1 2]	3,409[1 2]
1949	7,073	125	227	415	2,212	610	2,629	3,619
1950	7,774	131	295	558	1,924	706	2.432	4,468
1951	6,962	122	270	510	2,748	750	2,858	5,961
1952	7,876	127	267	508	2,396	930	2,717	5,897
1953	9,056	130	313	602	3,213	934	3,132	6,231
1954	7,283	115	278	546	2,963	869	3,202	6,592
1955	9,504	123	292	523	3,204	880	3,382	9,208
1956	8,681	107	275	506	3,411	648	3,418	7,055
1957	8,478	92	296	582	3,496	637	3,157	6,176
1958	9,815	105	296	568	3,670	737	3,668	7,681
1959	8,471	105	279	541	3,879	755	3,979	11,459
1960	6,794	93	232	431	3,813	622	3,818	7,818
1961	8,301	96	279	585	3,936	700	3,932	7,071
1962	9,497	93	285	597	3,263	663	3,561	7,148
1963	8,127	77	280	548	3,692	564	4,384	7,882
1964	8,586	86	252	466	3,957	624	3,823	7,966
1965	9,776	83	285	527	3,317	509	3,550	9,079
1966	9,400	83	253	477	3,510	621	3,860	11,259
1967	9,596	82	295	556	3,860	745	4,010	13,507
1968	9,590	75	258	390	3,991	639	3,960	11,457
1969	9,585	71	292	491	4,519	862	3,970	10,571

NETHERLANDS (thousands of metric tons)

	Wheat	Rye	Barley	Oats	Potatoes	Sugar Beet
1945	218	206	93	252	2,591	449
1946	359	456	176	425	4,245	1,705
1947	194	318	135	433	4,611	1,577
1948	306	382	155	356	5,870	1,893
1949	425	517	184	521	4,605	2,943
1950	295	421	232	382	4,048	2,913
1951	269	459	197	492	3,793	2,444
1952	326	498	238	483	4,356	2,782
1953	250	433	279	485	3,685	2,977
1954	397	515	208	467	3,999	3,061
1955	350	465	264	582	3,907	2,984
1956	309	492	273	483	3,206	2,525
1957	393	458	292	505	3,741	2,689
1958	402	427	315	446	3,606	2,878
1959	494	386	268	319	3,141[40] 3,315	3,098
1960	590	460	291	387	4,173	4,676
1961	482	301	385	431	3,720	3,854
1962	603	339	431	465	3,952	2,934
1963	530	313	387	424	3,854	2,691
1964	712	356	376	420	4,111	3,876
1965	691	250	373	363	3,230	3,573
1966	597	190	416	357	4,123	3,645
1967	739	239	447	365	4,840	5,074
1968	679	239	389	318	5,045	5,128
1969	677	207	389	322	4,704	5,002

NORWAY (thousands of metric tons)

	Wheat	Rye	Barley	Oats	Mixed Corn	Potatoes
1945	86	4	81	165	11	1,112
1946	80	5	94	186	12	1,204
1947	46	2	81	132	7	919
1948	76	3	89	177	10	1,454
1949	67	2	86	163	10	1,099
1950	66	2	99	180	10	1,116
1951	40	1	123	170	9	1,015
1952	40	1	148	161	8	1,187
1953	39	1	206	179	7	1,249
1954	41	2	224	161	6	1,130
1955	32	1	209	114	5	981
1956	56	3	297	182	6	1,392
1957	30	1	315	136	4	1,010
1958	17	1	340	127	4	1,202
1959	20	2	304	118	4	1,071
1960	23	4	400	173	6	1,247
1961	27	3	428	174	5	1,222
1962	20	4	343	107	2	919
1963	18	3	463	113	3	1,218
1964	20	2	480	126	2	804
1965	12	2	485	113	2	1,134
1966	4	1	405	91	2	1,090
1967	11	2	485	123	2	807
1968	16	4	621	176	3	912
1969	11	4	486	140	1	763

See p.296 for footnotes

D2 Output of Main Cereal, Potato, and Sugar Beet Crops (in thousands of hectolitres or metric tons)

1945–1969

POLAND (thousands of metric tons)

	Wheat	Rye	Barley	Oats	Potatoes	Sugar Beet
1945	751	3,766	967	1,556	21,870	3,460
1946	619	2,763	674	1,017	18,710	2,983
1947	985	4,306	1,035	1,763	30,821	3,493
1948	1,620	6,304	1,010	2,402	26,756	4,228
1949	1,781	6,759	1,028	2,333	30,901	4,789
1950	1,888	6,488	1,081	2,127	36,130	6,377
1951	1,363	6,148	1,009	1,981	26,696	5,363
1952	2,013	6,173	1,176	2,348	27,725	6,158
1953	1,870	4,853	1,134	2,169	31,800	6,881
1954	2,002	5,844	1,085	2,073	35,662	6,950
1955	2,134	7,003	1,239	2,287	27,021	7,286
1956	2,121	6,558	1,131	2,259	38,052	6,428
1957	2,319	7,437	1,227	2,541	35,104	7,621
1958	2,321	7,329	1,210	2,670	34,800	8,427
1959	2,484	8,113	1,043	2,483	35,698	5,975
1960	2,303	7,878	1,310	2,774	37,855	10,262
1961	2,792	8,356	1,339	2,940	45,203	11,555
1962	2,700	6,685	1,315	2,740	37,817	10,075
1963	3,067	7,124	1,479	2,830	44,868	10,661
1964	3,042	6,964	1,261	2,218	47,860	12,574
1965	3,422	8,202	1,468	2,541	43,263	12,314
1966	3,603	7,661	1,409	2,625	46,144	13,620
1967	3,934	7,645	1,412	2,818	48,620	15,521
1968	4,670	8,438	1,494	2,891	50,817	14,800
1969	4,710	8,167	1,948	3,063	44,935	11,321

PORTUGAL (thousands of metric tons)[13]

	Wheat	Rye	Barley	Oats	Maize	Rice	Potatoes
1945	315	122	48	78	363	45	743
1946	508	147	104	210	554	63	940
1947	348	151	73	112	474	86	1,024
1948	356	124	83	92	511	92	1,018
1949	405	149	94	104	342	78	790
1950	575	170	129	141	688	121	1,128
1951	580	194	137	148	615	141	1,390
1952	579	175	102	134	650	141	1,078
1953	690	183	105	131	499	140	1,120
1954	781	195	104	125	587	154	1,073
1955	508	155	72	82	583	183	1,104
1956	558	171	78	97	641	160	1,102
1957	797	203	101	128	427	162	1,196
1958	809	209	102	143	425	149	1,087
1959	623	175	66	89	487	163	866
1960	492	138	50	61	466	151	1,041
1961	430	119	52	65	632	177	1,056
1962	645	171	72	104	591	173	894
1963	592	216	61	98	523	166	1,145
1964	472	167	46	68	597	181	1,143
1965	612	209	72	99	459	137	888
1966	312	145	49	63	565	154	923
1967	637	175	73	111	577	146	1,296
1968	747	199	94	129	548	149	1,083
1969	454	167	54	79	553	176	1,126

ROMANIA (thousands of metric tons)

	Wheat	Rye	Barley	Oats	Maize	Rice	Potatoes	Sugar Beet
1945	1,066[33]	44[33]	267[33]	258[33]	1,099[33]	...	893[33]	201[33]
1946	1,609	62	233	282	1,007	...	675	342
1947	1,279[41]	66[41]	360[41]	...	5,279[41]	...	1,630[41]	600[41]
1948	2,397	85	280	375	2,260	11	717	597
1949	...	...	...	...	...		1,090[41]	...
1950	2,219	182	325	283	2,101	36	1,601	633
1951	3,521	229	526	389	3,100	45	2,141	1,430
1952	2,975	211	518	429	2,520	49	2,257	890
1953	3,964	262	612	494	3,225	55	2,355	1,300
1954	2,140	170	386	357	4,953	50	2,397	1,408
1955	3,006	214	445	374	5,877	35	2,608	2,000
1956	2,436	136	291	305	3,932	37	2,675	1,519
1957	3,701	152	417	392	6,338	36	3,058	2,043
1958	2,914	124	305	250	3,657	37	2,777	1,732
1959	4,001	128	449	315	5,680	55	2,897	3,446
1960	3,450	103	405	284	5,531	49	3,009	3,399
1961	3,990	104	468	275	5,740	31	2,875	2,911
1962	4,054	75	419	167	4,932	20	2,597	2,180
1963	3,799	78	351	123	6,023	51	2,692	2,298
1964	3,824	92	348	79	6,692	54	2,640	3,668
1965	5,937	125	485	124	5,877	46	2,195	3,275
1966	5,065	100	483	170	8,022	56	3,352	4,368
1967	5,820	71	531	163	6,858	69	3,096	3,830
1968	4,848	48	590	114	7,105	60	3,707	3,936
1969	4,349	47	544	137	7,676	68	2,165	3,783

RUSSIA (millions of metric tons)[14]

	Wheat	Rye	Barley	Oats	Maize	Potatoes	Sugar Beet
1945	13.4	...	...	...	...	58.3	5.5
1946	...	...	...	...	...	55.6	4.3
1947	...	...	...	...	...	74.5	14.0
1948	...	...	...	...	...	95.0	12.9
1949	...	...	...	...	...	89.6	15.7
1950	31.1	18.0	6.4	13.0	6.6	88.6	20.8
1951	...	...	...	...	...	58.8	23.6
1952	43.9	...	...	...	...	69.2	22.2
1953	41.3	14.5	7.9	10.1	3.7	72.6	23.2
1954	42.4	15.6	7.8	10.8	3.7	75.0	19.8
1955	47.3	16.5	10.4	11.8	11.6	71.8	31.0
1956	67.4	14.1	12.9	13.2	9.9	96.0	32.5
1957	58.1	14.5	8.5	12.7	4.6	87.8	39.7
1958	76.6	15.8	13.0	13.4	10.2	86.5	54.4
1959	69.1	16.9	10.2	13.5	5.7	86.6	43.9
1960	64.3	16.4	16.0	12.0	9.8	84.4	57.7
1961	66.5	16.7	13.3	8.9	17.1	84.3	50.9
1962	70.8	17.0	19.5	5.7	15.5	69.7	47.4
1963	49.7	11.9	19.8	4.0	11.1	71.8	44.1
1964	74.4	13.6	28.6	5.5	13.8	93.6	81.2
1965	59.7	16.2	20.3	6.2	8.0	88.7	72.3
1966	100.5	13.1	27.9	9.2	8.4	87.9	74.0
1967	77.4	13.0	24.7	11.6	9.2	95.5	87.1
1968	93.4	14.1	28.9	11.6	8.8	102.2	94.3
1969	79.9	10.9	32.7	13.1	12.0	91.8	71.2

See p.296 for footnotes

D2 Output of Main Cereal, Potato, and Sugar Beet Crops (in thousands of hectolitres or metric tons)

1945–1969

SPAIN (thousands of metric tons)

	Wheat	Rye	Barley	Oats	Maize	Rice	Potatoes	Sugar Beet
1945	2,263	277	1,031	297	472	206	2,664	958
1946	4,131	534	2,636	749	531	206	2,558	1,526
1947	3,180	431	1,725	469	490	237	2,835	1,213
1948	3,275	443	2,066	533	479	235	2,702	1,986
1949	3,035	489	1,635	448	331	263	2,814	1,512
1950	3,374	467	1,491	507	536	252	2,870	1,385
1951	4,266	514	2,151	552	607	285	4,550	2,436
1952	4,098	495	2,200	554	647	324	3,797	4,136
1953	3,026	406	1,476	435	707	393	3,717	2,379
1954	4,773	526	2,205	526	751	401	3,939	1,854
1955	3,991	493	1,718	506	616	389	4,081	2,267
1956	4,196	511	1,551	452	714	384	4,307	2,743
1957	4,900	496	1,881	535	771	388	3,954	2,285
1958	4,540	515	1,778	519	916	375	4,292	3,207
1959	4,635	533	2,092	524	959	386	4,588	3,919
1960	3,520	385	1,562	431	1,012	361	4,620	3,572
1961	3,431	351	1,744	495	1,067	394	4,918	4,423
1962	4,812	453	2,162	513	920	392	4,153	3,584
1963	4,860	424	2,071	466	1,171	399	5,075	2,750
1964	3,977	346	1,927	390	1,203	398	4,254	3,331
1965	4,715	349	1,892	370	1,142	350	4,079	3,678
1966	4,876	353	2,006	442	1,154	375	4,423	4,042
1967	5,650	336	2,576	492	1,195	366	4,490	4,282
1968	5,312	355	3,441	539	1,473	362	4,570	4,620
1969	4,624	320	3,969	547	1,507	417	4,789	4,980

SWEDEN (thousands of metric tons)

	Wheat	Rye	Barley	Oats	Mixed Corn	Potatoes	Sugar Beet
1945	588	276	169	755	463	1,659	1,814
1946	680	289	183	783	515	1,941	1,776
1947	399	142	176	678	432	1,758	1,493
1948	702	322	193	793	572	2,277	1,808
1949	698	277	178	840	648	1,720	1,770
1950	739	243	210	807	654	1,734	1,978
1951	471	169	248	794	665	1,630	1,732
1952	773	277	328	784	677	1,711	1,597
1953	987	297	469	945	716	1,727	1,997
1954	1,021	301	361	863	657	1,429	1,848
1955	717	170	407	597	528	1,285	1,663
1956	951	267	613	1,133	698	2,012	1,786
1957	711	230	557	847	548	1,498	2,103
1958	598	170	659	894	520	1,393	1,764
1959	836	211	664	787	486	1,411	1,733
1960	824	230	847	1,176	563	1,753	2,414
1961	839	164	945	1,394	545	1,526	2,264
1962	906	164	926	1,184	448	1,516	1,441
1963	696	75	1,155	1,156	428	1,908	1,574
1964	1,065	119	1,375	1,448	456	1,477	1,731
1965	1,038	169	1,437	1,340	410	1,542	1,340
1966	576	82	1,408	1,154	266	1,355	1,434
1967	1,130	195	1,564	1,396	259	1,399	1,798
1968	1,074	209	1,776	1,584	262	1,486	1,982
1969	917	182	1,575	1,129	177	931	1,470

SWITZERLAND (thousands of metric tons)

Wheat	Rye	Barley	Oats	Potatoes	Sugar Beet
258	28	76	110	1,613	213
237	29	64	89	1,080	171
218	25	55	74	1,230	161
225	27	54	65	1,141	185
290	30	65	88	764	204
253	38	44	52	1,132	235
261	37	51	63	968	209
279	39	61	70	1,192	203
245	37	63	78	986	213
346	45	62	67	1,312	219
338	29	63	59	934	210
217	36	94	69	1,288	224
304	30	70	56	1,264	245
337	39	71	47	1,311	282
349	40	76	48	1,302	261
378	47	76	44	1,291	230
316	34	92	47	1,239	224
318	65	125	49	1,127	168
299	50	95	35	1,246	297
388	63	105	38	1,206	362
352	51	95	30	906	298
348	46	107	33	1,049	366
426	63	117	32	1,125	423
416	58	112	30	1,098	453
379	43	132	37	979	392

D2 Output of Main Cereal, Potato, and Sugar Beet Crops (in thousands of hectolitres or metric tons)

1945–1969

U.K: GREAT BRITAIN (thousands of metric tons)

	Wheat	Barley	Oats	Potatoes	Sugar Beet
1945	2,209	2,130	2,908	8,842	3,948
1946	1,997	1,987	2,568	8,752	4,595
1947	1,693	1,640	2,280	6,850	3,007
1948	2,394	2,053	2,612	10,295	4,388
1949	2,237	2,157	2,683	7,727	4,026
1950	2,646	1,734	2,422	8,295	5,302
1951	2,352	1,967	2,358	7,201	4,607
1952	2,342	2,365	2,523	6,884	4,304
1953	2,705	2,554	2,590	7,249	5,360
1954	1,810	2,274	2,236	6,516	4,594
1955	2,640	2,977	2,525	5,610	4,629
1956	2,888	2,838	2,273	6,766	5,252
1957	2,722	2,989	1,972	5,111	4,612
1958	2,750	3,203	1,987	5,062	5,834
1959	2,827	4,046	2,032	6,293	5,598
1960	3,036	4,235	1,900	6,559	7,331
1961	2,609	4,957	1,708	5,728	6,031
1962	3,968	5,688	1,610	6,108	5,398
1963	3,043	6,533	1,324	6,024	5,338
1964	3,789	7,311	1,225	6,514	6,318
1965	4,165	7,956	1,142	7,067	6,813
1966	3,470	8,527	1,048	6,104	6,599
1967	3,898	9,012	1,307	6,673	6,884
1968	3,466	8,071	1,149	6,403	7,118
1969	3,360	8,481	1,250	5,820	6,034

YUGOSLAVIA (thousands of metric tons)

	Wheat	Rye	Barley	Oats	Maize	Potatoes	Sugar Beet
1945	...	...	...	...	...	...	...
1946	...	...	...	...	...	...	...
1947	...	...	...	...	...	...	...
1948	2,532	251	353	345	4,075	1,480	1,498
1949	2,523	269	381	384	3,709	2,100	1,095
1950	1,833	219	266	195	2,093	1,048	851
1951	2,283	277	359	293	4,040	1,654	1,937
1952	1,683	225	258	216	1,470	1,149	512
1953	2,514	309	458	352	3,840	2,096	1,514
1954	1,384	191	253	233	3,000	1,876	1,219
1955	2,436	263	390	278	3,900	2,270	1,380
1956	1,603	205	344	324	3,370	2,190	1,130
1957	3,103	280	604	484	5,660	3,310	2,030
1958	2,453	241	470	259	3,950	2,620	1,480
1959	4,134	265	575	404	6,670	2,760	2,420
1960	3,574	233	529	373	6,160	3,270	2,290
1961	3,174	191	571	432	4,550	2,690	1,730
1962	3,514	169	475	305	5,270	2,630	1,870
1963	4,143	156	524	345	5,380	3,030	2,670
1964	3,703	175	534	293	6,960	2,820	2,830
1965	3,462	156	682	338	5,920	2,380	2,620
1966	4,603	176	713	386	7,980	3,230	4,030
1967	4,823	171	606	363	7,200	2,800	3,680
1968	4,363	138	450	295	6,810	2,890	2,910
1969	4,882	135	459	308	7,821	3,440	3,636

D2 Output of Main Cereal, Potato, and Sugar Beet Crops (in thousands of hectolitres or metric tons)

1970–1975

ALBANIA (thousands of metric tons)

	Wheat	Rye	Barley	Oats	Maize	Other Cereals	Potatoes	Sugar Beet	Rice	Mixed Corn
1970	230	...	...	...	...					
1971	138	...	...	...	...					
1972	...	...	...	...	...					
1973	166	...	...	...	...					
1974	...	...	...	...	...					
1975	...	...	...	...	...					

AUSTRIA (thousands of metric tons)

	Wheat	Rye	Barley	Oats	Maize	Other Cereals	Potatoes	Sugar Beet	Rice	Mixed Corn
1970	810	363	913	272	612	101	2,704	1,947		
1971	974	448	1,016	284	721	102	2,717	1,590		
1972	863	402	977	255	726	95	2,341	2,148		
1973	939	400	1,087	284	966	112	2,117	2,220		
1974	1,102	415	1,238	290	857	111	1,996	2,386		
1975	945	347	1,006	306	981	122	1,579	3,134		

BELGIUM (thousands of metric tons)

	Wheat	Rye	Barley	Oats	Maize	Other Cereals	Potatoes	Sugar Beet	Rice	Mixed Corn
1970	708	61	526	194			1,373	3,868		21
1971	878	82	588	278			1,373	4,873		32
1972	916	72	637	244			1,106	4,319		29
1973	976	59	716	246			1,201	5,136		30
1974	1,004	46	699	222			1,460	4,465		31
1975	677	29	426	228			1,049	4,913		18

BULGARIA (thousands of metric tons)

	Wheat	Rye	Barley	Oats	Maize	Other Cereals	Potatoes	Sugar Beet	Rice	Mixed Corn
1970	3,032	28	1,167	98	2,375		374	1,714		
1971	3,095	24	1,253	102	2,518		404	1,516		
1972	3,582	21	1,427	75	2,974		382	1,951		
1973	3,258	19	1,368	51	2,586		328	1,719		
1974	2,911	21	1,636	67	1,626		345	1,611		
1975	2,771	18	1,699	56	2,822		318	1,758		

CZECHOSLOVAKIA (thousands of metric tons)

	Wheat	Rye	Barley	Oats	Maize	Other Cereals	Potatoes	Sugar Beet	Rice	Mixed Corn
1970	3,174	454	2,280	776	513		4,793	6,644		
1971	3,878	619	2,851	902	524		4,621	5,832		
1972	4,017	634	2,651	726	642		5,058	6,884		
1973	4,646	690	2,962	740	619		5,087	6,163		
1974	5,059	671	3,375	687	574		4,522	8,219		
1975	4,202	530	3,114	591	843		3,565	7,734		

D2 Output of Main Cereal, Potato, and Sugar Beet Crops (in thousands of hectolitres or metric tons)

1970–1975

DENMARK (thousands of metric tons)

	Wheat	Rye	Barley	Oats	Maize	Other Cereals	Potatoes	Sugar Beet	Rice	Mixed Corn	Buckwheat
1970	512	134	4,813	631			1,033	1,892		142	
1971	585	150	5,458	701			750	1,999		132	
1972	592	155	5,572	637			709	2,166		111	
1973	542	140	5,432	444			748	2,521		75	
1974	592	168	5,967	472			898	2,691		62	
1975	520	163	5,156	367			666	3,140		46	

FINLAND (thousands of metric tons)

	Wheat	Rye	Barley	Oats	Maize	Other Cereals	Potatoes	Sugar Beet	Rice	Mixed Corn	Buckwheat
1970	409	131	933	1,330			1,136	431		65	
1971	443	132	1,054	1,424			803	464		60	
1972	463	119	1,140	1,245			716	662		56	
1973	462	124	992	1,169			669	607		48	
1974	593	134	963	1,113			525	629		49	
1975	622	81	1,242	1,450			680	630		47	

FRANCE (thousands of metric tons)

	Wheat	Rye	Barley	Oats	Maize	Other Cereals	Potatoes	Sugar Beet	Rice	Mixed Corn	Buckwheat
1970	12,922	287	8,126	2,103	7,581		8,694	17,522			19
1971	15,482	294	8,910	2,540	8,954		8,829	19,951			19
1972	18,046	328	10,466	2,478	8,252		7,245	19,276			18
1973	17,850	327	10,948	2,208	10,692		7,209	22,688			14
1974	19,141	311	10,037	2,081	8,692		7,356	21,556			15
1975	15,013	292	9,344	1,948	8,194		6,495	23,656			13

WEST GERMANY (thousands of metric tons)

	Wheat	Rye	Barley	Oats	Maize	Other Cereals	Potatoes	Sugar Beet	Rice	Mixed Corn	Buckwheat
1970	5,662	2,665	4,754	2,484	507		16,250	13,329		1,226	
1971	7,142	3,032	5,774	3,037	594		15,176	14,410		1,367	
1972	6,608	2,917	5,997	2,888	564		15,038	14,656		1,270	
1973	7,134	2,576	6,622	3,045	573		13,677	15,858		1,226	
1974	7,761	2,560	7,048	3,482	521		14,549	16,499		1,282	
1975	7,014	2,125	6,970	3,445	531		10,853	18,203		1,170	

EAST GERMANY (thousands of metric tons)

	Wheat	Rye	Barley	Oats	Maize	Other Cereals	Potatoes	Sugar Beet	Rice	Mixed Corn	Buckwheat
1970	2,132	1,483	1,926	558			13,054	6,135		343	
1971	2,490	1,754	2,286	807			9,412	5,128		395	
1972	2,744	1,904	2,592	890			12,140	7,223		379	
1973	2,861	1,699	2,848	806			11,401	6,682		276	
1974	3,154	1,949	3,422	922			13,404	6,959		254	
1975	2,736	1,563	3,681	780			7,673	6,414		148	

D2 Output of Main Cereal, Potato, and Sugar Beet Crops (in thousands of hectolitres or metric tons)

1970–1975

GREECE (thousands of metric tons)

	Wheat	Rye	Barley	Oats	Maize	Other Cereals	Potatoes	Sugar Beet	Rice	Mixed Corn
1970	1,931	9	737	107	511		756			
1971	1,946	9	781	115	571		668			
1972	1,768	8	874	113	584		689			
1973	1,659	6	848	106	585		733			
1974	2,142	7	933	121	455		757			
1975	2,120	7	916	114	488		878			

HUNGARY (thousands of metric tons)

	Wheat	Rye	Barley	Oats	Maize	Other Cereals	Potatoes	Sugar Beet	Rice	Mixed Corn
1970	2,723	158	553	57	4,072		1,813	2,175		
1971	3,922	182	785	91	4,732		1,797	2,023		
1972	4,095	173	807	64	5,554		1,349	2,909		
1973	4,502	178	874	72	5,963		1,355	2,754		
1974	4,971	177	899	75	6,247		1,720	3,708		
1975	4,007	147	701	92	7,172		1,630	4,089		

IRELAND (thousands of metric tons)

	Wheat	Rye	Barley	Oats	Maize	Other Cereals	Potatoes	Sugar Beet	Rice	Mixed Corn
1970	368		600				1,468	966		
1971	364		725				1,428	1,199		
1972	239		748				1,070	1,095		
1973	183		608				1,332	1,295		
1974	209		682				1,111	908		
1975	189		677				1,000	1,407		

NORTHERN IRELAND (thousands of metric tons)

	Wheat	Rye	Barley	Oats	Maize	Other Cereals	Potatoes	Sugar Beet	Rice	Mixed Corn
1970	5		160	43			406			
1971	4		198	40			375			
1972	4		175	29			304			
1973	3		177	26			311			
1974	3		197	24			297			
1975	3		187	23			243			

ITALY (thousands of metric tons)

	Wheat	Rye	Barley	Oats	Maize	Other Cereals	Potatoes	Sugar Beet	Rice	Mixed Corn
1970	9,689	69	315	486	4,754		3,668	9,518	817	
1971	9,994	55	373	488	4,528		3,259	8,776	892	
1972	9,421	38	390	440	4,789		2,949	11,177	755	
1973	8,920	38	458	419	5,089		2,947	9,388	1,045	
1974	9,695	37	559	462	5,043		2,903	7,711	997	
1975	9,610	37	648	506	5,326		2,943	12,536	1,010	

D2 Output of Main Cereal, Potato, and Sugar Beet Crops (in thousands of hectolitres or metric tons)

1970–1975

NETHERLANDS (thousands of metric tons)

	Wheat	Rye	Barley	Oats	Maize	Other Cereals	Potatoes	Sugar Beet	Rice	Mixed Corn
1970	640	168	329	199			5,604	4,711		
1971	706	209	373	206			5,749	5,024		
1972	673	151	340	140			5,581	4,957		
1973	725	105	383	134			5,771	5,592		
1974	746	78	315	163			6,095	4,911		
1975	528	63	336	158			5,003	5,927		

NORWAY (thousands of metric tons)

	Wheat	Rye	Barley	Oats	Maize	Other Cereals	Potatoes	Sugar Beet	Rice	Mixed Corn
1970	12	5	580	228			857			1
1971	10	5	569	279			708			2
1972	12	5	522	271			634			1
1973	20	7	535	349			672			2
1974	62	11	649	404			847			2
1975	48	4	445	259			435			1

POLAND (thousands of metric tons)

	Wheat	Rye	Barley	Oats	Maize	Other Cereals	Potatoes	Sugar Beet	Rice	Mixed Corn
1970	4,608	5,433	2,149	3,209			50,301	12,742		
1971	5,456	7,827	2,451	3,195			39,801	12,557		
1972	5,147	8,149	2,750	3,212			48,735	14,341		
1973	5,807	8,268	3,159	3,220			51,928	13,664		
1974	6,408	7,882	3,909	3,244			48,519	12,971		
1975	5,207	6,270	3,638	2,920			40,429	15,707		

PORTUGAL (thousands of metric tons)

	Wheat	Rye	Barley	Oats	Maize	Other Cereals	Potatoes	Sugar Beet	Rice	Mixed Corn
1970	548	157	54	72	581		1,220		195	
1971	794	168	85	125	526		1,124		162	
1972	604	164	62	85	519		1,139		164	
1973	517	134	67	79	509		1,086		168	
1974	534	143	75	99	486		1,115		130	
1975	601	145	87	121	451		1,013		133	

ROMANIA (thousands of metric tons)

	Wheat	Rye	Barley	Oats	Maize	Other Cereals	Potatoes	Sugar Beet	Rice	Mixed Corn
1970	3,356	43	513	117	6,536		2,064	3,175	65	
1971	5,595	65	789	161	7,850		3,783	4,321	67	
1972	6,041	58	839	111	9,817		3,672	5,581	45	
1973	5,488	43	730	102	7,397		2,644	4,380	50	
1974	5,007	42	916	91	7,440		4,119	4,947	53	
1975	4,862	52	952	57	9,241		2,716	4,905	56	

RUSSIA (millions of metric tons)

	Wheat	Rye	Barley	Oats	Maize	Other Cereals	Potatoes	Sugar Beet	Rice	Mixed Corn
1970	99.7	13.0	38.2	14.2	9.4		96.8	78.9		
1971	98.8	12.8	34.6	14.7	8.6		92.7	72.2		
1972	86.0	9.6	36.8	14.1	9.8		78.3	76.4		
1973	109.8	10.8	55.0	17.5	13.2		108.2	87.0		
1974	83.9	15.2	54.2	15.3	12.1		81.0	77.9		
1975	66.2	9.1	35.8	12.5	7.3		88.7	66.3		

D2 Output of Main Cereal, Potato, and Sugar Beet Crops (in thousands of hectolitres or metric tons)

1970–1975

SPAIN

	Wheat	Rye	Barley	Oats	Maize	Other Cereals	Potatoes	Sugar Beet	Rice	Mixed Corn
1970	4,126	259	3,103	393	1,848		5,301	5,446	382	
1971	5,449	272	4,784	582	2,056		4,865	6,412	361	
1972	4,562	263	4,358	440	1,923		5,275	5,212	347	
1973	3,966	252	4,402	425	2,038		5,579	5,501	387	
1974	4,534	254	5,404	559	1,993		5,693	3,984	367	
1975	4,302	241	6,728	609	1,794		5,338	6,337	379	

SWEDEN (thousands of metric tons)

	Wheat	Rye	Barley	Oats	Maize	Other Cereals	Potatoes	Sugar Beet	Rice	Mixed Corn
1970	945	221	1,870	1,656			1,490	1,561		206
1971	977	296	1,993	1,834			1,242	1,706		198
1972	1,130	357	1,850	1,601			1,137	1,783		189
1973	1,312	316	1,736	1,188			947	1,781		160
1974	1,793	429	2,356	1,656			1,257	2,140		244
1975	1,455	322	1,903	1,321			837	1,992		165

SWITZERLAND (thousands of metric tons)

	Wheat	Rye	Barley	Oats	Maize	Other Cereals	Potatoes	Sugar Beet	Rice	Mixed Corn
1970	346	49	142	29			977	379		
1971	410	52	168	41			1,093	472		
1972	410	50	156	37			824	396		
1973	345	45	173	39			910	540		
1974	411	40	210	55			929	518		
1975	356	24	172	55			908	479		

U.K.: GREAT BRITAIN (thousands of metric tons)

	Wheat	Rye	Barley	Oats	Maize	Other Cereals	Potatoes	Sugar Beet	Rice	Mixed Corn
1970	4,231		7,369	1,175			7,076	6,412		
1971	4,811		8,360	1,321			7,021	7,869		
1972	4,775		9,070	1,219			6,222	6,216		
1973	5,000		8,830	1,054			6,497	7,427		
1974	6,127		8,936	931			6,494	4,587		
1975	4,486		8,324	771			4,308	4,864		

YUGOSLAVIA (thousands of metric tons)

	Wheat	Rye	Barley	Oats	Maize	Other Cereals	Potatoes	Sugar Beet	Rice	Mixed Corn
1970	3,792	127	402	309	6,933		2,964	2,948		
1971	5,605	134	464	312	7,443		2,952	2,961		
1972	4,844	120	487	260	7,930		2,406	3,294		
1973	4,751	118	676	298	8,253		2,974	3,338		
1974	6,283	119	794	353	8,031		3,127	4,350		
1975	4,396	98	703	368	9,392		3,191	4,220		

D2 Output of Main Cereals, Potatoes, and Sugar Beet (in thousands of hectolitres or metric tons)

NOTES

1. SOURCES:– The main sources were as for table D1. Portugese data for 1915 and 1916 were supplied by the Portugese National Institute of Statistics.

2. Unless conversion was done in the source, statistics which were collected in units of volume have been left in volume measure here. The appropriate ratios for converting measures of volume into measures of weight vary slightly each year, and from country to country. The following table gives a guide to the ratios which may be used to calculate approximate weights, showing the weight in kilograms of 1 hectolitre of various crops:–

	Current British Convention	French 19th Century	Italian 19th Century	Danish 1911	Hungarian 1897	Portugese 1916–18
wheat	78.6	...	75	77.3	74.9	77.7
rye	67.3	71	65	73.7	69.3	74.2
barley	69.8	64	65	67.6	62.7	58.0
oats	52.4	47	41	50.3	43.2	46.0
maize	74.8	70	72	...	73.4	75.6
mixed corn	...	...	...	55.7	67.2	...
buckwheat	62.3	65	...	61.1	...	...
rice	...	...	51	...	...	...
potatoes	66.1	76	...	71.9	70.7	...

3. P.A. Khromov, *Economic Development of Russia in the 19th and 20th Centuries, 1800–1917* (Moscow, 1950) gives the following statistics of the total grain harvest in the 50 provinces of European Russia (excluding Finland, Poland, and the Caucasus) in million chetverts:–

1800–13 average	155	1865	182	1874	271
1834–40 average	179	1866	220	1875	208
1841–48 average	210	1870	282	1876	237
1857–61 average	220	1871	219	1877	267
1861	216	1872	242	1878	276
1864	199	1873	241		

FOOTNOTES

[1] Up to 1880 (1833 for potatoes and 1885 for buckwheat) the unit of collection was the hectolitre. Conversion was made to a measure of weight by the French authorities, using the fixed ratios given above.

[2] Previous statistics are of the quantity used in factories in the season beginning in the year indicated. The break is negligible.

[3] Including spelt.

[4] Excluding Galicia, which had an output of 86 thousand tons in 1873.

[5] These are averages for 1871–80.

[6] Up to 1851 returns were made by mayors, who appear to have under-estimated in comparison with later returns made by cantonal commissioners.

[7] Millet is included with maize up to 1835 and from 1871 to 1880.

[8] From 1871 to 1919 the parts of Alsace and Lorraine ceded to Germany are excluded.

[9] Statistics to 1870 apply to the territory later constituting the German Empire, exclusive of Alsace-Lorraine, which is included for 1871–1917. From 1919 to 1944 the statistics apply to the boundaries of the day, but always excluding Austria, the Sudetenland, and territories in Poland, Lithuania, and France annexed in 1939–41. The main changes in this period were cessions to Czechoslovakia, Denmark, and Poland in 1919 and to Poland in 1922, and the return of Saarland in 1935.

[10] Figures to 1859 apply to the whole Kingdom (including Croatia and the military frontier). Later statistics, to 1918, apply to Transleithania (excluding Croatia-Slavonia. From 1920 they apply to the territory established by the treaty of Trianon.

[11] Figures to 1871 (1st line) exclude summer rye.

[12] Up to 1921 the statistics apply to the 1871 boundaries. For 1922–43 they apply to the 1924 boundaries. And from 1944 they apply to post-Second World War territory, except that Trieste is not included until 1949.

[13] Mainland only.

[14]The figures to 1894 (1st line) apply to the 50 provinces of European Russia (excluding Finland, Poland, and the Caucasus). From 1894 (2nd line) to 1909 (1st line) Poland is also included, except for sugar beet (see below). From 1909 (2nd line) to 1913 the statistics apply to the whole Russian Empire except Finland. For 1920–39 they apply to the U.S.S.R. as constituted in 1924, except that the figures for 1920 and 1921 (which, unlike the others, are not later revisions) exclude Turkestan, Transcaucasia, and the Far East. From 1940 the figures apply to the present territory of the U.S.S.R. The sugar beet statistics apply throughout to either the whole Empire except Finland or to the current territory of the U.S.S.R.

[15]Galicia is excluded in 1914 and 1915, and about three-quarters of it in 1916. Kustenland is excluded in 1915 and 1916, and part of it in 1914. Bukovina is excluded in 1914 and 1916. The output of these districts in 1913 was as follows:—

	Wheat	Rye	Barley	Oats	Maize	Other Corn	Potatoes	Sugar Beet
Galicia	503	592	326	689	30	53	333	11
Küstenland	20	3	4	4	53	2	12	–
Bukovina	20	27	72	79	45	1	45	7

[16]Subsequent statistics are for the Republic, though Burgenland is not included until 1922 (2nd line). Figures for 1913 on the same basis as for 1917 and for 1923 are as follows:—

	Wheat	Rye	Barley	Oats	Maize	Other Corn	Potatoes	Sugar Beet
1917 basis	290	604	179	466	78	42	1,508	404
1923 basis	351	634	221	488	103	42	1,605	605

In all statistics for the Republic spelt is included in wheat instead of rye.

[17]Spelt only.

[18]Figures for 1941–44 exclude Eupen and Malmedy. They are known to be underestimates owing to concealment by farmers.

[19]The method of collection was changed in 1936.

[20]Subsequent figures include southern Dobrudja.

[21]The method of collection was changed in 1927.

[22]Subsequently excludes Sub-Carpathian Russia (Ruthenia) and 12 villages in Slovakia ceded to the U.S.S.R.

[23]Subsequently includes South Jutland, acquired from Germany.

[24]Statistics for 1930–38 are for rural communes only. Figures including the towns are available for 1933, as follows:—

Wheat	Rye	Barley	Oats	Mixed Corn	Potatoes	Sugar Beet
319	255	974	1,013	808	1,349	1,781

[25]Subsequently excludes territory ceded to the U.S.S.R.

[26]From 1914 to 1919 the invaded departments are excluded.

[27]From 1939 to 1944 parts of Alsace-Lorraine annexed by Germany are excluded, and in 1943 and 1944 Corsica is excluded.

[28]Subsequently mixed corn only.

[29]The following are the changes in the area to which the statistics apply:— In 1913 new territories in the north and in the islands were acquired from Turkey. Macedonia was lost in 1915, and the western part of it recovered in 1917. In 1919 the postwar frontiers were achieved, but Thrace is not included in the statistics until 1922.

[30]Statistics for 1940–44 relate to the prewar boundaries, except for small areas incorporated in Germany. From 1945 they apply to the present territory.

[31]The following are the changes in the area to which the statistics apply:— 1914 Dobrudja acquired; 1918 Bessarabia acquired; 1920 Bukovina, Transylvania, part of the Banat, and parts of Hungary proper acquired.

[32]Exclusive of the output of intercropping, which normally constituted 10-20 per cent of the total.

[33]The following are the changes in the area to which the statistics apply:— Southern Dobrudja was ceded to Bulgaria in 1940. Bessarabia and northern Bukovina were ceded to the U.S.S.R. in 1940, but were temporarily reconquered in 1943 and are apparently included in the 1944 statistics. Northern Translyvania was ceded to Hungary in 1940 but reacquired by 1946.

[34]Previously excluding Memel.

[35]Output in 1855 in thousands of hectolitres was as follows:—
wheat 66,148; rye 8,993; barley 27,794.

[36]Subsequently including spelt.

[37]**Subsequently includes mixtures of oats and barley.**

[38]Subsequently includes Saarland.

[39]Subsequently includes West Berlin, which had a negligible effect on the statistics.

[40]Subsequently includes early potatoes.

[41]These statistics are described by the F.A.O. as 'doubtful'.

D3 AREA OF VINEYARDS AND OUTPUT OF WINE (in thousands of hectares and hectolitres)

1840–1889

	Austria[1]		France[2]		Germany		Hungary[9]	
	V	W	V	W	V	W[5]	V	W
1840	...	...	2,145	27,700	...	...	...	...
1841	...	...	...	...	...	...	...	...
1842	...	3,523	...	...	...	...	...	15,848
1843	...	3,599	...	...	...	...	...	...
1844	...	3,454	...	...	...	...	...	...
1845	...	3,859	2,169	30,100	...	...	...	...
1846	...	3,793	...	...	...	2,880	...	...
1847	...	3,880	...	54,300	...	2,940	...	...
1848	...	...	...	51,600	...	2,980	...	...
1849	...	...	2,193	35,600	...	2,180	...	...
1850	...	...	2,182	45,300	...	1,690	...	...
1851	...	3,990	2,180	39,400	...	1,070	...	15,869
1852	...	...	2.190	38,000	...	1,650	...	...
1853	...	...	2,168	22,700	...	1,630	382	...
1854	...	4,754	2,173	10,800	...	420	...	10,363
1855	...	...	2,175	15,200	...	1,050	...	...
1856	...	...	2,170	21,300	...	1,020	...	...
1857	...	6,418	2,180	35,400	...	1,960	...	10,193
1858	...	...	2,184	53,900	...	3,590	...	...
1859	...	5,959	2,173	29,900	...	3,190	...	9,329
1860	...	...	2,205[3]	39,600[3]	...	1,720	...	...
1861	...	...	2,220	29,700	...	1,090	...	4,016
1862	...	...	2,321	48,600	...	2,530	...	4,885
1863	...	...	2,274	51,400	...	2,480	...	3,979
1864	...	...	2,256	50,700	...	1,100	...	3,116
1865	...	...	2,293	68,900	...	1,650	...	3,533
1866	...	...	2,287	63,800	...	3,000	...	2,799
1867	...	...	2,315	39,100	...	2,960	...	4,677
1868	...	4,845	2,332	52,100	...	4,440	...	4,995
1869	205	3,730	2,350[4]	70,000[4]	...	2,090	...	4,407
1870	205	2,721	2,238	54,500	...	2,310[6]	...	4,087
1871	206	3,212	2,369	56,900	...	2,170	425	4,622
1872	209	2,221	2,373	50,200	...	1,540	425[9]	2,864[9]
1873	204	1,859	2,381	35,700	...	1,720	358	3,675
1874	207	3,158	2,447	63,100	...	3,500	358	1,998
1875	205	6,426	2,421	83,800	...	4,500	359	6,260
1876	207	2,389	2,370	41,800	...	3,230	360	1,858
1877	202	3,202	2,346	56,400	...	2,460	360	3,905
1878	207	6,731	2,296	48,700	119	3,060	362	8,100
1879	207	2,929	2,241	25,800	119	990	362	6,314
1880	207	1,731	2,209	29,700	116	520	362	2,427
1881	207	3,036	2,069	34,100	119	2,670	361	4,231
1882	207	3,367	2,197	33,500	119	1,600	367	4,113
1883	207	3,474	2,096	36,000	120	2,810	364	4,336
1884	207	3,286	2,041	34,800	120	2,970	368	4,411
1885	229	4,001	1,991	28,500	120	3,730	368	6,025
1886	233	3,722	1,959	25,100	120	1,500	364	4,370
1887	233	4,702	1,944	24,300	120	2,390	353	5,512
1888	233	4,155	1,843	30,100	121	2,860	343	4,344
1889	235	4,106	1,818	23,200	121	2,020	334	4,997

Abbreviations used throughout this table: V=Vineyards W=Wine

See p.303 for footnotes

D3 Area of Vineyards and Output of Wine (in thousands of hectares and hectolitres)

1840–1889

	Croatia-Slavonia		Italy[10]		Portugal[11]	Romania		Spain
	V	W	V	W	W	V	W	W
1840	...	...	...	...	...	...	...	...
1841	...	...	...	...	...	...	...	...
1842	...	...	...	...	...	...	...	...
1843	...	...	...	...	...	...	...	...
1844	...	...	...	...	...	...	...	...
1845	...	...	...	...	...	...	...	...
1846	...	...	...	...	...	...	...	...
1847	...	...	...	...	...	...	...	...
1848	...	...	...	...	...	...	...	...
1849	...	...	...	...	...	...	...	...
1850	...	...	...	...	...	...	...	...
1851	...	...	...	...	...	...	...	...
1852	...	...	...	...	...	...	...	...
1853	...	...	...	...	...	...	...	...
1854	...	...	...	...	...	...	...	...
1855	...	...	...	...	...	...	...	...
1856	...	...	...	...	...	...	...	...
1857	...	...	...	...	...	...	...	...
1858	...	...	...	...	...	...	...	...
1859	...	...	...	...	...	...	...	...
1860	...	...	...	...	...	80	1,300	...
1861	...		...	19,200	...	...		...
1862	...		...	23,460	...	...	1,149	...
1863	...		...	19,800	...	...	961	...
1864	...		...	21,486	...	...	535	...
1865	...	average	...	22.696	...	95	558	...
1866	...	783	...	23.906	...	...	1,821	...
1867	...		...	25,116	...	...	979	...
1868	...		...	26,326	...	...	1,242	...
1869	...		...	27,536	...	...	1,102	...
1870	...		...	25.800	...	102	678	...
1871	...		...	28,500	...	102	1,684	...
1872	65		...	26,400	...	102	1,037	...
1873	...	...	...	28,900	...	...	...	...
1874	...	...	...	28,095	...	...	...	...
1875	...	...	...	28,260	...	110	...	...
1876	...	...	...	22,500	...	...	...	...
1877	...	...	...	25,440	...	...	...	...
1878	...	...	...	26,520	...	...	...	...
1879	...	...		26,081	...	...	...	...
1880	...	...		28,643		...	...	...
1881	...	...	3,167	25,832	2,244	...	...	...
1882	...	...		33,500	2,812	...	...	...
1883	...	...		35,934	2,527	...	...	...
1884	...	...		28,728	3,257	...	...	...
1885	68	1,197	...	31,918	...	...	...	20,500
1886	68	1,593	...	38,227	...	163	2,600	...
1887	68	1,274	...	34,532	...	...	...	...
1888	68	1,089	...	32,846	...	...	...	...
1889	67	618	...	21,757	...	146	3,076	...

See p.303 for footnotes

D3 Area of Vineyards and Output of Wine (in thousands of Hectares and hectolitres)

1890–1944

	Austria[1]		Bulgaria		Czechoslovakia		France		Germany		Greece[7]		Hungary[9]	
	V	W	V	W	V	W	V	W	V	W[5]	V[8]	W[5]	V	W
1890	235	3,623	...	...	...	...	1,817	27,400	120	2,980	...	...	311	3,790
1891	245	2,998	...	.	...	...	1,764	30,200	119	750	...	...	254	1,367
1892	245	3,460	...	...	...	...	1,793	28,900	118	1,670	...	...	249	885
1893	251	4,535	...	...	...	...	1,821	50,700	116	3,820	...	...	226	1,044
1894	252	3,775	...	...	...	...	1,707	39,400	117	2,820	...	...	220	1,541
1895	253	3,583	...	...	...	...	1,661	26,900	116	2,010	...	1,600	203	2,143
1896	253	3.485	...	...	...	...	1,641	44,000	116	5,050	...	2,150	207	1,606
1987	253	2,775	...	...	...	...	1,624	31,900	117	2,780	...	1,200	205	1,256
1898	254	4,224	...	...	...	...	1,648	31,700	117	1,410	...	1,651	208	1,265
1899	255	3,368	111	...	...	...	1,632	46,800	117	2,000	...	1,254	214	1,918
1900	254	5,213	...	1,929	...	...	1,609	68,500	119	2,000	...	770	222	1,824
1901	254	4,796	...	...	...	...	1,618	60,100	120	2,000	...	1,100	227	2,901
1902	250	4,857	...	...	...	...	1,588	42,300	120	2,480	...	2,000	234	2,913
1903	250	3,766	81	1,078	...	...	1,588	35,200	120	3,790	...	1,300	239	2,705
1904	250	4,484	91	1,619	...	...	1,725	68,900	120	4,240	...	1,800	248	3,856
1905	249	5,337	91	1,462	...	...	1,744	57,900	120	3,860	...	1,100	258	3,519
1906	249	4,298	92	779	...	...	1,748	52,200	120	1,640	...	...	270	3,431
1907	238	4,250	89	867	...	...	1,649[14]	66,100[14]	119	2,490	...	...	276	3,408
1908	226	8,142	86	1,643	...	...	1,666	60,800	117	3,140	...	...	290	7,235
1909	230	6,253	85	1,319	...	...	1,637	54,600	115	2,020	...	...	298	3,649
1910	223	2,547	79	771	...	...	1,630	28,700	113	850	...		305	2,825
1911	222	3,837	68	551	...	...	1,606	45,000	110	2,923	97	3,231	312	4,616
1912	224	3,970	62	715	...	...	1,563	59,500	109	2,019	...	...	319	2,993
1913	219	4,353	54	609	...	...	1,550[15]	44,300[15]	106	1,005	...[17]	...[17]	324	3,316
1914	214[12]	3,615[12]	57	348	...	...	1,534	60,000	102	921	136[17]	3,845[17]	315	2,257
1915	198[12]	3,199[12]	52	476	...	...	1,533	20,400	97	2,699	108	3,392	315	3,039
1916	180[12]	1,697[12]	49	601	...	...	1,518	36,100	92	1,076	195[17]	2,747[17]	307	2,213
1917	39	1,046	49	660	...	...	1,516	38,300	94	1,956	172	3,027	305	5,609
1918	38	1,050[1]	47	678	...	...	1,512[14]	45,200[14]	92[6]	2,729	164[17]	3,174[17]	303[9]	5,701[9]
1919	38	288	43	781	...	...	1,505[4][15]	54,500[4][15]	69	1,741	178	2,667	...	...
1920	37[1]	295	44	426	19	333	1,518	59,300	73	2,440	140	1,749	190	2,450
1921	26	397	45	609	17	454	1,517	48,000	74	1,755	146[17]	1,873[17]	210	3,478
1922	25[1] / 30	827[1] / 938	48	669	17	595	1,527	76.800	74	3,406	122	1,794	216	4,614
1923	32	822	56	769	17	330	1,537	60,000	75	791	127	1,778	221	4,640
1924	32	305	63	959	16	262	1,550	70,900	74	1,804	124	2,301	222	1,363
1925	32	860	68	1,153	17	313	1,542	65,100	73	1,591	112	2,363	221	3,441
1926	34	462	73	1,526	17	140	1,525	42,600	73	989	114	2,692	221	1,293
1927	32	226	77	1,528	17	106	1,506	51,200	73	1,428	103	2,270	222	1,826
1928	38	775	79	1,713	17	323	1,516	60,300	73	2,053	122	3,075	222	3.083
1929	31	573	86	1,634	17	224	1,511	65,000	72	2,019	130[18] / 110	2,546	216	2,490
1930	35	1,202	88	1,556	18	474	1,527	45,600	71	2,814	123	2,209	213	4,022
1931	33	1,385	91	1,348	19	456	1,550	59,300	71	2,840	128	1,945	214	3,900
1932	30	1,078	93	1,415	19	434	1,541	49,600	72	1,722	142	3,950	212	3,557
1933	31	930	88	1,253	20	338	1,534	51,800	72	1,799	143	3,910	210	3,083
1934	32	909	93	1,511	21	329	1,555	78,100	73	4,525	145	3,700	211	2,542
1935	34	1,379	89	2,023	24	601	1,549	76,100	72	4,174	153	5,100	214	2,858
1936	38	984	88	825	25	525	1,511	43,700	72	3,315	152	1,940	214	4,539
1937	38	853	89	1,446	26[13]	432[13]	1,518	54,300	74	2,522	156	3,400	216	4,473
1938	40	1,045	89	2,346	...	...	1,513[16]	60,300[16]	73	2,445	157	4,680	218	3,309
1939	41	...	...	2,200	...	246	1,494	69,000	72	2,992	133	4,495	220	4,176
1940	39	270	135	777	16	181	1,470	49,400	67	1,086	...	...	223	863
1941	40	727	144	1,333	15	190	1,453	47,600	....	...	...	...	225	1,576
1942	40	512	146	2,042	16	225	1,434[16]	35,000[16]	...	...	...	...	229	4,205
1943	40	894	147	2,146	16	219	1,422	41,000	...	...	...	...	235	3,923
1944	40	625	151	2,241	16	189	1,403[16]	44,300[16]	...	...	...	...	...	...

See p.303 for footnotes

D3 Area of Vineyards and Output of Wine (in thousands of hectares and hectolitres)

1890–1944

	Hungary Croatia-Slavonia		Italy[10]		Portugal[11]		Romania		Spain		Switzerland		Serbia Yugoslavia	
	V	W	V	W	V	W	V	W	V	W	V	W	V	W
1890	54	333	3,430	29,457	...	...	146	3,081	...	18,500	...	...	...	...
1891	61	251	3,444	37,177	...	...	160	3,557	...	...	...	...	...	...
1892	57	187	3,466	34,346	186	3,606	139	3,122	...	...	...	...	...	...
1893	53	189	3,435	32,679	...	...	146	1,300	...	...	...	...	61	421
1894	46	245	3,451	26,385	...	...	...	...	...	21.800	...	...	...	...
1895	43	292	3,462	24,901	...	6,500	145	3,373	1,707	21,600	28	888	...	...
1896	41	140	3,446	29,544	...	3,280	144	4,628	...	29,900	...	1,270	...	...
1897	42	196	...	29,427	...	4,000	154	3,200	...	15,400	...	1,015	68	941
1898	40	186	...	34,389	...	5,000	139	3,900	...	28,100	31	855	...	...
1899	40	351	...	34,093	...	3,200	148	2,061	1,997	21,200	30	868	68	285
1900	38	334	...	36,648	...	5,500	146	3,498	1,460	37,800	30	2,103	...	100
1901	37	542	3,990	46,513	...	6,000	133	891	1,401	22,399	32	1,200	...	100
1902	38	676	4,000	43,628	...	4,800	143	1,043	1,384	12,184	31	1,191	37	200
1903	39	572	4,010	36,953	...	3,000	133	1,861	1,441	14,850	29	989	35	200
1904	41	873	3,991	43,036	...	6,200	104	836	1,411	21,856	19	1,267	34	400
1905	43	741	4,046	30,836	...	4,100	90	1,760	1,461	17,704	28	840	32	400
1906	44	623	3,779	31,357	...	...	87	1,761	1,399	13,575	28	1,300	35	600
1907	40	805	3,768	56,749	...	...	83	968	1,367	18,384	27	682	35	500
1908	40	1,676	3,759	54,481	...	6,900	79	2,284	1,310	18,557	26	925	40	900
1909	42	1,199	4,455	65,035	...	...	74	1,270	1,298	14,716	16	409	32	394
1910	45	247	4,455	32,642	...	...	74	1,713	1,293	11,283	24	244	34	154
1911	46	872	4,453	47,527	...	4,075[19]	71	993	1,290	14,747	24	749	...	...
1912	46	554	4,431	49,164	...	...	70	1,590	1,260	16,466	23	659	...	...
1913	48	1,096	4,429	58,210	...	...	73[20]	1,519[20]	1,250	17,105	22	181	...	...
1914	48	971	4,413	47,965	...	...	71	661	1,241	16,168	21	368	...	...
1915	48	437	4,412	21,233	...	4,837	69	1,997	1,247	10,112	21	666	...	...
1916	31	521	4,336	43,412	...	4,583	75	...	1,284	23,396	20	331	...	...
1917	...	833	4,317	54,279	...	4,406	...[20]	...[20]	1,294	23,763	18	608	...	...
1918	...	...	4,136	40,657	...	4,270	83	1,724	1,317	22,568	19	705	...	...
1919	incorporated in Yugoslavia		4,264	38,999	...	5,133	86[20]	2,209[20]	1,320	20,525	19	590	...	...
1920			4,236	47,123	...	3,384	102	2,371	1,332	26,771	18	606	173	3,460
1921			4,218[10]	35,551[8]	...	4,607	...	...	1,331	19,204	18	479	172	3,150
1922			4,274	38,247	...	5,794	...	...	1,341	25,672	15	1,019	168	4,615
1923			4,273	57,993	...	6,131	204	5,435	1,342	22,078	14	748	167	4,414
1924			4,277	48,089	...	5,246	210	6,114	1,341	21,745	14	306	165	2,918
1925			4,264	48,876	...	5,672	235	7,585	1,353	26,698	14	357	178	4,097
1926			4,283	40,940	...	3,666	220	5,065	1,382	15,754	14	454	175	2,912
1927			4,279	39,151	...	9,267	240	7,101	1,398	28,325	14	309	178	2,855
1928			4,399	52,460	...	4,525	240	7,127	1,417	22,085	14	609	176	4,318
1929			4,294	46,910	351	6,600	240	5,046	1,389	24,998	13	746	181	2,910
1930			4,240	40,761	...	5,785	240	8,385	1,440	18,228	12	572	184	4,016
1931			3,947	40,025	...	7,380	240	8,748	1,427	19,074	11	525	199	4,494
1932			3,944	49,103	...	6,150	273	7,815	1,433	21,188	11	388	192	4,387
1933			3,945	35,035	...	9,200	273	7,514	1,417	19,764	11	240	195	2,853
1934			3,962	32,146	...	10,805	273	8,704	1,451	21,719	11	847	199	3,867
1935			3,958	47,616	...	5,924	273	10,458	1,465	17,037	11	1,100	207	5,418
1936			3,918	34,110	...	3,709	273	6,707	...	...	12	488	214	3,865
1937			3,907	36,582	...	8,049	365	10,663	...	...	11	469	215	2,903
1938			3,910	41,780	...	10,955	365	9,924	...	...	12	345	219	4,672
1939			3,936	42,550	...	7,720	...[21]	11,542[21]	1,358	20,151	12	733	223	4,738
1940			3,934	30,494	...	5,187	229	2,120	1,456	14,168	11	462	...	...
1941			3,947	36,671	...	7,374	...	7,491	1,395	16,944	11	826	...	...
1942			3,927	37,987	...	8,335	...	3,188	1,367	20,350	11	750	...	...
1943			3,932[10]	37,830[10]	...	14,007	...	6,750	1,370	21,945	11	747	...	...
1944			3,889	33,270	...	14,507	...	5,548	1,371	21,180	11	1,051	...	...

See p.303 for footnotes

D3 **Area of Vineyards and Output of Wine** (in thousands of hectares and hectolitres)

1945–1975

	Austria[1]		Bulgaria		Czechoslovakia		France		West Germany		Greece[7]		Hungary[9]	
	V	W	V	W	V	W	V	W	V	W[5]	V[8]	W[5]	V	W
1945	36	881	155	2,361	16	236	1,434	28,600	...	...	129	2,400	239	3,335
1946	36	1,266	156	1,550	17	587	1,436	36,200	...	...	129	3,090	238	3,657
1947	35	1,053	...	4,300	19	419	1,440	44,200	...	...	...	3,770	237	2,364
1948	35	1,016	...	1,500	20	337	1,433	47,400	51	2,185	...	3,850	238	2,679
1949	35	971	...	426	19	290	1,437	42,900	51	1,363	...	4,140	...	3,173
1950	35	1,291	...	1,818	18	264	1,453	65,100	49	3,244	...	3,940	230	3,600
1951	36	1,104	...	2,270	19	267	1,450	52,900	53	3,114	...	3,500	228	3,226
1952	36	746	...	...	19	272	1,455	53,900	53	2,715	...	3,404	225	2,637
1953	37	826	146	...	18	266	1,455	59,100	55	2,457	...	3,860	216	1,786
1954	37	1,639	126	...	18	302	1,445	60,900	59	3,100	...	4,228	216	1,859
1955	37	1,164	121	...	19	328	1,435	61,100	60	2,408	...	3,575	201	3,368
1956	37	351	124	...	23	[304][22]	1,386	51,700	59	930	...	3,982	196	2,330
1957	37	1,415	129	...	32	370	1,335	33,300	59	2,264	...	4,016	196	3,260
1958	37	1,897	165	...	22	489	1,315	47,700	61	4,800	...	3,211	199	5,294
1959	35	728	174	...	24	257	1,323	60,300	64	4,303	...	3,274	201	3,257
1960	35	897	180	2,890	24	294	1,318	63,100	66	7,433	...	2,820	204	2,956
1961	36	1,328	182	2,800	24	325	1,285	48,600	67	5,094	142	3,350	204	3,508
1962	36	1,007	185	4,480	24	226	1,287	75,000	68	3,928	138	3,740	219	3,131
1963	40	1,827	189	4,620	25	346	1,271	57,500	69	6,034	134	2,567	229	4,243
1964	40	2,840	190	3,620	26	524	1,270	62,400	69	7,185	130	3,593	243	5,545
1965	45	1,387	192	4,740	27	281	1,263	68,417	69	5,035	129	4,057	247	2,425
1966	45	1,454	194	4,270	28	345	1,250	62,253	69	4,809	127	3,843	245	3,367
1967	46	2,594	200	3,511	29	746	1,240	62,026	69	6,069	125	3,948	240	4,789
1968	46	2,477	203	4,970	29	825	1,228	66,460	70	6,048	122	4,120	236	4,843
1969	46	2,265	201	4,913	31	987	1,208	51,290	71	5,947	125	5,160	234	5,614
1970	47	3,096	197	4,086	32	991	1,200	75,531	74	9,889	...	4,830	230	4,379
1971	48	1,813	195	4,087	34	1,025	1,173	62,287	76	6,027	...	4,560	222	4,289
1972	48	2,596	193	3,787	36	1,090	1,174	59,461	78	7,456	...	4,820	218	5,034
1973	48	2,404	193	5,204	37	1,115	1,181	83,505	81	10,697	...	4,610	213	6,231
1974	50	1,665	196	4,442	38	1,151	1,179	76,445	83	6,805	...	4,860	210	4,258
1975	50	2,704	196	3,468	40	1,237	1,186	66,509	85	9,241	...	4,340	206	4,951

	Italy[10]		Portugal		Romania		Spain		Switzerland		Yugoslavia	
	V	W	V	W	V	W	V	W	V	W	V	W
1945	3,878	29,298	...	10,167	215[21]	6,357[21]	1,373	13,852	11	613	...	...
1946	3,873	33,750	...	6,689	...	5,450	1,378	17,345	11	731	...	...
1947	3,848	36,446	...	10,111	220	3,640	1,394	20,955	11	881	...	...
1948	3,842[10]	40,393[10]	...	8,176	212	3,410	1,420	14,184	11	791	223	4,100
1949	3,853	41,037	...	7,927	202	4,090	1,431	14,324	11	551	232	4,040
1950	3,924	41,049	...	8,725	223	4,250	1,444	14,469	11	721	234	3,350
1951	3,931	49,761	...	9,490	223	4,550	1,481	16,074	11	1,041	250	6,058
1952	3,900	44,854	...	5,802	227	4,090	1,497	17,889	11	678	256	3,151
1953	3,886	52,542	...	11,736	222	4,100	1,510	23,465	12	682	261	3,825
1954	3,884	50,474	296	12,185	218	4,100	1,481	17,498	13	698	274	2,851
1955	3,849	58,441	291	11,336	213	5,764	1,497	16,847	13	801	280	5,300
1956	3,841	62,981	287	10,965	222	2,622	1,524	21,144	13	445	273	3,220
1957	3,791	42,509	289	9,576	230	...	1,541	17,365	13	413	271	4,210
1958	3,800	67,994	318	8,585	240	...	1,567	19,834	12	654	275	5,780
1959	3,769	66,374	321	8,924	257	...	1,583	17,278	12	1,061	277	4,600
1960	3,722	55,318	323	11,458	271	5,600	1,606	21,257	12	1,104	273	3,350
1961	3,675	52,760	325	7,420	278	4,800	1,617	20,482	12	862	272	4,260
1962	3,623	69,569	330	15,268	263	6,700	1,627	24,508	12	837	270	5,150
1963	3,524	53,640	339	12,979	247	6,100	1,524	25,836	12	942	266	5,900
1964	3,437	66,945	342	13,595	256	5,800	1,534	34,860	12	975	263	5,850
1965	3,353	68,206	345	14,749	242	5,211	1,544	26,452	12	966	262	5,150
1966	3,270	64,796	346	8,928	253	5,566	1,548	30,749	12	832	259	5,690
1967	3,199	74,725	348	9,941	264	5,240	1,584	23,310	12	961	257	5,230
1968	3,093	65,323	348	11,985	278	6,792	1,588	23,133	12	1,034	256	6,080
1969	2,772	71,658	348	8,329	288	6,848	1,592	24,619	12	796	255	7,060
1970	1,917	68,874	350	11,618	293	4,323	1,578	25,274	12	1,267	253	5,478
1971	1,918	64,271	...	9,069	299	6,350	1,476	24,325	12	1,004	252	5,546
1972	1,931	59,190	...	8,587	300	6,235	1,541	26,560	12	1,299	250	6,263
1973	1,919	76,716	...	11,270	300	9,223	1,574	39,999	13	755	249	7,701
1974	1,912	76,687	...	14,123	298	6,284	1,567	36,190	13	830	247	5,811
1975	1,910	69,814	...	9,380	296	6,763	1,611	32,365	13	1,194	...	5,419

See p.303 for footnotes

D3 Area of Vineyards and Output of Wine (in thousands of hectares and thousands of hectolitres)

NOTE

SOURCES: The main sources are as for table D1, with additional material for Hungary and Romania from *Magyarorszag Szoloszeti Statistikaya 1860–1873.* The Czechoslovak output in 1952 was furnished by the Federal Statistical Office of Czechoslovakia.

FOOTNOTES

[1] Cisleithania (excluding Lombardy and Venetia) to 1916. Subsequent figures apply to the Republic, though Burgenland is not included until 1922 (2nd line), and for 1917–20 (area) and 1917–18 (output) the whole of Carinthia and Styria is included (i.e. including parts later incorporated in Yugoslavia). Figures for 1913 comparable with those for 1922 (2nd line) and after are 48 thousand hectares and 677 thousand hectolitres.

[2] Various estimates were made for earlier periods. The following appear in official publications:— Area 1829; 2,003; 1835 2,119; Output 1788 25.0; 1808 28.0; 1827 36.8; 1829 31.0; 1830 15.3; 1835 26.5.
J.C. Toutain, *Le produit de l'agriculture francaise de 1700 à 1958,* (Cahiers de l'I.S.E.A., 1961) makes the following estimates of annual average output (in million hectolitres):— 1701–10 65.4; 1751–60 21.3 to 47.4; 1771–80 26.3: 1781–90 15.8 to 33.5; 1803–12 35.4.

[3] Subsequently includes Savoy and Nice.

[4] From 1870 to 1919 the parts of Alsace and Lorraine ceded to Germany are excluded.

[5] Wine must.

[6] Figures for 1871–1918 include Alsace-Lorraine. The area and output in 1913 without Alsace-Lorraine are 79 thousand hectares and 825 thousand hectolitres.

[7] In 1860 there were 65 thousand hectares of vineyards and an output of 213 thousand hectolitres.

[8] These figures are of vineyards for wine.

[9] Figures to 1872 apply to the whole Kingdom. From 1873 to 1918 they exclude Croatia-Slavonia. And from 1920 they apply to the territory established by the treaty of Trianon.

[10] Up to 1921 the statistics apply to the 1871 boundaries. For 1922–43 they apply to the 1924 boundaries. Since 1943 they apply to the 1954 boundaries, except that Trieste is not included until 1949.

[11] Mainland only.

[12] Part of Kustenland is excluded.

[13] Subsequently excluding Sub-Carpathian Russia (Ruthenia), which was ceded to the U.S.S.R. in 1945. Its area in 1937 was 4.6 thousand hectares and its output 140 thousand hectolitres.

[14] Figures to 1907 do not include Corsica.

[15] Figures for 1914–18 exclude the invaded departments.

[16] From 1939 to 1944 parts of Alsace-Lorraine annexed by Germany are excluded, and in 1943–44 Corsica is excluded.

[17] The following are the changes in the area to which the statistics apply:— In 1913 new territories in the north and in the islands were acquired from Turkey. In 1915 Macedonia was lost, and the western part of it was regained in 1917. In 1919 the postwar boundaries were achieved, but Thrace is not included in the statistics until 1922.

[18] Subsequently only vineyards in production.

[19] Excluding Santarem and Villa Real provinces.

[20] Southern Dobrudja was acquired in 1914, Bessarabia in 1918, and Bukovina, Transylvania, part of the Banat and part of Hungary proper in 1920.

[21] The wine-producing area was affected by the cession of northern Transylvania to Hungary in 1940. It was regained in 1946.

[22] Excluding production on state farms.

D4 **AREA AND OUTPUT OF MEDITERRANEAN CROPS** (in thousands of hectares and thousands of metric tons)

1861–1889

	Italy[1]				
	Olives		Citrus Fruits	Other F Fruits	Tobacco
	A	O	O	O	O
1861	...	1,055	237	436	...
1862	...	1,908	240	473	...
1863	...	1,294	261	336	...
1864	...	2,055	276	297	...
1865	...	2,281	248	332	...
1866	...	1,974	314	481	...
1867	...	1,421	298	565	...
1868	...	1,810	270	556	3.5
1869	...	2,325	286	661	3.9
1870	...	2,179	279	632	3.7
1871	...	2,778	342	588	3.8
1872	...	2,069	350	677	4.4
1873	...	2,851	330	718	4.9
1874	...	2,269	325	652	4.9
1875	...	2,632	372	576	4.4
1876	...	2,351	407	588	5.7
1877	...	2,128	390	627	4.5
1878	...	2,022	431	576	5.1
1879	...	2,671	420	622	4.9
1880	...	2,384	402	725	5.5
1881	...	958	490	686	5.7
1882	...	1,575	483	606	5.1
1883	...	1,146	565	561	5.4
1884	...	1,635	560	591	6.0
1885	...	1,679	471	595	6.1
1886	...	2,283	511	579	5.3
1887	...	1,421	542	624	4.1
1888	...	2,185	570	710	2.2
1889	...	1,126	470	877	1.8

Abbreviations used thoughout this table: A=Area O=Output

See p.308 for footnotes

D4 Area and Output of Mediterranean Crops (in thousands of hectares and thousands of metric tons)

1890–1944

	Bulgaria		**Greece**					**Italy**[1]				
	Tobacco		Cotton		Tobacco		Dried Grapes	Olives		CF	O.F.F.	Tobacco
	A	O	A	O	A	O	O	A	O	O	O	O
1890	...	...	...	...	...	...	...	...	2,266	620	965	2.3
1891	...	...	...	...	...	...	...	...	2,023	495	995	3.1
1902	...	...	...	...	...	...	...	...	1,263	491	820	4.5
1893	...	...	...	...	...	...	...	...	2,190	520	702	6.1
1894	...	...	...	...	...	...	...	...	1,600	556	711	5.9
1895	...	...	...	...	...	...	...	...	2,176	522	732	6.8
1896	...	...	...	...	...	...	...	...	1,468	543	799	5.9
1897	...	...	...	...	...	...	...	...	1,396	461	707	6.3
1898	...	...	...	...	...	...	...	...	1,918	529	761	5.7
1899	5	4	...	...	...	...	...	...	736	635	791	5.8
1900	...	4	...	...	...	...	...	...	1,220	668	899	6.2
1901	...	...	...	...	...	...	...	...	2,144	708	894	5.8
1902	...	...	...	...	...	...	...	...	1,240	775	847	5.0
1903	...	9	...	...	...	...	...	...	2,185	831	694	5.6
1904	...	5	...	...	...	...	...	...	1,133	662	892	6.2
1905	...	4	...	...	...	...	...	...	2,287	789	872	7.1
1906	...	6	...	...	...	...	...	...	746	740	1,228	7.0
1907	6	4	...	...	...	...	...	...	1,940	768	1,040	7.3
1908	5	3	...	...	...	...	...	...	424	902	1,125	6.8
1909	5	4	...	...	...	...	...	2,345	1,715	1,065	728	8.3
1910	8	6	...	...	...	...	...	2,331	723	966	1,070	9.1
1911	12	11	9.0	2.7	15	13	146	2,345	1,258	999	1,024	9.5
1912	9	6	... [3]	... [3]	... [3]	... [3]	... [3]	2,313	499	847	1,039	9.3
1913	6	5	...,	...				2,291	905	1,113	1,179	8.1
1914	20	15	12 [3]	3.3[3]	36[3]	25[3]	181[3]	2,298	928	1,018	1,156	8.7
1915	22	16	6.8	1.9	18	13	161	2,308	788	964	1,497	9.0
1916	15	12	6.9[3]	1.4[3]	29[3]	16[3]	146[3]	2,310	1,074	1,087	1,109	7.2
1917	25	15	4.9	1.3	40	28	142	2,301	1,100	803	1,583	4.9
1918	41	26	7.8[3]	1.7[3]	47[3]	30[3]	124[3]	2,295	1,503	878	952	7.0
1919	32	22	10	2.2	37	30	133	2,293	596	842	1,366	7.8
1920	39	29	7.0	1.3	39	32	137	2,292	1,061	799	1,393	9.8
1921	23	16	5.2[3]	1.2[3]	29[3]	23[3]	130[3]	2,290[1]	1,183[1]	780[1]	1,070[1]	14.9[1]
1922	34	26	7.5	1.8	32	26	202	2,310	2,007	858	1,172	19.0
1923	53	40	12	2.4	62	58	151	2,310	1,412	783	1,177	23.1
1924	49	49	16	3.1	82	50	185	2,284	1,658	832	1,387	27.9
1925	51	40	15	3.2	80	61	178	2,295	1,063	843	1,192	36.4
1926	32	27	15	3.9	81	61	174	2,294	1,351	1,041	1,413	39.3
1927	24	22	15	2.7	92	63	170	2,280	1,147	839	1,332	32.8
1928	22	16	15	3.3	93	59	171	2,329	1,718	840	1,380	37.2
1929	38	33	20	3.3	101	69	139	2,258	1,824	957	1,359	34.0
1930	32	27	20	3.5	97	66	171	2,265	770	1,016	1,134	42.2
1931	35	32	18	3.0	84	43	101	2,091	1,378	839	1,320	49.0
1932	20	17	20	4.8	63	29	189	2,091	1,255	1,300	1,543	40.8
1933	27	25	29	6.9	78	55	167	2,078	957	859	1,403	39.0
1934	22	21	37	7.8	73	42	207	2,077	1,249	834	1,289	39.6
1935	35	28	45	11	80	46	213	2,074	1,331	725	1,255	38.6
1936	43	42	62	13	111	81	177	2,171	966	732	1,083	42.2
1937	39	35	72	16	95	69	189	2,173	1,701	691	1,248	42.9
1938	31	26	68	14	84	48	188	2,176	1,042	836	1,076	42.1
1939	43	41	65	14	97	48	175	2,183	2,027	693	1,303	43.2
1940	53[2]	44[2]	...	...	...	...	...	2,187	1,024	744	1,313	51.3
1941	52	39	...	...	...	...	...	2,187	1,269	785	1,271	53.5
1942	48	42	...	...	...	...	...	2,188	1,128	705	1,199	48.6
1943	54	38	...	...	...	...	...	2,208 [1]	914[1]	684[1]	1,334[1]	33.5[1]
1944	44	32	...	...	...	...	...	2,195	985	521	1,325	23.5

See p.308 for footnotes

D4 Area and Output of Mediterranean Crops (in thousands of hectares and thousands of metric tons)

1890–1944

	Portugal	Romania		Spain									
	Olive Oil	Tobacco		Olives		Citrus Fruits		Sugar Cane		Cotton		Tobacco	
	O	A	O	A	O	A	O	A	O	A	O	A	O
1890	...	4.7	2.6	...	...	...	...	...	...	...	...	...	...
1891	...	4.4	3.1	...	...	...	...	...	...	...	...	...	...
1892	...	6.1	5.1	...	...	...	...	...	...	...	...	...	...
1893	...	5.8	3.4	...	...	...	...	...	...	...	...	...	...
1894	...	5.6	2.3	...	...	...	...	...	...	...	...	...	...
1895	...	...	...	...	...	...	...	...	...	...	...	...	...
1896	...	5.7	4.1	...	...	...	...	...	...	...	...	...	...
1897	...	4.5	3.8	...	...	...	...	...	...	...	...	...	...
1898	...	2.3	2.6	...	...	...	...	...	...	...	...	...	...
1899	...	2.2	1.2	...	...	...	...	...	...	...	...	...	...
1900	...	4.6	4.1	...	...	...	...	...	...	...	...	...	...
1901	...	4.1	3.0	...	...	...	...	...	...	...	...	...	...
1902	...	4.1	2.8	...	...	...	...	...	...	...	...	...	...
1903	...	5.8	4.6	...	...	...	...	...	...	...	...	...	...
1904	...	6.3	1.8	...	...	...	...	...	...	...	...	...	...
1905	...	7.7	3.9	...	...	...	...	...	...	...	...	...	...
1906	...	6.2	4.5	...	...	...	...	...	...	...	...	...	...
1907	...	8.8	7.1	...	...	...	...	...	...	...	...	...	...
1908	...	9.3	7.3	...	...	...	...	...	...	...	...	...	...
1909	...	8.3	5.5	1,395	1,398			...	...	...	...	...	...
1910		9.5	7.0	1,416	625	...	...	...	189	...	...	...	...
1911	23	10	9.3	1,444	2,220	...	...	...	234	...	...	...	...
1912	...	9.3	6.0	1,448	355	...	...	4.0	152	...	...	...	...
1913	...	11[4]	9.5[4]	1,453	1,487	...	...	4.0	139	...	...	...	...
1914	...	11	7.7	1,465	1,181	51	...	...	72	...	...	...	...
1915	26	13	8.4	1,482	1,773	...	...	1.9	64	...	...	...	...
1916	26	10	...	1,487	1,147	...	...	1.6	44	...	...	...	...
1917	38	...[4]	...[4]	1,504	2,208	...	...	1.7	64	...	...	...	...
1918	27	13	6.1	1.559	1,394	...	...	1.9	86	...	...	...	...
1919	28	15[4]	12[4]	1,572	1,813	...	...	1.9	65	...	...	...	...
1920	18	24	17	1,571	1,662	...	...	1.9	73	...	...	...	...
1921	23	17	10	1,614	1,523	...	...	2.3	129	...	...	0.1	0.2
1922	29	21	13	1,613	1,540	...	...	2.6	120	0.5	...	0.2	0.4
1923	44	18	9.7	1,624	1,613	...	...	2.3	93	0.4	...	...	...
1924	40	31	22	1,655	1,745	...	...	3.1	108	1.5	0.9	...	...
1925	38	37	16	1,679	1,868	56	...	...	120	2.2	1.1	...	...
1926	16	30	18	1,694	1,291	57	1,219	...	...	4.6	2.2	...	...
1927	89	31	20	1,713	3,517	63	1,091	...	...	4.6	1.6	...	1.4
1928	26	28	15	1,787	971	63	1,190	2.4	141	7.8	2.1	2.1	2.9
1929	76	31	26	1,818	3,341	69	1,490	2.7	167	7.8	2.1	2.7	4.7
1930	18	34	24	1,882	619	75	1,255	3.8	232	18	4.8	4.8	7.9
1931	64	16	11	1,911	1,806	75	1,257	3.8	259	5.8	2.4	3.6	5.9
1932	39	10	7.1	1,878	1,836	78	1,230	3.4	202	8.2	3.1	4.1	7.5
1933	74	10	6.3	1,901	1,647	80	1,027	3.2	209	7.8	2.7	4.3	7.5
1934	22	10	5.9	1,905	1,579	78	1,024	3.1	194	10	5.6	4.1	7.4
1935	52	18	13	1,921	2,251	80	961	3.1	197	25	7.9	4.1	7.1
1936	27	18	15	...	...	...	...	...	...	...	...	...	...
1937	97	14	10	...	...	...	...	...	...	...	...	...	...
1938	33	17	12	...	...	...	...	...	...	...	...	...	...
1939	76	22[5]	14[5]	1,918	1,150	81	757	2.8	188	16	4.3	3.8	5.3
1940	34	13	10	1,936	1,445	82	801	2.6	181	19	4.7	5.0	7.2
1941	90	14	11	1,974	1,946	82	903	2.5	144	22	9.1	5.4	10
1942	38	18	11	1,971	1,301	86	829	2.1	97	33	13	6.5	8.3
1943	86	...	...	1,971	2,057	85	917	2.3	113	49	14	8.5	11
1944	36	22	15	1,967	1,322	85	1,109	2.6	137	60	17	9.0	13

See p.308 for footnotes

D4 Area and Output of Mediterranean Crops (in thousands of hectares and thousands of metric tons)

1945–1969

	Bulgaria		Greece					Italy				
	Tobacco		Cotton		Tobacco		Dried Grapes	Olives		Citrus Fruits	Other F Fruits	Tobacco
	A	O	A	O	A	O	O	A	O	O	O	O
1945	46	23	28	6.9	46	23	60	2,195	663	554	1,237	17.1
1946	73	40	52	10	64	34	76	2,107	854	638	1,267	44.5
1947	62	48	42	12	80	45	112	2,263	1,592	735	1,692	76.4
1948	...	...	46	12	72	37	100	2,277[1]	679[1]	775[1]	1,499[1]	74.4[1]
1949	...	...	57	48	75	46	126	2,286	1,150	670	2,027	71.8
1950	...	...	77	79	103	58	117	2,294	1,012	998	1,869	78.7
1951	...	...	87	89	96	63	107	2,316	2,148	905	2,136	79.5
1952	...	...	82	77	76	42	114	2,214	1,099	958	2,376	73.0
1953	...	...	89	95	88	63	123	2,196	2,011	1,023	2,380	68.3
1954	96	55	109	128	106	67	113	2,215	1,730	1,005	2,220	66.1
1955	90	55	166	189	129	97	107	2,256	1,153	1,059	2,710	72.3
1956	89	72	160	154	118	82	132	2,240	981	1,053	2,777	71.2
1957	94	57	156	191	122	109	144	2,233	2,010	1,117	2,431	77.1
1958	108	83	162	187	112	84	125	2,247	1,462	1,273	3,285	79.8
1959	119	99	131	170	102	80	137	2,298	1,654	1,230	3,869	90.3
1960	87	62	165	184	94	64	120	2,311	2,106	1,238	3,906	79.5
1961	96	56	217	288	104	74	166	2,317	2,251	1,477	4,764	25.0
1962	120	107	278	270	122	89	201	2,321	1,741	1,238	4,766	46.3
1963	124	105	233	305	147	129	143	2,290	2,861	1,618	5,275	65.2
1964	131	150	141	225	143	134	163	2,294	1,878	1,804	5,511	78.9
1965	121	123	136	228	132	126	177	2,291	2,232	1,777	5,138	73.5
1966	117	132	133	260	126	104	183	2,287	1,808	2,029	6,002	73.1
1967	103	118	136	285	128	114	149	2,283	2,712	2,161	5,049	86.9
1968	114	115	141	228	112	89	195	5,285	1,933	2,510	5,285	74.1
1969	117	96	158	338	107	80	186	5,145	2,413	2,529	5,145	79.4

	Portugal	Romania		Spain									
	Olive Oil	Tobacco		Olives		Citrus Fruits		Sugar Cane		Cotton		Tobacco	
	O	A	O	A	O	A	O	A	O	A	O	A	O
1945	40	21[5]	11[5]	1,976	973	84	960	3.0	126	36	5.6	8.7	9.8
1946	44	25	7.9	1,989	2,000	81	634	3.2	144	58	20	10	15
1947	92	24	...	1,993	2,556	81	800	3.3	166	28	9.5	7.4	13
1948	28	27	14	2,001	733	81	877	3.5	210	53	20	9.9	16
1949	97	...	...	2,008	1,924	82	756	3.9	271	37	9.6	9.9	15
1950	39	29	14	2,023	902	84	967	4.2	302	34	13	10	15
1951	104	34	25	2,049	2,951	89	1,097	4.2	283	44	25	15	20
1952	51	33	15	2,062	1,499	92	1,435	4.8	353	67	52	19	30
1953	120	36	24	2,077	1,790	93	1,080	5.2	422	88	60	21	32
1954	48	32	19	2,084	1,456	96	1,363	5.1	369	108	67	22	34
1955	67	35	26	2,130	1,350	97	1,178	5.0	388	164	110	20	33
1956	92	35	26	2,113	1,858	96	506	5.1	406	200	148	18	27
1957	99	40	36	2,122	1,614	102	1,313	5.1	364	160	106	17	25
1958	61	47	31	2,123	1,644	102	1,346	5.0	323	169	121	16	23
1959	90	36	26	2,145	2,228	109	1,662	5.1	324	225	191	16	23
1960	85	22	16	2,148	2,367	115	1,617	5.1	320	250	217	18	30
1961	113	28	18	2,153	1,863	124	1,959	5.4	336	319	318	21	37
1962	52	38	26	2,167	1,641	132	1,407	5.3	363	346	335	19	32
1963	99	41	40	2,194	3,124	142[6]	2,082	5.0	354	263	285	18	27
1964	41	40	42	2,211	579	114	1,911	5.1	357	197	225	20	28
1965	72	38	35	2,220	1,658	117	2,023	5.1	458	198	249	21	34[6]
1966	38	38	40	2,154	2,108	124	2,308	5.3	430	234	267	13	21
1967	81	39	35	2,257	1,378	128	2,142	5.5	412	144	198	18	31
1968	53	36	33	2,224	2,282	132	1,893	5.5	407	136	229	14	26
1969	72	36	24	2,227	1,746	142	2,593	5	420	150	180	14	20

Other F Fruits: Other Fresh Fruits

See p.308 for footnotes

D4 Area and Output of Mediterranean Crops (in thousands of hectares and thousands of metric tons)

1970–1975

	Bulgaria		Greece					Italy				
	Tobacco		Cotton		Tobacco		Dried Grapes	Olives		Citrus Fruits	Other F Fruits	Tobacco
	A	O	A	O	A	O	O	A	O	O	O	O
1970	118	108	143	328	98	95	169	2,253	2,124	2,400	5,776	78.4
1971	115	120	139	360	91	88	161	2,222	2,385	2,585	5,319	79.3
1972	122	158	174	395	84	86	137	2,199	1,870	2,546	5,285	84.3
											5,271[7]	
1973	119	141	154	378	83	90	147	2,182	2,836	2,758	5,311	93.8
1974	123	145	153	357	83	85	180	2,180	2,323	2,934	5,154	92.7
1975	127	162	138	366	94	117	155	2,172	3,371	2,811	5,273	113.4

	Portugal	Romania		Spain									
	Olive Oil	Tobacco		Olives		Citrus Fruits		Sugar Cane		Cotton		Tobacco	
	O	A	O	A	O	A	O	A	O	A	O	A	O
1970	67	34	23	2,196	2,014	153	2,069	6	421	91	160	15	26
1971	42	33	30	2,095	1,648	169	2,323	5	423	78	124	16	27
1972	54	39	38	2,137	2,153	197	3,013	5	369	122	177	18	27
1973	42	52	38	2,122	2,115	195	2,924	5	332	92	140	16	26
1974	48	53	39	2,085	1,547	200	2,705	4	302	101	181	14	23
1975	58	57	40	2,102	2,203	212	2,896	4	273	62	140	14	26

NOTE

SOURCES:— As in Table D1

FOOTNOTES

[1] Up to 1921 the statistics apply to the boundaries of 1871. For 1922-43 they apply to the 1924 boundaries; and from 1944 onwards to the 1954 boundaries, except that Trieste is not included until 1949.

[2] Subsequently includes southern Dobrudja.

[3] The following are the changes in the area to which the statistics apply:— In 1913 new territories in the north and in the islands were acquired from Turkey. In 1915 Macedonia was lost, but the western part of it was regained in 1917. In 1919 the postwar boundaries were achieved, but Thrace is not included in the statistics until 1922.

[4] Southern Dobrudja was acquired in 1914, Bessarabia in 1918, and Bukovina, Transylvania, part of Banat, and parts of Hungary proper in 1920.

[5] Southern Dobrudja was ceded to Bulgaria in 1940. Bessarabia and northern Bukovina were ceded to the U.S.S.R. in 1940, and though temporarily reconquered in 1943, this does not appear to have affected these series. Northern Transylvania was ceded to Hungary in 1940, but was regained by 1946.

[6] There was a change in the basis of calculation.

[7] Subsequently excluding pomegranates and quinces.

D5 NUMBERS OF LIVESTOCK (in thousands)

1815–1869

	AUSTRIA[1]						BELGIUM				DENMARK				
	H	C	P	S	G	Po	H[2]	C	P	S	H	C	P	S	Po
1815	...	...	...	...	...	...	...	...	...	...	...	...	...	...	...
1816	...	...	...	...	...	...	254	981	...	970	...	...	...	...	...
1817	...	...	...	...	...	...	241	913	...	727	...	...	...	...	...
1818	...	...	...	...	...	...	240	895	...	677	...	...	...	...	...
1819	...	...	...	...	...	...	242	890	...	672	...	...	...	...	...
1820	...	...	...	...	...	...	241	894	...	680	...	...	...	...	...
1821	...	...	...	...	...	...	246	894	...	710	...	...	...	...	...
1822	...	...	...	...	...	...	246	889	...	735	...	...	...	...	...
1823	...	...	...	...	...	...	243	887	...	772	...	...	...	...	...
1824	...	...	...	...	...	...	255	897	...	805	...	...	...	...	...
1825	...	...	...	...	...	...	254	893	...	774	...	...	...	...	...
1826	...	...	...	...	...	...	256	887	...	...	...	...	...	...	...
1827	...	...	...	...	...	...	256	875	...	...	...	...	...	...	...
1828	...	...	...	...	...	...	258	878	...	...	...	...	...	...	...
1829	...	...	...	...	...	...	262[3]	899[3]	...	...[3]	...	...	...	...	...
1830	...	...	...	...	...	...	...	...	...	...	...	...	...	...	...
1831	...	...	...	...	...	...	...	...	...	...	...	...	...	...	...
1832	...	...	...	...	...	...	...	...	...	...	...	...	...	...	...
1833	...	...	...	...	...	...	...	...	...	...	...	...	...	...	...
1834	...	...	...	...	...	...	...	...	...	...	...	...	...	...	...
1835	...	...	...	...	...	...	...	...	...	...	...	...	...	...	...
1836	...	...	...	...	...	...	...	...	...	...	...	...	...	...	...
1837	...	...	...	...	...	...	...	...	...	...	...	...	...	...	...
1838	...	...	...	...	...	...	...	...	...	...	...	...	...	...	...
1839	...	...	...	...	...	...	...	...	...	...	...	...	...	...	...
1840	...	...	...	...	...	...	247	913	421	733	...	...	...	...	...
1841	...	...	...	...	...	...	...	...	...	...	...	...	...	...	...
1842	1,116	4,984	...	6,745	...	...	...	...	...	...	...	...	...	...	...
1843	1,143	5,048	...	6,503	...	...	...	...	...	...	...	...	...	...	...
1844	1,144	5,044	...	6,540	...	...	...	...	...	...	...	...	...	...	...
1845	1,145	5,049	...	6,532	...	...	295	1,204	496	663	...	...	...	...	...
1846	1,152	5,203	...	6,541			...	...	...	...	...	...	...	...	...
1847	1,155	5,223	...	6,474	...	...	...	...	...	...	...	...	...	...	...
1848	...	...	...	...	...	...	...	...	...	...	...	...	...	...	...
1849	...	...	...	...	...	...	...	...	...	...	...	...	...	...	...
1850	...	...	...	...	...	...	...	...	...	...	...	...	...	...	...
1851	1,123	5,126	2,156	5,640	1,068	...	...	...	...	...	...	...	...	...	...
1852	...	...	...	...	...	...	...	...	...	...	...	...	...	...	...
1853	...	...	...	...	...	...	...	...	...	...	...	...	...	...	...
1854	...	...	...	...	...	...	...	...	...	...	...	...	...	...	...
1855	...	...	...	...	...	...	...	...	...	...	...	...	...	...	...
1856	...	...	...	...	...	...	277	1,258	458	583	...	...	...	...	...
1857	1,295	8,013	3,410	5,285	1,028	...	...	...	...	...	...	...	...	...	...
1958	...	...	...	...	...	...	...	...	...	...	...	...	...	...	...
1859	...	...	...	...	...	...	...	...	...	...	...	...	...	...	...
1860	...	...	...	...	...	...	...	...	...	...	...	...	...	...	...
1861	...	.....	...	...	...	...	...	...	...	...	325	1,121	304	1,749	...
1862	...	...	...	...	...	...	...	...	...	...	...	...	...	...	...
1863	...	...	...	...	...	...	...	...	...	...	...	...	...	...	...
1864	...	...	...	...	...	...	...	...	...	...	...	...	...	...	...
1865	...	...	...	...	...	...	...	...	...	...	...	...	...	...	...
1866	...	...	...	...	...	...	283	1,242	632	586	353	1,194	382	1,875	...
1867	...	...	...	...	...	...	...	...	...	...	...	...	...	...	...
1868	...	...	...	...	...	...	...	...	...	...	...	...	...	...	...
1869	1,390	7,425	2,551	5,026	979	...	...	...	...	...	...	...	...	...	...

Abbreviations used throughout this table: H=Horses C=Cattle P=Pigs S=Sheep G=Goats Po=Poultry A & M=Asses and Mules R=Reindeer

See p.341 for footnotes

D5 Numbers of Livestock (in thousands)

1815–1869

	FRANCE					GERMANY					
	H	C	P	S	G	H	C	P	S	G	Po
1815	...	...	...	...	...	...	...	...	...	...	...
1816	...	...	...	...	...	...	9,317	3,243	...	...	...
1817	...	...	...	...	...	...	...	...	...	...	...
1818	...	...	...	...	...	...	...	...	...	...	...
1819	...	...	...	...	...	...	9,944	3,322	...	...	...
1820	...	...	...	...	...	...	...	...	...	...	...
1821	...	...	...	...	...	...	...	...	...	...	...
1822	...	...	...	...	...	...	9,877	3,593	...	...	...
1823	...	...	...	...	...	...	...	...	...	...	...
1824	...	...	...	...	...	...	...	...	...	...	...
1825	...	...	...	...	...	...	10,371	4,105	...	...	...
1826	...	...	...	...	...	...	...	...	...	...	...
1827	...	...	...	...	...	...	...	...	...	...	...
1828	...	...	...	...	...	...	10,424	3,832	...	...	...
1829	...	...	...	...	...	...	...	...	...	...	...
1830	...	...	...	...	...	...	...	...	...	...	...
1831	...	...	...	...	...	...	10,844	4,037	...	...	...
1832	...	...	...	...	...	...	...	...	...	...	...
1833	...	...	...	...	...	...	...	...	...	...	...
1834	...	...	...	...	...	...	11,661	4,514	...	...	...
1835	...	...	...	...	...	...	...	...	...	...	...
1836	...	...	...	...	...	...	...	...	...	...	...
1837	...	...	...	...	...	...	12,098	4,502	...	...	...
1838	...	...	...	...	...	...	...	...	...	...	...
1839	...	...	...	...	...	...	...	...	...	...	...
1840	2,818	11,762	4,911	32,151	964	...	12,755	5,245	...	...	...
1841	...	...	...	...	...	...	...	...	...	...	...
1842	...	...	...	...	...	...	...	...	...	...	...
1843	...	...	...	...	...	...	12,605	4,919	...	...	...
1844	...	...	...	...	...	...	...	...	...	...	...
1845	...	...	...	...	...	...	...	...	...	...	...
1846	...	...	...	...	...	...	13,155	5,116	...	...	...
1847	...	...	...	...	...	...	...	...	...	...	...
1848	...	...	...	...	...	...	...	...	...	...	...
1849	...	...	...	...	...	...	13,102	5,735	...	...	...
1850	...	...	...	...	...	...	...	...	...	...	...
1851	...	...	...	...	...	...	...	...	...	...	...
1852	2,866	11,911	5,246	33,282	1,338	...	13,107	4,751	...	...	...
1853	...	...	...	...	...	...	...	...	...	...	...
1854	...	...	...	...	...	...	...	...	...	...	...
1855	...	...	...	...	...	...	13,265	4,786	...	...	...
1856	...	...	...	...	...	...	...	...	...	...	...
1857	...	...	...	...	...	...	...	...	...	...	...
1858	...	...	...	...	...	...	13,160	5,884	...	...	...
1859	...[4]	...[4]	...[4]	...[4]	...[4]	...	...	...	...	...	...
1860	...	...	...	...	...	...	...	...	...	...	...
1861	...	...	...	...	...	...	13,417	5,995	...	...	...
1862	2,914	11,813	6,038	29,530	1,726	...	...	...	...	...	...
1863	...	...	...	...	...	...	...	...	...	...	...
1864	...	...	...	...	...	...	14,011	7,279	...	...	...
1865	...	...	...	...	...	...	...	...	...	...	...
1866	...	...	...	...	...	...	...	...	...	...	...
1867	...	...	...	...	...	...	13,536	8,349	...	...	...
1868	...	...	...	...	...	...	...	...	...	...	...
1869	...	...	...	...	...	...	...	...	...	...	...

See p.341 for footnotes

D5 Numbers of Livestock (in thousands)

1815–1869

	GREECE[5]						HUNGARY[6]				
	H	A & M	C	P	S	G	H	C	P	S	G
1815	...	...	...	...	...	...	...	...	...	...	...
1816	...	...	...	...	...	...	...	...	...	...	...
1817	...	...	...	...	...	...	...	...	...	...	...
1818	...	...	...	...	...	...	...	...	...	...	...
1819	...	...	...	...	...	...	...	...	...	...	...
1820	...	...	...	...	...	...	...	...	...	...	...
1821	...	...	...	...	...	...	...	...	...	...	...
1822	...	...	...	...	...	...	...	...	...	...	...
1823	...	...	...	...	...	...	...	...	...	...	...
1824	...	...	...	...	...	...	...	...	...	...	...
1825	...	...	...	...	...	...	...	...	...	...	...
1826	...	...	...	...	...	...	...	...	...	...	...
1827	...	...	...	...	...	...	...	...	...	...	...
1828	...	...	...	...	...	...	...	...	...	...	...
1829	...	...	...	...	...	...	...	...	...	...	...
1830	...	...	...	...	...	...	...	...	...	...	...
1831	...	...	...	...	...	...	...	...	...	...	...
1832	...	...	...	...	...	...	...	...	...	...	...
1833	...	...	...	...	...	...	...	...	...	...	...
1834	...	...	...	...	...	...	...	...	...	...	...
1835	...	...	...	...	...	...	...	...	...	...	...
1836	...	...	...	...	...	...	...	...	...	...	...
1837	...	...	...	...	...	...	...	...	...	...	...
1838	...	...	...	...	...	...	...	...	...	...	...
1839	...	...	...	...	...	...	...	...	...	...	...
1840	...	...	...	...	...	...	...	...	...	...	...
1841	...	...	...	...	...	...	...	...	...	...	...
1842	...	...	...	...	...	...	1,554[7]	5,607[7]	4,958[7]	20,017[7]	...
1843	...	...	...	...	...	...	...	...	...	...	...
1844	...	...	...	...	...	...	...	...	...	...	...
1845	...	...	...	...	...	...	...	...	...	...	...
1846	...	...	...	...	...	...	...	...	...	...	...
1847	...	...	...	...	...	...	...	...	...	...	...
1848	...	...	...	...	...	...	...	...	...	...	...
1849	...	...	...	...	...	...	...	...	...	...	...
1850	...	...	...	...	...	...	...	...	...	...	...
1851	...	...	...	...	...	...	...	...	...	...	...
1852	...	...	...	...	...	...	...	...	...	...	...
1853	...	...	...	...	...	...	...	...	...	...	...
1854	...	...	...	...	...	...	...	...	...	...	...
1855	...	...	...	...	...	...	...	...	...	...	...
1856	...	...	...	...	...	...	...	...	...	...	...
1857	...	...	...	...	...	...	1,964	4,291	4,088	11,087	402
1858	...	...	...	...	...	...	...	...	...	...	...
1859	...	...	...	...	...	...	...	...	...	...	...
1860	83	99	259	134	2,540	2,408	...	...	...	...	...
1861	...	...	...	...	...	...	...	...	...	...	...
1862	...	...	...	...	...	...	...	...	...	...	...
1863	...	...	...	...	...	...	...	...	...	...	...
1864	...	...	...	...	...	...	...	...	...	...	...
1865	...	...	...	...	...	...	...	...	...	...	...
1866	...	...	...	...	...	...	...	...	...	...	...
1867	...	...	...	...	...	...	...	...	...	...	...
1868	...	...	...	...	...	...	...	...	...	...	...
1869	...	...	...	...	...	...	...	...	...	...	...

See p.341 for footnotes

D5 Numbers of Livestock (in thousands)

1815–1869

	IRELAND					ITALY[8]					
	H	C	P	S	Po	H	A & M	C[9]	P	S	G
1815	...	...	...	...	...	...	...	...	...	...	...
1816	...	...	...	...	...	...	...	...	...	...	...
1817	...	...	...	...	...	...	...	...	...	...	...
1818	...	...	...	...	...	...	...	...	...	...	...
1819	...	...	...	...	...	...	...	...	...	...	...
1820	...	...	...	...	...	...	...	...	...	...	...
1821	...	...	...	...	...	...	...	...	...	...	...
1822	...	...	...	...	...	...	...	...	...	...	...
1823	...	...	...	...	...	...	...	...	...	...	...
1824	...	...	...	...	...	...	...	...	...	...	...
1825	...	...	...	...	...	...	...	...	...	...	...
1826	...	...	...	...	...	...	...	...	...	...	...
1827	...	...	...	...	...	...	...	...	...	...	...
1828	...	...	...	...	...	...	...	...	...	...	...
1829	...	...	...	...	...	...	...	...	...	...	...
1830	...	...	...	...	...	...	...	...	...	...	...
1831	...	...	...	...	...	...	...	...	...	...	...
1832	...	...	...	...	...	...	...	...	...	...	...
1833	...	...	...	...	...	...	...	...	...	...	...
1834	...	...	...	...	...	...	...	...	...	...	...
1835	...	...	...	...	...	...	...	...	...	...	...
1836	...	...	...	...	...	...	...	...	...	...	...
1837	...	...	...	...	...	...	...	...	...	...	...
1838	...	...	...	...	...	...	...	...	...	...	...
1839	...	...	...	...	...	...	...	...	...	...	...
1840	...	...	...	...	...	...	...	...	...	...	...
1841	...	1,863	1,413	2,106	8,459	...	...	...	...	...	...
1842	...	...	...	...	...	...	...	...	...	...	...
1843	...	...	...	...	...	...	...	...	...	...	...
1844	...	...	...	...	...	...	...	...	...	...	...
1845	...	...	...	...	...	...	...	...	...	...	...
1846	...	...	...	...	...	...	...	...	...	...	...
1847	558	2,591	622	2,186	5,691	...	...	...	...	...	...
1848	...	...	...	...	...	...	...	...	...	...	...
1849	526	2,771	795	1,777	6,328	...	...	...	...	...	...
1850	527	2,918	928	1,876	6,945	...	...	...	...	...	...
1851	522	2,967	1,085	2,122	7,471	...	...	...	...	...	...
1852	525	3,095	1,073	2,614	8,176	...	...	...	...	...	...
1853	540	3,383	1,145	3,143	8,661	...	...	...	...	...	...
1854	546	3,498	1,343	3,722	8,630	...	...	...	...	...	...
1855	556	3,564	1,178	3,602	8,367	...	...	...	...	...	...
1856	573	3,588	919	3,694	8,908	...	...	...	...	...	...
1857	600	3,621	1,255	3,452	9,491	...	...	...	...	...	...
1858	611	3,667	1,410	3,495	9,563	...	...	...	...	...	...
1859	629	3,816	1,266	3,593	10,252	...	...	...	...	...	...
1860	620	3,606	1,271	3,542	10,061	...	...	...	...	...	...
1861	614	3,472	1,102	3,556	10,371	432	839	3,230	2,092	8,038	2,151
1862	603	3,255	1,154	3,456	9,917	399	757	3,086	1,840	7,456	1,992
1863	580	3,144	1,067	3,308	9,649	374	693	2,975	1,626	6,979	1,862
1864	562	3,262	1,058	3,367	10,424	358	643	2,900	1,452	6,609	1,758
1865	548	3,498	1,306	3,694	10,682	350	620	2,858	1,317	6,347	1,680
1866	536	3,746	1,497	4,274	10,890	350	611	2,852	1,220	6,194	1,627
1867	524	3,708	1,235	4,836	10,335	417	642	3,270	1,534	6,443	1,649
1868	525	3,647	870	4,901	10,603	437	669	3,343	1,511	6,508	1,649
1869	528	3,734	1,082	4,651	10,802	466	716	3,454	1,539	6,685	1,676

See p.341 for footnotes

D5 Numbers of Livestock (in thousands)

1815–1869

	NETHERLANDS[10]					NORWAY				ROMANIA			
	H	C	P	S	Hens	H	C	P	S	H	C	P	S
1815	...	...	...	...	...	...	...	...	...	...	...	...	...
1816	189	975	...	677	...	...	...	...	...	...	...	...	...
1817	...	...	...	...	...	...	...	...	...	...	...	...	...
1818	...	...	...	...	...	...	...	...	...	...	...	...	...
1819	...	...	...	...	...	...	...	...	...	...	...	...	...
1820	209	1,027	...	692	...	...	...	...	...	...	...	...	...
1821	...	...	...	...	...	...	...	...	...	...	...	...	...
1822	...	...	...	...	...	...	...	...	...	...	...	...	...
1823	...	...	...	...	...	...	...	...	...	...	...	...	...
1824	...	...	...	...	...	...	...	...	...	...	...	...	...
1825	200	944	...	638	...	...	...	...	...	...	...	...	...
1826	...	...	...	...	...	...	...	...	...	...	...	...	...
1827	...	...	...	...	...	...	...	...	...	...	...	...	...
1828	...	...	...	...	...	...	...	...	...	...	...	...	...
1829	...	...	...	...	...	...	...	...	...	...	...	...	...
1830	193	967	...	638	...	...	...	...	...	...	...	...	...
1831	...	...	...	...	...	...	...	...	...	...	...	...	...
1832	...	...	...	...	...	...	...	...	...	...	...	...	...
1833	...	...	...	...	...	...	...	...	...	...	...	...	...
1834	...	...	...	...	...	...	...	...	...	...	...	...	...
1835	...	...	...	...	...	...	...	...	...	...	...	...	...
1836	...	...	...	...	...	113	644	80	1,029	...	...	...	...
1837	...	...	...	...	...	...	...	...	...	...	...	...	...
1838	...	...	...	...	...	...	...	...	...	...	...	...	...
1839	...	...	...	...	...	...	...	...	...	...	...	...	...
1840	217	1,066	...	781	...	...	...	...	...	...	...	...	...
1841	...	...	...	...	...	...	...	...	...	...	...	...	...
1842	...	...	...	...	...	...	...	...	...	...	...	...	...
1843	...	...	...	...	...	...	...	...	...	...	...	...	...
1844	220	1,057	...	613	...	...	...	...	...	...	...	...	...
1845	...	...	...	...	...	...	...	...	...	...	...	...	...
1846	...	...	...	...	...	132	843	89	1,447	...	...	...	...
1847	...	...	...	...	...	...	...	...	...	...	...	...	...
1848	...	...	...	...	...	...	...	...	...	...	...	...	...
1849	...	...	...	...	...	...	...	...	...	...	...	...	...
1850	...	...	...	...	...	...	...	...	...	...	...	...	...
1851	270	1,249	237	803	...	...	...	...	...	...	...	...	...
1852	239	1,251	239	836	...	...	...	...	...	...	...	...	...
1853	234	1,237	234	832	...	...	...	...	...	...	...	...	...
1854	240	1,145	240	858	...	...	...	...	...	...	...	...	...
1855	235	1,255	236	821	...	154	950	113	1,596	...	...	...	...
1856	235	1,260	239	782	...	...	...	...	...	...	...	...	...
1857	237	1,279	261	779	...	...	...	...	...	...	...	...	...
1858	236	1,213	251	768	...	...	...	...	...	...	...	...	...
1859	239	1,227	261	802	...	...	...	...	...	...	...	...	...
1860	243	1,288	271	866	...	...	...	...	...	461	2,608	1,051	4,410
1861	247	1,335	281	870	...	...	...	...	...	...	...	...	...
1862	250	1,374	279	882	...	...	...	...	...	...	...	...	...
1863	254	1,381	299	894	...	...	...	...	...	...	...	...	...
1864	255	1,335	295	930	...	...	...	...	...	...	...	...	...
1865	254	1,314	296	967	...	149	953	96	1,705	...	...	...	...
1866	254	1,272	322	1,076	...	...	...	...	...	...	...	...	...
1867	255	1,361	303	1,027	...	...	...	...	...	...	...	...	...
1868	253	1,368	290	950	...	...	...	...	...	...	...	...	...
1869	254	1,402	300	927	...	...	...	...	...	...	...	...	...

See p.341 for footnotes

D5 Numbers of Livestock (in thousands)

1815–1869

	RUSSIA[11]				SPAIN[12]					
	H	C	P	S	H	A & M	C	P	S	G
1815	...	...	...	...	...	...	...	...	...	...
1816	...	...	...	...	...	...	...	...	...	...
1817	...	...	...	...	...	...	...	...	...	...
1818	...	...	...	...	...	...	...	...	...	...
1819	...	...	...	...	...	...	...	...	...	...
1820	...	...	...	...	...	...	...	...	...	...
1821	...	...	...	...	...	...	...	...	...	...
1822	...	...	...	...	...	...	...	...	...	...
1823	...	...	...	...	...	...	...	...	...	...
1824	...	...	...	...	...	...	...	...	...	...
1825	...	...	...	...	...	...	...	...	...	...
1826	...	...	...	...	...	...	...	...	...	...
1827	...	...	...	...	...	...	...	...	...	...
1828	...	...	...	...	...	...	...	...	...	...
1829	...	...	...	...	...	...	...	...	...	...
1830	...	...	...	...	...	...	...	...	...	...
1831	...	...	...	...	...	...	...	...	...	...
1832	...	...	...	...	...	...	...	...	...	...
1833	...	...	...	...	...	...	...	...	...	...
1834	...	...	...	...	...	...	...	...	...	...
1835	...	...	...	...	...	...	...	...	...	...
1836	...	...	...	...	...	...	...	...	...	...
1837	...	...	...	...	...	...	...	...	...	...
1838	...	...	...	...	...	...	...	...	...	...
1839	...	...	...	...	...	...	...	...	...	...
1840	...	...	...	...	...	...	...	...	...	...
1841	...	...	...	...	...	...	...	...	...	...
1842	...	...	...	...	...	...	...	...	...	...
1843	...	...	...	...	...	...	...	...	...	...
1844	...	...	...	...	...	...	...	...	...	...
1845	...	...	...	...	...	...	...	...	...	...
1846	...	...	...	...	...	...	...	...	...	...
1847	...	...	...	...	...	...	...	...	...	...
1848	...	...	...	...	...	...	...	...	...	...
1849	...	...	...	...	...	...	...	...	...	...
1850	...	...	...	...	...	...	...	...	...	...
1851	...	...	...	...	...	...	...	...	...	...
1852	...	...	...	...	...	...	...	...	...	...
1853	...	...	...	...	...	...	...	...	...	...
1854	...	...	...	...	...	...	...	...	...	...
1855	...	...	...	...	...	...	...	...	...	...
1856	...	...	...	...	...	...	...	...	...	...
1857	...	...	...	...	...	...	...	...	...	...
1858	...	...	...	...	...	...	...	...	...	...
1859	...	...	...	...	382	1,415	1,869	1,608	18,687	3,145
1860	...	...	...	...	...	...	...	...	...	...
1861	...	...	...	...	...	...	...	...	...	...
1862	...	...	...	...	...	...	...	...	...	...
1863	...	...	...	...	...	...	...	...	...	...
1864	...	...	...	...	...	...	...	...	...	...
1865					673	...	2,905	4,265	22,055	4,430
1866	15.5	21.0	9.4	44.2	...	...	...	...	...	...
1867					...	...	...	...	...	...
1868					...	...	...	...	...	...
1869					...	...	...	...	...	...

See p.341 for footnotes

D5 Numbers of Livestock (in thousands)

1815–1869

	SWEDEN[13]				SWITZERLAND					UNITED KINGDOM: Great Britain				
	H	C	P	S	H	C	P	S	G	H	C	P	S	Po
1815	406	1,545	...	1,294	...	...	...	...	...	...	...	...	...	...
1816	...	...	...	...	...	...	...	...	...	...	...	...	...	...
1817	...	...	...	...	...	...	...	...	...	...	...	...	...	...
1818	...	...	...	...	...	...	...	...	...	...	...	...	...	...
1819	...	...	...	...	...	...	...	...	...	...	...	...	...	...
1820	417	1,601	...	1,347	...	...	...	...	...	...	...	...	...	...
1821	...	...	...	...	...	...	...	...	...	...	...	...	...	...
1822	...	...	...	...	...	...	...	...	...	...	...	...	...	...
1823					...	...	...	...	...	...	...	...	...	...
1824					...	...	...	...	...	...	...	...	...	...
1825	381	1,621	514	1,440	...	...	...	...	...	...	...	...	...	...
1826					...	...	...	...	...	...	...	...	...	...
1827					...	...	...	...	...	...	...	...	...	...
1828					...	...	...	...	...	...	...	...	...	...
1829					...	...	...	...	...	...	...	...	...	...
1830	385	1,658	525	1,413	...	...	...	...	...	...	...	...	...	...
1831					...	...	...	...	...	...	...	...	...	...
1832					...	...	...	...	...	...	...	...	...	...
1833					...	...	...	...	...	...	...	...	...	...
1834					...	...	...	...	...	...	...	...	...	...
1835	384	1,674	514	1,466	...	...	...	...	...	...	...	...	...	...
1836					...	...	...	...	...	...	...	...	...	...
1837					...	...	...	...	...	...	...	...	...	...
1838					...	...	...	...	...	...	...	...	...	...
1839					...	...	...	...	...	...	...	...	...	...
1840	391	1,700	514	1,453	...	...	...	...	...	...	...	...	...	...
1841					...	...	...	...	...	...	...	...	...	...
1842					...	...	...	...	...	...	...	...	...	...
1843					...	...	...	...	...	...	...	...	...	...
1844					...	...	...	...	...	...	...	...	...	...
1845	383[14]	1,788[14]	555[14]	1,531[14]	...	...	...	...	...	...	...	...	...	...
1846					...	...	...	...	...	...	...	...	...	...
1847					...	...	...	...	...	...	...	...	...	...
1848					...	...	...	...	...	...	...	...	...	...
1849					...	...	...	...	...	...	...	...	...	...
1850	382[14]	1,807[14]	555[14]	1,547[14]	...	...	...	...	...	...	...	...	...	...
1851					...	...	...	...	...	...	...	...	...	...
1852					...	...	...	...	...	...	...	...	...	...
1853					...	...	...	...	...	...	...	...	...	...
1854					...	...	...	...	...	...	...	...	...	...
1855	399[14]	1,919[14]	564[14]	1,592[14]	...	...	...	...	...	...	...	...	...	...
1856					...	...	...	...	...	...	...	...	...	...
1857					...	...	...	...	...	...	...	...	...	...
1858					...	...	...	...	...	...	...	...	...	...
1859	401	1,917	458	1,644[15]	...	...	...	...	...	...	...	...	...	...
1860					...	...	...	...	...	...	...	...	...	...
1861	435	1,987	379	1,741[15]	...	...	...	...	...	...	...	...	...	...
1862	438	2,000	379	1,737[15]	...	...	...	...	...	...	...	...	...	...
1863	439	2,010	378	1,764[15]	...	...	...	...	...	...	...	...	...	...
1864	442	2,035	384	1,775[15]	...	...	...	...	...	...	...	...	...	...
1865	428[14]	1,924[14]	380[14]	1,590[14]	...	...	...	...	...	...	...	...	...	...
1866	437[14]	1,983[14]	387[14]	1,645[14]	100	993	304	447	375	...	...	...	...	...
1867	434[14]	1,977[14]	362[14]	1,622[14]	...	...	...	...	...	...	4,993	2,967	28,919	...
1868	401[14]	1,742[14]	300[14]	1,409[14]	...	...	...	...	...	...	5,424	2,309	30,711	...
1869	421[14]	1,874[14]	339[14]	1,539[14]	...	...	...	...	...	...	5,313	1,930	29,538	...

See p.341 for footnotes

D5 Numbers of Livestock (in thousands)

1870–1919

	AUSTRIA[1]						BELGIUM			
	H	C	P	S	G	Po	H[2]	C	P	S
1870	...	...	...	...	...	...	...	...	...	...
1871	...	...	...	...	...	...	...	...	...	...
1872	...	...	...	...	...	...	...	...	...	...
1873	...	...	...	...	...	...	...	...	...	...
1874	...	...	...	...	...	...	...	...	...	...
1875	...	...	...	...	...	...	...	...	...	...
1876	...	...	...	...	...	...	...	...	...	...
1877	...	...	...	...	...	...	...	...	...	...
1878	...	...	...	...	...	...	...	...	...	...
1879	...	...	...	...	...	...	...	...	...	...
1880	1,463	8,584	2,722	3,841	1,007	...	272	1,383	646	365
1881	...	...	...	...	...	...	...	...	...	...
1882	...	...	...	...	...	...	...	...	...	...
1883	...	...	...	...	...	...	...	...	...	...
1884	...	...	...	...	...	...	...	...	...	...
1885	...	...	...	...	...	...	...	...	...	...
1886	...	...	...	...	...	...	...	...	...	...
1887	...	...	...	...	...	...	...	...	...	...
1888	...	...	...	...	...	...	...	...	...	...
1889	...	...	...	...	...	...	...	...	...	...
1890	1,548	8,644	3,550	3,187	1,036	...	...	...	...	...
1891	...	...	...	...	...	...	...	...	...	...
1892	...	...	...	...	...	...	...	...	...	...
1893	...	...	...	...	...	...	...	...	...	...
1894	...	...	...	...	...	...	...	...	...	...
1895	...	...	...	...	...	...	272	1,421	1,163	236
1896	...	...	...	...	...	...	...	...	...	...
1897	...	...	...	...	...	...	...	...	...	...
1898	...	...	...	...	...	...	...	...	...	...
1899	...	...	...	...	...	...	...	...	...	...
1900	1,716	9,511	4,683	2,621	1,020	26,672	242	1,657	1,006	...
1901	...	...	...	...	...	...	245	1,646	1,015	...
1902	...	...	...	...	...	...	247	1,647	1,137	...
1903	...	...	...	...	...	...	249	1,720	1,183	...
1904	...	...	...	...	...	...	246	1,782	1,155	...
1905	...	...	...	...	...	...	245	1,788	1,047	...
1906	...	...	...	...	...	...	245	1,780	1,148	...
1907	...	...	...	...	...	...	250	1,818	1,279	...
1908	...	...	...	...	...	...	253	1,861	1,162	...
1909	...	...	...	...	...	...	255	1,857	1,117	...
1910	1,803[1]	9,160[1]	6,432[1]	2,428[1]	1,257[1]	35,981[1]	317	1,880	1,494	185
1911	...	...	...	...	...	...	262	1,812	1,229	...
1912	...	...	...	...	...	...	263	1,831	1,349	...
1913	...	...	...	...	...	...	267	1,849	1,412	...
1914	...	...	...	...	...	...	...	...	...	...
1915	...	...	...	...	...	...	...	...	...	...
1916	...	...	...	...	...	...	...	...	...	...
1917	...	...	...	...	...	...	...	...	...	...
1918	...	1,842[16]	1,270[16]	...	...	...	...	...	...	...
1919	243[16]	1,719[16]	1,107[16]	...	...	...	162	1,286	770	...

See p.341 for footnotes

D5 **Numbers of Livestock** (in thousands)

1870–1919

	BULGARIA					DENMARK				
	H	C	P	S	Po	H	C	P	S	Po
1870	...	...	...	...	...	...	...	...	...	...
1871	...	...	...	...	...	317	1,239	442	1,842	...
1872	...	...	...	...	...	...	...	...	...	...
1873	...	...	...	...	...	...	...	...	...	...
1874	...	...	...	...	...	...	...	...	...	...
1875	...	...	...	...	...	...	...	...	...	...
1876	...	...	...	...	...	352	1,348	504	1,719	...
1877	...	...	...	...	...	...	...	...	...	...
1878	...	...	...	...	...	...	...	...	...	...
1879	...	...	...	...	...	...	...	...	...	...
1880	...	...	...	...	...	...	...	...	...	...
1881	...	...	...	...	...	348	1,470	527	1,549	...
1882	...	...	...	...	...	...	...	...	...	...
1883	...	...	...	...	...	...	...	...	...	...
1884	...	...	...	...	...	...	...	...	...	...
1885	...	...	...	...	...	...	...	...	...	...
1886	...	...	...	...	...	...	...	...	...	...
1887	...	...	...	...	...	...	...	...	...	...
1888	...	...	...	...	...	376	1,460	771	1,225	4,592
1889	...	...	...	...	...	...	...	...	...	...
1890	344	1,426	462	6,868	...	...	...	...	...	...
1891	...	...	...	...	...	...	...	...	...	...
1892	...	...	...	...	...	...	...	...	...	...
1893	...	...	...	...	...	411	1,696	829	1,247	5,856
1894	...	...	...	...	...	...	...	...	...	...
1895	...	...	...	...	...	...	...	...	...	...
1896	...	...	...	...	...	...	...	...	...	...
1897	...	...	...	...	...	...	...	...	...	...
1898	...	...	...	...	...	449	1,745	1,168	1,074	8,767
1899	...	...	...	...	...	...	...	...	...	...
1900	...	...	...	...	...	...	...	...	...	...
1901	495	1,596	368	7,015	...	...	...	...	...	...
1902	...	...	...	...	...	...	...	...	...	...
1903	...	...	...	...	...	487	1,840	1,457	877	11,555
1904	...	...	...	...	...	...	...	...	...	...
1905	538	1,696	465	8,131	...	...	...	...	...	...
1906	...	...	...	...	...	...	...	...	...	...
1907	...	...	...	...	...	...	...	...	...	...
1908	...	...	...	...	...	...	...	...	...	...
1909	...	...	...	...	...	535	2,254	1,468	727	11,816
1910	478	1,606	527	8,669	8,689	...	...	...	...	...
1911	...	...	...	...	...	...	...	...	...	...
1912	...	...	...	...	...	...	...	...	...	...
1913	...	...	...	...	...	...	...	...	...	...
1914	...	...	...	...	...	567	2,463	2,497	515	15,140
1915	...	...	...	...	...	526	2,416	1,919	533	...
1916	...	...	...	...	...	515[18]	2,290[18]	1,983[18]	254[18]	...
1917	...	...	...	...	...	572	2,458	1,651	480	12,288
1918	...	...	...	...	...	545	2,124	621	470	9,884
1919	...[17]	...[17]	...[17]	...[17]	...[17]	558	2,188	716	509	12,134

See p.341 for footnotes

D5 **Numbers of Livestock** (in thousands)

1870–1919

	FINLAND						FRANCE				
	H	C	P	S	Po[21]	R	H	C	P	S	G
1870	...	...	...	...	...	...	...[22]	...[22]	...[22]	...[22]	...[22]
1871	...	...	...	...	...	...	...	...	...	...	...
1872	...	...	...	...	...	...	...	...	...	...	...
1873	...	...	...	...	...	...	...	...	...	...	...
1874	...	...	...	...	...	...	...	...	...	...	...
1875	...	...	...	...	...	...	...	...	...	...	...
1876	...	...	...	...	...	...	...	...	...	...	...
1877	...	...	...	...	...	...	...	...	...	...	...
1878	...	...	...	...	...	...	...	...	...	...	...
1879	...	...	...	...	...	...	...	...	...	...	...
1880	...	...	...	...	...	...	...	...	...	...	...
1881	269	1,029	149	886	...	...	...	...	...	...	...
1882	273	1,070	151	921	...	...	2,838	12,997	7,147	23,809	1,851
1883	278	1,112	160	949	...	...	2,852	11,794	5,847	21,640	1,462
1884	282	1,140	165	961	...	...	2,886	12,018	5,881	22,328	1,553
1885	282	1,163	166	978	...	...	2,911	13,105	5,881	22,617	1,483
1886	286	1,222	178	1,020	...	...	2,938	13,275	5,775	22,688	1,426
1887	290	1,250	185	1,043	...	...	2,909	13,395	5,979	22,880	1,545
1888	285	1,254	178	1,021	...	...	2,892	13,379	5,847	22,631	1,546
1889	290	1,268	186	1,032	...	...	2,881	13,518	6,038	21,997	1,505
1890	293	1,305	194	1,054	...	...	2,862	13,562	6,017	21,658	1,505
1891	293	1,291	189	1,026	...	...	2,883	13,662	6,096	21,792	1,480
1892	290	1,287	176	996	310	106	2,795	13,719	7,421	21,116	1,485
1893	291	1,306	169	1,007	...	...	2,768	12,154	5,861	20,276	1,466
1894	297	1,364	178	1,028	...	...	2,807	12,879	6,038	20,722	1,485
1895	301	1,409	197	1,067	...	...	2,812	13,234	6,306	21,164	1,510
1896	303	1,456	215	1,092	...	...	2,850	13,334	6,402	21,191	1,499
1897	306	1,475	222	1,101	...	...	2,899	13,487	6,263	21,445	1,496
1898	307	1,485	224	1,080	...	...	2,894	13,418	6,231	21,278	1,502
1899	308	1,457	214	1,031	...	...	2,917	13,551	6,305	21,358	1,504
1900	311	1,428	211	985	...	...	2,903	14,521	6,740	20,180	1,558
1901	313	1,409	205	971	...	...	2,926	14,674	6,758	19,670	1,529
1902	316	1,406	210	942	...	...	3,028	14,929	7,209	18,477	1,532
1903	317	1,417	214	919	...	...	3,082	14,105	7,561	17,954	1,563
1904	315	1,451	216	936	...	...	3,139	14,137	7,522	17,801	1,462
1905	323	1,481	220	938	...	...	3,169	14,316	7,559	17,783	1,477
1906	326	1,475	219	912	...	...	3,165	13,968	7,049	17,461	1,457
1907	328[19]	1,491[20]	221	904	...	...	3,095	13,940	6,995	17,460	1,421
1908	281	1,149	...	...	...	...	3,216	14,240	7,202	17,456	1,425
1909	284	1,153	...	...	...	...	3,236	14,298	7,306	17,358	1,418
1910	301	1,199	422	1,330	...	...	3,198	14,532	6,900	17,111	1,418
1911	298	1,188	...	...	...	...	3,236	14,436	6,720	16,425	1,424
1912	298	1,189	...	...	...	...	3,222	14,706	6,904	16,468	1,409
1913	297	1,178	...	...	...	...	3,222[23]	14,788[23]	7,036[23]	16,131[23]	1,435[23]
1914	294	1,167	...	...	...	...	2,205	12,668	5,926	14,038	1,308
1915	288	1,150	...	...	...	...	2,209	12,520	4,910	12,262	1,231
1916	276	1,111	...	...	...	...	2,246	12,342	4,362	10,845	1,177
1917	271	1,106	...	...	...	...	2,303	12,242	4,165	9,881	1,161
1918	262	1,076	...	815	...	...	2,233[22][23]	12,251[22][23]	4,377[22][23]	9,061[22][23]	1,197[22][23]
1919	273	1,101	...	...	...	...	2,413	12,374	4,081	8,991	1,175

See p.341 for footnotes

D5 **Numbers of Livestock** (in thousands)

1870–1919

	GERMANY						GREECE[15]						
	H	C	P	S	G	Po	H	A & M	C	P	S	G	Po
1870	...	...	...	...	...	...	...	...	...	...	...	...	...
1871	...	...	...	...	...	...	...	...	...	...	...	...	...
1872	...	14,307	8,549	...	...	...	...	...	...	...	...	...	...
1873	3,352	15,777	7,124	24,999	2,320	...	...	...	...	...	...	...	...
1874	...	...	...	...	...	...	...	...	...	...	...	...	...
1875	...	...	...	...	...	...	...	...	...	...	...	...	...
1876	...	...	...	...	...	...	...	...	...	...	...	...	...
1877	...	...	...	...	...	...	...	...	...	...	...	...	...
1878	...	...	...	...	...	...	...	...	...	...	...	...	...
1879	...	...	...	...	...	...	...	...	...	...	...	...	...
1880	...	...	...	...	...	...	...	...	...	...	...	...	...
1881	...	...	...	...	...	...	...	...	...	...	...	...	...
1882	...	14,141	11,047	...	...	...	...	...	...	...	...	...	...
1883	3,523	15,787	9,206	19,190	2,641	...	...	...	...	...	...	...	...
1884	...	...	...	...	...	...	...	...	...	...	...	...	...
1885	...	...	...	...	...	...	...	...	...	...	...	...	...
1886	...	...	...	...	...	...	...	...	...	...	...	...	...
1887	...	...	...	...	...	...	...	...	...	...	...	...	...
1888	...	...	...	...	...	...	...	...	...	...	...	...	...
1889	...	...	...	...	...	...	...	..	...	...	...	...	...
1890	...	...	...	...	...	...	...	...	...	...	...	...	...
1891	...	...	...	...	...	...	...	...	...	...	...	...	...
1892	3,836	17,556[24]	12,174	13,590	3,092	...	...	...	...	...	...	...	...
1893	...	...	...	...	...	...	...	...	...	...	...	...	...
1894	...	...	...	...	...	...	...	...	...	...	...	...	...
1895	...	...	...	...	...	...	...	...	...	...	...	...	...
1896	...	...	...	...	...	...	...	...	...	...	...	...	...
1897	...	...	...	...	...	...	...	...	...	...	...	...	...
1898	...	...	...	...	...	...	...	...	...	...	...	...	...
1899	...	...	...	...	...	...	159	230	417	80	4,568	3,339	...
1900	4,195	18,940[24]	16,807	9,693	3,267	64,102	...	...	...	...	...	...	...
1901	...	...	...	...	...	...	...	...	...	...	...	...	...
1902	...	...	...	...	...	...	...	...	...	...	...	...	...
1903	...	...	...	...	...	...	...	...	...	...	...	...	...
1904	4,267	19,332[24]	18,921	7,907	3,330	...	...	...	...	...	...	...	...
1905	...	...	...	...	...	...	...	...	...	...	...	...	...
1906	...	...	...	...	...	...	...	...	...	...	...	...	...
1907	...	...	...	...	...	76,625	...	...	...	...	...	...	...
1908	...	...	...	...	...	...	...	...	...	...	...	...	...
1909	...	...	...	...	...	...	...	...	...	...	...	...	...
1910	...	...	...	...	...	...	...	...	...	...	...	...	...
1911	...	...	...	...	...	...	149	212	298	227	3,545	2,638	2,819
1912	...	...	...	...	...	82,164	...[5]	...[5]	...[5]	...[5]	...[5]	...[5]	...[5]
1913	4,558	20,994	25,659	5,521	3,548	...	...	...	...	...	...	...	...
1914	3,435	21,829	25,341	5,471	3,538	...	64[5]	207[5]	331[5]	138[5]	2,614[5]	1,650[5]	1,585[5]
1915	3,342	20,317	17,287	5,073	3,438	...	...	...	...	...	...	...	...
1916	3,304	20,874	17,002	4,979	3,940	65,178	212[5]	423[5]	435[5]	302[5]	4,796[5]	3,482[5]	4,663[5]
1917	3324	20.095[25]	11,052[25]	4,954[25]	4,315[25]	58,995[25]	218	395	571	351	5,548	3,575	3,794
	3,257	19,650[26]	10,778[26]	4,918[26]	4,210[26]	57,347[26]							
1918	3,425	17,650	10,271	5,347	4,321	51,305	186[5]	355[5]	649[5]	365[5]	5,468[5]	3,473[5]	4,453[5]
1919	3,465	16,318	11,518	5,341	4,140	...	...	...	...	...	...	...	...

See p.341 for footnotes

D5 Numbers of Livestock (in thousands)

1870–1919

	HUNGARY[6]					IRELAND				
	H	C	P	S	G	H	C	P	S	Po
1870	...	...	...	...	...	533	3,800	1,461	4,337	11,159
1871	...	...	...	...	...	538	3,976	1,621	4,233	11,717
1872	...	...	...	...	...	541	4,059	1,389	4,263	11,738
1873	...	...	...	...	...	532	4,147	1,044	4,485	11,863
1874	...	...	...	...	...	527	4,125	1,099	4,442	12,068
1875	...	...	...	...	...	526	4,115	1,252	4,254	12,139
1876	...	...	...	...	...	535	4,117	1,425	4,009	13,619
1877	...	...	...	...	...	553	3,998	1,469	3,988	13,566
1878	...	...	...	...	...	562	3,985	1,269	4,095	13,711
1879	...	...	...	...	...	572	4,068	1,072	4,018	13,783
1880	...	...	...	...	...	557	3,922	850	3,562	13,430
1881	...	...	...	...	...	548	3,957	1,096	3,256	13,972
1882	...	...	...	...	...	539	3,987	1,430	3,072	13,999
1883	...	...	...	...	...	534	4,097	1,348	3,219	13,382
1884	1,749	4,879	4,804	10,595	270	535	4,113	1,307	3,245	12,747
1885	...	...	...	...	...	547	4,229	1,269	3,478	13,851
1886	...	...	...	...	...	549	4,184	1,263	3,366	13,910
1887	...	...	...	...	...	557	4,157	1,408	3,378	14,461
1888	...	...	...	...	...	565	4,099	1,398	3,627	14,486
1889	...	...	...	...	...	574	4,094	1,381	3,789	14,857
1890	...	...	...	...	...	585	4,240	1,570	4,323	15,408
1891	...	...	...	...	...	593	4,449	1,368	4,723	15,276
1892	...	...	...	...	...	606	4,531	1,113	4,828	15,336
1893	...	...	...	...	...	614	4,464	1,152	4,421	16,097
1894	...	...	...	...	...	623	4,392	1,389	4,105	16,181
1895	1,997	5,830	6,447	7,527	...	630	4,358	1,338	3,913	16,370
1896	...	...	...	...	...	629	4,408	1,405	4,081	17,538
1897	...	...	...	...	...	610	4,465	1,327	4,158	17,777
1898	...	...	...	...	...	591	4,487	1,254	4,288	17,687
1899	...	...	...	...	...	580	4,507	1,363	4,365	18,234
1900	...	...	...	...	...	567	4,609	1,269	4,387	18,547
1901	...	...	...	...	...	565	4,673	1,219	4,379	18,811
1902	...	...	...	...	...	580	4,782	1,328	4,216	18,504
1903	...	...	...	...	...	596	4,664	1,384	3,945	18,154
1904	...	...	...	...	...	605	4,677	1,315	3,828	18,257
1905	...	...	...	...	...	609	4,645	1,164	3,749	18,549
1906	...	...	...	...	...	604	4,639	1,244	3,715	18,977[27]
1907	...	...	...	...	...	596	4,676	1,317	3,817	24,327
1908	...	...	...	...	...	605	4,792	1,218	4,126	24,031
1909	...	...	...	...	...	599	4,700	1,149	4,133	24,105
1910	...	...	...	...	...	613	4,689	1,200	3,980	24,339
1911	2,001	6,184	6,416	7,698	...	616	4,712	1,415	3,907	25,448
1912	...	...	...	...	...	618	4,848	1,324	3,829	25,526
1913	...	...	...	...	...	614	4,933	1,060	3,621	25,701
1914	...	...	...	...	...	619	5,052	1,306	3,601	26,919
1915	...	...	...	...	...	561	4,844	1,205	3,600	26,089
1916	...	...	...	...	...	599	4,970	1,290	3,764	26,473
1917	...	...	...	...	...	598	4,909	947	3,744	22,245
1918	...	...	...	...	...	619	4,863	974	3,627	24,424
1919	...[6]	...[6]	...[6]	...[6]	...	625	5,029	978	3,513	...

See p.341 for footnotes

D5 Numbers of Livestock (in thousands)

1870–1919

	ITALY[8]						NETHERLANDS[10]				
	H	A & M	C[9]	P	S	G	H	C	P	S	Hens
1870	505	782	3,606	1,618	6,975	1,730	252	1,411	329	900	...
1871	552	839	3,784	1,707	7,521	1,793	252	1,376	319	868	...
1872	579	884	3,932	1,777	7,596	1,839	248	1,377	320	855	...
1873	601	917	4,047	1,833	8,013	1,877	253	1,432	360	902	...
1874	615	940	4,132	1,874	8,173	1,906	259	1,469	352	936	...
1875	624	952	4,187	1,899	8,277	1,925	260	1,457	339	941	...
1876	626	953	4,209	1,910	8,323	1,936	268	1,439	352	891	...
1877	622	943	4,202	1,905	8,313	1,938	270	1,413	360	885	...
1878	622	940	4,162	1,886	8,245	1,931	275	1,471	360	909	...
1879	626	942	4,298	1,924	8,319	1,951	279	1,462	337	898	...
1880	633	952	4,505	1,983	8,436	1,979	278	1,470	335	848	...
1881	645	968	4,783	2,064	8,596	2,016	271	1,434	376	792	...
1882	660	1,014	4,930	2,094	8,611	2,027	270	1,428	404	745	...
1883	684	1,038	5,047	2,109	8,576	2,029	269	1,437	421	704	...
1884	702	1,055	5,133	2,109	8,488	2,023	269	1,474	427	753	...
1885	714	1,064	5,189	2,094	8,352	2,007	270	1,510	442	774	...
1886	721	1,064	5,215	2,065	8,163	1,983	273	1,531	458	803	...
1887	720	1,059	5,213	2,021	7,923	1,951	274	1,526	490	804	...
1888	714	1,045	5,175	1,962	7,633	1,909	274	1,494	485	778	...
1889	702	1,024	5,110	1,888	7,292	1,859	276	1,490	494	772	...
1890	684	995	5,014	1,800	6,900	1,800	273	1,533	579	819	...
1891	686	1,009	4,981	1,755	6,681	1,780	272	1,532	547	811	...
1892	688	1,023	4,965	1,725	6,524	1,775	271	1,529	544	752	...
1893	692	1,033	4,964	1,710	6,428	1,785	265	1,485	571	688	...
1894	696	1,043	4,979	1,709	6,393	1,811	264	1,509	640	665	...
1895	701	1,051	5,011	1,722	6,420	1,851	266	1,543	662	679	...
1896	708	1,056	5,060	1,750	6,504	1,907	269	1,583	656	706	...
1897	715	1,060	5,124	1,793	6,655	1,978	274	1,621	654	729	...
1898	723	1,063	5,204	1,850	6,865	2,064	280	1,641	714	737	...
1899	732	1,063	5,302	1,922	7,137	2,165	285	1,647	738	755	...
1900	742	1,062	5,415	2,008	7,478	2,282	295	1,656	747	771	4,343
1901	753	1,075	5,544	2,109	7,863	2,413	302	1,649	764	752	4,561
1902	764	1,086	5,690	2,224	8,317	2,560	304	1,647	823	709	4,673
1903	777	1,093	5,819	2,320	8,777	2,672	296	1,667	883	654	4,935
1904	790	1,098	5,931	2,396	9,243	2,750	295	1,690	862	607	...
1905	805	1,099	6,028	2,453	9,714	2,793	...	...	...	...	...
1906	843	1,150	6,108	2,491	10,191	2,802	...	...	...	...	...
1907	877	1,196	6,171	2,509	10,674	2,776	...	...	...	...	...
1908	907	1,235	6,218	2,508	11,163	2,715	...	...	...	...	...
1909	933	1,269	6,284	2,519	11,552	2,685	...[28]	...[28]	...[28]	...[28]	...[28]
1910	954	1,297	6,337	2,541	11,841	2,686	327	2,027	1,260	889	9,778[29]
1911	972	1,319	6,408	2,576	12,031	2,718	...	...	...	...	...
1912	986	1,335	6,487	2,622	12,120	2,781	...	...	...	...	...
1913	995	1,345	6,574	2,680	12,110	2,875	...	...	...	...	...
1914	1,000	1,350	6,668	2,750	12,000	3,000	...	...	...	...	...
1915	903	1,288	6,482	2,585	11,998	3,029	...	...	...	...	...
1916	837	1,252	6,338	2,461	11,956	3,052	...	...	...	...	...
1917	804	1,240	6,238	2,379	11,875	3,070	...	...	...	...	...
1918	803	1,253	6,180	2,337	11,752	3,083	378	2,049	600	642	...
1919	833	1,292	6,165	2,338	11,744	3,080	362	1,969	450	437	...

See p.341 for footnotes

D5 Numbers of Livestock (in thousands)

1870–1919

	NORWAY					ROMANIA				
	H	C	P	S	Po	H	C	P	S	Po
1870	...	...	...	...	...	...	...	...	...	...
1871	...	...	...	...	...	...	...	...	...	...
1872	...	...	...	...	...	...	...	...	...	...
1873	...	...	...	...	...	...	...	...	...	...
1874	...	...	...	...	...	...	...	...	...	...
1875	152	1,017	101	1,686	...	391	1,833	804	4,191	...
1876	...	...	...	...	...	...	...	...	...	...
1877	...	...	...	...	...	...	...	...	...	...
1878	...	...	...	...	...	...	...	...	...	...
1879	...	...	...	...	...	...	...	...	...	...
1880	...	...	...	...	...	...	...	...	...	...
1881	...	...	...	...	...	...	...	...	...	...
1882	...	...	...	...	...	...	...	...	...	...
1883	...	...	...	...	...	...	...	...	...	...
1884	...	...	...	...	...	533	2,376	886	4,655	...
1885	...	...	...	...	...	...	...	...	...	...
1886	...	...	...	...	...	...	...	...	...	...
1887	...	...	...	...	...	...	...	...	...	...
1888	...	...	...	...	...	564	2,406	797	4,973	...
1889	...	...	...	...	...	...	...	...	...	...
1890	151	1,007	121	1,418	808	595	2,520	926	5,002	...
1891	...	...	...	...	...	...	...	...	...	...
1892	...	...	...	...	...	...	...	...	...	...
1893	...	...	...	...	...	...	...	...	...	...
1894	...	...	...	...	...	...	...	...	...	...
1895	...	...	...	...	...	671	2,138	1,079	6,848	...
1896	...	...	...	...	...	...	...	...	...	...
1897	...	...	...	...	...	...	...	...	...	...
1898	...	...	...	...	...	...	...	...	...	...
1899	...	...	...	...	...	...	...	...	...	...
1900	173[30]	950[30]	165[30]	999[30]	1,659[30]	864	2,589	1,709	5,655	...
1901	...	...	...	...	...	...	...	...	...	...
1902	...	...	...	...	...	...	...	...	...	...
1903	...	...	...	...	...	...	...	...	...	...
1904	...	...	...	...	...	...	...	...	...	...
1905	...	...	...	...	...	...	...	...	...	...
1906	...	...	...	...	...	...	...	...	...	...
1907	164	1,088	307	1,390	1,411	...	...	...	...	...
1908	...	...	...	...	...	...	...	...	...	...
1909	...	...	...	...	...	...	...	...	...	...
1910	...	...	...	...	...	...	...	...	...	...
1911	...	...	...	...	...	825	2,667[40]	1,022	5,270	...
1912	...	...	...	...	...	...	...	...	...	...
1913	...	...	...	...	...	...	...	...	...	...
1914	...	...	...	...	...	...[31]	...[31]	...[31]	...[31]	...
1915	...	...	...	...	...	...	...	...	...	...
1916	...	...	...	...	...	1,219	2,873	1,382	7,811	...
1917	202	1,150	238	1,295	1,884	...	...	...	...	...
1918	211	1,046	207	1,400	1,676	...[32]	...[32]	...[32]	...[32]	...
1919	...	...	...	...	...	1,380	4,634[40]	2,290	7,791	...

See p.341 for footnotes

D5 Numbers of Livestock (in thousands)

1870–1919

RUSSIA (in millions)

	H	C	P	S
1870	15.6	21.4	9.1	45.3
1871	...	...	...	...
1872	...	...	...	...
1873	...	...	...	...
1874	...	...	...	...
1875	...	...	...	...
1876	...	...	...	...
1877	17.6	27.3	10.8	51.8
1878	...	...	...	...
1879	...	...	...	...
1880	...	...	...	...
1881	...	...	...	...
1882	20.0	23,8	9.2	47.5
1883	17.9	23.6	9.4	46.7
1884	...	...	...	...
1885	...	...	...	...
1886	...	...	...	...
1887	...	...	...	...
1888	19.7	24.6	9.2	44.5
1889	...	...	...	...
1890	19.8	25.5	9.6	46.1
1891	17.3	25.3	9.6	39.8
1892	16.6	24.0	8.8	40.0
1893	...	...	...	...
1894	16.7	24.1	8.8	37.3
1895	17.0	24.5	9.2	38.2
1896	18.8	29.5	13.3	46.4
1897	18.8	30.7	12.9	45.8
1898	19.1	30.2	12.0	46.3
1899	19.6	30.9	11.6	45.5
1900	19.7	31.7	11.8	47.6
1901	20.2	31.9	12.1	38.8
1902	20.5	32.2	11.6	47.8
1903	20.3	31.8	11.4	46.9
1904	20.7	31.9	12.0	46.5
1905	20.8	31.2	11.5	45.4
1906	20.5	30.5	11.9	42.2
1907	20.5	29.7	11.6	40.7
1908	20.6	29.7	11.4	39.9
1909	21.3	30.5	11.3	39.9
1910	21.9	31.3	12.0	40.7
1911	21.8	31.0	12.7	40.2
1912	22.1	31.0	12.6	39.6
1913	22.8	32.0	13.5	41.4
1914	21.3[11]	30.4[11]	13.0[11]	38.9[11]
1915	...	...	...	...
1916	34.2	51.7	17.3	82.5
1917	34.5	51.6	18.6	91.7
1918	33.9	50.8	19.3	80.2
1919	32.3	48.6	18.4	78.7

ESTONIA

	H	C	P	S
	included in Russia			
1914	...	...	...	...
1915	...	...	...	...
1916	...	...	...	...
1917	...	...	...	...
1918	...	...	...	...
1919	165[33]	407[33]	150[33]	420[33]

LATVIA

	H	C	P	S
	included in Russia			
1914	...	...	...	...
1915	...	...	...	...
1916	...	...	...	...
1917	...	...	...	...
1918	...	...	...	...
1919	...	...	...	...

LITHUANIA

	H	C	P	S
	included in Russia			
1914	...	...	...	...
1915	...	...	...	...
1916	...	...	...	...
1917	...	...	...	...
1918	...	...	...	...
1919	...	...	...	...

See p.341 for footnotes

D5 Numbers of Livestock (in thousands)

1870–1919

	SERBIA						SPAIN						
	H	C	P	S	G	Poultry	H	A & M	C	P	S	G	Hens
1870	...	...	...	...	...	...	...	...	...	...	...	...	...
1871	...	...	...	...	...	...	...	..	...	...	...	...	...
1872	...	...	...	...	...	...	...	...	...	...	...	...	...
1873	...	...	...	...	...	...	...	...	...	...	...	...	...
1874	...	...	...	...	...	...	...	...	...	...	...	...	...
1875	...	...	...	...	...	...	...	...	...	...	...	...	...
1876	...	...	...	...	...	...	...	...	...	...	...	...	...
1877	...	...	...	...	...	...	...	...	...	...	...	...	...
1878	...	...	...	...	...	...	...	...	...	...	...	...	...
1879	...	...	...	...	...	...	...	...	...	...	...	...	...
1880	...	...	...	...	...	...	...	...	...	...	...	...	...
1881	...	...	...	...	...	...	...	...	...	...	...	...	...
1882	...	...	...	...	...	...	...	...	...	....	...	...	...
1883	...	...	...	...	...	...	...	...	...	...	...	...	...
1884	...	...	...	...	...	...	...	...	...	...	...	...	...
1885	...	...	...	...	...	...	...	...	...	...	...	...	...
1886	...	...	...	...	...	...	...	...	...	...	...	...	...
1887	...	...	...	...	...	...	...	...	...	...	...	...	...
1888	...	...	...	...	...	...	310	995	1,460	1,162	13,773	2,650	...
1889	...	...	...	...	...	...	...	...	...	...	...	...	...
1890	163	819	909	2,964	510	...	...	...	...	...	...	...	...
1891	...	...	...	...	...	...	...	...	2,218	1,928	13,359	2,534	...
1892	...	...	...	...	...	...	...	...	...	...	...	...	...
1893	...	...	...	...	...	...	...	...	...	...	...	...	...
1894	...	...	...	...	...	...	...	...	...	...	...	...	...
1895	...	...	...	...	...	...	...	...	...	...	...	...	...
1896	170	915	904	3,094	...	...	...	...	...	...	...	...	...
1897	...	...	...	...	...	...	...	...	...	...	...	...	...
1898	...	...	...	...	...	...	...	...	...	...	...	...	...
1899	...	...	...	...	...	...	...	...	...	...	...	...	...
1900	...	...	...	...	...	...	...	...	...	...	...	...	...
1901	185	957	960	3,062	432	...	...	...	...	...	...	...	...
1902	...	...	...	...	...	...	...	...	...	...	...	...	...
1903	...	...	...	...	...	...	...	...	...	...	...	...	...
1904	...	...	...	...	...	...	...	...	...	...	...	...	...
1905	...	...	...	...	...	...	440	1,548	2,497	2,031	13,481	2,440	...
1906	174	963	908	3,160	510	...	...	...	...	...	...	...	...
1907	...	...	...	...	...	...	...	...	2,212	2,031	13,728	2,808	...
1908	...	...	...	...	...	...	...	...	2,452	2,120	16,119	3,355	...
1909	...	...	...	...	...	...	495	1,699	2,317	2,296	15,471	...	...
1910	153	957	866	3,819	631	...	520	1,754	2,369	2,424	15,117	...	...
1911	...	...	...	...	...	...	546	1,741	2,541	2,472	15,726	...	...
1912	...	...	...	...	...	...	526	1,758	2,562	2,571	15,830	...	...
1913	...	...	...	...	...	...	542	1,797	2,879	2,710	16,441	...	...
1914	...	...	...	...	...	...	525	1,825	2,743	2,810	16,128	...	...
1915			included in Yugoslavia				512	1,777	2,926	2,883	15,995	...	...
1916							489	1,752	3,071	2,814	16,012	...	...
1917							558	1,967	3,233	3,929	17,227	...	...
1918							577	1,966	3,174	4,107	17,735	...	...
1919							594	2,083	3,397	4,434	19,337	...	...

D5 **Numbers of Livestock** (in thousands)

1870–1919

	SWEDEN					SWITZERLAND					
	H	C	P	S	Po	H	C	P	S	G	Po
1870	428	1,966	354	1,595	...	...	...	...	...	...	...
1871	438	2,026	383	1,636	...	...	...	...	...	...	...
1872	446	2,103	401	1,660	...	...	...	...	...	...	...
1873	456	2,181	422	1,695	...	...	...	...	...	...	...
1874	447	2,094	399	1,565	...	...	...	...	...	...	...
1875	459	2,186	415	1,609	...	...	...	...	...	...	...
1876	461	2,189	432	1,589	...	101	1,036	335	368	396	...
1877	459	2,163	426	1,534	...	...	...	...	...	...	...
1878	465	2,211	431	1,536	...	...	...	...	...	...	...
1879	466	2,237	416	1,503	...	...	...	...	...	...	...
1880	465	2,228	419	1,457	...	...	...	...	...	...	...
1881	459	2,192	419	1,377	...	...	...	...	...	...	...
1882	470	2,257	431	1,388	...	...	...	...	...	...	...
1883	473	2,287	455	1,412	...	...	...	...	...	...	...
1884	476	2,327	477	1,410	...	...	...	...	...	...	...
1885	480	2,366	516	1,442	...	...	...	...	...	...	...
1886	485	2,381	548	1,444	...	89	1,213	395	342	416	...
1887	481	2,331	571	1,378	...	...	...	...	...	...	...
1888	482	2,349	610	1,350	...	...	...	...	...	...	...
1889	480	2,331	621	1,338	...	...	...	...	...	...	...
1890	487	2,399	645	1,351	...	...	...	...	...	...	...
1891	489	2,420	655	1,345	...	...	...	...	...	...	...
1892	494	2,483	682	1,352	...	...	...	...	...	...	...
1893	495	2,474	717	1,324	...	...	...	...	...	...	...
1894	501	2,516	769	1,319	...	...	...	...	...	...	...
1895	506	2,540	787	1,313	...	...	...	...	...	...	...
1896	512	2,555	789	1,299	...	109	1,307	567	272	416	...
1897	517	2,548	803	1,297	...	...	...	...	...	...	...
1898	523	2,582	816	1,291	...	...	...	...	...	...	...
1899	525	2,583	811	1,284	...	...	...	...	...	...	...
1900	533	2,583	806	1,261	...	...	...	...	...	...	...
1901	539	2,594	809	1,232	...	125	1,340	555	219	355	...
1902	542	2,577	808	1,196	...	...	...	...	...	...	...
1903	546	2,586	816	1,167	...	...	...	...	...	...	...
1904	547	2,546	797	1,106	...	...	...	...	...	...	...
1905	555	2,550	830	1,074	...	...	...	...	...	...	...
1906	564	2,600	872	1,051	...	135	1,498	549	210	362	...
1907	566	2,629	879	1,022	...	...	...	...	...	...	...
1908	575	2,685	895	1,010	...	...	...	...	...	...	...
1909	581	2,730	922	1,022	...	...	...	...	...	...	...
1910	587	2,748	957	1,004	...	...	...	...	...	...	...
1911	588	2,690	951	946	...	144	1,443	570	161	341	...
1912	...[37]	...[37]	...[37]	...[37]	...	...	...	...	...	...	...
1913	...	...	...	...	...	...	...	...	...	...	...
1914	660	3,069	1,023	1,205	...	...	...	...	...	...	...
1915	672	2,884	891	1,146	...	...	...	...	...	...	...
1916	701	2,913	1,065	1,198	...	137	1,616	545	173	359	...
1917	715	3,020	1,030	1,344	...	...	...	...	...	...	...
1918	715	2,584	634	1,409	...	129	1,531	366	230	356	2,386
1919	716	2,551	717	1,564	...	124	1,433	465	265	350	...

See p.341 for footnotes

D5 Numbers of Livestock (in thousands)

1870–1919

UNITED KINGDOM: Great Britain

	H	C	P	S	Poultry
1870	1,267	5,403	2,171	28,398	...
1871	1,254	5,338	2,500	27,120	...
1872	1,258	5,625	2,772	27,922	...
1873	1,276	5,965	2,500	29,428	...
1874	1,312	6,125	2,423	30,314	...
1875	1,340	6,013	2,230	29,167	...
1876	1,375	5,844	2,294	28,183	...
1877	1,389	5,698	2,499	28,161	...
1878	1,413	5,738	2,483	28,406	...
1879	1,433	5,856	2,092	28,157	...
1880	1,421	5,912	2,001	26,619	...
1881	1,425	5,912	2,048	24,581	...
1882	1,414	5,807	2,510	24,320	...
1883	1,411	5,963	2,618	25,068	...
1884	1,414	6,269	2,584	26,068	...
1885	1,409	6,598	2,403	26,535	...
1886	1,425	6,647	2,221	25,521	...
1887	1,428	6,441	2,299	25,959	...
1888	1,420	6,129	2,404	25,257	...
1889	1,421	6,140	2,511	26,632	...
1890	1,433	6,509	2,774	27,272	...
1891	1,488	6,853	2,889	28,733	...
1892	1,518	6,945	2,138	28,735	...
1893	1,525	6,701	2,114	27,280	...
1894	1,529	6,347	2,390	25,862	...
1895	1,545	6,354	2,884	25,792	...
1896	1,553	6,494	2,879	26,705	...
1897	1,526	6,500	2,342	26,340	...
1898	1,517	6,622	2,452	26,743	...
1899	1,517	6,796	2,624	27,239	...
1900	1,500	6,805	2,382	26,592	...
1901	1,511	6,764	2,180	26,377	...
1902	1,505	6,556	2,300	25,766	...
1903	1,537	6,705	2,687	25,640	...
1904	1,560	6,858	2,862	25,207	...
1905	1,572	6,987	2,425	25,257	...
1906	1,569	7,011	2,323	25,420	...
1907	1,556	6,912	2,637	26,115	...
1908	1,546	6,905	2,823	27,120	...
1909	1,553	7,021	2,381	27,618	...
1910	1,545	7,037	2,350	27,103	...
1911	1,481	7,114	2,822	26,495	...
1912	1,441[39]	7,026	2,656	25,058	...
	1,611				
1913	1,607	6,964	2,234	23,931	...
1914	1,609	7,093	2,634	24,286	...
1915	1,487	7,288	2,579	24,598	...
1916	1,567	7,442	2,314	25,007	...
1917	1,583	7,437	2,051	24,043	...
1918	1,586	7,410	1,825	23,353	...
1919	1,600	7,424	1,936	21,534	...

See p.341 for footnotes

D5 Numbers of Livestock (in thousands)

1920–1975

	AUSTRIA[1]						BELGIUM			
	H	C	P	S	G	Po	H[2]	C	P	S
1920	236[40]	2,190[40]	1,247[40]	450[40]	320[40]	...	205	1,487	977	...
1921	...	...	...	...	...	...	222	1,515	976	...
1922	...	...	...	...	...	...	230	1,517	1,139	...
1923	265[40]	2,038[40]	1,380[40]	591[40]	374[40]	5,418[40]	243	1,603	1,176	...
1924	...	...	...	...	...	...	252	1,628	1,139	...
1925	...	...	...	...	...	...	250	1,655	1,152	...
1926	...	...	...	...	...	...	250	1,712	1,144	...
1927	...	...	...	...	...	...	256	1,739	1,124	...
1928	...	...	...	...	...	...	253	1,751	1,139	...
1929	...	...	...	...	...	...	249	1,738	1,237	187
1930	...	...	...	...	...	...	246	1,759	1,250	...
1931	...	...	...	...	...	...	242	1,768	1,235	...
1932	...	...	...	...	...	...	238	1,784	1,245	...
1933	...	...	...	...	...	...	233	1,813	1,353	...
1934	261	2,349	2,823	263	326	9,072	232	1,840	1,258	...
1935	...	...	...	...	...	...	231	1,837	1,284	...
1936	...	...	...	...	...	...	263	1,783	1,054	...
1937	...	...	...	...	...	...	264	1,710	872	...
1938	247	2,579	2,868	315	349	9,304	265	1,690	960	...
1939	231	2,620	2,830	317	323	8,815	246	1,600	856	...
1940	226	2,582	2,190	342	305	7,622	(286)[42][43]	1,828[43]	633[43]	153[43]
1941	226	2,494	2,043	354	292	6,939	230	1,759	444	186
1942	221	2,505	1,772	402	300	5,972	230	1,407	526	216
1943	224	2,530	1,872	444	308	6,169	223	1,392	485	213
1944	240	2,536	1,697	460	281	5,648	238[43]	1,440[43]	635[43]	199[43]
1945	264	2,187	1,030	391	247	4,161	257	1,539	735	177
1946	274	2,206	1,490	399	272	4,326	262	1,652	776	144
1947	283	2,158	1,724	474	310	4,664	251	1,588	648	107
1948	284	2,109	1,618	454	316	4,140	240	1,688	912	113
1949	282	2,203	1,927	375	317	5,134	234	1,902	1,361	121
1950	283	2,281	2,523	362	323	6,972	227	2,020	1,234	116
1951	276	2,284	2,448	332	310	7,216	234	2,127	1,427	124
1952	267	2,347	2,701	319	311	8,002	227	2,151	1,382	114
1953	259	2,300	2,643	297	298	8,577	203	2,168	1,161	44
1954	245	2,304	2,803	278	280	9,193	191	2,207	1,240	38
1955	236	2,346	2,933	255	256	9,318	182	2,197	1,347	36
1956	222	2,325	2,727	227	227	9,401[41]	172	2,368	1,225	42
1957	200	2,297	2,917	207	209	9,767	165	2,422	1,267	44
1958	180	2,279	2,838	194	187	9,843	156[44]	2,495[44]	1,480[44]	47[44]
1959	163	2,308	2,845	185	175	10,155	157	2,538	1,559	69
1960	150	2,387	2,990	175	162	10,131	147	2,531	1,579	59
1961	135	2,457	2,995	169	149	10,278	139	2,639	1,882	64
1962	121	2,437	2,849	153	132	10,328	132	2,687	1,859	60
1963	109	2,311	2,925	145	120	10,609	120	2,480	1,563	58
1964	97	2,350	3,132	147	111	10,880	109	2,524	1,745	64
1965	85	2,441	2,639	142	98	10,574	98	2,619	1,885	67
1966	75	2,497	2,786	138	94	11,021	87	2,597	2,117	68
1967	66	2,480	2,932	130	88	11,092	79	2,611	2,392	65
1968	59	2,433	3,094	126	77	11,510	(81)[42]	2,674	2,504	84
1969	53	2,418	3,196	121	69	11,740	(76)[42]	2,713	3,094	85
1970	47	2,468	3,445	113	62	12,335	(67)[42]	2,715	3,835	66
1971	43	2,499	3,091	112	56	12,396	(60)[42]	2,643	3,925	66
1972	40	2,514	3,256	119	51	12,600	(58)[42]	2,750	4,298	69
1973	39	2,624	3,290	136	48	12,181	(55)[42]	2,896	4,720	74
1974	40	2,581	3,517	154	46	12,410	(53)[42]	2,889	4,666	81
1975	41	2,500	3,683	169	43	13,090	(53)[42]	2,805	4,679	83

See p.341 for footnotes

D5 Numbers of Livestock (in thousands)

1920–1975

	BULGARIA					CZECHOSLOVAKIA					
	H	C	P	S	Po	H	C	P	S	G	Po
1920	398	1,877	1,090	8,923	7,294	591[45]	4,377[45]	2,053[45]	986[45]	...[45]	...[45]
1921	...	...	...	...	...	...	...	...	...	...	...
1922	...	...	...	...	...	...	...	...	...	....	...
1923	...	...	...	...	...	...	...	...	....	...	...
1924	...	...	...	...	...	...	...	...	....	...	...
1925	...	...	...	...	...	740	4,691	2,539	861	1,245	17,886
1926	482	1,817	1,002	8,740	10,118	...	...	...	...	...	...
1927	...	...	...	...	...	...	...	...	...	...	...
1928	...	...	...	...	...	...	...	...	...	...	...
1929	...	...	...	...	...	...	...	...	...	...	...
1930	...	...	...	...	...	...	4,458	2,776	608	1,081	36,617
1931	...	...	...	...	...	...	4,451	2,576	531	...	...
1932	...	...	...	...	...	708	4,341	2,621	465	...	...
1933	...	...	...	...	...	701	4,405	3,430	476	877	...
1934	532	1,498	902	8,840	12,774	701	4,305	3,032	510	930	...
1935	...	...	...	...	...	695	4,283	2,745	547	957	39,232
1936	...	...	...	...	...	704	4,596	3,242	592	1,000	40,414
1937	...	...	...	...	...	...	4,938	3,900	644	1,072	43,493
1938	...	...	...	...	...	...	...	3,827	...	1.008	41,989
1939	507	1,449	752	9,413	...	641	4,728	3,123	519	1,052	37,577
1940	509[17]	1,511[17]	860[17]	9,182[17]	...	630	4,729	3,319	495	1,114	31,379
1941	591	1,639	1,095	10,128	...	631	4,609	2,766	466	1,127	26,664
1942	594	1,755	1,061	8,847	7,661	638	4,425	3,071	519	1,320	25,891
1943	522	1,492	498	7,471	7,039	602	4,383	2,933	490	1,408	26,275
1944	478	1,390	675	6,390	6,649	608	4,358	3,256	519	1,459	23,610
1945	476	1,391	836	7,178	6,399	649[46]	4,143[46]	2,362[46]	510[46]	1,509[46]	...[46]
1946	499	1,631	719	8,916	11,412	653	3,975	2,944	491	1,310	12,281
1947	549	1,711	1,028	8,837	11,613	630	3,275	2,566	386	1,115	13,478
1948	...	...	825	8,266	11,380	628	3,663	3,242	459	922	16,393
1949	...	...	...	8,853	...	629	4,213	4,218	531	982	17,794
1950	...	...	...	7,820	...	605	4,303	3,802	596	...	18,206
1951	...	...	...	7,569	...	572	4,376	4,234	800	...	18,690
1952	473	1,625	1,058	7,569	11,592	559	4,445	4,918	982	...	20,787
1953	471	1,638	1,337	7,759	12,610	544	4,082	4,174	1,017	...	21.094
1954	467	1,591	1,436	7,867	12,851	543	4,041	4,771	1,017	...	22,540
1955	468	1,607	1,316	7,802	13,611	543	4,107	5,285	1,000	899	23,367
1956	472	1,602	1,413	7,829	13,817	542	4,134	5,369	956	846	23,876
1957	460	1,529	1,468	7,596	14,117	517	4,091	5,435	889	790	24,250
1958	431	1,442	1,993	7,742	14,302	456	4,183	5,283	817	739	25,364
1959	382	1,356	2,052	8,619	15,236	389	4,303	5,687	727	696	27,569
1960	334	1,284	2,266	8,769	21,666	330	4,387	5,962	646	662	28,157
1961	312	1,452	2,553	9,333	23,366	292	4,518	5,895	603	616	28,805
1962	301	1,582	2,331	10,161	22,800	254	4,507	5,897	524	597	28,032
1963	277	1,582	2,066	10,107	20,969	227	4,480	5,845	527	588	30,093
1964	256	1,494	2,097	10,308	21,922	204	4,436	6,139	568	582	28,840
1965	249	1,474	2,607	10,440	21,883	188	4,389	5,544	614	559	27,752
1966	240	1,450	2,408	10,312	20,845	177	4,462	5,305	670	521	29,466
1967	229	1,385	2,276	9,998	23,637	166	4,437	5,601	770	477	31,208
1968	224	1,363	2,314	9,905	27,726	156	4,249	5,136	906	417	32,544
1969	199	1,297	2,140	9,652	24,874	144	4,223	5,037	977	364	34,871
1970	182	1,255	1,966	9,223	29,590	131	4,288	5,530	981	318	39,187
1971	169	1,279	2,369	9,678	33,706	118	4,349	5,935	932	285	38,238
1972	159	1,379	2,806	10,127	34,102	100	4,466	6,093	889	241	39,170
1973	148	1,441	2,598	9,921	34,788	84	4,556	6,266	842	212	41,232
1974	142	1,454	2,431	9,765	36,939	71	4,566	6,719	811	174	39,476
1975	137	1,554	3,422	9,791	35,089	62	4,555	6,683	805	140	40,130

See p.341 for footnotes

D5 Numbers of Livestock (in thousands)

1920–1975

	DENMARK					FINLAND					
	H	C	P	S	Po	H	C	P	S	Po[21]	R
1920	563[47] / 602	2,286[47] / 2,504	1,008[47] / 1,116	504[47] / 540	13,997[47] / 14,395	313[19] / 385	1,194[20] / 1,824	374	1,704	879	53
1921	598	2,591	1,430	522	17,803	393	1,792	375	1,572	...	...
1922	576	2,525	1,899	442	19,184	398	1,844	378	1,571	1,113	63
1923	562	2,523	2,855	374	20,029	400	1,865	382	1,550	1,151	61
1924	548	2,667	2,868	303	20,284	403	1,864	376	1,485	1,204	61
1925	536	2,758	2,517	261	20,093	402	1,871	378	1,451	1,239	62
1926	548	2,838	3,122	233	18,524	400	1,860	391	1,414	1,258	67
1927	525	2,913	3,731	...	...	396	1,872	418	1,368	1,298	66
1928	519	3,016	3,363	...	...	394	1,917	435	1,319	1,363	59
1929	521[48]	3,031[48]	3,616[48]	193[48]	22,075[48]	358	1,744	380	967	1,688	55
1930	495	3,057	4,872	...	...	357	1,810	395	1,024	1,907	64
1931	499	3,208	5,453	...	...	362	1,822	346	920	2,227	79
1932	496	3,237	4,886	...	...	360	1,806	414	965	2,741	84
1933	501	3,134	4,407	...	...	357	1,745	435	973	3,009	92
1934	506	3,062	3,061	...	...	358	1,767	496	982	2,975	96
1935	521	3,072	3,036	...	28,568	361	1,822	510	1,024	2,844	103
1936	536	3,108	3,497	...	...	369	1,879	459	1,025	2,879	100
1937	552	3,084	3,066	187	26,498	380	1,925	504	1,072	2,801	100
1938	565[48]	3,186[48]	2,842[48]	...	27,863[48]	390	1,954	531	1,073	2,766	107
1939	594	3,326	3,183	147	33,296	386	1,938	519	1,000	2,765	93
1940	575	3,279	3,269	...	[49] 24,568	[50] 348	[50] 1,470	[50] 311	[50] 729	[50] 1,865	[50] 77
1941	612	3,065	1,815	...	13,181	359	1,588	259	717	1,964	192
1942	613	2,919	1,211	186	10,507	358	1,551	213	677	1,403	172
1943	625	3,028	2,083	186	15,340	363	1,720	263	789	1,078	148
1944	639	3,188	2,084	203	16,836	358	1,859	364	965	1,082	118
1945	644	3,237	1,646	213	16,372	[51] 385	[51] 1,693	[51] 229	[51] 1,015	[51] 993	[51] 68
1946	653	3,167	1,768	170	17,890	381	1,674	254	1,099	1,172	84
1947	601	3,014	1,830	91	18,886	385	1,566	335	982	1,446	96
1948	574	2,826	1,448	77	22,806[49]	382	1,451	304	999	1,918	107
1949	532	2,949	2,684	65	25,868	402	1,538	409	1,067	2,668	138
1950	502	3,053	3,235	59	24,548	[52] 409	[52] 1,782	[52] 446	[52] 1,220	[52] 3,524[53]	[52] 87
1951	465	3,110	3,189	56	22,250	382	1,814	442	1,096	3,871	124
1952	422	3,051	3,588	48	23,429	369	1,851	414	1,126	3,851	125
1953	399	3,068	4,310	39	24,571	339	1,809	434	998	3,667	152
1954	358	3,151	4,852	37	25,013	326	1,885	546	908	4,003	141
1955	309	3,180	4,598	33	22,959	313	1,902	523	749	4,059[53][21] / 5,858	174
1956	282	3,168	4,630	34	24,704	297	1,839	494	566	5,887	152
1957	254	3,214	5,409	34	23,060	275	1,838	589	457	6,241	162
1958	237	3,273	5,347	36	26,272	261	1,935	597	407	6,476	170
1959	212	3,379	6,074	42	26,506	254	1,949	524	381	5,478	171
1960	171	3,397	6,147	44	24,485	251	1,921	483	341	5,743	181
1961	125	3,593	7,095	47	30,575	235	2,057	534	307	6,460	202
1962	100	3,504	7,181	52	29,047	228	2,152	626	279	6,509	188
1963	81	3,343	7,334	61	25,281	220	2,195	577	238	6,842	176
1964	64	3,277	8,011	71	24,982	207	2,146	600	222	6,581	197
1965	53	3,345	8,591	93	20,264	184	2,028	595	199	6,878	193
1966	46	3,374	8,120	112	20,527	165	2,049	651	175	6,960	168
1967	42	3,282	8,486	122	18,595	141	2,036	771	173	7,284	177
1968	40	3,141	7,963	110	18,448	126	2,071	720	155	6,940	185
1969	42	3,000	8,022	90	18,421	101[70]	1,981[70]	797[70]	159[70]	7,248[70]	238[70]
1970	45	2,842	8,361	70	17,847	90	1,873	1,047	187	8,264	145
1971	47	2,723	8,626	57	16,220	73	1,865	1,183	175	8,293	210
1972	48	2,779	8,929	52	18,419	60	1.835	1,093	155	9,600	229
1973	50	2,957	8,423	55	16,124	48	1,884	1,190	145	9,064	240
1974	55	3,100	7,763	59	15,417	49	1,905	1,098	146	8,638	234
1975	58	3,060	7,682	61	15,262	38	1,843	1,078	124	9,073	175

See p.341 for footnotes

D5 Numbers of Livestock (in thousands)

1920–1975

	FRANCE					GERMANY					
	H	C	P	S	G	H	C	P	S	G	Po
1920	2,635	13,217	4,942	9,406	1,341	3,588	16,807	14,179	6,150	4,459	60.955
1921	2,706	13,344	5,166	9,600	1,361	3,683[26]	16,851[26]	15,879[26]	5,890[26]	4,331[26]	68,015[26]
						3,666	16,791	15,818	5,891	4,296	67.760
1922	2,778	13,576	5,196	9,782	1,368	3,650	16,316	14,678	5,566	4,140	65,200
1923	2,848	13,749	5,406	9,925	1,353	...	16,653	17,226	6,094	4,658	...
1924	2,859	14,025	5,802	10,172	1,377	3,855	17,326	16,895	5,735	4,360	71,706
1925	2,880	14,373	5,793	10,537	1,378	3,917	17,202	16,200	4,753	3,796	71,504
1926	2,894	14,482	5,777	10,775	1,388	3,873	17,221	19,423	4,080	3,484	75,705
1927	2,927	14,941	6,019	10,693	1,405	3,810	18,011	22,899	3,819	3,225	79,418
1928	2,936	15,005	6,017	10,445	1,372	3,718	18,414	20,106	3,635	2,890	84,509
1929	2,986	15,631	6,102	10,452	1,885	3,617	18,033	19,944	3,480	2,625	92,154
1930	2,924	15,467	6,329	10,152	1,675	3,522	18,470	23,442	3,504	2,581	98,232
1931	2,919	15,434	6,398	9,845	1,488	3,451	19,124	23,080	3,499	2,516	92,449
1932	2,901	15,643	6,488	9,762	1,463	3,395	19,139	22,859	3,405	2,503	93,538
1933	2,878	15,830	6,769	9,730	1,448	3,397	19,739	23,891	3,387	2,588	96,901
1934	2,838	15,705	7,044	9,571	1,405	3,360[56]	19,198[56]	23,170[56]	3,483[56]	2,494[56]	94,416[56]
						3,370	19,266	23,298	3,487	2,556	94,972
1935	2,810	15,670	7,043	9,558	1,316	3,390	18,938	22,827	3,928	2,501	94,145
1936	2,774	15,762	7,089	9,808	1,359	3,410	20,088	25,892	4,341	2,634	97,036
1937	2,742	15,804	7,117	9,994	1,447	3,434	20,504	23,847	4,692	2,630	93,261
1938	2,692[54]	15,622[54]	7,127[54]	9,872[54]	1,416[54]	3,443	19,911	23,481	4,809	2,509	97,130
1939	2,123	14,189	6,380	8,948	1,277	3,023	19,948	25,240	4,852	2,306	97,117
1940	2,115	14,381	4,978	8,182	1,246	3,128	19,663	21,578	4,862	2,174	96,631
1941	2,193	15,515	4,750	7,771	1,065	3,093	19,432	18,303	4,984	2,030	82,117
1942	2,190[54]	15,806[54]	4,405[54]	7,092[54]	1,084[54]	3,096	19,102	15,025	5,196	2,213	74,248
1943	2,120	14,516	3,656	6,615	931	3,142	19,598	16,549	5,671	2,330	77,171
1944	2,046[54]	13,480[54]	3,667[54]	6,224[54]	851[54]	3,232	20,286	15,336	6,802	...	...
						WEST GERMANY					
1945	2,257	14,273	4,386	6,632	1,021	...	...	...	...	...	...
1946	2,354	15,100	5,334	7,259	1,146	...	...	...	...	...	...
1947	2,407	15,126	5,678	7,406	1,145	...	...	...	...	...	...
1948	2,418	15,434	6,424	7,510	1,236	1,617	10,569	6,755	2,491	1,428	28,221
1949	2,414[55]	15,432[55]	6,760[55]	7,480[55]	1,282[55]	1,629	10,883	9,698	2,020	1,445	44,218
1950	2,397	15,801	6,824	7,511	1,297	1,570	11,149	11,890	1,643	1,347	51,801
1951	2,380	16,235	7,222	7,585	1,294	1,455	11,375	13,603	1,666	1,302	54,271
1952	2,333	16,281	7,179	7,675	1,289	1,360	11,641	12,979	1,544	1,153	54,768
1953	2,287	16,911	7,287	7,839	1,278	1,271	11,641	12,435	1,352	1,024	59,097
1954	2,215	17,322	7,570	8,013	1,251	1,172	11,521	14,525	1,226	891	58,856
1955	2,161	17,572	7,729	8,216	1,280	1,099	11,553	14,593	1,188	766	56,040
1956	2,064	17,693	7,759	8,403	1,270	1,025	11,815	14,408	1,146	660	57,680
1957	1,982	17,924	8,131	8,573	1,240	967[56]	11,948[56]	15,418[56]	1,127[56]	567[56]	60,161[56]
						974	12,009	15,495	1,135	587	60,962
1958	1,903	18,466	8,469	8,749	1,199	912	12,127	14,734	1,113	498	62,327
1959	1,825	18,735	8,357	8,942	1,164	814	12,480	14,876	1,084	414	64,083
1960	1,729	19,501	8,603	9,063	1,172	710	12,867	15,776	1,035	352	63,983
1961	1,617	20,583	9,217	8,924	1,176	634[57]	13,277[57]	17,207[57]	1,010[57]	292[57]	69,267[57]
						636	13,281	17,218	1,011	292	69,447
1962	1,526	20,265	9,080	8,945	1,124	560	13,355	16,869	981	236	69,253
1963	1,357	20,041	8,967	8,626	1,069	493	13,014	16,643	899	189	76,014
1964	1,228	20,244	9,043	8,821	1,041	417	13,053	18,146	841	150	80,616
1965	1,114	20,640	9,239	9,056	1,014	360	13,680	17,723	797	122	85,246
1966	1,044	21,184	9,840	9,186	1,017	312	13,973	17,682	812	105	91,998
1967	874	21,679	10,693	9,510	924	283	13,981	19,033	810	89	91,388
1968	750	21,566	9,602	9,794	919	264	14,061	18,732	830	75	91,866
1969	697[75]	21,719[75]	10,463[75]	10,037[75]	925[75]	254	14,286	19,323	841	60	98,955
1970	626	21,723	11,483	10,239	924	253	14,026	20,969	843	50	101,545
1971	524	21,764	11,386	10,115	909	265	13,638	19,985	850	43	102,181
1972	447	22,509	11,387	10,442	899	283	13,892	20,028	908	40	102,174
1973	425	23,701	11,560	10,375	923	320	14,364	20,452	1,016	38	99,143
1974	413	24,119	12,031	10,568	959	325	14,430	20,234	1,040	...	91,538
1975	400	24,078	11,451	10,803	991	341	14,493	19,805	1,087	...	90,826

See p.341 for footnotes

D5 Numbers of Livestock (in thousands)

1920–1975

	EAST GERMANY						GREECE[5]						
	H	C	P	S	G	Po	H	A & M	C	P	S	G	Po
1920							201	364	659	416	5,811	3,418	5,073
1921							177[5]	371[5]	675[5]	404[5]	5,789[5]	3,717[5]	5,410[5]
1922							211	377	754	407	5,961	4,212	5,777
1923							194	355	671	334	5,643	3,674	5,956
1924							259	422	844	390	6,623	4,169	6,072
1925							270	437	854	452	6,636	4,103	7,860
1926							281	457	925	510	6,951	4,669	7,313
1927							277	464	909	453	6,442	4,579	7,738
1928							290	493	910	419	6,920	4,919	8,693
1929							323	528	831	276	5,806	4,179	...
1930							317	497	837	335	6,799	4,637	8,635
1931							325	512	868	423	7,072	4,626	9,037
1932							324	524	875	472	6,927	4,678	10,063
1933							341	544	914	507	7,427	4,952	11,502
1934							347	551	950	584	7,910	5,207	11,251
1935							361	556	957	624	8,185	5,286	11,246
1936							359	589	986	607	8,440	5,514	12,067
1937							372	597	998	465	8,451	5,288	12,330
1938							363	588	967	430	8,139	4,356	11,945
1939							...	...	1,103	358	7,795	3,499	11,945
1940							...	...	...	...	...	...	...
1941							...	...	...	...	...	...	...
1942							...	...	...	...	...	...	...
1943							...	...	...	...	...	...	...
1944							194	381	505	280	5,300	2,700	8,200
1945	...	...	...	...	...	...	200	411	533	330	5,600	2,900	7,816
1946	646	2,767	1,969	748	899	...	220	455	561	400	6,000	3,130	8,377
1947	649	2,782	2,074	686	1,072	...	241	504	693	480	7,116	3,535	8,324
1948	665	2,879	2,616	723	1,398	...	237	520	709	509	6,767	3,527	8,516
1949	695	3,317	4,322	900	...	...	246	562	751	537	6,785	3,629	8,748
1950	723	3,615	5,705	1,085	1,628	22,726	279	621	815	582	6,905	3,710	9,050
1951	745	3,808	7,088	1,240	1,578	26,584	292	651	846	636	7,326	3,958	10,010
1952	749	3,936	9,100	1,428	1,327	27,230	305	668	873	587	7,784	4,139	10,506
1953	727	3,796	8,208	1,550	1,136	25,834	315	692	904	603	8,254	4,510	11,278
1954	695	3,793	8,367	1,712	961	26,782	317	704	917	603	8,738	4,643	12,056
1955	669	3,760	9,029	1,807	860	27,300	326	716	957	621	8,970	4,795	12,748
1956	641	3,719	8,326	1,893	764	28,732	332	726	981	641	9,275	4,894	13,595
1957	624	3,744	8,255	2,019	694	31,391	333	731	1,005	640	9,195	4,939	14,122
1958	607	4,145	7,504	2,111	625	33,138	331	734	1,028	631	9,255	5,010	14,656
1959	560	4,465	8,283	2,115	547	38,604	328	731	1,046	638	9,374	5,066	13,873
1960	447	4,675	8,316	2,015	439[58]	36,910[58]	327	729	1,074	628	9,353	5,064	14,337
1961	403	4,548	8,864	1,930	446[59]	35,879[58]	337	715	1,069	547	8,962	4,603	15,030
1962	369	4,508	8,045	1,792	388[58]	35,626[58]	329	695	1,060	513	8,899	4,389	17,161
1963	341	4,614	9,289	1,899	397	39,581	318	687	1,034	483	8,513	4,153	17,851
1964	306	4,682	8,759	1,972	353	38,210	306	675	1,017	486	8,097	3,990	18,535
1965	272	4,762	8,878	1,963	302	37,988	294	654	1,046	558	7,819	3,895	22,424
1966	250	4,918	9,312	1,928	278	37,070	279	635	1,082	553	7,829	3,945	25,707
1967	219	5,019	9,254	1,818	236	37,976	265	635	1,094	492	7,874	4,042	25,626
1968													
1967	219	5,019	9,254	1,818	236	37,976	265	609	1,094	492	7,874	4,042	25,626
1968	188	5,109	9,523	1,794	204	38,802	267	587	1,038	392	7,724	4,005	25,916
1969	148	5,171	9,237	1,696	158	42,565	255	559	997	383	7,680	4,054	26,133
1970	127	5,190	9,648	1,598	135	43,034	232	537	952	446	7,535	4,130	24,558
1971	106	5,293	9,995	1,607	113	43,343	216	515	986	504	7,686	4,185	29,044
1972	94	5,379	10,361	1,657	96	43,658	194	487	1,055	590	7,906	4,261	31,049
1973	82	5,482	10,849	1,742	78	45,667	180	467	1,232	826	8,367	4,472	29,904
1974	76	5,585	11,519	1,847	65	47,530	166	442	1,240	761	8,274	4,476	30,366
1975	70	5,532	11,501	1,883	53	47,122	158	431	1,184	709	8,361	4,608	29,147

See p.341 for footnotes

D5 **Numbers of Livestock** (in thousands)

	HUNGARY				IRELAND			1920–1975	
	H	C	P	S	H	C	P	S	Po
1920	...	...	...	...	624	5,023	982	3,586	...
1921	...	...	...	...	...	5,197	977	3,708	...
						Southern Ireland			
1922	...	...	...	...	487	4,375	938	2,794	17,246
1923	...	...	...	...	487	4,278	1,286	2,666	17,278
1924	850	1,896	2,458	1,814	473	4,268	987	2,726	16,982
1925	876	1,920	2,633	1,891	460	3,991	732	2,813	17,279
1926	865	1,847	2,520	1,804	434	3,947	884	3,003	21,367
1927	903	1,805	2,387	1,611	424	4,047	1,178	3,120	21,584
1928	918	1,812	2,662	1,566	429	4,125	1,183	3,263	21,714
1929	892	1,819	2,582	1,573	433	4,137	945	3,375	22,089
1930	860	1,785	2,362	1,464	448	4,038	1,052	3,515	22,900
1931	865	1,814	2,715	1,440	450	4,029	1,227	3,575	22,782
1932	846	1,819	2,361	1,210	446	4,025	1,108	3,461	22,536
1933	820	1,697	1,899	1,056	441	4,137	931	3,405	22,505
1934	803	1,678	2,502	1,087	429	4,086	968	2,931	19,984
1935	807	1,756	3,176	1,228	420	4,019	1,088	3,042	19,485
1936	794	1,742	2,554	1,350	424	4,014	1,017	3,062	20,312
1937	798	1,756	2,624	1,484	429	3,955	934	3,000	19,491
1938	814	1,882	3,110	1,629	442	4,056	959	3,197	19,630
1939	...	...	...	...	445	4,057	931	3,048	19,551
1940	865	2,068	4,390	1,510	459	4,023	1,049	3,071	19,975
1941	844	2,049	3,949	1,254	459	4,150	764	2,909	17,393
1942	900	2,365	4,670	1,709	452	4,084	519	2,693	17,365
1943	...	...	...	...	454	4,136	434	2,560	17,097
1944	...	...	...	...	459	4,246	381	2,663	18,330
1945	329	1,070[9]	1,114	328	465	4,211	426	2,581	18,314
1946	399	1,100[9]	1,327	370	452	4,146	479	2,423	18,276
1947	490	1,479[9]	1,894	508	438	3,950	457	2,094	17,304
1948	651	1,993[9]	2,771	579	421	3,921	457	2,058	20,790
1949	600	1,942	3,316	910	402	4,127	675	2,192	22,077
1950	712	2,222	5,542	1,049	391	4,322	645	2,385	21,132
1951	697	2,009	4,298	1,143	367	4,376	558	2,616	18,838
1952	698	2,091	4,740	1,481	342	4,309	719	2,857	19,379
1953	681	2,236	4,977	1,637	329	4,397	882	2,930	19,114
1954	683	2,075	4,454	1,869	313	4,504	958	3,113	16,062
1955	711	2,128	5,818	1,857	296	4,483	799	3,269	16,076
1956	729	2,170	6,056	1,930	276	4,537	747	3,439	16,362
1957	720	1,973	4,996	1,873	258	4,417	900	3,720	14,502
1958	724	1,937	5,338	2,050	244	4,466	948	4,174	14,078
1959	717	2,004	6,225	2,155	234	4,684	852	4,412	13,904
1960	628	1,971	5,356	2,381	224	4,741	951	4,314	13,047
1961	463	1,957	5,921	2,643	207	4,713	1,056	4,528	12,843
1962	374	1,987	6,409	2,850	196	4,741	1,111	4,671	11,870
1963	339	1,906	5,428	3,043	190	4,860	1,102	4,691	11,888
1964	323	1,883	6,358	3,305	180	4,962	1,108	4,950	11,627
1965	321	1,964	6,963	3,400	172	5,359	1,266	5,014	11,405
1966	295	1,973	5,799	3,270	158	5,590	1,014	4,664	10,793
1967	287	2,014	6,005	3,274	143	5,586	985	4,239	10,593
1968	274	2,096	6,609	3,311	134	5,572	1,063	4,077	10,492
1969	249	2,006	5,970	3,277	125	5,688	1,116	4,006	10,335
1970	231	1,933	5,970	3,024	124	5,956	1,192	4,082	11,231
1971	219	1,917	7,510	2,657	117	6,134	1,323	4,189	11,777
1972	204	1,901	7,353	2,271	112	6,438	1,199	4,260	11,734
1973	189	1,965	6,980	2,259	103	6,970	1,108	4,261	11,339
1974	163[71]	2,017[71]	8,293[71]	2,021[71]	98	7,215	923	4,060	10,707
1975	140	2,041	7,885	2,039[71]	89	7,168	796	3,683	9,444

See p.341 for footnotes

D5 Numbers of Livestock (in thousands)

1920–1975

	NORTHERN IRELAND					ITALY					
	H	C	P	S	Po	H	A & M	C	P	S	G
1920	...	...	...	...	...	896	1,356	6,193	2,379	11,744	3,080
1921	...	...	...	...	...	990[8]	1,446[8]	6,264[8]	2,461[8]	11,754[8]	3,083[8]
1922	...	800	118	425	...	992	1,452	6,624	2,585	11,945	3,093
1923	122	748	196	464	6,682	1,000	1,460	7,000	2,750	12,100	3,100
1924	117	736	140	509	6,814	1,012	1,471	7,226	3,081	12,220	3,103
1925	112	667	112	484	6,733	1,029	1,484	7,346	3,229	12,303	3,103
1926	109	666	158	529	7,916	1,050	1,500	7,400	3,493	12,350	3,100
1927	107	697	236	600	7,898	1,042	1,487	7,297	3,574	12,109	2,641
1928	105	738	229	624	7,979	1,021	1,462	7,214	3,572	11,465	2,286
1929	104	700	192	655	8,309	988	1,423	7,149	3,487	10,851	2,037
1930	104	673	216	704	8,808	942	1,371	7,104	3,318	10,268	1,893
1931	103	681	236	794	8,691	919	1,342	7,080	3,287	9,716	1,854
1932	104	715	220	792	9,371	896	1,316	7,075	3,261	9,291	1,824
1933	102	734	271	750	10,150	874	1,291	7,090	3,239	8,933	1,804
1934	101	769	380	761	10,292	854	1,268	7,123	3,223	8,822	1,792
1935	100	799	458	818	10,085	834	1,247	7,176	3,212	8,778	1,789
1936	99	770	522	835	10,570	816	1,227	7,248	3,206	8,863	1,795
1937	98	730	570	829	10,182	796	1,224	7,300	2,814	9,095	1,804
1938	99	732	561	893	10,193	791	1,228	7,680	2,940	9,467	1,828
1939	97	753	627	895	10,220	781	1,221	7,892	3,303	9,875	1,867
1940	97	732	475	854	9,122	762	1,109	8,242	3,474	9,852	1,818
1941	97	787	351	812	12,933	743	998	8,501	3,645	9,829	1,770
1942	95	827	271	742	14,601	769	995	8,385	3,725	9,422	1,727
1943	90	832	257	683	15,430	710[9]	919[8]	7,326[8]	3,391[8]	8,194[8]	1,571[8]
1944	88	886	237	672	16,646	651	845	6,248	3,067	6,966	1,415
1945	85	919	249	654	17,471	628	806	5,885	3,044	6,845	1,411
1946	77	913	312	640	19,841	641	803	6,229	3,316	7,532	1,559
1947	75	934	334	527	21,029	691	840	7,277	3,894	8,727	1,859
1948	68	966	335	575	24,234	792[8]	1,123[8]	7,848[8]	3,949[8]	10,130[8]	2,360[8]
1949	61	980	458	645	24,242	799	1,157	8,180	4,404	10,366	2,594
1950	55	990	523	717	20,724	798	1,169	8,350	4,055	10,295	2,491
1951	45	961	585	672	17,838	769	1,166	8,395	3,512	10,142	2,255
1952	40	941	676	795	16,456	734	1,158	8,708	4,215	10,002	2,113
1953	37[60] 33	936	759	895	14,608	706	1,136	9,008	4,368	9,892	1,981
1954	30	942	820	930	11,386	669	1,126	8,831	3,745	9,452	1,798
1955	28	904	686	870	11,272	617	1,035	8,686	3,760	9,042	1,731
1956	24	918	653	873	11,536	573	965	8,440	3,863	8,568	1,679
1957	21	972	742	929	11,737	496	931	8,476	3,921	8,543	1,590
1958	19	980	700	980	12,250	474	919	8,649	3,900	8,626	1,549
1959	16	964	848	1,011	11,886	446	892	9,062	3,845	8,393	1,471
1960	13	998	985	1,099	10,393	430	860	9,399	4,148	8,343	1,440
1961	11	1,075	1,033	1,183	10,214	408	833	9,827	4,335	8,231	1,381
1962	...	1,109	1,182	1,209	9,595	390	780	9,520	4,478	8,065	1,309
1963	...	1,110	1,190	1,140	9,283	367	736	9,152	4,684	7,857	1,278
1964	...	1,112	1,152	1,094	10,557	348	701	8,608	5,029	7,762	1,236
1965	...	1,116	1,248	1,074	10,394	341	688	9,183	5,409	7,866	1,228
1966	...	1,189	1,057	1,054	10,864	331	627	9,386	5,176	8,000	1,139
1967	...	1,235	975	1,012	11,944	321	600	9,503	5,292	8,212	1,140
1968	...	1,207	1,012	962	12,059	319	548	9,539	6,186	8,285	1,124
1969	...	1,243	1,033	935	12,942	310	510	10,024	7,298	8,206	1,045
1970	...	1,320	1,069	966	13,966	296	481	9,563	9,224	8,138	1,031
1971	...	1,384	1,157	975	14,664	271	438	8,721	8,980	7,948	1,019
1972	...	1,444	1,047	1,004	14,870	254	400	8,611	8,196	7,846	976
1973	...	1,536	1,015	964	12,693	249	343	8,738	8,201	7,809	948
1974	...	1,620	839	937	11,818	250	311	8,408	8,814	7,995	958
1975	...	1,626	645	934	12,056	253	287	8,153	8,888	8,152	940

See p.341 for footnotes

D5 Numbers of Livestock (in thousands)

1920–1975

	NETHERLANDS					NORWAY				
	H	C	P	S	Hens	H	C	P	S	Po[62]
1920	...	...	...	...	...	...	...	...	...	...
1921	364	2,063	1,519	668	9,661	...	...	...	...	...
1922	...	...	...	...	...	...	...	...	...	...
1923	...	...	...	...	...	193	1,131	237	1,525	2,638
1924	...	...	...	...	...	186	1,114	249	1,507	3,018
1925	...	...	...	...	...	184	1,151	253	1,529	3,173
1926	...	...	...	...	...	183	1,200	303	1,595	3,053
1927	...	...	....	...	...	183	1,210	300	1,608	2,994
1928	...	...	...	...	...	182	1,221	283	1,654	3,092
1929	...	...	...	...	...	177	1,224	289	1,533	2,929
1930	299	2,366	2,018	485	24,637	177	1,251	339	1,588	3,098
1931	...	...	...	...	25,915	177	1,310	317	1,692	3,324
1932	...	...	2,736	...	26,671	179	1,342	304	1,736	3,503
1933	...	2,877	2,113	...	...	180	1,340	420	1,764	3,544
1934	269	2,830	2,082	642	34,540	181	1,295	550	1,698	3,513
1935	288	2,639	1,524	680	28,482	183	1,328	410	1,737	3,437
1936	295	2,570	1,679	655	27,788	186	1,348	410	1,749	3,472
1937	300	2,627	1,406	608	27,704	190	1,343	445	1,739	3,481
1938	312	2,763	1,538	654	29,646	193	1,399	429	1,778	3,526
1939	322	2,817	1,553	690	32,805	204	1,455	362	1,744	3,438[62]
1940	326	2,690	1,288	574	34,908	206	1,400	400	1,700	3,000
1941	319	2,659	948	508	7,740	207	1,280	270	1,660	2,340
1942	337	2,441	491	574	3,683	208	1,250	220	1,695	1,500
1943	309	2,058	545	451	3,868	218	1,220	145	1,715	1,200
1944	...	2,190	...	...	...	227	1,255	220	1,795	1,200
1945	302	2,277	769	489	...	231	1,220	195	1,760	1,200
1946	305	2,410	1,040	558	10,915	238	1,267	257	1,707	1,433
1947	316	2,367	857	460	13,959	225	1,225	259	1,698	2,047
1948	303	2,313	871	425	17,405	206	1,175	248	1,630	2,726
1949	279	2,543	1,301	465	20,288	198	1,224	419	1,736	3,711
1950	256	2,726	1,864	390	23,465	191	1,237	422	1,812	3,912
1951	254	2,867	1,939	360	25,361	184	1,231	386	1,929	3,321
1952	245	2,862	1,847	383	23,830	175	1,152	418	1,987	3,197
1953	249	2,934	1,968	424	27,558	168	1,150	379	1,985	3,385
1954	242	3,026	1,975	407	31,951	159	1,181	406	1,952	3,563
1955	222	2,995	2,378	381	30,673	150	1,171	464	1,922	3,482
1956	210	2,962	2,332	433	35,557	142	1,112	507	1,826	3,954
1957	201	3,105	2,529	496	35,154	133	1,103	459	1,821	3,838
1958	195	3,204	2,472	543	37,797	126[61]	1,116[61]	423[61]	1,810[61]	3,477[61]
1959	196	3,396	2,590	522	43,199	117	1,105	475	1,806	3,039
1960	187	3,507	2,955	456	42,410	109	1,129	492	1,842	3,108
1961	171	3,623	2,860	438	49,917	102	1,180	534	1,855	2,924
1962	162	3,817	2,800	482	45,890	94	1,159	550	1,864	2,717
1963	149	3,695	2,923	468	44,597	86	1,122	515	1,881	2,595
1964	137	3,567	3,268	443	45,551	77	1,102	536	1,941	2,502[62]
1965	123	3,751	3,752	484	42,279	67	1,059	568	1,989	3,278
1966	105	3,968	3,918	558	45,285	61	1,041	568	2,096	3,774
1967	89	4,030	4,295	529	44,511	53	996	590	2,067	3,876
1968	...	4,116	4,683	552	45,400	47	1,008	610	1,946	3,716
1969	...	4,277	4,755	554	49,091	42	973	658	1,874	3,872
1970	...	4,366	5,650	610	56,209					
1970	...	4,314[72]	5,533[72]	575[72]	55,375[72]	35	943	642	1,753	3,746
1971	...	4,201	6,158	572	60,125	31	932	682	1,681	3,804
1972	...	4,306	6,233	592	58,430	27	940	737	1,635	3,838
1973	...	4,675	6,425	657	60,328	25	966	766	1,648	3,997
1974	...	4,979	6,719	749	62,388	24	955	747	1,632	4,121
1975	...	4,956	7,279	760	68,053	22	915	669	1,639	3,822

See p.341 for footnotes

D5 **Numbers of Livestock** (in thousands)

1920–1975

	POLAND					PORTUGAL[65]					
	H	C	P	S	Po	H	A & M	C	P	S	G
1920	...	...	...	...	...	...	...	...	...	...	...
1921	3,289	8,063	5,287	2,193	...	...	...	...	...	...	...
1922	...	...	...	...	...	...	...	...	...	...	...
1923	...	...	...	...	...	...	...	...	...	...	...
1924	...	...	...	...	35,000	...	...	...	...	...	...
1925	...	...	...	...	...	80	325	768	1,117	3,684	1,557
1926	...	...	...	...	...	...	...	...	...	...	...
1927	4,069	8,601	6,329	1,918	...	...	...	...	...	...	...
1928	...	...	...	...	...	...	...	...	...	...	...
1929	4,047	9,057	4,829	2,524	...	...	...	...	...	...	...
1930	4,103	9,400	6,047	2,492	50,000	...	...	...	...	...	...
1931	4,124	9,786	7,321	2,599	...	...	...	...	...	...	...
1932	3,940	9,461	5,844	2,488	...	...	...	...	...	...	...
1933	3,773	8,985	5,753	2,557	...	...	...	...	...	...	...
1934	3,764	9,258	7,091	2,554	...	86	388	778	1,139	3,224	1,257
1935	3,760	9,759	6,723	2,802	...	...	...	...	...	...	...
1936	3,825	10,200	7,060	3,024	...	...	...	...	...	...	...
1937	3,889	10,572	7,696	3,188	...	...	...	...	...	...	...
1938	3,916	10,554	7,525	3,411	50,420	...	...	...	...	...	...
1939	...	...	...	...	...	...	...	...	...	...	...
1940	...	...	...	...	...	81	361	832	...	3,890	1,196
1941	...	...	...	...	...	...	...	...	...	...	...
1942	...	...	...	...	...	...	...	...	...	...	...
1943	...	...	...	...	...	...	...	...	...	...	...
1944	...[63]	...[63]	...[63]	...[63]	...[63]	...	...	...	...	...	...
1945	1,395[64]	3,323[64]	1,697[64]	707[64]	...	...	...	...	...	...	...
1946	1,730	3,911	2,674	727	19,365	...	...	...	...	...	...
1947	2,016	4,746	4,700	983	26,598	...	...	...	...	...	...
1948	2,297	5,748	5,100	1,410	46,061	...	...	...	...	...	...
1949	2,652	7,072	6,120	1,945	49,406	...	...	...	...	...	...
1950	2,800	7,200	9,350	2,199	46,240	...	...	...	...	...	...
1951	2,870	7,200	8,450	2,574	...	...	...	...	...	...	...
1952	2,745	7,255	8,648	2,895	...	...	...	...	...	...	...
1953	2,722	7,385	9,730	3,330	...	...	...	...	...	...	...
1954	2,650	7,687	9,788	4,170	...	...	...	...	...	...	...
1955	2,560	7,912	10,888	4,243	53,700	68	359	895	1,419	3,593	707
1956	2,547	8,353	11,561	4,223	...	...	...	...	...	...	...
1957	2,623	8,265	12,325	4,040	...	...	...	...	...	...	...
1958	2,733	8,210	11,959	3,882	...	...	...	...	...	...	...
1959	2,839	8,353	11,209	3,778	...	...	...	...	...	...	...
1960	2,805	8,695	12,615	3,662	71,858	...	...	...	...	...	...
1961	2,730	9,168	13,434	3,494	77,825	...	...	...	...	...	...
1962	2,657	9,590	13,617	3,251	75,770	...	...	...	...	...	...
1963	2,620	9,841	11,653	3,056	79,270	...	...	...	...	...	...
1964	2,593	9,940	12,918	3,022	81,434	...	...	...	...	...	...
1965	2,554	9,947	13,779	3,061	80,288	...	...	...	...	...	...
1966	2,590	10,391	14,251	3,164	81,026	...	...	...	...	...	...
1967	2,643	10,768	14,233	3,321	80,117	...	...	...	...	...	...
1968	2,673	10,940	13,911	3,328	84,269	...	...	...	...	...	...
1969	2,633	11,049	14,357	3,229	85,498	...	...	...	...	...	...
1970	2,585	10,844	13,446	3,199	87,561	...	...	...	...	...	...
1971	2,501	11,076	15,243	3,180	88,854	...	...	...	...	...	...
1972	2,422	11,453	17,347	3,110	92,875	31	266	1,123	1,994	2,403	731
1973	2,373	12,192	19,782	3,050	94,227	...	...	...	...	...	...
1974	2,312	13,023	21,496	3,023	96,583	...	...	...	...	...	...
1975	2,237	13,254	21,311	3,175	99,795	...	...	...	...	...	...

See p.341 for footnotes

D5 Numbers of Livestock (in thousands)

1920–1975

	ROMANIA					RUSSIA (in millions)			
	H	C	P	S	Po	H	C	P	S
1920	1,485	4,730	2,514	8,690	...	30.3	45.9	16.3	77.3
1921	1,687	5,521	3,132	11,194	...	28.7	43.7	15.4	75.7
1922	1,802	5,746	3,147	12,321	...	25.7	40.9	13.1	68.2
1923	1,828	5,549	2,925	12,481	...	23.3	41.8	10.4	62.9
1924	1,845	5,399	3,133	13,612	...	24.0	47.3	14.6	69.1
1925	1,815	5,049	3,088	12,950	...	25.2	51.2	18.4	78.6
1926	1,877	4,798	3,168	13,582	...	26.9	54.0	18.1	85.8
1927	1,942	4,553	3,076	12,941	...	29.1	56.5	18.7	90.3
1928	1,945	4,436	2,832	12,801	...	32.1	60.1	22.0	97.3
1929	1,959	4,334	2,413	12,406	...	32.6	58.2	19.4	97.4
1930	1,809[11]	3,834[11]	2,323[11]	11,921[11]	...	31.0	50.6	14.2	85.5
1931	1,988	4,080	3,222	12,356	...	27.0	42.5	11.7	62.5
1932	2,034	4,189	2,964	12,294	...	21.7	38.3	10.9	43.8
1933	...	...	...	...	...	17.3	33.5	9.9	34.0
1934	...	...	...	...	...	15.4	33.5	11.5	32.9
1935	2.167	4,327	2,970	11,838	...	14.9	38.9	17.1	36.4
1936	2,025	4,171	3,030	11,809	39,709	15.5	46.0	25.9	43.8
1937	2,065	4,184	3,170	12,372	38,282	15.9	47.5	20.0	46.6
1938	2,158	4,161	3,165	12,768	34,666	16.2	50.9	25.7	57.3
1939	2,043	4,254	2,926	12,851	35,406	17.2	53.5	25.2	69.9
1940	1,095[32]	2,643[32]	1,770[32]	8,288[32]	22,036[32]	17.7	47.8	22.5	66.6
1941	1,103	2,765	1,655	8,003	23,055	21.1	54.8	27.6	80.0[66]
1942	1,113	3,087[9]	2,001	8,093	22,151	10.0	31.6	8.3	70.5
1943	978[32]	3,315[9,32]	1,906[32]	7,478[32]	20,383	8.2	28.3	6.1	61.4
1944	...	...	...	...	...	7.8	33.8	5.5	63.2
1945	748[32]	2,484[32]	1,020[32]	5,628[32]	11,872[32]	9.9	44.1	8.8	70.5[66]
1946	768	3,048	1,406	7,088		10.7	47.6	10.6	58.5
1947	...	...	...	...	...	10.9	47.0	8.7	57.7
1948	932	4,183	1,591	10,634	15,263	11.0	50.1	9.7	63.3
1949	917	4,164	1,967	10,303	14,014	11.8	54.8	15.2	70.4
1950	971	4,309	2,211	9,834	17,507	12.7	58.1	22.2	77.6
1951	1,073	4,778	2,587	11,599	27,207	13.8	57.1	24.4	82.6
1952	1,073	4,674	3,654	10,914	27,223	14.7	58.8	27.1	90.5
1953	...	...	...	...	...	15.3	56.6	28.5	94.3
1954	1,067	4,477	4,088	10,145	27,500	15.3	55.8	33.3	99.8
1955	1,120	4,630	4,370	10,882	29,500	14.2	56.7	30.9	99.0
1956	1,150	4,800	4,950	11,120	33,000	13.0	58.8	34.0	103.3
1957	1,200	4,600	3,900	10,500	35,000	12.4	61.4	40.8	108.2
1958	1,309	4,470	3,249	10,374	35,000	11.9	66.8	44.3	120.2
1959	1,223	4,394	4,008	10,662	35,000	11.5	70.8	48.7	129.9
1960	1,110	4,450	4,300	11,200	37,000	11.0	74.2	53.4	136.1
1961	1,000	4,530	4,300	11,500	38,000	9.9	75.8	58.7	133.0
1962	1,013	4,707	4,665	12,285	44,692	9.4	82.1	66.7	137.5
1963	780	4,566	4,518	12,168	34,150	9.1	87.0	70.0	139.7
1964	709	4,637	4,658	12,400	38,358	8.5	85.4	40.9	133.9
1965	689	4,756	6,034	12,734	39,910	7.9	87.2	52.8	125.2
1966	689	4,935	5,365	13,125	40,085	8.0	93.4	59.6	129.8
1967	705	5,198	5,400	14,109	43.966	8.0	97.1	58.0	135.5
1968	715	5,332	5,752	14,380	47,148	8.0	97.2	50.9	138.4
1969	703	5,136	5,853	14,298	47,618	7.5	95.7	49.0	140.6
1970	668	5,216	6,359	13,818	54,333	7.4	95.2	56.1	130.7
1971	654	5,528	7,742	14,071	61,262	7.3	99.2	67.5	138.1
1972	631	5,767	8,785	14,455	64,496	7.1	102.4	71.4	139.9
1973	610	5,897	8,987	14,302	66,511	6.8	104.0	66.6	139.1
1974	557	5,983	8,566	13,929	67,672	6.7	106.3	70.0	142.6
1975	562	6,126	8,813	13,865	78,626	6.4	109.1	72.3	145.3

See p.341 for footnotes

D5 Numbers of Livestock (in thousands)

1920–1939

	ESTONIA					LATVIA				
	H	C	P	S	Po	H	C	P	S	Po
1920	165[33]	443[33]	261[33]	530[33]	...	261	768	481	978	...
1921	...	...	...	...	...	283	800	482	1,132	...
1922	199	527	272	745	...	303	811	402	1,162	...
1923	210	513	338	666	...	341	911	487	1,488	...
1924	208	502	288	609	...	340	905	458	1,235	...
1925	224	555	339	720	676	352	916	487	1,182	...
1926	226	599	333	666	748	365	955	521	1,152	...
1927	230	634	354	667	779	369	967	535	1,128	...
1928	228	651	327	659	810	365	961	535	1,090	...
1929	205	604	279	476	946	356	978	382	906	1,854[34]
1930	204	627	290	467	979	359	1,026	523	873	2,378
1931	207	669	323	479	1,034	366	1,117	712	923	2,708
1932	208	692	303	514	1,104	366	1,153	582	984	2,922
1933	210	682	277	541	1,115	370	1,156	586	1,114	2,995
1934	212	676	282	552	1,093	375	1,158	686	1,209	3,038
1935	218	725	289	593	1,109	384	1,275	803	1,347	3,634
1936	216	731	245	584	1,147	389	1,261	674	1,352	3,757
1937	209	639	379	651	1,465	392	1,210	739	1,334	3,668
1938	219	661	385	650	1,477	400	1,224	814	1,361	3,957
1939	219	706	442	696	1,614	415	1,272	892	1,470	4,322
	included in Russia					included in Russia				

1920–1940

	LITHUANIA				
	H	C	P	S	Po
1920	...	...	...	...	...
1921	409	849	1,343	1,073	...
1922	455	1,021	1,514	1,228	...
1923	505	1,285	1,697	1,413	...
1924	482	1,252	1,564	1,399	...
1925	497	1,339	1,488	1,455	...
1926	535	1,397	1,441	1,573	...
1927	617	1,128	1,010	1,410	...
1928	611	1,199	1,060	1,468	2,214
1929	588	1,160	944	1,125	2,010
1930	562	1,034	1,207	604[35]	2,262
1931	592	1,121	1,338	606	2,805
1932	589	1,154	1,234	625	3,083
1933	580[36]	1,156[36]	1,236[36]	630[36]	2,950
1934	545	1,152	1,232	1,258	2,200
1935	545	1,132	1,223	1,220	2,087
1936	547	1,149	1,210	1,275	2,177
1937	549	1,163	1,184	1,289	2,230
1938	550	1,164	1,187	1,241	2,240
1939	521	1,104	1,117	1,224	1,997
1940	557	1,189	1,161	1,263	2,237
	included in Russia				

See p.341 for footnotes

D5 Numbers of Livestock (in thousands)

1920–1975

	SPAIN							SWEDEN				
	H	A & M	C	P	S	G	Hens	H	C	P	S	Po
1920	..[12]	...[12]	...[12]	...[12]	...[12]	...[12]	...[12]	...	...	...	...	...
1921	722	2,433	3,718	5,152	20,522	4,298	25,103	...	...	...	...	...
1922	...	...	...	...	...	...	...	...	...	...	...	...
1923	626	2,132	3,435	4,728	18,550	3,804	...	...	...	...	...	...
1924	634	2,147	3,436	4,160	18,460	3,804	...	...	...	...	...	...
1925	698	2,363	3,794	5,267	20,067	4,749	26,777	...	...	...	...	...
1926	...	...	...	...	...	...	...	...	...	...	...	...
1927	...	...	...	...	...	...	...	620	2,899	1,387	708	9,504
1928	...	...	...	...	...	...	...	...	...	...	...	...
1929	598	2,160	3,660	4,773	19,370	4,525	...	...	...	...	...	...
1930	...	...	...	...	...	...	...	653	3,060	1,522	652	...
1931	563	2,179	3,654	5,102	20,047	4,008	...	656	3,109	1,614	635	...
1932	803	2,623	4,163	5,018	16,571	4,624	...	612	2,920	1,495	468	11,304
1933	568	2,190	3,569	5,412	19,093	4,575	...	611	2,890	1,563	443	...
1934	...	...	...	...	...	...	...	609	2,890	1,456	449	...
1935	808	2,655	4,215	5,134	17,526	4,692	29,799	611	2,919	1,293	444	...
1936	...	...	...	...	...	...	...	616	2,950	1,322	429	...
1937	...	...	...	...	...	...	...	633	2,986	1,425	353	...
1938	...	...	...	...	...	...	...	617	3,036	1,371	406	...
1939	555	1,922	3,739	6,942	21,779	6,692	29,591	616	2,976	1,316	373	11,192
1940	592	1,990	3,899	5,613	24,237	6,249	26,721	617	2,889	1,315	329	11,208
1941	...	...	...	...	...	...	...	612	2,757	1,001	403	10,697
1942	602	1,914	4,152	4,974	23,489	6,109	25,499	591	2,546	845	435	6,993
1943	...	...	...	...	...	...	...	594	2,790	989	520	8,049
1944	...	...	...	...	...	...	...	604	2,859	1,054	558	9,093
1945	...	...	...	...	...	...	...	599	2,843	1,079	516	9,696
1946	...	...	...	...	...	...	...	593	2,869	1,165	482	11,000
1947	...	...	...	...	...	...	...	551	2,797	1,189	421	12,395
1948	607[67]	1,826[67]	3,300[67]	2,668[67]	15,921[67]	4,272[67]	18,716	487	2,625	1,195	349	14,023
1949	...	...	...	...	...	...	...	465	2,584	1,238	311	12,448
1950	642[67]	1,821[67]	3,112[67]	2,688[67]	16,344[67]	4,135[67]	23,819	440	2,648	1,263[68]	279	12,241
1951	...	...	...	...	...	...	...	412	2,610	1,324[68]	228	12,329
1952	...	...	...	...	...	...	...	383	2,509	1,374[68]	223	11,722
1953	...	...	...	...	...	...	...	359	2,531	1,422[68]	209	11,591
1954	...	...	...	...	...	...	...	335	2,560	1,614[68]	202	11,819
1955	598[67]	1,754[67]	2,742[67]	2,793[67]	15,933[67]	3,097[67]	23,370	312	2,575	1,568[68]	177	11,697
1956	...	...	...	...	...	...	...	276	2,397	1,555[68]	154	11,302
1957	...	...	...	...	...	...	...	255	2,426	1,855[68]	143	11,274
1958	...	...	...	...	...	...	...	244	2,543	2,031[68]	139	11,307
1959	...	...	...	...	...	...	...	229[69]	2,580[69]	2,202[68][69]	146[69]	12,553
								211	2,471	2,161	129	
1960	506	1,844	3,640	6,032	22,622	3,300	32,388	192	2,392	1,830	140	11,925
1961	...	...	...	...	...	...	...	178	2,465	1,963	155	11,701
1962	440	1,897	3,683	6,118	20,099	2,599	40,032	163	2,551	1,998	165	10,061
1963	397	1,770	3,671	6,055	19,868	2,336	40,973	149	2,422	1,791	184	9,907
1964	345	1,382	3,723	5,011	17,617	2,284	35,211	133	2,311	1,865	218	9,997
												9,615[73]
1965	321	1,221	3,712	4,931	17,073	2,196	38,486	109	2,250	1,884	220	8,778
1966	304	1,118	3,721	5,770	16,761	2,279	42,736	93	2,211	1,898	238	8,048
1967	313	1,190	3,914	6,824	16,648	2,449	44,991	78	2,083	2,016	267	8,106
1968	308	1,102	4,021	6,673	16,726	2,504	47,911	69	2,062	2,086	327	9,898
1969	304	1,027	4,215	7,488	17,024	2,529	48,892	67	2,043	2,065	342	8,452
1970	282	901	4,282	7,621	17,005	2,551	...	61	1,926	2,074	335	7,836
1971	266	841	4,169	7,423	16,668	2,448	...	55	1,833	2,281	330	8,356
1972	261	736	4,235	8,048	15,950	2,368	...	53	1,829	2,428	332	8,277
1973	266	687	4,495	9,112	16,238	2,403	...	52	1,890	2,374	347	7,823
1974	256	630	4,438	8,671	15,599	2,230	43,099	...	1,910	2,375	372	8,004
1975	251	580	4,335	8,662	15,195	2,293	...	...	1,879	2,446	368	7,714

See p.341 for footnotes

D5 Numbers of Livestock (in thousands)

1920–1975

	SWITZERLAND						UNITED KINGDOM: Great Britain				
	H	C	P	S	G	Po	H	C	P	S	Po[38]
1920	130	1,382	546	241	334	...	1,580	6,713	2,122	19,744	...
1921	134	1,425	640	245	330	3,247	1,601	6,660	2,651	20,490	...
1922	...	...	...	...	...	...	1,552	6,869	2,450	20,122	...
1923	...	...	...	...	...	...	1,485	7,017	2,798	20,621	...
1924	...	...	...	...	...	...	1,426	7,059	3,427	21,729	...
1925	...	...	...	...	...	...	1,350	7,368	2,799	23,094	...
1926	140	1,587	637	170	289	4,116	1,307	7,451	2,345	24,062	...
1927	...	...	...	...	...	...	1,249	7,486	2,888	24,608	49,221
1928	...	...	...	...	...	...	1,204	7,240	3,167	23,968	49,399
1929	140	1,609	924	184	236	...	1,160	7,191	2,509	23,661	52,283
1930	...	...	...	...	...	...	1,118	7,086	2,454	23,965	58,219
1931	140	1,609	926	185	238	4,864	1,091	7,274	2,945	25,580	63,562
1932	...	...	...	...	...	...	1,067	7,591	3,350	26,412	69,297
1933	...	1.684	897	...	...	...	1,052	7,914	3,236	25,901	73,835
1934	...	1,660	1,003	...	...	...	1,034	7,973	3,526	24,183	73,642
1935	...	1,590	1,088	...	...	...	1,021	7,860	4,074	24,243	70,256
1936	140	1,569	878	176	220	5,544	1,013	7,853	4,040	24,205	70,005
1937	...	1,638	936	...	...	...	1,005	7,909	3,883	24,712	63,704
1938	...	1,701	923	...	...	...	1,002	8,030	3,822	25,882	64,053
1939	...	1,711	880	...	...	...	987	8,119	3,767	25,993	64,137
1940	...	1,695	959	...	...	4,641	959	8,361	3,631	25,465	62,121
1941	144	1,584	764	198	215	3,752	962	8,153	2,207	21,445	49,126
1942	144	1,493	670	196	207	3,042	917	8,248	1,872	20,764	43,212
1943	146	1,517	629	204	218	3,725	871	8,428	1,571	19,700	35,299
1944	147	1,497	600	209	218	3,775	829	8,616	1,631	19,435	38,481
1945	149	1,461	698	193	205	4,492	796	8,697	1,903	19,496	44,665
1946	152	1,472	655	196	208	5,051	756	8,716	1,644	19,718	47,276
1947	147	1,451	710	182	189	5,025	703	8,633	1,294	16,186	48,977
1948	142	1,424	767	183	187	5,800	635	8,840	1,816	17,589	61,138
1949	138	1,478	887	183	185	6,100	557	9,263	2,364	18,847	71,257
1950	134	1,530	908	170	180	6,300	494	9,630	2,463	19,714	75,385
1951	131	1,607	892	192	148	6,240	432	9,512	3,306	19,311	76,506
1952	131	1,682	1,007	190	145	6,260	374	9,303	4,287	20,860	78,519
1953	128	1,635	1,017	185	142	6,280	333	9,508	4,406	21,560	77,511
1954	126	1,593	950	195	145	6,260	300	9,777	5,431	21,943	72,258
1955	120	1,583	1,038	195	120	6,240	274	9,764	5,157	22,078	75,585
1956	117	1,646	1,162	201	113	6,420	233	9,989	4,821	22,721	80,928
1957	113	1,643	1,160	201	112	6,405	208	9,909	5,232	23,868	83,131
1958	108	1,664	1,190	202	110	6,420	189	9,976	5,695	25,125	87,474
1959	103	1,687	1,226	200	113	6,420	...	10,328	5,135	26,601	94,718
1960	100	1,746	1,351	210	...	5,980	157	10,772	4,739	26,772	92,612
1961	95	1,761	1,335	227	89	5,965	...	10,861	5,009	27,784	104,075
1962	90	1,782	1,235	227	89	5,880	...	10,749	5,540	28,289	99,436
1963	82	1,716	1,314	230	85	5,750	...	10,605	5,670	28,204	102,891
1964	76	1,698	1,426	240	82	5,800	...	10,515	6,227	28,563	107,820
1965	73	1,773	1,672	249	78	6,331	...	10,826	6,731	28,837	107,746
1966	67	1,796	1,514	266	75	6,586	...	11,017	6,282	28,903	108,076
1967	62	1,835	1,620	236	73	6,657	...	11,106	6,131	27,874	113,680
1968	59	1,855	1,849	280	72	6,211	...	10,944	6,375	27,042	115,400
1969	56	1,869	1,799	290	71	6,345	...	11,131	6,750	25,669	113,571
								----74	----74	----74	----74
1970	53	1,907	1,753	291	...	6,361	...	11,261	7,020	25,114	129,464
1971	50	1,823	1,836	292	...	5,963	...	11,420	7,567	25,006	124,352
1972	47	1,841	1,879	301	...	6,021	...	12,040	7,572	25,873	125,175
1973	47	1,911	2,136	336	69	6,698	...	12,910	7,965	26,979	131,386
1974	48	1,973	2,065	359	...	6,536	...	13,583	7,705	27,562	127,854
1975	47	1,965	1,964	366	...	6,121	...	13,091	6,686	27,336	124,515

See p.341 for footnotes

D5 **Numbers of Livestock** (in thousands)

1920–1975

YUGOSLAVIA

	H	C	P	S	G	Po
1920	...	...	...	...	...	...
1921	1,062	4,951	3,350	7,002	1,553	...
1922	1,044	4,058	2,887	8,462	1,801	...
1933	1,063	3,870	2,497	7,639	1,730	...
1934	1,054	3,784	2,518	7,619	1,718	...
1935	1,106	3,768	2,802	7,907	1,811	13,679
1926	1,117	3,706	2,806	7,933	1,721	13,697
1927	1,120	3,729	2,770	7,736	1,739	13,839
1928	1,109	3,654	2,663	7,722	1,750	13,810
1929	1,140	3,728	2,675	7,736	1,804	15,143
1930	1,161	3,812	2,924	7,953	1,731	16,272
1931	1,169	3,872	3,133	8,426	1,928	16,425
1932	1,157	3,812	2,863	8,510	1,872	16,820
1933	1,187	3,876	2,656	8,600	1,871	17,014
1934	1,206	3,990	2,792	8,868	1,881	17,858
1935	1,201	3,982	2,932	9,211	1,896	17,761
1936	1,216	4,074	3,126	9,568	1,906	18,356
1937	1,249	4,169	3,180	9,909	1,901	19,114
1938	1,264	4,267	3,451	10,137	1,890	19,419
1939	1,273	4,225	3,504	10,154	1,866	19,226
1940	...	...	...	...	...	...
1941	...	...	...	...	...	...
1942	...	...	...	...	...	...
1943	...	...	...	...	...	...
1944	...	...	...	...	...	...
1945	...	...	...	...	...	...
1946	...	...	...	...	...	...
1947	879	3,928	3,485	9,192	...	...
1948	973	4,246	3,439	9,970	...	...
1949	1,050	5,278	4,135	11,654	...	19,354
1950	1,097	5,248	4,295	10,046	...	20,207
1951	1,095	4,740	3,917	10,276	...	17,174
1952	1,103	4,834	3,999	10,522	...	20,440
1953	1,126	5,007	4,527	11,404	...	19,665
1954	1,193	5,097	4,310	12,112	...	25,450
1955	1,242	5,290	4,780	11,979	...	24,873
1956	1,296	5,206	4,655	11,360	...	25,938
1957	1,307	4,947	3,705	10,622	...	25,992
1958	1,296	4,860	4,226	10,626	...	28,508
1959	1,274	5,038	5,657	11,249	...	27,721
1960	1,272	5,297	6,210	11,449	...	30,343
1961	1,200	5,702	5,818	10,823	...	28,878
1962	1,226	5,884	5,161	11,143	...	28,304
1963	1,175	5,355	5,013	10,056	...	29,939
1964	1,140	5,094	6,100	9,707	...	32,473
1965	1,109	5,219	6,985	9,433	...	31,429
1966	1,131	5,584	5,118	9,868	...	31,685
1967	1,134	5,710	5,525	10,329	...	35,153
1968	1,126	5,693	5,865	10,346	...	35,974
1969	1,109	5,261	5,093	9,730	...	37,142
1970	1,076	5,029	5,544	8,974	...	40,854
1971	1,048	5,138	6,562	8,703	...	44,954
1972	1,015	5,148	6,216	8,326	...	44,584
1973	964	5,366	6,342	7,774	...	49,206
1974	945	5,681	7,401	7,852	...	54,685
1975	922	5,872	7,683	8,175	...	54,991

D5 Numbers of Livestock (in thousands)

NOTES

1. SOURCES:— The main sources were as for table D1. Bulgarian statistics for sheep in 1946—51 were supplied by Professor Michael Kaser's group at St. Antony's College, Oxford and are derived from B. Simov *et al, Virzstanoviavane; irazvitie na promishlenostta v N R B, 1944—1948* (Sofia, 1968). Dutch statistics for horses in 1865—69 and for cattle in 1965 and 1868—69 were supplied by the Netherlands Central Office of Statistics. Romanian statistics for 1949, 1950, 1954, and 1957 were supplied by Mr. G. Radulescu, Editor-in-Chief of the Enciclopedica Romana.

2. With some exceptions, indicated in footnotes, statistics were taken in either summer or winter, as follows:— SUMMER: Denmark, Finland, France, Great Britain, Hungary (to 1911), Ireland, Italy, Netherlands, (from 1910), Norway (from 1900), Poland, the Baltic States, Spain (from 1939) and Sweden.

WINTER: Austria, Belgium, Bulgaria, Czechoslovakia, Germany, Greece, Hungary (from 1945), Netherlands to 1904), Norway (to 1890), Romania, Russia, Spain (to 1935), Switzerland, and Yugoslavia.

FOOTNOTES

[1] Cisleithania (excluding Lombardy and Venetia) to 1910, and the Republic subsequently.
[2] Used in agriculture only.
[3] Figures to 1829 exclude the whole of Limburg and Luxembourg.
[4] Subsequently includes Savoy and Nice.
[5] Statistics apply to the territory of the day (see p.xi). However,Macedonia is excluded in 1916 and eastern Macedonia in 1917 and 1918, and Thrace is not included until 1922.
[6] Transleithania (excluding Croatia-Slavonia) to 1911. Later statistics are for the territory established by the treaty of Trianon. The following figures are available for Croatia-Slavonia (in thousands):—

	Horses	Cattle	Pigs	Sheep	Goats
1857	130	357	417	195	29
1895	311	909	883	596	22
1911	350	1,135	1,164	850	96

[7] These are estimates, of which that for sheep is believed to be excessive.
[8] Statistics up to 1921 apply to the 1871 boundaries. For 1922—43 they apply to the 1924 boundaries, and from 1944 they apply to the 1954 boundaries, except that Trieste is not included until 1949.
[9] Including buffaloes.
[10] The following earlier figures of cattle are available (in thousands):— 1804 903; 1807 978.
[11] Figures to 1914 are for the 50 provinces of European Russia (excluding Finland, Poland, and the Caucasus). From 1916 to 1939 they they are for the U.S.S.R. boundaries of 1924, and subsequently for the boundaries of the day.
[12] Statistics prior to 1921 are originally from a variety of sources and are clearly not always comprable with each other. Earlier statistics given in J.V. Vives, *An Economic History of Spain* (Princeton, 1969) are as follows (in thousands):—

	Horses	Asses & Mules	Cattle	Pigs	Sheep	Goats
1797	230	...	1,650	1,200	11,700	2,500
1803	140	450	2,680	2,100	12,000	...

[13] The following earlier statistics are available (in thousands):—

	Horses	Cattle	Sheep
1805	397	1,468	1,214
1810	405	1,516	1,243

[14] Excluding the town of Stockholm.
[15] Including goats, which numbered 173 thousands in 1851—5 and 133 thousand in 1865.
[16] The whole of Carinthia, Lower Austria, Styria, and Tirol is included in these figures, but Burgenland is not.
[17] Between 1910 and 1920 southern Dobrudja was ceded to Romania and rather larger areas were acquired from Turkey. From 1941 southern Dobrudja is again included.
[18] These statistics are for February instead of in the summer.
[19] From 1908 to 1920 (1st line) the statistics relate only to horses over three years old. This figure is not given for 1907, but the number of 'horses' (as opposed to 'colts') was 286 thousand.
[20] From 1908 to 1920 (1st line) the statistics relate only to cattle over two years old.This figure is not given for 1907, but the number of 'bulls' and 'cows' (as opposed to 'young cattle') was 1,185 thousand.
[21] Over six months old only, except from 1955 (2nd line).
[22] Figures for 1870—1918 exclude the parts of Alsace and Lorraine ceded to Germany.
[23] Figures for 1914—18 exclude the invaded departments.

[24]W.G. Hoffman, *Das Wachstum der Deutschen Wirtschaft seit der Mitte des 19 Jahrhunderts* (Berlin, etc., 1965) gives different figures for cattle as follows (in thousands):– 1892 15,690; 1900 16,906; 1904 16,917.

[25]Figures for 1872 to 1917 (1st line) include Alsace-Lorraine.

[26]Figures for 1917 (2nd line) to 1921 (1st line) apparently relate to the 1921 boundaries (i.e. including Eastern Upper Silesia, but excluding other territory ceded after the First World War). Statistics for 1913 for the comparable area to 1921 (2nd line) are as follows (in thousands):–

Horses	Cattle	Pigs	Sheep	Goats	Poultry
3,806	18,474	22,533	4,988	3,164	71,907 (in 1912).

[27]Subsequently the coverage of young poultry was much improved.

[28]Subsequent statistics were taken in late spring or summer, whereas earlier ones were at 31 December.

[29]*Jaarcijfers* for 1921 gives a figure of 6,710, whilst the one given here appears in later issues. It is likely, however, that the difference does not spring from a revision but from greater coverage of the later series.

[30]Subsequent statistics were taken in autumn or summer, and, until 1959, were for rural communes only, whereas earlier ones were at 31 December and included the towns.

[31]Dobrudja was acquired in 1913.

[32]Figures for 1919 to 1939 apply to the interwar territory. Southern Dobrudja was ceded to Bulgaria in 1940. Bessarabia and northern Bukovina were ceded to the U.S.S.R. in 1940, though temporarily reconquered in 1943. Northern Transylvania was ceded to Hungary from 1940 to 1945.

[33]Excluding the district of Petseri.

[34]Fowls over six months only.

[35]Figures to 1929 include goats.

[36]Subsequent figures were taken in June (as were those of fowls throughout), whereas earlier ones were taken in December.

[37]Subsequent statistics were taken in summer or early autumn, whereas earlier ones are for the years' end.

[38]The Scottish component excludes geese, and also, in 1968 and 1969, ducks.

[39]Earlier statistics are of horses used in agriculture, later ones of all horses on agricultural holdings.

[40]Excluding Burgenland, which had the following livestock in 1923 (in thousands):–

Horses	Cattle	Pigs	Sheep	Goats	Poultry
18	125	93	6	8	491

[41]Subsequently excluding turkeys and guinea fowl.

[42]This figure is of all horses. The comparable figure for 1941 is 269, and for 1967 it is 84.

[43]Figures for 1941–44 exclude Eupen and Malmédy, and are underestimates because of concealment by farmers.

[44]Previous statistics relate to holdings of one hectare or more, whilst there is no limit for later figures. However, some smallholdings are undoubtedly omitted.

[45]Figures exist for 1919 but are not available.

[46]Subsequently excludes Sub-Carpathian Russia (Ruthenia) and 12 villages in Slovakia, ceded to the U.S.S.R. in 1945.

[47]Subsequently includes South Jutland.

[48]For 1930–38 the statistics relate to rural communes only. Figures including the towns are available for 1933 as follows:– (in thousands)

Horses	Cattle	Pigs	Sheep	Fowls
520	3,185	4,477	179	26,625

[49]For 1940–48 the statistics for fowls relate to rural communes only. In 1949 the number of fowls in the towns was 706 thousand.

[50]Subsequent statistics apparently relate to a different time of year from the earlier ones.

[51]Subsequent statistics compare to ones taken on 1 September in 1932 and 1938, which differ from the continuous series given here, and are as follows (in thousands):–

	Horses	Cattle	Pigs	Sheep
1932	348	1,713	361	879
1938	381	1,849	487	1,022

[52]Figures for 1945–49 were taken at 1 March. Figures from 1950 have been taken at 15 June.

[53]Revised figures for 1950 and 1955 are given in the 1967 *Statistical Yearbook of Finland*, but not for the intervening years. The revised figures are 3,381 in 1950 and 3,945 in 1955.

[54]Parts of Alsace-Lorraine annexed by Germany are excluded from 1939 to 1945, and Corsica is excluded in 1943–44.

[55]Subsequently includes Tende and Brigue.

[56]Subsequently including Saarland.

[57]Subsequently including West Berlin.

[58]Excluding the Kleintierhaltung in Berlin.

[69]This is a mid-year rather than an end-year figure.

[60]Subsequently horses used for agricultural purposes only.

[61]Subsequent statistics include urban municipalities.

[62]Figures for 1940–64 are of hens only, and from 1965 they are of hens and cocks only.

[63]Subsequent figures are for the postwar territory.

[64]Unofficial estimates of doubtful validity.

[65]Mainland only.

[66]Figures for 1942–45 include goats.

[67]Excluding suckling animals.

[68]Subsequent statistics were collected in April rather than June.

[69]Subsequent statistics relate only to farms of two hectares and over.

[70]Previously on holdings above quarter of a hectare, and subsequently on those over 1 hectare.

[71]December instead of March.

[72]Subsequently excluding holdings of less than 10 Standard Farm Units.

[73]Subsequently only fowls and chickens.

[74]Changes in the basis of collection affected comparability, but only to a significant extent for pigs and poultry.

[75]Subsequent statistics were collected in December rather than summer or autumn.

D6 OUTPUT OF COWS' MILK (in thousands of tons)

1903–1949

	Austria*	Belgium	Bulgaria[1]	Czech*	Denmark[3]	Finland	France*	Germany*	East Germany*	Hungary*
1903	...	...	...	...	2,723	...	...	...	...	...
1904	...	...	...	...	...	...	...	...	...	...
1905	...	...	...	...	...	...	...	...	...	...
1906	...	...	...	...	...	...	...	...	...	...
1907	...	...	...	...	...	...	...	...	...	...
1908	...	...	...	...	...	...	...	...	...	...
1909	...	...	...	...	3,525	...	...	...	...	...
1910	...	...	...	...	...	...	...	...	...	...
1911	...	...	...	...	...	...	...	...	...	...
1912	...	...	...	...	...	...	...	...	...	...
1913	...	...	...	...	...	...	...	...	...	...
1914	...	...	...	...	3,602	...	...	...	...	...
1915	...	...	...	...	...	...	...	...	...	...
1916	...	...	...	...	...	...	...	...	...	...
1917	...	...	...	...	...	...	...	...	...	...
1918	...	...	...	...	...	...	...	...	...	...
1919	...	...	...	...	...	...	...	...	...	...
1920	...	...	...	...	2,703[4]	...	...	...	...	...
1921	...	...	...	...	3,333	...	...	...	...	...
1922	...	...	...	...	3,519	...	...	...	...	...
1923	...	...	...	...	3,833	...	12,067	...	...	...
1924	...	...	...	...	4,238	...	...	...	...	...
1925	...	..	...	...	4,348	...	13,098	...	...	...
1926	...	...	...	...	4,529	...	12,571	...	...	...
1927	...	...	...	...	4,678	...	...	...	...	...
1928	...	...	...	...	4,777	...	...	21,315	...	...
1929	...	2,914	...	...	5,075	2,133	14,282	22,826	...	...
1930	2,492	2,958	...	...	5,272	...	...	21,508	...	...
1931	...	2,975	...	...	5,565	...	...	23,610	...	...
1932	...	3,110	...	...	5,485	...	...	24,226	...	...
1933	...	3,150	...	...	5,390	...	...	24,720	...	...
1934	2,622	3,131	...	...	5,320	2,387	...	24,450	...	...
1935	...	3,104	...	...	5,120	2,435	14,692	24,200[7]	...	345[8]
1936	...	3,174	...	4,633	5,275	2,475	...	25,400	...	411[8]
1937	2,369	2,928	...	4,616	5,300	2,663	14,828	25,445	...	460[8]
1938	...	3,090	...	...	5,400	2,682	13,751	25,120	...	455[8]
1939	1,983	2,834	541	3,877	5,300	2,307	14,192	25,360	...	...
1940	1,925	...	533	3,194	4,622	2,028[5]	10,645[6]	24,440	...	...
1941	1,945	2,128	413	2,846	3,621	1,761	9,767[6]	...	...	...
1942	1,947	2,089	144	2,403	3,338	1,460	8,489[6]	22,531	...	...
1943	2,020	2,152	184	1,984	3,813	1,502	8,106[6]	22,810	...	...
1944	1,888	2,100	154	1,897[2]	4,010	1,633	7,412[6]	...	...	...
1945	1,375	1,121	113[1]	2,049	4,271	1,611	7,892[6]	...	...	...
1946	1,387	1,194	...	2,649	4,595	1,500	10,600	West Germany	...	...
1947	1,250	2,400	...	2,417	4,106	1,700	10,300	...	...	...
1948	1,553	2,580	...	2,258	4,058	1,930	11,100	8,555	2,025	866
1949	1,748	3,060	...	2,618	4,883	2,175	13,700	11,316	2,560	...

Abbreviations used where space demands:— Czech: Czechoslovakia; Switz: Switzerland: UK: United Kingdom

See p.346 for footnotes

D6 Output of Cows' Milk (thousands of tons)

1903–1949

	Ireland[9]	Italy*	Netherlands	Norway[11]	Poland	Russia (million tons)	Spain	Sweden	Switz	U.K.
1903	...	...	2,439	...	...	...	...	...	...	...
1904	...	...	2,314	...	...	...	...	...	...	...
1905	...	...	2,423	...	...	...	...	...	...	...
1906	...	...	2,535	...	...	...	...	...	...	...
1907	...	...	2,576	...	...	...	...	...	...	...
1908	...	...	2,619	...	...	...	...	...	...	...
1909	...	...	2,530	...	...	...	...	...	...	...
1910	...	...	2,706	...	...	...	...	...	...	...
1911	...	...	2,680	...	...	...	...	...	...	...
1912	...	...	2,877	...	...	...	...	...	...	...
1913	...	...	2,943	...	...	24.1[13]	...	...	...	...
1914	...	...	3,026	...	...	...	...	...	...	...
1915	...	...	3,125	...	...	...	...	...	...	...
1916	...	...	3,217	...	...	...	...	...	...	...
1917	...	...	2,650	...	...	24.2[13]	...	...	...	...
1918	...	...	1,944	...	...	...	...	...	...	...
1919	...	...	2,162	...	...	...	...	...	...	...
1920	...	...	2,513	...	...	...	...	...	...	...
1921	...	...	2,981	...	...	19.2[13]	...	...	...	...
1922	...	...	3,080	...	...	...	...	...	...	...
1923	...	...	3,401	...	...	...	...	...	2,452	...
1924	...	...	3,627	...	...	26.2	...	...	2,542	...
1925	...	...	3,726	...	...	...	...	...	2,574	...
1926	2,357	...	3,982	...	...	...	....	...	2,752	...
1927	...	...	4,167	...	...	...	...	...	2,709	...
1928	...	...	4,263	...	...	31.0	...	...	2,830	...
1929	2,376	...	4,351	...	...	29.8	...	1,990	2,688	...
1930	...	...	4,418	1,223	...	27.0	1,374	2,162	2,615	...
1931	...	...	4,544	...	...	23.4	...	2,165	2,625	...
1932	...	...	4,607	1,258	...	20.6	...	2,157	2,709	5,864
1933	...	...	4,732	...	9,265	19.2	1,499	2,196	2,784	5,958
1934	2,320	...	4,778	1,312	...	20.8	...	2,372	2,808	5,958
1935	2,357	...	4,996	1,302	...	21.4	...	2,455	2,732	5,958
1936	2,311	...	5,165	1,352	...	23.5	...	2,653	2,673	6,174
1937	2,292	...	5,340	1,364	...	26.1	...	2,778	2,706	6,165
1938	2,268	...	5,325	1,373	10,310	29.0	...	2,962	2,792	6,099[16]
1939	2,348	...	5,512	1,413	...	27.2	...	3,156	2,693	8,483
1940	2,184	...	5.194	1,522	...	26.6[14] / 33.6	...	3,102	2,618	7,752
1941	2,264	...	4,089	...	...	...	1,424	2,722	2,471	7,396
1942	2,212	...	3,117	...	...	...	...	2,516	2,261	7,522
1943	2,240	...	2,715	...	...	...	1,977	2,829	2,219	7,855
1944	2,217	...	2,583	...	...	...	...	3,106	2,115	8,019
1945	2,264	...	2,546	1,078	...[12]	26.4	...	3,375[15] / 4,284	2,120	8,241
1946	2,170	4,547	3,911	1,259	2,793	27.7	...	4,625	2,160	8,549
1947	2,020	3,704	3,918	1,319	3,399	30.2	...	4,489	2,060	8,348
1948	2,104	4,202[10]	4,687	1,393	...	33.4	...	4,402	2,285	9,174
1949	2,306	4,917	5,464	1,525	...	34.9	...	4,647	2,441	9,754

U.K.: United Kingdom

See p.346 for footnotes

D6 Output of Cows' Milk (thousands of tons)

1950–1975

	Austria*	Belgium	Bulgaria[1]	Czech*	Denmark[3]	Finland	France*	Germany*	East Germany*	Hungary*	Ireland[9]
1950	2,085	3,230	...	3,272	5,403	2,450	15,500	13,861	3,580	1,446	2,409
1951	2,296	3,280	...	3,555	5,233	2,652	16,500	15,171	3,805	1,452	2,278
1952	2,311	3,344	271	3,587	4,998	2,862	15,500	15,812	4,392	1,381	2,245
1953	2,424	3,535	267	3,244	5,378	2,946	17,500	16,741	4,239	1,323	2,381
1954	2,539	3,654	300	3,264	5,394	2,914	18,600	17,054	4,702	1,411	2,451
1955	2,533	3,707	381	3,521	5,124	2,865	18,035	16,907	5,077	1,526	2,437
1956	2,613	3,665	456	3,711	5,068	3,085	19,600	17,007	4,986	1,516	2,550
1957	2,732	3,725	524	3,742	5,344	3,153	20,660	17,263[7] 17,378	5,286	1,779	2,695
1958	2,752	3,747	593	3,764	5,147	3,155	21,115	17,977	5,656	1,949	2,629
1959	2,777	3,767	673	3,771	5,426	3,322	20,300	18,497	5,826	1,987	2,493
1960	2,842	3,904	745	3,830	5,399	3,486	22,972	19,250	5,730	1,955	2,671
1961	2,901	3,910	813	3,945	5,524	3,624	23,816	19,872[17] 19,996	5,612	1,897	2,784
1962	3,005	3,965	772	3,664	5,355	3,644	24,332	20,307	5,216	1,805	2,877
1963	3,049	3,830	797	3,535	5,086	3,758	25,363	20,714	5,569	1,803	2,892
1964	3,128	3,685	926	3,763	5,233	3,825	25,260	20,841	5,751	1,854	3,009
1965	3,209	3,765	1,000	3,924	5,367	3,769	26,780	21,183	6,371	1,761	3,142
1966	3,216	3,760	1,098	4,169	5,306	3,693	28,016	21,322	6,728	1,849	3,232
1967	3,260	3,865	1,211	4,335	5,193	3,559	29,355	21,717	6,904	1,975	3,461
1968	3,256	3,906	1,199	4,554	5,122	3,596	30,444	22,121	7,227	1,933	3,671
1969	3,241	3.912	1,206	4,751	4.872	3,599	30,031	22,216	7,232	1,888	3,684
1970	3,229	3,749	1,252	4,794	4,630	3,310	27,276[20]	21,856	7,091	1,863	3,633
1971	3,183	3,608	1,291	4,924	4,556	3,293	27,639	21,165	7,150	1,803	3,741
1972	3,187	3,647	1,308	5,123	4,636	3,286	28,846	21,490	7,515	1,810	3,936
1973	3,179	3,611	1,344	5,430	4,729	3,107	29,291	21,265	7,738	1,957	4,153
1974	3,185	3,709	1,411	5,503	4,818	3,056	29,470	21,508	8,076	2,020	4,045
1975	3,167	3,680	1,436	5,463	4,918	3,066	29,686	21,604	8,095	1,979	4,260

	Italy*	Netherlands	Norway[11]	Poland	Romania*	Russia (million tons)	Spain	Sweden	Switzerland	U.K.	Yugoslavia
1950	5,277	5,771	1,610	...	...	35.3	...	4,852	2,573[19] 2,521	10,479	1,440
1951	5,469	5,679	1,632	...	...	36.2	1,789	4,705	2,636	10,039	...
1952	5,450	5,601	1,558	9,091	1,573	35.7	1,967	4,438	2,648	10,156	1,283
1953	5,691	5,830	1,574	9,293	1,508	36.5	2,077	4,420	2,693	10,764	1,502
1954	6,122	5,863	1,540	9,613	1,698	38.2	2,068	4,275	2,791	10,974	1,548
1955	6,644	5,725	1,548	9,903	1,830	43.0	1,930	4,062	2,787	10,436	1,701
1956	6,459	5,822	1,541	10,278	1,714	49.1	2,076	3,935	2,814	11,616	1,857
1957	6,784	5,876	1,566	11,043	1,798	54.7	2,151	4,034	2,870	11,972	2,159
1958	6,913	6,134	1,514	11,859	2,007	58.7	2,045	3,980	2,890	11,429	2,192
1959	7,238[18] 9,571	6,299	1,537	12,302	2,794	61,7	1,950	3,860	2,967	11,092	2,300
1960	9,712	6,721	1,614	12,488	2,951	61.7	2,075	3,926	3,084	12,080	2,283
1961	9,914	6,952	1,603	12,759	3,083	62,6	2,221	3,977	3,066	12,642	2,249
1962	9,570	7,283	1,641	12,861	2,887	63.9	2,237	3,927	3,113	12,923	2,220
1963	8,553	7,020	1,656	12,641	2,734	61.2	2,364	3,782	3,092	12,600	2,170
1964	8,936	6,971	1,642	12,592	2,742	63.3	2,380	3,640	3,014	13,399	2,238
1965	9,457	7,151	1,643	13,331	2,972	72.6	2,418	3,655	3,095	12,862	2,303
1966	10,129	7,242	1,680	14,221	3,437	76.0	2,726	3,538	3,131	12,661	2,513
1967	9,772	7,520	1,709	14,480	3,835	79.9	3,014	3,318	3,252	13,059	2,607
1968	10,009	7,791	1,769	14,642	3,565	82.3	3,373	3,301	3,300	13,509	2,633
1969	9,617	7,915	1,731	14,758	3,511	81.5	3,180	3,180	3,193	13,750 12,747[21]	2,626
1970	9,354	8,238	1,704	14,948	3,549	82.9	3,664 4,456[18]	2,932	3,183	12,971	2,567
1971	9,312	8,392	1,744	15,147	3,593	83.1	4,395	2,879	3,140	13,305	2,581
1972	9,859	8,951	1,807	15,765	3,887	83.1	4,652	2,997	3,214	14,171	2,814
1973	9,690	9,354	1,803	16,243	4,110	88.3	4,940	3,033	3,274	14,402	3,105
1974	9,309	9,915	1,800	16,667	4,110	91.8	5,084	3,112	3,339	13,993	3,487
1975	9,113	10,221	1,810	16,375	4,226	90.7	5,139	3,168	3,375	13,937	3,654

Czech: Czechoslovakia U.K.: United Kingdom

See p.346 for footnotes

D6 **Output of Cows' Milk** (in thousands of tons)

NOTES

1. SOURCES:– Statistics for Denmark prior to 1929 are based on estimates in E. Jensen, *Danish Agriculture* (Copenhagen, 1937). All other statistics are taken from the official publications noted on p. xv or from the International Institute of Agriculture and the F.A.O. *Statistical Yearbooks.*

2. The basis on which the statistics are collected varies from country to country and over time, so that comparisons must be made with caution. In principle, the statistics include milk fed to young animals, except for countries marked with an asterisk.

3. Where necessary, conversions from liquid measure have been made on the assumption that the specific gravity of milk is 1.031.

FOOTNOTES

[1] Figures for 1939–45 are for deliveries to dairies only.
[2] Subsequently excludes Sub-Carpathian Russia (Ruthenia) and 12 villages in Slovakia ceded to the U.S.S.R. in 1945.
[3] The following earlier estimates are given in E. Jensen, *op. cit.* in note 1 (converted to thousands of tons):–

1861	758	1888	1,765
1871	1,090	1893	2,022
1881	1,438	1898	2,241

[4] Subsequently including South Jutland.
[5] Subsequently excluding milk produced in the towns.
[6] Excluding parts of Alsace-Lorraine annexed by Germany, and in 1943–44 Corsica.
[7] Saarland is excluded to 1935 and from 1948 to 1957 (1st line).
[8] These figures probably are only of deliveries to dairies.
[9] Statistics to 1944 are for years ended 31 May following that indicated.
[10] Subsequently including Trieste.
[11] Figures to 1940 are for years ended 30 June.
[12] There was a substantial change of territory in 1945.
[13] These figures are for the 1924 boundaries of the U.S.S.R.
[14] Statistics from 1940 (2nd line) are for the territory established after the Second World War.
[15] Previous statistics are of deliveries to dairies only.
[16] Previous statistics are for Great Britain only, and exclude milk fed to livestock.
[17] Subsequently includes West Berlin.
[18] Milk fed to livestock is not included previously.
[19] Previously including goats' milk.
[20] This break results from revisions in methods of assessment.
[21] Subsequently excluding milk fed to livestock.

D7 BUTTER OUTPUT (in thousands of metric tons)

1900–1949

	Austria	Belgium	Denmark[2]	Finland	France	Germany	Ireland	Italy	Neth'l	Norway	Russia	Sweden	Switz	U.K.
1900	...	...	...	...	...	...	...	...	...	...	...	...	...	...
1901	...	...	...	...	...	...	...	...	...	...	...	...	...	...
1902	...	...	...	...	...	...	...	...	...	...	...	...	...	...
1903	...	...	107	...	...	...	...	...	60	...	...	...	...	...
1904	...	...	...	...	...	...	...	...	54	...	...	...	...	...
1905	...	...	...	...	...	...	...	...	57	...	...	...	...	...
1906	...	...	...	...	...	...	...	...	60	...	...	...	...	...
1907	...	...	...	...	...	...	...	...	61	...	...	...	...	...
1908	...	...	...	...	...	...	...	...	62	...	...	...	...	...
1909	...	...	140	...	...	...	...	...	59	...	...	...	...	...
1910	...	...	...	...	...	...	...	...	65	...	...	...	...	...
1911	...	...	...	...	...	...	...	...	62	...	...	...	...	...
1912	...	55	...	...	...	...	...	...	67	...	...	...	...	...
1913	...	55	...	...	...	...	...	...	69	...	...	...	...	...
1914	...	...	139	...	...	...	...	...	70	...	...	...	...	...
1915	...	...	...	...	...	...	...	...	73	...	...	...	...	...
1916	...	...	...	...	...	...	...	...	74	...	...	...	...	...
1917	...	...	...	...	...	...	...	...	63	...	...	...	...	...
1918	...	...	79	...	...	...	...	...	46	...	...	...	...	...
1919	...	...	...	...	...	...	...	...	51	...	...	...	...	...
1920	...	46	110	...	...	...	...	...	57	...	...	...	...	...
1921	...	49	132	...	...	...	...	...	60	...	...	...	...	...
1922	...	49	142	...	...	...	...	...	65	...	...	...	...	...
1923	...	51	159	...	...	...	...	...	69	...	...	...	13	...
1924	...	52	174	...	...	...	...	...	73	...	...	...	12	...
1925	...	60	176	...	...	...	...	...	75	...	...	...	13	...
1926	...	61	185[3]	...	...	...	...	...	83	...	...	...	14	...
			152											
1927	...	62	162	...	...	...	...	...	85	...	...	...	13	...
1928	...	63	166	21	...	...	33	42	85	3	...	41	15	...
1929	...	60	179	24	220	310	36	42	87	4	...	48	16	...
1930	...	62	190	27	...	345	35	42	87	4	...	55	17	49[9]
														7
1931	...	61	195	28	219	380	31	43	85	6	...	54	14	...
1932	...	65	188	26	213	420	31	43	85	8	...	51	23	...
1933	...	70	185	24	218	448	34	44	85	9	...	55	24	...
1934	22	67	183	24	236	451[5]	39	45	88	9	...	62	28	12
1935	23	62	173	24	243	452	42	50	96	9	...	63	27	21
1936	23	65	180	28	...	496	43	45	100	11	...	67	25	27
1937	23	63	183	30	208	517	39	55	101	12	...	73	24	19
1938	...	64	189	33	...	508	39	58	101	15	...	80	29	21
1939	31	61[1]	183	34	196[4]	548	36	60	109	18	...	84	27	22
1940	42	...	163	24	170[4]	627	33	61	106	13	...	81	23	16
1941	45	24	124	20	154[4]	...	34	54	100	8	...	78	22	8
1942	44	28	109	14	145[4]	...	31	49	71	11	...	72	18	10
1943	43	33	125	16	149[4]	...	30	38[7]	55	9	...	79	19	9
1944	41	21	129	17	123[4]	...	29	35	49	7	...	87	19	10
						West Germany								
1945	20	19	132	25	125	...	31	37	39	4	...	94	18	8
1946	25	22	141	31	152	226	28	38	53	6[8]	...	100[8]	20	11[9]
										15		106		20
1947	21	25	125	32	143	174	26	45	53	17	...	101	16	15
1948	22	...	120	40	180	174	29	47	71	17	...	95	14	17
1949	25	26[1]	156	48	193	237[6]	35	53	84	19	...	101	15	19
		66				242								

Abbreviations used where space demands:— Neth'l: Netherlands; Switz: Switzerland; U.K.: United Kingdom

See p.349 for footnotes

D7 Butter Output (in thousands of metric tons)

1950–1975

	Austria	Belgium	Denmark[2]	Finland	France	Germany	Ireland	Italy	Neth'l	Norway	Russia	Sweden	Switz	U.K.
1950	25	72	179	53	225	259	37	58	94	19	...	111	19	25
1951	25	72	168	56	250	276	33	60	84	17	...	108	25	14
1952	29	74	154	62	235	271	33	60	74	16	...	95	22	16
1953	30	83	173	65	276	288	36	61	83	18	382	99	24	25
1954	32	91	181	65	305	303	40	62	82	14	389[8] 501	94	29	28
1955	30	91	164	59	300	290	38	65	74	16	575	86	26	25
1956	33	89	165	74	325	301	44	63	77	18	675	83	27	34
1957	40	89	175	78	345	311	50	63	77	21	754	88	29	44
1958	40	90	159	80	340	359[5] 362	48	62	92	18	779	87	31	36
1959	38	87	168	86	335	376	39	66	81	17	845	79	33	20
1960	39	89	167	93	385	406	46	67	100	20	848	84	35	45
1961	38	88	171	96	405	432	49	71	97	19	894	84	32	56
1962	39	97	167	96	405	449	50	70	102	20	940	92	35	65
1963	40	90	149	102	432	465	50	52	94	21	884	85	35	48
1964	42	85	156	105	427	472	56	56	88	20	952	80	30	28
1965	45	89	166	101	475	484	65	64	102	20	1,184	80	33	41
1966	45	85	160	101	492	489	67	70	99	24	1,157	75	34	34
1967	47	88	154	96	538	502	73	68	97	23	1,177	65	41	41
1968	46	98	160	102	575	524	78	68	118	26	1,165	66	38	54
1969	45	98	144	101	513	510	78	67	112	23	1,065	63	32	58
1970	42	92	131	87	481	494	73	67	121	19	1,067	50	29	65
1971	39	85	124	84	474	462	75	71	125	20	1,122	46	29	67
1972	43	92	136	83	539	489	78	79	163	22	1,176	56	31	96
1973	42	88	146	80	550	510	87	79	169	23	1,350	56	31	97
1974	42	92	137	78	543	508	76	71	172	21	1,360	58	34	54
1975	41	93	139	74	556	518	84	62	204	21	1,320	56	34	47

Neth'l: Netherlands Switz: Switzerland U.K.: United Kingdom

See p.349 for footnotes

D7 Butter Output (in thousands of metric tons)

NOTE

SOURCE:– Statistics for Denmark to 1926 are taken from E. Jensen, *Danish Agriculture* (Copenhagen, 1937). All others are from the International Institute of Agriculture and F.A.O. *Statistical Yearbooks,* or from the official publications noted on p. xv.

FOOTNOTES

[1] Figures for 1940 to 1949 (1st line) are of butter made in factories only.

[2] Earlier estimates are given in E. Jensen, *op cit.* above, and in E. Lindhard, 'Danmarks Landbrug, 1875–1925', *Lantbruck i Norden, 1875–1925* (Gothenburg, 1926), as follows (converted, where necessary, into thousands of tons):–

1861	24	1876	42	1888	65	1898	84
1871	36	1881	49	1893	75		

[3] This break is occasioned by a change in source.

[4] Excluding the parts of Alsace-Lorraine annexed by Germany and, in 1943–44, Corsica.

[5] Saarland is excluded to 1934 and from 1946 to 1958 (1st line).

[6] Figures from 1946 to 1949 (1st line) are for butter made in factories only.

[7] Subsequent figures are for the 1954 boundaries.

[8] Earlier figures are of butter made in factories only.

[9] Figures for 1930 (2nd line) to 1946 (1st line) are of butter made in factories only.

D8 MEAT OUTPUT (in thousands of metric tons)

1929–1975

	Austria	Belgium	Bulgaria	Czech	Denmark[4]	Finland	France[6]	Germany	Greece	Hungary	Ireland[10]	Italy
1929	...	257	...	474	...	63	1,310	3,151	...	...	...	800
1930	...	266	...	473	...	66	1,258	3,132	...	...	...	666
1931	...	277	...	483	...	70	1,229	3,232	...	...	...	703
1932	...	285	...	462	...	69	1,276	3,109	...	...	...	658
1933	...	307	46	435	...	72	1,342	3,151	...	...	...	679
1934	...	308	46	493	457	72	1,395[7] 1,610	3,515[10]	...	...	...	634
1935	...	312	45	407	424	78	1,688	3,429	...	...	158	...
1936	...	302	47	380	397	87	1,702	3,375	...	...	163	...
1937	...	316	44	...	429	93	1,648	3,586	...	...	156	...
1938	...	303	44	...	393	...	1,651[8]	3,677	...	...	148	...
1939	...	296	43	426	407	...	1,516	...	49	...	154	...
1940	...	243	43	341	379	...	984	...	...	...	166	...
1941	...	135	49	310	278[5]	...	779	...	...	...	193	...
1942	...	147	42	285	271	...	734[8]	...	...	...	179	...
1943	...	101	23	289	282	...	609	...	...	...	145	...
1944	...	90	20	257	...	...	611[8]	...	...	...	143	...
1945	...	90	31	240	332	...	822	...	50	...	143	320
								West Germany				
1946	...	129	16	282	388	...	1,293	...	54	...	146[12] 162	463
1947	...	152	25[2]	420	416	...	1,380	829	...	...	152	382
1948	...	187		259	298	...	1,500	833	...	...	135	478
1949	137	280	...	289	391[5] 370	107	1,805	1,097	64	...	140	511
1950	196	322	...	...	437	106	1,901	1,490	62	...	146	511
1951	233	322	...	...	493	118	1,835	1,697	64	...	153	491
1952	260	352	...	...	481	114	1,985	1,818	79	109	177	570
1953	280[1]	361	...	...	574	114	2,190	1,938	85	118	190	609
1954	331	373	...	312	625	135	2,370	2,916	94	118	215	620
1955	343	387	...	353	633	133	2,455	2,179	107	128[3]	183	646
1956	354	395	...	392	611	130	2,500	2,213	116	161	170	703
1957	357	390	209	413	669	136	2,515	2,352	120	166	202	700
1958	375	413	256	415[3] 709	666	133	2,470	2,461[10] 2,509	126	179	218	778
1959	376	413	231	716	713	131	2,673	2,519	134	376	224	853
1960	391	444	210	733	753	129	2,780	2,600	139	354	247	898
1961	410	441	243	761	756	131	2,928	2,709	140	393	289	1,010
1962	434	473	262	775	811	150	3,093	2,928	152	410	285	1,056
1963	466	515	242	775	826	157	2,994[9] 2,692	2,964	160	399	293	979
1964	436	441	263	831	845	167	2,605	3,007	169	391	280	979
1965	439	473	296	913	899	166	2,809	3,023	188	417	297	970
1966	435	517	311	881	928	159	2,862	3,065	206	406	310	1,049
1967	450	568	327	925	956	182	3,017	3,137	206	407	377	1,109 1,395[23]
1968	403	606	352	978	925	175	3,056	3,370	208	469	360	1,560
1969	410	628	326	925	881	201	2,869	3,406	221	439	386	1,610
1970	414	728	301	955	911	213	2,971	3,521	233	438	400	1,725
1971	437	767	324	1,005	960	242	3,152	3,673	246	501	437	1,782
1972	435	795	364	1,066	937	239	3,060	3,499	265	538	410	1,746
1973	437	841	361	1,083	960	223	3,048	3,486	287	530 834[25]	393	1,800
1974	475	921	352	1,141	983	245	3,416	3,754	335	940	514	1,860
1975	482	892	427	1,176	971	240	3,416	3,664	317	995	546	1,799

Czech: Czechoslovakia

See p.352 for footnotes

D8 Meat Output (in thousands of metric tons)

1929–1975

	Neth'l	Norway[14]	Poland	Portugal[15]	Rom	Russia[18] (million tons)	Spain	Sweden	Switz	U.K.[22]	Yugoslavia
1929	411	85	582	44	209	5.8	189	139	155	1,221	...
1930	412	...	586	44	187	4.3	184	159	151	1,154	...
1931	503	93	702	...	193	3.9	171	174	151	1,157	...
1932	512	...	690	51	169	2.8	161	174	159	1,217	...
1933	447	94	649	...	196	2.3	150	171	171	1,274	
1934	437	102	647	53	228	2.0	147	185	173	1,316	...
1935	408	97	683	51	230	2.3	152	177	173	1,383	...
1936	413	98	738	58	229	3.7	...	189	158	1,402	...
1937	369	100	800	52	220	3.0	...	212	154	1,360[22]	...
1938	365	101	...	56[15]	237	4.5	...	219	163	...	...
1939	419	63	...	68	234[17]	5.1	...	234	198	...	...
1940	347	64	...	67	172	3.9[19] 4.7	74	251	200	...	...
1941	240	...	...	60	81	...	65	214	170	...	...
1942	188	...	...	43	99[17]	...	55	113[21] 149	136	...	...
1943	...	...	...	49	119[17]	...	85	188	132	...	...
1944	...	...	...	63	...[17]	...	...	...	126	...	...
1945	...	...	...	61	34[16]	2.6	...	...	118	934	...
1946	174	73	...	49	...	3.1	62	246	119	901	...
1947	194	82	...	51	...	2.5	54	262	141	762	...
1948	158[12]	68	...	73	...	3.1	82	242	137	787	...
1949	219	90	...	81	...	3.8	110[20]	277	165	952	...
1950	331	102	...	75	...	4.9	432	291	179	1,133	...
1951	381	99	...	72	...	4.7	436	312	176	1,157	...
1952	370	103	...	78[16] 91	...	5.2	416	308	188	1,293	367
1953	397	100	...	93	...	5.8	398	305	198	1,348	310
1954	422	106	1,093	102	...	6.3	421	313	197	1,653	332
1955	467	122	1,213	99	...	6.3	413	334	198	1,559	364
1956	470	116	1,364	96[13] 141	...	6.6	424	308	210	1,637	382
1957	496	117	1,496	142	...	7.4	449	326	220	1,680	361
1958	489	112	1,607	136	...	7.7	451	353	217	1,718	367
1959	501	116	1,479	148	...	8.7	483	364	221	1,673	431
1960	583[13] 680	120	1,503	156	...	8.7	540	337	236	1,713	488
1961	640	127	1,623	162	...	8.7	532	338	246	1,867	475
1962	697	133	1,653	162	...	9.5	522	374	254	1,945	509
1963	752	121	1,571	150	260	10.2	587	375	255	1,981	490
1964	696	121	1,565	147	277	8.3	670	364	260	1,961	536
1965	786	130	1,733	162	302	10.0	577	368	276	1,993	622
1966	793	131 141[24]	1,785	173	322	10.7	699	395	284	2,011	549
1967	864	139	1,817	160	395	11.5	766	397	289	1,983	598
1968	944	144	1,826	184	425	11.6	793	397	320	1,988	647
1969	935	152	1,882	217	408	11.8	822	401	328	1,976	596
1970	1,065	149	1,825	210	380	12.3	940	398	337	2,100	619
1971	1,155	153	1,841	200	410 809[26]	13.3	935	401	350	2,149	675
1972	1,099	158	2,064	206	864	13.6	901	404	355	2,122	622
1973	1,130	163	2,270	221	985	13.5	1,104	394	370	2,073	625
1974	1,293	175	2,533	229	1,060	14.6	1,281	425	387	2,310	748
1975	1,303	172	2,569	228	1,046	15.0	1,204	431	381	2,301	766

Neth'l: Netherlands Rom: Romania Switz: Switzerland U.K.: United Kingdom

See p.352 for footnotes

D8 **Meat Output** (in thousands of metric tons)

NOTES

1. SOURCES:– International Institute of Agriculture and F.A.O. *Statistical Yearbooks,* and the official publications noted on p. xv.

2. W.G. Hoffman, *Das Wachstum der Deutschen Wirtschaft seit der Mitte des 19 Jahrhunderts* (Berlin, etc., 1965) gives the following estimates for Germany for the period 1816–1938, relating to the territory of Imperial Germany in 1914 for the period 1816–1913 (except that Alsace-Lorraine is only included from 1871), and to the boundaries of the day for 1924–39 (in thousands of metric tons):–

1816	338	1845	761	1862	1,019	1879	1,515	1896	2,482	1913	3,183
1819	368	1846	779	1863	1,093	1880	1,515	1897	2,523	1924	2,602
1822	390	1847	704	1864	1,239	1881	1,507	1898	2,611	1925	2,699
1825	453	1848	730	1865	1,195	1882	1,581	1899	2,764	1926	2,786
1928	458	1849	766	1866	1,189	1883	1,641	1900	2,803	1927	3,106
1831	485	1850	838	1867	1,113	1884	1,745	1901	2,712	1928	3,406
1834	545	1851	803	1868	1,153	1885	1,774	1902	2,575	1919	3,331
1835	611	1852	740	1869	1,198	1886	1,822	1903	2,704	1930	3,335
1836	641	1853	756	1870	1,172	1887	1,889	1904	2,901	1931	3,513
1837	624	1854	752	1871	1,245	1888	2,014	1905	2,878	1932	3,369
1838	637	1855	715	1872	1,242	1889	1,934	1906	2,847	1933	3,391
1839	659	1856	808	1873	1,317	1890	1,915	1907	2,835	1934	3,758
1840	664	1857	889	1874	1,440	1891	1,899	1908	3,177	1935	3,616
1841	696	1858	974	1875	1,443	1892	1,930	1909	3,199	1936	3,495
1842	785	1859	957	1876	1,453	1893	2,044	1910	3,200	1937	3,732
1843	641	1860	1,012	1877	1,389	1894	2,051	1911	3,357	1938	3,776
1844	687	1861	991	1878	1,480	1895	2,216	1912	3,274		

FOOTNOTES

[1] Figures from 1954 are ones which were revised later. From the size of the break here it appears that there were substantial revisions. The unrevised figure for 1954 is 285.

[2] Previous figures are of slaughterings in towns only.

[3] Previous figures are of commercial production only.

[4] Earlier estimates are given in E. Lindhard, 'Danmarks Landbrug, 1875–1925', *Landbrukt i Norden, 1975–1925* (Gothenburg, 1926), as follows (in thousands of tons):–

1871	116	1888	146	1903	242	1918	175
1876	124	1893	164	1909	261	1923	357
1881	129	1898	194	1914	359	1924	365

[5] Figures for 1942 to 1949 (1st line) include allowance for the weight of animals exported alive.

[6] Excluding horsemeat.

[7] Earlier figures are of meat on which slaughter tax was paid only.

[8] Figures for 1939–44 exclude the parts of Alsace-Lorraine annexed by Germany, and those for 1943–44 exclude Corsica.

[9] Earlier figures include lard.

[10] Up to 1934 and from 1947 to 1957 (1st line) Saarland is excluded. West Berlin is also excluded from 1947 to 1957 (1st line).

[11] Figures to 1944 are for years ended 31 May.

[12] Subsequent statistics do not include meat from imported animals.

[13] Subsequently including lard.

[14] Figures to 1940 are for years ended 30 June.

[15] Mainland only up to 1938.

[16] Earlier statistics are of slaughterings in public slaughterhouses only.

[17] Southern Dobrudja was ceded to Bulgaria in 1940. Bessarabia and northern Bukovina were ceded to the U.S.S.R. in 1940, but were reconquered temporarily in 1943, and may be included in the 1943 and 1944 figures. Northern Transylvania was ceded to Hungary in 1940 but regained by 1946.

[18] Earlier statistics are available as follows (in millions of tons):—

1913 (1924 boundaries)	4.1
1917	4.3
1921	3.3
1924	3.4
1928	4.9

[19] Figures from 1940 (2nd line) are for the territory established after the Second World War.

[20] Earlier figures are for commerical production in 50 provincial capitals only.

[21] Earlier figures relate only to inspected slaughterhouses.

[22] Figures to 1937 are for Great Britain only.

[23] Subsequent statistics include estimates of unregistered slaughterings.

[24] Revised figures in 1973 and later *Arbok*.

[25] There was a great increase in the recorded production of pig meat.

[26] Later statistics are from revised series published in the 1973 and later *Yearbooks*.

D9 LANDINGS OF FISH (in thousands of metric tons)

1860–1914

	Denmark	France	Germany	Iceland	Italy	Netherlands	Norway	Sweden	United Kingdom
1860	...	...	...	...	38	...	...	...	...
1861	...	...	...	...	40	...	...	...	...
1862	...	...	...	...	42	...	...	...	...
1863	...	...	...	...	42	...	...	...	...
1864	...	...	...	...	44	...	...	...	...
1865	...	...	...	...	43	...	...	...	...
1866	...	...	...	...	47	...	21	...	...
1867	...	...	...	...	47	...	22	...	...
1868	...	...	...	...	47	...	20	...	...
1869	...	...	...	...	47	...	19	...	...
1870	...	...	...	...	47	8	25	...	...
1871	...	...	...	...	47	10	25	...	...
1872	...	...	...	...	50	8	23	...	...
1873	...	...	...	...	47	12	25	...	...
1874	...	61	...	...	47	11	23	...	...
1875	...	57	...	...	47	10	24	...	...
1876	...	67	...	...	47	11	22	...	...
1877	...	67	...	...	51	14	29	...	...
1878	...	...	...	...	55	11	21	...	...
1879	...	71	...	...	55	17	21	...	...
1880	...	76	29	...	60	22	23	...	...
1881	...	...	29	...	62	20	20	...	...
1882	...	61	29	...	62	24	20	...	...
1883	...	78	30	...	61	24	24	...	...
1884	...	92	30	...	65	34	24	...	...
1885	...	93	31	...	72	29	19	...	...
1886	...	93	31	...	74	38	22	...	...
1887	...	...	32	...	73	37[2] / 48	15	...	...
1888	...	88	32	...	78	41	22	...	592
1889	...	100	34	...	84	54	23	...	653
1890	...	93	34	...	85	56	22	...	649
1891	...	...	32	...	89	43	26	...	611
1892	...	...	40	...	91	71	25	...	636
1893	...	...	41	...	91	67	24	...	689
1894	...	97[1] / 118	48	...	95	65	23	...	714
1895	...	128	62	...	88	58	22	...	715
1896	...	181	71	...	92	64	22	...	747
1897	...	158	59	...	98	41	25	...	706
1898	...	162	88	...	94	63	21	...	805
1899	...	133	67	...	80	34	24	...	760
1900	...	148	97	...	82	53	29	...	745
1901	...	156	122	...	77	70	28	...	805
1902	...	132	120	...	72	93	29	...	913
1903	...	128	144	...	83	107	29	...	943
1904	...	139	149	...	80	100	27	...	1,030
1905	...	137	140	46	82	76	31	...	1,024
1906	...	148	155	49	87	93	33	...	1,044
1907	...	137	179	55	90	107	39	...	1,205
1908	...	165	181	59	103	86	35[3] / 421	...	1,152
1909	...	151	185	56	124	101	522	...	1,136
1910	44	170	194	61	118	98	529	...	1,162
1911	53	129	190	66	109	86	581	...	1,198
1912	58	111	204	87	104	66	655	...	1,200
1913	61	127	217	93	100	99	597	...	1,224
1914	52	82	...	93	90	65	618	107	896

Abbreviations used where space demands:– F I: Faroe Islands; E Ger: East Germany; Neth'l: Netherlands; U.K.: United Kingdom

See p.356 for footnotes

D9 Landings of Fish (in thousands of metric tons)

1915–1969

	Denmark	F I	France	Germany	E Ger	Iceland	Italy	Neth'l	Norway	Poland	Portugal	Spain	Sweden	U.K.
1915	67	...	65	...	...	109	71	82	575	...	...	...	31	440
1916	93	...	65	...	...	128	64	95	515	...	...	...	45	418
1917	63	...	65	...	...	104	55	..	541	...	...	...	48	396
1918	65	...	67	...	...	98	66	13	611	...	...	...	84	445
1919	89	...	115	...	...	128	88	111	657	...	...	...	...	868
1920	64	...	126	...	...	137	102	86[2]	484	...	...	...	97	1,096
1921	62	...	111[4] 230	...	...	140	112[8]	84	438	...	...	...	68	856
1922	51	...	223	...	...	183	120	75	563	...	...	...	69	923[10]
1923	68	17	241	...	...	184	114	85	571	...	...	...	88	862
1924	69	16	251	274	...	254	109	108	617	...	...	...	75	1,054
1925	79	17	253	261	...	269	107	86	622	...	...	...	72	983
1926	76	20	267	294	...	201	113	102[2] 201	799	...	...	268	77	971
1927	84	21	270	298	...	323	118	213	792	...	165	231	80	1,021
1928	95	24	257	324	...	342	124	246	894	...	200	254	88	1,061
1929	89	27	286	337	...	348	129	231	976	...	150	182	82	1,111
1930	93	32	291	368	...	417	135	243	994	...	185	286	87	1,152
1931	88	31	307	388[6] 347	...	363	140	259	740	6	202	309	88	1,041
1932	90	29	309	339	...	345	144	210	910	9	175	320	87	1,025
1933	85	27	317	387	...	398	146	195	1,055	14	155[9]	322	102	985
1934	89	23	333	401	...	371	148	219	683	15	217	388	101	981
1935	87	21	294	478	...	310	167	197	924	17	223	...	107	1,044
1936	87	19	319	599	...	301	170	233	1,031	23	203	...	112	1,095
1937	88	28	358	672	...	368	173	263	904	14	190	...	121	1,142
1938	87	29	444[5]	718	...	352	175	236	1,065	13	241	299	144	1,097[11] 816
1939	101	...	187	542	...	307	177	171	1,043	...	201	370	133	607
1940	119	...	136	...	...	410	160	...	1,081	...	195	440	90	200
1941	156	...	147	...	...	309	127	96	811	...	192	435	113	144
1942	163	...	117	...	...	412	100	78	755	...	201	453	125	178
1943	192	...	93	...	...	463	85[8]	71	643	...	254	445	144	178
1944	173	...	81[5]	...	...	546	79	...	648	...	251	482	129	192
				West Germany										
1945	...	...	214[6]	...	...	366	100	_[6]	756[12]	3	244[6]	553	153[6]	324[11] 522
1946	197	...	245	265	...	413	115[6] 160	190	945	23	306	594	184	944
1947	206	97	317	302	...	506	160	295	1,196	40	282	581	179	1,037[11] 1,172
1948	226	92	438	409	...	516	157	294	1,504	47	292	547	194	1,206
1949	258	100	435	501	...	437	179[8]	264	1,297	49	281	598	182	1,159
1950	251	98	432	553	...	386	186	258	1,468	66	307	604	187	989
1951	293	93	464	679	...	440	185	294	1,839	88	307	619	183	1,086
1952	324	87	468	663	...	437	212	314	1,815	92	363	617	204	1,105
1953	343	89	497	764	62	458	208	343	1,557	107	425	643	200	1,122
1954	359	89	479	704	63	480	218	339	2,068	118	439	666	201	1,070
1955	425	106	497	815	69	518	218	320	1,813	127	425	770	220	1,100
1956	463	116	516	801	75	548	220	298	2,201	139	472	762	197	1,050
1957	533	106	492	792	97	517	212[6] 248	301	1,746	139	470	777	222	1,015
1958	598	107	501	743	93	605	246	314	1,442	145	456	845	238	999
1959	674	87	556	768	106	655	254	320	1,575	162	428	859	268	989
1960	581	109	571	674	114	610	250	315	1,543	184	475	970	254	924
1961	638	120	568[7] 751	619	130	716	282	346	1,523	186	500	988	267	893
1962	785	144	744	633	150	833	257	322	1,332	180	526	1,108	293	944
1963	848	137	742	647	189	785	290	361	1,388	227	540	1,332	341	961
1964	871	139	780	624[6]	225	973	325	388	1,623	264	604	1,213	387	974
1965	841	145	768	633	231	1,199	354	377	2,312	298	554	1,355	380	1,047
1966	851	165	805	657	223	1,240	369	353	2,872	335	506	1,380	330	1,068
1967	1,070	173	820	662	288	898	373	315	3,266	339	540	1,460	351	1,026
1968	1,467	166	803	683	302	601	364	323	2,856	407	506	1,533	328	1,040
1969	1,275	176	701	652	316	690	371	323	2,491	408	457	1,522	278	1,083

See p.356 for footnotes

D9 Landings of Fish (in thousands of metric tons)

1970–1975

	Denmark	F I	France	W Germany	E Ger	Iceland	Italy	Neth'l	Norway	Poland	Portugal	Spain	Sweden	U.K.
1970	1,226	208	764	613	322	734	387	301	2,980	469	498	1,539	295	1,099
1971	1,401	207	758	508	338	685	405	321	3,075	518	463	1,505	238	1,107
1972	1,443	208	797	419	336	727	430	348	3,186	544	442	1,531	227	1,082
1973	1,465	247	823	478	365	902	402	344	2,987	580	467	1,573	227	1,133
1974	1,835	247	808	526	363	945	426	326	2,645	679	429	1,513	214	1,087
1975	1,767	286	806	442	375	995	406	351	2,550	801	369	1,533	215	980

NOTES

1. SOURCES.– France to 1920, Iceland, Italy, Norway, and the U.K. from the official publications noted on p. xv. Germany from W.G. Hoffman, *Das Wachstum der Deutschen Wirtschaft seit der Mitte des 19 Jahrhunderts* (Berlin, 1965); Netherlands to 1920 from data supplied by the Netherlands Central Office of Statistics; all others from League of Nations and United Nations *Statistical Yearbooks.*

2. The definitions of fish landings vary from country to country, but except as indicated in footnotes they are consistent for each country. For France prior to 1961, the Netherlands since 1946, and the U.K. throughout, fish landed at foreign ports are not included; and for the Netherlands since 1946 fish landed at Dutch ports by foreign ships are included. Otherwise the statistics relate to fish caught by the ships of the country concerned.

FOOTNOTES

[1] Figures to 1894 (1st line) are of cod, herring and mackerel only.
[2] Statistics to 1887 (1st line) are of pickled herring only. From 1887 (2nd line) to 1920 they are of all salted herring. Subsequently all kinds of fish are included, but from 1921 to 1926 (1st line) they exclude coastal fisheries.
[3] Statistics to 1908 (1st line) are of the value of the catch in million kroner.
[4] Figures from 1894 (2nd line) to 1921 (1st line) are of cod, herring, mackerel, tunny, and sardines only.
[5] Figures for 1939–44 exclude some molluscs.
[6] There is a change in the method of estimation.
[7] Subsequently includes that part of the catch which was landed abroad.
[8] Figures to 1921 apply to the 1871 boundaries. For 1922-43 they apply to the 1924 boundaries, and from 1944 to the boundaries of 1954, except that Trieste is not included until 1950.
[9] Previous statistics exclude that part of the catch which was recorded in numbers not in weight.
[10] Subsequent statistics do not include southern Ireland. Statistics for Great Britain alone in 1922 and 1923 were respectively 902 and 860 thousand tons.
[11] Statistics for 1938 (2nd line) to 1945 (1st line) are for England and Wales only, and from 1945 (2nd line) to 1947 (1st line) they are for Great Britain.
[12] Subsequent statistics are converted to round fresh weight.

D10 EXTERNAL TRADE IN CORN (in thousands of metric tons or hectolitres)

1750–1799

	Great Britain[1] I (a)	Great Britain[1] E (a)	Sweden[17] I (a)[31]
1750	. .	2,764	3,439
1751	. .	1,929	2,030
1752	—	1,251	2,680
1753	—	876	4,369
1754	. .	1,039	4,691
1755	—	689	7,091
1756	. .	300	6,024
1757	413	35	3,843
1758	58	26	3,109
1759	. .	663	2,004
1760	. .	1,146	1,411
1761	—	1,286	1,638
1762	. .	858	5,267
1763	. .	1,251	5,988
1764	. .	1,155	9,816
1765	305	486	8,102
1766	32	480	5,875
1767	1,449	15	6,141
1768	1,015	20	8,097
1769	12	150	6,603
1770	. .	218	5,036
1771	9	29	3,815
1772	73	20	7,891
1773	166	23	5,734
1774	841	47	2,200
1775	1,632	265	1,060
1776	61	614	4,058
1777	678	256	5,339
1778	308	410	5,094
1779	15	646	5,717
1780	12	652	4,537
1781	465	300	9,274
1782	236	422	10,813
1783	1,699	151	15,052
1784	631	259	15,839
1785	323	387	11,745
1786	148	596	11,361
1787	172	352	8,135
1788	433	241	7,328
1789	329	407	9,350
1790	649	90	6,622
1791	1,364	207	4,429
1792	64	873	3,074
1793	1,425	224	3,306
1794	954	451	3,219
1795	913	55	728
1796	2,557	73	2,448
1797	1,344	160	5,394
1798	1,155	175	10,091
1799	1,347	113	7,176

1800–1849

	Austria-Hungary[2] I (b)	Austria-Hungary[2] E (b)	Denmark[3] I (a)	Denmark[3] E (a)	France[4] I (a)	France[4] E (a)
1800	...	...	...	...	...	...
1801	...	...	...	...	...	...
1802	...	...	...	...	...	...
1803	...	...	...	...	...	...
1804	...	...	...	...	...	...
1805	...	...	...	...	...	...
1806	...	...	...	...	...	...
1807	...	...	...	...	...	...
1808	...	...	...	...	...	...
1809	...	...	...	...	...	...
1810	...	...	...	...	...	....
1811	...	...	...	...	...	...
1812	...	...	...	...	...	...
1813	...	...	...	...	...	...
1814	...	...	...	...	...	...
1815	...	...	...	...	...	...
1816	...	...	...	...	...	...
1817	...	...	...	...	...	...
1818	...	...	...	...	...	...
1819	...	...	...	...	1,305	186
1820	...	...	...	1,745	662	173
1821	...	...	...	2,514	609	63
1822	...	...	...	2,041	1	72
1823	...	...	...	2,010	1	90
1824	...	...	...	2,814	1	218
1825	...	...	...	2,925	951	799
1826	...	...	...	2,560	90	541
					(000 tons)	
1827	...	...	...	2,428	5	20
1828	...	...	...	3,268	88	16
1829	...	...	...	2,308	130	17
1830	...	...	....	2,089	154	10
1831	...	...	...	1,877	85	20
1832	...	...	...	2,291	335	17
1833	...	...	...	3,021	1	18
1834	...	...	...	3,511	—	20
1835	...	...	...	2,560	—	21
1836	...	...	...	1,966	17	23
1837	...	...	...	2,239	21	25
1838	...	...	...	2,416[3] / 1,168	8	49
1839	...	...	...	1,769	88	59
1840	...	...	...	2,131	168	15
1841	...	...	...	1,784	12	64
1842	37	78	...	1,333	42	64
1843	74	67	138	1,798	152	22
1844	67	126	57	2,559	186	28
1845	65	73	62	2,674	56	33
1846	66	57	51	2,975	369	18
1847	98	84	366	2,758	757	15
1848	71	8	17	3,801	94	144
1849	...	...	40	4,430	. .	222

Abbreviations used throughout this table: I Imports E Exports (a) (000 hectolitres) (b) (000 tons)

See p.364 for footnotes

D10 External Trade in Corn (in thousands of metric tons or hectolitres)

1800–1849

	Norway[5]	Russia[6]	Sweden[17]		U.K.: Great Britain	
	I (b)	E (a)	I (a)[31]	E (a)[31]	I (a)	E (a)
1800	...	...	1,824	...	3,680	64
1801	...	...	8,692	...	4,145	81
1802	...	...	4,452	...	1,885	433
1803	...	...	3,696	...	1,088	224
1804	...	...	4,979	...	1,341	183
1805	...	...	1,140	...	2,679	227
1806	...	...	3,439	...	902	87
1807	...	...	1,798	...	1,178	73
1808	...	...	779	...	247	285
1809	...	...	4,409	...	1,327	90
1810	...	...	3,701	...	4,559	221
1811	...	...	4,600	...	977	285
1812	...	...	6,245	...	847	134
1813	...	...	13,061	...	1,626	...
1814	...	...	6,931 ----[17]	...	2,481	323
1815	...	...	2,853	63	1,117	663
1816	...	...	3,004	12	966	355
1817	...	...	2,467	1	3,171	925
1818	...	...	7,423	14	4,928	172
1819	...	...	5,853	55	1,821	131
1820	...	...	423	378	2,897	276
1821	...	...	60	425	2,057	582
1822	...	...	372	62	1,487	465
1823	...	...	29	11	1,233	425
1824	...	...	49	218	1,286	180
1825	...	...	39	115	2,292	113
1826	...	...	2,305	44	2,609	58
1827	...	...	5,120	137	2,071	166
1828	53	...	11	1,338	4,102	221
1829	[49][5]	...	13	675	6,371	218
1830	...	...	432	344	6,417	108
1831	...	...	1,553	664	8,343	192
1832	...	...	1,077	125	3,648	844
1833	...	...	51	2,013	3,392	279
1834	...	...	23	1,985	2,853	463
1835	72	...	739	1,390	2,185	390
1836	87	...	60	633	2,505	748
1837	108	...	1,182	372	3,226	896
1838	89	...	8,504	1	5,594	463
1839	110	...	1,911	496	9,050	125
1840	83	...	133	830	7,351 ----[7] 635	253
1841	78	...	757	1,680	596	...
1842	81	468	1,506	1,854	661	...
1843	76	586	463	983	251	...
1844	100	761	379	1,709	477	...
1845	59	699	744	4,468	354	...
1846	68	1,115	1,359	2,675	647	...
1847	83	2,755	153	2,665	1,749	...
1848	109	1,037	70	4,038	1,238	...
1849	117	925	317	6,081	1,758	...

See p.364 for footnotes

D10 **External Trade in Corn** (in thousands of metric tons or hectolitres)

1850–1899

	Austria-Hungary[2] I	Austria-Hungary[2] E	Denmark[3] I	Denmark[3] E	France[4] I	France[4] E	Germany[11] I
	(b)	(b)	(b)	(b)	(b)	(b)	(b)
1850	...	...	83	4,083	...	326	...
1851	156	56	152	3,288	8	364	...
1852	235	39	95	3,531	20	177	...
1853	[275][8]	[24][8]	180	3,437	359	78	...
1854	332	58	194	3,570	418	19	...
1855	225	122	124	4,575	276	14	...
1856	138	233	198	3,104	658	13	...
1857	125	169	208	3,364	291	30	...
1858	133[2]	117[2]	129	3,302	137	484	...
1859	123	108	115	4,003	105	613	...
1860	102[2]	352[2]	267	3,217	55	362	692
1861	111	435	482	3,662	1,027	92	547
1862	120	418	442	3,123	472	42	671
1863	116	212	411[3]	4,511[3]	185	62	360
1864	176	216	121	3,242	61	154	384[11]
1865	92[2]	487[2]	193	4,980	26	358	516[12]
1866	104	429	279	4,018	63	515	536
1867	105	1,029	333	3,813	694	43	1,357
1868	121	1,385	565	2,695	831	51	1,284
1869	110	819	393	3,359	139	66	876
1870	155	427	366	4,766	424[10]	31[10]	1,037[11]
1871	190	632	308	4,104	1,044	12	1,077[12]
1872	462	281	289	4,623	421	312	1,170
1873	619	340	675	3,241	519	223	1,639
1874	743	446	956	2,640	821	171	2,010
1875	202	592	882	2,732	354	492	1,891
1876	289	651	1,156	2,637	534	253	2,571
1877	529	947	2,473	1,512	349	388	3,155
1878	488	897	1,960	2,752	1,398	62	2,844
1879	521	961	1,643[7]	3,626[7]	2,234	33	3,217
			234	289			
1880	786	730	159	307	2,040	31	1,642
1881	652	687	143	192	1,319	33	1,878
1882	663	1,117	138	175	1,341	22	2,090
1883	528	755	213	155	1,073	28	2,175
1884	555	589	217	114	1,127	19	2,715
1885	651	695	197	150	688	20	2,195
1886	250	643	167	160	746	14	1,443
1887	216	780	235	129	924	8	2,025
1888	94	1,015	285	114	1,175	15	1,713
1889	97	794	281	88	1,185	17	2,801
1890	183	774	289	84	1,101	13	3,037
1891	109	764	255	90	2,066	10	3,002
1892	102	770	264	121	1,945	19	3,233
1893	203	852	317	95	1,026	30	2,783
1894	522	635	487	94	1,279	38	3,890
1895	395	485	470	45	500	21	3,795
1896	279	663	452[9]	66[9]	190	27	5,028
			447	52			
1897	678	576	619	50	549	28	4,914
1878	1,246	512	633	58	2,009	60	5,581
1899	296	665	650	61	159	31	4,922

See p.364 for footnotes

D10 External Trade in Corn (in thousands of metric tons or hectolitres)

1850–1899

	Italy[13]	Norway[5]	Romania[15]	Russia[6]	Spain[16]	Sweden[17]		U.K.
	I	I	E	E	I	I	E	I
	(b)	(b)	(b)	(b)	(b)	(a)[31]	(a)	(b)
1850	...	113	...	992	...	2,074	5,041	1,450
1851	...	105	....	1,153	...	5,721	3,278	1,551
1852	...	101	...	1,824	...	4,903	2,169	1,246
1853	...	95	...	2,556	...	2,384	3,790	1,712
1854	...	73	...	637	...	754	6,932	1,291
1855	...	88	...	145	...	702	10,705	1,060
1856	...	102	...	1,713	...	4,877[17]	6,710	1,577
1857	...	133	...	1,770	...	4,863	10,242	1,555
1858	...	100	...	2,142	...	1,169	15,787	1,876
1859	...	114	...	2,367	...	748	17,197	1,715
1860	...	127	...	2,343	...	1,216	16,499	2,401
1861	214	154	...	2,342[6] 2,437	...	6,959 63[7] 78[17]	19,363 94[7] 135[17]	2,709
1862	323	122	...	2,716	...	54	106	3,240
1863	450	150	...	1,744	...	54	150	2,590
1864	764	162	...	...	...	72[17]	149	2,030
1865	443	135	...	2,535	...	28	196	2,215
1866	379[13]	136	...	3,097	,...	46	167	2,782
1867	282	110	...	3,807	...	122	217	2,961
1868	224	154	...	3,090	...	148	129	3,033
1869	233	160	...	2,592	...	130	174	3,624
1870	270[14][13]	172	...	5,212	63	62	323	3,338
1871	290[14]	129	...	5,825	65	32	326	3,845
1872	330	152	...	4,065	...	72	262	4,737
1873	269	156	...	5,147	- -	94	253	4,259
1874	364	183	...	6,697	16	199	254	4,163
1875	311	188	...	5,703	22	133	242	4,867
1876	329	193	...	6,402	40	129	316	5,355
1877	210[13]	241	...	7,590	9	276	229	5,620
1878	346	210	...	10,621	60	226	307	6,021
1879	488	190	...	10,022	121	177	366	6,135
1880	230	191	...	5,897	30	149	322	5,996
1881	147	211	...	6,020	20	211	226	5,627
1882	165	190	...	8,639	276	223	292	5,673
1883	232	200	1,310	8,869	238	293	304	6,476
1884	355	197	1,034	9,223[7]	99	281	202	4,977
1885	724	229	1,375	5,301	112	328	251	6,170
1886	936	202	1,308[15]	4,258	150	244	285	5,367
1887	1,016	198	1,573	6,028	314	273	268	5,876
1888	670	256	1,673	8,394	243	223	191	6,234
1889	873	251	1,990	7,173	145	227	119	6,510
1890	645	220	1,937	6,425	160	211	72	6,773
1891	464	251	1,754	5,975	155	190	183	6,462
1892	697	206	1,709	2,945	139	238	112	6,616
1893	861	249	2,507	6,103	419	259	217	6,867
1894	487	268	1,805	9,694	425	371	139	7,707
1895	658	272	1,744	8,671	203	251	75	7,866
1896	737[13]	298	2,299	7,553	187	237	62	8,223
1897	456	296	1,692	7,227	142	193	21	7,702
1898	915	316	2,180	6,922	59	244	40	8,252
1899	516	338	874	4,907	373	342	39	8,240

See p.364 for footnotes

D10 External Trade in Corn (in thousands of metric tons or hectolitres)

1900–1949

	Austria-Hungary		Denmark[3]		France[4]		Germany[11]
	I	E	I	E	I	E	I
	(b)	(b)	(b)	(b)	(b)	(b)	(b)
1900	298	529	593	60	159	40	4,815
1901	379	533	548	53	194	27	5,503
1902	313	660	622	44	288	24	5,468
1903	388	770	558	51	505	18	5,753
1904	751	449	697	51	236	25	5,064
1905	758	616	631	57	201	44	6,375
1906	266	569	809	47	320	46	6,541[11]
1907	138	513	681	53	382	39	6,753
1908	131	417	567	61	85	52	5,393
1909	956	351	653	38	149	81	6,513
1910	438	390	635	75	653	37	6,765
1911	593	111	674	86	2,170	25	8,110
1912	844	212	759	93	727	40	7,390
1913	898	457	863	89	1,570	31	7,561
1914	882	154	578	91	1,790	92	...
1915	...	...	936	- -	2,105	157	...
1916	...	...	590	- -	2,921	48	...
1917	...	...	298	- -	2,406	37	...
1918	...	...	3	17	2,014[10]	25[10]	...
1919	...	...	252	12	2,382	35	...[11 20]
	Austria						
1920	321		269	22	2,415	33	1,482
1921	592		543	55	1,120	46	4,921[21]
1922	408		644	49	679	83	3,294
1923	468		948	26	1,429	85	...
1924	603		1,042[9]	72[9]	1,496	114	...
			1,063	72			
1925	646		941	61	1,223	15	3,962
1926	677		748	104	485	64	5,158
1927	658		1,288	65	2,178	11	7,791
1928	600		1,173	77	1,461	6	6,183
1929	636		815	79	1,431	6	4,832
1930	764		1,414	46	1,070	914	3,450
1931	922		1,897	46	2,388	626	2,585
1932	851		1,616	23	1,753	186	3,002
1933	910		1,207	33	488	194	1,517
1934	913		852	100	537	466	1,687
1935	721		824	76	545	916	1,000[20]
1936	679		852[9]	81[9]	438	400	353
			843	81			
1937	856		985[3]	178[3]	326	87	387
			996	178			
1938	692[2]		667	121	413[10]	135[10]	391
1939	...		343	94	526	801	...
1940	...		260	3	662	305	...
1941	...		5	29	427	19	...
1942	...		49	17	211	462	...
1943	...		- -	56	- -	301	...
1944	...		- -	11	150[10]	329[10]	...
							West Germany[20 22]
1945	...		- -	38	664	66	...
1946	...		42	87	2,000	43	...
1947	...		106	120	558	122	...
1948	354		287	221	1,180	83	...
1949	770		450[18]	175[18]	645[4]	268[4]	...
				195	1,780	388	

See p.364 for footnotes

D10 External Trade in Corn (in thousands of metric tons or hectolitres)

1900–1949

	Hungary[24]	Italy[13]	Norway[5]	Romania[15]	Russia[6]	Spain[16]	Sweden[17]	U.K.[1]
	E	I	I	E	E	I	I	I
	(b)	(b)	(b)	(b)	(b)	(b)	(b)	(b)
1900	...	732	318	1,376	5,947	223	374	8,128
1901	...	1,046	313	2,172[15] 2,300	6,702	144	246	8,404
1902	...	1,178	360	2,612	8,526	70	431	8,462
1903	...	1,173	455	2,408	9,532	91	435	9,200
1904	...	806	391	1,520	9,435	223	472	9,244
1905	...	1,172	383	2,385	7,056	885	381	9,055
1906	...	1,374[13]	379	3,156	8,506	526	345	8,986
1907	...	933	356	3,108	6,646	117	272	9,178
1908	...	790	356	1,698	5,605	79	352[17]	7,995
1909	...	1,332	348	2,135	11,226	96	378	8,972
1910	...	1,442	377	2,137	12,639	161	401	9,044
1911	...	1,391	387	3,859[15]	10,488	134	344	9,118
1912	...	1,790	304	2,787[15]	7,524	42[16] 218	490[17] 507	9,748
1913	...	1,811	326	2,745	9,084	782	350	9,939
1914	...	1,016	323	2,034	5,335	636	350	8,797
1915	...	2,252	309	677	300	579	585	8,392
1916	...	1,831	344	[1,791][25]	[343][26]	423	369	8,258
1917	...	1,916	270	...	...[6]	108	150	7,021
1918	...	1,542	161	...	2	197	116	4,493
1919	1	2,105[13]	330	1	—	554	233	5,673
1920	3	2,118	349	939	4	688	270	7,719
1921	444	2,800	310	1,453	3	915[16]	363	7,184
1922	181	2,681	386	1,165	1[27]	608	228	7,907
1923	363	2,789	409	1,708	728[27]	318	581	8,273[1]
1924	910	2,131	461	1,259	2,576[27]	301	597	9,503
1925	763	2,242	395	789	569[27]	545	455	7,548
1926	1,014	2,146	421	1,631	2,016[27]	385	460	7,481
1927	725	2,308	454	2,825	2,099[27]	309	576	8,875
1928	693	2,745	382	965	289[27]	654	694	7,977
1929	1,071	1,765[13]	365	1,595	178	634	565	8,412
1930	840	1,935	463	3,085	4,764	135	488	8,320
1931	576	1,485	540	3,182	5,056	175	660	10,001
1932	316	1,056	451	2,456	1,727	580	530	8,892
1933	968	466	493	1,741	1,684	106	426	9,413
1934	646	469	444	865	769	62	225	9,280
1935	415	550	458	1,091	1,517	53	120	9,212
1936	694	535	408	1,951	321	...	154	9,882
1937	736	1,658	492	2,118	1,277	...	295	9,546
1938	656	291	457	1,259	2,054	...	258	9,178
1939	1,179	648	551	[15]	277[6]	[385][28]	98	8,519
1940	487	691	162	1,080	1,155	712	186	8,506
1941	290	86	178	135	...	707	11	6,228
1942	243	83	134	34	...	407	119	3,676
1943	287	...	336	42	...	458	32	3,375
1944	161	...	77	92	...	388	23	2,988
1945	--[24]	...[13]	408	...	...	438[16]	66	4,337
1946	...	1,206	356	...	1,700	346	136	3,766
1947	23	1,062	280	...	800	307	167	4,968
1948	...	1,891	512	...	3,200	388	250	6,742
1949	317	1,667	450	...	2,400	296	195	6,108

See p.364 for footnotes

D10 External Trade in Corn (in thousands of metric tons or hectolitres)

1950–1975

	Austria[2]	Denmark[3]		France		W Germany[29]	E Germany[23]
	I	I	E	I	E	I	I
	(b)	(b)	(b)	(b)	(b)	(b)	(b)
1950	634	412	151	1,265	1,042	3,152	251
1951	940	296	105	1,294	849	4,502	364
1952	929	249	326	1,517	390	4,714	334
1953	652	157[19]	353[19]	1,161	496	3,388	349
1954	564	1,042	177	850	1,667	5,572	328
1955	892	859	253	747	2,913	4,236 / 4,280[29]	555
1956	658	952	341	2,500	1,754	6,045	606
1957	640	561	205	1,087	3,097	5,540	1,078
1958	658	920	469	988	1,868	4,982[20]	1,292
1959	858	1,463	246	1,097	1,364	5,589	1,335
1960	888	1,292	163	744	2,700	5,284	1,520
1961	523	826	185	872	4,193	5,614	1,250
1962	709	1,211	250	1,253	3,199	7,862	1,238
1963	590	647	334	1,319	5,240	5,073	1,023
1964	729	1,013	215	1,351	7,006	5,882	1,303
1965	955	950	498	1,600	7,144	6,641	1,225
1966	875	920	373	1,518	7,472	6,926	1,350
1967	524	834	265	1,353	7,148	6,966	1,184
1968	435	646	219	1,169	10,376	6,431	1,075
1969	277	346[18] / 242	469[18] / 405	1,266	12,374	6,456[29] / 6,233	1,311
1970	227	395	351	1,122	10,364	7,780	2,084
1971	367	746	228	887	11,651	8,081	1,867
1972	63	491	339	816	14,765	8,492	2,040
1973	102	427	352	710	10,440	8,267	1,594
1974	99	462	668	637	15,974	7,032	1,219
1975	97	262	1,013	1,277	11,671	6,501	1,130

	Hungary[24]	Italy[13]	Norway[5]	Romania[15]	Russia[6]	Spain[16]	Sweden[17]	U.K.[1]
	E	I	I	E	E	I	I	I
	(b)	(b)	(b)	(b)	(b)	(b)	(b)	(b)
1950	324	1,051	565	...	2,900	301	246	5,178
1951	383	1,557	478	...	4,100	283	448	6,498
1952	249	1,272	443	...	4,500	116	529	6,647
1953	260	1,133	548	...	3,100	584	121	7,055
1954	318	259	421	...	3,900	815	106	5,812
1955	419	761	526	...	3,700	96	409	7,080
1956	258	645	523	...	3,215	150	327	7,267
1957	24	534	377	...	7,413	278	205	7,328
1958	112	191	425	476	5,100	136	421	8,445
1959	109	59	451	223	7,009	278	616	8,453
1960	95	583	460	731	6,818	218	421	8,046
1961	167	2,434	481	1,208	7,481	1,576	303	8,219
1962	78	449	503	1,068	7,814	1,347[16] / 1,357	389[17] / 369	9,040
1963	79	301	503	1,409	6,260	1,541	396	7,873
1964	90	540	538	1,234	3,513	2,059	308	7,672
1965	200	926	537	882	4,330	2,359	184	7,969
1966	56	1,168	580	1,303	3,557	3,449	227	7,515
1967	204	847	582	2,339	4,248	3,308	153	7,788
1968	148	1,356	545	1,562	5,406	2,492	146	7,957
1969	488	1,427	519[30] / 547	1.377	7,205[30] / 8,049	2,436	95	8,567
1970	700[24] / 859	1,164	834	373	6,918	2,214	113	9,252
1971	159	1,607	649	704	9,573	3,171	73	8,669
1972	549	1,284	783	902[15] / 905	5,091	2,596	75	8,102
1973	550	2,030	879	1,128	5,812	2,978	148	7,467
1974	1,862	2,544	766	713	8,427	4,705	300	6,947
1975	1,310	1,612	634	1,164	4,383	4,772	110	7,189

See p.364 for footnotes

D10 External Trade in Corn (in thousands of metric tons or hectolitres)

NOTES

1. SOURCES:— Apart from France 1819–26, which comes from M. Block, *Statistique de la France* (Paris, 1860), all figures are taken from the official publications noted on p. xv. with gaps filled from League of Nations and United Nations, *International Trade Statistics,* International Institute of Agriculture, *Yearbook of Agricultureal Statistics,* and F.A.O., *Trade Yearbook.*

2. Except as indicated in footnotes, the statistics are of 'special' trade — i.e. exports of domestic produce or imports for consumption.

FOOTNOTES

[1] Figures to 1840 (1st line) are for Great Britain, and include trade with Ireland. Subsequently they are for the U.K., southern Ireland being treated as external from April 1923. Statistics to 1840 (1st line) are of wheat and flour only. Subsequently they are of barley, maize, oats, and wheat.

[2] All statistics relate to the boundaries of the day, except that Dalmatia was not included until 1861. All cereals are covered, together with cereal preparations from 1938.

[3] Figures to 1838 (1st line) include the Duchies of Schleswig, Holstein, and Lauenburg as part of Denmark. From 1838 (2nd line) to 1863 they are not included, but trade *with* them is ignored. Statistics for 1864–73 are for years ended 31 March following that indicated. Up to 1863 flour, meal, the minor grains, and peas are included. Subsequently (except as indicated in footnote 18) the statistics are of barley, maize, oats, rye, and wheat, and, from 1936 (2nd line), rice.

[4] Figures to 1949 (1st line) are of wheat and flour only. Subsequently they cover all cereals and preparations.

[5] All grains except rice. Data is lacking for Finmark and Nordland provinces in 1829.

[6] Figures to 1861 (1st line) are of barley, oats, rye, and wheat only. There were substantial territorial losses between 1917 and 1921 and gains between 1940 and 1945.

[7] Subsequently in thousands of metric tons.

[8] Earlier statistics are for years ended 31 October. The 1853 figures cover 14 months.

[9] Up to 1896 (1st line) and from 1924 (2nd line) to 1936 (1st line) the statistics are of 'general' rather than 'special' trade.

[10] Alsace-Lorraine is excluded to 1871–1918 and for 1939–44.

[11] Figures to 1 March 1906 apply to the Zollgebiet. Subsequently they are for the Empire or Republic. Schleswig-Holstein is included from 1865 and Alsace-Lorraine from 1871 to 1918. Statistics cover all grain except buckwheat and rice.

[12] From 1 July 1865 to December 1871 maize is not included.

[13] Wheat only. Transit trade is included in 1877 and probably earlier, but not subsequently. There were changes in the composition of 'special' trade in 1897, 1907, and 1930. The main territorial changes were the inclusion of Venetia in 1867, the Papal States in 1871, and the acquisitions from Austria-Hungary in 1920, and the loss of territory to Yugoslavia in 1945.

[14] Including oats and maslin.

[15] Barley, maize, rye, and wheat to 1901 (1st line), with oats from 1901 (2nd line) and all other cereals from 1972 (2nd line). Malt is also included from 1887 to 1911. There were substantial territorial gains in 1913 and 1920, and losses in 1940.

[16] Wheat only to 1912 (1st line). Barley, maize, oats, rye and wheat from 1912 (2nd line) to 1921. Barley, maize, and wheat from 1922 to 1945, with maslin also from 1946 to 1962 (1st line). Subsequently all cereals and preparations.

[17] Including Finland to 1814. Data for imports relate to barley, oats, rye, and wheat to 1861 (2nd line), with wheat flour and rye flour included from 1861 (3rd line). Malt is included from 1856 to 1863, but imports had been negligible for many years previously. Maize is included from 1908 although barley is excluded for 1908 to 1912 (1st line). From 1912 (2nd line) to 1962 (1st line) statistics are of all imports of grains and flour, and subsequently they are of all cereals. Exports are of oats only to 1861 (2nd line) and of barley, oats, rye, and wheat subsequently.

[18] From 1949 (2nd line) to 1969 (1st line) flour, meal etc. is included. There is no break in the import series in 1949.

[19] Subsequently does not include trade with the Faroe Islands and Greenland.

[20] Saarland is treated as external from 1920 to 18 February 1935 and from 1946 to 4 July 1959.

[21] From July 1922 eastern Upper Silesia was transferred to Poland.

[22] Excluding West Berlin.

[23] Wheat only.

[24] Barley, maize, oats, rye, wheat, and flour to 1945. Subsequently to 1970 (1st line) maize, wheat, and flour, and all grains and flour thereafter.

[25] January-September only.

[26] Exports across the European frontier only.

[27] Figures for 1922–28 are for economic years ending in the year indicated. Exports for October-December 1928 were 1 thousand tons.

[28] April–December only.

[29] All grain and flour to 1950 (1st line) and from 1969 (2nd line); all cereals and preparations in the intervening period.

[30] Subsequently all cereals and cereal preparations.

[31] The original data to 1861 (1st line) were given in barrels, and have been converted on the basis of 1.649 hectolitres to the barrel.

D11 EXPORTS OF AGRICULTURAL, FISHING AND FORESTRY PRODUCTS (in units as indicated)

1830–1869

	Denmark			Finland		France	Greece	
	Butter (a)	Eggs (b)	Meat (a)	Wood (f)	Wood Pulp (a)	Wine (c)	Currants (a)	Tobacco (a)
1830	1.9	...	...	...	...	875	...	...
1831	1.6	...	0.2	...	...	806	...	...
1832	1.4	...	0.1	...	...	1,303	...	...
1833	1.4	...	0.2	...	...	1,338	...	...
1834	1.5	...	0.2	...	...	1,393	...	...
1835	1.7	...	0.3	...	...	1,301	...	...
1836	2.2	...	0.4	...	...	1,305	...	...
1837	2.0	...	0.4	...	...	1,114	...	...
1838	2.1	...	0.4[1]	...	...	1,453	...	...
			1.3					
1839	1.9	...	2.2	...	...	1,194	...	...
1840	2.0	...	2.0	...	...	1,334	...	...
1841	2.0	...	1.9	...	...	1,478	...	...
1842	1.5	...	1.3	...	...	1,368	...	...
1843	1.2	...	1.1	...	...	1,430	...	...
1844	1.3	...	0.6	...	...	1,403	...	...
1845	1.2	...	1.0	...	...	1,491	...	...
1846	1.3	...	0.9	...	...	1,360	...	...
1847	1.5	...	0.9	...	...	1,488	...	...
1848	1.2	...	1.0	...	...	1,548	...	...
1849	1.5	...	1.0	...	...	1,872	...	...
1850	2.1	...	1.7	...	...	1,911	...	...
1851	1.4	...	1.4	...	...	2,269	...	...
1852	2.4	...	1.3	...	...	2,439	...	...
1853	1.1	...	1.2	...	...	1,976	...	...
1854	1.7	...	1.4	...	...	1,330	...	...
1855	1.4	...	1.4	...	...	1,215	...	...
1856	1.5	...	1.3	...	...	1,275	...	...
1857	1.2	...	1.6	...	...	1,124	...	...
1858	1.0	...	1.0	...	...	1,620	31	1.1
1859	0.9	...	1.6	...	...	2,519	28	0.6
1860	1.7	...	2.2	310	—	2,021	40	1.0
1861	2.4	8	1.7	339	- -	1,858	36	1.1
1862	2.9	10	1.7	303	- -	1,894	40	0.4
1863	4.4	15	2.1	452	- -	2,084	38	0.4
1864	4.0	26	3.1	406	—	2,336	36	1.3
1865	4.9	35	7.6	617	- -	2.868	52	1.3
1866	5.0	70	5.4	515	—	3,274	60	0.6
1867	4.5	31	5.1	474	- -	2,591	65	0.9
1868	4.0	27	5.4	597	- -	2,806	60	0.7
1869	6.3	32	5.5	617	- -	3,063	56	1.1

Abbreviations used throughout this table: (a) 000 tons (b) 000 score (c) 000 hectolitres (d) million cubic metres (e) millions (f) 000 cubic metres

See p.371 for footnotes

D11 Exports of Agricultural, Fishing and Forestry Products (in units as indicated)

1830–1869

	Italy		Norway				Spain		Sweden		
	Citrus Fruits (a)	Wine (c)	Fish (a)	Timber (d)	Paper (a)	Wood Pulp (a)	Oranges (e)	Wine (c)	Timber (d)	Paper (a)	Wood Pulp (a)
1830	...	...	56	...	...	...	...	...	...	...	...
1831	...	...	67	...	...	...	...	...	...	...	...
1832	...	...	79	...	...	...	...	...	...	...	...
1833	...	...	91	...	...	...	...	...	...	...	...
1834	...	...	80	...	...	...	...	...	...	...	...
1835	...	...	72	...	...	...	...	...	...	...	...
1836	...	...	68	1.2	...	...	...	...	...	...	...
1837	...	...	95	1.1	...	...	...	...	...	...	...
1838	...	...	61	1.2	...	...	...	...	...	...	...
1839	...	...	68	1.4	...	...	...	...	...	...	...
1840	...	...	93	1.3	...	...	...	...	...	...	...
1841	...	...	78	1.3	...	...	...	...	...	...	...
1842	...	...	83	1.3	...	...	...	...	...	...	...
1843	...	...	63	1.3	...	...	...	...	...	...	...
1844	...	...	102	1.3	...	...	...	...	...	...	...
1845	...	...	85	1.4	...	...	...	...	...	...	...
1846	...	...	104	1.4	...	...	...	...	...	...	...
1847	...	...	89	1.1	...	...	...	...	...	...	...
1848	...	...	78	0.9	...	...	...	...	...	...	...
1849	...	...	106	1.0	...	...	81	700	...	...	...
1850	...	...	84	1.1	...	...	55	615	...	...	...
1851	...	...	107	1.3	...	...	95	716	...	...	...
1852	...	...	88	1.3	...	...	53	752	...	...	...
1853	...	...	89	1.5	...	...	52[4]	934	...	...	...
							51				
1854	...	...	77	1.5	...	...	62	1,139			
1855	...	...	87	1.5	...	...	84	1,159	...	...	...
1856	...	...	93	1.5	...	...	217	1,224	...	...	...
1857	...	...	89	1.5	...	...	106	1,638	...	...	...
1858	...	...	84	1.5	...	...	122	941	...	...	...
1859	...	...	103	1.6	...	...	150	1,099	...	...	...
1860	...	...	113	1.6	...	...	209	1,385	...	0.2	...
1861	5	255	93	1.7	...	...	117	955	1.2	0.1	...
1862	46	217	126	1.8	...	...	243	1,225	1.3	0.6	...
1863	69	468	125	1.9	...	...	157	1,203	1.4	0.1	...
1864	66	236	119	2.0	...	...	101	1,357	1.6	0.2	...
1865	70	275	130	2.2	...	...	134	1,090[5]	2.0	0.4	...
								1,038			
1866	91[3]	359[3]	123	2.1	...	...	190	1,060	1.9	0.5	...
1867	67	299	125	2.0	...	...	298	1,248	2.1	1.1	...
1868	72	241	128	2.1	...	—	189	1,747	2.5	1.4	...
1869	88	287	168	2.1	...	...	272	1,725	2.4	1.5	...

See p.371 for footnotes

D11 Exports of Agricultural, Fishing and Forestry Products (in units as indicated)

1870–1919

	Denmark			Finland			France	Greece		Italy	
	Butter	Eggs	Meat	Wood[2]	Wood pulp	News-print	Wine	Currants	Tobacco	Citrus Fruits	Wine
	(a)	(a)	(a)	(f)	(a)	(a)	(c)	(a)	(a)	(a)	(c)
1870	7.6	56	9.4	522	- -	...	2,866[18]	47	0.4	77[3]	240[3]
1871	7.2	340	7.5	555	—	...	3,319	75	0.8	88	243
1872	10.6	690	5.6	783	—	...	3,430	62	1.6	88	609
1873	11.6	1,427	7.2	894	1	...	3,981	77	1.1	84	309
1874	14.8	1,184	7.9	1,127	3	...	3,232	79	1.4	72	272
1875	13.5	1,595	6.4	1,001	2	...	3,730	81	1.4	96	363
1876	16.0	1,398	5.8	1,553	3	...	3,331	...	...	93	507
1877	13.2	944	6.1	1,605	2	...	3,102	...	...	101	363
1878	11.4	1,201	5.9	1,043	3	...	2,795	...	...	98	537
1879	11,7	1,310	5.7	995	3	...	3,047	...	...	100	1,077
1880	12.5	1,992	7.2	1,570	3	...	2,488	...	...	93	2,206
1881	12.3	1,860	6.6	1,221	1	...	2,572	...[10]	...[10]	129	1,760
1882	14.3	2,390	7.5	1,461	2	...	2,618	...	...	120	1,332
1883	17.2	2,814	12.2	1,380	3	...	2,541	...	...	159	2,629
1884	16.6	3,643	16.8	1,444	6	...	2,472	...	...	173	2,381
1885	17.8	3,624	13.2	1,490	6	...	2,603	...	...	152	1,481
1886	20.2	4,652	15.2	1,207	7	...	2,709	...	...	125	2,354
1887	24.1	5,547	21.2	1,088	9	...	2,402	...	...	230	3,603
1888	30.2	5,039	36.0	1,238	8	...	2,118	...	...	165	1,829
1889	34.4	5,839	35.8	1,371	11	...	2,167	...	...	194	1,439
1890	44.6	6,686	30.9	1,263	14	...	2,162	...	...	191	936
1891	45.7	7,170	37.4	1,595	13	...	2,049	...	...	135	1,179
1892	45.3	7,939	43.6	1,486	13	...	1,845	116	2.6	171	2,449
1893	49.0	7,027	52.0	1,824	20	...	1,569	147	2.7	198	2,363
1894	59.0	7,950	53.4	2,262	21	...	1,721	161	2.4	215	1,943
1895	59.0	7,906	68.3	2,288	19	...	1,697	155	1.9	221	1,711
1896	60.6[6] 50.8	9,826[6] 9,624	82.0[6] 78.0	2,648	19	...	1,784	165	2.9	237	1,656
1897	53.0	12,228	69.4	2,958	17	...	1,775	111	2.3	224	2,396
1898	60.7	13,202	77.7	3,005	20	...	1,636	124	2.0	197	2,503
1899	61.2	15,058	84.7	3,164	18	...	1,717	126	2.9	239	2,430
1900	61.3	16,612	84.7	3,382	24	...	1,905	74	3.8	201	1,827
1901	66.8	19,014	79.0	3,374	26	...	2,022	109	4.3	244	1,335
1902	69.8	21,530	95.3	3,452	26	17	2,052	120	4.6	320	1,389
1903	80.1	23,244	101	4,467	37	18	1,726	119	5.7	310	2,163
1904	81.5	21,406	121	4,924	59	24	1,643	112	7.0	347	1,211
1905	79.9	20,733	110	4,550	61	25	2,606	112	5.9	310	987
1906	79.4	19,765	107	4,505	56	28	2,110	125	8.1	347	814
1907	85.7	20,106	122	4,330	61	33	2,788	123	6.8	382	1,041
1908	88.9	21,254	141	4,733	64	33	2,273	101	4.9	368	1,364
1909	89.2	19,207	129	4,718	71	36	2,280	105	6.0	369	1,588
1910	88.5	20,363	131	4,788	87	46	2,318	112	5.8	381	2,033
1911	89.6	21,513	146	5,109	114	54	1,569	125	8.5	389	1,179
1912	85.2	19,226	173	5,317	138	57	2,060	[11]		368	1,177
1913	91.0	22,734	163	6,687	127	70	1,659[9]	96[12]	10[12]	437	1,787
1914	95.3	22,863	188	3,533	97	72	1,155	...	...	442	2,045
1915	101.6	24,097	182	592	100	72	1,003	...	...	335	961
1916	95.8	24,058	135	714[2] 192	101[7] 94	78	689	...	...	316	623
1917	61.5	22,190	114	125	54	68	460	...	...	206	1,230
1918	14.7	16,388	20	268	80	16	434[8 9]	...	...	136[3]	2,780[3]
1919	36.6	16,935	13	3,108	130	34	1,180	...	...	210	725

See p.371 for footnotes

D11 Exports of Agricultural, Fishing and Forestry Products (in units as indicated)

1870–1919

	Norway				Portugal			Russia	Spain		Sweden		
	Fish (a)	Timber (d)	Paper (a)	Wood-pulp[18] (a)	Cork (a)	Pres Sardines (a)	Wine (c)	Sugar (a)	Oranges (a)	Wine (c)	Timber (d)	Paper (a)	Wood pulp (a)
1870	146	2.1	...	1	...	...	...	...	229	1,419	2.6	1.8	...
1871	114	2.3	...	2	...	...	...	...	445	1,584	2.7	1.9	...
1872	183	2.2	...	3	...	...	...	...	582	1,868	3.1	1.9	5.8
1873	134	2.3	...	4	17	...	402	...	507	2,548	3.1[14] / 3.4	2.5	6.7
1874	152	2.0	...	6	19	...	531	--	590	1,980	3.1	3.0	5.6
1875	158	1.6	...	9	12	...	583	--	440	1,968	2.9	3.4	5.2
1876	154	2.0	...	12	16	...	528	8	627	1,746	3.4	4.7	5.9
1877	146	1.7	1	15	14	...	571	64	677	2,169	3.6	4.0	6.1
1878	133	1.6	1	19	11	...	425	5	638	2,793	3.0	5.3	5.2
1879	140	1.5	2	21	11	...	419	3	683	3,699	3.3	7.0	9.8
1880	132	1.9	3	26	17	...	593	...	789	6,079	3.7	7.1	9.5
1881	172	1.8	2	43	19	...	701	1	600	6,872	3.8	5.4	9.0
1882	130	1.9	3	67	23	...	778	2	939[13] / 117	7,514	4.3	6.0	9.2
1893	109	2.0	3	81	20	...	870	--	99	7,524	4.5	6.5	10
1894	128	2.0	4	88	22	...	820	2	105	6,400	4.1	6.7	11
1885	130	1.8	4	103	21	2.6	1,501	48	71	7,078	4.3	7.8	16
1886	156	1.7	4	110	22	5.6	1,963	62	82	7,266	4.1	8.6	26
1887	179	1.8	4	139	23	7.4	1,467	75	86	8,234	4.3	9.8	29
1888	166	1.9	5	171	21	6.8	1,731	91	94	8,979	5.0	11.3	39
1889	178	2.0	5	185	24	4.7	1,475	81	98	8,589	5.1[15] / 5.2	11.3	52
1890	168	1.9	7	202	23	6.9	914	53	101	9,418	5.2	16	64
1891	141	1.9	10	228	22	9.4	826	124	65	11,307	5.5	19	86
1892	188	1.9	15	212	23	9.8	1,002	48	89	6,736	5.2	21	74
1893	210	1.7	19	231	23	7.9	770	37	91	5,165	5.3	19	82
1894	162	1.7	22	250	23	5.8	611	86	160	4,126	5.5	24	85
1895	167	1.7	28	260	27	8.7	682	93	235	5,348	5.5	25	122
1896	148	1.8	35	298	28	9.4	761	222	215	6,665	5.1	28	150
1897	205	2.1	39	313	32	10.0	782	133	277	5,343	6.4	29	151
1898	195	2.0	41	325	29	11.5	863	119	238	6,409	6.5	31	153
1899	160	2.0	44	365	25	8.3	830	127	311	4,842	6.6	39	186
1900	159	2.0	47	392	27	9.6	829	205	260	3,869	6.7	50	205
1901	162	1.8	48	390	29	10	791	128	285	2,339	6.0	58	209
1902	181	2.0	49	454	28	13	839	130	369	1,968	6.4	80	251
1903	169	2.1	53	453	31	15	780	240	396	2,431	6.6	93	316
1904	152	1.8	60	453	35	14	729	180	409	2,285	6.1	103	342
1905	152	1.8	69	453	27	16	900	100	314	3,072	6.0	122	336
1906	172	2.0	92	515	38	19	908	97	393	2,463	6.3	138	361
1907	197	1.9	94	568	41	17	910	179	469	2,385	5.9	146	456
1908	200	1.5	108	605	35	17	842	298	466	2,568	5.2	143	490
1909	263	1.3	124	612	36	18	863	204	468	2,346	4.7	137	491
1910	279	1.3	139	649	43	19	1,156	148	497	2,518	5.5	166	652
1911	272	1.2	126	637	43	23	1,165	452	442	2,987	5.5	176	736
1912	261	1.1	151	707	46	25	1,146	375	563	3,203[4]	5.8	204	812
1913	296	1.0	181	721	89	25	1,090	...	569		6.3	216	847
1914	257	0.9	182	746	...	...	...	...	478	2,422	5.1	190	800
1915	339	1.4	207	740	...	...	...	...	456	1,637	5.3	228	872
1916	309	1.4	100	701	...	...	...	...	383	4,433	6.2	265	870
1917	302	1.0	80	420	...	...	2,070	...	246	6,285	3.5	183	620
1918	228	0.7	112	525	...	...	1,505	--	173	2,620	3.7	155	624
1919	257	0.9	107	529	...	...	1,478	--	349	6,142	5.0	170	808

Pres Sardines: Preserved Sardines

See p.371 for footnotes

D11 Exports of Agricultural, Fishing and Forestry Products (in units as indicated)

1920–1975

	Denmark			Finland			France	Greece		Ireland	Italy	
	Butter	Eggs	Meat	Wood	Wood pulp	Newsprint	Wine	Currants	Tobacco	Meat	Citrus Fruits	Wine
	(a)	(b)	(a)	(f)	(a)	(a)	(c)			(a)	(a)	(c)
1920	74.8	27,310	68	4,049	170	90	2,136	104	27	...	236	874
1921	92.1	32,407	103	3,234	173	94	1,801	102	26	...	271	913
1922	95.5	36,756	146	4,921	235	130	1,034	87	37	...	225	891
1923	112	39,962	210	5,468	261	127	1,503	120	21	...	224	830
1924	123	41,624	216	5,969	377	135	2,251	109	42	...	301	2,559
1925	123	40,334	231	5,979	367	149	1,556	95	42	32.3	384	1,455
1926	133	41,610	221	5,950	406	144	1,834	95	55	32.8	372	1,051
1927	143	42,243	275	7,495	466	155	1,279	96	53	41.0	405	1,036
1928	148	39,450	292	6,611	611	172	1,375	95	49	53.6	304	922
1929	159	39,285	271	6,565	645	174	1,382	84	50	43.5	323	974
1930	169	43,112	350	5,299	633	188	1,088	86	49	34.7	405	1,032
1931	172	48,716	442	4,470	786	191	820	80	43	36.9	385	1,672
1932	158	55,236	434	4,363	937	201	703	88	35	25.4	308	803
1933	151	53,517	335	5,397	1,006	226	725	87	35	26.2	417	999
1934	150	56,279	261	6,162	1,051	260	725	98	37	28.4	343	993
1935	138	58,613	225	5,950	1,214	280	721	101	50	35.5	313	944
1936	146	70,088	200	6,405	1,359	342	825	101	40	34.6	269	1,438
1937	153	80,645	227	6,289	2,470	382	862	113	42	30.7	371	1,872
1938	158	77,916	214	5,069	1,246	358	1,032	104	49	31.7	356	1,441
1939	150	85,675	230	3,886	1,298	422	916	...	...	29.1	414	1,477
1940	108	67,172	174	1,328	266	61	482	...	...	38.6	353	1,697
1941	53	27,427	89	1,235	517	51	1,646	...	...	50.2	383	1,837
1942	36	5,371	38	1,348	281	58	1,589	...	...	25.2	240	1,300
1943	50	1,861	69	1,633	273	103	1,942	...	...	11.9	...	...
1944	53	2,500	121	579	186	44	937	...	...	12.2	...	...
1945	61	7,857	75	691	164	56	766	...	...	19.0	...[3]	...[3]
1946	78	9,811	96	2,387	450	208	728	...	...	15.1	85	323
1947	87	14,497[13]	90	3,386	633	246	582	...	...	7.1	201	489
1948	106	40.8	70	3,340	800	289	620	64	18	6.0	281	633
1949	138	80.5	154	3,830	921	348	744	85	28	12.1	357	684
1950	156	95.5	249	3,827	1,056	379	984	88	25	38.0	369	1,072
1951	140	85.4	299	4,840	1,191	382	1,892	65	32	49.4	344	980
1952	117	89.6	292	4,158	865	392	2,275	86	41	78.4	350	1,223
1953	137	97.2	370	3,560	991	402	2,786	106	49	86.9	330	1,207
1954	141	105.5	408	4,145	1,149	392	3,034	119	52	107.9	389	1,180
1955	129	107.7	428	4,788	1,312	470	3,024	104	55	63.9	354	1,185
1956	121	100.0	378	4,223	1,317	537	3,227	96	49	53.4	423	1,884
1957	118	103.0	451	4,449	1,336	551	2,282	121	69	70.4	451	1,912
1958	115	107.1	454	4,259	1,344	585	1,305	100	62	84.8	386	1,850
1959	118	107.7	484[21]	4,950	1,459	576	2,084	99	55	82.1	459	1,453
1960	118	84.7	526	5,635	1,594	691	3,282	106	61	104	403	2,156
1961	120	67.3	538	5,415	1,601	846	4,113	99	66	134	464	2,112
1962	115	50.7	594	4,541	1,709	870	3,528	124	47	130	443	2,313
1963	102	39.2	636	4,306[2] 4,594	1,927	882	4,358	137	62	135	415	2,471
1964	104	30.2	638	4,680	2,125	989	3,688	115	70	124	515	2,319
1965	116	23.4	688	4,124	1,999	1,101	3,493	125	73	136	562	2,636
1966	112	23.8	688	3,790	2,218	1,193	3,880	124	73	146	483	2,569
1967	104	22.8	712[21]	3,481	2,124	1,151	3,462	108	88	215	498	2,592
1968	107	21.0	711	3,962	2,224	1,161	3,620	110	70	194	534	2,851
1969	100	25.0	666	4,478	2,217	1,156	3,954	138	71	207	610	2,324
1970	87	20.3	679	4,702	2,057	1,187	4,132	125	63	217	508	4,831
1971	77	13.9	732	4,758	1,507	1,168	4,963	125	59	241	495	8,468
1972	87	11.3	803	4,910	1,611	1,310	5,869	142	74	226	455	13,348
1973	100	12.4	709	5,256	1,664	1,321	7,275	92	46	217	239	9,538
1974	101	10.1	697	4,323	1,338	1,137	6,596	106	67	275	371	9,579
1975	98	11.1	709	2,892	948	776	6,352	113	51	330	412	12,942

See p.371 for footnotes

D11 Exports of Agricultural, Fishing and Forestry Products (in units as indicated)

1920–1975

	Norway				Portugal			Russia	Spain		Sweden		
	Fish	Timber	Paper	Wood pulp[18]	Cork	Pres Sardines	Wine	Sugar	Oranges	Wine	Timber	Paper	Wood Pulp
	(a)	(d)	(a)	(a)	(a)	(a)	(c)	(a)	(a)	(c)	(d)	(a)	(a)
1920	375	0.9	184	607	...	...	1,029	..	258	4,930	5.4	299	881
1921	267	0.5	82	372	...	...	709	..	434	3,116	3.0	191	482
1922	281	1.0	216	612	123	38	2,536	..	401	2,960	5.9	295	1,047
1923	315	0.9	211	705	109	53	1,538	..	461	3,050	5.8	331	896
1924	283	0.8	196	672	110	44	1,360	15	671	3,470	5.3	378	1,221
1925	266	0.9	284	638	122	34	1,042	28	715	2,900	5.4	404	1,188
1926	284	0.8	257	726	137	32	947	25	717	2,990	4.9	420	1,303
1927	292	0.7	300	729	123	33	864	110	620	5,030	5.7	425	1,455
1928	282	0.8	309	792	123	35	1,499	136	859	5,952	5.9	411	1,327
1929	335	0.8	314	879	140	34	945	127	793	3,786	6.6	489	1,789
1930	329	0.6	294	850	100	35	818	102	1,085	3,489	5.4	444	1,641
1931	234	0.4[16]	172	648	93	45	756	320	855	3,349	3.9	485	1,567
1932	251	347	277	871	90	44	755	76	882	1,975	4.0	473	1,292
1933	260	271	257	836	123	29	767	38	978	2,503	4.7	516	1,916
1934	194	258	258	950	124	34	743	49	885	1,550	4.7	556	1,999
1935	219	257	286	753	136	40	854	76	700	1,313	3.6	609	2,103
1936	240	268	290	878	153	43	879	163	...	...	4.2	607	2,280
1937	254	290	322	958	...	...	799	134	...	...	4.5	664	2,552
1938	227	235	240	768	114	30	838	114	...[20]	...	3.6	474	1,981
1939	259	289	307	780	...	41	992	25	[111]	[263][20]	3.9	601	2,331
1940	224	161	121	421	...	36	701	34	325	419	2.3	...	1,044
1941	201	230	76	391	...	50	601	...	313	198	2.4	190	756
1942	183	64	29	198	...	33	791	...	231	271	1.8	237	659
1944	164	27	40	167	67	38	625	...	203	555	1.0	194	439
1944	179	55	20	67	53	34	484	...	249	699	0.8	207	297
1945	89	21	59	59	65	27	564	...	263	384	2.8	245	1,569
1946	259	123	245	249	82	36	1,303	28	139	358	3.2	521	1,804
1947	301	169	260	344	159	27	825	18	174	361	2.2	627	1,797
1948	350	151	279	505	139	31	999	15	274	831	2.8	682	1,680
1949	333	217	278	655	124	17	1,170	63	426	1,370	3.8	711	1,893
1950	221	213	299	776	177	17	1,009	97	421	768	4.0	865	2,091
1951	282	230	302	825	196	22	1,212	124	727	744	4.5	926	2,010
1952	287	237	244	779[18]	124	30	1,136	138	777	704	4.1	668	1,630
1953	237	304	213	593	126	32	1,067	195	1,004	1,030	4.9	841	2,166
1954	299	209	230	654	123	42	1,295	208	809	1,545	4.7	985	2,229
1955	329	216	216	669	132	53	1,626	210	1,000	1,190	5.3	1,086	2,302
1956	342	252	242	681	114	47	1,856	174	379	1,413	4.9	1,221	2,547
1957	323	317	255	674	102	40	1,808	191	459	1,481	5.5	1,301	2,470
1958	288	278	244	653	117	49	2,286	200	732	3,272	4.3	1,329	2,358
1959	310	206	294	683[18] 713	127	60	1,582	197	784	1,349	4.9	1,471	2,679
1960	271	208	300	814	138	54	1,605	243	941	1,200	4.8	1,700	2,932
1961	192	185	328	765	129	61	1,632	414	906	1,531	4.5	1,804	2,729
1962	216	152	302	772	131	59	1,502	792	1,121	1,769	4.6	1,881	2,839
1963	211	171[17] 319	354	791	143	53	1,748	802	670	1,825	4.9	2,086	3,209
1964	195	379	389	878	144	55	2,270	348	1,337	2,013	5.6	2,327	3,476
1965	218	335	402	869	139	61	2,455	604	1,155	2,185	5.3	2,293	3,333
1966	229	251	415	851	116	55[19] 73	2,768	993	1,278	2,426	5.0	2,398	3,614
1967	217	252	479	825	99	68	2,520	1,032	1,188	2,659	5.5	2,430	3,519
1968	227	194	595	921	92	62	2,418	1,300	1,021	2,384	6.4	2,784	3,588
1969	297	401	1,040	952	103	48	2,418	1,081	1,029	2,581	6.8	3,133	3,669
1970	338	258	1,072	993	99	45	2,051	1,079	1,441	3,244	6.9	3,328	3,742
1971	296	266	1,025	777	97	40	2,019	1,002	1,195	3,574	7.5	3,315	3,308
1972	317	286	1,034	827	108	42	1,965	50	1,400	3,682	8.4	3,600	3,685
1973	303	635	1,080	996	97	45	2,096	43	1,646	3,769	9.4	4,107	4,735
1974	262	595	1,118	977	86	30	1,870	95	1,540	4,290	7.4	4,301	4,613
1975	278	390	833	621	67	30	1,261	53	1,510	4,831	5.3	3,118	3,329

Pres Sardines: Preserved Sardines

See p.371 for footnotes

D11 Exports of Agricultural, Fishing and Forestry Products

NOTES

1. SOURCES:— The main sources were the official publications noted on p. xv with gaps filled from the League of Nations and United Nations, *International Trade Statistics,* and the F.A.O., *Trade Yearbook.* Finnish statistics of wood and pulp to 1916 (1st line) are taken from Erkki Pihkala, *Finland's Foreign Trade 1860–1917* (Bank of Finland, Helsinki, 1969).

2. Except as indicated in footnotes, the statistics are of 'special' trade, i.e. exports of domestic produce.

3. Swedish data for timber are available for 1738–1860 in *Historisk Statistik för Sverige,* vol. 3, but in a variety of units of measurement.

FOOTNOTES

[1] Figures to 1838 (1st line) include the Duchies of Schleswig, Holstein, and Lauenburg as part of Denmark. From 1838 (2nd line) to 1863 they are not included, but trade *with* them is ignored.

[2] Figures to 1916 (1st line) are of pitprops, square timber, sawn logs, and sawn timber. From 1916 (2nd line) to 1963 (1st line) they are of pitprops, square timber, deals, boards, etc., but not plywood or veneers. From 1963 (2nd line) they are of all sawn or planed wood.

[3] Venetia was included from 1867, the Papal States from 1871, and the territories acquired from Austria from 1919. Statistics from 1946 relate to the 1954 boundaries.

[4] Previously including lemons.

[5] From 1865 (2nd line) to 1912, full-bodied wines other than 'sherry and similar types' are excluded.

[6] Figures to 1896 (1st line) are of 'general' trade.

[7] This break is occasioned by a change of source (see note 1).

[8] The partsof Alsace and Lorraine ceded to Germany are excluded from 1871 to 1918.

[9] Figures for 1914–18 exclude the occupied departments.

[10] Arta and part of Thessaly were acquired in 1881.

[11] Subsequent statistics cover all dried grapes.

[12] Previous statistics are for Old Greece, subsequent ones for the enlarged country, though the boundaries were not fully stabilised until 1923.

[13] Subsequent statistics are in thousands of metric tons.

[14] Previously only covers beams, deals, planks, and rafters, but subsequently includes masts, spars, and pitprops.

[15] Subsequently including staves.

[16] Subsequent statistics are in thousands of cubic metres.

[17] Subsequently includes floated timber.

[18] Statistics to 1959 (1st line) are of mechanical and sulphite wood pulp only, mechanical pulp being reckoned at wet weight up up to 1952 and subsequently at dry weight. From 1959 (2nd line) the figures are of all pulp and waste paper.

[19] Subsequently covers all prepared and preserved fish.

[20] April–December only.

[21] From 1960 to 1968 excluding dried meat from animals other than pigs. This amounted to 6 thousand tons in 1960, and 5 thousand tons in 1968.

E. INDUSTRY

Apart from table E.1, which gives indices of industrial production, and table E.15, showing the numbers of cotton spindles, all the tables in this section consist of physical output and external trade statistics for major commodities which possess an adequate degree of homogeneity to allow aggregation and meaningful comparisons between countries. Inevitably, these are mostly basic commodities rather than finished goods; yarn and cloth rather than clothing, metals rather than machinery. The picture they give of industrial development is necessarily biased and partial. However, until very recent decades, there is little that could be added to them in the way of continuous statistical series for consumer industries; and even then, there is far more detail available for centrally-planned than for market economies.

Probably enough has been written about the problems of constructing indices of industrial production for most users to be aware of their pitfalls. Even given all the desired basic information, an index which accurately reflects the composition of industrial output in any year will not, in a changing world, have precisely the right weighting of activities for another year. Where the components of an index are expressed in terms of values rather than volume, changes in relative prices will be an added source of possible misrepresentation. Changing the weights and linking indices is one solution to this problem, and often the best one; but it takes away exact precision of comparability. Such precision, however, can easily become unreal and meaningless where new commodities and activities are added to, and sometimes displace, old ones. All worthwhile indices of industrial production, then, are compromises between relevance and exact comparability over time. The skill of the constructor is in picking the base-years and linking points which produce least distortion, and appear to represent best the reality of industrial activity and change. Judgement on these matters inevitably contains subjective elements, and it is safe to say that there is no objectively perfect index.

Technical problems have been compounded, until the interwar period, and perhaps later in some countries, by lack of sufficient basic information. As was mentioned above, statistics on the more complex products of industry were not generally collected until quite recently. And if one goes well back into the nineteenth century, it is often true to say that the only statistics which were collected were those concerned with taxation in one shape or another – customs collected, excise duties imposed, the output of state monopolies, certain mining records. Clearly such a sample is not unbiased, and in general it seems wise to view nineteenth century indices of industrial production with a certain amount of scepticsm and to use them with caution. Nor should this attitude be relaxed too much even for the twentieth century, especially where comparisons between countries are concerned. For whilst coverage and statistical technique have generally improved, the pace of economic change has quickened, and variations in the value of money have been much greater. These, indeed, have been the source of particular criticism of the official indices of the U.S.S.R., at any rate until the late 1950s or the 1960s, and various western scholars have tried to produce improved versions. The work of two of them is shown here alongside the official series. Yet another cause for caution in making comparisons between countries is their very different state of industrial development at various times. Clearly the absolute size of the industrial base at any time has an influence on the possible rates of change which can be achieved.

The remaining tables in this section are reasonably straightforward, though not always quite so much as they seem. Most of the commodities covered are fairly homogeneous, but hardly one is perfectly so. The main sources of such variation as is not obvious are referred to in the notes following each table, and in the footnotes.

E1 INDICES OF INDUSTRIAL PRODUCTION

1801–1849

	France (a)	United Kingdom (a)
1801	...	6.6
1802	...	6.9
1803	...	7.1
1804	...	7.3
1805	...	7.4
1806	...	7.6
1807	...	7.8
1808	...	7.9
1809	...	8.1
1810	...	8.2
1811	...	8.4
1812	...	8.5
1813	...	8.6
1814	...	8.8
1815	19.2	9.0
1816	19.5	9.2
1817	19.9	9.5
1818	21.3	9.8
1819	19.5	10
1820	20.7	10
1821	21.9	11
1822	21.4	11
1823	20.2	12
1824	21.8	12
1825	19.7	13
1826	20.8	13
1827	21.3	13
1828	20.9	14
1829	21.1	14
1830	21.0	15
1831	20.4	15
1832	21.5	16
1833	22.9	16
1834	23.1	17
1835	23.0	17
1836	23.2	18
1837	22.8	19
1838	24.2	19
1839	22.9	20
1840	24.3	20
1841	25.6	21
1842	26.7	22
1843	28.3	22
1844	28.4	23
1845	29.7	24
1846	30.6	24
1847	29.7	25
1848	26.7	26
1849	32.2	27

1850–1899

	Austria (a)	France (a)	Germany (a)	Italy (a)	Russia (a)	Sweden[2] (a)	U.K. (a)
1850	...	33.5	9.5	...	...	...	28
1851	...	31.1	9.8	...	...	...	29
1852	...	34.8	10.0	...	...	...	30
1853	...	36.5	9.9	...	...	...	31
1854	...	34.2	9.7	...	...	...	32
1855	...	37.3	10	...	...	...	33[3] 26.3
1856	...	38.1	11	...	...	...	28.1
1857	...	35.3	12	...	...	...	29.1
1858	...	38.2	12	...	...	...	28.5
1859	...	36.6	12	...	...	...	30.0
1860	...	39.1	13	...	8.8	...	31.7
1861	...	38.7	13	32	8.5	15	31.7
1862	...	37.0	13	32	6.8	16	32.4
1863	...	37.8	15	32	7.3	17	32.5
1864	...	41.2	15	32	7.6	17	35.0
1865	...	39.9	16	33	7.5	19	37.3
1866	...	40.4	17	35	9.8	18	38.7
1867	...	40.2	17	37	10.0	18	36.4
1868	...	43.8	18	37	9.7	20	36.4
1869	...	44.4	19	40	11	24	35.8
1870	...	40.0	19	40	11	25	40.2
1871	...	41.3	21[1]	39	12	19	43.5
1872	...	45.8	24	40	12	20	44.8
1873	...	43.8	26	44	12	20	45.3
1874	...	46.5	27	46	13	23	46.4
1875	...	47.1	27	46	14	24	46.7
1876	...	47.7	28	46	14	25	47.5
1877	...	46.5	27	46	14	25	47.4
1878	...	47.4	28	44	18	24	47.3
1879	...	46.0	27	44	18	25	45.6
1880	28.6	49.4	26	42	18	25	50.3
1881	31.8	54.1	27	47	22	29	53.5
1882	33.1	55.3	27	47	21	30	55.7
1883	37.0	54.5	29	47	23	29	56.5
1884	38.3	52.5	30	49	22	32	54.4
1885	36.4	52.0	31	51	24	34	52.1
1886	39.0	52.9	31	49	25	32	51.0
1887	40.3	53.7	33	53	28	34	55.1
1888	39.6	55.6	35	51	26	36	58.3
1889	42.9	58.4	39	51	29	37	62.4
1890	46.8	57.3	40	51	32	40	63.3
1891	50.0	60.3	41	47	34	43	64.1
1892	50.6	63.6	42	47	35	45	61.0
1893	51.9	61.5	43	47	40	48	60.0
1894	55.8	62.7	45	51	40	52	63.5
1895	57.8	59.5	49	53	44	51	66.5
1896	58.4	64.4	50	51	46	57	71.4
1897	59.1	66.7	53	53	49	58	73.4
1898	63.6	68.6	56	53	54	62	77.0
1899	64.3	71.3	58	56	60	66	80.1

UK: United Kingdom

(a) 1913=100

See p.380 for footnotes

E1 Indices of Industrial Production

1900–1949

	Austria (a)	Belgium (b)	Bulgaria (b)	Czech (b)	Denmark (b)	Finland (b)	France (a)	E.Germany (c)	Germany (a)	Greece (b)	Hungary (b)	Ireland (b)
1900	64.9	...	...	...	...	...	67.9	...	61	...	...	...
1901	68.2	52	...	...	...	...	67.7	...	59	...	...	...
1902	68.2	60	...	...	...	...	66.3	...	60	...	...	...
1903	68.8	62	...	...	...	...	70.8	...	65	...	...	...
1904	69.4	63	...	...	...	...	66.9	...	68	...	...	...
1905	73.3	64	...	...	...	...	74.6	...	70	...	...	...
1906	76.6	67	...	...	...	...	76.1	...	73	...	...	...
1907	87.7	69	...	...	...	...	79.3	...	79	...	...	...
1908	85.7	66	...	...	...	...	77.8	...	78	...	...	...
1909	83.8	72	...	...	...	...	83.1	...	81	...	...	...
1910	84.4	75	...	...	...	...	81.1	...	86	...	...	...
1911	89.0	79	...	...	...	...	88.8	...	91	...	...	...
1912	97.4	84	...	...	...	...	102.3	...	97	...	...	...
1913	100	83	...	...	...	...	100	...	100	...	...	...
1914	...	...	...	...	...	...	...	...	...	...	...	...
1915	...	...	...	...	...	...	...	...	...	...	...	...
1916	...	...	...	...	...	...	...	...	...	...	...	...
1917	...	...	...	...	...	...	...	...	...	...	...	...
1918	...	...	...	...	...	...	1937=100	...	...	...	...	...
1919	...	...	...	...	...	...	56[7]	...	...	...	...	...
1920	...	61	...	...	...	...	61	...	...	...	...	...
1921	...	54	...	62	...	...	54	...	...	...	...	...
1922	1937=100	67	...	57	...	...	77	...	...	...	...	...
1923	62	79	...	60	...	...	87	...	...	...	...	...
1924	64	87	...	79	...	...	108	...	...	...	...	...
									1937=100			
1925	74	82	...	82	...	...	107	...	68[10]	57	...	...
1926	74	96	...	80	...	56	125	...	61	55	...	63
1927	84	106	...	92	63	63	109	...	78	61	74	...
1928	92	115	...	99	68	69	126[8] / 111	...	78	65	75	...
1929	94	115	...	104	74	67	123	...	79	66	77	69
1930	80	97	...	93	79	61	123	...	69	68	73	...
1931	66	88	...	84	74	54	105	...	56	71	67	70
1932	58	73	...	66	67	56	91	...	48	67	63	...
1933	59	76	...	63	77	64	99	...	54	73	68	...
1934	66	76	...	69	87	78	92	...	67	83	76	...
1935	75	83	...	73	92	84	88	...	79	93	82	...
1936	81	90	103[5]	83	96	92	95	...	90	92	91	98
1937	100	100	100	100	100	100	100	...	100	100	100	100
1938	101[4]	81	108	...	100	103	92	...	110	109	98	103[12]
1939	...	86	115	...	107	99	...	...	...	116	...	...
1940	...	...	128	...	87	73	...	...	...	...	...	...
1941	...	...	136	...	83	75	...	...	...	...	...	...
1942	...	...	131	...	87	79	(56)[9]	...	...	...	...	...
1943	...	...	114[6]	...	89	89	(49)[9]	...	...	...	...	75
1944	...	...	...	...	88	83	(35)[9]	...	...	...	...	78
1945	...	...	...	...	75	87	(45)[9]	...	...	37[11]	...	89
1946	...	73	...	...	102	105	76	38	...	62	...	106
1947	...	91	...	...	117	117	89	49	WEST GERMANY	78	...	117
1948	92	100	230	108	128	133	103	64	63	85	...	133
1949	123	100	307	123	137	140	112	79	90	101	125	152

Czech: Czechoslovakia E.Germany: East Germany
(a) 1913=100 (b) 1937=100 (c) 1950=100

See p.380 for footnotes

E1 Indices of Industrial Production

1900–1949

	Italy	Netherlands	Norway	Poland	Romania	Russia		Spain	Sweden	U.K.[15]	Yugoslavia
	(a)	(b)	(b)	(b)	(b)	(b)		(d)	(a)	(a)	(b)
1900	61	...	...	...	...	63		...	68	80.1	...
1901	61	...	...	...	...	65		...	70	80.3	...
1902	67	...	...	...	...	69		...	73	81.7	...
1903	67	...	...	...	...	67		...	77	80.0	...
1904	70	..	...	...	...	69		...	80	81.0	...
1905	74	...	...	...	...	61		...	81	85.7	...
1906	79	...	...	...	...	69		54	89	89.3	...
1907	90	...	...	...	...	73		59	92	91.0	...
1908	93	...	...	...	...	74		61	90	83.7	...
1909	95	...	39	...	...	77		59	83	84.3	
1910	95	...	45	...	...	86		58	97	85.5	...
1911	95	...	46	...	...	91		59	99	91.5	...
1912	102	...	55	...	...	95		66	103	93.9	...
1913	100	...	59	...	...	100		67	100	100	...
	1937=100					(e)	(f)		1937=100		
	57					17	...		46		
1914	54	...	60	...	...	...	...	62	44	93.7	...
										1937=100	
										57.4	
1915	71	...	65	...	...	...	...	55	48	58.6[16]	...
1916	71	...	67	...	...	...	...	63	50	55.4	...
1917	63	...	56	...	...	12	...	65	42	51.7	
1918	61	...	51	...	...	...	...	65	35	50.0	
1919	59	...	53	...	...	...	...	58	39	55.1	
1920	59	...	60	...	...	...	...	63	44	61.2[15]	...
										60.0	
1921	54	...	43	...	...	5	...	65	34	48.9	...
1922	61	...	53	...	...	...	...	60	40	56.5	...
1923	66	...	59	...	...	...	...	72	44	59.9	
1924	73	...	63	...	...	8	...	83	50	66.5	...
1925	83	73	69	67	49	12	...	85	51	69.1	...
1926	83	75	61	66	57	17	...	94	56	65.3	...
1927	80	83	63	81	64	19	...	94	58	75.3	...
1928	88	95	69	92	71	22	37	96	63	73.3	...
1929	90	97	77	92	76	27	43	100	66	76.9	
1930	85	99	78	81	74	33	53	99	68	73.6	...
1931	77	93	60	71	78	40	57	93	64	68.9	...
1932	77	82	72	58	67	45	58	88	59	68.6	...
1933	82	88	72	63	78	48	61	84	60	73.1	...
1934	80	90	75	71	94	57	70	86	73	80.4	...
1935	86	88	83	77	93	70	83	87	81	86.6	...
1936	86	89	91	85	99	90	99	...	89	94.4	...
1937	100	100	100	100	100	100	100	...	100	100	100
1938	100	101	100	109	100	112	104	...	101	97.3	108
1939	109	110	107	...	...	130	111	...	110	...	115
1940	110	104[13]	92	...	...	131	116	86	100	...	...
1941	103	89[13]	90	...	...	...	...	101	98	...	...
1942	89	70[13]	82	...	...	...	...	112	103	...	...
1943	69	64[13]	78	...	...	...	...	120	108	...	...
1944	42	43[13]	64	...	...	136	...	122	115	...	...
1945	29	31[13]	57	...	...	120	77	114	113	...	...
1946	71	77	97	...	...	100	81	134	137	99.7	90
1947	91	98	115	...	...	122	93	137	140	105.0	138
1948	99	116	128	150	84	151	114	140	150	114.0	171
1949	109	129	137	177	...	185	137	133	155	120.7	192

U.K.: United Kingdom

(a) 1913=100 (b) 1937=100 (c) 1950=100 (d) 1929=100 (e) Soviet official index 1937=100 (f) Moorsteen Powell index 1937=100.

See p.380 for footnotes

E1 Indices of Industrial Production

1949–1975
1963=100

	Austria	Belgium	Bulgaria	Czech	Denmark	Finland	France	E.Germany (a)	W.Germany (b)	Greece (a)	Hungary	Ireland
1949	37	60	15	27	51	41	43	23	28	30	23	55
1950	43	61	18	31	56	44	45	29	35[17]	38	30	63
1951	49	69	22	35	58	51	51	36	41	44	38	64
1952	50	66	26	41	55	48	51	41	45	43	46	64
1953	51	64	29	45	58	52	52	46	48	49	52	68
1954	58	70	32	47	63	59	57	51	54	60	54	72
1955	67	75	34	52	64	65	64	55	63	63	54	74
1956	71	80	40	57	65	67	69	59	68	64	49	71
1957	75	80	46	63	69	69	75	63	71	69	56	68
1958	77	76	53	70	71	67	77	70	73	76	63	70
1959	81	77	64	78	80	72	78	79	79	77	70	76
1960	90	83	73	87	86	82	85	85	88	84	78	81
1961	94	88	81	95	90	91	90	90	93	89	87	88
1962	96	93	91	101	98	96	95	96	97	91	94	94
1963	100	100	100	100	100	100	100	100	100	100	100	100
1964	108	107	111	104	113	107	107	107	110	111	107	108
1965	113	109	127	112	120	115	109	113	116	121	111	113
1966	118	111	142	121	122	121	116	121	117	140	118	118
1967	119	113	161	129	126	125	119	129	114	146	125	127
1968	128	119	177	135	130	132	123	137	125	159	138	141
1969	142	131	194	141	147	151	136	146	141	178	139	152
1970	154	135	213	154	152	169	145	155	150	196	152	159
1971	163	139	232	164	155	171	154	164	153	218	162	165
1972	175	147	254	175	167	193	164	174	159	249	170	173
1973	185	157	277	187	175	207	175	186	170	288	182	192
1974	194	162	299	198	165	219	181	198	167	282	197	198
1975	182	147	335	212	156	205	165	212	158	296	206	186

(a) Soviet Official Index (b) Moorsteen-Powell Index 1937=100

E1 Indices of Industrial Production

1949–1975
1963=100

	Italy	Netherlands	Norway	Poland	Portugal	Romania	Russia (a)	Russia (b)	Spain	Sweden	Switzerland	U.K.[15]	Yugoslavia
1949	29	42	51	18	...	...	21	137	32	55	...	66	34
1950	33	47	56	23	...	16	26	156	37	57	...	70	35
1951	37	49	60	29	...	...	30	176	42	60	...	72	34
1952	39	49	60	34	...	...	33	189	48	58	...	71	33
1953	42	54	63	40	47	33	37	205	50	59	...	75	37
1954	46	59	67	44	...	...	42	228	52	61	...	79	42
1955	51	64	70	49	56	40	47	254	54	65	...	83	47
1956	54	68	74	54	61	45	52	279	59	67	...	83	52
1957	58	71	76	59	64	48	57	302	64	70	...	85	57
1958	60	71	76	65	69	53	63	345	66	71	71	84	63
1959	67	79	80	71	73	58	70	358	67	75	77	88	70
1960	77	87	87	79	80	68	77	379	72	83	84	95	77
1961	84	90	91	88	88	78	84	407	81	89	91	96	84
1962	92	95	95	95	92	89	93	...	91	94[18]	95	97	93
1963	100	100	100	100	100	100	100	...	100	100	100	100	100
1964	101	110	109	109	112	114	107	...	112	110	105	108	116
1965	109	116	115	119	119	129	117	...	126	118	108	112	125
1966	121	123	121	128	127	143	127	...	142	122	112	113	131
1967	131	129	126	138	134	163	139	...	151	125	116	114	130
1968	140	143	132	149	147	182	151	...	163	131	121	120	138
1969	145	156	139	163	158	200	162	...	188	140	131	123	153
1970	155	170	145	175	167	227	175	...	207	149	143	124	167
1971	154	180	150	189	180	255	189	...	215	151	146	125	185
1972	161	188	159	211	203	284	202	...	250	155	149	127	198
1973	177	200	168	233	227	325	216	...	289	166	157	137	212
1974	185	205	173	261	232	373	233	...	316	176	159	133	233
1975	168	195	185	289	220	418	251	...	295	172	139	126	245

(a) Soviet Official Index (b) Moorsteen-Powell Index 1937=100

See p.380 for footnotes

E1 Indices of Industrial Production

NOTES

1. SOURCES:– Austria 1880–1913 Richard Rudolph, 'The Role of Financial Institutions in the Industrialization of the Czech Crownlands, 1880–1914', unpublished doctoral dissertation, Department of History, University of Wisconsin (1968), p. 23. Belgium to 1937 – The I.R.E.S. index, quoted in C. Carbonnelle, 'Recherches sur l'évolution de la production en Belgique de 1900 à 1957', *Cahiers Economiques de Bruxelles* (1959). France to 1913 – F. Crouzet, 'Un indice de la production industrielle francaise au XIXe siecle', *Annales (Economies, Societes, Civilisations)* (1970). Germany to 1938 – W.G. Hoffman, *Das Wachstum der Deutschen Wirtschaft seit der Mitte des 19 Jahrhunderts* (Berlin, etc., 1965). Italy to 1947 – *Annali di Statistica,* serie VIII vol. 9. Russia to 1913 – R.W. Goldsmith, 'The Economic Growth of Tsarist Russia, 1860–1913', *Economic Development and Cultural Change* (1961). Russia 1928–61 (second column) – R. Moorsteen & R.P. Powell, *The Soviet Capital Stock, 1928–1962* (Homewood, Ill,. 1966). (This is a combined index of the separate indices published on pp. 622–4 of civilian industries, munitions industries, and construction, using their weights in 1937). U.K. to 1855– W.G. Hoffman, *British Industry, 1700–1950* (Oxford, 1955). U.K. 1955–1949 – C.H. Feinstein, *National Income, Expenditure and Output of the United Kingdom, 1855–1965* (Cambridge, 1972). All other statistics are from the official publications noted on p. xiii, or from the League of Nations and United Nations, *Statistical Yearbooks.*

2 Another index of industrial production in France, covering periods of years since the late 18th century, is given by T. Markovitch, *L'industrie francaise de 1789 a1964 – conclusions generales* (Cahiers de l'I.S.E.A., 1966), as follows (1938=100):–

1781–90	6.3	1865–74	28.8	1925–34	93.9
1803–12	7.1	1875–84	33.9	1935–38	97.5
1815–24	9.4	1885–94	39.4	1946–49	116.4
1825–34	12.4	1895–1904	47.8	1950–54	141.8
1835–44	16.5	1905–13	57.8	1955–59	187.7
1845–54	19.5	1920–24	67.9	1960–64	246.4
1855–64	24.6				

3. The bases of many official indices have been changed quite frequently in the last 20 or 30 years. Where this has happened, the old and the new indices have been crudely spliced together.

FOOTNOTES

[1] From 1871 to 1917 including Alsace-Lorraine.
[2] The index to 1913 is of the value of the output of manufactures and handicrafts at constant prices.
[3] This break is occasioned by the change of source (see note 1).
[4] First 9 months only.
[5] July-December only.
[6] January-July only.
[7] On the 1913=100 basis the 1919 figure is 57.
[8] A much more complete index begins in 1928.
[9] Excluding Alsace-Lorraine.
[10] On the 1913=100 basis the 1925 figure is 103.
[11] May-December only.
[12] A series published in the first U.N. *Statistical Yearbook,* but not given in the retrospective tables published in the Irish *Statistical Abstract,* gave the following figures for 1938–43:–

1938	98	1940	101	1942	77
1939	103	1941	94	1943	78.

[13] These are described as 'rough estimates'.
[15] The statistics from 1920 (2nd line) relate to Great Britain and Northern Ireland.
[16] On the 1913=100 basis the figure for 1915 is 95.5.
[17] On the all-Germany 1937=100 basis the 1950 figure for West Germany alone is 64.
[18] Previously does not include electricity and gas.
[19] The official index has been spliced onto Feinstein's.

E2 OUTPUT OF COAL (in thousands of metric tons)

1815–1869

	Austria[1]		Belgium	France[4]	Germany		Hungary[5]	
	HC	BC			HC	BC	HC	BC
1815	...		...	882	...	...	...	...
1816	...		...	...	...	...	...	...
1817	...		...	...	1,300	...	...	...
1818	...		...	...	1,300	...	...	...
1819	95		...	...	1,200	...	...	...
1820	125		...	1,094	1,300	...	...	...
1821	135		...	...	1,400	...	...	...
1822	138		...	...	1,500	...	...	...
1823	131		...	...	1,500	...	...	...
1824	151		...	...	1,600	...	...	...
1825	152		...	1,491	1,600	...	...	...
1826	173		...	...	1,600	...	...	...
1827	180		...	1,691	1,700	...	...	...
1828	172		...	1,774	1,700	...	...	...
1829	179		...	1,742	1,700	...	...	...
1830	214		...	1,863	1,800	...	...	...
1831	197		2,305	1,760	1,700	...	...	...
1832	214		2,281	1,964	1,900	...	...	...
1833	176		2,531	2,055	2,100	...	...	...
1834	237		2,437	2,490	2,100	...	...	...
1835	251		2,639	2,506	2,100	...	...	...
1836	274		3,056	2,842	2,300	...	...	...
1837	283		3,229	2,981	2,700	500	...	...
1838	335		3,260	3,113	2,900	600	...	...
1839	432		3,479	2,995	3,000	700	...	...
1840	473		3,930	3,003	3,200	700	...	...
1841	531		4,028	3,410	3,400	600	...	...
1842	561[1] / 497		4,141	3,592	3,800	1,000	19	
1843	490		3,982	3,693	3,600	900	21	
1844	612		4,445	3,783	3,800	1,000	44	
1845	689		4,919	4,202	4,400	1,200	21	
1846	768		5,037	4,469	4,600	1,300	15	
1847	797		5,664	5,153	4,800	1,500	39	
1848	884		4,863	4,000	4,400	1,700	...	
1849	852		5,252	4,049	4,600	1,800	...	
1850	877		5,821	4,434	5,100	1,800	...	
1851	665	361	6,234	4,485	5,700	2,100	61	98
1852	741	491	6,795	4,904	6,500	2,400	69	140
1853	788	614	7,173	5,938	7,000	2,500	86	101
1854	853	746	7,948	6,827	8,400	2,600	104	139
1855	1,014	806	8,409	7,453	9,900	2,900	112	135
1856	1,134	976	8,212	7,926	10,600	3,200	126	126
1857	1,289	1,020	8,384	7,902	11,200	3,800	126	181
1858	...[2]	...[2]	8,926	7,352	12,200	4,000	...[2]	...[2]
1859	1,599	1,128	9,161	7,483	11,400	4,300	206	193
1860	1,706	1,483	9,611	8,304	12,348	4,383	238	237
1861	2,007	1,556	10,057	9,423	14,133	4,622	258	237
1862	2,261	1,748	9,936	10,290	15,576	5,084	324	258
1863	2,211	1,751	10,345	10,710	16,907	5,460	340	265
1864	2,188[3]	1,869[3]	11,158	11,243	19,409	6,204	349[3]	244[3]
1865	2,475	1,975	11,841	11,600	21,795	6,758	362	258
1866	2,294	1,900	12,775	12,260	21,630	6,533	462	287
1867	2,921	2,440	12,756	12,739	23,808	6,995	403	534
1868	3,309	2,822	12,299	13,254	25,705	7,174	487	443
1869	3,476	3,133	12,943	13,464	26,774	7,570	494	562

Abbreviations used throughout this table: HC: Hard Coal BC: Brown Coal

See p.390 for footnotes

E2 Output of Coal (in thousands of metric tons)

1815–1869

	Italy[6]		Russia		Spain		Sweden	U.K.
	HC	BC	HC	BC	HC	BC		
1815	...	...	...		...	...	...	...
1816	...	...	...		...	...	...	16,200
1817	...	...	...		...	...	...	...
1818	...	...	...		...	...	...	...
1819	...	...	...		...	...	...	...
1820	...	...	...		...	...	...	17,700
1821	...	...	...		...	...	...	...
1822	...	...	...		...	...	...	...
1823	...	...	...		...	...	...	19,200
1824	...	...	...		...	...	...	...
1825	...	...	...		...	...	...	22,300
1826	...	...	...		...	...	...	...
1827	...	...	...		...	...	...	...
1828	...	...	...		...	...	...	...
1829	...	...	...		...	...	...	...
1830	...	...	...		...	...	...	22,800
1831	...	...	...		...	...	...	...
1832	...	...	...		...	...	...	...
1833	...	...	...		...	...	...	...
1834	...	...	...		...	...	...	...
1835	...	...	...		...	...	...	28,100
1836	...	...	...		...	...	...	...
1837	...	...	...		...	...	...	...
1838	...	...	...		...	...	...	...
1839	...	...	...		...	...	...	...
1840	...	...	...		...	...	...	34,200
1841	...	...	...		...	...	...	...
1842	...	...	...		...	...	...	...
1843	...	...	...		...	...	...	...
1844	...	...	...		...	...	...	...
1845	...	...	...		...	...	...	46,600
1846	...	...	...		...	...	...	...
1847	...	...	...		...	...	...	...
1848	...	...	...		...	...	...	...
1849	...	...	...		...	...	...	...
1850	...	...	...		...	...	...	50,200
1851	...	...	...		...	...	...	...
1852	...	...	...		...	...	...	...
1853	...	...	...		...	...	...	...
1854	...	...	...		...	...	...	65,699
1855	...	...	...		...	...	...	65,487
1856	...	...	...		...	...	...	67,714
1857	...	...	...		...	...	...	66,444
1858	...	...	...		...	...	...	66,052
1859	...	...	...		...	...	26	73,135
1860	...	...	300		322	18	26	81,327
1861	34		380		331	22	31	84,977
1962	43		350		360	29	31	82,948
1863	36		360		401	50	30	87,677
1864	38		400		388	39	29	94,277
1865	37		380		461	34	34	99,726
1866	50		450		393	40	35	103,262
1867	42		440		...	...	36	106,177
1868	51		450		...	...	45	104,796
1869	56		600		...	...	47	109,152

See p.390 for footnotes

E2 Output of Coal (in thousands of metric tons)

1870–1919

	Austria[1]		Belgium	Bulgaria		Czechoslovakia		France[4]	Germany		Greece[11]
	HC	BC		HC	BC	HC	BC		HC	BC	
1870	3,759	3,458	13,697	...	...	...	...	13,330[9]	26,398[10]	7,605[10]	...
1871	4,353	4,222	13,773	...	...	...	...	13,259	29,373	8,483	...
1872	4,148	4,823	15,659	...	...	...	...	15,803	33,306	9 018	...
1873	4,487	5,783	15,778	...	...	...	...	17,479	36,392	9,753	...
1874	4,471	6,409	14,669	...	...	...	...	16,908	35,919	10,740	...
1875	4,550	6,851	15,011	...	...	...	...	16,957	37,436	10,368	...
1876	4,928	6,940	14,330	...	...	...	...	17,101	38,454	11,096	...
1877	4,886	7,126	13,919	...	...	...	...	16,805	37,530	10,700	...
1878	5,078	7,241	14,899	...	...	...	...	16,961	39,590	10,930	...
1879	5,379	7,906	15,447	...	1	...	...	17,111	42,026	11,445	...
1880	5,890	8,421	16,867	...	1	...	...	19,362	46,974	12,145	...
1881	6,343	8,961	16,874	...	3	...	...	19,766	48,688	12,852	...
1882	6,559	8,996	17,591	...	3	...	...	20,604	52,119	13,260	...
1883	7,194	9,854	18,178	...	5	...	...	21,334	55,943	14,500	...
1884	7,191	10,009	18,051	...	5	...	...	20,024	57,224	14,880	...
1885	7,379	10,514	17,438	...	6	...	...	19,511	58,320	15,355	...
1886	7,421	10,931	17,286	...	6	...	...	19,910	58,057	15,626	...
1887	7,796	11,573	18,379	...	7	...	...	21,288	60,334	15,899	...
1888	8,274	12,860	19,218	...	14	...	...	22,603	65,386	16,574	...
1889	8,593	13,846	19,870	...	18	...	...	24,304	67,342	17,631	...
1890	8,931	15,329	20,366	...	25	...	...	26,083	70,238	19,013	...
1891	9,193	16,183	19,676	...	29	...	...	26,025	73,716	20,555	...
1892	9,241	16,190	19,583	...	33	...	...	26,179	71,372	20.978	...
1893	9,733	16,816	19,411	...	44	...	...	25,651	73,852	21,567	...
1894	9,573	17,333	20,535	...	58	...	...	27,417	76,741	22,103	...
1895	9,723	18,389	20,458	...	62	...	...	28,020	79,164	24,713	...
1896	9,900	18,883	21,252	...	76	...	...	29,190	85,690	26,798	...
1897	10,493	20,458	21,492	...	80	...	...	30,798	91,055	29,423	...
1898	10,948	21 083	22,088	...	105	...	...	32,356	96,310	31,649	...
1899	11,455	21,752	22,072	...	106	...	...	32,863	101,640	34,203	...
1900	10,993	21,540	23,463	...	123	...	...	33,404	109,290	40,279	...
1901	11,739	22,474	22,213	...	144	...	...	32,325	108,539	44,212	...
1902	11,045	22,140	22,877	...	135	...	...	29,997	107,474	43,001	...
1903	11,498	22,158	23,797	...	117	...	...	34,906	116,638	45,674	...
1904	11,868	21,988	24,173	...	147	...	...	34,168	120,816	48,633	...
1905	12,585	22,693	23,348	...	173	...	...	35,928	121,298	52,499	...
1906	13,473	24,168	25,150	...	144	...	...	34,196	137,118	56,415	...
1907	13,850	26,262	25,300	...	180	...	...	36,754	143,223	62,547	...
1908	13,875	26,729	23,135	...	175	...	...	37,384	148,537	66,746	...
1909	13,713	26,044	25,095	...	227	...	...	37,840	148,788	68,658	...
1910	13,774	25,133	25,523	...	227	...	...	38,350	152,828	69,474	1.5
1911	14,380	25,265	24,598	...	245	...	...	39,230	160,748	73,761	–
1912	15,798	26,284	24,511	...	245	...	...	41,145	174,875	80,935	–
1913	16,460	27,378	24,371[7] 22,842	11	358	(14,087)[8]	(23,137)[8]	40,844	190,109	87,233	0.2
1914	15,546	23,581	16,714	...	421	(13,458)[8]	(20,005)[8]	27,528	161,385	83,946	20
1915	16,290	22,064	14,178	...	533	(14,316)[8]	(18,388)[8]	19,533	146,868	87,948	40
1916	...	...	16,863	...	640	15,469	19,440	21,310	159,170	94,180	117
1917	...	...	14,931	...	761	14,548	18,267	28,915	167,747	95,453	158
1918	...[1]	...[1]	13,891	...	673	11,969	16,349	26,259[9]	158,254[10]	100,600[10]	213
1919	...	...	18,483	...	583	10,254	17,324	22,441	116,707[20]	93,648	183

See p.390 for footnotes

E2 Output of Coal (in thousands of metric tons)

1870–1919

	Hungary[5]		Italy		Netherlands		Norway[13]	Portugal	
	HC	BC	HC	BC	HC	BC		HC	BC
1870	537	603	59		32	–	–	...	–
1871	617	856	80		34	–	–	...	–
1872	641	945	94		35	–	–	...	–
1873	684	950	117		45	–	–	...	–
1874	625	774	127		43	–	–	...	–
1875	636	816	117		43	–	–	...	–
1876	667	884	116		42	–	–	...	–
1877	682	907	121		31	–	–	...	–
1878	687	909	124		32	–	–	...	–
1879	674	932	131		37	–	–	...	–
1880	805	1,013	139		39	–	–	...	–
1881	849	1,113	135		42	–	–	...	–
1882	799	1,260	165		45	–	–	...	–
1883	893	1,474	214		48	–	–	...	–
1884	940	1,585	223		50	–	–	...	–
1885	956	1,587	190		46	–	–	...	–
1886	859	1,568	243		42[12]	–	–	...	–
					79				
1887	786	1,723	328		89	–	–	...	–
1888	851	1,874	367		91	–	–	...	–
1889	937	1,952	390		101	–	–	...	–
1890	995	2,252	376		109	–	–	...	–
1891	1,019	2,428	289		100	–	–	...	–
1892	1,052	2,554	296		96	–	–	...	–
1893	983	2,918	317		101	–	–	...	–
1894	1,037	3,175	271		109	–	–	...	–
1895	1,068	3,475	305		127	–	–	...	–
1896	1,133	3,762	276		138	–	–	...	–
1897	1,118	3,871	314		150	–	–	...	–
1898	1,239	4,517	341		150	–	–	...	–
1899	1,239	4,293	389		213	–	–	...	–
1900	1,367	5,130	480		320	–	–	...	–
1901	1,365	5,180	426		311	–	–	...	–
1902	1,163	5,132	2	412	391	–	–	1	–
1903	1,233	5,272	3	344	458	–	–	8	–
1904	1,155	5,519	4	259	443	–	–	...	–
1905	1,088	6,089	2	411	468	–	–	...	–
1906	1,238	6,365	4	469	533	–	–	...	–
1907	1,274	6,491	5	448	723	–	1.5	...	–
1908	1,210	7,151	2	477	908	–	6	5	–
1909	1,397	7,659	2	553	1,121	–	4	...	–
1910	1,302	7,734	3	559	1,293	–	5	...	–
1911	1,290	8,155	3	555	1,477	–	22	11	–
1912	1,302	8,285	2	662	1,725	–	24	15	–
1913	1,320	8,954	1	700	1,873[12]	–	33	25	–
					1,902				
1914	1,116	8,059	1	780	1,983	–	38	29	...
1915	...	...	9	944	2,333	–	18	60	...
1916	1,204	7,880	19	1,287	2,656	–	19	143	...
1917	1,217[5]	7,610[5]	45	1,677	3,126	42	25	189	...
1918	...	...	32[6]	2,139[6]	3,548	1,484	55	185	...
1919	...	...	24	1,134	3,540	1,882	68	130	...

See p.390 for footnotes

E2 Output of Coal (in thousands of metric tons)

1870–1919

	Romania		Russia		Serbia		Spain		Sweden	U.K.
	HC	BC	HC	BC	HC	BC	HC	BC		
1870	...	...	690		...	...	...	...	37	112,203
1871	...	...	830		...	...	...	...	42	119,235
1872	...	...	1,090		...	...	...	...	39	125,479[17]
1873	...	...	1,170		...	...	...	...	50	130,745
1874	...	...	1,290		...	...	...	...	57	128,621
1875	...	...	1,700		...	...	610		64	135,445
1876	...	...	1,820		...	...	...		77	136,277
1877	...	...	1,790		...	...	...		94[16]	136,333
1878	...	...	2,520		...	...	...		93	134,740
1879	...	...	2,920		...	...	...		102	135,866
1880	...	...	3,290		...	...	826	21	101	149,327
1881	...	...	3,490		...	...	936		118	156,658
1882	...	...	3,780		...	...	1,196		143	159,011
1883	...	...	3,980		...	...	1,071		153	166,364
1884	...	...	3,930		...	...	979		165	163,338
1885	...	...	4.270		...	...	946		174	161,908
1886	...	...	4,580				1,001		170	160,046
1887	...	...	4,530		...	...	1,034		169	164,722
1888	...	...	5,190		...	...	1,037		169	172,662
1889	...	...	6,210		...	...	1,120		187	179,756
1890	...	...	6,010		...	...	1,168	42	188	184,528
1891	...	...	6,230		...	...	1,262	26	198	188,455
1892	...	...	6,950		...	...	1,430	35	199	184,704
1893	...	...	7,610		91	27	1,480	41	200	166,963
1894	...	...	8,760		2	82	1,659	48	196	191,299
1895	...	...	9,100		1	61	1,739	45	224	192,704
1896	...	...	9,380		12	75	1,868	55	226	198,496
1897	...	...	11,200		...	...	2,020	54	224	205,374
1898	...	67	12,310		13	81	2,434	66	236	205,297
1899	...	78	13,970		22	96	2,600	71	239	223,627
1900		86	16,160		56	100	2,584	91	252	228,794
1901	...	105	16,530		44	126	2,652	96	271	222,562
1902	...	...	16,470		36	118	2,723	84	305	230,739
1903	...	110	17,860		41	119	2,697	104	320	234,030
1904	...	125	19,610		44	140	3,023	101	321	236,158
1905	...	130	18,670		48	137	3,203	169	322	239,918
1906	...	128	21,730		61	211	3,209	189	297	255,097
1907	...	144	26,000		53	215	3,696	191	305	272,129
1908	...	161	25,910		61	232	3,885	233	305	265,726
1909	...	...	26,820		51	241	3,871	265	247	268,007
1910	...	...	25,430		40	237	3,812	246	303	268,676
1911	...	242	28,420		32	273	3,664	252	312	276,255
1912	...	...	31,130		313		3,852	284	360	264,595
1913	...	250	36,050[15]		...		3,971	277	364	292,042
			27,987	1,130						
1914	...	230	30,750	1,150	...		4,133	291	367	269,927
1915	—	254	30,040	1,400	...		4,359	328	412	257,269
1916	—	300	32,480	1,990	...		5,116	473	415	260,489
1917	...	...	28,960	2,350	...		5,367	638	443	252,487
1918	...[14]	...[14]	11,550	1,550	...		6,512	726	404	231,404
1919	205	1,353	7,740	1,710	...		5,704	540	430	233,467

U.K.: United Kingdom

See p.390 for footnotes

E2 Output of Coal (in thousands of metric tons)

1920–1975

	Austria[1]		Belgium	Bulgaria		Czechoslovakia		Denmark[11]	France[4]
	HC	BC		HC	BC	HC	BC		
1920	133	2,697	22,143	34	726	11,380	19,958	–	25,261
1921	138	2,479	21,807	40	902	12,023	21,335	–	28,960
1922	166	3,136	21,209	49	983	10,465	19,174	–	31,913
1923	158	2,686	22,922	63	1,013	12,347	16,266	–	38,556
1924	172	2,786	23,362	70	1,155	15,179	20,460	–	44,982
1925	145	3,027	23,097	57	1,166	12,559	18,605	–	48,091
1926	157	2,958	25,230	64	1,142	14,177	18,516	–	52,453
1927	176	3,064	27,551	69	1,168	14,016	19,621	–	52,875
1928	202	3,263	27,578	70	1,361	14,568	20,444	–	52,440
1929	208	3,525	26,940	79	1,573	16,548	22,534	–	54,977
1930	216	3,063	27,415	71	1,522	14,469	19,160	–	55,057
1931	228	2,982	27,042	86	1,437	13,165	17,869	–	51,046
1932	221	3,104	21,424	98	1,663	11,032	15,787	–	47,279
1933	239	3,105	25,300	81	1,493	10,627	14,968	–	47,981
1934	251	2,851	26,389	79	1,568	10,789[18]	15,071[18]	–	48,658
1935	261	2,971	26,506	104	1,566	10,893	15,114	–	47,119
1936	244	2,897	27,876	102	1,576	12,233	15,949	–	46,171
1937	230	3,242	29,859	121	1,732	16,778[19]	17,895[19]	–	45,364
1938	226	3,317	29,585	146	1,942	15,835	16,028	–	47,562[9]
1939	217	3,533	29,844	166	2,048	18,803	19,393	–	50,249
1940	228	3,714	25,539	215	2,550	20,966	22,282	226	40,984
1941	226	3,536	26,722	212	2,785	21,071	22,439	1,000	43,857
1942	225	3,523	25,055	219	3,448	22,771	24,129	1,800	43,828
1943	214	3,651	23,737	204	3,811	24,617	27,582	2,600	42,427
1944	195	3,677	13,529	125	2,890	23,238	26,848	2,200	26,577[9]
1945	72	2,066	15,833	128	3,435	11,716[19]	15,356[19]	2,300	35,017
1946	108	2,407	22,852	93	3,420	14,168	19,475	2,300	49,289
1947	178	2,839	24,436	4,170		16,216	22,362	2,800	47,309
1948	181	3,338	26,691	127	4,139	16,683	23,588	2,400	45,136
1949	183	3,816	27,854	172	5,060	17,002	26,527	1,600	53,048
1950	183	4,308	27,321	157	5,771	17,356	27,509	770	52,521
1951	196	4,989	29,651	190	6,224	17,302	30,168	1,582	54,978
1952	190	5,179	30,384	237	7,173	19,057	33,258	1,601	57,357
1953	162	5,574	30,060	269	8,077	18,925	34,350	798	54,544
1954	177	6,285	29,249	294	8,632	19,940	37,860	679	56,324
1955	171	6,619	29,920	293	9,135	20,643	40,751	801	57,389
1956	166	6,730	29,461	370	9,845	21,788	46,299	1,396	57,384
1957	152	6,877	29,001	385	10,730	22,543	51,016	2,560	59,089
1958	141	6,494	27,062	380	11,572	23,932	56,838	2,445	60,039
1959	134	6,221	22,757	503	13,866	25,124	53,703	2,687	59,781
1960	132	5,973	22,469	570	15,416	26,214	58,403	2,673	58,237
1961	106	5,661	21,539	591	16,966	26,233	65,308	2,494	55,264
1962	99	5,712	21,204	636	19,104	27,149	69,485	2,556	55,241
1963	104	6,053	21,416	658	20,275	28,180	73,303	2,512	50,229
1964	103	5,761	21,305	609	23,751	28,201	75,605	2,195	55,271
1965	59	5,450	19,786	552	24,490	27,624	73,216	2,129	54,037
1966	20	5,283	17,499	491	24,653	26,731	74,108	1,982	50,338
1967	14	4,604	16,435	468	26,739	25,946	71,363	1,302	47,624
1968	–	4,177	14,806	439	28,282	25,927	74,885	760	41,911
1969	–	3,841	13,200	370	28,632	27,068	79,337	431	40,583
1970	–	3,670	11,362	397	28,854	28,064	81,783	135	37,354
1971	–	3,770	10,956	388	26,620	28,702	84,791	–	33,014
1972	–	3,756	10,500	384	26,894	27,822	85,566	–	29,763
1973	–	3,634	8,842	351	26,459	27,669	81,829	–	25,682
1974	–	3,629	8,111	307	23,998	27,891	82,790	–	22,896
1975	–	3,397	7,479	330	27,515	28,007	87,086	–	22,411

See p.390 for footnotes

E2 Output of Coal (in thousands of metric tons)

1920–1975

	Germany		East Germany		Greece[11]	Hungary		Italy[6]	
	HC	BC	HC	BC		HC	BC	HC	BC
1920	107,528	111,888	...	...	197	840	4,788	152	1,588
1921	113,898	123,064	...	...	169	726	5,516	114	1,029
1922	119,145[21]	137,208[21]	...	...	132	857	6,183	195	751
1923	62,225	118,249	...	...	118	793	6,895	174	959
1924	118,829	124,360	...	...	131	744	6,342	127	921
1925	132,729	139,804	...	...	142	805	5,519	189	1,008
1926	145,363	139,877	...	...	153	828	5,822	209	1,192
1927	153,595	150,852	...	...	143	786	6,244	169	925
1928	150,876	166,260	...	...	121	783	6,510	128	704
1929	163,437	174,458	...	...	156	826	7,044	223	783
1930	142,699	146,010	...	...	130	812	6,176	231	558
1931	118,640	133,311	...	...	105	776	6,111	236	365
1932	104,741	122,647	...	...	138	895	5,931	255	378
1933	109,692	126,795	...	...	99	800	5,907	334	384
1934	124,857[20]	137,274	...	...	101	756	6,199	374	409
1935	143,003	147,072	...	...	93	823	6,718	443	547
1936	158,283	161,397	...	...	106	827	7,105	806	770
1937	184,513	184,709	...	...	131	917	8,055	964	1,060
1938	186,186	194,985	...	...	108	1,042	8,306	1,014	1,339
1939	187,956	212,109	...	...	139	1,107	9,407	1,113	2,011
1940	184,354	225,016	...	...	250	1,207	10,161	986	3,411
1941	186,531	236,127	...	...	180	1,301	10,955	1,192	3,248
1942	187,920	245,918	...	...	365	1,250	11,234	1,386	3,522
1943	190,482	253,429	...	...	370	1,373	10,789	1,041	2,316
1944	166,035	229,385	...	...	190	1,260	8,398	194	948
	West Germany								
1945	35,484	24,252	...	...	70	711	3,574	80[6]	1,476[6]
1946	53,940	51,588	2,509	108,400	128	722	5,631	146	2,651
1947	71,124	58,727	2,750	101,700	133	1,060	7,749	155	3,070
1948	87,033	64,855	2,848	109,960	127	1,238	9,377	111	1,766
1949	103,238	73,845	3,019	124,000	180	1,378	10,458	90	1,882
1950	110,755	77,403	2,805	137,050	180	1,400	11,868	80	1,734
1951	118,925	84,878	3,204	151,252	177	1,619	13,651	96	1,954
1952	123,278	85,152	2,754	158,462	256	1,718	16,846	92	1,853
1953	124,472	86,236	2,638	172,752	444	1,994	19,016	74	1,817
1954	128,035	89,540	2,648	181,913	700	2,435	19,101	64	1,656
1955	130,728	92,154	2,682	200,612	782	2,692	19,623	48	1,508
1956	134,407	97,030	2,743	205,866	798	2,371	18,219	54	1,480
1957	133,156	98,669	2,753	212,595	998	2,277	18,926	55	1,362
1958	132,582[20]	95,512[20]	2,903	214,970	1,193	2,626	21,623	44	1,511
1959	141,832	95,432	2,841	214,783	1,536	2,734	22,622	31	1,930
1960	142,297	97,971	2,721	225,465	2,550	2,847	23,676	20	1,512
1961	142,741	98,957	2,671	236,926	2,519	3,071	25,104	24	2,243
1962	141,135	103,011	2,575	246,992	2,644	3,341	25,311	16	2,452
1963	142,116	108,499	2,483	254,219	3,586	3,710	26,769	14	1,937
1964	142,201	112,814	2,340	256,926	3,873	4,125	27,423	9	1,665
1965	135,077	103,641	2,212	250,839	5,091	4,362	27,075	6	1,402
1966	125,970	99,249	1,987	249,040	5,007	4,360	25,988	—	1,645
1967	112,043	97,656	1,789	242,027	5,267	4,056	22,976	—	2,912
1968	112,012	102,350	1,579	247,113	5,850	4,242	22,972	—	2,094
1969	111,630	108,187	1,334	254,553	6,686	4,133	22,365	—	2,236
1970	111,271	108,437	1,049	261,482	7,680	4,151	23,679	—	2,689
1971	110,795	104,546	857	262,814	10,888	3,941	23,483	—	2,583
1972	102,470	110,415	815	248,451	11,318	3,671	22,171	—	1,543
1973	97,339	118,658	753	246,245	13,118	3,410	23,371	—	2,151
1974	94,876	126,044	594	243,468	14,263	3,209	22,552	—	2,003
1975	92,393	123,377	539	246,706	17,907	3,021	21,867	—	2,050

See p.390 for footnotes

E2 Output of Coal (in thousands of metric tons)

1920–1975

	Netherlands		Norway	Poland		Portugal		Romania	
	HC	BC		HC	BC	HC	BC	HC	BC
1920	4,116	1,396	77	31,690	248	145	25	187	1,400
1921	4,243	122	109	29,894	270	133	20	210	1,595
1922	4,866	29	208	34,631	220	129	14	255	1,862
1923	5,595	54	230	36,098	171	137	16	292	2,229
1924	6,180	191	266	32,280	89	125	8	297	2,479
1925	7,117	208	286[13]	29,081	66	108	17	314	2,615
1926	8,843	211	278	35,747	76	202	31	322	2,731
1927	9,488	201	319	38,084	78	179	26	373	2,850
1928	10,920	197	275	40,616	74	201	27	398	2,630
1929	11,581	157	251	46,236	74	197	29	371	2,675
1930	12,211	144	188	37,506	55	212	34	299	2,071
1931	12,901	122	243	38,265	41	201	26	287	1,632
1932	12,756	124	256	28,835	33	186	16	188	1,464
1933	12,574	97	295	27,356	33	208	12	195	1,314
1934	12,341	92	314	29,233	26	203	15	228	1,624
1935	11,878	86	309	28,545	18	211	20	278	1,667
1936	12,803	89	309	29,747	14	217	21	293	1,672
1937	14,321	143	297	36,218	18	259	23	303	1,880
1938	13,488	171	299	38,104	10	308	18	345	2,478
1939	12,861	197	312	23,184[22]	6[22]	299	35	286	2,179
1940	12,145	199	269	47,000[23]	...	369	64	298	2,385
1941	13,356	199	146	58,000[23]	...	435	84	264	2,194
1942	12,330	281	—	65,000[23]	...	498	108	285	2,367
1943	12,497	383	—	70,000[23]	...	391	108	306	2,604
1944	8,313	233	—	54,000[23] [24]	... [24]	410	126	202	2,069
1945	5,097	130	6	20,183[25]	...	436	163	211	1,820
1946	8,314	483	96	47,288	1,455	380	141	167	1,784
1947	10,104	474	336	59,130	4,766	370	108	163	2,105
1948	11,032	279	436	70,262	5,040	387	103	215[26]	2,720[26]
								2,040	906
1949	11,705	205	457	74,081	4,621	443	115	...	...
1950	12,247	194	364	78,001	4,836	419	94	2,773	1,159
1951	12,424	249	470	82,000	4,899	417	85	3,227	1,401
1952	12,532	235	453	84,440	5,076	442	77	3,377	1,847
1953	12,297	252	428	88,719	5,633	478	71	3,325	2,172
1954	12,071	172	341	91,619	5,909	432	65	3,191	2,363
1955	11,895	255	322	94,476	6,045	404	88	3,353	2,751
1956	11,836	270	390	95,149	6,183	414	146	3,458	3,014
1957	11,376	288	384	94,096	5,954	499	184	3,636	3,419
1958	11,880	255	288	94,981	7,541	567	156	3,906	3,482
1959	11,978	199	252	99,106	9,258	527	159	4,148	3,829
1960	12,498	4	404	104,438	9,327	435	156	4,481	3,682
1961	12,621	—	369	106,606	10,338	470	158	4,902	3,801
1962	11,573	—	473	109,604	11,091	405	153	5,319	4,270
1963	11,509	—	382	113,150	15,344	416	142	5,655	4,612
1964	11.480	—	442	117,354	20,280	444	101	5,892	5,231
1965	11,446	—	426	118,831	22,626	428	90	6,036	6,059
1966	10,052	—	434	121,979	24,508	420	51	6,310	7,142
1967	8,065	—	427	123,881	23,922	443	39	6,716	8,303
1968	6,663	—	324	128,634	26,878	397	31	7,184	9,836
1969	5,564	—	385	135,010	30,865	416	8	7,534	11,618
1970	4,334	—	461	140,101	32,766	271	—	8,087	14,748
1971	3,609	—	435	145,491	34,517	253	—	8,505	14,446
1972	2,812	—	455	150,697	38,221	252	—	8,073	17,198
1973	1,722	—	415	156,630	39,215	221	—	8,294	18,370
1974	758	—	461	162,002	39,826	230	—	8,523	20,684
1975	—	—	389	171,625	39,865	222	—	...	...

See p.390 for footnotes

E2 Output of Coal (in thousands of metric tons)

1920–1975

	Russia[15]		Spain		Sweden	U.K.	Yugoslavia	
	HC	BC	HC	BC			HC	BC
1920	6,730	2,020	5,421	552	440	233,215	66	2,830
1921	7,500	2,020	5,012	409	377	165,871[27]	78	3,006
1922	9,318	2,006	4,436	330	379	253,612	102	3,587
1923	10,524	2,176	5,971	394	420	280,430	136	3,960
1924	14,584	1,744	6,128	412	438	271,404	130	4,039
1925	14,903	1,617	6,117	403	264	247,078	179	3,975
1926	23,353	2,417	6,536	400	384	128,305	191	3,988
1927	29,452	2,823	6,563	430	398	255,264	284	4,461
1928	32,453	3,057	6,371	423	359	241,283	354	4,697
1929	36,589	3,478	7,108	439	395	262,046	409	5,245
1930	43,289	4,491	7,120	388	398	247,796	366	4,906
1931	50,741	6,011	7,091	341	343	222,981	406	4,450
1932	57,471	6,889	6,854	336	333	212,083	368	4,108
1933	67,467	8,866	5,999	301	349	210,436	379	3,797
1934	82,777	11,383	5,932	299	415	224,269	387	3,926
1935	95,336	14,298	6,946	321	424	225,819	390	4,002
1936	109,257	17,569	3,272	199	456	232,119	441	4,035
1937	109,878	18,090	2,084	208	460	244,268	428	4,574
1938	114,728	18,535	5,649	166	431	230,636	450	5,287
1939	124,957	21,251	6,606	194	444	235,050	446	5,622
1940	139,974	25,949	8,862	569	498	227,898	420	6,916
1941	...	...	8,771	827	557	209,655	...	...
1942	...	...	9,307	1,141	582	208,233	...	...
1943	....	...	9,672	1,162	558	202,112	...	...
1944	...	...	10,447	1,209	570	195,842	...[28]	...
1945	99,428	49,905	10,635	1,342	615	185,709	206	3,405
1946	114,295	49,768	10,685	1,336	488	193,119	757	6,047
1947	132,249	51,000	10,489	1,275	416	199,947	1,062	8,229
1948	150,012	58,230	10,423	1,398	374	210,886	952	9,692
1949	169,100	66,407	10,637	1,330	317	218,550	1,275	10,833
1950	185,225	75,864	11,043	1,344	309	219,780	1,154	11,712
1951	202,464	79,464	11,348	1,489	279	225,824	992	11,050
1952	215,009	85,866	12,056	1,598	347	227,557	1,011	11,087
1953	224,315	96,107	12,194	1,790	285	227,106	925	10,321
1954	243,681	103,428	12,398	1,755	267	227,208	988	12,675
1955	276,615	113,253	12,426	1,828	282	225,107	1,137	14,070
1956	304,002	125,172	12,851	1,935	294	225,569	1,232	15,869
1957	328,502	134,968	13,931	2,519	304	227,217	1,227	16,780
1958	353,030	140,206	14,445	2,672	319	219,285	1,208	17,778
1959	365,220	138,066	13,541	2,102	272	209,413	1,298	19,809
1960	374,925	134,698	13,783	1,762	251	196,712	1,283	21,430
1961	377,019	129,345	13,796	2,089	200	193,521	1,313	22,760
1962	386,432	130,976	12,695	2,488	148	200,605	1,189	23,506
1963	395,132	136,590	12,908	2,591	99	198,937	1,286	26,136
1964	408,870	145,127	12,196	2,604	84	196,734	1,262	28,247
1965	427,881	149,850	12,943	2,773	59	190,508	1,169	28,788
1966	439,195	146,434	12,873	2,654	40	177,384	1,133	28,160
1967	451,422	143,815	12,364	2,666	11	174,906	908	25,558
1968	455,881	138,299	12,322	2,832	20	166,713	835	25,897
1969	467,316	140,486	11,627	2,740	22	152,790	682	25,815
1970	476,406	147,708	10,751	2,831	12	144,600	643	27,779
1971	487,539	153,342	10,715	3,081	12	147,100	707	30,195
1972	499,469	155,719	11,098	3,068	10	119,500	599	30,342
1973	510,621	156,960	10,002	3,003	12	130,200	576	31,874
1974	523,867	160,641	10,452	2,852	11	109,200	601	32,982
1975	537,647	163,633	10,816	3,380	11	127,700	598	34,939

U.K.: United Kingdom

See p.390 for footnotes

E2 Output of Coal (in thousands of metric tons)

NOTES

1. SOURCES:– Belgium 1831–1913 – A. Wibail, 'L'évolution économique de l'industrie charbonnière Belge depuis 1831', *Bulletin de l'Institute des Sciences Economiques* vol. IV no. 1 (1934). Germany 1817–1959 – based on the indices in W.G. Hoffman, *Das Wachstum der Deutschen Wirtschaft seit der Mitte des 19 Jahrhunderts* (Berlin, etc., 1965). Russia to 1921 (except 1913 (2nd line) – W. Nutter, *The Growth of Industrial Production in the Soviet Union* (Princeton, 1962). U.K. to 1850 – estimates by B.R. Mitchell from a forthcoming publication. U.K. 1854–1938 – based on B.R. Mitchell & Phyllis Deane *Abstract of British Historical Statistics* (Cambridge, 1962). U.K. 1938–69 – based on Ministry of Fuel and Power (later Ministry of Power) *Statistical Digest* and its *Supplement* for 1945. All other figures are taken from the official publications noted on p. xv with a few gaps filled from the U.N. *Statistical Yearbook.*

2. Lignite is counted as brown coal, except as indicated in footnote [4]. Where there is no other indication, output was of hard coal entirely.

3. The calorific power of different types of coal varies quite substantially, even within the two broad categories of hard and brown coal. The relation between these two is conventionally taken to be that brown coal has 60 per cent of the heating value of hard coal in Czechoslovakia, France, and Hungary, but only 50 per cent in other countries.

FOOTNOTES

[1] Figures to 1842 (1st line) include Hungary and the Italian provinces. From 1842 (2nd line) to 1918 they apply to the Kingdom of Austria, and subsequently to the Republic. The outputs of the Austrian provinces in Italy prior to 1866 were as follows (all brown coal, (in thousands of tons):–

1842	7	1848	19	1854	26	1860	7
1843	10	1849	16	1855	21	1861	7
1844	9	1850	...	1856	19	1862	16
1845	12	1851	11	1857	19	1863	7
1846	17	1852	20	1858	...	1864	11
1847	19	1853	55	1859	7	1865	7

Lombardy was lost after 1859, and the statistics for the rest of the period are for Venetia alone.

[2] Total output of hard and brown coal for the whole Austro-Hungarian Empire was 2,911 thousand tons.

[3] Previous statistics are for years ended 31 October. Total output for the whole Austro-Hungarian Empire in November and December 1865 was 510 thousand tons of hard coal and 438 thousand tons of brown coal.

[4] Hard coal and lignite. Earlier figures are given in M. Block, *Statistique de la France* (Paris, 1860) as follows (in thousands of tons):– 1787 215; 1802 844; 1811 774.

[5] Hungarian output is included with Austrian prior to 1842. From 1842 to 1917 the statistics apply to the whole Kingdom of Hungary.

[6] Statistics to 1918 apply to the boundaries of 1871. From 1919 to 1945 they apply to the boundaries of 1924, and subsequently to the boundaries of 1954.

[7] This break is probably occasioned by a change from unscreened to screened production figures, and by the exclusion in later years of colliery consumption.

[8] This production is also included in the statistics for Austria.

[9] From 1871 to 1918 and from 1939 to 1944 parts of Alsace and Lorraine ceded to Germany are excluded.

[10] From 1871 to 1918 parts of Alsace-Lorraine are included.

[11] The ouput is entirely of lignite.

[12] Figures to 1886 (1st line) relate to state-owned mines only, and from 1886 (2nd line) to 1913 (1st line) they relate to Limburg province only.

[13] The entire output comes from Spitzbergen. Up to 1925 the statistics cover only coal shipped from the island.

[14] Coal mines in Transylvania were acquired in 1919.

[15] Figures from 1913 (2nd line) to 1940 apply to the 1923 boundaries of the U.S.S.R.

[16] Previous statistics are for years ended 31 October.

[17] The figures for 1854–72 were based on voluntary returns, and it appears that by the end of the period they were understating output by between 1 and 2 million tons.

[18] One mine was transferred from the brown to the hard coal category.

[19] For 1938–45 Sudetenland is excluded.

[20] From 1920 to 1934 and from 1945 to 1958 Saarland is excluded. Statistics for that district are as follows (in thousands of tons):—

1920	9,410	1928	13,107	1945	3,463	1952	16,236
1921	9,575	1929	13,579	1946	7,898	1953	16,418
1922	11,240	1930	13,236	1947	10,541	1954	16,818
1923	9,192	1931	11,367	1948	12,567	1955	17,329
1924	14,032	1932	10,438	1949	14,262	1956	17,090
1925	12,990	1933	10,561	1950	15,091	1957	16,455
1926	13,681	1934	11,318	1951	16,279	1958	16,423

[21] From July 1922 eastern Upper Silesia is excluded.

[22] First half-year only.

[23] These are rough estimates, and include most of the Ostrava-Karvina coalfield, which was part of Czechoslovakia prior to 1940 and after 1944.

[24] Up to 1944 the statistics apply to the boundaries of 1923, and subsequently to the postwar territory.

[25] April-December only.

[26] This break is apparently caused by the transfer of the Jin Valley coalfields from the brown to the hard coal category.

[27] Southern Ireland is subsequently excluded.

[28] There were coal mines in the territory acquired from Italy in 1945, and the 1939 output of the postwar territory was 1,410 thousand tons.

E3 OUTPUT OF CRUDE PETROLEUM (in thousands of metric tons)

1857–1909

	Austria[1]	Germany	Hungary[2]	Italy	Romania	Russia
1857		...	...	...	0.3	...
1858	—	...	...	...	0.5	...
1859	—	...	...	...	0.6	...
1860	—	...	...	...	1.2	4
1861	—	...	...	..	2.4	4
1862	—	...	...	..	3.2	4
1863	0.2	...	...	..	3.9	6
1864	0.2	...	...	..	4.6	9
1865	0.3	...	...	0.3	5.4	9
1866	0.3	...	...	0.1	5.9	13
1867	0.3	...	...	0.1	7.1	17
1868	0.4	...	...	0.1	7.7	29
1869	0.4	...	...	..	8.1	42
1870	0.4	...	...	..	12	33
1871	0.4	...	...	..	13	26
1872	0.5	4	...	..	13	27
1873	0.5	2	...	0.1	14	68
1874	0.6	1	...	0.1	14	106
1875	0.6	1	...	0.1	15	153
1876	0.6	1	...	0.4	15	213
1877	0.6	1	...	0.4	16	276
1878	0.6	1	...	0.4	15	358
1879	1.0	2	...	0.4	15	431
1880	1.0	1	...	0.3	16	382
1881	1.2	4	1.9	0.2	17	701
1882	1.9	8	0.7	0.2	19	870
1883	1.8	4	—	0.2	19	1,039
1884	2.3	6	..	0.4	29	1,533
1885	2.2	6	..	0.3	27	1,966
1886	53	10	..	0.2	23	1,936
1887	56	10	..	0.2	25	2,405
1888	65	12	..	0.2	30	3,074
1889	79	10	..	0.2	41	3,349
1890	99	15	1.0	0.4	54	3,864
1891	94	15	0.7	1.2	75	4,610
1892	95	14	..	2.5	83	4,775
1893	102	14	..	2.7	75	5,620
1894	119	17	2.1	2.9	69	5,040
1895	195	17	2.1	3.6	80	6,935
1896	269	20	2.2	2.5	82	7,115
1897	282	23	2.3	1.9	105	7,566
1898	310	26	2.5	2.0	180	8,635
1899	315	27	2.1	2.2	226	9,264
1900	349	50	2.2	1.7	247	10,684
1901	407	44	3.3	2.2	298	11,987
1902	524	50	4.3	2.6	325	11,621
1903	675	63	3.0	2.5	412	11,099
1904	827	90	2.1	3.5	531	11,665
1905	797	79	4.7	6.1	681	8,310
1906	740	81	2.7	7.5	971	8,885
1907	1,128	106	2.4	8.3	1,147	9,760
1908	1,721	141	2.4	7.1	1,139	10,388
1909	2,088	137	2.6	5.9	1,356	11,248

See p. 395 for footnotes

E3 Output of Crude Petroleum (in thousands of metric tons)

1910–1969

	Austria[1]	Bulgaria	Czech.	France	Germany	Hungary[2]	Italy
1910	1,768	–	...	–	140	2.5	7.1
1911	1,490	–	...	–	137	2.2	10
1912	1,146	–	...	–	135	2.8	7.5
1913	1,115	–	...	–	121	2.1	6.6
1914	700[1]	–	2	–	110	4.4	5.5
1915	578[1]	–	4	–	99	6.2	6.1
1916	...	–	5	–	93	5.9	7.0
1917	...[1]	–	9	–	91[3]	9.5[3]	5.7
1918	...	–	8	–	38	...	4.9
1919	...	–	7	47	37	–	4.9
1920	–	–	10	55	35	–	4.9
1921	–	–	14	56	38	–	4.5
1922	–	–	18	70	42	–	4.3
1923	–	–	11	70	51	–	4.7
1924	–	–	11	74	59	–	5.2
1925	–	–	23	65	79	–	7.9
1926	–	–	22	67	95	–	5.4
1927	–	–	16	73	97	–	6.1
1928	–	–	14	74	92	–	6.0
1929	–	–	14	75	103	–	5.9
1930	–	–	23	76	174	–	7.8
1931	- -	–	20	74	229	–	16
1932	0.1	–	18	75	230	–	27
1933	0.9	–	18	79	239	–	27
1934	4.2	–	26	78	318	–	20
1935	6.6	–	20	76	427	–	16
1936	7.5	–	19	70	445	–	16
1937	33	–	18	70	451	2	14
1938	57	–	20	72	552	43	13
1939	144	–	21	70	741	144	12
1940	413	–	31	...	1,056	254	11
1941	652	–	35	58	901	422	12
1942	871	–	36	65	743	666	13
1943	1,104	–	36	68	710	839	11
1944	1,213	–	32	59	720	833[4]	7
					West Germany		
1945	445	–	14	29	543	655	7
1946	845	–	25	52	649	685	11
1947	910	–	32	50	577	567	10
1948	951	–	31	52	636	480	9
1949	1,150	–	44	58	842	506	9
1950	1,700	–	63	128	1,119	512	8
1951	2,283	–	73	291	1,367	499	18
1952	2,765	–	113	350	1,755	598	64
1953	3,221	–	122	367	2,189	846	85
1954	3,432	...	125	505	2,666	1,217	72
1955	3,666	150	107	878	3,147	1,601	204
1956	3,428	247	108	1,264	3,506	1,202	570
1957	3,186	285	108	1,410	3,960	675	1,262
1958	2,836	222	106	1,386	4,432	830	1,546
1959	2,458	192	123	1,618	5,103	1,036	1,695
1960	2,448	200	137	1,977	5,530	1,217	1,998
1961	2,356	207	154	2,163	6,204	1,457	1,972
1962	2,394	199	177	2,370	6,776	1,641	1,808
1963	2,620	173	180	2,522	7,383	1,757	1,784
1964	2,663	160	195	2,846	7,673	1,801	2,669
1965	2,855	229	192	2,988	7,884	1,803	2,207
1966	2,757	404	190	2,932	7,868	1,706	1,757
1967	2,685	499	200	2,832	7,927	1,686	1,615
1968	2,724	475	205	2,688	7,982	1,807	1,506
1969	2,758	325	210	2,496	7,876	1,754	1,479

See p. 395 for footnotes

E3 Output of Crude Petroleum (in thousands of metric tons)

1910–1969

	Netherlands	Poland	Romania	Russia	U.K.	Yugoslavia
1910	—	...	1,326	11,283	—	...
1911	—	...	1,625	10,547	—	...
1912	—	...	1,899	10,408	—	...
1913	—	...	1,848	10,281[8]	—	...
				9,234		
1914	—	...	1,810	9,176	—	...
1915	—	...	1,588	9,442	—	...
1916	—	...	899	9,970	—	...
1917	—	...	724	8,800	—	...
1918	—	...	969	4,146	—	...
1919	—	...	856	4,448	—	...
1920	—	765	1,109	3,851	—	...
1921	—	705	1,168	3,781	—	—
1922	—	713	1,373	4,658	—	—
1923	—	737	1,512	5,277	—	—
1924	—	771	1,860	6,064	—	—
1925	—	812	2,317	7,061	—	—
1926	—	796	3,244	8,318	—	—
1927	—	723	3,669	10,285	—	—
1928	—	743	4,282	11,625	—	—
1929	—	675	4,837	13,684	—	—
1930	—	663	5,792	18,451	—	—
1931	—	631	6,756	22,392	—	—
1932	—	557	7,348	21,414	—	—
1933	—	551	7,377	21,489	—	—
1934	—	529	8,466	24,218	—	—
1935	—	515	8,394	25,218	—	—
1936	—	511	8,704	27,427	—	—
1937	—	501	7,153	28,501	—	1
1938	—	507	6,610	30,186	—	1
1939	—	(260)[5]	6,240	30,259	4	1
1940	—	...	5,810	31,121[8]	17	1
1941	—	...	5,453	...	30	...
1942	—	...	5,665	...	83	...
1943	—	...	5,273	...	115	...
1944	2	...[6]	3,525	...	97	...
1945	6	(82)[7]	4,640	19,436	73	...
1946	63	117	4,193	21,746	56	29
1947	213	128	3,810	26,022	48	33
1948	496	140	4,149	29,249	45	36
1949	621	152	4,700	33,444	47	63
1950	705	162	5,047	37,878	47	110
1951	714	181	6,211	42,253	46	148
1952	715	215	8,002	47,311	56	152
1953	820	189	9,058	52,777	56	172
1954	939	184	9,741	59,281	60	216
1955	1,024	180	10,556	70,793	55	257
1956	1,097	184	10,920	83,806	67	294
1957	1,523	181	11,180	98,346	83	396
1958	1,621	175	11,336	113,216	81	462
1959	1,773	175	11,438	129,557	84	592
1960	1,918	194	11,500	147,859	87	944
1961	2,046	203	11,582	166,068	108	1,341
1962	2,157	202	11,864	186,244	113	1,525
1963	2,215	212	12,233	206,069	125	1,611
1964	2,270	282	12,395	223,603	129	1,799
1965	2,395	340	12,571	242,888	83	2,063
1966	2,366	400	12,825	265,125	78	2,222
1967	2,265	450	13,206	288,068	88	2,374
1968	2,147	475	13,285	309,150	81	2,494
1969	2,020	439	13,246	328,373	77	2,699

See p. 395 for footnotes

E3 Output of Crude Petroleum (in thousands of metric tons)

1970–1975

	Austria[1]	Bulgaria	Czech.	France	Germany	Hungary[2]	Italy
1970	2,798	334	203	2,309	7,535	1,937	1,405
1971	2,516	305	194	1,861	7,420	1,955	1,291
1972	2,478	248	191	1,486	7,098	1,977	1,152
1973	2,578	190	171	1,254	6,638	1,989	1,047
1974	2,238	144	149	1,080	6,191	1,997	1,031
1975	2,037	122	142	1,024	5,741	2,006	1,029

	Netherlands	Poland	Romania	Russia	U.K.	Yugoslavia
1970	1,919	424	13,377	353,039	83	2,854
1971	1,714	395	13,793	377,075	83	2,961
1972	1,597	347	14,128	400,440	83	3,200
1973	1,492	392	14,287	429,037	88	3,332
1974	1,461	550	14,486	458,948	88	3,458
1975	1,419	553	14,590	491,000	1,223	3,692

NOTES

1. SOURCES The official publications noted on p. xv with a few gaps filled from U.N. *Statistical Yearbooks.* Czechoslovak figures for 1947, 1949, and 1950 were supplied by the Federal Statistical Office of Czechoslovakia.

2. Output from oil shale is not included in this table.

FOOTNOTES

[1] Cisleithania to 1917, except in 1914 and 1915 when the statistics are for Galicia only. Later statistics are for the Republic.
[2] Transleithania (including Croatia-Slavonia) to 1917, and subsequently the territory established by the treaty of Trianon.
[3] Previously includes Alsace-Lorraine.
[4] First 9 months only.
[5] First half-year only.
[6] The territory in Galicia ceded to the U.S.S.R. in 1945 contained the main Polish oilfields.
[7] April-December only.
[8] Figures to 1913 (1st line) apply to the Russian Empire. From 1913 (2nd line) to 1940 they apply to the 1923 territory of the U.S.S.R., and subsequently to the post-Second World War Boundaries.

E4 OUTPUT OF NATURAL GAS (in millions of cubic metres)

1894–1929

	Austria	Bulgaria	Czech	France	Germany	Hungary	Italy	Neth'l	Poland	Romania	Russia	U.K.	Yugoslavia
1894	...	—	...	...	...	—	..	—	...	...	...	—	...
1895	...	—	...	...	...	—	..	—	...	...	...	—	...
1896	...	—	...	...	...	—	..	—	...	...	...	—	...
1897	...	—	...	...	...	—	..	—	...	...	...	—	...
1898	...	—	...	...	...	—	..	—	...	...	...	—	...
1899	...	—	...	...	...	—	1	—	...	...	...	—	...
1900	...	—	...	...	...	—	1	—	...	...	...	—	...
1901	...	—	...	...	...	—	1	—	...	...	...	—	...
1902	...	—	...	...	...	—	2	—	...	...	...	—	...
1903	...	—	...	...	...	—	2	—	...	...	...	—	...
1904	...	—	...	...	...	—	3	—	...	...	...	—	...
1905	...	—	...	...	...	—	3	—	...	...	...	—	...
1906	...	—	...	...	...	—	6	—	...	...	...	—	...
1907	...	—	...	...	...	—	6	—	...	...	...	—	...
1908	...	—	...	...	...	—	7	—	...	...	...	—	...
1909	...	—	...	...	...	—	8	—	...	...	...	—	...
1910	...	—	...	...	...	—	9	—	...	...	...	—	...
1911	...	—	...	...	...	—	9	—	...	...	...	—	...
1912	...	—	...	...	...	—	7	—	...	...	...	—	...
1913	...	—	...	...	...	—	6	—	...	...	29	—	...
1914	...	—	...	...	...	—	6	—	...	...	...	—	...
1915	...	—	...	...	...	—	6	—	...	...	...	—	...
1916	...	—	...	...	...	—	6	—	...	...	...	—	...
1917	...	—	...	...	...	—	7	—	...	...	...	—	...
1918	...	—	...	...	...	—	7	—	...	...	...	—	...
1919	...	—	...	...	...	—	9	—	...	144	...	—	...
1920	...	—	...	...	...	—	8	—	405	171	...	—	...
1921	...	—	...	...	...	—	8	—	400	181	...	—	...
1922	...	—	...	...	...	—	7	—	403	250	22	—	...
1923	...	—	...	...	...	—	7	—	390	287	25	—	...
1924	...	—	...	...	...	—	7	—	438	362	28	—	...
1925	...	—	...	...	...	—	7	—	535	370	140	—	...
1926	...	—	...	...	...	—	6	—	481	377	228	—	...
1927	...	—	...	...	...	—	6	—	454	439	271	—	...
1928	...	—	..	..	...	—	6	—	460	613	304	—	...
1929	...	—	2	..	...	—	7	—	467	807	331	—	2

Czech: Czechoslovakia Neth'l: Netherlands U.K.: United Kingdom

E4 Output of Natural Gas (in millions of cubic metres)

1930–1975

	Austria	Bulgaria	Czech	France	E Germany	W Germany	Hungary	Italy	Neth'l	Poland	Romania	Russia[7]	U.K.	Yugoslavia
1930	—	—	3	..	...	...	—	9	—	487	1,206	520	—	5
1931	—	—	1	..	...	...	—	12	—	474	1,383	847	—	6
1932	..	—	1	..	...	...	2	13	—	437	1,456	1,049	—	2
1933	..	—	1	..	...	...	2	14	—	462	1,500	1,066	—	1
1934	15	—	1	..	...	12	2	15	—	469	1,814	1,533	—	1
1935	..	—	1	..	...	14	3	12	—	485	1,914	1,791	—	1
1936	..	—	1	..	...	22	3	13	—	483	2,130	2,053	—	2
1937	..	—	2	..	...	21	4	15	—	531	2,007	2,179	—	2
1938	1	—	2	..	...	18	8	17	—	584	1,860	2,200	—	2
1939	...	—	1	..	...	30	13	20	—	(332)[4]	1,702	2,200	—	3
1940	...	—	2	..	...	...	32	28	—	...	1,661	3,219[7]	—	...
1941	...	—	2	..	...	...	38	42	—	...	1,575	...	—	...
1942	...	—	1	3	...	...	47	55	—	...	1,791[6]	...	—	...
											1,333			
1943	...	—	1	46	...	...	70	55	—	...	1,412	...	—	...
1944	149	—	1	66	...	...	78	49	—	...	930	...	—	...
						West Germany								
1945	...	—	2	85	...	71	77	42	—	(102)[5]	1,304	3,278	—	3
1946	...	—	3	110	...	109	91	64	—	149	1,332	3,750	—	9
1947	...	—	...	147	...	78	101[3]	94	1	148	1,176	4,590	—	12
1948	241	—	...	174	...	67	320	117	6	157	2,346	5,070	—	8
1949	...	—	...	228	...	54	370	249	7	136	...	5,240	—	8
1950	470	—	37	246	...	68	379	510	8	182	3,350	5,761	—	15
1951	483	—	81	282[1]	...	84[2]	405	966	9	277	4,044	6,252	—	13
						57								
1952	448	—	125	258	...	57	500	1,433	16	313	4,952	6,384	—	14
1953	555	—	168	233	...	58	549	2,280	25	319	5,595	6,869	—	24
1954	625	—	172	251	...	87	558	2,967	100	358	5,826	7,512	—	28
1955	748	—	173	256	...	240	545	3,627	145	393	6,169	8,981	—	34
1956	745	—	274	306	...	367	452	4,466	169	436	6,756	12,067	—	38
1957	759	—	772	439	...	357	411	4,987	166	419	7,460	18,583		42
1958	820	—	1,248	682	24	344	379	5,175	208	384	8,506	28,085	1	46
1959	1,128	—	1,490	1,645	23	388	334	6,118	226	418	9,305	35,391	1	50
1960	1,469	—	1,442	2,846	26	448	342	6,447	330	541	10,143	45,303	1	53
1961	1,556	—	1,410	4,010	38	481	324	6,862	449	723	10,914	58,981	3	69
1962	1,635	—	1,195	4,740	53	616[2]	340	7,150	499	791	12,907	73,525	4	95
						807								
1963	1,699	...	1,114	4,861	101	1,171	611	7,267	569	945	14,262	89,832	6	191
1964	1,764	...	1,021	5,090	108	1,808	784	7,684	835	1,180	15,483	108,566	6	274
1965	1,724	73	965	5,048	133	2,639	1,108	7,800	1,743	1,312	17,281	127,666	13	330
1966	1,874	109	1,070	5,161	116	3,390	1,552	8,767	3,311	1,290	18,616	142,962	3	402
1967	1,797	329	1,017	5,563	107	4,338	2,045	9,300	6,991	1,463	20,502	157,445	472	462
1968	1,630	506	1,108	5,682	143	6,487	2,687	10,408	14,056	2,402	21,737	169,101	2,019	584
1969	1,483	525	1,185	6,506	343	8,912	3,235	11,960	21,848	3,672	22,740	181,121	5,043	730
1970	1,897	474	1,204	6,880	1,232	12,645	3,469	13,171	31,617	4,975	23,629	197,945	11,063	977
1971	1,891	327	1,223	7,149	2,853	15,365	3,705	13,348	43,742	5,164	25,251	212,398	18,290	1,151
1972	1,963	220	1,162	7,517	5,055	17,690	4,110	14,142	58,385	5,601	26,212	221,386	16,460	1,242
1973	2,270	222	1,042	7,546	7,012	19,378	4,821	14,062	70,815	5,811	27,753	236,326	28,850	1,329
1974	2,207	180	975	7,628	7,732	20,195	5,101	15,228	83,703	5,528	28,643	260,553	34,820	1,447
1975	2,359	111	1,150	7,356	8,000	18,280	5,175	14,562	90,852	5,963	29,015	298,000	36,250	1,548

Czech: Czechoslovakia Neth'l: Netherlands U.K.: United Kingdom

See p. 398 for footnotes

E4 Output of Natural Gas (in millions of cubic metres)

NOTES

1. SOURCES:– The official publications noted on p. xv and the League of Nations and United Nations *Statistical Yearbooks,* and U.N., *World Energy Supplies.*

2. Except as incidated in footnotes, the statistics in this table relate to natural gas from gasfields only, and exclude methane from coalfields.

FOOTNOTES

[1] This break is unexplained, but may be due to the earlier inclusion of methane from coal mines.

[2] From 1951 (1st line) to 1962 (2nd line) natural gas from oil wells is excluded.

[3] Previously excludes repressured gas.

[4] First half-year only.

[5] April–December only.

[6] This break is unexplained, but may be due to the subsequent exclusion of gas from oil wells.

[7] Figures to 1940 apply to the 1923 boundaries of the U.S.S.R., and later figures to the post-Second World War boundaries.

E5 OUTPUT OF MAIN NON-FERROUS METAL ORES (in thousands of metric tons)

1750–1784			1785–1819		
	Copper[1]	Tin[3]		Copper[1]	Tin
	United Kingdom			United Kingdom	
1750	9.6	2.9	1785	4.5	2.9
1751	11.2	2.3	1786	4.9	3.5
1752	12.3	2.6	1787	...	3.3
1753	13.2	2.6	1788	...	3.4
1754	14.2	2.8	1789	...	3.5
1755	14.4	2.8	1790	...	3.2
1756	16.3	2.8	1791	...	3.5
1757	17.3	2.8	1792	...	3.9
1758	15.2	2.8	1793	...	3.3
1759	17.0	2.7	1794	...	3.4
1760	16.1	2.8	1795	...	3.5
1761	17.3	2.4	1796	5.1	3.1
1762	16.4	2.6	1797	5.3	3.3
1763	18.2	2.8	1798	5.7	2.9
1764	21.8	2.7	1799	5.0	2.9
1765	17.1	2.8	1800	5.3	2.6
1766	21.6	3.1	1801	5.4	2.4
1767	18.8	2.9	1802	5.3	2.7
1768	24.1	2.7	1803	5.7	3.0
1769	27.1	2.9	1804	5.5	3.0
1770	31.3	3.0	1805	6.3	2.8
1771	28.3[2]	2.9	1806	7.0	2.9
	3.4				
1772	3.5	3.2	1807	6.8	2.5
1773	3.4	2.9	1808	6.9	2.4
1774	3.7	2.5	1909	6.9	2.5
1775	3.7	2.7	1810	5.8	2.0
1776	3.6	2.7	1811	6.2	2.4
1777	3.5	2.8	1812	6.8	2.4
1778	3.1	2.6	1813	7.0	2.4
1779	3.8	2.7	1814	6.5	2.7
1780	2.9	3.0	1815	6.6	3.0
1781	3.6	2.7	1816	6.8	3.4
1782	3.5	2.6	1817	6.6	4.2
1783	4.4	2.6	1818	6.9	4.1
1784	4.5	2.7	1819	6.9	3.4

See p. 405 for footnotes

E5 Output of Main Non-Ferrous Metal Ores (in thousands of metric tons)

1820–1869

	Copper			Lead			Tin	Zinc	
	Germany	Spain[4]	U.K.[1]	Germany	Spain[4]	U.K.	U.K.	Germany	Italy
1820	...	...	7.6	...	...	...	3.0	...	...
1821	...	...	8.6	...	...	...	3.4	...	...
1822	....	...	9.2	...	...	...	3.3	...	...
1823	...	...	8.0	...	...	...	4.3	...	...
1824	...	...	7.9	...	...	...	5.1	...	...
1825	...	...	8.3	...	...	...	4.4	...	...
1826	...	...	9.1	...	...	...	4.7	...	...
1827	...	...	10.5	...	...	...	5.6	...	...
1828	...	...	10.1	...	...	...	5.0	...	...
1829	...	...	9.9	...	...	...	4.5	...	...
1830	...	...	11.1	...	...	...	4.5	...	...
1831	...	...	12.4	...	...	...	4.4	...	...
1832	...	...	12.3	...	...	...	4.4	...	...
1833	...	...	11.4	...	...	...	4.1	...	...
1834	...	...	11.4	...	...	...	4.0	...	...
1835	...	...	12.5	...	...	...	4.3	...	...
1836	...	...	11.8	...	...	...	4.1	...	...
1837	32	...	11.0	...	...	...	4.9	51	...
1838	33	...	11.7	...	...	...	...	56	...
1839	36	...	12.7	...	...	...	...	52	...
1840	30	...	11.2	...	...	...	...	53	...
1841	32	...	10.2	...	...	...	...	66	...
1842	36	...	10.1	...	...	...	...	82	...
1843	37	...	11.1	...	...	...	...	96	...
1844	37	...	11.4	...	...	...	...	110	...
1845	35	...	13.1	...	...	53.5	...	127	...
1846	40	...	12.1	...	...	51.0	...	139	...
1847	43	...	12.2	...	...	56.6	...[5]	131	...
1848	41	...	13.1	...	...	55.8	10.3	127	...
1849	40	...	12.3	...	...	59.6	10.9	131	...
1850	45	...	12.0	...	47.6	65.5	10.5	151	...
1851	56	...	12.4	...	...	66.1	9.6	154	...
1852	70	...	11.9	...	...	66.0	9.8	185	...
1853	71	...	12.0	...	...	62.0	9.0[5] 5.9	165	...
1854	70	...	12.2[2] 20.2	...	...	65.0	6.0	182	...
1855	72	...	21.6	...	42.1	66.5	6.1	219	...
1856	80	...	24.6	...	...	74.3	6.3	231	...
1857	74	...	17.7	...	...	68.5	6.7	223	...
1858	74	...	14.7	...	...	69.4	7.0	250	...
1859	80	...	16.1	...	...	64.2	7.2	284	...
1860	93	2.7	16.3	...	64.5	64.3	6.8	310	...
1861	106	1.7	15.5	...	62.4	66.6	7.6	334	0.2
1862	124	2.9	15.0	...	62.8	70.1	8.6	334	0.2
1863	142	3.3	14.4	...	72.3	69.3	10.2	292	0.3
1864	157	2.9	13.5	...	65.4	68.2	10.3	313	0.2
1865	153	3.6	12.1	...	62.0	68.3	10.2	335	0.7
1866	164	3.5	11.4	...	67.9	68.5	10.2	353	1.5
1867	179	...	10.4	96	...	69.5	8.8	369	6.4
1868	202	...	10.8	95	...	72.1	9.4	370	51.0
1869	217	...	8.4	101	...	74.5	9.9	405	80.5

U.K.: United Kingdom

See p. 405 for footnotes

E5 Output of Main Non-Ferrous Metal Ores (in thousands of metric tons)

1870–1919

	Bauxite	Copper		
	France	Germany	Spain[4]	United Kingdom
1870	...	207	...	7.3
1871	...	217	...	6.4
1872	...	282	...	5.8
1873	...	292	...	5.3
1874	...	263	...	5.0
1875	...	279	...	4.7
1876	...	305	...	4.8
1877	...	344	...	4.6
1878	...	374	...	4.1
1879	...	399	...	3.6
1880	...	481	...	3.8
1881	...	524	...	4.0
1882	...	567	...	3.6
1883	...	613	...	2.6
1884	...	593	...	3.5
1885	...	621	...	2.8[6]
1886	...	496	...	...
1887	...	508	...	...
1888	...	531	...	...
1889	...	573	...	...
1890	...	596	...	...
1891	...	588	...	...
1892	...	568	...	...
1893	...	585	...	...
1894	...	588	...	...
1895	...	633	...	...
1896	...	717	6	...
1897	...	701	7	...
1898	...	703	6	...
1899	...	734	4	...
1900	...	748	5	...
1901	77	777	7.9	...
1902	97	762	7.3	...
1903	134	773	7.7	...
1904	76	798	8.1	...
1905	103	794	8.2	...
1906	118	769	9.1	...
1907	158	771	9,9	...
1908	171	727	14.6	...
1909	130	799	17.5	...
1910	196	926	17.4	...
1911	255	869	18.3	...
1912	259	969	22.5	...
1913	309	942	24.0	...
1914	...	884	13.3	...
1915	...	1,023	22.3	...
1916	...	1,282	20.8	...
1917	...	1,140	25.6	...
1918	...	1,009	21.7	...
1919	159	630	23.4	...

See p. 405 for footnotes

E5 Output of Main Non-Ferrous Metal Ores (in thousands of metric tons)

1870–1919

	Lead			Tin	Zinc	
	Germany	Spain[4]	U.K.	U.K.	Germany	Italy
1870	106	85.8	74.6	10.4	367	92.8
1871	97	...	70.2	11.1	335	56.4
1872	94	...	61.4	9.7	420	80.9
1873	101	...	55.1	10.1	445	79.0
1874	104	...	59.7	10.1	451	64.7
1875	114	119.6	58.3	9.8	468	62.0
1876	121	...	59.6	8.6	534	66.0
1877	147	...	62.4	9.7	577	88.8
1878	153	...	58.9	10.3	597	62.7
1879	149	...	52.4	9.7	590	73.4
1880	160	79.8	57.8	9.1	633	85.3
1881	165	...	49.4	8.8	660	72.2
1882	178	88.3	51.1	9.3	695	91.4
1883	170	99.3	44.1	9.5	678	100.6
1884	163	83.3	40.7	9.7	632	105.0
1885	158	89.0	38.3	9.5	681	107.9
1886	159	106.0	40.1	9.5	705	107.5
1887	158	119.0	38.5	9.4	901	93.1
1888	162	129.0	38.2	9.4	668	87.3
1889	170	136.9	36.2	9.1	709	97.1
1890	168	140.3	34.1	9.8	759	110.9
1891	159	145.7	37.7	9.5	794	120.7
1892	163	152.3	30.0	9.4	800	129.7
1893	168	157.1	30.2	9.0	788	132.8
1894	163	152.6	30.2	8.5	729	132.8
1895	162	160.8	29.5	6.8	706	121.2
1896	158	167.0	31.3	4.9	730	118.2
1897	150	166.4	27.0	4.5	664	122.2
1898	149	167.4	25.8	4.7	642	132.1
1899	144	162.6	24.0	4.1	665	150.6
1900	148	172.5	24.8	4.3	639	139.7
1901	153	169.2	20.3	4.6	648	135.8
1902	168	177.6	18.0	4.5	703	132.0
1903	166	175.0	20.3	4.4	683	157.5
1904	164	185.8	20.1	4.2	716	148.4
1905	153	185.6	20.9	4.5	731	147.8
1906	141	185.4	22.7	4.6	705	155.8
1907	147	186.5	24.9	4.5	698	160.5
1908	157	188.1	21.3	5.1	706	152.3
1909	160	180.0	22.9	5.3	724	129.9
1910	149	190.5	21.8	4.9	718	146.3
1911	140	189.9	18.3	5.0	700	139.7
1912	143	232.6	19.5	5.3	770	149.8
1913	145	193.9	18.4	5.4	773	158.3
1914	129	143.6	19.7	5.1	637	145.9
1915	121	171.5	15.7	5.0	585	80.6
1916	137	174.4	12.8	4.8	630	94.0
1917	125	172.9	11.5	4.0	630	79.5
1918	125	169.7	11.1	4.0	535	67.1
1919	85	101.5	10.5	3.3	342	65.6

U.K.: United Kingdom

See p. 405 for footnotes

E5 Output of Main-Non-Ferrous Metal Ores (in thousands of metric tons)

1920–1975

	Bauxite			Copper		
	France	Hungary	Yugoslavia	Germany	Spain[4]	Yugoslavia
1920	267	...	...	575	11.3	54
1921	95	--	10	623[3]	22.0	76[3]
				15.5		4.0
1922	236	--	31	17.5	10.0	5.2
1923	394	--	33	18.2	13.2	6.8
1924	389	--	19	22.7	16.6	8.1
1925	502	--	79	23.8	21.3	7.3
1926	511	4	132	27.7	23.9	9.7
1927	653	340	100	27.3	28.7	12.9
1928	636	396	49	26.2	27.8	16.3
1929	678	389	103	29.0	28.5	16.3
1930	609	32	95	27.0	23.0	24.5
1931	404	90	65	29.8	25.7	22.7
1932	401	112	67	30.7	15.6	15.0
1933	491	72	81	31.5	17.3	28.0
1934	529	185	85	28.0	13.8	32.8
1935	513	211	216	30.2	11.8	32.2
1936	650	329	292	29.1	22.7	30.2
1937	691	533	354	29.9	17.1	41.9
1938	684	540	406	30.0[7]	23.2	45.0
1939	709	496	319	23.9	10.4	51.2
1940	489	558	283	24.8	7.2	44.1
1941	587	781	...	23.6	8.2	...
1942	640	889	...	24.0	14.4	...
1943	916	998	...	24.4	17.9	...
1944	666	...	...	25.0[7]	18.3	...
				East Germany[8]		
1945	258	44	...	...	14.7	8.0
1946	449	101	71	3.0	19.0	24.3
1947	680	340	88	4.0	17.0	33.4
1948	804	446	144	5.9	19.3	40.5
1949	785	861	347	7.6	20.4	37.7
1950	808	578	206	8.3	19.5	43.3
1951	1,146	753	498	8.5	20.8	36.9
1952	1,119	1,207	613	11.0	24.9	37.0
1953	1,156	1,394	478	15.8	22.7	35.3
1954	1,287	1,260	687	20.7	24.2	32.2
1955	1,494	1,241	791	19	27.3	29.1
1956	1,462	892	881	18	31.9	31.8
1957	1,690	907	888	21	33.6	33.5
1958	1,830	1,049	733	23	47.7	35.2
1959	1,757	938	816	24	58.4	34.6
1960	2,067	1,190	1,025	24	54.9[11]	33.3
1961	2,225	1,366	1,232	25	70	37.9
1962	2,194	1,468	1,332	26	72	51.7
1963	2,029	1,363	1,285	24	80	62.1
1964	2,433	1,477	1,293	23	71	63.2
1965	2,662	1,477	1,574	22	90	62.6
1966	2,811	1,429	1,887	19	87	62.2
1967	2,813	1,650	2,131	19	106	63.2
1968	2,713	1,959	2,072	19	129	70.5
1969	2,773	1,934	2,128	15	133	81.7
1970	2,992	2,022	2,098	18	141	90.8
1971	3,117	2,090	1,959	15	155	94.4
1972	3,281	2,358	2,197	20	179	103.1
1973	3,299	2,600	2,167	18	190	111.8
1974	2,938	2,751	2,370	18	225	112.1
1975	2,563	2,890	2,306	...	240	114.9

See p. 405 for footnotes

E5 Output of Main Non-Ferrous Metal Ores (in thousands of metric tons)

1920–1975

	Lead			Tin	Zinc			
	Germany	Spain[4]	U.K.	U.K.	Germany	Italy	Poland	Yugoslavia
1920	97	121.4	11.2	3.1	353	96.0	43	...
1921	84[9]	135.9	5.3	0.7	355[9]	63.5[2]	70	...
						27.6		
1922	63		8.5	0.4	98[2]	40.2	94	...
	[2]				40.1			
1923	23.0	127.5	9.7	1.0	31.7	52.9	104	...
1924	36.5	141.8	11.1	2.0	58.4	58.9	101	...
1925	42.8	153.6	12.0	2.4	69.3	69.6	124	...
1926	53.9	149.5	14.7	2.4	104.4	74.7	129	...
1927	57.6	144.0	15.7	2.6	141.6	85.4	108	...
1928	57.6	131.0	14.3	2.8	144.4	84.8	100	4.8
1929	60.5	142.8	18.0	3.3	142.5	87.0	105	4.7
1930	68.7	123.3	19.6	2.5	138.7	79.6	100	7.5
1931	54.3	109.6	22.8	0.6	105.2	47.1	60	15.5
1932	51.0	105.4	31.8	1.4	75.3	32.2	27	23.1
1933	53.7	88.4	38.3	1.6	104.4	29.1	42	28.5
1934	58.9	72.2	51.9	2.0	131.7	46.1	55	31.2
1935	60.0	71.4	39.8	2.1	140.9	62.2	53	31.0
1936	64.0	41.1	29.5	2.1	156.5	68.2	55	30.5
1937	75.0	32.0	25.5	2.0	165.6	73.7	72	47.7
1938	89.3[7]	31.8	28.8[10]	2.0	196.4[7]	107.7	70	44.6
			30.2					
1939	96.0	26.0	16.8	1.7	190.2	106.0	...	33.1
1940	95.6	46.0	13.8	1.6	261.8	81.6	...	31.8
1941	101.5	46.9	8.1	1.5	287.0	70.7	...	...
1942	102.4	37.9	5.5	1.4	277.7	75.9	...	...
1943	107.4[7]	33.6	4.2	1.4	297.5[7]	67.9	...	...
1944	...	30.4	4.0	1.3	...	21.2	...	...
	West Germany				West Germany			
1945	...	27.1	2.9	1.2	...	10.3	...	7.7
1946	...	29.6	2.6	0.8	...	25.4	67	22.4
1947	...	32.1	2.9	0.9	...	57.8	82	35.0
1948	25.6	22.1	2.3	0.9	53.6	73.5	95.5	36.7
1949	40.9	27.4	2.2	0.9	57.8	74.3	108	43.9
1950	44.8	34.9	3.1	0.9	70.2	87.0	114	48.4
1951	50.4	41.2	4.2	0.9	75.3	101.9	123	44.1
1952	51.6	41.8	6.0	0.9	80.7	111.8	142	47.8
1953	63.0	48.8	8.4	1.1	116.1	106.2	161.6	60.0
1954	67.7	56.1	9.3	1.0	120.7	117.7	176.2	57.2
1955	68.1	61.2	8.3	1.1	120.2	119.6	172.2	55.7
1956	66.3	58.8	8.0	1.1	121.8	123.3	151.5	57.5
1957	72.0	61.2	8.7	1.0	126.4	130.1	131.2	58.1
1958	61.9	69.8	4.6	1.1	117.2	137.0	122.7	60.0
1959	53.0	68.6	2.4[6]	1.3	105.7	132.5	129.3	60.7
1960	50.0	71.6	...	1.2	114.5	130.6	144.1	56.4
1961	49.7	77.7	...	1.2	122.0	136.4	139.6	59.9
1962	49.8	72.2	...	1.2	112.8	131.1	145.1	61.1
1963	52.8	67.3	...	1.2	108.1	105.2	147.1	88.3
1964	48.9	58.0	...	1.2	111.3	116.1	150.8	91.8
1965	48.5	53.8	...	1.3	108.7	113.7	185.0	91.8
1966	55.4	65.9	...	1.3	106.6	117.6	189.8	85.2
1967	59.4	52.6	...	1.5	114.1	124.6	218.4	90.0
1968	52.5	64.1	...	1.8	117.5	141.7	218.8	95.5
1969	39.3	78.4	...	1.6	116.5	132.1	229.0	96.7
		71.7						
1970	40.5	72.7	...	1.7	127.4	109.1	241.7	101.1
1971	41.1	70.2	...	1.8	131.8	105.1	236.3	98.7
1972	38.5	69.4	...	3.3	121.5	119.3	222.4	96.7
1973	34.5	64.5	...	3.6	122.8	78.6	210.0	97.4
1974	30.5	64.1	...	3.2	116.0	97.6	200.0	94.7
1975	32.3	58.5	...	3.3	116.1	87.2	190.0	103.4

U.K.: United Kingdom

See p. 405 for footnotes

E5 Output of Main Non-Ferrous Metal Ores (in thousands of metric tons)

NOTES

1. SOURCES:— Germany 1837–59 – based on indices in W.G. Hoffman, *Das Wachstum der Deutschen Wirtschaft seit der Mitte des 19 Jahrhunderts* (Berlin, etc., 1965). Great Britain 1750–1938 – B.R. Mitchell & Phyllis Deane, *Abstract of British Historical Statistics* (Cambridge, 1962), where the original sources are given. All other statistics are taken from the official publications noted on p. xv or from the League of Nations and United Nations *Statistical Yearbooks.*

2. So far as possible, the statistics in this table are of metal content. Specific deviations from this are indicated in the footnotes.

FOOTNOTES

[1] Prior to 1854 the statistics relate only to copper sold publicly in Cornwall and Devon.
[2] Statistics up to this point are of crude ore.
[3] This series is available almost continuously back to the mid-16th century, and then at wider intervals to 1199.
[4] These statistics are of refined metal from native ores up to 1969 (1st line) and subsequently of the content of concentrates.
[5] The figures for 1848 to 1853 (1st line) are of crude ore.
[6] The quantities are insignificant after this date.
[7] Figures for 1939–44 include Austria and annexed territories in the East (which include the Polish lead and zinc mines.)
[8] Output in West Germany is small.
[9] Subsequently excluding eastern Upper Silesia, ceded to Poland in mid-1922.
[10] Subsequently including metal from lead concentrates.
[11] Subsequent figures include small amounts of metal from imported ores.

E6 OUTPUT OF MAIN NON-METALLIC MINERALS (in thousands of metric tons)

1861–1914

	Germany	Italy
	Potassium Salts	Sulphur
1861	2	166
1862	20	165
1863	59	183
1864	117	181
1865	93	172
1866	145	198
1867	153	199
1868	181	201
1869	232	201
1870	292[1]	204
1871	375	200
1872	490	239
1873	451	274
1874	430	251
1875	529	207
1876	581	276
1877	812	260
1878	770	305
1879	662	376
1880	666	360
1881	906	373
1882	1,201	446
1883	1,189	447
1884	969	411
1885	921	426
1886	945	374
1887	1,080	342
1888	1,235	377
1889	1,186	371
1890	1,275	369
1891	1,371	396
1892	1,351	419
1893	1,526	418
1894	1,644	406
1895	1,522	371
1896	1,781	426
1897	1,946	497
1898	2,209	502
1899	2,493	564
1900	3,051	554
1901	3,535	563
1902	3,285	539
1903	3,631	554
1904	4,085	528
1905	5,044	569
1906	5,542	500
1907	5,749	427
1908	6,099	445
1909	7,042	435
1910	8,312	430
1911	9,607	414
1912	11,161	389
1913	11,957	386
1914	8,230	378

See p. 407 for footnotes

1915–1975

	France	Germany	East Germany	Italy
	Potash	Potassium Salts	Potash	Sulphur
1915	—	6,980	...	358
1916	—	8,730	...	269
1917	—	8,953	...	212
1918	—	9,283[1]	...	234
1919	...	7,888	...	226
1920	...	11,390	...	264
1921	145	9,196	...	274
1922	212	13,079	...	167
1923	262	11,351	...	256
1924	272	8,105	...	295
1925	312	12,085	...	264
1926	367	9,415	...	271
1927	371	11,080	...	306
1928	407	12,499	...	296
1929	492	13,328	...	324
1930	506	11,967	...	351
1931	368	8,051	...	353
1932	326	6,416	...	350
1933	332	7,363	...	377
1934	356	9,617	...	343
1935	347	11,673	...	312
1936	369	11,765	...	328
1937	490	14,460	...	344
1938	581	16,442	...	380
1939	614	15,900	...	356
1940	230	16,200	...	331
1941	673	17,230	...	299
1942	619	16,810	...	227
1943	664	16,970	...	138
1944	467	16,100	...	78
		West Germany		
1945	145	...	...	75
1946	574	...	...	144
1947	633	...	...	158
1948	684	5,270	...	175
1949	799	7,291	...	201
1950	902	8,927	1,336	213
1951	872	10,847	1,409	216
1952	928	12,585	1,346	231
1953	904	12,587	1,378	218
1954	1,081	15,576	1,463	197
1955	1,189	16,107	1,552	185
1956	1,327	15,544	1,556	171
1957	1,402	16,200	1,604	179
1958	1,479	16,664	1,650	157
1959	1,462	17,422	1,644	121
1960	1,535	18,642	1,666	81
1961	1,712	19,509	1,675	70
1962	1,722	18,413	1,752	54
1963	1,722	18,537	1,845	43
1964	1,807	20,588	1,857	29
1965	1,808	22,209	1,926	36
1966	1,736	21,483	2,006	14
1967	1,780	19,850	2,206	10
1968	1,683	20,187	2,293	7
1969	1,770	20,310	2,346	1
1970	1,742	21,030	2,420	2
1971	1,870	22,306	2,445	14
1972	1,620	23,023	2,458	34
1973	2,039	24,950	2,556	30
1974	2,079	26,202	2,864	16
1975	1,918	22,006	3,019	20

E6 Output of Main Non-metallic Minerals (in thousands of metric tons)

NOTES

1. SOURCES:— The official publications noted on p. xv. The German figures for 1914–16 and 1939–44 were calculated by means of the index in W.G. Hoffman, *Das Wachstum der Deutschen Wirtschaft seit der Mitte des 19 Jahrhunderts* (Berlin, etc. 1965).

2 Statistics of potash derived from potassium salts mined in Germany are available in the source for part of the period covered here. The weight of potash averages a little over 12 per cent of the weight of the salts.

FOOTNOTE

[1] Figures for 1870–1918 include Alsace.

E7 OUTPUT OF IRON ORE (in thousands of metric tons)

1822–1869

	Austria[1]	France	Germany	Italy[2]	Lux	Norway	Spain	Sweden	U.K.
1822	...	...	175	...	...	...	...	...	...
1823	...	...	163	...	...	...	...	...	...
1824	...	...	149	...	...	...	...	...	...
1825	...	...	192	...	...	...	...	...	...
1826	...	...	229	...	...	...	...	...	...
1827	...	...	220	...	...	...	...	...	...
1828	...	...	235	...	...	...	...	...	...
1829	...	...	206	...	...	...	...	...	....
1830	...	...	235	...	...	...	...	...	...
1831	...	...	263	...	...	...	...	...	...
1832	...	...	266	...	...	...	...	...	...
1833	...	...	260	...	...	...	...	...	...
1834	...	...	263	...	...	...	...	...	...
1835	...	830	280	...	...	...	...	...	...
1836	...	897	286	...	...	...	...	236	...
1837	...	973	343	...	...	...	...	256	...
1838	...	1.013	372	...	...	...	...	248	...
1839	...	1,032	401	...	...	...	...	258	...
1840	...	995	429	...	...	...	...	261	...
1841	...	1,044	486	...	...	...	...	265	...
1842	...	2,566	486	...	...	...	...	285	...
1843	...	2,418	401	...	...	...	...	256	...
1844	...	2,382	372	...	...	...	...	247	...
1845	...	2,460	429	...	...	...	...	234	...
1846	...	...	601	...	...	...	...	264	...
1847	...	3,464	629	...	...	...	...	288	...
1848	...	...	687	...	...	...	...	289	...
1849	...	1,766	658	...	...	...	...	294	...
1850	...	1,821	830	...	...	...	...	281	...
1851	502	1,774	715	...	...	...	...	322	...
1852	525	2,081	801	...	...	...	...	324	...
1853	547	3,319	887	...	...	...	...	317	...
1854	581	3,847	1,230	...	...	...	...	317	...
1855	599	3,876	1,345	...	...	...	...	359	9,707
1856	663	4,608	1,716	...	...	...	...	376	10,651
1857	695	4,495	1,945	...	...	...	...	364	9,777
1858	...	3,933	1,602	...	...	...	...	368	8,170
1859	...	...	1,087	...	...	...	...	361	8,006
1860	...	3,033	1,259	...	...	...	173	395	8,153
1861	...	3,198	1,545	83	...	24	130	429	7,332
1862	...	3,366	1,831	105	...	24	213	430	7,683
1863	...	3,278	2,003	137	...	19	223	448	8,752
1864	...	3,137	2,117	134	...	44	253	464	10,227
1865	...	3,011	2,546	142	...	50	192	497	10,069
1866	...	3,162	2,489	154	...	25	180	483	9,820
1867	696	2,772	2,603	141	...	19	254	485	10,182
1868	681	2,684	2,918	117	722	20	385	535	10,332
1869	688	3,131	3,147	112	924	17	311	596	11,694

Lux: Luxembourg U.K.: United Kingdom

See p. 411 for footnotes

E7 Output of Iron Ore (in thousands of metric tons)

1870–1919

	Austria[1]	France	Germany	Italy[2]	Lux	Norway	Romania	Russia[6]	Spain	Sweden	U.K.
1870	835	2,614[3]	2,918[4]	89	912	21	...	...	436	616	14,602
1871	864	1,852	3,376	86	990	7	...	...	586	663	16,902
1872	928	2,782	4,720	163	1,174	33	...	...	722	732	16,089
1873	1,040	3,051	4,835	259	1,332	29	...	...	812	832	15,833
1874	906	2,517	3,690	280	1,443	30	...	...	423	926	15,083
1875	705	2,506	3,690	228	1,091	29	...	...	520	822	16,075
1876	555	2,393	3,519[5]	232	1,197	21	...	...	885	797	16,998
1877	539	2,426	3,717	230	1,263	17	...	...	1,578	739	16,965
1878	666	2,470	4,051	190	1,411	12	...	...	1,706	677	15,978
1879	628	2,271	4,245	187	1,614	8	...	...	1,754	645	14,611
1880	697	2,874	5,065	289	2,173	7	...	...	3,565	775	18,315
1881	619	3,032	5,439	421	2,162	6	...	...	3,503	826	17,726
1882	903	3,467	5,787	242	2,477	2	...	...	4,726	893	18,321
1883	882	3,298	6,181	204	2,576	2	...	...	4,526	885	17,662
1884	974	2,977	6,554	225	2,451	—	...	...	3,907	910	16,397
1885	931	2,318	6,509	201	2,648	- -	...	...	3,933	873	15,665
1886	796	2,286	6,051	209	2,434	—	...	...	4,167	872	14,336
1887	847	2,579	6,701	231	2,650	2	...	...	5,556	903	13,308
1888	1,009	2,842	7,402	177	3,262	1	...	...	4,618	960	14,825
1889	1,115	3,070	7,832	173	3,171	1	...	...	4,854	986	14,779
1890	1,362	3,472	8,047	221	3,359	1	...	1,736	6,055	941	14,002
1891	1,231	3,579	7,555	216	3,102	1	...	1,940	5,123	987	12,983
1892	993	3,707	8,169	214	3,370	1	...	1,986	5,134	1,294	11,495
1893	1,109	3,517	8,106	191	3,352	1	...	2,041	5,450	1,484	11,383
1894	1,215	3,772	8,434	188	3,958	—	...	2,411	5,352	1,927	12,565
1895	1,385	3,680	8,437	183	3,913	1	...	2,851	5,514	1,904	12,817
1896	1,449	4,062	9,404	204	4,759	2	...	3,130	6,763	2,039	13,921
1897	1,614	4,582	10,117	201	5,349	4	...	4,024	7,420	2,087	14,009
1898	1,734	4,731	10,552	190	5,349	4	...	4,444	7,197	2,303	14,404
1899	1,725	4,986	11,975	237	6,014	5	...	5,790	9,398	2,435	14,693
1900	1,894	5,448	12,793	247	6,171	18	...	6,001	8,676	2,610	14,253
1901	1,963	4,791	12,115	232	4,455	42	...	4,652	7,907	2,795	12,472
1902	1,744	5,004	12,834	241	5,130	54	...	3,925	7,905	2,897	13,641
1903	1,716	6,220	15,221	375	6,010	53	...	4,219	8,304	3,678	13,936
1904	1,719	7,023	15,699	409	6,348	45	...	5,193	7,985	4,085	13,995
1905	1,914	7,395	16,848	367	6,596	63	...	4,976	9,077	4,366	14,825
1906	2,254	8,481	19,505	384	7,229	109	...	5,345	9,449	4,503	15,749
1907	2,540	10,008	20,204	518	7,493	141	...	5,452	9,896	4,480	15,984
1908	2,632	10,057	18,426	539	5,799	120	...	5,578	9,272	4,713	15,272
1909	2,490	11,890	19,712	505	5,794	40	...	5,171	8,786	3,886	15,042
1910	2,628	14,606	22,446	551	6,263	102	...	5,742	8,667	5,549	15,470
1911	2,766	16,639	23,820	374	6,060	221	...	6,995	8,774	6,151	15,768
1912	2,927	19,160	27,200	582	6,511	408	...	6,935	9,139	6,699	14,011
1913	3,039	21,918	28,608	603	7,333	545	...	9,537[6] 9,214	9,862	7,476	16,254
1914	2,281	11,252	20,505	706	4,900	652	...	7,660	6,820	6,589	15,107
1915	2,547	620	17,710	680	6,140	715	...	5,940	5,618	6,883	14,463
1916	...	1,681	21,334	942	6,958	418	...	7,250	5,857	6,987	13,712
1917	...	2,035	22,465	994	4,502	303	...	5,330	5,551	6,217	15,084
1918	...[1]	1,672[3]	18,392[4]	694[2]	3,131	96	...	590	4,693	6,624	14,847
1919	...	9,413	6,154	613	3,112	91	113	90	4,640	4,981	12,451

Lux: Luxembourg U.K. United Kingdom

See p. 411 for footnotes

E7 Output of Iron Ore (in thousands of metric tons)

1920–1975

	Austria[1]	France	Germany	Italy[2]	Lux	Norway	Poland	Romania	Russia[6]	Spain	Sweden	U.K.	Yugoslavia
1920	...	13,922	6,362	390	3,704	79	184	80	170	4,768	4,519	12,911	10
1921	711	14,201	5,907	279	3,032	57	306	91	140	2,602	6,464	3,534	16
1922	1,112	21,106	5,928	311	4,489	259	410	95	190	2,772	6,201	6,978	37
1923	1,211	23,349	5,118	341	4,080	386	455	99	410	3,456	5,588	11,050	245
1924	714	29,044	4,457	219	5,334	522	288	103	940	4,613	6,500	11,228	347
1925	1,030	35,598	5,923	496	6,678	425	210	107	2,220	4,443	8,169	10,306	139
1926	1,094	39,318	4,793	505	7,756	213	317	103	3,430	3,182	8,466	4,160	369
1927	1,599	45,482	6,626	503	7,266	479	546	97	4,810	4,960	9,661	11,387	336
1928	1,928	49,191	6,475	625	7,027	531	736	84	6,133	5,771	4,669	11,443	440
1929	1,891	50,728	6,374	715	7,571	746	659	90	7,997	6,547	11,468	13,427	428
1930	1,181	48,571	5,741	718	6,649	772	477	93	10,663	5,517	11,236	11,813	431
1931	512	38,559	2,621	561	4,765	575	285	62	10,591	3,190	7,071	7,748	133
1932	307	27,599	1,340	412	3,313	374	77	8	12,086	1,760	3,299	7,446	27
1933	267	30,245	2,592	508	3,362	474	164	14	14,455	1,815	2,699	7,582	53
1934	467	32,015	4,343	485	3,828	567	247	84	21,509	2,094	5,253	10,757	180
1935	775	32,046	5,290	551	4,134	765	332	92	26,845	3,983	7,933	11,070	233
1936	1,024	33,302	6,652	839	4,896	847	469	107	27,834	2,266	11,250	12,905	451
1937	1,885	37,795	8,522	998	7,766	1,008	780	129	27,770	1,270	14,953	14,443	629
1938	2,670	33,132	11,145[7]	990	5,141	1,425	872	139	26,585	2,545	13,928	12,049	607
1939	2,998	32,993[3]	13,211	948	5,853	1,340	...	140	26,921	3,594	13,787	14,718	667
1940	3,186	12,731	17,177	1,179	4,886	615	813	150	29,866	2,627	11,295	17,986	...
1941	2,895	10,570	15,566	1,340	6,882	567	906	160	...	2,274	10,528	19,278	...
1942	2,997	12,758	13,325	1,085	5,109	284	808	213	...	2,154	9,727	20,225	...
1943	3,189	16,879	12,552	836	5,262	219	717	252	...	2,135	10,820	18,791	...
1944	3,015	9,372[3]	10,269[7]	390	2,923	264	681	203	...	2,199	7,253	15,720	...
			West Germany										
1945	324	7,713	...	134[2]	1,406	79	...	102	15,864	1,936	3,930	14,402	...
1946	462	16,232	3,877	132	2,247	60	424	107	19,327	2,384	6,867	12,368	399
1947	885	18,719	4,444	227	1,992	128	544	121	23,340	2,383	8,894	11,269	739
1948	1,197	23,061	7,275	549	3,399	199	659	209	27,985	2,515	13,286	13,299	879
1949	1,488	31,428	9,112	589	4,137	275	699	324	32,570	2,769	13,729	13,612	835
1950	1,860	30,016	10,883	479	3,845	298	790	392	39,651	3,039	13,611	13,171	731
1951	2,370	35,203	12,923	553	5,625	332	876	469	44,926	3,327	15,383	15,014	582
1952	2,653	40,802	15,404	812	7,245	769	999	640	52,583	3,798	16,949	16,492	676
1953	2,756	42,447	14,619	991	7,170	1,186	1,309	688	59,650	4,010	16,983	16,072	795
1954	2,721	43,826	13,036	1,091	5,887	1,095	1,575	599	64,346	3,847	15,325	15,807	1,111
1955	2,839	50,311	15,684	1,394	7,205	1,256	1,856	637	71,862	4,802	17,355	16,435	1,398
1956	3,258	52,704	16,928	1,674	7,594	1,550	1,973	694	78,079	5,790	18,947	16,506	1,725
1957	3,496	57,785	18,320	1,581	7,843	1,547	1,994	644	84,339	5,238	19,924	17,173	1,876
1958	3,410	59,484	17,984	1,292	6,638	1,601	2,173	743	88,616	5,033	18,312	14,846	1,997
1959	3,382	60,938	18,063	1,249	6,509	1,546	2,014	1,064	94,015	4,609	18,351	15,109	2,095
1960	3,542	66,964	18,869	1,261	6,977	1,657	2,182	1,460	105,857	5,638	21,690	17,361	2,200
1961	3,693	66,606	18,866	1,236	7,458	1,670	2,386	1,737	117,633	6,063	23,593	16,783	2,184
1962	3,751	66,301	16,643	1,151	6,507	1,939	2,436	1,738	128,111	5,761	22,526	15,522	2,190
1963	3,734	57,883	12,898	1,024	6,990	1,999	2,609	2,286	137,502	5,149	23,637	15,151	2,297
1964	3,563	60,938	11,613	876	6,680	2,123	2,680	1,932	145,856	5,078	26,619	16,588	2,307
1965	3,536	59,531	10,847	785	6,315	2,464	2,862	2,479	153,432	5,788	29,354	15,662	2,504
1966	3,475	55,059	9,467	828	6,528	2,451	3,054	2,681	160,271	5,069	27,987	13,877	2,493
1967	3,473	49,221	8,553	737	6,304	3,378	3,077	2,797	168,246	5,085	28,337	12,944	2,579
1968	3,482	55,238	7,714	738	6,398	3,704	3,050	2,747	176,616	6,190	32,419	13,936	2,720
1969	3,982	55,425	7,451	763	6,311	3,854	2,768	2,999	186,134	6,250	33,185	12,298	2,721
1970	3,997	56,805	6,762	757	5,722	4,008	2,554	3,206	195,492	7,000	31,509	12,018	3,694
1971	4,171	55,862	6,391	684	4,507	4,056	2,078	3,467	203,008	7,310	34,367	10,228	3,724
1972	4,132	54,246	6,117	616	4,116	3,881	1,656	3,361[8] 842	208,127	6,490	33,979	9,049	3,960
1973	4,210	54,232	6,429	526	3,782	3,970	1,413	838	216,104	6,900	34,727	7,105	4,671
1974	4,245	54,260	5,671	598	2,686	3,904	1,296	837	224,831	7,800	36,153	3,602	5,034
1975	3,833	49,647	4,274	632	2,315	4,109	1,192	786	232,803	8,320	30,867	4,490	5,232

Lux: Luxembourg U.K.: United Kingdom

See p. 411 for footnotes

E7 Output of Iron Ore (in thousands of metric tons)

NOTES

1. SOURCES:— Germany 1817–76 – based on the index in W.G. Hoffman, *Das Wachstum der Deutschen Wirtschaft seit der Mitte des 19 Jahrhunderts* (Berlin, etc., 1965). Luxembourg 1868–75 – data supplied by the Service Central de la Statistique et des Etudes Economiques. Russia 1913 (2nd line) to 1927 – G.W. Nutter, *Growth of Industrial Production in the Soviet Union* (Princeton, 1962). U.K. 1855–1938 – based on B.R. Mitchell and Phyllis Deane, *Abstract of British Historical Statistics* (Cambridge, reprinted edition, 1971), where the original sources are given and discussed (see pp. 128–9). All other statistics are taken from the official publications noted on p. xv with a few gaps. filled from the British Iron & Steel Federation *Statistical Year Books.*

2. These statistics relate to the weight of crude ores, not to their metal content. Figures of the latter for recent years are available in the U.N. *Statistical Yearbooks.*

FOOTNOTES

[1] Cisleithania (excluding the Italian provinces) to 1918, and the Republic subsequently.

[2] Statistics to 1918 apply to the 1871 boundaries. For 1919–45 they apply to the 1924 boundaries, and from 1946 to the boundaries of 1954.

[3] From 1871 to 1918 and from 1940 to 1944 the parts of Alsace and Lorraine ceded to Germany are excluded.

[4] For 1871–1918 includes Alsace-Lorraine.

[5] The figures to 1876 are based on an index (see note 1), and the last digit cannot be regarded as accurate.

[6] Figures to 1913 (1st line) apply to the Russian Empire. From 1913 (2nd line) to 1940 they apply to the 1923 boundaries of the U.S.S.R., and subsequently to the post-Second World War territory.

[7] For 1939–44 includes Polish Upper Silesia.

E8 OUTPUT OF PIG IRON (in thousands of metric tons)

1780–1814

	Russia[1]	U.K.
1780	110	...
1781	106	...
1782	109	...
1783	112	...
1784	109	...
1785	116	...
1786	122	...
1787	124	...
1788	125	69
1789	123	
1790	128	...
1791	137	...
1792	121	...
1793	134	...
1794	130	...
1785	135	...
1786	123	127
1787	130	...
1788	138	...
1789	154	...
1800	160	...
1801	167	...
1802	160	...
1803	153	...
1804	160	...
1805	149	...
1806	146	248
1807	144	...
1808	145	...
1809	146	...
1810	144	...
1811	145	...
1812	134	...
1813	130	...
1814	123	...

1817–1869

	Austria[2]	Belgium	Finland	France
1817	...	...	...	...
1818	...	...	...	...
1819	...	...	...	113
1820	...	...	...	...
1821	...	...	...	...
1822	...	...	...	...
1823	...	...	...	...
1824	...	...	...	198
1825	...	...	...	199
1826	...	...	...	206
1827	...	...	...	216
1828	73	...	...	221
1829	...	...	...	217
1830	...	...	...	266
1831	...	90	...	225
1832	...	93	...	225
1833	...	95	...	236
1834	...	100	...	269
1835	...	115	...	295
1836	...	135	...	308
1837	...	150	...	332
1838	...	132	...	348
1839	...	100	...	350
1840	...	95	...	348
1841	113	90	...	377
1842	114	96	...	399
1843	115	98	...	423
1844	130	107	...	427
1845	134	135	...	439
1846	151	189	...	522
1847	156	248	7	592
1848	146	162	5	472
1849	141	149	6	414
1850	155	145	5	406
1851	159	168	6	446
1852	172	179	7	523
1853	182	230	10	661
1854	197	285	8	771
1855	213	294	11	849
1856	228	322	9	923
1857	244	302	12	992
1858	...[3]	324	13	872
1859	221	319	12	864
1860	225	320	15	898
1861	230	312	9	967
1862	250	357	12	1,091
1863	237	392	13	1,157
1864	202[4]	450	13	1,213
1865	191	471	14	1,204
1866	178	482	18	1,260
1867	215	423	14	1,229
1868	263	436	17	1,235
1869	278	534	19	1,381

U.K.: United Kingdom

See p. 418 for footnotes

E8 **Output of Pig Iron** (in thousands of metric tons)

1817–1869

	Germany	Hungary[7]	Italy[8]	Luxembourg	Norway	Russia[1]	Spain	Sweden	U.K.
1817	...	...	...	...	...	132	...	...	...
1818	...	...	...	...	...	127	...	...	330
1819	...	...	...	...	...	132	...	...	...
1820	...	...	...	...	...	135	...	...	374
1821	...	...	...	...	...	159	...	...	...
1822	...	...	...	...	...	153	...	...	...
1823	85	...	...	...	...	149	...	...	462
1824	85	...	...	...	...	140	...	...	...
1825	95	...	...	...	...	158	...	...	591
1826	100	...	...	...	...	157	...	...	...
1827	105	...	...	...	...	184	...	...	702
1828	105	...	...	...	...	178	...	...	714
1829	120	...	...	...	...	188	...	...	...
1830	110	...	...	...	...	187	...	...	688
1831	120	...	...	...	...	194	...	...	...
1832	130	...	...	...	...	174	...	...	...
1833	135	...	...	...	...	159	...	...	711
1834	140	...	...	...	...	167	...	...	...
1835	155	...	...	...	...	175	...	...	1,016
1836	160	...	...	...	...	181	...	107	...
1837	175	...	...	...	...	191	...	109	...
1838	170	...	...	...	...	181	...	110	...
1839	185	...	...	...	...	182	...	116	1,269
1840	190	...	...	...	...	189	...	125	1,419
1841	185	24	...	...	...	179	...	121	1,524
1842	180	28	...	12	...	188	...	122	1,117
1843	185	28	...	...	...	190	...	133	1,235
1844	180	28	...	...	...	185	...	117	...
1845	190	32	...	13	...	187	...	98	1,537
1846	230	30	...	14	...	215	...	127	...
1847	230	40	...	24	...	195	...	138	2,032
1848	210	...	...	18	...	198	...	143	...
1849	190	...	...	19	...	190	...	119	...
1850	210	...	...	13	...	228	...	142	2,285
1851	230	38	...	11	...	207	...	145	...
1852	270	37	...	...	...	215	...	150	2,744
1853	310	59	...	14	...	238	...	146	...
1854	390	58	...	...	...	231	...	146	3.119
1855	420	63	...	...	...	251	...	188	3,270
1856	500	72	...	15	...	259	...	159	3,644
1857	540	87	...	17	...	213	...	151	3,718
1858	500	...[3]	...	...	...	277	...	177	3,511
1859	460[5]	97	...	...	...	271	...	183	3,773
1860	529	88	...	...	...	298[1] / 336	41	185	3,888
1861	592	85	27	7	...	320	67	170	3,772
1862	696	98	29	...	...	251	89	200	4,006
1863	813	108	24	17	...	279	98	187	4,582
1864	905	117[4]	21	...	...	300	95	241	4,845
1865	988[6]	101	17	27	...	300	92	227	4,882
1866	977	97	20	46[9] / 70	6	305	72	230	4,597
1867	1,034	95	22	80	7	289	...	254	4,837
1868	1,184	132	20	80	5	325	...	263	5,050
1869	1,313	127	18	100	4	330	...	292	5,533

U.K.: United Kingdom

See p. 418 for footnotes

E8 Output of Pig Iron (in thousands of metric tons)

1870–1919

	Austria[2]	Belgium	Czech	Finland	France	Germany	Hungary[7]	Italy[8]
1870	279	565	...	20	1,178[11]	1,261[11]	124	20
1871	292	609	...	21	860	1,424	133	17
1872	313	656	...	19	1,218	1,828	147	24
1873	371	607	...	24	1,382	1,991	163	29
1874	332	533	...	25	1,416	1,666	162	29
1875	303	542	...	21	1,448	1,759	160	28
1876	273	491	...	26	1,435	1,615	127	19
1877	259	471	...	22	1,507	1,718	129	16
1878	293	465	...	14	1,521	1,899	141	19
1879	286	453	...	18	1,400	1,965	118	12
1880	320	608	...	22	1,725	2,468	144	17
1881	380	625	...	22	1,886	2,620	164	28
1882	435	727	...	22	2,039	3,004	176	25
1883	522	783	...	18	2,069	3,135	176	24
1884	540	751	...	23	1,872	3,235	195	18
1885	499	713	...	24	1,631	3,268	216	16
1886	485	702	...	17	1,517	3,128	235	12
1887	512	756	...	20	1,568	3,532	193	12
1888	586	827	...	20	1,683	3,813	204	12
1889	617	832	...	15	1,734	3,963	239	13
1890	666	788	...	24	1,962	4,100	299	14
1891	617	684	...	23	1,897	4,096	305	12
1892	631	753	...	24	2,057	4,351	310	13
1893	663	745	...	21	2,003	4,428	319	8
1894	742	819	...	21	2,070	4,700	330	10
1895	779	829	...	23	2,004	4,770	349	9
1896	817	959	...	26	2,340	5,564	401	7
1897	888	1,035	...	33	2,484	6,009	420	8
1898	958	980	...	27	2,525	6,367	469	12
1899	996	1,025	...	27	2,578	7,160	471	19
1900	1,000	1,019	...	31	2,714	7,550	456	24
1901	1,030	764	...	31	2,389	6,964	451	16
1902	992	1,069	...	30	2,405	7,450	435	31
1903	971	1,216	...	23	2,841	8,800	416	75
1904	988	1,283	...	16	2,974	8,860	388	89
1905	1,120	1,311	...	22	3,077	9,507	421	143
1906	1,222	1,363	...	16	3,314	10,833	420	135
1907	1,384	1,378	...	15	3,590	11,390	440	112
1908	1,467	1,270	...	12	3,401	10,505	523	113
1909	1,465	1,616	...	9	3,574	11,092	530	208
1910	1,505	1,852	...	8	4,038	13,111	502	353
1911	1,596	2,046	...	9	4,470	13,845	518	303
1912	1,760	2,301	...	10	4,939	15,600	553	380
1913	1,758	2,485	(1,228)[10]	9	5,207	16,761	623	427
1914	1,353	1,454	(928)[10]	10	2,736	12,481	494	385
1915	1,429	68	(953)[10]	8	584	10,190	388	378
1916	1,477	128	(1,218)[10]	9	1,311	11,327	453	467
1917	1,933	8	(1,061)[10]	9	1,408	11,601	447	471
1918	...[2]	—	781	6	1,293	10,680[11]	...[7]	314[8]
1919	60	251	663	7	1,333[11] 2,412	6,284	...	240

Czech: Czechoslovakia

See p. 418 for footnotes

E8 Output of Pig Iron (in thousands of metric tons)

1870–1919

	Lux	Norway	Poland	Romania	Russia[1]	Spain	Sweden	U.K.
1870	130	4	...	...	359	...	300	6,059
1871	140	3	...	...	359	...	299	6,733
1872	160	2	...	...	400	...	339	6,850
1873	250	1	...	...	380	...	346	6,671
1874	240	1	...	...	379	...	328	6,087
1875	270	2	...	...	428	...	351	6,467
1876	231	1	...	...	443	...	352	6,661
1877	215	1[12]	...	...	400	...	345	6,715
1878	248	1	...	...	418	...	341	6,483
1879	261	1	...	...	433	...	343	6,091
1880	261	1	...	...	449	135	406	7,873
1881	294	1	...	...	471	118	430	8,275
1882	377	1	...	...	479	126	399	8,725
1883	335	1	...	...	482	142	423	8,666
1884	366	1	...	...	510	126	431	7,937
1885	420	—	...	...	528	...	465	7,534
1886	301	—	...	...	531	...	442	7,122
1887	492	1	...	...	613	...	457	7,681
1888	524	1	...	...	667	...	457	8,127
1889	562	- -	....	...	741	...	441	8,457
1890	560	1	...	...	928	261	456	8,031
1891	545	- -	...	...	1,005	359	490	7,525
1892	587	1	...	...	1.073	205	486	6,817
1893	558	- -	...	...	1,150	252	453	7,089
1894	680	- -	...	...	1,333	281	463	7,546
1895	695	- -	...	...	1,455	240	463	7,827
1896	899	- -	...	...	1,624	267	494	8,799
1897	870	- -	...	...	1,883	323	538	8,937
1898	955	- -	...	...	2,244	283	532	8,748
1899	983	- -	...	...	2,713	295	498	9,572
1900	971	- -	...	...	2,937	295	526	9,104
1901	916	- -	...	...	2,870	335	528	8,056
1902	1,080	1	...	...	2,601	259	538	8,818
1903	1,218	1	...	...	2,491	313	507	9,078
1904	1,198	- -	...	...	2,975	294	529	8,834
1905	1,368	- -	...	...	2,736	316	539	9,762
1906	1,460	...	...	...	2,722	315	604	10,347
1907	1,485	—	...	...	2,822	355	616	10,276
1908	1,300	—	...	...	2,827	404	568	9,202
1909	1,553	—	...	...	2,900	429	445	9,685
1910	1,683	—	...	...	3,047	373	604	10,173
1911	1,729	- -	...	...	3,598	409	634	9,679
1912	2,252	- -	...	...	4,203	403	699	8,891
1913	2,548	- -	...	...	4,641	425	730[13]	10,425
					4,216[1]		742	
1914	1,827	7	...	...	4,137	431	652	9,067
1915	1,591	9	...	...	3,764	440	777	8,864
1916	1,951	6	...	...	3,804	498	758	9,062
1917	1,529	6	...	...	2,964	358	857	9,488
1918	1,267	9	...	—	597	387	779	9,253
1919	617	2	407	12	117	294	509	7,536

Neth'l: Netherlands Switz: Switzerland U.K.: United Kingdom

See p. 418 for footnotes

E8 **Output of Pig Iron** (in thousands of metric tons)

1920–1975

	Austria	Belgium	Bulgaria	Czech	Denmark	Finland	France	Germany	E. Germany	Hungary[7]	Italy[8]
1920	100	1,116	—	737	—	10	3,434	7,044[6]	...	...	88
1921	226	876	—	577	—	10	3,417	7,845	...	71	61
1922	321	1,613	—	335	—	12	5,229	9,396[16]	...	98	158
1923	342	2,148	—	817	—	9	5,432	4,936	...	124	236
1924	267	2,844	—	983	—	11	7,693	7,812	...	116	304
1925	380	2,543	—	1,166	—	11	8,494	10,177	...	93	482
1926	332	3,368	—	1,088	—	9	9,432	9,644	...	189	513
1927	433	3,709	—	1,260	—	10	9,273	13,103	...	300	489
1928	458	3,857	—	1,569	—	9	9,981	11,804	...	285	507
1929	459	4,041	—	1,645	—	7	10,300	13,240	...	368	671
1930	297	3,365	—	1,437	—	3	10,035	9,695	...	257	537
1931	145	3,198	—	1,165	—	5	8,199	6,063	...	160	510
1932	95	2,749	—	450	—	7	5,537	3,932	...	66	461
1933	88	2,710	—	499	—	5	6,234	5,247	...	93	518
1934	133	2,953	—	600	—	2	6,151	8,717[15]	...	140	529
1935	193	3,030	—	811	—	6	5,789	12,846	...	186	633
1936	248	3,161	—	1,140	—	4	6,230	15,302	...	306	762
1937	388	3,843	—	1,675[14]	—	16	7,855	15,960	...	358	801
1938	551	2,426	—	1,627	—	28	6,012	18,045	...	335	864
1939	...	3,059	—	...	—	29	7,376	17,478	...	409	1,005
1940	679	1,790	—	1,582	—	25	3,683	13,955	...	427	1,062
1941	646	1,422	—	1,528	—	22	3,351	15,441	...	448	1,038
1942	784	1,269	—	1,576	—	28	3,838	15,332	...	418	887
1943	961	1,631	—	1,679	—	42	4,921	15,972	...	417	648
1944	928	719	—	1,565[14]	—	99	2,893	13,369	...	296	233[8]
								W. Germany			
1945	102	735	—	576	12	35	1,177	...	...	44	65
1946	58	2,161	—	961	18	77	3,444	2,083	124	160	177
1947	279	2,817	—	1,423	23	66	4,886	2,265	132	301	318
1948	613	3,929	1	1,645	31	90	6,559	4,663	274	384	449
1949	838	3,749	3	1,885	39	99	8,345	7,140	313	420[17]	393
1950	883	3,695	3	1,951	51	64	7,761	9,473	337	465	504
1951	1,049	4,868	5	2,057	33	101	8,750	10,697	342	534	953
1952	1,173	4,790	9	2,306	36	108	9,769	12,877	660	631	1,102
1953	1,321	4,232	6	2,781	36	79	8,666	11,654	1,078	734	1,222
1954	1,354	4,625	7	2,790	40	74	8,841	12,512	1,318	857	1,256
1955	1,506	5,385	8	2,982	55	114	10,960	16,482	1,517	883	1,625
1956	1,737	5,770	10	3,282	56	103	11,480	17,577	1,574	768	1,873
1957	1,960	5,581	54	3,563	59	128	11,916	18,358	1,663	837	2,072
1958	1,818	5,519	91	3,774	44	101	11,967	16,659[15]	1,775	1,100	2,060
1959	1,837	5,967	177	4,244	59	108	12,472	21,602	1,898	1,121	2,098
1960	2,232	6,553	192	4,696	73	137	14,145	25,739	1,995	1,259	2,683
1961	2,262	6,454	206	4,971	66	152	14,566	25,431	2,031	1,320	3,056
1962	2,118	6,740	223	5,177	69	331	13,959	24,251	2,075	1,397	3,556
1963	2,106	6,899	265	5,254	69	332	14,306	22,909	2,150	1,399	3,741
1964	2,204	8,044	457	5,716	73	597	15,863	27,182	2,260	1,499	3,498
1965	2,200	8,367	695	5,868	75	940	15,770	26,990	2,338	1,584	5,488
1966	2,195	8,230	930	6,269	76	936	15,590	25,413	2,448	1,640	6,289
1967	2,140	8,902	1,028	6,822	76	1,025	15,710	27,366	2,525	1,669	7,294
1968	2,474	10,371	1,111	6,918	76	811	16,455	30,305	2,333	1,659	7,826
1969	2,816	11,211	1,134	7,009	77	1,231	18,215	33,764	2,098	1,760	7,781
1970	2,964	10,845	1,252	7,548	68	1,164	19,228	33,627	1,994	1,835	8,332
1971	2,849	10,403	1,378	7,961	68	1,029	18,354	29,990	2,027	1,984	8,536
1972	2,846	11,777	1,562	8,360	41	1,183	19,016	32,002	2,151	2,070	9,415
1973	3,006	12,655	1,610	8,534	...	1,412	20,304	36,828	2,202	2,110	10,032
1974	3,443	13,020	1,528	8,905	...	1,381	22,519	40,221	2,280	2,298	11,686
1975	3,056	9,069	1,560	9,281	...	1,368	17,921	30,074	2,456	2,226	11,350

Czech: Czechoslovakia E. Germany: East Germany W. Germany: West Germany

See p. 418 for footnotes

E8 Output of Pig Iron (in thousands of metric tons)

1920–1975

	Lux'bg	Neth'l	Norway	Poland	Romania	Russia[1]	Spain	Sweden	Switzerland	U.K.	Yugoslavia
1920	693	—	3	412	19	116	251	484	—	8,164	6
1921	970	—	2	444	33	117	347	320	—	2,658	12
1922	1,679	—	2	480[16]	31	180	210	274	—	4,981	16
1923	1,407	—	4[13] 26	520	39	314	400	301	—	7,560	24
1924	2,157	69	64	336	46	670	497	533	—	7,424	15
1925	2,363	118	87	315	64	1,309	528	459	—	6,362	3
1926	2,559	143	97	327	63	2,203	487	495	—	2,497	19
1927	2,732	204	123	618	63	2,961	590	455	—	7,410	23
1928	2,770	258	141	684	70	3,282	557	438	—	6,716	29
1929	2,906	254	154	706	72	4,021	749	524	—	7,711	31
1930	2,473	273	145	478	69	4,964	616	496	—	6,291	35
1931	2,053	257	119	347	26	4,871	473	418	—	3,834	38
1932	1,960	236	103	199	9	6,161	296	282	—	3,631	10
1933	1,888	253	112	306	2	7,110	330	346	—	4,202	31
1934	1,955	258	127	382	62	10,430	363	558	—	6,065	33
1935	1,872	254	130	396	82	12,490	341	613	—	6,527	21
1936	1,987	274	168	586	97	14,400	226	632	—	7,845	44
1937	2,513	312	181	720	127	14,487	132	693	—	8,629	50
1938	1,551	267	174	880	133	14,650	436	714	—	6,869	116
1939	1,838	284	191	(652)[19] [21]	119	14,520	473	691	—	8,108	113
1940	1,059	169	147	(915)[20]	122	14,902	579	787	5	8,337	122
1941	1,343	176	123	1,081	118	...	536	749	10	7,512	...
1942	1,692	152	111	1,128	162	...	535	770	12	7,850	...
1943	2,268	94	145	1,169	226	...	584	828	15	7,302	...
1944	1,348	99	124	1,095[21]	141	...	551	887	29	6,845	...
1945	317	25	51	219	54	8,803	479	785	3	7,221	12
1946	1,365	187	135[18]	726	66	9,862	491	719	12	7,886	8
1947	1,818	288	146	867	...	11,223	503	725	12	7,910	171
1948	2,624	442	202	1,134	186	13,742	522	803	36	9,425	183
1949	2,372	434	234	1,391	...	16,389	615	860	32	9,651	202
1950	2,499	454	226	1,533	320	19,175	664	837	34	9,788	226
1951	3,157	524	245	1,616	336	21,909	650	905	40	9,824	262
1952	3,076	539	273	1,836	381	25,071	763	1,103	40	10,900	288
1953	2,722	593	278	2,359	448	27,415	800	1,057	41	11,354	281
1954	2,800	610	246	2,663	429	29,972	877	1,001	35	12,074	368
1955	3,085	670	355	3,112	570	33,310	964	1,247	54	12,670	531
1956	3,316	662	452	3,506	583	35,754	913	1,412	41	13,381	647
1957	3,368	701	565	3,682	686	37,040	962	1,543	45	14,512	735
1958	3,285	917	523	3,864	737	39,600	1,302	1,414	34	13,183	779
1959	3,444	1,139	623	4,374	846	42,972	1,675	1,501	40	12,785	900
1960	3,786	1,346	720	4,563	1,014	46,757	1,886	1,627	50	16,016	1,016
1961	3,834	1,456	757	4,770	1,099	50,893	2,077	1,895	50	14,984	1,042
1962	3,597	1,571	724	5,311	1,511	55,265	2,101	1,957	50	13,912	1,103
1963	3,587	1,708	749	5,395	1,706	58,691	1,911	2,017	42	14,825	1,060
1964	4,191	1,947	894	5,643	1,924	62,377	1,903	2,354	30	17,551	1,076
1965	4,145	2,364	1,090	5,760	2,019	66,184	2,338	2,451	25	17,740	1,177
1966	3,963	2,209	1,139	5,855	2,198	70,264	2,107	2,397	25	15,962	1,217
1967	3,963	2,588	1,232	6,581	2,456	74,812	2,687	2,567	24	15,396	1,256
1968	4,308	2,821	1,431	6,676	2,992	78,788	2,783	2,702	22	16,696	1,286
1969	4,872	3,460	1,491	6,856	3,477	81,634	3,300	2,768	25	16,653	1,288
1970	4,814	3,594	1,251	7,111	4,210	85,933	4,165	2,842	28	17,677	1,377
1971	4,588	3,759	1,313	7,331	4,381	89,256	4,825	2,815	32	15,416	1,630
1972	4,671	4,289	1,372	7,579	4,890	92,327	5,928	2,587	28	15,317	1,949
1973	5,091	4,707	1,506	7,896	5,713	95,933	6,271	2,782	26	17,031	2,109
1974	5,469	4,804	1,583	7,952	6,081	99,868	6,904	3,181	35	14,115	2,316
1975	3,889	3,970	1,512	7,926	6,602	102,968	6,842	3,508	35	12,132	2,193

Lux'bg: Luxembourg Neth'l: Netherlands U.K.: United Kingdom

See p. 418 for footnotes

E8 Output of Pig Iron (in thousands of metric tons)

NOTES

1. SOURCES:– Germany to 1859 – based on the index in W.G. Hoffman, *Das Wachstum der Deutschen Wirtschaft seit der Mitte des 19 Jahrhunderts* (Berlin, etc. 1965). German wartime statistics, and those for most East European countries, and all statistics for Luxembourg from 1866 onwards are taken from the British Iron and Steel Federation (later British Steel Corporation), *Statistics of the Iron and Steel Industries* (later *Statistical Year Book).* Earlier statistics for Luxembourg were supplied by the Groupement des Industries Sidérurgiques Luxembourgeoises. Finnish statistics to 1899 were supplied by the Central Statistical Office of Finland, those for 1846–70 being taken from Eevert Laine, *Suomen Vuoritiomi, 1809–1884.* Russian statistics to 1860 (1st line) are from S.G. Strumilin, *Istoriia Chernoi Metallurgii v S.S.S.R.* I (Moscow, 1954), and those from 1860 (2nd line) to 1913 (1st line) are from P.A. Khromov, *Economic Development of Russia in the 19th and 20th Centuries, 1800–1917* (Moscow, 1950). All other statistics are taken from the official publications noted on p. xv.

2. Output of ferro-alloys is normally included in these statistics.

3. T.J. Markovitch, *L'industrie francaise de 1789 à 1964* (Cahiers de l'I.S.E.A., 1966) gives the following averages of French output (in thousands of tons):– 1781–90 141; 1803–12 200: 1815–24 150. S.G. Strumilin, *op. cit.* above, gives the following statistics for years before his continuous series begins (in thousands of tons):– 1720 10; 1730 16; 1740 25; 1750 33; 1760 60; 1770 84.

FOOTNOTES

[1] Figures to 1860 (1st line) apply to the 50 provinces of European Russia (excluding Finland, Poland, and the Caucasus). From 1860 (2nd line) to 1913 (1st line) they are for the whole Russian Empire. From 1913 (2nd line) to 1940 they are for the 1923 boundaries of the U.S.S.R., and later figures are for the post-Second World War boundaries.

[2] Figures to 1918 are for Cisleithania (excluding Lombardy and Venetia), and later figures are for the Republic. Decennial averages for 1819–48 for the whole Austro-Hungarian Empire are available as follows (in thousands of tons):– 1819–28 73; 1829–38 103; 1839–48 164. Statistics for Lombardy and Venetia are available as follows (in thousands of tons):–

1841	6.4	1845	6.3	1849	8.1	1853	9.4
1842	6.3	1846	10.2	1850	...	1854	8.6
1843	6.4	1847	7.5	1851	14.3	1855	8.5
1844	5.4	1848	7.4	1852	10.9	1856	10.4
						1857	9.9

[3] Output for the whole Austro-Hungarian Empire was 373 thousand tons.

[4] Statistics to 1864 are for years ended 31 October. Output for the whole Austro-Hungarian Empire in November and December 1864 was 56 thousand tons.

[5] Previous figures are based on an index (see note 1) and are rounded to the nearest 5 to 1844 and the nearest 10 from 1845–59.

[6] Previously including Luxembourg.

[7] Figures to 1918 are for Transleithania (including Croatia-Slavonia), and later figures are for the territory established by the treaty of Trianon.

[8] Figures to 1918 are for the boundaries of 1871. For 1919–45 they apply to the 1924 boundaries, and from 1946 to the 1954 boundaries.

[9] Previous statistics apparently relate to wrought and cast iron. Earlier figures are available as follows (in thousand tons):– 1806 24; 1811 14.

[10] This is also included in Austrian output.

[11] From 1871 to 1919 (1st line) the parts of Alsace and Lorraine ceded in 1871 are excluded from France, and (except in 1919) are included in Germany. The output of this district can be derived from German sources as follows (in thousands of tons):–

1881	305	1890	640	1900	1,524	1910	2,723
1882	359	1891	635	1901	1,447	1911	2,908
1883	371	1892	734	1902	1,630	1912	3,149
1884	410	1893	726	1903	1,974	1913	3,864
1885	432	1894	804	1904	2,070		
1886	429	1895	829	1905	2,169		
1887	516	1896	920	1906	2,423		
1888	543	1897	928	1907	2,512		
1889	563	1898	994	1908	2,182		
		1899	1,290	1909	2,315		

[12] Previously including castings.
[13] Previously does not include ferro-alloys.
[14] From 1938 to 1944 Teschen is excluded.
[15] From 1921 to 1924 and 1946 to 1958 Saarland is excluded. The output of this district was as follows (in thousand tons):—

1921	896	1930	1,912	1946	247	1953	2,382
1922	1,157	1931	1,515	1947	653	1954	2,497
1923	929	1932	1,349	1948	1,134	1955	2,879
1924	1,345	1933	1,592	1949	1,582	1956	3,031
1925	1,450	1934	1,827	1950	1,684	1957	3,166
1926	1,625			1951	2,370	1958	3,103
1927	1,771			1952	2,550		
1928	1,936						
1929	2,105						

[16] Eastern Upper Silesia was transferred from Germany to Poland from July 1922.
[17] Ferro-maganese and ferro-silicon are not previously included.
[18] Subsequently excluding production for use in the producer's own works, and also excluding ferro-silicon converted to 45%Si.
[19] First half-year only.
[20] Excluding central Poland.
[21] From 1940 to 1944 Teschen (previously and subsequently part of Czechoslovakia) is included. Figures from 1945 are for the postwar boundaries, which include what was formerly German Silesia.

E9 OUTPUT OF CRUDE STEEL (in thousands of metric tons)

1860–1909

	Austria[1]	Belgium	France	Germany	Italy	Lux'bg	Russia[3]	Spain	Sweden	U.K.
1860	...	...	...	...	...	–	1.6	–	...	...
1861	...	...	...	...	...	–	1.9	–	...	...
1862	...	...	...	...	...	–	2.0	–	...	...
1963	...	...	...	...	...	–	2.0	–	...	...
1864	...	...	...	...	...	–	3.5	–	...	...
1865	...	...	...	...	...	–	4	–	...	...
1866	...	...	...	...	...	–	4	–	...	...
1867	...	...	...	...	...	–	6	–	...	...
1868	...	...	...	...	...	–	10	–	...	...
1869	...	...	...	...	...	–	8	–	...	...
1870	22	...	84	126	...	–	9	–	12	...
1871	36	...	80	143	...	–	7	–	9	334
1872	55	...	130	189	...	–	9	–	16	417
1873	77	...	156	248	...	–	9	–	16	582
1874	97	...	217	325	...	–	9	–	21	640
1875	89	54	239	318	...	–	13	–	19	719
1876	90	80	231	340	...	–	18	–	21	841
1877	97	100	250	391	...	–	44	–	17	901
1878	85	120	282	463	...	–	64	–	19	998
1879	86[2]	110	339[2]	510	...	–	210	–	20[2]	1,025
1880	124	132	389	690	3	–	307	–	37	1,316
1881	134	142	422	900	4	–	293	–	49	1,807
1882	155	183	458	1,070	3	–	248	–	58	2,143
1883	165	179	522	1,060	3	–	222	–	65	2,040
1884	320	186	503	1,140	5	–	207	–	67	1,802
1885	289	155	554	1,203	3	–	193	20	77	1,917
1886	268	155	428	1,315	24	21	242	30	78	2,300
1887	310	216	493	1,681	73	57	226	50	111	3,093
1888	402	232	592	1,793	118	70	222	60	114	3,357
1889	433	254	626	1,999	158	97	259	70	136	3,628
1890	516	221	683	2,135	108	97	378	80	168	3,636
1891	495	222	744	2,452	76	111	434	90	172	3,208
1892	516	260	825	2,653	57	103	515	90	160	2,967
1893	578	273	790	3,034	71	129	631	90	167	2,997
1894	671	406	818	3,617	55	131	703	95	168	3,161
1895	753	408	876	3,891	50	135	879	100	197	3,312
1896	898	599	1,181	4,697	66	137	1,022	102	257	4,198
1897	949	617	1,325	4,887	64	144	1,225	102	274	4,558
1898	1,084	654	1,434	5,279	87	170	1,619	112	264	4,639
1899	1,146	731	1,499	5,872	109	166	1,897	112	272	4,933
1900	1,170	655	1,565	6,461	116	185	2,216	122	300	4,980
1901	1,099	516	1,425	6,137	129	257	2,228	152	269	4,983
1902	1,167	769	1,568	7,466	135	315	2,184	163	286	4,988
1903	1,162	969	1,840	8,430	187	372	2,434	203	318	5,115
1904	1,257	1,091	2,096	8,564	201	366	2,766	196	333	5,108
1905	1,459	1,227	2,255	9,669	270	398	2,266	265	368	5,905
1906	1,608	1,395	2,451	10,700	391	435	2,496	290	398	6,566
1907	1,731	1,467	2,767	11,619	430	444	2,671	298	420	6,628
1908	2,018	1,198	2,723	10,726	537	461	2,698	301	438	5,381
1909	1,963	1,580	3,039	11,515	662	535	2,940	308	313	5,976

Lux'bg: Luxembourg U.K.: United Kingdom

See p. 424 for footnotes

E9 Output of Crude Steel (in thousands of metric tons)

1910–1949

	Austria[1]	Belgium	Bulgaria	Czech	Denmark	Finland	France	Germany	E.Germany	Hungary	Italy
1910	2,174	1,892	—	...	—	...	3,413	13,100	...	...	732
1911	2,348	2,028	—	...	—	...	3,837	14,303	...	...	736
1912	2,708	2,442	—	...	—	...	4,429	16,355	...	...	918
1913	2,611	2,403[4]	—	(1,229)[5]	—	7	4,687	17,609	...	...	934
		2,467									
1914	...	1,396	—	...	—	...	2,802	13,810	...	...	911
1915	...	99	—	...	—	...	1,111	12,278	...	...	1,009
1916	...	99	—	...	—	...	1,784	14,871	...	...	1,269
1917	...	10	—	...	—	...	1,991	15,501	...	...	1,332
1918	...[1]	11	—	...	—	...	1,800	14,092	...	...	933[11]
1919	...	334	—	786	—	...	1,293[7]	8,710[7]	...	...	732
							2,156	7,847			
1920	...	1,253	—	973	—	6	2,706	9,278[8]	...	62	774
1921	297	789	—	918	—	15	3,099	9,997[9]	...	166	700
1922	481	1,565	—	721	—	24	4,538	11,714	...	257	983
1923	500	2,297	—	1,180	—	25	5,222	6,305	...	283	1,142
1924	370	2,875	—	1,350	—	29	6,670	9,835	...	239	1,359
1925	464	2,549	—	1,475	—	29	7,464	12,195	...	231	1,786
1926	474	3,339	—	1,345	—	28	8,617	12,342	...	325	1,780
1927	551	3,680	—	1,689	—	12	8,349	16,311	...	472	1,596
1928	636	3,905	—	1,973	—	30	9,479	14,517	...	486	1,960
1929	632	4,110	—	2,193	—	26	9,716	16,245	...	514	2,122
1930	468	3,354	—	1,817	—	28	9,444	12,536	...	369	1,743
1931	323	3,105	—	1,514	—	18	7,816	8,291	...	316	1,409
1932	205	2,790	—	672	—	35	5,638	5,771	...	180	1,396
1933	226	2,731	—	734	—	36	6,577	7,617	...	228	1,771
1934	309	2,944	—	940	—	38	6,155	11,923[8]	...	315	1,850
1935	364	3,023	—	1,178	—	45	6,255	16,447	...	446	2,209
1936	418	3,168	—	1,538	20	42	6,686	19,208	...	553	2,025
1937	650	3,863	—	2,301[6]	20	48	7,893	19,849	...	665	2,087
1938	673	2,279	—	1,800	26	76	6,137	22,656[10]	...	647	2,323
1939	780	3,104	—	2,421	...	77	7,950	23,733[10]	...	733	2,283
1940	766	1,894	—	2,265	...	77	4,413	21,540	...	750	2,258
1941	804	1,624	—	2,316	...	62	4,310	20,836	...	782	2,063
1942	897	1,380	—	2,332	...	84	4,488	20,480	...	784	1,934
1943	1,054	1,670	—	2,514	...	97	5,127	20,758	...	776	1,727
1944	1,013	634	—	2,543[6]	...	93	3,092	18,318[10]	...	694	1,026
								W. Germany[8]			
1945	172	749	—	993	46	86	1,661	...	...	129	395[11]
1946	187	2,297	—	1,677	52	89	4,408	2,555	153	343	1,153
1947	357	2,882	—	2,286	58	77	5,733	3,060	...	597	1,691
1948	648	3,920	5	2,621	72	103	7,236	5,561	398	770	2,125
1949	835	3,849	5	2,806	76	111	9,152	9,156	643	860	2,055

Czech: Czechoslovakia E.Germany: East Germany W.Germany: West Germany

See p. 424 for footnotes

E9 Output of Crude Steel (in thousands of metric tons)

1910–1949

	Lux'bg	Norway	Poland	Portugal	Romania	Russia[3]	Spain	Sweden	Switz	U.K.	Yugoslavia
1910	598	...	...	–	...	3,314	316	472	–	6,476	...
1911	716	...	...	–	...	3,949	323	471	–	6,566	...
1912	947	...	...	–	...	4,503	330[18] 297	515	–	6,905	...
1913	1,326[12]	...	...	–	...	4,918[3] 4,231	242	591	–	7,787	...
1914	1,136	...	...	–	...	4,466	356	507	–	7,971	...
1915	980	...	...	–	...	4,120	387	600	–	8,687	
1916	1,312	...	...	–	...	4,276	323	614	–	9,136	...
1917	1,087	...	...	–	...	3,080	470	581	–	9,873	...
1918	888	...	...	–	...	402	303	545	–	9,692	...
1919	369	...	...	–	...	199	241	491	–	8,021	...
1920	585	...	981[13]	–	40	194	...	437	–	9,212	23
1921	754	...	841[13]	–	45	220	306[18] 360	212	–	3,762	27
1922	1,394	...	1,004[13]	–	68	318	231	311	–	5,975	44
1923	1,201	7	1,135	–	82	615	463	271	–	8,618	51
1924	1,887	7	681	–	87	993	540	501	–	8,333	41
1925	2,086	8	782	–	101	1,868	626	475	–	7,504	53
1926	2,244	9	788	–	112	2,911	608	495	–	3,654	64
1927	2,471	11	1,244	–	130	3,592	671	499	–	9,243	73
1928	2,567	17	1,438	–	153	4,251	777	576	–	8,657	84
1929	2,702	25	1,377	–	161	4,854	1,007	694	–	9,791	98
1930	2,270	22	1,237	–	157	5,761	929	611	–	7,444	86
1931	2,035	11	1,037	–	113	5,620	648	539	–	5,286	92
1932	1,956	26	564	–	103	5,927	534	528	–	5,345	71
1933	1,845	31	883	–	145	6,889	508	630	–	7,138	90
1934	1,932	32	856	–	175	9,693	647	862	–	8,992	90
1935	1,837	52	949	–	213	12,588	595	896	–	10,017	100
1936	1,981	59	1,149	–	220	16,400	373	977	–	11,974	125
1937	2,510	70	1,468	–	239	17,730	167	1,105	–	13,192	169
1938	1,437	68	1,441	–	276	18,057	574	972	5	10,565	227
1939	1,762	68	504[14]	–	268	17,564	584	1,151	–	13,433	235
1940	1,042	69	[15] 1,168[16]	–	261	18,317[3]	804	1,145	40	13,183	258
1941	1,249	59	2,005	1	...	...	689	1,156	74	12,510	...
1942	1,569	63	2,091	1	...	...	644	1,228	82	13,150	...
1943	2,159	65	2,440	1	351	...	676	1,214	92	13,240	...
1944	1,269	50	1,950[15]	1	...	...	657	1,197	113	12,337	...
1945	259	37	488[17]	1	118	12,252	576	1,203	107	12,014	67
1946	1,295	58	1,219	1	157	13,346	641	1,203	34	12,899	202
1947	1,714	66	1,579	2	183	14,534	608	1,191	102	12,929	311
1948	2,453	74	1,955	2	353	18,639	624	1,257	120	15,116	368
1949	2,279	77	2,304	2	459	23,291	720	1,370	124	15,803	401

Lux'bg: Luxembourg Switz: Switzerland U.K.: United Kingdom

See p. 424 for footnotes

E9 Output of Crude Steel (in thousands of metric tons)

1950–1975

	Austria	Belgium	Bulgaria	Czech	Denmark	Finland	France	W.Germany	E.Germany	Hungary	Ireland	Italy
1950	947	3,777	5	3,122	123	102	8,652	12,121	999[19]	1,048	—	2,362
									1,257			
1951	1,028	5,054	7	3,455	161	127	9,835	13,506	1,748	1,290	14	3,063
1952	1,058	5,067	6	3,754	176	147	10,867	15,806	2,249	1,459	15	3,535
1953	1,283	4,497	18	4,366	180	147	9,997	15,420	2,573	1,543	16	3,500
1954	1,653	4,973	62	4,270	199	175	10,627	17,434	2,701	1,491	15	4,207
1955	1,823	5,852	74	4,474	237	177	12,592	21,336	2,816	1,629	18	5,395
1956	2,078	6,312	130	4,882	240	194	13,398	23,189	3,046	1,415	19	5,908
1957	2,509	6,233	159	5,166	262	204	14,096	24,507	3,277	1,375	22	6,787
1958	2,393	5,980	211	5,509	255	186	14,616	22,785[8]	3,430	1,627	25	6,271
1959	2,512	6,410	230	6,136	292	232	15,219	29,435	3,615	1,759	23	6,762
1960	3,163	7,141	253	6,768	317	254	17,281	34,100	3,750	1,887	30	8,229
1961	3,101	6,960	340	7,043	323	277	17,570	33,458	3,867	2,053	28	9,124
1962	2,970	7,297	423	7,639	367	304	17,240	32,563	4,048	2,333	19	9,490
1963	2,947	7,279	461	7,600	359	326	17,556	31,597	4,051	2,374	20	10,157
1964	3,194	8,796	475	8,377	396	371	19,780	37,339	4,264	2,365	53	9,793
1965	3,221	9,229	588	8,599	412	359	19,604	36,821	4,313	2,520	53	12,660
1966	3,193	8,917	699	9,124	405	347	19,585	35,316	4,485	2,649	56	13,639
1967	3,023	9,716	1,239	10,002	401	411	19,655	36,744	4,592	2,739	65	15,890
1968	3,467	11,573	1,461	10,555	457	729	20,410	41,159	4,695	2,902	68	16,963
1969	3,926	12,837	1,515	10,802	482	967	22,511	45,316	4,824	3,033	81	16,428
1970	4,079	12,609	1,800	11,480	473	1,167	23,773	45,040	5,053	3,108	80	17,277
1971	3,960	12,444	1,947	12,064	471	1,025	22,859	40,314	5,350	3,111	80	17,452
1972	4,070	14,532	2,121	12,727	498	1,456	24,054	43,706	5,670	3,274	77	19,815
1973	4,238	15,523	2,246	13,158	449	1,615	25,264	49,521	5,892	3,327	116	20,995
1974	4,699	16,224	2,188	13,640	535	1,656	27,023	53,232	6,165	3,467	110	23,803
1975	4,068	11,584	2,265	14,323	559	1,618	21,530	40,415	6,480	3,673	82	21,836

	Lux'bg	Neth'l	Norway	Poland	Portugal	Romania	Russia[3]	Spain	Sweden	Switz	U.K.	Yugoslavia
1950	2,451	490	81	2,515	2	555	27,329	815	1,437	130	16,554	428
1951	3,077	554	88	2,787	2	644	31,350	818	1,504	144	15,890	434
1952	3,002	685	98	3,179	3	698	34,492	904	1,666	156	16,681	442
1953	2,659	862	111	3,604	3	717	38,128	897	1,759	157	17,892	515
1954	2,828	929	121	3,949	2	628	41,434	1,100	1,840	150	18,817	616
1955	3,225	981	171	4,426	3	766	45,272	1,213	2,127	166	20,109	805
1956	3,456	1,051	290	5,014	4	779	48,698	1,243	2,399	171	20,991	887
1957	3,493	1,185	350	5,304	4	864	51,176	1,346	2,483	234	22,047	1,049
1958	3,379	1,438	371	5,663	4	934	54,920	1,560	2,407	244	19,880	1,119
1959	3,663	1,670	426	6,160	4	1,420	59,971	1,823	2,821	251	20,510	1,299
1960	4,084	1,942	490	6,681	5	1,806	65,294	1,919	3,189	275	24,695	1,442
1961	4,113	1,971	499	7,234	6	2,126	70,756	2,340	3,530	297	22,440	1,532
1962	4,010	2,087	488	7,684	5	2,451	78,307	2,311	3,573	318	20,820	1,596
1963	4,032	2,342	542	8,004	222	2,704	80,231	2,492	3,837	322	22,881	1,588
1964	4,559	2,646	614	8,573	250	3,039	85,038	3,150	4,447	345	26,651	1,677
1965	4,585	3,138	676	9,088	273	3,426	91,021	3,516	4,689	347	27,439	1,769
1966	4,390	3,256	730	9,850	271	3,670	96,907	3,847	4,727	428	27,706	1,867
1967	4,481	3,402	795	10,454	316	4,088	102,224	4,521	4,737	445	24,279	1,832
1968	4,834	3,707	812	11,007	313	4,751	106,537	4,971	5,043	453	26,277	1,997
1969	5,521	4,721	849	11,251	399	5,541	110,330	5,981	5,346	500	26,846	2,220
1970	5,462	5,042	869	11,750	385	6,517	115,889	7,394	5,462	524	28,316	2,228
1971	5,241	5,083	885	12,388	409	6,803	120,660	7,794	5,235	532	24,174	2,453
1972	5,457	5,585	918	13,131	431	7,401	125,592	9,564	5,225	543	25,321	2,588
1973	5,294	5,625	950	13,204	497	8,161	131,481	10,809	5,625	584	26,649	2,676
1974	6,448	5,840	956	14,220	357	8,840	136,206	11,646	5,941	593	22,426	2,836
1975	4,886	4,822	919	14,574	384	9,549	141,325	11,125	5,585	420	20,098	2,916

Czech: Czechoslovakia E. Germany: East Germany Lux'bg: Luxembourg Neth'l: Netherlands Switz: Switzerland U.K.: United Kingdom

See p. 424 for footnotes

E9 Output of Crude Steel (in thousands of metric tons)

NOTES

1. SOURCES:– The same as for table D7, except that Austria-Hungary 1880–1913 and Spain 1884–1904 are taken from I. Svennilson, *Growth and Stagnation in the European Economy* (Geneva, 1954), and Russia to 1950 is taken from G.W. Nutter, *Growth of Industrial Production in the Soviet Union* (Princeton, 1962).

2. Except as indicated in footnote 2, and except for Russia to 1913 (1st line), which includes wrought iron, the statistics in this table relate to the types of steel produced by the Bessemer, Siemens-Martin, and later-invented processes. The following statistics of the output of crucible steel and wrought iron for France for the period 1824–69 (in thousands of tons) were supplied by the Ministry of Industrial and Scientific Development:–

1824	142	1836	210	1848	283	1859	543
1825	144	1837	225	1849	252	1860	562
1826	151	1838	226	1850	257	1861	669
1827	149	1839	233	1851	268	1862	781
1828	151	1840	240	1852	320	1863	807
1829	154	1841	271	1853	474	1864	834
1830	148	1842	292	1854	535	1865	811
1831	146	1843	318	1855	579	1866	868
1832	148	1844	326	1856	588	1867	835
1933	158	1845	355	1857	586	1868	894
1834	183	1846	373	1858	553	1869	1,014
1835	210	1847	390				

The following averages of the output of steel and steel manufactures for Sweden for the period 1833–65 (in thousands of tons) were supplied by the Swedish Central Office of Statistics:–

1833	8	1846–50	11	1856–60	20
1836–40	9	1851–55	18	1861–65	28
1841–45	11				

FOOTNOTES

[1] Figures to 1918 are for the whole Austro-Hungarian Empire, Hungary's proportion growing from about 20 per cent in 1880 to about 30 per cent in 1913. After 1918 the figures are for the Republic.

[2] Previous figures are of Bessemer steel only.

[3] Figures to 1913 (1st line) are for the whole Russian Empire except Finland. From 1913 (2nd line) to 1940 they apply to the 1923 territory of the U.S.S.R. Later figures are for the post-Second World War territory.

[4] This break occurs on a change of source (see note 1 to table E8).

[5] This is also included in the Austro-Hungarian output.

[6] From 1938 to 1944 Teschen is excluded.

[7] Up to 1918 the parts of Alsace-Lorraine ceded to Germany in 1871 are included in Germany rather than in France. Subsequently they are included in France.

[8] From 1921 to 1934 and from 1946 to 1958 Saarland is excluded. Its output during these periods was as follows (in thousands of tons):–

1921	987	1928	2,073	1946	291	1953	2,684
1922	1,313	1929	2,209	1947	708	1954	2,805
1923	1,064	1930	1,935	1948	1,228	1955	3,165
1924	1,485	1931	1,538	1949	1,757	1956	3,374
1925	1,582	1932	1,463	1950	1,898	1957	3,439
1926	1,737	1933	1,676	1951	2,603	1958	3,460
1927	1,895	1934	1,950	1952	2,823		

[9] In July 1922 eastern Upper Silesia was transferred from Germany to Poland.

[10] For 1939–44 includes Sudetenland, and for 1940–44 parts of Poland also.

[11] Figures to 1918 apply to the boundaries of 1971. For 1919–45 they apply to the boundaries of 1924, and from 1946 to the boundaries of 1954.

[12] Previous figures do not include castings.
[13] It is not clear whether or not the output of eastern Upper Silesia prior to July 1922 is included here.
[14] First half-year only.
[15] For 1940–44 includes Teschen, which was previously and subsequently part of Czechoslovakia. From 1945 the figures apply to the postwar territory.
[16] Excluding central Poland.
[17] February-December only.
[18] Figures from 1912 (2nd line) to 1921 (1st line) are of rolled iron and steel.
[19] Previously steel ingots only.

E10 OUTPUT OF ALUMINIUM[1] (in thousands of metric tons)

1890–1929

	France	Germany	Italy	Norway	U.K.
1890	- -[2]	...	—	—	—
1891	- -	...	—	—	—
1892	0.1	...	—	—	—
1893	0.1	...	—	—	—
1894	0.3	...	—	—	—
1895	0.4	...	—	—	—
1896	0.4	...	—	—	—
1897	0.5	...	—	—	—
1898	0.6	...	—	—	—
1899	0.8	...	—	—	—
1900	1.0	...	—	—	—
1901	1.2	...	—	—	—
1902	1.4	...	—	—	—
1903	1.6	...	—	—	—
1904	1.6	...	—	—	—
1905	1.9	...	—	—	—
1906	3.4	...	—	—	—
1907	4.7	...	0.3	—	—
1908	4.7	...	0.6	—	—
1909	6.1	...	0.8	—	—
1910	6.4	...	0.8	—	—
1911	7.4	...	0.8	—	—
1912	10	...	0.8	—	—
1913	13	0.8	0.9	—	7.6
1914	10	...	0.9	—	...
1915	6	...	0.9	—	...
1916	10	...	1.1	—	...
1917	11	...	1.7	—	
1918	12	...	1.7	—	...
1919	10	...	1.7	—	...
1920	12	19	1.2	—	8.1
1921	8	19	0.7	—	5.1
1922	7	16	0.8	—	7.1
1923	14	16	1.5	13	9.1
1924	16	19	2.1	20	8.1
1925	18	26	1.9	21	9.7
1926	24	31	1.9	24	3.1
1927	25	28	2.5	21	9.7
1928	26	32	3.5	25	9.7
1929	29	33	7.4	29	8.1

U.K.: United Kingdom

See p. 427 for footnotes

1930–1975

	France	Germany	Italy	Norway	U.K.
1930	25	31	8.0	27	13
1931	18	27	11	21	14
1932	14	19	13	18	10
1933	14	19	12	15	11
1934	15	37	13	15	13
1935	22	71	14	15	15
1936	30	98	16	15	16
1937	35	128[3]	23	23	19
1938	42	166	26	29	23
1939	53	199	34	31	25
1940	60	211	39	28	19
1941	64	234	48	18	23
1942	45	264	44	20	48
1943	46	250	46	24	57
1944	26	244[3]	17	20	36
		W.Germany			
1945	37	...	43[4]	5	32
1946	48	...	11	17	32
1947	53	...	25	22	29
1948	64	...	33	31	30
1949	54	29	26	36	30
1950	61	28	37	47	30
1951	90	74	49	52	28
1952	106	100	52	53	28
1953	113	107	55	56	31
1954	120	129	58	64	32
1955	129	137	62	75	25
1956	150	147	63	99	28
1957	160	154	77	104	30
1958	169	137	74	126	27
1959	173	151	75	148	25
1960	238	169	84	168	29
1961	279	173	83	175	33
1962	294	178	81	209	35
1963	298	209	91	219	31
1964	316	220	116	268	32
1965	341	238	124	276	36
1966	364	244	129	330	37
1967	361	253	128	361	39
1968	366	257	142	468	38
1969	372	263	145	502	34
1970	381	309	146	522	40
1971	384	427	136	530	119
1972	394	448	149	557	171
1973	359	533	184	620	252
1974	393	689	212	648	293
1975	383	678	190	591	308

E10 Output of Aluminium (in thousands of metric tons)

NOTES

1. SOURCES:– The official publications noted on p. xv supplemented (for Germany) by the League of Nations *Statistical Yearbooks.*

2. Secondary production has, in recent years, been much more important than primary production in the United Kingdom. Figures of this for 1942–65 can be found in B.R. Mitchell & H.G. Jones, *Second Abstract of British Historical Statistics* (Cambridge, 1971).

FOOTNOTES

[1] Primary production, excluding metal derived from scrap.
[2] Output began in 1862, but did not exceed 15 tons per year until 1890.
[3] Figures for 1938–44 include Austria and the annexed territories in the East.
[4] Subsequent figures are for the boundaries of 1954.

E11 IMPORTS AND EXPORTS OF COAL BY MAIN SURPLUS AND DEFICIENT COUNTRIES (in thousands of metric tons)

1827–1869

	Austria		Belgium		Denmark[10]	Finland	France	
	I	E[2]	I[4]	E[4]	I[5]	I	I[5]	E[5]
1827	...	...	...	...	...	...	542	5
1828	...	...	...	...	...	...	584	5
1829	...	...	...	...	...	...	554	6
1830	...	...	...	...	...	...	637	6
1831	...	...	3	470	...	...	548	7
1832	...	...	12	319	...	...	576	22
1833	...	...	12	576	...	...	702	23
1834	...	...	24	648	...	...	747	23
1835	...	...	16	696	...	...	803	21
1836	...	...	22	774	...	...	999	26
1837	...	...	28	789	...	...	1,144	34
1838	...	...	35	776	...	...	1,227	35
1839	...	...	28	746	...	...	1,219	33
1840	...	...	30	779	...	...	1,291	37
1841	...	...	28	1,015	...	...	1,619	49
1842	29	21	35	1,015	...	...	1,669	58
1843	24	36	31	1,086	51	...	1,663	62
1844	28	39	11	1,243	60	...	1,756	52
1845	33	44	9	1,543	79	...	2,207	66
1846	36	7	11	1,356	85	...	2,194	54
1847	40	53	10	1,827	65	...	2,549	53
1848	36	40	10	1,461	118	...	2,144	49
1849	...	...	11	1,665	102	...	2,394	38
1850	...	...	9	1,987	128	...	2,833	42
1851	85	59	10	2,057	118	...	2,927	35
1852	121	58	8	2,104	126	...	3,096	41
1853	[179][3]	[72][3]	13	2,332	136	...	3,530	46
1854	64	109	53	2,626	173	...	4,130	100
1855	63	129	69	2,974	171	...	4,952	112
1856	90	138	89	2,866	245	...	5,070	100
1857	156	117	146	2,887	250	...	5,368	120
1858	208	189	108	3,091	185	...	5,672	131
1859	222[1]	198[7]	110	3,145	236	...	5,759	178
1860	234[1]	279[1]	97	3,450	205	14	6,160	200
1861	268	294	93	3,379	295	27	6,290	283
1862	317	370	79	3,289	256	27	6,218	260
1863	343	323	73	3,328	285	29	6,120	315
1864	344	397	67	3,783	244	18	6,633	343
1865	367[1]	386[1]	75	4,071	383	23	7,213	343
1866	287	481	184	4,520	353	26	8,230	406
1867	394	731	444	4,081	345	23	7,983	356
1868	587	809	253	4,295	409	33	7,975	394
1869	687	821	223	4,269	356	26	8,304	381

Abbreviations used throughout this table: I Imports E Exports NI Nett Imports

See p. 436 for footnotes

E11 Imports and Exports of Coal by Main Surplus and Deficient Countries (in thousands of metric tons)

1816–1869

	Greece	Italy	Neth'l	Norway	Russia	Spain	Sweden	Switz	U.K.
	I	I[5]	NI[5]	I[5]	I[7]	I	I[7]	I[4]	E
1816	...	...	...	...	...	...	...	...	242
1817	...	...	...	...	...	...	...	...	257
1818	...	...	...	...	...	...	...	...	276
1819	...	...	...	...	...	...	...	...	242
1820	...	...	...	...	...	...	...	...	255
1821	...	...	...	...	...	...	...	...	267
1822	...	...	...	...	...	...	...	...	292
1823	...	...	...	...	...	...	...	...	258
1824	...	...	...	...	...	...	...	...	287
1825	...	...	...	...	...	...	...	...	318
1826	...	...	...	...	...	...	...	...	354
1827	...	...	...	...	...	...	...	...	375
1828	...	...	...	...	...	...	...	...	364
1829	...	...	...	4	...	...	...	...	377
1830	...	...	...	3	...	...	...	...	512
1831	...	...	...	2	...	...	...	...	519
1832	...	...	...	...	...	...	...	...	597[8]
1833	...	...	...	...	...	...	...	...	639
1834	...	...	...	...	...	...	...	...	620
1835	...	...	...	6	...	...	...	...	741
1836	...	...	...	7	...	...	...	...	926
1837	...	...	...	9	...	...	...	...	1,124
1838	...	...	...	19	...	...	...	...	1,324
1839	...	...	...	15	...	...	...	...	1,455
1840	...	...	...	17	...	...	15	...	1,618
1841	...	...	...	22	...	...	15	...	1,861
1842	...	...	...	27	...	...	30	...	2,007
1843	...	...	...	24	...	...	22	...	1,849
1844	...	...	...	25	...	...	22	...	1,725
1845	...	...	...	37	...	...	33	...	2,482
1846	...	...	1,082	37	...	...	31	...	2,428
1847	...	...	1,458	39	...	...	30	...	2,028
1848	...	...	1,375	50	...	...	52	...	2,742
1849	...	...	1,256	40	...	164	58	...	2,775
1850	...	...	1,182	52	...	276	76	...	3,264
1851	...	...	1,175	56	...	346	82	...	3,352
1852	...	...	1,419	56	...	298	81	...	3,535
1853	...	...	1,571	62	...	400	86	...	3,818
1854	...	...	2,241	89	...	325	105	...	4,186
1855	...	...	1,752	97	...	296	119	...	4,839
1856	...	...	1,780	114	...	351	180	...	5,728
1857	...	...	1,589	115	...	459	231	...	6,587
1858	...	...	1,398	101	...	624	193	55	6,393
1859	...	...	1,328	123	...	662	260	78	6,893
1860	...	...	1,808	126	...	645	259	114	7,163
1861	...	240	1,660	162	...	316	336	160	7,682
1862	...	446	2,138[6]	140	...	326	343	177	8,140
1863	...	390	1,536	137	...	286	343	177	8,133
1864	...	555	1,273	180	...	334	363	216	8,674
1865	...	456	1,443	178	...	314	375	263	9,003
1866	...	524	1,579	195	650	331	385	260	9,800
1867	64	516	1,510	233	803	361	355	254	10,214
1868	32	580	1,580	237	577	377	416	290	10,666
1869	73	650	1,630	207	803	390	363	280	10,397

Neth'l: Netherlands Switz: Switzerland U.K.: United Kingdom

See p. 436 for footnotes

E11 Imports and Exports of Coal by Main Surplus and Deficient Countries (in thousands of metric tons)

1870–1919

	Austria		Belgium		Bulgaria	Denmark[10]	Finland	France	
	I	E	I[4]	E[4]	I[4]	I[5]	I	I[5]	E[5]
1870	927	925	229	3,753	...	431	33	6,045[11]	395[11]
1871	1,364	1,047	204	4,186	...	448	41	5,950	329
1872	1,588	1,167	219	5,357	...	429	33	7,709	577
1873	1,785	1,681	696	4,960	...	433	31	8,029	695
1874	1,627	2,161	464	4,501	...	468	45	7,433	747
1875	1,628	2,703	725	4,710	...	550	30	8,282	672
1876	1,576	2,750	833	4,399	...	581	33	8,221	727
1877	1,499	2,755	678	4,091	...	574	40	7,882	614
1878	1,665	2,921	721	4,466	...	545	46	8,201	594
1879	[2,272][4]	[3,278][4]	740	4,832	...	616	27	8,880	539
1880	2,204	3,700	934	5,375	...	702	34	9,941	603
1881	2,148	3,643	1,040	5,392	...	743	33	10,222	601
1882	2,146	3,469	1,059	5,387	...	797	41	10,868	457
1883	2,368	4,047	1,302	5,438	...	916	38	11,707	510
1884	2,478	4,103	1,257	5,473	...	912	49	11,678	500
1885	2,508	4,102	1,260	5,187	...	955	76	10,917	506
1886	2,664[9]	4,489[9]	1,025	5,181	...	915	43	10,381	610
	2,723	4,540							
1887	2,885	4,783	1,036	5,518	...	939	42	10,565	595
1888	3,271	6,162	1,063	5,528	...	1,056	37	10,551	629
1889	3,423	6,542	1,025	5,817	...	1,128	51	9,981	943
1890	3,628	7,505	1,787	5,914	...	1,081	69	11,603	941
1891	3,937	7,687	1,766	6,043	...	1,163	71	11,690	906
1892	3,625	7,490	1,684	5,882	...	1,157	61	11,557	896
1893	4,171	7,520	1,583	6,281	...	1,130	60	11,401	898
1894	4,502	7,643	1,707	5,992	...	1,282	71	11,644	801
1895	5,052	7,903	1,896	5,992	...	1,328	74	11,510	963
1896	5,664	8,338	1,955	5,973	...	1,744[10]	95	11,594	904
						1,626			
1897	5,674	8,956	2,288	5,973	...	1,743	176	11,975	1,021
1898	6,022	9,371	2,386	6,124	...	1,810	164	11,917	1,101
1899	5,881	9,795	3,152	6,104	...	1,979	255	13,370	1,026
1900	6,931	8,942	3,601	6,939	17	1,940	204	16,177	927
1901	6,461	9,129	3,102	6,363	27	2,020	134	15,441	719
1902	6,342	8,815	3,497	6,574	20	2,074	125	15,132	843
1903	6,457	9,063	3,908	6,388	28	2,159	167	14,802	959
1904	6,768	8,758	4,085	6,485	36	2,329	171	14,562	1,207
1905	7,008	9,227	4,659	6,161	42	2,265	189	14,007	1,858
1906	8,009	9,596	5,858	6,288	44	2,466	203	18,742	1,448
1907	10,394	10,049	5,801	6,020	77	2,198	302	19,431	1,224
1908	17,920	11,120	5,876	6,161	134	2,727	496	19,166	1,162
1909	10,877	9,546	6,338	6,651	112	3,017	447	20,023	1,256
1910	18,593	10,952	7,211	6,551	114	2,771	362	19,892	1,370
1911	11,611	7,974	8,402	6,826	184	2,951	456	21,445	1,432
1912	12,099	8,447	9,524	6,697	158	3,499	519	20,704	1,952
1913	14,656	8,125	10,451	6,738	108	3,590	586	25,323	1,500
1914	10,762	6,263	...	...	219	3,618	229	18,057	737
1915	...	...	...	...	- -	3,890	7	19,735	114
1916	...	...	...	...	6	3,705	30	20,422	117
1917	...	...	...	...	23	2,125	16	17,453	126
1918	...	...	...	...	180	2,228	27	16,835[11]	1,851[11]
1919	...	...	...	...	1	2,323	43	22,100	523

Czech: Czechoslovakia

See p. 436 for footnotes

E11 Imports and Exports of Coal by Main Surplus and Deficient Countries (in thousands of metric tons)

1870–1919

	Germany		Greece	Italy	Neth'l	Norway
	I[4]	E[4]	I	I[5]	NI[5]	I[5]
1870	...	...	76	942	1,810	235
1871	...	...	112	791	1,820	227
1872	2,268	3,820	66	1,037	1,950	243
1873	1,456	4,022	73	960	1,860	242
1874	1,809	4,197	56	1,031	1,710	301
1875	1,876	4,523	60	1,060	1,960	380
1876	2,105	5,287	...	1,454	2,260	334
1877	2,026	5,009	...	1,330	2,300	450
1878	1,931	5,825	...	1,325	2,440	404
1879	1,894	6,012	...	1,524	2,630	423
1880	2,059[14] 5,140	7,236	...	1,738	2,910	462
1881	5,017	7,458	...	2,073	2,921	477
1882	5,112	7,632	...	2,180	2,950	524
1883	5,500	8,705	...	2,351	3,269	564
1884	5,763	8,817	...	2,605	3,262	575
1885	6,024	8,956	...	2,957	3,416	661
1886	6,645	8,655	...	2,927	3,448	644
1887	7,099	8,781	...	3,583	3,496	623
1888	8,464	9,460	...	3,873	3,898	718
1889	10,207	8,847	...	3,999	3,784	820
1890	10,671	9,145	...	4,355	3,647	767
1891	11,839	9,536	...	3,917	4,256	891
1892	11,138	8,971	139	3,878	4,029	903
1893	11,370	9,677	120	3,724	4,069	900
1894	11,674	9,739	122	4,696	4,107	1,061
1895	12,298	10,361	117	4,305	4,081	1,121
1896	13,115	11,599	141	4,081	4,395	1,136
1897	14,183	12,390	133	4,260	4,604	1,230
1898	14,270	13,989	170	4,432	4,530	1,233
1899	14,837	13,943	89	4,860	4,605	1,478
1900	15,344	15,276	155	4,947	5,001	1,520
1901	14,406	15,266	155	4,839	4,873	1,413
1902	14,308	16,101	124	5,406	4,771	1,547
1903	14,729	17,390	149	5,547	5,054	1,529
1904	14,968	17,997	131	5,905	5,417	1,508
1905	17,345[12]	18,157[12]	102	6,474	5,541	1,513
1906	...	19,551	95	7,673	6,011	1,544
1907	22,685	20,061	159	8,300	6,049	1,749
1908	20,244	21,191	273	8,452	5,996	2,073
1909	20,365	23,351	210	9,304	6,158	2,096
1910	18,594	24,257	270	9,339	6,331	2,159
1911	17,983	27,406	341	9,596	6,613	2,187
1912	17,646	31,145	...	10,057	7,433	2,474
1913	17,527	34,598	504[15]	10,834	8,264	2,483
1914	...	...	...	9,759	7,334	2,764
1915	...	...	...	8,369	6,712	3,095
1916	...	...	...	8,065	5,610	2,833
1917	...	...	...	5,038	...	1,226
1918	...[13]	...[13]	...	5,841	1,326	1,574
1919	...	...	...	6,227	3,506	1,791

Neth'l: Netherlands

See p. 436 for footnotes

E11 Imports and Exports of Coal by Main Surplus and Deficient Countries (in thousands of metric tons)

1870–1919

	Portugal	Romania	Russia[7]		Spain	Sweden	Switz	UK
	I[5]	I	I	E	I	I	I	E
1870	...	...	845	...	513	465	321	11,341
1871	...	...	1,238	...	502	495	393	12,404
1872	182	...	1,062	...	331	601	459	12,916
1873	260	...	833	...	428	599	436	12,272
1874	186	...	1,037	...	409	643	440	13,596
1875	426	...	1,041	...	473	788	465	14,203
1876	418	...	1,498	...	655	832	542	15,942
1877	239	...	1,481	...	766	870	514	15,120
1878	228	...	1,821	...	759	723	487	15,240
1879	253	...	1,486	...	771	723	521	15,993
1880	317	...	1,922	...	883	959	603	18,178
1881	322	...	1,791	...	983	908	559	19,061
1882	381	62	1,730	...	1,108	1,033	619	20,246
1883	405	131	2,267	...	1,263	1,049	690	22,019
1884	428	144	1,913[7]	...	1,342	1,157	702	22,713
			1,922					
1885	394	139[9]	1,823	...	1,317	1,253	740	23,074
1886	433	155	1,867	...	1,407	1,224	749	22,462
1887	446	170	1,575	...	1,382	1,244	813	23,632
1888	482	203	1,742	...	1,488	1,414	827	26,043
1889	559	195	2,081	...	1,615	1,643	914	27,946
1890	600	241	1,748	...	1,718	1,657	994[14]	29,199
							1,116	
1891	622	335	1,748	...	1,863	1,757	1,276	29,970
1892	604	301	1,669	...	1,870	1,746	1,252	29,514
1893	529	341	2,006	...	1,765	1,747	1,024	28,153
1894	632	312	2,265	...	1,841	1,984	1,290	32,266
1895	599	313	2,246	...	1,725	1,968	1,385	32,224
1896	615	327	2,351	...	1,883	2,050	1,514	33,477
1897	652	367	2,529	...	1,853	2,300	1,598	35,921
1898	745	414	2,995	...	1,441	2,458	1,714	35,621
1899	764	319	4,481	...	1,783	3,135	1,851	41,841
1900	883	158	4,500	...	1,992	3,130	2,057	44,796
1901	861	221	3,671	...	2,163	2,870	1,871	42,549
1902	950	180	3,378	...	2,309	2,984	1,888	43,852
1903	918	177	3,500	...	2,266	3,288	2,052	45,671
1904	939	168	3,890	...	2,307	3,481	2,160	46,998
1905	914	170	4,145	...	2,352	3,411	2,267	48,239
1906	1,060	184	4,394	...	2,427	3,856	2,511	56,492
1907	1,158	346	4,093	...	2,136	4,402	2,924	64,622
1908	1,156	281	4,416	...	2,219	4,693	2,921	63,551
1909	1,173	228	4,363	...	2,353	4,341	2,947	64,089
1910	1,191	240	4,709	...	2,315	4,453	2,838	63,081
1911	1,148	253	5,303	...	2,372	4,288	3,145	65,636
1912	1,337	...	6,088[7]	...	2,678[9]	4,774	3,197	65,478
			5,305					
1913	1,392	419	7,748	...	3,098	5,375	3,387	74,578
1914	1,211	...	4,552	...	2,876	5,077	3,111	59,987
1915	1,071	...	658	...	1,905	5,056	3,312	44,234
1916	950	...	948	...	2,151	5,333	3,152	38,967
1917	402	...	753	...	1,167	2,024	2,270	35,558
1918	215	...	17	—	528	2,486	2,142	32,263
1919	647	...	...	...	901	2,210	1,736	35,816

Switz: Switzerland UK: United Kingdom

See p. 436 for footnotes

E11 Imports and Exports of Coal by Main Surplus and Deficient Countries (in thousands of metric tons)

1920–1975

	Austria[1]	Belgium		Bulgaria	Czechoslovakia		Denmark[10]	Finland	France	
	I	I[4]	E[4]	I	I[4]	E[4]	I[5]	I	I[5]	E[5]
1920	3,995[14]	2,184	2,056	1	1,299	4,289	2,711	90	32,516	345
1921	5,749	6,160	7,666	4	1,097	6,258	2,561	87	25,336	2,171
1922	5,085	5,623	4,585	8	626	4,990	3,638	243	32,211	2,655
1923	5,023	9,089	3,634	14	919	4,606	3,967	525	33,451	2,929
1924	5,765	10,041	3,377	23	1,068	5,129	4,651[10]	619	34,785	2,775
							4,651			
1925	5,272	11,498	3,997	18	1,775	4,660	4,041	612	30,460	2,801
1926	5,125	10,633	5,328	12	1,737	6,298	3,945	567	29,109	3,006
1927	5,601	12,569	4,481	7	2,015	5,722	5,023	1,034	30,422	2,675
1928	5,712	12,098	5,868	7	2,827	5,593	4,588	1,076	29,985	3,202
1929	6,658	15,295	5,271	9	2,861	5,961	5,552	1,170	36,575	4,080
1930	4,823	13,809	5,467	9	2,247	4,756	5,059	917	36,420	2,911
1931	4,625	12,279	7,270	4	2,239	4,146	5,303	1,068	32,714	2,831
1932	3,508	9,190	5,039	4	1,959	3,301	4,983	1,060	25,464	2,086
1933	3,118	7,463	4,975	4	1,399	3,353	4,937	1,137	25,619	1,921
1934	3,083	7,290	5,177	3	1,479	3,703	5,180	1,298	24,535	1,885
1935	3,028	6,490	5,647	4	1,506	3,416	5,437	1,222	22,002	1,528
1936	2,925	6,916	6,511	3	1,370	3,513	5,838[10]	1,724	22,907	1,333
							5,800			
1937	3,393	9,939	5,636	3	1,443	5,130	6,016	2,232	30,890	1,034
1938	...	6,899	6,576	4	1,921	...	5,396	1,778	22,724	1,215
1939	...	...	...	3	...	...	6,015	1,421	18,078	1,185
1940	...	...	...	1	...	...	4,117	690	8,020	304
1941	...	...	...	4	...	...	3,700	1,064	2,120	700
1942	...	...	...	...	...	...	2,995	901	3,137	702
1943	...	...	...	...	...	...	3,535	1,308	4,758	19
1944	...	...	...	...	...	...	3,737	905	3,682	56
1945	...	...	...	...	...	...	1,499	111	5,326	53
1946	2,367	...	...	...	...	...	3,836	938	10,973	409
1947	3,831	7,557	2,082	...	1,049	1,604	4,296	1,499	17,195	460
1948	5,872	5,873	1,551	...	2,221	2,936	3,582	2,415	21,020	415
1949	6,212	3,687	1,796	---26	3,335	3,583	4,919	1,200	22,575	1,160
1950	5,678	3,594	3,154	36	3,966	3,461	6,676	1,929	14,861	2,401
1951	6,039	5,844	2,527	36	4,313	2,387	6,114	2,384	20,098	2,093
1952	5,057	5,465	3,578	41	4,063	2,706	6,250	2,601	20,110	1,718
1953	4,550	5,702	5,031	43	4,785	2,588	6,302	2,026	16,231	2,564
1954	5,960	7,410	6,577	45	4,406	2,530	6,788	2,319	17,044	3,072
1955	5,300	7,843	8,339	49	4,060	2,924	7,673	2,642	18,179	6,440
1956	5,646	9,185	6,008	40	3,451	3,085	5,805	2,708	24,382	2,551
1957	6,049	9,863	5,384	142	2,292	3,475	4,609	3,085	26,671	2,421
1958	6,166	9,726	3,860	174	2,576	3,817	4,439	2,484	21,306	2,074
1959	4,627	9,154	3,049	289	2,355	4,115	4,139	2,862	17,588[5]	1,735[5]
									16,314	1,691
1960	5,295	8,645	3,166	320	2,402	4,955	5,478	3,166	15,979	1,613
1961	4,815	8,809	3,560	812	3,355	5,301	5,159	3,047	16,778	1,505
1962	5,125	9,359	3,477	1,219	4,023	5,501	5,508	2,985	16,508	1,557
1963	5,778	12,015	3,144	1,568	4,346	5,883	5,594	2,543	22,813	1,176
1964	5,465	11,837	2,980	2,293	5,044	5,886	5,119	3,307	19,713	1,103
1965	5,292	11,550	2,490	2,820	4,538	5,398	4,486	3,349	17,150	1,092
1966	4,962	10,425	1,741	3,183	4,030	5,617	4,657	2,772	15,896	989
1967	4,735	10,110	2,033	3,524	4,162	5,632	4,341	2,792	15,449	925
1968	4,885	11,714	1,595	3,594	4,623	5,860	4,709	2,754	15,763	1,088
1969	4,752	12,403	1,425	4,288	4,624	6,488	4,251	3,224	16,376	2,047
1970	5,515	13,359	1,191	5,308	4,569	6,720	3,812	4,064	17,600	2,095
1971	4,325	10,274	1,124	6,230	5,447	6,895	2,451	3,645	16,830	1,511
1972	4,700	10,795	1,180	6,113	5,535	6,982	2,357	3,385	15,171	1,608
1973	4,804	12,104	1,102	6,122	5,299	7,318	3,196	3,804	16,467	1,958
1974	5,113	14,837	1,019	6,301	5,168	7,627	3,831	4,916	21,325	1,775
1975	4,284	10,159	923	6,593	5,188	7,648	4,279	4,734	20,413	1,291

See p. 436 for footnotes

E11 Imports and Exports of Coal by Main Surplus and Deficient Countries (in thousands of metric tons)

1920–1975

	Germany		E.Germany	Greece	Hungary		Italy	S Ireland	Neth'l	Norway
	I	E[4]	I[5]	I	I[5]	E[5]	I[5]	I	NI	I[5]
1920	2,704 [13]	7,305 [13]	...	212 [15]	...	...	5,620	...	3,125	1,827
1921	3,580 [13]	... [13]	...	244	603	191	7,471	...	3,977	1,066
1922	14,614 [13]	5,062 [13]	...	227	788	309	8,834	...	4,822	2,070
1923	[26,808] [17]	[1,209] [17]	...	321	838	267	9,134	...	3,916	2,165
1924	[15,280] [17]	[2,795] [17]	...	461	1,133	271	11,170	2,521	4,482	2,444
1925	9,903	13,646	...	630	1,189	512	10,513	2,275	4,187	2,375
1926	4,882	38,035	...	551	1,219	677	12,258	1,784	2,592	1,970
1927	7,894	26,878	...	714	1,513	309	14,059	2,537	3,191	2,678
1928	10,176	23,895	...	695	1,661	288	12,698	2,444	2,269	2,607
1929	10,691	26,769	...	785	1,860	409	14,603	2,501	2,834	2,976
1930	9,150	24,383	...	827	1,237	385	12,937	2,540	1,892 [21] 3,710	2,737
1931	7,568	23,123	...	778	869	381	11,094	2,452	2,623	2,424
1932	5,662	18,312	...	734	384	346	8,778	2,341	1,655	2,538
1933	5,738	18,444	...	596	330	232	9,562	2,302	684	2,635
1934	6,639 [13]	21,937 [13]	...	757	419	179	12,737	2,375	1,006	2,669
1935	5,930	26,774	...	744	367	214	14,590	2,281	473	2,810
1936	6,104	29,493	...	869	465	207	9,264	2,514	414	3,040
1937	6,651	39,659	...	895	580	253	12,927	2,604	89	3,462
1938	6,412	30,769	...	897	524	287	12,140	2,524	373	2,929
1939	...	...	...	...	...	...	11,276	2,922	1,936	3,561
1940	...	...	...	...	...	...	12,530	2,802	...	1,853
1941	...	...	...	...	...	...	11,582	1,512	...	1,361
1942	...	...	...	...	...	...	10,793	1,065	...	1,427
1943	...	...	...	...	...	...	...	1,032	...	1,709
1944	...	...	...	...	...	...	...	746	...	1,420
	West Germany[18]									
1945	...	...	...	...	...	...	...	935	...	1,124
1946	...	5,145	...	...	...	...	5,713	1,297	2,740	1,826
1947	...	5,974	...	...	...	...	9,154	1,533	3,285	2,380
1948	1,957	9,453	...	247	...	...	8,610	1,724	2,788	2,015
1949	3,099 [18]	13,189 [18]	...	290	940	120	8,952	1,658	3,340	1,745
1950	5,089	15,740	9,038	284	944 [20] 899	47	8,597	1,994	3,891	1,832
1951	10,148	13,665	8,726	382	944	126	11,036	2,203	4,540	1,790
1952	12,407	12,700	9,865	292	1,427	211	9,484	1,843	4,538	1,174
1953	10,103	14,168	12,351	283	1,673	428	9,320	1,773	4,288	1,166
1954	9,121	17,003	13,503	255	2,017	698	9,195	1,831	5,297	1,018
1955	16,931	13,186	13,086	323	1,996	527	10,403	1,947	5,761	1,285
1956	19,757	12,844	12,487	236	1,895	217	10,820	1,518	−685	1,469
1957	22,567	13,573	12,592	282	3,525	31	11,760	1,275	6,375	1,133
1958	17,210 [13]	11,645 [13]	15,098	250	2,276	94	9,323	1,401	4,519	966
1959	9,576	14,986	16,535	192	2,245	58	8,288	1,616	3,043	861
1960	8,072	17,974	16,086	235	2,402	63	10,417	1,687	3,057	1,040
1961	8,281	17,297	16,731	236	2,614	137	10,344	1,810	2,678	990
1962	9,029	18,311	17,574	213	2,623	143	11,152	1,506	4,670	927
1963	9,986	16,806	17,866	287	3,703	278	11,780	1,474	5,642	1,051
1964	8,659	14,123	19,169	302	4,366	189	10,935	1,323	4,795	1,044
1965	8,451	13,577	17,887	430	3,687	184	11,295	1,307	2,422	1,045
1966	8,156	16,015	17,477	398	2,434	196	12,550	1,353	2,654	1,114
1967	7,998	17,615	14,885 [19] 11,153	238	2,793	218	11,134	1,278	2,834	1,055
1968	7,079	20,408	9,127	286	2,664	241	11,132	1,245	3,766	1,234
1969	7,959	17,705	9,527	370	2,751	335	11,937	1,167	3,695	1,283
1970	10,241	15,906	11,315	448	3,158	93	12,224	1,230	2,836	1,309
1971	8,574	14,278	11,018	398	3,054	105	11,856	1,052	1,937	1,088
1972	8,233	13,249	10,678	531	2,781	135	11,044	910	1,400	944
1973	8,360	14,072	11,540	696	2,597	141	11,011	861	2,185	997
1974	7,200	17,683	10,242	887	2,544	110	12,550	901	3,435	1,260
1975	7,894	14,709	9,411	763	2,676	103	12,580	697	3,881	1,111

E Germany: East Germany S Ireland: Southern Ireland Neth'l Netherlands

See p. 436 for footnotes

E11 Imports and Exports of Coal by Main Surplus and Deficient Countries (in thousands of metric tons)

1920–1975

	Poland		Portugal	Romania	Russia		Spain	Sweden	Switz	UK	Yugoslavia
	I[5]	E[5]	I[7]	I	I	E[7]	I	I	I	E	I[7]
1920	2,691	147	600	...	37	—	369	3,172	2,647	25,332	...
1921	3,525[22]	335[22]	643	...	251	—	1,080	1,693	1,634	25,057	...
1922	2,477	5,439	934	40	605[24]	—	1,644	3,156	2,220	65,228	316
1923	267	12,913	794	195	496[24]	—	1,196	3,879	2,783	80,734	308
1924	389	11,416	939	228	319[24]	—	1,430	4,715	2,602	62,640	334
1925	243	8,158	988	273	48[24]	—	1,667	4,240	2,739	51,632	546
1926	122	14,437	879	201	306[24]	—	1,013	3,967	2,707	20,927	441
1927	237	11,226	1,076	187	472[24]	—	2,005	5,837	3,045	51,970	449
1928	248	13,035	1,146	159	...	—	1,888	5,175	3,029	50,854	531
1929	315	14,071	1,139	238	66	1,400	2,084	6,259	3,462	61,234	664
1930	164	12,697	1,236	168	64	1,900	1,681	5,970	3,148	55,755	585
1931	142	14,073	1,100	116	107	1,700	1,200	5,974	3,290	43,436	450
1932	147	10,425	916	105	53	1,800	918	5,826	3,280	39,523	354
1933	174	9,274	1,099	68	15	1,800	798	6,054	3,165	39,695	292
1934	150	10,251	1,110	79	26	2,200	1,125	6,747	3,118	40,296	343
1935	173	9,214	1,161	59	36	2,200	1,155	7,000	3,088	39,335	430
1936	169	8,720	1,080	62	...	1,800	...	7,694	3,178	35,073	305
1937	95	11,372	1,318	77	...	1,300	...	8,938	3,486	40,985	413
1938	180	11,947	960	90	—	400	...	7,713	3,337	36,431	...
1939	...	...	1,177	...	- -	200	...	8,682	3,967	37,509	...
1940	...	...	763	...	3,414	- -	125	5,721	2,677	19,961	...
1941	...	...	686	...	...	...	141	4,803	2,216	5,166	...
1942	...	...	491	...	...	...	182	3,890	1,909	3,631	...
1943	...	...	515	...	...	...	174	4,803	1,945	3 683	...
1944	...[23]	...[23]	574	...	...	...	90	3,562	1,369	2,648	...
1945	...	...	471	...	...	...	55	362	239	3,378	...
1946	...	...	536	...	7,900	500	75	3,455	1,536	4,526	...
1947	...	[19,338][16]	927	...	8,300	1,000	17	5,064	2,522	1,074	...
1948	102	32,222	767	...	7,800	800	507	7,017	2,638	10,674	...
1949	—	28,131	871	[26]	9,400	1,200	998	5,949	2,021	14,139	...
1950	—	32,089	693	90	8,800	1,000	726	7,145	2,675	13,768	...
1951	—	31,197	642	135	8,000	100	538	8,442	3,378	7,932	...
1952	—	30,116	464	248	8,700	200	993	8,011	2,805	11,940	...
1953	—	30,134	580	337	8,900	2,300	1,168	5,841	2,345	14,196	689
1954	—	30,505	469	504	9,800	2,800	975	5,190	2,796	13,936	835
1955	—	30,444	512	665	8,700	2,900	647	5,869	2,790	12,429	1,121
1956	15	25,964	480	702	6,400	4,100	336	5,519	3,323	8,679	1,466
1957	551	19,398	558	765	3,400	7,000	628	5,187	3,484	7,140	1,749
1958	1,128	23,465	400	705	3,800	8,100	1,108	3,387	2,481	4,291	1,147
1959	2,209	23,843	332	822	4,400	9,200	844	3,299	2,393	3,535	1,535
1960	1,185	25,038	392	1,006	4,800	10,500	346	3,767	2,710	5,226	1,688
1961	1,502	25,064	566	873	4,700	12,900	503	3,462	2,375	5,687	1,672
1962	1,552	25,111	548	1,397	4,900	15,900	1,851	3,454	2,442	4,787	1,616
1963	1,742	24,979	668	1,524	5,100	16,800	1,918	3,405	2,964	8,002	1,691
1964	1,831	26,898	652	1,569	5,100	19,200	1,951	3,645	2,090	5,964	2,219
1965	1,846	28,567	645	1,543	6,800	18,800	1,722	3,110	1,770	3,856	2,298
1966	1,621	29,825	760	1,715	7,300	18,600	1,452	3,154	1,397	3,752	2,008
1967	1,436	30,090	689	1,773	7,800	19,200	1,554	2,697	1,052	2,625	1,581
1968	1,392	32,414	623	2,119	6,900	21,137	2,279	2,807	986	3,558	1,868
1969	1,389	30,755	687	2,518	7,200	23,239	2,378	2,672	873	4,486	1,952
1970	1,405[25] 1,096	35,072	739	2,903	7,100	24,300	3,651	2,868	827	3,363	2,022
1971	1,264	36,260	470	2,935	8,400	24,800	3,040	2,642	568	2,695	2,259
1972	1,157	39,062	545	3,000	9,700	24,400	3,306	2,193	391	1,749	2,191
1973	1,165	43,605	470	4,025	10,000	24,400	3,506	2,522	371	2,693	2,468
1974	1,203	48,284	322	4,189	9,700	26,000	3,737	3,100	536	1,850	2,658
1975	1,096	45,058	410	4,810	9,800	25,951	4,391	2,834	322	2,182	2,809

Switz: Switzerland UK: United Kingdom

See p. 436 for footnotes

E11 **Imports and Exports of Coal by Main Surplus and Deficient Countries** (in thousands of metric tons)

NOTES

1. SOURCES:— Belgium to 1912 — A. Wibail, L'evolution economique de l'industrie charbonniere Belge depuis 1831 *'Bulletin de l'Institut des Sciences Economiques* VI 1 (1934). Bulgaria and Romania from 1950, U.N., *World Energy Supplies.* Czechoslovakia 1949–52 — supplied by the Federal Statistical Office of Czechoslovakia. Finland 1943 and 1945 — supplied by the Central Statistical Office of Finland. U.K. to 1938 — based on B.R. Mitchell & Phyllis Deane *Abstract of British Historical Statistics* (Cambridge, 1962) where the original sources are given. All other statistics are taken from the official publications noted on p. xv, with gaps filled from the League of Nations, *International Trade Statistics* and the United Nations, *Yearbook of International Trade Statistics.*
2. Exports from England & Wales for 1697–1791 and from Great Britain for 1792–1808 can be found in E.B. Schumpeter, *English Overseas Trade Statistics, 1697–1808* (Oxford, 1960), and, in uniform Imperial measure, in B.R. Mitchell & Phyllis Deane, *op. cit.* They include shipments to Ireland, however.
3. Where no indication is given in the footnotes, statistics in this table are of hard coal only.

[1] Figures to 1914 apply to the Austro-Hungarian custom area. This included Lombardy to 1859, and Venetia to 1865. It did not include Dalmatia until 1861. Figures from 1920 are for the Republic of Austria.
[2] Lignite is included, but not coke.
[3] These figures are for the 14 months from 1 November 1852, previous statistics being for years ended 31 October.
[4] Coke is included.
[5] Coke and lignite are included (converted to coal equivalent in the case of France prior to 1959).
[6] Re-exports are not deducted prior to 1863, but they were extremely small.
[7] Figures to 1884 (1st line) relate to European Russia (except Finland) and include coke, lignite and peat. From 1884 (2nd line) to 1912 (1st line) they are for the Empire (except Finland), still including coke, lignite and peat. From 1912 (2nd line) to 1918 they are for the Empire, but are of coal only. From 1920 the figures are for the U.S.S.R.
[8] Coke is not subsequently included.
[9] Coke is subsequently included.
[10] Figures from 1896 (2nd line) to 1924 (1st line) and from 1936 (2nd line) onwards are net of re-exports.
[11] Figures for 1871–1918 treat Alsace-Lorraine as foreign.
[12] Prior to March 1906 the statistics exclude trade via the free ports.
[13] Significant changes in the area covered by the statistics were as follows:— Alsace-Lorraine was lost in 1918; West Prussia, Posen, and the Saarland were lost in 1921, and eastern Upper Silesia in July 1922. Saarland was recovered in February 1935, excluded again in 1945, and reincorporated in West Germany in 1959.
[14] Lignite is subsequently included.
[15] There were major territorial acquisitions between 1913 and 1920.
[16] Excluding lignite.
[17] These are incomplete figures owing to the French occupation of the Ruhr.
[18] Figures for 1946–49 exclude the French Occupied Zone.
[19] Lignite is subsequently excluded.
[20] Subsequently only coke-oven coke is included.
[21] Bunker coal is not subsequently included with exports.
[22] Eastern Upper Silesia was acquired in July 1922.
[23] There were major territoial changes, including the acquisition of the whole of Silesia.
[24] These figures are for the economic years, ended 30 September.
[25] Subsequently excluding briquettes.
[26] Subsequent statistics are expressed in coal equivalent.

E12 IMPORTS AND EXPORTS OF PETROLEUM BY MAIN SURPLUS AND DEFICIENT COUNTRIES

(in thousands of metric tons)

1856–1899

	Austria[1]		Bulgaria	Denmark	Finland	Germany	Italy	Netherlands
	I	E	I	I	I	I	I	I
1856	...	...	...	...	...	—	...	—
1857	...	...	...	...	...	—	...	—
1858	...	...	...	...	...	—	...	—
1859	...	...	...	...	...	—	...	—
1860	...	...	...	...	- -	—	...	—
1861	...	...	...	...	—	—	—	—
1862	...	...	...	...	—	—	—	—
1863	...	...	...	0.5	- -	—	—	3.9
1864	3.4	0.3	...	1.7	- -	—	1.2	8.2
1865	3.3[1]	0.7[1]	...	2.2	- -	12	8.4	5.6
1866	4.8	0.5	...	2.2	0.1	33	12	9.7
1867	6.4	0.5	...	3.8	0.1	61	19	12
1868	12	0.6	...	4.8	0.3	72	35	16
1869	20	0.7	...	5.0	0.4	91	30	15
1870	32	0.9	...	5.3	0.9	96	39	18
1871	41	1.2	...	5.4	1.0	125	43	20
1872	47	0.9	...	5.9	0.8	121	42	21
1873	65	0.8	...	7.5	2	172	35	28
1874	69	0.8	...	10	2	155	44	29
1975	81	0.4	...	8	1	201	45	34
1876	109	0.4	...	10	2	212	44	34
1877	104	0.4	...	14	3	250	50	41
1878	105	0.3	...	9	2	251	47	42
1879	93	0.3	...	19	2	252	59	44
1880	115	1.0	...	8	3	213	58	49
1881	148	0.7	...	18	4	291	60	54
1882	125	2.2	...	16	4	343	61	60
1883	110	2.1	...	17	5	370	64	68
1884	135	5.1	...	21	4	463	74	75
1885	141	3.1	...	19	6	482	93	77
1886	129	2.6	...	25	5	438	72	85
1887	113	1.6	8	21	6	509	76	90
1888	120	2.0	6	25	7	564	70	90
1889	140	3.4	9	29	9	626	71	99
1890	129	4.2	13	29	9	647	71	104
1891	140	2.6	12	39	10	676	86	114
1892	150	2.4	11	38[2]	10	743	84	123
				33				
1893	164	4.4	14	45	12	765	91	129
1894	143	6.0	17	37	10	785	90	141
1895	137	14	11	45	13	811	83	150
1896	87	43	12	47[3]	15	854	96	152
				35				
1897	92	37	16	37	16	895	91	160
1898	81	29	14	40	17	906	89	169
1899	98	32	12	44	20	911	85	162

Abbreviations used throughout this table: I Imports E Exports

See p. 444 for footnotes

E12 Imports and Exports of Petroleum by Main Surplus and Deficient Countries (in thousands of metric tons)

1856–1899

	Norway	Portugal	Romania	Russia	Spain	Sweden	Switz	U.K.[5]
	I	I	E	E	I	I	I	I
1856	—	...	...	...	...	—	...	0.3
1857	—	...	...	...	...	—	...	2.9
1858	—	...	...	...	...	—	...	3.3
1859	—	...	...	...	...	—	...	0.6
1860	—	...	...	...	...	—	...	- -
1861	—	...	...	...	...	—	...	1.3
1862	- -	...	...	...	...	—	...	20
1863	0.1	...	...	...	...	—	...	29
1864	0.2	...	...	...	...	0.7	...	17
1865	0.3	...	...	...	...	0.9	...	12
1866	0.6	...	...	...	...	1.6	...	25
1867	0.8	...	...	...	...	1.6	...	18
1868	1.1	...	...	...	...	3.4	...	17
1869	1.5	...	...	...	...	3.3	...	21
1870	2.3	...	...	...	...	5.0	15	27
1871	3.5	...	...	...	...	5.4	22	35
1872	3.1	...	...	...	...	6.6	19	25
1873	5.2	...	...	...	...	8.4	27	65
1874	5.5	...	...	...	38	9.0	...	84
1875	5.2	...	...	...	28	9.1	15	76
1876	5.9	...	...	...	33	10	18	98
1877	8.9	...	...	...	47	11	18	132
1878	5.5	...	...	...	34	11	21	118
1879	6.6	...	...	...	43	14	21	169
1880	7.4	...	...	...	50	12	23	152
1881	9.3	...	...	...	69	17	26	231
1882	7.7	7.9	...	...	59	18	28	233
1883	9.0	5.4	18	59	62	19	27	275
1884	11	9.6	22	113	65[4]	24	33	207
					44			
1885	10	9.1	21	177	57	25	27	289
1886	11	9.4	15	246	45	28	32	278
1887	10	9.4	16	311	43	28	33	302
1888	13	10	18	573	59	26	36	369
1889	15	11	19	734	33	45	39	402
1890	14	12	12	788	51	38	41	411
1891	16	12	18	889	55	42	44	510
1892	23	14	20	939	45	42	48	509
1893	24	14	17	987	55	49	52	606
1894	29	15	17	880	44	47	53	637
1895	28	14	16	1,059	54	59	56	692
1896	36	13	17	1,058	40	52	63	742
1897	40	14	21	1,046	35	66	66	725
1898	37	14	27	1,115	33	64	66	857
1899	42	15	48	1,392	33	74	69	938

Switz: Switzerland U.K.: United Kingdom

See p. 444 for footnotes

E12 Imports and Exports of Petroleum by Main Surplus and Deficient Countries (in thousands of metric tons)

1900–1949

	Austria[1]		Belgium		Bulgaria	Czech	Denmark	Finland	France[11]			Germany		
	I	E	I	E[7]	I	I	I	I	COI	ROI	E	COI	ROI	E
1900	44	51	...	...	16	...	42	19	...	...	...	938	...	...
1901	41	37	...	...	15	...	45	21	...	...	...	927	...	...
1902	41	55	...	...	12	...	46	22	...	...	...	939	...	...
1903	39	89	...	...	15	...	49	23	...	...	...	980	...	...
1904	43	136	...	...	21	...	53	24	...	...	...	980	...	...
1905	44	209	...	...	14	...	53	28	...	...	...	959[12]	...	...
1906	35	245	...	...	20	...	52	25	...	...	...	971	...	...
1907	37	227	...	...	14	...	58	28	...	...	...	1,021	...	...
1908	21	378	...	...	18	...	61	30	...	...	...	1,052	...	...
1909	23	505	...	...	21	...	74	32	...	...	...	983	...	...
1910	36	451	...	...	22	...	89	33	...	...	...	1,014	...	...
1911	39	400	...	...	20[8]	...	98	34	...	...	...	987	...	...
1912	39	610	...	...	18	...	110	35	...	...	...	1,118	...	...
1913	51	494	389	...	26	...	125	36	...	...	...	1,034	...	...
1914	41	309	...	...	25	...	124	26	...	...	...	...	...	...
1915	...	145	...	...	13	...	120	29	...	...	...	...	...	...
1916	...	344	...	...	7	...	129	32	...	...	...	...	...	...
1917	...	...	...	...	2	...	64	25	...	...	...	...	...	...
1918	...[1]	...[1]	...	...	6	...	18	- -	...	...	...	...	...	...
1919	...	...	...	...	20	...	132	41	...	...	...	...	...	...
1920	80	...	...	...	6	...	169	12	...	...	...	...	...	...
1921	96	...	...[6]	...	22	52	145	17	...	...	...	...	...	...
1922	104	...	208	...	31	65	218	21	...	...	...	...	...	...
1923	104	...	308	...	39	120	260	27	...	...	...		492	...
1924	160	...	358	...	36	146	319 / 301[3] [9]	33	...	...	...		772	...
1925	142	...	381	...	44	133	312	29	...	...	...		1,167	...
1926	169	...	378	...	48	144	374	30	...	...	...		1,388	...
1927	183	...	366	...	51	173	387	35	106	2,233	117		1,684	144
1928	238	...	632	...	60	196	419	44	188	2,867	141		2,001	142
1929	260	...	706	...	77	194	438	36	198	3,069	113		2,531	199
1930	314	...	733	...	79	356[8] / 404	527	38	460	3,397	107		3,271	298
1931	312	...	759	...	75	411	555	32	450	3,724	80		2,935	355
1932	257	...	821	...	64	399	575	44	985	3,523	144		2,453	288
1933	327	...	832	...	66	362	565	36	2,799	3,018	280		2,647	286
1934	259	...	1,038	...	66	370	604	43	3,977	1,801	554		3,094	216
1935	284	...	879	...	76	400	573	46	5,316	1,074	586		3,863	...
1936	294	...	1,190	...	75	423	656[3] / 644	68	6,018	1,485	556		4,246	...
1937	269	14	1,186	...	89	485	686	209	6,140	1,623	663		4,335	...
1938	...	...	1,124	404	88	...	833	234	6,968	1,325	664		4,986	...
1939	...	...	...	...	100	...	852	260	6,149	1,177	496		...	...
1940	...	...	...	...	102	...	154	100	3,655	656	338		...	...
1941	...	...	...	...	73	...	60	83	18	284	82		...	...
1942	...	...	...	...	...	...	69	96	—	227	8		...	...
1943	...	...	...	...	...	...	51	97	—	166	1		...	...
1944	...	...	...	...	...	...	47	50	—	125	—		...	...
												West Germany		
1945	...	...	...	...	...	...	150	25	299	1,789	32	...	...	...
1946	...	...	...	...	1,842	...	623	149	2,686	2,694	384	...	...	...
1947	14	...	2,094	776	1,430	318	1,123	318[10] / 357	5,029	2,102	753	...	...	...
1948	54	14	2,224	741	...	395	1,148	514	7,729	1,202	1,063	2,523	...	...
1949	93	38	2,048	488	...	574	1,212[9] / 1,325	408	11,812	665	2,332	1,087	...	...

Czech: Czechoslovakia

COI = Crude Oil Imports ROI = Refined Oil Imports

See p. 444 for footnotes

E12 Imports and Exports of Petroleum by Main Surplus and Deficient Countries (in thousands of metric tons)

1900–1949

	Greece	Hungary		Italy		Netherlands		Norway	Poland		Portugal
	I	I	E[7]	I	E[7]	I	E[7]	I	I	E	I
1900	...	...	...	86	...	169	...	40	...	...	14
1901	...	...	...	69	...	180	...	47	...	...	20
1902	...	...	...	69	...	190	...	45	...	...	18
1903	...	...	...	68	...	193	...	59	...	...	21
1904	...	...	...	69	...	181	...	51	...	...	18
1905	...	...	...	67	...	189	...	44	...	...	19
1906	...	...	...	65	...	200	...	42	...	...	19
1907	...	...	...	78	...	199	...	44	...	...	21
1908	...	...	...	91	...	197	...	65	...	...	21
1909	...	...	...	101	...	197	...	63	...	...	22
1910	...	...	...	99	...	198	...	65	...	...	22
1911	...	...	...	143	...	201	...	72	...	...	22
1912	...	...	...	141	...	204	...	82	...	...	22
1913	...	...	...	150	...	214	...	80	...	...	32
1914	...	...	...	161	...	360	...	91	...	...	28
1915	...	...	...	169		175	...	63	...	...	27
1916	...	...	...	216	...	152	...	108	...	...	29
1917	...	...	...	232	...	104	...	59	...	...	29
1918	...	...	...	287	...	5	...	44	...	...	11
1919	...	5	...	241	...	418	...	120	...	...	31
1920	...	17	...	247	...	481	...	85	1	93	30
1921	...	43	...	204	...	422	...	88	1	231	20
1922	...	60	...	291	...	501	...	150	...	292	39
1923	...	83	...	349	...	621	...	152	15	317	60
1924	...	93	...	376	...	686	...	185	3	355	64
1925	74	77	...	428	...	674	...	185	5	273	62
1926	88	133	...	466	...	777	...	181	2	381	74
1927	111	166	...	537	...	935	...	202	3	196	87
1928	127	192	...	607	...	915	...	222	4	187	113
1929	148	208	...	699	...	897	...	270	7	185	111
1930	161	249	...	739	...	1,010	...	270	8	122	126
1931	165	165	...	702	...	1,119	...	303	5	148	126
1932	182	147	...	674	...	954	...	373	– –	161	125
1933	183	175	...	642	...	1,015	...	433	3	155	141
1934	209	234	...	725	...	953	...	484	...	148	163
1935	244	174	...	842	...	1,094	27	460	...	118	197
1936	281	258	...	692	...	1,240	50	470	...	110	175
1937	324	280	...	1,376	...	1,505	69	542	...	77	192
1938	81	209	...	1,682	...	1,724	70	581	7	...	193
1939	...	...	...	2,031	...	...	...	679	...	...	209
1940	...	...	...	1,262	...	...	...	242	...	...	219
1941	...	...	...	348	...	...	...	186	...	...	181
1942	...	...	...	527	...	...	...	163	...	...	43
1943	...	...	...	...	...	...	...	156	...	...	87
1944	...	...	...	...	...	...	...	161	...[13]	...[13]	110
1945	...	...	...	...	...	...	...	172	...	...	186
1946	...	...	...	357	...	...	...	577	190	...	359
1947	...	...	...	1,787	...	2,315	103	949	238	...	566
1948	159	...	...	2,420	...	2,664	285	1,299	384	...	587
1949	197	11	29	3,188	...	3,641	1,289	1,306	337	...	527

E Germany: East Germany

See p. 444 for footnotes

E12 Imports and Exports of Petroleum by Main Surplus and Deficient Countries (in thousands of metric tons)

1900–1949

	Romania		Russia		Spain		Sweden	Switz	United Kingdom			Yugoslavia
	E	I	COI	ROE	I	E[7]	I	I	COI	ROI	E	I
1900	49	...		1,442	49	...	80	71	996		...	...
1901	58	...		1,558	37	...	78	72	991		...	...
1902	76	...		1,534	37	...	84	74	1,113		...	...
1903	126	...		1,783	34	...	96	74	1,117		...	...
1904	164	...		1,837	31	...	97	75	1,180		...	...
1905	220	...		945	29	...	105	73	1,172		...	...
1906	333	...		661	52	...	107	76	1,169		...	...
1907	428	...		733	25	...	112	79	1,188		...	...
1908	463	...		797	30	...	144	83	1,342		...	...
1909	424	...		796	40	...	141	81	1,399		...	...
1910	582	...		859	33	...	140	85	1,350		...	...
1911	674	...		855	33	...	165	87	1,428		...	...
1912	851	...		839	33	...	152	91	1,618		...	...
1913	1,056	...		947	41[4]	...	180	87	1,907		...	...
					88							
1914	640	...		528	76	...	144	56	2,526		...	...
1915	...	...		78	92	...	149	45	2,299		...	...
1916	...	...		41	91	...	163	39	1,764		...	...
1917	...	...		34	72	...	51	28	3,230		...	...
1918	...	- -		2	56	...	40	20	5,174		...	...
1919	...	...		- - -	109	...	163	...	2,788		...	...
1920	246	- -		- -	161	...	190	68	17	3,436	257	...
1921	362	...		7	139	...	145	43	413	4,111	109	...
1922	433	...		52[14]	136	...	178	85	883	3,820	351	74
1923	413	...		84[14]	154	...	218	92	1,360	3,798	484	72
1924	436	...		712[14]	217	...	255	107	1,888	4,224	634	74
1925	785	5		1,373[14]	238	...	302	88	2,313	3,967	872	100
1926	1,494	...		1,474[14]	263	...	330	90	2,185	5,185	609	112
1927	1,913	...		2,086[14]	345	...	358	169	2,702	5,250	631	133
1928	2,344	...		2,783[14]	411	...	441	201	2,024	6,038	633	143
1929	2,817	...		3,859	461	...	479	240	1,980	6,341	805	154
1930	3,784	2	295	4,418	610	...	577	265	1,874	7,202	668	206
1931	4,572	...	382	4,842	725	...	639	308	1,400	6,894	520	107
1932	4,975	...	629	5,489	727	...	714	367	1,498	6,941	521	152
1933	5,594	1	536	4,394	652	...	773	381	1,596	7,563	521	137
1934	6,222	...	459	3,856	924	...	814	418	1,935	8,407	637	128
1935	6,221	...	207	3,162	878	...	931	418	1,985	8,502	736	119
1936	6,228	...	218	2,448	...	...	1,008	400	2,080	8,864	680	158
1937	5,168	...	68	1,861	...	...	1,185	393	2,143	9,279	772	143
1938	4,126	142	188	1,200	...	...	1,335	414	2,308	9,541	601	...
1939	...	76	26	500	...	...	1,488	428	2,201	8,873	541	...
1940	...	69	—	874	...	...	541	284	1,589	10,161	221	...
1941	...	...	...	...	...	...	131	111	992	12,275	54	...
1942	...	...	...	...	...	...	108	87	600	9,942	67	...
1943	...	...	...	...	...	...	147	72	535	14,684	38	...
1944	...	...	...	...	...	...	137	58	695	19,891	80	...
1945	...	...	...	...	608	39	196	30	964	15,056	171	...
1946	...	500	- -	500	528	5	1,836	394	2,214	12,428	410	...
1947	...	1,000	- -	800	1,727	...	3,098	726	2,514	10,762	654	...
1948	...	800	- -	700	1,840	...	3,334	883	4,715	13,408	347	...
1949	...	1,700	100	800	2,214	...	3,048	875	6,145	11,637	508	...

Switz: Switzerland

COI=Crude Oil Imports; ROE= Refined Oil Exports; ROI=Refined Oil Imports

See p. 444 for footnotes

E12 Imports and Exports of Petroleum by Main Surplus and Deficient Countries (in thousands of metric tons)

1950–1975

	Austria		Belgium		Bulgaria	Czech	Denmark	Finland	France		
	I	E	I	E[7]	I	I	I	I	COI	ROI	E
1950	86	48	2,448	466	...	393	1,860	542	14,135	412	3,448
1951	82	23	3,706	764	...	563	1,989	609	18,073	633	5,123
1952	55	34	4,543	1,966	...	652	2,007	719	21,222	728	7,201
1953	45	79	4,978	2,005	...	605	2,161	801	22,000	482	7,235
1954	109	96	5,809	1,664	343	935	2,596	943	23,640	751	6,498
1955	381	163	7,101	1,863	331	1,060	3,249	1,118[16] 682	24,832	952	6,111
1956	318	399	8,320	2,350	378	1,176	3,701	944	25,013	1,285	5,668
1957	425	307	8,617	2,170	479	1,609	3,868	1,480	24,062	2,744	4,546
1958	792	220	9,540	2,697	518	1,645	4,380	1,803	28,318	1,749	6,666
1959	945	182	9,576	3,289	698	2,076	4,537	1,861	29,171	2,125	6,512
1960	1,210	151	10,078	3,389	915	4,969[15]	5,154	2,624	31,023	2,687	7,074
1961	1,703	94	11,147	3,202	1,182	2,785	5,889[9] 5,816	2,923	35,018	2,462	8,178
1962	2,272	210	12,779	3,523	1,661	...	7,336	3,465	37,161	3,070	7,526
1963	2,750	225	16,387	5,136	2,152	4,217	8,078	3,554	43,257	4,047	6,956
1964	3,000	211	18,073	5,116	3,154	...	9,858	5,390[16] 5,489	49,192	4,415	7,822
1965	2,847	202	19,955	5,385	3,576	6,096	10,690	5,476	58,556	3,719	10,022
1966	3,712	104	21,874	5,562	4,072	6,512	12,438	7,114	62,752	4,916	13,007
1967	3,735	103	23,288	5,504	4,820	7,449	13,024	8,223	72,348	4,809	12,594
1968	4,999	121	29,554	7,937	5,833	7,810	14,472	9,071	77,176	5,198	11,491
1969	5,446	161	34,336	11,560	7,446	9,375	17,798	10,220	86,306	5,315	11,785
1970	6,834	142	36,492	10,209	8,338[25] 8,239	9,798	20,727	12,946	100,163	6,371	10,733
1971	7,855	139	38,721	9,601	9,735	11,505	20,518	12,065	104,749	8,081	11,840
1972	8,588	156	51,452	13,430	10,312	12,571	21,620	13,143	121,065	8,947	12,407
1973	9,759	151	44,369	14,796	11,171	14,176	21,224	13,865	136,511	7,264	13,449
1974	8,896	206	39,419	11,445	12,144	14,655	19,961	13,925	130,351	6,900	11,212
1975	8,530	149	35,415	13,552	12,344	15,839	18,676	11,002	107,041	7,861	11,370

	W.Germany			E Germany	Greece	Hungary		Italy		Netherlands	
	COI	ROI	E	I	I	I	E[7]	I	E	I	E[7]
1950	1,950	...	...	406	244	32	8	5,289	...	6,220	3,340[20]
1951	3,206	509	...	433	262	218	28	7,461	1,376	7,309	3,976
1952	3,574	683	540	451	1,252	293	52	9,978	2,890	7,962	4,698
1953	4,560	963	1,008	723	1,255	403	61	12,922	5,145	8,615	5,178
1954	5,985	1,369	1,585	1,016	1,449	359	43[18] 63	15,939	6,578	11,527	7,440
1955	7,111	2,847	2,130	1,105	1,533	312	154	17,590	5,874	13,770	8,721
1956	7,999	5,108	2,680	1,156	1,539	461	89	18,915	5,773	15,622	9,495
1957	8,158	5,709	2,053	1,424	1,618	1,221[19] 1,249	176	19,981	5,742	15,988	9,839
1958	10,889	6,478	2,498	1,479	1,828	1,211	273	22,826	6,687	18,508	11,514
1959	16,895	5,531	2,856	2,025	1,955	1,324	357	25,560	8,304	17,874	10,172
1960	23,056	6,725	3,531	2,579[17] 2,677	2,314	1,557	487	30,628	9,222	21,744	12,786
1961	29,293	6,959	5,561	3,183	2,402	1,643	486	35,788	10,438	24,600	13,272
1962	33,202	12,634	5,268	3,484	2,586	1,790	577	43,345	11,635	25,283	13,848
1963	40,078	14,425	6,628	4,171	3,627	2,234	475	49,890	12,809	26,063	12,354
1964	51,276	14,388	7,795	5,380	3,017	2,579	553	57,513	14,926	30,077	13,296
1965	59,068	15,674	7,128	6,550	4,777	2,621	483	70,014	21,154	33,192	14,497
1966	67,687	17,547	7,660	7,274	4,637	3,360	639	79,586	26,440	36,921	16,507
1967	71,999	19,103	8,250	7,799	5,231	3,503	882	90,570	26,082	40,163	18,161
1968	85,702	20,455	9,886	9,338	5,024	3,773	1,044	91,523	27,454	42,642	19,420
1969	89,551	25,118	9,696	10,321[15] 9,272	6,032	4,391	1,026	105,468	30,770	54,278	27,592
1970	98,786	30,367	10,674	10,334	6,208	5,276	806[18] 844	115,732	32,255	75,216	38,809
1971	100,230	33,524	10,722	10,919	6,544	5,631	337	119,685	32,373	79,980	40,991
1972	102,600	36,228	10,588	14,858	9,283	6,696	555	125,145	33,158	98,627	50,654
1973	110,493	40,289	11,488	16,045	13,840	7,476	484	130,878	33,550	109,803	53,304
1974	102,543	35,531	11,334	16,434	12,954	7,818	336	123,954	27,442	69,192	44,258
1975	88,414	36,336	8,233	16,997	13,662	9,231	378	106,212	18,431	64,393	42,859

Czech: Czechoslovakia

COI= Crude Oil Imports ROI= Refined Oil Imports

See p. 444 for footnotes

E12 Imports and Exports of Petroleum by Main Surplus and Deficient Countries (in thousands of metric tons)

1950–1975

	Norway	Poland		Portugal	Romania	Russia		
	I	I	E	I	E	I	COE	ROE
1950	1,390	473	1	565	...	2,300	300	800
1951	1,775	755	7	742	...	2,600	900	1,600
1952	1,985	844	24	961	...	3,600	1,300	1,800
1953	2,158	950	50	977	...	4,600	1,500	2,700
1954	2,248	1,186	59	1,297	...	3,800	2,100	4,400
1955	2,819	1,431	125[21] / 155	1,462	...	3,800	2,900	5,100
1956	3,003	1,489	137	1,503	...	3,800	3,900	6,200
1957	2,944	1,786	69	1,644	...	2,900	5,900	7,800
1958	3,019	1,874	142[21] / 178	1,705	5,050	3,200	9,100	8,679
1959	3,183	2,204		1,829	5,796	3,300	12,500	12,462
1960	3,633	2,504	196	1,941	5,869	3,200	17,800	14,902
1961	4,423	3,034	274	1,992	6,012	2,700	23,400	17,220
1962	5,138	3,703	555[21] / 573	2,067	5,793	2,300	26,300	18,574
1963	5,559	4,250	589	2,245	5,740	2,300	30,200	20,676
1964	5,982	4,637	586	2,483	6,090	2,100	36,700	19,500
1965	5,800	5,464	1,027	2,562	5,636	1,900	43,400	20,600
1966	6,705	5,689	521	2,405	5,642	1,700	50,300	22,900
1967	6,936	6,482	677	2,710	5,426	1,400	54,100	24,500
1968	7,871	8,117	1,481	2,948	5,493	1,100	59,200	26,400
1969	8,764	8,907	1,709	3,389	4,994	1,100	63,900	26,900
1970	10,799	9,435	1,316	4,338	5,220	1,100	66,800	29,000
1971	9,710	10,254	1,069	4,782	5,176	1,500[24]	74,800	30,400
1972	10,735	12,035	1,723	4,934	4,988	1,300[24]	76,200	30,900
1973	11,575	14,219	1,332	5,041	4,842	1,500[24]	85,300	33,100
1974	10,613	13,601	1,177	6,637	6,456	1,000[24]	80,600	35,700
1975	8,781	16,439	1,601	5,695	6,007	1,060[24]	93,070	37,378

	Spain		Sweden	Switz	United Kingdom			Yugoslavia
	I	E[7]	I	I	COI	ROI	E	I
1950	...	...	3,767	1,057	9,394[23]	10,055[23]	1,212	...
1951	4,615	1,860	4,892	1,119	16,970	9,943	3,467	...
1952	4,468	1,978	5,083	1,238	23,195	6,057	5,528	...
1953	4,591	1,975	5,538	1,322	26,163	6,113	7,510	557
1954	4,864	2,095	6,476	1,617	28,526	6,718	7,955	529
1955	4,161	1,043	8,084	1,892	28,301	8,652	6,375	534
1956	4,734	1,213	9,771	2,508	29,067	9,571	7,838	621
1957	7,106	1,394	9,400	2,548	28,416	11,003	6,388	689
1958	7,497	1,390	10,597	2,953	34,289	11,191	8,525	683
1959	7,925	1,424	10,862	3,063[22]	39,868	12,957	8,353	746
1960	7,337	1,670	13,210	3,940	45,331	14,023	9,215	628
1961	8,183	1,753	13,340	4,317	49,744	11,996	7,825	495
1962	10,596	1,984	14,606	5,018	53,189	15,946	9,893	1,067
1963	11,243	1,924	16,129	6,787	54,732	18,511	9,880	999
1964	13,064	1,821	17,975	7,047	60,349	18,914	9,232	1,216
1965	14,048	1,687	19,089	8,241	66,707	20,531	10,797	1,503
1966	16,949	1,799	22,500	8,879	71,489	21,988	12,160	2,614
1967	21,799	3,285	22,596	9,426	74,641	24,281	11,676	3,328
1968	28,978	6,262	26,214	10,809	83,014	22,317	14,320	3,743
1969	28,305	5,540	29,178	11,628	94,568	20,473	14,296	4,027
1970	31,358	5,527	32,664	12,920	103,434	20,656	17,658	5,544
1971	36,293	4,624	31,110	13,366	109,697	19,818	18,354	5,960
1972	39,739	5,067	29,610	13,431	107,259	20,606	19,349	5,355
1973	42,329	5,213	29,668	14,604	116,438	20,432	19,717	9,610
1974	45,556	4,804	28,879	13,363	113,645	15,717	16,075	8,794
1975	42,616	2,570	30,581	12.238	88,749	14,593	15,015	8,369

Switz: Switzerland

COI= Crude Oil Imports ROI= Refined Oil Imports COE= Crude Oil Exports ROE= Refined Oil Exports

See p. 444 for footnotes

E12 Imports and Exports of Petroleum by main Surplus and Deficient Countries (in thousands of metric tons)

NOTES

1. SOURCES:– Finland to 1917 – Erkki Pihkala, *Finland's Foreign Trade 1960–1917* (Bank of Finland, Helsinki, 1969). Finland 1943 and 1945 – supplied by the Central Statistical Office of Finland. Netherlands imports 1914–21 – supplied by the Netherlands Central Office of Statistics. Poland imports 1928–48 and exports 1950–58 – supplied by the Polish Central Statistical Office. U.K. to 1965 – based on B.R. Mitchell & H.G. Jones, *Second Abstract of British Historical Statistics* (Cambridge, 1971), where the original sources are given. All other statistics are taken from the official publications noted on p. xv , with gaps filled from the League of Nations, *International Trade Statistics* and the United Nations, *Yearbook of International Trade Statistics.*

2. Except as indicated in headings or footnotes, crude oil and refined products are aggregated.

FOOTNOTES

[1] Figures to 1916 are for the Austro-Hungarian customs area, which excluded Venetia from 1866. Later figures are for the Republic of Austria.
[2] Figures to 1892 (1st line) include other oils than petroleum.
[3] From 1896 (2nd line) onwards, except for 1924–36, the statistics are of net imports.
[4] Figures from 1884 (2nd line) to 1913 (1st line) are of crude oil only.
[5] Converted, where necessary, from the original fluid measure on the basis of 1 metric tons = 256 gallons.
[6] Subsequently including Luxembourg.
[7] Refined products only.
[8] Previously refined products only.
[9] From 1924 (2nd line), except for 1949–61, lubricating oils are excluded.
[10] A broader classification is used subsequently.
[11] Prior to 1927 statistics are available only in value terms in official sources. T.J. Markovitch, *L'industrie francaise de 1789 à 1964* (Cahiers de l'I.S.E.A., 1966) gives the following annual averages of net imports of crude oil (in thousands of tons):–

1855–64	15	1885–94	192	1920–24	352
1865–74	22	1895–1904	230	1925–34	1,560
1875–84	67	1905–13	117		

[12] Prior to 1909 excludes trade of the Free Ports.
[13] The Galician oilfields were in the part of Poland ceded to the U.S.S.R. in 1945.
[14] These figures are for economic years, ended 30 September, Exports in October–December 1928 were 796 thousand tons.
[15] Subsequently crude oil only.
[16] From 1955 (2nd line) to 1964 (1st line) motor spirit and kerosene are excluded.
[17] Figures to 1960 (1st line) do not include heating oil.
[18] Figures to 1954 (1st line) are of gasoil only.
[19] Figures from 1949 to 1957 (1st line) for imports and 1970 (1st line) for exports do not include kerosene.
[20] Figures to 1950 do not include lubricating oil.
[21] Figures to 1955 (1st line) and from 1959 to 1962 (1st line) are of fuel oil and motor fuel only.
[22] A new classification brought more items under the heading "petroleum products" from 1960.
[23] Refinery feedstocks were transferred from the "refined" to the "crude" category from 1950.
[24] Imports of crude oil were as follows: 1971, 5,100; 1972, 7,800; 1973, 13,200; 1974, 4,400; 1975, 6,499.
[25] Subsequently excluding lubricating oils, etc.

E13 IMPORTS AND EXPORTS OF IRON ORE BY MAIN TRADING COUNTRIES (in thousands of metric tons)

1847–1909

	Belgium[1]	France		Germany	Norway	Spain	Sweden	United Kingdom
	I	I	E	I	E	E	E	I
1847	...	14	—	...	...	...	...	...
1848	...	11	—	...	...	...	...	...
1849	...	30	—	...	...	...	...	...
1850	...	34	—	...	...	3.3	...	...
1851	...	18	—	...	...	1.2	...	...
1852	...	21	—	...	...	0.5	...	...
1853	...	27	—	...	...	4.4	...	...
1854	...	47	—	...	...	8.5	...	...
1855	...	55	—	...	...	12	...	11
1856	...	102	1	...	...	16	...	..
1857	−61	165	15	...	...	18	...	17
1858	−69	154	31	...	...	19	...	29
1859	−97	164	31	...	...	21	1.9	29
1860	−120	268	70	1	...	19	2.3	23
1861	−93	309	64	−4	0.3	40	5.7	23
1862	−66	375	65	−67	1.2	56	6.1	37
1863	−16	436	67	−143	0.4	72	5.6	63
1864	38	458	92	−155	2.5	62	7.7	75
1865	74	477	153	−160	2.2	57	17	78
1866	150	450	137	−78	5.7	53	14	58
1867	171	492	150	−50	6.0	64	10	88
1868	260	554	195	132	10	116	12	116
1869	387	592	239	−189	16	...	10	133
1870	389	489[2]	145[2]	216[2]	17	253	13	211
1871	432	378	136	247	3	391	12	329
1872	612	670	337	124	15	747	19	815
1873	524	722	354	356	19	800	24	984
1874	630	807	215	−68	29	700	25	766
1875	663	833	180	−386	22	336	27	466
1876	505	844	106	−473	14	682	15	683
1877	567	979	81	−476	6.0	1,258	13	1,159
1878	593	933	80	−821	1.2	1,356	14	1,192
1879	424	943	67	−744	0.5	1,062	13	1,102
1880	611	1,177	123	−656	0.1	2,822	30	2,675
1881	802	1,308	106	−817	0.2	3,122	24	2,490
1882	863	1,432	129	−836	0.4	4,025	20	3,338
1883	1,245	1,501	105	−1,087	5.7	4,226	32	3,242
1884	1,297	1,413	120	−918	0.7	3,968	40	2,775
1885	1,237	1,420	90	−859	1.4	3,797	26	2,868
1886	1,262	1,159	104	−1,019	0.2	4,188	19	2,924
1887	1,452	1,155	281	−709	2.5	5,216	42	3,826
1888	1,693	1,312	296	−1,049	0.4	4,464	117	3,619
1889	1,650	1,447	266	−945	1.1	5,052	119	4,096
1890	1,473	1,612	288	−685	0.4	5,709	188	4,544
1891	1,342	1,438	299	−576	0.8	4,344	174	3,232
1892	1,454	1,684	305	−620	0.1	4,800	320	3,842
1893	1,514	1,631	302	−780	0.5	4,785	484	4,131
1894	1,684	1,638	248	−466	1.6	4,976	831	4,485
1895	1,532	1,651	237	−463	1.5	5,175	800	4,521
1896	1,680	1,862	239	−55	2.1	6,273	1,151	5,525
1897	2,134	2,138	300	−44	4.2	6,885	1,401	6,065
1898	1,869	2,032	236	583	4.6	6,558	1,440	5,556
1899	2,303	1,951	292	1,045	13	8,613	1,628	7,168
1900	2,108	2,119	372	860	27	7,823	1,620	6,399
1901	1,441	1,663	259	1,980	39	6,894	1,761	5,638
1902	2,182	1,563	423	1,089	49	7,560	1,729	6,543
1903	2,654	1,833	714	1,881	42	7,692	2,827	6,415
1904	2,918	1,739	1,219	2,620	45	7,292	3,066	6,199
1905	2,940	2,152	1,356	2,386	61	8,545	3,317	7,463
1906	3,113	2,016	1,759	3,778[3]	81	9,272	3,661	7,949
1907	3,096	2,000	2,148	4,572	133	8,636	3,522	7,765
1908	2,896	1,455	2,384	4,665	110	7,253	3,654	6,155
1909	3,912	1,204	3,908	5,512	39	8,545	3,196	6,431

Abbreviations used throughout this table: I Imports E Exports

See p. 447 for footnotes

E13 Imports and Exports of Iron Ore by Main Trading Countries (in thousands of metric tons)

1910–1975

	Belgium	Czech	France		Germany	E Germany	Norway	Poland	Spain	Sweden	UK
	I	I	I	E	I	I	E	I	E	E	I
1910	4,588	...	1,319	4,895	6,864	...	89	...	8,246	4,414	7,134
1911	5,155	...	1,352	6,177	8,239	...	181	...	7,282	5,087	6,449
1912	5,527	...	1,455	8,324	9,810	...	441	...	8,469	5,521	6,708
1913	6,360[1] 7,085	...	1,412	10,068	11,406[1] 14,019	... ...	569	...	8,907	6,440	7,561
1914	...	...	702	4,829	...	...	468	...	6,083	4,787	5,797
1915	...	...	271	95	...	...	426	...	4,508	5,992	6,296
1916	...	...	628	75	...	...	405	...	5,148	5,537	7,045
1917	...	...	508	127	...	...	198	...	5,138	5,818	6,289
1918	...	...	119[2]	68[2]	...[2]	...	97	...	4,292	4,464	6,688
1919	...	...	304	1,697	...		33	...	3,703	2,417	5,284
1920	2,450	656	485[6]	4,910[6]	5,915[6]		226	...	4,631	3,729	6,605
1921	1,680[4]	561	460	5,301	6,521	...	180	...	1,825	4,337	1,918
1922	3,594	318	380	9,468	11,014[7]	...	285	240	2,752	5,322	3,529
1923	6,523	1,065	534	9,854	[2,377][8]	...	359	668	3,371	4,958	5,954
1924	9,034	1,003	725	12,287	[3,076][8]	...	525	259	3,827	5,948	6,022
1925	9,050	1,084	1,242	9,227	11,540	...	425	294	3,618	8,800	4,452
1926	10,847	1,034	1,368	11,234	9,553	...	128	273	1,857	7,656	2,122
1927	12,678	1,067	1,047	14,665	17,409	...	380	710	4,758	10,716	5,247
1928	13,727	1,669	998	17,055	13,794	...	546	504	5,421	5,093	4,511
1929	14,057	2,079	1,141	16,389	16,953	...	735	...	5,595	10,899	5,780
1930	12,915	1,862	1,012	15,080	13,890	...	632	...	3,724	9,387	4,204
1931	10,675	1,604	782	12,407	7,071	...	348	...	1,873	4,496	2,153
1932	9,482	379	335	10,061	3,452	...	343	112	1,310	2,219	1,824
1933	9,836	389	561	10,986	4,572	...	481	...	1,411	3,151	2,751
1934	10,261	520	941	12,641	8,265	...	683	137	1,778	6,870	4,429
1935	10,583	791	443[6]	16,632[6]	14,061[6]	...	786	270	1,893	7,719	4,620
1936	10,718	822	392	18,252	18,469	...	995	381	1,744	11,198	6,057
1937	12,407	1,945	921	19,321	20,621	...	1,026	625	848	13,565	7,152
1938	9,394	1,360[5]	437	15,515	21,927	...	1,497	665	1,145	12,685	5,247
1939	10,113	1,205	...	...	...		1,182	...	1,261	13,650	5,393
1940	3,209	900	...	...	...	...	239	...	800	10,137	4,635
1941	1,470	1,278	...	...	...	...	505	...	559	9,539	2,332
1942	1,127	1,085	...	...	...	...	568	...	672	8,625	1,953
1943	4,631	1,279	...	...	...	...	342	...	591	10,257	1,924
1944	736	563	...	...	...	...	243	...[10]	528	4,598	2,207
					W Germany						
1945	1,845	55[5]	...	...	...	...	4	...	261	1,229	4,136
1946	5,984	...	102	5,582	...	...	5	...	789	5,316	6,707
1947	6,784	...	199[6]	6,636[6]	51	...	51	1,200	730	8,504	6,955
1948	9,511	1,824	261	6,312	2,429	...	183	1,616	817	11,518	8,876
1949	9,404	1,963	469	7,587	4,518[9]	...	204	1,617	990	12,783	8,832
1950	8,620	2,195	195	8,009	4,870	5	283	1,918	936[11] 1,550	12,943	8,527
1951	11,808	2,560	353	10,599	7,371	145	269	2,170	2,254	15,246	8,887
1952	11,058	2,986	436	10,013	9,642	398	679	2,625	2,434	15,878	9,847
1953	11,862	3,038	989	10,391	10,048	622	1,010	3,097	2,097	14,686	11,157
1954	12,819	3,700	312	11,484	8,754	812	993	4,105	1,628	14,221	11,797
1955	15,054	3,926	553	14,144	14,325	1,237	1,306	4,407	2,838	15,813	13,065
1956	15,749	3,903	645	14,398	17,825	695	1,338	4,776	4,352	17,474	14,560
1957	16,078	4,923	982	14,651	19,122	815	1,324	5,914	4,616	17,661	16,167
1958	16,872	5,164	1,004	15,568	16,962	910	1,224	5,750	1,952[12]	14,935	13,106
1959	18,305	6,385	957[6]	20,379[6]	20,036[6]	1,019	1,017	6,213	1,005	15,617	13,564
1960	20,752	7,211	1,520	27,155	33,654	1,190	1,310	7,320	3,148	19,888	18,257
1961	20,652	7,970	1,713	25,855	32,673	1,096	1,209	7,670	853	20,434	15,206
1962	21,204	8,319	1,915	25,683	29,140	1,260	1,348	8,104	892	19,599	13,104
1963	19,765	9,333	3,505	21,204	27,081	1,334	1,287	8,806	1,202	20,486	14,164
1964	23,012	9,309	3,642	22,091	35,097	1,405	1,629	9,087	1,556	24,689	18,290
1965	23,899	9,553	3,985	20,747	35,567	1,452	1,444	9,274	872	24,885	18,594
1966	21,552	9,336	4,304	18,195	31,519	1,456	1,505	9,429	–65	22,545	16,199
1967	22,006	10,366	4,889	17,537	32,180	1,550	2,506	10,056	216	23,396	16,333
1968	26,490	11,147	5,051	18,271	40,024	1,424	2,880	11,106	575	29,037	17,873
1969	27,517	10,716	6,973	18,515	43,813	1,320	2,872	11,575	697	31,986	18,468
1970	29,169	12,724	9,694	18,643	48,128	1,490	3,117	11,843	–394	27,972[13]	20,189
1971	28,152	12,592	9,438	18,304	40,684	1,561	2,902	12,430	–903	26,549	17,755
1972	28,078	13,152	11,648	19,072	40,845	1,601	3,083	12,548	–2,251	28,069	17,712
1973	32,417	13,211	11,644	19,454	50,489	1,775	3,163	13,668	–3,455	33,293	23,156
1974	33,430	13,985	15,953	19,833	57,770	1,802	2,809	15,609	–2,319	33,503	20,292
1975	25,520	14,802	13,276	15,991	44,828	2,118	3,267	15,423	–4,175	23,511	16,075

Czech: Czechoslovakia E Germany: East Germany W Germany: West Germany UK: United Kingdom

See p. 447 for footnotes

E13 **Imports and Exports of Iron Ore by Main Trading Countries** (in thousands of metric tons)

NOTES

1. SOURCES:– Belgium to 1913 – A. Wibail, "L'évolution économique de la sidérurgie Belge de 1830 à 1913", *Bulletin de l'Institut des Sciences Evonomiques* V, 1 (1933). France 1866–1922 – supplied by the Direction Nationales des Statistiques de Commerce Extérieur. Poland 1828–34 and 1950–53 – supplies by the Polish Central Statistical Office. Sweden 1867–1883 – L. Jörberg, *Growth and Fluctuations of Swedish Industry, 1869–1912* (Lund) 1961). All other statistics are taken from the official publications noted on p. xv with gaps filled from League of Nations, *International Trade Statistics,* United Nations, *Yearbook of International Trade,* and the British Iron & Steel Federation, *Statistical Year Book.*

2. The statistics are of crude weight, not iron content.

FOOTNOTES

[1] Figures to 1913 (1st line) are of net imports.
[2] From 1871 to 1918 Alsace-Lorraine was part of Germany rather than France.
[3] Up to March 1906 the free ports were not included with Germany.
[4] Including Luxembourg from 1 May 1922.
[5] From 16 March 1939 to 30 April 1939 Sudetenland is excluded, and the Czech lands and Slovakia were treated as independent of each other. The figures given here are aggregates of the separate statistics of each.
[6] From 1921 to February 1935 and from April 1948 to July 1959, Saarland was included with France rather than Germany.
[7] Eastern Upper Silesia was transferred from Germany to Poland in July 1922.
[8] These figures are incomplete owing to the French occupation of the Ruhr.
[9] Figures for 1947–49 are of the American and British Occupation Zones only.
[10] Poland acquired the whole of Silesia in 1945.
[11] Figures to 1950 do not include exports of iron concentrates.
[12] Figures from 1958 are of net exports. Prior to that date imports were negligible.
[13] Excluding a negligible amount of pyrites.

E14 RAW COTTON CONSUMPTION INDICATORS (in thousands of metric tons)

1750–1799

	France[2]	Sweden[1]	United Kingdom[3]
1750	...	--	1.0
1751	...	--	1.3
1752	...	--	1.5
1753	...	--	1.9
1754	...	0.1	1.4
1855	...	--	1.7
1756	...	--	1.2
1757	...	--	0.8
1758	...	--	0.9
1759	...	--	1.0
1760	...	--	0.8
1761	...	--	1.2
1762	...	--	1.3
1763	...	--	1.1
1764	...	--	1.7
1765	...	--	1.7
1766	...	--	3.1
1767	...	--	1.6
1768	...	--	1.8
1769	...	--	1.8
1770	...	--	1.5
1771	...	--	1.1
1772	...	--	2.2
1773	...	--	1.1
1774	...	--	2.4
1775	...	--	2.8
1776	...	0.1	2.7
1777	...	0.1	2.9
1778	...	--	2.7
1779	...	0.1	2.5
1780		0.1	3.0
1781		--	2.3
1782		0.1	5.2
1783		0.1	4.3
1784		0.1	5.1
1785	average 4.0	0.1	8.2
1786		0.1	8.7
1787		0.1	10.1
1788		0.1	8.9
1789		0.1	15
1790		0.1	14
1791	...	0.1	13
1792	...	0.1	15
1793	...	0.1	8
1794	...	0.1	10
1795	...	0.1	11
1796	...	0.2	14
1797	...	0.1	10
1798	...	--	14
1799	...	--	19

See p. 454 for footnotes

E14 **Raw Cotton Consumption Indicators** (in thousands of metric tons)

1800–1849

	Austria	Belgium[1]	Finland[1]	France[2]	Germany[2]	Neth'l[2]	Russia[6]	Spain	Sweden[1]	UK[3]
1800	...	...	...	...	...	...	...	...	0.1	24
1801	...	...	...	...	...	...	...	...	0.1	24
1802	...	...	...	...	...	...	...	...	0.1	25
1803	...	...	...		...	...	...	...	0.2	24
1804	...	...	...		...	...	...	...	0.2	28
1805	...	...	...		...	...	...	...	0.1	27
1806	...	...	...		...	...	...	...	0.1	26
1807	...	...	...		...	...	...	...	0.1	33
1808	...	...	...	average	...	...	...	...	- -	19
1809	...	...	...	8.0	...	...	...	...	0.8	40
1810	...	...	...		...	...	...	...	1.8	56
1811	...	...	...		...	...	...	...	0.4	40[3]
1812	...	...	...		...	...	1.4	...	0.1	33
1813	...	...	- -	...	...	...	0.7	...	0.1	35
1814	...	...	- -	...	...	...	0.5	...	...	33
1815	...	...	- -		...	...	0.8	...	0.1	37
1816	...	...	- -		...	...	0.6	...	- -	40
1817	...	...	- -		...	...	0.8	...	0.1	49
1818	...	...	0.1		...	...	1.1	...	0.1	50
1919	...	...	0.1		...	...	1.6	...	0.2	49
1820	...	...	- -	average 19.0	...	...	0.6	...	0.2	54
1821	...	...	- -		...	...	1.0	...	0.2	59
1822	...	...	- -		...	...	1.6	...	0.1	66
1823	...	...	- -		...	...	1.3	...	0.2	70
1824	...	...	- -		...	...	0.9	...	0.1	75
1825	...	...	- -		...	...	1.0	...	0.1	76
1826	...	...	0.1		...	...	1.7	...	0.2	68
1827	...	...	- -		...	...	1.1	...	0.2	89
1828	4.7	...	- -	average	...	...	1.5	...	0.2	99
1829	5.9	...	- -	34	...	...	2.2	...	0.2	99
1830	6.4	...	- -		...	...	1.9	...	0.2	112
1831	5.6	1.0	- -	28	...	...	1.7	...	0.3	119
1832	8.7	2.5	0.1	34	...	...	2.1	...	0.4	126
1833	8.1	3.1	- -	36	...	...	2.3	...	0.3	130
1834	8.2	2.2	- -	37	...	...	2.5	3.4	0.3	137
1835	8.7	4.8	- -	39	...	...	3.6	2.9	0.4	144
1836	12	6.7	- -	44		...	4.2	3.6	0.5	157
1837	13	7.0	0.1	44		...	4.3	4.3	0.4	166
1838	13	6.9	0.1	51	average	...	5.4	5.2	0.6	189
1839	12	4.1	- -	40	8.9	...	5.8	3.8	0.6	173
1840	12	9.1	0.1	53		...	6.5	8.4	0.8	208
1841	14	7.6	...	56		...	5.1	8.4	0.8	199
1842	18	6.1	...	57		...	8.4	4.9	1.2	197
1843	21	7.5	...	60		...	7.7	2.6	1.1	235
1844	19	7.2	...	59	average 13	...	9.6	7.0	1.4	247
1845	24	8.7	0.3	60		...	12	17	1.4	275
1846	25	6.2	0.3	64		−1.7	12	...	1.4	279
1847	24	7.6	0.3	45		1.6	14	...	2.1	200
1848	16	8.2	0.4	45	average	2.8	20	...	3.4	262
1849	25	13	0.4	64	16	0.4	26	12	2.8	286

Neth'l: Netherlands UK: United Kingdom

See p. 454 for footnotes

E14 Raw Cotton Consumption Indicators (in thousands of metric tons)

1850–1899

	Austria[4]	Belgium[1]	Finland[1]	France[2]	Germany[2]	Italy[1]	Neth'l[2]	Portugal[1]	Russia[6]	Spain	Sweden[1]	Switz[1]	UK[3]
1850	29	10	0.3	59		...	−0.2	...	20	16	2.0	...	267
1851	24	10	...	58		...	1.2	...	23	15	3.4	...	299
1852	35	12		72		...	2.0	...	30	16	3.7	...	336
1853	32	11	0.7	75	average	...	5.0	...	32	16	4.5	...	345
1854	32	11	0.5	72	26	...	0.8	...	27	17	6.7	...	352
1855	34	11	0.6	76		...	−1.0	...	25	17	6.7	...	381
1856	39	13	- -	84		...	−1.3	...	36	28	7.6	...	404
1857	36	11	0.9	73	average	...	3.1	...	40	17	5.5	...	375
1858	40	12	0.1	80	40	...	−3.9	...	44	21	4.5	...	411
1859	37[4]	13	0.4	82	48	...	9.7	...	48	24	6.9	...	443
1860	45[4]	15	1.4[7]	115	67	...	3.6	...	47	24	8.2	33	492
			1.8										
1861	44	15	1.6	110	74	12.4	−2.3	...	43	27	7.7	29	457
1862	19	5	0.3	28	38	3.8	−1.4	...	14	13	1.3	19	205
1863	16	7	0.5	45	40	4.1	6.6	...	18	17	0.7	20	230
1864	18	7	0.5	56	37	3.2	1.4	...	27	14	1.7	23	251
1865	22[4]	12	0.8	61	46	2.8	−1.8	...	26	15	3.2	24	328
1866	25	15	0.9	99	57	6.0	4.5	...	48	19	4.7	34	400
1867	37	16	1.3	74	67	9.9	4.4	...	54	21	5.7	34	439
1868	40	16	1.2	99	73	11	4.5	...	42	22	4.9	41	450
1869	42	16	1.8	94	64	12	3.0	...	53	20	5.6	42	426
1870	45	16	1.4[8]	59[5]	81[5]	15	5.0	...	46	27	6.4	38	489
1871	58	26	1.6[8]	99	112	27	13	...	68	35	10	54	547
1872	48	24	1.8[8]	80	111	20	18	2.0	59	28	5.7	42	536
1873	43	18	1.7[8]	55	118	24	5.2	2.0	58	27	8.2	38	565
1874	48	20	2.2	94	127	31	5.8	1.6	76	38	10	41	579
1875	52	18	2.3	101	114	19	5.5	2.1	85	34	6.0	22	557
1876	56	19	1.9	103	135	20	10	2.0	77	39	10	24	581
1877	57	20	2.0	85	117	24	5.2	2.7	73	34	8.8	19	558
1878	57	22	2.3	80	111	27	12	2.4	118	36	7.0	16	541
1879	66	22	2.3	90	123	37	9	2.8	106	37	6.8	23	522
1880	64	23	3.0	89	137	47	14	3.4	94	45	9.2	22	617
1881	72	30	2.8	109	139	49	10	3.3	149	45	10	25	649
1882	67	25	3.1	111	138	63	9	3.3	127	46	10	23	661
1883	95	24	3.0	116	169	67	18	4.0	147	54	13	29	692
1884	85	25	3.3	97	160	66	13	3.7	121	53	10	27	672
1885	72	17	2.6	108	156	79	17	4.2	124	49	11	23	589
1886	83	21	3.3	111	161	68	9	5.1	137	46	11	20	658
1887	95	23	3.2	121	198	76	12	5.0	184	46	11	27	680
1888	83	21	2.8	95	179	75	9	5.5	137	42	12	22	692
1889	87	14	4.2	124	225	90	8	6.0	171	64	12	29	709
1890	105	32	4.4	125	227	102	12	8.2	136	50	13	27	755
1891	106	34	4.1	154	237	93	14	7.2	152	61	15	25	756
1892	108	21	4.7	179	219	98	12	7.4	164	61	13	24	702
1893	110	35	2.9	138	227	99	11	11	187	59	11	22	650
1894	119	35	5.6	160	254	120	11	11	190	68	18	25	727
1895	122	22	4.4	141	267	108	12	13	201	71	14	26	755
1896	117	29	5.2	134	242	113	16	10	224	59	14	24	743
1897	123	38	6.7	189	273	120	14	13	225	76	18	24	740
1898	143	43	5.8	176	322	133	20	15	233	65	19	26	799
1899	132	35	6.2	175	295	131	19	16	264	86	16	24	799

Neth'l: Netherlands Switz: Switzerland UK: United Kingdom

See p. 454 for footnotes

E14 Raw Cotton Consumption Indicators (in thousands of metric tons)

1900–1949

	Austria[4]	Belgium[1]	Bulgaria[1]	Czech[2]	Finland[1]	France[2]	W.Germany[2]	E Germany	Greece[1]	Hungary[1]	Italy[1]
1900	127	35	...	...	6.4	159	279	...	...	...	123
1901	138	33	...	...	5.6	185	327	...	...	...	135
1902	147	45	...	...	5.9	187	336	...	...	...	147
1903	152	54	...	...	5.3	219	370	...	...	...	154
1904	156	40	...	...	5.9	176	382	...	...	...	155
1905	164	48	...	...	6.3	202	394	...	...	...	165
1906	168	54	...	...	7.8	205	385	...	...	...	183
1907	206	62	...	...	8.1	229	454	...	...	...	218
1908	181	49	...	...	7.7	232	429	...	...	...	207
1909	193	67	1.2	...	7.7	260	448	...	...	...	191
1910	173	63	0.7	...	6.8	158	383	...	...	...	175
1911	201	126	0.8	...	8.0	252	437	...	...	...	190
1912	224	141	0.9	...	8.7	276	507	...	...	...	214
1913	210	140	0.4	...	8.8	271	478	...	...	...	202
1914	172	...	0.5	...	6.9	160	...	...	...	...	191
1915	123	...	--	...	8.9	219	...	...	...	...	291
1916	...	...	--	...	12.4	226	...	...	...	...	254
1917	...	...	--	...	4.0	254	...	...	...	...	179
1918	...[4]	...	0.2	...	0.6	136[5]	...[5]	...	...	...	130
1919	...	51	--	...	6.4	201	...	...	...	--	179
1920	10	101	0.2	62	6.5	202	139	...	...	0.2	179
1921	23	61	--	89	7.2	189	...	...	...	0.9	158
1922	24	65	--	71	7.5	240	218	...	...	2.2	178
1923	22	76	0.2	75	7.3	235	215	...	...	3.1	185
1924	24	72	0.2	104	5.9	281	316	...	...	3.0	201
1925	34	95	0.4	137	8.1	317	413	...	...	5.2	237
1926	26	92	0.8	101	8.8	344	327	...	...	5.5	239
1927	34	115	1.4	148	9.6	327	508	...	...	7.6	209
1928	31	111	1.7	125	9.0	315	388	...	...	9.1	233
1929	26	111	1.9	123	7.7	358	393	...	...	13	245
1930	22	100	2.7	113	7.1	361	346	...	...	15	205
1931	22	101	3.1	93	7.2	222	303	...	...	16	171
1932	20	80	3.8	81	7.6	244	358	...	...	18	190
1933	25	101	4.8	71	9.2	349	419	...	...	23	220
1934	28	100	7.2	79	14	223	349	...	...	26	187
1935	33	121	6.3	78	13	222	356	...	...	24	149
1936	38	128	8.3	95	13	329	318	...	...	29	101
1937	39	136	10.4	111	15	293	350	...	...	27	166
1938	...	124	12.0	71[9]	14	288	353	...	...	27	159
1939	...	64	9.5	44	12	239	...	...	...	26	111
1940	...	45	5.3	10	10	282	...	...	...	16	108
1941	...	1	1.7	10	4	...	...	...	...	7.2	4
1942	...	1	--	2	--	...	...	...	...	0.3	1
1943	...	--	0.9	0.5	--	...	...	...	...	3.9	...
1944	...	--	0.5	--[9]	--	...	...	...	...	0.8	...
1945	...	52	2.3	4	6	218	...	...	5	0.2	...
1946	—	67	13	20	9	188	...	...	13	12	187
							W Germany[2]				
1947	11[4]	98	...[1]	60[2]	11	221		...	3[1]	26[1]	206
1948	14	71[1]	...	54	10[1]	190[2]	94	...	19	26	205[2]
		88			12	242					180
1949	17	80	...	60	8	231	127	...	18	30	207

Czech: Czechoslovakia E Germany: East Germany W Germany: West Germany

See p. 454 for footnotes

E14 **Raw Cotton Consumption Indicators** (in thousands of metric tons)

1900–1949

	Neth'l [2]	Poland [1]	Portugal [1]	Romania [1]	Russia [6]	Spain	Sweden [1]	Switz [1]	UK [3]	Yugoslavia [1]
1900	18	...	16	...	262	66	17	24	788[10]	...
1901	20	...	13	...	264	78	17	25	712	...
1902	22	...	15	...	286	85	18	25	741	...
1903	19	...	14	...	295	80	18	26	733	...
1904	21	...	15	...	299	71	17	27	674	...
1905	24	...	16	...	273	76	19	26	822	...
1906	22	...	13	...	296	87	21	26	841	...
1907	29	...	17	...	319	92	21	28	900	...
1908	29	...	16	...	347	95	21	26	870	...
1909	22	...	15	0.4	349	71	17	27	827	...
1910	20	...	16	0.3	362	73	21	24	740	...
1911	29	...	18	0.5	351	90	20	27	858	...
1912	35	...	18	0.4	421	93	22	30	972	...
1913	36	...	18	0.3	424[6]	88	22	31	988	...
					223					
1914	29	...	15	0.4	...	84	23	24	942	...
1915	40	...	18	0.1	...	143	121	38	876[11]	...
1916	38	...	16	...	...	102	28	27	894	...
1917	10	...	14	–	...	97	7	22	816	...
1918	- -	...	15	–	...	60	7	8	680	...
1919	32	...	7	0.2	...	74	17	27	692	...
1920	29	23	12		...	80	23	23	783	14
1921	31	37	14	0.5	...	82	13	26	484	38
1922	31	65	14	1.4	...	83	18	23	639	42
1923	32	58	16	1.8	...	83	19	28	618	45
1924	25	43	13	1.9	...	79	21	31	621	50
1925	42	55	14	1.5	...	86	20	34	730	57
1926	45	66	16	1.1	...	82	23	30	684	69
1927	53	79	17	2.7	...	96	24	36	706	69
1928	49	76	17	...	208	74	25	32	689	70
1929	53	66	16	3.3	238	76	22	32	679	76
1930	52	61	18	3.3	257	99	23	31	577	88
1931	52	55	15	3.0	338	95	24	26	447	81
1932	35	51	21	3.7	395	106	25	29	570	86
1933	39	61	22	5.0	379	98	23	34	534	105
1934	42	68	22	5.7	420	102	32	32	600	146
1935	40	66	23	6.0	437	99	28	29	572	149
1936	50	71	21	9.4	596	...	32	30	631	168
1937	63	72	30	17	717	...	34	38	649[12]	207
1938	53	...	28	20	893	...	36	31	503	216
1939	61	...	19	13	...	...	47	42	597	181
1940	...	...	24	13	849[6]	74	20	22	630	...
1941	...	...	23	7.9	...	52	16	12	438	...
1942	...	...	23	0.4	...	66	32	1.7	426	...
1943	...	...	18	1.4	...	88	18	0.1	401	...
1944	...	...	33	1.0	...	84	35	0.2	365	...
1945	...	...	24	...	312	116	12	19	325	...
1946	53	...	39	...	...	70	19	38	369	...
1947	54	69	26	...	...	57	17	32	370	...
1948	45[2]	[1]	33[1]	[1]	...	75	26[1]	26[1]	443	...[1]
	48	73	33	18			25	31		30
1949	53	78	33	13	821	91	25	29	443	34

Neth'l: Netherlands Switz: Switzerland UK: United Kingdom

See p. 454 for footnotes

E14 Raw Cotton Consumption Indicators (in thousands of metric tons)

1950–1975

	Austria[4]	Belgium[1]	Bulgaria[1]	Czech[2]	Finland[1]	France[2]	W.Germany[3]	E Germany	Greece[1]	Hungary[1]	Italy[1]
1950	20	87	...	60	11	252	189	...	21	30	203
1951	21	103	22	65	12	272	235	43	25	30	214
1952	21	88	26	69	13	266	209	54	24	33	193
1953	17	80	29	59	13	249	233	65	23	50	187
1954	20	93	33	65	14	290	265	75	26	51	190
1955	23	92	33	72	13	275	271	87	25	51	174
1956	23	90	34	76	14	264	286	87	23	43	166
1957	23	98	35	80	16	298	310	89	26	34	192
1958	26	81	36	89	14	305	311	92	28	44	187
1959	25	82	41	92	15	254	294	98	28	43	189
1960	26	90	48	98	18	298	319	100	26	51	222
1961	28	93	47	102	17	303	325	102	30	55	226
1962	28	86	50	106	16	285	303	104	31	59	227
1963	25	86	52	105	16	278	283	100	34	62	231
1964	25	87	54	103	16	283	285	93	35	65	227
1965	26	79	56	104	17	258	286	93	38	73	191
1966	25	75	61	108	15	267	282	92	44	76	218
1967	23	66	65	111	17	268	255	91	46	78	241
1968	21	65	72	111	16	243	258	89	44	74	223
1969	23	66	74	108	16	244	255	89	46	69	221
1970	23	70	75	111	13	248	254	93	49	72	221
1971	23	66	76	115	14	237	234	92	53	76	201
1972	23	62	80	119	14	235	240	91	61	72	200
1973	22	57	81	119	13	231	233	91	77	74	187
1974	22	58	82	122	13	233	238	92	82	75	195
1975	19	46	80	125	12	202	209	91	90	79	180

	Neth'l[2]	Poland[1]	Portugal[1]	Romania[1]	Russia[6]	Spain	Sweden[1]	Switz[1]	UK[3]	Yugoslavia[1]
1950	61	87	36	17	953	59	28	30	461	35
1951	65	90	35	22	1,265	53	29	34	464	30
1952	58	90	39	24	1,360[6] 911	68	27	36	311	26
1953	64	91	38	50	965	75	26	32	377	26
1954	70	92	42	51	1,019	69	29	36	404	27
1955	72	94	46	54	1,106	76	30	38	354	34
1956	73	95	44	49	1,084	86	29	36	330	38
1957	74	92	43	46	1,171	100	30	40	344	42
1958	72	101	45	50	1,236	103	30	42	292	42
1959	71	108	46	51	1,301	103	28	34	289	43
1960	77	116	55	52	1,344	121	28	39	278	48
1961	82	125	66	56	1,344	126	28	42	250	52
1962	77	128	66	65	1,355	139	27	42	221	54
1963	78	125	69	67	1,366	119	23	41	226	72
1964	76	132	74	69	1,431	114	21	41	237	72
1965	77	145	80	71	1,496	114	21	43	230	81
1966	71	150	83	73	1,550	126	20	40	212	89
1967	67	150	78	74	1,626	126	17	40	181	90
1968	62	143	80	76	1,691	98	17	40	180	90
1969	62	141	85	80	1,713	119	15	41	177	91
1970	59	145	90	80	1,756	113	14	42	172	92
1971	55	150	93	82	1,843	111	12	43	161	90
1972	52	152	104	82	1,908	119	9	43	138	90
1973	47	150	109	85	1,919	124	9	41	141	92
1974	46	152	120	87	1,951	119	9	41	121	94
1975	37	147	106	91	1,984	115	8	38	111	98

Neth'l: Netherlands Switz: Switzerland UK: United Kingdom

See p. 454 for footnotes

E14 Raw Cotton Consumption Indicators (in thousands of metric tons)

NOTES

1. SOURCES:— Statistics prior to 1948 are taken from the official publications noted on p. xv with occasional gaps filled from League of Nations sources, with the following exceptions:— Finland to 1860 (1st line) — Per Schybergson, *Hantverk och fabriker. Finlands konsumtionsvaruindustrii 1815–1870* (transcribed by the Central Statistical Office of Finland). Finland 1860 (2nd line) to 1917 — Erkki Pihkala, *Finland's Foreign Trade 1860–1917* (Bank of Finland, Helsinki, 1969). France to 1830 — T.J. Markovitch, *L'industrie francaise de 1789 à 1964* (Cahiers de l'I.S.E.A., 1966). Russia to 1913 (1st line) — P.A. Khromov, *Economic Development of Russia in the 19th and 20th Centuries, 1800–1917* (Moscow, 1950). Russia 1913 (2nd line) to 1953 (1st line) — G.W. Nutter, *The Growth of Industrial Production in the Soviet Union* (Princeton, 1962). U.K. to 1936 — based on B.R. Mitchell & Phyllis Deane, *Abstract of British Historical Statistics* (Cambridge, 1962), where the original sources are given. Statistics from 1948 (except Russia to 1953) are taken from the United Nations, *Statistical Yearbooks,* the original source being the International Cotton Federation.

2. Where statistics of cotton consumption are available they have been preferred. Otherwise statistics of imports minus re-exports are given, or, failing that, "special" trade imports — i.e. imports *intended* for home consumption. In the last resort statistics of total imports have been given.

3. Estimates of consumption in thousands of bales are available back to 1907 in publications of the International Federation of Master Cottonspinners, though with a gap for the wars and immediate postwar periods. They were given in measure of weight for the year ended 31 July 1939 in the U.N. *Statistical Yearbook* as follows (in thousands of tons):—

Austria	39	Germany	234	Romania	20
Belgium	70	Greece	18	Spain	30
Bulgaria	16	Hungary	28	Sweden	30
Czechoslovakia	43	Italy	144	Switzerland	31
Finland	13	Netherlands	56	United Kingdom	583
France	281	Poland	76	Yugoslavia	20
		Portugal	22		

FOOTNOTES

[1] Figures to 1947 or 1948 (1st line) are of "special" imports, and subsequently of estimated consumption for years ended 31 July.

[2] Figures to 1947 or 1948 (1st line) are of net imports, and subsequently of estimated consumption for years ended 31 July.

[3] Figures to 1810 are of net imports, and subsequently they are of estimated consumption.

[4] Figures to 1915 are for the whole Austro-Hungarian customs area. Lombardy was excluded from 1860 and Venetia from 1866, and Dalmatia was not included until 1861. Figures from 1920 are for the Republic of Austria. Austro-Hungarian statistics are of net imports. Republic statistics are of "special" imports to 1947 and subsequently of estimated consumption for years ended 31 July.

[5] For 1871–1918 Alsace-Lorraine is included with Germany rather than France.

[6] Figures to 1859 are of total imports of raw cotton. From 1860 to 1913 (1st line) they are said to be raw cotton consumption, though to begin with they are the same as imports. From 1913 (2nd line) to 1953 (1st line) the figures are of ginned cotton consumption, and subsequently they are of raw cotton consumption for years ended 31 July. The figures to 1913 (1st line) apply to the Russian Empire (excluding Finland). From 1913 (2nd line) to 1940 they are for the 1923 boundaries of the U.S.S.R., and subsequently for the postwar territory.

[7] This break occurs on a change of source (see note 1).

[8] These figures exclude imports by rail.

[9] From March 1939 to 1944 the Sudetenland is excluded.

[10] Figures for 1900–14 are for years ended 31 August.

[11] Subsequent figures are for years ended 31 July.

[12] Subsequent figures are for 52 week periods as close to the calendar year as possible.

E15 COTTON SPINDLES (in thousands)

1834–1970

	Austria[1]	Belgium	Czechoslovakia	France	Germany	East Germany[2]	Italy
1834	800	200	...	2,500	626[8]	...	...
1852	1,400	400	...	4,500	900	...	...
1861	1,800	612	...	5,500	2,235	...	...
1867	1,500	625	...	6,800[7]	2,000[7]	...	...
1877	1,558	800	...	5,000	4,700	...	450
1882/3	1,950	840	...	4,800	4,800	...	880
1886/7	2,070	...	...	...	5,060	...	1,150
1891/2	2,400	930	...	5,040	6,071	...	...
1904	3,450	880[6]	...	6,150	8,434	...	1,686
1908	4,000	1,200	...	6,700	9,900	...	2,435
1913	4,909[1]	1,492	...	7,400[7]	11,186[7]	...	4,200
							4,600
1920[3]	1,140	1,572	3,584	9,400	9,400	...	4,515
1921	...	1,548	3,082	9,600	9,400	...	4,506
1922	...	1,630	3,549	9,600	9,500	...	4,580
1923	1,023	1,683	3,508	9,600	9,605	...	4,570
1924	1,051	1,741	3,460	9,359	9,464	...	4,570
1925	1,038	1,788	3,471	9,428	9,500	...	4,771
1926	1,032	1,854	3,568	9,511	10,480	...	4,833
1927	1,025	1,936	3,629	9,567	10,800	...	5,086
1928	1,014	2,070	3,663	9,770	11,153	...	5,189
1929	955	2,156	3,673	9,880	11,250	...	5,210
1930	817	2,172	3,636	10,250	11,070	...	5,342
1931	768	2,164	3,638	10,350	10,591	...	5,397
1932	767	2,156	3,622	10,144	10,233	...	5,384
1933	758	2,087	3,627	10,144	9,850	...	5,338
1934	774	2,106	3,627	10,170	10,109	...	5,493
1935[4]	765	2,091	3,625	10,157	...	...	5,477
1936	776	2,008	3,611	10,016	...	...	...
1937	777	1,995	3,548	9,932	10,247	...	...
1938	742	1,993	3,357	9,783	10,323	...	5,395
1939	742	1,984	3,330	9,794	12,225[9]	...	5,324
					West Germany		
1950	546	1,802	2,331	8,148	5,785	750	5,566
1951	561	1,844	2,340	8,110	6,168	850	5,661
1952	571	1,857	2,380	8,110	6,244	890	5,736
1953	577	1,833	2,380	7,964	6,279	890	5,781
1954	607	1,835	2,420	7,698	6,100	980	5,750
1955[3]	608	1,752	2,450	7,618	6,005	1,000	5,698
1956	596	1,661	2,480	5,547	5,954	1,000	5,726
1957	607	1,601	1,893	6,257	5,855	1,100	5,574
1958[5]	579	1,581	1,900	6,280	6,120	1,150	5,212
1959	579	1,521	1,950	6,071	5,948	1,150	4,854
1960	576	1,493	1,950	5,802	5,909	1,150	4,611
1961	565	1,470	2,055	5,467	5,817	1,150	4,522
1962	563	1,463	2,089	5,418	5,605	1,357	4,453
1963	559	1,446	2,066	4,645	5,403	1,518	4,449
1964	557	1,387	2,042	4,563	5,214	1,586	4,466
1965	503	1,337	2,102	4,299	5,091	1,586	4,424
1966	480	1,215	2,151	4,189	4,926	1,586	4,287
1967	453	1,121	2,124	4,105	4,672	1,586	4,324
1968	435	1,080	2,133	3,788	4,529	1,625	4,325
1969	416	1,068	2,124	3,621	4,349	1,625	4,125
1970	415	985	2,095	3,588	4,262	1,675	4,121

See p. 457 for footnotes

E15 Cotton Spindles (in thousands)

1834–1970

	Netherlands	Poland[2]	Portugal	Russia[2]	Spain	Switzerland	United Kingdom
1834	...	...	...	700[12]	...	580	10,000
1852	...	...	...	...	...	900	20,977[17]
1861	40	...	...	1,000[13]	...	1,350	30,387
1867	...	...	...	2,500[14]	...	1,000	34,215
1877	...	...	...	...	...	1,854[16]	44,207[18]
1882/3	250	...	110	4,400	1,865	1,900	...
1886/7	...	...	...	...	...	...	44,348[19]
1891/2	260	...	160[11]	6,000	2,050	1,722	44,509[20]
1904	...	...	230	7,146[21]	2,600	1,600	47,857[21] [22]
1908	386	...	378	7,900	1,850	1,500	52,818
1913	479	...	480	9,212 [15]	2,000	1,398	55,653
1920[3]	598	1,400	482	7,200	1,800	1,536	58,692
1921	630	1,161	400	...	1,806	1,531	56,141
1922	720	1,200	487	...	1,806	1,519	56,605
1923	669	1,200	487	7,246	1,813	1,513	56,583
1924	686	1,101	503	...	1,813	1,515	56,750
1925	817	1,172	503	...	1,813	1,517	57,116
1926	921	1,375	503	...	1,817	1,529	57,286
1927	1,002	1,372	503	6,945	1,873	1,518	57,325
1928	1,111	1,544	503	7,311	1,897	1,525	57,136
1929	1,160	1,557	503	7,465	1,875	1,504	55,917
1930	1,167	1,554	503	7,624	1,875	1,446	55,207
1931	1,215	1,555	503	...	2,070	1,381	54,246
1932	1,213	1,706	453	...	2,070	1,346	51,891
1933	1,224	1,818	446	9,200	2,070	1,303	49,001
1934	1,236	1,696	452	9,800	2,070	1,295	45,893
1935[4]	1,219	1,684	452	9,800	2,070	1,287	43,756
1936	1,218	1,683	464	9,800	2,070	1,236	42,307
1937	1,221	1,704	471	9,900	2,070	1,272	39,938
1938	1,206	1,715	469	10,050	2,070	1,248	37,340
1939	1,241	1,764 [10]	444	10,350	2,000	1,249	36,322
1950	1,170	1,067	536	9,483	2,210	1,156	29,580
1951	1,170	1,085	782	9,750	2,210	1,162	28,968
1952	1,170	1,185	949	9,900	2,206	1,165	27,933
1953	1,234	1,220	875	9,900	2,226	1,158	27,232
1954	1,232	1,260	886	10,150	2,240	1,158	26,454
1955[3]	1,099	1,275	896	10,150	2,335	1,189	25,183
1956	1,077	1,310	962	10,100	2,364	1,188	23,972
1957	1,059	1,340	998	10,147	2,364	1,199	22,487
1958[5]	1,041	1,925	1,055	10,712	2,608	1,192	19,889
1959	1,032	1,954	1,088	10,800	2,700	1,177	14,104
1960	1,020	2,001	1,101	10,800	2,589	1,169	9,710
1961	1,013	2,019	1,125	11,500	2,711	1,168	9,465
1962	985	1,955	1,138	12,202	2,648	1,126	8,053
1963	987	1,973	1,155	12,300	2,580	1,120	6,475
1964	960	1,965	1,112	12,000	2,612	1,132	6,077
1965	907	1,967	1,198	12,707	2,580	1,114	5,345
1966	821	2,076	1,212	13,427	2,420	1,040	5,092
1967	656	2,086	1,249	14,173	2,176	1,027	3,790
1968	637	2,042	1,323	14,507	2,117	978	3,822
1969	552	2,083	1,335	14,604	2,101	965	3,635
1970	563	2,108	1,357	14,694	2,210	941	3,486

See p. 457 for footnotes

E15 **Cotton Spindles** (in thousands)

NOTES

1. SOURCES:—1834–67, all countries except Russia in 1840 and 1857, the U.K. in 1850, 1861 and 1867, and Italy in 1867 – D.S. Landes in the *Cambridge Economic History of Europe,* vol. V1, part 1. Russia in 1840 – M.G.Mulhall, *Dictionary of Statistics* (4th edition, London, 1899). Russia in 1857, Switzerland in 1876, and all statistics for 1904 – S.J. Chapman, *The Cotton Industry and Trade* (London, 1905). Italy in 1867 – *L'Industria Tessile Cotoniera in Italia dai suoi Inizia ad Oggi* (Rome, 1952). 1877, all countries except Switzerland and the U.K. – *Annali di Staistica,* serie II, vol. 13. 1882/3, all countries except the U.K. – T. Ellison, *The Cotton Trade of Britain* (London, 1886). 1891–2, all countries except the U.K. – F. Merttens in *Transactions of the Manchester Statistical Society* (April 1894). 1904 – all countries except the U.K. – J.A. Todd, *The Cotton World* (London, 1927) U.K. in 1850–1903 – *Reports of H.M. Inspectors of Factories,* published in the Sessional Papers of Parliament. 1908–1970 – publications of the International Federation of Cotton and Allied Textile Industries (under various names).

2. In principle, the statistics in this table relate to spinning spindles, except as indicated in footnotes. Rayon spinning spindles are included.

FOOTNOTES

[1] The figures to 1913 apply to the whole Austro-Hungarian Empire.
[2] Statistics from 1950 are estimated. (From 1920 in the case of Russia).
[3] From 1920 to 1934 and 1955 to 1957 the count was made on 31 July.
[4] From 1935 to 1954 the count was made on 31 January.
[5] From 1958 the count was made on 31 December.
[6] In 1898.
[7] From 1871 to 1918 Alsace-Lorraine is included in Germany rather than France.
[8] In 1836.
[9] This figure probably applies to Greater Germany (i.e. including Austria and Sudetenland).
[10] There were substantial territorial changes in 1945.
[11] In 1894.
[12] *Circa* 1840.
[13] In 1857.
[14] In 1870.
[15] Figures to 1913 are for the whole Russian Empire, including Finland.
[16] In 1876.
[17] In 1850.
[18] In 1878. According to Ellison (*op. cit.* in sources) this figure may have related to machines in use only.
[19] In 1885. According to Ellison (*op, cit.* in sources) this figure may have related to machines in use only.
[20] In 1890.
[21] In 1903.
[22] Figures to 1903 include doubling spindles, which numbered 3,952 thousand in 1903.

E 16 OUTPUT OF COTTON YARN (in thousands of metric tons)

1920–1975

	Austria	Belgium	Bulgaria	Czechoslovakia	France	Germany[3]	East Germany[6]	Greece	Hungary[6]	Italy
1920	...	...	...	...	...	...	...	...	...	148
1921	...	...	...	...	...	...	...	...	...	133
1922	...	...	...	...	...	...	...	...	...	156
1923	18.1	...	...	...	...	...	...	6.2	...	164
1924	16.6	...	...	...	...	...	...	6.0	...	173
1925	26.6	...	...	...	...	316	...	...	...	199
1926	23.0	...	...	...	...	267	...	7.7	...	199
1927	29.0	...	...	...	...	366	...	...	...	179
1928	27.2	74.3	...	...	...	355	...	7.9	...	196
1929	23.7	68.8	1.3	...	280	...	...	8.2	...	220
1930	19.9	61.3	2.2	...	238	...	...	9.6	...	184
1931	17.7	51.7	2.7	...	193	...	...	10.1	...	153
1932	18.0	44.6	3.1	...	180	...	...	10.1	...	169
1933	18.4	46.4	4.5	...	235	350	...	12.5	...	191
1934	22.9	43.4	6.5	83.9	...	...[4]	...	14.2	...	173
1935	26.9	61.3	6.2	...	...	359	...	13.5	...	171
1936	31.4	66.3	8.8	41.2[1]	...	369	...	15.2	...	140
1937	32.5	72.5	10.1	88.7	...	369	...	15.8	...	187
1938	31.0	75.1	...	...	250	411	...	15.8	21.0	178
1939	...	...	11.5	...	...	...	...	17.1	...	192
1940	...	...	...	...	...	...	...	...	...	178
1941	...	...	...	...	60[2]	...	...	...	...	115
1942	...	...	...	...	36	...	...	...	...	76
1943	...	...	...	...	28	...	...	...	...	49
1944	...	...	...	...	14	...	...	0.9	...	17
						West Germany				
1945	...	...	...	...	63[2]	...	...	8.2	...	[10][8]
1946	4.6	62.8	...	37.0	172	44	...	14.1	8.9	135
1947	8.7	74.5	...	54.7	204	79	...	15.4	18.8	180
1948	12.4	85.9	15.9	68.1	224	119	...	15.4	23.9	189
1949	18.1	89.7	16.5	75.8	228	228	...	18.0	28.6	209
1950	19.4	106.3	16.4	77.4	251	282	24.0	19.8	32.8	216
1951	21.8	117.7	19.8	75.2	271	324	39.4	21.7	37.9	231
1952	17.4	91.2	25.0	68.1	256	292	51.1	20.3	43.9	203
1953	18.9	99.8	26.4	63.3	270	343	58.9	21.6	42.7	193
1954	21.2	112.5	27.7	67.4	295	369	61.8	23.9	44.9	203
1955	23.5	107.6	30.2	76.2	265	373	63.1	23.5	47.2	175
1956	23.9	108.6	31.3	81.7	281	396	62.2	23.7	37.7	190
1957	25.8	111.4	33.2	87.5	313	418	60.6	27.0	45.1	212
1958	26.5	86.3	36.3	94.5	308	393	64.2	23.4	46.4	199
1959	25.2	97.5	46.8	98.2	282	398[4]	66.9	22.4	48.0[7]	214
									38.5	
1960	26.6	103.2	49.0	102.2	315	421	72.6	23.9	47.0	239
1961	28.4	103.4	49.9	106.4	315	403	79.6	26.5	51.1	239
1962	27.0	94.9	52.7	109.9	296	383	82.9	29.3	53.0	249
1963	25.4	93.9	55.7	106.9	298	373	78.6	30.5	57.2	251
1964	25.7	94.4	57.7	105.5	300	381	81.0	31.4	59.5	240
1965	24.4	85.2	60.6	108.1	267	382[5]	79.0	34.9	63.9	201
						295				
1966	22.9	79.9	63.7	112.2	289	281	77.6	36.8	63.6	251
1967	20.1	70.7	67.3	112.3	268	251	77.0	38.5	64.8	247
1968	19.5	72.5	69.8	112.0	257	255	73.3	36.2	62.8	233
1969	20.6	75.3	71.1	110.6	267	252	69.4	39.8	57.6	254
1970	20.8	74.8	73.7	113.9	270	239	68.5	41.9	56.7	247
1971	21.4	69.7	75.3	118.6	266	221	66.9	46.4	55.5	225
1972	21.3	66.8	78.8	121.5	275	222	61.8	51.9	55.8	238
1973	20.6	65.4	80.2	123.6	280	215	59.1	65.3	57.5	237
1974	20.4	64.7	79.7	126.0	279	214	57.9	69.5	57.9	236
1975	16.4	44.3	78.9	129.1	232	192	59.1	79.4	61.2	200

See p. 460 for footnotes

E 16 Output of Cotton Yarn (in thousands of metric tons)

1913–1975

	Netherlands	Poland[12]	Portugal	Romania	Russia	Spain	Sweden[12]	Switzerland	U.K.[12]	Yugoslavia
1913	...	...	...	...	271	...	...	...	...	...
1917	...	...	...	...	211	...	...	...	...	...
1918	...	...	...	...	118	...	...	...	...	...
1919	...	...	...	...	19	...	...	...	...	...
1920	...	...	...	...	15	32.1	...	...	...	...
1921	...	...	...	...	22	27.3	...	...	...	...
1922	...	...	...	...	72	35.4	...	...	...	...
1923	...	...	...	...	87	26.6	...	...	...	...
1924	...	...	...	...	116	33.4	...	...	...	...
1925	...	...	...	...	197	33.4	...	...	...	...
1926	39.4	...	...	...	252	29.5	...	...	...	...
1927	44.2	...	...	...	284	34.5	...	...	...	...
1928	48.3	60	...	...	324	30.3	22.1	...	...	...
1929	50.0	51	...	...	354	30.8	20.7	...	...	...
1930	49.2	47[7] 60	...	...	287	33.0	21.4	...	...	...
1931	43.5	55	...	...	314	32.2	19.0	...	...	...
1932	32.7	54	...	...	355	32.5	23.7	...	...	...
1933	37.9	62	...	...	367	30.5[11]	23.7	...	...	...
1934	38.7	70	...	...	388	...	27.7	...	...	...
1935	39.9	72	...	...	384	...	26.6	...	557	...
1936	45.3	78	...	...	480	...	29.0	...	594	...
1937	55.5	78	...	...	533	...	28.7	...	616	...
1938	51.7	64	20.8	16.5	529	...	27.5	...	476	...
1939	57.8	...	21.6	...	562	...	28.5	...	495	18.9
1940	47.1	...	22.6	...	650	49	28.2	...	540	...
1941	21.5	...	25.3	...	...	42	22.6	...	409	...
1942	15.1	...	21.0	...	...	57	20.7	...	363	...
1943	13.5	...	17.3	...	...	73	19.3	...	355	...
1944	...	...[9]	19.4	...	...	65	20.1	...	334	...
1945	...	[14][10]	24.8	...	303	75	24.2	...	301	2.4
1946	34.4	47	28.9	...	...	85	24.5	...	336	23.7
1947	46.9	59	29.0	...	...	60	22.7	24.3	336	28.7
1948	54.9	82	31.9	21.4	568	65	24.3	26.5	413	27.8
1949	62.1	91	30.7	...	...	60	26.3	25.4	417	29.2
1950	67.6	92	**35.6**	29.2	663	58	28.1	28.7	433	29.9
1951	69.7	95	**31.7**	34.2	...	52	28.3	31.2	439	26.9
1952	62.8	95	**35.8**	38.5	...	64	25.7	29.4	314	25.9
1953	74.0	104	**34.9** 36.3[13]	41.9	899	68	26.2	28.3	376	27.7
1954	78.3	109	**42.7**	42.7	971	64	27.9	32.5	399	34.1
1955	79.6	115	**44.6**	45.6	1,038	65	26.9	32.9	356	38.2
1956	80.8	116	**42.9**	43.0	977	70	27.2	32.6	337	38.9
1957	82.9	123	**44.6**	44.5	1,016	75	28.1	37.3	347	42.6
1958	79.0	135	**47.1**	47.1	1,063	96	26.7[7]	35.1	304	45.2
1959	81.6	146	**46.5**	48.2	1,124	90	25.3	31.1	292	47.0
1960	87.3	153	**56.5**	51.6	1,169	95[7] 116	25.4	36.2	285	50.6
1961	87.2	165	**62.3**	59.6	1,165	132	25.2	38.8	266	55.3
1962	84.3	163	**63.7**	69.7	1,192	134	23.4	37.5	237	68.6
1963	84.5	160	**70.0**	70.5	1,220	128	20.8	37.1	238	74.9
1964	88.4	179	**74.1**	74.0	1,274	127	19.6	38.5	247	82.0
1965	81.7	187	**79.7**	78.3	1,292	121	18.7	39.2	237	86.0
1966	79.9	193	**80.6**	80.4	1,323	132	17.2	36.4	225	92.5
1967	68.8	194	**79.6**	84.3	1,373	129	15.4	36.2	190	93.1
1968	70.5	194	**84.4**	93.0	1,421	111	14.1	37.2	190	94.7
1969	69.0[7] 54	198	88.0	102.0	1,438	144	13.2	39.4	191	96.0
1970	52	208	91.5	109.0	1,435	143	11.5	40.7	184	102
1971	47	214	82.6	121.3	1,495	139	9.5	39.5[7]	162	100
1972	44	212	92.3	129.6	1,505	142	8.3	39.9	154	101
1973	40	215	147	144	1,535	144	8.2	39.2	153	103
1974	39	214	113	157	1,557	146	7.4	39.9	140	108
1975	30	212	95.8	145	1,573	138	6.5	33.0	125	107

U.K.: United Kingdom

See p. 460 for footnotes

E16 **Output of Cotton Yarn** (in thousands of metric tons)

NOTES

1. SOURCES:– The official publications noted on p. xv with gaps filled from League of Nations and United Nations, *Statistical Yearbooks,* and Russian statistics to 1945 and in 1950 taken from G.W. Nutter, *The Growth of Industrial Production in the Soviet Union* (Princeton, 1962).

2. Except as indicated in footnotes, tyre cord yarns are excluded, and yarn made from waste and from mixed fibres of more than 50 per cent cotton are included.

FOOTNOTES

[1] Subsequently including tyre cord yarn.
[2] Alsace-Lorraine is excluded from 1941 to June 1945.
[3] The following statistics are available for Germany before 1914 (in thousands of tons): 1907 359; 1908 355; 1909 369.
[4] Prior to 1935 and from 1946 to 1959 Saarland is excluded.
[5] Previously mixed yarns of less than 50 per cent cotton are included.
[6] Excluding yarn made from waste.
[7] The cause of this break is not given.
[8] May-December.
[9] There were substantial territorial changes in 1945.
[10] April–December.
[11] Figures to 1934 are for Catalonia only.
[12] **Including tyre cord yarn.**
[13] **Subsequently including yarns of mixed fibres, including tyre cord yarns of these materials.**

E17 OUTPUT OF COTTON TISSUES (in units shown)

1920–1975

	Austria	Belgium	France	Germany	Greece	Italy	Netherlands	Portugal	Spain	Sweden
	Thousands of metric tons									
1920	...	...	...	...	...	...	...	...	...	...
1921	...	...	...	...	...	94	...	...	...	...
1922	...	...	...	...	...	101	...	...	...	...
1923	...	...	...	...	...	105	...	...	...	...
1924	...	...	...	...	...	122	...	...	...	...
1925	...	...	...	...	...	134	...	...	...	...
1926	...	...	...	...	...	130	...	...	...	...
1927	...	...	...	...	...	116	...	...	...	...
1928	...	63.1	177	288	...	126	...	...	...	14.9
1929	...	61.4	181	...	...	135	...	...	...	14.9
1930	...	49.0	177	...	20	110	...	...	...	15.7
1931	...	45.0	148	...	22	95	...	...	...	14.1
1932	...	38.7	145	...	22	95	...	...	...	18.1
1933	...	38.6	167	284	24	110	...	...	...	15.7
1934	86.9	34.0	138	...	27	103	...	...	...	18.1
1935	93.0	51.0	138	...	27	104	...	...	...	18.6
1936	99.8[1]	51.9	158	271[3]	27	84	...	...	...	20.0
	12.0			204						
1937	13.0	53.2	151	...	29	90	...	...	...	20.1
1938	12.0	49.5	149	222	28	94	57.0	16.8	...	19.9
1939	...	...	...	...	40	85	...	...	...	20.2
1940	...	...	...	...	...	75	...	17.5	42.7	20.7
1941	...	...	...	...	...	27	...	19.1	36.0	14.4[8]
1942	...	...	...	...	...	10	...	17.9	49.0	15.4
1943	...	...	...	...	...	9	...	14.4	63.4	13.9
1944	...	...	...	...	...	1	...	15.5	55.8	13.8
				West Germany						
1945	...	...	31	...	19	[7][4]	...	19.8	64.5	17.5
1946	...	54.7	101	28	30	82	30.9	23.3	73.8	18.5
1947	5.6	68.7	134	51	45	100	44.5	23.0	51.6	18.3
1948	8.4	62.7	150	76	55	113	45.5	25.7	56.4	20.3
1949	12.1	59.5	155	145	61	110	53.0	24.6	51.5	22.0
1950	13.4	73.5	195	189	92	118	58.9	28.8	50.0	23.5
1951	14.4	79.1	206	217	98	123	60.1	27.3	45.2	23.7[7]
										23.4
1952	12.0	61.9	192	209	87	112	55.0	30.1	55.3	21.9
1953	12.8	66.6	202	238	96	108	59.9	30.3	52.0	21.9
1954	13.8	77.1	218	252	110	115	63.5	34.5	46.1	22.8
1955	15.1	74.1	193	259	99	101	62.9	35.1	45.9	23.0
1956	15.5	79.6	197	277	105	106	64.8	34.5	47.9[7]	23.0
									69.6	
1957	16.8	84.6	226	287	119	117	66.0	34.5	67.7	24.2
1958	17.6	67.2	234	274	124[1]	114[5]	60.6	35.5	71.7	23.5[7]
					14					
1959	16.7	74.7	225	275	13	126	63.3	36.5	69.6	22.6
1960	18.4	84.4	240	289	15	139	71.3	40.4	79.1[7]	22.6
									92.6	
1961	19.7	81.6	236	280[3]	17	136	70.3	42.2	102.1	22.8
				238						
1962	18.8	79.4	233	223	18	143	65.7[6]	42.2	108.3	22.0
							62.9			
1963	18.7	82.3	233	208	19	146	63.1	46.1	104.0	19.8
1964	18.9	85.8	231[2]	206	19	135	64.5	49.4	109.5	20.6
			242							
1965	19.1	75.4	210	206	24	103	58.5	52.2	109.3	19.0
1966	20.4	74.0	224	199	22	133	55.2	51.3	119.5	16.8
1967	18.6	68.4	210	178	22	128	52.6	52.5	122.9	15.4
1968	18.3	68.7	199	186	23	120	48.5	57.3	104.9	14.2
1969	19.0	70.8	206	190	23	117	47.6	56.2	119.5	13.1
1970	17.9	70.3	197	182	19	115	44.6	44.9	120.7	11.0
1971	17.9	71.7	197	179	21	109	38.2	50.5	119.4	10.0
1972	18.8	73.8	205	189	24	108	37.1	50.5	123.3	9.1
1973	16.6	72.5	208	188	25	111	36.9	66.3	129.9	9.3
1974	15.6	67.7	205	182	28	119	38.2	61.0	132.5	8.8
1975	13.7	55.1	175	166	30	109	29.7	53.2	128.0	7.6

See p. 463 for footnotes

E17 Output of Cotton Tissues (in units shown)

1913–1975

	millions of linear metres					millions of square metres			
	Bulgaria	Czech	Poland	Russia	UK	E Germany	Hungary	Romania	Yugoslavia
1913	...	...	...	2,582	...	...	...	...	...
1917	...	...	...	1,205	...	...	...	...	...
1918	...	...	...	932	...	...	...	...	...
1919	...	...	...	153	...	...	...	...	...
1920	...	...	...	120	...	...	...	...	...
1921	...	...	...	151	...	...	...	...	...
1922	...	...	...	347	...	...	...	...	...
1923	...	...	...	642	...	...	...	...	...
1924	...	...	...	923	...	...	...	...	...
1925	...	...	...	1,678	...	...	...	...	...
1926	...	...	...	2,273	...	...	...	...	...
1927	...	...	...	2,480	...	...	...	...	...
1928	...	...	42.6	2,678	...	...	...	...	...
1929	...	...	36.3	2,996	...	...	...	...	...
1930	...	...	32.6[7]	2,351	...	...	...	...	...
			40.1						
1931	...	...	35.1	2,242	...	...	...	...	...
1932	...	...	30.4	2,694	...	...	...	...	...
1933	...	...	36.1	2,732	...	...	...	...	...
1934	...	43.6[9]	41.0	2,733	...	...	...	...	...
1935	...	...	45.1	2,640	2,805	...	...	...	...
1936	...	...	49.7	3,270	...	...	...	...	...
1937	...	...	51.5	3,448	3,328	...	...	...	...
1938	...	...	...	3,460	...	...	...	104	111
1939	34	...	...	3,763	...	...	...	...	...
1940	...	...	...	3,954	...	...	...	...	...
1941	...	...	...	...	1,966	...	...	...	...
1942	...	...	...	...	1,620	...	...	...	...
1943	...	...	...	...	1,640	...	...	...	...
1944	...	...	...[10]	...	1,507	...	...	...	...
1945	...	...	[11][11]	1,616	1,407	...	...	...	...
1946	...	...	207	1,901	1,487	...	...	...	89
1947	...	...	258	2,541	1,484	...	...	...	148
1948	58	264	349	3,150	1,768	...	147	91	161
1949	...	318	406	3,601	1,833	...	166	...	153
1950	83	347	436	3,899	1,941	74	177	140	146
1951	94	363	468	4,768	2,014	122	204	173	123
1952	106	359	468	5,044	1,546	153	212	200	112
1953	114	328	494	5,285	1,704	169	207	197	132
1954	119	329	521	5,589	1,823	198	224	210	166
1955	132	342	561	5,904	1,629	201	234	243	174
1956	142	351	556	5,456	1,474	211	181	192	183
1957	153	370	570	5,587	1,493	205	208	188	207
1958	170	404	599	5,788	1,307	217	218	207	219
1959	209	424	637	6,149	1,223	241	226[7]	218	229
							213		
1960	218	446	667	6,387	1,183	254	225	248	257
1961	227	467	710	6,425[12]	1,129	264	247	282	269
				5,246					
1962	243	478	693	5,300	957	289	265	299	312
1963	251	467	696	5,478	927	267	275	301	348
1964	269	463	761	5,814	946	250	293	302	378
1965	291	478	811	5,975	928	244	305	319	394
1966	299	494	844	6,173	837	244	317	339	416
1967	307	492	823	6,426	681	247	313	357	378
1968	319	480	834	6,638	668	250	290	377	401
1969	335	469	845	6,725	662	237	270	410	415
1970	319	501	881	6,653	628	248	258	437	390
1971	324	524	904	6,934	559	244	267	482	391
1972	323	537	901	6,984	513	242	275	531	374
1973	333	548	868	7,137	453	243	308	571	361
1974	347	594	884	7,196	410	248	318	612	365
1975	372	592	928	7,240	405	246	317	591	376

Czech: Czechoslovakia UK: United Kingdom E Germany: East Germany

See p. 463 for footnotes

E17 Output of Cotton Tissues

NOTES

1. SOURCES:— The official publications noted on p. xv with gaps filled from League of Nations and United Nations, *Statistical Yearbooks* and O.E.C.D., *Statistical Bulletins,* and Russian statistics to 1934 taken from G.W. Nutter, *The Growth of Industrial Production in the Soviet Union* (Princeton, 1962).

2. Except as indicated in footnotes, fabrics of mixed fibres with cotton predominating are included in this table.

FOOTNOTES

[1] Previous figures are in million square metres.
[2] Subsequent figures include cloth of mixed fibres, which has previously been excluded.
[3] Figures for 1928, 1933, and 1936 (1st line) are of total output in cotton factories. Figures from 1936 (2nd line) to 1961 (1st line) are of cotton yarn input to weaving mills. From 1961 (2nd line) the figures are of output of cloth containing 50 per cent or more of cotton.
[4] May—December.
[5] Figures to 1958 do not include cloth of mixed fibres.
[6] Figures to 1962 (1st line) are of cotton and mixed yarn input to weaving mills.
[7] The reason for this break is not given.
[8] Previous statistics are known to be not quite complete.
[9] This figure is in thousands of metric tons.
[10] Previous statistics are in thousands of metric tons. There were substantial territorial changes in 1945.
[11] April—December.
[12] Subsequent statistics are in million square metres.

E18 RAW WOOL CONSUMPTION INDICATORS (in thousands of metric tons)

1772–1819

	Germany	United Kingdom[1]	
	O	O	NI
1772	...	...	0.7
1773	...	...	0.7
1774	...	...	1.0
1775	...	36	0.7
1776	...		0.9
1777	...		1.3
1778	...		0.2
1779	...		0.3
1780	...		0.8
1781	...		1.1
1782	...		0.5
1783	...		1.2
1784	...		0.7
1785	...		1.4
1786	...	average	0.7
1787	...	41	1.9
1788	...		1.9
1789	...		1.2
1790	...		1.5
1791	...		1.3[1]
1792	...		2.0
1793	...		0.9
1794	...		2.0
1795	...		2.2
1796	...		1.6
1797	...		2.1
1798	...		1.1
1799	...		2.3
1800	...		3.8
1801	...		3.4
1802	...		3.5
1803	...		2.7
1804	...		3.7
1805	...		3.9
1806	...		3.3
1807	...		5.3
1808	...		1.1
1809	...	average	3.1
1810	...	45	5.0
1811	...		2.2
1812	...		3.2
1813	...		...
1814	...		7.1
1815	...		6.8
1816	11.1		3.7[1]
			3.4
1817	...		6.4
1818	...		11.2
1819	12.6		7.3

Abbreviations used throughout this table:— O=Output I=Imports NI=Net Imports C=Consumption

See p. 468 for footnotes

E18 Raw Wool Consumption Indicators (in thousands of metric tons)

1820–1869

	Austria/Hungary		Belgium	France	Germany	Italy		United Kingdom	
	O	NI	I	C	O	O	I	O	NI
1820	...	...	...	...	...	...	...		4.4
1821	...	...	...	...	...	...	...		7.4
1822	...	...	...	...	14.3	...	...	average 50	8.6
1823	...	...	...	...	...	...	...		8.7
1824	...	...	...	...	...	...	...		10.1
1825	...	...	...	...	17.0	...	...		19,5
1826	...	...	...	...	...	...	...		6.8
1827	...	...	...	...	...	...	...	average 52	12.8
1828	...	...	...	...	18.1	...	...		13.2
1829	...	...	...	...	...	...	...		9.0
1830	...	...	...	...	...	...	...		13.0
1831	...	...	...	...	17.8	...	...		12.3
1832	...	...	...	...	...	...	...	average 54	10.6
1833	...	...	...	...	...	...	...		14.8
1834	...	...	...	...	19.5	...	...		19.7
1835		...	...	...	...	...	...		15.2
1836		...	...	...	...	...	...		27.1
1837		...	...	...	23.5	...	...	average 54	19.5
1838		...	...	...	...	...	...		20.3
1839	average 31	...	...	...	...	...	...		23.6
1840		...	2.9	...	25.9	...	...		19.8
1841		...	3.9	...	...	...	...		20.5
1842		−3.3	4.1	...	...	...	...	average 57	15.3
1843		−3.1	3.8	...	26.5	...	...		17.2
1844		−4.5	3.9	...	...	...	...		24.9
1845		−4.1	4.7	...	...	...	...		29.5
1846		−1.8	3.4	...	27.9	...	...		25.6
1847		−2.8	4.1	...	...	...	...	average 59	23.7
1848		−1.7	3.3	...	...	...	...		27.4
1849	average 27	...	4.6	...	27.7	...	...		24.1
1850		0.2	4.2	...	...	...	...		21.7
1851		1.3	5.2	...	...	...	...		27.7
1852		11	5.7	...	28.9	...	...	average 61	31.1
1853		−4.3[2]	5.6	...	...	...	...		45.8
1854		6.7	5.9	...	...	...	...		31.2
1855		0.9	8.3	...	27.0	...	...		24.3
1856		−2.5	10.3	...	...	...	...		34.1
1857		2.5	11.2	...	...	...	...	average 64	35.5
1858		−1.3	10.2	...	28.1	...	...		39.2
1859	average 29	−4.6	13.2	...	...	...	...		43.2
1860		−1.3	14.0	...	...	...	...		48.2
1861		0.2	16.4	...	32.5	8.0	8.2		35.0
1862		−3.2	18.6	99	...	7.7	3.7	average 66	51.5
1863		−7.1	14.4	...	...	7.0	3.5		47.8
1864		−5.8	20.9	...	36.6	6.6	4.9		65.0
1865		−7.2	28.0	...	...	6.4	4.9	68	54.7
1866		−5.7	29.9	...	...	6.2	4.6	66	74.0
1867	average 35	2.7	35.1	...	36.2	6.4	6.7	74	83.5
1868		−0.1	47.4	...	...	6.5	4.6	78	62.6
1869		0.9	47.0	...	...	6.7	6.7	75	58.7

See p. 468 for footnotes

E18 Raw Wool Consumption Indicators (in thousands of metric tons)

1870–1919

	Austria/Hungary		Belgium	France	Germany		Italy		United Kingdom	
	O	NI	I	C	O	NI	O	I	O	NI
1870		1.1	41.7	...[5]	...[5]	...	7.0	4.7	72	73.3
1871		4.7	52.5	...	...	...	7.5	4.4	69	79.9
1872	average	6.6	53.4	...	34.2	...	7.8	6.0	71	73.2
1873	35	−4.5	53.4	...	...	...	8.0	5.2	75	85.3
1874		3.4	51.1	...	...	...	8.2	6.3	76	86.2
1875		1.8	45.8	163	...	...	8.4	6.8	74	82.8
1876		3.9	51.9	...	...	...	8.7	8.4	71	94.3
1877		7.1	49.0	...	...	...	9.1	8.2	69	96.6
1878		10.8	46.5	...	...	...	9.5	6.5	69	87.8
1879	average	11.7	43.3	...	...	...	9.6	8.5	69	71.7
1880	22	7.3	49.3	173	...	53.4	9.7	7.3	68	94.8
1881		12.1	45.5	...	...	65.3	9.9	9.5	63	77.3
1882		15.4	57.0	168	30.1	75.1	9.9	7.5	59	95.6
1883		13.6	48.4	...	...	78.2	10.7	9.5	58	90.4
1884		15.8	36.4	...	...	93.8	10.6	10.1	60	105
1885		13.8	43.8	200	...	88.7	10.4	11.1	62	97
1886		9.5	39.2	227	...	95.7	10.2	12.1	62	119
1887		19.6	44.4	211	...	100.9	10.1	11.1	61	109
1888		15.2	38.1	205	...	118.7	9.9	9.4	61	126
1889	average	15.4	44.2	218	...	129.0	9.8	9.8	60	143
1890	20	16.1	35.0	210	...	119.6	9.7	8.2	63	124
1891		19.7	42.2	227	...	136.6	9.6	9.0	67	145
1892		21.8	32.8	230	23.8	151.4	10.0	9.8	69	134
1893		20.1	44.9	237	...	139.7	9.7	8.9	69	143
1894		23.7	37.8	241	...	150.3	9.6	9.4	64	157
1895		23.7	48.5	230	...	172.0	9.8	12.4	61	158
1896		23.5	49.3	266	...	161.1	10.1	10.8	62	166
1897		22.9	41.8	243	...	152.8	10.3	10.9	63	149
1898		24.1	46.3	262	...	167.8	10.6	10.2	63	183
1899	average	22.9	62.4	265	...	168.6	10.7	13.4	64	160
1900	19	21.7	42.0	203	18.3	130.2	10.8	12.7	64	203
1901		26.7	53.4	262	...	140.7	11.0	14.5	63	171
1902		31.0	55.2	241	...	150.4	11.2	16.9	62	145
1903		27.8	53.9	243	...	155.0	11.4	15.4	60	129
1904		30.4	52.8	214	15.8	158.6	12.0	15.6	60	125
1905		26.8	63.9	221	15.9	154.3	12.6	14.9	59	139
1906		29.6	61.2	244	15.9	162.0	13.2	16.3	59	158
1907		33.1	67.2	244	16.2	171.7	13.9	18.5	59	190
1908		35.7	59.5	231	15.7	166.6	14.5	21.2	61	163
1909	average	40.3	59.6	276	15.3	178.7	15.0	22.0	64	161
1910	19	40.5	161.3	273	14.8	181.5	15.4	23.3	65	196
1911		42.2	154.2	271	14.2	183.4	15.6	23.2	62	211
1912		42.0	156.8	255	13.6	200.7	15.8	27.2	...	193
1913		33.5	149[4] 50	266	13.3	182.2	15.7	28.6	...	214
1914	...	36.4	...	210	...	...	15.6	20.8	...	174
1915	...	...	...	88	...	...	15.6	60.8	...	354
1916	...	...	...	93	...	...	15.5	61.4	...	257
1917	...	...	...	78	...	...	15.5	41.1	...	268
1918	...	...	...	60[4]	...	...	15.9	42.8	average	180
1919	...	...	...	174	...	...	16.4	33.6	48	390

See p. 468 for footnotes

E18 Raw Wool Consumption Indicators (in thousands of metric tons)

1920–1975

	Belgium	France	Germany		Italy		United Kingdom	
	I	C	O	NI	O	I	O	NI
1920	...	168	...	...	16.4	33.1		288
1921	...	155	...	...[7]	16.5	22.2	average	178
1922	33	305	...	191	16.7	45.7	48	273
1923	51	260	...	133	16.9	42.3		124
1924	49	225	14.3	147	17.0	42.1	48	160
1925	43	246	11.9	134	17.2	41.7	50	153
1926	52	286	10.2	147	17.3	53.2	52	191
1927	62	303	9.6	208	17.0	47.8	54	190
1928	57	269	9.1	171	16.1	59.7	52	180
1929	68	199	8.7	169	15.2	64.7	51	182
1930	65	306	8.1	156	14.4	60.3	50	210
1931	47	250	8.1	141	13.6	53.9	51	250
1932	39	254	8.1	144	13.0	77.3	54	254
1933	36	301	8.0	158	12.6	91.8	54	243
1934	30	193	8.1	143	12.4	71.8	52	217
1935	55	221	9.1	124	12.3	57.5	49	239
1936	63	197	10.1	103	11.5	21.0	49	269
1937	64	194	11.1	103	11.8	45.1	49	235
1938	65	232	12.1	139[7]	12.3	37.7	50	265
1939	...	207	12.1	...	12.8	32.1	51[6] / 31	305
1940	...	118	...	...	13.0	22.6	41	784
1941	...	...	...	...	12.8	2.9	36	141
1942	...	...	...	...	12.2	0.9	33	185
1943	...	...	...	...	10.2	...	28	121
1944	...	...	...	...	9.1	...	27	230
			West Germany					
	C[6]			C[6]		C[6]		
1945	...	56	...	...	8.7	...	26	188
1946	...	280	...	...	9.6	...	28	158
1947	38	215	...	14	11.2	59	23	202[10] / 186
1948	30	190	...	21[8]	13.6	62	23	219
1949	32	179	5.1	41	16.0	54	25	223
1950	37	190[6] / 115	4.1	58	16.0	57	26	235
1951	28	90	4.2	53	15.5	44	25	180
1952	26	97	3.9	60	15.1	57	28	172
1953	32	114	3.4	70	15.0	60	29	221
1954	29	116	3.1	69	14.2	54	32	209
1955	29	111	3.0	76	13.8	51	30	216
1956	35	126	2.9	80	12.2	58	31	216
1957	37	141	2.9	82	12.2	73	34	218
1958	33	113	2.9	63	12.5	68	35	202
1959	36	121	2.9[9] / 4	68	12.7	75	38	231
1960	40	129	4	69	12.7	90	35	218
1961	38	127	4	68	12.7	85	39	214
1962	46	123	4	67	12.3	93	39	203
1963	44	125	4	70	12.3	89	37	208
1964	43	111	4	65	12.0	84	38	190
1965	44	107	3	66	12.0	86	38	183
1966	43	119	3	68	12.3	110	39	176
1967	36	98	3	56	12.2	99	39	163
1968	40	109	3	67	11.9	96	36	178
1969	42	121	3	75	12.0	107	31	175
1970	40	125	3	68	11.7	93	31	153
1971	30	136	3	74	11.3	88	31	141
1972	31	138 / 146[11]	2	77	11.0	97 / 103[11]	31	152
1973	23	117	2	54	11.1	93	32	137
1974	20	105	2	39	11.4	87	33	113
1975	24	107	2	56	11.6	88	33	111

See p. 468 for footnotes

E18 **Raw Wool Consumption Indicators** (in thousands of metric tons)

NOTES

1. SOURCES:– Germany, output to 1959 – W.G. Hoffman, *Das Wachstum der Deutschen Wirtschaft seit der Mitte des 19 Jahrhunderts* (Berlin, etc., 1965). U.K., output to 1927 and net imports to 1938 – B.R. Mitchell & Phyllis Deane, *Abstract of British Historical Statistics* (Cambridge, 1962), where the original sources are given. All other statistics are taken from the official publications noted on p. xv with gaps filled from League of Nations, *International Trade Statistics* and *Statistical Yearbooks* and United Nations *Statistical Yearbooks.*

2. Except as indicated in footnotes, the output figures relate to the weight unwashed, and the trade figures to all kinds of unmanufactured wool and animal hair. Belgian import statistics include wool tops.

FOOTNOTES

[1] Figures to 1791 apply to England and Wales only. From 1792 to 1816 (1st line) they apply to Great Britain. Trade with Ireland is included in these two periods.

[2] Previous statistics are for years ended 31 October. This figure is for 14 months ended 31 December 1853.

[3] T.J. Markovitch, *L'industrie francaise de 1789 à 1964* (Cahiers de l'I.S.E.A., 1966) gives the following estimates of average raw wool consumption for periods before the continuous official series begins (in thousands of tons):–

1781–90	36.0	1825–34	66.5	1855–64	110.4
1803–12	44.0	1835–44	81.7	1865–74	146.8
1815–24	53.8	1845–54	90.6	1875–84	183.9

[4] Subsequent figures are of net imports.

[5] From 1871 to 1918 Alsace-Lorraine is included in Germany rather than France.

[6] Subsequent statistics are of virgin clean wool only.

[7] Figures for 1922–1938 are of gross imports, but exports were very small.

[8] Figures for 1947–48 are for the British and American Occupation Zones only.

[9] The reason for this break is not given.

[10] **Subsequent statistics are of the consumption of virgin clean wool.**

[11] **Subsequently including consumption outside the wool industry.**

E19 OUTPUT OF WOOL YARN (in thousands of metric tons)

1925–1975

	Austria	Belgium	Bulgaria	Czechoslovakia	France	Germany	East Germany	Greece	Hungary
1925	...	...	...	...	...	123	...	...	...
1926	...	...	...	...	...	...	...	...	...
1927	...	...	...	...	...	...	...	...	...
1928	...	...	...	...	...	136	...	...	...
1929	...	...	0.4	...	...	...	...	...	...
1930	...	...	0.9	...	...	...	...	0.5	...
1931	...	...	0.6	...	...	...	...	0.4	...
1932	...	...	0.6	...	...	...	...	0.5	...
1933	...	...	0.5	...	...	136	...	0.6	...
1934	...	...	0.4	35.0	...	...	...	0.7	...
1935	...	...	0.3	...	...	133	...	0.7	...
1936	...	...	0.5	15.9	...	138	...	1.1	...
1937	13.5	...	0.6	27.2	...	155	...	0.9	...
1938	10.8	25.8	...	...	118	177	...	0.8	11.6
1939	...	...	0.8	...	...	...	...	1.8	...
1940	...	...	...	...	...	...	...	0.9	...
1941	...	...	...	...	...	...	...	0.9	...
1942	...	...	...	...	[43][1]	...	...	...	...
1943	...	...	...	...	[33][1]	...	...	...	...
1944	...	...	...	...	20	...	...	...	...
						West Germany			
1945	...	...	...	...	39	...	...	...	...
1946	...	30.9	...	...	92	20	...	2.0	1.8
1947	3.8	42.3	...	29.5	116	28	...	2.0	6.0
1948	6.8	34.1	5.2	32.0	132	38	...	2.7	7.9
1949	9.3	35.6	6.2	35.4	123	65	...	3.4	8.3
1950	11.0	40.2	7.0	34.4	127	92	9.8	6.2	12.1
1951	11.5	34.1	6.7	32.3	120	95	14.2	5.1	13.7
1952	9.3	29.8	7.7	35.2	110	90	14.1	4.5	11.7
1953	10.5	37.6	8.3	31.8	120	106	20.1	5.0	8.7
1954	10.9	38.8	8.7	29.2	128	105	27.1	4.1	11.4
1955	11.8	41.6	9.4	32.2	129	115	19.5	3.8	13.4
1956	12.4	45.3	11.1	31.8	142	118	21.5	4.1	9.8
1957	12.2	47.1	11.0	33.0	154	124	20.9[5]	4.7	12.1
							69.0		
1958	10.4	38.1	11.7	37.2	134	106	73.0	4.8	13.1
1959	11.5	46.5	15.6	38.5	136	113	79.7	7.3	13.0
1960	12.5	50.8	16.4	39.3	143	118	80.1	10.0	14.9
1961	13.4	54.1	15.5	41.1	147	114	78.0	9.4	15.7
1962	13.6	58.6	16.3	42.0	146	114	79.1	9.4	16.5
1963	13.8	64.4	17.4	40.9	158	115	76.0	11.0	16.7
1964	13.2	62.3	17.3	40.1	147	117	73.3	11.7	16.9
1965	12.9	64.6	17.4	41.7	130	120[2]	71.7	8.2	16.7
						91			
1966	13.7	69.7	18.4	42.9	146	91	70.9	9.5	17.6
1967	12.5	61.0	19.6	42.9	127	70	71.0	8.9	18.0
1968	12.8	72.6	20.6	42.5	130	79	66.9	7.5	16.4
1969	13.5	81.3	23.1	43.2	145	87	67.3	8.3	14.7
1970	12.3	81.2	24.3	45.5	143	79	68.2	11.1	14.2
1971	12.3	90.3	25.4	47.3	152	85	64.4	10.7	14.7
1972	12.4	89.1	27.1	48.1	155	87	62.4	12.4	13.5
1973	12.0	84.0	29.0	49.3	152	65	62.8	10.7	13.2
1974	10.3	78.7	30.5	50.3	143	55	58.7	10.9	11.8
1975	8.8	71.2	31.5	54.2	135	51	62.4	15.4	10.1

See p. 471 for footnotes

E19 **Output of Wool Yarn** (in thousands of metric tons)

1925–1975

	Italy	Netherlands	Poland	Romania	Russia[4]	Spain	Sweden	U.K.	Yugoslavia
1925	...	...	...	...	29	...	...	...	...
1926	...	...	...	...	36	...	...	...	...
1927	...	...	...	...	44	...	...	...	...
1928	...	...	31.8	...	50	...	10.5	...	...
1929	...	...	29.8	...	57	...	10.3	...	...
1930	...	...	23.2	...	71	...	10.2	...	...
1931	...	8.5	25.3	...	73	...	8.7	...	...
1932	...	8.4	21.3	...	71	...	9.6	230	...
1933	...	9.1	23.6	...	68	...	10.8	228	...
1934	...	8.4	26.4	...	61	...	12.6	239	...
1935	...	7.0	30.1	...	66	...	12.3	...	...
1936	...	8.5	33.0	...	73	...	13.3	...	...
1937	...	9.4	34.2	...	77	...	14.0	249	...
1938	71	9.7	...	7.0	80	...	10.5	212	...
1939	...	14.0	...	...	90	...	11.7	...	6.2
1940	...	15.0	...	...	83	14.7	15.1	...	...
1941	...	13.3	...	...	...	14.9	11.9[6]	...	...
1942	...	9.6	...	...	...	15.1	12.6	...	...
1943	...	7.4	...	...	...	15.2	12.6	...	...
1944	...	...	...	...	...	15.0	13.5	...	...
1945	...	...	[7.6][3]	...	40	13.5	15.6	...	...
1946	60	15.0	22.2	...	50	17.5	16.8	184	8.9
1947	83	19.0	23.8	...	64	16.8	16.8	200	10.8
1948	83	21.9	33.2	8.2	82	13.6	18.7	228	13.0
1949	93	23.5	38.6	...	96	8.8	18.8	240	13.3
1950	108	23.7	41.9	12.8	102	10.0[5] / 11.3	18.3	252	13.9
1951	103	18.7	45.8	15.6	115	8.3	16.1	227	13.4
1952	106	19.7	44.4	15.6	125	10.7	13.4	206	10.3
1953	115	21.8	50.2	17.0	137	13.8	15.8	243	7.7
1954	124	23.1	50.1	16.9	159	11.6	14.9	244	8.7
1955	129	23.9	52.0	17.7	168	12.5	14.1	244	10.7
1956	130	24.9	53.0	17.3	180	13.8	14.1	241	12.2
1957	146[2] / 112	24.1	54.7	17.4	188	13.7	15.1	244	14.8
1958	107	21.8	56.5	17.5	201	14.1	13.7	224	16.7
1959	134	24.9	58.6	17.2	213	12.2	12.9	247	17.3
1960	161	24.5	58.5	19.4	221	13.0[5] / 19.3	13.2	249	20.6
1961	156	24.7	60.3	21.9	232	24.6	12.6	239	19.8
1962	168	24.6	62.4	20.5	241	25.7	12.5	236	19.3
1963	172	25.9	59.7	22.5	243	27.5	12.2	251	26.4
1964	165	25.0	63.9	24.1	236	29.0	12.2	254	26.7
1965	159	23.2	65.5	24.8	236	31.0	10.7	249	31.8
1966	192	24.0	69.2	26.3	258	31.7	9.7	243	35.2
1967	178	20.9	75.1	28.3	282	32.3	9.4	228	32.1
1968	173	20.7[7] / 15	77.7	30.4	302	32.9	8.2	246	29.6
1969	173	17	81.6	32.3	322	36.9	7.2	243	33.9
1970	167	16	84.4	35.7	350	36.5	5.1	227	37.9
1971	166	14	87.7	38.4	371	37.4	4.4	224	39.4
1972	180	15	87.4	41.5	377	37.0	4.0	232	42.4
1973	200[3] / 54	14	88.8	46.0	393	37.3	3.0	235	41.9
1974	49	12	92.3	49.2	408	34.0	2.6	210	40.4
1975	50	11	102.7	50.6	417	28.5	2.4	188	41.8

U.K.: United Kingdom

See p. 471 for footnotes

E19 **Output of Wool Yarn** (in thousands of metric tons)

NOTES

1. SOURCES:– The official publications noted on p. xv with gaps filled from League of Nations and United Nations, *Statistical Yearbooks,* and the Russian statistics to 1936 taken from G.W. Nutter, *The Growth of Industrial Production in the Soviet Union* (Princeton, 1962).

2. In principle, the output of mixed yarn with more than 50 per cent wool content is included in this table.

FOOTNOTES

[1] Excluding Alsace-Lorraine.

[2] Certain mixed yarns are not subsequently included.

[3] April–December.

[4] G.W. Nutter, *op. cit.* in note 1, gives the following figures for earlier years, the first figure for 1913 applying to the Russian Empire and the second to the U.S.S.R. territory of 1923:–

1893	18	1908	70	1913	110 / 47
1895	29	1910	74	1918	25
1900	55	1911	75	1919	10
1905	65	1912	82		

[5] The reason for this break is not given. The figure for 1950 comparable to the later series for East Germany is 51.8

[6] Previous statistics do not include yarn spun on commission.

[7] Subsequently only yarns for industrial use.

E20 OUTPUT OF WOOL TISSUES (in units stated)

1925–1975

Thousands of metric tons

	Austria	Belgium	France	Germany	Italy	Netherlands	Portugal	Sweden
1925	...	...	...	...	...	...	...	...
1926	...	...	...	...	...	...	...	...
1927	...	...	...	...	...	...	...	...
1928	...	...	...	...	...	...	...	8.0
1929	...	...	...	...	...	...	...	8.1
1930	...	...	...	...	...	...	...	8.4
1931	...	...	...	...	...	...	...	7.2
1932	...	...	...	...	...	...	...	8.0
1933	...	...	...	...	...	...	...	8.3
1934	...	...	...	...	...	...	...	10.4
1935	...	...	...	...	...	...	...	10.2
1936	...	...	...	60.0	...	...	...	11.5
1937	10.8	...	...	...	...	...	...	11.6
1938	6.0	12.8	71.8	64.8	45.3	17.4	...	9.5
1939	...	...	...	...	...	...	...	10.7
1940	...	...	...	...	...	...	7.0	12.9
1941	...	...	...	...	...	...	8.0	10.4
1942	...	...	...	...	...	...	7.5	9.2
1943	...	...	...	...	...	...	5.0	9.5
1944	...	...	...	...	...	...	6.2	9.9
				West Germany				
1945	...	...	...	...	...	...	7.0	11.1
1946	...	19.5	46.5	13.2	39.9	17.0	7.2	12.3
1947	2.7	22.5	64.8	18.7	45.0	21.6	8.6	12.9
1948	4.3	19.4	77.0	25.6	49.4	25.8	9.7	14.2
1949	6.3	21.4	76.1	43.4	47.2	25.8	8.3[2]	15.1
							2.5	
1950	7.2	26.4	75.0	60.2	59.1	24.2	3.2	14.2
1951	7.8	25.0	72.2	65.1	51.5	20.2	4.1	13.8
1952	6.1	20.2	67.0	58.4	64.8	21.4	3.6	11.3
1953	5.2	24.2	62.6	68.1	64.4	23.2	4.2	13.3
1954	5.5	25.1	66.0	65.9	79.9	25.0	4.2	11.8
1955	5.9	28.5	63.5	71.7	77.7	26.7	4.1	11.0
1956	5.7	30.8	67.6	72.0	82.6	27.3	4.1	11.6
1957	5.2	30.0	76.6	74.8	85.8	26.3	4.3	11.2
1958	4.6	24.7	73.1	63.9	76.4	25.2	4.2	10.1
1959	4.6	29.2	67.7	67.1[1]	84.5	28.8[1]	4.5	10.6[3]
				162		71		6.6
1960	4.9	29.3	67.8	171	82.4	68	5.0	6.5
1961	5.1	33.4	69.2	169	78.6	70	4.9	6.0
1962	5.8	35.2	69.8	169	80.1	68	5.0	5.8
1963	6.2	36.3	77.2	151	77.4	71	5.5	5.3
1964	5.8	38.9	75.6	148	70.8	72	5.8	4.8
1965	5.7	38.3	60.1	157	52.5	67	6.0	4.6
1966	6.6	40.8	67.0	152	99.2	69[3]	5.9	3.8
						35		
1967	6.1	36.1	63.5	122	92.3	28	6.1	4.0
1968	6.8	35.0	54.4	142	98.2	30	6.8	3.9
1969	6.9	37.6	69.9	142	98.7	30	7.3	3.6
1970	6.0	39.2	63.6	126	99.6	27	8.3	2.7
1971	5.9	41.7	68.0	131	97.0	29	8.8	1.6
1972	6.6	43.9	71.3	141	107.5[8]	26	9.2	1.6
					147.6			
1973	6.8	37.3	71.6	124	165.9	24	10.7	1.0
1974	6.4	30.5	67.5	99	158.9	21	10.3	0.7
1975	5.7	30.1	63.2	99	...	19	8.3	0.5

See p. 474 for footnotes

E20 Output of Wool Tissues (in units stated)

1925–1975

	millions of linear metres				millions of square metres				
	Bulgaria	Czech	Poland	Russia[7]	E Germany	Hungary	Romania	U.K.	Yugoslavia
1925	...	...	...	...	...	...	...	...	...
1926	...	...	...	...	...	...	...	...	...
1927	...	...	...	103	...	...	...	...	...
1928	...	...	15.8	117	...	...	...	...	...
1929	...	...	11.7	129	...	...	...	...	...
1930	...	...	8.6[5] 14.4	115	...	...	...	...	...
1931	...	...	13.2	108	...	...	...	...	...
1932	...	...	10.3	89	...	...	...	...	...
1933	...	...	11.7	86	...	...	...	...	...
1934	...	12.1	14.5	78	...	...	...	...	...
1935	...	...	17.7	84	...	...	...	268	...
1936	...	7.8	21.6	102	...	...	...	...	...
1937	...	17.2	20.9	108	...	...	...	290	...
1938	...	...	...	113	...	20	12.3	...	...
1939	5.3	...	...	122	...	...	...	...	12.4
1940	...	...	...	120	...	...	...	...	...
1941	...	...	...	...	...	...	...	...	...
1942	...	...	...	...	...	...	...	...	...
1943	...	...	...	...	...	...	...	216	...
1944	...	...	...	...	...	...	...	178	...
1945	...	...	[5.1][6]	54	...	...	...	177	...
1946	...	...	23[4]	71	...	...	...	204	16
1947	...	19.6[4]	33	95	...	...	...	212	22
1948	5.4	40	42	124	...	20	11.8	244[2] 347	29
1949	...	48	50	149	...	23	...	367	26
1950	8.9	48	56	155	...	27	23	376	24
1951	8.2	47	61	176	...	31	28	350	23
1952	9.2	48	63	190	...	23	27	316	20
1953	10.4	40	71	209	...	16	29	344	17
1954	10.0	35	71	243	43	21	30	346	20
1955	11	39	76	252	32	26	31	343	26
1956	13	37	76	268	27	20	31	332	28
1957	13	38	76	284	29	24	29	330	34
1958	14	43	78	303	34	25	28	292	33
1959	19	46	80	326	43	24	28	305	38
1960	19	46	79	369	48	27	32	307	46
1961	17	48	78	382	49	29	37	295	43
1962	18	48	83	396	48	30	34	274	42
1963	19	46	84	403[1] 636	39	29	38	272	48
1964	19	43	90	618	39	30	41	272	53
1965	20	44	91	607	39	29	41	270	55
1966	22	45	91	669	40	31	44	253	58
1967	22	46	90	723	39	32	50	246	52
1968	23	45	94	774	36	36	52	246	50
1969	26	46	99	814	36	24	55	239	49
1970	27	49	99	849	37	27	63	215	57
1971	28	53	99	888	37	26	70	186	59
1972	29	57	100	890	37	24	74	184	59
1973	30	56	107	919	37	23	83	192	60
1974	33	63	117	940	37	24	94	175	66
1975	38	68	124	956	37	20	96	151	66

Czech' Czechoslovakia E Germany: East Germany U.K.: United Kingdom

See p. 474 for footnotes

E20 Output of Wool Tissues

NOTES

1. SOURCES:— The official publications noted on p. xv with gaps filled from League of Nations and United Nations, *Statistical Yearbooks,* and the Russian statistics to 1934 taken from G.W. Nutter, *The Growth of Industrial Production in the Soviet Union* (Princeton, 1962). The Czech figures for 1949 and 1950 were supplied by the Federal Statistical Office of Czechoslovakia.

2. Except as indicated in footnote 5, statistics in this table include cloths of mixed yarns in which wool predominates.

FOOTNOTES

[1] Subsequent statistics are in million square metres.
[2] Previous statistics are in million linear metres.
[3] The reason for this break is not given.
[4] Previous statistics are in thousands of metric tons.
[5] Previous statistics are of pure wool cloth only.
[6] April–December.
[7] G.W. Nutter, *op. cit.* in note 1, gives an estimate for 1913 for the 1923 territory of the U.S.S.R. of 105 million metres.
[8] Subsequently including woollen blankets.

E21 OUTPUT OF ARTIFICIAL AND SYNTHETIC FIBRES (in thousands of metric tons)

1910–1969

	Austria	Belgium	Czech	Finland	France	Germany	E Germany	Italy	Netherlands
1910	...	...	...	...	1.2	...		...	...
1911	...	...	...	...	...	...		...	...
1912	...	...	...	...	...	...		...	...
1913	0.7	1.4	...	...	2.9	2.1		0.2	...
1914	...	...	...	...	...	...		...	...
1915	...	...	...	...	...	...		...	...
1916	...	...	...	...	...	...		...	...
1917	...	...	...	...	...	...		...	...
1918	...	...	...	...	...	...		- -	...
1919	...	...	...	...	...	...		0.3	...
1920	...	...	...	...	1.5	...		0.7	...
1921	....	...	...	...	...	...		1.5	...
1922	0.7	3.0	0.3	...	2.9	5.0		2.6	1.1
1923	1.1	3.5	0.9	...	4.0	6.5		4.8	1.8
1924	1.0	4.0	0.6	...	6.0	10.5		10.5	2.0
1925	1.5	5.0	1.0	...	6.5	11.8		13.9	2.7
1926	1.3	6.0	0.9	...	7.9	11.2		16.7	4.5
1927	1.7	7.5	1.5	...	9.5	18.7		24.4	5.8
1928	1.5	6.6	1.7	...	13.6	22.2		25.0	6.8
1929	1.4	6.1	2.0	...	19.0	28.1		32.3	8.0
1930	0.8	5.8	2.3	...	23.2	29.3		30.1	8.0
1931	...	4.4	2.8	...	20.7	30.6		34.3	8.5
1932	0.4	4.3	2.6	...	24.0	28.2		32.5	9.0
1933	0.4	5.1	2.7	...	26.9	32.8		38.3	8.7
1934	0.9	5.9	3.6	...	27.9	46.2		48.7	9.9
1935	0.9	6.3	2.8	—	30.2	62.0		69.6	9.6
1936	0.9	6.6	3.4	—	30.0	88.3		89.0	10.0
1937	1.0	7.8	4.3	—	35.1	157		119	10.9
1938	1.1	5.8	2.7	- -	32.9	219		119	9.3
1939	5.9	6.8	2.7	0.8	32.5[2]	273		140	...
1940	20.8	6.2	5.4	0.2	26.6	308		163	...
1941	32.7	9.4	6.2	- -	49.3	373		181	...
1942	32.7	8.6	7.4	0.9	54.1	401		144	...
1943	31.8	12.3	13.1	2.5	55.1	401		102	12.0
1944	21.1	6.1	15.0	5.2	26.5	300		30.6	9.4
						West Germany[3]			
1945	1.5	5.0	3.6	3.6	22.4[2]		...	3.3	...
1946	2.3	20.3	12.5	5.4	46.4	21.8	...	42.9	9.5
1947	4.2	20.9	18.9	5.9	56.6	28.7	...	74.0	20.5
1948	10.8	21.6	22.4	6.3	74.4	103	44.2	65.8	25.8
1949	17.6	19.0	25.9	6.2	73.3	129	...	86.6	29.8
1950	32.8	23.1	26.2	7.8	84.1	163	87.4	104	33.3
1951	43.7	30.2	27.9	8.7	106.8	185	97.5	133	36.7
1952	32.7	19.4	32.8	9.3	77.7	144	106	79	32.8
1953	30.9	28.4	36.6	11.3	97.8	175[3]	114	110	38.1
1954	39.0	32.2	37.5	16.1	112	196	120	133	42.8
1955	41.9	33.1	49.1	17.0	121	229	123	140	46.3
1956	44.7	34.4	49.2	17.1	121	243	126	162	45.5
1957	50.3	36.7	47.7	19.9	140	258	138	162	47.8
1958	50.9	28.8	54.8	15.2	149	228	143	156	48.8
1959	55.8	30.9	58.0	14.1	142	262	147	181	52.6
1960	58.1	34.0	61.9	16.4	164	282	145	195	58.4
1961	51.4	37.0	68.0	18.5	175	296	151	216	60.4
1962	55.7	40.3	73.1	18.3	191	337	156	253	64.8
1963	60.5	42.1	75.5	22.1	223	373	157	278	75.5
1964	64.7	45.6	80.8	25.4	241	422	159	314	89.2
1965	67.9	49.3[1]	80.3	29.4	217	456	161	297	102.5
1966	66.3	55.7	85.3	33.4	235	493	173	324	110.4
1967	66.8	57.2	91.4	30.6	219	496	184	335	97.2
1968	76.4	57.9	91.9	35.4	249	622	189	387	113
1969	81.5	57.7	94.3	35.0	288	715	194	442	128

See p. 477 for footnotes

E21 Output of Artificial and Synthetic Fibres (in thousands of metric tons)

1910–1969

	Norway	Poland	Romania	Russia	Spain	Sweden	Switz	U.K.	Yugoslavia
1910	—	...	—	...	—	—	...	...	...
1911	—	...	—	...	—	—	...	...	...
1912	—	...	—	...	—	—	...	...	...
1913	—	...	—	...	—	—	0.1	5.2	...
1914	—	...	—	...	—	—	...	...	...
1915	—	...	—	...	—	—	...	...	...
1916	—	...	—	...	—	—	...	...	...
1917	—	...	—	...	—	—	...	...	...
1918	—	...	—	...	—	—	...	...	...
1919	—	...	—	...	—	—	...	...	...
1920	—	...	—	...	—	—	...	...	...
1921	—	...	—	...	—	—	...	...	...
1922	—	0.2	—	...	—	—	0.9	5.9	...
1923	—	0.4	—	...	—	..	1.7	6.9	...
1924	—	0.5	—	...	—	0.1	1.5	10.0	...
1925	—	0.6	—	...	—	0.1	2.4	12.2	...
1926	—	0.9	—	...	—	0.1	3.3	10.4	...
1927	—	1.6	—	...	—	0.1	4.1	15.8	...
1928	—	2.4	—	0.2	0.5	0.2	4.5	20.6	...
1929	—	2.6	—	...	0.9	0.2	4.6	21.4	...
1930	—	2.7	—	...	1.2	0.2	4.6	21.2	...
1931	—	3.6	—	...	1.4	0.3	4.6	23.8	...
1932	—	3.5	—	2.8	1.8	0.3	4.0	31.5	...
1933	—	3.8	—	...	2.5	0.3	4.2	36.6	...
1934	—	4.7	—	...	2.6	0.5	4.6	40.5	...
1935	—	5.7	—	...	3.2	0.7	3.7	53.9	...
1936	—	5.9	0.3	8.0	1.8	1.0	5.0	63.1	...
1937	0.1	7.5	0.6	8.6	1.4	2.1	5.5	67.3	...
1938	0.1	10.2[4]	0.8	0.9	0.9	2.5	5.5	61.1	...
1939	0.2	8.1	1.2	11.5	1.5	2.9	5.5	77.0	...
1940	0.3	11.8	0.9	11.1	3.1	3.6	5.5	76.7	...
1941	0.3	14.5	1.0	...	4.1	5.0	8.4	61.9	...
1942	0.5	17.2	1.2	...	5.5	8.4	15.6	54.9	...
1943	0.5	20.0	2.0	...	6.6	12.7	17.7	56.4	...
1944	0.5	16.8	1.1	...	8.3	16.5	18.2	60.1	...
1945	0.3	...	1.4	1.1	7.4	13.6	16.4	62.8	...
1946	2.4	8.7	1.3	3.2	14.8	14.9	16.7	80.9	...
1947	3.3	11.9	1.4	6.7	16.4	11.2	17.0	91.8	...
1948	7.1	18.0	1.3	11.1	16.4	12.1	17.5	106	...
1949	11.8	22.3	1.4	17.0	18.6	12.8	16.8	131	...
1950	13.5	24.9	1.4	24.2	24.5	14.1	17.3	168	...
1951	14.3	27.4	1.9	34.1[5]	23.6	17.4	18.8	174	...
1952	11.6	32.0	2.5	49.4	31.9	11.9	19.1	128	...
1953	14.4	41.3	2.2	62.3	32.3	14.0	22.6	190	...
1954	16.5	48.2	2.5	78.9	39.5	17.5	22.7	203	...
1955	15.7	54.0	2.6	110	46.9	18.5	24.7	214	...
1956	14.4	59.0	2.6	129	50.1	22.7	25.6	219	...
1957	16.1	62.9	2.7	149	51.5	26.1	25.5	225	—
1958	13.4	65.9	3.0	166	51.5	26.4	23.4	224	10.1
1959	14.5	68.6	3.4	180	49.4	28.6	26.0	234	19.7
1960	14.3	77.6	4.1	211	59.7	28.5	29.0	269	21.1
1961	12.9	82.5	4.6	251	52.9	30.8	29.9	259	19.8
1962	17.3	84.6	4.9	277	63.6	31.8	33.4	284	21.0
1963	20.3	87.3	5.7	309	72.2	31.9	38.3	326	21.1
1964	23.8	94.3	6.3	361	80.5	36.6	41.3	374	22.0
1965	26.0	102	20.9	408	71.8	38.4	47.5	391	22.2
1966	24.3	108	34.3	458	75.0	35.1	46.0	400[6]	28.6
1967	26.2	115	47.3	511	70.4	38.7	51.8	434	29.3
1968	29.4	122	53.6	554	88.2	38.7	58.0	539	36.5
1969	30.6	129	56.5	584	113	35.3	58.9	554	38.5

Switz: Switzerland U.K.: United Kingdom

See p. 477 for footnotes

E21 OUTPUT OF ARTIFICIAL AND SYNTHETIC FIBRES (in thousands of metric tons)

1970–1975

	Austria	Belgium	Czech.	Finland	France	W Germany	E Germany	Italy	Netherlands
1970	86.5	57.4	100	39.6	256	723	209	425	126
1971	102	56.9	109	38.8	345	785	210	488	142
1972	107	54.5	117	39.8	369	801	229	498	149
1973	116	54.5	125	38.5	400	980	255	547	...
1974	122	49.5	131	38.7	364	940	266	492	...
1975	101	23.1	140	30.1	293	734	282	411	...

	Norway	Poland	Romania	Russia	Spain	Sweden	Switz.	U.K.	Yugoslavia
1970	28.0	136	76.6	623	118	34.8	604	599	40.8
1971	28.2	149	95.3	676	137	36.4	70.1	613	54.7
1972	28.9	160	99.6	746	176	37.2	79.8	647	77.0
1973	29.4	176	116	830	200	36.8	80.8	731	84.1
1974	28.9	192	143	887	197	35.1	75.6	628	88.2
1975	18.4	207	148	855	171	19.6	75.9	563	82.4

NOTE

SOURCES.– The official publications noted on p. xv with gaps filled from the League of Nations and United Nations, *Statistical Yearbooks,* and from O.E.C.D., *Statistical Bulletins.*

FOOTNOTES

[1] Subsequently including tow for cigarette filters.
[2] From 1940 to 1945 Alsace-Lorraine is excluded.
[3] Figures for 1946–53 are of production for sale only.
[4] Subsequent figures apply to the boundaries established in 1945.
[5] Previously excluding synthetic fibres, which amounted to 2.3 thousand tons in 1953.
[6] Previously the statistics of continuous filament were of deliveries rather than output. The effect of the change is to raise the series by about 1 per cent.
[7] Subsequently excluding acetate fibres.

E22 LINEN INDUSTRY INDICATORS (in thousands of metric tons)

1760–1814

	France	U.K.[1]
	Flax & Hemp Input	Flax & Hemp Input
1760	...	26
1761	...	36
1762	...	38
1763	...	39
1764	...	41
1765	...	40
1766	...	37
1767	...	37
1768	...	41
1769	...	43
1770	...	47
1771	...	58[1]
1772	...	43
1773	...	43
1774	...	47
1775	...	43
1776	...	45
1777	...	47
1778	...	48
1779	...	54
1789		47
1781		48
1782		59
1783		42
1784		52
1785	average	48
1786	81.9	49
1787		55
1788		66
1789		62
1780		56
1781		56[1]
1782		73
1783		70
1784		72
1795		72
1796		76
1797		66
1798		76
1789		85
1800		78
1801		85
1802		74
1803		89
1804		94
1805		85
1806		89
1807	average	92
1808	80.0	70
1809		96
1810		99
1811		74
1812		93
1813		...
1814		86

1815–1864

	Austria/Hungary	Belgium	France	Germany	U.K.
	Flax & Hemp Input	Flax & Hemp Input	Flax & Hemp I	Linen Yarn Output	Flax & Hemp Input
1815	...	...		...	100
1816	...	...		...	79
1817	...	...		...	93
1818	...	...		...	103
1819	...	...	average	...	83
1820	...	...	84.7	...	82
1821	...	...		...	80
1822	...	...		...	101
1823	...	...		...	107
1824	...	...		...	99
1825	...	...		...	104
1826	...	...		...	85
1827	...	...		...	102
1828	...	...		...	98
1829	...	...	average	...	94
1830	...	...	100.8	...	103
1831	...	...		...	102
1832	...	...		...	110
1833	...	...		...	116
1834	...	...		...	104
1835	...	...		...	101
1836	....	...		...	144
1837	...	...		...	122
1838	...	...		...	158
1839	...	...	average	...	147
1840	...	...	113.9	...	133[3]
					131
1841	...	...		...	136
1842	164	...		...	121
1843	154	...		...	148
1844	158	...		...	166
1845	160	...		...	157
1846	149	...		...	139
1847	154	...		...	129
1848	...	...		...	157
1849	...	...	average	...	188
1850	...	...	118.1	50	189
1851	158	...		53	163[4]
		...			157
1852	...	...		51	155
1853	...	...		50	170
1854	138	...		51	128
1855	...	...		51	130
1856	...	12		51	154
1857	154	...		49	164
1858	...[2]	...		51	132
1859	145	...	average	50	138
1860	...	...	138.8	50	143
1861	...	...		50	144
1862	...	...		55	165
1863	143	...		48	148
1864	...	...		46	168

Abbreviations used throughout this table: U.K.: United Kingdom

Other abbreviations used where space demands: Flax & Hemp I: Flax & Hemp Input

See p. 480 for footnotes

E 22 Linen Industry Indicators (in thousands of metric tons)

1865–1919

	Austria/ Hungary	Belgium	France	Germany	U.K.
	Flax & Hemp I	Flax & Hemp I	Flax & Hemp I	Linen Yarn Output	Flax & Hemp I
1865	...	...		47	171
1866	152[2]	39		47	147
1867	169	...		47	144
1868	156	...		52	170
1869	158	...	average	49	151
1870	148	...	158.7[5]	55[5]	200
1871	143	...		47	213
1872	...	...		45	175
1873	137	...		54	200
1874	133	...		54	205
1975	110	...		50	173
1876	139	...		44	149
1877	131	...		47	188
1878	150[4]	...		50	159
1879	137	...	average	49	159
1880	148	61	156.6	44	172
1881	141	60		41	173
1882	133	54		46	178
1883	140	35		48	155
1884	145	32		47	151
1995	135	23		43	160
1886	133	20		38	132
1887	153	38		41	149
1888	126	54		41	175
1889	131	52	average	44	174
1890	142	55	131.3	46	171
1891	140	61		43	149
1892	151	63		26	145
1893	150	52		42	145
1894	138	64		42	161
1895	153	74		44	203
1896	150	62		41	156
1897	140	55		37	161
1898	151	59		39	167
1899	148	73	average	40	148
1900	151	...	124.8	33	141
1901	154	...		31	145
1902	155	...		36	139
1903	183	...		42	163
1904	150	...		32	161
1905	188	...		42	168
1906	209	...		31	155
1907	176	...		32	186
1908	161	...		30	172
1909	158	...	average	30	164
1910	161	...	136.3	29	167
1911	138	155		30	170
1912	158	176		34	202
1913	146	140		31	196
1914	112	...	...	...	170
1915	...	...	...	...	179
1916	...	...	...	...	189
1917	...	...	...	...	164
1918	...	...	...[5]	...[5]	139
1919	...	62	...	...	86

See p. 480 for footnotes

1920–1975

	Belgium	France	Germany	U.K.
	Flax & Hemp I	Flax & Hemp I	Linen Yarn Output	Flax & Hemp I
1920	125		19	135
1921	62		21	54
1922	63	average	23	85[8]
1923	91	57.3	20	99[8]
1924	119		20	124
		Linen & Hemp Yarn Output		
1925	136	41.6	18	105
1926	163	47.8	11	112
1927	164	47.2	19	129
1928	212	45.4	13	107
1929	177	39.0	7	121
1930	137	40.4	7	107
1931	96	37.4	6	107
1932	97	32.7	8	94
1933	66	35.0	11	94
1934	68	29.7	20	125
1935	146	26.8	19	120
1936	154	27.2	17	137
1937	166[6]	28.6	20	138
1938	205	29.3	23	123
1939	...	...	...	149
1940	...	...	...	181
1941	...	18.9[11]	...	128
1942	...	17.4[11]	...	117
1943	...	14.1[11]	...	110
1944	...	8.4[11]	...	140
			West Germany[7]	
1945	...	7.7[11]	...	111
1946	...	17.0	...	97
1947	91	18.2	...	118
1948	82	20.7	...	127
1949	104	19.5	5	92
1950	122	24.0	5	127
1951	135	29.7	7	139
1952	156[6]	31.0	7	118
1953	138	28.5	8	125
1954	159	31.0	9	126
1955	189	28.3	10	142
1956	196	29.3	9	129
1957	196	31.0	10	140
1958	123	30.3	9	118
1959	120	26.6	9[7]	130
1960	134	30.5	9	133
1961	184	30.7	9	113
1962	180	28.8	9	126
1963	205	26.0	8	126
1964	257	24.9 12.9[12]	7	124
1965	247	20.8	8	110
1966	191	22.5	6	98
1967	152	17.5	6	88
1968	141	15.9	6	85
1969	107	15.5	5	84
1970	55	16.7	5	85[10] 39
1971	59	16.2	5	27
1972	81	14.2	4	33
1973	94	14.0	4	30
1974	76[9]	14.3	4	23
1975	62	11.4	3	19

E 22 **Linen Industry Indicators** (in thousands of metric tons)

NOTES

1. SOURCES:— France to 1924 — T.J. Markovitch, *L'industrie francaise de 1789 à 1964* (Cahiers de l'I.S.E.A., 1966). Germany to 1938 — based on the 1907 census output (given in *Statistisches Jahrbuch, 1913)* and the index in W.G. Hoffman, *Das Wachstum der Deutschen Wirtschaft seit der Mitte des 19 Jahrhunderts* (Berlin, etc., 1965), pp. 368–70. U.K. hemp component — E.B. Schumpeter, *English Overseas Trade, 1697–1808* (Oxford, 1960), the *Return relating to Flax and Hemp* (P.P. 1854 LXV and similar previous returns), and the *Annual Statement of Trade.* U.K. flax component to 1935 — based on the 1913 net imports and domestic output (from *Annual Statement of Trade* and *Agricultural Statistics* respectively) and the index in the endpapers of W.G. Hoffman, *British Industry, 1700–1950* (Oxford, 1955). All other statistics are from the official publications noted on p. xv.

2. Except as indicated in footnotes, input of raw material in any year is taken to be domestic output plus imports minus exports and re-exports. No allowance can be made for stock changes or for wastage.

FOOTNOTES

[1] Figures to 1771 apply to England & Wales only. From 1772 to 1791 they are for Great Britain only.
[2] Lombardy was excluded from 1859 and Venetia from 1866.
[3] Figures to 1840 (1st line) have not had the small re-exports of hemp deducted.
[4] Previous statistics include jute.
[5] From 1871 to 1918 Alsace-Lorraine is included in Germany rather than France. German statistics for 1920–38 apply to the 1924 territory.
[6] Only from 1938 to 1952 are the small re-exports of hemp deducted.
[7] Saarland is excluded from 1949 to 1959.
[8] Southern Ireland is excluded from 1 April 1923.
[9] The 1975 figure excludes hemp, of which 4 thousand tons were imported in 1974.
[10] Subsequently the hemp component comprises true hemp only, not sisal etc.
[11] Linen only.
[12] Tow appears to have been excluded subsequently. Comparable figures back to 1952 are as follows:—

1952	18.6	1956	17.8	1960	16.2
1953	16.1	1957	18.1	1961	14.8
1954	18.1	1958	16.6	1962	13.1
1955	15.5	1959	13.7	1963	13.0

E 23 OUTPUT OF SULPHURIC ACID (in thousands of metric tons)

1860–1919

	Austria[1]	Belgium	France	Germany	Italy[3]	Neth'l	Russia[4]	Spain[15]	Sweden	Switz	U.K.[5]
1860	...	...	...	...	...	...	5	...	...	...	...
1865	...	...	...	...	...	...	7	...	...	...	380
1866	...	...	...	...	...	...	...	...	...	...	...
1867	...	...	125	75	...	...	...	...	...	...	...
1868	...	...	...	...	...	...	...	...	...	...	...
1969	...	...	...	...	...	...	...	...	...	...	...
1870	...	...	...	...	...	...	8	...	...	...	590
1871	...	...	...	43	...	...	...	...	...	...	...
1872	...	...	...	47	...	...	...	...	...	...	...
1873	...	...	...	45	...	...	...	...	...	...	...
1874	...	...	...	55	...	...	...	...	...	...	...
1875	...	...	...	86	...	...	16	...	...	...	730
1876	...	...	...	85	...	...	...	...	...	...	...
1877	...	...	...	86	...	...	...	...	...	...	...
1878	23	30	200	92	...	...	...	...	...	...	...
1879	...	...	...	112	...	...	...	...	...	...	...
1880	...	...	...	130	...	...	23	...	...	...	900
1881	...	...	...	214	...	...	...	...	...	...	...
1882	...	...	...	237	...	...	...	...	...	...	...
1883	...	...	...	245	...	...	...	...	...	...	...
1884	...	...	...	285	...	...	...	...	...	...	...
1885	...	...	...	283	...	...	37	...	...	...	890
1886	...	...	...	292	...	...	...	...	...	...	...
1887	...	...	...	316	...	...	...	...	10	...	...
1888	...	...	...	330	...	...	44	...	16	...	...
1889	...	...	...	389	...	...	...	...	13	...	...
1890	49	...	...	420	...	...	40	...	17	...	870
1891	...	...	...	423	...	...	...	...	18	...	...
1892	...	...	...	446	...	...	37	...	28	...	...
1893	...	...	...	477	59	...	44	...	27	...	...
1894	...	...	...	511	72	...	...	...	31	...	...
1895	...	...	...	504	96	...	52	...	35	...	770
1896	...	...	...	553	111	...	...	...	40	...	...
1897	...	...	...	584	129	...	60	...	37	...	...
1898	...	...	...	636	139	...	...	...	39	...	...
1899	...	...	...	689	165	...	...	...	36	...	...
1900	100	165	625	703	230	...	106	...	35	...	1,010
1901	...	...	...	708	235	...	...	...	41	...	...
1902	...	...	...	798	252	...	...	1	42	...	...
1903	...	...	...	836	263	...	...	1	59	...	...
1904	...	...	...	998	278	...	...	1	48	...	...
1905	...	...	...	1,059	302	...	178	2	53	...	...
1906	113	...	...	1,129	365	...	...	5	95	...	...
1907	...	...	...	1,159	425	...	...	8	117	...	...
1908	...	...	...	1,151	524	...	...	9	64	...	...
1909	...	...	...	1,223	590	...	...	7	46	...	...
1910	...	...	...	1,381	645	...	250	10	73	...	...
1911	...	...	...	1,500	596	...	275	12	79	...	...
1912	...	...	...	1,650	635	...	284	26	79	...	...
1913	350	420	900	1,727	645	320	292[4]	21[15]	84	30	1,082
							121				
1914	...	...	...	1,506	630	...	...	26	84	...	...
1915	...	...	...	1,138	626	...	...	39	76	...	...
1916	...	...	...	...	...	...	...	110	76	...	...
1917	...	...	...	1,104	...	...	...	131	55	...	...
1918	...	...	...	1,009[2]	624[3]	...	...	61	45	...	...
				848							
1919	...	...	...	442	365	...	17	57	65	...	...

Abbreviations used throughout this table: Czech: Czechoslovakia; E Germany: East Germany; Neth'l: Netherlands; Switz: Switzerland; U.K.: United Kingdom

See p. 484 for footnotes

E23 Output of Sulphuric Acid (in thousands of metric tons)

1920–1975

	Austria	Belgium	Bulgaria	Czech	Denmark	Finland	France	Germany	E Germany	Greece	Hungary	Ireland[12]
1920	...	...	...	...	...	...	...	792[8] / 367	...	...	...	...
1921	...	...	...	...	...	...	...	954[9] / 862	...	...	...	...
1922	...	...	...	...	...	1.2	...	1,040	...	...	...	...
1923	...	...	...	...	...	7.8	...	...	...	...	...	...
1924	...	...	...	...	...	10	...	744	...	...	...	...
1925	44	462	...	114	...	11	1,500	961	...	...	50	...
1926	...	...	...	...	...	11	...	1,239	...	...	...	...
1927	...	...	...	...	3	11	...	1,448	...	...	...	42
1928	...	...	...	...	3	21	...	1,555	...	...	...	48
1929	...	496	...	221	3	19	1,032	1,704	...	...	...	58
1930	...	585	...	...	3	15	...	1,475	...	25	...	57
1931	...	396	...	...	3	12	...	1,105	...	16	...	45
1932	...	344	...	...	3	15	...	939	...	14	...	40
1933	...	...	...	...	3	18	...	1,213	...	15	...	37
1934	...	625	...	...	4	20	...	1,307[8]	...	29	...	40
1935	...	...	...	...	4	22	...	1,574	...	46	...	44
1936	...	...	...	...	5	24	...	1,765	...	49	...	52
1937	28	...	...	165	5	25	...	2,050	...	43	...	54
1938	32	749	...	...	7	29	1,272	2,272	...	52	40	55
1939	35	...	...	...	6	27	...	2,716	...	58	...	...
1940	22	...	...	...	5	25	...[6]	2,140	...	...	...	...
1941	24	...	...	...	3	14	458	2,362	...	...	...	...
1942	24	...	...	...	4	18	365	2,514	...	...	...	...
1943	43	...	...	...	4	26	342	2,543	...	...	...	...
1944	54	...	...	...	6	26	153	2,199	...[10]	...	...	...
								West Germany[10]				
1945	6	122	...	...	5	30	277[6]	...	...	14	...	...
1946	4	545	...	123	4	54	840	342	108	35	...	50
1947	6	729	...	192	5	61	1,069	517	...	41	20	55
1948	6	829	...	215	5	66	1,275	761[10]	190	39	33	53
1949	8	780	...	219	7	89	1,151	1,139	...	50	59	53
1950	9	880	...	252	11	94	1,215	1,466	300	41	67	62
1951	10	934	8	258	9	117	1,450	1,703	354	71	87	70
1952	16	846	12	278	8	120	1,191	1,740	370	60	117	58
1953	28	767	14	311	9	135	1,180	1,897	446	59	150	51
1954	35	966	15	341	10	133	1,378	2,092	531	96	131	66
1955	69	1,143	19	383	10	133	1,473	2,279	592	119	143	66
1956	74	1,116	29	422	10	153	1,535	2,530	611	88	117	65
1957	80	1,073	40	445	10	163	1,600	2,723	640	106	132	60
1958	117	1,133	64	463	9	148	1,786[7] / 1,824	2,917	650	90	148	54
1959	121	1,249	91	513	13	168	1,890	2,938[11]	689	141	168	73
1960	140	1,423	123	553	18	187	2,046	3,170	730	135	178	95
1961	150	1,322	192	599	12	229	2,205	3,103	819	131	200	129
1962	160	1,233	247	643	12	238	2,271	3,101	861	125	224	...
1963	200	1,249	269	725	13	333	2,394	3,316	919	120	283	...
1964	217	1,348	291	893	17	356	2,702	3,602	937	138	340	...
1965	193	1,488	318	933	24	383	2,916	3,751	985	236	393	...
1966	229	1,362	353	982	16	480	3,073	3,834	973	379	417	...
1967	241	1,484	360	1,012	14	549	3,227	3,778	988	504	450	...
1968	269	1,746	472	977	16	597	3,349	4,210	1,078	551	468	...
1969	277	1,837	498	1,034	22	678	3,527	4,481	1,104	665	477	...
1970	289	1,794	502	1,110	22	843	3,682	4,435	1,099	623	484	...
1971	286	1,932	514	1,174	17	783	3,923	4,388	1,076	728	491	...
1972	300	2,460	514	1,176	16	1,004	4,114	4,735	1,045	813	594	...
1973	303	2,595	561	1,209	15	937	4,383	5,069	1,058	912	670	...
1974	...	2,590	761	1,211	16	1,229	4,689	5,130	1,005	886	683	...
1975	...	1,844	854	1,245	21	1,034	3,758	4,157	1,002	920	659	...

See p. 484 for footnotes

E 23 Output of Sulphuric Acid (in thousands of metric tons)

1920–1975

	Italy	Neth'l	Norway	Poland	Portugal	Romania	Russia[4]	Spain[15]	Sweden	Switz	U.K.	Yugoslavia
1920	352	...	...	...	...	...	...	98	91	...	...	...
1921	420	...	...	...	...	...	11	163	63	...	...	...
1922	485	...	...	...	...	...	...[14]	138	61	...	...	...
1923	767	...	...	...	...	...	45	173	79	...	...	...
1924	632	...	...	...	...	...	89	179	88	...	...	...
1925	800	350	...	...	...	...	100	202[15]	114	30	848	...
1926	823	...	...	...	...	...	145	219	111	...	...	...
1927	820	...	...	185	...	25	176	178	108	...	861	...
1928	704	...	...	222	...	25	211[14]	179	121	...	900	...
1929	835	375	...	233	...	27	265	110	129	...	930	...
1930	831	320	...	165	...	48	396	151	140	...	813	...
1931	633	380	...	120	...	40	464	128	130	...	682	...
1932	562	430	...	99	...	...	552	114	121	...	763	...
1933	678	460	...	121	...	38	627	127	127	...	772	...
1934	774	380	...	139	...	39	782	162	127	...	864	...
1935	804	280	...	112	...	39	994	261	152	...	912	...
1936	957	360	...	135	...	39	1,197	81	147	...	1,012	...
1937	1,026	430	...	181	...	39	1,369	...	163	...	1,068	...
1938	1,076	474	40	189	78	44	1,544	87	167	120	960	...
1939	1,284	460	...	...	82	45	1,625	118	171	...	1,086	25
1940	1,255	195	...	...	80	...	1,587[4]	168	158	...	1,215	11
1941	1,136	57	...	...	73	...	...	158	148	...	1,219	...
1942	766	72	...	...	84	...	...	[128][16]	144	...	1,305	...
1943	547	92	...	...	58	...	...	[74][16]	185	...	1,271	...
1944	175	...	...	...	107	...	...	125[15] 276	221	...	1,289	...
1945	122	...	...	[36][13]	113	...	781	369	229	...	1,236	5
1946	525	276	30	124	113	...	725	288	262	120	1,349	26
1947	845	312	35	155	116	...	996	367	242	120	1,354	32
1948	975	376	40	222	136	28	1,479	353	281	140	1,577	44
1949	1,160	396	57	276	141	...	1,845	403	305	150	1,687	45
1950	1,276	438	69	...	148	52	2,125	456	333	119	1,832	40
1951	1,460	542	68	277	194	60	2,372	565	342	147	1,632	39
1952	1,505	559	67	348	186	60	2,662	640	327	120	1,530	36
1953	1,601	584	67	370	204	68	2,919	650	342	84	1,905	40
1954	1,824	687	79	419	209	74	3,292	721	395	120	2,075	59
1955	1,943	690	78	450	228	92	3,798	799	397	180	2,131	72
1956	2,046	720	83	481	202	95	4,323	859	399	128	2,287	107
1957	2,064	715	77	499	239	122	4,569	980	422	125	2,373	124
1958	2,031	761	71	573	266	144	4,803	1,072	387	121	2,277	125
1959	2,145	812	88	610	311	199	5,081	1,141	404	129	2,467	128
1960	2,299	860	87	685	320	226	5,398	1,132	410	160	2,745	130
1961	2,446	827	90	794	341	248	5,718	1,236	421	163	2,705	234
1962	2,551	818	90	852	352	326	6,132	1,499	448	122	2,775	286
1963	2,711	854	104	888	417	343	6,885	1,462	475	148	2,927	391
1964	2,890	976	110	1,001	408	417	7,647	1,528	524	159	3,185	472
1965	2,979	1,090	124	1,062	413	541	8,518	1,616	579	194	3,358	435
1966	3,369	1,058	139	1,139	412	619	9,367	1,781	603	169	3,168	542
1967	3,524	1,170	214	1,213	403	679	9,734	1,796	604	164	3,234	552
1968	3,489	1,376	262	1,314	430	773	10,159	2,067	632	149	3,335	549
1969	3,465	1,511	310	1,516	430	838	10,665	2,152	703	164	3,287	649
1970	3,327	1,562	312	1,901	463	994	12,059	2,021	709	168	3,352	696
1971	3,097	1,496	314	2,252	398	1,047	12,775	2,454	769	165	3,459	752
1972	3,033	1,537	355	2,568	379	1,162	13,685	2,325	945	165	3,449	791
1973	3,036	1,546	382	2,914	326	1,311	14,855	2,595	938	...	3,886	882
1974	3,219	1,674	381	3,333	420	1,358	16,663	2,919	940	...	3,855	863
1975	3,006	1,292	333	3,413	399	1,448	18,645	2,740	793	...	3,166	871

See p. 484 for footnotes

E 23 **Output of Sulphuric Acid** (in thousands of metric tons)

NOTES

1. SOURCES:– Austria 1878–1906 and U.K. 1865–1900 – L.F. Haber, *The Chemical Industry during the Nineteenth Century* (Oxford, 1952), quoting, for Austria, J. Glaser, *Die Chemische Industrie Österreichs und ihre Entwicklung.* Czechoslovakia 1925–51 – supplied by the Federal Statistical Office of Czechoslovakia. Germany 1867, France 1867–1925, Belgium 1867–1925, Netherlands 1913–25 – T.J. Kreps, *The Economics of the Sulphuric Acid Industry* (Stanford, 1938), where the original sources are cited. Austria, Hungary, and Switzerland in 1925 – League of Nations, *The Chemical Industry* (Geneva, 1927). Russia to 1950 – G.W. Nutter, *The Growth of Industrial Production in the Soviet Union* (Princeton, 1952). Sweden to 1907 – supplied by the Swedish Central Office of Statistics. All other statistics are taken from the official publications noted on p. xv, with gaps filled from League of Nations and United Nations, *Statistical Yearbooks.*

2. So far as possible, except as indicated in footnote [3], output is given in terms of 100% H_2SO_4.

3. With the exceptions of Germany, Italy, and Spain, all statistics prior to 1914 are estimates.

FOOTNOTES

[1] Figures to 1913 apply to the whole Austro-Hungarian Empire.

[2] Subsequently excluding Alsace-Lorraine and Posen.

[3] Figures to 1918 are of acid of unknown grade, but clearly not 100% H_2SO_4. If the figure for 1918 were on the same basis as 1919 it would be 390 thousand tons when converted to the 100% H_2SO_4 basis.

[4] Figures to 1913 (1st line) apply to the whole Russian Empire. From 1913 (2nd line) to 1940 they apply to the 1923 territory of the U.S.S.R., and subsequently to the territory established after the Second World War.

[5] It is not clear whether the estimates to 1900 are in thousands of Imperial or metric tons, but in view of their tentative nature it is not of much concern. Considerably lower estimates are given in T.J. Kreps, 1900, (*op cit.* in note 1) for 1867 and 1878, *viz.* 155 and 600 thousand tons respectively.

[6] From 1941 to 1945 Alsace-Lorraine is excluded.

[7] Subsequent figures include residual acid.

[8] From 1920 (2nd line) Saarland, Danzig, and Memel are excluded. Saarland is reincluded from 1 March 1935.

[9] From 1921 (2nd line) eastern Upper Silesia is excluded.

[10] Figures to 1946–48 are for the American and British Occupation Zones only.

[11] From 1945 to 1959 Saarland is excluded.

[12] Years ended 30 June.

[13] May-December. There were substantial boundary changes in 1945.

[14] Figures for 1923 to 1928 are for years ended 30 September.

[15] Figures to 1944 (1st line) are of production for sale. Estimates of total production in 1913/4 and in 1924/5 by T.J. Kreps, *op. cit.* in note 1, are 60 and 320 thousand tons respectively.

[16] Excluding Valencia and Alicante provinces.

E 24 TIMBER INDUSTRY INDICATORS (in units shown)

1848–1909

	Finland	Germany	Sweden	
	Wood Pulp[1]	Working Wood output	Timber Cut	Wood Pulp
	(a)	(b)	(c)	(a)
1848	...	5.5	...	–
1849	...	4.9	...	–
1850	...	5.7	...	–
1851	...	5.6	...	–
1852	...	6.1	...	...
1853	...	5.8	...	...
1854	...	6.0	...	...
1855	...	6.1	...	–
1856	...	7.3	...	–
1857	...	7.6	...	–
1858	...	7.6	...	
1859	...	6.7	...	...
1860	...	7.0	...	–
1861	...	7.9	...	–
1862	...	8.7	...	–
1863	...	9.2	...	–
1864	...	8.8	...	...
1865	...	8.6	...	–
1866	...	8.1	...	–
1867	...	7.8	...	–
1868	...	9.0	...	–
1869	...	11.7	...	3
1870	...	10.8[2]	498	3
1871	...	10.7	577	4
1872	...	12.0	553	5
1873	...	12.5	635	8
1874	...	12.6	508	7
1875	...	11.5	401	8
1876	...	13.0	621	10
1877	...	10.2	592	12
1878	...	10.5	499	7
1879	...	10.4	359	11
1880	...	10.8	1,125	17
1881	...	11.6	884	23
1882	...	12.3	945	21
1883	...	13.7	952	19
1884	--	14.5	845	27
1885	--	14.5	1,063	28
1886	--	14.2	871	36
1887	1	15.4	907	47
1888	1	15.5	1,112	52
1889	4	16.2	1,248	79
1890	5	17.3	988	95
1891	5	17.8	1,108	117
1892	6	19.9	1,214	117
1893	8	16.2	1,094	140
1894	9	20.8	1,308	181
1895	9	17.6	1,322	215
1896	9	20.1	1,709	277
1897	10	19.7	1,900	313
1898	13	19.3	2,139	335
1899	13	20.0	2,130	341
1900	14	19.8	2,258	318
1901	19	19.7	1,766	334
1902	18	20.9	1,877	395
1903	25	24.0	2,056	437
1904	23	23.7	1,860	459
1905	30	22.7	2,100	525
1906	57	23.2	2,148	560
1907	64	23.5	2,337	577
	181[1]			
1908	146	24.1	2,224	750
1909	184	26.1	2,572	680

(a) = 000 metric tons (b) = million cubic metres (c) = 000 cubic metres (d) = 000 standards

See p. 487 for footnotes

E 24 Timber Industry Indicators (in units shown) 1910–1969

	Finland		Germany		Norway			Russia	Sweden	
	Rough Sawn Timber (d)	Wood Pulp (a)	Working Wood (b)	Wood Pulp (a)	Sawn & Planed (b)	Wood Pulp (a)	Timber Floated (b)	Sawn Wood (b)	Timber Cut (c)	Wood Pulp (a)
1910	...	231	31.3	...	...	...	...	...	3,194	941
1911	758	240	28.2	...	...	...	...	...	3,214	967
1912	...	273	28.7	...	...	...	...	...	3,331	1,135
1913	...	299	...	620	...	681	...	14	3,813	1,186
1914	628	282	...	...	...	...	...	...	3,914	1,135
1915	417	307	...	...	...	...	...	...	4,823	1,216
1916	320	342	...	...	...	...	...	...	4,937	1,324
1917	219	246	...	...	...	...	...	...	4,361	1,024
1918	131	157	...[2]	...	...	...	...	...	4,802	920
1919	261	228	...	...	...	...	...	...	4,160	949
1920	464	324	...	400	...	654	...	...	3,418	1,299
1921	609	352	...	390	...	371	6,057	...	1,927	777
1922	726	458	...	430	...	612	1,507	...	3,967	1,303
1923	963	542	...	1,134	...	697	2,780	...	3,921	1,372
1924	952	566	22.2	1.307	...	659	4,841	...	3,869	1,696
1925	997	624	25.7	1,650	...	812	4,683	...	4,664	1,733
1926	1,153	675	23.6	1,698	...	755	4,048	...	4,542	1,927
1927	1,282	777	24.9	1,891	1,258	819	4,257	13	4,384	2,103
1928	1,229	896	25.8	1,986	1,502	882	4,202	14	4,876	1,900
1929	1,059	973	24.3	2,056	1,484	958	5,262	17	5,180	2,540
1930	819	1,076	23.7	2,088	1,374	931	5,321	22	5,360	2,447
1931	691	1,084	19.5	1,805	1,110	551	2,736	24	5,099	2,198
1932	706	1,263	15.9	1,709	1,023	900	2,016	24	4,973	1,996
1933	897	1,379	23.1	1,769	946	855	3,332	27	5,778	2,563
1934	1,137	1,568	27.7	2,011	1,133	983	4,145	31	5,378	2,870
1935	960	1,728	27.7	2,153	1,177	861	4,022	34	4,995	2,978
1936	1,016	1,976	34.4	2.367	1,284	993	3,372	40	5,190	3,180
1937	1,151	2,191	39.3	2,564	1,384	1,096	4,184	34	5,084[6]	3,524
									44.0	
1938	848[3]	2,110[3]	47.2	2,553	1,396	900	5,630	...	39.8	3,061
	662	1,612								
1939			...	...	1,525	965	2,281	34	39.1	3,137
1940	309	657	...	...	1,765	581	3,357	35	42.1	1,967
1941	359	678	...	...	1,806	597	2,999	...	44.9	1,302
1942	369	662	...	...	1,490	494	2,572	...	44.2	1,751
1943	450	830	...	...	1,089	432	2,376	...	51.3	1,278
1964	368	664	...	...	905	320	2,451	...	38.8	1,298
			West Germany							
1945	490	781	...	...	759	254	1,732	15	48.9	1,999
1946	565	1,195	...	239	1,247	510	2,658	16	44.4	2.736
1947	687	1,458	...	344	1,491	631	3,467	19	45.8	2,825
1948	764	1,621	29.1	529	1,600	816	3,768	30	36.7	3,003
1949	804	1,572	26.5	774	1,945	893	4,713	...	40.8	2,881
1950	892	1,912	21.7	918	1,938	1,015	3,663	50	34.0	3,160
1951	1,040	2,190	22.3	997	1,767	1,086	3,740	56	38.7	3,369
1952	746	1,879	21.8	901	2,115	1,009	4,874	61	41.7	3,029
1953	842	1,928	18.9	1,034	2,179	1,078	4,260	66	34.7	3,210
1954	977	2,420	18.6	1,192	2,213	1,035	3,985	69	41.5	3,641
1955	1,017	2,750	23.4	1,274	2,251	1,259	3,746	76	41.6	3,883
1956	772	2,841	19.3	1,337	2,372	1,247	3,922	77	41.9	4,105
1957	835	3,065	20.5	1,376	2,348	1,313	4,253	82	41.7	4,251
1958	987	3,063	20.7	1,340	2,265	1,282	3,865	94	40.9	4,083
1959	1,034	3,181	21.8	1,385	2,034	1,381	3,348	104	36.3	4,389
1960	1,341	3,699	20.4	1,451	2,237	1,533	3,434	106	43.1	4,949
1961	1,295	4,297	21.9	1,440	2,039	1,525	3,134	104	44.3	5,178
1962	1,137	4,419	23.0	1,403	1,926	1,500	2,808	105	46.3	5,190
1963	1,195[4]	4,825	18.5	1,435	1,970	1,594	2,462	106	43.3	5,676
	5,582									
1964	5,779	5,330	21.0	1,390	2,499	1,798	2,481	111	49.7	6,366
1965	5,708[5]	5,575	21.7	1,390	2,598	1,826	2,238	111	49.7	6,678
1966	4,944	5,498	23.6	1,410	2,403[8]	1,794	1,648	107	48.9	6,543
					1,649					
1967	5,130	5,508	23.6	1,444	1,816	1,798	1,490	109	54.2	6,792
1968	4,993	5,704	20.9	1,559	1,747	2,000	1,326	110	48.0	7,081
1969	5,689	6,062	23.8	1,672	1,910	2,088	1,042	112	51.8	7,627

See p. 487 for footnotes

E24 Timber Industry Indicators (in units shown)

1970–1975

	Finland		Germany		Norway			Russia	Sweden	
	Rough Sawn Timber (d)	Wood Pulp (a)	Working Wood (b)	Wood Pulp (a)	Sawn Wood (b)	Wood Pulp (a)	Timber Floated (b)	Sawn Wood (b)	Timber Cut (c)	Wood Pulp (a)
1970	6,224	6,222	25.4 28.2[7]	1,732	1,969	2,182	1,005	116	58.8	8,142
1971	7,515	5,991	28.3	1,677	1,969	1,977	1,036	119	63.5	7,734
1972	7,475	6,284	23.8	1,707	2,017	2,061	888	119	56.4	8,314
1973	8,140	6,678	30.7	1,760	2,312	2,124	769	117	58.5	9,462
1974	7,700	6,592	32.0	1,849	2,288	2,203	809	115	60.2	9,745
1975	4,950	5,174	26.1	1,531	2,130	1,734	972	115	55.3	8,344

NOTE

SOURCES.— Finland to 1923 – supplied by the Central Statistical Office of Finland, Germany to 1938– W.G. Hofman, *Das Wachstum der Deutschen Wirtschaft seit der Mitte des 19 Jahrhunderts* (Berlin, etc., 1965). Russia to 1956 – G.W. Nutter, *The Growth of Industrial Production in the Soviet Union* (Princeton, 1962). Sweden to 1899 – supplied by the Swedish Central Office of Statistics. All other statistics are taken from the official publications noted on p. xv, with gaps filled from the League of Nations and United Nations, *Statistical Yearbooks.*

FOOTNOTES

[1] Figures of mechanical pulp are not included until 1907 (2nd line). The only earlier figure available for this type is for 1904, when output was 67 thousand tons.
[2] From 1871 to 1918 Alsace-Lorraine was included.
[3] Subsequently excluding Viipuri and Petsamo, ceded to the U.S.S.R. in 1940.
[4] Subsequently in million cubic metres.
[5] The method of collecting the statistics was changed.
[6] Figures to 1937 (1st line) are for state forests only. From 1937 (2nd line) they include private forests, exclude bark which was previously included, and are in million cubic metres.
[7] Subsequently including wood for fuel.
[8] Subsequently sawn wood only.

E 25 OUTPUT OF MOTOR VEHICLES (in thousands)

1900–1949

	Czechoslovakia		France[1]		Germany		East Germany		Italy	
	C V	P C	C V	P C	C V	PC	C V	P C	C V	P C
1900	...	...	2		...	...	...	...	...	...
1901	...	...	...		...	...	...	...	...	...
1902	...	...	...		...	...	...	...	...	...
1903	...	...	...		...	...	...	...	...	...
1904	...	...	...		...	...	...	...	...	...
1905	...	...	14		...	...	...	...	...	...
1906	...	...	...		...	...	...	...	...	...
1907	...	...	...		0.4	3.9	...	...	...	...
1908	...	...	...		0.4	4.6	...	...	...	...
1909	...	...	...		0.6	7.3	...	...	...	...
1910	...	...	38		0.8	9.4	...	...	...	...
1911	...	...	...		1.4	11.7	...	...	...	...
1912	...	...	...		1.8	16.1	...	...	...	...
1913	...	...	45		...	...	...	...	...	...
1914	...	...	...		...	...	...	...	...	...
1915	...	...	...		...	...	...	...	...	...
1916	...	...	...		...	...	...	...	...	...
1917	...	...	...		...	...	...	...	...	...
1918	...	...	...		...	...	...	...	...	...
1919	...	...	...		...	...	...	...	...	...
1920	...	...	40		...	...	...	...	...	...
1921	...	...	14	41	...	...	...	...	...	...
1922	...	...	26	49	...	...	...	...	...	...
1923	...	...	38	72	...	...	...	...	...	...
1924	5		48	97	...	...	...	...	...	...
1925	5		56	121	10	39	...	...	3.6	46
1926	7		33	159	5	32	...	...	3.3	61
1927	2	8	46	145	12	85	...	...	3.6	51
1928	3	10	36	187	21[3]	102[3]	...	...	3.7	54
					30	108				
1929	3	12	42	212	32	96	...	...	3.2	52
1930	4	13	38	194	19	77	...	...	4.5	42
1931	4	12	34	167	15	63	...	...	2.6	26
1932	3	10	28	136	8	43	...	...	3.1	27
1933	1	8	30	159	13	92	...	...	3.5	38
1934	1	8	24	157	27	147	...	...	4.4	41
1935	1	7	22	143	42	205	...	...	9.5	41
1936	1	10	24	180	57	244	...	...	17	36
1937	2	13	25	177	62	269	...	...	16	61
1938	2	11	45[1]	182[1]	63	275	...	...	12	59
1939	...	...	...	...	...	...	...	...	13	56
1940	...	...	...[2]	...[2]	...	...	...	...	26	22
1941	...	...	44	11	...	...	...	...	28	11
1942	...	...	36	3	...	...	...	...	21	9
1943	...	...	19	--	...	...	...	...	17	4
1944	...	...	10[2]	--[2]	...	...	...	...	12	2
					West Germany[4]					
1945	...	...	33	2	...	...	...	...	8	2
1946	3.0	3.8	65	30	13	10	...	...	18	11
1947	8.4	9.4	70	66	13	10	...	...	17	25
1948	7.2	18.0	98	100	27[4]	30[4]	0.4	2.6	15	44
1949	5.8	20.8	98	188	55	104	1.2	3.5	21	65

Abbreviations used throughout this table: C V: Commercial Vehicles; P C: Private Cars

See p. 491 for footnotes

E 25 **Output of Motor Vehicles** (in thousands)

	Poland		Russia		Spain		Sweden		1900–1949 United Kingdom	
	C V	P C	C V	P C	C V	P C	C V	P C	C V	P C
1900	–	–	...	...	–	–	–		...	...
1901	–	–	...	...	–	–	–		...	...
1902	–	–	...	...	–	–	–		...	...
1903	–	–	...	...	–	–	–		...	...
1904	–	–	...	...	–	–	–		...	...
1905	–	–	...	...	–	–	–		...	...
1906	–	–	...	...	–	–	–		...	...
1907	–	–	...	...	–	–	–		...	...
1908	–	–	...	...	–	–	–		...	...
1909	–	–	...	...	–	–	–		...	...
1910	–	–	...	...	–	–	–		...	...
1911	–	–	...	...	–	–	–		...	...
1912	–	–	...	...	–	–	–		...	...
1913	–	–	...	...	–	–	–		...	...
1914	–	–	...	...	–	–	–		...	...
1915	–	–	...	...	–	–	–		...	...
1916	–	–	...	...	–	–	–		...	...
1917	–	–	...	...	–	–	–		...	...
1918	–	–	...	...	–	–	–		...	...
1919	–	–	...	...	–	–	–		...	...
1920	–	–	...	...	–	–	–		...	...
1921	–	–	...	...	–	–	–		...	...
1922	–	–	...	...	–	–	–		...	...
1923	–	–	...	...	–	–	–		24	71
1924	–	–	- -	...	–	–	–		30	117
1925	–	–	- -	...	–	–	0.3		35	132
1926	–	–	- -	...	–	–	0.3		44	154
1927	–	–	- -	...	–	–	0.8		47	165
1928	–	–	1	0.1	–	–	1.2		47	165
1929	–	–	2	0.2	–	–	1.3	0.5	57	182
1930	–	–	4	0.2	–	–	2.3		67	170
1931	–	–	4	–	–	–	2.3		67	159
1932	–	–	24	- -	–	–	2.9		61	171
1933	–	–	39	10	–	–	2.7		66	221
1934	–	–	55	17	–	–	3.2		86	257
1935	–	–	78	19	–	–	3.4		92	338
1936	–	–	132	4	–	–	3.0	1.5	114	354
1937	–	–	182	18	–	–	4.8	1.8	114	390
1938	–	–	184	27	–	–	4.8	2.2	104	341
1939	–	–	182	20	–	–	7.6		97 I	305 I
1940	–	–	140	6	–	–	...	1.8	132	1.9
1941	–	–	...	...	–	–	...	0.1	140	5.1
1942	–	–	...	...	–	–	...	0.1	155	5.5
1943	–	–	...	...	–	–	...	0.2	148	1.6
1944	–	–	...	...	–	–	...	0.3	131	2.1
1945	–	–	70	5	–	–	...	0.5	123	17
1946	–	–	96	6	–	–	6.0	2.0	146	219
1947	–	–	123	10	–	–	8.0	4.0	155	287
1948	–	–	177	20	–	–	7.8	4.2	173	335
1949	0.2	–	277	46	0.2	–	5.7	5.3	216	412

See p. 491 for footnotes

E 25 Output of Motor Vehicles (in thousands)

1950–1975

	Czechoslovakia		France[1]		W Germany		E Germany		Italy		Netherlands	
	C V	P C	C V	P C	C V	P C	C V	P C	C V	P C	C V	P C
1950	6.0	24.5	100	257	82	219	6.2	7.2	29	100	...	...
1951	11.5	17.1	133	314	93	277	11	11	30	118	...	...
1952	10.1	6.3	130	370	106	318	12	12	25	114	...	...
1953	11.4	7.3	130	368	96	388	18	14	32	143	1.3	...
1954	12.9	5.4	163	437	113	561	20	20	36	181	1.5	...
1955	10.5	12.5	172	553	140	762	22[5]	22[5]	39	231	1.9	...
1956	11.0	25.1	179	649	159	911	24	28	36	280	2.5	...
1957	10.3	34.6	204	724	166	1,040	20	36	34	318	1.8	...
1958	11.5	43.4	204	924	181	1,307	16	38	34	369	1.6	—
1959	11.5	50.6	198	1,085	208	1,503	16	53	30	471	3.0	3.9
1960	13.3	56.2	234	1,136	230	1,817	13	64	49	596	4.1	15
1961	16.4	58.8	217	1,028	235	1,904	12	70	66	694	5.1	13
1962	17.2	64.3	230	1,307	234	2,109	8	72	69	878	5.0	24
1963	15.4	56.5	255	1,482	240	2,414	10	84	75	1,105	5.4	17
1964	13.9	42.1	264	1,351	247	2,650	12	93	62	1,029	6.5	30
1965	16.5	77.7	242	1,374	230	2,733	15	103	72	1,104	6.1	30
1966	18.0	92.7	263	1,761	205	2,830	21	107	84	1,282	7.2	33
1977	19.9	111.7	258	1,752	172	2,296	23	112	104	1,439	7.1	49
1968	22.6	125.5	243	1,833	229	2,862	25	115	119	1,545	9.0	58
1969	23.6	132.4	291	2,168	274	3,437	27	121	119	1,477	11.1	61
1970	24.5	142.9	292	2,458	296	3,529	27	127	135	1,720	11.7	67
1971	25.1	149.0	316	2,694	265	3,692	28	134	116	1,701	13.0	78
1972	25.6	154.5	335	2,993	276	3,513	30	140	107	1,732	12.3	87
1973	27.5	164.4	394	3,202	277	3,643	33	147	135	1,825	12.8	95
1974	30.1	168.7	418	3,045	228	2,840	37	155	142	1,631	12.4	69
1975	33.8	175.4	355	2,951	247	2,906	38	159	110	1,349	10.6	60

	Poland		Russia		Spain		Sweden		United Kingdom[1]	
	C V	P C	C V	P C	C V	P C	C V	P C	C V	P C
1950	0.8	—	294	65	0.2	—	7.8	8.9	261	523
1951	2.6	0.1	235	54	0.4	—	9.9	13	258	476
1952	6.9	1.6	248	60	0.3	—	11	11	242	448
1953	11	1.6	300	77	0.4	0.5	11	19	240	595
1954	13	1.7	354	95	0.4	6.1	16	28	269	769
1955	13	4.0	400	108	1.7	14	18	33	340	898
1956	13	5.8	441	98	4.7	18	19	38	297	708
1957	15	8.0	467	114	7.1[6]	23	19	52	288	861
1958	14	12	490	122	16	33	22	69	313	1,052
1959	18	14	480	125	18	39	17	96	371	1,190
1960	24	13	501	139	17	42	20	109	458	1,353
1961	25	14	533	149	30	56	22	108	460	1,004
1962	29	16	561	166	41	71	22	126	425	1,249
1963	34	18	590	173	53	83	21	147	404	1,608
1964	35	20	604	185	61	124	23	162	465	1,868
1965	34	26	613	201	74	160	25	182	455	1,722
1966	38	28	655	230	89	255	25	174	439	1,604
1967	40	27	697	251	86	279	20	194	385	1,552
1968	45	39	750	280	76	317	21	222	409	1,816
1969	52	48	785	294	74	380	28	245	466	1,717
1970	53	65	815	344	77	455	32	272	458	1,641
1971	60	86	862[7]	529	68	460	31	292	459	1,742
1972	67	91	651	730	84	612	34	321	408	1,921
1973	77	115	687	917	104	719	38	345	417	1,747
1974	80	133	729	1,119	115	721	43	331	403	1,534
1975	85	164	765	1,201	101	712	51	319	381	1,268

See p. 491 for footnotes

E 25 Output of Motor Vehicles (in thousands)

NOTES

1. SOURCES:– The official publications noted on p. xv with gaps, filled from the League of Nations and United Nations, *Statistical Yearbooks* and O.E.C.D. *Statistical Bulletins.* Russian statistics to 1947 are taken from G.W. Nutter, *The Growth of Industrial Production in the Soviet Union* (Princeton, 1962) and Swedish statistics for 1925–28, 1930–36, and 1939 are based on data supplied by the Swedish Central Office of Statistics.

2. Except as indicated in footnotes, the statistics relate to the production of complete vehicles, other than motor cycles. They do not include the assembly of imported parts.

FOOTNOTES

[1] Figures to 1938 or 1939 are for years ended 30 September.
[2] Figures for 1941–44 exclude Alsace-Lorraine.
[3] Chassis production for export is not included until 1929 (2nd line).
[4] Figures to 1946–48 are for the American and British Occupation Zones only.
[5] Subsequently excluding military vehicles.
[6] Previously excluding three-wheeled vehicles.
[7] Subsequently excluding wheeled tractors.

E 26 OUTPUT OF BEER (in thousands of hectolitres)

1750–1799

	France	U.K.[1]
1750	...	948
1751	...	955
1752	...	939
1753	...	1,098
1754	...	927
1755	...	918
1756	...	942
1757	...	889
1758	...	915
1759	...	940
1760	...	1,003
1761	...	988
1762	...	945
1763	...	918
1764	...	920
1765	...	890
1766	...	897
1767	...	879
1768	...	896
1769		897
1770	...	898
1771	...	900
1772	...	898
1773	...	904
1774	...	864
1775	...	897
1776	...	922
1777	...	938
1778	...	956
1779	...	981
1780	...	1,021
1781		1,009
1782		1,053
1783		931
1784		1,000
1785	average	985
1786	800	963
1787		1,023[1]
		1,064
1788		1,051
1789		1,059
1790		1,089
1791	...	1,144
1792	...	1,221
1793	...	1,244
1794	...	1,207
1795	...	1,211
1796	...	1,302
1797	...	1,369
1798	...	1,372
1799	...	1,378

1800–1849

	Austria[2]	Belgium	France	Germany	U.K.[1]
1800	...	...	...	...	1,169
1801	...	...	...	...	1,107
1802	...	...	...	...	1,151
1803	...	...		...	1,244
1804	...	...		...	1,206
1805	...	...		...	1,230
1806	...	...		...	1,238
1807	...	...	average	...	1,254
1808	...	...	2,800	...	1,249
1809	...	...		...	1,233
1810	...	...		...	1,267
1811	...	...		...	1,293
1812	...	...		...	1,276
1813	...	...		...	1,171
1814	...	...		...	1,210
1815	...	...		...	1,313
1816	...	...		...	1,284
1817	...	...		...	1,147
1818	...	...		...	1,162
1819	...	...	average	10,200	1,215
1820	...	...	2,972	11,100	1,156
1821	...	...		11,300	1,202
1822	...	...		11,500	1,236
1823	...	...		11,300	1,300
1824	...	...		11,900	1,298
1825	...	...		12,300	1,369[1]
1826	...	...		12,400	1,476
1827	...	...		12,000	1,423
1828	...	...		11,700	1,358
1829	...	...	average	11,100	1,394
1830	...	...	3,145	11,100	1,264
1831	...	4,687		12,800	...
1832	...	4,755		11,400	...
1833	...	5,114		12,000	...
1834	...	5,570		12,200	...
1835	...	5,575	3,381	12,700	...
1836	...	5,632	...	12,800	...
1837	...	5,639	...	13,200	...
1838	...	5,772	...	12,900	...
1839	...	5,577	...	12,900	...
1840	...	5,309	4,241	13,100	...
1841	4,424	5,161	...	13,800	...
1842	4,662	5,221	...	15,000	...
1843	4,450	4,843	...	13,600	...
1844	4,714	5,731	...	13,100	...
1845	5,016	5,537	4,700	14,400	...
1846	...	5,338	...	13,600	...
1847	3,816	4,550	...	11,600	...
1848	4,228	5,230	...	13,000	...
1849	...	5,277	...	14,000	...

Abbreviations used where space demands:—Czech: Czechoslovakia; E Ger: East Germany; Neth'L: Netherlands; Switz: Switzerland; U.K.: United Kingdom

See p. 499 for footnotes

E 26 Output of Beer (in thousands of hectolitres)

1850–1899

	Austria[2]	Belgium	Bulgaria	Denmark[3]	France	Germany	Hungary[7]	Italy[8]
1850	...	5,544	...	...	4.048	14,600	...	...
1851	5,771	5,669	...	...	4,449	14,500	...	...
1852	...	5,586	...	...	4,523	13,400	...	...
1853	...	5,382	...	...	5,048	13,800	...	...
1854	4,790	5,089	...	...	4,959	12,500	...	...
1855	4,885	5,130	...	...	5,871	12,700	...	...
1856	5,835	5,603	...	...	6,649	13,300	...	...
1857	6,733	6,235	...	...	7,088	15,400	...	...
1858	6,950	6,996	...	...	6,807	16,500	...	...
1859	7,133[2]	7,167	...	...	6,697	17,400	...	...
1860	6,507	6,555	...	...	6,573	17,000	626	...
1861	5,806	6,503	...	...	6,798	17,200	490	...
1862	7,037	6,424	...	...	6,963	18,800	572	...
1863	7,831	6,911	...	...	7,051	20,700	489	...
1864	7,374	7,217	...	...	7,212	21,800	464	...
1865	7,295	7,562	...	...	7,686	23,700	597	...
1866	7,144	7,289	...	...	8,078	23,600	552	...
1867	6,855	6,951	...	...	7,007	22,700	439	...
1868	7,291	7,393	...	...	7,327	21,900	539	...
1869	7,915	7,267	...	...	7,528	23,900	589	...
1870	9,304	7,794	...	...	6,499[4]	23,700[4]	689	...
1871	10,028	7,721	...	...	6,400	26,500	799	...
1872	11,445	8,789	...	...	7,146	31,800[5] 32,945	759	...
1873	12,685	9,189	...	...	7,414	36,989	765	...
1874	11,744	9,360	...	...	7,345	38,194	580	...
1875	11,536	9,674	...	...	7,356	38,936	597	...
1876	11,671	9,688	...	...	7,604	38,857	506	...
1877	11,101	9,268	...	...	7,743	38,269	438	...
1878	10,815	9,171	...	...	7,565	37,425	508	...
1879	10,707	8,683	...	...	7,375	37,184	474	112
1880	10,530	9,239	...	...	8,227	38,497[6] 38,572	427	116
1881	11,530	9,317	...	...	8,625	39,109	456	127
1882	11,655	9,094	...	...	8,306	39,324	487	131
1883	11,877	9,312	...	...	8,619	40,873	547	122
1884	12,392	9,703	...	...	8,493	42,374	645	144
1885	12,486	9,367	...	...	8,010	41,857	669	168
1886	11,961	9,461	...	...	7,979	45,068	630	145
1887	12,718	10,160	...	...	8,234	47,100	631	175
1888	12,621	10,160	...	...	7,952	47,696	522	138
1889	12,938	10,631	...	...	8,383	54,420	503	158
1890	13,570	10,771	...	...	8,491	52,830	547	156
1891	14,038	10,770	...	730	8,306	53,205	645	132
1892	15,151	10,927	...	737	8,937	54,780	1,239	99
1893	16,248	11,383	...	743	8,938	55,623	1,322	94
1894	16,514	11,551	...	790	8,443	55,369	1,587	95
1895	17,275	12,230	35	825	8,867	60,695	1,416	115
1896	18,621	12,778	38	909	8,991	61,621	1,676	107
1897	19,060	13,186	32	956	9,233	66,378	1,597	109
1898	19,207	13,707	52	982	9,558	67,968	1,604	133
1899	19,574	14,280	59	1,042	10,396	69,500	1,566	145

See p. 499 for footnotes

E 26 Output of Beer (in thousands of hectolitres)

1850–1899

	Norway[9]	Romania[10]	Russia[11]	Serbia	Sweden	Switzerland	U.K.
1850	...	...	...	...	...	...	...
1851	...	...	...	...	...	...	...
1852	...	...	...	...	...	...	...
1853	...	...	...	...	...	...	...
1854	...	...	...	...	...	...	...
1855	...	...	...	...	...	...	...
1856	...	...	...	...	...	...	...
1857	...	...	...	...	...	...	...
1858	...	...	...	...	...	...	...
1859	...	...	...	...	...	...	...
1860	...	...	...	...	...	...	...
1861	...	...	...	...	...	...	...
1862	...	...	...	...	...	...	...
1863	...	...	...	...	...	...	...
1864	...	...	...	...	...	...	...
1865	...	...	...	...	...	...	...
1866	...	...	...	...	...	...	...
1867	...	...	...	...	...	...	...
1868	...	...	...	...	...	...	...
1869	...	...	...	...	...	...	...
1870	208	...	...	...	...	...	...
1871	232	...	...	...	...	...	...
1872	247	...	...	...	...	...	...
1873	315	...	...	...	...	...	...
1874	358	...	...	...	...	...	...
1875	431	...	...	...	...	...	...
1876	414	...	...	...	...	...	...
1877	423	...	...	...	...	...	...
1878	426	...	...	...	...	...	...
1879	366	...	...	...	...	...	...
1880	363	...	...	...	...	...	...
1881	355	24	...	...	...	...	44,955
1882	356	20	...	...	...	...	45,057
1883	381	20	...	...	...	...	44,784
1884	369	24	...	...	...	...	46,036
1885	374	18	...	...	950	895	45,176
1886	300	18	...	...	1,040	1,004	45,239
1887	302	24	...	...	1,070	1,115	46,216
1888	350	28	...	42	1,285	1,102	46,507
1889	347	23	...	39	1,340	1,158	49,755
1890	427	26	...	46	1,305	1,295	52,100
1891	492	30	...	43	1,475	1,383	52,757
1882	467	...	...	50	1,480	1,460	52,470
1883	480	32	...	55	1,525	1,522	52,520
1884	475	36	...	66	1,608	1,512	52,743
1895	420	42	...	61	1,744	1,702	53,574
1896	414	42	5,364	55	2,102	1,880	56,284
1897	457	53	5,657	55	2,253	2,003	57,791
1898	555	63	5,374	68	2,531	2,118	59,218
1899	606	91	5,913	70	2,958	2,143	61,214

See p. 499 for footnotes

E 26 Output of Beer (in thousands of hectolitres)

1900–1949

	Austria[2]	Belgium	Bulgaria	Czech	Denmark[3]	Finland	France	Germany	Greece	Hungary[7]	Ireland[25]
1900	20,023	14,617	41	...	1,018	...	10,712	70,857	...	1,448	...
1901	20,104	14,660	45	...	1,072	...	10,423	71,157	...	1,415	...
1902	19,628	14,431	52	...	950	...	10,410	67,699	...	1,238	...
1903	19,227	14,804	61	...	949	...	10,944	68,976	...	1,317	...
1904	19,820	15,317	69	...	983	...	11,392	70,241	...	1,516	...
1905	19,099	15,750	90	...	907[3]	...	10,705	72,755[19] 68,591	...	1,501	...
1906	20,420	16,399	122	...	2,588	...	11,594	69,031	...	1,688	...
1907	20,915	16,283	156	...	2,549	...	11,349	69,535	...	1,882	...
1908	21,885	15,932	145	...	2,646	...	11,749	66,961	...	2,157	...
1909	19,735	15,354	140	...	2,441	...	11,352	63,754	...	1,908	...
1910	20,849	16,019	160	...	2,579	...	12,239	64,465	...	2,185	...
1911	22,149	17,032	...	...	2,663	...	14,350	70,353	...	2,706	...
1912	22,709	16,899	213	...	2,449	...	12,656	67,872	...	2,951	...
1913	21,082	16,727	166	...	2,466	...	12,844[14]	69,200	...	2,988	...
1914	20,076	...	242	...	2,527	...	9,056	59,373	...	3,074	...
1915	16,040	8,139	216	...	2,425	...	5,824	45,862	...	3,054	...
1916	11,910	7,086	161	...	2,581	...	7,705	36,835	...	2,972	...
1917	[2]	5,391	73	...	2,306	...	7,115	23,837[4]	...	977	...
1918	1,179	4,930	12	...	1,669	...	6,375[14]	24,825[20]	...	1,262[7]	...
1919	...	9,488	20	4,420	2,374	...	10,785	29,458[21]	...	...	...
1920	3,049	10,408	139	5,889	2,662	...	11,548	23,438	...	491	...
1921	3,040	12,536	219	6,554	2,471	...	12,254[4]	33,993[22]	119	443	...
1922	3,371	15,643	204	6,123	2,133	...	16,802	...	85	768	...
1923	3,000	14,491	222	7,273	2,294	...	20,235	...	62	354	...
1924	4,590	14,919	217	8,581	2,264	...	20,396	38,149	128	421	...
1925	5,054	14,650	125	9,215	2,415	...	19,688	47,560	160	612	3,998
1926	5,330	13,960	91	9,713	2,258	...	19,121	48,342	97	455	3,741
1927	5,210	13,257	77	9,998	2,132	...	19,237	51,619	95	690	3,519
1928	5,256	14,928	72	11,062	2,014	...	16,312	54,995	80	671	3,370
1929	5,275	15,377	84	11,611	2,119	...	21,145	58,078	98	601	3,524
1930	5,385	16,662	51	11,417	2,291	...	20,761	48,560	87	446	3,710
1931	4,385	18,377	47	10,377	2,212	...	21,000[15]	37,137	76	310	3,357
1932	3,058	15,558	91	9,556	2,005	105	16,250[15]	33,570	63	184	2,861
1933	2,522	14,667	60	7,952	2,024	141	[19,195][15]	34,144[21] 34,891	58	165	3,013
1934	2,419	14,717	46	7,996	2,161	191	29,211	36,858	73	167	3,034
1935	2,287	14,109	32	7,744	2,209	233	24,709	39,762	85	185	3,193
1936	2,304	14,384	39	7,562	2,332	297	23,133	39,897	93	220	3,089
1937	2,136	14,228	69	8,316[12]	2,353	368	24,250	43,602	95	241	2,895
1938	...	13,835	96	6,283	2,267	405	23,080[16]	48,108[23]	97	288	2,365
1939	...	12,912	129	6,634	2,356	373	18,231	51,268[23]	93	...	2,346
1940	...	10,232	...	5,989	1,865	473	18,148[16]	48,723[23]	83	...	2,240
1941	...	5,791	...	6,248	2,083	423	14,902	47,024	19	...	2,574
1942	...	5,097	...	6,273	1,957	411	13,137	42,512	...	...	2,110
1943	...	4,860	...	5,748	2,217	534	14,168	43,363	...	...	2,066
1944	...	4,817	...	5,585[12]	2,492	582	13,044[17][16] [18]	...	...	...	2,319
								West Germany			
1945	...	7,870	...	7,421[13]	2,831	591	9,256	...	45	343	2,705
1946	2,004	10,802	...	7,426	2,764	593	10,491	... [24]	86	166	2,746
1947	1,374	12,595	...	8,846	3,159	605	12,866	11,989	89	371	2,430
1948	1,745	11,340	298	8,160	3,236	669	8,325	10,685	107	494	2,708
1949	2,232	10,494	...	9,695	3,433	705	8,717	13,424	137	472	2,944

See p. 499 for footnotes

E 26 Output of Beer (in thousands of hectolitres)

1900–1949

	Italy[8]	Netherlands	Norway[9]	Poland	Portugal	Romania[10]
1900	163	...	589	...	...	81
1901	162	...	559	...	...	53
1902	176	...	529	...	...	48
1903	217	...	437	...	...	60
1904	220	...	417	...	...	78
1905	305	...	428	...	...	86
1906	360	...	426	...	...	112
1907	447	...	419	...	...	135
1908	548	...	418	...	...	178
1909	567	...	450	...	...	186
1910	598	...	462	...	...	186
1911	721	...	502	...	...	265
1912	673	...	529	...	...	324
1913	652	...	514	...	...	299[26]
1914	526	...	550	...	...	324
1915	600	...	511	...	...	329
1916	620	...	615	...	...	...
1917	411	...	564	...	...	...
1918	505[8]	...	412	...	...	...[26]
1919	949	...	583	...	...	41
1920	1,157	...	894	...	...	169
1921	1,369	...	869	1,659	...	314
1922	1,188	...	847	1,840	...	792
1923	1,465	...	809	...	...	[786][10]
1924	1,281	...	712	1,641	...	737
1925	1,218	1,944	746	1,651	...	642
1926	1,296	2,033	667	1,690	...	872
1927	983	2,058	558	2,097	...	929
1928	1,127	...	502	2,511	...	985
1929	902	2,319	502	2,786	...	771
1930	672	2,280	506	2,516	...	595
1931	433	2,103	415	1,928	...	419
1932	422	1,807	420	1,400	...	[358][10]
1933	372	1,609	391	1,058	...	342
1934	289	1,512	397	1,172	...	510
1935	497	1,373	406	1,065	...	514
1936	577	1,262	443	1,179	...	506
1937	613	1,298	481	1,407	64	596
1938	709	1,382	480	1,502	65	605
1939	830	1,508	504	...	69	637[26]
1940	815	1,764	607	...	82	770
1941	633	2,247	477	...	115	1,274
1942	299	2,076	65	...	126	1,062
1943	...	2,286	—	...	132	1,003[26]
1944	347	1,848	2	...	142	...
1945	696[8]	1,157	25	...	158	...
1946	898	1,873	446	...	150	...
1947	919	1,852	518	1,529	170	...
1948	892	1,514	471	1,615	183	418
1949	1,200	1,336	550	2,532	163	...

See p. 499 for footnotes

E 26 Output of Beer (in thousands of hectolitres)

1900–1949

	Russia[11]	Serbia	Spain	Sweden[18]	Switzerland	United Kingdom[1]	Yugoslavia
1900	5,872	71	...	2,894	2,166	60,010[19]	...
1901	5,744	63	...	3,125	1,963	59,144	...
1902	5,706	71	...	2,941	1,999	58,674	...
1903	6,682	76	...	3,062	2,079	58,160	...
1904	6,674	76	...	3,176	2,115	56,971	...
1905	7,291	68	...	3,208	2,265	55,403	...
1906	8,796	82	...	3,293	2,393	56,506	...
1907	9,300	90	...	3,152	2,436	56,360	...
1908	8,760	108	...	3,120	2,441	54,885	...
1909	9,253	112	...	2,734	2,346	53,843	...
1910	10,198	...	...	2,583	2,507	54,777	...
1911	10,990	...	...	2,776	3,003	57,113	...
1912	10,666	...	...	2,658	2,997	56,682	...
1913	11,612[11] 8,064	...	...	2,745	2,969	58,836	...
1914	...	...	...	2,827	2,811	56,870	...
1915	...	...	...	2,619	2,130	48,564	...
1916	...	...	...	2,631	1,703	44,959	...
1917	...	...	279	2,372	1,241	27,088	...
1918	...	...	266	1,499	842	21,294	...
1919	...	...	297	1,542	922	36,108	...
1920	...		303	2,040	1,068	44,846	...
1921	...		349	2,072	1,362	40,403	550
1922	...		349	1,824	1,355	34,808	620
1923	...		419	1,960	1,451	32,666[27]	...
1924	2,276		438	2,070	1,581	33,928	...
1925	2,513		442	1,417	1,835	34,144	...
1926	4,084		616	1,455	2,044	32,949	...
1927	4,141		601	1,502	2,058	32,569	...
1928	3,907		603	1,470	2,338	41,019	1,301
1929	3,400		744	1,503	2,541	40,749	1,189
1930	3,700		794	1,642	2,610	39,765	1,582
1931	3,920		859	1,614	2,621	35,415	1,204
1932	4,210		719	1,563	2,526	30,147[28]	824
1933	4,315		745	1,265	2,419	31,761	558
1934	4,568		763	1,205	2,471	33,996	485
1935	5,186		793	1,302	2,321	35,685	451
1936	7,436		...	1,349	2,047	36,659	483
1937	8,960		...	1,481	2,136	39,127	700
1938	10,310		...	1,588	2,135	40,153	886[29]
1939	10,740[11]		770	1,752	2,185	41,785	427
1940	12,130		611	1,563	2,461	41,731	...
1941	...		82	1,294	2,010	47,626	...
1942	...		583	1,236	1,401	47,740	...
1943	...		616	1,350	1,018	49,026	...
1944	...[11]		645	1,285	868	51,507	...
1945	4,050		669	1,376	1,059	53,463	...
1946	5,690		465	1,478	1,183	50,046	54
1947	6,840		861	1,660	1,693	48,774	682
1948	7,075		503	1,670	1,732	46,126	1,187
1949	9,835		460	1,721	1,895	43,002	1,411

See p. 499 for footnotes

E 26 **Output of Beer** (in thousands of hectolitres)

1950–1975

	Austria[2]	Belgium	Bulgaria	Czech	Denmark	Finland	France	Germany	E Ger	Greece	Hungary	Ireland
1950	2,877	10,140	381	10,779	3,540	776	7,851	17,057	3,800	203	777	3,035
1951	3,051	9,929	322	11,144	3,370	878	7,617	22,533	5,739	242[19] 183	981	3,071
1952	3,821	10,171	388	11,438	3,125	881	8,388	25,849	6,992	226	1,250	3,089
1953	4,211	10,210	422	10,982	3,287	896	8,396	28,768[19] 25,869	8,391	204	1,686	3,036
1954	4,087	9,667	549	10,204	3,257	889	8,834[18]	27,247	10,617	233	1,989	3,130
1955	4,305	9,998	584	10,486	3,388	932	12,575	30,912	11,772	286	2,354	3,208
1956	4,612	9,769	584	11,099	3,374	902	13,064	33,917	11,073	301	2,408	3,385
1957	4,942	10,185	599	12,472	3,525	908	15,153	38,886	12,954	333	2,735	3,192
1958	5,120	10,148	750	12,577	3,528	860	17,573	40,941	12,885	357	3,065	3,253
1959	4,885	10,600	873	13,604	3,938	894	18,734	44,300[24]	13,658	376	3,318	3,252
1960	5,269	10,110	1,075	14,093	4,023	917	17,261	47,324	13,424	435	3,555	3,391
1961	5,703	10,514	1,220	14,911	4,236	966	18,154	51,492	13,682	444	3,781	3,622
1962	5,885	10,309	1,322	15,705	4,273	935	18,205	55,215	13,078	411	3,826	3,461
1963	6,397	10,734	1,460	16,581	4,439	986	17,850	59,156	13,180	361	4,080	3,396
1964	6,671	11,330	1,376	17,827	4,765	996	20,252	66,521	13,772	401	4,228	3,463
1965	6,896	11,092	1,717	18,801	4,567	1,180	19,795	67,439	13,633	530	4,440	3,466
1966	7,286	11,278	1,935	19,375	5,561	1,178	20,220	70,206	14,004	723	4,635	3,478
1967	7,623	11,723	2,169	19,393	6,007	1,395	20,647	71,342	14,582	772	4,801	3,468
1968	7,305	11,894	2,402	20,066	6,019	1,581	19,962	73,231	15,014	783	4,814	3,774
1969	7,365	12,478	2,726	20,817	6,523	2,399	20,781	78,795	15,982	735	4,896	3,727
1970	7,391	13,015	3,047	21,178	7,122	2,485	20,871	81,609	16,642	777	5,006	3,885
1971	7,697	12,876	3,234	22,274	7,815	2,383	20,955	84,474	18,057	807	5,027	4,155
1972	8,038	13,495	3,390	22,498	8,445	2,553	20,395	85,881	18,445	922	4,963	4,400
1973	8,208	14,691	3,760	22,270	9,023	2,600	22,664	87,450	19,412	1,175	5,860	4,600
1974	7,765	14,604	4,242	22,138	8,408	2,728	22,098	87,688	19,308	1,480	6,456	5,050
1975	7,757	13,797	4,516	21,790	8,881	2,457	22,660	88,426	20,400	1,286	6,619	6,120

	Italy[8]	Neth'l	Norway[9]	Poland	Portugal	Romania[10]	Russia[11]	Spain	Sweden[8]	Switz	U.K.[1]	Yugoslavia
1950	1,383	1,413	598	3,458	129	871	13,080	604	1,756	1,993	41,182	1,144
1951	1,299	1,603	664	3,790	126	954	15,170	744	1,753	2,110	41,056	1,188
1952	1,581	1,611	687	4,231	135	1,184	16,080	1,157	1,785	2,361	40,914	922
1953	1,495	1,832	651	4,978	150	1,245	18,330	1,299	1,969	2,362	40,888	568
1954	1,690	1,978	655	5,246	150	1,362	18,890	1,375	2,041	2,340	39,058	801
1955	1,566	2,321	750	5,170	205	1,308	18,470	1,683	2,238	2,572	39,850	804
1956	1,833[8]	2,485	764	5,195	204	1,312	18,070	1,827	2,121	2,686	39,801	770
1957	1,697	2,733	759	5,692	218	1,557	19,650	2,371	2,089	2,966	40,505	1,043
1958	1,959	2,941	782	6,106	297	1,512	19,910	2,897	2,777	3,156	39,376	1,230
1959	2,071	3,398	817	6,590	328	1,480	23,190	3,295	2,752	3,293	41,634	1,262
1960	2,489	3,552	843	6,732	379	1,633	24,979	3,433	2,795	3,127	43,369	1,630
1961	3,055	3,802	904	7,055	415	1,927	26,667	4,100	2,798	3,748	45,333	1,860
1962	3,779	3,965	874	6,563	322	2,128	28,184	4,667	2,724	4,004	45,660	1,788
1963	3,689	4,408	977	7,254	373	2,256	28,088	5,688	2,959	4,136	46,276	2,241
1964	4,268	4,965	981	7,580	501	2,384	28,296	6,906	2,987	4,580	48,472	2,669
1965	4,547	5,402	1,071	7,735	502	2,665	31,690	7,497	3,039	4,396	48,447	2,995
1966	5,179	5,695	1,137	8,297	660	3,028	34,371	8,352	3,141	4,586	49,470	4,051
1967	5,553	6,571	1,226	8,956	749	3,311	36,126	9,418	3,279	4,685	50,210	4,367
1968	5,384	6,849	1,338	9,453	857	3,511	38,300	10,260	3,755	4,510	51,433	4,752
1969	5,748	7,841	1,442	9,992	1,000	3,707	39,706	10,755	4,251	4,657	53,861	5,344
1970	5,938	8,772	1,517	10,372	1,345	4,375	41,857	12,307	4,374	4,733	55,165	6,665
1971	6,285	9,492	1,656	11,211	1,365	4,951	44,131	12,184	4,469	4,821	56,850	8,327
1972	6,524	9,875	1,687	11,809	1,504	5,051	45,861	12,332	4,406	4,494	57,737	9,345
1973	8,598	11,066	1,821	12,788	2,529	5,621	50,809	14,755	4,507	4,710	60,582	9,704
1974	8,064	11,642	1,869	12,442	3,015	6,480	54,003	15,483	4,349	4,631	63,057	9,429
1975	6,493	12,430	1,875	12,901	3,143	7,449	57,100	16,620	4,527	4,325	64,565	8,454

See p. 499 for footnotes

E26 Output of Beer (in thousands of hectolitres)

NOTES

1. SOURCES:– Belgium 1868 and 1869 – supplied by the Belgian National Institute of Statistics. France to 1834 – T.J. Markovtich, *L'industrie francaise de 1789 à 1964* (Cahiers de l'I.S.E.A., 1966) Germany to 1872 (1st line) – W.G. Hoffman, *Das Wachstum der Deutschen Wirtschaft seit der Mitte des 19 Jahrhunderts* (Berlin, etc., 1965), using the index of beer output. Greece to 1928 – estimated from data supplied by the National Statistical Service of Greece. Russia to 1955 – G.W. Nutter, *The Growth of Industrial Production in the Soviet Union* (Princeton, 1962). All other statistics are taken from the official publications noted on p. xv with gaps filled from the League of Nations and United Nations, *Statistical Yearbooks*.

2. Except as indicated in footnotes, all types of beer have been aggregated in this table, though for the U.K. from 1881 to 1932 the statistics are expressed in the source in terms of standard barrels of 36 gallons at a gravity of 1,055 degrees.

3. Home-brewed beer is not covered in this table.

FOOTNOTES

[1] Figures to 1787 (1st line) apply to England & Wales, and from 1787 (2nd line) to 1830 to Great Britain. They are for years ended 24 June in 1750–52; years ended 5 July from 1753 to 1825; and years ended 5 January from 1826 to 1830.

[2] Figures to 1859 apply to the whole Austro-Hungarian Empire. From 1860 to 1917 they apply to Cisleithania, and subsequently to the Republic. Up to 1937 they are for years ended 31 August.

[3] Figures to 1905 are for taxed beer only. Figures for tax-free beer are for years ended 31 May, and are as follows (in thousands of hectolitres):–

1892	1,200	1896	1,333	1900	1,516	1903	1,495
1893	1,236	1897	1,389	1901	1,490	1904	1,556
1894	1,267	1898	1,400	1902	1,534	1905	1,591
1895	1,282	1899	1,503				

[4] From 1871 to 1917 Alsace-Lorraine is included in Germany rather than France, though not included in the French statistics until 1922

[5] This break occurs on a change of source (see note 1).

[6] Small areas outside the main tax districts are included for the first time from 1880 (2nd line).

[7] Figures to 1918 apply to Transleithania, and subsequently to the territory established by the treaty of Trianon. Up to 1938 they are for years ended 31 August.

[8] Figures to 1918 apply to the boundaries of 1871. For 1919–45 they apply to the boundaries of 1924, and subsequently to the boundaries of 1954. Up to 1956 they are for years beginning 1 July.

[9] Strong beer only.

[10] From 1881 to 1922 and from 1934 to 1943 the figures are for years ended 31 March following that indicated. The figure for 1923 is for 9 months beginning 1 April, and that for 1932 is for 15 months ended 31 March 1933.

[11] Figures to 1913 (1st line) apply to the Russian Empire. From 1913 (2nd line) to 1939 they apply to the territory of the U.S.S.R. in 1923. In 1940 they include territories incorporated in 1939–40, and from 1945 they apply to the present territory.

[12] Figures to 1938–44 are for the Czech lands only.

[13] Year beinnning 1 July.

[14] Figures to 1914–18 exclude the invaded departments.

[15] The figures to 1931 and 1932 are for years ended 31 March following that indicated, and the figure to 1933 is for 9 months beginning 1 April.

[16] Figures for 1939–44 exclude Haut Rhin, together with for 1941–44 the rest of Alsace-Lorraine.

[17] Excluding Corsica.

[18] Figures for 1945–54 are known to be incomplete.

[19] The method of measurement was changed.

[20] Subsequently excluding Eupen, Malmedy, etc., Rosen, West Prussia, and Danzig.

[21] Subsequently excluding Memel, northern Schleswig, and (until 1933) Saarland.

[22] Subsequently excluding eastern Upper Silesia.

[23] From 1939 to 1944 includes Memel, and from June 1940 to 1944 Eupen, Malmedy, etc.

[24] From 1947 to 1959 Saarland is excluded.

[25] Years ended 30 September.

[26] Southern Dobrudja is included from 1914 to 1939; Bessarabia and Bukovina from 1920 to 1939; and Transylvania and the Banat from 1920, except for certain parts of northern Transylvania in 1940–43.

[27] Southern Ireland is excluded from 1 April 1923.

[28] See note 2.

[29] Figures to 1938 are of consumption rather than production.

E 27 OUTPUT OF ELECTRIC ENERGY (in giga Watt hours)

1884—1929

	Austria[1]	Belgium	Bulgaria[2]	Czech[1]	Denmark	Finland[1, 3]	France	Germany[1]	Greece[1]	Hungary[1, 7]	Ireland[1, 8]
1884	...	...	...	...	...	...	...	...	...	...	...
1885	...	...	...	...	...	...	...	...	...	...	...
1886	...	...	...	...	...	...	...	...	...	...	...
1887	...	...	...	...	...	...	...	...	...	...	...
1888	...	...	...	...	...	...	...	...	...	...	...
1889	...	...	...	...	...	...	...	...	...	...	...
1890	...	...	...	...	...	...	...	...	...	...	...
1891	...	...	...	...	...	...	...	...	...	...	...
1892	...	...	...	...	...	...	...	...	...	...	...
1893	...	...	...	...	...	...	...	...	...	...	...
1894	...	...	...	...	...	...	...	...	...	...	...
1895	...	...	...	...	...	...	...	...	...	...	...
1896	...	...	...	...	...	...	...	...	...	...	...
1897	...	...	...	...	...	...	...	...	...	...	...
1898	...	...	...	...	...	...	...	...	...	...	...
1899	...	...	...	...	...	...	...	...	...	...	...
1900	...	...	...	...	...	...	...	1.00	...	...	...
1901	...	...	...	...	...	...	0.34	1.30	...	...	...
1902	...	...	...	...	...	...	0.37	1.40	...	...	...
1903	...	...	...	...	...	...	0.43	1.60	...	...	...
1904	...	...	...	...	...	...	0.48	2.20	...	...	...
1905	...	...	...	...	...	...	0.53	2.60	...	...	...
1906	...	...	...	...	...	...	0.60	2.70	...	...	...
1907	...	...	...	...	...	...	0.67	3.20	...	...	...
1908	...	...	...	...	...	...	0.75	3.90	...	...	...
1909	...	...	...	...	...	...	0.85	4.80	...	...	...
1910	...	...	...	...	...	...	1.02	5.40	...	...	...
1911	...	...	...	...	...	...	1.23	6.00	...	...	...
1912	...	...	...	...	...	...	1.48	7.40	...	...	...
1913	...	...	...	[0.96]	...	...	1.80	8.00	...	...	...
1914	...	...	...	...	...	...	2.15	8.80	...	...	...
1915	...	...	...	...	...	...	1.90	9.80	...	...	...
1916	...	...	...	...	...	...	2.18	11.00	...	...	...
1917	...	...	...	...	...	...	2.40	12.00	...	...	...
1918	...	...	...	...	...	...	2.70[4]	13.00[4, 6]	...	...	...
1919	...	...	...	1.16	...	...	2.90	13.50	...	...	...
1920	1.77	1.20	...	1.37	0.25	...	3.50[5] / 5.80	15.00	0.08	...	...
1921	1.78	1.30	...	1.40	0.26	...	6.50	17.00	0.09	...	...
1922	1.84	1.41	...	1.36	0.27	...	7.30	17.00	0.10	...	...
1923	1.91	1.59	...	1.48	0.31	0.33	8.17	15.40	0.11	0.34	...
1924	2.02	1.83	0.02	1.76	0.34	0.53	9.95	17.30	0.12	0.36	...
1925	2.14	2.19	0.03	1.96	0.38	0.54	11.14	20.33	0.13	0.44	...
1926	2.19	2,70	0.04	2.10	0.42	0.61	12,44	21.22	0.14	0.52	...
1927	2.31	3.13	0.05	2.38	0.46	0.69	12.58	25.14	0.16	0.60	...
1928	2.40	3.60	0.07	2.75	0.50	0.76	14.25	27.87	0.18	0.65	...
1929	2.55	4.14	0.09	2.50	0.56	1.00[3] / 1.11	15.60	30.66	0.17	0.70	0.06

Abbreviations used where space demands: Czech: Czechoslovakia; Neth'l: Netherlands; Switz: Switzerland; U.K.: United Kingdom E. Ger: East Germany

See p. 504 for footnotes

E 27 Output of Electric Energy (in giga Watt hours)

1884–1929

	Italy[1,9]	Neth'l[1]	Norway[10]	Poland[1,11]	Portugal	Romania[1]	Russia[12]	Spain[1]	Sweden[13]	Switz[14]	U.K.[15]	Yugoslavia[1]
1884	0.001	...	...	...	...	...	...	...	...	...	...	...
1885	0.002	...	...	...	...	...	...	...	...	...	...	...
1886	0.003	...	...	...	...	...	...	...	...	...	...	...
1887	0.003	...	...	...	...	...	...	...	...	...	...	...
1888	0.004	...	...	...	...	...	...	...	...	...	...	...
1889	0.005	...	...	...	...	...	...	...	...	...	...	...
1890	0.006	...	...	...	...	...	...	...	...	...	...	...
1891	0.008	...	...	...	...	...	...	...	...	...	...	...
1892	0.02	...	...	...	...	...	...	...	...	...	...	...
1893	0.02	...	...	...	...	...	...	...	...	...	...	...
1894	0.03	...	...	...	...	...	...	...	...	...	...	...
1895	0.03	...	...	...	...	...	...	...	...	...	...	...
1896	0.05	...	...	...	...	...	...	...	...	...	0.1	...
1897	0.05	...	...	...	...	...	...	...	...	...	0.1	...
1898	0.08	...	...	...	...	...	...	...	...	...	0.1	...
1899	0.10	...	...	...	...	...	...	...	...	...	0.2	...
1900	0.14	...	...	...	...	...	...	...	...	...	0.2	...
1901	0.16	...	...	...	...	...	...	0.19	0.1	...	0.4	...
1902	0.22	...	...	...	...	...	...	0.20	0.1	...	0.5	...
1903	0.30	...	...	...	...	...	...	0.21	0.1	...	0.6	...
1904	0.40	...	...	...	...	...	...	0.22	0.2	...	0.8	...
1905	0.45	...	...	...	...	...	...	0.23	0.2	...	1.0	...
1906	0.55	...	...	...	...	...	...	0.24	0.2	...	1.2	...
1907	0.70	...	...	...	...	...	...	0.25	0.3	...	1.43[15]	...
1908	0.95	...	...	...	...	...	...	0.29	0.4	...	1.6	...
1909	1.15	...	...	...	...	...	...	0.33	0.6	...	1.7	...
1910	1.30	...	...	...	...	...	...	0.36	0.8	...	1.9	...
1911	1.50	...	...	...	...	...	...	0.42	0.8	...	2.1	...
1912	1.80	...	...	...	...	...	...	0.46	1.2	...	2.4	...
1913	2.00	...	...	...	...	...	2.04[12] 1.95	0.50	1.45[13]	...	2.5	...
1914	2.20	...	...	...	...	...	...	0.53	...	...	3.0	...
1915	2.58	...	...	...	...	...	...	0.57	...	...	3.5	...
1916	2.93	...	...	...	...	...	2.58	0.71	...	...	4.1	...
1917	3.43	...	...	...	...	...	...	0.85	...	...	4.7	...
1918	4.00[9]	...	...	...	...	...	...	0.82	...	...	4.9	...
1919	4.30	0.61	...	...	...	...	..	0.67	2.43	...	4.9	...
1920	4.00	0.71	5.30	...	0.10	...	0.50	0.96	2.61	2.80	5.4[15] 8.54	...
1921	4.69	0.77	5.60	...	0.11	...	0.52	0.87	2.22	2.65	8.41	...
1922	4.54	0.91	6.00	...	0.12	...	0.78	1.04	2.68	3.00	9.27	...
1923	4.73	1.05	6.20	1.52	0.13	0.15	1.15	1.19	2.99	3.30	10.27	
1924	5.61	1.19	6.60	1.51	0.14	0.16	1.56	1.35	3.52	3.70	11.26	...
1925	6.45	1.33	7.00	1.67	0.15	0.24	2.93	1.54	3.67	3.99	12.11	...
1926	7.26	1.49	7.30	1.96	0.17	0.39	3.51	1.62	4.01	4.40	12.74	...
1927	8.39	1.72	7.70	2.32	0.19	0.42	4.21	1.77	4.39	4.73	14.50	...
1928	8.74	1.96	8.10	2.62	0.22	0.54	5.01	2.41	4.41	5.04	15.63	...
1929	9.63	2.26	7.80	3.05	0.24	0.57	6.22	2.43	4.97	5.28	16.98	0.75

See p. 504 for footnotes

E 27 Output of Electric Energy (in giga Watt hours)

1930–1975

	Austria[1]	Belgium	Bulgaria[2]	Czech[1]	Denmark	Finland[1]	France	Germany[1]	E Ger[1]	Greece[8]	Hungary[1, 7]	Ireland[1, 8]
1930	2.50	4.29	0.10	...	0.58	1.21	16.85	29.10	...	0.22	0.72	0.12
1931	2.40	4.11	0.11	...	0.66	1.26	15.67	25.79	...	0.26	0.71	0.15
1932	2.30	3.75	0.12	...	0.66	1.48	14.95	23.46	...	0.28	0.69	0.17
1933	2.39	3.79	0.13	2.24	0.75	1.69	16.40	25.66	...	0.29	0.73	0.19
1934	2.46	3.91	0.14	2.43	0.83	1.85	16.74	30.66	...	0.31	0.81	0.21
1935	2.60	4.33	0.14	2.59	0.87	2.10	17.47	35.70[6] 36.71	...	0.37	0.90	0.24
1936	2.68	4.80	0.17	2.97	0.98	2.32	18.47	42.49	...	0.40	0.98	0.28
1937	2.89	5.39	0.20	3.55[17] 4.12[18]	1.10	2.79	20.08	48.97	...	0.44	1.06	0.31
1938	2.99	5.13	0.23	[2.16]	1.14	3.11	20.80	55.33	...	0.47	1.11	0.38
1939	3.42	5.43[16]	0.27	[2.47]	1.07	3.11	22.10[4]	61.38	...	0.50[20] 0.31	1.23	0.41
1940	3.81	4.19	0.30	[2.65]	0.87	1.71	20.68	62.96	...	0.29	...	0.44
1941	4.20	4.82	0.30	...	1.00	1.78	20.28	70.00	...	0.22	....	0.45
1942	4.68	4.99	0.32	...	1.09	1.93	20.03	71.50	...	0.18	...	0.41
1943	5.10	5.06	0.34	...	1.13	3.14	21.07[6]	73.94	...	0.16	1.81	0.44
1944	5.81	3.71	0.31	...[18]	1.05	2.73	16.03[6, 4]	...	...	0.15	...	0.41
								West Germany				
1945	3.18	3.53[16]	0.40	4.46	0.98	2.96	18.37	...	...	0.21	0.69	0.48
1946	4.34	6.11	0.44	5.62	1.38	2.94	22.83	22.00	11.54	0.29[20] 0.31	1.16[7]	0.57
1947	3.90	7.05	0.48	6.66	1.68	2.87	25.81	27.75	...	0.41	...	0.62
1948	5.33	7.69	0.55	7.52	1.84	2.96	28.85	34.08	14.60	0.51	2.23	0.71
1949	5.51	7.95	0.70	8.28	1.98	3.57	29.93	40.65	...	0.61	2.36	0.79
1950	6.35	8.27	0.82[2]	9.28	2.22	4.18	33.03	46.10	19.47	0.70	3.00	0.97
1951	7.38	9.25	1.02	10.30	2.55	4.61	38.15	53.73	21.46	0.85	3.51	1.03
1952	8.03	9.26	1.35	11.63	2.69	4.77	40.57	58.67	23.18	0.97	4.20	1.16
1953	8.76	9.59	1.56	12.36	2.77	5.40	41.46	62.88	24.25	1.03	4.62	1.29
1954	9.85	10.34	1.73	13.61	3.28	5.71	45.57	70.46	26.04	1.17	4.82	1.46
1955	10.75	10.95	2.07	15.01	3.88	6.84	49.63	78.87	28.70	1.35	5.43	1.57
1956	11.72	11.85	2.39	16.59	4.02	6.66	53.83	87.82	31.18	1.55	5.20	1.64
1957	12.46	12.61	2.66	17.72	3.70	7.74	57.43	94.65	32.74	1.69	5.45	1.77
1958	13.56	12.52	3.02	19.62	3.87	7.97	61.60	98.24	34.87	1.86	6.48	1.90
1959	14.79	13.18	3.87	21.88	4.37	7.92	64.51	106.20	37.25	2.04	7.09	2.09
1960	15.97	14.12	4.66	24.45	5.18	8.63	72.12	116.42[19] 118.99	40.31	2.28	7.62	2.26
1961	16.63	14.97	5.41	26.96	4.97	10.44	76.49	127.29	42.52	2.52	8.38	2.45
1962	17.81	16.41	6.04	28.73	5.78	11.59	83.09	138.36	45.06	2.81	9.12	2.71
1963	18.44	17.76	7.18	29.86	6.99	11.58	88.25	150.39	47.45	3.22	9.67	2.89
1964	20.36	19.43	8.70	31.98	7.32	12.46	93.78	164.84	51.03	3.86	10.58	3.36
1965	22.24	20.37	10.24	34.19	7.38	13.61	101.44	172.34	53.61	4.40	11.18	3.67
1966	23.82	21.52	11.76	36.47	9.31	15.51	106.11	177.88	56.87	5.76	11.86	3.98
1967	24.44	22.60	13.63	38.62	9.48	16.40	111.64	184.68	59 69	6.67	12.49	4.40
1968	25.71	25.06	15.45	41.63	12.10	17.36	117.92	203.28	63.23	7.43	13.16	4.90
1969	26.35	27.63	17.23	43.13	16.57	19.28	131.52	226.05	65.46	8.43	14.07	5.40
1970	30.04	28.96	19.51	46.16	18.86	21.19	140.71	242.61	67.65	9.40	14.54	6.09
1971	28.75	31.60	21.02	47.24	17.54	20.84	149.00	259.63	69.42	11.04	14.99	6.47
1972	29.39	35.66	22.27	51.40	19.37	22.30	163.65	274.77	72.83	13.12	16.32	6.92
1973	31.32	39.12	21.95	53.47	18.00	24.94	174.48	299.00	76.91	14.82	17.64	7.47
1974	33.88	40.76	22.81	56.03	17.65	26.52	180.40	311.71	80.29	14.20	18.98	7.90
1975	35.20	38.97	25.24	59.28	17.55	25.26	178.51	301.80	84.51	15.15	20.47	7.73

See p. 504 for footnotes

E 27 Output of Electric Energy (in giga Watt hours)

1930–1975

	Italy[1,9]	Neth'l[1]	Norway[10]	Poland[1,11]	Portugal	Romania[1]	Russia[12]	Spain[1]	Sweden[13]	Switz[14]	U.K.[15]	Yugoslavia[1]
1930	10.38	2.47	7.63	2.91	0.26	0.55	8.37	2.61	5.12	5.17	17.69	...
1931	10.67	2.58	7.40	2.60	0.27	0.52	10.69	2.68	5.09	5.05	18.22	0.78
1932	10.47	2.59	7.20	2.26	0.29	0.54	13.54	2.80	4.90	4.79	19.46	0.78
1933	10.59	2.66	7.25	2.40	0.30	0.59	16.36	2.90	5.34	4.93	21.20	...
1934	11.65	2.80	7.14	2.62	0.33	0.75	21.01	3.03	6.03	5.35	23.42	0.72
1935	12.60	2.84	7.84	2.82	0.36	0.87	26.23	3.27	6.90	5.69	25.93	0.63
1936	13.80	3.12	7.99	3.08	0.37	0.96	32.84	2.80	7.43	6.05	28.87	0.80
1937	13.65	3.49	8.33[10] 9.19	3.63	0.42	1.08	36.17	2.47	7.98	6.84	31.93	0.91
1938	15.43	3.69	9.78	3.98	0.43	1.15	39.37	2.75	8.16	7.04	33.77	1.09
1939	15.54	4.06	10.47	[2.06][21]	0.45	1.21[22]	43.20	3.11	9.05	7.13	35.81[23] 26.28	1.10
1940	18.42	3.78	9.22	...	0.46	1.13	48.31[12]	3.62	8.62	8.05	28.35	...
1941	19.43	3.65	9.42	...	0.48	1.17	...	3.89	9.12	8.29	31.75	...
1942	20.76	3.61	...	...	0.47	1.27[22]	...	4.44	9.80	7.97	34.88	...
1943	20.23	3.57	...	...	0.48	...	...	4.78	11.04	8.68	36.12	...
1944	18.25	2.97	...	...	0.51	...	...	4.72	12.43	8.52	37.41	...
1945	13.55[9]	1.83	...	...[11]	0.55	...	43.26	4.17	13.54	9.60	36.40	0.83
1946	12.61	3.70	11.31	5.71	0.64	...	48.57	5.41	14.20	10.07	40.34[23] 49.50	1.14
1947	17.49	4.64	11.99	6.61	0.72	...	56.49	5.97	13.46	9.77	50.80	1.45
1948	20.57	5.58	12.07	7.51	0.81	1.50	66.34	6.11	14.08	10.43	54.80	2.06
1949	22.69	6.34	15.00	8.15	0.87	1.86	78.26	5.63	16.04	9.76	57.40	2.19
1950	20.78	7.42	16.92	9.42	0.94	2.11	91.23	6.92	18.18	10.48	63.30	2.41
1951	24.78	7.91	17.65	10.51	1.04	2.47	104.02	8.30	19.35	12.25	69.37	2.55
1952	29.22	8.60	18.48	11.98	1.34	2.89	119.12	9.42	20.55	12.89	71.48	2.70
1953	30.84	9.60	18.80	13.68	1.38	3.44	134.33	10.05	22.44	13.47	75.10	2.98
1954	32.62	10.59	21.27	15.47	1.66	3.70	150.70	10.48	23.96	13.18	81.88	3.44
1955	35.57	11.19	22.60	17.75	1.89	4.34	170.23	11.92	24.72	15.45	89.10	4.34
1956	38.12	12.45	23.11	19.50	2.18	4.93	191.65	13.67	26.63	14.90	95.77	5.05
1957	40.59	13.37	25.72	21.16	2.17	5.44	209.69	14.52	28.97	15.89	99.97	6.25
1958	42.73	13.85	27.34	23.96	2.67	6.18	235.35	16.35	30.35	16.89	107.34	7.36
1959	45.49	14.97	28.51	26.38	2.99	6.82	265.11	17.35	32.23	18.18	114.80[25]	8.11
1960	49.35	16.52	31.12	29.31	3.26	7.65	292.27	18.61	34.72	19.07	129.07	8.93
1961	56.24	17.62	33.59	32.25	3.61	8.66	327.61	20.88	38.32	22.30	137.51	9.92
1962	60.57	19.26	37.74	35.38	3.83	10.09	369.28	22.91	40.62	21.34	150.80	11.28
1963	64.86	20.98	39.46	36.96	4.30	11.68	412.42	25.90	40.66	22.01	162.62	13.54
1964	71.34	22.98	43.94	40.61	4.76	13.85	458.90	29.53	45.40	22.86	170.95	14.19
1965	76.74	25.01	48.95	43.80	4.63	17.22	506.67	31.72	49.11	24.46	182.77	15.52
1966	82.97	27.87	48.35	47.39	5.59	20.81	544.57	37.70	50.66	27.96	188.47	17.17
1967	89.99	30.06	52.87	51.26	5.93	24.77	587.70	40.64	53.84	30.55	194.25	18.70
1968	96.83	33.62	59.70	55.52	6.22	27.83	638.66	45.85	56.25	30.55	207.14	20.64
1969	104.01	37.14	57.02	60.05	6.84[24]	31.51	689.05	52.12	58.08	29.67	221.12	23.37
1970	110.45	40.86	57.61	64.53	7.49	35.09	740.93	56.49	60.64	33.17	230.30	26.02
1971	117.42	44.90	63.56	69.89	7.93	39.45	800.36	62.52	66.55	32.78	237.27	29.51
1972	124.86	49.55	67.61	76.47	8.90	43.44	857.43	68.90	71.68	31.30	244.08	33.23
1973	135.26	52.63	73.05	84.30	9.82	46.78	914.61	76.27	78.08	36.54	262.00	35.06
1974	145.52	55.35	76.70	91.60	10.75	49.06	975.75	80.86	75.13	37.25	253.58	39.46
1975	148.91	54.26	77.56	97.17	10.73	53.72	1,038.63	82.39	80.57	42.28	252.67	40.04

See p. 504 for footnotes

E 27 Output of Electric Energy (in giga Watt hours)

NOTES

1. SOURCES:– Germany 1900–24 is based on the index in W.G. Hoffman, *Das Wachstum der Deutschen Wirtschaft seit der Mitte des 19 Jahrhunderts* (Berlin, etc., 1965). Sweden 1900–12 is based on capacity figures in L. Jorberg, *Growth and Fluctuations of Swedish Industry, 1869–1912* (Lund, 1961). U.K. to 1920 (1st line) is based on the 1907 Census of Production and statistics drawn from Garcke's *Manual of Electricity Undertakings* (London, 1896–1921). All other statistics are taken from the official publications noted on p xv with gaps filled from the League of Nations and United Nations, *Statistical Yearbooks,* and O.E.C.D., *Statistical Bulletins.*

2. Except as indicated in footnotes, the statistics are of net output (i.e. exclusive of electricity consumed in the power stations).

FOOTNOTES

[1] Statistics are of gross output (to 1969 2nd line in the case of Finland).
[2] Figures to 1950 are of public supply only.
[3] Figures to 1929 (1st line) are of public supply only.
[4] Alsace-Lorraine is included in Germany up to 1918, and in France from 1919 onwards, except in 1940–44.
[5] Previous figures are rough estimates based on major companies only.
[6] From 1919 to 1935 (1st line) Saarland is excluded.
[7] Figures to 1946 are of public supply only.
[8] Figures are of public supply only, and are for years ended 31 March following that indicated.
[9] Figures to 1918 apply to the 1871 boundaries. For 1919–45 they apply to the 1924 boundaries, and from 1946 to the 1954 boundaries. They are for years ended 30 June.
[10] Figures to 1937 (1st line) are of consumption rather than production.
[11] There were major territorial changes in 1945. Statistics up to then exclude production at plant with less than 100 kWh capacity. Subsequently they exclude production at plant with less than 1,000 kWh capacity.
[12] Figures for 1913 (1st line) are for the Russian Empire. From 1913 (2nd line) to 1940 they are for the U.S.S.R. territory of 1923, and subsequently for the present territory.
[13] Figures to 1912 are rough estimates based on capacity installed.
[14] Years ended 30 September.
[15] Figures to 1920 (1st line) are rough estimates of sales, except for the Census of Production figure for 1907.
[16] For 1940–45 output for own industrial use is measured gross instead of net, making the statistics about 3 per cent higher.
[17] Previously excluding output from small power stations.
[18] The figures for 1938–40 exclude the Sudetenland. A series for 1937–45 for Slovakia is given in *Statisticka Prirueka Slovanska* (1947) as follows:–

1937	0.43	1940	0.51	1943	0.71
1938	0.41	1941	0.59	1944	0.64
1939	0.48	1942	0.64	1945	0.33

[19] West Berlin is included from 1960 (2nd line).
[20] Figures from 1939 (2nd line) to 1946 (1st line) are of public supply only.
[21] First half-year only.
[22] Southern Dobrudja, Bessarabia, and northern Bukovina are excluded from 1940, and northern Transylvania is excluded for 1940–42.
[23] Figures from 1939 (2nd line) to 1946 (1st line) are of the output of authorised undertakings and of railways in Great Britain only.
[24] Subsequently includes the Azores and Madeira.
[25] This break results from a revision in the production statistics of industrial producers. The reduction in 1960 amounted to 0.28. A revised figure was also published for 1955, viz. 88.43.

F. EXTERNAL TRADE

Because it has long been an important source of revenue to governments, external trade provides more statistical material at an earlier date for most countries than does any other economic activity. Some statistics, indeed, go back to mediaeval times. Unfortunately, however, it was the standard practice until some time in the nineteenth century, to record the aggregate values of trade in terms of officially fixed values for each commodity (or, at any rate, for most comodities). Since these were not always kept up-to-date, the aggregates tended to become increasingly misleading as a representation of the actual values of imports and exports[1]. For this reason, the statistics are only shown here from the time when declared or computed actual values were used, or from which estimates of these values have been made.

Most continental European countries have recorded their external trade in two forms; "general" trade and "special" trade. The former includes all commodities entering or leaving the country; the latter relates only to commodities intended to internal use or to commodities which have been, in some sense, produced within the country. It is the latter, the "special" trade, which has been shown in this section wherever possible. It must be noted, however, that the exact definition of "special" trade has not been rigidly fixed, though the scope for major variations is obviously lacking. Moreover, statements of origin or intention to sell can be both honestly and dishonestly mistaken. These sources of unreliability or lack of comparability in the figures are not, however, likely to be of very great significane. Perhaps more important, at any rate in the early part of the nineteenth century, is the inherent defect in trade statistics which results from smuggling. Probably this has never been entirely absent wherever there have been sizeable tariffs on articles which are valuable in relation to their bulk. For the eighteenth century and the early nineteenth century, when tariffs were generally quite high and preventive staff were neither well-paid nor efficient, the tales of extensive smuggling seem well-justified. The approach to free trade in the middle of the nineteenth century must have rendered much of this activity redundant; and by the time tariffs were once again raised, policing was much more effective than it had been earlier. For practical purposes, then, it seems possible to take the statistics in this section as reasonably, though not perfectly, accurate, certainly from the middle of the nineteenth century onwards.

It is clear that one major influence on the course of these statistics has been the changes which have taken place in price levels, above all since 1914. It has not been found practicable to include a list showing variations in the exchange rates of European countries, though these obviously have a bearing on any analysis of external trade. An idea of changing price levels in each country, for at least the crucial last half-century or so of our period, can be got from section H, below. And alterations in the internal value of the currency unit are listed in the introduction, p xiii.

Table F.2, showing the trade of each country with others which have at various times been its chief trading partners, presents its own peculiar problems. The main one of these is that the records of no two countries tell precisely the same story about their trade with each other. The chief cause of this is confusion between countries of shipment, of consignment, and of origin. Different systems have been used at various times in most countries; and even when allowance is made for this, it is clear that the system supposedly in use has not always been followed with precise accuracy in every case.

It would be extremely useful to have statistics showing a breakdown of the trade of the various countries by major commodity groups. Unfortunately, changes in definition occur in the published statistics of every country with very great frequency, and to produce reasonably consistent and comparable series for even one country is a considerable enterprise.[2] Reluctantly, therefore, such commodity statistics have been omitted. They are available for recent periods in the publications as international trade of the United Nations and of O.E.C.D.

[1] This problem in relation to the English statistics is admirably set out in G.N. Clark, *Guide to English Commercial Statistics, 1696–1782* (London, 1938). Belgium, France, the Netherlands, and the Scandinavian countries operated similar systems up to some point in the first half of the nineteenth century.

[2] As I discovered when compiling tables 7–9 of the Overseas Trade section of the *Abstract of British Historical Statistics* (Cambridge, 1962).

F 1 EXTERNAL TRADE AGGREGATE CURRENT VALUE (in millions)

1796–1849

	Austria/Hungary[1] (kronen)		Belgium[2] (francs)		Finland (marks)		France[3] (francs)		Greece[4] (drachmas)	
	I	E	I	E	I	E	I	E	I	E
1796	...	...	...	...	...	...	...	...	...	...
1797	...	...	...	...	...	...	...	...	...	...
1798	...	...	...	...	...	...	...	...	...	...
1799	...	...	...	...	...	...	253	300	...	...
1800	...	...	...	...	...	...	323	272	...	...
1801	...	...	...	...	...	...	415	305	...	...
1802	...	...	...	...	...	...	465	325	...	...
1803	...	...	...	...	...	...	430	347	...	...
1804	...	...	...	...	...	...	441	380	...	...
1805	...	...	...	...	...	...	492	375	...	...
1806	...	...	...	...	...	...	477	456	...	...
1807	...	...	...	...	...	...	393	376	...	...
1808	...	...	...	...	...	...	320	331	...	...
1809	...	...	...	...	...	...	288	332	...	...
1810	...	...	...	...	...	...	339	366	...	...
1811	...	...	...	...	...	...	299	328	...	...
1812	...	...	...	...	2	5	308	419	...	...
1813	...	...	...	...	6	6	251	354	...	...
1814	...	...	...	...	6	7	239	346	...	...
1815	...	...	...	...	5	7	199	422	...	...
1816	...	...	...	...	6	9	243	548	...	...
1817	...	...	...	...	7	10	332	464	...	...
1818	...	...	...	...	7	10	336	502	...	...
1819	...	...	...	...	6	9	295	460	...	...
1820	...	...	...	...	4	7	335	543	...	...
1821	...	...	...	...	4	6	394	405	...	...
1822	...	...	...	...	5	6	426	385	...	...
1823	...	...	...	...	5	7	362	391	...	...
1824	...	...	...	...	5	8	455	441	...	...
1825	...	...	...	...	6	9	534[3]	667[3]	...	...
							401	544		
1826	...	...	...	...	7	9	436	461	...	...
1827	...	...	...	...	5	11	414	507	...	...
1828	...	...	...	...	6	9	454	511	...	...
1829	...	...	...	...	7	9	483	504	...	...
1830	...	...	...	...	8	9	489	453	...	...
1831	137	160	...	...	6	8	374	456	...	...
1832	159	179	...	...	9	9	505	507	...	...
1833	163	182	...	...	9	10	491	560	...	...
1834	162	172	...	...	10	10	504	511	...	...
1835	184	177	...	...	12	11	520	577	...	...
1836	199	193	...	...	13	11	565	629	...	...
1837	195	180	...	...	13	12	569	514	..	...
1838	207	211	...	...	11	15	657	659	...	...
1839	207	212	...	...	11	12	651	677	...	...
1840	222	217	...	...	13	13	747	695	...	...
1841	213	224	...	...	17	14	805	761	...	...
1842	223	217	...	...	15	14	847	644	...	...
1843	235	219	...	...	16	15	846	687	...	...
1844	242	230	...	...	16	16	867	790	...	...
1845	244	226	...	...	18	15	856	848	...	...
1846	266	214	217	149	20	14	920	852	...	...
1847	269	236	241	171	19	15	956	720	...	...
1848	176	97	182	151	20	13	474	690	...	...
1849	185	125	207	179	22	15	724	938	21	13

Abbreviations used throughout this table: I: Imports; E: Exports; R: Re-exports; D E: Domestic Exports

Other abbreviations used where space demands: tho m drachmas: thousand million drachmas; tho m lire: thousand million lire;

See p. 521 for footnotes

F 1 External Trade Aggregate Current Value (im millions)

1796–1849

	Netherlands (gulden)		Russia (paper rubels)		Spain (pesetas)		Sweden (kronor)		United Kingdom (pounds)		
	I	E	I	E	I	E	I	E	I	DE	R
1796	...	...	...	...	...	...	...	...	40	30	9
1797	...	...	...	...	...	...	...	...	34	28	9
1798	...	...	...	...	...	...	...	...	50	32	11
1799	...	...	...	...	...	...	...	...	51	37	9
1800	...	...	...	...	...	...	...	...	62	38	15
1801	...	...	...	...	...	...	...	...	69	41	13
1802	...	...	46	63	...	...	...	...	55	46	13
1803	...	...	45	67	...	...	...	...	54	37	9
1804	...	...	43	59	...	...	...	...	57	38	11
1805	...	...	46	72	...	...	...	...	61	38	10
1806	...	...	43	63	...	...	...	...	53	41	9
1807	...	...	33	54	...	...	...	...	54	37	8
1808	...	...	...	...	...	...	...	...	52	37	7
1809	...	...	...	...	...	...	...	...	74	47	14
1810	...	...	...	...	...	...	...	...	89	48	13
1811	...	...	...	...	...	...	...	...	51	33	7
1812	...	...	76	139	...	...	...	...	56	42	9
1813	...	...	122	132	...	...	...	...	...	...	...
1814	...	...	113	194	...	...	...	...	81	46	25
1815	...	...	114	219	...	...	...	...	71	52	17
1816	...	...	129	200	...	...	...	...	50	42	13
1817	...	...	167	295	...	...	...	...	61	42	10
1818	...	...	181	256	...	...	...	...	81	47	12
1819	...	...	177	215	...	...	...	...	56	35	10
1820	...	...	245	223	...	...	...	...	54	36	10
1821	...	...	208	200	...	...	...	...	46	37	10
1822	...	...	157	188	...	...	...	...	45	37	8
1823	...	...	160	198	...	...	...	...	52	35	7
1824	...	...	179	205	...	...	...	...	51	38	8
1825	...	...	191	245	...	...	...	...	74	39	8
1826	...	...	194	190	...	...	...	...	50	32	7
1827	...	...	208	238	...	...	...	...	59	37	7
1828	...	...	201	206	...	...	...	...	57	37	7
1829	...	...	216	227	...	...	...	...	54	36	7
1830	...	...	198	272	...	...	...	...	56	38	6
1831	...	...	177	244	...	...	...	...	62	37	7
1832	...	...	196	261	...	...	21	22	53	37	7
1833	...	...	193	249	...	...	21	25	59	40	7
1834	...	...	218	229	...	...	22	24	65	42	8
1835	...	...	223	227	...	...	23	28	68	47	9
1836	...	...	237	282	...	...	26	28	84	53	9
1837	...	...	252	264	...	...	25	26	70	42	9
1838	...	...	248	313	...	...	29	33	80	50	9
1839	...	...	249	341	...	...	29	32	91	53	10
			million new paper rubels[5]								
1840	...	...	78.1	85.4	...	...	27	31	91	51	10
1841	...	...	80.8	89.3	...	...	31	34	84	52	10
1842	...	...	84.6	85.0	109	77	29	27	76	47	8
1843	...	...	75.0	82.2	109	78	26	25	71	52	8
1844	...	...	78.5	93.4	...	...	26	32	79	59	8
1845	...	...	83.2	92.2	144	105	26	37	88	60	9
1846	162	118	87.0	102	149	126	28	37	87	58	9
1847	169	126	89.2	148	...	...	31	46	112	59	12
1848	181	124	90.8	88.0	135	117	35	32	88	53	8
1849	180	127	96.2	95.9	147	120	38	36	101	64	12

See p. 521 for footnotes

F 1 External Trade Aggregate Current Value (in millions)

1850–1899

	Austria/Hungary[1] (kronen)		Belgium[2] (francs)		Bulgaria (leva)		Denmark (kroner)		Finland (marks)	
	I	E	I	E	I	E	I	E	I	E
1850	334	220	237	264	...	...	...	...	23	16
1851	316	273	218	200	...	...	...	...	31	19
1852	419	292	267	230	...	...	...	...	20	20
1853	[415][8]	[457][8]	298	294	...	...	...	...	24	20
1854	438	458	343	389	...	...	...	...	18	9
1855	497	488	385	344	...	...	...	...	25	13
1856	602	528	435	370	...	...	...	...	38	21
1857	586	485	435	414	...	...	...	...	44	23
1858	617	551	440	381	...	...	...	...	31	22
1859	538	585	451	413	...	...	...	...	31	25
1860	458[1]	614[1]	517	470	...	...	...	...	38	27
1861	472	615	556	453	...	...	...	...	49	33
1862	430	666	587	502	...	...	...	...	63	34
1863	525	606	610	534	...	...	...	...	61	39
1864	545	703	684	596	...	...	...	...	51	38
1865	558	730	756	602	...	...	...	...	65	41
1866	490	761	747	643	...	...	...	...	51	38
1867	589	815	775	597	...	...	...	...	58	43
1868	775	858	864	657	...	...	...	...	62	48
1869	841	876	904	692	...	...	160	118	70	50
1870	872	791	921	690	...	...	174	158	68	50
1871	1,082	935	1,277	889	...	...	196	148	76	61
1872	1,228	776	1,278	1,051	...	...	200	177	93	68
1873	1,166	847	1,423	1,159	...	...	197	174	107	89
1874	1,255	1,006	1,293	1,115			233[10]	180[10]	137	94
							209	157		
1875	1,099	1,102	1,307	1,102			210	154	197	174
1876	1,069	1,190	1,449	1,064	...	...	208	160	146	86
1877	1,111	1,333	1,426	1,082	...	...	205	144	128	100
1878	1,104	1,309	1,473	1,112	...	...	175	137	138	106
1879	1,113	1,368	1,526	1,190	32	20	182	141	118	89
1880	1,227	1,352	1,681	1,217	48	33	208	177	105	95
1881	1,284	1,463	1,630	1,303	58	32	224	162	127	124
1882	1,308	1,563	1,608	1,326	42	34	226	161	142	108
1883	1,250	1,500	1,552	1,343	49	46	255	167	153[11]	120[11]
									147	118
1884	1,225	1,383	1,426	1,338	51	35	246	150	137	112
1885	1,116	1,344	1,347	1,200	44	45	223	133	108	89
1886	1,078	1,397	1,335	1,182	64	50	188	139	97	77
1887	1,137	1,346	1,432	1,241	65	46	221	154	105	76
1888	1,066	1,458	1,534	1,244	66	64	245	157	111	90
1889	1,178	1,532	1,556	1,459	73	81	268	173	132	102
1890	1,221	1,543	1,672	1,437	85	71	268	195	140	92
1891	1,227	1,573	1,800	1,519	81	71	294	209	146	103
1892	1,245	1,445	1,537	1,369	77	75	280	208	145	93
1893	1,341	1,611	1,575	1,356	91	91	284	198	126	113
1894	1,400	1,591	1,575	1,304	99	73	307	222	138	135
1895	1,445	1,484	1,680	1,385	69	78	312	217	150	142
1896	1,412	1,548	1,777	1,468	77	109	319	219	172	158
1897	1,511	1,532	1,873	1,626	84	60	326	243	202	167
1898	1,640	1,615	2,045	1,787	73	67	367	239	237	178
1899	1,609	1,862	2,260	1,949	60	53	400	270	251	183

See p. 521 for footnotes

F 1 **External Trade Aggregate Current Value** (in millions)

1850–1899

	France (francs)		Germany[13] (marks)		Greece[4] (drachmas)		Italy[15] (lire)		Netherlands (gulden)	
	I	E	I	E	I	E	I	E	I	E
1850	791	1,068	.	...	...	...	...	...	188	137
1851	765	1,158	...	...	23	12	...	...	200	144
1852	989	1,257	...	...	22	9	...	...	205	157
1853	1,196	1,542	...	...	18	8	...	...	204	154
1854	1,292	1,414	...	...	19	6	...	...	244	193
1855	1,594	1,558	...	...	24	10	...	...	249	217
1856	1,990	1,893	...	...	27	23	...	...	294	225
1857	1,873	1,866	...	...	33	22	...	...	300	231
1858	1,563	1,887	...	...	36	22	...	...	313	231
1859	1,641	2,266	...	...	41	22	...	...	288	242
1860	1,897	2,277	...	...	48	24	...	...	316	251
1861	2,442	1,926	...	...	43	25	821	478	335	273
1862	2,199	2,243	...	...	39	25	830	576	329	253
1863	2,426	2,643	...	...	50[4]	20[4]	902	633	351	287
1864	2,528	2,924	...	...	49	22	984	573	381	344
1865	2,642	3,088	...	...	67	37	965	558	403	344
1866	2,794	3,181	...	...	69	37	869	613	425	338
1867	3,027	2,826	...	...	67	43	884	732	439	340
1868	3,304	2,790	...	...	66	36	895	786	469	368
1869	3,153	3,075	...	...	75	42	935	791	461	391
1870	2,867[12]	2,802[12]	...	...	76	34	895	755	507	399
1871	3,567	2,873	...	...	87	56	961	1,075	586	460
1872	3,570	3,762	...	...	88	50	1,183	1,162	617	514
1873	3,555	3,787	...	...	82	57	1,261	1,131	682	508
1874	3,508	3,701	...	...	88	58	1,296	978	718	538
1875	3,537	3,873	...	...	102	67	1,207	1,022	713	533
1876	3,989	3,576	...	...	87	53	1,307	1,208	750	541
1877	3,680	3,436	...	...	96	52	1,142[15]	934[15]	809	563
1878	4,176	3,180	...	...	91	57	1,062	1,021	847	582
1879	4,595	3,231	...	...	102	56	1,252	1,072	840	630
1880	5,033	3,468	2,814	2,923	98[4]	60[4]	1,187	1,104	840	630
1881	4,863	3,561	2,962	3,030	116	70	1,240	1,165	920	690
1882	4,822	3,574	3,099	3,224	143	76	1,227	1,152	992	752
1883	4,804	3,452	3,221	3,259	121	83	1,288	1,188	1,073	684
1884	4,343	3,232	3,236	3,190	116	74	1,319	1,071	1,129	841
1885	4,088	3,088	2,923	2,854	114	76	1,460	951	1,092	891
1886	4,208	3,249	2,874	2,976	117	79	1,458	1,028	1,103	950
1887	4,026	3,246	3,109	3,136	132	103	1,605	1,002	1,137	992
1888	4,107	3,247	3,253	3,207	109	96	1,175	892	1,272	1,115
1889	4,317	3,704	4,015	3,167	133	108	1,391	951	1,245	1,094
1890	4,437	3,753	4,162	3,335	121	96	1,319	896	1,300	1,088
1891	4,768	3,570	4,151	3,176	140	107	1,127	877	1,356	1,141
1892	4,188	3,461	4,010	2,954	119	82	1,173	958	1,282	1,134
1893	3,854	3,236	3,962	3,092	91	88[14]	1,191	964	1,409	1,117
1894	3,850	3,078	3,942	2,961	110	74	1,095	1,027	1,461	1,115
1895	3,720	3,374	4,119	3,318	108	73	1,187	1,038	1,444	1,178
1896	3,799	3,401	4,307	3,525	116	72	1,180[15]	1,052[15]	1,635	1,338
1897	3,956	3,598	4,681	3,635	116	82	1,192	1,092	1,706	1,479
1898	4,472	3,511	5,076	3,757	138[14]	88	1,413	1,204	1,796	1,516
1899	4,518	4,153	5,463	4,217	131	94	1,507	1,431	1,917	1,583

See p. 521 for footnotes

F 1 External Trade Aggregate Current Value (in millions)

1850–1899

	Norway (kroner)		Portugal[18] (milreis or escudos)		Romania[20] (piastres)		Russia (rubels)		Spain[6] (pesetas)	
	I	E	I	E	I	E	I	E	I	E
1850	...	...	...	...	...	...	93.9	98.1	168	122
1851	43	43	...	...	...	...	104	97.4	172	124
1852	43	42	...	...	...	...	101	115	188	142
1853	49	46	...	...	...	...	102	148	184[21]	209[21]
1854	55	42	...	...	...	...	70.4	65.3	203	248
1855	61	45	...	...	...	...	72.7	39.5	256	315
1856	67	48	...	...	...	...	123	160	326	266
1857	63	46	...	...	...	...	152	170	389	292
1858	45	42	...	...	...	...	149	151	376	243
1859	56	48	...	...	...	...	159	166	315	257
1860	63	53	...	...	...	...	159	181	37	275
1861	79	49	27	14	...	...	167	177	505	317
1862	75	55	...	...	...	274	153	180	420	278
1863	80	61	...	...	175	308	155	155	475	305
1864	77	50	...	...	143	366	175	187	497	353
1865	90[17]	54[17]	25	20	...	...	164	209	407	322
1866	105	69	27	19	108	94	205	223	328	310
1867	97	70	26	17	132	124	265	245	400	295
1868	105	69	25	18	150	189	261	227	574	277
1869	93	78	23	18	133	169	342	264	442	267
					(lei)					
1870	103	81	25	20	72	158	336	360	522	400
1871	102	81	27	21	90	173	369	369	569	442
1872	137	105	29	23	85	159	435	327	527	510
1873	167	121	34	24	92	136	443	364	532	588
1874	186	121	28	23	123	135	471	432	572	466
1875	177	103	36	24	101	145	531	382	570	452
1876	167	118	35	23	166	235	478	401	554	445
1877	190	109	32	25	336	141	321	528	538	516
1878	140	92	32	20	307	217	596	618	541	480
1879	132	89	34	21	254	239	588	628	605	528
1880	151	109	35	25	255	219	623	499	712	650
1881	165	121	36	21	275	207	518	506	651	671
1882	160	123	37[19]	25[19]	269	245	567	618	817	765
1883	161	116	31	23	360	221	562	640	893	719
1884	159	112	33	22	295	184	537	590	780	619
1885	146	102	33	23	269	248	435	538	765	698
1886	135	103	37	26	296	255	427	484	855	727
1887	134	107	37	21	315	266	400	617	811[6]	722[6]
1888	158	122	38	23	310	256	386	784	683	763
1889	192	133	42	23	368	274	432	751	782	827
1890	209	131	44	22	363	276	407	692	851	868
1891	223	130	40	21	437	275	372	707	916	847
1892	200	126	31	25	381	285	400	476	795	709
1893	205	136	38	23	430	371	400	599	715	660
1894	206	132	36	24	422	294	554	669	754	628
1895	223	137	40	27	305	265	526	689	769	754
1896	240	148	40	26	338	324	586	689	842	968
1897	264	168	40	27	356	224	560	730	851	1,028
1898	280	159	49	31	390	283	618	733	662	865
1899	310	159	51	29	333	149	661	627	990	815

See p. 521 for footnotes

F 1 External Trade Aggregate Current Value (in millions)

1850–1899

	Sweden (kronor)		Switzerland (francs)		United Kingdom (pounds)			Serbia/Yugoslavia (dinars)	
	I	E	I	E	I	DE	R	I	E
1850	36	36	...	...	103	71	12	...	...
1851	42	40	...	...	110	74	13	...	...
1852	44	41	...	...	110	78	13	...	...
1853	52	52	...	...	149[7]	99	17[7]	...	...
1854	79	79	...	...	152	97	19	...	...
1855	85	96	...	...	144	96	21	...	...
1856	106	92	...	...	173	116	23	...	...
1857	85	78	...	...	188	122	24	...	...
1858	57	59	...	...	165	117	23	...	...
1859	74	79	...	...	179	130	25	...	...
1860	79	86	...	...	211	136	29	...	...
1861	107	80	...	...	217	125	35	...	...
1862	97	87	...	...	225	124	42	...	...
1863	96	92	...	...	249	147	50	...	...
1864	95	94	...	...	275	160	52	...	...
1865	105	108	...	...	271	166	53	...	...
1866	112	106			295	189	50		
1867	133	127	...	...	275	181	45	26	25
1868	134	118	...	...	295	180	48	30	38
1869	132	123	...	...	295	190	47	27	34
1870	140	152	...	...	303	200	44	28	31
1871	163	159	...	...	331	223	61	28	28
1872	207	200	...	...	355	256	58	29	33
1873	261	219	...	...	371	255	56	27	32
1874	297	225	...	...	370	240	58	32	35
1875	261	204	...	...	374	223	58	31	35
1876	283	223	...	...	375	201	56	...	...
1877	300	215	...	...	394	199	53	...	...
1878	232	184	...	...	369	193	53	...	...
1879	213	185	...	...	363	192	57	42	39
1880	271	236	...	...	411	223	63	46	35
1881	282	222	...	...	397	234	63	43	40
1882	293	254	...	...	413	241	65	48	40
1883	328	256	...	...	427	240	66	50	40
1884	320	239	...	...	390	233	63	51	40
1885	337	246	756	666	371	213	58	40	38
1886	296	228	799	667	350	213	56	52	41
1887	291	247	837	671	362	222	59	36	36
1888	323	282	827	673	388	235	64	35	39
1889	372	302	907	695	428	249	67	35	39
1890	376	304	954	703	421	264	65	38	46
1891	368	323	932	672	435	247	62	43	52
1892	359	328	869	658	424	227	64	37	46
1893	332	328	828	646	405	218	59	41	49
1894	345	298	826	621	408	216	58	35	46
1895	343	311	916	663	417	226	60	28	43
1896	357	340	994	688	442	240	56	33	53
1897	399	358[22]	1,027	693	451	234	60	45	56
1898	446	345	1,065	724	471	233	61	41	57
1899	503	358	1,160	796	485	255[24]	65	46	66
						264			

See p. 521 for footnotes

F 1 External Trade Aggregate Current Value (in millions)

1900–1949

	Albania (gold francs)		Austria/Hungary (kronen)		Belgium[2] (francs)		Bulgaria[9] (leva)		Czechoslovakia (koruna)	
	I	E	I	E	I	E	I	E	I	E
1900	...	...	1,696	1,942	2,216	1,923	46	54	...	...
1901	...	...	1,653	1,885	2,221	1,828	70	83	...	...
1902	...	...	1,720	1,914	2,381	1,926	71	104	...	...
1903	...	...	1,877	2,130	2,656	2,110	82	108	...	...
1904	...	...	2,048	2,089	2,782	2,183	130	158	...	...
1905	...	...	2,146	2,244	3,068	2,334	122	148	...	...
1906	...	...	2,341	2,380	3,454	2,794	108	115	...	...
1907	...	...	2,502	2,457	3,774	2,334	125	126	...	...
1908	...	...	2,398	2,255	3,327	2,848	130	112	...	...
1909	...	...	2,746	2,319	3,704	2,810	160	111	...	...
1910	...	...	2,853	2,419	4,265	3,407	177	129	...	...
1911	...	...	3,192	2,404	4,509	3,580	199	185	...	...
1912	...	...	3,557	2,734	4,958	3,952	213	156	...	...
1913	...	...	3,407	2,770	5,050	3,716	189	93	...	...
1914	...	...	2,902	2,095	...	...	...	...	...	...
1915	...	...	3,800	1,335	...	...	...	...	...	...
1916	...	...	6,009	1,540	...	...	...	...	...	...
1917	...	...	...	...	...	...	...	...	...	...
1918	...	...	...	...	...	...	...	...	...	...
1919	...	...	...	...	5,246	2,300	964	552	...	...
			(schilling)							
1920	18	2	2,450	1,342	12,942	8,862	2,255	2,056	23,912	28,515
1921	18	2	2,446	1,302	10,198	7,273	2,976	2,801	23,685	29,458
1922	12	3	2,529	1,589	9,229[2]	6,234[2]	4,066	5,926	13,498	19,633
1923	23	8	2,765	1,616	13,205	9,725	5,154	4,343	10,821	13,903
1924	20	12	3,448	1,970	17,712	13,865	5,678	5,876	15,855	17,035
1925	22	17	2,833	1,923	17,881	14,807	7,284	6,242	17,618	18,821
1926	25	12	2,766	1,703	23,063	19,999	6,247	5,618	15,277	17,857
1927	25	11	3,082	2,036	29,139	26,697	6,129	6,627	17,962	20,135
1928	32	15	3,230	2,200	32,060	30,954	7,041	6,231	19,208	21,224
1929	39	15	3,263	2,189	35,624	31,880	8,325	6,397	19,988	20,499
1930	33	12	2,699	1,851	31,094	26,159	4,587[9]	6,191[9]	15,715	17,474
							4,588	6,191		
1931	30	8	2,161	1,291	23,971	23,179	4,659	5,934	11,801	13,149
1932	23	5	1,384	764	16,343	15,123	3,383	3,383	8,158	7,392
1933	16	6	1,148	775	15,243	14,288	2,846	2,846	6,125	5,923
1934	12	4	1,153	857	14,022	13,795	2,247	2,535	6,392	7,288
1935	14	6	1,206	895	17,446	16,126	3,009	3,253	6,743	7,947
1936	17	7	1,249	952	21,707	19,745	3,151	3,910	7,915	8,036
1937	19	10	1,454	1,217	27,892	25,516	4,662	5,020	10,982	11,983
1938	23	10	...	...	23,069	21,671	4,930	5,578	[6,889][25]	[8,511][25]
	(leks)									
1938	1,004	339								
1939	...	...	...	...	19,811	21,934	5,197	6,065	[25]	[25]
1940	...	...	...	...	8,292[2]	10,808[2]	7,028	7,019	[25]	[25]
1941	...	...	...	...	7,283	5,308	10,239	9,234	[25]	[25]
1942	...	...	...	...	6,357	4,598	12,929	13,437	[25]	[25]
1943	...	...	...	...	6,209	8,421	15,131	16,271	[25]	[25]
1944	...	...	...	...	3,588	5,289	6,478	11.357	[25]	[25]
1945	81	22	...	...	13,763[2]	3,986[2]	5,820	12,397	[777][25]	[500][25]
1946	102	95	...	...	57,184	29,836	17,514	14,942	10,308	14,283
1947	1,513	237	1,191	842	85,559	61,655	21,416	24,533	28,920[26]	28,550
									(new koruna)	
1948	909	417	3,900	1,984	87,518	74,121	37,741	36,351	4,906	5,422
1949	645	291	6,366	3,229	81,858	80,092	...	...	5,170	5,805

See p. 521 for footnotes

F 1 External Trade Aggregate Current Value (in millions)

1900–1949

	Denmark (kroner)		Finland (marks)		France (francs)		Germany[13] (marks)		E Germany (valuta marks)	
	I	E	I	E	I	E	I	E	I	E
1900	416	282	270	195	4,698	4,109	5,769	4,611	...	...
1901	397	291	215	184	4,369	4,013	5,421	4,431	...	...
1902	434	318	233	199	4,394	4,252	5,631	4,678	...	...
1903	444	352	268	212	4,802	4,252	6,003	5,015	...	...
1904	466	359	267	215	4,502	4,451	6,354	5,223	...	...
1905	483	391	268	247	4,779	4,867	7,129	5,732	...	...
1906	559	394	314	280	5,627	5,265	8,021[29]	6,359[29]	...	...
1907	601	417	379	265	6,223	5,596	8,745	6,847	...	...
1908	551	440	364	243	5,640	5,051	7,663	6,399	...	...
1909	567	444	367	255	6,246	5,718	8,519	6,597	...	...
1910	577	485	384	288	7,174	6,234	8,927	7,475	...	...
1911	623	537	445	318	8,066	6,077	9,683	8,106	...	...
1912	739	597	470	338	8,231	6,713	10,674	8,967	...	...
1913	777	637	495	402	8,421	6,880	10,751	10,097	...	...
1914	718	780	380	282	6,402	4,869	...	...	...	...
1915	1,029	979	578	256	11,036	3,937	...	...	...	...
1916	1,250	1,177	963	498	20,640	6,214	...	...	...	...
1917	1,024	970	1,232	440	27,554	6,013	...	...	...	...
1918	910	710	505	227	22,306[12]	4,723[12]	...[12]	...[12]	...	...
1919	2,394	740	2,510	880	35,799	11,880	...[30 31]	...[30 31]	...	...
1920	2,943	1,591	3,627	2,926	49,905	26,894	3,929	3,709	...	...
1921	1,549	1,410	3,586	3,389	22,754	19,772	5,732	[2,976][32]	...	...
1922	1,456	1,176	3,970	4,468	24,275[11]	21,379[11]	6,301	6,188	...	...
1923	1,907	1,539	4,600	4,393	32,859	30,867	4,808[31]	5,338[31]	...	...
							6,150	6,102[33]		
1924	2,218	1,976	4,716	4,971	40,163	42,369	9,132	6,674	...	...
1925	1,937	1,789	5,520	5,574	44,095	45,755	12,429	9,284	...	...
1926	1,528	1,406	5,668	5,637	59,598	59,678	9,984	10,415	...	...
1927	1,578	1,447	6,386	6,324	53,050	54,925	14,114	10,801	...	...
1928	1,647	1,541	8,013	6,245	53,436	51,375	13,931	12,055	...	...
1929	1,715	1,616	7,001	6,430	58,221[28]	50,139[28]	13,359	13,486	...	...
1930	1,656	1,524	5,226	5,404	52,511	42,835	10,349	12,036	...	...
1931	1,410	1,260	3,457	4,457	42,206	30,436	6,713	9,592	...	...
1932	1,104	1,086	3,502	4,631	29,808	19,705	4,653	5,741	...	...
1933	1,225	1,164	3,926	5,298	28,431	18,474	4,199	4,872	...	...
1934	1,307	1,176	4,775	6,226	23,097	17,850	4,448[30]	4,178[30]	...	...
1935	1,287	1,213	5,332	6,240	20,974	15,496	4,156	4,270	...	...
1936	1,442	1,327	6,211	7,223	25,414	15,492	4,228	4,778	...	...
1937	1,649[27]	1,541[27]	9,162	9,380	42,391	23,939	5,495	5,919	...	...
	1,674	1,569								
1938	1,625	1,535	8,488	8,398	46,065	30,590	5,449	5,264	...	...
1939	1,740	1,578	7,568	7,710	43,785	31,590	5,207	5,653	...	...
1940	1,377	1,517	9,164	2,875	45,770	17,511	5,012	4,868	...	...
1941	1,311	1,278	10,200	4,321	24,936	15,777	6,925	6,840	...	...
1942	1,210	1,053	11,731	5,991	25,952	29,664	8,691	7,560	...	...
1943	1,225	1,338	12,874	8,713	13,960	35,407	8,258	8,588	...	...
1944	1,167	1,361	8,910	6,332	9,769	25,557	...	...	...	...
							West Germany			
1945	696	904	6,793	5,228	57,027	11,399	...	...	...	...
			million new marks							
1946	2,848	1,618	243	231	264,737	101,388	...	...	...	...
1947	3,090	2,313	470	432	397,135	223,321	...	...	...	...
1948	3,424	2,731	664	553	672,673	434,047	3,164	1,817	...	...
1949	4,211	3,560	663	644	926,326	783,906	7,330	3,806	1,315	1,387

See p. 521 for footnotes

F1 External Trade Aggregate Current Value (in millions)

1900–1949

	Greece[4] (drachmae)		Hungary (pengos)		Ireland (pounds)		Italy[15] (lire)		Netherlands (gulden)	
	I	E	I	E	I	E	I	E	I	E
1900	131	103	...	...	...	...	1,700	1,338	1,968	1,695
1901	141	94	...	...	...	...	1,718	1,374	2,047	1,734
1902	137	80	...	...	...	...	1,723	1,464	2,172	1,828
1903	137	86	...	...	...	...	1,813	1,483	2,278	1,951
1904	137	91	...	...	...	...	1,878	1,564	2,420	1,986
1905	142	84	...	...	...	...	2,016	1,694	2,584	1,994
1906	145	124	...	...	...	...	2,514[15]	1,894[15]	2,524	2,084
1907	149	118	...	...	...	...	2,881	1,938	2,692	2,212
1908	155	111	...	...	...	...	2,913	1,718	2,824	2,181
1909	138	102	...	...	...	...	3,112	1,855	3,137	2,455
1910	161[19]	145[19]	...	...	...	...	3,246	2,065	3,265	2,632
1911	174	141	...	...	...	...	3,389	2,190	3,333	2,732
1912	158	146	...	...	...	...	3,702	2,383	3,613	3,113
1913	178[4]	119[4]	...	...	...	...	3,646	2,497	3,918	3,083
1914	319	179	...	...	...	...	2,923	2,195	2,889	2,505
1915	289	218	...	...	...	...	4,704	2,512	2,111	1,749
1916	399	155	...	...	...	...	8,390	3,053	1,883	1,347
1917	223	113	...	...	...	...	13,990	3,276	970	821
1918	734[4]	297[4]	...	...	...	...	16,039	3,305	618	386
1919	1,522	764	...	...	...	...	16,623	6,004	2,835	1,426
1920	2,177	682	484	191	...	...	26,822	11,628	3,345	1,722
1921	1,764	944	604	295	...	...	16,914	8,043	2,267	1,385
1922	3,170[4]	2,489[4]	626	383	...	...	15,741	9,160	2,032	1,230
1923	6,076	2,544	491	392	...	...	17,157	10,950	2,017	1,312
1924	8,039	3,266	815	667	69	51	19,373	14,270	2,366	1,689
1925	10,177	4,574	865	848	63	44	26,200	18,170	2,455	1,809
1926	9,967	5,440	941	877	61	42	25,879	18,544	2,443	1,749
1927	12,600	6,040	1,182	808	61	44	20,375	15,519	2,550	1,900
1928	12,417	6,331	1,211	826	60	46	21,920	14,444	2,688	1,990
1929	13,276	6,960	1,064	1,039	61	47	21,303[15]	14,767[15]	2,766	2,005
1930	10,524	5,799	823	912	57	45	17,347	12,119	2,427	1,728
1931	8,763	4,165	539	570	50	36	11,643	10,210	1,896	1,315
1932	7,870	4,576	329	335	43	26	8,268	6,812	1,306	850
1933	8,426	5,155	313	391	36	19	7,432	5,991	1,254	754
1934	8,831	5,474	345	404	39	18	7,675	5,224	1,079	736
1935	10,766	7,095	402	452	37	20	7,790	5,238	978	711
1936	11,847	7,384	437	504	40	23	6,039	5,542	1,071	796
1937	15,548	9,546	484	588	44	23	13,943	10,444	1,605	1,204
1938	14,759	10,149	417	522	41	24	11,273	10,497	1,460	1,079
1939	12,281	9,200	493	604	43	27	10,309	10,823	1,560	1,006
1940	12,243	9,079	603	516	47	33	13,220	11,519	1,023	649
1941	4,384	3,899	740	799	30	32	11,467	14,514	744	635
1942	12,589	5,405	946	1,152	35	33	14,038	16,047	482	617
1943	28,182	10,202	1,148	1,300	26	28	...	...	420	641
1944	...	11,328	809	950	29	30	...	...	...	...
1945	2,830	1,225	...[34]	...[34]	41	36	...	...	...	...
	(tho m drachmae)		(forints)							
1946	515	202	371	420	72	39	...	...	2,205	816
							(tho m lire)			
1947	930	387	1,459	1,045	131	40	937	341	4,279	1,893
1948	1,822[4]	470[4]	1,975	1,933	137	49	844	576	4,965	2,719
1949	2,048	575	3,382	3,293	130	61	883	641	5,332	3,851

See p. 521 for footnotes

F 1 External Trade Aggregate Current Value (in millions)

1900–1949

	Norway (kroner)		Poland[35] (zlotys)		Portugal (escudos)		Romania (lei)		Russia (rubels)	
	I	E	I	E	I	E	I	E	I	E
1900	311	173	...	...	60	31	217	280	626	716
1901	287	165	...	...	58	28	292	354	593	762
1902	290	181	...	...	56	28	283	375	599	860
1903	293	193	...	...	59	31	270	356	682	1,001
1904	292	193	...	...	62	31	311	262	651	1,006
1905	312	218	...	...	61	29	338	457	635	1,077
1906	344[17]	246[17]	...	...	60	31	422	491	801	1,095
1907	362	229	...	...	61	30	431	554	847	1,053
1908	355	219	...	...	67	28	414	379	913	998
1909	366	243	...	...	65	31	368	465	906	1,428
1910	402	283	...	...	70	36	410	617	1,084	1,449
1911	469	298	...	...	68	34	570	692	1,162	1,591
1912	526	336	...	...	75	34	638	642	1,172	1,519
1913	552	393	...	...	89	35	590	671	1,374	1,520
1914	567	410	...	...	69	27	504	452	...	...
1915	868	677	...	...	76	34	333	570	1,131	397
1916	1,354	988	...	...	129	56	...	...	2,675	579
1917	1,661	791	...	...	137	55	...	...	...	...
									(new rubels)	
1918	1,253	755	...	...	178	83	...	...	82.5	6.4
1919	2,584	782	...	...	229	107	3,762	104	2.5	0.1
1920	3,033	1,247	...	...	691	222	6,980	3,448	22.5	1.1
1921	1,464	638	...	...	933	225	12,145	8,263	165	15.8
1922	1,314	787	845	655	1,252	444	12,325	14,039	[213][39]	[49.8][39]
1923	1,343	831	1,117	1,196	2,299	684	19,514	24,575	117[39]	105[39]
1924	1,537	1,066	1,479	1,266	2,958	949	26,265	28,361	183[39]	293[39]
1925	1,379	1,048	1,666	1,397	2,484	861	30,098	29,025	567[39]	453[39]
1926	1,093	812	1,549[19] 1,547	2,253[19] 2,253	2,342	736	37,128	38,224	593[39]	552[39]
1927	977	685	2,892	2,515	2,662	723	33,840	38,111	560[39]	633[39]
1928	1,023	683	3,362	2,506	2,679	1,029	[31,641][38]	[27,030][38]	741[39]	621[39]
1929	1,073	752	3,111	2,813	2,529	1,073	29,626	28,960	691	724
1930	1,065	684	2,246	2,433	2,408	945	22,951	28,517	830	813
1931	861	467	1,468	1,879	1,675	812	15,426	22,189	867	636
1932	690	569	862	1,084	1,722	792	11,451	16,710	552	451
1933	665	558	827	960	1,918	802	11,739	14,166	273	389
1934	737	578	799	975	1,973	909	13,209	13,656	182	328
1935	825	605	861	925	2,296	924	10,848	16,756	189	288
1936	927	685	1,003	1,026	1,997	1,030	12,638	21,703	242	243
1937	1,293	823	1,254	1,196	2,362	1,203	20,163	31,359	229	295
1938	1,193[17]	787[17]	1,300	1,185	2,304	1,142	18,694	21,525	245	230
1939	1,366	808	[766][36]	[781][36]	2,078	1,338	...	...	168	104
1940	948	612	...	...	2,449	1,619	...	...	246	240
1941	1,125	575	...	...	2,469	2,973	30,576	41,286	278	179
1942	944	492	...	...	2,500	3,941	44,907	52,816	182	66
1943	1,008	539	...	...	3,342	4,035	89,988	71,132	173	67
1944	722	517	...	...	3,939	3,166	...	...	199	115
1945	1,206	326	...[37]	...[37]	4,083	3,237	...	...	260	302
1946	2,197	1,202	583	506	6,896	4,586	334,253	102,569	692	588
1947	3,820	1,820	1,281	985	9,494	4,310	...	...	670	694
1948	3,721	2,061	2,066	2,125	10,362	4,295	...	...	1,102	1,177
1949	4,221	2,137	2,530	2,475	9,047	4,094	...	...	1,340	1,303

See p. 521 for footnotes

F 1 **External Trade Aggregate Current Value** (in millions)

1900–1949

	Spain[6] (pesetas)		Sweden (kronor)		Switzerland[23] (francs)		United Kingdom (pounds)			Serbia/Yugoslavia (dinars)	
	I	E	I	E	I	E	I	DE	R	I	E
1900	945	794	526	391	1,111	836	523	291	63	54	66
1901	909	757	460	353[22]	1,050	837	522	280	68	44	66
1902	887	814	502	392	1,129	874	528	283	66	45	72
1903	934	901	530	441	1,196	889	543	291	70	58	60
1904	921	918	572	415	1,240	891	551	301	70	61	62
1905	1,059	954	574	450	1,380	969	565	330	78	56	72
1906	1,015	898	638	504	1,469	1,071	608	376	85	44	72
1907	948	944	674	525	1,687	1,153	646	426	92	71	81
1908	982	896	598	482	1,487	1,038	593	377	80	76	78
1909	957	926	614	473	1,602	1,098	625	378	91	74	93
1910	1,000	971	669	493	1,745	1,196	678	430	104	85	98
1911	995	976	690	664	1,802	1,257	680	454	103	115	117
1912	1,052	1,046	783	760	1,979	1,358	745	487	112	106	84
1913	1,309	1,079	847	817	1,920	1,376	769	525	110	...	78
1914	1,051	881	727	772	1,478	1,187	697	431	95	...	...
1915	1,207	1,258	1,143	1,316	1,680	1,670	852	385	99	...	...
1916	1,281	1,378	1,139	1,556	2,379	2,448	949	506	98	...	...
1917	1,326	1,325	759	1,350	2,405	2,323	1,064	527	70	...	...
1918	624	1,009	1,233	1,350	2,401	1,963	1,316	501	31	...	...
1919	1,084	1,311	2,534	1,576	3,533	3,298	1,626	799	165	...	687
1920	1,431	1,025	3,314	2,278	4,243	3,277	1,933	1,334	223	3,466	1,321
1921	2,836	1,585	1,259	1,097	2,296	2,140	1,086	703	107	4,122	2,461
	(gold pesetas)										
1922	2,719	1,319	1,114	1,154	1,914	1,762	1,003	720	104	6,422	3,691
1923	2,927	1,526	1,295	1,142	2,243	1,760	1,096[40]	767[40]	119[40]	8,310	8,049
1924	2,947	1,791	1,424	1,261	2,504	2,070	1,277	801	140	8,222	9,539
1925	2,250	1,585	1,446	1,360	2,633	2,039	1,321	773	154	8,753	8,905
1926	2,154	1,606	1,490	1,420	2,415	1,836	1,241	653	125	7,632	7,818
1927	2,586	1,895	1,584	1,617	2,564[23]	2,023[23]	1,218	709	123	7,286	6,400
1928	3,005	2,183	1,708	1,575	2,719	2,133	1,196	724	120	7,835	6,445
1929	2,737	2,113	1,783	1,812	2,731	2,098	1,221	729	110	7,595	7,922
1930	2,448	2,457	1,662	1,550	2,564[23]	1,762[23]	1,044	571	87	6,960	6,780
1931	1,178	990	1,428	1,122	2,251	1,349	861	391	64	4,800	4,801
1932	976	742	1,155	947	1,763[23]	801[23]	702	365	51	2,860	3,056
1933	837	673	1,096	1,079	1,594	853	675	368	49	2,883	3,378
1934	855	613	1,305	1,302	1,435	844	731	396	51	3,573	3,878
1935	876	588	1,476	1,297	1,283	822[23]	756	426	55	3,700	4,030
1936	...	...	1,633	1,514	1,266	882	848	441	61	4,077	4,376
1937	...	...	2,123	2,000	1,807	1,286	1,028	521	75	5,234	6,272
1938	...	...	2,082	1,843	1,607	1,317	920	471	62	4,975	5,047
1939	...	...	2,499	1,889	1,889	1,298	886	440	46	4,757	5,521
1940	621	394	2,004	1,328	1,854	1,316	1,152	441	26	...	...
1941	550	521	1,674	1,345	2,024	1,463	1,145	365	13	...	...
1942	609	631	1,780	1,319	2,049	1,572	1,206	391	11	...	...
1943	914	878	1,814	1,172	1,727[23]	1,629	1,885	337	13	...	...
1944	827	957	1,677	853	1,186	1,132	2,360	327	18	...	...
1945	869	881	1,084	1,758	1,225	1,474	1,517	436	51	...	...
										(new dinars)	
1946	923	813	3,386	2,547	3,423	2,676	1,301[11]	915[11]	50	509	676
1947	1,214	938	5,220	3,240	4,820	3,268	1,798	1,142	60	2,076	2,046
1948	1,441	1,114	4,945	3,979	4,999	3,435	2,075	1,578	65	3,831	3,712
1949	1,399	1,177	4,333	4,250	3,791	3,457	2,278	1,787	59	3,685	2,484

See p. 521 for footnotes

F 1 External Trade Aggregate Current Value (in millions)

1950–1975

	Albania (leks)		Austria (schillings)		Belgium (francs)		Bulgaria (leva)		Czechoslovakia (koruna)	
	I	E	I	E	I	E	I	E	I	E
1950	1,103	324	9,209	6,510	97,835	82,823	...	...	4,603	5,608
1951	1,978	458	14,027	9,635	127,517	132,671	...	...	6,456	6,086
							(new leva)			
1952	1,590	654	13,958	10,797	123,114	122,703	185	200	6,307	6,294
1953	2,001	549	13,269	13,187	121,523	113,444	234	241	6,330	7,153
1954	1,292	509	16,987	15,851	127,863	115,690	229[26]	272	6,716	7,238
1955	2,141	650	23,068	18,169	142,737	139,139	292	276	7,579	8,467
1956	1,940	950	25,319	22,076	164,392	158,614	294	353	8,537	9,988
1957	2,666	1,452	29,339	25,442	172,199	159,850	389	433	9,985	9,776
1958	3,930	1,461	27,912	23,864	156,693	152,708	429	437	9,772	10,895
1959	4,265	1,701	29,760	25,161	172,621	165,335	678	547	11,537	12,435
1960	4,054	2,428	36,813	29,129	198,469	189,560	740	669	13,072	13,892
1961	3,612	2,429	38,604	31,262	211,162	196,500	779	775	14,570	14,733
1962	3,229	2,046	40,348	32,851	228,435	216,613	918	904	14,904	15,793
1963	3,537	2,404	43,557	34,475	256,421	242,012	1,092	976	15,554	17,723
1964	4,906	2,996	48,433	37,601	296,511	280,028	1,243	1,146	17,489	18,545
1965	...	...	54,614	41,600	325,074	319,684	1,378	1,376	19,242	19,357
1966	...	...	60,519	43,773	359,104	341,578	1,730	1,527	19,699	19,764
1967	...	...	60,046	47,029	364,337	354,132	1,839	1,706	19,296	20,622
1968	...	...	64,896	51,707	419,758	408,559	2,085	1,890	22,155	21,638
1969	...	...	73,460	62,723	501,053	504,466	2,047	2,100	23,718	23,900
1970	...	...	92,266	74,270	570,447	579,981	2,142	2,345	26,605	27,305
1971	...	...	104,476	78,997	629,063	620,238	2,480	2,553	28,870	30,095
1972	...	...	120,576	89,747	681,773	710,980	2,772	2,837	30,912	32,588
1973	...	...	137,863	101,977	856,129	870,119	3,172	3,201	35,805	35,322
1974	...	...	168,228	133,356	1,160,685	1,099,825	4,196	3,721	43,974	41,213
1975	...	...	163,344	130,862	1,127,336	1,056,998	5,236	4,541	50,716	46,651

	Denmark (kroner)		Finland (marks)		France (francs)		Germany (marks)		East Germany (valuta marks)	
	I	E	I	E	I	E	I	E	I	E
1950	5,890	4,592	891	815	1,073,158	1,077,785	11,374	8,362	1,973	1,705
1951	6,993	5,793	1,554	1,869	1,615,253	1,484,268	14,726	14,577	2,552	2,993
1952	6,645	5,874	1,822	1,568	1,591,894	1,416,131	16,203	16,909	3,246	3,102
1953	6,914	6,178	1,219	1,315	1,457,874	1,406,353	16,010	18,526	4,127	4,064
1954	8,083	6,648	1,510	1,565	1,522,099	1,509,501	19,337	22,035	4,619	5,402
1955	8,139	7,303	1,770	1,813	1,674,314	1,735,659	24,472	25,717	4,952	5,437
1956	9,057	7,677	2,036	1,779	1,976,229[28]	1,622,569[28]	27,964	30,861	5,620	5,942
					1,978,089	1,623,477				
1957	9,383	8,106	2,279	2,124	2,267,468	1,889,262	31,697	35,968	6,864[34]	7,702[34]
1958	9,303	8,747	2,333	2,479	2,357,243	2,152,808	31,133	36,998	7,153	8,042
	9,435[27]	8,897[27]			(new francs)					
1959	11,064	9,677	2,673[34]	2,672[34]	25,150	27,721	35,823[30]	41,184[30]	8,472	8,994
1960	12,469	10,316	3,403	3,165	31,016	33,901	42,723	47,946	9,217	9,271
1961	12,938	10,620	3,690	3,374	32,992	35,668	44,363	50,978	9,453	9,582
1962	14,715	11,525	3,929	3,533	37,134	36,356	49,498	52,975	10,111	9,987
1963	14,703	13,176	3,867	3,678	43,100	39,916	52,277	58,310	9,788	11,395
1964	18,077	14,651	4,817	4,132	49,719	44,408	58,839	64,920	11,061	12,312
1965	19,495	16,025	5,265	4,566	51,042	49,619	70,448	71,651	11,800	12,893
1966	20,739	16,944	5,524	4,817	58,629	53,807	72,670	80,628	13,503	13,461
1967	21,940	17,660	5,794	5,231	61,108	56,171	70,183	87,045	13,771	14,515
1968	24,274	19,799	6,711	6,874	68,756	62,564	81,179	99,551	14,250	15,923
1969	28,594	22,654	8,505	8,345	89,126	77,009	97,972	113,557	17,318	17,443
1970	33,056	25,172	11,071	9,687	105,101	98,531	109,606	125,276	20,357	19,240
1971	34,209	27,325	11,734	9,897	116,957	113,004	120,119	136,011	20,831	21,321
1972	35,535	31,445	13,107	12,082	134,742	130,368	128,744	149,023	22,851	23,931
1973	46,969	37,549	16,601	14,605	164,262	158,065	145,417	178,396	27,330	26,171
1974	60,480	46,922	25,617	20,680	250,160	217,181	179,733	230,578	33,870	30,443
1975	59,675	50,053	27,983	20,241	229,644	220,751	184,313	221,589	39,290	35,105

See p. 521 for footnotes

F 1 **External Trade Aggregate Current Value** (in millions)

1950–1975

	Greece[4] (tho m drachmae)		Hungary (forints)		Ireland (pounds)		Italy (tho m lire)		Netherlands (gulden)	
	I	E	I	E	I	E[10]	I	E	I	E
1950	2,141	452	3,706	3,857	159	72	926	753	7,811	5,368
1951	5,975	1,524	4,626	4,646	205	82	1,355	1,030	9,700	7,409
1952	5,193	1,798	5,394	5,143	172	102	1,460	867	8,449	8,015
1953	7,156	3,397	5,722	5,849	182	114	1,513	942	9,026	8,180
	(new drachmae)									
1954	9,901	4,556	6,241	6,096	180	115	1,524	1,024	10,860	9,172
1955	11,464	5,484	6,507	7,055	204[41] 208	110	1,695	1,160	12,191	10,211
1956	13,911	5,698	5,649	5,717	183	108	1,984	1,341	14,156	10,876
1957	15,734	6,588	8,011	5,728	184	131	2,296	1,595	15,599	11,770
1958	16,946	6,953	7,407	8,025	199	131	2,010	1,611	13,774	12,227
1959	17,009	6,127	9,309	9,035	213	131	2,105	1,821	14,968	13,703
1960	21,060	6,096	11,455	10,260	226	153	2,953	2,280	17,217	15,305
1961	21,422	6,700	12,040	12,080	261	181	3,265	2,614	18,652	15,712
1962	21,037	7,503	13,485	12,906	274	174	3,797	2,918	19,358	16,596
1963	24,129	8,703	15,327	14,156	308	197	4,745	3,159	21,601	17,962
1964	26,552	9,256	17,546	15,870	349	222	4,533	3,724	25,548	21,025
1965	34,012	9,833	17,849	17,721	372	221	4,611	4,500	27,010	23,144
1966	36,685	12,179	18,379	18,705	373	244	5,368	5,024	29,024	24,443
1967	35,588	14,856	20,841	19,971	392	285	6,142	5,441	30,181	26,380
1968	41,831	14,047	21,163	21,004	497	333	6,429	6,366	33,638	30,197
1969	47,825	16,609	22,631	24,462	590	372	7,792	7,330	39,797	36,074
1970	58,750	19,276	29,410	27,197	655	433	9,356	8,254	48,603	42,622
1971	62,943	19,874	35,098	29,355	755	539	9,901	9,362	52,294	49,775
1972	70,374	26,126	34,093	35,583	838	647	11,265	10,849	55,422	53,879
1973	102,747	42,812	37,299	42,039	1,138	869	16,343	12,989	66,560	66,879
1974	131,555	60,891	51,010	46,927	1,627	1,122	26,604	19,684	87,424	87,926
1975	172,012	74,174	61,537	52,170	1,704	1,447	25,087	22,758	87,346	88,594

	Norway (kroner)		Poland[35] (zlotys)		Portugal (escudos)		Romania (new lei)		Russia (rubels)	
	I	E	I	E	I	E	I[20]	E[20]	I	E
1950	4,846[42]	2,789[42]	2,673	2,537	7,882	5,341	1,460	1,274	1,310	1,615
1951	6,266	4,427	3,697	3,047	9,491	7,561	...	...	1,792	2,062
1952	6,239[43]	4,039[43]	3,452	3,102	9,991	6,845	...	...	2,256	2,511
1953	6,514	3,632	3,097	3,324	9,547	6,284	...	...	2,492	2,653
1954	7,277	4,167	3,615	3,475	10,084	7,297	...	...	2,864	2,901
1955	7,783	4,522	3,727	3,679	11,452	8,189	2,771	2,530	2,755	3,084
1956	8,653	5,517[44]	4,087	3,939	12,724	8,621	...	...	3,251	3,254
1957	9,103	5,867	5,006	3,900	14,422	8,289	...	...	3,544	3,943
1958	9,360[17]	5,315[17]	4,907	4,238	13,791	8,306	2,890	2,810	3,915	3,869
1959	9,449	5,789	5,678	4,581	13,679	8,351	3,012	3,135	4,566	4,905
1960	10,446	6,291	5,980	5,302	15,693	9,408	3,887	4,302	5,066	5,007
1961	11,543	6,652	6,747	6,014	18,857	9,373	4,888	4,755	5,245	5,399
1962	11,885	6,942	7,542	6 585	16,829	10,632	5,647	4,908	5,810	6,328
1963	13,013	7,664[45]	7,916	7,080	18,865	12,023	6,132	5,490	6,353	6,545
1964	14,169	9,219	8,289	8,386	22,376	14,830	7,009	6,000	6,963	6,915
1965	15,787	10,309	9,361	8,911	26,551	16,572	6,463	6,609	7,253	7,357
1966	17,170	11,168	9,976	9,088	29,406	17,811	7,279	7,117	7,112	7,957
1967	19,627	12,411	10,579	10,106	30,451	20,164	9,277	8,372	7,863	8,687
1968	19,331	13,841	11,412	11,431	33,856	21,909	9,654	8,811	8,469	9,571
1969	21,011	15,741	12,839	12,566	37,261	24,526	10,443	9,799	9,294	10,490
1970	26,443	17,549	14,430	14,191	45,493	27,296	11,761	11,105	10,559	11,520
1971	28,715	18,003	16,151	15,489	52,416	30,248	12,616	12,606	11,232	12,426
1972	28,808	21,625	19,613	18,133	60,684	35,255	14,465	14,373	13,309	12,734
1973	36,041	27,085	26,303	21,355	74,776	45,410	17,418	18,576	15,544	15,802
1974	46,556	34,732	34,799	27,605	114,700	58,014	25,563	24,226	18,834	20,738
1975	50,541	37,778	41,424	34,063	97,589	49,335	26,548	26,547	26,669	24,030

See p. 521 for footnotes

F 1 External Trade Aggregate Current Value (in millions)

1950–1975

	Spain[6] (pesetas)		Sweden (kronor)		Switzerland (francs)		United Kingdom[7] (pounds)			Yugoslavia (new dinars)	
	I	E	I	E	I	E	I	DE	RE	I	E
1950	1,195 23,344[46]	1,239 23,363[46]	6,102	5,707	4,536	3,911	2,607[11] 3,892	2,174[11] 2,566	85	2,883	1,929
1951	25,460	28,930	9,184	9,225	5,911	4,690			127	4,796	2,234
1952	34,300	27,479	8,947	8,134	5,193	4,748	3,465	2,567	142	4,663	3,082
1953	35,770[47]	28,930[47]	8,161[47]	7,657[47]	5,054	5,163	3,328	2,558	103	4,941	2,325
1954	36,828	27,871	9,192	8,196	5,587	5,264	3,359	2,650	98	4,242	3,005
1955	37,044	26,774	10,337	8,933	6,397	5,616	3,861	2,877	116	5,512	3,207
1956	46,001	26,519	11,434	10,067	7,590	6,195	3,862	3,143	144	5,927	4,042
1957	51,724	28,557	12,567	11,062	8,442	6,702	4,044	3,295	130	8,266	4,939
1958	52,332	29,145	12,249	10,799	7,330	6,615	3,748	3,176	141	8,563	5,517
1959	47,687	30,047	12,488	11,424	8,263	7,233	3,983	3,330	131	8,590	5,958
1960	43,286	43,564	15,006	13,273	9,641	8,074	4,541	3,555	141	10,330	7,077
1961	65,535	42,575	15,151	14,198	11,635	8,773	4,395	3,681	159	11,378	7,111
1962	94,166	44,165	16,154	15,129	12,977	9,524	4,487	3,791	158	11,097	8,631
1963	117,305	44,134	17,552	16,568	13,978	10,378	4,813	4,081	154	13,208	9,879
1964	134,637	57,265	19,946	19,014	15,512	11,367	5,507	4,253	153	16,540	11,164
1965	180,206	57,989	22,644	20,541	15,929	12,861	5,751	4,728	173	16,099	13,644
1966	214,339	75,213	23,704	22,071	17,004	14,204	5,947	5,047	194	19,623	15,251
1967	211,008	84,660	24,319	23,422	17,786	15,165	6,434	5,029	185	21,342	15,646
1968	245,150	111,244	26,516	25,553	19,425	17,349	7,890	6,183	220	22,460	15,796
1969	294,111	133,012	30,546	29,445	22,734	20,009	8,315	7,040	259	26,672	18,431
1970	330,045	167,087	36,235	35,137	27,873	22,140	9,037	8,061		35,925	20,989
1971	345,531	205,645	36,181	38,159	29,642	23,617	9,821	9,181		48,781	27,217
1972	435,523	245,215	38,604	41,739	32,340	26,091	11,138	9,746		54,957	38,033
1973	558,168	302,670	46,311	53,135	36,588	29,948	15,840	12,454		76,689	48,494
1974	883,661	407,894	72,758	70,485	42,929	35,353	23,117	16,494		127,837	64,678
1975	922,205	441,091	74,050	72,239	34,172	33,250	24,028	19,762		130,845	69,228

See p. 521 for footnotes

F 1 External Trade Aggregate Current Values

NOTES

1. SOURCES:– Finland to 1859 – Kauko E. Joustela, *Suomen Venäjänkauppa autonomisen ajan alkupuoliskolla vv. 1809–65* (Helsinki, 1963). Finland 1860– 1917 Erkki Pihkala, *Finland's Foreign Trade, 1860–1917* (Bank of Finland, Helsinki, 1969). Germany to 1939 – W.G. Hoffman, *Das Wachstum der Deutschen Wirtschaft seit der Mitte des 19 Jahrhunderts* (Berlin, etc., 1965). Germany 1940–49 – supplied by the Federal German Statistical Office. Russia to 1913 – P.A. Khromov, *Economic Development of Russia in the 19th and 20th Centuries, 1800–1917* (Moscow, 1950). Sweden 1832–42 – supplied by the Swedish Central Office of Statistics. U.K. imports and re-exports to 1953 – estimates in A.H. Imlah, *Economic Elements in the Pax Britannica* (Cambridge, Mass., 1958. All other statistics are taken from the official publications noted on p. xv with gaps filled from the League of Nations, *International Trade Statistics* and the United Nations, *Yearbook of International Trade.*

2. Except as indicated in footnotes, statistics are of merchandise trade only, and are of 'special' rather than 'general' trade – i.e. imports for domestic consumption, and exports of domestic origin plus re-exports of commodiites originally entered for domestic consumption.

3. Imports are normally valued c.i.f., and exports f.o.b.

FOOTNOTES

[1]The Austro-Hungarian customs area did not include Dalmatia until 1861, and it excluded Bosnia-Hercegovina throughout. Otherwise it conformed to the boundaries of the day of the Hapsburg Empire. Statistics from 1920 apply to the Republic of Austria.

[2]From May 1922 to 31 August 1940, and since 1 May 1945, the statistics apply to the Belgium-Luxembourg customs area. Gold movements are included.

[3]E. Levasseur, *Histoire du Commerce de la France* (Paris, 1912) quotes the following statistics from Arnould, *De la balance du commerce* for period averages during the *ancien régime* (in million livres):–

	I	E		I	E		I	E
1716–20	92.3	122.5	1740–48	182.6	238.5	1765–76	333.3	391.6
1721–32	115.8	148.4	1749–55	275.5	341.2	1777–83	345.7	337.8
1733–35	123.3	154.2	1756–63	174.6	148.9	1784–88	567.7	493.9
1736–39	167.6							

Statistics to 1825 (1st line) are of 'general' trade.

[4]The following are the main boundary changes affecting the trading area of Greece:– 1864 Ionian Islands acquired; 1881 Arta and much of Thessaly acquired; 1914 Crete, Epiros, and part of Macedonia acquired; 1919 Thrace acquired, but the eastern part was returned to Turkey in 1923; 1949 Dodecanese Islands acquired.

[5]The revaluation of the paper rouble in terms of silver was approximately four times.

[6]Gold is included, and, prior to 1888, the transit trade.

[7]The values of imports and re-exports to 1853 are estimates (see note 1). All imports and included, whether for home consumption or for re-export.

[8]These figures are for the 14 months beginning 1 November 1852. Previous statistics are for years ended 31 October.

[9]Statistics are of 'general' trade, though re-exports are in fact regligible. Gold movements are included up to 1930 (1st line).

[10]Figures to 1874 (1st line) are of 'general' trade.

[11]There is probably a slight break owing to changes in the method of valuation.

[12]From 1871 to 1918 Alsace Lorraine was included in Germany rather than France.

[13]Statistics are available back to 1871, but not on a consistent basis, and incomplete statistics go back to 1834 for the Zollverein.

[14]Previous statistics are based on officially determined, but variable values.

[15]Transit trade is included in 1877 and probably earlier. It is excluded subsequently, but there were alterations in definition affecting the composition of 'special' trade in 1897, 1907, and 1930.

[16]Including very small amounts of re-exports.

[17]Figures to 1938 and from 1959 are of 'general' trade. For the period to 1865 they are calculated on the basis of fixed estimated prices. Up to 1906 in-transit trade for Sweden is included in both imports and exports.

[18]Including Maderia and the Azores.

[19]Previous statistics include gold movements.

[20]Figures to 1910 and from 1950 are of 'general' trade, but in 1910 they did not differ from those of 'special' trade.

[21]Figures for 1849–53 exclude trade in tobacco.

[22] Statistics of exports to Norway are incomplete for the period 1898–1901.

[23] After 1930 re-exports (though not direct transit trade) are included in both imports and exports. All gold movements are included to 1927. From 1928 gold for banking purposes is excluded, and from 1936 (exports) and 1944 (imports) all gold is excluded. From 1933 to 1939 the repair and finishing trades are included.

[24] The value of new ships sold abroad is subsequently included.

[25] The 1938 figures are for January–September and the 1945 figures for May–December. For the intervening period the following statistics are available for the separate parts of the country (in million koruna):–

Czechoslovakia (less Sudetenland)	Imports	Exports	Protectorate (continued)	Imports	Exports
Oct-Dec 1938	1,501	1,723	1944	1,829	4,701
Jan–15 March 1939	2,194	2,292	Jan–Apri 1945	213	432
Bohemia, Moravia, Silesia Protectorate			Slovakia		
16 Mar-Dec 1939	4,103	4,312	16 Mar-Dec 1939	1,555	2,200
1940	4,764	4,215	1940	2,873	3,175
1941	3,654	4,248	1941	3,486	3,191
1942	2,695	4,085	1942	4,751	4,704
1943	2,583	5,149	1943	5,183	5,832

[26] Imports as well as exports are subsequently valued f.o.b.

[27] Strictly speaking the statistics to 1937 (1st line) are not of 'special' trade, but of 'general' imports less re-exports (at import value) and 'general' exports less re-exports (at export value). Statistics from 1958 (2nd line) are of 'general' trade.

[28] There were slight changes in the basis of collection.

[29] Prior to 1 March 1906 the free ports of Hamburg, Cuxhaven, Bremerhaven, and Geestemunde were not included in the German customs area.

[30] From 1920 to March 1935 and from 1945 to July 1959 Saarland is not included in Germany (or West Germany).

[31] Figures for 1920 to 1923 (1st line) are in 1913 values instead of current values.

[32] May-December only.

[33] Reparations in kind are not previously included. In 1924 they amounted to 122 thousand gold marks.

[34] The figures are subsequently of 'general' trade.

[35] Figures to 1939 include the Free City of Danzig.

[36] January to July only.

[37] Statistics are subsequently of 'general' trade, both imports and exports being valued f.o.b. at official exchange rates.

[38] Including bullion.

[39] The figure for 1922 is for 9 months to 30 September, and the statistics for 1923–28 are for years ended 30 September. In the last quarter of 1928 (not shown here) imports were 159 and exports 170 million roubles.

[40] Trade with southern Ireland is treated as external from 1 April 1923.

[41] Revised estimates for the parcel post were not carried back beyond 1955.

[42] Spitzbergen is subsequently treated as an integral part of Norway.

[43] Partly worked gold, and coins of gold and silver, are subsequently no longer included.

[44] Subsequently including whale-oil etc. delivered direct from fishing grounds.

[45] Subsequently includes floated timber.

[46] Previously in million gold pesetas, subsequently in million paper pesetas.

[47] Subsequently including the Canary Islands, Ceuta and Melilla.

[48] Subsequently includes unmanufactured gold and silver, and coins.

F2 EXTERNAL TRADE (by value) WITH MAIN TRADING PARTNERS

1890–1919

AUSTRIA-HUNGARY (in million kronen)

	Germany		British East Indies		Italy		Russia[1]		U.K.		U.S.A.	
	I	E	I	E	I	E	I	E	I	E	I	E
1890	...	...	...	...	...	...	...	...	...	...	...	...
1891	448	855	96	9	68	94	56	36	129	107	47	21
1892	462	804	93	10	84	107	48	33	123	92	50	28
1893	493	856	104	15	102	115	62	47	134	135	58	24
1894	516	835	88	14	100	105	86	58	149	142	63	26
1895	518	767	80	13	95	125	94	54	151	127	75	34
1896	515	804	85	14	94	120	88	55	147	148	85	35
1897	541	798	83	24	110	119	112	52	138	141	112	34
1898	565	841	84	33	118	116	136	64	139	149	134	29
1899	599	983	87	36	119	143	87	81	148	165	125	32
1900	635	1,016	84	46	114	147	89	72	149	201	153	38
1901	635	978	95	60	104	136	86	73	137	187	129	33
1902	652	988	89	46	110	148	96	75	143	173	136	40
1903	697	1,091	112	34	122	153	114	80	155	227	163	46
1904	767	1,037	130	62	105	157	120	72	155	182	182	41
1905	804	1,114	125	69	107	161	138	65	157	200	204	53
1906	906	1,133	164	73	116	178	151	69	189	231	215	59
1907	979	1,177	185	51	123	193	138	78	239	222	239	67
1908	995	1,047	136	56	118	228	127	72	216	231	222	58
1909	1,068	1,045	174	58	123	233	181	77	219	241	231	84
1910	1,154	1,062	214	69	131	228	167	91	229	224	237	81
1911	1,263	1,038	220	52	142	222	209	96	229	216	290	58
1912	1,406	1,213	199	63	162	239	229	91	245	257	349	64
1913	1,367	1,211	233	95	169	216	202	103	217	270	323	70
1914	1,190	1,009	196	47	182	190	135	70	148	132	224	63
1915	1,648	975	24	—	204	35	26	25	6	—	221	17
1916	2,384	1,153	4	—	5	—	134	77	2	—	19	4
1917	...	...	...	...	...	...	...	...	...	...	...	...
1918	...	...	...	...	...	...	...	...	...	...	...	...
1919	...	...	...	...	...	...	...	...	...	...	...	...

See p. 605 for footnotes

F2 External Trade (by value) with Main Trading Partners

AUSTRIA (in million schillings) 1920–1944

	Czechoslovakia		Germany		Hungary		Italy		Poland		Switzerland		U.K.		U.S.A.		Yugoslavia	
	I	E	I	E	I	E	I	E	I	E	I	E	I	E	I	E	I	E
1920	...	...	...	...	...	...	...	...	...	...	...	...	...	...	...	...	...	...
1921	...	...	...	...	...	...	...	...	...	...	...	...	...	...	...	...	...	...
1922	596	163	575	248	282	206	131	168	118	147	130	75	59	56	207	22	104	199
1923	633	168	508	228	301	134	193	167	171	129	159	119	66	73	176	29	142	213
1924	780	217	537	279	402	174	250	205	259	194	197	131	108	85	192	41	151	205
1925	566	215	479	316	318	162	122	208	249	164	127	93	105	72	222	42	134	176
1926	554	208	483	222	361	172	144	180	252	73	130	108	103	69	151	61	166	153
1927	565	240	543	412	298	203	140	192	270	106	157	114	135	76	192	64	176	157
1928	593	279	667	440	279	191	114	196	301	123	167	138	146	81	217	76	131	165
1929	591	303	704	374	328	168	119	207	291	107	149	124	120	99	198	75	132	169
1930	480	228	581	333	285	122	107	176	217	84	116	110	93	102	144	49	149	150
1931	367	156	495	224	198	93	94	109	178	57	94	95	76	93	96	25	96	100
1932	213	83	290	139	136	72	68	76	106	33	49	61	37	29	56	15	108	58
1933	158	63	236	130	135	81	51	87	77	52	44	64	37	35	62	19	104	57
1934	160	67	209	145	129	98	50	91	73	35	45	64	51	47	62	13	98	53
1935	156	66	204	145	115	96	57	127	77	38	40	51	54	39	71	17	82	54
1936	144	71	216	157	118	95	59	129	74	49	39	47	55	53	78	23	77	49
1937	160	88	238	184	132	112	80	173	67	53	48	70	67	65	87	31	115	67
1938	...	...	...	...	...	...	...	...	...	...	...	...	...	...	...	...	...	...
1939	...	...	...	...	...	...	...	...	...	...	...	...	...	...	...	...	...	...
1940	...	...	...	...	...	...	...	...	...	...	...	...	...	...	...	...	...	...
1941	...	...	...	...	...	...	...	...	...	...	...	...	...	...	...	...	...	...
1942	...	...	...	...	...	...	...	...	...	...	...	...	...	...	...	...	...	...
1943	...	...	...	...	...	...	...	...	...	...	...	...	...	...	...	...	...	...
1944	...	...	...	...	...	...	...	...	...	...	...	...	...	...	...	...	...	...

F2 External Trade (by value) with Main Trading Partners

AUSTRIA (in million schillings) **1945–1975**

	Czechoslovakia		Germany		Hungary		Italy		Poland		Switzerland		U.K.		U.S.A.		Yugoslavia	
	I	E	I	E	I	E	I	E	I	E	I	E	I	E	I	E	I	E
1945	...	....	...	...	...	...	...	...	...	...	...	...	...	...	...	...	...	...
1946	...	...	...	...	...	...	...	...	...	...	...	...	...	...	...	...	...	...
1947	156	78	210	37	34	36	89	138	63	23	160	212	109	45	40	44	26	18
1948	270	149	228	115	117	73	288	369	120	29	220	264	143	148	173	102	223	97
1949	391	233	764 [2]	250 [2]	202	140	574	766	242	122	214	187	287	137	1,843	96	179	217
1950	399	398	1,528	996	199	237	722	1,214	425	199	380	341	713	244	2,138	363	214	262
1951	464	509	2,351	1,369	282	151	742	1,348	528	421	604	586	1,642	845	3,116	577	341	288
1952	434	417	3,009	2,171	242	214	878	1,528	541	385	521	554	1,341	754	2,553	551	619	556
1953	287 [3]	227 [3]	3,737 [3]	2,609 [3]	173 [3]	166 [3]	970 [3]	2,158 [3]	557 [3]	403 [3]	581 [3]	593 [3]	1,376 [3]	1,181 [3]	1,652 [3]	820 [3]	348 [3]	564 [3]
	247	227	3,762	2,510	125	167	967	2,306	527	407	564	549	766	908	1,655	765	248	544
1954	224	195	6,106	3,728	363	305	1,436	2,829	533	465	766	694	817	616	1,488	734	439	634
1955	395	279	8,173	4,557	502	392	1,837	3,059	634	464	1,001	837	1,035	665	2,431	898	386	558
1956	459	494	8,602	5,159	496	507	2,057	3,685	668	712	1,252	1,222	1,068	792	3,262	1,154	391	597
1957	490	587	11,094	6,119	391	614	2,321	4,467	857	832	1,443	1,374	1,218	630	3,659	984	489	677
1958	472	486	10,915	6,052	529	510	2,104	4,062	772	815	1,204	994	1,213	578	2,818	1,177	458	681
1959	546	472	11,979	6,671	619	677	2,339	4,140	730	521	1,305	1,142	1,375	647	2,032	1,484	535	708
1960	598	764	14,706	7,810	693	695	2,963	4,847	813	526	1,594	757	1,819	820	2,703	1,284	719	1,011
1961	608	835	16,553	8,585	546	678	3,060	4,764	721	691	1,808	825	1,942	958	2,287	1,200	621	902
1962	651	798	17,071	9,177	784	734	3,302	5,036	848	759	2,003	2,369	2,039	934	2,249	1,273	654	874
1963	732	706	18,006	9,093	848	991	3,377	5,750	1,052	526	2,238	2,337	2,342	1,347	2,064	1,311	778	882
1964	770	751	20,215	10,481	703	1,125	3,606	4,624	1,037	612	2,632	2,963	2,581	1,716	2,497	1,493	690	990
1965	988	967	22,815	11,899	814	1,102	4,512	4,481	1,180	829	3,018	3,109	2,987	1,616	2,400	1,739	725	1,013
1966	913	1,146	25,670	11,707	983	1,012	4,575	4,712	1,106	931	3,623	3,556	3,470	1,846	2,624	2,005	1,168	998
1967	972	1,072	25,014	10,444	884	1,252	4,717	5,580	958	1,042	4,387	4,067	3,614	2,613	2,096	2,010	1,200	1,501
1968	1,207	1,207	26,879	12,094	1,052	1,351	4,657	5,332	1,061	1,015	4,856	4,746	3,995	3,280	2,171	2,393	1,174	1,948
1969	1,596	1,566	30,352	15,197	1,254	1,598	4,829	6,345	1,198	1,097	5,598	5,956	4,859	3,566	2,193	2,855	1,176	2,323
1970	1,753	1,606	38,053	17,357	1,549	2,089	6,032	7,189	1,506	1,161	6,820	7,698	6,252	4,552	3,155	3,043	1,296	3,444
1971	2,123	1,733	42,844	18,111	1,548	2,222	6,973	7,329	1,361	1,249	7,740	8,820	6,914	5,661	3,869	3,185	1,186	3,332
1972	2,000	1,648	50,480	20,120	1,975	2,162	8,700	8,625	1,586	1,825	8,743	10,362	7,310	6,993	3,902	4,040	1,224	2,870
1973	2,214	1,984	57,460	22,186	2,551	2,581	10,137	10,731	1,710	2,492	10,255	11,162	7,127	7,744	4,225	4,243	1,432	3,956
1974	3,092	2,872	67,455	26,227	3,256	5,072	11,893	12,760	2,388	4,345	11,549	13,341	7,151	8,528	4,835	4,646	1,712	6,819
1975	3,330	3,324	65,345	28,601	2,420	4,702	13,210	10,413	2,555	5,784	11,000	10,233	6,508	7,342	4,787	3,248	1,418	5,983

See p. 605 for footnotes

F2 External Trade (by value) with Main Trading Partners

BELGIUM (in million francs)[4] 1844–1879

	Argentina		France		Germany		India		Netherlands		Russia		U.K.		U.S.A.	
	I	E	I	E	I	E	I	E	I	E	I	E	I	E	I	E
1844	...	...	...	...	...	...	...	...	...	...	...	...	...	...	...	...
1845	2	—	43	82	27	33	...	...	37	33	23	1	42	16	20	3
1846	1	—	47	69	32	29	...	...	34	22	22	1	27	13	13	3
1847	2	—	45	72	31	36	...	...	41	28	32	1	37	13	17	6
1848	2	—	38	49	21	27	...	...	38	27	15	1	27	29	12	5
1849	3	—	43	56	23	31	...	...	36	29	13	1	39	34	20	7
1850	4	—	51	67	25	40	...	...	39	31	13	2	37	37	17	10
1851	3	1	55	66	25	37	...	...	40	31	12	2	41	32	12	10
1852	6	1	55	80	28	44	...	...	45	36	22	3	49	36	20	9
1853	6	1	62	99	37	45	...	...	51	42	28	4	47	60	21	15
1854	8	2	57	119	48	46	...	...	68	52	18	1	47	119	27	18
1855	12	2	60	132	66	36	...	...	75	49	2	—	67	78	23	11
1856	22	2	73	146	61	47	...	...	78	57	19	2	77	59	28	15
1857	37	2	76	158	46	69	...	...	82	58	27	5	73	67	31	15
1858	23	1	106	139	38	62	...	...	84	59	30	6	86	59	19	13
1859	34	2	110	150	41	60	...	...	93	59	26	8	78	77	22	11
1860	41	4	110	162	59	74	...	...	102	62	28	6	83	95	24	10
1861	42	3	97	174	72	69	...	...	114	60	33	7	91	76	27	5
1862	45	2	139	178	76	75	...	...	109	63	31	7	85	103	23	12
1863	28	3	150	187	73	76	...	...	112	74	22	11	109	103	26	6
1864	36	3	179	217	81	84	...	...	129	82	24	4	119	115	29	9
1865	83	4	203	239	72	83	...	...	113	70	40	14	146	134	19	7
1866	72	4	197	265	89	81	...	...	88	80	30	8	141	130	38	10
1867	56	3	196	236	102	91	...	...	97	68	48	15	131	122	37	9
1868	71	2	201	273	112	108	...	...	122	75	47	13	142	120	36	7
1869	67	3	233	258	116	121	...	...	134	81	46	22	145	129	39	11
1870	50	3	233	231	122	139	...	...	141	82	43	22	159	147	42	11
1871	63	5	247	297	230	209	...	...	171	103	64	12	233	193	87	9
1872	77	8	316	321	169	240	...	...	165	121	63	12	230	238	81	14
1873	71	7	336	380	172	266	...	...	179	132	73	13	263	242	136	16
1874	50	5	326	343	167	243	...	...	171	157	92	15	204	222	123	19
1875	48	4	356	344	172	244	...	...	170	150	81	18	249	209	71	17
1876	58	4	353	314	196	244	...	...	185	165	115	19	249	192	111	11
1877	64	8	354	296	215	223	...	...	197	166	82	25	213	228	122	11
1878	54	7	323	329	237	220	...	...	187	146	130	23	194	250	176	9
1879	40	7	309	372	220	248	...	...	202	156	145	17	200	230	230	20

See p. 605 for footnotes

F2 External Trade (by value) with Main Trading Partners

BELGIUM (in million francs) 1880–1914

	Argentina		France		Germany		India		Netherlands		Russia		U.K.		U.S.A.	
	I	E	I	E	I	E	I	E	I	E	I	E	I	E	I	E
1880	39	5	335	399	245	234	18	—	237	151	127	13	255	247	271	36
1881	33	11	336	415	229	251	50	—	245	160	118	11	240	254	223	43
1882	46	12	318	441	243	227	72	2	238	163	139	10	198	262	185	45
1883	48	10	307	415	233	229	81	3	210	177	134	8	198	274	160	43
1884	62	17	277	412	185	236	65	3	188	176	124	8	185	252	161	40
1885	55	11	259	322	176	215	69	3	197	186	93	6	164	238	120	33
1886	60	15	251	330	152	196	69	4	200	175	74	9	172	236	160	41
1887	69	18	283	335	157	210	47	4	199	168	96	6	188	240	165	49
1888	55	22	289	343	179	212	56	5	216	172	150	6	183	256	120	52
1889	57	42	323	353	174	258	64	9	205	217	113	11	198	300	118	43
1890	75	17	316	359	182	265	77	10	206	208	114	10	213	268	157	51
1891	87	12	327	379	180	313	122	9	197	229	116	8	199	266	200	55
1892	68	14	300	311	168	313	61	13	179	190	74	6	183	235	207	53
1893	83	15	278	310	180	301	71	15	201	177	98	17	198	242	135	50
1894	90	14	282	285	185	294	76	16	174	155	105	22	178	235	126	42
1895	93	14	300	284	199	311	53	20	175	165	117	22	193	267	133	47
1896	85	19	311	288	215	327	55	21	177	171	110	31	206	291	174	49
1897	68	17	297	298	234	363	47	17	155	184	139	41	276	302	232	60
1898	100	21	311	332	245	451	92	18	165	203	126	41	284	307	303	52
1899	148	20	390	346	285	486	85	15	169	215	132	44	312	361	280	65
1900	119	21	375	426	324	427	40	18	196	218	126	31	301	359	267	79
1901	100	21	351	351	300	415	71	25	199	201	106	29	227	342	336	78
1902	104	14	386	357	331	429	85	22	208	218	148	33	241	359	276	89
1903	185	22	412	393	340	459	117	21	229	233	219	38	248	365	266	93
1904	199	42	466	347	351	505	142	26	241	269	212	27	255	392	222	86
1905	240	48	518	372	410	570	104	35	245	261	238	33	284	366	242	92
1906	238	66	605	548	465	642	104	28	260	273	234	36	352	410	299	108
1907	243	72	652	530	460	701	175	29	299	304	211	38	395	411	318	80
1908	311	60	517	465	450	680	96	29	290	282	203	38	353	364	341	73
1909	320	90	563	499	495	730	168	35	283	311	326	41	362	409	277	107
1910	278	129	747	669	576	881	188	32	293	328	364	67	419	458	231	117
1911	272	84	739	695	602	959	268	35	298	352	318	67	436	498	341	114
1912	306	93	908	752	703	1,007	...	...	357	368	272	83	506	595	414	145
1913	317	91	1,000	762	762	940	241	48	357	321	267	88	519	545	420	106
1914	...	...	...	...	...	...	...	...	...	...	...	...	...	...	...	...

F2 External Trade (by value) with Main Trading Partners

1915–1944

BELGIUM[4] (in million francs)

	Argentina		France		Germany		India		Netherlands		Russia		U.K.		U.S.A.	
	I	E	I	E	I	E	I	E	I	E	I	E	I	E	I	E
1915	...	...	...	...	...	...	...	...	...	...	...	...	...	...	...	...
1916	...	...	...	...	...	...	...	...	...	...	...	...	...	...	...	...
1917	...	...	...	...	...	...	...	...	...	...	...	...	...	...	...	...
1918	...	...	...	...	...	...	...	...	...	...	...	...	...	...	...	...
1919	211	10	938	590	100	667	108	7	383	448	28	7	1,416	241	1,087	50
1920	833	142	2,318	2,527	952	1,282	621	113	778	1,037	19	3	2,185	1,454	2,280	316
1921	714[4]	108[4]	1,785[4]	1,639[4]	1,409[4]	1,097[4]	359[4]	102[4]	952[4]	954[4]	28[4]	6[4]	1,198[4]	1,343[4]	1,615[4]	222[4]
1922	[467][5]	[138][5]	[1,347][5]	[1,114][5]	[870][5]	[609][5]	[122][5]	[104][5]	[703][5]	[456][5]	[6][5]	[1][5]	[931][5]	[769][5]	[747][5]	[147][5]
1923	956	362	2,866	2,019	916	458	388	231	1,381	1,206	38	2	2.212	1.902	1.479	874
1924	1,469	434	3,791	2,196	1,614	1,576	636	359	1,815	1,704	120	4	2,400	2,916	1,985	1,087
1925	1,420	438	3,727	2,189	1,640	1,829	686	307	1,890	1,589	148	82	2,232	2,902	2,174	1,208
1926	1,681	516	4,912	2,834	2,504	2,487	761	463	2,385	2,274	238	8	2,668	3,839	2,625	2,277
1927	2,348	772	5,925	3,071	3,610	4,521	664	694	3,104	2,893	218	8	3,334	4,877	3,200	2,421
1928	2,230	1,109	6,666	3,967	3,994	4,246	821	793	3,707	4,120	205	51	3,613	5,246	3,098	2,422
1929	2,347	941	6,939	4,016	4,908	3,812	882	797	4,134	4,043	210	103	3,980	5,806	3,407	2,155
1930	1,551	712	5,516	4,121	5,181	2,987	797	575	4,047	3,348	605	77	2,838	4,998	3,106	1,289
1931	1,268	407	4,172	4,070	4,047	2,390	428	467	3,514	2,969	470	56	1,955	4,917	2,099	1,149
1932	1,034	306	2,658	2,930	2,748	1,553	296	441	2,327	1,946	366	33	1,413	2,367	1,411	715
1933	910	331	2,581	2,934	2,473	1,448	368	289	1,742	1,767	462	52	1,372	1,792	1,201	720
1934	949	453	2,339	2,410	2,004	1,628	347	280	1,437	1,549	384	117	1,098	2,002	1,004	594
1935	1,259	591	2,725	2,960	2,133	1,583	439	360	1,636	1,845	562	189	1,393	2,400	1,296	991
1936	1,189	597	2,898	3,520	2,476	2,064	637	391	1,936	2,360	632	298	1,959	2,888	1,475	1,572
1937	1,766	388	3,443	4,401	3,175	2,779	412	428	2,275	2,818	748	449	2,307	3,455	2,368	1,909
1938	951	687	3,310	3,324	2,599	2,648	642[6] 597	364[6] 357	2,075	2,610	783	444	1,833	2,973	2,489	1,443
1939	1,222	775	3,073	2,862	2,378	1,999	408	334	1,868	3,444	253	148	1,610	3,027	1,928	1,983
1940	535[4]	247[4]	1,285[4]	2,089[4]	1,322[4]	1,181[4]	157[4]	166[4]	1,009[4]	2,071[4]	... [4]	... [4]	695[4]	1,116[4]	834[4]	705[4]
1941	—	—	1,266	1,201	3,979	2,369	—	—	883	1,331	...	...	7	—	39	—
1942	—	—	1,913	1,052	2,988	2,894	1	—	716	835	...	...	1	—	7	—
1943	—	—	2,092	1,085	2,798	6,453	—	—	600	670	—	—	—	—	3	—
1944	—	—	1,116	445	1,630	4,266	—	—	409	355	—	—	6	—	4	—

See p. 605 for footnotes

F2 **External Trade (by value) with Main Trading Partners**

1945–1975

BELGIUM[4] (in million francs)

	Argentina		France		Germany		India				Netherlands		Russia		U.K.		U.S.A.	
	I	E	I	E	I	E	I		E		I	E	I	E	I	E	I	E
							India	Pakistan	India	Pakistan								
1945	528[4]	9[4]	2,061[4]	1,360[4]	519[4]	1[4]	173[4]		—[4]		460[4]	847[4]	12[4]	—[4]	3,314[4]	67[4]	2,526[4]	748[4]
1946	2,149	1,044	7,718	4,454	1,483	173	588		100		2,970	4,495	52	9	9,669	1,934	11,618	3,230
1947	2,865	1,855	9,698	7,638	2,282[2]	945[2]	1,501		697		5,022	7,867	377	82	7,932	6,055	22,662	2,711
1948	3,666	3,878	7,665	6,971	4,881	3,268	1,043	216	1,022	129	7,189	11,444	2,199	886	8,478	6,665	15,647	4,452
1949	2,197	2,145	8,248	5,983	5,281	8,381	780	363	1,171	542	7,587	11,727	248	1,313	7,218	7,494	14,781	4,188
1950	1,468	501	11,042	7,626	7,892	5,631	917	420	696	432	9,779	18,561	552	1,027	9,426	6,462	15,253	6,992
1951	1,375	1,843	13,104	12,141	11,186	8,042	1,400	1,129	869	728	13,916	23,789	854	669	10,627	13,319	20,558	10,501
1952	1,050	1,208	12,451	9,096	13,289	11,719	966	707	945	519	16,216	18,745	579	742	10,050	13,588	18,070	9,213
1953	2,421	248	13,405	9,062	14,868	10,513	779	866	1,021	487	16,620	20,121	836	827	10,955	8,785	12,438	11,544
1954	2,921	1,008	15,259	11,109	17,358	11,116	594	896	1,228	409	17,068	24,174	1,398	1,216	10,680	7,252	13,129	9,275
1955	1,220	1,163	17,693	13,897	19,703	16,335	1,237	1,084	1,146	473	18,811	28,766	1,471	846	12,059	8,928	15,673	12,183
1956	1,685	769	19,482	16,904	24,340	16,059	786	1,011	2,449	714	21,363	34,659	1,792	1,586	13,227	10,090	20,429	15,090
1957	2,047	2,778	20,428	17,564	26,730	16,286	689	984	1,969	489	24,302	36,215	1,746	1,410	14,079	8,884	21,247	13,113
1958	2,232	3,144	18,137	16,141	26,840	17,606	595	892	1,870	536	24,581	31,515	1,262	883	11,572	8,690	15,497	14,076
1959	2,368	2,121	21,552	14,719	28,226	22,103	534	784	778	441	27,171	35,008	1,637	375	14,342	9,743	16,252	21,786
1960	2,280	1,365	26,898	19,620	33,701	29,803	692	748	1,196	900	29,390	40,149	1,432	951	14,583	10,481	19,551	17,891
1961	2,390	1,445	31,051	22,072	37,637	30,153	791	928	875	839	32,299	45,939	1,764	1,367	15,912	10,325	18,740	18,055
1962	3,511	905	33,246	26,824	42,565	38,184	799	1,106	778	329	33,665	49,309	2,298	1,280	18,353	10,807	22,553	20,696
1963	3,285	444	38,461	35,248	49,226	44,801	766	960	1,130	493	37,696	54,648	2,550	660	21,071	13,877	23,597	20,554
1964	3,091	544	43,814	42,303	58,682	57,927	935	1,199	1,097	526	43,986	64,123	2,484	735	22,706	13,824	26,238	22,514
1965	3,127	663	49,764	46,403	69,079	69,712	1,261	1,166	1,552	758	48,255	70,366	2,314	1,139	24,383	15,328	27,533	26,606
1966	3,943	421	55,808	55,178	77,629	71,992	1,338	1,340	1,935	665	52,481	75,973	3,034	1,322	26,567	16,086	28,479	29,565
1967	4,159	428	55,844	63,169	78,074	69,777	1,518	1,062	1,988	616	54,224	75,790	2,976	2,015	25,121	16,718	29,563	29,420
1968	3,746	559	63,562	75,760	86,564	85,476	1,983	1,195	1,770	615	60,770	85,902	3,307	2,371	30,111	17,846	34,456	38,507
1969	3,977	948	79,445	105,760	115,891	115,233	2,142	1,063	2,044	1,014	71,225	97,384	2,936	2,551	34,753	20,242	38,323	34,754
1970	4,721	998	97,636	115,160	133,466	140,042	1,619	1,061	2,066	686	83,321	112,649	3,899	2,710	33,156	21,430	50,181	35,150
1971	4,159	1,135	111,459	123,046	158,105	157,366	1,697	1,127	1,728	366	103,385	123,046	5,042	3,236	38,882	22,408	40,220	41,338
1972	3,653	1,431	132,956	144,332	166,357	179,510	1,780	891	2,355	493	108,997	132,148	4,638	4,051	43,610	31,518	38,422	43,367
1973	4,353	1,224	160,594	180,696	212,352	205,862	1,946	403	2,316	1,004	137,790	155,224	6,936	8,218	55,921	40,308	48,381	48,819
1974	4,596	2,335	199,863	219,701	257,315	236,481	2,287	580	3,690	1,309	191,685	188,778	10,538	14,308	66,823	59,340	75,469	61,619
1975	3,299	3,033	196,759	202,073	248,443	235,402	1,965	681	5,736	1,719	192,307	181,157	11,028	12,812	70,155	68,395	71,718	43,106

See p. 605 for footnotes

F2 External Trade (by value) with Main Trading Partners

1884—1914

BULGARIA (in million leva)[7]

	Austria-Hungary		Czechoslovakia		France		Germany		Italy		Russia		Turkey		U.K.	
	I	E	I	E	I	E	I	E	I	E	I	E	I	E	I	E
1884	...	...	...	...	...	...	...	...	...	...	...	...	...	...	...	...
1885	11	1	...	...	2	5	2	1	1	2	3	—	5	9	11	12
1886	17	2	...	...	4	10	2	—	1	1	4	—	11	29	18	5
1887	15	4	...	...	4	6	3	—	1	1	3	—	10	25	22	6
1888	18	3	...	...	4	14	4	—	1	1	3	—	10	28	20	10
1889	22	4	...	...	3	18	4	1	1	2	5	—	10	31	21	13
1890	33	6	...	...	3	19	4	—	1	2	5	—	10	22	20	15
1891	34	3	...	...	4	24	5	1	1	1	5	—	10	17	16	17
1892	28	3	...	...	3	20	8	13	2	3	3	—	10	22	18	7
1893	33	2	...	...	4	14	12	16	2	2	3	—	10	25	20	17
1894	35	3	...	...	4	9	12	12	3	1	5	—	13	27	20	12
1895	22	3	...	...	3	13	9	13	2	1	3	—	9	23	15	14
1896	22	3	...	...	3	14	9	20	3	2	4	—	10	22	18	33
1897	22	4	...	...	4	9	11	8	3	1	4	—	9	11	23	17
1898	20	10	...	...	4	7	9	7	3	2	3	—	7	17	17	10
1899	18	4	...	...	3	5	9	4	3	1	2	—	6	21	12	10
1900	13	6	...	...	3	5	6	6	3	1	4	—	5	18	8	6
1901	17	7	...	...	4	5	10	9	4	3	4	—	10	24	14	16
1902	18	8	...	...	4	8	9	11	5	3	3	—	11	22	15	24
1903	23	10	...	...	3	8	11	9	6	3	4	—	12	23	15	20
1904	38	14	...	...	11	8	20	12	8	5	6	—	17	26	19	25
1905	33	19	...	...	7	9	21	12	7	4	3	—	17	21	20	13
1906	28	8	...	...	5	9	16	15	6	4	5	—	18	22	20	15
1907	35	8	...	...	7	7	20	17	6	3	5	—	18	27	21	21
1908	36	6	...	...	7	6	21	12	5	4	6	—	19	33	23	10
1909	39	12	...	...	11	5	29	14	5	3	6	—	21	37	27	8
1910	48	8	...	...	15	9	34	14	7	2	7	—	21	44	23	15
1911	48	11	...	...	25	11	40	23	9	4	7	—	16	29	30	24
1912	51	16	...	...	15	8	44	25	13	9	10	—	14	17	32	16
1913	55	14	...	...	13	5	37	17	7	4	32	1	6	4	17	8
1914	...	...	...	...	...	...	...	...	...	...	...	...	...	...	...	...

See p. 605 for footnotes

F2 External Trade (by value) with Main Trading Partners

1915–1944

BULGARIA (in million leva)[7]

	Austria-Hungary		Czechoslovakia		France		Germany		Italy		Russia		Turkey		U.K.	
	I	E	I	E	I	E	I	E	I	E	I	E	I	E	I	E
1915	...	...	...	...	...	...	...	...	...	...	...	...	...	...	...	...
1916	...	...	...	...	...	...	...	...	...	...	...	...	...	...	...	...
1917	...	...	...	...	...	...	...	...	...	...	...	...	...	...	...	...
1918	Austria		...	...	...	...	...	...	...	...	...	...	...	...	...	...
1919	—	18	39	81	6	21	...	...	346	68	...	...	147	64	105	21
1920	66	149	73	203	198	100	...	...	625	284	24	1	408	79	311	53
1921	263	107	148	155	301	135	...	...	611	303	3	59	116	528	449	16
1922	340	216	155	105	279	309	870	713	497	522	14	122	299	1,034	604	30
1923	423	512	165	158	495	514	1,014	286	846	521	20	4	199	532	812	28
1924	590	531	316	385	419	632	1,126	867	789	502	19	1	176	225	724	26
1925	702	461	570	350	493	311	1,430	1,131	1,020	771	32	2	199	224	959	28
1926	541	429	748	407	481	321	1,369	1,095	865	679	27	—	131	112	709	42
1927	502	1,058	600	313	447	383	1,290	1,529	894	486	20	—	151	173	736	66
1928	567	915	757	183	540	349	1,494	1,739	1,070	686	18	1	159	296	732	121
1929	635	803	748	304	680	329	1,850	1,912	888	670	27	1	189	161	739	100
1930	311[7]	478[7]	430[7]	396[7]	425[7]	321[7]	1,065[7]	1,621[7]	623[7]	514[7]	22[7]	—[7]	94[7]	80[7]	376[7]	128[7]
1931	335	993	431	274	328	234	1,084	1,748	638	542	3	—	90	80	617	59
1932	208	507	292	104	227	90	900	880	344	424	12	—	75	48	358	86
1933	137	277	106	99	96	93	841	1,025	281	258	11	1	27	18	152	50
1934	107	135	85	91	86	53	902	1,083	176	233	10	—	30	36	143	53
1935	193	149	294	224	43	60	1,608	1,562	94	285	7	1	19	16	141	142
1936	181	116	244	128	39	80	1,940	1,860	19	142	4	—	25	25	146	454
1937	166	202	244	279	164	81	2,699	2,163	246	211	1	—	25	32	232	695
1938	...	...	292	255	182	83	2,563[8]	3,284[8]	370	422	2	—	44	32	348	267
1939	...	...	227	217	62	53	3,403	4,110	357	368	5	—	42	39	...	...
1940	...	...	...	...	...	...	...	...	...	...	...	...	...	...	...	...
1941	...	...	...	...	...	...	...	...	...	...	...	...	...	...	...	...
1942	...	...	...	...	...	...	...	...	...	...	...	...	...	...	...	...
1943	...	...	...	...	...	...	...	...	...	...	...	...	...	...	...	...
1944	...	...	225	134	24	76	4,676	9,965	26	1	1	112	181	74	...	...

See p. 605 for footnotes

F2 External Trade (by value) with Main Trading Partners

1945–1975

BULGARIA (in million leva)[7]

	Austria		Czechoslovakia		France		Germany				Italy		Russia		Turkey		U.K.	
	I	E	I	E	I	E	I		E		I	E	I	E	I	E	I	E
1945	...	...	3	8	2	3	269		60		1	—	4,632	11,626	315	282	...	...
1946	...	...	[789][7]	[1,223][7]	[17][7]	[476][7]	[61][7]		[21][7]		[29][7]	[76][7]	[9,850][7]	[8,064][7]	[341][7]	[278][7]	...	...
							East	West	East	West								
1947	...	...	...	...	...	...					...	...	...	...	...	...	...	...
1948	20	62	106	88	13	17	15	—	41	—	23	17	510	437	6	6	15	6
1949	...	...	...	...	...	...	...	...	...	...	...	...	...	...	...	...	...	...
1950	...	...	...	...	...	...	...	...	...	...	...	...	...	...	...	...	...	...
1951	...	...	...	...	...	...	...	...	...	...	...	...	...	...	...	...	...	...
1952	50	48	136	145	5	1	77	8	75	12	4	5	614	665	4	9	21	22
1953	...	...	...	...	...	...	...	...	...	...	...	...	...	...	...	...	...	...
1954	28	68	183	144	6	7	169	38	201	39	6	14	613	734	9	11	39	35
1955	38	35	283	173	9	11	157	42	221	37	7	6	807	812	8	9	32	13
1956	46	37	246	219	29	25	226	54	269	53	13	11	706	1,001	8	8	50	21
1957	43	46	220	319	36	30	219	98	174	65	32	42	1,190	1,366	7	12	35	13
1958	31	31	246	277	37	33	267	104	202	84	30	36	1,314	1,364	8	9	21	22
1959	73	44	360	288	62	28	348	322	319	102	113	64	1,949	1,765	7	5	69	27
	million new leva		million new leva		million new leva		million new leva		million new leva		million new leva		million new leva		million new leva		million new leva	
1960	11	13	72	64	9	6	82	44	66	22	8	11	389	360	2	3	13	8
1961	21	10	65	71	12	6	99	25	89	25	12	9	416	394	1	2	9	7
1962	26	10	71	75	13	15	79	26	94	34	17	22	518	454	1	3	14	10
1963	31	10	95	82	18	11	114	39	95	41	21	23	586	522	3	4	20	11
1964	25	20	74	86	30	11	105	60	96	37	29	37	656	610	3	4	17	15
1965	36	15	90	107	30	8	99	80	127	48	38	46	689	718	5	4	22	21
1966	37	27	91	74	56	16	122	154	126	48	48	68	827	776	5	7	37	25
1967	46	25	115	94	41	25	148	79	138	65	74	65	916	904	4	6	23	26
1968	38	25	97	104	57	21	176	84	142	63	67	51	1,107	1,046	6	6	24	31
1969	36	24	93	119	29	25	179	53	174	63	65	57	1,139	1,146	6	5	23	34
1970	42	19	113	102	52	44	184	57	203	60	67	67	1,118	1,261	6	5	52	29
1971	46	26	151	118	59	27	213	69	219	59	71	71	1,297	1,399	6	7	38	44
1972	34	26	175	135	29	28	271	91	219	73	71	81	1,448	1,597	8	4	41	29
1973	49	26	183	132	35	38	278	138	267	88	71	95	1,646	1,750	10	9	48	29
1974	83	33	170	150	71	41	380	291	284	92	100	77	1,831	1,872	16	18	70	35
1975	93	28	165	206	125	49	347	410	317	76	135	62	2,653	2,481	13	39	74	25

See p. 605 for footnotes

F2 External Trade (by value) with Main Trading Partners

1919–1944

CZECHOSLOVAKIA (in million koruna)

	Austria		Germany		Hungary		Poland		Romania		Russia		U.K.		U.S.A.	
	I	E	I	E	I	E	I	E	I	E	I	E	I	E	I	E
1919	...	...	...	...	...	...	...	...	...	...	...	...	...	...	...	...
1920	3,042	9,678	5,604	3,331	656	2,512	399	1,425	308	732	138	126	1,009	813	4,111	544
1921	1,983	7,835	5,862	3,061	926	3,066	384	1,424	482	1,175	72	133	1,342	2,104	4,547	771
1922	986	3,969	3,700	4,118	684	1,589	324	605	430	523	21	93	652	1,347	2,286	932
1923	667	2,639	4,488	3,205	353	714	376	358	186	405	6[9] 80	9[9] 73	337	1,219	714	557
1924	1,244	3,524	6,435	4,131	880	1,135	723	558	467	796			448	1,586	889	719
1925	1,296	3,252	7,140	5,347	1,121	1,178	1,238	659	369	850	33	404	654	1,535	1,174	756
1926	1,131	2,904	5,635	4,780	1,028	1,228	1,097	364	481	835	80	156	605	1,540	765	845
1927	1,280	3,069	6,539	5,721	963	1,622	1,023	662	663	908	154	190	800	1,520	1,232	1,012
1928	1,442	3,124	7,410	5,670	849	1,468	1,264	851	537	871	191	279	830	1,478	1,148	1,170
1929	1,565	3,074	7,675	4,691	967	1,306	1,299	888	473	700	257	259	817	1,423	1,089	1,472
1930	1,211	2,439	6,011	3,572	930	1,004	880	639	562	596	302	328	579	1,378	786	977
1931	851	1,796	4,791	2,493	134	289	619	379	566	341	278	489	434	1,356	484	805
1932	450	1,039	2,869	1,454	121	201	375	189	335	302	164[9] 113	121[9] 77	339	406	926	507
1933	299	721	1,774	1,170	167	190	191	167	177	221			280	360	464	428
1934	325	769	1,707	1,618	128	154	235	145	186	271	96	32	331	466	355	494
1935	310	754	1,536	1,224	133	139	252	264	260	383	73	104	367	547	400	615
1936	355	716	1,834	1,230	144	157	221	169	362	380	91	181	475	723	483	729
1937	457	877	1,904	1,801	161	227	279	315	532	654	125	94	695	1,039	961	1,112
1938	...	...	...	...	...	...	...	...	...	...	...	...	...	...	...	...
1939	...	...	...	...	...	...	...	...	...	...	...	...	...	...	...	...
1940	...	...	...	...	...	...	...	...	...	...	...	...	...	...	...	...
1941	...	...	...	...	...	...	...	...	...	...	...	...	...	...	...	...
1942	...	...	...	...	...	...	...	...	...	...	...	...	...	...	...	...
1943	...	...	...	...	...	...	...	...	...	...	...	...	...	...	...	...
1944	...	...	...	...	...	...	...	...	...	...	...	...	...	...	...	...

See p. 605 for footnotes

F2 External Trade (by value) with Main Trading Partners

1945–1975

CZECHOSLOVAKIA (in million koruna)

	Austria		Germany				Hungary		Poland		Romania		Russia		U.K.		U.S.A.	
	I	E	I		E		I	E	I	E	I	E	I	E	I	E	I	E
1945	...	...	...		...		...	...	...	...	...	...	...	...	...	...	...	...
1946	407	627	107		998		589	382	28	141	192	189	1,352	1,713	916	420	853	1,083
1947	507	1,023	276		526		569	801	690	479	246	391	1,946	1,395	3,376	1,840	2,955	1,250
1948	898	1,539	858		1,264		1,037	1,111	2,024	2,643	1,471	1,190	5,888	6,006	3,816	1,358	1,820	1,168
			East	West	East	West												
1949	177	281	151	105	146	200	203	236	385	518	271	273	1,272	1,358	420	129	...	...
1950	208	185	215	112	297	180	245	240	417	631	153	273	1,384	1,425	302	284	...	...
1951	232	199	392	131	256	90	348	355	644	617	233	266	1,815	1,833	242	295	...	...
1952	180	168	353	67	371	126	447	548	595	702	270	294	2,298	2,092	220	204	...	...
1953	113	103	438	61	441	106	529	507	722	733	259	794	2,476	2,313	167	208	—	14
1954	97	93	542	121	584	127	558	484	581	607	271	305	2,522	2,510	159	192	3	20
1955	120	135	705	119	574	124	555	461	548	740	300	270	2,631	2,900	202	163	4	25
1956	155	144	851	280	1,010	364	467	424	554	714	205	252	2,808	3,085	193	178	5	39
1957	180	148	1,039	431	952	395	528	547	432	563	192	267	3,856	2,866	261	248	10	44
1958	150	140	1,167	445	1,134	386	651	557	515	683	161	272	3,253	3,579	233	211	7	54
1959	160	163	1,260	417	1,282	439	626	620	590	827	306	436	4,305	4,229	353	256	13	72
1960	271	195	1,427	428	1,408	489	676	804	796	924	463	458	4,539	4,742	390	274	40	89
1961	264	215	1,656	450	1,583	512	978	750	1,016	1,181	389	554	4,723	5,136	442	311	61	68
1962	254	201	1,644	440	1,655	483	1,004	900	1,044	1,447	433	634	5,626	5,964	438	292	51	71
1963	253	210	1,675	333	1,599	545	944	1,099	1,052	1,408	381	725	6,067	6,886	601	362	76	98
1964	255	244	1,829	506	1,915	594	1,057	1,138	1,392	1,388	537	669	6,572	6,924	663	419	98	99
1965	349	306	2,073	633	1,995	664	1,234	952	1,502	1,791	679	496	6,874	7,364	528	434	139	147
1966	446	282	2,291	584	2,141	678	1,237	952	1,294	1,703	664	500	6,585	6,627	691	485	307	203
1967	381	333	2,305	595	2,294	739	1,086	1,097	1,434	1,691	623	644	6,950	7,035	520	480	133	195
1968	505	384	2,877	729	2,362	861	1,305	1,205	1,785	1,668	787	718	7,460	7,257	575	507	118	163
1969	635	518	2,988	1,060	2,590	1,309	1,375	997	1,873	1,787	1,001	769	7,957	8,096	564	557	133	129
1970	735	544	3,208	1,513	3,285	1,501	1,313	1,438	1,942	2,196	976	1,122	8,703	8,795	669	575	196	169
1971	761	698	3,578	1,781	3,319	1,662	1,428	1,789	1,925	2,507	890	1,076	9,780	9,529	769	621	209	157
1972	738	720	3,891	1,721	3,552	1,689	1,759	1,732	2,358	3,019	1,017	1,169	10,266	11,061	694	659	417	174
1973	969	776	4,550	2,101	3,948	2,086	2,171	1,898	2,911	3,608	1,291	1,165	10,737	11,188	810	813	788	220
1974	1,479	1,142	5,269	3,030	4,470	2,488	2,621	2,272	3,557	3,742	1,413	1,247	11,997	12,258	1,336	1,247	796	320
1975	1,618	1,110	6,188	3,271	5,725	2,579	2,662	2,738	4,847	4,127	1,424	1,516	16,276	15,387	1,133	979	756	180

F2 External Trade (by value) with Main Trading Partners

1873–1909

DENMARK (in million kroner)

	France		Germany		Norway		Sweden		U.K.		U.S.A.	
	I	E	I	E	I	E	I	E	I	E	I	E
1873	...	...	...		...	...	...	...	...	...	...	...
1874	4	—	83	59	10	15	26	24	58	71	4	—
1875	5	—	84	50	8	18	26	22	64	73	2	—
1876	4	—	88	53	6	16	27	26	59	76	4	—
1877	3	1	85	53	5	12	24	26	54	64	8	—
1878	3	2	76	48	5	11	20	21	41	63	8	—
1879	3	2	73	54	5	9	19	20	47	64	11	1
1880	4	1	80	67	6	16	28	27	53	76	18	1
1881	5	1	91	62	6	18	25	28	59	64	19	2
1882	4	1	97	60	7	12	32	27	59	73	12	4
1883	5	2	102	59	7	11	42	30	65	82	17	4
1884	5	1	99	58	8	10	39	27	63	68	15	4
1885	6	2	94	52	6	9	36	23	54	63	16	2
1886	4	2	76	50	6	8	30	23	49	72	13	2
1887	5	2	91	60	5	7	36	22	57	77	15	3
1888	5	1	100	36	6	7	38	18	62	111	10	2
1889	8	2	100	41	7	7	41	20	73	126	14	2
1890	7	2	100	59	6	7	43	22	68	129	21	2
1891	9	2	111	68	6	9	47	23	69	132	19	2
1892	10	1	104	67	5	9	49	26	68	136	29	1
1893	5	1	110	47	4	7	44	24	69	144	20	1
1894	6	2	119	66	5	8	50	23	69	153	14	1
1895	7	1	122	66	6	7	47	22	71	155	10	2
1896	8	2	126	58	6	9	51	22	78	170	17	2
1897	11	2	129	66	7	10	52	27	79	171	48	2
1898	9	1	134	56	8	10	53	33	97	200	64	2
1899	11	1	144	67	7	11	52	35	101	216	78	7
1900	15	2	154	68	8	12	53	38	108	233	78	7
1901	13	1	147	68	9	13	47	40	88	249	87	9
1902	14	3	166	79	8	13	56	40	88	269	71	16
1903	16	4	190	90	10	14	56	37	95	294	80	17
1904	16	1	214	105	9	13	54	40	90	283	74	16
1905	14	2	207	128	10	15	59	42	100	280	100	21
1906	18	2	234	124	12	14	63	48	111	291	129	26
1907	17	1	258	129	14	19	67	53	135	312	124	27
1908	16	1	238	122	11	22	58	46	109	337	113	25
1909	16	1	256	133	11	19	58	40	114	330	86	31

F2 External Trade (by value) with Main Trading Partners

DENMARK (in million kroner) **1910–1939**

	France		Germany		Norway		Sweden		U.K.		U.S.A.	
	I	E	I	E	I	E	I	E	I	E	I	E
1910	16	3	242	125	7	11	56	23	117	341	52	9
1911	17	3	266	160	8	16	67	31	115	353	63	8
1912	19	3	314	182	9	19	69	33	136	373	69	9
1913	21	3	328	179	9	19	71	34	135	410	87	9
1914	18	6	265	301	17	23	83	38	145	432	84	12
1915	13	6	200	487	28	32	93	68	253	385	314	12
1916	20	2	265	691	40	56	117	63	337	351	311	9
1917	14	2	244	490	31	79	135	113	286	265	214	4
1918	4	2	316	308	47	128	235	187	196	52	38	2
1919	53	8	335	265	48	137	195	231	814	164	599	29
1920	65	22	532	326	73	184	190	358	888	672	754	91
1921	43	30	462	211	41	82	98	139	305	826	343	43
1922	46	38	477	89	33	86	105	94	341	763	224	15
1923	61	17	651	105	40	76	115	131	407	1,063	254	29
1924	81	14	649	364	41	64	129	169	446	1,187	294	29
1925	72	13	583	402	43	76	114	148	307	1,088	337	10
1926	67	10	504	291	30	65	98	112	186	859	263	12
1927	59	9	509	321	22	50	106	108	217	877	251	9
1928	64	12	567	342	28	68	109	108	240	919	227	10
1929	69	12	591	340	38	67	125	109	263	967	239	19
1930	69	16	591	262	41	77	123	102	251	951	194	10
1931	53	21	491	179	22	68	91	85	219[10] / 255	815[10] / 729	154	6
1932	29	15	296	150	24	33	63	66	255	729	88	5
1933	36	14	287	158	29	31	89	58	356	781	76	8
1934	41	15	288	189	28	42	103	76	407	740	82	11
1935	36	12	292	206	33	55	90	82	479	732	70	9
1936	16	20	376	280	43	53	101	84	542	744	79	12
1937	20[11]	10[11]	407[11]	298[11]	38[11]	79[11]	103[11]	102[11]	642[11]	825[11]	93[11]	29[11]
	18	10	404	297	38	71	102	82	638	824	87	29
1938	20	22	399[12]	304[12]	41	41	107	74	562	861	128	17
1939	28	16	470	369	40	56	127	77	573	827	128	21

See p. 605 for footnotes

F2 External Trade (by value) with Main Trading Partners

DENMARK (in million kroner) **1940–1975**

	France		Germany		Norway		Sweden		U.K.		U.S.A.	
	I	E	I	E	I	E	I	E	I	E	I	E
1940	5	2	770	1,089	48	45	67	56	150	190	93	2
1941	—	—	1,021[12]	977[12]	58	99	99	66	1	—	1	—
1942	1	1	848	693	59	77	136	75	—	—	—	—
1943	1	1	869	990	68	79	97	73	—	—	—	10
1944	2	—	908[12]	1,090[12]	57	68	38	62	—	—	—	—
1945	4	29	159	183	91	115	153	72	107	310	23	34
1946	76	62	118	73	143	102	201	173	1,289	514	256	51
1947	101	60	108	37	158	125	213	209	671	627	605	99
			West Germany									
1948	109	116	119	39	149	176	226	205	889	831	494	147
1949	202	170	105	232	157	188	289	188	1,339	1,564	672	112
1950	503	136	571	787	206	163	471	273	1,869	1,931	544	119
1951	402	296	895	729	262	249	594	307	1,818	2,224	745	164
1952	322	178	1,032	732	248	244	592	301	1,830	2,262	552	279
1953	302	184	1,268	708	249	211	646	323	1,994	2,492	309	409
1954	365	124	1,562	841	279	253	744	429	2,157	2,400	396	490
1955	441	157	1,517	1,220	268	304	722	517	2,077	2,413	635	531
1956	339	245	1,754	1,398	321	310	809	524	2,206	2,340	904	562
1957	396	195	1,801	1,553	335	300	840	706	2,286	2,229	924	662
1958	317[13]	255[13]	1,845[13]	1,725[13]	328[13]	416[13]	935[13]	640[13]	2,111[13]	2,228[13]	842[13]	790[13]
1959	408	229	2,350	1,924	370	440	1,073	700	2,359	2,519	1,042	969
1960	549	167	2,728	2,061	406	461	1,183	914	1,820	2,701	1,220	695
1961	588	297	2,877	2,142	518	525	1,395	970	1,834	2,573	1,037	789
1962	589	239	3,145	2,193	612	588	1,722	1,106	2,045	2,787	1,219	860
1963	558	402	3,082	2,217	526	532	1,755	1,377	2,134	3,007	1,296	830
1964	743	490	3,713	2,353	597	801	2,310	1,703	2,482	3,380	1,566	884
1965	724	437	4,125	2,700	738	906	2,570	1,971	2,583	3,502	1,657	1,064
1966	746	502	4,203	2,395	801	1,046	2,808	2,103	2,842	3,812	1,628	1,312
1967	858	483	4,196	2,077	977	1,269	3,160	2,395	3,034	3,998	1,881	1,219
1968	1,030	528	4,562	2,396	1,024	1,425	3,627	2,959	3,294	4,080	2,054	1,577
1969	1,207	612	5,440	2,831	1,183	1,532	4,438	3,561	3,917	4,362	2,195	1,853
1970	1,415	594	6,128	3,125	1,281	1,735	5,188	4,096	4,513	4,605	2,426	1,948
1971	1,365	639	5,895	3,105	1,258	1,852	5,272	4,009	4,312	4,841	2,672	1,987
1972	1,376	728	5,697	3,178	1,419	1,844	4,851	4,054	3,739	5,055	2,156	2,118
1973	1,872	1,277	9,525	6,200	2,182	2,520	7,443	5,293	5,222	7,214	3,163	2,712
1974	2,140	1,509	10,500	7,548	2,519	2,746	7,815	7,126	5,264	7,548	3,437	2,559
1975	2,247	1,589	11,775	6,648	2,892	3,285	8,489	7,483	6,117	9,414	3,615	2,579

See p. 605 for footnotes

F2 External Trade (by value) with Main Trading Partners

1827–1864

FINLAND (in million marks)

	Germany		Russia[14]		Sweden		U.K.		U.S.A.	
	I	E	I	E	I	E	I	E	I	E
1827	...	...	2	2	...	...	...	...	...	...
1828	...	...	2	2	...	...	...	...	...	...
1829	...	...	3	2	...	...	...	...	...	...
1830	...	...	4	2	...	...	...	...	...	...
1831	...	...	3	2	...	...	...	...	...	...
1832	...	...	5	3	...	...	...	...	...	...
1833	...	...	3	3	...	...	...	...	...	...
1834	...	...	4	3	...	...	...	...	...	...
1835	...	...	5	3	...	...	...	...	...	...
1836	...	...	6	3	...	...	...	...	...	...
1837	...	...	9	3	...	...	...	...	...	...
1838	...	...	6	3	...	...	...	...	...	...
1839	...	...	5	3	...	...	...	...	...	...
1840	...	...	7	5	2	2	...	...	...	...
1841	...	...	8	5	2	2	...	...	...	...
1842	...	...	6	5	3	2	...	...	...	...
1843	...	...	8	5	2	2	...	...	...	...
1844	...	...	9	5	2	2	...	...	...	...
1845	...	...	9	7	2	1	...	...	...	...
1846	...	...	9	6	2	1	...	...	...	...
1847	...	...	8	6	2	1	...	...	...	...
1848	...	...	8	6	2	1	...	...	...	...
1849	...	...	9	6	2	1	...	...	...	...
1850	...	...	10	7	2	1	...	...	...	...
1851	...	...	11	9	1	2	...	...	...	...
1852	...	...	11	9	2	2	...	...	...	...
1853	...	...	12	10	2	1	...	...	...	...
1854	...	...	12	6	4	3	...	...	...	...
1855	...	...	17	7	6	6	...	...	...	...
1856	15	2	18	7	8	4	3	5	1	—
1857	14	2	24	8	5	3	4	5	3	—
1858	12	2	14	9	3	2	4	5	2	—
1859	10	2	14	11	3	3	5	4	5	—
1860	11	2	15	12	4	3	5	6	6	—
1861	14	2	22	13	4	5	5	7	9	—
1862	16	3	33	14	5	4	4	7	8	—
1863	16	2	33	18	5	3	6	9	6	—
1864	14	3	27	18	4	3	4	9	7	—

See p. 605 for footnotes

F2 External Trade (by value) with Main Trading Partners

1865–1899

FINLAND (in million marks)

	Germany		Russia[14]		Sweden		U.K.		U.S.A.	
	I	E	I	E	I	E	I	E	I	E
1865	18	3	34	17	5	3	4	11	8	——
1866	10	3	28	12	5	2	4	9	7	—
1867	12	2	36	26	4	3	4	8	5	——
1868	11	3	36	26	5	4	5	9	5	—
1869	15	5	31	26	6	4	13	9	6	—
1870	16	4	22	21	8	5	9	10	5	—
1871	18	5	20	16	7	5	9	10	7	——
1872	22	6	23	16	9	5	15	14	7	——
1873	24	9	34	26	10	8	20	20	9	——
1874	37	6	63	37	13	8	21	24	8	——
1875	39	6	68	41	13	6	21	18	11	——
1876	34	9	65	36	10	9	16	24	2	—
1877	35	7	77	35	9	9	16	21	1	—
1878	28	5	67	41	8	6	13	27	2	—
1879	25	6	57	50	6	5	12	14	3	——
1880	35	7	58	51	10	10	15	18	4	——
1881	41	5	68	50	11	8	17	32	4	——
1882	43	8	72	55	14	8	16	23	2	—
1883	40	7	67	48	13	10	17	24	3	—
1884	34	7	68	44	11	11	21	25	——	—
1885	30	4	50	40	9	8	13	18	2	—
1886	24	5	47	34	8	7	12	14	1	—
1887	28	6	46	31	8	31	15	13	——	——
1888	35	8	50	32	8	9	14	18	1	—
1889	38	8	54	37	9	9	19	23	4	—
1890	45	6	47	36	12	7	23	18	2	—
1891	47	7	53	36	10	6	22	19	5[15]	——[15]
1892	42	8	61	33	9	5	17	21	1	—
1893	36	8	50	40	7	5	14	25	1	—
1894	49	9	48	44	9	5	17	33	1	—
1895	53	10	51	49	9	6	19	36	——	—
1896	59	11	55	48	10	5	24	47	——	——
1897	66	13	73	48	12	6	29	51	——	—
1898	75	15	82	51	15	8	38	54	1	—
1899	81	17	86	55	14	7	41	54	——	——

See p. 605 for footnotes

F2 External Trade (by value) with Main Trading Partners

1900–1934

FINLAND (in million marks)

	Germany		Russia		Sweden		U.K.		U.S.A.	
	I	E	I	E	I	E	I	E	I	E
1900	90	17	101	57	13	7	34	58	1	—
1901	67	16	87	55	11	6	26	52	——	——
1902	85	19	94	59	11	6	22	61	——	——
1903	98	20	103	53	11	8	27	64	2	—
1904	95	20	105	58	12	7	27	64	——	—
1905	101	27	95	68	13	8	29	75	——	—
1906	124	29	96	33	16	9	36	86	——	——
1907	153	31	111	73	19	10	46	84	——	—
1908	146	26	99	68	20	9	47	82	——	—
1909	145	32	117	72	18	10	41	78	——	—
1910	160	35	110	80	19	12	46	86	——	——
1911	173	47	138	89	21	14	62	88	——	—
1912	187	49	132	99	25	15	68	88	——	—
1913	203	52	140	113	28	17	61	109	——	—
1914	118	21	145	126	40	24	34	68	——	——
1915	7	—	385	204	164	62	5	——	——	—
1916	——	—	607	480	324	30	1	——	——	—
1917	——	—	626	428	580	16	1	1	——	—
1918	101	98	48	18	140	27	30	15	6	21
1919	157	82	6	1	321	71	676	377	639	21
1920	611	139	1	8	385	239	1,003	1,252	795	193
1921	1,206	372	1	56	267	406	709	1,142	614	275
1922	1,316	388	19	139	248	292	867	1,653	609	291
1923	1,564	271	216	85	264	253	848	1,816	584	343
1924	1,411	454	221	221	294	248	884	2,001	629	301
1925	1,760	747	74	430	358	237	937	2,062	812	296
1926	1,975	715	108	220	418	219	727	2,162	801	365
1927	2,075	999	209	319	523	194	924	2,539	981	341
1928	2,962	988	126	269	657	138	990	2,208	1,179	409
1929	2,683	925	119	211	540	126	912	2,441	873	453
1930	1,937	674	132	243	390	142	715	2,103	638	412
1931	1,210	375	96	99	287	132	435	1,991	372	413
1932	1,003	386	178	70	345	120	641	2,166	269	444
1933	1,081	521	184	100	387	116	808[16]	2,429[16]	289	462
1934	988	631	274	101	501	161	1,090	2,913	412	429

See p. 605 for footnotes

F2 External Trade (by value) with Main Trading Partners

1935–1954

FINLAND (in million marks)

	Germany		Russia		Sweden		U.K.		U.S.A.	
	I	E	I	E	I	E	I	E	I	E
1935	1,088	595	161	67	599	306	1,291	2,905	405	561
1936	1,201	719	125	37	785	392	1,502	3,462	518	667
1937	1,804	1,228	133	58	1,127	463	2,062	4,189	775	740
1938	1,723	1,244	106	44	1,111	405	1,862	3,701	774	773
1939	1,663	1,276	64	27	1,203	484	1,449	2,793	763	984
1940	1,888	1,554	194	9	2,232	274	623	85	1,251	150
1941	5,601	2,343	131	56	1,857	377	34	—	615	42
1942	8,654	3,982	2	—	969	262	1	—	22	—
1943	9,851	5,978	—	—	688	210	—	—	2	—
1944	6,464	4,273	—	—	712	442	—	—	2	—
1945	106	—	1,293	1,546	3,501	832	727	1,839	3	99
	million new marks		million new marks		million new marks		million new marks		million new marks	
1946	—	—	52	46	24	22	52	62	47	16
1947	—	1	53	56	23	26	82	136	111	52
1948	5[2]	5[2]	83	83	32	31	168	160	80	54
1949	6	20	75	100	44	27	147	178	51	50
1950	39	45	71	62	59	34	207	190	53	76
1951	147	133	119	155	87	58	327	575	97	128
1952	226	145	220	275	106	63	347	373	140	86
1953	93	92	261	335	53	41	192	290	61	95
1954	102	116	271	337	69	43	286	352	70	90

See p. 605 for footnotes

F2 External Trade (by value) with Main Trading Partners

1955–1975

FINLAND (in million marks)

	Germany		Russia		Sweden		U.K.		U.S.A.	
	I	E	I	E	I	E	I	E	I	E
1955	159	165	260	317	87	34	359	435	93	104
1956	240	154	283	342	110	38	416	382	132	119
1957	259	188	403	424	134	66	402	460	128	107
1958	386	269	419	428	193	89	401	548	125	115
1959	481	292	475	448	243	86	420	623	136	154
	------[13]	------[13]	------[13]	------[13]	------[13]	----[13]	------[13]	------[13]	------[13]	------[13]
1960	660	366	500	450	354	153	539	776	195	158
1961	784	437	503	409	422	192	563	748	208	148
1962	795	422	538	628	474	203	596	716	201	189
1963	695	442	653	590	458	209	592	791	189	191
1964	831	477	846	498	612	266	711	951	233	238
1965	996	512	755	725	737	343	808	944	265	273
1966	942	535	856	682	781	423	887	989	252	308
1967	939	450	931	896	892	508	880	1,091	227	303
1968	1,034	722	1,135	1,062	1,066	751	1,023	1,421	233	401
1969	1,410	836	1,097	1,173	1,434	1,157	1,391	1,537	347	498
1970	1,881	1,029	1,377	1,151	1,924	1,543	1,735	1,715	483	453
1971	1,974	1,029	1,624	1,050	2,130	1,611	1,808	1,906	505	470
1972	2,360	1,247	1,520	1,492	2,489	2,142	1,817	2,218	577	578
1973	3,075	1,511	2,002	1,705	3,270	2,223	1,875	2,880	788	652
1974	3,946	1,779	4,640	2,835	4,719	3,394	2,263	3,971	1,901	766
1975	4,414	1,740	4,737	4,069	5,105	3,687	2,497	2,967	2,114	642

See p. 605 for footnotes

F2 External Trade (by value) with Main Trading Partners

1842–1874

FRANCE (in million francs)

	Algeria		Belgium		Germany		Italy		Spain		U.K.		U.S.A.	
	I	E	I	E	I	E	I	E	I	E	I	E	I	E
1842	3	45	99	52	90	76	127	101	39	72	154	159	176	82
1843	2	41	91	44	56	67	115	64	26	62	86	87	144	66
1844	2	63	104	46	58	75	117	68	32	74	90	99	134	102
1845	3	89	117	58	54	81	103	74	32	68	85	110	141	96
1846	4	94	102	49	56	81	149	80	36	74	79	113	141	100
1847	3	83	111	59	62	76	119	80	36	71	72	127	128	132
1848	2	73	64	66	24	49	65	68	21	64	29	190	101	117
1849	14	79	91	84	34	57	103	85	27	69	59	200	147	147
1850	5	76	104	101	38	62	101	94	35	71	69	226	123	178
1851	16	94	101	124	38	64	106	103	31	61	66	278	122	134
1852	18	103	124	122	48	56	133	107	32	65	86	250	168	163
1853	25	118	140	123	66	57	148	101	44	69	92	317	158	217
1854	33	118	133	124	61	56	135	86	51	67	133	280	193	182
1855	37 [7]	156 [7]	146 [7]	131 [7]	84 [7]	69 [7]	147 [7]	99 [7]	66 [7]	93 [7]	244 [7]	251 [7]	205 [7]	204 [7]
	53	104	197	151	118	77	155	105	97	81	285	317	176	247
1856	39	108	204	182	121	108	218	146	107	96	337	372	223	324
1857	31	89	176	168	144	142	166	136	106	102	322	387	189	258
1858	29	97	149	166	105	147	168	155	49	112	262	426	178	210
1859	34	147	160	169	124	172	140	189	54	101	278	591	200	308
1860	58	153	177	167	134	182	173	184	69	105	308	599	240	250
1861	61	131	224	157	194	184	180	189	73	129	438	456	363	82
1862	41	125	259	206	141	231	194	183	55	137	526	620	96	100
1863	52	127	268	211	156	235	207	247	55	170	592	800	81	94
1864	76	129	285	229	176	248	231	285	57	169	567	891	69	75
1865	71	136	304	258	186	256	242	284	54	157	600	991	49	108
1866	67	130	305	262	221	225	237	238	63	124	637	1,141	192	173
1867	68	115	381	255	286	259	321	187	90	103	578	907	141	156
1868	72	144	354	272	303	253	329	178	88	109	580	879	150	126
1869	64	130	316	295	256	305	321	230	104	97	551	910	175	193
1870	47	110	272	311	103	104	235	201	74	91	525	851	218	307
1871	80	132	476	410	161	199	442	153	107	102	839	819	190	313
1872	138	141	440	479	358	410	375	229	124	113	666	936	205	333
1873	149	140	475	470	311	463	346	230	141	110	597	925	200	291
1874	113	136	409	524	316	414	289	204	130	139	596	992	242	296

See p. 605 for footnotes

F2 External Trade (by value) with Main Trading Partners

1875–1904

FRANCE (in million francs)

	Algeria		Belgium		Germany		Italy		Spain		U.K.		U.S.A.	
	I	E	I	E	I	E	I	E	I	E	I	E	I	E
1875	109	146	439	527	349	427	323	219	94	141	627	1,074	190	264
1876	123	149	404	446	389	431	415	216	96	155	652	1,038	265	230
1877	122	138	409	446	373	395	342	186	109	133	576	1,063	258	217
1878	120	129	411	410	419	344	349	170	149	138	582	919	488	207
1879	122	139	415	429	413	344	358	180	183	150	601	834	716	276
1880	127	162	457	465	438	363	398	181	343	159	665	914	731	332
1881	92	161	472	453	455	383	434	210	371	168	703	901	506	319
1882	96	165	508	457	477	339	361	200	367	158	724	966	390	365
1883	96	155	492	471	462	326	427	177	372	171	697	907	353	350
1884	102	147	463	457	417	328	369	172	298	153	617	844	280	275
1885	124	168	405	437	374	300	263	177	361	162	537	832	272	254
1886	125	189	419	448	335	298	309	193	398	173	526	858	293	282
1887	134	153	414	481	322	316	308	192	357	149	476	820	325	271
1888	158	174	419	473	333	308	181	119	378	172	529	864	248	256
1889	201	179	475	571	338	342	134	144	355	195	538	996	307	274
1890	208	195	501	538	351	342	122	150	353	153	627	1,026	317	329
1891	187	207	487	500	366	364	124	126	412	81	589	1,013	486	248
1892	195	190	387	502	337	355	132	133	278	35	530	1,027	534	240
1893	142	185	395	505	323	336	151	128	208	14	493	965	317	205
1894	208	199	372	478	310	325	122	98	176	109	481	916	327	186
1895	246	203	288	497	310	334	115	134	213	109	496	1,002	283	289
1896	197	218	282	501	308	340	127	115	288	100	511	1,033	314	225
1897	238	216	288	513	309	380	132	151	247	99	486	1,136	438	242
1898	224	226	315	549	334	394	138	143	326	82	506	1,024	623	210
1899	271	260	332	606	360	457	159	192	239	148	591	1,242	427	255
1900	166	259	422	598	427	465	149	156	220	135	675	1,230	510	255
1901	198	259	358	562	402	444	140	155	157	121	602	1,201	457	253
1902	254	269	330	634	418	487	154	175	148	125	567	1,283	425	248
1903	263	287	325	631	444	513	152	172	167	122	556	1,195	540	255
1904	234	315	306	678	429	555	151	190	164	111	524	1,217	483	251

F2 External Trade (by value) with Main Trading Partners

1905–1939

FRANCE (in million francs)

	Algeria		Belgium		Germany		Italy		Spain		U.K.		U.S.A.	
	I	E	I	E	I	E	I	E	I	E	I	E	I	E
1905	216	327	313	764	477	629	154	213	180	111	593	1,260	512	295
1906	244	355	377	804	583	640	182	247	171	131	751	1,299	588	402
1907	291	393	427	861	638	650	194	264	169	126	884	1,373	671	396
1908	273	399	410	749	608	617	165	242	149	128	794	1,183	657	315
1909	272	397	439	903	661	726	165	293	180	124	888	1,266	728	474
1910	447	439	470	1,004	861	804	189	344	195	141	931	1,279	614	456
1911	426	490	543	1,024	980	795	190	278	231	136	994	1,220	827	380
1912	427	569	541	1,144	999	822	209	302	230	140	1,049	1,365	890	431
1913	331	553	556	1,108	1,069	867	241	306	282	151	1,116	1,457	895	423
1914	313	445	318	602	614	511	174	215	193	112	857	1,165	795	377
1915	547	368	23	36	8	—	433	388	581	140	3,038	1,101	3,028	446
1916	539	520	7	57	6	—	717	782	884	190	5,969	1,123	6,163	622
1917	683	524	5	69	6	—	815	971	1,348	207	6,808	1,018	9,771	682
1918	624	604	5	36	5	—	818	780	578	183	6,396	1,083	7,140	420
1919	1,224	959	1,111	1,534	755	1,560	1,017	678	1,464	388	8,803	2,117	9,218	893
1920	1,054	2,290	3,325	4,479	2,668	1,502	1,283	1,249	1,052	970	10,318	4,238	10,866	2,256
1921	1,112	1,415	1,732	3,250	2,615	1,877	616	686	490	563	2,943	3,192	3,539	2,193
1922	984	1,716	1,796[18]	4,015[18]	1,446	1,970	774	797	366	518	3,273	3,979	3,845	2,007
			1,880	4,194										
1923	1,284	2,128	2,533	5,721	1,174	1,080	1,140	1,173	651	899	5,040[19]	6,363[19]	4,851	2,473
1924	1,653	2,613	2,734	7,222	2,051	3,959	1,481	1,481	900	1,168	4,773	7,899	5,586	3,151
1925	1,727	2,981	3,349	7,742	2,346	3,833	1,727	2,225	877	1,456	5,688	9,266	6,377	3,094
1926	2,702	3,369	4,876	9,525	4,925	4,384	2,231	2,623	1,073	1,765	6,142	10,594	7,820	3,673
1927	2,601	3,426	3,980	8,263	4,170	6,630	1,550	2,064	1,444	1,622	6,330	9,000	6,807	3,152
1928	2,832	3,965	4,040	7,955	5,004	5,623	1,525	2,129	1,619	1,694	5,309	7,935	6,177	3,033
1929	2,990	4,501	3,920	7,224	6,613	4,743	1,516	2,209	1,442	1,588	5,859	7,625	7,160	3,335
1930	3,300	4,564	4,199	5,442	7,937	4,155	1,527	1,681	1,508	1,129	5,298	6,894	6,148	2,435
1931	3,428	3,976	3,633	3,582	6,142	2,749	1,437	992	1,405	685	3,851	5,088	3,800	1,543
1932	3,291	3,271	2,447	2,240	3,613	1,699	630	595	717	387	2,464	1,983	2,900	957
1933	3,865[3]	3,310[3]	1,965[3]	2,140[3]	3,037[3]	1,714[3]	621[3]	496[3]	686[3]	377[3]	2,178[3]	1,695[3]	2,857[3]	868[3]
1934	2,813	3,083	1,469	1,978	2,226	1,989	484	552	498	396	1,649	1,565	2,190	836
1935	2,330	2,578	1,406	1,816	1,738	1,051	405	596	339	300	1,583	1,639	1,788	718
1936	2,843	2,693	1,643	1,857	1,774	667	215	138	473	288	1,803	1,958	2,526	880
1937	3,807	3,290	3,060	3,146	3,492	1,565	571	632	315	425	3,389	2,753	4,033	1,535
1938	4,864	3,780	3,160	4,181	3,153	1,851	578	485	192	389	3,239	3,559	5,277	1,683
1939	4,760	3,702	3,046	3,921	2,089	1,036	500	317	79	138	2,978	4,153	5,841	2,268

See p. 605 for footnotes

F2 External Trade (by value) with Main Trading Partners

FRANCE (in million francs) **1940–1975**

	Algeria		Belgium		Germany		Italy		Spain		U.K.		U.S.A.	
	I	E	I	E	I	E	I	E	I	E	I	E	I	E
1940	4,879	2,817	2,666	1,820	99	652	821	258	429	230	3,679	2,137	8,485	1,209
1941	6,612	3,046	1,699	2,038	3,915	6,247	503	500	262	224	146	113	505	125
1942	5,707	3,354	1,471	3,188	7,519	17,795	422	299	542	205	13	137	142	3
1943	36	—	1,717	3,651	8,380	29,189	143	45	235	199	33	151	65	—
1944	39	16	811	1,938	4,807	22,418	25	—	224	90	30	75	1,407	—
1945	1,933	2,682	1,583	2,809	1,665	114	103	—	247	171	5,064	323	27,175	593
1946	24,627	13,358	10,267	20,263	12,785	2,342	2,349	653	218	60	15,095	5,339	83,860	6,399
1947	36,897[20]	31,645[20]	19,238[20]	26,286[20]	15,160[20]	5,850[20]	2,736[20]	2,165[20]	20[20]	3[20]	12,466[20]	15,452[20]	120,082[20]	5,979[20]
					West Germany									
1948	80,496	67,308	25,248	31,261	35,964	23,376	11,379	4,606	4,209	863	18,834	31,828	118,679	15,813
1949	80,822	107,770	32,212	45,129	68,444	39,292	17,091	15,833	12,672	7,009	32,819	70,109	162,657	15,739
1950	92,357	121,818	49,131	68,955	69,792	84,311	37,251	28,014	9,814	11,355	39,950	98,809	131,607	43,687
1951	97,874	163,502	77,038	85,602	101,531	69,831	47,769	35,229	13,379	14,244	56,897	133,720	181,723	88,430
1952	114,387	178,658	62,167	79,609	114,676	78,888	33,910	37,961	17,889	19,334	60,107	85,192	159,731	54,839
1953	108,012	159,364	59,501	85,259	109,961	98,535	22,527	45,447	16,804	24,001	66,606	76,031	134,968	63,523
1954	115,791	172,615	70,656	100,324	120,328	123,329	27,587	57,532	16,577	19,842	70,030	84,422	133,377	54,056
1955	132,921	208,048	91,772	119,000	154,026	176,943	36,808	66,544	15,569	31,063	75,822	125,413	160,465	72,882
1956	133,357	215,967	107,291	124,869	199,030	166,179	49,843	65,363	12,442	25,251	108,448	97,241	238,601	78,273
1957	161,016	298,762	117,821	140,628	250,132	201,846	56,468	75,478	15,784	25,685	97,429	103,122	300,509	89,857
1958	190,390	412,376	126,379	136,464	274,202	224,522	55,453	72,756	29,368	34,683	84,306	105,149	236,683	126,442
1959	167,648	471,109[20]	132,980	186,857[20]	364,781	363,409[20]	87,689	131,957[20]	17,679	29,636[20]	97,782	123,713[20]	211,618	229,188[20]
	million new francs		million new francs		million new francs		million new francs		million new francs		million new francs		million new francs	
1960	2,535	5,392	1,837	2,531	4,888	4,656	1,247	1,979	315	414	1,133	1,711	3,677	1,954
1961	2,930	4,374	1,999	2,957	5,626	5,408	1,509	2,412	369	591	1,476	1,809	3,638	2,059
1962	3,246	2,777	2,453	3,127	6,536	6,278	2,046	2,734	465	812	1,922	1,717	3,825	2,102
1963	2,817	2,735	3,252	3,626	7,760	6,622	2,552	3,690	517	1,085	2,565	1,963	4,449	2,077
1964	3,011	2,444	3,874	4,328	9,114	7,727	3,133	3,429	641	1,359	2,682	2,257	5,610	2,322
1965	2,811	2,525	4,237	4,818	9,435	9,578	3,585	3,619	656	1,659	2,577	2,290	5,371	2,935
1966	2,750	2,156	5,111	5,463	11,271	10,368	4,690	4,439	840	1,940	2,875	2,459	5,922	3,256
1967	2,620	1,996	5,724	5,589	12,317	9,729	5,304	5,178	830	1,911	2,916	2,872	6,020	3,276
1968	2,751	2,326	7,168	6,359	14,733	11,634	6,556	5,773	908	1,739	3,038	2,981	6,511	3,778
1969	3,073	2,355	10,238	8,371	20,039	15,884	9,020	8,062	1,166	2,152	4,004	3,158	7,586	4,217
1970	3,539	3,124	11,918	10,928	23,427	20,487	9,806	11,107	1,491	2,456	4,800	3,829	10,533	5,298
1971	1,294	2,771	12,933	12,683	26,375	24,310	11,693	12,425	2,022	2,787	5,292	5,186	9,988	6,100
1972	1,702	2,383	15,437	15,011	30,196	27,785	13,838	15,108	2,654	3,268	6,648	7,036	11,021	6,970
1973	2,115	3,337	19,315	18,396	37,661	30,919	14,994	18,752	3,584	4,577	7,690	10,104	13,758	7,499
1974	4,610	6,195	25,742	24,914	48,873	37,917	19,009	25,692	5,116	6,546	10,816	14,351	19,763	10,740
1975	3,215	8,129	22,019	22,775	43,548	36,896	20,342	11,588	5,381	5,912	10,965	14,389	17,483	8,748

See p. 605 for footnotes

F2 External Trade (by value) with Main Trading Partners

GERMANY (in million marks) 1879–1914

	Austria-Hungary		Belgium		France		Italy		Netherlands		Russia		Sweden		U.K.		U.S.A.	
	I	E	I	E	I	E	I	E	I	E	I	E	I	E	I	E	I	E
1879	...	...	...	...	...	...	...	...	...	...	...	...	...	...	...	...	...	...
1880	402	291	195	164	246	285	63	52	190	227	336	213	23	61	351	438	...	...
1881	433	316	215	169	253	319	57	71	247	240	333	183	26	59	365	449	...	...
1882	503	326	238	171	245	342	53	74	271	259	391	193	28	63	397	513	115	192
1883	476	336	273	174	248	313	62	84	239	256	410	184	28	72	480	552	136	144
1884	426	325	293	163	244	283	83	87	236	230	414	169	31[21] / 18	73[21] / 59	507	514	125	176
1885	384	284	280	147	218	248	76	85	213	225	345	151	21	59	452	453	122	155
1886	404	286	277	155	222	249	90	84	212	230	264	148	20	52	453	443	106	212
1887	422	296	278	161	213	219	91	99	231	234	362	132	27	50	461	491	143	231
1888	446[22]	299[22]	271[22]	172[22]	214[22]	219[22]	111[22]	81[22]	247[22]	271[22]	456[22]	200[22]	35[22]	54[22]	496[22]	480[22]	153[22]	236[22]
1889	530	319	336	137	271	209	149	102	284	249	552	197	50	71	665	647	317	395
1890	583	332	314	151	258	231	140	93	307	258	542	206	46	91	601	690	397	417
1891	570	331	249	153	251	237	133	87	270	268	581	263	52	73	565	679	403	358
1892	564	321	207	141	255	201	134	90	209	234	383	240	55	67	548	629	535	347
1893	572	339	188	148	239	201	149	84	212	240	353	185	61	71	565	670	427	354
1894	572	353	170	150	211	188	125	81	188	243	544	195	63	73	512	632	450	270
1895	513	374	177	159	223	202	138	82	161	245	569	221	63	76	536	676	483	368
1896	547	400	173	168	230	201	132	89	159	262	635	364	74	78	551	713	528	383
1897	583	406	182	189	246[23] / 243	210[23] / 210	146	88	181	263	708[24] / 700	372[24] / 346	87	92	568	699	652	397
1898	627	426	197	187	261	205	161	92	181	278	727	410	103	105	566	741	876	333
1899	716	450	243	207	298	216	193	112	197	321	702	397	104	135	673	801	894	377
1900	704	486	215	253	303	277	181	123	209	364	717	325	104	137	719	862	1,004	440
1901	684	464	183	236	272	249	178	123	192	372	716	318	84	110	553	907	986	385
1902	696	480	194	261	304	253	189	125	195	392	760	344	80	118	557	958	893	449
1903	724	500	206	268	330	272	196	131	187	417	826	379	90	131	594	982	935[25]	469[25]
1904	703	555	231	277	365	274	187	141	212	410	819	315	99	147	615	985	943	495
1905	752	580	273	312	402	293	211	164	246	433	1,091	368	119	156	718	1,042	992	542
1906	811[22]	649[22]	291[22]	356[22]	434[22]	383[22]	241[22]	231[22]	242[22]	443[22]	1,070[22]	406[22]	150[22]	177[22]	825[22]	1,067[22]	1,237[22]	637[22]
1907	813	717	297	343	454	449	285	303	228	452	1,108	438	172	187	977	1,060	1,320	653
1908	752	737	262	323	420	438	236	311	231	454	946	450	145	174	697	997	1,283	508
1909	755	767	290	349	485	455	288	289	253	454	1,364	445	142	156	723	1,015	1,263	606
1910	759	822	326	391	509	543	275	324	259	499	1,387	547	164	191	767	1,102	1,188	633
1911	739	918	340	413	524	599	285	348	298	532	1,634	625	183	192	809	1,140	1,343	640
1912	830	1,035	387	493	552	689	305	401	345	609	1,528	680	214	197	843	1,161	1,586	698
1913	827	1,105	345	551	584	790	318	394	333	694	1,425	880	224	230	876	1,438	1,711	713
1914	...	...	...	...	...	...	...	...	...	...	...	...	...	...	...	...	...	...

See p. 605 for footnotes

F2 External Trade (by value) with Main Trading Partners

1915–1944

GERMANY (in million marks)

	Austria-Hungary		Belgium		France		Italy		Netherlands		Russia		Sweden		U.K.		U.S.A.	
	I	E	I	E	I	E	I	E	I	E	I	E	I	E	I	E	I	E
1915	...	...	...	...	...	...	...	...	...	...	...	...	...	...	...	...	...	...
1916	...	...	...	...	...	...	...	...	...	...	...	...	...	...	...	...	...	...
1917	...	...	...	...	...	...	...	...	...	...	...	...	...	...	...	...	...	...
1918	...	...	...	...	...	...	...	...	...	...	...	...	...	...	...	...	...	...
1919	...	...	...	...	...	...	...	...	...	...	...	...	...	...	...	...	...	...
1920	...	...	...	...	...	...	...	...	...	...	...	...	...	...	...	...	...	...
1921	...	...	...	...	...	...	...	...	...	...	...	...	...	...	...	...	...	...
	Austria																	
1922	...	...	...	...	...	...	...	...	...	...	...	...	...	...	...	...	...	...
1923	131[26]	305[26]	85[26]	112[26]	186[26]	67[26]	150[26]	245[26]	201[26]	685[26]	92[26]	73[26]	95[26]	271[26]	1,015[26]	557[26]	1,172[26]	475[26]
1924	134	313	204	106	694	114	372	240	426	648	126	89	121	286	827 [27]	612 [27]	1,709	491
1925	176	320	415	344	558	489	496	425	743	996	205	250	269	342	944	937	2,196	604
1926	116	311	343	418	378	670	388	486	543	1,127	323	266	234	401	576	1,163	1,603	744
1927	211	366	548	441	806	562	528	462	698	1,119	433	330	370	409	963	1,178	2,073	776
1928	232	425	474	489	741	693	467	547	710	1,175	379	403	253	431	894	1,180	2,026	796
1929	202	441	447	609	642	935	443	602	701	1,355	426	354	350	476	865	1,306	1,790	991
1930	181	360	325	601	519	1,149	365	484	561	1,206	436	431	304	494	639	1,219	1,307	685
1931	114	275	222	464	342	834	268	341	384	955	304	763	158	424	453	1,134	791	488
1932	65	160	146	302	190	483	181	223	273	633	271	626	95	228	259	446	592	281
1933	58	121	139	278	184	395	166	227	232	613	194	282	103	191	238	406	483	246
1934	66	107	161	236	177	282	185	246	264	482	210	63	134	198	206	383	373	158
1935	71	108	126	202	154	253	188	278	196	404	215	39	153	207	256	375	241	170
1936	77	109	139	212	99	255	209[28]	241[28]	169	396	93	126	192	230	264	406	232	172
1937	93	123	198[29]	288[29]	156[29]	313[29]	221[29]	311[29]	216[29]	468[29]	65[29]	117[29]	232[29]	277[29]	309[29]	432[29]	282[29]	209[29]
1938	...	...	154	190	159	229	284	349	208	460	53	34	267	275	309	374	455	157
1939	...	...	129	161	78	129	287	362	177	504	30[30] 129	31[30] 134	262	377	181	228	198	125
1940	...	...	243	131	...	...	508	724	406	440	396	217	346	403	—	—	16	11
1941	...	...	562	385	752	315	938	1,192	640	695	325	272	477	455	—	—	8	3
1942	...	...	705	293	1,404	546	1,022	1,305	857	534	—	—	410	423	—	—	—	—
1943	...	...	681	308	1,416	560	781	950	824	427	—	—	386	477	—	—	—	—
1944	...	...	...	...	...	...	...	...	...	...	...	...	...	...	...	...	...	...

See p. 605 for footnotes

F2 External Trade (by value) with Main Trading Partners

WEST GERMANY (in million marks) **1945–1975**

	Austria		Belgium		France		Italy		Netherlands		Russia		Sweden		U.K.		U.S.A.	
	I	E	I	E	I	E	I	E	I	E	I	E	I	E	I	E	I	E
1945	...	...	...	...	...	...	...	...	...	...	...	...	...	...	...	...	...	...
1946	...	...	...	...	...	...	...	...	...	...	...	...	...	...	...	...	...	...
1947	...	...	...	...	...	...	...	...	...	...	...	...	...	...	...	...	...	...
1948	32	121	80	263	11	223	68	69	122	224	...	...	...	...	...	...	...	...
1949	44	229	418	403	91	514	318	217	402	368	4	—	94	75	129	256	1,574	102
											3	—	295	241	182	380	2,588	160
1950	178	312	405	677	690	612	507	486	1,246	1,164	1	—	637	531	489	361	1,735	430
1951	237	500	610	987	621	973	549	674	1,022	1,456	2	—	803	974	498	878	2,722	989
1952	369	627	943	1,196	606	1,077	643	632	1,170	1,345	17	1	927	1,239	525	955	2,505	1,044
1953	407	668	850	1,308	780	1,084	744	1,240	1,251	1,657	66	7	811	1,173	645	788	1,655	1,243
1954	565	1,034	867	1,580	965	1,194	843	1,341	1,526	2,059	93	53	904	1,476	847	858	2,228	1,227
1955	697	1,359	1,385	1,733	1,445	1,458	1,044	1,434	1,770	2,422	151	112	1,103	1,779	866	1,026	3,202	1,611
1956	781	1,417	1,343	2,106	1,345	1,947	1,223	1,656	2,002	2,876	224	289	1,276	1,956	1,147	1,257	3,970	2,074
1957	902	1,761	1,316	2,145	1,547	2,253	1,553	2,000	2,258	3,246	409	250	1,486	2,169	1,135	1,407	5,629	2,494
1958	916[31]	1,847[31]	1,409[31]	2,453[31]	1,595[31]	2,164[31]	1,698[31]	1,853[31]	2,500[31]	2,995[31]	386[31]	303[31]	1,411[31]	2,266[31]	1,361[31]	1,460[31]	4,193[31]	2,642[31]
1959	998	1,960	1,776	2,489	2,761	2,970	2,182	2,202	3,124	3,465	443	383	1,533	2,285	1,630	1,661	4,576	3,776
1960	1,152	2,444	2,441	2,890	3,998	4,202	2,631	2,847	3,638	4,210	673	778	1,804	2,593	1,956	2,147	5,974	3,723
1961	1,247	2,686	2,355	3,262	4,618	4,777	3,043	3,385	3,762	4,755	796	823	1,930	2,614	1,965	2,122	6,097	3,454
1962	1,376	2,757	2,765	3,583	5,270	5,440	3,735	4,106	4,196	4,883	861	826	2,000	2,670	2,351	1,954	7,033	3,858
1963	1,369	2,938	3,359	4,142	5,495	6,432	3,700	5,462	4,789	5,718	835	614	2,014	2,981	2,472	2,212	7,942	4,195
1964	1,524	3,295	4,305	4,879	6,270	7,424	4,468	4,593	5,350	6,736	937	774	2,304	3,259	2,782	2,717	8,066	4,785
1965	1,712	3,798	5,416	5,558	7,843	7,792	6,562	4,499	6,826	7,371	1,101	586	2,742	3,573	3,141	2,804	9,196	5,741
1966	1,695	4,219	5,607	6,421	8,617	9,216	6,680	5,657	6,870	7,988	1,153	541	2,389	3,574	3,155	3,129	9,177	7,178
1967	1,477	4,097	5,436	6,439	8,488	10,050	6,436	6,890	7,275	8,628	1,100	792	2,167	3,534	2,932	3,472	8,556	7,859
1968	1,766	4,420	6,799	7,444	9,778	12,242	8,066	7,568	8,810	10,114	1,175	1,094	2,489	3,850	3,407	4,028	8,850	10,835
1969	2,190	4,857	8,987	9,277	12,697	15,118	9,491	9,260	11,256	11,522	1,306	1,582	2,897	4,369	3,913	4,591	10,253	10,633
1970	2,313	5,685	10,389	10,294	13,899	15,480	10,836	11,172	13,313	13,314	1,254	1,547	3,148	4,688	4,264	4,456	12,066	11,437
1971	2,455	6,363	11,638	11,582	15,919	16,975	12,692	11,451	15,769	14,522	1,277	1,608	3,139	4,631	4,413	5,449	12,420	13,140
1972	2,657	7,474	12,964	12,301	18,157	19,406	13,899	12,556	17,578	15,178	1,386	2,295	3,195	5,028	4,582	7,046	10,765	13,798
1973	2,958	8,440	14,219	14,660	18,964	23,132	14,041	14,980	20,707	18,262	1,993	3,114	3,602	5,851	5,155	8,400	12,223	15,089
1974	3,516	10,152	15,917	17,584	20,898	27,345	14,976	18,731	25,219	23,470	3,269	4,774	4,280	7,873	6,267	11,011	13,972	17,343
1975	3,788	9,824	15,743	16,866	22,147	25,962	17,228	16,190	25,731	22,192	3,240	6,948	4,253	8,098	6,939	10,095	14,226	13,146

See p. 605 for footnotes

F2 External Trade (by value) with Main Trading Partners

1950–1975

EAST GERMANY (in million valuta marks)[32]

	Bulgaria		Czechoslovakia		West Germany[33]		Hungary		Poland		Russia	
	I	E	I	E	I	E	I	E	I	E	I	E
1950	...	...	...	...	255	333	...	...	...	...	...	...
1951	...	...	...	...	183	148	...	...	...	...	...	...
1952	...	...	...	...	193	139	...	...	...	...	...	...
1953	76	84	245	238	263	293	144	179	470	456	1,926	1,821
1954	104	100	323	307	436	440	202	197	470	562	1,918	2,465
1955	130	89	297	394	551	573	261	194	482	520	1,773	2,166
1956	144	136	443	461	614	647	165	200	440	584	2,340	3,391
1957	112	125	499	590	772	860	198	266	432	635	3,092	3,401
1958	128	155	610	662	799	888	305	275	356	641	2,941	3,553
1959	191	213	666	733	960	965	347	368	440	784	3,883	3,955
1960	230	290	785	807	898	1,014	393	396	457	773	4,024	3,884
1961	277	352	916	962	857	922	436	418	430	875	4,497	3,830
1962	320	268	944	912	823	885	414	473	455	979	5,234	4,590
1963	305	411	907	964	829	1,021	400	512	456	1,050	4,926	5,361
1964	338	366	1,049	1,056	1,078	1,113	472	522	608	988	5,087	5,811
1965	394	409	1,103	1,226	1,107	1,235	521	532	589	1,132	5,061	5,505
1966	455	442	1,234	1,301	1,469	1,288	637	592	649	1,175	5,815	5,361
1967	480	525	1,336	1,328	1,288	1,249	644	771	692	1,195	5,954	5,913
1968	514	637	1,381	1,689	1,228	1,410	720	813	942	1,224	6,269	6,583
1969	617	641	1,545	1,741	1,954	1,535	889	779	1,103	1,324	7,326	6,962
1970	714	665	1,920	1,850	2,162	1,888	931	1,124	1,230	1,673	8,170	7,315
1971	761	749	1,987	1,973	2,153	2,142	1,066	1,286	1,275	1,920	7,954	8,139
1972	768	912	2,122	2,240	2,624	2,204	1,274	1,219	1,543	2,282	8,009	9,615
1973	959	1,034	2,360	2,637	2,436	2,499	1,618	1,155	2,236	2,576	8,638	9,889
1974	992	1,189	2,517	3,035	2,987	3,010	1,685	1,703	2,408	2,640	10,147	9,956
1975	...	...	...	...	...	...	...	...	...	...	...	...

See p. 605 for footnotes

F2 External Trade (by value) with Main Trading Partners

1851–1884

GREECE (in million drachmae)

	Austria-Hungary		France		Germany		Italy		Russia		Turkey		U.K.		U.S.A.	
	I	E	I	E	I	E	I	E	I	E	I	E	I	E	I	E
1851	4	3	2	—	...	...	...	...	1	—	8	1	6	7	—	—
1852	3	2	2	2	...	...	...	...	1	1	10	1	4	3	—	—
1853	3	[2] [34]	2	[1] [34]	...	...	...	...	—	[1] [34]	6	[1] [34]	5	[2] [34]	—	—
1854	...	...	2	—	—	—	—	—	1	—	8	1	6	7	—	—
1855	...	...	...	...	...	...	...	...	...	...	...	...	...	...	...	...
1856	...	...	...	...	...	...	...	...	...	...	...	...	...	...	...	...
1857	9	5	5	2	...	...	...	...	1	1	8	3	9	11	1	—
1858	8	4	7	3	...	...	...	...	1	1	8	4	10	11	1	—
1859	8	3	7	3	...	...	...	...	2	—	11	4	10	11	1	1
1860	8	4	8	2	...	...	...	...	4	1	10	4	14	13	1	—
1861	8	3	9	2	...	...	...	...	4	—	9	4	12	14	1	—
1862	7	3	10	1	...	...	...	...	2	—	9	6	11	13	—	—
1863	8	3	11	1	...	...	...	...	4	1	12	4	15	12	—	—
1864	9	3	10	1	...	...	...	...	2	1	11	5	16	12	—	—
1865	10	7	11	3	...	...	...	...	6	2	15	7	24	20	1	—
1866	...	...	...	...	...	...	...	...	...	...	...	...	...	...	...	...
1867	...	...	...	...	...	...	...	...	...	...	...	...	...	...	...	...
1868	...	...	16	7	...	...	12	7	...	...	13	8	29	26	...	...
1869	...	...	...	...	...	...	...	...	...	...	...	...	...	...	...	...
1870	...	...	...	...	...	...	...	...	...	...	...	...	...	...	...	...
1871	...	...	13	6	...	...	8	2	16	5	17	7	34	45	...	...
1872	...	...	...	...	...	...	...	...	...	...	...	...	...	...	...	...
1873	...	...	...	...	...	...	...	...	...	...	...	...	...	...	...	...
1874	16	8	18	3	...	...	7	2	14	2	21	8	39	46	...	...
1875	...	...	...	...	...	...	...	...	...	...	...	...	...	...	...	...
1876	...	...	...	...	...	...	...	...	...	...	...	...	...	...	...	...
1877	...	...	...	...	...	...	...	...	...	...	...	...	...	...	...	...
1878	...	...	...	...	...	...	...	...	...	...	...	...	...	...	...	...
1879	...	...	...	...	...	...	...	...	...	...	...	...	...	...	...	...
1880	...	...	...	...	...	...	...	...	...	...	...	...	...	...	...	...
1881	...	...	...	...	...	...	...	...	...	...	...	...	...	...	...	...
1882	...	...	...	...	...	...	...	...	...	...	...	...	...	...	...	...
1883	34	9	18	24	—	1	6	3	17	2	18	6	37	36	...	...
1884	...	...	...	...	...	...	...	...	...	...	...	...	...	...	...	...

See p. 605 for footnotes

F2 External Trade (by value) with Main Trading Partners

1885–1914

GREECE (in million drachmae)

	Austria-Hungary		France		Germany		Italy		Russia		Turkey		U.K.		U.S.A.	
	I	E	I	E	I	E	I	E	I	E	I	E	I	E	I	E
1885	...	...	...	...	...	...	...	...	...	...	...	...	...	...	...	...
1886	...	...	...	...	...	...	...	...	...	...	...	...	...	...	...	...
1887	17	7	10	22	3	4	6	2	34	1	17	4	31	42	...	4
1888	16	8	11	18	4	3	4	1	25	1	13	4	29	41	2	5
1889	19	9	12	33	5	3	5	3	26	2	25	10	10	33	3	3
1890	17	9	10	21	6	2	5	2	21	1	19	10	33	33	2	6
1891	19	7	13	6	7	3	4	2	27	3	21	8	40	50	3	4
1892	16	6	11	15	9	3	4	3	15	2	22	5	34	33	2	5
1893	13	7	7	14	8	5	2	2	17	2	15	3	25	36	2	6
1894	14	8	8	10	9	2	3	5	29	5	9	8	30	22	3	2
1895	14	6	7	8	8	5	2	7	28	5	10	7	31	17	4	2
1896	12	7	9	7	10	3	3	4	24	8	14	8	29	18	5	3
1897	12	8	12	8	8	5	3	5	29	2	9	5	29	27	4	4
1898	17	8	12	10	11	5	5	4	33	2	16	7	42	28	5	4
1899	15	8	10	11	10	5	6	4	33	1	16	7	26	27	4	6
1900	15	8	13	7	12	10	6	4	32	1	11	4	27	39	4	8
1901	17	9	14	9	12	7	6	4	31	1	12	5	31	29	3	6
1902	21	9	11	8	11	6	6	5	31	2	12	6	29	20	3	4
1903	19	10	12	12	11	5	6	4	31	—	14	5	29	22	2	5
1904	20	11	10	9	13	7	7	4	27	3	16	7	30	21	2	4
1905	19	8	10	7	14	8	6	4	28	1	16	5	28	24	3	6
1906	17	11	10	8	15	11	7	5	27	5	14	7	28	38	4	9
1907	19	11	11	8	14	11	6	8	25	2	13	6	31	33	7	11
1908	18	13	11	11	15	10	6	9	22	2	14	6	36	27	7	6
1909	17	10	10	8	12	10	6	6	27	1	12	6	31	25	5	9
1910	20	12	10	15	14	15	7	14	36	4	11	5	35	33	4	11
1911	24	14	10	14	13	16	7	4	34	3	9	5	41	34	4	13
1912	28	17	9	20	14	15	7	12	24	2	9	6	38	28	4	13
1913	29	13	11	14	13	12	6	4	35	3	4	1	43	28	3	9
1914	...	...	...	...	...	...	...	...	...	...	...	...	...	...	...	...

F2 External Trade (by value) with Main Trading Partners

1915–1944

GREECE (in million drachmae)

	France		Germany		Italy		Russia		Turkey		U.K.		U.S.A.	
	I	E	I	E	I	E	I	E	I	E	I	E	I	E
1915	...	...	...	...	...	...	...	...	...	...	...	...	...	...
1916	...	...	...	...	...	...	...	...	...	...	...	...	...	...
1917	...	...	...	...	...	...	...	...	...	...	...	...	...	...
1918	...	...	...	...	...	...	...	...	...	...	...	...	...	...
1919	135	41	——	6	165	43	3	16	61	87	411	193	350	81
1920	222	36	26	53	215	56	14	——	60	54	532	136	456	99
1921	135	30	88	140	156	53	4	——	35	50	294	201	393	175
1922	201	125	184	524	276	205	1	——	90	55	445	422	677	660
1923	429	123	275	474	448	319	94	——	199	30	863	703	1,221	243
1924	663	156	468	860	883	490	82	1	209	28	1,273	480	1,111	594
1925	860	286	826	840	1,001	879	234	7	245	56	1,534	621	1,826	1,078
1926	840	339	756	1,189	739	1,079	255	4	253	34	1,168	635	1,621	1,284
1927	979	359	936	1,286	833	1,276	339	7	268	33	1,709	627	2,007	1,312
1928	867	314	1,071	1,627	646	1,039	340	2	259	19	1,795	828	1,957	1,256
1929	903	426	1,250	1,613	753	1,272	281	5	339	14	1,688	816	2,088	1,118
1930	780	403	1,099	1,392	659	838	356	20	392	11	1,365	748	1,651	875
1931	573	259	1,072	588	537	696	583	27	481	13	1,153	629	842	724
1932	395	236	758	690	450	786	794	19	265	9	1,076	1,113	1,089	485
1933	364	433	864	918	478	721	649	30	274	23	1,210	973	492	642
1934	588	147	1,291	1,231	430	534	438	69	253	51	1,470	952	552	805
1935	184	192	1,997	2,109	394	423	487	71	218	61	1,658	897	667	1,202
1936	224	250	2,674	2,681	59	132	552	66	177	40	1,889	899	846	1,057
1937	266	241	4,134	2,960	437	601	244	69	202	56	1,668	922	652	1,580
1938	229	296	4,256	3,904	501	525	365	32	273	66	1,926	843	1,070	1,731
1939	...	...	...	...	...	...	...	...	...	...	...	...	...	...
1940	...	...	...	...	...	...	...	...	...	...	...	...	...	...
1941	...	...	...	...	...	...	...	...	...	...	...	...	...	...
1942	...	...	...	...	...	...	...	...	...	...	...	...	...	...
1943	...	...	...	...	...	...	...	...	...	...	...	...	...	...
1944	...	...	...	...	...	...	...	...	...	...	...	...	...	...

F2 External Trade (by value) with Main Trading Partners

1945–1975

GREECE (in million drachmae)

	France I	France E	Germany I	Germany E	Italy I	Italy E	Russia I	Russia E	Turkey I	Turkey E	U.K. I	U.K. E	U.S.A. I	U.S.A. E
1945	...	...	...	...	...	...	...	...	...	...	...	...	...	...
1946	...	...	...	...	...	...	...	...	...	...	...	...	...	...
1947	[2,197][35]	[1,945][35]	[2,271][35]	–	[7,829][35]	[10,044][35]	–	–	[11,384][35]	[292][35]	[14,916][35]	[19,999][35]	[41,480][35]	[14,104][35]
	thousand million drachmae		thousand million drachmae		thousand million drachmae		thousand million drachmae		thousand million drachmae		thousand million drachmae		thousand million drachmae	
1948	29	26	85	14	83	67	–	––	56	10	137	121	859	66
1949	95	62	79	60	84	42	...	...	97	4	186	120	847	109
1950	75	24	171	90	132	22	...	...	54	6	265	68	695	75
1951	311	170	561	305	547	138	...	...	122	13	576	221	1,767	209
			West Germany											
1952	409	157	630	539	614	113	–	––	73	45	515	290	1,136	228
1953	496	199	958	868	1,195	310	5	43	210	78	771	396	1,146	406
	million new drachmae		million new drachmae		million new drachmae		million new drachmae		million new drachmae		million new drachmae		million new drachmae	
1954	652	333	1,602	1,113	1,538	585	44	110	65	37	1,098	578	1,376	454
1955	711	484	1,927	1,371	1,313	803	58	66	69	38	1,271	541	2,098	708
1956	724	761	2,220	1,133	1,260	632	145	205	105	24	2,010	538	2,344	677
1957	937	444	2,957	1,702	1,549	543	318	271	70	19	1,743	589	2,571	906
1958	920	893	3,442	1,422	1,497	418	428	503	39	12	1,677	531	2,324	947
1959	633	448	3,273	1,254	1,193	452	537	353	82	13	2,022	571	1,757	790
1960	959	290	3,351	1,129	1,215	377	850	565	53	11	2,150	577	2,845	818
1961	1,316	339	3,859	1,262	1,387	227	597	563	41	27	2,273	522	2,431	971
1962	1,668	397	3,986	1,366	1,610	637	610	577	103	49	2,512	725	2,017	576
1963	1,499	316	4,404	1,681	1,800	447	852	672	102	43	2,517	680	2,538	1,646
1964	1,869	496	5,260	1,977	2,154	549	822	725	95	14	2,842	679	3,029	1,346
1965	2,885	515	5,866	2,238	3,094	501	1,096	807	233	6	3,106	760	3,381	936
1966	2,581	723	6,335	2,415	3,680	603	1,142	849	182	5	3,601	707	3,935	1,279
1967	2,836	1,367	6,732	2,343	3,683	1,477	1,125	915	122	5	3,266	743	3,003	1,953
1968	3,161	460	7,708	2,750	4,307	1,872	814	743	100	13	4,047	583	3,203	1,428
1969	3,265	1,118	9,216	3,296	4,299	1,610	910	901	271	36	4,267	765	4,557	1,623
1970	4,274	1,086	10,901	3,887	4,916	1,933	1,087	1,035	181	19	5,064	1,147	3,479	1,448
1971	4,640	1,864	12,264	4,008	5,781	1,710	937	611	167	21	4,617	851	4,172	1,783
1972	5,751	2,175	14,688	5,639	7,703	2,635	1,271	1,072	360	145	4,912	862	4,367	2,550
1973	7,771	2,837	20,061	9,245	9,379	4,064	1,320	1,310	666	496	5,794	2,998	8,619	2,757
1974	9,354	3,633	21,418	12,861	11,282	5,201	1,798	2,421	746	421	6,248	3,501	12,102	3,687
1975	10,294	5,396	27,206	15,614	14,171	6,130	3,328	2,824	23	98	8,290	3,626	12,689	3,767

See p. 605 for footnotes

F2 External Trade (by value) with Main Trading Partners

HUNGARY (in million pengos) **1919–1944**

	Austria		Czechoslovakia		Germany		Poland		Romania		Russia	
	I	E	I	E	I	E	I	E	I	E	I	E
1919	...	...	...	...	...	...	...	...	...	...	...	...
1920	244	115	91	26	41	21	...	...	4	3	...	...
1921	227	157	176	47	78	27	1	1	21	14	...	...
1922	180	145	149	57	104	35	28	10	45	44	...	...
1923	126	171	118	45	70	24	31	7	50	34	...	...
1924	188	242	204	160	102	53	45	17	64	35	...	...
	---[36]	---[36]	---[36]	---[36]	---[36]	---[36]	---[36]	---[36]	---[36]	---[36]		
1925	193	283	209	198	132	89	42	38	69	34	...	...
1926	186	325	212	171	157	114	49	14	76	35	...	...
1927	207	281	286	157	216	107	54	28	85	37	...	...
1928	196	282	272	145	237	98	49	27	96	45	...	...
1929	140	316	229	170	213	121	51	17	96	47	...	...
1930	95	256	173	153	175	94	30	12	73	29	...	...
1931	67	170	49	24	131	73	25	7	65	20	...	...
1932	51	101	34	23	74	51	7	3	41	11	...	...
1933	62	106	32	29	62	44	4	4	24	13	...	...
1934	81	99	24	20	63	90	4	3	30	20	...	...
1935	76	86	19	21	91	108	4	4	54	24	...	...
1936	72	87	22	20	113	115	5	4	59	24	...	...
1937	87	99	30	21	125	141	5	5	48	25	...	...
1938	47	95	27	22	124	143	6	5	40	21	...	...
1939	...	...	...	...	...	...	...	...	...	...	—	—
1940	...	...	...	...	...	...	...	...	...	...	...	...
1941	...	...	...	...	...	...	...	...	...	...	...	...
1942	...	...	...	...	...	...	...	...	...	...	...	...
1943	...	...	...	...	...	...	...	...	...	...	...	...
1944	...	...	...	...	...	...	...	...	...	...	...	...

See p. 605 for footnotes

F2 External Trade (by value) with Main Trading Partners

1945–1975

HUNGARY

	Austria		Czechoslovakia		Germany				Poland		Romania		Russia	
	I	E	I	E	I		E		I	E	I	E	I	E
					East	West	East	West						
1945	...	...	...	...	...		...		...	...	...	...	...	...
1946	...[13]	...[13]	...[13]	...[13]	...[13]		...[13]		...[13]	...[13]	...[13]	...[13]	...[13]	...[13]
	million forints		million forints		million forints				million forints		million forints		million forints	
1947	...	...	...	...	...		...		...	...	...	...	...	...
1948	...	...	...	...	...		...		...	...	...	...	...	...
1949	229	230	348	333	26	189	61	239	179	135	138	184	725	820
1950	210	198	382	407	96	367	284	287	365	316	261	298	908	1,115
1951	128	197	606	614	263	201	157	218	425	376	206	171	1,180	1,516
1952	212	192	857	677	464	194	353	200	395	420	262	220	1,387	1,741
1953	188	152	819	822	476	186	422	187	332	378	240	301	1,664	2,198
1954	302[37]	242	788[37]	885	616	322[37]	574	238	298[37]	341	194[37]	178	1,719[37]	2,018
1955	326	313	662	928	602	462	762	353	336	375	220	228	1,178	1,795
1956	257	242	648	734	533	313	452	410	291	266	152	142	1,271	1,418
1957	291	195	925	890	825	344	582	351	415	257	200	142	2,779	1,244
1958	236	277	897	1,085	838	416	885	401	376	394	161	177	2,281	1,864
1959	351	320	1,035	1,023	1,063	455	1,056	570	469	458	267	213	3,002	2,449
1960	405	377	1,313	1,103	1,185	648	1,182	525	582	535	487	304	3,556	3,011
1961	371	304	1,214	1,617	1,231	642	1,295	614	681	700	286	335	4,183	3,896
1962	433	407	1,480	1,608	1,375	582	1,231	626	786	831	459	428	4,892	4,600
1963	571	403	1,761	1,557	1,560	744	1,255	676	937	921	421	399	5,076	5,023
1964	587	401	1,815	1,750	1,564	943	1,431	796	1,118	991	487	494	5,839	5,755
1965	607	463	1,579	2,105	1,540	909	1,586	934	1,037	1,233	456	337	6,496	6,168
1966	565	572	1,562	2,012	1,780	1,080	1,849	1,001	1,076	1,234	387	353	6,073	6,184
1967	754	556	1,786	1,798	2,278	1,218	1,924	868	1,309	1,193	463	436	6,949	7,201
1968	643[78]	477[78]	1,882[78]	2,083[78]	2,304[78]	900[78]	2,016[78]	905[78]	1,321[78]	1,133[78]	477[78]	429[78]	7,593[78]	7,910[78]
1969	734	642	1,684	2,343	2,234	971	2,636	1,191	1,390	1,379	571	533	8,400	8,462
1970	956	759	2,333	2,381	3,074	1,549	2,644	1,630	1,701	1,623	814	632	9,767	9,272
1971	1,126	749	2,945	2,328	3,813	2,197	2,842	1,613	1,797	2,209	956	793	11,984	10,249
1972	1,045	935	2,909	2,955	3,600	2,568	3,481	1,955	1,789	2,525	807	821	11,821	12,839
1973	1,321	1,303	3,058	3,714	3,232	4,707	3,220	2,608	1,823	2,587	1,135	1,272	12,710	14,034
1974	2,526	1,638	3,819	4,300	4,845	4,873	4,767	2,819	2,354	2,730	1,233	1,866	14,522	14,989
1975	2,301	1,226	4,606	4,371	6,363	4,400	5,649	2,729	3,027	2,727	2,176	1,459	21,504	20,278

See p. 605 for footnotes

F2 External Trade (by value) with Main Trading Partners

1923–1975

IRELAND (in million pounds)

	Germany		Great Britain		Northern Ireland		U.S.A.	
	I	E	I	E	I	E	I	E
1923	...	...	...	...	...	...	...	...
1924	0.7	0.1	48	43	7.9	7.5	3.7	0.2
1925	0.9	0.1	44	37	6.8	6.5	3.2	0.3
1926	2.3	0.2	40	35	6.5	5.7	5.0	0.3
1927	1.5	0.4	41	38	6.4	5.1	4.7	0.5
1928	1.8	0.3	40	39	6.2	5.3	3.8	0.3
1929	1.6	0.7	42	39	6.1	5.2	4.8	1.0
1930	1.3	0.7	40	36	5.8	4.8	3.9	1.2
1931	1.2	0.1	36	31	5.0	3.9	2.0	0.4
1932	1.3	0.1	29	22	3.8	3.0	1.3	0.1
1933	1.8	0.2	23	16	2.1	2.2	1.1	0.2
1934	2.3	0.2	24	14	2.0	2.3	1.9	0.1
1935	1.3	0.5	25	16	1.8	2.0	1.4	0.2
1936	1.3[3]	0.6	27[3]	19	1.6[3]	2.3	1.9[3]	0.3
	1.4		21		0.5		3.1	
1937	1.4	0.8	21	20	0.6	2.2	2.9	0.2
1938	1.5	0.9	20	20	0.6	2.5	4.7	0.1
1939	...	...	23	23	0.8	2.7	3.6	0.3
1940	...	...	24	28	0.6	3.4	4.1	0.5
1941	...	—	21	28	0.6	3.4	2.3	0.7
1942	...	—	19	27	1.0	5.1	3.0	0.3
1943	...	—	13	23	0.5	4.9	3.6	0.3
1944	...	—	13	24	0.8	5.7	3.0	0.3

	Germany		Great Britain		Northern Ireland		U.S.A.	
	I	E	I	E	I	E	I	E
1945	...	—	19	28	0.9	6.9	4.0	0.4
1946	...	—	36	29	1.6	7.2	8.5	0.6
1947	...	—	52	27	2.2	7.5	29	0.3
1948	...	0.1	71	35	2.2	7.6	11	0.4
1949	0.5	0.4	72	46	2.3	8.4	19	0.5
1950	1.9	1.5	82	54	2.4	8.5	21	1.3
1951	4.6	1.2	93	58	2.7	11	25	3.2
1952	5.4	0.9	85	73	2.6	14	18	3.2
1953	5.3	0.9	90	86	2.4	17	16	2.4
1954	7.3	1.8	97	86	2.7	17	12	2.2
1955	9.6	1.5	105	81	3.0	15	18	3.0
1956	8.0	2.3	101	68	3.4	15	14	3.2
1957	7.0	3.3	96	79	8.6	22	11	4.0
1958	8.0	2.8	104	80	8.4	21	14	7.5
1959	10	3.5	101	77	8.9	19	14	9.9
1960	12	3.7	105	92	7.4	20	19	11
1961	14	5.6	119	111	14	23	20	13
1962	19	5.3	125	105	11	23	21	14
1963	20	5.8	142	111	14	30	18	14
1964	24	9.0	162	129	16	29	27	10
1965	24	12.0	174	127	15	27	30	9
1966	22	9.5	179	141	14	28	35	17
1967	25	6.9	179	170	18	35	32	26
1968	36	8.1	237	195	21	43	38	49
1969	43	10.8	289	201	25	50	55	57
1970	46	13	322	235	30	57	49	60
1971	55	14	348	289	26	66	65	60
1972	64	30	397	327	31	67	63	61
1973	93	54	534	393	43	82	78	86
1974	126	66	706	530	52	104	105	109
1975	120	115	768	628	64	154	122	88

See p. 605 for footnotes

F2 External Trade (by value) with Main Trading Partners

1860–1896

ITALY (in million lire)

	Austria-Hungary		France		Germany		Switzerland		U.K.		U.S.A.	
	I	E	I	E	I	E	I	E	I	E	I	E
1860	...	...	...	...	...	...	...	...	...	...	...	...
1861	158	66	219	184	8	1	84	146	191	26	31	3
1862	139	56	233	188	4	5	81	136	192	95	16	17
1863	147	70	267	235	5	4	74	115	203	88	6	10
1864	152	78	294	204	4	2	72	91	179	93	9	16
1865	121	78	346	187	6	5	64	76	184	86	8	3
1866	94[38]	60[38]	315	215	5	6	59	97	190	93	18	25
1867	146	125	258	280	6	4	62	105	179	73	33	21
1868	169	140	230	290	8	5	61	121	205	85	41	31
1869	155	106	261	266	10	3	49	122	232	117	38	30
1870	147	133	224[39]	203[39]	13	5	49	135	240[40]	116[40]	39	35
1871	172	197	201	393	13	8	52	157	283	143	51	32
1872	215	220	326	442	15	8	49	176	294	135	45	29
1873	225	222	363	446	24	14	41	160	302	111	50	29
1874	250	208	391	366	28	19	41	108	281	132	48	28
1875	233	191	367	382	37	24	31	109	298	140	43	29
1876	264	187	412	542	40	21	33	150	309	134	49	21
1877	234[41]	154[41]	322[39 41]	401[39 41]	25[41]	17[41]	26[41]	80[41]	296[40 41]	126[40 41]	40[41]	27[41]
1878	196	173	268	464	39	21	32	98	237	97	54	36
1879	194	207	295	438	46	24	29	107	256	95	72[42]	61[42]
1880	181	166	300	476	88	78	34	102	259	84	76	55
1881	218	151	329	524	66	68	36	135	307	83	63	57
1882	189	147	310	458	85	73	44	130	290	92	69	61
1883	200	135	300	500	109	86	52	123	298	92	58	59
1884	200	108	282	415	110	109	66	118	300	89	60	55
1885	222	93	288	367	119	104	71	109	314	71	72	46
1886	223	93	311	446	129	108	81	88	275	71	55	52
1887	249	92	326	405	166	115	65	88	306	79	64	66
1888	137	84	156	170	145	80	58	214	264	115	77	61
1889	159	90	167	165	156	91	62	230	314	113	75	76
1890	144	84	163	161	141	119	55	169	320	111	82	77
1891	122	93	144	150	134	131	48	150	262	115	74	74
1892	122	106	169	147	144	145	49	173	245	113	79	100
1893	120	120	159	148	147	146	51	188	252	104	96	82
1894	115	126	131	144	140	143	43	206	249	122	107	91
1895	133	114	162	136	144	170	46	187	235	115	124[42]	102[42]
1896	132	121	134	153	145	160	45	170	230	110	122	86

See p. 605 for footnotes

F2 External Trade (by value) with Main Trading Partners

ITALY (in million lire) **1897–1934**

	Austria-Hungary		France		Germany		Switzerland		U.K.		U.S.A.	
	I	E	I	E	I	E	I	E	I	E	I	E
1897	134[41]	137[41]	161[41]	116[41]	150[41]	179[41]	42[41]	185[41]	223[41]	114[41]	125[41]	93[41]
1898	130	144	116	146	157	192	40	185	254	117	166	107
1899	161	159	152	202	194	236	49	247	300	148	168	118
1900	191	144	167	169	203	221	57	207	359	154	226	121
1901	178	131	179	175	206	235	57	205	279	151	234	140
1902	176	127	184	168	222	246	57	260	287	143	211	177
1903	176	154	193	171	236	226	59	274	282	132	212	166
1904	187	137	188	171	252	206	49	258	319	134	239	191
1905	195	144	205	182	287	222	50	320	348	130	238	226
1906	226[41]	140[41]	228[41]	213[41]	394[41]	252[41]	65[41]	366[41]	450[41]	132[41]	311[41]	240[41]
1907	249	158	256	198	527	301	73	349	523	156	393	236
1908	301	145	276	204	521	245	80	297	501	132	405	204
1909	309	156	329	199	504	307	80	217	491	168	390	272
1910	290	165	334	218	525	293	84	216	476	210	363	264
1911	289	185	327	206	550	301	78	204	510	223	415	247
1912	294	219	390	223	626	328	85	219	577	264	515	262
1913	265	221	283	231	613	343	87	249	592	261	523	268
1914	234	197	206	174	503	319	77	232	505	306	443	262
1915	46	119	240	438	230	204	118	314	849	391	1,749	283
1916	1	—	595	738	12	—	209	632	1,977	447	3,415	315
1917	——	—	993	912	18	—	249	605	2,165	483	6,192	244
1918	2	—	1,234	1,207	16	—	191	410	2,666	727	6,641	169
	Austria											
1919	106	275	760	1,403	88	85	370	786	2,444	773	7,350	630
1920	654	621	1,904	1,696	1,097	574	575	1,505	4,609	1,379	8,689	939
1921	445	510	1,070	967	1,293	814	287	831	1,680	795	5,711	1,084
1922	327	222	1,151	1,365	1,246	972	331	1,208	2,022	1,117	4,398	1,018
1923	326	335	1,324	1,581	1,308	697	372	1,201	2,204	1,211	4,608	1,523
1924	467	686	1,474	1,823	1,524	1,565	408	1,612	2,169	1,493	4,648	1,239
1925	673	666	2,358	2,024	2,253	2,025	521	1,635	2,728	1,852	6,196	1,896
1926	634	562	2,136	2,111	2,956	2,215	592	1,509	1,881	1,755	5,608	1,934
1927	507	485	1,799	1,284	2,108	2,233	539	1,255	1,826	1,528	3,958	1,641
1928	464	434	2,060	1,362	2,303	1,856	546	988	1,794	1,404	4,012	1,521
1929	483	427	2,044	1,304	2,737	1,777	549	1,051	2,040	1,461	3,561	1,718
	[41]	[41]	[41]	[41]	[41]	[41]	[41]	[41]	[41]	[41]	[41]	[41]
1930	412	378	1,504	1,234	2,258	1,555	548	929	1,677	1,190	2,538	1,327
1931	291	315	825	1,119	1,588	1,091	401	771	1,099	1,201	1,327	1,046
1932	186	190	482	517	1,151	778	310	578	743	736	1,108	688
1933	175	131	413	459	1,143	729	721	483	727	689	1,115	529
1934	190	122	437	352	1,248	834	293	438	707	529	957	388

See p. 605 for footnotes

F2 External Trade (by value) with Main Trading Partners

1935–1954

ITALY (in million lire)

	Austria		France		Germany		Switzerland		U.K.		U.S.A.	
	I	E	I	E	I	E	I	E	I	E	I	E
1935	272	134	471	305	1,427	851	246	338	568	431	879	423
1936	370	193	128	190	1,617	1,086	233	345	52	156	895	550
1937	632	289	491	442	2,589[43]	1,503[43]	412	508	561	641	1,539	784
1938	...	...	254	328	3,016	2,202	376	495	728	587	1,338	782
1939	...	...	154	243	3,030	1,899	336	530	568	518	979	773
1940	...	...	125	290	5,139	3,558	470	718	419	276	1,219	393
1941	...	...	207	219	6,890	7,106	534	1,087	3	—	91	5
1942	...	...	119	181	8,374[43]	7,639[43]	519	627	2	—	18	—
1943	...	...	...	...	...	...	...	...	...	...	...	...
1944	...	...	...	...	...	...	...	...	...	...	...	...
1945	...	...	...	...	...	...	...	...	...	...	...	...
1946	...	...	...	...	...	...	...	...	...	...	...	...
1947	...	...	...	...	...	...	...	...	...	...	...	...
1948	13,050	10,283	7,893	23,058	17,590	16,577	25,764	44,232	27,812	45,490	317,701	51,337
1949	20,016	18,492	21,470	36,188	39,726	54,284	26,732	35,598	34,593	67,018	311,041	26,392
1950	25,481	19,977	41,764	65,313	75,887	73,799	33,465	47,813	51,129	85,755	217,884	47,699
1951	32,164	21,049	58,511	92,656	99,906	80,246	42,022	57,731	50,075	138,551	284,477	70,535
1952	42,159	24,019	58,942	56,734	136,730[2]	87,977[2]	55,134	56,106	83,384	71,153	307,529	87,185
					135,485	86,685						
1953	55,142	25,703	75,909	49,121	179,619	103,865	63,447	64,047	116,934	67,751	202,821	90,080
1954	64,457	35,628	97,534	60,449	203,679	115,159	58,260	73,988	102,633	80,967	186,510	80,221

See p. 605 for footnotes

F2 External Trade (by value) with Main Trading Partners

ITALY (in million lire) **1955–1975**

	Austria		France		Germany		Switzerland		U.K.		U.S.A.	
	I	E	I	E	I	E	I	E	I	E	I	E
1955	70,283	42,858	108,367	67,539	214,733	145,664	57,344	84,415	90,545	84,065	253,094	99,585
1956	82,854	48,319	100,203	95,912	247,558	179,983	63,556	100,217	107,163	86,621	325,368	125,897
1957	98,902	53,102	121,425	101,087	281,161	224,706	66,329	121,932	121,845	99,224	427,060	161,904
1958	93,262	45,761	94,690	84,558	243,321	226,850	64,163	122,302	109,213	109,213	357,981	177,463
1959	91,949	51,084	162,082	112,089	292,911	295,072	70,966	131,549	116,655	135,741	234,053	215,978
1960	112,133	69,614	248,679	172,116	418,835	375,761	86,259	152,614	151,856	156,312	418,360	239,662
1961	110,996	72,943	299,505	199,671	509,370	465,487	93,423	179,196	179,730	175,730	539,691	238,786
1962	116,145	78,159	334,283	269,066	642,051	562,036	104,327	206,695	239,922	174,779	553,281	275,592
1963	131,866	82,114	460,587	328,058	813,232	564,231	121,170	212,673	290,911	169,112	651,598	298,180
1964	105,814	87,776	446,498	406,490	738,468	707,188	114,999	227,452	248,097	207,833	615,781	316,927
1965	101	104	452	464	681	953	107	244	214	211	621	387
1966	107	110	542	583	858	1,007	125	252	251	239	657	465
1967	127	116	655	676	1,060	960	142	259	271	263	665	540
1968	122	109	728	801	1,148	1,189	156	286	273	281	748	681
1969	145	117	968	1,061	1,462	1,440	185	328	313	264	886	795
					(in thousand million lire)							
1970	167	143	1,235	1,065	1,861	1,780	209	390	353	313	967	846
1971	176	173	1,399	1,267	1,998	2,129	212	441	362	362	892	918
1972	205	273	1,772	1,536	2,286	2,486	243	488	395	463	931	1,062
1973	333	290	2,442	1,880	3,302	2,821	371	607	560	648	1,352	1,111
1974	451	399	3,509	2,498	4,734	3,662	549	825	809	1,025	2,037	1,504
1975	393	483	3,355	3,025	4,316	4,293	583	862	840	1,047	2,194	1,490

F2 External Trade (by value) with Main Trading Partners

1845–1879

NETHERLANDS (in million florins)

	Belgium		Dutch East Indies		Germany		Russia		U.K.		U.S.A.	
	I	E	I	E	I	E	I	E	I	E	I	E
1845	...	...	...	...	...	...	...	...	...	...	...	...
1846	10	15	48	11	21	29	8	6	35	25	6	2
1847	14	20	48	9	20	31	16	10	32	26	5	4
1848	13	16	51	9	19	33	9	4	47	34	5	4
1849	15	18	55	8	23	30	12	3	35	35	7	3
1850	23	21	50	10	27	27	10	3	37	39	4	5
1851	31	22	52	12	23	33	9	3	40	38	4	5
1852	23	21	63	16	24	37	12	3	40	41	6	4
1853	21	20	53	19	28	32	17	2	45	47	5	4
1854	36	26	61	25	37	48	12	——	53	54	6	3
1855	22	40	63	18	44	56	——	——	51	56	6	4
1856	28	29	74	22	50	63	15	5	56	59	8	5
1857	42	29	67	37	51	29	18	5	57	60	7	4
1858	51	30	69	23	52[44]	69[44]	14	4	60	54	8	7
1859	42	34	70	25	50	67	13	5	56	61	9	5
1860	39	33	73	32	56	70	19	5	67	64	11	5
1861	30	40	76	39	62	80	19	5	79	61	12	3
1862	35	34	76	28	68	80	18	3	68	62	6	3
1863	41	44	66	23	74	95	9	8	91	72	6	2
1864	40	54	78	53	83	98	13	4	94	91	5	2
1865	48	55	73	27	97	121	11	4	118	98	3	4
1866	46	40	79	41	99	121	14	8	125	89	4	3
1867	44	38	79	44	90	122	23	4	130	84	6	3
1868	56	53	83	31	99	136	15	4	147	94	7	5
1869	55	62	76	28	109	136	15	4	131	108	8	4
1870	56	67	81	32	103	144	23	4	174	106	10	3
1871	79	65	80	31	104	183	33	5	195	112	26	4
1872	97	74	67	35	113	201	23	6	220	109	22	5
1873	91	76	82	45	131	230	27	3	247	115	30	4
1874	87	77	77	36	137	222	39	8	228	117	30	5
1875	105	80	77	41	155	227	37	21	242	125	21	4
1876	102	86	73	42	154	221	43	15	225	124	30	5
1877	107	90	74	48	186	217	57	8	206	132	39	4
1878	117	90	69	53	193	232	63	10	217	131	52	3
1879	112	94	56	42	208[44]	259[44]	83	8	219	129	54	9
					221	270						

See p. 605 for footnotes

F2 External Trade (by value) with Main Trading Partners

1880–1914

NETHERLANDS (in million florins)

	Belgium		Dutch East Indies		Germany		Russia		U.K.		U.S.A.	
	I	E	I	E	I	E	I	E	I	E	I	E
1880	104	101	56	47	246	266	46	9	212	147	81	16
1881	111	109	53	42	289	304	47	7	244	160	61	16
1882	124	113	53	40	312	349	77	9	276	156	43	38
1883	141	115	81	36	322	333	90	5	258	132	61	19
1884	146	130	76	43	302	407	94	4	317	187	66	22
1885	162	128	97	45	297	401	77	5	269	229	56	26
1886	158	138	90	45	314	414	75	5	262	255	67	46
1887	161	131	114	41	302	420	95	3	246	293	79	49
1888	157	146	118	47	318	530	126	5	341	298	62	38
1889	177	140	143	69	269	511	113	5	297	285	76	22
1890	195	148	160	53	271	517	121	6	284	271	98	24
1891	186	150	225	64	271	552	119	4	270	296	93	21
1892	184	160	177	63	271	504	39	3	267	326	149	23
1893	176	168	193	57	279	551	89	6	264	256	155	22
1894	161	155	225	54	285	557	175	5	246	260	132	22
1895	166	154	202	52	293	596	198	5	238	268	111	38
1896	174	164	239	53	302	700	223	6	256	290	167	47
1897	186	166	218	60	304	790	249	7	270	322	234	45
1898	209	161	261	64	342	814	164	8	269	338	279	44
1899	206	159	289	68	335	834	205	8	277	349	297	61
1900	208	176	273	64	386	911	145	11	288	383	284	65
1901	226	175	324	62	466	901	160	8	248	426	303	79
1902	233	193	349	61	565	895	210	10	237	457	234	107
1903	228	213	337	62	603	972	230	8	257	461	232	106
1904	259	221	376	68	555	1,039	333	11	253	433	232	97
1905	254	227	400	71	638	1,066	319	12	264	410	241	81
1906	264	260	337	68	614	1,058	216	10	309	466	315	86
1907	286	285	437	82	599	1,159	209	12	325	446	294	86
1908	471	281	405	89	692	1,081	280	13	296	490	322	81
1909	290	289	425	88	743	1,279	558	14	293	500	291	100
1910	301	330	494	114	820	1,319	433	16	325	545	295	85
1911	324	319	456	126	902	1,357	367	18	339	555	331	105
1912	344	371	496	154	1,046	1,555	292	25	354	605	362	136
1913	352	340	529	163	1,133	1,478	366	31	341	684	443	131
1914	246	219	395	143	877	1,125	188	22	327	602	301	164

F2 External Trade (by value) with Main Trading Partners

1915–1944

NETHERLANDS (in million florins)

	Belgium		Dutch East Indies		Germany		Russia		U.K.		U.S.A.	
	I	E	I	E	I	E	I	E	I	E	I	E
1915	63	114	379	132	608	714	——	1	396	476	331	117
1916	59	53	388	111	566	520	2	1	358	396	273	102
1917	22	63	...	...	246	317	...	...	192	306	199	37
1918	13	20	5	11	321	154	...	...	52	74	24	14
1919	225	177	329	163	433	578	21	29	588	208	549	57
1920	321	181	240	264	903	421	5	2	555	328	526	77
1921	229	172	129	206	649	254	3	5	318	357	392	47
1922	191	176	103	132	609	168	6	5	327	307	271	62
1923	220	142	114	111	501	187	22	3	310	368	256	69
1924	255	153	135	107	577	495	46	10	306	414	271	58
1925	276	166	137	137	594	470	35	17	394	468	276	71
1926	273	146	145	128	668	381	39	3	232	483	258	80
1927	270	158	117	130	654	466	31	4	252	460	268	65
1928	302	174	141	182	730	468	23	4	259	437	266	69
1929	286	207	147	187	842	451	38	3	263	406	272	71
1930	259	195	97	144	768	360	59	4	230	380	211	49
1931	198	174	72	89	620	252	72	89	160	317	148	34
1932	135	118	60	47	400	179	36	5	118	160	86	29
1933	131	106	51	31	396	161	35	5	113	128	78	32
1934	114	86	58	31	312	180	27	8	102	137	69	28
1935	112	80	57	32	249	131	23	11	96	148	65	42
1936	129	101	79	44	247	119	22	17	114	170	73	58
1937	192	142	126	94	338	179	40	22	146	253	137	74
1938	171	114	102	100	311	157	32	23	127	238	154	46
1939	231	98	91	101	369	139	22	22	127	230	147	46
1940	152	63	54	42	324	311	4	11	56	78	135	12
1941	89	63	6	—	518	502	——	1	——	—	2	——
1942	52	44	——	—	327	485	——	——	——	—	——	—
1943	41	44	——	—	285	536	3	1	——	—	——	—
1944	...	...	...	...	...	...	...	...	...	...	...	...

F2 External Trade (by value) with Main Trading Partners

NETHERLANDS (in million florins) **1945–1975**

	Belgium		Dutch East Indies		West Germany		Russia		U.K.		U.S.A.	
	I	E	I	E	I	E	I	E	I	E	I	E
1945	...	...	...	...	...	...	...	...	...	...	...	...
1946	302	170	20	26	56	52	1	—	372	89	536	59
1947	522	296	197	133	97	58	...	...	422	243	1,198	61
1948	732	424	334	200	267	160	9	11	492	393	862	85
1949	762	511	406	392	361	411	59	19	621	627	879	130
1950	1,437	727	510	300	961	1,109	9	2	820	790	899	271
1951	1,774	1,095	755	402	1,205	1,029	53	6	845	1,178	1,071	449
1952	1,451	1,251	543	440	1,184	1,118	97	19	782	1,002	1,085	536
1953	1,556	1,266	494	291	1,441	1,150	119	86	897	879	900	694
1954	1,841	1,293	528	233	1,832	1,459	88	125	936	1,060	1,284	627
1955	2,205	1,411	369	258	2,155	1,755	115	59	1,039	1,263	1,652	602
1956	2,680	1,543	440	315	2,547	1,979	160	30	1,158	1,273	1,976	679
1957	2,816	1,826	454	274	2,902	2,191	150	73	1,255	1,280	2,049	604
1958	2,459	1,830	308	111	2,691	2,337	156	41	1,017	1,455	1,554	688
1959	2,747	2,009	272	98	3,098	2,964	240	46	1,132	1,470	1,651	787
1960	3,155	2,184	236	100	3,712	3,452	169	45	1,183	1,676	2,279	754
1961	3,549	2,373	149	48	4,313	3,630	144	72	1,335	1,564	2,073	702
1962	3,804	2,444	73	37	4,469	4,025	132	116	1,405	1,755	2,199	724
1963	4,163	2,694	55	33	5,247	4,649	171	86	1,577	1,727	2,348	736
1964	4,911	3,207	344	43	6,200	5,661	129	54	1,830	1,923	2,813	812
1965	5,299	3,438	400	118	6,392	6,428	192	106	1,758	2,011	2,768	882
1966	5,509	3,690	353	120	7,211	6,576	175	91	1,771	2,009	3,295	1,112
1967	5,568	3,886	355	166	7,670	6,885	187	241	1,674	2,330	3,208	1,241
1968	6,047	4,320	216	136	8,876	8,393	196	169	1,844	2,579	3,671	1,579
1969	7,046	5,031	189	164	10,626	10,718	247	202	2,319	2,754	3,862	1,631
1970	8,187	5,942	178	171	13,164	13,873	210	165	2,815	2,981	4,737	1,832
1971	7,334	6,960	174	183	14,386	16,438	228	163	2,967	3,553	5,126	1,960
1972	8,584	8,130	168	190	15,021	18,273	256	205	2,874	3,962	4,519	2,019
1973	9,763	9,694	221	262	18,542	21,812	357	218	3,439	5,278	5,937	2,373
1974	11,665	12,362	225	317	23,232	26,515	632	455	4,790	8,018	7,944	3,509
1975	11,510	12,280	314	409	22,354	26,941	768	523	5,097	8,121	8,771	2,440

F2 External Trade (by value) with Main Trading Partners

1865–1899

NORWAY (in million kroner)

	Canada[45]		Denmark		France		Germany		Netherlands		Sweden		Great Britain/U.K.[46]		U.S.A.	
	I	E	I	E	I	E	I	E	I	E	I	E	I	E	I	E
1865	...	...	...	...	...	...	...	...	...	...	...	...	...	...	...	...
1866	...	...	14	3.9	5.8	9.3	31	10	3.0	6.5	5.8	5.5	28	19	0.4	0.4
1867	...	...	17	3.7	3.2	8.7	30	10	2.6	5.7	4.9	6.4	24	21	0.1	0.1
1868	...	...	19	3.8	3.8	8.2	33	12	2.6	6.2	6.1	4.6	24	21	0.1	—
1869	...	...	18	4.6	3.9	9.5	29	13	2.8	7.0	5.3	5.9	21	22	—	—
1870	...	...	18	4.5	2.8	7.8	27	12	3.1	6.4	8.5	7.9	26	24	0.1	0.1
1871	...	...	15	5.0	2.6	6.6	25	13	3.4	6.2	9.7	7.9	28	25	0.1	—
1872	...	...	22	6.2	6.0	10.5	31	18	4.4	7.4	11	11	41	30	0.1	0.1
1873	...	...	19	6.0	10.1	12.4	42	20	5.8	8.7	12	12	53	40	0.4	0.2
1874	...	...	20	7.8	8.9	10.7	49	19	6.8	7.3	13	15	55	38	2.0	—
1875	...	...	21	5.9	8.7	7.7	47	18	5.9	6.2	13	13	52	29	2.4	0.1
1876	...	...	19	5.9	10.6	10.5	45	19	6.9	6.7	14	15	45	36	2.1	—
1877	...	...	18	5.0	9.4	9.3	54	18	7.9	6.5	14	12	50	34	3.9	—
1878	...	...	15	4.3	4.7	6.6	42	16	6.3	4.7	12	9	36	28	3.8	0.1
1879	...	...	14	5.0	3.9	6.2	35	17	5.3	5.6	12	9	37	25	2.3	0.3
1880	...	...	18	5.9	6.2	8.5	39	14	5.9	6.0	13	14	42	39	1.9	0.2
1881	...	...	20	6.6	9.7	8.3	45	16	6.6	7.3	15	14	42	41	2.9	0.1
1882	...	...	15	7.1	5.4	10.2	50	16	5.6	6.6	19	15	43	38	2.6	0.2
1883	...	...	13	5.6	5.9	8.8	47	17	5.3	5.4	19	14	42	40	6.2	0.3
1884	...	...	13	6.1	5.5	9.5	46	15	5.4	5.4	17	13	42	37	6.4	0.3
1885	...	...	11	4.9	4.6	7.8	42	12	4.8	5.4	16	13	37	34	7.4	0.4
1886	...	...	10	4.4	3.6	7.5	38	13	4.7	5.3	17	14	34	34	6.0	1.5
1887	...	...	9	4.7	3.4	7.6	35	14	5.0	5.1	17	14	35	35	7.2	1.1
1888	...	...	9	6.0	3.2	8.9	43	16	5.8	5.7	19	17	44	40	6.3	1.4
1889	...	...	9	4.8	4.7	8.0	48	17	7.5	6.4	22	21	60	44	7.9	1.9
1890	...	...	9	5.3	5.8	7.1	55	18	8.1	6.2	23	20	66	42	9.2	2.1
1891	...	...	12	5.1	5.7	9.9	56	16	8.2	6.0	25	19	63	43	14.7	1.7
1892	...	...	11	4.4	7.4	7.2	55	16	9.0	5.9	27	20	53	44	9.5	1.8
1893	...	...	10	4.5	3.7	8.1	56	16	8.9	6.2	28	21	56	48	10.4	2.0
1894	...	...	9	4.4	3.6	7.9	56	15	8.1	6.5	29	21	58	45	8.9	1.1
1895	...	...	9	4.8	4.4	6.1	59	17	8.5	6.7	34	23	64	48	7.8	0.7
1896	...	...	11	4.8	5.2	7.0	64	18	9.9	7.6	38	23	63	56	11	0.8
1897	...	...	13	7.2	4.1	7.4	71	22	9.6	8.9	42	26	68	65	12	0.9
1898	...	...	14	6.9	5.1	6.9	82	23	12.0	9.3	24	15	81	66	14	1.3
1899	...	...	17	6.5	4.2	6.9	88	22	14.0	9.3	26	16	89	66	19	0.9

See p. 605 for footnotes

F2 External Trade (by value) with Main Trading Partners

1900–1934

NORWAY (in million kroner)

	Canada[45]		Denmark		France		Germany		Netherlands		Sweden		Great Britain/U.K.[46]		U.S.A.	
	I	E	I	E	I	E	I	E	I	E	I	E	I	E	I	E
1900	...	...	17	7.3	5.2	8.2	85	23	15	11	27	15	93	74	17	2.0
1901	...	...	19	6.8	4.4	8.3	77	20	13	10	24	15	79	70	18	1.5
1902	...	...	18	7.6	5.3	9.3	79	25	15	11	24	16	77	75	12	2.2
1903	...	...	17	8.6	5.6	7.1	79	25	13	16	31	16	68	79	12	2.4
1904	...	...	17	8.2	4.3	7.3	83	27	14	18	34	14	75	77	9	3.6
1905	...	...	21	9.7	4.5	9.9	87	31	14	20	38	15	78	82	8	4.6
1906	...	...	20	11.3[47]	6.0	10.0[47]	88	36[47]	15	24[47]	41[47]	16[47]	96[46, 47]	95[46, 47]	14	5.4[47]
1907	...	...	25	12.1	6.6	8.9	101	35	18	14	23	15	105	88	15	7.1
1908	...	...	27[48]	9.4[48]	7.3[48]	10[48]	112[48]	33[48]	17[48]	14[48]	20[48]	12[48]	94[48]	85[48]	18[48]	5.9[48]
1909	0.5	0.4	20	6.0	9.5	12	117	35	13	8	21	17	89	78	28	18.0
1910	0.5	0.8	20	6.9	11	11	133	43	14	11	25	22	103	84	29	24
1911	0.5	0.8	22	7.6	12	11	148	51	17	12	31	20	127	82	31	26
1912	0.6	1.2	27	8.4	15	13	168	55	20	18	35	21	148	88	34	29
1913	0.8	1.2	28	9.2	12	14	176	67	21	18	46	26	146	98	39	30
1914	1.1	1.0	29	18	11	10	151	76	22	16	47	35	159	105	73	45
1915	0.3	0.7	33	30	14	28	155	193	37	18	75	67	254	187	184	33
1916	—	0.8	69	41	23	79	176	292	47	14	132	68	374	274	338	32
1917	3.2	0.5	104	20	31	82	156	150	45	10	162	56	431	302	551	22
1918	—	—	129	42	14	113	138	85	22	26	221	97	363	311	200	7
1919	24	1.5	140	46	54	44	156	205	52	14	190	71	781	221	753	34
1920	56	1.7	192	76	79	86	323	137	84	29	189	80	995	389	691	98
1921	35	2.3	96	37	30	32	271	84	62	11	126	50	377	174	277	80
1922	4	2.4	104	36	29	55	283	76	59	14	128	52	294	229	243	90
1923	21	3.9	90	41	32	53	308	78	66	14	91	52	294	251	224	112
1924	31	5.3	76	47	34	67	312	104	81	23	99	65	366	289	211	132
1925	41	3.3	84	46	36	72	280	107	75	28	93	62	311	302	195	111
1926	24	4.0	82	30	43	49	223	81	54	16	83	52	212	229	156	95
1927	27	4.3	53	22	31	23	197	86	53	16	79	39	199	198	134	73
1928	31	4.4	73	27	26	29	217	93	61	16	87	37	197	178	121	65
1929	19	4.2	65	32	21	38	261	98	49	19	97	42	222	200	112	74
1930	14	2.8	74	37	23	38	229	82	44	26	89	44	274	171	103	55
1931	11	2.0	70	19	24	27	198	54	35	18	89	30	174[46]	129[46]	66	33
1932	10	1.8	34	25	24	35	147	69	29	20	58	32	149	144	58	51
1933	16	2.2	32	24	21	32	139	70	29	25	56	38	152	114	46	60
1934	19	2.6	42	23	22	27	141	79	25	19	80	44	169	140	64	55

See p. 605 for footnotes

F2 **External Trade (by value) with Main Trading Partners**

1935–1954

NORWAY (in million kroner)

	Canada[45]		Denmark		France		Germany		Netherlands		Sweden		Great Britain/U.K.[46]		U.S.A.	
	I	E	I	E	I	E	I	E	I	E	I	E	I	E	I	E
	[3]	[3]	[3]	[3]	[3]	[3]	[3]	[3]	[3]	[3]	[3]	[3]	[3]	[3]	[3]	[3]
1935	33	2.9	43	25	29	28	140	79	20	14	82	50	147	146	67	65
1936	37	2.7	37	30	30	42	163	90	24	17	105	55	165	162	78	80
1937	39	2.6	59	29	43	44	219[43]	107[43]	33	28	138	66	236	207	110	80
							225	113								
1938	46[49]	2.5[49]	42[49]	34[49]	36[49]	52[49]	220[49]	122[49]	39[49]	21[49]	137[49]	69[49]	193[49]	194[49]	119[49]	61[49]
1939	57	2.3	50	34	44	36	259	118	35	27	140	86	230	195	147	84
1940	21	0.5	35	36	14	15	340	283	13	10	95	79	98	79	108	15
1941	—	—	76	45	4	6	757	340	10	22	73	55	—	—	4	—
1942	—	—	62	48	18	8	623	357	9	7	60	47	—	—	1	—
1943	—	—	83	62	6	6	683	388	5	3	67	48	—	—	1	—
1944	—	—	59	50	5	5	458	418	2	1	48	30	—	—	—	—
1945	60	0.3	149	83	—	18	69[43]	116[43]	2	4	362	50	223	10	143	8
1946	133	6.1	107	130	65	86	123	64	49	52	225	143	425	125	477	63
1947	102	23.5	183	141	152	115	70	49	117	93	322	194	737	264	950	89
1948	127	6.0	185	122	169	136	101	113	125	112	492	180	682	325	497	158
1949	118	6.5	182	150	217	130	163[2]	155[2]	154	83	593	194	900	388	553	149
							133	137								
1950	88	8.6	185	198	314	129	199	315	219	126	701	217	1,073	505	589	273
1951	228	21	229	236	286	229	423	341	273	189	756	371	1,442	876	785	316
1952	275	25	248	225	228	172	698	354	260	127	863	388	1,246	813	698	312
1953	279	17	207	231	223	136	1,047	332	296	122	855	341	1,365	708	554	414
1954	283	13	248	270	235	171	1,109	426	429	154	1,144	397	1,471	797	611	359

See p. 605 for footnotes

F2 External Trade (by value) with Main Trading Partners

NORWAY (in million kroner) 1955–1975

	Canada		Denmark		France		Germany		Netherlands		Sweden		Great Britain/U.K.[46]		U.S.A.	
	I	E	I	E	I	E	I	E	I	E	I	E	I	E	I	E
1955	314	16	292	238	272	187	1,086	506	416	158	1,260	409	1,579	980	667	416
1956	407	25	293	289	323	257	1,525	653	404	189	1,214	546	1,639	1,055	825	466
1957	412	20	288	328	338	261	1,556	780	526	242	1,474	589	1,588	1,171	803	398
1958	423	22	414	323	308	212	1,892	746	645	196	1,494	520	1,447	1,028	639	476
			416[50]	330[50]												
1959	451[49]	29[49]	421[49]	379[49]	297[49]	181[49]	1,903[49]	852[49]	653[49]	188[49]	1,525[49]	554[49]	1,262[49]	1,182[49]	661[49]	597[49]
1960	510	26	429	400	337	162	2,030	864	595	238	1,663	763	1,570	1,422	873	428
															875[51]	428[51]
1961	533	32	528	525	352	215	2,275	898	603	223	1,884	811	1,811	1,375	798	549
1962	492	42	547	606	447	248	2,108	1,050	574	206	2,041	924	1,781	1,183	850	738
1963	487	41	778	540	474	270	2,207	1,168	662	244	2,492	1,048	2,083	1,361	893	751
1964	510	49	793	629	481	371	2,234	1,353	715	310	2,704	1,309	1,876	1,849	1,058	853
1965	588	68	862	741	689	321	2,497	1,416	715	353	3,349	1,620	1,903	1,834	1,104	914
1966	671	88	997	791	532	335	2,757	1,497	758	314	3,227	1,709	2,350	2,111	1,283	990
1967	590	82	1,228	978	589	340	2,676	1,545	763	346	3,816	1,944	2,782	2,398	1,257	1,004
1968	821	91	1,314	977	651	342	2,673	1,816	616	391	3,711	2,098	2,390	2,666	1,473	1,140
1969	801	88	1,374	1,146	793	505	3,136	2,288	755	483	3,986	2,456	2,809	2,713	1,644	1,081
1970	1,251	89	1,646	1,262	777	634	3,796	3,148	864	573	5,317	2,840	3,257	3,145	1,922	1,007
1971	1,315	134	1,846	1,329	807	809	4,067	2,792	850	532	5,502	3,063	3,459	3,364	1,721	1,268
1972	1,019	209	1,979	1,561	1,057	695	3,955	2,708	1,255	684	5,394	3,405	3,359	4,089	1,713	1,560
1973	1,084	360	2,305	2,054	1,794	872	5,034	2,994	1,916	916	6,248	4,080	3,722	4,886	2,216	1,444
1974	1,316	276	2,631	2,822	1,445	1,164	6,696	3,636	1,955	1,301	8,780	6,083	4,678	5,768	3,787	1,847
1975	976	304	2,934	2,745	1,898	1,371	7,920	3,727	2,280	1,266	9,725	6,011	4,898	9,184	3,609	2,191

See p. 605 for footnotes

F2 External Trade (by value) with Main Trading Partners

1920–1944

POLAND (in million zloty)

	Czechoslovakia		Germany		Russia		U.K.		U.S.A.	
	I	E	I	E	I	E	I	E	I	E
1920	...	...	...	...	...	...	...	...	...	...
1921	...	...	...	...	...	...	...	...	...	...
1922	55	31	312	324	3	21	59	27	132	6
1923	54	58	487	605	5	23	91	70	171	7
1924	85	100	510	547	5	11	110	133	184	7
1925	91	157	511	559	9	39	133	115	230	10
1926	78[53]	196[53]	367[53]	573[53]	13[53]	42[53]	161[53]	386[53]	270[53]	15[53]
1927	167	253	737	805	100	45	271	306	373	19
1928	213	296	903	859	39	39	314	227	467	19
1929	228	296	850	877	40	81	265	288	384	31
1930	170	216	606	627	46	129	178	294	271	22
1931	100	144	359	315	36	125	104[10]	318[10]	155	13
1932	46	90	173	176	19	29	75	178	104	10
1933	36	48	146	168	18	60	83	185	110	16
1934	33	50	109	162	18	26	86	192	121	23
1935	35	53	124	140	15	11	117	181	123	43
1936	36	49	143	145	16	9	142	222	119	67
1937	44	52	182	173	15	4	149	219	149	101
1938	41	43	299[8]	286[8]	10	1	148	216	158	63
1939	...	...	...	...	...	...	...	...	...	...
1940	...	...	...	...	...	...	...	...	...	...
1941	...	...	...	...	...	...	...	...	...	...
1942	...	...	...	...	...	...	...	...	...	...
1943	...	...	...	...	...	...	...	...	...	...
1944	...	...	...	...	...	...	...	...	...	...

See p. 605 for footnotes

F2 External Trade (by value) with Main Trading Partners

1945–1975

POLAND (in million zloty)

	Czechoslovakia		Germany				Russia		U.K.		U.S.A.	
	I	E	I		E		I	E	I	E	I	E
			East	West	East	West						
1945	...	...	...		...		...	...	...	...	...	...
1946	[54]	[54]	[54]		[54]		[54]	[54]	[54]	[54]	[54]	[54]
1947	25	59	34		42		318	282	109	54	204	6
1948	212	173	124		164		472	443	166	174	119	3
1949	278	213	189	45	259	75	474	481	338	251	58	17
1950	352	233	308	66	352	55	770	616	255	213	20	45
1951	338	350	542	77	353	59	965	722	414	271	6	33
1952	371	334	478	66	410	51	1,100	989	252	173	—	45
1953	329	381	512	60	445	64	1,054	1,098	232	242	2	53
1954	320	309	546	74	450	60	1,347	1,316	270	215	6	73
1955	319	301	487	92	500	113	1,254	1,122	279	312	10	92
1956	412	305	541	226	430	212	1,377	1,081	260	317	10	95
1957	309	244	660	221	501	200	1,688	1,034	358	255	223	107
1958	378	290	622	269	426	284	1,336	1,061	332	275	407	107
1959	452	323	749	267	548	312	1,809	1,252	346	347	284	122
1960	509	452	746	268	499	274	1,861	1,561	355	396	337	126
1961	651	587	811	251	439	310	1,959	1,940	407	416	484	142
1962	795	583	940	237	470	301	2,311	2,275	473	416	314	169
1963	772	579	1,014	219	482	321	2,589	2,470	418	451	347	165
1964	773	783	943	271	658	337	2,570	2,887	329	514	453	221
1965	976	834	1,085	326	613	404	2,914	3,126	386	510	121	275
1966	933	713	1,121	239	642	440	3,167	2,965	640	580	178	317
1967	941	811	1,168	375	703	425	3,684	3,607	712	591	204	348
1968	914	982	1,185	472	917	471	4,043	4,168	700	588	193	340
1969	979	1,082	1,280	505	1,111	510	4,801	4,486	736	554	196	368
1970	1,242	1,059	1,599	573	1,314	723	5,445	5,003	764	609	233	371
1971	1,429	1,094	1,832	790	1,239	800	5,701	5,549	780	611	324	425
1972	1,696	1,338	2,211	1,570	1,530	977	5,856	6,683	910	685	404	471
1973	1,985	1,676	2,412	3,069	2,187	1,431	6,363	6,914	1,247	855	1,045	632
1974	2,067	2,056	2,558	4,155	2,080	1,743	7,817	7,875	1,675	1,234	1,573	861
1975	2,249	2,742	3,131	3,360	3,151	1,778	10,557	10,766	2,227	968	1,959	778

See p. 605 for footnotes

F2 External Trade (by value) with Main Trading Partners

PORTUGAL (in million escudos) **1860–1896**

	France		Germany		Portugese Colonies		Spain		U.K.		U.S.A.	
	I	E	I	E	I	E	I	E	I	E	I	E
1860	...	...	...	...	...	...	...	...	...	...	...	...
1861	3.0	0.4	0.3	0.2	0.8	0.6	2.4	1.3	14	8	0.8	0.1
1862	...	...	...	...	...	...	...	...	...	...	...	...
1863	...	...	...	...	...	...	...	...	...	...	...	...
1864	...	...	...	...	...	...	...	...	...	...	...	...
1865	...	...	...	...	...	...	...	...	...	...	...	...
1866	...	...	...	...	...	...	...	...	...	...	...	...
1867	...	...	...	...	...	...	...	...	...	...	...	...
1868	...	...	...	...	...	...	...	...	...	...	...	...
1869	3.1	1.0	0.3	0.2	0.6	0.6	1.9	1.4	10	10	1.1	0.2
1870	2.4	0.8	0.4	0.2	1.0	0.8	1.8	1.8	13	12	1.7	0.2
1871	2.2	0.9	0.3	0.4	0.5	0.7	2.0	1.6	16	12	1.5	0.4
1872	3.8	0.4	0.5	0.7	0.8	0.6	2.8	1.8	15	13	1.2	0.2
1873	4.1	1.0	1.0	0.5	0.8	0.5	2.5	1.8	19	14	0.9	0.2
1874	4.4	1.0	0.6	0.9	0.8	0.9	1.3	1.4	13	12	1.3	0.3
1875	5.9	1.3	0.8	0.8	0.8	1.1	2.3	1.3	18	14	2.3	0.4
1876	5.5	2.2	0.6	0.9	0.8	1.0	2.1	1.3	18	12	2.1	0.4
1877	5.2	2.1	1.1	0.9	0.8	0.8	2.1	1.6	14	12	2.1	0.8
1878	4.7	1.0	1.2	0.6	0.4	0.7	2.5	1.2	15	11	2.3	0.3
1879	4.3	1.2	1.6	0.8	0.7	0.7	2.5	1.1	13	11	6.0	0.3
1880	4.1	1.5	1.9	1.1	0.7	0.8	2.1	1.8	15	11	5.3	0.6
1881	4.4	2.6	2.5	0.7	0.7	0.6	2.2	1.6	15	9	5.5	0.6
1882	4.1	2.8	2.7	0.9	0.7	0.6	2.0	1.5	15	12	5.7	0.7
1883	...	...	...	...	...	...	...	...	...	...	...	...
1884	...	...	...	...	...	...	...	...	...	...	...	...
1885	4.5	6.5	3.7	1.1	0.7	0.6	1.6	1.2	12	6.0	4.6	0.6
1886	5.1	9.5	4.7	1.3	0.8	0.6	2.6	1.2	12	6.7	5.0	0.6
1887	5.0	4.8	4.5	1.6	0.7	0.6	2.3	1.2	12	6.8	5.3	0.6
1888	5.0	5.2	4.7	1.9	0.8	0.9	2.6	0.9	12	7.8	4.9	0.6
1889	6.0	3.8	5.4	2.0	0.8	1.0	3.2	1.1	14	8.5	3.7	0.5
1890	6.9	1.5	6.3	2.1	0.8	1.1	2.9	0.9	13	8.0	5.1	0.7
1891	5.3	1.3	5.2	2.3	0.9	1.3	2.5	0.9	12	7.5	5.3	0.8
1892	3.4	1.0	2.8	2.2	0.9	1.6	1.7	1.4	10	8.7	6.0	0.9
1893	3.8	0.9	4.4	2.0	1.0	2.1	2.9	1.4	11	6.6	7.3	0.8
1894	3.8	0.8	4.3	2.1	1.0	2.2	3.0	2.5	10	6.7	5.8	0.5
1895	4.0	0.7	5.2	2.1	1.1	2.6	3.8	3.2	11	7.2	6.8	0.5
1896	3.9	0.6	5.6	2.0	1.1	2.9	3.8	3.2	12	7.2	4.4	0.5

F2 External Trade (by value) with Main Trading Partners

PORTUGAL (in million escudos)

1897–1934

	France		Germany		Portugese Colonies		Spain		U.K.		U.S.A.	
	I	E	I	E	I	E	I	E	I	E	I	E
1897	3.5	0.9	5.3	2.2	1.0	3.5	4.2	3.9	12	7.4	4.6	0.6
1898	4.7	1.0	6.6	2.2	1.2	5.0	4.5	4.1	16	8.8	7.0	0.5
1899	4.4	0.7	7.3	2.1	1.2	5.5	3.6	3.4	17	7.8	8.1	0.5
1900	5.0	1.0	8.6	2.2	1.5	5.5	4.6	4.7	19	7.9	9.0	0.6
1901	5.7	0.8	9.0	2.1	1.4	3.8	5.3	4.4	18	8.3	7.6	0.6
1902	5.7	0.8	9.2	2.1	1.6	3.4	6.0	4.6	17	8.3	4.0	0.7
1903	5.6	0.9	9.9	2.0	1.7	4.9	5.4	5.4	17	8.0	6.2	0.7
1904	6.0	0.8	10.5	2.4	1.8	5.3	5.6	6.0	18	7.0	4.4	0.6
1905	6.1	0.7	9.6	2.3	1.9	4.9	5.2	4.1	17	7.3	3.5	0.5
1906	6.4	1.0	10.0	2.5	1.6	4.5	4.3	5.0	17	7.9	4.7	0.4
1907	6.7	0.7	11.0	2.5	2.0	4.5	4.1	4.9	19	7.4	6.1	0.6
1908	6.2	0.7	10.0	2.3	2.1	4.1	4.8	5.4	18	7.0	7.2	0.6
1909	5.8	0.8	10.0	2.3	2.1	5.2	4.6	5.5	17	7.3	6.9	0.9
1910	6.2[56]	0.9[56]	11.0[56]	3.3[56]	2.6[56]	6.3[56]	4.7[56]	5.1[56]	20[56]	8.0[56]	7.4[56]	1.1[56]
1911	5.2	1.4	12.0	3.3	2.6	4.7	5.1	5.8	19	6.9	5.8	0.8
1912	6.9	1.7	12.0	3.0	1.9	4.9	4.5	5.2	21	7.3	7.8	1.0
1913	7.6	1.3	16.0	3.4	2.9	5.0	3.8	5.5	23	7.6	9.9	1.2
1914	5.5	1.1	10.0	1.5	3.1	5.2	2.1	2.2	21	8.2	9.0	1.4
1915	4.7	3.0	0.6	0.1	4.0	7.5	3.9	2.5	30	9.4	15	1.5
1916	6.4	13	0.1	...	6.7	10	8.6	3.4	58	13	27	2.8
1917	9.3[56]	17[56]	0.8[56]	—[56]	28[56]	13[56]	15[56]	10[56]	58[56]	12[56]	42[56]	7.7[56]
1918	8.7[56]	22[56]	0.8[56]	—[56]	22[56]	16[56]	29[56]	13[56]	65[56]	30[56]	63[56]	3.7[56]
1919	11	21	0.3	0.1	20	10	20	3.0	98	28	46	4.9
1920	53	28	26	2.8	24	32	35	10.6	26	51	118	16
1921	78	21	61	10	42	31	53	9.5	292	49	164	17
1922	101	107	127	18	52	74	46	15	437	85	116	24
1923	185	130	248	27	111	100	69	23	768	152	257	45
1924	109	73	466	84	197	130	105	25	979	255	303	42
1925	231	89	340	64	172	102	82	33	720	252	227	39
1926	269	64	395	53	160	83	114	29	574	218	318	46
1927	283	51	364	71	181	87	163	27	689	210	326	28
1928	250	163	349	117	205	112	72	32	822	220	298	59
1929	237	119	382	118	199	136	71	46	679	251	340	77
1930	206	130	354	90	192	103	114	30	516	203	324	53
1931	125	150	265	82	178	81	54	22	396	189	167	37
1932	114	125	237	76	178	110	57	42	401	165	191	51
1933	98	78	250	76	200	121	71	41	542	180	181	56
1934	95	89	269	107	216	104	71	44	451	216	193	49

See p. 605 for footnotes

F2 External Trade (by value) with Main Trading Partners

1935—1954

PORTUGAL (in million escudos)

	France		Germany		Portugese Colonies		Spain		U.K.		U.S.A.	
	I	E	I	E	I	E	I	E	I	E	I	E
1935	122	92	287	126	189	114	92	42	592	215	260	54
1936	101	115	281	124	201	106	68	27	418	273	229	74
1937	110	123	354	131	262	154	25	57	427	258	248	94
1938	141	94	387	149	233	140	12	55	393	236	266	61
1939	140	66	276	121	253	173	6	26	395	359	219	121
1940	100	120	39	29	476[56]	293[56]	16	93	422	471	586	235
1941	47	36	200	565	655[56]	400[56]	66	49	375	526	629	547
1942	35	37	313	960	1,016[56]	566[56]	99	76	309	1,147	388	226
1943	36	51	481	855	1,109[56]	562[56]	132	99	516	1,229	464	388
1944	18	11	314	361	1,257[56]	742[56]	178	111	433	788	476	714
1945	36	211	14	1	1,527[56]	759[56]	159	55	445	573	778	551
1946	203	163	34	3	2,068[56]	1,036[56]	182	83	943	659	1,714	685
1947	391	103	51	13	740	1,103	141	76	1,122	635	2,993	495
1948	350	156	37	65	869	1,143	82	63	2,313	756	2,351	437
1949	589	236	74	125	1,059	1,050	79	43	2,206	759	1,615	418
1950	397	256	298	195	1,286	1,332	68	88	1,353	925	1,235	690
1951	509	317	516	352	1,104	1,711	160	106	1,459	1,483	1,434	1,016
1952	472	287	724	426	1,528	1,728	79	51	1,592	831	1,367	990
1953	510	216	1,037	450	1,392	1,659	67	33	1,452	787	935	1,036
1954	694	282	1,378	504	1,716	1,788	52	134	1,507	1,092	838	753

See p. 605 for footnotes

F2 **External Trade (by value) with Main Trading Partners**

PORTUGAL (in million escudos) **1955–1975**

	France		Germany		Portugese Colonies		Spain		U.K.		U.S.A.	
	I	E	I	E	I	E	I	E	I	E	I	E
1955	877	436	1,665	637	1,569	1,927	63	47	1,615	1,262	1,102	839
1956	957	548	2,039[2]	615[2]	1,515	2,109	96	144	1,729	1,238	1,313	786
1957	1,190	425	2,408	566	1,687	2,156	99	94	1,909	1,163	1,561	703
1958	1,062	548	2,431	641	2,031	2,262	58	60	1,780	940	970	687
1959	1,029	356	2,416	700	1,931	2,397	143	80	1,753	949	830	816
1960	1,307	319	2,677	857	2,239	2,384	138	95	1,868	1,284	1,152	1,049
1961	1,462	401	2,982	810	2,354	2,153	228	120	2,907	1,263	1,431	1,111
1962	1,584	507	2,684	855	2,110	2,364	197	275	2,500	1,277	1,499	1,392
1963	1,511	607	2,867	904	2,680	2,829	255	266	2,588	1,627	1,671	1,411
1964	1,579	740	3,400	1,125	3,297	3,673	453	456	3,007	2,340	2,364	1,559
1965	1,998	764	4,322	1,339	3,616	4,111	721	453	3,448	2,922	2,151	1,755
1966	2,208	905	4,486	1,134	3,901	4,179	740	426	4,024	3,327	2,347	2,032
1967	2,092	937	4,591	1,074	4,290	4,781	1,361	360	4,164	4,330	2,094	2,027
1968	2,348	1,007	5,290	1,258	5,265	5,416	1,407	343	4,410	4,611	2,469	2,309
1969	2,675	1,278	5,861	1,570	5,496	6,027	1,597	423	5,168	5,158	1,814	2,314
1970	3,176	1,245	7,050	1,728	6,717	6,688	1,983	442	6,369	5,570	3,251	2,374
1971	3,469	1,357	8,204	1,889	6,944	6,490	2,501	515	7,150	6,751	3,614	2,928
1972	3,848	1,825	8,983	2,550	7,045	5,165	3,021	732	7,884	8,048	5,391	3,785
1973	5,192	2,344	10,794	3,417	7,539	6,740	4,061	1,011	8,516	10,792	6,117	4,430
1974	9,160	3,449	15,863	4,647	12,415	6,372	5,365	1,200	10,930	13,234	11,088	5,761
1975	7,484	3,264	10,980	5,024	4,855	3,574	4,140	1,329	8,740	10,468	12,342	3,559

F2 External Trade (by value) with Main Trading Partners

1871–1899

ROMANIA (in million lei)

	Austria-Hungary		Czechoslovakia		France		Germany		Russia		U.K.	
	I	E	I	E	I	E	I	E	I	E	I	E
1871	30	27	...	...	9	21	7	1	1	7	25	20
1872	...	...	...	...	...	...	...	...	...	...	...	...
1873	34	34	...	...	15	19	10	8	4	5	19	17
1874	48	56	...	...	16	10	6	—	3	2	33	13
1875	40	39	...	...	16	24	5	—	2	2	25	19
1876	79	74	...	...	28	32	15	1	5	4	27	41
1877	180	90	...	...	39	6	40	—	27	5	37	12
1878	168	67	...	...	16	19	20	1	28	5	53	40
1879	125	69	...	...	16	18	19	2	11	6	51	38
1880	126	83	...	...	18	28	24	1	6	4	57	56
1881	135	72	...	...	23	19	32	2	6	5	51	82
1882	135	75	...	...	23	27	30	6	9	8	45	98
1883	154[57]	72[57]	...	...	37[57]	19[57]	44[57]	5[57]	9[57]	8[57]	79[57]	89[57]
1884	130	70	...	...	24	17	43	—	10	9	58	62
1885	121	84	...	...	14	12	42	3	9	13	52	85
1886	94	35	...	...	15	29	73	3	10	13	71	117
1887	54	21	...	...	25	20	90	9	9	8	87	154
1888	51	14	...	...	28	19	83	7	7	5	85	144
1889	49	17	...	...	33	13	108	16	10	5	102	141
1890	53	9	...	...	40	17	109	13	9	5	98	161
1891	71	23	...	...	42	10	140	31	14	3	115	144
1892	89	32	...	...	31	11	114	33	8	3	84	121
1893	110	37	...	...	35	8	118	131	11	4	94	80
1894	115	43	...	...	34	10	117	58	9	7	84	79
1895	86	42	...	...	26	6	81	26	10	9	59	75
1896	93	33	...	...	26	9	96	17	8	6	73	112
1897	97	55	...	...	24	5	99	7	8	4	79	55
1898	109	86	...	...	26	7	111	13	8	5	76	38
1899	96	38	...	...	22	6	91	10	7	6	60	11

See p. 605 for footnotes

F2 External Trade (by value) with Main Trading Partners

1900–1934

ROMANIA (in million lei)

	Austria-Hungary		Czechoslovakia		France		Germany		Russia		U.K.	
	I	E	I	E	I	E	I	E	I	E	I	E
1900	69	44	...	...	16	8	56	19	6	5	31	17
1901	71	49	...	...	19	10	84	40	6	6	56	24
1902	70	44	...	...	17	11	80	20	6	6	55	41
1903	74	49	...	...	16	10	78	15	9	6	43	31
1904	93	53	...	...	18	9	92	20	8	6	45	26
1905	96	41	...	...	17	19	92	35	9	4	51	32
1906	119	32	...	...	19	28	142	24	10	3	63	53
1907	105	33	...	...	20	32	148	56	9	6	70	86
1908	95	26	...	...	23	28	141	25	13	8	67	40
1909	86	115	...	...	24	28	125	27	11	4	58	35
1910	98	37	...	...	26	47	138	24	12	6	57	34
1911	137	63	...	...	35	49	184	33	14	7	86	56
1912	139	95	...	...	39	50	240	43	17	6	88	43
1913	138	96	...	...	34	64	238	52	13	4	56	45
1914	133	135	...	...	28	27	183	47	11	3	56	36
1915	93	339	...	...	17	—	89	176	29	2	21	—
1916	...	...	...	...	...	...	...	...	...	...	...	...
1917	...	...	...	...	...	...	...	...	...	...	...	...
1918	...	...	...	...	...	...	...	...	...	...	...	...
	Austria											
1919	168	6	35	22	438	11	4	—	—	—	529	—
1920	770	254	250	142	971	138	134	41	—	—	1,394	224
1921	2,050	392	1,065	407	1,653	929	1,087	353	1	—	1,681	994
1922	1,968	995	1,156	1,124	728	1,355	2,422	822	—	245	1,096	332
1923	3,057	2,569	1,619	1,082	1,292	2,613	4,429	1,788	2	2	1,801	1,174
1924	4,421	3,913	3,028	2,630	2,123	1,778	5,051	1,615	5	—	2,583	1,645
1925	4,948	4,347	4,273	2,742	2,333	1,665	4,996	2,462	—	—	3,152	2,369
1926	...	...	...	...	...	...	...	...	...	...	...	...
1927	4,500	5,025	4,716	2,031	2,618	1,364	7,645	7,096	33	—	2,841	2,232
1928	...	...	...	...	...	...	...	...	...	...	...	...
1929	3,715	2,733	4,020	1,789	1,641	1,296	7,135	8,005	43	1	2,160	1,867
1930	2,679	2,589	1,370	1,985	1,707	1,959	5,777	5,364	42	—	1,874	3,230
1931	1,395	2,368	1,923	1,557	1,244	2,411	4,589	2,543	40	—	1,305	2,246
1932	583	1,063	1,458	1,161	1,681	2,170	2,832	2,054	—	—	1,285	2,324
1933	1,078	933	1,155	679	1,238	1,753	2,181	1,503	—	—	1,744	2,182
1934	1,303	1,243	1,312	741	1,463	1,322	2,048	2,264	—	—	2,147	1,368

F2 External Trade (by value) with Main Trading Partners

1935–1954

ROMANIA (in million lei)

	Austria		Czechoslovakia		France		Germany		Russia		U.K.	
	I	E	I	E	I	E	I	E	I	E	I	E
1935	1,175	2,108	1,408	990	783	689	2,580	2,802	—	—	1,064	1,615
1936	1,695	1,874	1,449	1,528	747	1,760	4,566	3,855	6	—	929	3,132
1937	1,722	2,138	3,267	2,590	1,243	1,813	5,853	6,054	38	52	1.907	2,783
1938	...	...	2,465	2,059	1,444	1,006	6,908[8]	5,707[8]	22	20	1,529	2,386
1939	...	...	...	...	...	...	...	...	...	...	...	...
1940	...	...	...	...	...	...	...	...	...	...	...	...
1941	...	...	...	...	...	...	...	...	...	...	...	...
1942	...	...	...	...	...	...	...	...	...	...	...	...
1943	...	...	...	...	...	...	...	...	...	...	...	...
1944	...	...	...	...	...	...	...	...	...	...	...	...
1945	...	...	...	...	...	...	...	...	...	...	...	...
1946	...	...	...	...	...	...	...	...	...	...	...	...
1947	...	...	...	...	...	...	...	...	...	...	...	...
1948	...	...	...	...	...	...	...	...	...	...	...	...
1949	... —[13]	... —[13]	... —[13]	... —[13]	... —[13]	... —[13]	... —[13]	... —[13]	... —[13]	... —[13]	... —[13]	... —[13]
1950	...	...	...	...	...	...	...	...	...	...	...	...
1951	...	...	...	...	...	...	...	...	...	...	...	...
1952	...	...	...	...	...	...	...	...	...	...	...	...
1953	...	...	...	...	...	...	...	...	...	...	...	...
1954	...	...	...	...	...	...	...	...	...	...	...	...

See p. 605 for footnotes

F2 External Trade (by value) with Main Trading Partners

ROMANIA (in million lei) **1955–1975**

	Austria		Czechoslovakia		France		East Germany		West Germany		Russia		U.K.	
	I	E	I	E	I	E	I	E	I	E	I	E	I	E
1955	...	...	...	...	...	...	...	...	...	...	...	...	...	...
1956	...	...	...	...	...	...	...	...	...	...	...	...	...	...
1957	...	...	...	...	...	...	...	...	...	...	...	...	...	...
1958	34	36	234	136	94	92	217	181	134	158	1,523	1,412	45	39
1959	31	40	295	210	61	84	269	213	113	144	1,408	1,500	65	52
1960	59	94	383	376	149	117	311	323	277	263	1,596	1,689	107	90
1961	88	101	458	341	152	131	352	318	380	300	1,793	2,107	308	138
1962	109	89	532	350	124	168	334	280	480	310	2,223	2,060	264	131
1963	107	134	609	330	143	193	386	251	458	323	2,396	2,477	300	145
1964	153	145	579	451	272	158	411	426	527	322	2,958	2,531	250	190
1965	143	146	418	572	295	131	375	430	663	379	2,437	2,631	263	183
1966	183	128	418	554	341	308	506	400	889	445	2,365	2,459	274	270
1967	321	141	541	522	481	327	555	419	1,537	579	2,379	2,597	307	385
1968	279	176	603	677	484	298	545	463	1,031	634	2,562	2,734	603	337
1969	297	183	652	845	564	321	507	728	1,027	724	2,789	2,730	611	294
1970	357	329	951	791	674	364	691	635	959	1,004	3,005	3,173	593	307
1971	365	298	896	735	807	503	920	781	887	1,253	2,908	2,399	690	305
1972	373	284	964	825	784	529	1,044	1,364	956	1,369	3,203	3,869	789	367
1973	452	450	987	1,091	839	611	1,125	1,322	2,096	1,722	3,449	4,120	635	480
1974	645	732	1,047	1,184	839	804	1,340	1,510	3,921	2,350	3,757	4,085	1,442	1,204
1975	895	598	1,284	1,162	940	748	1,569	1,339	2,846	2,191	4,577	5,276	879	624

F2 External Trade (by value) with Main Trading Partners

1832–1864

RUSSIA (in million rubels)[58]

	Austria-Hungary		China		Czechoslovakia		France		Germany		Hungary		Poland		Romania		U.K.	
	I	E	I	E	I	E	I	E	I	E	I	E	I	E	I	E	I	E
1832	12	14	...	...	...	...	13	11	36	25	...	...	...	...	...	...	60	96
1833	11	15	8	7	...	...	13	11	30	20	...	...	...	...	...	...	58	111
1834	11	11	7	7	...	...	13	11	44	18	...	...	...	...	...	...	64	106
1835	12	11	7	7	...	...	14	8	36	17	...	...	...	...	...	...	71	90
1836	11	15	5	9	...	...	16	11	35	22	...	...	...	...	...	...	79	130
1837	12	12	8	4	...	...	18	10	42	22	...	...	...	...	...	...	81	114
1838	12	14	8	8	...	...	19	10	39	18	...	...	...	...	...	...	79	85
1839	12	14	9	9	...	...	22	13	43	25	...	...	...	...	...	...	73	80
1840	11	13	9	9	...	...	31	16	46	21	...	...	...	...	...	...	76	134
1841	...	...	...	...	...	...	...	...	...	...	...	...	...	...	...	...	...	...
1842	...	...	...	...	...	...	...	...	...	...	...	...	...	...	...	...	...	...
1843	...	...	...	...	...	...	...	...	...	...	...	...	...	...	...	...	...	...
1844	...	...	...	...	...	...	...	...	...	...	...	...	...	...	...	...	...	...
1845	...	...	...	...	...	...	...	...	...	...	...	...	...	...	...	...	...	...
1846	...	...	...	...	...	...	...	...	...	...	...	...	...	...	...	...	...	...
1847	3	5	...	...	...	...	9	21	14	14	...	...	...	...	...	...	22	47
1848	3	3	...	...	...	...	8	3	14	5	...	...	...	...	...	...	26	40
1849	3	5	...	...	...	...	9	5	14	6	...	...	...	...	...	...	27	41
1850	3	5	...	...	...	...	8	4	13	7	...	...	...	...	...	...	25	42
1851	7	5	...	...	...	...	8	3	20	10	...	...	...	...	...	...	27	39
1852	6	6	...	...	...	...	9	7	19	12	...	...	...	...	...	...	25	43
1853	6	8	4	4	...	...	8	15	22	16	...	...	...	...	...	...	28	66
1854	5	8	7	6	...	...	4	3	24	20	...	...	...	...	...	...	9	12
1855	7	6	7	7	...	...	1	—	43	18	...	...	...	...	...	...	1	—
1856	9	7	6	6	...	...	6	17	41	23	...	...	...	...	...	...	22	64
1857	7	7	8	6	...	...	9	14	38	22	...	...	...	...	...	...	39	72
1858	8	6	7	6	...	...	11	16	33	18	...	...	...	...	...	...	41	66
1859	7	7	8	6	...	...	10	13	36	21	...	...	...	...	2	1	45	76
1860	8	6	7	6	...	...	11	12	37	25	...	...	...	...	2	3	44	85
1861	8	6	8	5	...	...	12	20	38	25	...	...	...	...	2	3	48	76
1862	7	6	9	5	...	...	11	11	42	31	...	...	...	...	1	2	36	82
1863	5	5	7	3	...	...	9	11	39	27	...	...	...	...	1	2	43	67
1864	8	6	6	4	...	...	10	15	42	28	...	...	...	...	1	2	53	87

See p. 605 for footnotes

F2 External Trade (by value) with Main Trading Partners

RUSSIA (in million rubels)[58] **1865–1899**

	Austria-Hungary		China		Czechoslovakia		France		Germany		Hungary		Poland		Romania		U.K.	
	I	E	I	E	I	E	I	E	I	E	I	E	I	E	I	E	I	E
1865	6	7	5	5	...	...	10	16	58	32	...	...	...	...	2	3	49	98
1866	8	6	5	5	...	...	10	17	78	35	...	...	...	...	1	3	59	102
1867	13	7	6	4	...	...	15	18	105	42	...	...	...	...	1	2	75	108
1868	11	9	...	...	...	...	13	21	120	46	...	...	...	...	1	3	79	106
1869	11	10	6	3	...	...	21	22	137	56	...	...	...	...	3	7	98	123
1870	10	14	8	4	...	...	19	34	136	76	...	...	...	...	3	3	107	170
1871	17	14	7	3	...	...	12	34	163	75	...	...	...	...	3	2	97	172
1872	24	20	...	...	...	...	19	22	171	77	...	...	...	...	4	3	120	143
1873	20	25	12	4	...	...	25	27	167	110	...	...	...	...	4	1	129	129
1874	21	33	11	3	...	...	20	33	181	136	...	...	...	...	2	2	128	136
1875	26	17	11	3	...	...	33	38	221	110	...	...	...	...	2	2	134	131
1876	23	27	...	...	...	...	18	30	198	120	...	...	...	...	3	2	104	132
1877	20	50	...	...	...	...	10	24	148	197	...	...	...	...	1	3	93	148
1878	27	40	...	...	...	...	20	83	263	175	...	...	...	...	1	5	162	191
1879	20	33	...	...	...	...	20	83	267	187	...	...	...	...	2	9	146	184
1880	23	33	...	...	...	...	21	53	274	138	...	...	...	...	2	10	150	148
1881	23	28	...	...	...	...	20	53	220	149	...	...	...	...	1	8	108	156
1882	30	33	...	...	...	...	20	51	214	178	...	...	...	...	2	7	125	210
1883	26	25	...	...	...	...	23	39	169	189	...	...	...	...	2	5	134	210
1884	21	31	...	...	...	...	19	39	176	183	...	...	...	...	2	8	123	152
1885	22	27	...	...	...	...	14	34	144	142	...	...	...	...	3	4	95	154
1886	17	24	...	...	...	...	12	25	135	119	...	...	...	...	2	3	108	140
1887	12	24	...	...	...	...	13	36	113	152	...	...	...	...	2	4	92	182
1888	15	23	3	...	...	...	13	53	122	182	...	...	...	...	1	5	6	279
1889	18	28	1	...	...	...	18	35	124	190	...	...	...	...	1	7	96	258
1890	17[58]	27[58]	14[58]	...[58]	...	...	16[58]	42[58]	114[58]	176[58]	...	...	...	...	1[58]	7[58]	87[58]	192[58]
	18	30	29	3			17	49	115	178					2	7	93	204
1891	16	34	29	5	...	...	17	49	103	193	...	...	...	...	2	9	83	180
1892	15	24	28	5	...	...	18	35	102	138	...	...	...	...	1	5	101	119
1893	23	35	33	4	...	...	29	72	101	133	...	...	...	...	1	6	118	155
1894	27	40	39	4	...	...	28	56	143	148	...	...	...	...	2	8	133	175
1895	24	35	42	5	...	...	23	50	176	179	...	...	...	...	2	10	120	175
1896	23	30	41	6	...	...	23	58	190	184	...	...	...	...	2	8	111	161
1897	19	39	39	6	...	...	25	64	180	175	...	...	...	...	1	11	104	151
1898	24	42	40	6	...	...	27	69	202	179	...	...	...	...	2	13	115	140
1899	31	27	44	8	...	...	28	60	231	164	...	...	...	...	2	7	130	129

See p. 605 for footnotes

F2 External Trade (by value) with Main Trading Partners

1900–1934

RUSSIA (in million rubels)[58]

	Austria-Hungary		China		Czechoslovakia		France		Germany		Hungary		Poland		Romania		U.K.	
	I	E	I	E	I	E	I	E	I	E	I	E	I	E	I	E	I	E
1900	27	26	46	7	...	...	31	57	217	188	...	...	...	...	2	5	127	146
1901	25	30	47	10	...	...	28	61	211	179	...	...	...	...	2	10	103	157
1902	24	36	52	9	...	...	27	55	208	203	...	...	...	...	2	16	99	189
1903	27	37	56	22	...	...	28	76	242	233	...	...	...	...	2	16	114	218
1904	21	41	52	23	...	...	27	62	228	235	...	...	...	...	2	10	103	230
1905	20	46	61	32	...	...	26	64	240	255	...	...	...	...	1	10	97	249
1906	21	45	97	58	...	...	29	77	298	285	...	...	...	...	1	18	106	225
1907	24	43	90	26	...	...	29	73	337	291	...	...	...	...	2	14	115	229
1908	27	49	93	23	...	...	36	65	348	279	...	...	...	...	3	13	120	221
1909	27	61	75	22	...	...	50	89	363	387	...	...	...	...	2	16	128	289
1910	35	50	79	20	...	...	61	94	450	391	...	...	...	...	2	15	154	315
1911	34	68	82	26	...	...	57	91	488	491	...	...	...	...	3	30	155	337
1912	33	73	76	31	...	...	56	98	532	454	...	...	...	...	2	20	142	328
1913	28	51	59	23	...	...	45	79	512	356	...	...	...	...	1	17	136	210
1914	...	...	...	...	...	...	...	...	...	...	...	...	...	...	...	...	...	...
1915	...	...	...	...	...	...	...	...	...	...	...	...	...	...	...	...	...	...
1916	...	...	...	...	...	...	...	...	...	...	...	...	...	...	...	...	...	...
1917	...	...	...	...	...	...	...	...	...	...	...	...	...	...	...	...	...	...
1918	...	...	5	—	—	—	2	—	—	1	—	—	—	—	—	—	9	2
1919	...	...	—	—	—	—	—	—	—	—	—	—	—	—	—	—	—	—
1920	...	...	—	—	—	—	—	—	5	—	—	—	—	—	—	—	5	—
1921	...	...	—	—	—	—	6	—	43	—	—	—	—	—	—	—	48	7
1922	...	...	[—][59]	[—][59]	[1][59]	[—][59]	[1][59]	[—][59]	[66][59]	[7][59]	[—][59]	[—][59]	[6][59]	[1][59]	[3][59]	[—][59]	[42][59]	[14][59]
1923	...	...	—	—	—	—	—	1	48	34	—	—	7	3	—	—	29	23
1924	...	...	9	4	2	—	2	12	36	52	—	—	2	2	—	2	38	66
1925	...	...	13	7	17	—	7	17	81	69	—	—	8	3	—	—	87	152
1926	...	...	24	14	15	—	15	31	138	88	—	—	8	3	—	1	102	173
1927	...	...	24	15	9	2	17	42	127	138	—	—	10	15	—	1	79	173
1928	...	...	36[59]	19[59]	14[59]	3[59]	28[59]	32[59]	195[59]	152[59]	1[59]	—[59]	6[59]	12[59]	—[59]	1[59]	37[59]	122[59]
1929	...	...	27	18	14	7	25	33	153	169	1	—	15	10	—	—	43	159
1930	...	...	19	22	21	3	23	35	197	161	—	—	30	11	—	1	63	220
1931	...	...	13	20	28	4	12	22	322	101	1	—	24	6	—	1	58	209
1932	...	...	14	19	8	1	3	23	257	79	—	—	4	4	—	1	72	109
1933	...	...	17	14	4	1	4	18	116	67	—	—	10	4	—	—	24	68
1934	...	...	7	5	2	1	9	17	23	77	—	—	4	3	—	—	25	54

See p. 605 for footnotes

F2 **External Trade (by value) with Main Trading Partners**

RUSSIA (in million rubels)[58] **1935–1954**

	China		Czechoslovakia		France		Germany				Hungary		Poland		Romania		U.K.	
	I	E	I	E	I	E	I		E		I	E	I	E	I	E	I	E
1935	6	5	5	1	14	14	17		52		1	——	2	3	——	——	18	68
1936	7	7	8	2	8	18	55		21		——	——	2	3	——	——	17	65
1937	7	6	2	3	5	15	34		18		——	——	1	2	——	1	11	95
1938	14	7	3	2	6	9	11		15		—	——	——	1	——	——	30	64
1939	18	6	3	1	3	5	10		11		—	——	——	1	—	——	19	23
1940	17	9	4	1	——	——	71		125		—	1	—	—	—	1	2	——
1941	...	...	...	...	...	...	...		...		...	...	...	...	...	...	...	...
1942	...	...	...	...	...	...	...		...		...	...	...	...	...	...	...	...
1943	...	...	...	...	...	...	...		...		...	...	...	...	...	...	...	...
1944	...	...	...	...	...	...	...		...		...	...	...	...	...	...	...	...
							East	West	East	West								
1945	...	...	...	...	...	...	...	...	...	...	...	...	...	...	...	...	...	...
1946	56	11	29	26	1	34	45	—	37	—	10	9	98	96	20	27	8	28
1947	72	69	35	40	——	10	20	—	39	—	16	15	123	94	25	34	32	39
1948	81	112	122	128	——	7	56	—	82	—	26	31	156	120	82	43	24	123
1949	129	180	185	185	2	3	132	—	105	1	60	75	168	123	90	100	33	61
1950	170	349	181	198	4	3	144	—	167	—	75	114	189	217	125	103	36	92
1951	298	431	228	261	7	8	295	—	269	—	103	110	238	280	125	129	70	142
1952	372	499	269	327	10	8	329	——	390	—	127	135	316	326	176	203	112	117
1953	427	628	281	314	19	16	435	3	455	2	155	142	331	296	207	199	48	81
1954	521	683	286	316	32	41	556	10	434	10	150	138	304	372	175	191	47	100

See p. 605 for footnotes

F2 External Trade (by value) with Main Trading Partners

1955–1975

RUSSIA (in million rubels)[58]

	China		Czechoslovakia		France		East Germany		West Germany		Hungary		Poland		Romania		U.K.	
	I	E	I	E	I	E	I	E	I	E	I	E	I	E	I	E	I	E
1955	579	674	348	320	33	54	456	431	21	26	132	104	258	389	189	241	64	152
1956	688	660	357	336	46	63	564	514	61	38	109	114	255	322	212	191	67	133
1957	664	490	347	496	43	60	688	776	56	65	96	225	230	388	171	226	101	159
1958	793	571	461	402	73	78	734	720	65	59	146	181	239	339	210	226	66	131
1959	990	859	524	543	90	79	801	927	108	80	186	234	285	438	225	209	82	149
1960	763	735	587	568	117	66	836	947	179	107	223	280	348	442	252	235	97	173
1961	496	331	628	587	108	72	788	1,088	161	107	294	323	429	478	307	263	115	204
1962	465	210	742	694	139	77	966	1,235	184	121	350	370	508	535	314	337	106	192
1963	372	169	856	764	64	93	1,173	1,183	134	118	381	399	553	596	369	359	117	194
1964	283	122	872	811	62	95	1,195	1,247	178	112	433	443	646	594	379	444	93	215
1965	203	173	932	833	103	100	1,156	1,227	120	129	464	491	703	654	397	363	137	262
1966	129	158	828	805	144	117	1,114	1,266	125	167	461	454	660	723	365	348	152	297
1967	51	45	884	871	170	130	1,271	1,275	147	173	537	527	812	821	382	355	178	273
1968	33	53	891	934	265	124	1,445	1,356	205	189	602	608	928	945	411	375	246	330
1969	26	25	1,003	999	126	127	1,466	1,565	298	199	647	630	1,012	1,079	405	429	216	384
1970	20	22	1,111	1,083	287	126	1,557	1,738	321	223	722	758	1,135	1,215	474	445	223	418
1971	63	65	1,109	1,122	260	179	1,591	1,581	401	242	718	811	1,131	1,190	469	393	184	373
1972	98	89	1,220	1,110	312	172	1,823	1,479	508	236	877	800	1,330	1,157	518	416	166	328
1973	104	103	1,445	1,392	455	280	2,167	1,908	785	495	1,118	1,003	1,598	1,485	628	534	179	556
1974	101	103	1,447	1,441	518	379	2,050	2,064	1,326	840	1,094	1,082	1,664	1,753	584	552	190	658
1975	113	97	1,977	2,110	837	518	2,763	3,114	2,036	968	1,689	1,732	2,515	2,557	861	734	385	618

See p. 605 for footnotes

F2 External Trade (by value) with Main Trading Partners

1883–1919

SERBIA (in million dinars)

	Austria-Hungary		Czechoslovakia		Germany		Italy		Russia		U.K.		U.S.A.	
	I	E	I	E	I	E	I	E	I	E	I	E	I	E
1883	...	...	...	...	...	...	...	...	...	...	...	...	...	...
1884	32	34	...	...	7.6	0.1	1.3	—	0.4	—	4.1	—	...	...
1885	30	32	...	...	2.3	0.1	1.3	0.1	0.9	—	3.4	0.2	...	...
1886	37	36	...	...	2.0	0.1	0.7	0.1	0.7	—	4.1	0.1	...	...
1887	27	32	...	...	1.3	0.5	0.5	0.1	0.8	—	3.2	—	...	...
1888	24	33	...	...	1.5	1.1	0.5	—	1.1	—	3.5	0.1	...	...
1889	23	34	...	...	2.1	0.8	0.5	—	1.1	—	3.7	0.2	...	...
1890	23	39	...	...	2.9	0.8	0.4	—	1.1	—	4.9	0.2	...	...
1891	26	46	...	...	4.3	0.9	1.0	—	0.8	—	5.2	—	...	...
1892	22	41	...	...	3.8	1.2	0.7	—	0.7	—	3.8	—	...	...
1893	24	43	...	...	4.1	1.7	1.5	0.1	0.7	—	4.5	—	...	...
1894	21	41	...	...	2.8	2.0	0.6	—	0.7	—	3.6	—	...	...
1895	17	39	...	...	1.9	1.6	0.4	—	1.3	—	2.4	—	...	...
1896	19	47	...	...	3.6	2.5	0.5	—	0.4	—	4.1	—	...	...
1897	26	49	...	...	4.8	3.7	0.5	—	0.5	—	6.5	—	...	...
1898	23	51	...	...	4.3	2.2	0.7	—	0.3	—	3.8	—	...	...
1899	27	55	...	...	4.8	5.9	0.9	—	0.7	—	5.7	—	...	...
1900	26	57	...	...	15	3.9	0.8	—	0.2	0.1	3.8	0.6	...	...
1901	23	56	...	...	6.8	4.1	0.9	—	0.7	0.9	3.9	0.6	...	...
1902	25	58	...	...	6.8	5.5	1.0	0.1	0.7	0.1	4.8	1.1	...	...
1903	35	51	...	...	7.1	3.1	1.2	0.3	0.7	—	4.9	0.3	...	...
1904	37	55	...	...	8.1	2.6	1.0	0.1	1.1	—	5.0	—	...	...
1905	33	65	...	...	6.3	2.1	0.8	0.1	0.8	—	5.3	—	...	...
1906	22	30	...	...	10	19	0.9	0.6	1.2	0.2	4.6	0.1	...	...
1907	26	13	...	...	20	33	2.3	4.9	0.4	3.1	10.2	2.3	...	...
1908	32	22	...	...	21	14	2.3	3.5	1.0	—	8.8	0.5	...	...
1909	18	29	...	...	29	16	2.3	3.0	1.9	—	7.6	0.1	...	...
1910	16	18	...	...	35	22	3.6	1.1	1.8	—	11.4	1.7	...	...
1911	47	48	...	...	31	29	4.9	4.4	3.4	0.1	9.5	0.1	...	...
1912	48	36	...	...	31	18	3.4	3.8	1.3	0.1	8.5	—	1.3	3.9
1913	...	...	...	...	...	...	...	...	...	...	...	...	...	...
1914	...	...	...	...	...	...	...	...	...	...	...	...	...	...
1915	...	...	...	...	...	...	...	...	...	...	...	...	...	...
1916	...	...	...	...	...	...	...	...	...	...	...	...	...	...
1917	...	...	...	...	...	...	...	...	...	...	...	...	...	...
1918	...	...	...	...	...	...	...	...	...	...	...	...	...	...
1919	...	...	...	...	...	...	...	...	...	...	...	...	...	...

F2 External Trade (by value) with Main Trading Partners

1848–1879

SPAIN[60] (in million pesetas)

	Argentina		Cuba		France		Germany		U.K.		U.S.A.	
	I	E	I	E	I	E	I	E	I	E	I	E
1848	...	...	...	...	...	...	...	...	...	...	...	...
1849	5 2	2.2	26	23	32	24	1.7	1.9	25	40	15	7
1850	2.4	1.9	22	25	53	33	2.6	0.6	29	35	21	6
1851	2.4	1.6	25	28	48	31	2.6	1.0	37	32	20	7
1852	3.1	2.3	35	32	48	36	1.8	1.0	37	40	22	7
1853	1.4[61]	3.3	26[61]	37	53[61]	48	1.9[61]	2.6	38[61]	64	22[61]	15
1854	2.6	8.2	36	39	43	60	1.1	5.3	40	76	28	14
1855	3.4	5.6	45	47	86	84	—	2.3	37	105	30	10
1856	2.5	7.1	40	47	121	68	1.5	4.2	48	70	41	15
1857	2.6	6.9	37	57	135	86	2.7	7.4	81	63	39	17
1858	3.3	6.6	42	57	117	68	3.7	3.1	84	49	37	13
1859	1.7	8.3	39	59	89	57	1.6	3.3	73	64	39	16
1860	2.3	8.2	41	56	95	62	0.7	2.3	93	80	52	19
1861	3.8	9.0	46	59	180	81	0.5	3.2	141	94	36	6
1862	11.2	11	53	58	156	63	0.4	3.3	105	77	12	10
1863	3.7	10	59	62	190	64	1.5	11.1	108	95	15	9
1864	3.0	13	55	63	185	101	1.3	6.5	133	103	15	7
1865	3.4	11	54	56	141	89	0.6	6.4	107	94	15	8
1866	3.1	8	45	58	110	93	0.2	3.2	72	95	14	10
1867	2.9	10	40	52	175	83	0.1	7.1	86	85	21	9
1868	2.2	11	43	54	212	70	0.1	2.4	116	88	24	11
1869	...	...	...	...	...	...	...	...	...	...	...	...
1870	...	...	...	...	...	...	...	...	...	...	...	...
1871	3.2	12	40	70	129	78	2.4	6.7	206	177	66	23
1872	8.5	18	37	67	117	89	1.2	7.9	148	218	55	28
1873	12.7	15	40	68	99	123	4.5	10.6	216	230	48	22
1874	8.2	16	51	61	144	104	5.9	8.7	180	165	70	20
1875	10.5	21	28	86	150	74	3.5	5.7	195	156	61	16
1876	8.2	10	38	70	164	91	7.3	7.9	144	179	60	12
1877	3.6	14	27	82	142	91	14	6.1	168	210	61	16
1878	3.5	13	23	63	173	120	13	6.7	141	175	65	15
1879	4.7	16	33	68	170	162	28	5.8	142	174	97	14

See p. 605 for footnotes

F2 External Trade (by value) with Main Trading Partners

SPAIN (in million pesetas)[60]

1880–1909

	Argentina		Cuba		France		Germany		U.K.		U.S.A.	
	I	E	I	E	I	E	I	E	I	E	I	E
1880	4.9	15	29	70	270	232	43	7.2	135	211	95	22
1881	6.3	17	23	63	207	255	51	8.7	135	200	83	21
1882	6.6	16	23	68	221	310	83	7.1	171	235	92	28
1883	7.7	17	27	59	235	303	87	10.1	187	204	101	21
1884	8.4	19	20	53	192	255	89	7.6	164	168	90	18
1885	**10.3**	18	40	65	199	316	95	12	119	162	91	15
1886	**9.3**	19	39	69	245	339	103	12	113	156	95	19
1887	6.0[60]	19[60]	37[60]	61[60]	235[60]	309[60]	83[60]	10[60]	114[60]	185[60]	100[60]	22[60]
1888	8.0	17	36	65	212	352	58	12	122	179	76	14
1889	8.6	23	35	83	264	386	54	15	161	207	102	15
1890	11	15	45	86	292	426	44	11	195	218	79	25
1891	11	8	37	115	327	457	43	10	238	176	87	15
1892	14	10	50	145	231	259	23	11	194	174	91	16
1893	13	10	30	128	204	206	20	14	155	179	87	16
1894	18	8	22	117	206	175	22	9	153	177	93	13
1895	14	10	30	136	235	238	34	6	155	198	85	13
1896	9[3]	10[3]	56[3]	256[3]	218[3]	282[3]	44[3]	9[3]	155[3]	226[3]	73[3]	11[3]
1897	14	11	27	253	147	254	53	21	155	264	99	12
1898	6	13	19	67	118	322	44	18	142	252	94	10
1899	25	13	21	74	158	250	65	26	241	281	120	13
1900	31	13	5	57	147	217	78	32	249	277	106	17
1901	25	13	3	58	145	179	80	35	199	274	120	19
1902	21	11	6	52	153	175	89	46	188	310	116	18
1903	22	17	7	66	161	220	95	41	185	316	118	26
1904	28	24	5	81	143	213	94	45	173	310	102	28
1905	44	30	5	73	160	208	85	37	168	318	119	35
1906	36	44	4	61	168	177	93	47	175	292	141	35
1907	24	40	4	63	158	198	99	60	181	296	136	39
1908	26	50	5	50	203	212	106	54	197	270	139	41
1909	35	52	4	54	198	239	115	48	206	267	122	62

See p. 605 for footnotes

F2 External Trade (by value) with Main Trading Partners

1910–1939

SPAIN (in million pesetas)[60]

	Argentina		Cuba		France		Germany		U.K.		U.S.A.	
	I	E	I	E	I	E	I	E	I	E	I	E
1910	41	64	4	56	198	260	116	56	204	263	110	66
1911	27	69	2	55	164	281	129	61	168	237	130	58
1912	40	71	3	64	183	258	138	74	201	236	155	67
1913	111	70	2	65	204	328	185	74	245	232	167	72
1914	38	41	6	52	134	251	108	42	219	233	147	64
1915	86	68	10	58	94	531	21	—	363	264	298	63
1916	60	85	19	71	110	567	3	—	326	285	454	96
1917	48	95	16	63	145	588	1	—	100	202	777	106
1918	85	113	12	43	88	343	—	—	67	168	142	50
1919	122	67	14	44	111	492	4	5	183	206	392	98
1920	134	97	17	81	219	280	86	16	214	219	331	78
1921	212	127	32	57	362	361	276	43	368	401	767	135
1922	123	99	89	56	198	211	279	45	448	326	481	156
1923	...	...	...	...	...	...	...	...	...	...	...	...
1924	119	100	10	105	349	346	233	99	441	424	514	175
1925	173	94	9	83	281	256	180	104	289	360	432	164
1926	137	80	10	73	344	266	181	86	216	360	401	212
1927	107	85	11	70	382	413	230	173	294	374	513	212
1928	166	121	29	64	419	522	286	158	311	375	513	211
1929	152	128	14	78	351	457	288	157	356	399	436	258
1930	53	175	20	65	270	470	284	181	301	387	412	227
1931	35	56	12	20	107	194	147	87	132	212	201	74
1932	59	39	9	15	74	133	100	66	99	192	161	52
1933	20	27	9	12	64	132	96	60	84	157	137	54
1934	18	22	9	14	66	96	99	68	86	142	147	52
1935	22	32	8	15	51	69	123	75	95	128	147	56
1936	...	...	...	...	...	...	...	...	...	...	...	...
1937	...	...	...	...	...	...	...	...	...	...	...	...
1938	...	...	...	...	...	...	...	...	...	...	...	...
1939	...	...	...	...	...	...	...	...	...	...	...	...

See p. 605 for footnotes

F2 **External Trade (by value) with Main Trading Partners**

1940–1975

SPAIN (in million pesetas)[60]

	Argentina		Cuba		France		Germany		U.K.		U.S.A.	
	I	E	I	E	I	E	I	E	I	E	I	E
1940	88	6	23	6	20	31	24	14	19	90	87	47
1941	106	5	4	4	14	16	51	162	21	40	39	42
1942	58	10	2	2	14	35	117	137	30	72	16	24
1943	75	23	1	3	15	9	171	227	31	122	93	77
1944	85	37	3	5	13	17	81	153	24	239	112	135
1945	89	34	22	11	12	12	17	2	36	257	158	178
1946	92	21	28	17	5	4	2	1	78	119	162	160
1947	259	46	29	22	1	—	2	4	77	130	107	76
1948	352	29	32	25	130	57	—	8	130	165	96	105
1949	188	37	15	19	89	125	12	29	117	184	126	65
1950	32[60]	37[60]	10[60]	23[60]	94[60]	79[60]	49[60]	27[60]	85[60]	176[60]	158[60]	189[60]
1951	32	12	19	37	125	121	59	84	112	304	209	203
1952	21	5	22	29	162	147	160	127	177	247	292	49
1953	28	1	22	29	188	116	214	192	190	231	221	158
1954	12	5	26	28	164	96	212	157	195	237	346	149
1955	3	3	39	34	205	110	192	198	192	223	351	143
1956	6	7	36	31	156	89	246	159	215	205	615	181
1957	6	9	44	36	140	100	219	201	229	246	688	134
1958	20	9	57	37	181	149	231	151	207	235	577	144
1959	19[62]	8[62]	23[62]	24[62]	135[62]	80[62]	255[62]	196[62]	167[62]	241[62]	573[62]	180[62]
1960	272	314	620	592	3,376	3,445	4,455	6,540	3,639	7,535	8,426	4,337
1961	387	499	554	264	5,730	3,385	7,276[2] / 7,115	6,465[2] / 6,283	4,917	7,218	16,493	4,225
1962	1,575	397	511	82	8,945	4,052	12,402	6,570	8,954	7,059	18,641	4,721
1963	3,323	511	1,302	549	12,715	4,322	15,713	5,386	11,615	7,070	19,178	4,744
1964	1,404	1,045	3,934	1,881	16,627	6,817	18,804	7,794	13,177	8,217	21,172	5,785
1965	3,488	863	1,868	2,293	19,596	6,429	25,374	7,928	16,588	7,795	31,602	6,932
1966	6,818	1,836	2,289	4,713	23,818	8,323	31,626	8,504	20,102	8,140	36,537	8,818
1967	7,709	2,069	2,317	1,692	24,197	8,504	29,361	8,728	18,238	8,567	35,562	12,362
1968	6,046	1,491	2,837	1,298	24,014	9,740	32,061	11,495	19,698	11,336	41,313	19,529
1969	7,452	3,073	2,969	2,751	30,067	12,836	39,634	14,291	22,481	11,962	50,965	19,957
1970	7,451	3,441	2,457	2,562	33,154	17,281	41,930	19,717	23,520	14,741	62,752	23,566
1971	10,400	3,070	1,942	2,012	34,161	22,283	42,152	25,066	27,294	17,375	54,000	31,540
1972	5,429	2,636	3,213	1,204	42,294	28,921	53,756	28,709	33,906	20,604	69,360	40,006
1973	8,788	3,322	3,241	2,267	57,660	38,711	76,565	35,586	35,679	24,325	90,540	41,888
1974	14,527	3,652	9,909	3,590	75,547	51,497	99,681	45,147	45,330	37,377	137,370	47,866
1975	10,821	3,005	17,988	10,160	77,670	60,254	95,515	47,194	49,841	33,596	148,067	46,308

See p. 605 for footnotes

F2 External Trade (by value) with Main Trading Partners

1830–1864

SWEDEN (in million kronor)

	Denmark		France		Germany		Netherlands		Norway		U.K.		U.S.A.	
	I	E	I	E	I	E	I	E	I	E	I	E	I	E
1830	2.2	2.6	0.4	3.0	4.5	2.1	0.3	0.8	2.8	0.9	2.6	5.9	1.2	3.7
1831	...	...	...	...	...	...	...	...	...	...	...	...	...	...
1832	1.8	2.8	0.6	2.1	4.4	2.8	0.3	0.6	2.4	0.8	2.2	4.4	1.6	4.5
1833	2.2	3.1	0.6	2.2	4.3	3.1	0.4	1.1	2.6	1.1	2.1	6.1	1.7	5.0
1834	2.2	2.6	0.4	3.0	4.6	2.9	0.3	0.8	2.8	0.9	2.6	5.9	1.2	3.7
1835	2.3	2.8	0.6	2.5	5.1	2.6	0.4	1.0	2.4	1.1	2.9	7.0	1.6	6.0
1836	1.6	2.8	0.5	1.8	7.6	3.0	0.4	0.9	2.7	1.0	2.5	6.9	2.1	7.3
1837	2.5	2.8	0.5	3.0	5.8	4.1	0.4	1.1	3.5	1.5	2.4	6.4	1.6	3.1
1838	3.0	3.3	0.5	3.1	8.0	7.2	0.4	1.4	2.9	1.0	2.3	6.9	1.9	5.2
1839	2.0	3.3	0.5	2.4	8.2	3.8	0.5	1.1	2.6.	1.5	3.1	6.9	1.9	6.8
1840	2.0	4.1	0.4	2.1	7.4	5.0	0.3	0.7	4.2	1.4	2.8	7.3	1.7	3.9
1841	2.5	3.5	0.5	2.2	7.9	6.1	0.8	1.5	4.0	1.5	4.0	7.4	1.7	4.3
1842	2.5	3.7	0.6	2.5	8.4	10.5	0.6	0.7	3.6	1.2	4.9	6.4	2.0	2.4
1843	1.9	3.6	0.8	2.9	5.6	7.7	0.5	0.7	2.6	1.2	4.1	5.6	1.2	1.5
1844	1.7	3.6	0.6	2.8	7.9	5.3	0.5	0.8	3.9	2.1	4.5	8.5	0.9	2.7
1845	2.0	4.2	0.6	3.9	12.3	4.8	0.5	0.7	3.2	2.0	3.6	13	1.3	2.5
1846	2.5	4.9	0.7	5.3	8.1	5.6	0.5	0.6	3.9	1.6	4.2	11	1.3	1.5
1847	2.5	7.8	0.6	4.2	18.1	7.3	0.6	0.7	4.4	2.2	5.3	15	1.7	3.3
1848	2.4	4.2	0.6	1.5	7.9	11.2	0.7	0.6	4.4	2.6	5.0	10	2.9	3.8
1849	2.4	4.4	0.9	2.6	7.9	7.4	1.1	1.0	4.7	2.2	5.7	12	4.0	2.7
1850	2.6	5.5	0.7	3.1	8.2	5.3	0.8	0.7	3.5	1.2	5.0	12	2.5	3.8
1851	3.6	5.7	0.5	3.1	10	6.0	0.8	0.6	4.6	0.9	6.3	16	3.6	2.9
1852	3.3	6.0	0.8	4.3	10	7.0	0.6	0.5	4.1	0.8	6.8	15	3.0	2.0
1853	4.8	10.7	1.1	6.0	27	11	0.9	1.7	6.4	1.4	13	35	5.5	2.6
1854	3.9	10.7	1.1	4.6	34	12	0.9	2.1	6.0	3.4	14	35	4.9	3.3
1855	4.7	11.5	1.2	5.4	31	14	1.9	8.6	8.4	6.3	18	40	2.9	2.9
1856	6.7	9.1	1.4	6.3	30	23	2.7	2.9	8.7	4.0	19	33	6.9	3.5
1857	4.8	8.2	1.4	8.4	24	20	1.5	1.1	8.9	2.7	15	25	6.4	3.0
1858	4.4	5.4	1.1	5.6	20	8	1.2	1.9	5.2	2.3	11	24	2.9	2.0
1859	4.7	6.8	2.4	7.7	23	13	1.6	2.0	5.4	3.6	16	32	5.5	2.9
1860	5.9	7.1	1.8	7.7	27	8	3.3	2.8	5.6	4.5	17	42	6.5	2.7
1861	7.2	6.6	1.5	10.4	30	7	4.7	2.0	5.6	3.1	23	36	6.4	0.8
1862	8.2	7.7	1.8	9.8	39	8	3.5	2.0	5.8	2.3	20	40	0.2	1.1
1863	10.4	7.7	2.6	9.4	35	8	2.4	4.1	4.6	2.2	22	46	0.1	1.2
1864	8.4	6.6	2.3	9.4	28	7	4.4	2.8	5.7	2.2	24	49	0.9	2.5

F2 **External Trade (by value) with Main Trading Partners**

SWEDEN (in million kronor) **1865–1899**

	Denmark		France		Germany		Netherlands		Norway		U.K.		U.S.A.	
	I	E	I	E	I	E	I	E	I	E	I	E	I	E
1865	10	7.7	3.7	11	33	8	4.6	4.4	5.9	3.6	31	53	0.7	1.1
1866	10	7.7	3.2	13	32	9	4.2	4.0	6.6	4.2	36	54	0.7	2.8
1867	26	11	4.2	18	31	12	4.4	4.4	7.4	3.6	29	63	1.0	3.9
1868	...	...	...	...	...	...	...	...	...	...	...	...	...	...
1869	...	...	...	...	...	...	...	...	...	...	...	...	...	...
1870	31	9	4.1	17	33	9	10.2	4.4	10	7.0	32	84	1.1	4.9
1871	25	15	4.1	14	43	11	8.9	6.7	9	7.2	52	79	6.0	6.7
1872	31	19	5.9	18	55	15	6.8	6.1	12	6.5	77	105	2.9	8.6
1873	37	22	9.4	19	62	18	9.9	5.3	13	7.4	95	121	8.0	7.0
1874	54	32	10.7	20	63	14	11.3	5.2	15	7.5	91	127	8.3	2.1
1875	49	25	10.1	25	55	13	9.2	4.9	15	7.1	92	109	2.5	1.1
1876	51	24	11.6	25	58	16	10.9	11.7	17	7.0	98	120	5.8	0.8
1877	49	22	9.3	25	67	14	12.1	10.6	15	6.7	87	117	6.9	0.7
1878	42	21	8.0	26	57	12	10.7	5.1	12	7.1	63	93	7.6	0.5
1879	48	21	5.5	28	52	13	9.2	5.7	11	6.4	59	92	6.2	1.1
1880	56	24	6.5	29	62	17	8.4	6.1	17	8.0	78	124	11.8	2.9
1881	52	22	7.8	28	77	21	7.7	10.4	17	8.2	74	107	9.8	0.4
1882	52	25	7.6	33	84	18	9.1	7.7	19	10.6	78	127	6.2	1.6
1883	57	32	7.6	31	91	19	9.3	9.9	21	9.2	86	129	9.5	0.3
1884	53	33	8.5	29	89	18	6.6	8.9	22	11	89	112	5.4	1.7
1885	50	31	8.2	24	101	19	6.7	9.0	24	10	85	122	8.6	0.8
1886	42	26	6.8	21	92	21	6.1	9.3	23	11	77	111	8.7	2.6
1887	47	32	6.2	27	89	24	5.5	8.5	23	12	74	110	6.6	2.8
1888	42	35	6.7	30	94	27	6.9	14	28	14	94	130	4.2	1.1
1889	45	34	7.6	24	116	36	9.0	13	34	16	111	142	5.9	1.4
1890	44	33	7.9	24	118	37	9.6	16	33	18	109	137	8.2	0.9
1891	45	37	9.1	34	120	38	8.5	13	34	17	99	146	13	0.7
1892	44	40	9.6	19	116	48	9.2	17	35	18	95	150	13	2.4
1893	40	37[63]	6.2	29[63]	113	44[63]	7.0	17[63]	31	16[63]	86	151[63]	11	0.7[63]
1894	40	38	8.5	32	120	39	3.7	18	27	15	98	124	12	—
1895	38	41	7.9	25	116	43	8.3	18	29	18	98	131	11	0.1
1896	46	42	7.2	29	118	44	8.8	20	29	20	99	144	9	0.7
1897	49	43	7.6	31	135	46	8.5	24	33	21[64]	121	150	7	0.2
1898	59	43	8.0	28	158	50	10	25	21	6	139	149	10	0.1
1899	61	43	9.0	29	184	55	10	26	20	6	155	157	10	—

See p. 605 for footnotes

F2 External Trade (by value) with Main Trading Partners

1900–1934

SWEDEN (in million kronor)

	Denmark		France		Germany		Netherlands		Norway		U.K.		U.S.A.	
	I	E	I	E	I	E	I	E	I	E	I	E	I	E
1900	63	48	9.7	30	188	65	11	30	22	7	177	169	9	—
1901	65	47	8.9	26	169	60	12	23	23	7[64]	132	150	11	...
1902	63	55	9.3	28	197	63	13	24	24	24	130	150	10	...
1903	64	61	9.5	31	206	71	16	24	25	32	139	162	13	...
1904	73	58	10.3	30	222	72	18	24	23	35	149	149	9	...
1905	40	50	16	30	220	85	14	23	23	31	140	159	41	10
1906	42	55	20	37	231	97	15	26	25	35	159	171	60	12
1907	46	58	23	40	238	109	17	17	23	25	177	182	61	14
1908	43	46	19	37	210	103	15	15	21	25	152	169	60	10
1909	40	45	23	36	213	97	16	14	21	24	157	156	48	16
1910	45	55	28	42	230	124	18	16	21	29	164	191	53	23
1911	46	66	31	49	240	134	19	24	20	38	161	196	55	24
1912	50	67	33	53	274	171	20	19	24	43	189	223	60	32
1913	54	71	35	66	290	179	21	19	26	54	207	238	77	34
1914	52	73	29	33	239	175	19	19	29	49	184	258	78	41
1915	70	80	24	31	251	486	27	43	51	76	214	330	322	34
1916	80	94	24	97	420	438	22	61	61	115	164	320	214	75
1917	113	113	16	64	288	352	23	80	52	163	65	216	96	50
1918	203	182	13	86	448	293	42	113	98	211	149	253	83	19
1919	249	160	63	126	269	131	60	61	77	200	669	512	646	62
1920	313	137	96	187	500	185	78	95	90	183	915	825	779	129
1921	120	88	45	52	325	119	45	42	43	107	218	327	243	97
1922	90	84	32	105	314	103	39	55	37	80	268	285	167	133
1923	108	81	38	89	342	90	52	35	36	73	284	359	214	128
1924	124	83	45	93	353	133	57	48	40	55	308	363	227	153
1925	124	84	49	84	378	206	59	56	49	65	291	367	219	143
1926	122	91	55	90	460	189	59	41	47	64	221	386	199	173
1927	133	100	54	67	485	271	58	59	42	78	264	448	201	175
1928	119	103	59	90	531	198	69	70	45	86	275	393	252	166
1929	130	118	52	102	548	275	74	70	50	96	309	450	261	198
1930	114	112	56	93	533	225	66	57	52	95	263	395	229	161
1931	91	83	49	69	472	114	61	39	40	72	201	300	178	133
1932	76	62	30	56	339	90	47	32	38	61	194	242	125	100
1933	66	74	30	68	320	115	48	42	37	55	197	285	113	131
1934	80	88	39	68	350	186	63	46	44	84	255	328	154	128

See p. 605 for footnotes

F2 External Trade (by value) with Main Trading Partners

SWEDEN (in million kronor) **1935–1954**

	Denmark		France		Germany		Netherlands		Norway		U.K.		U.S.A.	
	I	E	I	E	I	E	I	E	I	E	I	E	I	E
1935	101	78	49	56	358	187	73	40	50	67	285	322	189	156
1936	105	84	50	72	399	241	84	44	53	103	314	374	223	188
1937	127	87	65	92	485[65]	315[65]	106	61	64	140	403	479	318	221
1938	125	91	62	61	499	335	115	69	65	123	380	451	339	166
1939	121	103	77	62	651	371	134	94	88	139	452	439	420	179
1940	72	50	25	18	794	494	50	45	77	112	170	120	310	55
1941	55	79	9	14	911	579	30	47	43	84	24	21	139	14
1942	53	110	7	9	842	550	25	27	36	69	13	28	91	25
1943	61	77	9	11	932	552	21	18	42	59	15	2	60	1
1944	72	39	6	3	819[65]	349[65]	17	12	21	28	16	6	51	2
1945	79	143	8	67	90	. .	19	69	51	331	75	282	201	239
1946	141	175	117	161	7	—	98	175	125	185	487	426	919	190
1947	175[3,66]	155[3,66]	200[3]	184[3]	110[3]	21[3]	184[3]	198[3]	166[3]	245[3]	701[3]	527[3]	1,814[3]	365[3]
	155	135	189				173	194	158		444	491	1,640	349
1948	154	159	257	203	151	151	252	244	153	365	860	671	692	292
1949	156	208	238	191	314	338	213	226	169	417	743	726	416	247
1950	214	336	389	250	697	733	274	345	181	513	1,215	812	524	356
1951	233	414	467	522	1,314	989	432	501	301	542	1,491	1,752	863	475
1952	226	443	323	480	1,662[2]	1,036[2]	472	411	350	632	1,282	1,353	858	463
					1,587	962								
1953	256	437	384	361	1,492	881	507	454	292	620	1,337	1,451	657	513
1954	327[67]	540[67]	453	390	1,867	1,008	640	485	331	805	1,464	1,524	724	381
	325	538												

See p. 605 for footnotes

F2 External Trade (by value) with Main Trading Partners — 1955–1975

SWEDEN (in million kronor)

	Denmark		France		Germany		Netherlands		Norway		U.K.		U.S.A.	
	I	E	I	E	I	E	I	E	I	E	I	E	I	E
1955	375	518	501	465	2,260	1,183	731	548	330	867	1,413	1,749	1,009	440
1956	389	558	433	635	2,515	1,377	797	625	425	824	1,583	1,789	1,171	512
1957	520	587	387	572	2,769	1,569	849	671	463	1,090	1,741	1,980	1,608	529
1958	491	640	450	478	2,856	1,536	928	527	412	1,137	1,718	1,757	1,296	629
1959	492	738	493	435	2,850	1,725	964	558	434	1,141	1,717	1,713	1,317	910
1960	648	872	589	515	3,210	2,017	1,166	680	571	1,212	1,950	2,122	1,889	848
1961	696	1,071	570	610	3,359	2,234	1,110	789	620	1,385	2,141	2,118	1,718	704
1962	769	1,198	666	670	3,555	2,310	1,248	825	698	1,457	2,320	1,997	1,640	847
1963	986	1,273	681	781	3,771	2,341	1,280	839	792	1,861	2,623	2,238	1,765	920
1964	1,241	1,650	810	956	4,288	2,727	1,145	977	959	2,026	3,007	2,647	2,002	1,034
1965	1,417	1,851	940	1,001	4,880	2,967	1,221	1,065	1,227	2,409	3,326	2,722	2,150	1,241
1966	1,488	1,981	1,024	1,202	4,774	2,839	1,282	1,091	1,303	2,329	3,646	2,803	2,215	1,522
1967	1,694	2,211	1,180	1,092	4,693	2,577	1,181	1,010	1,450	2,799	3,569	3,123	2,258	1,720
1968	1,908	2,420	1,193	1,189	4,959	2,960	1,215	1,176	1,542	2,661	3,595	3,784	2,457	1,984
1969	2,339	2,939	1,310	1,534	5,809	3,447	1,315	1,315	1,793	2,911	4,218	3,839	2,615	1,856
1970	2,808	3,442	1,502	1,766	6,856	4,142	1,626	1,581	2,108	3,808	5,000	4,403	3,155	2,096
1971	2,888	3,794	1,407	1,941	6,847	4,302	1,468	1,680	2,249	3,924	5,097	5,170	2,884	2,494
1972	3,114	3,844	1,763	2,078	7,268	4,476	1,586	1,643	2,493	3,978	5,018	6,136	2,763	2,937
1973	3,538	5,250	1,892	2,712	9,153	5,392	2,281	2,131	3,182	5,021	5,727	7,860	3,055	3,217
1974	5,098	5,953	2,786	3,697	13,157	6,939	3,413	3,104	4,784	7,354	7,777	9,330	4,590	3,744
1975	5,285	6,213	3,129	3,443	14,348	7,196	3,479	2,909	4,960	8,032	8,183	7,851	4,887	3,760

F2 External Trade (by value) with Main Trading Partners

1884–1914

SWITZERLAND (in million francs)

	Austria-Hungary		France		Germany		Italy		U.K.		U.S.A.	
	I	E	I	E	I	E	I	E	I	E	I	E
1884	...	...	...	...	...	...	...	...	...	...	...	...
1885	66	38	179	140	249	158	112	60	52	99	18	78
1886	92	36	188	139	261	160	119	58	46	104	21	87
1887	88	38	212	131	264	165	117	65	46	103	29	81
1888	96	33	203	142	254	165	116	51	44	105	22	87
1889	107	39	262	142	270	185	141	54	51	106	25	76
1890	102	39	226	124	295	182	129	50	52	107	29	83
1891	87	36	214	125	293	164	136	47	46	113	31	72
1892	68	37	179	103	227	162	140	46	42	117	41	76
1893	76	40	112	74	238	168	147	43	44	118	38	80
1894	80	39	110	73	243	157	144	38	43	118	35	72
1895	68	39	139	75	274	164	158	39	47	131	39	91
1896	71	40	178	81	305	172	137	39	52	147	39	71
1897	67	41	192	84	306	176	150	39	54	146	52	71
1898	66	42	204	83	315	194	156	39	51	148	73	74
1899	77	46	214	96	345	199	191	42	56	166	62	92
1900	69	46	207	110	350	202	162	44	62	176	57	96
1901	64	45	206	109	317	192	158	46	47	189	61	88
1902	71	47	217	112	324	203	178	51	54	186	62	109
1903	78	48	222	114	356	202	181	52	57	178	57	117
1904	82	52	239	108	377	211	169	54	58	172	54	106
1905	92	54	274	120	441	232	177	57	67	175	57	125
1906	92	64	281	109	480	277	201	70	84	176	59	136
1907	103	66	298	121	551	282	230	83	118	189	70	160
1908	99	65	284	117	513	240	172	92	87	179	61	112
1909	102	70	306	121	534	254	185	83	91	182	64	146
1910	111	80	347	130	566	270	203	86	113	200	69	144
1911	114	85	340	133	581	275	181	85	100	213	75	142
1912	122	89	376	138	647	307	193	91	117	230	84	136
1913	109	78	348	141	631	306	207	89	113	236	118	136
1914	103	67	221	115	481	275	194	83	76	234	108	122

F2 External Trade (by value) with Main Trading Partners

1915–1944

SWITZERLAND (in million francs)

	Austria-Hungary		France		Germany		Italy		U.K.		U.S.A.	
	I	E	I	E	I	E	I	E	I	E	I	E
1915	66	157	189	221	418	457	259	90	112	355	324	107
1916	45	195	236	401	472	709	390	150	160	424	565	133
1917	44	93	305	462	483	699	369	136	269	362	459	120
1918	61	101	280	466	620	445	222	97	248	269	354	99
1919	69	242	407	502	483	698	273	209	363	347	788	183
	Austria											
1920	72	106	603	522	809	253	325	166	466	646	865	283
1921	32	88	321	239	440	195	200	74	156	349	385	586
1922	25	48	303	240	366	193	225	93	174	348	190	215
1923	31	65	395	214	417	124	232	101	182	363	178	210
1924	34	90	454	206	486	328	288	94	188	397	207	206
1925	41	70	499	173	471	368	266	104	281	422	227	192
1926	40	66	496	154	465	267	252	113	150	300	188	201
1927	46[53]	81[53]	475[53]	135[53]	542[53]	398[53]	226[53]	115[53]	192[53]	311[53]	220[53]	210[53]
1928	57	71	491	157	624	386	200	141	203	308	244	195
1929	55	68	490	182	698	349	203	158	169	290	239	208
1930	51[68]	55[68]	447[68]	183[68]	709[68]	278[68]	185[68]	120[68]	139[68]	265[68]	205[68]	144[68]
1931	43	45	362	156	660	198	180	94	99[10] 96	237[10] 236	164	92
1932	28	24	272	123	500	111	143	82	79	86	115	55
1933	36	23	244	142	461	139	134	80	91	88	90	58
1934	36	24	230	122	389	183	116	76	91	84	76	48
1935	29	22[53]	207	121[53]	338	170[53]	91	73[53]	76	78[53]	70	48[53]
1936	27	25	187	115	314	171	83	62	77	98	72	70
1937	44	38	245	140	403	200	117	102	113	144	126	112
1938	33	31	229	121	373	206	117	91	95	148	125	91
1939	...	...	275	140	440	192	135	81	109	165	133	130
1940	...	...	139	112	411	285	165	142	88	95	199	140
1941	...	...	76	93	656	577	245	186	14	23	151	108
1942	...	...	77	67	660	656	154	159	20	22	235	102
1943	...	...	78[53]	52	532[53]	598	131[53]	94	4[53]	36	56[53]	153
1944	...	...	52	24	433	293	29	5	1	34	21	141

See p. 605 for footnotes

F2 External Trade (by value) with Main Trading Partners

1945–1975

SWITZERLAND (in million francs)

	Austria		France		Germany		Italy		U.K.		U.S.A.	
	I	E	I	E	I	E	I	E	I	E	I	E
1945	2	1	130	165	54	11	47	11	22	32	137	385
1946	42	20	355	282	45	8	228	156	197	58	548	453
1947	89	39	459	298	133	16	321	210	323	117	1,032	395
1948	106	73	391	329	323	69	299	227	356	140	954	456
1949	57	65	353	240	332	313	251	260	276	158	766	430
1950	63	82	511	858	497	362	324	520	370	137	626	515
1951	102	125	620	392	914	422	398	348	399	229	943	597
1952	97	107	512	330	959	496	379	442	336	233	837	703
1953	94	118	515	367	1,040	609	462	504	341	246	619	852
1954	108	135	643	389	1,253[2]	680[2]	546	466	317	267	710	641
					1,216	641						
1955	128	169	770	385	1,507	755	613	463	336[19]	303[19]	828	650
									333	298		
1956	177	184	844	542	1,853	864	726	503	411	329	1,001	762
1957	208	210	886	578	2,193	961	936	541	450	366	1,197	765
1958	153	202	757	494	1,954	1,080	870	520	413	372	837	658
1959	176	220	932	501	2,808	1,242	951	593	617	414	875	815
1960	209	260	1,212	544	2,841	1,493	1,013	671	573	472	1,096	807
1961	287	306	1,489	664	3,664	1,578	1,212	746	681	510	1,199	817
1962	365	344	1,740	778	4,087	1,668	1,355	870	811	560	1,270	911
1963	359	369	2,006	915	4,419	1,722	1,454	1,052	927	645	1,206	961
1964	440	448	2,310	998	4,703	1,864	1,523	1,007	1,113	781	1,353	1,039
1965	471	535	2,312	1,052	4,795	2,203	1,628	1,020	1,158	901	1,351	1,242
1966	545	643	2,394	1,223	4,997	2,142	1,684	1,180	1,287	918	1,534	1,528
1967	625	777	2,454	1,383	5,102	2,024	1,751	1,303	1,374	1,131	1,488	1,555
1968	732	843	2,521	1,496	5,737	2,463	1,937	1,513	1,422	1,291	1,737	1,780
1969	957	1,005	2,753	1,718	6,643	3,035	2,201	1,753	1,833	1,383	1,922	1,884
1970	1,251	1,152	3,362	1,807	8,349	3,289	2,623	2,074	2,167	1,585	2,372	1,963
1971	1,434	1,345	3,729	2,073	8,801	3,586	2,929	2,085	2,340	1,719	2,121	1,998
1972	1,671	1,543	4,381	2,330	9,681	3,922	3,129	2,174	2,364	2,036	2,234	2,263
1973	1,812	1,800	5,117	2,647	11,063	4,201	3,417	2,495	2,240	2,276	2,333	2,445
1974	2,109	2,326	5,886	3,109	12,479	4,843	3,930	2,823	2,502	2,539	2,806	2,501
1975	1,489	1,852	4,754	2,965	9,553	4,944	3,386	2,306	2,105	2,051	2,587	2,135

See p. 605 for footnotes

F2 External Trade (by value) with Main Trading Partners

1827–1864

UNITED KINGDOM (in million pounds)

	Argentina		Australia		Canada		France		Germany		India		Netherlands		New Zealand		Russia		U.S.A.	
	I	E	I	E	I	E	I	E	I	E	I	E	I	E	I	E	I	E	I	E
1827	...	...	...	0.3	...	1.4	...	0.4	...	4.8	...	3.7	...	...	...	...	...	1.4	...	7.0
1828	...	...	...	0.4	...	1.7	...	0.5	...	4.6	...	...	...	...	...	...	...	1.3	...	5.8
1829	...	...	...	0.3	...	1.6	...	0.5	...	4.7	...	...	...	...	...	...	...	1.4	...	4.8
1830	...	...	...	0.3	...	1.9	...	0.5	...	4.6	...	...	...	...	...	...	...	1.5	...	6.1
1831	...	...	...	0.4	...	2.1	...	0.6	...	3.8	...	...	...	...	...	...	...	1.2	...	9.1
1832	...	...	...	0.5	...	2.1	...	0.7	...	5.3	...	...	...	...	...	...	...	1.6	...	5.5
1833	...	...	...	0.6	...	2.1	...	0.8	...	4.5	...	2.6	...	2.2	...	...	...	1.5	...	7.6
1834	...	...	...	0.7	...	1.7	...	1.1	...	4.7	...	3.2	...	2.5	...	...	...	1.4	...	6.8
1835	...	...	...	0.7	...	2.2	...	1.5	...	4.8	...	4.3	...	2.6	...	...	...	1.8	...	10.6
1836	...	...	...	0.8	...	2.7	...	1.6	...	4.6	...	3.6	...	2.5	...	...	...	1.7	...	12.4
1837	...	...	...	0.9	...	2.1	...	1.6	...	5.0	...	3.6	...	3.0	...	...	...	2.0	...	4.7
1838	...	...	...	1.3	...	1.9	...	2.3	...	5.1	...	3.9	...	3.5	...	...	...	1.7	...	7.6
1839	...	...	...	1.7	...	3.0	...	2.3	...	5.4	...	4.7 [70]	...	3.6	...	...	...	1.8	...	8.8
1840	...	...	...	2.1	...	2.8	...	2.4	...	5.6	...	5.2	...	3.4	...	...	...	1.6	...	5.3
1841	...	...	...	1.3	...	2.9	...	2.9	...	6.0	...	4.8	...	3.6	...	...	...	1.6	...	7.1
1842	...	...	...	1.0	...	2.3	...	3.2	...	6.6	...	4.4	...	3.6	...	...	...	1.9	...	3.5
1843	...	...	...	1.3	...	1.8	...	2.5	...	6.7	...	5.7	...	3.6	...	...	...	1.9	...	5.0
1844	...	...	...	0.8	...	3.0	...	2.7	...	6.7	...	6.9	...	3.1	...	...	...	2.1	...	7.9
1845	...	...	...	1.2	...	3.6	...	2.8	...	7.1	...	5.9	...	3.4	...	...	...	2.2	...	7.1
1846	...	——	...	1.5 [71] / 1.4	...	3.3	...	2.7	...	7.2	...	5.8	...	3.6	...	——	...	1.7	...	6.8
1847	...	0.2	...	1.6	...	3.2	...	2.6	...	6.8	...	4.8	...	3.0	...	0.1	...	1.8	...	11.0
1848	...	0.4	...	1.4	...	2.0	...	1.0	...	5.3	...	4.6	...	2.8	...	0.1	...	1.9	...	9.6
1849	...	1.4	...	2.0	...	2.3	...	2.0	...	6.1	...	6.2	...	3.5	...	0.1	...	1.6	...	12
1850	...	0.8	...	2.5	...	3.2	...	2.4	...	7.5	...	7.2	...	3.5	...	0.1	...	1.5	...	15
1851	...	0.5	...	2.6	...	3.8	...	2.0	...	7.7	...	7.0	...	3.5	...	0.2	...	1.3	...	14
1852	...	0.8	...	4.1	...	3.1	...	2.7	...	7.9	...	6.5	...	4.1	...	0.1	...	1.1	...	17
1853	...	0.6	...	14.3	...	4.9	...	2.6	...	8.2	...	7.3	...	4.5	...	0.2	...	1.2	...	24
1854	1.3	1.3	4.3	11.6	7.1	6.0	10	3.2	16	8.5	11	9.1	6.7	4.6	——	0.3	4.3	0.1	30	21
1855	1.1	0.7	4.5	6.0	4.7	2.9	9	6.0	16	9.9	13	9.9	6.5	4.6	——	0.2	0.5	–	26	17
1856	1.0	1.0	5.6	9.6	6.9	4.1	10	6.4	11	12	17	11	7.4	5.7	0.1	0.3	12	1.6	36	22
1857	1.6	1.3	5.8	11	6.4	4.3	12	6.2	14	13	19	12	7.2	6.4	0.2	0.4	13	3.1	34	19
1858	1.2	1.0	5.0	10	4.7	3.2	13	4.9	9	13	15	17	6.3	5.5	0.3	0.5	12	3.1	34	15
1859	1.6	1.0	5.5	11	5.5	3.6	17	4.8	11	12	15	20	6.7	5.4	0.3	0.6	14	4.0	34	23
1860	1.1	1.8	6.0	9	6.8	3.7	18	5.3	15	14	15	17	8.3	6.1	0.4	0.6	16	3.3	45	22
1861	1.5	1.4	6.4	10	8.7	3.7	18	8.9	14	13	22	16	7.7	6.4	0.5	0.9	13	3.0	49	9
1862	1.1	0.9	6.5	11	8.5	4.0	22	9.2	15	13	34	15	7.9	6.0	0.6	1.2	15	2.1	28	14
1863	1.2	1.3	6.4	11	8.2	4.8	24	8.7	14	14	48	20	8.7	6.3	0.7	2.0	12	2.7	20	15
1864	1.2	1.8	8.9	10	6.9	5.6	26	8.2	15	16	52	20	12.0	6.9	1.1	1.9	15	2.8	18	17

See p. 605 for footnotes

F2 External Trade (by value) with Main Trading Partners

UNITED KINGDOM (in million pounds) 1865–1899

	Argentina		Australia		Canada		France		Germany		India		Netherlands		New Zealand		Russia		U.S.A.	
	I	E	I	E	I	E	I	E	I	E	I	E	I	E	I	E	I	E	I	E
1865	1.0	2.0	9.0	12	6.4	4.7	32	9.1	17	18	37	18	12	8.1	1.3	1.6	17	2.9	22	21
1866	1.1	2.8	9.9	12	6.9	6.8	37	12	19	16	37	20	12	9.0	1.6	2.2	20	3.2	47	29
1867	0.9	2.8	11	8	6.8	5.9	34	12	19	21	26	22	11	9.4	1.7	1.5	22	3.9	41	22
1868	1.5	1.9	11	10	6.8	4.8	34	11	18	23	30	21	11	10.4	1.5	1.7	20	4.3	43	21
1869	1.3	2.3	11	12	7.7	5.2	34	11	18	23	33	18	13	10.8	1.6	1.9	17	6.5	43	25
1870	1.5	2.3	12	8	8.5	6.8	38	12	15	20	25	19	14	11.2	2.1	1.5	21	7.0	50	28
1871	2.0	2.5	12	9	9.3	8.3	30	18	19	27	31	18	14	14.1	2.5	1.4	24	6.6	61	34
1872	1.9	3.9	13	12	9.1	10.2	42	17	19	32	34	19	13	16.2	2.7	2.3	24	6.6	55	41
1873	2.6	3.7	14	14	11	8.6	43	17	20	27	30	21	13	16.7	3.2	3.4	21	9.0	72	34
1874	1.3	3.1	15	15	12	9.3	47	16	20	25	31	24	15	14.4	3.5	4.4	21	8.8	74	28
1875	1.4	2.4	17	16	10	9.0	47	15	22	23	30	24	15	13.1	3.5	3.9	21	8.1	70	22
1876	1.7	1.5	19	15	11	7.4	45	16	21	20	30	22	17	11.8	3.5	3.2	18	6.2	76	17
1877	1.7	2.1	18	16	12	7.6	46	14	26	20	31	25	20	9.6	3.7	3.3	22	4.2	78	16
1878	1.1	2.3	17	15	10	6.4	41	15	24	20	28	23	22	9.3	4.0	4.3	18	6.6	89	15
1879	0.8	2.1	17	13	10	5.4	39	15	22	19	25	21	22	9.4	4.5	3.6	16	7.6	92	20
1880	0.9	2.5	20	14	13	7.7	42	16	24	17	30	31	26	9.2	5.2	2.9	16	8.0	107	31
1881	0.6	3.3	22	18	11	8.4	40	17	24	17	33	29	23	8.9	5.1	3.7	14	6.2	103	30
1882	1.2	4.2	20	20	10	9.7	39	17	26	19	40	29	25	9.4	4.7	4.3	21	5.8	88	31
1883	0.9	4.9	20	20	12	9.2	39	18	28	19	39	32	25	9.5	5.8	3.9	21	5.0	89	27
1884	1.2	5.8	22	20	11	8.7	37	17	24	19	34	31	26	10.2	6.0	3.7	16	5.0	86	24
1885	1.9	4.7	18	21	10	7.2	36	15	23	16	32	29	25	8.9	5.1	3.9	18	4.2	87	22
1886	1.6	5.2	16	19	10	7.9	37	14	21	16	32	31	25	8.2	4.7	3.3	14	4.4	82	27
1887	2.2	6.2	18	17	11	8.1	37	14	25	16	31	31	25	8.2	5.7	3.1	16	4.2	83	30
1888	2.7	7.7	20	23	9	7.6	39	15	27	16	31	33	26	8.5	5.9	3.0	26	4.8	80	29
1889	2.0	10.7	20	20	12	8.1	46	15	27	19	36	31	27	9.7	6.8	3.2	27	5.3	96	30
1890	4.1	8.4	21	20	12	7.2	45	17	26	19	33	34	26	10.1	8.3	3.3	24	5.8	97	32
1891	3.5	4.2	23	22	13	7.2	45	16	27	19	32	31	27	9.5	8.2	3.4	24	5.4	104	28
1892	4.5	5.7	23	16	15	7.4	44	15	26	18	31	28	29	8.8	7.8	3.5	15	5.4	108	27
1893	4.8	5.5	22	12	13	7.2	44	13	26	18	26	29	29	9.2	8.1	3.3	19	6.4	92	24
1894	6.2	4.5	24	13	13	6.3	44	14	27	18	28	29	28	8.8	8.3	3.0	24	6.9	90	19
1895	9.1	5.4	25	14	13	5.8	48	14	27	21	26	25	28	7.4	8.4	3.1	25	7.0	87	28
1896	9.0	6.6	21	18	16	5.5	50	14	28	22	25	30	29	8.3	8.1	4.0	23	7.2	106	20
1897	5.8	4.8	21	17	20	6.2	53	14	26	22	25	27	29	8.9	8.6	4.0	22	7.5	113	21
1898	7.8	5.6	20	17	21	7.3	51	14	29	23	28	30	29	8.6	9.0	4.0	20	9.2	126	15
1899	11	6.2	24	18	21	8.1	53	15	30	26	28	31	31	9.4	9.7	4.5	19	11.7	120	18

F2 External Trade (by value) with Main Trading Partners

1900–1934

UNITED KINGDOM (in million pounds)

	Argentina		Australia		Canada		France		Germany		India		Netherlands		New Zealand		Russia		U.S.A.	
	I	E	I	E	I	E	I	E	I	E	I	E	I	E	I	E	I	E	I	E
1900	13	7.1	24	22	22	8.1	54	20	31	28	27	30	31	10.9	12	5.5	22	11.0	139	20
1901	12	6.8	24	21	20	11	51	17	32	24	27	35	33	9.1	11	5.6	22	8.7	141	18
1902	14	5.9	20	20	24	12	51	16	34	23	29	33	35	8.4	11	5.7	26	8.6	127	24
1903	19	8.0	17	16	27	11	49	16	35	24	32	35	35	8.7	14	6.4	31	9.1	122	23
1904	23	11	24	17	23	11	51	15	34	25	37	41	35	8.2	13	6.3	31	8.2	119	20
1905	25[72]	13[72]	27[72]	17[72]	26[72]	12[72]	53[72]	16[72]	36[72]	30[72]	36[72]	43[72]	36[72]	10[72]	13[72]	6.4[72]	33[72]	8.2[72]	116[72]	24[72]
	25	13	27	17	26	12	47	16	54	30	36	43	15	10	13	6.4	35	8.2	115	24
1906	24	19	29	20	29	14	47	20	56	34	38	45	16	12	16	7.4	32	8.9	131	28
1907	27	18	34	24	26	18	46	23	57	41	44	52	16	14	18	8.7	33	11	134	31
1908	36	16	29	23	25	13	42	22	55	33	30	49	17	12	15	8.8	30	13	124	21
1909	33	19	33	24	26	16	44	21	58	32	35	44	17	12	18	7.4	38	11	118	30
1910	29	19	39	28	26	21	44	23	62	37	43	46	19	13	21	8.7	44	12	118	31
1911	27	19	39	31	25	20	42	24	65	39	45	52	19	13	18	9.8	43	14	123	28
1912	41	21	36	35	28	24	46	26	70	40	52	58	21	14	20	10.4	41	14	135	30
1913	43	23	38	35	32	25	46	29	80	41	48	70	24	15	20	10.8	40	18	142	29
1914	37	15	37	34	32	18	38	26	47	23	43	63	24	13	23	9.4	28	14	139	34
1915	64	12	45	29	42	14	31	70	—	...	62	46	23	18	30	9.4	21	13	238	26
1916	52	14	36	36	61	19	27	93	—	–	72	53	22	24	32	12.1	18	25	292	33
1917	48	13	64	22	85	17	23	112	—	–	67	60	20	21	29	7.0	18	49	376	33
1918	63	18	45	26	125	15	35	131	—	–	89	49	8	15	25	7.7	7	0.3	515	23
1919	82	21	111	26	118	17	49	147	1	15	108	71	22	34	53	9.6	16	13	542	34
1920	128	43	112	63	97	44	76	136	30	22	96	181	39	48	48	27	34	12	563	77
1921	68	28	68	46	64	20	53	44	21	18	44	109	39	27	49	15	3	2.2	275	44
1922	57	23	65	60	57	26	49	49	27	32	48	92	34	35	49	16	8	3.6	222	56
1923	65[73]	28[73]	49[73]	58[73]	56[73]	28[73]	59[73]	49[73]	35[73]	43[73]	67[73]	86[73]	37[73]	30[73]	43[73]	21[73]	9[73]	2.5[73]	211[73]	60[73]
1924	79	27	59	61	68	30	67	42	37	43	79	91	43	25	47	20	20	3.9	241	54
1925	69	29	73	60	73	29	65	31	48	44	80	86	46	25	51	23	25	6.2	245	52
1926	68	23	61	61	66	27	59	20	73	26	58	82	50	18	47	21	24	5.9	229	49
1927	77	27	53	61	57	30	63	24	60	42	66	85	45	21	47	20	21	4.5	200	45
1928	77	31	54	56	59	36	61	25	64	41	65	84	43	22	47	19	22	2.7	188	47
1929	82	29	56	54	48	36	57	32	69	37	63	78	42	22	48	21	27	3.7	196	46
1930	57	25	46	32	40	30	49	30	66	27	51	53	40	19	45	18	34	6.8	154	29
1931	53	15	46	15	35	21	41	23	64	18	37	32	35	14	38	11	32	7.3	104	18
1932	51	11	46	20	45	17	19	18	31	15	32	34	22	12	37	10	20	9.2	84	15
1933	42	13	49	21	48	18	19	18	30	15	37	33	19	12	37	10	18	3.3	76	19
1934	47	15	50	26	53	21	19	17	31	14	42	37	21	12	40	11	17	3.6	82	18

See p. 605 for footnotes

F2 External Trade (by value) with Main Trading Partners

UNITED KINGDOM (in million pounds) **1935–1954**

	Argentina		Australia		Canada		France		Germany		India		Netherlands		New Zealand		Russia		U.S.A.	
	I	E	I	E	I	E	I	E	I	E	I	E	I	E	I	E	I	E	I	E
1935	44	15	54	29	58	22	22	17	32	20	41	38	23	12	38	13	22	3.5	88	23
1936	45	15	61	32	77	24	26	18	35	21	52	34	25	12	44	17	19	3.5	93	28
1937	60	20	72	38	92	29	26	21	39	23	65	39	32	15	50	20	29	3.1	114	31
1938	39	19	72	38	81	24	24	15	32	22	56[74] / 50	36[74] / 34	29	13	47	19	20[75] / 29	6.5[75] / 11	118	21
1939	47	20	62	32	82	23	27	14	19	12	49	30	30	14	42	16	17	8	118	28
1940	61	18	97	46	153	33	15	16	—	—	73	33	12	6	56	17	2	1	276	33
1941	52	16	46	38	194	39	—	—	—	—	57	32	—	—	56	15	1	23	409	32
1942	49	13	40	64	178	33	—	—	—	—	60	22	—	—	60	25	3	67	536	26
1943	58	10	33	44	285	32	—	—	—	—	60	18	—	—	50	19	2	54	1,104	20
1944	81	4	54	51	390	27	—	7	—	—	70	24	—	—	57	17	2	50	1,391	19
1945	48	6	53	50	323	28	2	27	2	3	68	33	1	6	63	15	4	28	610	19
1946	67	21	67	55	201	34	14	34	6	18	69	80	12	31	74	28	5	10	230	36
1947	131	35	97	72	239	45	31	24	19	21	95	92	26	31	90	43	8	12	297	48
1948	122	53	169	145	223	73	46	34	30	25	108[76] / 96	114[76] / 96	44	45	109	53	27	5	183	66
1949	77	51	213	189	225	80	75	33	38	27	99	117	65	53	117	65	16	9	222	57
1950	96	39	220	256	180	126	110	44	42	44	98	97	86	72	134	87	34	12	211	113
1951	86	28	254	324	261	137	135	55	78[2] / 75	50[2] / 50	153	115	128	74	165	111	60	4	380	137
1952	53	21	227	221	320	130	87	62	90	51	115	113	102	71	166	115	58	4	315	146
1953	99	15	294	213	306	157	82	66	70	59	113	115	89	94	170	100	40	3	253	159
1954	81	23	236	278	273	132	97	64	78	71	148	115	110	100	176	126	42	10	282	150

See p. 605 for footnotes

F2 External Trade (by value) with Main Trading Partners

1955–1975

UNITED KINGDOM (in million pounds)

	Argentina		Australia		Canada		France		Germany		India		Netherlands		New Zealand		Russia		U.S.A.	
1955	I	E	I	E	I	E	I	E	I	E	I	E	I	E	I	E	I	E	I	E
1955	87	24	264	284	344	141	137	72	91	77	159	130	133	106	180	139	63	23	420	183
1956	92	17	236	240	348	178	112	89	110	92	141	168	137	119	197	127	55	26	408	243
1957	108	33	248	236	320	195	110	88	125	105	158	176	132	118	183	140	71	37	483	244
1958	104	33	199	235	309	188	101	72	136	123	139	161	159	98	161	128	60	24	352	273
1959	106	40	223	223	312	208	104	77	144	142	143	171	160	113	183	98	63	27	371	361
1960	98	42	197	260	375	215	132	88	182	163	149	151	180	116	183	121	75	37	566	326
1961	75	51	174	201	349	222	143	112	194	171	145	152	173	138	160	124	85	43	484	280
1962	93	47	185	228	349	188	131	138	194	199	136	117	197	151	169	107	84	42	476	327
1963	89	25	206	236	369	173	154	181	208	213	141	137	209	168	173	115	91	55	498	340
1964	78	28	250	256	452	187	184	185	266	219	141	127	235	192	208	117	90	38	639	356
1965	71	27	219	281	458	201	191	177	265	255	128	114	271	193	208	125	119	47	672	498
1966	71	23	208	255	425	215	212	197	302	253	119	95	291	196	187	126	125	50	723	625
1967	72	25	174	254	456	213	255	204	339	247	126	82	329	194	186	99	123	63	812	615
1968	52	34	211	317	513	259	312	235	436	323	135	72	393	242	197	103	158	103	1,064	879
1969	79	47	236	315	507	299	325	290	467	362	107	61	408	278	216	120	196	96	1,133	866
		47[79]		323[79]		311[79]		313[79]		419[79]		67[79]		298[79]		122[79]		96[79]		912[79]
1970	66	44	260	346	682	288	368	339	549	505	105	73	459	377	203	129	211	102	1,174	945
1971	57	54	277	365	637	349	445	394	647	535	111	138	508	405	228	146	200	89	1,095	1,096
1972	77	51	283	318	605	380	604	512	841	591	112	141	614	451	252	147	219	90	1,180	1,220
1973	106	42	341	404	735	414	979	679	1,351	790	148	133	911	604	276	167	327	97	1,622	1,525
1974	99	49	312	599	984	488	1,349	914	1,902	1,026	203	127	1,637	983	248	256	396	110	2,265	1,777
1975	54	68	280	632	856	539	1,628	1,165	1,999	1,304	237	165	1,873	1,115	268	254	408	210	2,352	1,789

F2 External Trade (by value) with Main Trading Partners

1920–1944

YUGOSLAVIA (in million dinars)

	Austria		Czechoslovakia		Germany		Italy		Russia		U.K.		U.S.A.	
	I	E	I	E	I	E	I	E	I	E	I	E	I	E
1920	714	563	322	68	50	99	1,271	358	2	...	244	3	82	5
1921	1,161	882	843	101	174	397	864	633	––	––	246	18	99	5
1922	1,861	848	1,278	299	462	311	1,005	1,126	1	–	459	70	225	17
1923	2,238	2,328	1,538	629	724	339	1,488	2,424	2	––	823	172	306	29
1924	1,626	2,333	1,650	944	682	389	1,688	2,757	8	1	874	132	321	51
1925	1,604	1,652	1,559	834	866	637	1,644	2,249	9	––	713	86	342	77
1926	1,533	1,610	1,427	939	918	724	1,054	1,960	9	6	439	68	309	50
1927	1,424	1,449	1,399	727	899	679	940	1,590	2	11	511	84	255	48
1928	1,355	1,154	1,402	580	1,067	779	939	1,680	3	4	447	102	385	60
1929	1,324	1,238	1,329	426	1,188	675	823	1,971	10	5	426	107	360	126
1930	1,171	1,199	1,225	556	1,221	791	783	1,919	8	–	412	104	285	58
1931	730	727	872	744	925	543	494	1,199	2	–	316	96	200	49
1932	384	676	447	403	506	345	362	705	2	5	213	65	127	29
1933	463	732	349	366	379	471	459	726	4	–	280	90	148	64
1934	442	634	418	437	497	598	555	798	6	2	331	181	230	157
1935	441	577	517	540	598	752	371	672	13	–	373	212	229	225
1936	420	640	626	540	1,088	1,039	102	137	5	–	347	432	260	214
1937	538	848	580	493	1,695	1,361	430	587	6	–	409	465	312	291
1938	342	306	530	398	1,618	1,814	445	324	3	–	431	485	299	256
1939	450	520	314	801	1,818	1,242	557	584	3	3	242	367	248	281
1940	...	...	...	...	...	...	...	...	...	...	...	...	...	...
1941	...	...	...	...	...	...	...	...	...	...	...	...	...	...
1942	...	...	...	...	...	...	...	...	...	...	...	...	...	...
1943	...	...	...	...	...	...	...	...	...	...	...	...	...	...
1944	...	...	...	...	...	...	...	...	...	...	...	...	...	...

F2 External Trade (by value) with Main Trading Partners

1945–1975

YUGOSLAVIA (in million dinars)

	Austria		Czechoslovakia		Germany				Italy		Russia		U.K.		U.S.A.	
	I	E	I	E	I		E		I	E	I	E	I	E	I	E
					East	West	East	West								
1945	...	...	...	...	...	...	...	...	...	...	...	...	...	...	...	...
1946	607	438	1,827	4,324	302	—	17	—	784	920	2,418	7,022	43	168	222	152
1947	1,556	2,498	8,964	9,560	2,099	—	1,383	—	3,988	7,152	11,274	8,514	2,767	1,325	2,020	1,045
1948	4,420	5,595	16,103	13,962	3,938	—	1,576	—	9,229	7,879	10,223	13,640	4,361	6,177	3,217	2,363
1949	7,635	6,741	5,647	2,616	1,179	6,548	204	3,372	9,472	6,207	1,167	2,789	9,326	13,340	9,263	5,049
1950	5,242	4,788	—	—	—	11,909	—	5,960	6,148	5,097	—	—	5,026	8,779	14,591	6,443
1951	4,549	4,959	—	—	—	13,434	—	9,222	9,784	5,951	—	—	9,187	10,155	43,968	8,080
1952	7,696	7,819	—	—	—	22,678	—	17,493	9,407	10,778	—	—	7,624	10,437	21,609	10,843
1953	6,273	3,594	.....	.....	4,089	20,701	.....	9,366	8,470	8,756	—	—	7,382	6,550	40,754	7,801
1954	6,562	5,941	332	866	67	17,172	275	14,204	7,107	10,516	318	439	7,129	6,814	28,446	6,869
1955	5,849	4,525	2,197	2,177	662	16,611	622	10,193	12,892	11,547	4,333	5,385	6,432	6,069	43,250	8,311
1956	5,804	5,179	3,616	2,455	950	14,216	1,308	14,746	12,309	13,712	21,139	12,669	9,787	5,867	38,767	8,223
1957	7,517	5,748	5,685	2,584	2,278	22,640	3,122	15,755	23,640	16,091	20,709	14,675	12,560	7,162	52,121	10,022
1958	7,608	5,661	8,213	5,853	7,881	24,065	7,907	12,529	20,279	16,173	17,345	10,922	10,839	10,366	40,198	9,889
1959	7,898	6,289	6,946	4,918	8,661	28,932	8,000	13,437	19,189	17,316	17,288	14,154	10,637	10,216	42,004	9,344
1960	11,237	8,990	7,874	7,724	11,207	36,973	13,915	15,230	28,545	22,431	17,081	15,803	13,624	12,988	26,549	11,589
1961	9,730	7,680	5,943	5,067	11,286	42,824	9,052	17,366	39,815	21,103	9,601	15,269	13,893	14,347	54,357	10,961
1962	9,619	8,060	7,728	6,404	10,906	29,933	10,601	21,360	31,378	28,902	17,742	12,988	14,573	14,768	54,862	15,669
1963	9,517	8,502	12,916	6,958	14,775	29,400	11,363	24,444	33,887	47,499	21,860	25,612	15,182	13,039	55,833	13,893
1964	10,435	9,222	24,662	13,453	21,805	34,002	18,952	24,124	52,341	39,581	30,034	34,840	20,609	16,576	51,908	15,397
	77	77	77	77	77	77	77	77	77	77	77	77	77	77	77	77
1965	430	355	882	887	789	1,463	951	1,195	1,719	1,803	1,349	2,345	780	453	2,376	776
1966	471	559	1,165	845	1,099	1,934	805	1,423	2,106	2,163	1,822	2,422	1,098	549	2,498	936
1967	881	723	1,420	752	1,033	4,289	946	1,443	3,421	3,376	2,458	3,289	1,367	688	1,860	1,189
1968	1,420	757	1,752	932	1,164	5,450	940	2,061	4,567	3,002	3,200	3,528	1,481	1,032	1,535	1,518
1969	1,733	790	2,038	1,068	1,320	6,605	748	2,752	5,434	3,858	2,859	3,509	2,030	1,444	1,572	1,586
1970	2,580	860	2,576	1,516	1,262	9,642	868	3,358	6,426	4,328	3,285	4,106	3,036	1,644	2,723	1,521
1971	2,594	792	2,603	1,963	1,559	10,486	1,168	3,576	6,737	3,843	4,782	4,558	3,342	1,923	3,343	1,854
1972	2,442	1,008	2,556	2,179	1,704	10,271	1,383	4,485	6,800	5,237	4,811	5,600	2,788	1,818	3,374	2,555
1973	3,572	1,332	3,182	2,152	2,445	14,558	1,391	5,448	9,022	7,926	6,915	6,946	2,801	1,419	3,174	3,953
1974	6,087	1,624	5,035	3,486	2,932	23,126	2,303	6,181	15,141	7,288	12,781	11,422	3,882	1,172	6,023	5,367
1975	5,384	1,273	5,409	4,155	3,798	24,437	3,217	5,368	14,772	6,323	13,712	17,211	4,036	1,070	7,096	4,498

See p. 605 for footnotes

F 2 External Trade (at Current Values) with Main Trading Partners

NOTES

1. SOURCES:— Finland to 1882 (plus trade with Sweden to 1885 and with the U.S.A. to 1891); the French statistics for 1842 (together with statistics of trade with Algeria in 1868 and 1871); the German statistics for 1940–49; the Polish statistics for 1951–54; and the Swedish statistics for 1832–41 were supplied by their respective central statistical offices, or the Direction Nationale des Statistiques de Commerce Exterieur in the case of France. Data for Bulgaria in 1939–46 were kindly supplied by Prof. Kaser's group, and are derived from P. Shapkerev, *Spisanie na Bulgarskoto ikonomichksko Dryzhestvo* 9–19 (1946). All other statistics are taken from the official publications noted on page xv. with gaps filled from the League of Nations, *International Trade Statistics,* and the United Nations, *Yearbook of International Trade.*

2. In this table no attention is drawn to the changes of boundary in the trading partners of each country shown. (see page ix).

3. Except as indicated in footnotes, statistics are of merchandise trade only, and are of 'special' rather than 'general' trade — i.e. imports for home consumption, and exports of home origin plus re-exports of commodities originally entered for home consumption.

4. Except as indicated in footnotes, statistics are of countries of first or last consignment.

FOOTNOTES

[1] Including Finland to 1913.
[2] Subsequently West Germany only.
[3] Subsequent statistics are of countries of origin or consumption.
[4] From 1 May 1922 to 31 August 1940 and since 1 May 1945 the statistics are for the Belgium—Luxembourg customs area. Gold movements are included.
[5] May—December only.
[6] Subsequently excludes Burma.
[7] Gold movements are included to 1930. The statistics for 1946 are for the first 9 months only and are in the pre-war currency.
[8] Including Austria.
[9] For 1924–32 the statistics relate to European Russia only.
[10] Eire is included with the U.K. to 1931.
[11] Strictly speaking, the statistics up to 1937 (1st line) are not of 'special' trade, but of 'general' imports less re-exports (at import value), and 'general' exports less re-exports (at export value).
[12] Including Austria from July 1938 to May 1945, and the Protectorate of Bohemia, Moravia, and Silesia in 1942–44.
[13] Subsequently 'general' trade, and countries of origin or consumption.
[14] Statistics of Finnish trade with Russia are available back to 1812 as follows (in million marks):—

	Imports	Exports		Imports	Exports		Imports	Exports
1812	0.4	0.4	1817	2.9	0.7	1822	2.2	1.4
1813	2.8	0.4	1818	3.1	0.9	1823	1.7	1.5
1814	2.4	0.4	1819	3.6	0.9	1824	2.3	1.9
1815	1.4	0.4	1820	1.5	1.1	1825	3.3	1.9
1816	2.1	0.5	1821	1.4	1.3	1826	3.2	2.0

[15] Figures to 1891 relate to the American continent, not the U.S.A.
[16] Eire is included with the U.K. to 1933.
[17] Figures to 1855 (1st line) are in officially fixed values.
[18] Subsequently Belgium—Luxembourg.
[19] Previously including Cyprus, Gibraltar, and Malta.
[20] From 1948 to July 1959 Saarland is included as part of France.
[21] Previously including Norway.
[22] The Hanse towns were treated as foreign in 1888, and the free port areas to March 1906. From this last date statistics relate to countries of origin or consumption (and consignment only if this is unknown).
[23] Previously including Algeria and Tunisia.
[24] Previously including Finland.
[25] Porto Rico is included from 1904, and the Panama Canal Zone from 1906, to 1913.
[26] Figures for 1923 are in post-inflation values.
[27] Eire is included with the U.K. to 1924.
[28] Eithiopia and Libya are included in 1937–39.
[29] Austria was part of Germany in 1938–9.
[30] Subsequently including the Baltic States.

[31] Saarland was incorporated in West Germany from 6 July 1959. Whilst it had been part of the French customs area from 1948, trade between West Germany and Saarland is not here included with trade with France.
[32] Trade was expressed in rubels to 1959, but the statistics have been converted on the basis of 1 rubel = 1.0502 valuta marks to 1957 and 4.6671 valuta marks for 1958–9.
[33] Including West Berlin.
[34] Excluding the value of currants.
[35] The figures for 1947 are in thousands of U.S. dollars.
[36] The original statistics were given in gold crowns up to 1924, were converted into paper crowns by the Hungarian statistical office retrospectively, and are here converted further into pengos.
[37] Imports are valued f.o.b. from 1955.
[38] Venetia is included as part of Italy from 1867.
[39] Algeria is included with France for 1871–77.
[40] Gibraltar and Malta are included with the U.K. to 1877, and British Asian possessions are included for 1871–77.
[41] Transit trade is included in 1877 and probably earlier. It is excluded subsequently, but there are alterations in definition affecting the composition of 'special' trade in 1897, 1907, and 1930.
[42] Canada is included with the U.S.A. for 1880–96.
[43] Austria is included with Germany for 1938–45.
[44] Statistics relate to trade with the Zollverein to 1858, but with Prussia only from 1859 to 1879 (1st line)
[45] Including Newfoundland throughout.
[46] U.K. up to 1906 and from 1932 onwards; Great Britain for 1907–31.
[47] Direct in-transit trade for Sweden is included in both imports and exports to 1906, and exports of transit goods from Sweden are included in other countries.
[48] For 1909–34 countries of purchase or sale.
[49] Statistics are of 'general' trade to 1938 and from 1959 onwards.
[50] Subsequently including the Faroë Islands and Greenland.
[51] Subsequently including Hawaii.
[52] Countries of origin or consumption.
[53] Gold movements are included up to 1927. In the case of Switzerland, gold other than for banking purposes continued to be included until 1935 (for exports) and 1943 (for imports).
[54] Subsequently 'general' trade, with both imports and exports valued f.o.b.
[55] Exclusive of the value of coal sent under special agreement.
[56] Figures to 1910 are by countries of origin and first destination (and consignment only if these are unknown). For 1911–37 they are by countries of purchase or sale. From 1938 they are by countries or origin or consumption, though there is apparently no break between 1937 and 1938. The Azores and Madeira are included as part of Portugal. The statistics for 1917 and 1918, supplied by the National Institute of Statistics, include re-exports, as do those for the colonies for 1940–46.
[57] Gold movements are included to 1883.
[58] Figures to 1890 (1st line) are for trade over the European frontier only. Statistics to 1840 are in paper rubels, and from 1847 to 1913 in silver or gold rubels. All figures for the Soviet period are in millions of new (1961) rubels.
[59] The figures for 1922 are for the 9 months to 30 September. Figures for 1923–28 are for years ended 30 September. Statistics for the last quarter of 1928 have been omitted.
[60] Including Ceuta and Melilla and the Canary Islands from 1951. Prior to 1888 transit trade cannot be excluded. Gold movements are included.
[61] Figures to 1853 exclude tobacco.
[62] Values to 1959 are in gold pesetas, which in terms of the official exchange rate of that year were equal to about 20 paper pesetas.
[63] A revaluation of exports in 1894 revealed overestimation previously.
[64] Exports to Norway are incomplete for 1898–1901.
[65] Austria is included with Germany for 1938–44.
[66] Iceland is included with Denmark to 1947 (1st line).
[67] The Faroe Islands are included with Denmark to 1954 (1st line).
[68] Re-exports (though not direct transit trade) are subsequently included in both imports and exports.
[69] Statistics of exports to the U.S.A. are available back to 1805 as follows (in million pounds):—

1805	11.0	1811	1.8	1817	6.9	1822	6.9
1806	12.4	1812	...	1818	9.5	1823	5.5
1807	11.8	1813	...	1819	4.9	1824	6.1
1808	5.2	1814	- -	1820	3.9	1825	7.0
1809	7.3	1815	13.3	1821	6.2	1826	4.7
1810	10.9	1816	9.6				

[70] Ceylon is included with India to 1839.
[71] Previously all British possessions in the Pacific.
[72] Previously countries of purchase or sale.
[73] Southern Ireland is treated as foreign from 1 April 1923.
[74] Burma is included with India to 1938 (1st line).
[75] The Baltic states are included with Russia from 1938 (2nd line)
[76] Subsequently excluding Pakistan.
[77] Subsequent figures are in million new dinars, and there was also a change in the system of valuation.
[78] Subsequently countries of origin or destination instead of by the domicile of the contractor.
[79] Subsequently including re-exports.

G. TRANSPORT AND COMMUNICATIONS

Government has generally been involved more intimately in the provision of means of transport and communication than in agriculture or industry, at any rate until very recently. As a consequence, there is usually more statistical material available from the past than on any subject except external trade. Shipping was a matter of close concern to all major maritime powers. The railways were of obvious military, as well as economic importance, and were under government surveillance, if not control, from the beginning. The same has applied to civil aviation. Postal services were long recognised as a government function, though nowhere organised on modern lines until Hill's example of the penny post in the United Kingdom in 1840. Telegraphs fell naturally into the same niche, where they were not simply an adjunct of the railways, and telephones generally followed. And in Europe, unlike North America, the potential influence of radio led to its direct control by governments, to a consequent desire to find finance from users of radio services, and hence to the almost universal use of licensing systems, which produced a useful statistical by-product. The principal absentees from this list of government influence are inland navigation and road transport, which remain, in market economies at any rate, the fields about which least data are available.

Table G.1, showing the length of railway line in each country, is fairly straightforward, and has the merit of being an almost complete record from the beginning of railway operation. Up to about 1870, there is a great diversity of figures given for many countries in the various secondary sources which provided continent-wide comparisons. Part of this was due to boundary changes, and part to misinformation about opening dates of some stretches of line. Where the source of discrepancies could not be identified, the national statistical offices of the countries concerned have generally been most helpful in supplying definitive statistics. The other two tables on railways do not generally give figures from the very beginning of operation, but some sort of national statistics were compiled from an early date in most countries. Initially these tended to be simple totals of freight and passengers carried, and governments generally seemed to be more interested in financial statistics, though these tend to require careful interpretation. By the later part of the nineteenth century, however, the more sophisticated figures of unit distance carried came increasingly to be collected. In tables G.2 and G.3 both types of measure are shown, as available.

The principle problems in using the shipping statistics in Table G.4 arise from changes in the size of ships covered and from changes in the method of measuring capacity. In most countries, there has been a lower limit of size below which vessels are not included in the register; but this has changed from time to time, and differed between countries. So far as aggregate capacity, especially of mechanically-propelled vessels is concerned, this limit, and the changes in it, have made little impact, though the numbers, particularly of sailing ships, have sometimes fluctuated violently with changes in the limit. These are usually easily apparent and it is hoped that all are indicated in footnotes. Changes in methods of measuring capacity are a more difficult problem. The two basic methods—gross and net, representing the inclusion and exclusion respectively of space which cannot be used for carrying cargo—are readily distinguished, especially in the case of mechanically-propelled vessels. In this table the net measure has been preferred wherever such a series is readily available, which has, however, become increasingly less common since the Second World War. A less easily identifiable change, however, took place in the British measurement system (which has been generally used internationally) in the middle of the nineteenth century. The original system, established in 1773, was based on length and breadth only. In 1836, a new Act changed the system, to cubic capacity, but it was optional. Old ships did not have to be re-measured, and new ones did not have to use the new Act, until a further legal change in 1855. It is not clear, in the British statistics, how much change there was during the period 1836–55. G.S. Graham writes that "....although lengths were somewhat increased after 1836, the same general type of ship continued to be built until the new measurement law came into force in 1855."[1] This implies that most of the change of system was concentrated in 1855, and if this was so, one can only conclude that it had remarkably little effect on the tonnage recorded. Whatever the effect on the British statistics, it is often completely unclear whether the statistics of other countries before 1855 are expressed in terms of the old or the new system of measurement. Probably, since most series were published retrospectively, it is best to assume that it was on the new.

Table G.5 presents a selection of statistics on inland waterway traffic for those countries for which the data are both available and significantly large. It is quite straightforward.

The statistics of motor vehicles in use, shown in table G.6, are reasonably uniform in definition, so far as their main constituents are concerned, though there are a good many minor variations at different times. They are, unfortunately, rather patchy so far as eastern Europe is concerned since the Second World War. The official statistics of these countries, however, contain quite extensive information about both goods and passenger traffic on the state-owned road transport networks. This is not generally available for the market economies.

Postal statistics (and even those of telegrams), which one might perhaps expect to be reasonably uniform and homogeneous, exhibit instead very considerable divergencies between countries and over time. Mail is generally broken down into various categories—letters, postcards, newspapers, samples, packets, official communications, and so forth. Whether or not some of these are excluded from officially published statistics (and especially the summary statistics which have often been the only ones available) has varied much from country to country and from time to time. Another source of variation has been the treatment of international mail, and especially of mail in transit for other countries. It is hoped that all these sources of difference have been noted; but even where known they are a serious adverse influence on direct comparability.

[1] G.S. Graham, "The Ascendancy of the Sailing Ship 1850–85", *Economic History Review* (1956).

G 1 LENGTH OF RAILWAY LINE OPEN (in kilometres)

1825–1869

	Austria-Hungary	Belgium	Denmark	Finland[2]	France	Germany	Greece	Ireland	Italy
1825	–	–	–	–	–	–	–	–	–
1826	–	–	–	–	–	–	–	–	–
1827	–	–	–	–	–	–	–	–	–
1828	–	–	–	–	17	–	–	–	–
1829	–	–	–	–	17	–	–	–	–
1830	–	–	–	–	31	–	–	–	–
1831	–	–	–	–	31	–	–	...	–
1832	–	–	–	–	52	–	–	...	–
1833	–	–	–	–	73	–	–	...	–
1834	–	–	–	–	141	–	–	...	–
1835	–	20	–	–	141	6	–	...	–
1836	–	44	–	–	141	6	–	...	–
1837	14	142	–	–	159	21	–	...	–
1838	32	258	–	–	159	140	–	...	–
1839	144	312	–	–	224	240	–	...	8
1840	144	334	–	–	410	469	–	21	20
1841	351	379	–	–	548	683	–	...	20
1842	378	439	–	–	645	931	–	...	49
1843	378	558	–	–	743	1,311	–	...	82
1844	473	577	–	–	822	1,752	–	...	133
1845	728	577	–	–	875	2,143	–	...	152
1846	900	594	–	–	1,049	3,281	–	...	259
1847	1,048	691	30	–	1,511	4,306	–	...	286
1848	1,071	780	30	–	2,004	4,989	–	585	379
1849	1.250	796	30	–	2,467	5,443	–	795	564
1850	1,357	854	30	–	2,915	5,856	–	865	620
1851	1,392	870	30	–	3,248	6,143	–	1,005	702
1852	1,392	901	30	–	3,654	6,605	–	1,140	705
1853	1,392	948	30	–	3,954	7,147	–	1,343	808
1854	1,433	1,072	30	–	4,315	7,571	–	1,444	1,081
1855	1,588	1,333	30	–	5,037	7,826	–	1,589	1,207
1856	1,790	1,417[1] / 1,442	109	–	5,852	8,617	–	1,702	1,360
1857	1,982	1,511	109	–	6,868	8,991	–	1,725	1,580
1858	2,401	1,692	109	–	8,094	9,650	–	1,913	1,777
1859	2,641	1,714	109	–	8,840[3]	10,593	–	2,037	2,236[3]
1860	2,927	1,729	109	–	9,167	11,089	–	2,195	2,404
1861	3,181	1,824	109	107	9,626	11,497	–	2,291	2,773
1862	3,351	1,906	168	107	10,522	12,048	–	2,573	3,109
1863	3,516	2,012	228	110	11,533	12,651	–	2,803	3,725
1864	3,554	2,094	307	110	12,362	13,114	–	2,889	4,162
1865	3,698	2,285	419	111	13,227	13,900	–	2,960	4,591
1866	3,965	2,511	478	111	13,915	14,787	...	3,074	5,258
1867	4,145	2,598	478	111	15,000	15,679	...	3,105	5,559
1868	4,533	2,730	592	111	15,835	16,316	...	...	5,933
1869	5,273	2,816	680	170	16,465[7]	17,215	9	...	6,124

Abbreviations used where space demands: Czech: Czechoslovakia; Neth'l: Netherlands; Switz: Switzerland; U.K.: United Kingdom

See p. 616 for footnotes

G 1 Length of Railway Line Open (in kilometres)

1825–1869

	Netherlands	Norway	Portugal[4]	Russia[16]	Spain	Sweden	Switzerland	U.K.: Great Britain
1825	–	–	–	–	–	–	–	43
1826	–	–	–	–	–	–	–	61
1827	–	–	–	–	–	–	–	66
1828	–	–	–	–	–	–	–	72
1829	–	–	–	–	–	–	–	82
1830	–	–	–	–	–	–	–	157[5]
1831	–	–	–	–	–	–	–	225
1832	–	–	–	–	–	–	–	267
1833	–	–	–	–	–	–	–	335
1834	–	–	–	–	–	–	–	480
1835	–	–	–	–	–	–	–	544
1836	–	–	–	–	–	–	–	649
1837	–	–	–	–	–	–	–	870
1838	–	–	–	27	–	–	–	1,196
1839	17	–	–	...	–	–	–	1,562[5]
1840	17	–	–	...	–	–	–	2,390[22]
1841	17	–	–	...	–	–	–	2,858
1842	17	–	–	...	–	–	–	3,122
1843	98	–	–	...	–	–	–	3,291
1844	109	–	–	...	–	–	–	3,600
1845	153	–	–	144	–	–	–	3,931[6]
1846	153	–	–	278	–	–	–	4,889[6]
1847	176	–	–	368	–	–	25	6,352[6]
1848	176	–	–	382	28	–	25	8,022
1849	176	–	–	...	28	–	25	8,918
1850	176	–	–	501	28	–	25	9,797
1851	176	–	–	1,004	77	–	25	10,090
1852	176	–	–	...	112	–	25	10,673
1853	204	–	–	1,049	214	–	25	10,958
1854	204	68	36	...	290	–	39	11,525
1855	311	68	36	...	443	–	210	11,744
1856	335	68	36	...	533	66	346	12,318
1857	335	68	36	1,170	612	209	519	12,919
1858	335	68	36	...	823	326	704	13,452
1859	335	68	36	1,336	1,088	447	937	14,069
1860	335	68	67	1,626	1,649	527	1,053	14,603
1861	...	68	67	2,238	2,362	571	...	15,210
1862	...	185	204	3,516	2,728	908	1,156	16,027
1863	...	185	455	3,521	3,568	1,014	...	17,038
1864	645	234	694	3,616	4,022	1,143	...	17,704
1865	776	270	694	3,842	4,761	1,305	1,322	18,439
1866	...	313	694	4,573	5,081	1,567	1,322	19,234
1867	...	313	694	5,038	5,123	1,687	1,322	19,837
1868	...	359	694	6,786	5,240	1,687	1,354	...
1869	...	359	694	8,166	5,250	1,727	...	...

See p. 616 for footnotes

G 1 Length of Railway Line Open (in kilometres)

1870–1919

	Austria-Hungary	Belgium	Bulgaria	Czech	Denmark	Finland[2]	France	Germany	Greece	Ireland	Italy
1870	6,112	2,897	224	...	770	483	15,544	18,876[7]	12	...	6,429
1871	7,350	3,119	224	...	882	489	15,632	21,471	12	3,201	6,710
1872	8,508	3,224	224	...	905	489	17,438	22,426	12	3,367	7,044
1873	9,344	3,333	224	...	905	492	18,139	23,890	12	3,383	7,223
1874	9,668	3,432	224	...	1,121	492	18,744	25,487	12	3,425	7,707
1875	10,331	3,499	244	...	1,252	638	19,357	27,970	12	3,459	8,018
1876	10,775	3,589	224	...	1,367	852	20,034	29,305	12	3,473	8,422
1877	11,250	3,644	244	...	1,445	852	20,534	30,718	12	3,547	8,664
1878	11,297	3,741	224	...	1,445	852	21,435	31,471	12	3,638	8,755
1879	11,374	4,012	224	...	1,561	852	22,249	33,250	12	3,679	8,898
1880	11,429	4,112	224	...	1,584	852	23,089	33,838	12	3,816	9,290
1881	11,707	4,182	224	...	1,621	852	24,249	34,381	12	3,931	9,506
1882	11,937	4,294	224	...	1,762	852	25,576	35,081	12	3,969	9,753
1883	12,240	4,319	224	...	1,810	1,158	26,692	35,993	22	4,029	10,149
1884	13,153	4,366	224	...	1,936	1,158	28,722	36,780	70	4,066	10,591
1885	13,329	4,410	224[7]	...	1,936	1,178	29,839	37,571	222	4,146	11,003
1886	13,633	4,420	...	...	1,959	1,520	30,696	38,525	474	4,238	11,823
1887	14,164	4,446	...	...	1,865	1,553	31,446	39,785	540	4,306	12,277
1888	14,810	4,447	693	...	1,965	1,559	32,128	40,827	602	4,401	13,037
1889	15,111	4,470	693	...	1,965	1,842	32,914	41,793	640	4,494	13,537
1890	15,273	4,526	803	...	2,005	1,895	33,280	42,869	697	4,496	13,629
1891	15,583	4,517	803	...	2,033	1,897	33,878	43,424	715	4,610	13,964
1892	15,670	4,525	803	...	2,085	1,974	34,881	44,177	906	4,662	14,487
1893	15,927	4,527	838	...	2,122	2,098	35,350	44,340	916	4,816	15,004
1894	16,299	4,541	838	...	2,185	2,242	35,971	45,462	916	4,902	15,492
1895	16,420	4,572	861	...	2,231	2,391	36,240	46,500	916	5,109	15,970
1896	16,727	4,589	861	...	2,236	2,391	36,472	47,433	949	5,117	16,053
1897	17,315	4,590	985	...	2,465	2,473	36,934	48,449	970	5,101	16,243
1898	18,124	4,534	994	...	2,526	2,516	37,255	49,830	1,003	5,114	16,352
1899	18,780	4,562	1,436	...	2,754	2,649	37,494	50,702	1,018	5,114	16,407
1900	19,229	4,562	1,566	...	2,914	2,650	38,109	51,678	1,033	5,125	16,429
1901	19,531	4,543	1,566	...	2,986	2,653	38,274	52,933	1,033	5,166	16,451
1902	19,939	4,552	1,566	...	3,024	2,746	38,547	53,843	1,117	5,175	16,723
1903	20,369	4,557	1,567	...	3,078	2,962	39,105	54,775	1,132	5,266	16,825
1904	20,621	4,539	1,567	...	3,207	3,046	39,363	55,817	1,335	5,307	16,912
1905	21,002	4,550	1,567	...	3,207	3,046	39,607	56,739	1,351	5,333	17,078
1906	21,594	4,574	1,567	...	3,353	3,053	39,775	57,584	1,372	5,415	17,380
1907	21,701	4,604	1,591	...	3,365	3,056	39,963	58,291	1,372	5,414	17,583
1908	21,921	4,663	1,591	...	3,404	3,140	40,186	59,241	1,427	5,415	17,723
1909	22,377	4,668	1,694	...	3,403	3,252	40,285	60,389	1,548	5,460	17,913
1910	22,642	4,679	1,897	...	3,445	3,356	40,484	61,209	1,573	5,476	18,090
1911	22,749	4,679	1,934[8]	...	3,691	3,421	40,635	61,978	1,573	5,478	18,394
1912	22,879	4,677	2,109	...	3,707	3,421	40,838	62,734	1,584	5,480	18,632
1913	22,981	4,676	2,109	...	3,868	3,560	40,770	63,378[11] 61,159	1,584	5,491	18,873
1914	...	...	2,124	...	3,951	3,683	37,400	61,749	[7]	...	19,125
1915	...	...	2,124	...	3,977	3,685	36,400	62,091	2,303	...	19,652
1916	...	...	2,148	...	4,113	3,793	36,600	62,347	2,328	...	20,046
1917	Austria	...	2,148[7]	...	4,257	3,828	36,700	62,443[11] 64,635	2,346	...	20,198
1918	...	...	2,203	13,077	4,251	3,906	36,400[7]	...[7]	2,373	...	20,262
1919	6,263	4,727	2,203	13,065	4,263[10]	3,984	37,700	57,935	2,383	5,531	20,304

See p. 616 for footnotes

G 1 Length of Railway Line Open (in kilometres)

1870–1919

	Netherlands	Norway[13]	Portugal[4]	Romania[14]	Russia[16]	Serbia	Spain	Sweden	Switzerland	U.K.: G.B.
1870	1,419	359	714	248	10,731	–	5,295	1,727	1,421	...
1871	1,488	414	774	316	13,641	–	5,328[1] 5,328	1,817	1,439	21,558
1872	1,499	493	782	...	14,360	–		1,935	1,470	22,097
1873	1,551	493	795	...	16,206	–	5,331	2,321	1,470	22,513
1874	1,620	493	...	648	18,220	–	5,597	3,361	1,617	23,062
1875	1,620	549	954	921	19,029	–	5,923	3,679	1,962	23,365
1876	1,629	580	977	921	19,623	–	6,129	4,298	2,275	23,695
1877	1,694	811	...	921	21,092	–	6,420	4,837	2,451	23,951
1878	1,781	887[13]	1,078	921	22,371	–	6,655	5,193	2,557	24,273
1879	1,849	1,023	...	921	22,680	–	7,010	5,677	2,571	24,815
1880	1,841	1,057	1,144	921	22,865	–	7,490	5,876	2,571	25,060
1881	1,961	1,115	1,222	951	23,091	–	7,848	6,170	2,618	25,336
1882	2,007	1,327	1,482	1,089	23,429	–	7,908	6,305	2,829	25,751
1883	2,119	1,452	1,485	1,200	24,145	–	8,241	6,400	2,883	26,052
1884	2,247	1,562	1,524	1,271	25,007	253	8,684	6,600	2,890	26,309
1885	2,392	1,562	1,528	1,359	26,024	253	8,933	6,890	2,890	26,720
1886	2,453	1,562	1,529	1,402	27,345	398	9,222	7,277	2,927	26,891
1887	2,547	1,562	1,745	1,896	28,240	540	9,422	7,388	2,961	27,220
1888	2,598	1,562	1,871	2,135	29,428	540	9,583	7,527	3,010	27,501
1889	2,600	1,522	...	2,409	29,933	540	9,774	7,888	3,142	27,619
1890	2,610	1,562	1,932	2,424	30,596	540	10,002	8,018	3,243	27,827
1891	2,623	1,562	1,991	2,429	30,723	540	10,347	8,279	3,323	27,902
1892	2,623	1,562	2,104	2,470	31,202	540	10,874	8,461	3,412	28,067
1893	2,661	1,562	2,134	2,496	32,870	540	11,315	8,782	3,487	28,429
1894	2,661	1,611	2,151	2,513	35,206	540	11,757	9,234	3,544	28,765
1895	2,661	1,726	2,152	2,534	37,058	540	12,364	9,756	3,596	28,986
1896	2,742	1,752	2,156	2,818	39,546	562	12,872	9,896	3,655	29,144
1897	2,742	1,952	2,159	2,880	41,585	562	12,948	10,226	3,724	29,411
1898	2,777	1,952	2,159	2,916	44,622	562	13,032	10,360	3,798	29,762
1899	2,770	1,981	2,159	3,081	49,870	571	13,132	10,708	3,859	29,828
1900	2,771	1,981	2,168	3,100[14]	53,234	571	13,214	11,303	3,867[1] 3,544	30,079
1901	2,819	2,057	2,171	3,149	56,452	593	13,379[1] 13,168	11,574	3,688	30,385
1902	2,851	2,105	2,183	3,177	57,599	593	13,325	11,951	3,767	30,495
1903	2,911	2,303	2,201	3,179	58,362	675	13,425	12,362	3,925	30,860
1904	2,924	2,383	2,280	3,178	59,616	707	13,687	12,543	4,031	31,139
1905	3,031	2,490	2,294	3,179	61,085	707	13,942	12,647	4,086	31,456
1906	3,046	2,548	2,328	3,181	63,623	707	14,155	13,088	4,121	31,722
1907	3,046	2,561	2,374	3,186	65,500	695	14,503	13,248	4,224	31,796
1908	3,070	2,582	2,360	3,187	65,919	692	14,569	13,364	4,311	31,951
1909	3,070	2,847	2,439	3,186	66,345	695	14,655	13,604	4,385	32,026
1910	3,190	2,976	2,448	3,437	66,581	892	14,684	13,829	4,463	32,184
1911	3,190	3,085	2,868	3,479	68,027	949	14,783	13,942	4,534	32,223
1912	3,256	3,085	2,868	3,532	68,954	976[7] 1,598	15,049	14,171	4,640	32,266
1913	3,305	3,085	2,958	3,549	70,156[15][16] 58,500		15,088	14,377	4,832	32,623
1914	3,339	3,165	2,976[4] 3,115	3,588	62,300	...	15,256	14,360	4,876	...
1915	3,400	3,174	3,149	3,702	65,100	...		14,561	4,941	...
1916	3,400	3,177	3,161	3,169	69,300	...	...	14,648	5,037	...
1917	3,400	3,180	3,185	1,330	70,300	...	...	14,760	5,066	...
1918	3,403	3,236	3,207	3,123	71,300	...	...	14,852	5,079	...
1919	3,451	3,250	3,231	4,968	71,400	...	...	14,855	5,078	32,703

See p. 616 for footnotes

G 1 Length of Railway Line Open (in kilometres)

1920–1975

	Austria	Belgium	Bulgaria	Czechoslovakia	Denmark[10]	Finland[2]	France
1920	6,639	4,938	2,205	[9] 13,430	4,328	3,988	38,200
1921	6,639	4,964	2,205	13,448	4,976	3,990	41,800
1922	6,640	4,984	2,256	13,468	4,974	4,091	41,900
1923	6,625	5,018	2,256	13,465	4,969	4,240	42,000
1924	6,625	5,035	2,296	13,456	4,968	4,295	42,000
1925	6,638	5,085	2,296	13,491	5,067	4,524	42,100
1926	6,644	5,101	2,308	13,497	5,073	4,664	42,100
1927	6,677	5,100	2,309	13,533	5,126	4,827	42,200
1928	6,688	5,096	2,380	13,567	5,201	4,936	42,200
1929	6,687	5,099	2,417	13,608	5,243	5,040	42,300
1930	6,710	5,125	2,441	13,610	5,294	5,128	42,400
1931	6,729	5,097	2,992	13,624	5,289	5,136	42,500
1932	6,717	5,134	3,030	13,621	5,291	5,224	42,500
1933	6,716	5,154	3,079	13,624	5,123	5,318	42,600
1934	6,701	5,145	3,143	13,612	5,176	5,455	42,600
1935	6,700	5,145	3,220	13,595	5,177	5,501	42,600
1936	6,702	5,138	3,236	13,595	5,152	5,510	42,600
1937	...	5,134	3,245	13,548	5,061	5,651	42,600
1938	...	5,128	3,352	...	5,000	5,740	42,600
1939	...	5,140	...	...	4,915	5,864	42,500
1940	...	5,038	...	...	4,915	4,596	40,600
1941	...	4,960	...	...	4,858	5,222	39,500
1942	...	4,890	...	...	4,861	5,670	39,800
1943	...	4,888	...	...	4,861	5,686	39,400
1944	...	5,102	...	...	4,861	4,220	39,400
1945	...	5,096	...	... [8]	4,861	4,513	40,500
1946	6,062	5,086	3,732	13,095	4,878	4,607	40,600
1947	...	5,049	...	13,095	4,878	4,713	41,100
1948	6,742	5,041	...	13,095	4,879	4,711	41,300
1949	...	5,050	...	13,124	4,822	4,641	41,300
1950	6,734	5,046	3,967	13,124	4,815	4,726	41,300
1951	6,738	5,046	...	13,132	4,770	4,815	41,200
1952	6,738	5,056	...	13,167	4,772	4,843	41,200
1953	6,703	5,041	...	13,162	4,740	4,880	41,200
1954	6,697	5,034	...	13,141	4,690	4,845	41,000
1955	6,698	4,935	4,091	13,168	4,575	4,918	39,800
1956	6,685	4,910	...	13,168	4,556	5,031	39,800
1957	6,612	4,854	4,108	13,168	4,441	5,100	39,600
1958	6,610	4,829	...	13,124	4,364	5,107	39,500
1959	6,600	4,715	4,146	13,139	4,343	5,284	39,400
1960	6,596	4,632	4,136	13,139	4,301	5,323	39,000
1961	6,586	4,620	4,163	13,139	4,220	5,327	38,700
1962	6,570	4,566	4,125	13,147	4,215	5,357	38,600
1963	6,566	4,544	...	13,165	4,020	5,363	38,500
1964	6,583	4,485	4,160	13,197	3,975	5,398	38,200
1965	6,580	4,485	4,094	13,301	3,901	5,470	37,890
1966	6,569	4,441	4,094	13,330	3,901	5,555	37,810
1967	6,542	4,364	4,158	13,332	3,438	5,619	37,460
1968	6,534	4,336	4,158	13,317	3,475	5,725	37,404
1969	6,510	4,282	4,196	13,315	3,198	5,724	36,742
1970	6,506	4,263	4,196	13,308	2,890	5,841	36,532
1971	6,495	4,165	4,231	13,296	2,890	5,910	35,624
1972	6,478	4,144	4,243	13,299	2,522	5,924	35,180
1973	6,477	4,081	4,245	13,293	2,493	5,936	34,812
1974	6,475	4,048	4,282	13,241	2,493	5,948	34,834
1975	6,468	4,004	4,290	13,215	2,493	5,957	34,787

See p. 616 for footnotes

G 1 Length of Railway Line Open (in kilometres)

1920–1975

	Germany		Greece	Hungary	Ireland	Italy
	[7]					
1920	57,545		2,396	...	5,542	20,385
1921	57,652[7]		2,463	8,141	...	20,556
1922	57,245		2,463	8,566	...	20,760
					Southern Ireland[21]	
1923	57,327		2,463	8,504	...	20,911
1924	57,546		2,463	8,508	...	21,010
1925	57,716		2,681	8,498	...	21,106
1926	57,864		2,681	8,522	...	21,349
1927	57,980		2,681	8,506	...	21,473
1928	58,223		2,679	8,617	...	21,598
1929	58,183		2,679	8,671	...	21,855
1930	58,176		2,678	8,676	4,294	22,119
1931	58,178		2.677	8,676	4,299	22,571
1932	58,208		2,687	8,675	4,297	22,808
1933	58,185		2,687	8,662	4,271	22,892
1934	58,232[7]		2,687	8,659	4,253	23,158
	58,378					
1935	58,841		2,692	8,655	4,113	23,046
1936	58,967		...	8,657	4,083	22,890
1937	59,126		...	8,671	4,041	22,931
1938	59,882[17]		2,976	8,671	4,041	22,955
1939	61,940[17]		...	...	4,041	22,955
1940	...		...	...	4,012	22,992
1941	...		...	...	4,010	23,062
1942	...		...	...	4,010	23,227
1943	...		...	...	4,012	...
1944	...		...	...	4,012	...
						[7]
1945	...		...	...	3,993	18,655
	East	West				
1946	...	...	...	...	3,993	20,637
1947	...	...	...	...	3,927	20,983
1948	...	...	...	...	3,927	21,399
1949	...	36,930	2,531	...	3,927	21,639
1950	12,895	36,924	2,553	8,756	3,927	21,550
1951	...	36,863	2,554	8,812	3,927	21,711
1952	...	36,853	2,546	8,875	3,824	21,743
1953	...	36,853[18]	2,522	8,852	3,779	21,822
1954	15,500	37,136	2,585	8,874[1]	3,642	21,852
		[19]		10,164		
1955	16,134	37,009	2,605	10,298	3,636	21,923
1956	16,094	36,514	2,664	10,285	3,636	21,723
1957	16,121	36,060[20]	2,628	10,280	3,574	21,584
		36,602				
1958	16,093	36,518	2,628	10,297	3,536[22]	21,516
1959	16,150	36,291	2,545	10,276	3,529	21,310
1960	16,174	36,019	2,583	10,307	2,911	21,277
1961	16,160	35,921	2,583	10,290	2,812	21,143
1962	16,159	35,638	2,583	10,336	2,663	20,972
1963	16,114	35,492	2,576	10,218	2,353	21,014
1964	16,108	35,374	2,576	10,274	2,346	20,885
1965	15,930	35,229	2,583	10,069	2,346	20,812
1966	15,730	34,476	2,573	10,075	2,342	20,381
1967	15,513	34,314	2,573	9,941	2,147	20,566
1968	15,237	34,037	2,571	9,692	2,147	20,358
1969	14,909	33,724	2,571	9,579	2,145	20,301
1970	14,658	33,010	2,571	9,514	2,190	20,212
1971	14,525	32,744	2,542	9,394	2,189	20,239
1972	14,384	32,604	2,543	9,289	2,190	20,198
1973	14,317	32,303	2,543	9,193	2,190	20,174
1974	14,252	31,987	2,532	8,989	2,189	20,176
1975	14,298	31,892	2,532	8,740	2,007	20,176

See p. 616 for footnotes

G 1 Length of Railway Line Open (in kilometres)

1920–1975

	Neth'l	Norway[13]	Poland	Portugal[4]	Romania[14]	Russia[16]	Spain	Sweden	Switz	U.K.: G.B.	Yugoslavia
	[12]										
1920	3,606	3,286	13,763[23]	3,268	4,968[7]	71,600	15,886	14,869	5,078	32,707	9,321
1921	3,653	3,286	15,356[7]	3,269	10,585	71,800	...	14,893	5,080	32,691	9,340
1922	3,663	3,445	18,323	3,269	10,578[14]	71,900[27]	...	15,109	5,083	32,717	9,340
1923	3,663	3,456	19,307	3,224	10,925	72,300[27]	...	15,211	5,098	32,743	9,364
1924	3,623	3,456	19,318	3,224	10,925	74,500[27]	...	15,424	5,101	32,767	9,547
1925	3,623	3,589	19,281	3,225	11,001	74,500[27]	...	15,695	5,102	32,849	9,758
1926	3,627	3,603	19,260	3,225	11,109	75,700[27]	...	15,793	5,135	32,857	9,803
1927	3,675	3,627	19,377	3,385	11,086	76,900[27]	...	15,985	5,137	32,839	9,840
1928	3,676	3,835	19,495	3,386	11,060	76,900	...	16,415	5,136	32,846[29] 32,641	10,014
1929	3,677	3,835	19,533	3,407	11,130	76,900	...	16,436	5,136	32,641	9,996
1930	3,677	3,835	19,600	3,407	11,133	77,900	17,063	16,523	5,142	32,632	10,041
1931	3,639	3,835	19,891	3,420	11,120	81,000	...	16,474	5,136	32,638	10,252
1932	3,639	3,873	20,016	3,465	11,213	81,800	...	16,454	5,135	32,604	10,218
1933	3,621	3,873	20,142	3,468	11,206	82,600	...	16,543	5,136	32,580	10,208
1934	3,576	3,873	20,063	3,468	11,213	83,500	...	16,661	5,137	32,553	10,225
1935	3,484	3,964	20,085	3,475	11,194	84,400	...	16,596	5,132[28]	32,450	10,244
1936	3,387	3,998	20,181	3,491	11,216	85,100	...	16,532	5,163	32,400	10,293
1937	3,342	3,998	20,245	3,522	11,259	84,900	...	16,707	5,249	32,334	10,335
1938	3,315	3,988	20,438	3,581	11,310[26] 9,990	85,000	...	16,710	5,240	32,216	10,419
1939	3,314	3,968	...	3,582	...	86,400[16]	...	16,599	5,228	32,176	10,521
1940	3,314	3,968	...	3,586	...	106,100	17,446	16,610	5,221	32,094	...
1941	3,351	4,155	...	3,586	...	...	...	16,581	5,223	32,050	...
1942	3,170	4,155	...	3,586	...	62,900	...	16,583	5,216	32,031	...
1943	3,159	4,175	...	3,586	...	81,700	...	16,567	5,213	32,028	...
1944	...	4,276	...[7]	3,586	...	110,700	...	16,569	5,218	32,012	...[7]
1945	2,824	4,276	[17,938][24]	3,584	...	112,900	...	16,552	5,217	31,984	...
1946	3,079	4,376	23,218	3,584	10,020	114,100	...	16,552	5,222	31,981	9,900
1947	3,251	4,376	24,049	3,584[25] 3,561	...	115,500	...	16,552	4,219	31,968[30]	10,614
1948	3,347	4,471	24,259	3,561	10,677	115,800	...	16,528	5,181	31,540	11,331
1949	3,208	4,471	26,076	3,590	...	116,000	...	16,533	5,171	31,500	11,448
1950	3,204	4,469	26,312	3,590	10,853	116,900	18,098	16,516	5,152	31,336	11,541
1951	3,210	4,469	26,386	3,596	...	117,800	...	16,476	5,152	31,152	11,581
1952	3,210	4,470	26,606	3,597	...	118,600	...	16,459	5,125	31,022	11,548
1953	3,186	4,470	26,762	3,597	...	119,300	...	16,456	5,124	30,935	11,619
1954	3,186	4,454	26,999	3,597	...	120,300	...	16,396	5,119	30,821	11,622
1955	3,178	4,454	26,985	3,597	10,967	120,700	...	16,357	5,106	30,676	11,652
1956	3,220	4,485	27,003	3,597	...	120,700	...	16,177	5,106	30,618	11,735
1957	3,223	4,504	26,974	3,597	10,976	121,200	...	16,093	5,106	30,521	11,760
1958	3,227	4,474	27,040	3,597	10,989	122,800	...	16,019	5,114	30,333	11,787
1959	3,229	4,493	27,017	3,597	10,998	124,400	...	15,790	5,117	29,747[31]	11,882
1960	3,253	4,493	26,904	3,597	10,981	125,800	18,033	15,399	5,117	29,562	11,867
1961	3,250	4,467[13]	26,827	3,597	10,986	126,600	...	14,794	5,118	28,812	11,867
1962	3,251	4,408	26,928	3,597	11,005	127,700	...	14,254	5,112	28,133[31]	11,792
1963	3,245	4,408	26,920	3,597	10,998	128,600	...	14,063	5,112	27,330	11,857
1964	3,238	4,360	26,898	3,597	10,985	129,300	17,782	13,721	5,098	25,735	11,847
1965	3,238	4,348	26,862	3,597	10,979	131,400	17,733	13,433	5,074	24,011	11,839
1966	3,232	4,349	26,739	3,618	11,007	132,500	17,351	13,067	5,071	22,082	11,580
1967	3,227	4,294	26,638	3,617	11,023	133,300	...	12,907	5,059	21,198	11,351
1968	3,148	4,294	26,628	3,617	11,016	133,600	17,425	12,807	5,051	20,031	10,688
1969	3,148	4,294	26,574	3,592	11,006	134,600	...	12,543	5,018	19,170	10,456
1970	3,148	4,292	26,678	3,563	11,012	135,200	...	12,203	5,010	18,969	10,289
1971	3,148	4,292	26,717	3,563	11,012	135,400	...	12,171	5,010	18,738	10,332
1972	2,834	4,256	26,737	3,563	11,023	136,300	...	12,104	5,007	18,417	10,417
1973	2,832	4,257	26,587	3,563	11,019	136,800	...	12,104	4,992	18,227	10,398
1974	2,832	4,257	26,709	3,563	11,086	137,500	...	12,102	4,990	18,168	10,319
1975	2,832	4,257	26,702	3,563	11,039	138,300	...	12,065	4,994	18,118	10,068

See p. 616 for footnotes

G 1 **Length of Railway Line Open** (in kilometres)

NOTES

1. SOURCES:— In addition to the official publications noted on p. xv the following have been used:— Belgium to 1856 (1st line) and Spain to 1871 — G. Stürmer, *Geschichte der Eisenbahnen* (Bromberg, 1872); Belgium 1856 (2nd line) to 1867 — A. Scheler, *Annuaire Statistique et Historique Belge;* Great Britain to 1938 and Ireland to 1913 — B.R. Mitchell & Phyllis Deane, *Abstract of British Historical Statistics* (Cambridge, 1962) where the original sources are given; Hungary to 1889 — *Statistisches Nachrichten über die Eisenbahnender Österreichisch—Ungarischen Monarchie* (1890—1). Russia to 1913 — P.A. Khromov, *Economic Development of Russia in the 19th and 20th Centuries, 1800—1917* (Moscow, 1950). The following data were supplied by their respective national statistical offices:— France to 1841; Greece 1950; Germany 1870—1914; Norway to 1914; Spain 1901 (2nd line) to 1914; and Sweden to 1914.

2. Except where otherwise indicated, the statistics are for the geographical length of line open at the end of each year. Narrow gauge lines are, in general, included, but not rack and similar mountain railways.

3. Statistics up to 1914 are, so far as possible, and except as indicated in footnotes, for 1913 boundaries.

FOOTNOTES

[1] These breaks occur on a change of source.
[2] Subsequently (throughout for Finland) statistics are of average length in use during the year.
[3] 1938.
[4] Sub-Carpathian Russia (Ruthenia) was ceded to the U.S.S.R. in 1945.
[5] Subsequent statistics are at 31 March.
[6] 104km. of Savoy railways were transferred from Italy to France.
[7] These breaks occur as a result of territorial changes: See Introduction.
[8] Saarland, with 146 km, was reincorporated in 1935. In 1957 it was again included in West Germany, having then 542 km.
[9] It is probable that this included railways in some of the territories annexed in 1938-9.
[10] The Hamburg Dock Railway and the Salzgitter line, with 485 km., are included after 1950.
[11] 1921.
[12] Southern Ireland after 1920, though including the lines in the North run by companies based in the South.
[13] The state railways component is subsequently for years ended 31 March following that indicated.
[14] For 1878-1960 at 30 June.
[15] The figures to 1913 are of the average length of line (excluding local lines) open during the year. Subsequent figures are of all lines open at year-end.
[16] For 1900-1922 at 31 March following the year indicated.
[17] The figure for 1938 (2nd line) is for the postwar territory.
[18] The statistics to 1913 (1st line) are for the Russian Empire (exclusive of Finland). From 1913 (2nd line) to 1939 they are for the 1923 territory of the U.S.S.R., and from 1946 onwards for the postwar territory.
[19] By 1913 an additional 1,590 km. had been built, the exact date of construction of which was (and is) unknown.
[20] 1940.
[21] A new method of measurement was used subsequently.
[22] For 1831-39 and 1841-47 Ireland is included.
[23] At 30 June.
[24] Subsequently excluding London Passenger Transport Board lines.
[25] Subsequently state railways only.
[26] 135 km. was transferred to docks authorities in 1959 and 16km was transferred back in 1962. This 16km has here been included in the 1960 figure.

G 2 FREIGHT TRAFFIC ON RAILWAYS (in thousands of metric tons and millions of ton/kilometres)

1834–1869

	Austria/ Hungary[1]	Belgium		Denmark	France		Germany
	a	a	b	a	a	b	b
1834	26	–	...	...	...	...	...
1835	48	–	...	...	...	...	...
1836	67	–	...	...	...	...	...
1837	64	–	...	...	...	...	...
1838	70	4	...	...	...	...	...
1839	82	50	...	...	...	...	...
1840	118	102	...	...	...	...	...
1841	181	166	...	...	1,060[2]	38[2]	...
1842	230	194	...	...	1,480	...	...
1843	301	333	...	...	1,530	...	...
1844	332	560	...	...	1,940	81	...
1845	383	691	...	...	2,310	100	...
1846	592	778	...	...	2,520	119	...
1847	931	1,005	...	...	3,600	...	...
1848	867	939	...	...	2,920	...	...
1849	1,062	1,035	...	...	3,420	...	...
1850	1,442	1,261	...	...	4,270	...	230
1851	1,807	1,271	72	...	4,630[2]	462[2]	360
1852	2,344	1,480	72	...	5,380	...	530
1853	2,608	1,841	85	...	7,170	813	640
1854	3,336	2,345	104	...	8,870	1,143	970
1855	3,447	2,715	111	...	10,650	1,517	1,250
1856	4,046	2,617	115	...	12,870	1,868	1,210
1857	4,085	2,858	102	...	14,970	2,142	1,480
1858	5,183	3,270	148	...	17,670	2,391	1,480
1859	5,619	3,397	153	...	19,950	2,729	1,440
1860	7,174	3,766	160	...	[3] 23,140	[3] 3,120	1,630
1861	8,837	...	...		27,900[2]	3,809[2]	1,970
1862	8,808	...	...	...	27,300	3,884	2,420
1863	8,534	...	...	...	28,890	4,074	2,750
1864	9,632	5,256	...	...	31,120	4,626	3,150
1865	10,525	5,899	...	...	34,020	5,172	3,660
1866	10,854	6,533	...	...	37,370	5,826	3,680
1867	13,340[1] 12,560	6,529	...	203	38,570	5,845	4,380
1868	15,841	6,645	...	237	42,380	6,310	5,040
1869	17,194	7,102	...	272	44,010	6,271	5,330

Abbreviations used throughout this table: a: 000 tons; b: million ton/kilometres
Other abbreviations used where space demands: U.K.: G.B.; United Kingdom: Great Britain

See p. 627 for footnotes

G 2 **Freight Traffic on Railways** (in thousands of metric tons and millions of ton/kilometres)

1834–1869

	Hungary[4]	Ireland	Norway		Russia	Sweden	U.K.: Great Britain
	a	a	a	b	a	a	a
1834	...	...	...	...	...	...	...
1835	...	...	...	...	...	...	...
1836	...	...	...	...	...	...	...
1837	...	...	...	...	...	...	...
1838	...	...	...	...	...	...	...
1839	...	...	...	...	...	...	...
1840	...	...	...	...	...	...	...
1841	...	...	...	...	...	...	...
1842	...	...	...	...	...	...	...
1843	...	...	...	...	...	...	...
1844	...	...	...	...	...	...	...
1845	...	...	...	...	...	...	...
1846	...	...	...	...	...	...	...
1847	...	...	...	...	...	...	...
1848	...	...	...	...	...	...	...
1849	...	...	...	...	...	...	...
1850	...	...	...	...	...	...	...
1851	...	...	...	...	...	...	...
1852	...	...	...	...	...	...	...
1853	...	...	...	...	...	...	...
1854	...	...	...	...	...	...	...
1855	...	...	83	...	...	...	...
1856	...	1,033	117	4	...	...	64,769
1857	...	1,125	139	5	...	...	71,342
1858	...	1,220	142	5	...	...	73,077
1859	...	1,440	154	5	...	...	78,587
1860	...	1,497	144	5	...	...	89,803
1861	...	1,709	174	6	...	...	94,046
1862	...	1,747	196	7	...	...	93,419
1863	...	1,775	...	...	...	...	100,400
1864	...	1,875	...	...	...	...	110,256
1865	...	2,049	...	...	...	285	114,384
1866	...	2,324	...	...	...	332	123,801
1867	...	2,584	274	16	5,188	460	134,683
1868	1,365	...[5]	302	18	7,208	776	...[5]
1869	1,612	...	356	21	...	1,626	...

See p. 627 for footnotes

G 2 Freight Traffic on Railways (in thousands of metric tons and millions of tons/kilometres)

1870–1919

	Austria/Hungary		Belgium		Bulgaria		Czechoslovakia		Denmark		Finland	
	a	b	a	b	a	b	a	b	a	b	a	b
1870	21,037	...	7,614	...	...	...	...	...	326	...	...	...
1871	[25,624][6]	...	10,999	...	...	...	...	...	419	...	...	18
1872	29,410	...	13,077	...	...	...	...	...	480	...	...	24
1873	36,948	...	13,775[7] 28,756	...	...	...	...	...	542	...	...	27
1874	36,009	...	24,658	...	...	...	...	...	626	...	...	32
1875	38,029	3,912	26,622	...	...	...	...	...	698	...	...	39
1876	40,689	4,088	26,325	...	...	...	...	...	867	...	...	46
1877	43,848	4,668	26,622	...	...	...	...	...	871	...	...	51
1878	44,808	4,590	27,672	...	...	...	...	...	815	...	...	44
1879	45,098	4,551	29,646	...	...	...	...	...	795[11]	...	...	41
1880	47,874	4,767	32,770	...	...	...	...	...	976	...	...	49
1881	51,929	5,015	34,077	...	...	...	...	...	1,081	...	...	51
1882	56,037	5,661	36,097	...	...	...	...	...	1,203	...	...	68
1883	62,417	5,942	36,588	...	...	...	...	...	1,230	...	484	59
1884	61,218	5,810	35,153	...	...	...	...	...	1,391	...	516	60
1885	61,556	6,071	33,588	...	...	...	...	...	1,448	...	595	70
1886	62,635	6,128	34,775	...	...	...	...	...	1,425	...	607	68
1887	65,716	6,539	37,064	...	...	...	...	...	1,473	...	631	72
1888	73,540	7,282	40,352	...	...	...	...	...	1,524	...	743	89
1889	79,091	7,618	42,597	...	...	...	...	...	1,738	...	854	97
1890	84,371	8,214	42,990	...	...	...	...	...	1,786	...	948	103
1891	84,557	8,002	42,262	...	...	...	...	...	1,827	...	1,034	119
1892	85,272	7,710	41,158	...	...	...	...	...	1,962	...	957	126
1893	90,904	8,350	43,918	...	...	...	...	...	2,166	128	1,077	145
1894	92,865	8,398	45,521	...	383	...	...	...	2,291	139	1,104	150
1895	93,879	8,516	46,664	...	437	...	...	...	2,436	154	1,219	158
1896	100,000	9,017	49,582	...	707	...	...	...	2,740	173	1,435	179
1897	104,492	9,557	51,814	...	728	...	...	...	3,018	191	1,662	212
1898	110,982	10,451	47,428	...	805	55	...	...	3,555	220	1,889	240
1899	114,512	10,678	52,177	...	725	47	...	...	3,804	236	2,209	285
1900	118,952	11,128	55,108	...	661	50	...	...	4,157	267	2,454	340
1901	120,511	11,158	54,225	...	981	68	...	...	4,318	268	2,308	304
1902	119,576	11,104	56,923	...	856	74	...	...	4,514	273	2,313	317
1903	121,727	11,448	59,297	...	897	89	...	...	5,091	321	2,800	378
1904	125,250	11,694	60,477	...	1,255	129	...	...	5,317	333	2,918	376
1905	134,006	12,314	64,439	...	1,279	121	...	...	5,748	361	2,787	351
1906	144,523	13,347	70,231	...	1,207	123	...	...	6,181	383	3,077	376
1907	152,212	14,710	71,407	...	1,301	149	...	...	6,504	398	3,457	425
1908	155,397	14,982	67,943	...	1,324	140	...	...	6,949	421	3,548	435
1909	152,486	15,217	71,002	...	1,603	188	...	...	6,858	416[7] 462	3,669	443
1910	137,912	15,152	76,176	...	1,671	196	...	...	6,919	465	3,840	462
1911	146,457	16,365	80,818	...	2,292	270	...	...	7,323	492	4,470	558
1912	159,554	17,287	87,249	...	1,987	215	...	...	7,821	533	4,618	586
1913	...	...	88,427	5,729	1,947[8]	176[8]	...	...	8,812	578	4,933	649
1914	...	...	...	...	2,536	...	...	...	9,306	601	4,419	685
1915	...	...	...	...	2,002	...	...	...	9,954	705	5,167	1,279
1916	...	...	...	...	2,834	...	...	...	11,605	932	6,161	1,483
1917	...	...	...	...	3,455	...	...	...	11,530	902	4,904	1,216
1918	...	...	...	...	2,926[9]	...[9]	...	...	10,370	748	1,941	298
1919	...	...	...	...	1,782	...	[59,185][10]	[4,720][10]	11,451	760	4,139	616

See p. 627 for footnotes

G 2 Freight Traffic on Railways (in thousands of metric tons and millions of ton/kilometres)

1870–1919

	France a	France b	Germany a	Germany b	Greece a	Greece b	Hungary a	Hungary b	Ireland a
1870	37,070[1,2]	5,057[1,2]	...	5,300[1,2]	...	...	1,952	...	...
1871	37,840[2]	5,509[2]	...	6,400	...	...	2,996	...	2,961
1872	53,370	7,725	...	8,200	...	...	3,460	...	3,111
1873	57,480	8,251	...	9,900	...	...	4,074	...	3,208
1874	56,680	7,926	...	10,100	...	...	3,705	...	3,171
1875	58,930	8,136	...	10,400	...	...	4,114	...	3,408
1876	61,840	8,326	...	10,800	...	...	4,366	...	3,576
1877	61,600	8,185	...	11,000	...	...	5,382	...	3,732
1878	63,090	8,400	...	11,100	...	...	5,585	...	3,626
1879	68,990	8,999	...	11,900	...	...	6,707	...	3,694
1880	80,770	10,350	...	13,500	...	...	6,475	...	3,654
1881	84,650[2]	10,750[2]	...	14,300	...	...	7,734	...	3,630
1882	88,750	10,840	...	15,600	...	...	8,717	...	3,900
1883	89,060	11,070	...	16,400	...	...	9,391	...	4,078
1884	80,360	10,480	...	16,800	...	...	10,649	...	3,887
1885	75,190	9,791	...	16,600	...	...	10,887	...	3,788
1886	73,380	9,314	...	17,200	...	...	12,112	...	3,703
1887	77,290	9,917	...	18,700	...	...	12,870	...	3,833
1888	82,360	10,410	199,507	20,400	...	...	13,632[4]	2,795	3.835
							22,620		
1889	87,040	11,050	213,814	22,100	131	...	23,970	2,716	4,231
1890	92,510	11,760	217,745	22,500	...	...	25,755	3,136	4,366
1891	96,550[2]	12,290[2]	230,949	23,400	...	...	27,790	3,429	4,482
1892	95,710	12,120	232,811	23,500	232	...	29,685	3,669	4,390
1893	97,020	12,270	...	24,700	242	...	35,014	4,212	4,261
1894	99,110	12,480	...	25,000	...	...	40,758	4,535	4,711
1895	100,800	12,900	260,499	26,600	268	...	31,894	4,395	4,835
1896	104,000	13,220	283,938	28,100	...	...	34,991	4,638	4,789
1897	108,400	13,790	301,179	30,300	...	...	35,724	4,772	5,128
1898	114,400	14,870	320,840	32,700	344	...	38,624	4,942	5,195
1899	120,400[2]	13,720[2]	341,491	35,100	337	...	39,933	5,020	5,292
1900	83,400	16,000	360,165	37,000	333	...	42,577	5,315	5,236
1901	80,400	15,800	352,536	35,400	419	...	43,027	5,381	5,219
1902	81,000	15,700	365,955	36,800	434	30	44,725	5,414	5,359
1903	85,300	16,100	392,205	39,600	523	...	46,424	5,582	5,657
1904	85,500	16,200	408,221	41,200	559	...	52,684	5,669	5,769
1905	91,000	17,400	444,037	44,600	534	...	51,948	6,041	5,808
1906	95,100	18,200	479,227	48,300	538	36	55,778	6,426	5,935
1907	102,000	19,300	514,908	51,300	613	...	61,497	6,935	6,185
1908	103,000	20,000	496,920	49,900	600	40	61,862	7,068	6,101
1909	107,000	20,800	526,213	52,800	601	...	66,896	7,557	6,263
1910	113,000	21,500	575,330	56,400	638	45	68,806	8,095	6,630
1911	121,000	22,700	616,772	62,000	717	49	78,760	8,999	6,724
1912	131,000	24,200	667,707	66,200	659	45	83,629	9,666	6,810
1913	136,000	25,200	676,627	67,700	743	50	87,175	9,914	6,775[5]
1914	88,200	17,800	528,882	...	771	56	...[4]	...[4]	5,686
1915	71,500	16,500	367,600	...	747	58	67,903	...	...
1916	79,700	18,900	415,600	...	789	65	78,163	11,778	...
1917	83,700	20,200	...[1,2]	...	616	54	74,775	10,054	...
1918	64,700	20,100	387,000	...	756	51	74,519	9,911	...
1919	77,000	20,700	287,200	...	766	56	...	...	...

See p. 627 for footnotes

G 2 **Freight Traffic on Railways** (in thousands of metric tons and millions of ton/kilometres)

1870–1919

	Italy		Netherlands		Norway		Poland	Portugal	Romania	
	a	b	a	b	a	b	a	a	a	b[18]
1870	4,757	...	...	...	350	20	...	...	...	...
1871	5,210	...	...	...	344	19	...	...	...	...
1872	6,374	...	...	...	434	24	...	...	...	...
1873	7,360	...	...	...	528	30	...	...	...	...
1874	7,062	...	...	...	587	31	...	...	...	...
1875	7,228	...	...	...	587	33	...	...	...	...
1876	7,151	...	...	...	681	42	...	...	...	...
1877	7,506	...	...	...	686	44	...	...	836	...
1878	7,507	...	2,700	...	[283][16]	[19][16]	...	...	871	...
1879	8,372	...	2,800	...	514	33	...	...	818	...
1880	9,329[13] / 9,832	...	4,000	...	605	38	...	663	792	...
1881	10,344	...	4,400	408	642	43	...	739	970	...
1882	11,005	...	5,000	472	792	57	...	880	1,130	...
1883	12,486	...	5,200	518	851	64	...	...	1,345	...
1884	13,415	...	5,200	523	918	68	...	886	1,153	...
1885	14,009	1,695	5,200	523	943	68	...	955	1,550	...
1886	14,660	1,779	5,100	541	957	68	...	1,050	1,634	...
1887	15,801	1,976	5,800	587	970	67	...	1,102	2,056	...
1888	16,466	1,852	6,400	648	1,023	70	...	1,316	2,255	...
1889	17,202	1,972	6,900	658	1,207	84	...	1,561	2,645	...
1890	17,458	2,038	...	...	1,326	89	...	2,316	3,108	...
1891	17,154	1,394	6,600	735	1,337	89	...	1,977	3,376	...
1892	17,026	1,976	6,600	766	1,337	88	...	1,568	3,342	...
1893	16,858	1,946	7,500	842	1,389	94	...	1,482	4,168	...
1894	17,468	1,983	7,100	791	1,392	93	...	1,564	3,706	...
1895	18,569	2,028	7,800	873	1,434	96	...	1,725	3,501	...
1896	19,321	2,151	8,000	926	1,570	110	...	1,899	4,215	...
1897	20,430	2,296	8,600	976	1,825	125	...	1,954	3,889	...
1898	21,748	2,438	8,300	1,044	2,126	141	...	2,035	4,779	...
1899	23,853[14]	2,624[14]	9,300	1,090	2,236	149	...	2,431	3,612	...
1900	17,996	2,126	9,600	1,051	1,594	111	...	2,706	3,988	...
1901	19,460	2,234	10,300	1,163	2,307	154	...	2,831	4,632[19]	...
1902	21,987	2,440	10,800	1,216	2,190	146	...	3,445	4,731	...
1903	23,688[14]	2,573[14]	10,800	1,219	2,488	158	...	3,752[17] / 3,579	4,998	...
1904	...[15]	...[15]	11,400	1,294	3,579	205	...	3,607	4,209	...
1905	25,703	4,893	11,600	1,281	3,720	209	...	3,776	5,748	...
1906	29,752	5,219	12,500	1,337	4,273	235	...	4,043	6,084	...
1907	32,636	5,621	12,500	1,320	4,361	240	...	4,153	6,780	...
1908	34,142	5,755	12,700	1,346	4,501	257	...	4,315	6,384	...
1909	35,601	6,065	13,100	1,354	6,081	339	...	4,527	6,948	...
1910	37,564	6,185	13,700	1,422	4,889	294	...	4,845	8,244	...
1911	39,101	6,486	15,400	1,851	5,790	336	...	...	9,377	...
1912	40,881	6,819	17,000	1,736	6,490	363	...	...	8,816	...
1913	41,422	7,070	17,500	1,802	7,218	401	...	...	9,043	1,443
1914	37,660	7,144	15,100	1,622	7,724	419	...	5,609	8,129[20] / 9,872	...
1915	38,283	8,874	13,500	1,693	6,761	434	...	5,881	9,286	...
1916	40,535	11,083	14,000	1,712	6,413	502	...	6,551	4,322	...
1917	38,653	10,627	12,100	...	6,757	533	...	5,996	2,368	...
1918	38,994	10,266	12,000	...	5,907	486	...	5,550	1,656	...
1919	39,727	9,795	12,700	...	6,095	450	12,000	4,597	3,548	...

See p. 627 for footnotes

G 2 Freight Traffic on Railways (in thousands of metric tons and millions of ton/kilometres)

1870–1919

	Russia[21]		Serbia	Spain		Sweden		Switzerland		U.K.:G.B.	
	a	b	a	a	b	a	b	a	b	a	b
1870	...	...	...	...	...	2,083	...	...	...	...	...
1871	...	...	...	3,738	...	2,113	...	...	...	169,122	...
1872	14,110	...	...	4,777	...	2,512	...	...	...	179,068	...
1873	18,718	...	...	3,895	...	3,013	...	...	...	190,810	...
1874	22,158	...	...	3,123	...	3,538	...	...	...	188,403	...
1875	25,454	...	...	4,358	...	5,086	...	...	...	199,346	...
1876	26,652	...	...	5,335	...	4,691	...	...	...	205,694	...
1877	...	...	...	6,548	...	4,749	...	...	...	211,650	...
1878	...	...	...	6,097	...	4,971	...	...	...	206,427	...
1879	...	...	...	5,824	...	4,548	...	...	...	211,899	...
1880	...	...	...	8,088	...	5,889	...	5,808	...	235,427	...
1881	...	...	...	...	...	6,667	...	5,674	...	245,291	...
1882	45,137	...	...	...	...	7,349	...	6,357	...	256,428	...
1883	49,908	...	...	...	...	7,551	...	7,080	...	266,579	...
1884	42,409	...	...	9,499	...	7,528	...	7,333	...	259,602	...
1885	42,858	...	...	9,221	...	7,635	...	7,477	...	257,630	...
1886	42,428	...	...	9,860	...	7,443	...	7,581	...	255,008	...
1887	50,100	...	...	9,808	...	7,591	...	8,316	...	269,410	...
1888	65,219	...	...	9,860	...	8,487	...	8,857	...	282,435	...
1889	75,143	...	...	...	...	9,892	...	9,387	...	298,049	...
1890	68,493	...	279	...	...	10,608	...	9,368	...	303,617	...
1891	70,631	...	330	...	...	11,226	...	9,651	...	310,823	...
1892	73,506	...	318	...	...	11,301	...	9,466	...	310,204	...
1893	79,425	...	388	...	...	12,009	...	10,291	...	292,771	...
1894	88,852	...	310	...	...	13,090	...	10,557	...	324,953	...
1895	91,587	...	342	...	...	14,838	...	11,107	...	334,759	...
1896	100,708	...	395	...	...	16,653	...	12,186	...	357,400	...
1897	111,754	27.6	356	...	...	18,510	...	13,015	...	375,270	...
1898	120,059[21]	30.0[21]	449	...	...	19,209	1,261	13,632	...	379,444	...
	122,825	30.9									
1899	...	33.3	456	...	...	19,601	1,333	14,341	...	414,969	...
	m tons										
1900	154	38.9	514	...	...	21,643	1,450	14,456	...	426,514	...
1901	155	39.2	526	...	...	21,465	1,460	13,819	...	417,409	...
1902	161	40.3	509	...	...	22,336	1,474	12,407	...	438,972	...
1903	179	44.8	558	...	...	25,651	1,847	12,223	...	445,161	...
1904	181	47.7	614	...	...	27,624	1,989	12,771	...	451,287	...
1905	169	45.4	677	...	...	29,058	2,063	13,926	...	462,730	...
1906	191	49.3	754	...	...	31,961	2,237	15,455	1,077	490,700	...
1907	204	54.2	...	24,567	...	33,738	2,365	17,342	1,211	517,981	...
1908	209	53.5	...	26,116	...	33,087	2,343	16,784	1,151	494,398	...
1909	225	58.1	...	25,593	...	31,134	2,167	16,124	1,180	501,669	...
1910	235	65.8	...	27,547	...	36,991	2,663	17,279	1,249	516,053	...
1911	...	...	...	29,090	...	38,053[22]	2,797[22]	18,152	1,366	525,256	...
						35,000	2,628				
1912	...	...	...	31,818	...	38,500	2,913	19,565	1,437	521,818	...
1913	[21]	76.8[21]	...	31,526	3,179	41,000	3,184	19,301	1,458	570,544[9]	...
	132	65.7								370,272	
1914	123	62.9	...	28,968	2,954	39,500	3,132	17,068	1,391	...	...
1915	126	75.6	...	30,706	3,301	47,500	4,422	19,313	1,551	...	...
1916	147	91.2	...	35,118	3,808	53,400	5,538	21,376	1,661	...	...
1917	115	63.0	...	35,512	3,781	48,700	4,584	20,319	1,360	...	...
1918	37	14.1	...	35,245	3,852	44,100	3,992	19,299	1,173	...	...
1919	31	17.5	...	35,149	3,736	38,100	3,123	19,298	1,388	309,753	...

See p. 627 for footnotes

G 2 Freight Traffic on Railways (in thousands of metric tons and millions of ton/kilometres)

1920–1975

	Austria[23]		Belgium		Bulgaria		Czechoslovakia		Denmark		Finland	
	a	b	a	b	a	b	a	b	a	b	a	b
1920	...	...	70,418	...	2,423	478	78,833	6,240	12,437	885	5,405	932
1921	...	...	66,948	...	2,907	535	81,415	6,636	11,948	849	5,163	835
1922	27,360	...	78,316	5,044	3,345	601	74,743	7,072	9,809	649	6,884	1,135
1923	...	...	88,016	5,888	3,541	635	76,984	7,735	10,263	650	8,276	1,351
1924	22,746	...	97,874	7,011	4,091	706	89,964	9,808	10,741	681	8,171	1,337
1925	25,283	3,751	96,770	7,037	3,607	672	89,528	9,874	11,462	715	8,905	1,442
1926	...	3,940	109,406	8,272	3,794	660	88,906	10,249	10,107	647	10,068	1,630
1927	27,807	4,257	104,171	7,810	3,988	702	95,117	11,191	9,380	633	11,143	1,768
1928	29,119	4,240	109,634	7,808	4,374	741	104,259	11,980	9,672	647	11,479	1,837
1929	30,720	4,444	118,969	8,386	4,763	880	108,714	12,381	9,612	667	10,707	1,804
1930	27,223	3,813	105,344	7,133	4,612	853	94,300	10,476	10,244	723	9,574	1,592
1931	23,610	3,154	94,045	6,027	4,467	852	81,500	9,228	9,532	696	8,522	1,444
1932	19,209	2,584	76,207	4,534	4,301	813	62,639	7,218	8,487	647	8,761	1,481
1933	18,510	2,556	74,872	4,440	4,235[9]	809[9]	55,697	6,501	6,681	540	10,491	1,674
1934	22,026	2,743	75,452	4,483	[3,051]	[591]	60,768	7,141	7,301	579	12,554[7]	1,966[7]
1935	22,952	2,844	76,862	4,757	4,366	835	65,287	7,886	7,129	596	13,718	2,020
1936	22,256	2,877	85,112	5,331	4,620	875	68,500	8,563	6,989	603	15,174	2,239
1937	...	4,151	96,430	6,230	5,183	984	72,501	10,871	7,279	647	17,577	2,639
1938	...	...	82,513	5,144	5,741	1,078	...	9,308	7,225	651	15,329	2,305
1939	...	...	84,705	5,556	5,987	1,191	...	...	7,095	673	13,860	2,197
1940	...	...	40,222	3,332	7,000	1,489	...	...	8,216	853	10,443	2,173
1941	...	...	45,787	3,632	...	...	...	...	...	...	11,842	...
1942	...	...	40,501	3,168	...	...	...	...	...	...	13,331	...
1943	...	...	39,690	3,060	...	...	...	...	...	...	14,591	...
1944	...	...	15,561	1,096	...	...	...	...	20,234	1,969	11,558	...
1945	...	...	26,159	2,049	...	...	...	...	18,179	1,671	13,223	2,492
1946	...	...	51,958	4,695	...	...	57,448	9,268	15,094	1,363	16,157	3,221
1947	...	12,619	61,073	5,868	...	1,262	64,420	11,405	12,966	1,294	17,317	3,499
1948	27,410	17,341	63,964	6,153	9,766	1,717	74,432	14,279	12,142	1,383	17,125	3,495
1949	34,512	18,822	60,218	5,666	...	...	82,060	16,416	10,757	1,320	15,386	3,041
1950	35,929	18,820	60,844	5,462	14,000	2,580	96,013	18,634	9,296	1,228	16,828	3,465
1951	39,120	19,238	72,201	6,628	...	2,939	107,934	21,475	9,610	1,310	20,553	4,445
1952	37,372	19,261	66,576	6,067	17,873	3,140	118,888	24,404	10,151	1,446	17,955	3,960
1953	36,437	18,969	62,544	5,721	...	3,682	123,381	26,328	8,475	1,283	16,343	3,692
1954	41,275	20,843	61,919	5,635	...	3,840	128,136	28,457	7,994	1,249	18,911	4,118
1955	44,528	23,286	69,591	6,618	23,700	4,118	140,222	31,702	7,923	1,294	20,080	4,500
1956	45,717	24,103	70,565	6,922	25,509	4,484	149,020	34,279	7,796	1,298	18,830	4,437
1957	46,906	24,818	66,769	6,586	27,641	4,928	159,857	39,541	8,383	1,350	18,639	4,349
1958	41,955	23,972	57,806	5,830	...	5,243	174,353	42,674	8,170	1,325	16,875	4,076
1959	41,444	24,345	58,476	6,062	35,100	6,289	180,510	44,101	8,732	1,420	17,695	4,211
1960	45,388	26,685	60,835	6,303	38,400	6,981	194,077	47,407	8,392	1,417	19,828	4,873
1961	43,490	26,931	61,383	6,455	40,500	7,447	205,695	50,674	8,439	1,436	19,658	4,727
1962	43,902	27,908	62,273	6,467	40,400	7,876	206,872	52,224	8,439	1,494	19,289	4,917
1963	45,863	28,875	65,327	6,825	43,500	8,573	201,955	51,662	8,844	1,610	18,902	4,936
1964	45,267	29,081	66,594	6,925	51,500	9,969	213,946	55,391	8,679	1,498	19,991	4,871
1965	44,862	29,215	63,879	6,758	56,000	10,784	218,527	56,904	8,960	1,532	21,561	5,192
1966	44,736	29,836	59,313	6,234	60,700	11,449	224,069	57,652	8,279	1,488	21,865	5,619
1967	42,770	29,806	59,431	6,082	63,100	11,719	226,123	55,781	8,100	1,480	22,569	5,603
1968	43,323	29,431	63,274	6,675	62,800	12,198	227,341	56,710	7,772	1,453	22,324	5,633
1969	45,903	30,906	69,226	7,416	62,700	12,618	225,616	56,760	7,733	1,490	23,374	6,032
1970	49,988	33,181	71,171	7,816	68,183	13,858	236,876	60,995	8,499	1,729	24,839	6,279
1971	48,863	33,752	66,418	7,328	70,218	14,918	249,603	63,464	8,873	1,875	23,537	5,764
1972	49,528	34,419	69,333	7,490	72,946	15,825	259,516	65,512	8,673	1,907	25,197	6,514
1973	51,517	35,138	75,524	8,183	75,683	16,640	260,569	64,943	8,968	2,034	27,549	7,018
1974	54,081	36,883	82,092	9,146	78,013	17,309	266,400	67,951	9,634	2,227	28,259	7,493
1975	46,358	33,988	59,201	6,757	78,793	17,285	271,413	69,271	8,787	1,997	23,408	6,443

See p. 627 for footnotes

G 2 Freight Traffic on Railways (in thousands of metric tons and millions of ton/kilometres)

1920–1975

	France		Germany		East Germany		Greece		Hungary		Ireland	
	a	b	a	b	a	b	a	b	a	b	a	b
1920	103,000[12]	25,900[12]	[24] 337,200	...	...	...	739[32]	57[32]	[4] ...	[4] ...	...	...
1921	137,000	26,000	354,000[25]	...	...	...	1,128	...	19,634	1,594	...	...
1922	157,000	28,600	470,200	68,734	...	...	1,031	...	26,109	2,288	...	...
1923	174,000	33,300	[289,500][26]	42,700	...	...	1,157	77	34,099	2,906	...[33]	...
1924	199,000	37,200	[342,600][26]	47,900	...	...	1,622	115	37,689	3,155	...	...
1925	195,000	37,100	442,500	60,200	...	...	1,754	153	35,361	3,029	...	...
1926	208,000	40,400	472,300	65,400	...	...	1,837	157	33,488	2,909	3,067	...
1927	194,000	36,600	529,100	73,300	...	...	1,737	150	39,107	3,399	3,600	...
1928	208,000	39,200	522,400[27] 525,500	73,900	...	...	1,701	150	40,577	3,420	3,551	...
1929	223,000	41,800	531,400	77,100	...	...	2,046	182	40,700	3,445	3,582	...
1930	224,000	40,900	438,200	61,600	...	...	2,532	211	38,755	3,345	3,412	...
1931	193,000	37,100	357,100	51,700	...	...	2,390	198	32,861	2,868	3,301	...
1932	161,000	31,900	307,600	44,800	...	...	2,128	180	23,935	2,487	2,880	...
1933	153,000	31,000	338,200	48,200	...	...	1,895	166	17,057	2,082	2,612	...
1934	148,000	29,700	402,700[24]	57,600[24]	...	...	2,106	188	19,627	2,449	3,106	...
1935	139,000	27,100	448,500	64,100	...	...	2,140	203	19,356	2,390	3,282	...
1936	148,000	29,500	496,900	71,400	...	...	2,364	244	21,419	2,635	3,247	...
1937	157,000[23]	31,800[23]	547,300	80,600	...	...	...	265	24,063	3,015	3,177	...
1938	133,000	26,500	574,500	89,000	...	...	2,557	324	25,188	3,056	2,925	...
1939	141,000	29,300	...	...	...	...	...	353	...	...	3,271	...
1940	102,000	24,000	...	...	...	...	...	397	...	...	3,409	...
1941	112,000	28,400	...	...	...	...	...	...	...	...	3,884	...
1942	103,000	27,400	...	...	...	...	...	...	...	...	3,931	...
1943	95,000	24,100	...	...	...	...	...	...	...	...	4,260	...
1944	42,200	9,590	...	...	...	...	...	...	...	...	4,462	...
1945	69,300	17,800	...	...	...	...	...	...	...	...	4,385	...
			West Germany									
1946	126,000	32,400	...	24,900	...	...	...	...	...	...	4,046	...
1947	141,000	37,100	183,900	32,700	...	...	...	114	16,910	2,556	3,915	...
1948	158,000	41,300	236,500[28]	41,900[28]	...	...	1,089	108	24,032	3,276	3,622	...
1949	161,000	41,100	288,074	43,578	110,987	12,398	1,430	146	33,417	4,549	3,609	404
1950	152,000	38,900	291,044	43,054	128,504	15,064	1,870	195	41,762	5,424	3,586	414
1951	177,000	45,400	323,910	49,889	153,214	17,291	2,357	264	48,588	6,276	3,504[34]	409[34]
1952	174,000	44,000	330,744	49,890	158,287	19,077	2,467	317[39] 278	60,610	7,447	3,114	356
1953	163,000	40,300	313,128[30]	45,921[29] 46,577[30]	182,257	22,112	2,328	335	69,628	8,179	3,362	382
1954	169,000	41,600	325,295[31]	47,642[31]	191,437	23,182	2,568	351	66,234	8,174	3,180	370
1955	192,000	46,900	366,764	52,904	207,514	25,222	2,453	303	70,787	8,807	3,193	383
1956	205,000	50,300	388,253[28] 414,019	56,422[28] 57,582	210,207	27,334	2,137	342	63,973	8,170	2,796	325
1957	217,000	53,700	422,908	57,754	220,335	28,635	2,360	373	73,683	9,496	2,566[33]	309[33]
1958	212,000	52,900	386,049	51,559	227,199	30,101	2,250	363	79,470	10,242	2,281	306
1959	213,000	53,400	396,010	53,640	229,197	31,648	2,145	361	87,410	11,703	2,400	317
1960	227,000	56,900	429,271	57,061	237,789	32,860	2,164	362	97,094	13,346	2,550	338
1961	230,000	58,800	423,753	58,191	248,714	34,733	2,540	410	99,684	13,865	2,410	332
1962	231,000	61,200	419,028	59,999	259,818	37,410	2,686	417	102,352	14,560	2,502	337
1963	240,000	63,000	430,840	64,538	261,097	37,591	2,849	445	106,166	15,371	2,511	340
1964	248,000	65,300	442,040	63,555	267,039	39,113	3,250	546	114,658	17,037	2,398	335
1965	239,000	64,600	422,246	60,986	260,430	38,868	3,289	570	114,809	17,297	2,439	377
1966	232,700	64,100	374,353	59,272	262,523	39,685	3,331	552	118,848	17,904	2,658	412
1967	228,700	62,900	319,452	57,359	253,083	38,473	3,400	563	117,651	18,512	2,907	480
1968	229,060	62,960	345,934	61,070	252,942	38,506	2,499	548	115,378	18,340	3,272	527
1969	242,680	67,210	380,269	69,447	251,955	39,445	2,529	587	112,709	18,420	3,195	505
1970	250,400	70,410	392,123	73,590	262,901	41,513	2,953	688	117,791	19,821	3,449	546
1971	239,700	67,040	362,241	67,188	268,473	44,033	3,358	748	119,641	20,322	3,748	578
1972	246,400	68,610	366,403	66,700	274,448	44,710	3,082	756	119,110	20,061	3,691	564
1973	258,100	73,870	386,020	69,304	280,585	46,829	3,291	798	123,055	21,318	3,731	568
1974	265,500	77,060	404,224	71,343	286,301	49,168	3,955	902	130,157	23,123	[2,209][34]	[452][34]
1975	218,900	64,040	329,042	57,254	288,980	49,681	4,034	931	132,059	23,541	3,398	561

See p. 627 for footnotes

G 2 **Freight Traffic on Railways** (in thousands of metric tons and millions of ton/kilometres)

1920–1975

	Italy		Netherlands		Norway		Poland		Portugal		Romania	
	a	b	a	b	a	b	a	b	a	b	a	b
1920	38,806	8,620	16,700	...	6,103	498	17,000	...	4,952	...	5,291[19]	...[19]
1921	41,678	8,598	15,800	...	7,006	483	30,900	...	5,749	...	...	...
1922	48,423	9,877	14,700	...	7,906	493	43,900	10,041	6,356	...	...	...
1923	54,146	10,463	14,600	...	9,059	550	76,000	10,521	5,881	...	16,483	2,560
1924	63,171	11,911	16,200	...	7,551	512	60,000[38] 63,000	10,984	6,061	...	17,303	3,457
1925	65,275	12,532	16,600	...	10,321	634	63,000	12,634	5,648	...	20,130	3,151
1926	64,982	12,386	20,000	...	9,923	611	69,000	16,227[39] 15,020	5,800	...	22,483	3,551
1927	61,869	10,995	20,400	...	9,802	610	79,000	17,560	5,600	...	23,688	3,713
1928	64,489	11,666	22,000	...	8,468	590	86,000	20,161	6,700	...	21,901	3,339
1929	65,274	12,246	24,300	...	9,878	468	91,000	21,242	7,000	...	23,020	3,541
1930	55,369	10,991	22,700	...	11,647	717	74,000	18,296	7,800	...	23,200	3,552
1931	46,536	9,584	22,000	...	8,320	550	67,000	18,291	6,300	...	20,972	3,450
1932	40,713	8,612	18,300	...	6,019	455	51,000	13,539	7,040	...	20,934	3,523
1933	40,457	7,976	18,100	...	5,692	467	51,000	14,182	7,180	...	20,759	3,798
1934	43,010	7,883	17,400	...	5,799	465	57,000	16,234	7,760	...	23,551	4,208
1935	47,257	10,090	14,100	...	8,449	598	58,000	15,730	[4,075][40]	...	24,558	4,370
1936	51,672	10,441	13,900	...	9,508	643	61,000	16,351	[4,256][40]	[588][40]	25,710	4,633
1937	57,614	11,524	16,100	2,256	11,888	771	76,000	19,889[38] 22,100	[4,197][40]	[586][40]	26,770	4,934
1938	54,375	11,554	14,600	2,040	13,264	825	78,000	22,442	6,180	523	27,600	4,950
1939	64,867	15,032	15,700	2,196	11,330	736	...	...	6,870	591	27,800[19]	4,888[19]
1940	70,211	19,981	19,000	2,664	7,829	616	...	...	7,510[17] 4,317	611	...	4,597
1941	72,698	24,080	19,300	2,700	5,096	651	...	...	4,464	657	...	5,516
1942	71,342	27,625	17,800	2,484	5,311	672	...	...	5,040	710	...	5,214
1943	35,073	...	17,000	2,376	6,580	739	...	...	5,132	711	...	4,942
1944	15,041[35]	...	10,600	1,488	6,253	715	...	...	5,300	729	...	3,679[19]
1945	28,388	8,903	5,300	2,040	4,305	592	...	...	5,199	688	...	...
1946	36,973	10,117	13,500	1,914	7,007[36]	842[36]	73,100	19,500	5,712	784	18,575	3,857[18] 4,794
1947	42,201[15] 48,880	9,851[15] 10,939	16,100	2,267	10,035	1,062	93,700	21,300	4,599	733	...	...
1948	49,426	11,154	18,500	2,541	12,308	1,227	121,000	28,300	4,076	644	24,102	5,655
1949	50,627	10,478	19,900	2,787	13,579	1,386	140,000	32,700	3,609	569	...	...
1950	50,520	10,419	21,200	3,016	14,637[37] 14,942	1,379[37] 1,409	160,000	35,100	3,344	521	35,069	7,598
1951	58,046	11,733	22,600	3,256	16,055	1,541	176,000	38,500	3,511	585	38,116	8,743
1952	57,903	12,406	22,100	3,067	16,055	1,541	187,000	40,300	3,795	678	45,194	10,791
1953	58,059	12,618	23,700	3,252	15,214	1,377	211,000	44,600	3,536	642	53,137	12,554
1954	59,010	12,981	25,100	3,373	14,954	1,368	222,000	48,200	3,708	685	50,376	12,619
1955	64,591	14,685	25,600	3,440	15,676	1,448	236,000	52,000	3,889	723	58,963	14,675
1956	66,411	14,202	26,500	3,562	16,598	1,498	239,000	52,100	4,011	761	62,015	15,955
1957	65,869	14,395	25,200	3,398	16,437	1,532	249,000	55,300	3,987	773	65,272	17,044
1958	57,694	13,154	23,600	3,124	16,828	1,445	250,000	57,200	3,771	738	66,643	17,018
1959	61,387	14,422	24,600	3,210	15,660	1,421	265,000	61,700	3,768	751	68,974	17,475
1960	68,688	15,860	26,400	3,409	18,242[16] 19,328	1,579[16] 1,638	287,000	66,500	3,730	762	77,492	19,821
1961	67,161	15,518	26,400	3,391	19,557	1,725	298,000	69,700	3,673	736	85,260	22,207
1962	66,818	16,684	27,800	3,702	20,031	1,766	306,000	72,700	3,664	730	92,022	24,419
1963	69,005	17,076	31,000	4,093	20,328	1,817	313,000	74,400	3,825	766	99,616	26,755
1964	62,428	14,728	30,300	3,885	23,009	1,972	331,830	79,061	3,803	763	110,105	29,386
1965	61,654	15,289	27,400	3,522	25,254	2,136	341,251	81,013	3,721	755	114,354	30,981
1966	60,801	16,022	25,200	3,272	24,481	2,208	353,581	85,014	3,302	677	126,630	34,541
1967	58,530	17,096	25,500	3,235	26,971	2,409	365,588	88,543	3,434	727	137,132	37,297
1968	58,137	17,280	25,800	3,274	31,200	2,597	377,841	92,637	3,609	771	148,098	40,705
1969	57,589	17,282	26,300	3,433	30,234	2,717	373,660	95,025	3,519	737	155,364	44,031
1970	60,879	18,129	26,700	3,532	30,075	2,845	382,307	99,262	3,232	643	171,312	48,045
1971	56,692	17,284	23,300	3,232	28,834	2,610	398,105	104,334	3,364	670	184,787	50,840
1972	56,308	17,187	21,800	3,071	29,597	2,659	415,887	109,777	3,740	695	193,740	53,280
1973	57,250	17,637	23,600	3,463	31,868	2,846	431,485	116,442	4,106	700	205,955	57,103
1974	55,895	18,217	22,600	3,370	32,059	2,952	452,872	125,156	4,552	713	218,000	61,618
1975	45,707	14,940	17,700	2,721	25,756	2,626	464,248	129,230	4,856	754	228,000	64,803

See p. 627 for footnotes

G 2 **Freight Traffic on Railways** (in thousands of metric tons and millions of ton/kilometres)

1920–1975

	Russia[21]		Spain		Sweden		Switzerland		U.K.: Great Britain		Yugoslavia	
	a	b	a	b	a	b	a	b	a	b	a	b
	m tons											
1920	40	14.4	33,106	3,775	39,100	3,287	22,021	1,401	323,158	**31,351**	...	...
1921	37	15.7	32,773	3,781	27,100	2,371	16,895	1,081	272,180	**21,730**	...	...
1922	[40][41]	[16.1][41]	39,910	3,826	29,700	2,730	17,877	1,219	306,466	**27,469**	15,518	1,551
1923	58[41]	23.5[41]	35,848	4,105	32,700	2,877	19,633	1,274	348,775	**31,004**	18,105	2.019
1924	68[41]	33.7[41]	43,303	4,424	36,400	3,192	22,311	1,930	340,881	**31,171**	21,093	2,268
1925	84[41]	47.4[41]	41,489	4,483	38,100	3,446	22,428	1,904	321,021	**29,976**	21,427	2,435
1926	117[41]	68.9[41]	41,870	4,682	37,700	3,575	22,790	1,812	219,057	**22,961**	21,324	2,921
1927	136[41]	81.7[41]	45,659	4,845	41,700	3,932	24,303	2,005	327,014[5]	**30,863**[5]	21,903[42]	3,194[42]
											23,137	3,252
1928	156	93.4	49,441	5,226	34,600	3,133	25,527	2,223	311,012	**28,983**	23,699	3,933
1929	188	113	49,868	5,700	46,100	4,585	26,517	2,358	334,835	**30,816**	24,703	4,298
1930	239	134	48,136	5,450	42,000	4,256	25,469	2,209	309,218	**29,080**	21,683	3,849
1931	258	152	...	5,115	30,800	3,465	24,946	2,043	272,652	**26,676**	19,255	3,411
1932	268	169	...	5,142	24,400	2,497	21,700	1,673	253,618	**24,420**	15,897	3,020
1933	268	170	...	4,803	25,000	2,517	21,356	1,678	255,076	**24,557**	15,650	3,048
1934	317	206	...	4,636	31,400	3,344	21,556	1,801	274,354	**26,506**	16,457	3,222
1935	389	258	29,658	4,683	35,100	3,885	20,768	1,830	275,225	**26,820**	17,451	3,305
1936	483	323	...	...	39,100	4,543	19,097	1,543	285,218	**28,501**	17,933	3,334
1937	517	355	...	...	46,100	5,607	23,458	2,164	301,919	**30,061**	20,506	3,987
1938	516	371	...	...	41,200	5,206	20,741	1,710	268,571	**26,598**	22,058	4,315
1939	554[21]	392[21]	...	...	45,600	6,054	24,801	2,137	292,900	...	21,133	4,784
1940	593	415	...	...	44,600	7,210	28,379	3,180	299,100	...	...	...
1941	549	402	...	...	45,500	7,969	33,334	3,879	291,300	...	...	...
1942	290	228	26,490	4,271	48,300	8,477	32,773	3,668	299,800	**38,953**	...	...
1943	313	256	27,451	4,316	51,400	8,818	30,243	2,972	305,700	**39,829**	...	...
1944	371	297	23,950	4,574	47,700	8,121	26,291	1,433	297,300	**39,970**	...	...
1945	395	314	25,992	4,676	43,700	6,996	20,101	1,406	270,700	**36,011**	...	...
1946	453	335	26,914	4,881	47,500	8,087	24,766	1,846	266,600	**33,748**	19,518	...
1947	491	351	28,357	5,175	44,400	8,128	26,533	1,995	261,400[23]	**33,014**[23]	26,870	...
1948	620	446	29,041	6,396	46,000	8,459	25,016	2,080	277,600	**35,421**	36,176	7,434
1949	735	524	29,179	6,412	42,600	8,107	21,694	1,858	284,700	35,990	48,424	9,642
1950	834	602	29,758	7,305	44,100	8,640	24,043	2,229	285,800	36,194	46,072	9,944
					(million tons)							
1951	909	677	30,330	7,889	48	10,027	28,486	2,680	289,400	37,449	41,917	8,704
1952	997	741	33,513	8,536	46	9,633	26,263	2,476	289,500	36,613	37,939	8,383
1953	1,067	798	34,482	8,632	43	9,017	26,017	2,647	293,900	37,226	39,335	8,817
1954	1,131	857	36,665	9,472	43	9,235	28,118	2,868	288,000	36,119	43,668	9,571
1955	1,267	971	34,963	8,693	47	10,320	31,161	3,275	278,600	34,916	50,205	11,577
1956	1,371	1,079	36,884	9,099	49	10,969	35,590	3,537	281,400	35,112	52,099	11,869
1957	1,488	1,213	40,250	9,746	48	10,396	34,464	3,725	278,700	34,142	56,595	12,984
1958	1,617	1,302	41,023	9,777	43	9,475	31,869	3,500	246,800	30,130	57,248	13,031
1959	1,764	1,430	36,702	9,035	44	9,685	34,183	3,798	237,700	28,960	60,686	13,974
1960	1,885	1,504	34,302	7,820	50	10,928	38,964	4,346	252,500	30,496	65,237	15,191
1961	1,988	1,567	35,375	7,996	50	11,100	41,148	4,651	242,000	28,764	64,244	14,941
1962	2,077	1,646	36,212[39]	8,451	49	11,064	43,379	4,907	232,100	26,333	63,588	15,033
1963	2,158	1,749	41,992	8,704	52	12,015	46,365	5,238	238,700	25,178	71,777	17,345
1964	2,289	1,854	43,102	9,156	59	12,919	49,120	5,271	243,400	26,248	76,527	18,258
1965	2,415	1,950	43,860	9,208	61	13,883	50,458	5,585	232,200	25,229	74,781	18,036
1966	2,482	2,016	41,786	8,901	59	14,062	50,668	5,784	216,900	24,241	71,616	17,518
1967	2,605	2,161	43,004	9,636	59	13,538	51,662	5,974	203,900	22,253	68,730	16,390
1968	2,706	2,275	43,448	9,256	65	14,798	52,710	6,113	210,600	24,026	68,409	16,372
1969	2,759	2,367	43,520	9,692	68	16,021	56,214	6,557	210,500	25,276	70,198	17,691
1970	2,896	2,495	43,137	10,339	71	17,311	60,199	7,035	208,700	26,807	75,374	19,253
1971	3,049	2,637	43,328	10,112	64	15,658	59,942	7,072	198,300	24,279	75,630	19,653
1972	3,172	2,761	46,506	10,744	65	16,214	61,300	7,178	178,400	23,357	72,339	19,179
1973	3,346	2,958	49,449	12,002	72	18,260	62,968	7,610	198,900	25,514	74,516	20,447
1974	3,497	3,098	51,223	12,009	77	19,598	61,241	7,451	178,300	24,168	81,506	23,081
1975	3,621	3,237	46,800	11,079	61	16,057	46,936	5,518	176,500	23,474	77,730	21,638

See p. 627 for footnotes

G 2 Freight Traffic on Railways (in thousands of metric tons and millions of ton/Kilometres)

NOTES

1. SOURCES:— Germany ton/kms to 1938 — W.G. Hoffman, *Das Wachstum derDeutschen Wirtschaft seit der Mitte des 19 Jahrhunderts* (Berlin, etc., 1965); Great Britain to 1938 and Ireland to 1913 — based on B.R. Mitchell & Phyllis Deane, *Abstract of British Historical Statistics* (Cambridge, 1962), where the original sources are given; Greece 000 tons in 1938 and 1948–55 — supplied by the National Statistical Service of Greece; Poland 1921 and 1922 — supplied by the Polish Central Statistical Office; Russia 1941 and 1942 — E.W. Williams, *Freight Transportation in the Soviet Union* (Princeton, 1962). All other statistics are taken from the official publications noted on p. xv.

2. It is not always clear whether traffic for the servicing of the railway is included or not, though there appears to be an indication whenever a change in this respect occurs.

FOOTNOTES

[1] Excluding the Italian provinces and, from 1867 (2nd line) purely Hungarian lines, though mixed lines continue to be included. (see also footnote [4].)

[2] Revised figures are given here for 1900. In the source they are given at decennial intervals for the period 1841–91 as follows:—

	thousand tons	million tons/kms		thousand tons	million tons/kms
1841	1,010	37	1871	27,800	5,530
1851	4,340	488	1881	56,200	10,600
1861	23,500	3,790	1891	63,100	11,800

[3] Savoy and Nice included.

[4] Transleithania to 1918. The figures to 1888 (1st line) are for purely Hungarian lines only. Subsequently they include traffic on mixed Austro-Hungarian lines, which is also included in the Austrian statistics (see footnote [1]). Statistics for 1915–1918 are for years ended 30 June.

[5] New bases of collection were adopted in 1869, 1913, and 1928. In addition, Manchester Ship Canal traffic is excluded from 1913 (2nd line).

[6] Excluding the Kaschau-Oderberger line, which carried 274 thousand tons in 1870.

[7] Previously state-operated lines only.

[8] The territorial changes of the Balkan Wars were effective from 1914.

[9] For 1919–33 figutes are for years ended 31 March following that indicated. The 1934 figures are for 9 months.

[10] Excluding the Kosice–Bohumin line.

[11] Previously excluding a small amount of traffic in Lolland-Falster.

[12] Alsace-Lorraine is excluded from France for 1870–1921 and included in Germany for 1871–1917.

[13] Figures to 1880 (1st line) relate to goods trains only. Subsequently express traffic is included.

[14] Figures for 1899–1903 are of freight charged at full car load rate only.

[15] Statistics for 1905–1947 (1st line) are for years beginning 1 July and are for state-operated lines only. Figures are available for privately-operated lines as follows (calendar years throughout):—

	thousand tons	million ton/kms		thousand tons	million ton/kms		thousand tons	million ton/kms
1906	3,683	104	1930	9,137	109	1938	8,760	256
1907	3,898	101	1931	7,161	154	1939	9,830	284
1908	4,543	116	1932	6,493	141	1940	12,150	...
1909	5,073	127	1933	5,967	131	1941	14,160	...
1910	5,698	142	1934	5,770	143			
1927	9,250	...	1935	5,950	143	1944	7,410	...
1928	9,945	217	1936	7,530	185	1945	4,700	...
1929	10,418	227	1937	9,350	271	1946	7,120	...

Figures for the state lines for the calendar year 1947 were as follows:— 41,202 thousand tons and 10,746 million ton/kilometres.

[16] First half-year only. Subsequent figures to 1960 (1st line) are for years ended 30 June.

[17] The reason for this break is not given.

[18] State-operated lines only. All remaining private lines were nationalised in 1946.

[19] For 1901–20 the figures are for years ended 31 March following that indicated. The newly-acquired territories are included after 1920. Bessarabia, northern Bukovina, and southern Dobrudja are excluded from 1940, and northern Transylvania is excluded for 1940–44.

[20]Subsequently including traffic for the servicing of the railways, which had previously been excluded.
[21]Figures to 1898 (1st line) apply to European Russia (exclusive of Finland). From 1898 (2nd line) to 1913 (1st line) they apply to the whole Empire, except Finland. From 1913 (2nd line) to 1939 they apply to the territory of the U.S.S.R. in 1923, and subsequently to the present territory.
[22]This break occurs on a change of source (see note 1).
[23]Subsequently state-operated lines only.
[24]Memel, Danzig, Posen, West Prussia, parts of Pomerania and Schleswig, Eupen, Malmédy, etc. and Saarland are excluded from 1920, though Saarland is reincorporated from 1935.
[25]Eastern Upper Silesia is excluded from July 1922.
[26]Excluding the occupied Rhineland.
[27]Previously excluding some private narrow gauge lines.
[28]Saarland is excluded from 1949 to 1956 (1st line).
[29]From 1946 to 1953 (1st line) the ton/km. statistics are for state-operated lines only.
[30]Subsequently including the Hamburg Dock line.
[31]Subsequently including the Salzgitter line.
[32]The territorial gains in the north are subsequently included.
[33]Subsequent statistics relate to railway systems based in southern Ireland, though their traffic in Northern Ireland is included. From 1958 the latter ceased when the state took over the southern part of the Great Northern Railway.
[34]Subsequent statistics to 1973 for the state lines are for years ended 31 March following that indicated. From 1958 this covered all lines in southern Ireland. The 1974 figures are for the period April–December, and those for 1975 are for the calendar year.
[35]Excluding Allied military traffic.
[36]From 1946/7 goods carried jointly by state and private lines are counted twice.
[37]Previously excluding freight carried free of charge.
[38]Tonnage figures to 1924 (1st line) and ton/kilometrage figures to 1937 (1st line) relate to standard gauge lines only.
[39]It is not clear whether there is a break here. Revised figures in the 1973 *Anuario Estadistico* were not carried back beyond 1963.
[40]These figures are for the six main companies only.
[41]The figure for 1922 is for 9 months to 30 September, and the figures for 1923–27 are for years ended 30 September.
[42]Figures to 1927 (1st line) are for state-operated lines plus the Southern Railway only.

G 3 PASSENGER TRAFFIC ON RAILWAYS (in millions)

1834–1869

	Austria/Hungary[1]		Belgium		Denmark		Finland		France		Germany	
	P	PK	P	PK	P	PK	P	PK	P	PK	P	PK
1834	0.002	...	...	...	...	...	—	—	...	...	...	...
1835	0.047	...	0.421	...	...	...	—	—	...	...	...	...
1836	0.079	...	0.871	...	...	...	—	—	...	...	...	...
1837	0.082	...	1.4	...	...	...	—	—	...	...	...	...
1838	0.272	...	2.2	...	...	...	—	—	...	...	...	...
1839	0.378	...	2.0	...	...	...	—	—	...	...	...	...
1840	0.353	...	2.2	...	...	...	—	—	...	...	...	...
1841	2.2	...	2.6	...	...	...	—	—	6.4[2]	112	...	...
1842	1.9	...	2.7	...	...	...	—	—	6.2	...	...	...
1843	2.7	...	3.1	...	...	...	—	—	7.4	...	...	...
1844	2.7	...	3.4	...	...	...	—	—	8.1	283	...	...
1845	2.6	...	3.5	...	...	...	—	—	8.9	247	...	...
1846	3.4	...	3.7	...	...	...	—	—	10.4	328	...	...
1847	4.9	...	3.7	...	...	...	—	—	12.8	...	...	...
1848	4.1	...	3.6	...	...	...	—	—	11.9	...	...	...
1849	4.7	...	3.9	...	...	...	—	—	14.8	...	...	...
1850	6.5	...	4.2	...	...	...	—	—	18.7	...	...	56
1851	8.0	...	4.4	...	...	...	—	—	19.9[2]	797	...	...
1852	8.2	...	4.5	...	...	...	—	—	22.6	...	...	87
1853	8.3	...	4.7	...	...	...	—	—	24.7	1,155	...	...
1854	9.1	...	4.9	...	...	...	—	—	28.1	1,375	...	1,050
1855	9.5	...	5.3	...	...	...	—	—	32.9	1,822	...	1,250
1856	9.9	...	6.0	...	...	...	—	—	36.4	1,845	...	1,260
1857	10.5	...	6.5	...	...	...	—	—	41.6	1,994	...	1,450
1858	11.2	...	6.6	...	...	...	—	—	45.4	2,107	...	1,490
1859	15.7	...	7.1	...	...	...	—	—	52.4[3]	2,707[3]	...	1,640
1860	12.2	...	7.4	...	....	...	—	—	56.5	2,521	...	1,740
1861	12.2	...	...	...	...	...	—	—	61.9[2]	2,689	...	1,950
1862	12.9	...	...	...	...	...	; -	...	65.1	2,853	...	2,080
1863	13.2	...	...	...	...	...	0.1	...	70.2	3,006	...	2,360
1864	12.7	...	9.4	...	...	...	0.1	...	73.4	3,164	...	2,590
1865	12.8	...	10.7	...	...	...	0.1	...	81.5	3,328	...	2,700
1866	15.7	...	11.6	...	...	...	0.1	...	87.3	3,407	...	3,140
1867	12.1[1] 11.6	...	12.6	...	1,9	...	0.1	...	101.6	4,301	...	2,970
1868	13.8	...	12.8	...	2.1	...	0.1	...	102.9	3,899	...	3,210
1869	16.8	...	13.6	...	2.6	...	0.1	...	111.2[16]	4,108[16]	...	3,530

Abbreviations used throughout this table: P: Passengers; PK: Passenger Kilometres

See p. 639 for footnotes

G 3 Passenger Traffic on Railways (in millions)

1834–1869

	Hungary[4]	Ireland	Italy		Norway		Russia[7]	Spain	Sweden	U.K.: Great Britain	
	P	P	P	PK	P	PK	P	P	P	P	PK
1834	...	...	...	...	...	...	...	...	...	...	...
1835	...	...	...	...	...	...	...	...	...	...	...
1836	...	...	...	...	...	...	...	...	...	...	...
1837	...	...	...	...	...	...	...	...	...	...	...
1838	...	...	...	...	...	...	...	...	...	5.4	...
1839	...	...	...	...	...	...	...	...	...	...	...
1840	...	...	...	...	...	...	...	...	...	...	...
1841	...	...	...	...	...	...	...	...	...	...	...
1842	...	...	...	...	...	...	...	...	...	... [5]	...
1843	...	2.1	...	...	...	...	...	...	...	21.7	...
1844	...	2.6	...	...	...	...	...	...	...	25.2	...
1845	...	3.4	...	...	...	...	...	...	...	30.4	...
1846	...	3.6	...	...	...	...	...	...	...	40.2	...
1847	...	3.8	...	...	...	...	...	...	...	47.9	...
1848	...	3.8 [5]	...	...	...	...	...	...	...	54.4 [5]	...
1849	...	6.1	...	...	...	...	...	...	...	57.8	...
1850	...	5.5	...	...	...	...	...	...	...	67.4	...
1851	...	5.6	...	...	...	...	...	...	...	79.7	...
1852	...	6.2	...	...	...	...	...	...	...	82.8	...
1853	...	7.1	...	...	...	...	...	...	...	95.2	...
1854	...	6.9	...	...	...	...	...	...	...	104.3	...
1855	...	7.2	...	...	0.128	...	...	...	...	111.4	...
1856	...	7.9	...	...	0.161	5	...	...	...	121.4	...
1857	...	8.4	...	...	0.174	6	...	...	...	130.6	...
1858	...	8.4	...	...	0.168	5	...	...	...	130.7	...
1859	...	9.4	...	...	0.170	6	...	...	...	140.3	...
1860	...	10.0	...	...	0.152	5	...	...	...	153.5	...
1861	...	10.7	...	...	0.142	5	...	...	...	163.0	...
1862	...	10.4	...	...	0.160	6	...	8.2	0.8	170.0	...
1863	...	11.5	...	...	...	...	...	10.5	1.0	192.2	...
1864	...	11.9	...	...	...	...	...	11.4	1.0	217.4	...
1865	...	13.2	...	...	0.300	...	...	11.4	1.1	238.7	...
1866	...	13.1	...	...	...	...	...	11.0	1.3	261.2	...
1867	...	14.0	14.9	...	0.386	13	9	...	1.5	273.7	...
1868	0.7	... [6]	17.5	...	0.388	14	10	...	...	... [6]	...
1869	1.2	13.3	...	...	0.613	19	...	...	2.4	298.6	...

See p. 639 for footnotes

G 3 **Passenger Traffic on Railways** (in millions)

1870–1919

	Austria/Hungary		Belgium		Bulgaria		Czechoslovakia		Denmark		Finland	
	P	PK	P	PK	P	PK	P	PK	P	PK	P	PK
1870	19.4	...	14.1	...	...	...	...	...	2.9	...	0.4	...
1871	[23.7] [9]	...	18.3[11]	...	...	...	...	...	3.1	...	0.6	32
1872	31.7	...	23.2	...	...	...	...	...	3.5	...	0.8	42
1873	37.7	...	26.4[12] / 40.2	...	...	...	...	...	3.9	...	0.9	44
1874	35.8	...	42.2	...	...	...	...	...	4.5	...	1.1	48
1875	35.8	...	48.4	...	...	...	...	...	5.0	...	1.2	59
1876	35.4	1,608	51.4	...	...	...	...	...	6.0	...	1.5	66
1877	32.8	1,522	52.0	...	...	...	...	...	6.2	...	1.4	67
1878	33.2	1,659	53.6	...	...	...	...	...	6.0	...	1.6	69
1879	33.7	1,614	53.9	...	...	...	...	...	5.8	...	1.8	68
1880	34.7	1,668	56.3	...	...	...	...	...	5.9	...	1.8	66
1881	36.8	1,628	57.2	...	...	...	...	...	6.2	...	1.7	64
1882	41.6	1,886	61.5	...	...	...	...	...	6.8	...	1.8	68
1883	47.4	2,660	63.7	...	...	...	...	...	7.6	...	1.8	68
1884	52.2	2,170	64.5	...	...	...	...	...	8.0	...	1.8	71
1885	55.6	2,246	65.5	...	...	...	...	...	8.3	...	1.8	76
1886	56.8	2,217	65.9	...	...	...	...	...	8.0	...	1.9	81
1887	57.3	2,255	68.8	...	...	...	...	...	9.2	...	2.1	93
1888	59.9	2,345	73.4	...	...	...	...	...	9.2	...	2.1	102
1889	64.0	2,437	76.3	...	...	...	...	...	9.5	...	2.2	104
1890	74.9	2,789	82.4	...	...	...	...	...	9.7	...	2.5	126
1891	85.0	3,078	86.5	...	...	...	...	...	10.3	...	2.6	137
1892	92.1	3,228	88.2	...	...	...	...	...	10.5	...	2.5	128
1893	97.3	3,513	92.1	...	...	...	...	...	12.1	303	2.6	132
1894	102.9	3,670	96.9	...	0.3	25	...	...	13.0	330	2.5	136
1895	106.4	3,847	99.6	...	0.4	27	...	...	13.4	336	3.0	149
1896	105.2	3,933	106.8	...	0.4	29	...	...	14.7	367	3.6	179
1897	109.5	4,034	114.4	...	0.5	36	...	...	15.2	387	4.3	222
1898	126.1	4,440	115.4	...	0.6	41	...	...	17.1	456	5.6	283
1899	142.3	4,894	129.0	...	0.6	45	...	...	19.5	522	6.2[12]	319
1900	158.1	5,194	139.1	...	0.7	64	...	...	20.8	546	7.1	337
1901	169.6	5,323	139.8	...	0.7	55	...	...	22.6	590	7.5	338
1902	173.6	5,518	142.5	...	0.9	69	...	...	24.4	613	7.6	342
1903	176.5	5,339	148.9	...	1.0	76	...	...	24.1	607	8.7	382
1904	182.5	5,603	152.9	...	1.2	91	...	...	24.5	625	9.2	390
1905	189.9	5,864	163.4	...	1.4	100	...	...	24.2	631	10.1	426
1906	207.1	6,353	169.8	...	1.6	126	...	...	25.2	665	11.8	523
1907	223.7	6,789	181.2	...	1.8	132	...	...	27.2	705	12.4	518
1908	228.3	7,058	176.8	...	2.2	149	...	...	27.9	723	12.8	495
1909	242.0	7.446	178.4	...	2.8	197	...	...	28.6	747[11] / 869	13.4	528
1910	254.6	7,522	193.1	4,306	3.1	210	...	...	29.4	917	14.3	555
1911	276.6	7,955	198.9	...	3.5	234	...	...	30.2	923	15.0	593
1912	290.9	8,321	211.0	...	3.3	230	...	...	31.7	958	16.2	622
1913	...	...	224.3	6,242	1.9[13]	136[13]	...	...	32.5	950	18.1	704
1914	...	...	...	...	4.2	303	...	...	33.9	969	19.3	735
1915	...	...	...	...	3.5	285	...	...	34.3	959	17.6	773
1916	...	...	...	...	1.5	140	...	...	38.0	1,049	23.3	1,074
1917	...	...	...	...	1.6	126	...	...	42.2	1,191	29.0	1,194
1918	...	...	...	...	2.7	231	...	...	38.1	1,151	12.4	585
	Austria[10]											
1919	...	...	112.7	...	5.4[14]	443[14]	[215.2] [15]	[6,429] [15]	42.3	1,231	13.0	679

See p. 639 for footnotes

G 3 Passenger Traffic on Railways (in millions)

1870–1919

	France		Germany		Greece		Hungary[4]		Ireland	
	P	PK	P	PK	P	PK	P	PK	P	PK
1870	102.6	4,272	...	4,400[16]	...	...	2.1	...	14.3	...
1871	95.7[2]	4,589	...	5,000	...	...	3.7	...	15.5	...
1872	111.5	4,278	...	5,000	...	...	5.4	...	16.3	...
1873	116.5	4,347	...	5,700	...	...	5.9	...	16.3	...
1874	121.1	4,446	...	5,800	...	...	6.0	...	16.5	...
1875	131.3	4,786	...	6,000	...	...	5.5	...	16.9	...
1876	137.0	4,962	...	6,100	...	...	5.3	...	17.4	...
1877	138.8	4,870	...	6,100	...	...	5.0	...	17.3	...
1878	152.8	5,779	...	6,200	...	...	5.5	...	17.9	...
1879	150.5	5,254	...	6,100	...	...	5.8	...	16.4	...
1880	165.1	5,863	...	6,500	...	...	5.8	...	17.3	...
1881	179.7[2]	6,323[2]	...	6,800	...	...	6.2	...	17.6	...
1882	194.9	6,761	...	7,100	...	...	6.4	...	18.7	...
1883	207.2	7,040	...	7,400	...	...	7.1	...	19.3	...
1884	211.9	6,883	...	7,700	...	...	8.3	...	19.6	...
1885	214.5	7,025	...	7,900	...	...	9.1	...	19.1	...
1886	216.6	7,137	...	8,400	...	...	8.6	...	18.7	...
1887	217.8	7,212	...	8,700	...	...	8.1	...	19.5	...
1888	224.8	7,345	340	8,300	...	...	8.8[4]	742	19.9	...
							14.1			
1889	244.2	8,628	377	10,200	3.4	...	19.0	940	21.0	...
1890	241.1	7,943	426	11,300	...	...	29.2	1,237	21.4	...
1891	255.7[2]	8,286[2]	464	11,800	...	...	35.9	1,504	22.2	...
1892	288.1	9,243	488	11,900	5.0	...	41.1	1,672	22.6	...
1893	317.8	10,010	...	12,700	4.5	...	45.6	1,869	23.7	...
1894	336.5	10,330	...	12,900	...	...	49.6	2,027	24.5	...
1895	348.9	10,660	592	14,000	4.7	...	53.2	2,091	26.2	...
1896	363.0	11,150	646	15,200	...	...	57.5	2,207	26.6	...
1897	374.8	11,440	692	16,300	...	...	57.0	2,126	25.9	...
1898	385.9	11,820	756	17,700	5.7	...	60.3	2,248	26.6	...
1899	401.8[2]	12,340[2]	805	18,800	6.2	...	61.6	2,292	27.4	...
1900	430	14,000	856	20,200	6.2	...	64.4	2,320	27.7	...
1901	406	12,900	876	20,700	6.3	...	67.0	2,433	26.9	...
1902	410	13,100	891	21,200	6.8	129	68.6	2,431	28.2	...
1903	413	13,200	958	22,600	7.0	...	72.4	2,540	28.6	...
1904	420	13,600	1,030	24,000	7.3	...	78.5	2,738	29.0	...
1905	429	14,100	1,116	25,800	7.8	...	86.5	2,950	29.0	...
1906	445	14,700	1,209	27,900	8.2	156	96.1	3,356	29.2	...
1907	459	15,200	1,295	29,800	8.5	...	107.2	3,667	29.7	...
1908	464	15,900	1,362	31,300	8.3	157	111.7	3,756	29.0	...
1909	476	16,200	1,470	33,800	8.7	...	124.2	4,032	29.6	...
1910	492	16,800	1,541	35,700	9.0	181	140.0	4,404	30.7	...
1911	494	17,500	1,643	38,200	9.1	182	153.8	4,772	30.8	...
1912	509	18,100	1,744	40,200	10.4	233	164.1	5,055	29.2[6]	...
1913	529	19,300	1,798	41,400	12.6	297	166.1	5,022	31.3	...
1914	355	13,700	...	...	12.3	254	...[4]	...[4]	...	...
1915	209	8,800	...	...	13.4	279	160	...	...	...
1916	325	10,000	...	...	17.1	431	204.3	10,746	...	...
1917	352	10,100	...	...	14.1	334	237.3	10,671	...	...
1918	377	11,900	...[16]	...[16]	14.7	402	263.0	12,031	...	...
1919	463	20,200	...	...	15.0	450	...	...	...	...

See p. 639 for footnotes

G 3 Passenger Traffic on Railways (in millions)

1870–1919

	Italy		Netherlands		Norway		Poland		Portugal		Romania[22]	
	P	PK	P	PK	P	PK	P	PK	P	PK	P	PK
1870	22.2	...	...	...	0.551	17	...	...	...	...	...	...
1871	22.4	...	...	...	0.584	19	...	...	...	...	...	...
1872	25.5	...	...	...	0.771	23	...	...	...	...	...	...
1873	26.3	...	...	...	1.5	46	...	...	...	...	...	...
1874	27.3	...	...	...	1.7	46	...	...	...	...	...	...
1875	28.0	...	...	...	1.5	43	...	...	...	...	...	...
1876	28.1	...	...	...	1.5	41	...	...	...	...	...	...
1877	28.1	...	...	...	1.4	41	...	...	...	...	1.3	...
1878	29.0	...	13.1	417	[0.608][18]	[19][18]	...	...	...	...	1.2	...
1879	30.4	...	13.4	421	1.4	44	...	...	...	...	0.7	...
1880	32.5	...	14.5	454	1.6	51	...	...	2.1	...	0.8	...
1881	34.0	...	15.2	469	1.8	56	...	...	2.2	...	1.0	...
1882	34.4	...	15.8	487	2.3	72	...	...	2.3	...	1.2	...
1883	36.8	...	16.0	542	2.7	84	...	...	2.5	...	1.4	...
1884	36.4	...	16.8	554	3.2	93	...	...	2.6	...	1.4	...
1885	40.8	...	16.6	543	3.1	89	...	...	2.6	...	1.4	...
1886	42.7	...	16.8	547	3.1	92	...	...	2.9	...	1.6	...
1887	45.5	...	17.7	567	3.2	93	...	...	3.7	...	2.0	...
1888	49.3	...	18.5	581	3.2	92	...	...	4.4	...	2.1	...
1889	51.0	...	19.5	633	3.6	99	...	...	5.0	...	2.4	...
1890	50.9	...	...	...	4.0	107	...	...	6.0	...	2.9	...
1891	49.4	2,191	22.2	640	4.3	117	...	...	5.7	...	4.3	...
1892	50.1	2,175	22.5	648	4.7	126	...	...	5.9	...	5.4	...
1893	50.3	2,184	23.5	694	4.7[19]	126[19]	...	...	6.2	...	5.8	...
					5.7	134						
1894	51.7	2,275	24.4	709	6.0	138	...	...	6.7	...	6.0	...
1895	52.6	2,302	25.3	738	6.3	146	...	...	7.2	...	5.9	...
1896	53.0	2,332	24.8	716	6.8	160	...	...	8.3	...	6.5	...
1897	54.0	2,407	25.0	724	7.4	172	...	...	9.6	...	5.7	...
1898	55.5	2,526	26.0	763	8.4	199	...	...	11.4	...	5.8	...
1899	57.9	2,571	27.9	815	9.4	220	...	...	11.4	...	7.1	...
1900	59.7	2,801	30.8	843	7.0	171	...	...	11.9	...	5.5	...
1901	61.1	2,775	32.7	962	9.9	234	...	...	12.6	...	5.3[21]	...
1902	64.5	2,913	34.1	987	10.1	243	...	...	12.8	...	5.7	...
1903	67.7	3,041	35.9	1,043	9.9	235	...	...	13.5[20]	...	5.6	...
									12.5			
1904	...[17]	...[17]	38.2	1,104	9.9	241	...	...	13.1	...	5.6	...
1905	85.1	4,178	38.8	1,170	9.8	235	...	...	13.4	...	6.6	...
1906	82.4	4,269	40.7	1,233	10.1	248	...	...	13.5	...	7.6	...
1907	88.8	4,365	41.0	1,248	10.4	257	...	...	13.2	...	8.2	...
1908	91.0	4,524	42.0	1,240	10.7	269	...	...	14.6	...	8.3	...
1909	92.5	4,532	43.2	1,271	15.4	386	...	...	15.2	...	9.2	...
1910	95.5	4,448	46.2	1,368	13.1	335	...	...	14.9	...	10.2	...
1911	99.2	4,500	44.9	1,176	14.3	371	...	...	...	...	11.4	...
1912	102.9	4,858	49.3	1,299	16.0	405	...	...	...	...	12.2	...
1913	106.0	5,000	54.1	1,433	17.8	462	...	...	...	...	11.1	...
1914	98.7	4,595	48.6	1,275	18.6	482	...	...	18.9	...	11.6	871
1915	93.2	5,028	60.0	1,458	18.7	508	...	...	20.0	...	...	...
1916	90.6	5,239	76.4	1,776	21.4	573	...	...	21.6	...	...	...
1917	82.1	5,201	64.4	...	25.8	678	...	...	17.9	...	...	...
1918	92.4	5,838	60.6	...	26.6	701	...	...	16.8	...	4.9	...
1919	118.3	6,407	60.2	...	30.2	773	61	...	19.1	...	14.2	...

See p. 639 for footnotes

G 3 Passenger Traffic on Railways (in millions)

1870–1919

	Russia[7]		Serbia		Spain		Sweden		Switzerland		U.K.: Great Britain	
	P	PK	P	PK	P	PK	P	PK	P	PK	P	PK
1870	...	...	...	...	...	...	2.5	...	...	...	322.2	...
1871	21	...	...	...	11.5	...	2.6	...	...	...	359.7	...
1872	24	...	...	...	11.9	...	3.1	...	...	...	406.5	...
1873	27	...	...	...	10.8	...	4.0	...	...	...	439.0	...
1874	...	...	...	...	10.6	...	5.3	...	...	...	461.3	...
1875	28	...	...	...	12.2	...	6.5	...	...	...	490.1	...
1876	29	...	...	...	14.0	...	6.8	...	...	...	517.1	...
1877	...	...	...	...	13.2	...	7.3	...	...	...	532.3	...
1878	...	...	...	...	13.3	...	7.2	...	...	...	547.1	...
1879	...	...	...	...	14.2	...	6.2	...	...	...	546.3	...
1880	...	...	...	...	14.8	...	7.0	...	21.5	...	596.6	...
1881	...	...	...	...	...	...	7.1	...	21.7	...	608.4	...
1882	37	...	...	...	...	...	7.8	...	22.5	...	636.1	...
1883	38	...	...	...	...	...	8.6	...	23.9	...	664.4	...
1884	37	...	...	...	18.5	...	9.0	...	23.3	...	675.4	
1885	37	...	...	...	17.7	...	9.7	...	24.0	...	678.1	...
1886	37	...	...	...	20.2	...	9.6	...	24.6	...	706.9	...
1887	37	...	...	...	20.1	...	10.1	...	25.6	...	714.2	...
1888	43	...	...	...	23.1	...	10.1	...	26.9	...	722.6	...
1889	43	...	...	...	24.7	...	11.1	...	29.2	...	754.2	...
1890	44	...	0.3	27	25.8	...	12.7	...	32.1	...	796.3	...
1891	48	...	0.4	33	27.9	...	13.6	...	34.6	...	823.3	...
1892	49	...	0.5	40	24.8	...	14.0	...	37.0	...	841.8	...
1893	52	...	0.5	40	33.7	...	14.8	...	39.7	...	849.5	...
1894	56	...	0.8	54	34.0	...	16.8	...	42.4	...	886.9	...
1895	61	...	0.7	43	34.3	...	18.3	...	45.0	...	903.5	...
1896	68	...	0.6	44	34.1	...	20.4	...	48.7	...	953.8	...
1897	75	9.2	0.6	39	25.7	...	22.7	...	52.5	...	1,004.5	...
1898	84[21] / 85	10.0[7] / 10.7	0.6	45	27.0	...	25.5	675	56.5	...	1,036.3	...
1899	94	11.3	0.7	51	29.0	...	28.7	761	60.1	...	1,079.3	...
1900	104	13.0	0.8	56	32.0	...	30.8	823	62.2	...	1,114.6	...
1901	113	13.3	0.7	50	33.4	...	33.3	875	60.1	...	1,145.5	...
1902	115	13.4	0.8	54	37.4	...	33.2	885	60.6	...	1,160.0	...
1903	123	14.6	0.8	55	39.6	...	36.3	968	68.2	...	1,166.6	...
1904	128	18.7	0.9	65	42.7	...	39.4	1,043	74.7	...	1,169.8	...
1905	122	19.5	1.0	75	42.6	...	41.7	1,097	81.6	...	1,170.0	...
1906	136	20.6	1.0	78	45.1	...	46.5	1,264	90.0	1,849	1,211.1	...
1907	149	18.9	...	...	47.3[23] / 46.0		52.0	1,415	96.7	1,955	1,229.8	...
1908	162	20.4	...	...	47.2	...	54.2	1,441	101.5	2,027	1,249.1	...
1909	175	21.4	...	...	46.0	...	53.8	1,463	104.1	2,081	1,235.5	...
1910	195	23.2	...	...	48.9	...	58.3	1,573	109.1	2,307	1,276.0	...
1911	212	...	...	...	50.3	...	60.3	1,637	116.2	2,431	1,295.5	...
1912	245[7]	...[7]	...	...	54.0	...	63	1,728	122.4	2,518	1,265.2	...
1913	185	25.2	...	...	57.5	2,139[23]	67	1,848	127.7	2,685	1,423.5[6] / 1,199.3	...
1914	235	...	...	...	57.9	2,159	69	2,010	114.2	2,385	...	...
1915	264	...	...	...	62.6	2,136	70[24]	2,145	107.1	1,980	...	...
1916	348	...	...	...	67.6	2,340	76	2,403	121.7	2,222	...	...
1917	354	...	...	...	71.0	2,419	77	2,404	119.2	2,080	...	...
1918	386	...	...	...	75.5	2,567	79	2,243	103.3	1,936	...	...
1919	202	...	...	...	83.6	2,936	86	2,451	113.9	2,124	1,522.6	...

See p. 639 for footnotes

G 3 Passenger Traffic on Railways (in millions)

1920–1975

	Austria		Belgium		Bulgaria		Czechoslovakia		Denmark		Finland	
	P	PK	P	PK	P	PK	P	PK	P	PK	P	PK
1920	...	...	223.3	5,205	6.9	469	280.2	8,687	45.6	1,365	17.2	775
1921	78.7	2,628	240.2	...	8.2	529	294.1	10,467	45.0	1,389	18.0	683
1922	97.9	3,495	248.9	6,157	9.1	568	294.2	8,271	42.0	1,258	21.2	911
1923	84.6	3,055	262.5	6,609	8.3	509	291.3	8,171	42.2	1,290	25.0	1,024
1924	108.7	3,643	251.1	6,194	9.0	571	320.9	8,953	43.1	1,293	28.4	1,062
1925	117.7	3,990	245.0	6,049	8.4	539	325.0	9,305	45.0	1,364	21.6	908
1926	110.5	3,719	244.5	6,259	8.5	578	325.0	9,264	45.5	1,384	22.0	940
1927	108.1	3,612	237.8	5,781	8.1	536	314.9	8,483	42.8	1,298	22.3	983
1928	110.8	3,821	255.2	6,270	9.0	610	338.1	9,070	40.8	1,238	23.5	1,084
1929	104.9	3,666	264.8	6,365	9.4	647	343.6	9,178	42.1	1,263	23.2	1,094
1930	101.0	3,454	262.3	6,964	8.2	550	334.5	8,821	43.7	1,318	21.5	1,045
1931	89.1	3,137	242.0	5,810	7.7	532	293.8	7,829	44.4	1,366	19.6	907
1932	70.5	2,527	208.8	5,157	8.0	566	265.8	7,092	42.7	1,351	18.7	830
1933	60.0	2,284	202.9	5,058	7.2	510	240.5	6,492	39.0	1,223	17.5	817
1934	57.0	2,131	193.8	4,873	[5.4][14]	[395][14]	244.4	6,755	41.3	1,364	18.7[11]	890[11]
1935	55.8	2,185	198.7	5,648	7.2	518	236.5	6,429	49.2	1,454	10.6	954
1936	52.4	2,160	207.1	5,635	8.7	579	240.9	6,776	55.0	1,613	21.4	1,012
1937	...	2,407	221.9	6,148	10.2	685	268.7	9,239	61.2	1,654	23.3	1,149
1938	...	...	213.4	5,965	11.1	739	...	8,647	61.7	1,651	24.2	1,234
1939	...	...	191.9	5,394	12.2	784	...	...	62.2	1,729	24.7	1,372
1940	...	...	89.3	2,803	16.0	1,022	...	...	64.2	1,876	...	...
1941	...	...	139.8	4,137	16.5	1,322	...	...	...	...	...	...
1942	...	...	193.2	5,721	...	...	...	...	...	...	...	...
1943	...	...	206.4	6,055	...	...	...	...	...	...	...	...
1944	...	...	132.8	3,097	...	...	...	...	99.0	3,316	...	...
1945	...	...	219.2	4,977	...	...	...	...	113.7	3,483	63.2	3,239
1946	...	...	237.6	6,776	...	...	309.9	13,190	101.0	2,957	61.7	3,021
1947	...	3,545	240.4	7,210	...	2,628	350.6	14,654	120.1	3,420	61.7	2,908
1948	123.9	4,211	233.6	7,088	50.0	2,560	415.3	14,977	116.3	3,486	49.9	2,256
1949	111.9	4,115	223.6	7,116	...	...	429.4	15,264	112.7	3,476	44.8	2,091
1950	115.2	4,293	219.1	7,047	48.9	2,292	441.5	15,615	111.0	3,392	46.3	2,189
1951	123.9	4,673	226.7	7,253	...	2,278	480.9	17,253	112.5	3,301	45.6	2,310
1952	130.3	4,664	231.8	7,546	51.8	2,489	496.5	17,649	112.7	3,175	39.6	2,073
1953	135.7	5,037	228.7	7,528	...	2,405	488.8	17,852	118.9	3,339	37.1	2,060
1954	135.0	5,179	229.4	7,562	...	2,535	508.6	17,906	122.9	3,313	38.4	2,140
1955	147.5	5,575	235.4	7,846	58.7	2,784	524.0	18,791	123.5	3,319	39.5	2,261
1956	148.8	5,754	247.3	8,333	61.0	2,807	530.0	18,628	119.6	3,259	35.8	2,250
1957	150.0	5,909	253.3	8,555	60.8	2,707	541.3	19,048	120.2	3,204	34.0	2,249
1958	158.0	6,195	263.5	9,057	...	3,088	536.7	18,682	122.2	3,267	30.9	2,118
1959	159.3	6,317	255.0	8,519	71.5	3,243	557.6	18,574	125.1	3,308	34.0	2,273
1960	163.7	6,622	261.4	8,578	79.0	3,617	580.6	19,335	124.9	3,303	36.6	2,343
1961	166.0	6,577	265.1	8,693	81.8	3,839	587.5	19,978	123.0	3,363	39.2	2,603
1962	178.3	6,630	272.8	8,958	81.1	3,912	577.3	19,769	123.0	3,410	37.3	2,357
1963	180.9	6,649	276.3	9,009	82.5	4,021	564.2	19,037	120.7	3,374	30.9	1,953
1964	178.7	6,606	275.3	9,041	85.7	4,341	562.1	19,232	122.4	3,443	31.7	2,038
1965	176.3	6,453	273.5	8,975	90.0	4,655	569.1	19,748	125.2	3,473	31.2	2,050
1966	172.7	6,333	269.9	8,708	96.7	5,119	568.7	19,382	125.0	3,514	31.5	2,131
1967	164.8	5,747	265.0	8,534	100	5,429	578.1	19,750	123.8	3,505	29.8	2,153
1968	163.7	5,630	254.8	8,177	101	5,707	549.1	18,965	122.7	3,348	27.6	2,201
1969	158.0	6,210	247.8[6]	8,238	105	6,061	517.7	18,569	120.0	3,309	25.6	2,154
1970	158.1	6,296	246.8	8,260	106	6,223	486.1	16,884	119.8	3,477	23.4	2,156
1971	164.8	6,522	245.5	8,425	100	6,223	480.6	16,966	121.4	3,461	24.9	2,349
1972	178.3	6,584	240.3	8,168	101	6,700	443.9	15,798	121.0	3,723	27.8	2,594
1973	174.3	6,530	236.6	8,093	103	7,071	444.2	15,670	118.4	3,572	29.6	2,773
1974	174.4	6,590	237.3	8,279	105	7,453	418.8	15,066	115.1[43]	3,414[43]	32.8	3,047
1975	169.1	6,486	232.1	8,258	104	7,569	410.0	15,433	112.5	3,440	35.5	3,135

See p. 639 for footnotes

G 3 Passenger Traffic on Railways (in millions)

1920–1975

	France		Germany		E Germany		Greece		Hungary		Ireland	
	P	PK	P	PK	P	PK	P	PK	P	PK	P	PK
1920	500[11]	22,100[11]	...[25]	...[25]			15.8[30]	447[30]	...[4]	...[4]	...	...
1921	661	25,700	...	...			17.9	...	111.8	2,534	...	...
1922	720	27,300	2,979[26]	75,600[26]			21.9	...	103.8	2,916	...	...
											Southern Ireland[32]	
1923	767	29,300	[2,382][27]	...			22.4	...	113.8	3,469	...	...
1924	772	28,400	[1,963][27]	44,600			26.7	...	111.1	3,423	...	...
1925	802	29,800	2,168	50,100			28.5	751	92.8	2,837	...	...
1926	777	28,300	1,877	44,000			27.0	720	104.9	2,838	23.3	...
1927	724	26,000	1,970	46.600			26.1	666	111.3	2,945	22.2	...
1928	745	27,000	2,071[28]	48,800			26.3	656	121.0	3,165	21.4	...
			2,088									
1929	765	28,200	2,057	48,100			28.1	679	125.4	3,171	22.5	...
1930	790	29,200	1,900	44,300			28.1	661	120.6	3,110	20.9	...
1931	773	29,000	1,636	37,700			26.8	608	110.8	2,744	20.1	...
1932	705	25.600	1,352	31,500			24.5	548	91.8	2,272	19.3	...
1933	661	24,600	1,284	30,700			24.3	531	55.4	1,783	17.7	...
1934	621	23,400	1,408[25]	35,500[25]			25.2	544	59.1	1,879	19.6	...
1935	582	22,600	1,542	40,300			26.5	612	61.3	1,911	22.6	...
1936	577	23,300	1,667	44,300			28.8	714	66.1	2,045	20.5	...
1937	614[10]	27,000[10]	1,874	51,100			...[31]	775	72.1	2,221	20.0	...
1938	540	22,100	2,049	57,100			10.2	811	78.0	2,376	19.3	...
1939	481	20,500	...	...			...	842	...	...	19.8	...
1940	347	17,100	...	...			...	750[31]	...	...	19.9	...
1941	454	17,100	...	...			...	...	...	...	25.2	...
1942	579	23,200	...	...			...	...	...	...	23.6	...
1943	686	28,200	...	...			...	...	...	...	26.2	...
1944	433	15,000	...	...			...	...	...	...	26.4	...
			West Germany[29]									
1945	596	26,100	...	...	...	...	...	...	...	...	26.1	...
1946	696	31,500	...	...	...	...	...	...	...	...	24.1	...
1947	649	31,100	...	...	...	...	...	394	127	3,876	23.8	...
1948	645	30,600	...	...	...	...	...	310	177	4,800	22.2	...
1949	597	29,500	1,530	30,739	880	...	...	353	201	5,785	20.5	...
1950	545	26,400	1,472	30,264	954	18,576	...	616	257	7,142	17.4	...
1951	549	28,100	1,407	29,973	1,006	19,527	...	748	340	10,597	17.3[33]	...
1952	543	28,600	1,385	29,493	1,056	20,801	...	793	356	10,641	16.8	...
1953	496	25,900	1,398	31,754	997	20,529	...	870	364	10,669	16.5	...
1954	500	26,600	1,447	33,207	1,008	22,632	...	892	365	10,505	16.0	...
1955	509	27,800	1,555	35,919	1,016	22,905	13.9	1,002	367	10,277	16.8	...
1956	526	30,800	1,621[29]	38,811[29]	1,022	22,560	12.9	955	329	9,222	15.8	...
			1,670	39,748								
1957	552	32,600	1,685	41,384	1,011	22,785	11.9	916	356	10,417	16.5[32]	...
1958	553	32,300	1,562	39,718	980	21,399	11.1	867	399	11,889	11.7	525
1959	568	32,000	1,396	39,278	958	21,388	11.7	998	438	12,848	12.3	554
1960	570	32,000	1,399	38,402	943	21,288	11.4	1,030	485	14,324	11.1	567
1961	576	33,600	1,303	38,469	830	19,540	11.5	1,029	492	14,460	10.2	554
1962	579	35,800	1,246	38,415	691	16,791	11.5	1,044	523	15,560	9.8	542
1963	599	36,800	1,196	37,328	666	16,263	11.0	1,007	510	15,560	9.8	533
1964	608	37,800	1,178	37,378	685	17,378	11.2	1,078	527	16,223	9.3	536
1965	620	38,300	1,165	38,567	684	17,446	11.5	1,131	536	16,347	9.0	542
1966	628	38,400	1,066	35,672[12]	668	17,386	11.7	1,151	549	16,692	9.3	557
				36,483								
1967	624	38,380	1,018	33,877	649	17,462	11.7	1,150	561	16,772	8.9	546
1968	579	35,900	1,009	34,985	634	17,098	11.2	1,333	561	16,514	9.5	579
1969	607	39,060	1,024	37,156	636	17,610	11.8	1,437	549	16,391	10.0	589
1970	613	40,980	1,054	38,129	626	17,666	12.6	1,531	526	16,339	10.3	755
1971	608	41,140	1,053	36,892	630	18,407	13.3	1,635	505	15,888	11.0	783
1972	626	43,230	1,053	39,638	641	19,932	12.9	1,563	502	16,143	11.9	844
1973	620	44,700	1,093	39,765	633	20,851	12.7	1,571	493	16,038	12.7	875
1974	642	47,310	1,124	40,568	622	20,792	12.3	1,594	483	16,467	[11.4][33]	[694][33]
1975	658	50,700	1,079	37,727	634	21,305	12.5	1,553	463	15,823	13.9[33]	899[33]

See p. 639 for footnotes

G 3 Passenger Traffic on Railways (in millions)

1920–1975

	Italy		Netherlands		Norway		Poland		Portugal		Romania	
	P	PK	P	PK	P	PK	P	PK	P	PK	P	PK
1920	112.8	6,430	54.8	...	32.2	824	67	...	22.9	...	13.6[21]	...[21]
1921	111.3	6,640	55.4	...	28.4	741	130	...	23.6	...	...	...
1922	112.1	6,540	51.7	...	27.3	688	148	9,362	24.6	...	...	...
1923	115.1	7,028	49.4	...	27.9	695	169	9,552	24.9	...	17.2	3,331
1924	120.0	8,200	47.9	...	26.7	669	177[36] 178	6,897	23.2	...	56.4	3,804
1925	129.0	8,000	47.2	...	23.7	623	164	6,366	24.9	...	50.7	3,412
1926	127.0	8,428	48.1	...	22.8	586	148	5,965	...	...	46.0	3,455
1927	123.3	8,144	52.3	...	20.1	530	161	6,307	30.0	...	40.4	3,150
1928	139.5	8,137	57.6	...	19.2	524	176	7,077	33.1	...	40.7	3,170
1929	143.7	8,071	58.8	...	18.1	502	167	7,073	33.3	...	38.8	3,047
1930	125.8	7,370	59.0	...	17.9	520	154	6,717	32.9	...	35.1	2,917
1931	108.0	6,528	56.2	...	17.6	532	136	5,474	30.2	...	31.6	2,630
1932	105.2	6,293	49.6	...	18.3	517	115[20]	4,695	28.4	...	26.0	2,204
1933	106.6	6,991	50.1	...	18.7	529	139	4,754	28.3	...	27.1	2,297
1934	112.6	7,698	48.1	...	17.8	517	147	5,275	30.2	...	30.5	2,526
1935	126.5	8,579	46.0	...	17.8	532	145	5,530	24.8	...	35.0	2,848
1936	136.1	9,806	44.5	...	19.6	597	174	5,941	25.7	848	39.1	3,141
1937	157.5	11,064	47.1	3,348	21.0	654	212	6,948	26.1	742	45.7	3,577
1938	167.0	11,773	47.8	3,423	21.8	703	228	7,493	21.7	714	48.7	3,788
1939	194.2	13,547	61.4	4,015	22.7	740	...	...	30.6	705	51.2	4,382
1940	222.6	17,135	62.3	4,236	17.7	596	...	...	26.3	768	...	5,094[21]
1941	284.6	21,932	66.0	4,641	25.5	767	...	...	25.5	738	...	3,266
1942	391.1	31,058	102.9	6,222	31.9	918	...	...	29.0	891	...	4,307
1943	217.9[34]	17,291	158.7	8,391	40.3	1,045	...	...	34.5	1,274	...	5,718
1944	114.0[34]	8,481	121.7	5,847	46.4	1,087	...[37]	...[37]	39.4	1,418	...	...[21]
1945	189.4[34]	12,552	43.0	2,026	47.7	1,069	...	...	42.0	1,233	...	...
1946	284.6[34]	18,467	127.0[19] 174.1	6,177	47.4[35]	1,305[35]	249	15,700	45.2	1,318	40.8	5,436[22]
1947	322.3[34][17] 536.6	21,262[17] 24,960	180.0	6,776	42.2	1,485	336[38]	18,100[38]	68.0	1,677	...	...
1948	544.6	26,594	177.6	6,839	40.6	1,466	422	20,400	69.2	1,699	74.7	6,476
1949	514.0	23,850	166.6	6,478	42.9	1,694	488	21,540	61.5	1,476	...	...
1950	527.1	23,578	158.4	6,228	40.1	1,531	613	27,124	57.5	1,385	117	8,155
1951	522.3	24,476	156.8	6,291	39.9	1,558	714	31,557	60.3	1,443	173	9,873
1952	537.8	25,107	155,4	6,392	38.7	1,533	831	38,117	62.3	1,551	181	9,185
1953	557.4	25,784	160.7	6,621	38.5	1,519	849	36,477	63.8	1,574	222	11,971
1954	556.5	24,888	172.2	7,061	38.9	1,548	905	36,226	67.1	1,628	232	11,929
1955	564.8	26,071	184.5	7,573	40.1	1,628	940	36,981	69.6	1,673	252	12,460
1956	559.5	27,711	189.0	7,687	40.0	1,709	956	37,596	72.3	1,715	264	13,054
1957	531.5	28,114	189.4	7,612	40.2	1,738	956	38,262	78.4	1,840	265	13,323
1958	538.1	28,869	186.6	7,466	39.5	1,713	963	38,085	85.1	1,933	233	11,619
1959	539.6	28,953	187.3	7,416	39.1	1,752	905	34,894	91.6	2,037	214	10,558
1960	574.4	30,723	196.4	7,821	38.7[18] 42.4	1,735[18] 1,831	817	30,942	98.8	2,156	215	10,737
1961	542.5	31,449	200.5	7,991	41.4	1,830	836	30,850	104.3	2,307	224	11,457
1962	525.4	31,465	198.2	7,878	40.3	1,843	867	31,246	107.9	2,439	239	12,325
1963	503.5	32,026	198.8	7,911	39.1	1,762	895	32,139	114.1	2,606	253	12,836
1964	471.7	30,617	195.1	7,854	35.9	1,716	929	33,270	120.0	2,780	261	13,331
1965	448.7	29,034	192.0	7,715	34.5	1,716	972	34,318	126.5	2,970	262	13,535
1966	444.3	29,886	189.2	7,603	34.3	1,749	995	34,877	131.9	3,124	281	14,651
1967	446.4	30,385	183.7	7,412	32.6	1,712	1,012	35,447	138.0	3,266	302	15,775
1968	446.1	31.311	180.3	7,355	30.7	1,647	1,030	35,870	141.8	3,309	303	16,142
1969	444.0	31,946	179.8	7,502	29.3	1,568	1,048	37,035	144.7	3,441	306	16,719
1970	456.0	34,764	187.9	8,011	29.4	1,573	1,056	36,891	144.8	3,540	328	17,793
1971	462.5	36,298	187.6	8,114	29.4	1,600	1,066	37,228	145.7	3,569	338	18,811
1972	468.4	37,839	183.8	8,039	29.5	1,622	1,081	38,782	153.7	3,761	361	20,184
1973	482.4	38,805	181.3	8,173	29.5	1,640	1,088	39,647	166.3	4,106	367	21,228
1974	517.2	40,665	183.0	8,589	32.6	1,884	1,111	41,670	178.7	4,552	378	22,406
1975	490.7	39,055	176.3	8,501	33.5	1,948	1,118	42,819	182.5	4,856	367	22,380

See p. 639 for footnotes

G 3 Passenger Traffic on Railways (in millions)

1920–1975

	Russia[7]		Spain		Sweden		Switzerland		U.K.: Great Britain[42]		Yugoslavia	
	P	PK	P	PK	P	PK	P	PK	P	PK	P	PK
1920	143	...	97.8	3,242	84	2,408	128.5	2,405	1,579.0	...	...	...
1921	84	11.3	105.0	3,428	75	2,161	120.0	2,223	1,229.4	...	...	...
1922	[77][39]	[9.9][39]	107.9	3,559	66	1,999	119.3	2,215	1,194.7	...	36.5	1,534
1923	122[39]	13.9[39]	115.0	3,629	64	2,045	127.5	2,351	1,235.6	...	38.0	1,628
1924	154[39]	15.4[39]	118.4	2,645	66	2,009	140.0	2,640	1,236.2	...	40.0	1,580
1925	212[39]	19.0[39]	117.9	3,680	66	2,038	146.4	2,819	1,232.6	...	40.0	1,629
1926	263[39]	23.4[39]	117.9	3,625	66	2,094	146.8	2,805	1,069.0	...	42.0	1,973
1927	254[39]	22.1[39]	114.6	3,491	66	2,166	157.8	3,017	1,174.7	...	46.2[41]	2,110[41]
									1,195.9[6]		47.6	2,137
1928	291	24.5	113.4	3,515	67	2,221	166.5	3,225	847.1	...	50.4	2,274
1929	365	32.0	114.6	3,809	69	2,294	175.2	3,434	869.9	...	49.6	2,210
1930	558	51.8	117.1	3,844	70	2,435	176.5	3,528	844.3	...	47.6	2,297
1931	724	61.8	...	3,530	68	2,323	171.7	3,416	795.2	...	43.2	2,154
1932	967	83.7	...	3,540	65	2,261	161.0	3,219	777.3	...	36.4	1,800
1933	927	75.2	...	3,553	65	2,268	158.9	3,311	798.9	...	32.9	1,703
1934	945	71.4	...	3,443	69	2,479	157.5	3,286	829.7	...	31.6	1,647
1935	919	67.9	58.3	3,425	73	2,702	151.5	3,134	856.2	...	39.7	2,224
1936	992	77.2	...	...	76	2,890	145.5	3,042	875.7	...	45.9	2,441
1937	1,143	90.9	...	...	80	3,103	152.4	3,296	906.1	...	54.7	2,860
1938	1,173	84.9	...	...	82	3,160	153.1	3,297	850.2	...	59.3	3,068
1939	1,267[7]	93.7[7]	...	...	88	3,565	159.4	3,561	844.9	30,566[40]	58.3	3,191
1940	1,344	98.0	...	...	98	4,494	169.5	3,659	691.1	...	...	...
1941	...	...	...	...	103	5,023	196.7	4,431	778.3	...	...	...
1942	...	...	107.8	7,529	117	5,743	217.5	4,800	944.4	...	...	...
1943	...	...	115.4	7,437	132	6,384	242.8	5,493	1,036.7	51,938	...	...
1944	...	...	114.4	7,343	145	6,580	262.5	5,915	1,039.1	51,583	...	...
1945	844	65.9	100.5	6,222	154	6,441	284.8	6,569	1,055.7	56,726	...	...
1946	1,078	97.9	99.0	6,867	154	6,405	285.7	6,315	901.1	47,043	78.4	3,969
1947	1,095	95.1	109.5	7,496	154	6,514	295.5	6,560	768.9[10]	37,039[10]	111	5,129
1948	1,049	82.5	115.1	7,567	151	6,578	285.3	6,724	700.3	34,213	136	6,102
1949	1,080	81.3	110.1	7,291	151	6,725	278.3	6,462	710.5	34,018	151	7,194
1950	1,164	88.0	107.5	7,093	150	6,637	267.6	6,428	704.0	32,472	179	8,304
1951	1,315	98.5	108.4	7,284	141	6,508	277.3	6,674	719.6	33,463	170	7,579
1952	1,441	107	114.6	7,851	134	6,333	284.1	6,878	710.8	32,926	104	4,815
1953	1,504	118	115.7	7,978	129	6,134	279.4	6,904	710.5	33,117	131	6,015
1954	1,574	129	114.4	7,879	126	6,138	280.4	6,954	744.7	33,333	148	6,536
1955	1,641	141	117.2	8,020	122	6,163	284.5	7,132	730.2	32,683	164	7,533
1956	1,658	142	123.3	8,552	118	6,237	290.9	7,307	740.1	34,010	159	7,314
1957	1,754	153	124.3	8,608	110	5,642	300.0	7,643	788.1	36,357	171	8,059
1958	1,835	158	127.6	8,730	103	5,312	304.3	7,843	777.3	35,647	184	8,877
1959	1,883	164	124.3	8,488	95	5,052	307.7	7,955	749.2	35,840	191	9,250
1960	1,950	171	108.8	7,341	91	5,180	310.7	7,974	721.3	34,677	212	10,449
1961	1,962	176	114.9	7,773	89	5,310	320.5	8,427	707.8	33,894	195	10,089
1962	2,037	189	128.5	8,789	87	5,353	330.2	8,812	670.5	31,749	193	9,908
1963	2,139	192	147.4	10,093	81	5,237	336.0	9,048	646.7	30,947	201	10,673
1964	2,250	195	168.6	11,820	77	5,371	344.5	9,659	629.0	31,984	226	12,308
1965	2,301	202	174.1	12,198	73	5,344	334.1	9,004	580.5	30,116	236	12,800
1966	2,450	219	176.2	12,523	67	5,133	332.0	9,027	547.3	29,697	213	12,196
1967	2,592	234	155.6	12,437	59	4,778	318.8	8,794	537.2	29,111	196	10,753
1968	2,746	254	148.0	11,836	61	4,603	320.2	8,992	532.3	28,703	183	10,284
1969	2,837	261	158.9	12,647	64	4,792	323.7	9,239	516.6	29,612	163	10,470
1970	2,930	265	164.4	13,293	64	4,693	322.6	9,339	526.4	30,408	157	10,939
1971	3,053	275	166.3	13,467	60	4,125	323.4	9,435	499.5	30,127	146	10,566
1972	3,167	286	177.9	14,391	69	4,553	316.6	9,502	445.8	29,100	141	10,578
1973	3,306	297	193.3	15,640	72	4,775	318.8	9,639	427.9	29,800	137	10,578
1974	3,389	306	198.7	16,079	82	5,619	313.8	9,538	436.5	30,900	135	10,429
1975	3,471	313	199.6	16,146	81	5,861	303.9	9,223	432.5	30,300	129	10,285

See p. 639 for footnotes

G 3 Passenger Traffic on Railways (in millions)

NOTE

SOURCES:— Finland to 1909 — supplied by the Central Statistical Office of Finland; Sweden in 1862 — supplied by the Swedish Central Office of Statistics; Great Britain to 1938 and Ireland to 1913 — B.R. Mitchell & Phyllis Deane, *Abstract of British Historical Statistics* (Cambridge, 1962), where the original sources are given. All other statistics are taken from the official publications noted on p. xv.

FOOTNOTES

[1] Excluding the Italian provinces, and, from 1867 (2nd line) purely Hungarian lines, though mixed lines continue to be included (see also footnote 4).

[2] Revised figures are given here for 1900. In the source they are given at decennial intervals for the period 1841–91 as follows (in millions):—

	Passengers		Passengers	Passenger/ Kilometres
1841	6.3	1871	94.1	no change
1851	19.6	1881	174	6,290
1861	61.1	1891	248	8,240

[3] Savoy and Nice included.

[4] Transleithania to 1918. The figures to 1888 (1st line) are for purely Hungarian lines only. Subsequently they include traffic on mixed Austro-Hungarian lines, which is also included in the Austrian statistics (see footnote [1]). Statistics for 1915–1918 are for years ended 30 June.

[5] For 1843–48 the figures are for years ended 30 June.

[6] New bases of collection were adopted subsequently.

[7] Figures to 1898 (1st line) apply to European Russia (exclusive of Finland). From 1898 (2nd line) to 1913 (1st line) they apply to the whole Empire, except Finland. From 1913 (2nd line) to 1939 they apply to the territory of the U.S.S.R. in 1923, and subsequently to the present territory.

[8] In thousand million passenger/kilometres.

[9] Excluding the Kaschau–Odernerger line, which carried 92 thousand passengers in 1870.

[10] Subsequently state-operated lines only.

[11] Passengers on return tickets were only counted once up to this date.

[12] Previously state-operated lines only.

[13] The territorial changes of the Balkan Wars were effective from 1914.

[14] From 1919–33 the figures are for years ended 31 March following that indicated. The 1934 figures are for 9 months.

[15] Excluding the Kosice–Бohumin line.

[16] Alsace-Lorraine is excluded from France for 1871–1920, and included in Germany for 1871–1917.

[17] Statistics for 1905–1947 (1st line) are for years beginning 1 July and are for state-operated lines only. Figures for private lines are available as follows (in millions):—

	Passengers	Passenger/ Kilometres		Passengers	Passenger/ Kilometres		Passengers	Passenger/ Kilometres
1906	19.6	412	1930	69.2	1,146	1938	102.0	1,653
1907	23.7	414	1931	63.5	1,121	1939	116.6	1,901
1908	28.2	476	1932	59.7	1,054	1940	136.2	...
1909	29.8	525	1933	61.0	1,081	1941	180.4	...
1910	32.5	550	1934	57.5	1,118			
1927	66.5	...	1935	72.9	1,211	1944	236.5	...
1928	69.1	1,208	1936	84.6	1,429	1945	220.0	...
1929	71.0	1,234	1937	92.2	1,490	1946	227.6	...

Figures for the state lines for the calendar year 1947 are as follows (in millions):— 311.4 passengers and 20,769 passenger/kilometres.

[18] First half-year only. Subsequent figures to 1960 (1st line) are for years ended 30 June.

[19] Previously excluding season ticket holders.

[20] The nature and size of this break is not given.

[21] For 1901–20 the figures are for years ended 31 March following that indicated. The newly acquired territories are included after 1920. Bessarabia, northern Bukovina, and southern Dobrudja are excluded from 1941, and northern Transylvania for 1941–44.

[22] State-operated lines only. All remaining private lines were nationalised in 1946.

[23] Subsequently on standard gauge lines only.

[24] Subsequently paying passengers only.

[25] Memel, Danzig, Posen, West Prussia, parts of Pomerania and Schleswig, Eupen, Malmédy, etc., and Saarland are excluded from 1920, though Saarland is reincorporated in 1935.

[26] Eastern Upper Silesia is excluded from July 1922.
[27] Excluding the occupied Rhineland.
[28] Previously excluding some private narrow gauge lines.
[29] Saarland is excluded from West Germany to 1956 (1st line).
[30] The territorial gains in the north are subsequently included.
[31] Subsequently excluding the Franco-Hellenic line.
[32] Subsequent statistics relate to railway systems based in southern Ireland, though including their traffic in Northern Ireland. From 1958 the latter ceased when the state took over the southern part of the Great Northern Railway.
[33] Subsequently to 1973 for the state lines are for years ended 31 March following that indicated. From 1958 this covered all lines in southern Ireland. The 1974 figures are for the period April–December, and those for 1975 cover the calendar year.
[34] Excluding Allied military traffic.
[35] From 1946/7 passengers carried jointly on a single journey by state and private lines are counted twice.
[36] Previously excluding narrow gauge lines.
[37] The territory of Poland was greatly altered in 1945.
[38] Subsequently including traffic on electric suburban lines.
[39] The figure for 1922 is for 9 months to 30 September, and the figures for 1923–27 are for years ended 30 September.
[40] Year ended 31 August.
[41] Figures to 1927 (1st line) are for state-operated lines plus the Southern Railway only.
[42] The Passenger-Kilometres series includes estimates for season ticket holders, whereas the passenger-journeys series does not.
[43] Subsequently excluding local ferry crossings.

G 4 MERCHANT SHIPS REGISTERED

1788–1819

	Norway				Sweden		United Kingdom			
	Number of Ships		Thousand Tons		Number of Ships	Thousand Tons	Number of Ships		Thousand Tons	
	Sail	Steam	Sail	Steam			Sail	Steam	Sail	Steam
1788	...		...		...	...	12,464		1,278	
1789	...		...		...	...	12,801		1,308	
1790	...		...		...	...	13,557		1,383	
1791	...		...		...	...	13,960		1,415	
1792	...		...		...	...	14,334		1,437	
1793	...		...		...	...	14,440		1,453	
1794	...		...		...	...	14,590		1,456	
1795	...		...		721	83	14,317		1,426	
1796	...		...		...	...	14,458		1,361	
1797	...		...		...	...	14,405		1,454	
1798	...		...		...	...	14,631		1,494	
1799	...		...		...	...	14,883		1,551	
1800	1,156		121		800	88	15,734		1,699	
1801	...		...		...	...	16,552		1,797	
1802	...		...		...	...	17,207		1,901	
1803	...		...		...	...	18,068		1,986	
1804	...		...		...	...	18,870		2,077	
1805	...		...		864	96	19,027		2,093	
1806	...		...		...	...	19,315		2,080	
1907	...		...		...	...	19,373		2,097	
1808	...		...		...	...	19,580		2,130	
1809	...		...		...	...	19,882		2,167	
1810	...		...		852	94	20,253		2,211	
1811	...		...		...	...	20,478		2,247	
1812	...		...		...	...	20,637		2,263	
1813	...		...		...	...	20,951		2,349	
1814	...		...		...	...	21,449	1	2,414	--
1815	1,673		148		994	117	21,861	8	2,477	1
1816	...		...		...	...	22,014	12	2,503	1
1817	...		...		...	...	21,761	14	2,420	1
1818	...		...		...	...	22,005	19	2,450	2
1819	...		...		...	...	21,973	24	2,449	3

G 4 Merchant Ships Registered

1820–1869

	Austria-Hungary[1]				Belgium				Denmark			
	Number of Ships		Thousand Tons		Number of Ships		Thousand Tons		Number of Ships		Thousand Tons	
	Sail	Steam	Sail	Steam	Sail	Steam	Sail	Steam	Sail	Steam	Sail	Steam
1820	...	...	...	...	...	...	...	...	...	...	...	...
1821	...	...	...	...	...	...	...	...	...	...	...	...
1822	...	...	...	...	...	...	...	...	...	...	...	...
1823	...	...	...	...	...	...	...	...	...	...	...	...
1824	...	...	...	...	...	...	...	...	...	...	...	...
1825	...	...	...	...	...	...	...	...	...	...	...	...
1826	...	...	...	...	...	...	...	...	...	...	...	...
1827	...	...	...	...	...	...	...	...	...	...	...	...
1828	...	...	...	...	...	...	...	...	...	...	...	...
1829	2,946	–	188	–	...	...	...	...	...	...	...	...
1830	2,927	–	190	–	...	...	...	...	...	...	...	...
1831	3,239	–	200	–	...	...	...	...	...	...	...	...
1832	3,157	–	195	–	...	...	...	...	1,626		65	
1833	3,276	–	192	–	...	...	...	...	1,645		66	
1834	3,231	–	187	–	...	...	...	...	1,626		64	
1835	3,255	–	179	–	...	...	...	...	1,620		62	
1836	3,266	–	166	–	...	...	...	...	1,624		61	
1837	3,175	7	163	1	151	4	22	1	1,589		61	
1838	3,283	10	164	2	146	5	22	2	1,611		62	
1839	3,201	10	189	2	154	5	22	2	1,558		65	
1840	3,228	10	197	2	155	6	22	1	1,634		69	
1841	3,208	10	202	2	139	5	22	1	1,633		74	
1842	3,400	11	205	2	145	7	23	5	1,650		76	
1843	3,409	11	206	2	134	8	22	5	1,691		77	
1844	3,382	13	208	3	134	...	23	...	1,770	11	77	1
1845	3,334	20	205	4	136	5	24	2	1,723	11	76	1
1846	3,393	20	215	4	137	6	25	3	1,767	15	77	1
1847	3,456	21	227	5	140	3	25	2	1,895	19	83	1
1848	3,465	26	234	6	151	4	29	2	1,983	17	85	1
1849	3,540	31	241	7	149	5	31	2	1,990	15	86	1
1850	3,564	32	252	8	156	5	33	2	2,002	16	90	1
1851	3,376[2]	35	238[2]	10	157	6	35	1	2,067	21	97	2
	9,868		262									
1852	9,645	39	272	11	155	5	34	1	2,077	26	101	2
1853	9,637	47	285	14	152	5	34	1	2,160	25	102	2
1854	9,843	50	305	15	151	7	37	1	2,403	25	113	2
1855	9,932	48	320	14	150	8	38	5	2,497	25	121	2
1856	9,600	53	339	18	140	8	36	6	2,624	27	130	2
1857	9,573	61	356	22	142	5	40	2	2,651	32	136	3
1858	9,596	60	352	22	136	6	39	3	2,698	35	139	4
1859	9,644	59	328	21	131	4	36	2	2,750	40	142	4
1860	...	...	...	...	108	8	29	4	2,727	43	135	4
1861	9,744	59	321	21	103	8	27	4	2,719	44	134	4
1862	9,766	59	310	21	96	7	26	3	2,719	44	133	4
1863	9,584	59	310	21	91	6	25	3	2,693[3]	47[3]	135[3]	4[3]
1864	9,428	63	312	24	99	8	31	4	3,028	51	144	5
1865	9,427	64	306	26	104	8	36	4	3,121	65	153	6
1866	9,045[1]	65[1]	318[1]	29[1]	91	7	33	5	3,054	77	163	8
	7,629		282									
1867	7,698	71	277	34	81	9	31	6	3,052[4]	80[4]	166[4]	10
									2,686	76	164	
1868	7,756	74	290	34	68	11	23	9	2,867	79	168	10
1869	7,741	80	299	38	67	12	24	9	2,719	89	168	10

See p. 660 for footnotes

G 4 Merchant Ships Registered

1820–1869

	Finland				France				Germany			
	Number of Ships		Thousand Tons		Number of Ships		Thousand Tons		Number of Ships		Thousand Tons	
	Sail	Steam	Sail	Steam	Sail	Steam	Sail	Steam	Sail	Steam	Sail	Steam
1820	...	...	...	...	...	...	...	...	...	...	...	...
1821	...	...	...	...	...	...	...	...	...	...	...	...
1822	...	...	...	...	...	...	...	...	...	...	...	...
1823	...	...	...	...	...	....	...	...	...	...	...	...
1824	...	...	...	...	...	...	...	...	...	...	...	...
1825	...	...	...	...	...	...	...	...	...	...	...	...
1826	...	...	...	....	...	...	...	...	...	...	...	...
1827	...	...	...	...	...	...	...	...	...	...	...	...
1828	...	...	...	...	...	...	...	...	...	...	...	...
1829	...	...	...	...	...	...	...	...	...	...	265	
1830	...	...	...	...	...	...	...	...	...	...	...	
1831	...	...	...	...	...	...	...	...	...	...	...	
1832	...	...	...	...	...	...	...	...	...	...	...	
1833	...	...	...	...	...	...	...	...	...	...	...	
1834	...	...	...	...	...	...	...	...	...	...	282	
1835	...	...	...	...	...	...	...	...	...	...	...	
1836	...	...	...	...	...	...	...	...	...	...	...	
1837	...	...	...	...	15,326		697		...	...	...	
1838	...	...	...	...	15,546	71	670	10	...	...	...	
1839	...	4	...	...	15,657	85	663	10	...	...	352	
1840	...	6	...	...	15,511	89	653	10	...	...	...	
1841	...	...	...	...	13,276	107	580	10	...	...	...	
1842	1,286	8	120	--	13,301	108	580	10	...	...	...	
1843	1,356		117		13,552	104	590	10	...	...	...	
1854	1,330	8	114	--	13,578	101	595	9	...	...	406	
1845	1,348		115		13,722	103	602	9	...	...	...	
1846	...		...		13,937	109	622	11	...	...	...	
1847	1,428		128		14,204	117	658	13	...	...	...	
1848	1,359	7	126	1	14,235	118	670	13	...	...	...	
1849	1,391		132		14,245	119	667	13	...	...	513	
1850	1,349	9	131	1	14,229	126	674	14	3,655	22	496	4
1851	...	10	...	1	14,418	139	685	19	3,712	22	514	4
1852	...	10	...	1	14,456	151	699	22	3,682	20	519	3
1853	1,354	8	137	1	14,545	174	736	26	3,730	26	540	6
1854	...	...	...	...	14,199	197	785	35	3,853	32	595	11
1855	...	...	...	...	14,023	225	827	45	3,947	39	619	12
1856	...	...	...	...	14,448	273	935	64	4,118	49	673	14
1857	1,379		135		14,845	330	980	72	4,484	73	715	21
1858	...	24	...	...	14,863	324	983	67	4,636	80	752	29
1859	...	24	...	1	14,708	324	961	65	4,781	83	750	25
1860	1,523	27	169	1	14,608	314	928	68	4,672	70	754	23
1861	...	34	...	2	14,738	327	911	73	4,673	72	764	25
1862	...	34	...	2	14,794	338	904	79	4,842	73	811	26
1863	1,604	25	195	1	14,746	346	900	85	4,997	76	864	29
1864	1,526	35	187		14,820	364	901	98	4,879	81	861	29
1865	1,548	48	202		14,867	384	900	108	4,974	85	894	34
1866	1,675	56	225		15,230	407	915	128	5,078	88	889	41
1867	1,607	65	233		15,182	420	916	133	4,922	98	887	51
1868	1,641[5]	62[5]	241[5]		15,182	433	923	135	4,991	114	891	56
1869	...	...	...		15,324	454	932	143	4,876	126	890	67

See p. 660 for footnotes

G 4 Merchant Ships Registered

1820–1869

	Greece				Italy			
	Number of Ships		Thousand Tons		Number of Ships		Thousand Tons	
	Sail	Steam	Sail	Steam	Sail	Steam	Sail	Steam
1820	...	...	...	...	...	...	...	...
1821	...	...	...	...	...	...	...	...
1822	...	...	...	...	...	...	...	...
1823	...	...	...	...	...	...	...	...
1824	...	...	...	...	...	...	...	...
1825	...	...	...	...	...	...	...	...
1826	...	...	...	...	...	...	...	...
1827	...	...	...	...	...	...	...	...
1828	...	...	...	...	...	...	...	...
1829	...	...	...	...	...	...	...	...
1830	...	...	...	...	...	...	...	...
1831	...	...	...	...	...	...	...	...
1832	...	...	...	...	...	...	...	...
1833	...	...	...	...	...	...	...	...
1834	2,891	–	...	...	...	...	...	...
1835	...	...	...	...	...	...	...	...
1836	...	...	...	...	...	...	...	...
1837	...	...	...	...	...	...	...	...
1838	...	...	...	...	...	...	...	...
1839	...	...	...	...	...	...	...	...
1840	3,814	–	111	–	...	...	...	...
1841	...	...	...	...	...	...	...	...
1842	...	...	...	...	...	...	...	...
1843	...	...	...	...	...	...	...	...
1844	...	...	...	...	...	...	...	...
1845	3,581	–	164	–	...	...	...	...
1846	...	...	...	...	...	...	...	...
1847	...	...	...	...	...	...	...	...
1848	...	...	...	...	...	...	...	...
1849	3,970	–	265	–	...	...	...	...
1850	4,046	–	266	–	...	...	...	...
1851	...	...	...	...	...	...	...	...
1852	...	...	...	...	...	...	...	...
1853	4,230	–	248	–	...	...	...	...
1854	4,230	–	250	–	...	...	...	...
1855	...	...	...	...	...	...	...	...
1856	...	...	...	...	...	...	...	...
1857	4,339	...	295	...	...	...	...	...
1858	3,918	2	268	...	...	...	...	...
1859	3,984	–	274	–	...	...	...	...
1860	4,070	–	263	–	...	...	...	...
1861	4,152	1	256	- -	...	...	...	...
1862	4,334	1	257	- -	9,356	57	644	10
1863	4,451	1	262	- -	10,264	82	661[6]	17
1864	4,527	1	280	- -	13,809	90	573	20
1865	5,743	1	327	- -	15,633	95	656	22
1866	5,501	11	324	5	16,111	99	695	22
1867	5,368	11	322	5	17,690	98	792	23
1868	5,411	11	330	5	17,858	101	860	23
1869	...	...	...	...	17,562	105	925	25

See p. 660 for footnotes

G 4 Merchant Ships Registered

1820–1869

	Netherlands				Norway				Russia[7]			
	Number of Ships		Thousand Tons		Number of Ships		Thousand Tons		Number of Ships		Thousand Tons	
	Sail	Steam	Sail	Steam	Sail	Steam	Sail	Steam	Sail	Steam	Sail	Steam
1820	...	...	...	...	1,672		125		...	...	...	...
1821	...	...	...	...	...		...		...	...	...	...
1822	...	...	...	...	...		...		...	...	...	...
1823	...	...	...	...	...		...		...	...	...	...
1824	...	...	...	...	...		...		...	...	...	...
1825	...	...	...	...	1,761		113		...	...	...	...
1826	1,176		148		...		...		...	...	...	...
1827	...		...		...		...		...	...	...	...
1828	1,302		169		...		...		...	...	...	...
1829	1,346		178		...		...		...	...	...	...
1830	...		...		2,031		135		...	...	...	...
1831	...		...		...		...		...	...	...	...
1832	...		...		...		...		...	...	...	...
1833	...		...		...		...		...	...	...	...
1834	...		...		...		...		...	...	...	...
1835	...		...		2,272		151		...	...	...	...
1836	...		...		2,293		153		...	...	...	...
1837	...		...		...		...		...	...	...	...
1838	...		...		2,427		170		...	...	...	...
1839	...		...		...		...		...	...	...	...
1840	...		...		2,509		205		...	...	...	...
1841	...		...		...		...		...	...	...	...
1842	...		...		...		...		...	...	...	...
1843	...		...		...		...		...	...	...	...
1844	...		...		...		...		...	...	...	...
1845	...		...		3,348		233		...	...	...	...
1846	1,931	5	378	2	...		...		...	...	...	...
1847	2,055	6	394	2	3,526		259		...	...	...	...
1848	2,140	6	408	2	...		...		...	...	...	...
1849	2,300[6]	10	430[6]	3	...		...		...	...	...	...
1850	1,781	12	331	3	3,696		284		...	...	...	...
1851	1,848	12	352	3	3,762		297		...	...	...	...
1852	1,958	13	375	3	4,089		320		...	...	...	...
1853	2,022	15	401	4	4,200		341		...	...	...	...
1854	2,139	17	435	4	4,309		375		...	...	...	...
1855	2,210	20	460	5	4,464		405		...	...	...	...
1856	2,312	31	492	9	4,851		456		...	...	...	...
1857	2,388	40	512	11	5,152		496		...	...	...	...
1858	2,397	41	512	11	5,247		514		...	...	...	...
1859	2,365	41	504	12	5,278		526		1,416		173	
1860	2,318	42	485	11	5,287		532		...		...	
1861	2,292	40	474	11	5,493		552		...		...	
1862	2,251	38	458	11	5,541		567		...		...	
1863	2,191	40	445	12	5,621		604		...		...	
1864	2,184	43	445	13	5,678		635		...		...	
1865	2,161	42	443	13	5,407		706		2,045	87	181	
1866	2,135	43	443	14	6,155	60	790	6	...	...	...	
1867	2,114	45	443	14	6,381	76	830	7	...	...	...	
1868	2,074	43	438	14	6,811	98	894	10	...	...	...	
1869	2,016	43	433	14	6,727	106	921	11	2,534	114	230	

See p. 660 for footnotes

G 4 Merchant Ships Registered

1820--1869

	Spain				Sweden				United Kingdom			
	Number of Ships		Thousand Tons		Number of Ships		Thousand Tons		Number of Ships		Thousand Tons	
	Sail	Steam	Sail	Steam	Sail	Steam	Sail	Steam	Sail	Steam	Sail	Steam
1820	...	...	...	...	819		94		21,935	34	2,436	3
1821	...	...	...	...	...		...		21,593	59	2,350	6
1822	...	...	...	...	...		...		21,153	85	2,307	9
1823	...	...	...	...	...		...		20,941	101	2,293	10
1824	...	...	...	...	...		...		21,164	116	2,338	12
1825	...	...	...	...	700		87		20,442	153	2,313	16
1826	...	...	...	...	...		...		20,738[6]	230[6]	2,387[6]	24[6]
1827	...	...	...	...	...		...		19,269	255	2,154	27
1828	...	...	...	...	...		...		19,372	274	2,165	28
1829	...	...	...	...	...[8]		...[8]		18,821	289	2,170	30
1830	...	...	...	...	1,841		131		18,876	298	2,168	30
1831	...	...	...	...	1,917		133		19,126	324	2,192	33
1832	...	...	...	...	1,948		130		19,312	352	2,226	36
1833	...	...	...	...	1,882		126		19,302	387	2,233	39
1834	...	...	...	...	1,809		124		19,545	430	2,268	44
1835	...	...	...	...	1,740		118		19,797	503	2,307	53
1836	...	...	...	...	1,809		116		19,827	561	2,289	60
1837	...	...	...	...	1,828		121		19,912	624	2,264	70
1838	...	...	...	...	1,882		129		20,234	678	2,346	75
1839	...	...	...	...	2,068		146		20,947	723	2,491	80
1840	...	...	...	...	2,171		159		21,883	771	2,680	88
1841	...	...	...	...	2,196		163		22,668	793	2,839	96
1842	...	...	...	...	2,171		167		23,121	833	2,933	108
1843	...	...	...	...	2,112		165		23,040	858	2,898	110
1844	...	...	...	...	2,044		160		23,116	900	2,931	114
1845	...	...	...	...	2,093		160		23,471	917	3,004	119
1846	...	...	...	...	2,062		155		23,808	963	3,069	131
1847	...	...	...	...	2,409		173		24,167	1,033	3,167	141
1848	...	...	...	...	2,440		182		24,520	1,118	3,249	151
1849	...	...	...	...	2,624		195		24,753	1,149	3,326	160
1850	4,531	23	240	5	2,744		204		24,797	1,187	3,397	168
1851	...	...	...	...	2,771		207		24,816	1,227	3,476	187
1852	...	...	...	...	2,846		211		24,814	1,272	3,550	209
1853	...	...	...	...	2,826		208		25,224	1,385	3,780	250
1854	...	...	...	...	2,783		214		25,335	1,524	3,943	306
1855	...	...	...	...	2,874		229		24,274	1,674	3,969	381
1856	...	...	...	...	3,020		252		24,480	1,697	3,980	387
1857	5,118	57	345	5	3,190		268		25,273	1,824	4,141	417
1858	...	...	...	...	3,300		275		25,615	1,926	4,205	452
1859	...	...	...	...	3,364		287		25,784	1,918	4,226	437
1860	4,716	84	400	15	3,200		281		25,663	2,000	4,204	454
1861	4,739	101	347	21	3,313		289		25,905	2,133	4,301	506
1862	4,704	124	356	33	3,108		280		26,212	2,228	4,396	538
1863	4,732	127	356	39	3,236		283		26,339	2,298	4,731	597
1864	4,614	135	359	42	3,198		287		26,142	2,490	4,930	697
1865	4,593	140	368	42	2,867	288	254	12	26,069	2,718	4,937	823
1866	4,355	145	356	43	3,030	293	286		26,140	2,831	4,904	876
1867	4,363	151	345	46	2,991	310	303		25,842	2,931	4,853	901
1868	...	...	...	...	2,924	344	303		25,500	2,944	4,878	902
1869	...	...	...	...	2,999	358	337		24,187	2,972	4,765	948

See p. 660 for footnotes

G 4 Merchant Ships Registered

1870–1919

	Austria/Hungary[1]				Belgium				Denmark					
	Number of Ships		Thousand Tons		Number of Ships		Thousand Tons		Number of Ships			Thousand Tons		
	Sail	Steam	Sail	Steam	Sail	Steam	Sail	Steam	Sail	Steam	Motor	Sail	Steam	Motor
1870	7,750[1]	83[1]	316[1]	47[1]	55	12	21	10	2,648	87	...	170	12	...
	7,367	83	310	47										
1871	7,232	91	259	49	48	12	17	9	2,655	91	...	173	16	...
1872	6,528	95	224	53	40	19	16	16	2,629	109	...	176	22	...
1873	6,593	99	217	56	41	28	16	30	2,723[3]	123[3]	...	185[3]	27[3]	...
1874	6,556	99	204	58	33	24	15	30	2,822	135	...	196	29	...
1875	6,832	94	201	56	32	27	15	35	2,909	167	...	205	39	...
1876	...	...	...	...	25	23	15	30	2,966	178	...	211	44	...
1877	7,010	95	201	57	22	28	11	38	2,966	187	...	207	45	...
1878	7,290	91	200	58	24	34	10	50	2,971	189	...	205	47	...
1879	7,629	101	201	60	25	39	12	60	2,953	192	...	203	49	...
1880	7,608	107	198	64	24	42	10	65	2,881	201	...	198	52	...
1881	7,829	106	193	67	18	41	7	70	2,857	226	...	192	61	...
1882	8,166	112	184	74	16	46	7	76	2,829	239	...	186	71	...
1883	8,574	117	178	72	15	47	6	80	2,857	258	...	185	81	...
1884	8,589	118	179	75	13	51	6	75	2,854	274	...	182	91	...
1885	8,768	120	165	78	11	54	5	80	2,881	280	...	180	90	...
1886	9,124	128	155	86	12	55	6	81	2,874	279	...	176	88	...
1887	9,104	131	137	86	10	55	6	81	2,877	281	...	172	90	...
1888	9,291	135	121	85	9	50	4	73	2,889	290	...	167	96	...
1889	9,414	141	113	86	9	42	4	66	2,938	305	...	177	104	...
1890	9,778	135	108	87	10	46	4	72	3,054	322	...	182	112	...
1891	9,977	135	104	90	8	47	2	71	3,094	343	...	188	117	...
1892	10,151	141	99	89	6	47	1	69	3,114	349	...	193	119	...
1893	10,887	144	90	97	6	56	1	74	3,116	362	...	195	129	...
1894	11,140	139	85	96	5	50	1	78	3,009	377	...	186	142	...
1895	11,467	148	81	107	5	54	1	86	3,010	401	...	179	144	...
1896	11,658	162	75	122	5	54	1	85	3,000	418	...	173	163	...
1897	11,499	175	68	143	5	56	1	85	2,996	436	...	163	181	...
1898	12,134	174	62	146	6	60	2	89	3,020	476	...	158	223	...
1899	11,928	183	58	162	6	67	3	106	3,047	497	...	155	255	...
1900	12,440	199	54	191	4	69	1	113	3,017	483	...	147	247	...
1901	12,713	211	54	227	6	66	1	109	3,026	497	...	143	257	...
1902	12,792	229	58	244	5	68	1	105	3,087	502	...	144	270	...
1903	12,917	232	55	253	4	67	1	102	3,121	508	...	138	292	...
1904	13,304	250	52	262	4	65	3	100	3,130	549	...	136	318	...
1905	13,642	266	51	276	4	67	3	97	3,126	572	...	130	331	...
1906	13,680	278	51	284	2	73	1	112	3,161	606	...	122	373	...
1907	13,983	296	50	310	3	74	1	119	3,266[9]	641	...	121[9]	402	...
1908	14,189	316	47	335	4	84	3	149	2,497	645	690	108	402	8
1909	14,629	357	45	343	4	97	3	184	2,441	652	738	107	406	9
1910	15,114	359	46	368	5	99	3	188	2,251	643	754	101	412	9
1911	15,847	382	47	390	8	93	6	161	2,147	640	775	94	412	8
1912	16,370	394	49	422	8	97	8	174	2,062	642	860	91	415	16
1913	...	...	...	...	12	112	13	222	1,970	642	941	90	421	30
1914	...	...	...	...	...	...	...	...	1,906	672	1,060	86	434	42
1915	...	...	...	...	...	...	...	...	1,874	664	1,128	96	432	59
1916	...	...	...	...	...	...	...	...	1,773	634	1,163	121	412	62
1917	...	...	...	...	...	...	...	...	1,592	536	1,269	97	339	64
1918	...	...	...	...	...	...	...	...	1,559	496	1,311	96	313	61
1919	...	...	...	...	...	...	...	...	1,584	514	1,463	103	334	82

See p. 660 for footnotes

G 4 Merchant Ships Registered

1870–1919

	Finland				France				Germany			
	Number of Ships		Thousand Tons		Number of Ships		Thousand Tons		Number of Ships		Thousand Tons	
	Sail	Steam	Sail	Steam	Sail	Steam & Motor	Sail	Steam & Motor	Sail	Steam & Motor	Sail	Steam & Motor
1870	1,538	78	240		14,929	457	921	151	4,589	132	872	67
1871	...	...	...		14,786	473	917	160	4,354	175	856	80
1872	1,689	97	240	6	15,062	512	912	177	4,311	216	835	106
1873	1,512	100	239	6	15,043	516	883	185	4,242	253	831	137
1874	1,837	117	276	7	15,002	522	843	195	4,303	299	844	156
1875	1,813	134	293	7	14,904	537	823	205	4,426	319	865	151
1876	1,812	138	299	8	14,861	546	793	218	4,491	318	886	148
1877	1,836	161	294	9	14,884	565	758	231	4,469	336	898	150
1878	1,827	176	294	10	14,939	588	730	246	4,453	351	911	147
1879	1,673	201	275	10	14,434	599	678	256	4,403	374	936	161
1880	1,500	203	262	10	14,406	652	642	278	4,246	414	927	177
1881	1,574	205	265	11	14,391	735	603	312	4,051	458	905	206
1882	1,670[5]	207[5]	272[5]	12[5]	14,368	832	567	416	3,855	515	878	255
1883	...	...	...	...	14,327	895	536	467	3,712	603	859	307
1884	...	...	...	...	14,414	938	523	511	3,607	650	845	339
1885	1,750	301	247	17	14,329	937	508	492	3,471	664	788	345
1886	1,835	318	251	17	14,400	951	493	500	3,327	694	798	372
1887	1,796[5]	312[5]	235[5]	17[5]	14,253	984	466	507	3,094	717	739	386
1888	...	...	...	...	14,263	1,015	451	510	2,885	750	702	412
1889	...	...	...	...	14,128	1,066	440	493	2,779	815	675	507
1890	...	...	...	...	14,001	1,110	444	500	2,757	896	682	593
1891	...	...	...	...	13,890	1,157	426	522	2,698	941	676	627
1892	1,776	417	232	26	14,117	1,161	407	499	2,742	986	696	645
1893	1,858	417	233	28	14,190	1,186	397	499	2,713	1,016	670	675
1894	1,964	404	238	28	14,332	1,196	399	492	2,622	1,043	635	732
1895	1,955	418	237	29	14,386	1,212	387	501	2,524	1,068	593	796
1896	1,921	447	237	36	14,301	1,235	390	504	2,552	1,126	576	862
1897	2,031	453	252	38	14,352	1,212	421	499	2,522	1,171	569	945
1898	2,171	495	276	44	14,406	1,209	415	496	2,490	1,223	586	1,010
1899	2,282	540	275	51	14,262	1,227	451	507	2,466	1,293	576	1,124
1900	2,411	588	287	54	14,313	1,272	510	528	2,493	1,390	584	1,319
1901	2,606	584	296	50	14,393	1,299	564	547	2,496	1,463	578	1,476
1902	2,594	595	292	50	14,691	1,330	669	549	2,500	1,545	574	1,591
1903	2,622	633	290	60	14,910	1,383	650	585	2,534	1,622	576	1,713
1904	2,696	662	294	62	15,057	1,457	653	696	2,567	1,657	574	1,743
1905	2,750	663	301	60	15,284	1,471	676	711	2,558	1,762	551	1,883
1906	2,793	709	303	64	15,488	1,511	677	723	2,597	1,833	532	2,063
1907	2,843	729	308	66	15,639	1,554	663	740	2,649	1,922	535	2,230
1908	3,025	805	327	74	15,768	1,608	648	808	2,685	1,955	517	2,280
1909	3,076	819	333	76	15,878	1,670	638	806	2,708	1,950	510	2,332
1910	3,171	828	333	78	15,895	1,726	636	816	2,702	1,973	507	2,383
1911	3,252	845	333	77	15,849	1,780	625	838	2,724	2,009	510	2,501
1912	3,349	852	349	77	15,813	1,857	614	904	2,752	2,098	498	2,643
1913	3,401	895	368	82	15,824	1,895	602	980	2,765	2,170	488	2,832
1914	3,569	950	393	86	15,682	1,935	586	1,043	...	...	...	...
1915	3,834	946	386	81	15,161	1,939	561	1,066	...	...	...	...
1916	4,094	988	418	87	14,470	1,942	520	1,027	...	...	...	...
1917	4,214	1,014	446	85	13,777	1,880	417	886	...	...	...	...
1918	4,401	1,120	436	102	13,378	1,842	409	850	...	...	...	...
1919	4,544	1,122	435	107	13,137	1,969	427	879	...	...	...	...

See p. 660 for footnotes

G 4 Merchant Ships Registered

1870–1919

	Greece				Hungary [12]				Italy			
	Number of Ships		Thousand Tons		Number of Ships		Thousand Tons		Number of Ships		Thousand Tons	
	Sail	Steam	Sail	Steam	Sail	Steam	Sail	Steam	Sail	Steam & Motor	Sail	Steam & Motor
1870	...	...	...	...	...	...	...	...	18,083 [13]	118	980 [13]	32
1871	...	...	...	...	565	1	83	1	11,270	121	994	38
1872	...	...	...	...	...	...	...	...	10,951	118	993	38
1873	...	16	227	6	...	...	...	...	10,712	133	998	49
1874	5,182	20	242	8	...	...	...	...	10,791	138	980	52
1875	5,410	27	254	27	...	...	...	...	10,828	141	987	57
1876	...	...	...	...	505	5	68	--	10,903	142	1,020	58
1877	...	...	...	...	...	...	...	...	10,742 [6]	151	1,010 [6]	58
1878	...	...	...	...	...	3	...	--	8,438	152	966	63
1879	...	...	...	...	...	3	...	--	7,910	151	933	73
1880	...	...	...	...	...	6	...	--	7,822	158	922	77
1881	...	...	...	...	465	6	67	--	7,639	176	895	94
1882	...	...	...	...	...	14	...	6	7,528	192	885	105
1883	...	...	...	...	...	17	...	6	7,270	201	866	107
1884	[3,141] [10]	72	[225] [10]	36	...	20	...	6	7,072	215	849	122
1885	...	...	...	...	...	24	...	7	7,111	225	829	125
1886	...	...	...	...	458	25	57	7	6,992	237	801	144
1887	5,074	83	227	31	...	28	...	10	6,727	254	732	163
1888	5,731	98	217	32	...	28	...	10	6,544	266	698	175
1889	5,809	82	223	41	457	30	48	10	6,442	279	642	186
1890	5,744	97	227	45	...	...	...	...	6,442	290	634	187
1891	5,675	105	214	55	445	40	41	13	6,312	305	626	200
1892	5,732	162	234	77	426	46	37	17	6,308	316	610	201
1893	6,002 [11]	161 [11]	231 [11]	84 [11]	433	59	36	32	6,341	327	588	208
1894	...	...	...	...	409	64	30	37	6,231	328	572	208
1895	1,164	112	251	81	440	64	28	38	6,166	345	556	221
1896	1,059	107	246	89	444	67	25	39	6,002	351	528	238
1897	1,165	109	246	92	432	70	22	46	5,872	366	527	260
1898	1,147	100	238	87	432	69	19	44	5,764	384	538	278
1899	972	108	197	91	424	80	16	47	5,665	409	558	315
1900	927 [11]	122 [11]	184 [11]	115 [11]	360	78	13	56	5,511	446	568	377
	673	122	176	143								
1901	630	134	148	163	347	79	11	63	5,337	471	575	425
1902	595	184	145	201	333	91	8	85	5,205	485	570	448
1903	604	167	145	199	361	90	6	86	5,153	501	584	461
1904	560	179	146	200	339	95	3	92	5,083	513	570	462
1905	551	183	145	226	382	95	3	92	5,020	514	541	484
1906	571	201	147	247	379	97	3	93	4,981	548	503	498
1907	567	212	145	258	385	104	3	109	4,874	589	469	527
1908	701	224	146	295	381	113	3	113	4,701	626	453	567
1909	882	261	165	292	378	116	2	114	4,723	680	440	631
1910	804	298	145	313	341	114	2	110	4,741	718	433	674
1911	813	322	145	350	388	128	2	132	4,713	757	411	697
1912	807	346	142	407	400	133	2	137	4,693	839	375	762
1913	788	389	137	434	411	134	2	143	4,696	931	356	877
1914	...	450	...	493	412	137	2	148	4,773	949 [14]	349	933 [14]
1915	784	474	107	550	...	...	...	...	4,737	644	332	934
1916	...	...	...	...	407	130	2	144	4,464	659	262	1,036
1917	...	...	...	...	416	126	3	144	4,084	559	218	896
1918	700	205	120	291	...	...	...	...	...	448 [14]	...	699 [14]
1919	1,056	282	133	430	...	...	...	...	...	408	...	632

See p. 660 for footnotes

G 4 Merchant Ships Registered

1870–1919

	Netherlands				Norway						Russia[7]			
	Number of Ships		Thousand Tons		Number of Ships			Thousand Tons			Number of Ships		Thousand Tons	
	Sail	Steam & Motor	Sail	Steam & Motor	Sail	Steam	Motor	Sail	Steam	Motor	Sail	Steam	Sail	Steam
1870	1,937	48	430	17	6,875	118	...	961	13	...	...	...	...	...
1871	1,846[15]	56[15]	414[15]	26[15]	6,923	140	...	993	19	...	...	...	...	...
	1,843	59	417	31										
1872	1,790	66	400	39	7,019	170	...	1,038	29	...	2,325	189	260	
1873	1,731	73	390	51	7,248	199	...	1,149	37	...	...	...	...	...
1874	1,747	80	392	63	7,453	211	...	1,235	40	...	...	...	...	...
1875	1,749	86	400	68	7,596	218	...	1,310	42	...	...	...	...	...
1876	1,702[16]	84[16]	401[16]	64[16]	7,651	258	...	1,390	46	...	2,163	218	302	74
1877	1,168	79	307	58	7,791	273	...	1,446	47	...	3,051	222	271	69
1878	1,100	79	299	59	7,942	306	...	1,475	52	...	3,643	259	308	74
1879	1,044	76	289	59	7,823	324	...	1,456	55	...	4,120	296	368	91
1880	917	79	264	64	7,761	334	...	1,461	58	...	4,276	326	379	89
1881	802	78	233	72	7,618	359	...	1,455	65	...	...	...	...	...
1882	751	86	217	85	7,506	407	...	1,447	83	...	...	...	...	...
1883	701	96	207	102	7,459	440	...	1,455	92	...	4,411[29]	379[29]	401[29]	99[29]
1884	673	107	198	110	7,397	487	...	1,478	105	...	2,608	342	351	120
1885	634	106	194	108	7,154	510	...	1,449	114	...	2,632	360	358	127
1886	586	106	177	109	6,942	502	...	1,411	113	...	2,614	369	362	130
1887	516	105	155	101	6,755	514	...	1,382	122	...	...	...	...	...
1888	502	107	140	105	6,697	536	...	1,397	138	...	...	...	...	...
1889	500	110	137	110	6,693	592	...	1,443	168	...	...	...	...	...
1890	500	118	127	128	6,760	672	...	1,503	203	...	...	...	...	...
1891	478	143	131	161	6,798	735	...	1,500	239	...	...	...	...	...
1892	447	150	123	169	6,739	767	...	1,494	251	...	...	...	...	...
1893	442	154	118	176	6,702	810	...	1,452	239	...	...	...	...	...
1894	424	157	110	183	6,453	859	...	1,335	264	...	...	...	...	...
1895	405	162	102	188	6,355	915	...	1,284	321	...	2,135	522	323	206
1896	440	172	98	196	6,230	962	...	1,215	352	...	2,207	567	336	241
1897	441	171	95	201	6,143	1,004	...	1,169	383	...	2,294	604	344	262
1898	429	176	88	214	5,981	1,068	...	1,121	437	...	2,143	657	254	300
1899	432	192	84	235	5,698	1,128	...	1,053	482	...	2,259	714	268	334
1900	425	213	78	268	5,642	1,171	...	1,003	505	...	2,293	745	269	364
1901	417	235	75	306	5,445	1,223	...	936	531	...	2,378	810	273	392
1902	436	257	73	331	5,569	1,290	...	884	567	...	2,489	840	285	397
1903	439	268	58	337	5,807	1,396	...	840	604	...	2,500	832	277	390
1904	463	269	58	341	5,843	1,477	...	809	642	...	2,533[18]	834[18]	284	383
1905	479	271	55	357	5,853	1,734	...	814	664	...	2,523	847	267	375
1906	492	283	53	377	5,813	1,493	305	793	752	3	...	...	...	...
1907	435	292	50	398	5,773	1,599	508	751	814	5	2,544	906	260	441
1908	403	283	44	414	5,742	1,645	1,165	725	847	9	2,465	898	258	443
1909	426	303	47	464	5,219[17]	1,671[17]	1,027[17]	702[17]	861[17]	9[17]	2,494	925	261	459
1910	440	324	46	488	1,205	1,738	104	630	893	3	2,504	943	260	463
1911	428	347	42	523	1,170	1,813	126	658	984	4	2,516	1,015	254	488
1912	413	367	41	577	1,106	1,973	153	633	1,081	4	2,577	1,068	257	500
1913	400	387	40	647	1,029	2,052	209	606	1,155	6	2,597	1,103	257[19]	526[19]
													184[7]	790[7]
1914	402	407	47	720	947	2,107	271	561	1,214	9	...	...	...	...
1915	390	397	45	726	867	2,200	393	505	1,254	18	...	...	...	...
1916	364	422	35	726	740	2,142	613	428	1,273	29	...	...	...	...
1917	331	468	31	723	602	1,837	978	294	995	52	...	...	...	...
1918	332	575	32	770	547	1,763	1,164	257	898	69	...	...	...	...
1919	283	570	28	804	457	1,826	1,382	232	979	105	...	...	...	...

See p. 660 for footnotes

G 4 Merchant Ships Registered

1870–1919

	Spain				Sweden				United Kingdom			
	Number of Ships		Thousand Tons		Number of Ships		Thousand Tons		Number of Ships		Thousand Tons	
	Sail	Steam	Sail	Steam	Sail	Steam & Motor	Sail	Steam & Motor	Sail	Steam	Sail	Steam
1870	...	...	...	...	3,008	368	319	28	23,189	3,178	4,578	1,113
1871	4,326		360		3,089	406	345	24	22,510	3,382	4,374	1,320
1872	...	...	...	...	3,185	479	354	35	22,103	3,673	4,213	1,538
1873	[20]	[20]	[20]	[20]	3,335	565	383	52	21,698	3,863	4,091	1,714
1874	2,674	212	510	115	3,585	627	411	82	21,464	4,033	4,108	1,871
1875	2,886	212	625	115	3,573	664	424	83	21,291	4,170	4,207	1,946
1876	2,752	388	452	159	3,700	681	443	82	21,144	4,335	4,258	2,005
1877	...	...	...	...	3,701	691	447	84	21,169	4,564	4,261	2,139
1878	2,063	339	374	164	3,563	752	454	82	21,058	4,826	4,239	2,316
1879	...	...	...	...	3,550	752	447	84	20,538	5,027	4,069	2,511
1880	1,889	347	326	234	3,581	752	462	81	19,938	5,247	3,851	2,724
1881	...	...	...	...	3,397	754	450	79	19,325	5,505	3,688	3,004
1882	1,555	252	316	248	3,356	785	440	88	18,892	5,814	3,622	3,335
1883	1,461	407	247	347	3,252	823	424	95	18,415	6,260	3,514	3,728
1884	1,395	430	231	383	3,158	886	422	108	18,053	6,601	3,465	3,944
1885	1,379	431	225	388	3,090	878	407	110	17,018	6,644	3,457	3,973
1886	1,336	431	216	384	3,033	903	386	115	16,179	6,653	3,397	3,965
1887	1,326	432	212	397	2,954	949	377	123	15,473	6,663	3,250	4,085
1888	1,277	421	205	393	2,885	959	375	125	15,025	6,871	3,114	4,350
1889	1,238	415	195	411	2,859	963	370	135	14,640	7,139	3,041	4,718
1890	1,342	411	210	408	2,858	1,016	370	141	14,181	7,410	2,936	5,043
1891	1,313	438	204	436	3,006	1,181	380	152	13,823	7,720	2,972	5,307
1892	1,233	474	197	455	2,927	1,209	377	172	13,578	7,950	3,080	4,565
1893	1,228	492	197	480	2,844	1,229	369	177	13,239	8,088	3,038	5,740
1894	1,237	502	199	489	2,914[21]	1,248[21]	371[21]	179[21]	12,943	8,263	2,987	5,969
1895	1,260	523	193	526	2,030	733	302	181	12,617	8,386	2,867	6,122
1896	1,256	543	192	564	2,013	756	291	206	12,274	8,522	2,736	6,284
1897	1,125	562	159	499	2,002	786	289	234	11,911	8,590	2,590	6,364
1898	...[20]	...[20]	...[20]	...[20]	2,004	817	291	266	11,566	8,838	2,388	6,614
1899	175	422	53	642	2,040	872	289	298	11,167	9,029	2,247	6,917
1900	163	469	51	735	2,076	911	289	325	10,773	9,209	2,096	7,208
1901	150	459	48	736	2,160	943	299	342	10,572	9,484	1,991	7,618
1902	136	459	44	721	2,035	952	279	357	10,455	9,803	1,951	8,104
1903	124	455	41	714	1,983	987	272	376	10,330	10,122	1,869	8,400
1904	119	450	38	689	1,950	1,019	266	408	10,210	10,370	1,803	8,752
1905	118	461	38	684	1,915	1,066	263	460	10,059	10,522	1,671	9,065
1906	110	468	35	673	1,852	1,090	254	488	9,857	10,907	1,555	9,612
1907	82	469	24	677	1,827	1,141	239	533	9,648	11,394	1,461	10,024
1908	80	479	23	687	1,751	1,187	213	564	9,542	11,626	1,403	10,139
1909	68	511	19	747	1,689	1,211	193	583	9,392	11,797	1,301	10,285
1910	65	526	17	758	1,635	1,214	177	593	9,090	12,000	1,113	10,443
1911	64	526	16	756	1,539	1,219	155	610	8,830	12,242	981	10,718
1912	60	547	15	826	1,539	1 254	154	651	8,510	12,382	903	10,992
1913	93	554	24	875	1,509	1,313	152	721	8,336	12,602[6]	847	11,273[6]
1914	94	548	25	875	1,509	1,336	152	749	8,203	12,862	794	11,622
1915	...	...	...	...	1,422	1,278	137	689	8,019	12,771	779	11,650
1916	...	...	...	...	1,378	1,267	130	666	7,669	12,405	715	11,037
1917	93	490	35	729	1,304	1,240	123	633	7,186	11,534	625	9,608
1918	149	452	47	692	1,295	1,238	119	621	6,856	11,334	604	9,497
1919	240	456	75	705	1,279	1,260	117	658	6,555	11,791	593	10,335

See p. 660 for footnotes

G 4 Merchant Ships Registered

1920–1975

	Belgium						Denmark					
	Number of Ships			Thousand Tons			Number of Ships			Thousand Tons		
	Sail	Steam	Motor	Sail	Steam	Motor	Sail	Steam	Motor	Sail	Steam	Motor
1920	13	180	...	7	337	...	1,595	571	1,583	101	392	100
1921	12	195	...	7	382	...	1,511[4]	615[4]	1,671[4]	94[19,4]	453[19,4]	122[19,4]
							574	609	714	92	764	179
1922	7	183	...	4	365	...	489	622	766	81	789	179
1923	3	180	...	3	379	...	396	623	816	60	770	209
1924	1	156	4	2	343	6	336	644	866	49	823	218
1925	1	150	5	2	328	12	285	659	931	40	841	236
1926	1	145	6	2	320	12	252	638	980	37	811	260
1927	1	142	6	2	301	12	204	617	1,007	31	762	286
1928	1	139	8	2	291	22	160	602	1,047	27	733	336
1929	1	149	10	2	321	33	136	595	1,081	21	734	351
1930	1	140	10	2	319	37	100	599	1,141	15	735	417
1931	1	137	10	2	315	37	73[4]	606[4]	1,202[4]	11[4]	736[4]	468[4]
1932	—	117	10	—	265	37	76	610	1,403	10	721	506
1933	—	103	10	—	230	37	59	591	1,410	8	672	512
1934	—	96	11	—	217	39	42	583	1,418	4	662	522
1935	—	91	11	—	206	39	34	563	1,449	4	629	555
1936	—	89	11	—	201	40	26	549	1,497	2	602	586
1937	—	76	16	—	183	54	18	521	1,514	1	570	616
1938	—	67	28	—	164	88	16	518	1,558	2	584	647
1939	—	56	31	—	149	96	18	499	1,621	2	565	679
1940	—	59	34	—	159	94	15	465	1,607	1	526	679
1941	—	56	34	—	147	97	14	437	1,625	1	479	649
1942	—	...	...	—	...	...	...	...	...	...	...	...
1943	—	...	...	—	...[19]	...[19]	14	408	1,681	1	443	550
1944	—	30	22	—	109	90	...	...	...	...	...	...
1945	—	28	24	—	96	107	5	349	1,761	- -	362	576
1946	—	34	27	—	118	130	5	339	1,778	- -	348	593
1947	—	47	31	—	204	146	5[22]	383[22]	1,854[22]	- -[22]	450[22]	648[22]
1948	—	52	39	—	216	176	4	373	1,920	- -	469	746
1949	—	48	46	—	205	204	3	358	1,958	- -	471	836
1950	—	45	49	—	199	226	2	344	2,010	- -	447	939
1951	—	43	47	—	207	224	2	311	2,001	- -	404	1,055
1952	—	40	51	—	200	237	2	268	2,017	- -	370	1,162
1953	—	39	51	—	191	229	2	252	2,024	- -	342	1,279
1954	—	32	50	—	198	232	2	218	2,015	- -	282	1,395
1955	—	32	50	—	221	230	2	192	2,022	- -	245	1,527
1956	—	34	52	—	241	262	2[23]	165	2,083[23]	- -[23]	195	1,686[23]
1957	—	34	57	—	249	282	1,565	149	620	90	175	1,785
1958	—	34	65	—	266	354	1,609	140	685	92	162	1,932
1959	—	31	67	—	260	370	1,658	118	769	94	164	2,028
1960	—	27	70	—	283	394	1,708	99	882	95	159	2,135
1961	—	22	69	—	229	396	1,733	87	990	96	172	2,227
1962	—	21	76	—	239	429	1,724	74	1,044	95	182	2,250
1963	—	18	81	—	217	481	1,719	66	1,069	93	238	2,197
1964	—	15	85	—	219	509	1,717	55	1,132	93	287	2,281
1965	—	10	87	—	169	591	1,714	48	1,204	92	315	2,341
1966	—	9	80	—	161	610	1,720	45	1,294	91	465	2,487
1967	—	9	84	—	161	674	1,722	43	1,384	92	516	2,594
1968	—	9	83	—	161	724	1,700	43	1,465	89	669	2,566
1969	—	9	88	—	161	797	1,664	42	1,514	86	872	2,528
1970	—	9	80	—	161	812	1,629	35	1,569	85	800	2,530
1971	—	9	80	—	161	915	1,579	37	1,623	81	1,276	2,500
1972	—	9	86	—	161	930	1,542	36	1,683	79	1,465	2,605
1973	—	8	80	—	136	954	1,521	39	1,724	78	1,651	2,522
1974	—	8	82	—	136	1,115	1,506	36	1,753	77	1,979	2,706
1975	—	5	89	—	82	1,274	1,518	32	1,787	78	1,897	2,750

See p. 660 for footnotes

G 4 Merchant Ships Registered

1920–1975

	Finland						France			
	Number of Ships			Thousand Tons			Number of Ships		Thousand Tons	
	Sail	Steam	Motor	Sail	Steam	Motor	Sail	Steam & Motor	Sail	Steam & Motor
1920	4,064[5]	1,144[5]	123	380[5]	108[5]	22	13,292	2,246	433	1,085
	788	809		108	144					
1921	701	795	127	97	91	19	13,508	2,519	452	1,388
1922	633	637	125	92	88	17	13,693	2,693	451	1,698
1923	615	598	116	94	89	16	13,640	2,696	386	1,759
1924	590	575	107	88	93	14	13,602	2,690	357	1,750
1925	543	568	96	97	176	13	13,665	2,809	356	1,766
1926	520	547	91	81	110	11	13,650	2,911	291	1,784
1927	513	558	103	80	130	13	13,550	3,008	268	1,778
1928	481	564	144	79	145	17	13,378	3,072	237	1,797
1929	439	570	154	76	155	17	13,409	3,126	232	1,775
1930	328	538	149	66	157	24	13,294	3,290	233	1,831
1931	279	520	152	67	163	14	13,075	3,442	226	1,870
1932	256	530	163	67	211	19	12,764	3,551	220	1,839
1933	242	535	161	73	386	29	12,612	3,602	219	1,804
1934	206[24]	545	168[24]	66[24]	428	30[24]	12,423	3,620	214	1,593
1935	298	528	31	72	418	14	12,125	3,713	199	1,588
1936	280	547	36	63	469	17	11,780	3,776	207	1,524
1937	262	567	37	56	537	17	11,320	3,842	200	1,484
1938	249	562	46	54	552	38	9,841	4,911	178	1,486
1939	227	560	50	49	557	43	9,079	5,373	171	1,546
1940	196	470	47	44	488	47	6,979	1,364	131	1,476
1941	180	429	42	31	379	30	8,517	5,437	158	1,608
1942	174	405	41	31	336	25	8,600	5,594	157	1,583
1943	172	400	42	31	336	25	8,585	5,668	156	1,579
1944	134[24]	362	41[24]	22[24]	288	22[24]	8,444	5,655	154	1,574
1945	15	312	167	14	232	21	8,257	5,781	153	1,546
1946	13	333	203	13	280	37	7,775	5,796	144	1,358
1947	11	386	247	13	411	66	7,403	6,258	94	1,671
1948	12[24]	385	256[24]	15[24]	423	83[24]	7,330	6,590	91	1,490
1949	162	387	108	27	429	79	7,218	7,040[25]	86	1,540[19, 25]
								1,236		3,070
1950	153	376	123	20	458	90	...	1,234	...	3,207
1951	145	375	128	16	468	107	...	1,246	...	3,367
1952	131	360	135	13	473	147	...	1,251	...	3,638
1953	128	338	147	12	441	223	...	1,260	...	3,826
1954	125	327	150	12	425	285	...	1,257	...	3,841
1955	117	316	162	12	436	305	...	1,220	...	3,922
1956	117	293	173	12	424	331	...	1,201	...	3,943
1957	116	274	186	12	401	364	...	1,230	...	4,010
1958	103	252	183	10	362	329	...	1,307	...	4,338
1959	98	223	196	10	312	396	...	1,409	...	4,538
1960	88	216	217	9	314	478	...	1,456	...	4,809
1961	83	200	250	8	295	516	...	1,488	...	5,117
1962	78	192	287	8	298	575	...	1,462	...	5,162
1963	53	179	335	6	295	644	...	1,498	...	5,216
1964	38	157	369	5	268	690	...	1,532	...	5,116
1965	30	140	390	4	240	747	...	1,558	...	5,198
1966	25	123	393	3	211	793	...	1,539	...	5,260
1967	17	101	407	2	170	925	...	1,538	...	5,577
1968	14	78	414	2	109	972	...	1,495	...	5,796
								570[40]		5,500[40]
1969	12	59	437	2	67	1,174	...	554	...	5,725
1970	9	53	447	1	65	1,304	...	538	...	5,921
1971	5	44	441	1	51	1,366	...	550	...	6,982
1972	3	37	456	–	41	1,572	...	531	...	7,440
1973	3	28	435	–	21	1,492	...	498	...	8,177
1974	–	27	422	–	14	1,610	...	514	...	9,476
1975		442			2,090		...	525	...	10,291

See p. 660 for footnotes

G 4 Merchant Ships Registered

1920–1975

	Germany						East Germany[10]		Greece			
	Number of Ships			Thousand Tons			Number of Ships	Thousand Tons	Number of Ships		Thousand Tons	
	Sail	Steam	& Motor	Sail	Steam	& Motor			Sail	Steam	Sail	Steam
1920	...	...		...	...		...	...	1,079	335	138	494
1921	...	...		...	...		...	...	1,093	440	152	685
1922	...	...		...	...		...	...	1,089	418	133	737
1923	2,282	1,956		288	1,546		...	...	1,060	431	122	762
1924	2,283	1,987		287	1,633		...	...	1,018	437	114	829
1925	2,164	1,987		260	1,675		...	...	814	467	68	913
1926	2,075	1,970		241	1,811		...	...	735	472	60	930
1927	1,964	2,017		215	1,979		...	...	726	504	59	1,111
1928	1,892	2,064		200	2,166		...	...	729	528	59	1,257
1929	1,852	2,087		190	2,312		...	...	718	547	58	1,350
1930	1,839	2,074		183	2,373		...	...	708	559	56	1,413
1931	1,767	2,009		158	2,360		...	...	698	575	56	1,488
1932	1,700	1,890		140	2,153		...	...	697	558	56	1,430
1933	1,689	1,825		139	2,062		...	...	699	565	56	1,572
1934	1,699	1,837		135	2,020		...	...	709	600	56	1,755
1935	1,692	1,825		132	2,006		...	...	700	600	54	1,759
1936	1,667	1,912		129	2,109		...	...	714	605	55	1,794
1937	1,636	2,032		127	2,243		...	...	...	615	...	1,875
1938	1,646	2,135		126	2,364		...	...	716	607	56	1,874
1939	...	...		...	...		...	...	...	577	...	1,837
1940	...	...	...	...	...	...	...	...	...	...	...	...
1941	...	...	...	...	...	...	...	...	...	...	...	...
1942	...	...	...	...	...	...	...	...	...	...	...	...
1943	...	...	...	...	...	...	...	...	...	...	...	...
1944	...	...	...	...	...	...	...	...	...	...	...	...
	West Germany[10]											
1945	...	...	...	...	...	...	...	...	...	...	...	...
1946	...	...	...	...	...	...	...	...		138		502[19]
1947	...	...	...	...	...	...	...	...		270		1,204
1948	...	168	...	...	92	...	...	...		305		1,304
1949	847	186	381	87	143	73	...	...		327		1,335
1950	829	278	630	100	408	262	...	...		337		1,304
1951	751	288	844	87	494	604	...	...		331		1,259
1952	512	298	1,198	62	553	904	1	1		489		1,270
1953	484	283	1,337	60	621	1,249	2	1		461		1,187
1954	463	266	1,437	55	662	1,642	3	8		478		1,263
1955	438	257	1,616	52	719	2,127	9	10		486		1,296
1956	430	274	1,761	54	831	2,582	17	14		516		1,425
1957	413	263	1,929	49	858	2,981	21	35		549		1,563
1958	388	244	2,104	42	952	3,448	31	104		616[26]		1,905[26]
1959	366	224	2,175	40	1,039	3,664	33	148		827		3,344
1960	347	177	2,182	38	995	3,729	47	197		1,043		5,384
1961	304	160	2,240	35	1,026	3,972	61	238		1,165		6,393
1962	283	140	2,303	34	1,012	4,167	82	351		1,232		6,774
1963	254	116	2,321	29	1,033	4,277	97	421		1,314		6,938
1964	227	99	2,321	26	1,023	4,368	110	494		1,442		7,249
1965	177	82	2,383	21	971	4,764	127	570		1,570		7,256
1966	163	75	2,423	18	1,016	4,989	150	658		1,739		7,856
1967	150	70	2,473	17	1,052	5,478	162	756		1,848		8,050
1968	134	68	2,490	14	1,130	5,923	162	777		1,945		9,216
1969	128	57	2,547	13	1,084	6,381	169	878		2,104		11,139
1970	96	51	2,543	9	1,392	7,040	175	940		2,319		13,539
1971	1	42	2,288	...	1,357	7,059	179	961		2,543		15,441
1972	—	42	2,024	—	1,460	6,361	194	1,028		2,826		19,093
1973		58	1,803		1,676	6,167	190	1,008		3,113		23,400
1974		63	1,551		2,663	5,634	194	1,152		3,145		24,080
1975		59	1,494		3,026	5,663	198	1,200		3,216		24,820

G 4 **Merchant Ships Registered**

1920–1975

	Southern Ireland						Italy			
	Number of Ships			Thousand Tons			Number of Ships		Thousand Tons	
	Sail	Steam	Motor	Sail	Steam	Motor	Sail	Steam & Motor	Sail	Steam & Motor
1920	...	...	...	...	...	...	...	495	...	835
1921	...	...	...	...	...	...	...	603	...	1,075
1922	...	...	...	...	...	...	...	856	...	1,509
1923	...	...	...	...	...	...	...	880[14]	...	1,636[14]
1924	...	...	...	...	...	...	3,432	1,304	191	1,589
1925	...	...	...	...	...	...	3,216	1,370	168	1,764
1926	166	152	232	9	52	4	3,089	1,410	155	1,877
1927	160	150	246	8	51	4	3,000	1,424	152	1,946
1928	151	150	253	7	51	5	2,827	1,454	144	2,010
1929	142	150	252	7	52	5	2,690	1,396	135	1,918
1930	116	152	249	6	48	6	2,629	1,434	128	1,990
1931	110	155	251	6	42	6	2,562	1,443	121	2,043
1932	105	152	260	5	41	6	2,482	1,407	120	2,051
1933	100	140	312	5	50	7	2,353	1,342	116	1,867
1934	95	147	329	5	50	7	2,261	1,301	112	1,776
1935	90	144	328	5	62	7	2,197	1,295	109	1,848
1936	88	136	334	5	61	7	2,093	1,284	104	1,832
1937	92	141	352	5	61	8	2,161	1,335	102	1,876
1938	93	137	364	5	59	51	2,263	1,346	99	1,940
1939	92	111	357	5	22	13	2,367	1,361	99[19]	1,998[19]
1940	85	87	360	5	16	9	2,403	1,341	145	3,353
1941	73	83	349	5	25	7	2,405	1,246	139	2,906
1942	66	88	345	5	40	7	2,442	1,129	133	2,431
1943	61	85	330	5	34	6	...	...	...	...
1944	58	85	323	4	34	6	...	...	...	...
1945	54	82	310	4	35	6	1,654	253	71	546
1946	50	76	313	4	28	6	2,569	646	106	1,160
1947	49	75	309	4	25	6	2,797	901	116	1,863
1948	50	78	320	4	30	12	2,993	1,074	118	2,287
1949	46	78	324	4	27	12	3,071	1,132	119	2,536
1950	46	82	340	4	30	12	3,072	1,189	112	2,809
1951	47	82	357	4	30	13	3,244	1,247	115	3,156
1952	43	76	368	4	30	14	3,310	1,275	116	3,413
1953	42	70	375	4	32	14	3,106	1,290	112	3,611
1954	41	68	381	4	31	15	2,946	1,323	105	3,933
1955	40	69	388	4	31	15	2,830	1,346	103	4,055
1956	39	67	396	4	35	21	2,643	1,437	98	4,407
1957	39	64	399	4	38	28	2,595	1,489	97	4,859
1958	39	63	409	4	44	34	2,539	1,474	105	5,019
1959	37	62	434	4	48	35	2,427	1,451	104	4,961
1960	37	58	426	4	40	36	2,360	1,479	104	5,161
1961	37	56	440	4	40	43	2,300	1,537	105	5,332
1962	34	53	467	3	39	57	2,293	1,643	108	5,369
1963	30	48	505	3	35	67	2,188	1,799	112	5,498
1964	30	47	537	3	36	67	2,151	1,819	119	5,472
1965	32	41	565	3	21	65	2,090	1,837	132	5,691
1966	33	40	609	3	20	66	2,100	1,879	139	5,864
1967	33	39	660	3	18	64	2,053	1,931	147	6,360
1968	34	38	755	3	18	70	2,001	1,968	154	6,710
1969	34	38	837	3	18	70	2,017	1,997	161	6,978
1970	35	38	920	3	18	90	2,028	2,108	170	7,467
1971	35	38	1,027	3	18	90	2,034	2,201	180	7,880
1972	35	37	1,111	3	14	92	2,022	2,297	182	8,304
1973	34	37	1,186	3	14	130	1,939	2,113	176	9,068
1974	24	3	1,317	1	1	144	1,932 / 1,699[38]	2,118 / 1,641[39]	172 / 163[38]	9,984 / 9,973[39]
1975	26	3	1,384	1	1	144	1,663	1,626	160	10,673

See p. 660 for footnotes

G 4 Merchant Ships Registered

1920–1975

	Netherlands				Norway					
	Number of Ships		Thousand Tons		Number of Ships			Thousand Tons		
	Sail	Steam & Motor	Sail	Steam & Motor	Sail	Steam	Motor	Sail	Steam	Motor
1920	241[27]	606[27]	24[27]	969[27]	409	1,922	1,497	204	1,199	125
	231	503	22	961						
1921	217	570	20[19]	1,167[19]	387	1,950	1,503	185	1,318	136
			25	1,869						
1922	214	577	24	2,069	361	1,906	1,473	172	1,300	147
1923	199	571	23	2,112	306	1,908	1,454	121	1,297	156
1924	173	575	20	2,089	256	1,928	1,451	62	1,324	181
1925	168	599	19	2,108	222	1,966	1,510	40	1,352	269
1926	149	645	17	2,116	216	1,956	1,547	30	1,325	340
1927	85[28]	681[28]	11[28]	2,115[28]	204	1,931	1,563	22	1,317	405
	231	545	33	2,152	187	1,893	1,608	13	1,315	515
1928	200	586	30	2,256	181	1,938	1,654	13	1,380	613
1930	161	638	24	2,397	181	1,991	1,781	12	1,414	868
1931	155	677	24	2,389	163	1,974	1,864	11	1,444	1,036
1932	152	665	24	2,228	158	1,944	1,921	9	1,392	1,059
1933	137	636	21	2,040	150	1,874	1,951	9	1,307	1,073
1934	140	617	22	1,968	140	1,776	2,002	8	1,169	1,125
1935	131	622	21	1,907	127	1,733	2,081	7	1,153	1,220
1936	119	657	19	1,930	113	1,715	2,187	6	1,122	1,334
1937	123	698	19	2,039	88	1,680	2,413	5	1,094	1,563
1938	115	755	16	2,218	76	1,659	2,573	4	1,074	1,708
		1,028[27]		2,650[27]						
1939		1,102		2,764	64	1,590	2,737	3[19]	1,015[19]	1,815[19]
								5	1,758	3,083
1940		...		...	57	1,435	2,777	4	1,531	2,898
1941		...		...	46	1,307	2,824	3	1,299	2,702
1942		...		...	31	1,202	2,821	3	1,114	2,244
1943		...		...	30	1,161	2,895	3	1,013	2,019
1944		...		...	28	1,090	2,954	2	931	1,958
1945		...		...	28	1,078	3,036	2	892	2,134
1946		855		1,946	27	1,130	3,318	3	1,096	2,338
1947		921		2,366	23	1,198	3,636	2	1,495	2,677
1948		937		2,584	17	1,202	3,917	2	1,615	3,062
1949		1,035		2,796	14	1,172	4,212	1	1,640	3,659
1950		1,108		2,958	15	1,131	4,321	2	1,579	4,100
1951		1,141		2,983	...	1,057	4,500	...	1,448	4,527
1952		1,200		3,072	...	985	4,666	...	1,366	4,883
1953		1,226		3,166	...	935	4,856	...	1,332	5,304
1954		1,272		3,287	...	893	5,059	...	1,238	5,863
1955		1,338		3,608	...	834	5,272	...	1,204	6,562
1956		1,425		3,900	...	791	5,486	...	1,241	7,104
1957		1,549		4,242	...	707	5,691	...	1,330	7,710
1958		1,544		4,489	...	680	5,899	...	1,483	8,613
1959		1,533[29]		4,534[29]	...	644	5,996	...	1,657	9,320
		1,501		4,486						
1960		1,476		4,661	...	590	6,078	...	1,627	9,775
1961		1,482		4,787	...	545	6,109	...	1,686	10,479
1962		1,496		5,021	...	499	6,190	...	1,853	11,094
1963		1,455		4,950	...	464	6,195	...	1,985	11,875
1964		1,441		4,911	...	391	6,205	...	2,099	12,718
1965		1,402		4,686	...	348	6,155	...	2,140	13,836
1966		1,349		4,560	...	322	6,203	...	2,403	14,750
1967		1,297		4,545	...	268	6,275	...	2,249	16,902
1968		1,218		4,256	...	231	6,304	...	1,970	17,532
1969		1,088		4,089	...	206	6,250	...	2,143	16,703
1970		1,017		3,955	...	200	6,128	...	2,926	17,203
1971		941		3,878	...	199	6,029	...	3,743	18,556
1972		786		3,326	...	196	5,973	...	4,472	18,240
1973		702		3,355	...	184	5,790	...	5,575	18,156
1974		649		3,303	...	184	5,681	...	6,709	18,090
1975		615		3,223	...	173	5,599	...	7,811	17,970

See p. 660 for footnotes

G 4 Merchant Ships Registered

1920–1975

	Poland		Portugal[32]		Russia	
	Number of Ships	Thousand Tons	Number of Ships	Thousand Tons	Number of Ships	Thousand Tons
1920	...	...	...	236[31]	25	510
1921	...	...	...	250	9	404
1922	...	...	...	237	...	...
1923	...	...	...	261	...	...
1924	...	...	...	264	8	331
1925	–	–	...	267	8	314
1926	6	11	...	251	8	315
1927	10	15	...	229	8	301
1928	18	22	...	219	3	374
1929	25	41	...	219	3	437
1930	31	65	...	239	3	529
1931	33	68	...	254	3	601
1932	39	66	...	245	3	682
1933	56	65	...	243	...	840
1934	57	65	...	241	...	939
1935	63	80	...	238	...	1,111
1936	58	95	...	238	...	1,215
1937	59	95	...	243	...	1,254
1938	71	102	...	250	...	1,273
1939	...	...	...	257	...	1,306
1940	...	...	...	...	...	...
1941	...	...	...	...	...	...
1942	...	...	...	...	...	...
1943	...	...	...	...	...	...
1944	...	...	...	...	...	...
1945	...	...	...	...	...	...
1946	26	94	232	179	...	...
1947	42	156	251	163	...	...
1948	43	160	270	263	...	2,097
1949	45	159	249	264	...	...
1950	52	171	216	230	...	2,125
1951	65	237	221	246	...	2,222
1952	69	249	216	258	...	2,261
1953	72	250	206	262	...	2,292
1954	78	265	205	271	...	2,371
1955	83	288	199	251	...	2,506
1956	83	287	189	255	...	2,636
1957	92	253	190	264	...	2,790
1958	106	407	185	275	...	2,966
1959	122	492	180	272	...	3,155
1960	138	578	178	286	...	3,429
1961	155	650	175	313	...	4,066
1962	178	764	170	322	...	4,684
1963	191	825	170	343	...	5,434
1964	196	853	164	342	...	6,958
1965	196	886	158	336	...	8,238
1966	211	991	157	357	...	9,492
1967	227	1,103	143	365	...	10,617
1968	237	1,191	147	384	...	12,062
1969	250	1,261	141	428	...	13,705
1970	259	1,319	142	433	...	14,832
1971	278	1,494	151	525	...	16,194
1972	283	1,610	156	547	...	16,774
1973	289	1,709	148	654	...	17,397
1974	307	2,083	148	704	...	18,176
1975	315	2,577	134	680	...	19,236

See p. 660 for footnotes

G 4 Merchant Ships Registered

1920–1975

	Spain						Sweden			
	Number of Ships			Thousand Tons			Number of Ships		Thousand Tons	
	Sail	Steam	Motor	Sail	Steam	Motor	Sail	Steam & Motor	Sail	Steam & Motor
1920	314	548	...	83	875	...	1,316	1,274	121	712
1921	274	595	...	81	1,002	...	1,323	1,250	118	690
1922	263	630	...	79	1,072	...	1,337	1,296	121	766
1923	253	637	...	74	1,091	...	1,310	1,342	112	823
1924	248	642	...	73	1,109	...	1,266	1,364	101	854
1925	236	642	...	68	1,083	...	1,200	1,367	89	904
1926	236	642	...	67	1,073	...	1,152	1,382	83	925
1927	231	646	...	65	1,052	...	1,078	1,444	78	953
1928	214	637	4	59	1,040	12	1,054	1,457	73	1,025
1929	205	642	11	56	1,052	31	1,009	1,476	70	1,082
1930	179	626	32	43	1,035	79	997	1,502	72	1,144
1931	134	721	60	26	1,043	156	990	1,506	70	1,192
1932	130	774	83	24	1,016	184	964	1,482	67	1,156
1933	119	753	93	21	977	202	916	1,455	62	1,127
1934	119	732	100	20	936	220	906	1,409	62	1,074
1935	118	731	106	20	925	233	897	1,375	61	1,041
1936	...	...	...	...	...	...	900	1,348	62	1,022
1937	...	...	...	...	...	...	923	1,342	62	1,020
1938	105	618	101	20	723	171	927	1,332	63	1,042
1939	...	...	...	...	...	...	922	1,320	63	1,055
1940	105	682	101	19	790	189	922	1,280	64	983
1941	106	708	106	20	846	191	893	1,227	62	949
1942	109	710	106	21	835	164	875	1,214	60	907
1943	122	720	105	19	823	168	847	1,229	59	923
1944	133	746	127	22	844	172	829	1,263	58	1,022
1945	150	759	155	26	834	209	814[34]	1,262	58[34]	1,052
1946	164	831	198	29	852	219	772	1,301	55	1,146
1947	168	847	235	30	858	232	754	1,378	55	1,274
1948	174	872	285	31	865	265	726	1,449	54	1,365
1949	181	888	323	33	874	291	702	1,493	52	1,394
1950	169	895	355	30	869	306	679[19,35]	1,522[19,35]	59[19,35]	1,432[19,35]
1951	173	884	392	31	852	331	644	1,260	67	2,261
1952	180	902	418	32	850	360	624	1,258	66	2,407
1953	175	906	448	31	870	401	599	1,260	63	2,590
1954	175[33]	901[33]	462[33]	30[33]	869[33]	445[33]	559	1,240	58	2,675
1955	171	911	490	29	879	472	516	1,123	55	2,735
1956	168	912	520	28	880	517	474	1,131	51	2,904
1957	165	912	569	27	878	602	432	1,151	46	3,141
1958	162	907	624	26	859	709	398	1,165	43	3,430
1959	164	896	682	26	820	797		1,508		3,628
1960	162	894	769	26	797	957		1,486		3,851
1961	167	893	857	27	780	1,098		1,409		3,978
1962	168	897	972	27	777	1,195		1,373[21,35]		4,161[21,35]
								1,073		4,139
1963	164	880	1,071	26	757	1,267		1,001		4,095
1964	154	820	1,191	25	693	1,303		943		4,136
1965	143	727	1,508	22	573	1,606		900		4,117
1966	142	682	1,679	22	561	1,800		872		4,454
1967	76	618	1,965	11	596	2,046		833		4,561
1968	84	567	2,103	13	561	2,346		819		4,746
1969	72	513	2,216	10	748	2,579		795		4,750
1970	71	456	2,330	10	579	2,992		763		4,634
1971	62	418	2,401	9	539	3,332		719		4,950
1972	58	382	2,522	8	459	4,031		688		5,351
1973	65	341[41]	2,634	10	635[41]	4,196		650		5,788
1974		1,041			4,331			629		6,991
1975		1,032			5,200			613		7,711

See p. 660 for footnotes

G 4 Merchant Ships Registered

1920–1975

	United Kingdom						Yugoslavia			
	Number of Ships			Thousand Tons			Number of Ships		Thousand Tons	
	Sail	Steam	Motor	Sail	Steam	Motor	Sail	Steam & Motor	Sail	Steam & Motor
1920	6,309	12,307	...	584	10,777	...	...	...	...	...
1921	6,272	12,660	...	610	10,932	...	...	...	...	...
1922	6,184[36]	12,787[36]	...[36]	574[36]	11,223[36]	...[36]	...	...	...	...
1923	5,962	10,813	1,624	551	10,897	263	...	...	...	...
1924	5,842	10,690	1,823	522	10,810	385	...	...	...	...
1925	5,785	10,526	1,965	520	10,965	499	...	...	...	...
1926	5,678	10,262	2,170	517	10,760	629	...	...	...	...
1927	5,609	10,032	2,340	507	10,577	770	...	...	...	...
1928	5,408	9,959	2,681	496	10,754	1,009	702	224	12	284
1929	5,249	9,855	2,940	480	10,675	1,214	729	248	11	304
1930	5,098	9,729	3,237	468	10,561	1,425	700	253	9	314
1931	4,960	9,529	3,483	462	10,233	1,579	710	223	11	338
1932	4,773	9,248	3,650	472	9,774	1,617	704	246	13	376
1933	4,632	8,900	3,863	466	9,062	1,642	711	237	13	351
1934	4,435	8,622	4,168	432	8,621	1,692	705	238	14	327
1935	4,351	8,306	4,494	414	8,253	1,819	699	244	14	356
1936	4,288	8,032	4,888	419	8,114	2,057	669	253	12	350
1937	4,185	7,702	5,294	415	7,902	2,236	667	256	12	361
1938	4,019	7,441	5,789	402	7,819	2,481	677	[25] 262	13	[25] 404
1939	...	13,303		...	10,511		185		401	
1940	...	13,254		...	10,412		...		...	
1941	...	12,822		...	9,674		...		...	
1942	...	12,185		...	9,000		...		...	
1943	...	12,169		...	9,119		...		...	
1944	...	12,525		...	9,994		...		...	
1945	...	12,700		...	10,341		...		...	
1946	3,610	12,581		408	10,315		...		...	
1947	3,250	12,481		380	10,371		86		141	
1948	3,193	12,795		370	10,461		99		164	
1949	3,149	13,103		367	10,453		107		181	
1950	3,104	13,429		365	10,738		115		201	
1951	3,056	13,473		349	10,606		124		223	
1952	3,065	13,598		343	10,663		134		246	
1953	2,835	13,649		321	10,811		147		248	
1954	2,771	13,685		317	10,978		176		256	
1955	2,676	13,671		316	10,966		207		284	
1956	2,637	13,764		312	11,053		222		291	
1957	2,600	13,837		312	11,207		227		300	
1958	2,588	14,045		304	11,349		251		395	
1959	2,496	14,202		294	11,627		268		451	
1960	2,482	14,532		291	11,797		290		575	
1961	2,493	15,008		279	12,001		318		718	
1962	2,550	15,580		276	11,501		325		806	
1963	2,596	16,115		270	11,462		343		912	
1964	2,622	16,722		266	11,315		346		930	
1965	2,829	17,483		272	11,426		357		968	
1966	...	18,413		...	11,668		360		996	
1967	...	19,277		...	11,736		354		1,138	
1968	...	20,317		...	12,671		356		1,183	
1969	...	21,647		...	13,574		355		1,367	
1970	...	23,250		...	14,700		365		1,434	
		1,977[42]			24,061[42]		381		1,460	
1971	...	1,875		...	25,177		390		1,514	
1972	...	1,798		...	26,940		389		1,522	
1973	...	1,776		...	29,106		387		1,600	
1974	...	1,767		...	30,795		415		1,776	
1975	...	1,682		...	31,489		426		1,865	

See p. 660 for footnotes

G 4 Merchant Ships Registered

NOTES

1. SOURCES:– The official publications noted on p. xv except for the U.K. to 1964, which is taken from B.R. Mitchell & Phyllis Deane, *Abstract of British Historical Statistics* (Cambridge, 1962) and B.R. Mitchell & H.G. Jones, *Second Abstract of British Historical Statistics* (Cambridge, 1971), where the original sources are cited, and except also for the following material supplied by the respective national statistical offices:– Finland to 1863, Poland to 1955, Portugal to 1969, and Sweden to 1859.

2. Statistics relate to 31 December, except where otherwise indicated.

3. Tonnage figures refer to net capacity, British measure, except where otherwise indicated.

4. The minimum size of vessel included on the register has varied from time to time and from country to country. Where possible changes are indicated in footnotes. Where no limits are indicated the presumption is that all vessels are included.

FOOTNOTES

[1] Venetia is included to 1866 (1st line). From 1870 (2nd line) Hungary is excluded and shown separately.

[2] From 1851 (2nd line) fishing vessels are included.

[3] Figures for 1864–70 are for 31 March in the year following that indicated.

[4] From 1867 (2nd line) to 1921 (1st line) only ships of 4 net tons and over are included, and from 1921 (2nd line) only ships of 20 gross tons and over are included. Iceland and Faroe Islands ships are excluded from 1921 (2nd line) though the latter are reincluded from 1932, when they numbered 202 ships of 21 thousand GRT.

[5] The size of vessel included has varied as follows:– To 1868, ships of 5 lasts or over (approximately 9 net tons); for 1870–72, ships of 10 lasts or over; for 1874–82, ships of 50 net tons or over; for 1885–87, ships of 25 net tons or over. from 1892 to 1920 (1st line), all ships; and since 1920 (2nd line), ships of 19 net tons or over.

[6] This break is caused by a revision of the register.

[7] Vessels over 25 tons. Statistics to 1913 (1st line) are for the Russian Empire (exclusive of Finland), and subsequently they are for the U.S.S.R.

[8] Statistics prior to 1830 relate only to ships registered in the 'staple towns' (i.e. the main ports).

[9] Motor ships are previously included with sail.

[10] Vessels of 60 net tons or over.

[11] From 1895 to 1900 (1st line) only ships of 50 net tons or over are included, and from 1900 (2nd line) only ships of 60 net tons or over are included.

[12] i.e. Fiume.

[13] Subsequently excluding ships which did not have a deed of nationality.

[14] For 1915–18 steamships of less than 250 net tons are not included, and for 1919–23 steamships of less than 50 net tons are not included.

[15] Three ships were transferred from 'sail' to 'steam'.

[16] Statistics prior to 1877, when the register was revised, were later said to contain many errors.

[17] In principle, to 1909 only vessels of 4 net tons or over are included, though ships as low as 1 ton were said to have been included "in some years". Subsequently only sailing ships of 50 gross tons or over and steamships of 25 gross tons or over are included.

[18] At 31 August.

[19] Subsequently in gross measure.

[20] From 1874 to 1897 only vessels of 50 net tons or over are included. Subsequently only vessels of 100 net tons or over are included.

[21] The size of vessel has varied as follows:– To 1894, ships of 10 net tons or over; from 1895 to 1962 (1st line), ships of 20 net tons or over, and subsequently ships of 100 net tons or over.

[22] At 30 September.

[23] Motor-assisted sailing vessels are subsequently transferred from the 'motor' to the 'sail' category.

[24] Motor-assisted sailing vessels are included with the 'motot' category to 1935 and from 1945 to 1948, but with the 'sail' category at other times.

[25] Subsequently vessels of 100 gross tons or over.

[26]Subsequently including ships with provisional registration papers.
[27]From 1920 (2nd line) to 1938 (1st line) tugs and dredgers are excluded. Ships registered in the colonies are included for the first time from 1938 (2nd line).
[28]Some motor-assisted vessels were transferred from the 'motor' to the 'sail' category.
[29]The reason for this break is not given.
[30]Mechanically-propelled vessels, in gross measure.
[31]Subsequently mechanically-propelled vessels in gross measure at June.
[32]Statistics are for the mainland only.
[33]At 1 November.
[34]Subsequently only motor-assisted vessels.
[35]For 1951–1962 (1st line) fishing vessels are excluded.
[36]Ships registered in southern Ireland are subsequently excluded.
[37]In gross measure.
[38]Motor-assisted sailing vessels are included, most of which comprised the fishing fleet. From 1974 (2nd line) the series relates entirely to the fishing fleet.
[39]Subsequently excluding certain recreational vessels.
[40]Subsequently commercial ships only.
[41]Subsequently excluding fishing vessels. The equivalent figures for 1973 are 1,032 ships and 4,002 thousand GRT.
[42]Subsequent statistics relate only to vessels of 500 GRT and over, and the tonnage figures are gross.

G 5 INLAND NAVIGATION TRAFFIC

1835–1869

	Austria[1]		France	Germany[2]		Netherlands[3]
	a	b	c	c	c	d
	000 tons	000 tons	m ton/kms	m ton/kms	000 tons	million tons
1835	2	...	...	...	...	...
1836	4	...	...	...	...	...
1837	5	...	...	...	...	...
1838	18	...	...	...	...	...
1839	20	...	...	...	...	...
1840	21	...	...	750	...	...
1841	29	...	...	...	...	...
1842	33	...	...	...	...	...
1843	47	...	...	...	...	...
1844	61	...	...	...	...	...
1845	86	...	1,813	850	...	...
1846	107	...	...	...	...	...
1847	178	...	...	...	...	...
1848	145	...	...	...	...	...
1849	70	...	...	...	...	...
1850	263	...	1,666	900	...	0.8
1851	404	...	...	...	...	0.9
1852	597	...	...	...	...	1.0
1853	505	...	2,002	...	...	1.0
1854	771	...	...	...	...	1.2
1855	953	...	...	1,200	...	1.1
1856	712	...	...	...	...	1.2
1857	869	...	...	...	...	1.1
1858	949	...	...	...	...	1.2
1859	1,459[1]	...	...	...	...	1.2
1860	845	...	1,901	1,350	...	1.4
1861	850	...	1,936	...	...	1.6
1862	872	...	2,092	...	...	1.6
1863	986	...	2,132	...	...	1.7
1864	1,083	...	2,082	...	...	1.6
1865	963	...	2,059	1,550	...	1.6
1866	1,213	...	2,225	...	...	1.9
1867	1,188	...	2,024	1,700	...	2.0
1868	1,241	...	2,172	1,750	...	2.2
1869	1,247	...	1,999	1,800	...	1.9

Abbreviations used throughout this table: a = Goods carried by Danube Steamship Co.; b = Goods Passing Customs on River Elbe; c = Goods carried by Inland Navigation; d= Loaded Ships Passing Customs on Rhine; e = Goods carried on River Danube.

Other abbreviations used where space demands: m ton/kms: million ton kilometres; m tons: million tons; thou m ton/kms: thousand million ton/kilometres

See p. 666 for footnotes

G 5 Inland Navigation Traffic

1870–1919

	Austria		Belgium	France	Germany		Netherlands[3]	Russia	
	a	b	c	c	c	c	d	c	c
	000 tons	000 tons	m ton/kms	m ton/kms	m ton/kms	000 tons	m tons	thou m ton/kms	m tons
1870	1,015	567	...	1,448[6]	1,650[6]	...	1.9	...	...
1871	918	456	...	1,558	1,730	...	2.1	...	...
1872	1,150	452	...	1,836	2,070	...	2.8	...	...
1873	1,011	408	...	1,847	2,199	12,300	3.0	...	...
1874	1,049	386	...	1,795	2,111	...	2.6	...	...
1875	1,189	562	...	1,964	2,373	...	2.9	...	...
1876	1,346	271	...	1,953	2,338	...	3.1	...	...
1877	1,271	405	...	2,034	2,486	...	3.3	...	...
1878	1,459	681	...	2,005	2,406	16,500	3.6	...	...
1879	1,356	948	...	2,023	2,558	...	3.8	...	...
1880	1,342	1,315	722	2,007	3,124	...	4.1	...	...
1881	1,444	1,267	703	2,174	2,920	...	4.5	...	...
1882	1,675	1,354	717	2,265	3,178	...	4.6	...	...
1883	1,644	1,337	726	2,383	3,524	21,900	5.0	...	...
1884	1,571	1,827	748	2,452	3,581	...	5.3	...	...
1885	1,694	1,649	760	2,453	3,801	...	5.2	...	...
1886	1,695	1,861	764	2,798	4,202	...	5.3	...	...
1887	1,710	1,851	857[5]	3,073	4,206	...	5.6	...	...
1888	1,855	2,375	588	3,180	4,693	28,000	6.1	...	...
1889	1,925	2,197	582	3,238	5,017	...	6.0	...	...
1890	[2,106][4]	2,765	578	3,216	5,586	...	6.6	...	...
1891	1,983	2,739	624	3,537	5,615	...	6.9	...	...
1892	1,830	2,543	623	3,609	5,193	...	7.3	...	...
1893	2,179	2,166	645	3,604	5,606	33,800	8.1	...	...
1894	2,030	3,035	696	3,912	6,339	...	9.3	...	...
1895	1,963	2,535	713	3,766	6,130	...	9.1	...	...
1896	2,241	2,969	800	4,191	7,447	...	12.4	...	...
1897	2,001	3,182	815	4,365	8,010	...	12.1	...	...
1898	1,910	3,001	882	4,577	8,413	46,200	14.0	...	...
1899	1,797	3,229	829	4,489	8,953	...	14.6	...	...
1900	2,012	2,740	894	4,675	9,371	...	15.6[3]	...	...
							13		
1901	2,073	3,028	852	4,380	9,257	...	13	...	...
1902	2,054	2,932	918	4,465	9,451	...	14	...	...
1903	1,997	3,964	1,035	4,955	11,644	56,200	18	...	...
1904	2,040	2,551	1,092	4,968	10,085	...	18	...	...
1905	2,256	3,422	1,143	5,085	11,692	...	21	...	...
1906	2,366	3,497	1,154	5,102	12,498	67,800	22	...	...
1907	2,218	3,435	1,198	5,371	12,674	68,900	23	...	...
1908	2,009	3,146	1,112	5,321	13,075	64,900	21	...	...
1909	2,249	3,350	1,200	5,471	13,470	73,365	25	...	...
1910	2,265	3,203	1,327	5,197	15,439	76,633	30	...	...
1911	2,436	2,161	1,404	5,767	12,953	79,962	31	...	...
1912	2,548	3,260	1,570	5,850	17,074	93,481	35	...	...
1913	2,311	3,096	1,636	6,185	17,888	99,625	38	28.5[7]	32.7[7]
1914	1,760	2,544	...	...	...	75,194	26	...	...
1915	981	1,629	...	2,167	...	40,491	9	...	...
1916	676	1,471	...	2,728	...	45,580	10	...	...
	Goods carried on River Danube								
	000 tons	m ton/kms							
1917	...	...	...	2,829	...	...	7	15.0	20.0
1918	295	...	...	3,268[6]	...[6]	...[6]	5	...	...
1919	...	...	649	2,682	...	33,683	6	...	...

See p. 666 for footnotes

G 5 Inland Navigation Traffic

1920–1975

	Austria		Belgium	Czechoslovakia		France
	e	e	c	c	c	c
	000 tons	m ton/kms	m ton/kms	000 tons	m ton/kms	m ton/kms
1920	443	...	998	...	...	3,173
1921	830	...	942	...	...	2,799
1922	875[8]	...	1,322	...	...	4,691
1923	1,408	...	1,532	1,829	...	5,005
1924	1,387	...	1,610	3,297	...	5,229
1925	1,227	...	1,723	3,543	...	5,277
1926	1,584	...	1,766	3,799	1,724	5,720
1927	1,835	...	2,045	4,177	1,865	5,947
1928	2,308	...	2,266	4,167	1,777	6,980
1929	1,919	...	2,185	3,513	1,492	6,809
1930	2,508	...	2,407	3,586	1,572	7,266
1931	1,873	...	2,507	4,102	2,200	7,379
1932	1,622	...	2,513	2,952	1,554	7,589
1933	1,435	...	2,610	2,311	1,230	7,795
1934	1,507	...	2,785	2,465	1,127	8,377
1935	1,553	...	2,841	2,532	1,185	8,033
1936	1,833	...	2,831	2,951	1,400	8,093
1937	...	...	3,237	3,876	2,261	7,882
1938	...	...	2,939	3,787	...	8,256
1939	...	...	2,931	3,677	...	6,908
1940	...	...	...	3,278	...	2,763
1941	...	...	1,892	3,258	...	3,084
1942	...	...	...	3,545	...	3,543
1943	...	...	2,105	3,503	...	3,749
1944	...	...	1,174	1,212	...	1,603
1945	...	...	1,389	817	...	2,616
1946	...	...	1,757	1,456	724	4,071
1947	...	...	2,020	1,532	...	4,767
1948	...	...	2,209	926	629	5,726[9]
1949	...	...	2,629	1,133	788	6,074
1950	...	...	2,998	1,336	764	6,693
1951	...	...	3,474	1,705	995	7,536
1952	...	...	3,389	1,943	1,138	7,772
1953	...	...	3,928	2,061	1,002	7,923
1954	2,558	430	4,116	2,058	1,260	8,282
1955	3,112	507	4,617	2,836	1,485	8,917
1956	4,113	546	4,493	2,651	1,472	9,265
1957	4,721	639	4,602	2,928	1,604	9,771
1958	5,058	698	4,326	3,247	1,784	9,425
1959	4,965	748	4,813	3,128	1,736	9,506
1960	6,202	962	5,226	3,530	1,962	10,773
1961	5,493	904	5,473	3,747	1,899	11,262
1962	5,390	919	5,421	3,925	1,975	11,234
1963	5,792	995	5,202	4,062	1,915	11,358
1964	5,907	1,032	6,107	4,498	2,170	12,470
1965	5,985	977	6,087	4,056	2,172	12,510
1966	6,741	2,104	5,970	4,346	2,412	12,652
1967	6,424	2,071	6,262	4,197	2,243	12,965
1968	8,067	2,500	6,651	4,340	2,360	13,235
1969	7,238	2,184	6,870	3,851	1,942	14,601
1970	7,593	2,367	6,734	4,464	2,434	14,183
1971	6,215	2,011	6,729	4,451	2,367	13,773
1972	6,684	2,076	6,758	4,868	2,626	14,156
1973	7,322	2,496	6,494	4,812	2,467	13,792
1974	7,273	7,012	6,853	4,924	2,812	13,738
1975	7,004	6,119	5,124	5,654	2,580	11,905

See p. 666 for footnotes

G 5 Inland Navigation Traffic

1920–1975

	Germany		East Germany		Netherlands	Russia	
	c	c	c	c	d	c	c
	m ton/kms	000 tons	m ton/kms	000 tons	million tons	thou m ton/kms	m tons
1920	...[10]	43,260[10]	...	...	13	...	...
1921	...	41,649	...	...	16	...	...
1922	...	58,823	...	...	21	...	...
1923	...	34,267	...	...	12	...	...
1924	11,531	70,900	...	...	32	10.5	14.6
1925	13,277	85,723	...	...	40	8.8	13.5
1926	14,736	102,359	...	...	52	12.0	17.2
1927	16,274	111,447	...	...	55	15.5	21.7
1928	15,170	107,745	...	...	51	16.5	23.4
1929	15,106	110,669	...	...	55	17.5	25.5
1930	14,702	105,152	...	...	52	20.7	32.0
1931	12,413	86,893	...	...	43	...	41.1
1932	10,927	73,513	...	...	33	...	...
1933	11,375	77,960	...	...	34	...	...
1934	13,532[10]	94,184[10]	...	...	41	...	...
1935	14,274	101,369	...	...	42	...	...
1936	17,112	116,051	...	...	46	...	...
1937	18,621	133,080[11]	...	...	58	...	...
		170,937					
1938	18,653	177,257	...	...	56	...	...
1939	...	170,305	...	...	42	...	...
1940	...	143,374	...	...	8	36.1	73.1
1941	...	...	...	...	19	...	...
1942	...	...	...	...	16	...	...
1943	...	...	...	...	16	...	...
1944	...	...	...	...	7	...	...
1945	...	...	...	...	2	18.8	36.9
	West Germany						
1946	...	...	...	...	7	20.4	39.9
1947	...	...	...	...	9	25.1	48.2
1948	...	...	...	...	16	32.1	63.5
1949	12,853	57,849	1,123	8,240	21	38.8	78.0
1950	16,752	71,855	1,579	10,001	29	46.2	91.8
1951	21,047	88,111	1,797	10,950	35	51.5	102.8
1952	22,452	95,270	1,707	12,539	37	58.2	110.2
1953	23,041	101,381	1,738	12,843	37	58.9	116.1
1954	25,054	109,385	1,742	11,619	41	62.4	128.2
1955	28,624	124,612	2,168	12,903	50	67.4	139.1
1956	32,270	135,920	2,268	13,455	58	70.5	147.1
1957	33,953	142,331	2,498	14,444	61	76.4	159.2
1958	32,768	137,000	2,398	14,863	59	85.5	178.3
1959	33,390	142,141	2,376	14,478	55	93.6	192.0
1960	40,390	171,362	2,252	12,633	71	99.6	210.3
1961	40,214	172,216	2,202	11,944	68	106.0	223.9
1962	39,936	170,775	2,162	11,440	66	109.9	230.3
1963	39,513	167,327	2,003	10,985	67	114.5	239.5
1964	40,609	183,795	2,138	12,023	73	124.5	252.3
1965	43,553	195,695	2,196	12,129	81	133.9	269.4
1966	45,072	207,894	2,556	13,370	88	137.7	279.0
1967	45,785	214,439	2,576	13,682	99	143.9	301.8
1968	47,932	233,328	2,443	13,142	110	155.4	322.5
1969	47,650	233,800	2,143	12,406	109	160.1	332.7
1970	48,813	240,001	2,358	13,660	112	174.0	357.8
1971	44,991	229,985	2,331	13,566	105	183.8	381.2
1972	43,969	228,499	2,304	13,242	102	180.3	395.7
1973	48,480	245,831	1,884	12,667	117	189.5	419.2
1974	50,972	252,108	2,326	14,718	128	212.3	452.4
1975	47,565	227,330	2,362	14,586	119	221.7	475.5

See p. 666 for footnotes

G 5 Inland Navigation Traffic

NOTE

SOURCES:– The official publications noted on p.xv with German data to 1908 and Netherlands to 1900 (1st line) supplied by their respective national statistical offices.

FOOTNOTES

[1] The series to 1859 differs from that which follows. The latter is approximately half the former in the two years for which comparison is possible – 1850 and 1855. The figures in the later series for these years are 137 and 532 thousand tons respectively. It is probable that inland traffic was only counted once in the later series, whilst it was double-counted in the earlier one.
[2] Information is available for earlier years but not in summary form.
[3] Data to 1900 (1st line) relate to the capacity of loaded shipping (in million river-tons). Subsequently they are of goods carried (in million tons).
[4] Thirteen months ended 31 December. Previous figures are for years ended 30 November.
[5] Previous statistics include some traffic by sea-going ships.
[6] Alsace was part of Germany for 1871–1918.
[7] Data are for the boundaries of the interwar period.
[8] Inland traffic is subsequently counted twice.
[9] Figures to 1948 are of goods embarked. Subsequently they are of goods discharged.
[10] Saarland is excluded for 1920–1934.
[11] Earlier figures are calculated according to goods.
[12] Earlier figures are calculated according to goods classification, whilst later ones are derived from harbour records.

G 6 MOTOR VEHICLES IN USE (thousands)

1900–1949

	Austria		Belgium		Czechoslovakia		Denmark		Finland	
	P C	C V	P C	C V[7]	P C	C V	P C[12]	V C	P C	V C
1900	...	...	...		...	...	...		...	...
1901	...	...	...		...	...	...		...	...
1902	...	...	...		...	...	...		...	...
1903	...	...	...		...	...	...		...	...
1904	...	...	...		...	...	...		...	...
1905	...	...	...		...	...	...		...	...
1906	...	...	...		...	...	...		...	...
1907	...	...	...		...	...	...		...	...
1908	...	...	...		...	...	...		...	...
1909	...	...	...		...	...	0.7		...	...
1910	...	...	...		...	...	1.0		...	...
1911	7.7[1]	...	...		...	...	...		...	...
1912	...	...	...		...	...	1.6		...	...
1913	12.2[1]		9.6		...	...	...		...	...
1914	...	...	...		...	...	3.1	0.4	...	...
1915	...	...	...		...	...	3.8	0.6	...	...
1916	...	...	...		...	...	5.0	0.7	...	...
1917	...	...	...		...	...	6.4[13]	0.9[13]	...	...
1918	...[2]	...[2]	...		...	...	...	...	...	...
1919	...	...	...		...	...	...	...	...	...
1920	6.4	2.8	...		...	...	13.9[13]	3.8[13]	...	...
1921	7.8[3]	3.3[3]	20.7		...	...	17.6[10]	4.7[10]	...	...
1922	8.4	3.5	31.7		5.3[8]	2.1[8]	...	...	...	...
1923	10.1	4.1	47.3		...	...	...	...	1.9[1]	...
1924	9.7	5.1	67.8		...	...	37.9[14]	9.8[14]	3.3[1]	...
1925	11.0	6.2	86.7		12.7[9]	5.4[9]	46.4[14]	13.1[14]	6.6[1]	3.9[1]
1926	12.2	7.7	92.2		17.3[10]	7.1[10]	[15]	[15]	11.5	5.4
1927	14.1	9.6	96.9		[11]	[11]	59.1[8] [16]	16.5[8] [16]	17.0	7.5
1928	16.8	12.1	79.0	41.4	25.1	11.5	62.6	26.3	22.1	9.6
1929	19.6[4]	14.9[4]	92.2	51.2	32.1	15.9	69.2	29.1	24.5	11.7
1930	17.4	14.6	99.3	58.7	41.0	21.6	78.5[16]	31.8[16]	24.3	12.4
1931	22.3	16 6	110	64.8	48.6	25.8	85.2	35.1	23.8	12.1
1932	23.2	16.5	116	68.0	...	...	83.0	34.3	22.9	11.7
1933	23.3	16.1	123	69.1	67.8[11] / 74.9	31.9[11] / 32.5	84.1	35.5	20.7	11.9
1934	24.0	16.0	121	73.1	83.6	33.0	88.1	37.5	20.4	12.9
1935	26.8	16.4	124	73.3	88.3[1]	33.3[1]	91.7	38.9	20.9	14.2
1936	30.1	16.2	132	74.5	85.0	30.4	95.3	40.1	21.7	15.7
1937	32.4[5]	16.2[5]	144	78.3	90.9	31.5	101	41.7	24.4	18.8
1938	...	...	154	78.6	...	...	108	42.6	25.9	20.0
1939	...	...	155	79.0	...	...	117	45.3	30.1	23.2
1940	...	...	110	58.8	...	...	7.0[17]	23.3[17]	...	...
1941	...	...	15.4	30.7	...	...	7.6[18][16]	24.1[18][16]	...	...
1942	...	...	10.8	27.8	...	...	7.4	23.4	...	...
1943	...	...	8.8	25.4	...	...	7.2	21.7	...	...
1944	...	...	13.0	28.4	...	...	6.5[16]	21.2[16]	...	...
1945	...	...	46.1	60.5	...	...	44.5	28.3	...	...
1946	...	...	86.0	91.8	63.0	51.2	100	42.1	8.6	13.7
1947	...[6]	...[6]	129	112	...	...	104[19]	49.0[19]	12.9	28.1
1948	31.8	35.9	127	128	119	75.7	108	53.4	18.6	30.5
1949	41.2	41.2	227	133	...	...	111	57.8	23.2	28.9

Abbreviations used throughout this table:— P C: Private Cars; C V: Commercial Vehicles

See p. 673 for footnotes

G 6 Motor Vehicles in Use (thousands)

1895–1949

	France		Germany		Greece		Hungary		Southern Ireland	
	PC	CV	PC	CV	PC	CV	PC	CV	PC	CV
1895	0.3	...	...	...	...	...	...	...	...	...
1896	0.5	...	...	...	...	...	...	...	...	...
1897	1.2	...	...	...	...	...	...	...	...	...
1898	1.5	...	...	...	...	...	...	...	...	...
1899	1.7	...	...	...	...	...	...	...	...	...
1900	2.9	...	...	...	...	...	...	...	...	...
1901	6.4	...	...	...	...	...	...	...	...	...
1902	9.2	...	...	...	...	...	...	...	...	...
1903	13.0	...	...	...	...	...	...	...	...	...
1904	17.1	...	...	...	...	...	...	...	...	...
1905	21.5	...	...	...	...	...	...	...	...	...
1906	26.3	...	10.1	1.2	...	...	...	...	...	...
1907	31.3	...	14.7	1.8	...	...	...	...	...	...
1908	37.6	...	18.5	2.3	...	...	...	...	...	...
1909	44.8	...	24.6	3.0	...	...	...	...	...	...
1910	53.7	...	31.7	4.2	...	...	...	...	...	...
1911	64.2	...	39.9	5.5	...	...	...	...	...	...
1912	76.8	...	49.8	7.7	...	...	...	...	...	...
1913	91.0	...	60.9[21]	9.7[21]	...	...	...	...	...	...
1914	108	...	55.3	9.1	...	...	...	...	...	...
1915	102	...	...	...	...	...	...	...	...	...
1916	101	...	...	...	...	...	...	...	...	...
1917	98.5	...	...	...	...	...	...	...	...	...
1918	94.9	...	...	...	...	...	...	...	...	...
1919	93.3	...	...	...	...	...	...	...	...	...
1920	157	79.4	...	...	...	...	1.4	0.3	...	...
1921	197[20]	92.9[20]	60.6[22]	30.3[22]	...	...	2.2	0.4	...	...
1922	243	121	80.9	45.5	...	...	2.3	0.5	...	...
1923	294	155	98.6	53.5	4.0	1.4	3.1	0.7	9.2	3.5
1924	374	201	130	62.4	5.6	2.8	4.0	1.0	13.4	4.5
1925	476	245	171	83.6	8.2	3.8	4.9[27]	1.5[27]	16.2	5.1[28]
1926	541	267	201	95.1	10.0	4.3	5.8	3.1	19.8	5.5
1927	643	307	261	108.6	12.3	5.0	8.2	4.4	22.4	6.0
1928	758	332	343	130.4	14.5	6.3	10.2	5.3	26.3	6.5
1929	930	366	422	155	17.1	8.0	11.6	6.8	29.4	7.2
1930	1,109	412	489	169	18.7	9.4	11.5	7.1	32.6	7.7
1931	1,252	438	511	173	19.8	11.2	9.8	6.9	35.7	8.3
1932	1,272	434	486	164	20.1	11.5	9.0	6.5	35.7	8.3
1933	1,397	458	511	167	20.3	11.7	5.8	5.7	36.7	8.4
1934	1,480	459	596[23]	180[23]	20.6	12.4	7.6	6.1	35.5	8.3
			662	205	[26]	[26]				
1935	1,547	458	787[24]	255[24]	...	...	8.9	6.5	38.0	8.7
			796	258						
1936	1,639	457	945	286[25]	...	...	10.9	6.9	40.8	9.3
1937	1,721	451	1,108	337	...	...	13.2	7.3	44.5	9.9
1938	1,818	451	1,272	384	...	...	15.7	7.6	48.6	11.2
1939	1,900	500	1,416	...	8.7	8.6	...	...	52.4	11.6
1940	1,800	500	...	...	...	...	...	...	50.2	11.7
1941	...	...	...	...	...	...	...	...	31.8	11.7
1942	...	...	...	...	...	...	...	...	8.0	12.1
1943	...	...	...	...	...	...	...	...	6.2	9.6
1944	680	230	...	...	...	...	...	...	6.6	9.6
1945	975	600	...	...	...	...	...	...	7.8	10.5
			West Germany							
1946	1,700		...	...	...	...	...	...	44.5	15.5
1947	1,750		...	...	4.6	15.2	36.4	11.9	52.2	19.7
1948	1,850		215	266	5.7	17.0	...	...	60.5	23.7
1949	1,950		352	329	8.2	21.1	...	...	71.9	24.9

See p. 673 for footnotes

G 6 Motor Vehicles in Use (thousands)

1900–1949

	Italy		Netherlands		Norway		Poland		Portugal	
	PC	CV	PC	CV	PC	CV	PC	CV	PC	CV
1900	...	...	...	...	- -		...	...	...	...
1901	...	...	...	...	- -		...	...	...	...
1902	...	...	...	...	- -		...	...	...	...
1903	...	...	...	...	- -		...	...	...	...
1904	...	...	...	...	- -		...	...	...	...
1905	...	...	...	...	- -		...	...	...	...
1906	...	...	...	...	0.1		...	...	...	...
1907	...	...	...	...	0.1		...	...	...	...
1908	...	...	...	...	0.1		...	...	...	...
1909	...	...	...	...	0.2		...	...	...	...
1910	...	...	...	...	0.3		...	...	...	...
1911	...	...	...	...	0.4		...	...	...	...
1912	...	...	...	...	0.5		...	...	...	...
1913	...	...	4.0		0.7		...	...	...	...
1914	22.0	2.0	...		1.0	0.1	...	...	...	...
1915	22.7	2.1	4.7		1.3	0.2	...	...	...	...
1916	21.1	2.6	5.4		2.1	0.4	...	...	...	...
1917	17.1	4.0	5.2		2.5	0.6	...	...	...	...
1918	6.8	5.8	1.6		2.6	0.7	...	...	...	...
1919	23.9	10.9	6.6		3.9	1.2	...	...	...	...
1920	31.5	18.0	11		6.7	2.4	...	...	...	...
1921	34.1	23.4	15		8.2	3.1	...	...	...	...
1922	41.0	24.5	18		9.6	3.7	...	...	...	...
1923	53.8	24.5	23		12.8	4.9	...	...	...	...
1924	57.0	27.7	31		14.7	5.8	7.4[31]	2.4[31]	...	...
1925	84.8	32.8	19[29]	12[29]	17.6	7.6	8.8	6.0	...	...
1926	105	36.5	29[10]	18[10]	21.5[30]	8.9[30]	9.6	7.0	...	...
1927	119	34.1	45	26	17.4	15.3	12.8	9.1	...	...
1928	144	40.1	52	30	18.5	18.5	15.7	14.0	...	...
1929	170	52.7	60	36	20.3	21.5	18.9	18.5	...	...
1930	183	62.1	68	44	22.4	24.0	19.9	19.5	...	...
1931	186	65.0	75	48	24.2	25.5	14.0	14.7	25.1	7.9
1932	188	68.0	81	50	25.2	26.3	11.7	14.3	24.2	8.7
1933	219	74.4	85	51	27.3	27.1	13.7	13.4	25.4	8.9
1934	236	80.5	90	51	29.6	28.9	13.8	12.1	27.9	10.0
1935	244	82.1	88	48	32.1	30.8	13.9	11.9	31.0	10.5
1936	222	81.9	89	48	36.1	33.7	15.9	12.7	33.2	11.1
1937	271	82.1	91	49	43.0	36.6	19.5	14.8	36.4	11.4
1938	289	83.6	94	50	51.1	39.5	24.6	17.4	38.0	11.5
1939	290	101	100	53	56.2	42.9	...	...	39.5	11.3
1940	270	87.5	...	...	48.8	38.7	...	...	39.1[32]	11.0[32]
									61.4	
1941	97.6	86.5	...	...	45.9	38.0	...	...	61.6	
1942	73.8	75.0	...	...	44.4	38.4	...	...	52.2	
1943	...	...	...	...	43.1	37.9	...	...	47.8	
1944	...	...	...	..	38.0	36.2	...	...	47.4	
1945	...	...	...	...	41.9	40.6	...	...	47.0	
1946	150	137	47	42	49.7	47.4	...	...	29.9	15.5
1947	184	188	68	59	55.4	52.6	23.0	...	40.0	19.8
1948	219	196	86	67	56.6	54.1	23.1	30.1	49.6	24.0
1949	267	214	113	75	58.2	54.5	36.5	40.0	56.5	26.0

See p. 673 for footnotes

G 6 Motor Vehicles in Use (thousands)

1900–1949

	Romania		Spain		Sweden		Switzerland		U.K. : G.B.		Yugoslavia	
	P C	C V	P C	C V	P C	C V	P C	C V	P C	C V	P C	C V
1900	...	...	...	...	...	...	...	...	...	...	...	...
1901	...	...	...	...	...	...	...	...	...	...	...	...
1902	...	...	...	...	...	...	...	...	...	...	...	...
1903	...	...	...	...	...	...	...	...	...	...	...	...
1904	...	...	...	...	...	...	...	...	8	9	...	...
1905	...	...	...	...	...	...	...	...	16	16	...	...
1906	...	...	...	...	...	...	...	...	23	22	...	...
1907	...	...	...	...	...	...	...	...	32	26	...	...
1908	...	...	...	...	...	...	...	...	41	33	...	...
1909	...	...	...	...	...	...	...	...	48	38	...	...
1910	...	...	...	...	...	...	2.3	0.3	53	54	...	...
1911	...	...	...	...	...	...	...	...	72	73	...	...
1912	...	...	...	...	...	...	...	...	88	88	...	...
1913	...	...	...	...	...	...	4.7	0.8	106	103	...	...
1914	...	...	...	...	...	...	5.4	0.9	132	133	...	...
1915	...	...	...	...	...	...	...	...	139	129	...	...
1916	...	...	...	...	3.0				142	133	...	...
1917	...	...	...	...	3.8		5.1	1.2	110	112	...	...
1918	...	...	...	...	4.1		...	...	78	83	...	...
1919	...	...	...	...	8.5		...	...	110	106	...	...
1920	...	...	...	...	21.3		8.9	3.3	187[34]	176[34]	...	...
1921	...	...	...	...	30.4		...	...	243	211	...	...
1922	...	...	...	...	39.9		15.0	5.8	315	229	...	...
1923	...	...	...	...	37.8	12.6	16.7	6.3	384	259	...	...
1924	...	...	...	...	46.6	16.3	22.5	8.3	474	297	...	...
1925	...	...	...	...	59.1	20.5	28.7	8.3	580	323	...	...
1926	11.3	3.6	...	...	70.5	24.1	36.1	9.4	684	358	...	...
1927	15.0	5.7	...	...	81.5	28.1	42.4	10.9	787	378	...	...
1928	21.2	7.5	...	...	94.3	32.9	50.2	11.9	885	401	...	...
1929	25.9	9.3	...	...	99.1	37.1	55.1	14.4	981	428	8.4	3.8
1930	26.0	9.4	...	...	104	40.9	60.7	15.5	1,056	449	8.5	3.5
1931	24.5	8.6	...	...	105	44.0	63.9	18.0	1,083	448	8.7	4.0
1932	21.7	8.4	...	...	102	43.5	...	...	1,128	455	8.3	4.2
1933	21.5	8.1	...	...	98.9	42.3	66.4[33]	19.8[33]	1,203	472	7.8	4.3
1934	22.2	8.4	...	...	102	45.0	69.7	19.8	1,308	498	7.6	3.5
1935	23.2	8.8	...	...	109	46.0	70.8	19.7	1,477	520	7.3	3.1
1936	23.2	8.8	...	...	119	49.1	69.1	19.6	1,643	545	9.9	3.9
1937	24.7	9.7	...	...	134	57.7	71.5	20.6	1,798	565	11.3	4.3
1938	25.4	10.4	...	...	157	62.6	74.9	21.1	1,944	583	13.6	5.2
1939	...	...	...	...	181	68.1	77.9	21.6	2,034	578	...	...
1940	...	...	...	...	34.6	46.7	65.9	18.1	1,423	525	...	...
1941	...	...	...	...	31.9	42.5	16.2	18.2	1,503	535	...	...
1942	...	...	...	...	36.7	42.3	16.8	19.8	858	538	...	...
1943	...	...	...	...	36.2	41.9	17.0	20.2	718	536	...	...
1944	...	...	...	...	39.1	42.1	17.5	19.7	755	538	...	...
1945	...	...	...	...	50.1	45.9	18.3	21.7	1,487	572	...	...
1946	...	...	...	...	138	64.2	63.0	27.2	1,770	665	...	...
1947	...	...	...	...	161	76.9	82.2	30.6	1,944	784	...	14.0
1948	...	...	83	74	180	82.8	106	31.5	1,961	896	7.2	16.7
1949	...	...	86	80	194	86.5	123	35.8	2,131	978	7.2	17.0

See p. 673 for footnotes

G 6 Motor Vehicles in Use (thousands)

1950–1975

	Austria		Belgium		Czechoslovakia		Denmark		Finland	
	PC	CV	PC	CV	PC	CV	PC	CV	PC	CV
1950	48.5	43.9	274	145	...	...	118	61.4	26.8	34.4
1951	56.6	46.3	304[35]	154[35]	...	...	122	67.0	36.2	40.0
1952	62.8	46.9	320[36]	150[36]	...	...	133	75.6	52.6	48.6
1953	71.8	48.5	368[36][37]	162[36][37]	...	...	158	85.0	59.2	49.1
1954	89.0	53.8	440[36]	135[36]	...	...	194	96.5	70.8	49.9
1955	140	61.1	...[38]	...[38]	140	105	221	103	85.4[40] / 110	56.1[40] / 61.2
1956	185	64.0	537	149	...	...	249	112	127	58.0
1957	230	65.4	...	...	...	...	280	118	139	60.8
1958	283	68.2	633	161	...	...	310	131	160	65.2
1959	337	70.9	...	...	...	...	354	150		
1960	400	73.9	753	177	247	126	408	170	183	75.2
1961	471[6] / 553	78.0[6] / 83.1	...	...	287	133	470	189	217	85.8
1962			915	200	318	139	548	205	259	90.5
1963	623	87.1	...	...	352	141	605	217	303	92.9
1964	698	91.4	1,152	221	382	150	675	232	376	93.2
1965	786	95.6	...	...	413	153	744	237	455	90.0
1966	877	101	1,436[39] / 1,503	236[39] / 320	456	160	813	247	506	96.2
1967	960	104	...	...	521	171	888	254	551	104
1968	1,056	107	1,813	349	599	179	955	259	581	106
1969	1,119[46]	113	1,921	359	700	192	1,023	262	643	110
1970	1,197	121	2,060	376	826	218	1,077	252	712	116
1971	1,325	128	2,154	385	938	228	1,147	220	753	127
1972	1,460	138	2,273	395	1,084	238	1,203	204	818	130
1973	1,541	140	2,390	406	1,193	248	1,245	222	894	134
1974	1,636	144	2,502	419	1,328	265	1,328	221	937	140
1975	1,721	146	2,614	428	1,505	285	1,295	228	996	144

	France		West Germany		East Germany		Greece		Hungary		Southern Ireland	
	PC	CV	PC	CV	PC	CV	PC	CV	PC		PC	CV
1950		2,150	516	372	75.7	95.4	9.3	22.4	13.1	8.2[49]	85.1	26.6
1951	1,700	740	682[42]	431[42]	71.0	75.6	9.3	22.4	8.5	—	96.7	28.7
1952	1,800	876	900	512	...	...	10.1	23.4	9.5	—	105	29.5
1953	2,020[41]	1,038[41]	1,126	577	...	...	10.5	24.1	9.4	—	109	34.4
1954	2,677	1,125	1,393[24] / 1,422	597[24] / 612	...	...	16.6	25.5	10.1	—	117	38.3
1955	3,113	1,225	1,693	606	117	98.7	...	...	10.1	22.3	128	41.5
1956	3,477	1,278	2,065[43] / 2,140	620[43] / 644	...	...	24.7	28.1	10.5	—	136	43.3
1957	3,972	1,371	2,584	688	...	...	31.2	29.8	12.7	—	135	44.6
1958	4,512	1,464	3,097	676	194	124	36.4	31.9	17.9	—	143	44.8
1959	5,018	1,543	3,684	660	...	...	39.7	34.2	24.8	—	154	45.1
1960	5,546	1,634	4,489	703	299	127	43.2	37.0	31.3	46.7	170	45.0
1961	6,158	1,723	5,343	751	383	124	48.8	47.0	39.9	—	186	45.3
1962	7,010	1,823	6,335	796	446	135	56.9	51.8	53.1	—	207	46.4
1963	7,953	1,936	7,305	829	507	139	67.6	57.1	71.3	—	229	46.9
1964	8,800	2,069	8,274	862	581	144	81.6	65.8	86.2	—	254	48.5
1965	9,600	2,181	9,267	895	662	159	104	73.4	99.4	79.2	281	49.9
1966	10,400	2,302	10,302	931	721	156	122	81.4	117	87.1	196	48.6
1967	11,200	2,412	11,016	923	827	164	144	89.3	145	98.7	314	47.8
1968	11,800	2,407	11,683	941	920	174	170	97.7	164	121	337	48.0
1969	12,400	2,560	12,585	978	1,039	187	195	107	192	133	375	51.5
1970	12,900	2,745	13,941	1,038	1,160	203	227	118	240	389	389	51.2
1971	13,400	2,921	15,115	1,084	1,267	215	264	129	295	165	414	47.0
1972	13,900	3,092	16,055	1,110	1,400	224	303	143	340	165	440	47.2
1973	14,500	3,330	17,023	1,139	1,539	235	347	163	409	162	477	51.7
1974	15,500	3,565	17,341	1,135	1,703	245	380	184	491	173	489	55.6
1975	15,300	3,705	17,898	1,121	1,880	260	439	211	580	189	512	55.2

See p. 673 for footnotes

G 6 Motor Vehicles in Use (thousands)

1950–1975

	Italy		Netherlands		Norway		Poland		Portugal	
	PC	CV	PC	CV	PC	CV	PC	CV	PC	CV
1950	342	229	139	82	60.1	56.3	40.1	46.4	60.5	28.8
1951	425	249	157	89	64.4	64.9	33.3	41.6	66.2	30.3
1952	510	274	173	94	73.3	73.9	37.5	49.2	70.8	32.8
1953	613	305	188	95	85.3	80.2	38.1	63.2	77.3	33.8
1954	744	339	219	100	102	85.6	36.1	62.9	87.1	35.9
1955	879	367	268	112	116	90.1	40.3	73.2	95.2	40.2
1956	1,031	360	328	127	128	94.2	44.8	82.8	106	42.8
1957	1,231	373	376	134	147	99.7	61.9	93.5	116	44.9
1958	1,393	385	421	140	166	106	83.9	102	130	47.6
1959	1,644	426	457	148	186	112	105	107	145	48.7
1960	1,995	456	522	157	219	119	117	120	158	50.4
1961	2,444	489	616	172	269	124	135	132	171	51.3
1962	3,030	538	730	185	314	129	162	146	190	53.6
1963	3,913	596	866	205	357	133	188	164	196	55.1
1964	4,675	630	1,059	220	408	137	211	174	211	68.5
1965	5,473	650	1,273	235	458	139	246	183	319	61.9
1966	6,357	684	1,502	254	509[44] 516	142[44] 135	289	197	359	65.9
1967	7,311	718	1,725	275	569	138	332	210	401	76.1
1968	8,266	793	1,990	285	619	140	375	226	450	77.9
1969	9,174	851	2,290[50]	315[50]	700	146	423	245	514	81.7
1970	10,181	904	2,600[50]	302[50]	748 695[48]	152 140[48]	479	260	551	147
1971	11,299	972	2,800[50]	320[50]	742	146	557	274	621	163
1972	12,484	1,015 979[47]	3,050[50]	325[50]	788	156	657	293 311[51]	697	185
1973	13,424	1,028	2,957	326	838	156	781	346	770	214
1974	14,295	1,081	3,153	336	890	153	920	386	854	238
1975	15,061	1,128	3,399	345	954	147	1,078	425	937	259

	Romania	Spain		Sweden		Switzerland		United Kingdom		Yugoslavia	
	CV	PC	CV	PC	CV	PC	CV	PC	CV	PC	CV
1950	...	89	83	252	94.5	147	38.5	2,258	1,032	6.4	17.1
1951	...	97[45]	87[45]	313	97.3	168	40.8	2,380	1,070	6.9	16.5
1952	...	102	89	361	105	188	42.7	2,508	1,097	8.5	19.3
1953	...	108	92	431	111	211	45.2	2,762	1,112	10.2	21.4
1954	...	118	114	536	116	238	48.9	3,100	1,140	11.3	22.4
1955	...	132	102	637	118	271	53.1	3,526	1,211	12.6	23.4
1956	5.2	153	111	735	121	309	58.6	3,888	1,273	14.7	23.8
1957	6.9	167	117	863	124	347	64.1	4,187	1,313	21.6	29.2
1958	9.1	188	124	972	126	386	68.7	4,549	1,364	28.4	32.4
1959	11.8	240	133	1,088	128	430	77.1	4,966	1,418	39.0	36.2
1960	22.1	291	159	1,194	130	485	82.3	5,526	1,491	53.3	38.7
1961	23.9	359	187	1,304	135	550	91.9	5,979	1,542	75.6	37.6
1962	23.9	441	220	1,424	138	630	108	6,556	1,563	97.9	43.8
1963	27.9	530	261	1,556	141	700	124	7,375	1,625	113	49.2
1964	31.2	652	315	1,666	144	779	144	8,247	1,673	142	56.3
1965	33.3	807	387	1,793	142	845	162	8,917	1,699	188	66.8
1966	34.0	1,053	467	1,890	143	919	180	9,513	1,647	253	80.0
1967	36.8	1,335	550	1,977	149	979	198	10,303	1,697	356	96.9
1968	38.1	1,634	620	2,072	150	1,061	219	10,816	1,644	430	103
1969	43.9	1,999	883	2,194	155	1,146	243	11,230	1,643	563	109
1970	45.1	2,378	741	2,289	159	1,239	255	11,515	1,694	721	122
1971	...	2,785	793	2,357	156	1,458[52]	152[52]	12,059	1,696	875	139
1972	...	3,255	852	2,458	160	1,557	162	12,717	1,721	1,002	158
1973	...	3,804	924	2,503	164	1,652	170	13,497	1,799	1,141	158
1974	...	4,310	988	2,639	170	1,723	176	13,639	1,841	1,333	171
1975	...	4,807	1,040	2,760	171	1,794	179	13,747	1,855	1,537	179

See p. 673 for footnotes

G 6 Motor Vehicles in Use

NOTES

1. SOURCES:– The official publications noted on p.xv with gaps filled from the League of Nations, *Statistical Yearbook,* except for Great Britain, which are taken from British Road Federation, *Basic Road Statistics,* and Greece 1923–34, which were supplied by the National Statistical Service of Greece.

2. So far as possible, and except as indicated in footnotes, buses and taxis are included with commercial vehicles.

3. Unless otherwise indicated, statistics relate to the year-end.

FOOTNOTES

[1] At 30 June.
[2] Previous figures are for Cisleithania, subsequent ones for the Republic.
[3] At 30 September for 1922–37.
[4] Buses (2.1 thousand in 1930) are included with private cars to 1929.
[5] Taxis (4.3 thousand in 1937) are included with private cars to 1937.
[6] At 31 October for 1948–61.
[7] Including tractors.
[8] In March.
[9] In August/September.
[10] At 1 October.
[11] In February for 1928–1933 (1st line).
[12] Including taxis.
[13] At 1 September previously, except 1917 which is at 20 May.
[14] At 1 July.
[15] Buses (0.9 thousand in 1927) are included with passenger cars to 1925.
[16] At 30 September for 1928–30 and 1942–44.
[17] At 1 September for 1931–40.
[18] At 1 December.
[19] At 31 October for 1945–47.
[20] Alsace-Lorraine is included from 1922.
[21] At 1 July subsequently. The 1914 figure is for the 1924 boundaries.
[22] Buses (1.8 thousand in 1922) are included with passenger cars to 1921.
[23] Figures to 1934 (1st line) are of vehicles operating on the roads; later figures are of all vehicles registered.
[24] Saarland is included to 1935 (2nd line) to 1939 and from 1954 (2nd line).
[25] Fuel lorries (1.4 thousand in 1936) are excluded in 1937 and 1938.
[26] The reason for this break is not given.
[27] Buses and taxis (1.1 thousand in 1926) are included with passenger cars to 1925.
[28] Previously including tractors.
[29] In January.
[30] Buses and taxis (3.7 thousand in 1927) are included with passenger cars to 1926.
[31] Buses are included with private cars in 1924.
[32] Previous figures are of vehicles registered, subsequently they are of all vehicles in existence.
[33] At 30 September subsequently.
[34] In March to 1920, and subsequently in August or September.
[35] Previous figures are of total vehicles taxed during the year.
[36] At 15 December.
[37] Dual purpose vehicles are included with commercial vehicles to 1953 and with private cars subsequently.
[38] At 1 August subsequently.
[39] Previous figures are of taxed vehicles only.
[40] Station wagons are included with commercial vehicles to 1955.
[41] A note in the source indicates that destroyed vehicles are subsequently deducted.
[42] Tax-exempt vehicles are not included in 1948–51.
[43] Subsequently including West Berlin.
[44] Taxis (7.8 thousand in 1966) are subsequently included with private cars.
[45] Previously including Spanish Morocco.
[46] Taxis (6.6 thousand in 1969) are subsequently included with private cars.
[47] Subsequently excluding buses.
[48] Subsequently excluding vehicles whose licences were cancelled during the year.
[49] Lorries only.
[50] Estimates (including special vehicles in commercial vehicles – 10 thousand in 1968 and 1973).
[51] Subsequently including special vehicles.
[52] The basis of classification was changed.

G 7 COMMERCIAL AVIATION INDICATORS

1920–1969

	Belgium[11] Regular Services		Czechoslovakia		Denmark Copenhagen Airport Traffic		Finland Civil Airports Traffic		France	
	P (a)	F (b)	P (a)	F (b)	P (c)	F (d)	P (c)	F (d)	P (a)	F (b)
1920	...	...	...	...	...	...	...	...	0.6	29
1921	...	...	...	...	...	...	...	...	4.1	106
1922	...	...	...	...	...	...	...	...	3.5	210
1923	...	...	...	...	0.4	5	...	...	4.2	383
1924	0.2	11	...	...	1.4	11	...	...	5.4	333
1925	0.4	47	...	...	3.4	9	...	...	6.3	319
1926	0.6	52	...	...	8.8	33	...	...	6.6	361
1927	0.8	52	...	...	9.2	63	3.1	39	7.7	445
1928	1.5	73	...	...	7.2	76	3.8	49	9.9	682
1929	1.6	87	...	...	9.2	109	5.8	84	12	888
1930	2.3	111	...	...	8.6	102	4.4	58	15	900
1931	3.2	140	...	...	11	130	4.5	42	18	810
1932	3.3	95	...	...	12	72	4.9	77	22	605
1933	4.4	112	...	...	21	86	6.6	130	30	829
1934	5.0	109	...	...	33	128	10	119	30	757
1935	8.0	158	...	...	36	162	12	128	38	812
1936	11.3	208	...	...	43	164[2]	14	223	43	729
1937	14.5	229	19	600	57	360	24	350	60	959
1938	18.1	405	...	...	65	457	25	419	73	1,022
1939	12.8	252	...	...	72	491	25	427	...	...
1940	5.5	99	...	...	45	605	18	432	...	...
1941	5.4	36	...	...	...	...	12	336	...	...
1942	8.9	64	...	...	45	341	24	644	...	...
1943	9.8	72	...	...	38	234	33	821	...	...
1944	14.8	77	...	...	30	226	30	586	...	...
1945	28.6	136	...	...	53	101	17	230	123	1,179
1946	153	788	46	1,700	233	666	31	289	334	5,983
1947	215	3,065	61	2,000	283	1,998	47	693	681	14,494
1948	173	3,019	55	2,812	291	2,232	74	1,205	1,040	45,126
1949	194	3,705	41	2,247	310	2,841	78	1,434	1,337	55,984
1950	235	6,591	46	2,682	345	4,719	97	1,698	1,595	59,634
1951	277	9,226	67	2,794	392[1]	5,908	91	...	1,839	70,788
1952	344	11,807	64	2,289	440					
					555	7,437	116	...	2,146	81,542
1953	448	15,534	74	2,750	657	8,378	173	...	2,470	80,241
1954	489	17,998	77	2,382	704	8,217	239	...	3,015[3]	96,313[3]
									2,645	73,450
1955	578	20,426	94	3,167	838	9,383	557	6,791	3,010	80,597
1956	679	23,070	117	3,566	1,042	11,203	663	8,424	3,596	89,228
1957	929	26,135	135	4,612	1,242	12,853	768	12,014	4,010	97,005
1958	1,198	27,045	193	6,838	1,396	15,482	742	9,720	4,318[4]	103,469[4]
1959	1,065	28,713	269	9,160	1,566	19,862	770	11,198	4,723	111,186
1960	1,264	33,254	390	13,780	1,884	26,239	914	12,456	5,437	120,421
1961	1,178	37,977	457	16,467	2,012	30,527	896	12,469	6,461[5]	151,926[5]
1962	1,384	35,218	575	27,924	2,265	36,385	1,034	14,538	6,205	140,633
1963	1,346	39,920	628	32,099	2,574	43,322	1,103	17,289	6,354	139,512
1964	1,488	46,923	702	29,327	2,964	46,810	1,052	16,808	7,023	146,692
1965	1,635	58,872	790	28,053	3,489	54,730	1,170	18,468	7,779	185,108
1966	1,654	63,647	924	28,585	3,995	60,912	1,275	21,243	9,259	221,862
1967	1,954	92,396	962	27,165	4,756	65,852	1,493	22,170	10,367	261,135
1968	1,977	118,747	960	26,576	5,333	82,524	1,539	23,693	10,241	319,145
1969	2,206	169,912	1,133	28,855	5,842	112,030	1,823	29,608	12,387	448,977

Abbreviations used throughout this table:— P: Passengers; F: Freight

Other abbreviations used where space demands:— (a) = kms millions; (b) = ton/kms thousands; (c) = thousands; (d) = tons

See p. 677 for footnotes

G 7 Commercial Aviation Indicators

1920–1969

	Germany		East Germany		Italy		Netherlands		Norway	
									Regular Services	
	P (a)	F (b)	P (c)	F (d)	P (a)	F (b)	P (a)	F (d)	P (c)	F & P (f)
1920	4.0	6			...	...	0.4	...	...	...
1921	6.8	32			...	...	1.3	...	...	...
1922	7.7	38			...	...	1.3	...	...	...
1923	8.5	40			...	...	2.8	...	...	...
	P (c)	F (d)								
	2.1	9.5								
1924	3.3	33			...	...	4.7	...	...	...
1925	10.6	119			...	...	8.5	...	...	...
1926	14.6	219			8	...	11	...	...	...
1927	27.0	554			20	...	15	...	...	...
1928	28.7	735			24	335	18	...	...	...
1929	23.8	756			40	746	19	...	...	...
							P(c)			
							7	...		
1930	23.8	816			63	988	4	—	...	...
1931	25.7	897			54	936	5	—	...	...
1932	28.2	873			73	1,108	7	0.3	...	...
1933	38.3	1,063			72	1,232	14	0.4	...	...
1934	62.7	1,445			78	1,521	23	0.4	...	...
1935	85.9	2,135			99	1,640	26	0.5	1.0	...
1936	124	2,758			109	1,645	36	0.6	1.2	...
1937	121	2,344			187	2,858	46	0.8	1.1	...
1938	128	2,633			209	3,343	60	1.2	2.4	0.3
1939	114	2,241			246	4,360	61	1.1	2.2[7]	...
1940	59	1,762			...	...	19	0.2	...	...
1941	...	...			...	...	17	0.2	...	...
1942	...	...			...	...	12	—	...	...
1943	...	...			...	...	17	...	...	...
1944	...	...			...	...	17	...	...	...
1945	...	...			...	...	31	0.1	...	...
	West Germany									
	(a)	(e)								
1946	...	...	...	...	...	...	346	3.7	33	3.5
1947	...	...	...	...	292	3,061	473	8.0	85	4.7
1948	...	...	...	...	439	9,094	723	15.6	99	10.8
						(e)				
1949	...	...	...	...	480	13	608	13.5	135	16.2
1950	333	6.3	...	...	550	15	772	24.3	162	21.1
1951	535	24.5	...	...	542	15	876	28.2	200	27.7
1952	721	36.2	...	...	580	16	1,013	34.8	222	29.5
1953	1,147	58.4	...	...	649	21	1,179	38.1	260	33.2
1954	1,078	49.0	...	...	792	24	1,362	44.4	265	31.8
1955	1,439	46.1	—	—	973	29	1,485	51.0	327	38.0
1956	1,801	40.5	3.0	480	1,220	36	1,725	61.1	402	45.5
1957	2,052	32.3	44.3	1,755	1,456	41[6]	1,975	66.9	497	55.5
						15				
1958	2,397	26.6	116	2,299	1,847	18	1,986	71.0	566	62.6
1959	2,725	34.5	128	2,814	2,326	24	2,229	86.8	592	66.2
1960	3,521	43.9	165	4,655	2,911	34	2,672	104	685	76.8
1961	3,900	53.7	159	5,027	3,765	47	2,795	118	690	78.9
1962	4,635	56.1	299	8,318	4,755	59	2,847	127	780	88.7
1963	5,454	65.0	306	9,379	5,710	70	2,563	128	864	99.7
1964	6,261	74.3	312	11,024	6,428	76	3,012	151	1,014	111
1965	7,679	92.8	373	13,060	7,349	88	3,367	199	1,180	123
1966	8,495	118	484	15,797	8,432	105	3,902	227	1,212	144
1967	9,406	135	606	21,773	9,664	119	4,311	247	1,440	169
1968	10,818	174	730	24,090	11,248	153	4,605	304	1,608	199
1969	12,849	214	843	23,319	13,457	198	4,799	355	1,737	224

Other abbreviations used where space demands:— (a) = thousands; (b) = tons; (c) = kms millions; (d) = ton/kms thousands; (e) = thousand tons; (f) = ton/kms millions.

See p. 677 for footnotes

G 7 Commercial Aviation Indicators

1920–1969

	Portugal Regular Services		Spain Regular Services		Sweden Regular Services		Switzerland[9]		United Kingdom	
	P (a)	F (b)	P (c)	F (d)	P (c)	F (d)	P (a)	F (e)	P (c)	F (d)
1920	...	...	...	...	...	...	...	...	...	...
1921	...	...	...	...	...	...	...	...	...	...
1922	...	...	...	...	...	...	0.6	—	...	...
1923	...	...	...	...	...	...	1.5	—	...	...
1924	...	...	...	...	...	...	4.0	6.7	...	...
1925	...	...	...	...	...	...	9.7	93.8	4.3	216
1926	...	...	...	...	...	...	7.9	32.5	6.0	232
1927	...	...	...	...	...	...	13.1	83.0	6.9	223
1928	...	...	...	...	1.0	45	19.6	279	10.4	315[10]
							(c) 3.5	(d) 59		292
1929	...	...	2.1	9.7	1.2	39	3.5	65	11.5	358
1930	...	...	3.0	35.0	1.1	40	3.6	91	9.7	321
1931	...	...	3.0	15.5	0.8	41	4.6	130	11.3	328
1932	...	...	3.0	11.5	1.9	64	5.8	102	25.8	413
1933	...	...	2.1	10.8	3.1	89	7.2	111	34.8	534
1934	...	...	3.4	24.1	4.6	127	10.6	112	46.9	744
1935	...	...	7.1	...	6.2	169	14.3	198	68.2	1,200
1936	...	...	...	...	5.7	154	15.4	202	66.2	1,074
1937	...	...	1.2	...	11.8	346	17.9	284	79.6	1,309
1938	...	...	11.3	...	13.9	441	23.3	456	86.0	1,587
1939	...	...	21.0	...	18.2	556	18.5	328	90.7	1,380
1940	...	...	18.1	...	13.5	509	...	...	67.8	1,526
1941	...	...	...	...	11.5	385	...	...	91.5	2,866
1942	17	406	...	...	14.4	497	...	...	164	8,322
1943	13	453	...	...	12.8	564	...	...	201	13,198
1944	12	563	14.6	76.3	11.8	350	...	...	288	23,066
1945	18	268	21.8	69.1	39.5	1,322	7.6	80	486	27,735
1946	76	243	49.9	170	82.5	2,102	93.7	631	584	12,829
1947	69	291	78.2	192	150	2,522	158	1,572	710	16,680
1948	75	453	102	264[8]	137	1,820	203	2,284	892	25,377
1949	78	459	116	366[8]	183	2,991	282	3,436	989	29,572
1950	97	609	181	...	245	5,273	324	5,593	1,278	35,862
1951	95	637	221	1,159	258	6,597	389	7,049	1,714	45,422
1952	105	817	245	1,184	293	6,457	451	8,258	2,000	44,719
1953	114	881	286	1,385	346	6,848	622	11,004	2,308	49,661
	(c) 44	(d) 565								
1954	61	696	320	1,547	379	7,938	780	13,510	2,439	51,790
1955	81	787	403	1,965	474	9,213	904	17,076	2,899	70,399
1956	108	1,087	537	2,652	568	10,132	1,050	20,745	3,383	72,841
1957	122	1,233	554	3,156	741	13,017	1,382	26,401	3,898	82,467
1958	162	1,359	610	3,974	849	15,173	1,614	33,449	4,138	85,311
1959	195	1,683	661	4,772	881	17,612	1,640	40,760	4,974	101,741
1960	243	2,100	782	5,632	1,012	21,152	2,004	54,873	6,372	118,111
1961	356	3,162	947	7,018	1,059	24,796	2,415	62,887	7,292	133,761
1962	400	2,782	1,236	9,396	1,177	28,712	2,816	67,907	7,838	165,163
1963	477	3,549	1,468	14,380	1,231	32,674	3,130	78,855[9]	8,767	196,355
								50,643		
1964	571	4,117	1,952	19,512	1,420	35,325	3,610	57,205	10,389	237,887
1965	716	6,139	2,395	26,302	1,492	41,558	4,147	70,895	11,937	303,727
1966	923	8,548	2,699	32,918	1,560	47,821	4,682	83,727	13,361	385,340
1967	1,160	12,611	3,071	41,090	1,825	55,683	5,241	85,396	14,070	399,591
1968	1,495	20,294	3,879	58,837	2,027	77,431	5,927	117,609	14,095	421,425
1969	1,929	29,567	4,837	82,731	2,181	97,176	6,794	175,298	16,261	531,713

Other abbreviations used where space demands:— (a) = thousands; (b) = thousand tons; (c) = kms/millions; (d) = ton/kms thousands; (e) = tons;

See p. 677 for footnotes

G 7 Commercial Aviation Indicators

1970–1975

	Belgium[11] Regular Services		Czechoslovakia		Denmark Copenhagen Airport Traffic		Finland Civil Airports Traffic		France	
	P (a)	F (b)	P (a)	F (b)	P (c)	F (d)	P (c)	F (d)	P (a)	F (b)
1970	2,447	183,990	1,236	34,402	6,791	112,873	2,249	35,971	13,937	478,437
1971	2,720	202,385	1,361	38,213	7,690	110,825	2,579	19,779	14,471	496,302
1972	3,093	224,514	1,588	45,431	8,192	125,045	2,987	21,891	17,740	628,742
1973	3,644	238,636	1,660	46,163	8,409	137,955	3,635	24,228	19,928	770,955
1974	3,975	286,101	1,827	47,987	8,449	142,395	4,098	26,850	22,016	884,980
1975	3,796	281,156	1,828	45,096	8,492	129,615	4,524	25,214	23,671	1,014,137

Other abbreviations used where space demands:— (a) = kms millions; (b) = ton/kms thousands; (c) = thoudands; (d) = tons

	Germany		East Germany		Italy		Netherlands		Norway Regular Services	
	P (a)	F (b)	P (c)	F (d)	P (a)	F (b)	P (a)	F (d)	P (c)	F & P (f)
1970	15,381	239	947	26,647	15,963	217	5,769	377	1,954	244
1971	17,441	248	1,073	29,719	18,545	231	6,444	408	2,135	263
1972	18,023	268	1,099	29,229	19,037	242	7,925	461	2,444	303
1973	16,874	285	1,120	30,757	20,455	284	9,211	499	2,757	337
1974	17,593	291	1,315	42,835	21,227	305	9,389	609	2,738	346
1975	18,131	265	1,490	52,568	21,922	272	10,323	587	2,880	354

Other abbreviations used where space demands:— (a) = thousands; (b) = tons; (c) = kms millions; (d) = ton/kms thousands; (e) = thousand tons (f) = ton/kms millions.

	Portugal Regular Services		Spain Regular Services		Sweden Regular Services		Switzerland[9]		United Kingdom	
	P (a)	F (b)	P (c)	F (d)	P (c)	F (d)	P (a)	F (e)	P (c)	F (d)
1970	2,453	36,987	5,874	90,806	2,449	98,512	7,733	187,600	17,432	493,820
1971	3,005	48,500	7,067	131,600	2,630	100,064	8,441	201,000	18,664	541,006
1972	3,419	55,300	8,074	154,900	3,007	119,591	9,704	218,500	22,169	680,434
1973	3,936	90,500	9,513	172,000	3,413	127,993	11,051	258,800	26,187	795,776
1974	4,211	105,000	10,105	199,500	3,478	143,024	11,376	295,000	25,397	785,950
1975	3,312	67,500	10,695	214,700	3,630	134,358	12,136	308,500	27,544	724,790

Other abbreviations used where space demands:— (a) = thousands; (b) = thousand tons; (c) = kms/millions; (d) = ton/kms thousands; (e) = tons.

NOTES

1. SOURCES:— The official publications noted on p.xv with gaps filled from the United Nations, *Statistical Yearbooks.*

2. Comparisons between different countries are especially difficult because of lack of uniformity in methods of collecting statistics, especially of freight, even in recent years.

FOOTNOTES

[1] Previous figures are of scheduled services only.
[2] Previously excluding transit traffic.
[3] Subsequently excluding the Moroccan, Tunisian, and Indo-Chinese companies.
[4] Subsequently excluding the African companies.
[5] Subsequently excluding the Algerian companies.
[6] Subsequently does not include free baggage.
[7] To 31 August.
[8] The reason for this break is not given. The figure for 1948 comparable to the post-1950 series is 505.
[9] Including the operations of foreign airlines at Swiss airports, except for freight from 1963 (2nd line), which relates to scheduled services of Swiss lines only.
[10] Previously including mail.
[11] Sabena traffic only.

G 8 POST, TELEGRAPH, AND TELEPHONE SERVICES

1830–1869

	Austria[1]		Belgium		Denmark[3]		Finland		France	
	(a)	(b)	(c)	(d)	(e)[4]	(f)	(g)[6]	(h)[7]	(i)[4]	(j)
1830	18.6	–	...	–	...	...	...	...	104	...
1831	20.5	–	...	–	...	...	...	...	109	...
1832	24.0	–	...	–	...	...	...	...	143	...
1833	24.5	–	...	–	...	...	...	...	120	...
1834	25.6	–	...	–	...	...	...	...	120	...
1835	24.2	–	...	–	...	...	...	...	124	...
1836	24.7	–	...	–	...	...	...	...	125	...
1837	24.9	–	...	–	...	...	...	...	134	...
1838	26.3	–	...	–	...	...	...	...	136	...
1839	26.8	–	...	–	...	...	...	...	142	...
1840	29.3	–	...	–	...	...	...	...	147	...
1841	30.7	–	...	–	...	...	...	...	153	...
1842	30.1	–	...	–	...	...	...	...	158	...
1843	27.0	–	...	–	...	...	...	...	160	...
1844	28.7	–	...	–	...	...	...	...	169	...
1845	30.2	–	...	–	...	...	0.3	...	176	...
1846	32.2	–	...	–	...	...	...	...	189	...
1847	33.0	–	...	–	...	...	...	...	217	...
1848	32.1[1] / 20.7	8	...	–	...	...	...	...	252	...
1849	23.2	9	...	–	...	...	...	...	305	...
1850	26.1	14	22.6	–	...	...	...	...	254	...
1851	29.2	56	27.7	[14][2]	...	...	...	...	199	...
1852	32.1	85	31.9	27	...	...	...	...	276	...
1853	37.4	147	34.1	52	...	...	...	...	286	...
1854	43.4	231	36.6	60	...	...	...	...	329	...
1855	46.4	270	41.9	61	...	...	0.6	...	358	...
1856	47.7	343	45.7	99	...	...	...	...	380	...
1857	50.0	397	47.9	119	...	...	...	...	398	...
1858	54.5	464	49.0	145	...	...	...	...	406	464
1859	66.5[1]	728	56.0	196	...	...	...	...	426	599
1860	60.4	727	57.0	226	...	...	...	...	444	720
1861	65.6	920	59.7	269	6.7	...	...	...	464	920
1862	73.4	1,022	63.1	292	6.8	...	...	...	487	1,518
1863	73.8	1,106	65.5	416	7.2	...	...	...	505	1,755
1864	81.3	1,693	67.3	546	8.6[5] / 9.2	...	...	...	568	2,167
1865	81.1[1] / 86.1	1,900	74.5	674	9.3	203	0.7	...	592	2,539
1866		2,659	88.2	1,128	9.0	238	...	124	616	2,941
1867	107	2,443	90.3	1,289	9.3	316	...	...	652	3,286
1868	114	2,433	94.5	1,503	9.9	357	...	...	679	3,581
1869	128	3,081	100	1,723	10.7[6] / 12.1	420	...	...	692	4,754

Abbreviations used:– (a) = Total unregistered mail items (millions); (b) = Telegrams (thousands); (c) = Total mail items (millions); (d) = Telegrams (thousands); (e) Total unregistered mail items (millions); (f) Telegrams (thousands); (g) = Total mail items (millions); (h) = Telegrams (thousands); (i) = Total mail items (millions); (j) = Telegrams (thousands).

See p. 698 for footnotes

G 8 Post, Telegraph, and Telephone Services

1830–1869

	Germany		Greece		Hungary[8]		Italy		Netherlands		Norway	
	(a)[4]	(b)	(c)	(d)	(e)	(f)	(g)[4]	(h)[10]	(i)	(j)	(k)	(l)
1830	...	...	...	—	...	...	...	...	...	—	...	...
1831	...	...	...	—	...	...	...	...	...	—	...	...
1832	...	...	...	—	...	...	...	...	...	—	...	...
1833	...	...	...	—	...	...	...	...	...	—	...	...
1834	...	...	...	—	...	...	...	...	...	—	...	...
1835	...	...	...	—	...	...	...	...	...	—	...	...
1836	...	...	...	—	...	...	...	...	...	—	...	...
1837	...	...	...	—	...	...	...	...	...	—	...	...
1838	...	...	...	—	...	...	...	...	...	—	...	...
1839	...	...	...	—	...	...	...	...	...	—	...	...
1840	...	...	0.8	—	...	...	...	...	...	—	...	...
1841	...	...	...	—	...	...	...	...	...	—	...	...
1842	...	...	...	—	...	...	...	...	...	—	...	...
1843	...	...	...	—	...	...	...	...	...	—	...	...
1844	...	...	...	—	...	...	...	...	...	—	...	...
1845	...	...	0.7	—	...	...	...	...	...	—	...	...
1846	...	...	...	—	...	...	...	...	...	—	...	...
1847	...	...	...	—	...	...	...	...	...	—	...	...
1848	...	...	...	—	...	...	...	...	...	—	1.0	...
1849	...	...	...	—	3.2	...	...	...	6	—	...	...
1850	85.9	0.04	0.8	—	5.5	...	...	...	7	—	1.5	...
1851	89.5	0.05	...	—	5.9[9]	...	...	...	11	—	...	...
1852	99.0	0.07	...	—	8.8	...	...	...	12	1	...	...
1853	111	0.15	...	—	10.6	...	...	...	13	46	...	...
1854	123	0.21	...	—	11.7	...	...	...	14	102	...	...
1855	133	0.32	1.0	—	14.3	...	...	...	15	104	2.3	23
1856	147	0.35	1.0	—	15.2	...	...	...	16	190	...	...
1857	155	0.44	1.1	—	16.3	...	...	...	17	225	...	...
1858	163	0.53	1.1	—	15.8	...	...	...	18	264	...	91
1859	170	0.57	1.2	5.5	54.7	...	...	...	19[11] 26	389	...	117
1860	179	0.73	1.3	20	...	...	...	...	27	413	3.3	130
1861	187	0.81	1.3	29	...	...	108	0.1	28	479	...	128
1862	197	0.98	2.1	...	26.1	...	133	0.1	29	527	...	139
1863	210	1.32	2.1	57	26.7	...	154	0.1	30	653	3.9	167
1864	233	1.75	2.4	62	28.0	...	153	1.1	31	802	...	200
1865	253	2.65	2.7	85	28.0	...	156	1.3	33	966	...	218
1866	269	3.37	2.8	103	30.8	...	164	1.6	36	1,088	4.7	269
1867	307	4.26	2.9	107	38.2	...	174	1.4	...	1,113	...	310
1868	344	5.16	3.0	101	38.0	998	176	1.8	...	1,497	5.4	355
1869	371	6.07	3.1	112	45.0	1,207	183	1.9	...	1,632	...	392

Abbreviations used:— (a) = Total unregistered mail items (millions); (b) = Telegrams (millions); (c) = Total mail items (millions); (d) = Telegrams (thousands); (e) Total unregistered mail items (millions); (f) = Telegrams (thousands); (g) = Total letter post items (millions); (h) = Telegrams (millions); (i) = Total unregistered letter post items (millions); (j) = Telegrams (thousands); (k) = Total letter post items (millions); (l) = Telegrams (thousands).

See p. 698 for footnotes

G 8 Post, Telegraph, and Telephone Services

1830–1869

	Portugal	Russia	Spain		Sweden		Switzerland		United Kingdom
	(b)	(c)	(d)	(e)	(f)	(g)	(h)[4]	(i)	(j)
1830	...	...	...	—	...	...	...	—	...
1831	...	...	...	—	...	...	...	—	...
1832	...	...	...	—	...	...	...	—	...
1833	...	...	...	—	...	...	...	—	...
1834	...	...	...	—	...	...	...	—	...
1835	...	...	...	—	...	...	...	—	...
1836	...	...	...	—	...	...	...	—	...
1837	...	...	...	—	...	...	...	—	...
1838	...	...	...	—	...	...	...	—	...
1839	...	...	...	—	...	...	...	—	82
1840	...	...	...	—	...	...	...	—	169
1841	...	...	...	—	...	...	...	—	196
1842	...	...	...	—	...	...	...	—	208
1843	...	...	...	—	...	...	...	—	219
1844	...	...	...	—	...	...	...	—	243
1845	...	...	...	—	...	...	...	—	272
1846	...	...	19.0	—	...	...	...	—	300
1847	...	...	19.8	—	...	...	...	—	321
1848	...	...	20.2	—	...	...	...	—	329
1849	...	...	20.5	—	...	...	...	—	338
1850	...	...	20.5	—	3.9	...	11.4	—	346
1851	...	...	20.8	—	4.0	...	16.2	—	361
1852	...	...	22.0	—	4.1	...	18.7	3	379
1853	...	...	23.2	—	4.4	...	21.0	...	411
1854	...	...	25.2	—	4.7	...	21.9	127	443
1855	...	...	28.8	3	4.8	61	23.1	159	457[14]
1856	...	...	30.2	...	5.3	117	25.2	210	552
1857	...	...	38.7	...	5.7	175	26.1	238	582
1858	...	...	42.6	...	5.8	174	27.3	228	602
1859	...	...	47.5	...	6.1	171	28.3	260	627
1860	...	...	54.4	316	6.3	159	28.8	277	646
1861	...	...	59.4	454	6.6	169	30.8	...	678
1862	...	...	63.5	496	6.9	210	31.3	...	692
1863	...	...	64.6	555	7.4	228	38.5	...	731
1864	...	927	68.8	747	8.2[13]	243	40.0	...	775
					10.0				
1865	...	1,044	70.4	956	11	328	43.4	560	817
1866	...	1,416	74.7	855	11	419	45.6	...	849
1867	...	1,589	72.9	742	12	490	48.7	...	877
1868	176	2,029	...	752	12	497	51.5	...	914
1869	454	2,399	...	748	13	561	49.3	...	933

Abbreviations used:— (a) = All mail items (millions); (b) = Telegrams (thousands); (c) = Telegrams (thousands); (d) = Total mail items (millions); (e) = Telegrams (thousands); (f) = Total mail items (millions); (g) = Telegrams (thousands); (h) = Total mail items (millions); (i) = Telegrams (thousands); (j) = Total mail items (millions).

See p. 698 for footnotes

G 8 Post, Telegraph, and Telephone Services

1870–1919

	Austria[1]			Belgium			Denmark[3]			Finland		
	(a)[4]	(b)	(c)	(d)	(e)	(f)	(g)[4]	(h)	(i)	(j)[4]	(k)[7]	(l)[20]
1870	148	3,388	–	111	1,998	...	13.0	525	...	...	131	...
1871	169	4,194	–	121	2,380	...	13.3	553	...	...	145	...
1872	205	4,852	–	131	2,407	...	15.2	600	...	...	184	...
1873	267	5,353	–	140	2,570	...	17.0	650	...	...	217	...
1874	245	4,678	–	154	2,750	...	18.8	763	...	...	299	...
1875	242	4,907	–	169	2,872	...	20.7	887	...	...	493	...
1876	257	5,444	–	174	2,911	...	23.5	941	...	...	540	...
1877	263	5,788	–	181	2,900	...	25.2	937	...	...	598	...
1878	295	5,989	–	177	2,961	...	26.8	916	...	...	541	...
1879	302	5,767	–	186[16] 197	3,243	...	28.3	969	...	2.6	521	...
1880	324	6,165	–	215	3,424	...	29.6	1,087	...	3.0	662	...
1881	342	6,678	–	239	3,791	...	32.7	1,161	...	3.1	892	...
1882	357	7,077	–	259	3,979[17] 6,896	...	34.7	1,192	...	3.2	1,001[7] 157	...
1883	384	7,021	–	268	7,030	...	35.9	1,247	...	3.6	162	...
1884	415	7,158	1.9	284	6,788	...	40.7	1,252	...	3.7	...	...
1885	437	7,199	2.5	295	6,799	...	41.0	1,256	...	4.3	178	...
1886	440	7,394	3.8	290	6,632	...	42.8	1,250	...	4.9	165	...
1887	449	7,715	4.8	286	6,799	...	45.4	1,293	...	5.5	171	...
1888	480	8,387	5.9	299	7,253	...	46.4	1,525	...	6.0[5] 7.7	...	...
1889	504	8,736	7.7	318	7,737	...	49.2	1,495	...	8.7	200	...
1890	538	9,082	12.8	326	8,063	13.3	53.6	1,503	...	10.0[16] 10.7	205	...
1891	568	9,661	17.0	341	8,446	...	55.3	1,629	...	11.2	209	...
1892	608	10,835	22.4	355	7,976	...	56.8	1,637	...	13.1	221	...
1893	647	12,069	38.7	360	8,312	...	62.4	1,765	...	13.6	225	...
1894	780	12,603	57.3	365	8,307	...	64.9	1,758	...	14.0	224	...
1895	788	13,235	62.8	388	8,515	19.5	67.9	1,811	...	15.1	218	...
1896	846	13,214	75.3	382	8,447	22.3	71.9	1,796	...	16.4	231	...
1897	923	13,771	91.2	410	9,189	26.6	74.6	1,860	...	17.7	251	...
1898	999	14,158	101.0[15] 82.2	444	10,282	29.8	80.8	1,953	...	19.2	269	...
1899	1,112	14,698		470	12,338	33.5	84.9	2,057	...	21.1	...	...
1900	1,193	15,057	94.1	502	14,277	38.4[19]	90.4	2,154	52.9	23.0	279	...
1901	1,239	15,380	104	530	14,193[18] 14,000	37.2	95.8	2,125	59.2	24.7	261	...
1902	1,298	16,137	114	568		37.0	100	2,245	73.4	27.2	261	...
1903	1,373	16,464	134	582	14,101	43.0	106	2,323	80.9	30.0	275	...
1904	1,421	17,221	158	604	15,585	47.7	112	2,406	97.6	32.4	283	...
1905	1,421	18,247	166	648	18,571	55.0	122	2,582	109	34.4	285	...
1906	1,436	18,846	185	667	19,194	64.5	134	2,728	125	38.6	328	...
1907	1,518	19,633	156	689	20,140	73.0	149	2,908	143	44.1	345	...
1908	1,598	19,837	182	708	18,078	88.0	157	2,982	149	47.4	349	...
1909	1,710	20,510	215	747	17,934	100	163	3,177	164	49.2	366	...
1910	1,797	20,965	270	808	20,688	112	172	3,302	186	53.1	388	...
1911	1,909	22,967	327	848	22,084	123	174	3,527	210	55.8	424	...
1912	1,968	23,866	361	873	23,722	135	185	3,760	227	56.5	454	...
1913	2,050	23,343	388	934	25,825	145	193	3,787	257	58.1	477	...
1914	...	21,048	403	...	...	...	199	4,517	283	53.9	483	...
1915	...	22,599	384	...	...	...	194	4,560	309	65.0	479	...
1916	...	20,639	374	...	...	...	203	4,593	345	67.3	531	...
1917	...	...	...	...	...	...	211	3,834	385	69.8	578	...
1918	...[1]	...[1]	...	...	...	...	214	3,814	422	61.5	445	...
1919	...	...	...	739	18,507	23	237	5,593	448	70.1	738	0.1

Abbreviations used:– (a) = Total unregistered mail items (millions); (b) = Telegrams (thousands); (c) = Telephone calls (millions); (d) = Total mail items (millions); (e) = Telegrams (thousands); (f) = Telephone calls (millions); (g) = Total unregistered mail items (millions); (h) = Telegrams (thousands); (i) = Telephone calls (millions); (j) = Total mail items (millions); (k) = Telegrams (thousands); (l) = Telephone calls (millions).

G 8 Post, Telegraph, and Telephone Services

1870–1919

	France			Germany			Greece		Hungary[8]		
	(a)[4]	(b)	(c)	(d)[4]	(e)	(f)	(g)	(h)	(i)	(j)	(k)
1870	733[21]	5,664[21]	...	382[21]	8.66[21]	...	3.1	127	48.1	1,489	...
1871	593	4,963	...	463	8.88	...	3.3	145	58.3	3,911	...
1872	649	6,224	...	500	9.71	...	3.4	189	67.9	4,355	...
1873	672	6,919	...	563	10.8	...	3.5	195	74.4	4,409	...
1874	719	6,897[22]	...	617	10.7	...	3.7	201	78.4	3,701	...
		7,283									
1875	743	8,001	...	654	11.0	...	3.9	240	80.5	3,722	...
1876	834	8,519	...	689	10.6	...	4.4	244	92.2	4,591	...
1877	866	9,590	...	717	11.3	...	4.6	...	95.8	4,735	...
1878	975	11,185[23]	...	761	11.4	...	5.5	...	104	5,640	...
1879	1,122	14,283	...	794	12.4	...	5.5	367	111	5,288	...
1880	1,231	16,662	...	843	13.5	...	6.0	370	116	5,132	...
1881	1,361	19,559	...	905	14.3	...	7.1	481	132	5,335	...
1882	1,324	20,126	...	950	14.8	...	7.8	494	153	5,716	...
1883	1,390	21,202	...	1,042	15.2	8	8.3	543	162	5,889	...
1884	1,421	22,111	...	1,083	15.7	16	9.3	564	175	5,776	...
1885	1,524	23,263	...	1,150	15.8	34	10.1	550	183	5,789	...
1886	1,494	24,133	...	1,223	16.9	57	13.1	756	195	6,010	...
1887	1,527	24,913	...	1,303	17.9	84	11.4	734	242	6,197	...
1888	1,794	25,926	...	1,367	19.7	130	12.8	905	233	6,756	...
1889	1,743	27,721	...	1,493	21.3	155	11.1	875	245	7,140	...
1890	1,763	27,032	...	1,634	22.2	182	11.4	984	237	7,612	...
1891	1,802	28,337	...	1,736	24.5	200	12.1	899	250	8,329	...
1892	1,826	30,027	21	1,828	26.0	238	12.7	1,036	269	9,970	...
1893	1,902	31,424	30	1,917	27.8	285	12.7	1,163	280	11,603	...
1894	1,911	31,175	44	2,016	28.6	326	12.8	1,141	306	12,126	...
1895	2,046	33,834	78	2,104	32.0	382	12.8	...	318	12,933	...
1896	2,088	34,130	94	2,211	32.4	434	13.6	1,171	351	13,448	...
1897	2,223	34,127	106	2,357	34.1	500	13.9	1,209	373	13,397	...
1898	2,345	35,850	142	2,504	36.3	563	13.5	1,162	401	13,584	...
1899	2,361	37,646	170	2,724	38.3	621	13.4	...	441	13,920	...
1900	2,433	40,097	193	3,280	39.7	691	...	...	488	14,370	...
1901	2,391	36,939	178	3,557	38.9	766	19.3	1,205	512	14,667	42.6
1902	2,227	40,690	189	3,800	38.4	843	21.0	...	520	15,417	49.0
1903	2,626	39,897	203	4,019	39.3	927	23.0	1,308	559	15,865	54.5
1904	2,812	41,888	219	4,232	40.2	1,069	24.8	1,311	592	17,109	62.8
1905	3,006	43,028	236	4,423	42.7	1,207	23.9	1,413	638	17,759	83.0
1906	3,217	45,179	239	4,831	43.6	1,353	25.0	1,541	683	18,933	104
1907	3,220	46,173	266	5,339	45.8	1,467	27.1	1,608	752	20,380	120
1908	3,419	46,547	237	5,488	45.0	1,519	28.1	1,429	773	20,573	125
1909	3,466	48,042	254	5,821	46.8	1,670	30.1	1,516	806	22,192	136
1910	3,758	50,150	264	5,677	48.2	1,851	30.8	1,734	865	23,587	161
1911	3,781	50,501	331	5,994	49.6	2,074	...	1,701	922	25,253	183
1912	3,897	...	396	6,461	52.3	2,327	...	1,702	954	26,498	202
1913	3,724	...	430	7,024	52.3	2,518	...	...	1,020	26,572	234
1914	3,128	52,217	375	...	...	...	...	...	1,076	30,715	245
1915	...	45,473	227	...	...	...	53.3	2,931	...	41,444	...
1916	...	46,795	254	...	...	...	29.1	2,916	1,597	44,837	231
1917	...	44,798	...	...	...	...	33.5	3,450	1,648	42,328	260
1918	...[21]	51,614[21]	...[21]	...[21]	...[21]	...[21]	43.3	4,452	...	...	...
1919	4,039	54,799	...	...	...	...	55.6	4,773	...	...	...

Abbreviations used :— (a) = Total mail items (millions); (b) = Telegrams (thousands); (c) = Telephone calls (millions); (d) = Total unregistered mail items (millions); (e) = Telegrams (millions); (f) = Telephone calls (millions); (g) = Total mail items (millions); (h) = Telegrams (thousands); (i) = Total unregistered mail items (millions); (j) = Telegrams (thousands); (k) = Telephone calls (millions).

See p. 698 for footnotes

G 8 Post, Telegraph, and Telephone Services

1870–1919

	Italy[24]			Netherlands			Norway			Poland		
	(a)[4]	(b)	(c)	(d)	(e)	(f)	(g)	(h)	(i)	(j)	(k)	(l)
1870	195	2.0	...	52	1,838	...	...	444	...	...	...	...
1871	230	2.6	...	66	2,038	...	...	604	...	...	...	...
1872	232	3.9	...	71	2,019	...	7.5	702	...	...	...	...
1873	234	4.5	...	78	2,064	...	...	615	...	...	...	...
1874	214	4.7	...	84	2,086[11] / 2,104	...	...	688	...	...	...	...
1875	239	4.7	...	...	2,215	...	...	709	...	...	...	...
1876	262	4.9	...	96	2,377	...	11.2	723	...	...	...	...
1877	315	4.9	...	103	2,405	...	13.0	794	...	...	...	...
1878	335	5.0	...	110	2,413	...	13.6	718	...	...	...	...
1879	307	5.3	...	117	2,705	...	14.3	680	...	...	...	...
1880	321	5.9	...	123	3,109	...	15.5	773	...	...	...	...
1881	362	6.0	...	131	3,282	...	17.5	847	...	...	...	...
1882	379	6.3	...	138	3,365	...	18.5	876	...	...	...	...
1883	401[24] / 414	6.4[24] / 6.9	...	148	3,380	...	20.4	874	...	...	...	...
1884	414	6.9	...	155	3,184	...	21.3	891	...	...	...	...
1885	431	7.0	...	165	3,183	...	22.2	860	...	...	...	...
1886	447	7.7	...	167	3,213	...	23.9	857	...	...	...	...
1887	364	7.9	...	166	3,375	...	24.5	830	...	...	...	...
1888	381	7.8	...	175	3,553	...	27.0	1,246	...	...	...	...
1889	388	8.0	...	182	3,695	...	28.4	1,373	...	...	...	...
1890	397	8.3	...	189	3,798	...	30.8	1,454	——	...	...	...
1891	418	8.2	...	195	4,014	...	32.3	1,594	...	...	...	...
1892	451	8.4	...	208	3,924	...	36.4	1,650	...	...	...	...
1893	484	7.9	...	218	4,021	0.1	37.9	1,729	...	...	...	...
1894	493	7.9	...	225	4,034	0.1	39.5	1,697	...	...	...	...
1895	522	8.1	...	243	4,237	0.1	42.4	1,799	——	...	...	...
1896	551	8.6	...	261	4,259	0.1	44.4	1,818	...	...	...	...
1897	597	8.6	...	268	4,459	0.2	47.8	1,941	...	...	...	...
1898	628	8.9	...	286	4,724	0.3	51.5	2,049	...	...	...	...
1899	628	9.2	...	302	4,923	0.5	56.6	2,049	...	...	...	...
1900	677	9.4	...	315	5,067	0.7	57.5	[2,677][25]	...	...	...	...
1901	747	9.6	...	340	5,392	0.9	60.9	2,195	1.5[25]	...	...	...
1902	807	9.9	...	356	5,503	1.1	63.9	2,157	1.7	...	...	...
1903	906	10.1	...	393	5,671	1.2	70.0	2,221	1.9	...	...	...
1904	926	10.5	0.2	418	5,608	1.5	73.7	2,276	2.1	...	...	...
1905	873	11.1	...	441	5,919	1.9	77.0	2,250	2.2	...	...	...
1906	903	11.5	2.4	449	5,974	2.4	80.4	2,390	2.4	...	...	...
1907	994	11.7	2.9	483	5,970	2.8	90.0	2,520	2.5	...	...	...
1908	1,052	12.4	3.8	502	5,943	3.0	87.5	2,725	2.9	...	...	...
1909	1,137	12.7	4.6	527	6,171	3.7	90.4	2,774	3.2	...	...	...
1910	1,239	15.2	5.6	538	6,173	4.5	104	3,035	3.9	...	...	...
1911	1,464	18.9	5.5	558	6,404	5.5	109	3,270	4.3	...	...	...
1912	1,478	20.0	6.9	584	6,544	6.7	117	3,616	5.0	...	...	...
1913	1,515	21.0	7.3	610	6,477	7.3	124	3,727	5.6	...	...	...
1914	1,531	22.0	7.1	...	7,348	8.1[5]	112	3,866	6.3	...	...	...
1915	2,052	22.3	4.6	673	8,195	8.1	127	4,572	6.9	...	...	...
1916	2,202	20.3	7.4	685	7,982	8.8	145	5,688	8.2	...	...	...
1917	2,533	19.8	8.1	705	7,256	9.1	138	6,283	9.2	...	...	...
1918	2,372	18.2	7.6	774	7,814	9.5	160	6,204	9.6	...	...	...
1919	2,127	21.9	8.6	838	10,259	11.0	174	6,560	10.3	256	2,979	...

Abbreviations used:— (a) = Total letter post items (millions); (b) = Telegrams (millions); (c) = Telephone calls (millions); (d) = Total unregistered letter post items (millions); (e) = Telegrams (thousands); (f) = Telephone calls (millions); (g) = Total letter post items (millions); (h) = Telegrams (thousands); (i) = Telephone calls (millions); (j) = Total letter post items (millions) (k) = Telegrams (thousands); (l) = Telephone calls (millions).

See p. 698 for footnotes

G 8 Post, Telegraph, and Telephone Services

1870–1919

	Portugal			Romania			Russia		Serbia		
	(a)	(b)	(c)	(d)	(e)	(f)[12]	(g)	(h)	(i)	(j)	(k)
1870	...	612	...	...	...	...	...	2,716	...	...	...
1871	...	674	...	...	...	...	...	3,048	...	...	...
1872	...	792	...	...	...	...	...	3,264	...	...	...
1873	...	908	...	...	...	...	...	3,432	...	...	...
1874	...	738	...	4.0	805	...	120	3,800	...	...	...
1875	...	865	...	6.0	872	...	128	4,179	...	...	...
1876	...	1,055	...	...	...	...	141	4,598	...	...	...
1877	...	...	...	11	960	...	188	5,370	...	...	...
1878	24	...	...	...	1,116	...	204	5,762	...	...	...
1879	26	1,117	...	...	...	...	200	6,385	...	...	...
1880	28	1,078	...	...	950	...	220	7,290	...	...	...
1881	34	1,122	...	13	1,150	...	239	8,904	...	...	...
1882	32	1,148	...	16	1,214	...	252	9,800	...	...	...
1883	34	1,206	...	17	1,244	...	255	10,226	...	...	...
1884	36	1,136	...	16	1,204	...	271	10,484	...	...	...
1885	39	1,191	...	19	1,224	...	292	10,885	...	...	...
1886	41	1,237	...	18	1,231	...	307	10,291	8.3[28]	...	...
1887	43	1,105	...	19	1,257	...	329	9,949	8.6[28]	396[28]	...
1888	46	1,241	...	25	1,318	...	355	...	8.9[28]	471[28]	...
1889	51	1,355	...	...	1,328	...	371	...	11.3[28]	458[28]	...
1890	57	[2,172][26]	...	...	1,358	...	384	10,981	14.7[29]	...	...
1891	60	[2,124][26]	...	28	1,523	...	418	12,134	14.5	617	...
1892	59	1,870	...	29	1,539	...	440	12,783	16.9	653	...
1893	56	1,711	...	34	1,593	...	464	13,297	17.3	888	...
1894	55	1,762	...	39	1,804	...	503	13,975	17.9[5]	885	...
									14.4		
1895	65	1,808	...	52	2,131	...	545	14,547	15.0	885	...
1896	61	1,762	...	55	2,195	0.4	593	15,593	15.7	901	...
1897	66	1,820	...	67	2,158	0.8	653	16,371	16.6	970	...
1898	64	1,961	...	73	2,399	1.0	711	17,595	17.4	1,018	...
1899	67	2,119	...	68	2,086	1.9	770	18,377	18.3	1,078	...
1900	67	2,199	...	62	2,063	1.5	849	19,557	21	1,172	...
1901	73	2,227	...	61	2,108	4.0	948	19,703	21	1,083	...
1902	77	2,337	...	89	2,342	2.0	1,007	20,113	21	1,169	0.6
1903	86	2,404	...	103	2,317	2.8	1,140	20,868	26	1,176	0.8
1904	91	2,641[27]	...	102	2,212	2.5	1,378	24,917	31	1,233	1.2
		1,515									
1905	94	1,533	...	222	2,651	3.2	1,529	26,058	40	1,332	2.4
1906	96	1,596	...	225	3,018	4.9	1,503	28,280	44	1,417	3.0
1907	107	1,611	...	151	2,925	9.4	1,634	30,025	55	1,563	4.7
1908	108	1,985	...	165	2,777	6.7	1,777	30,195	53	1,629	3.9
1909	104	1,821	...	153	2,937	12.4	1,944	33,516	55	1,814	4.1
1910	112	1,954	...	158	3,197	13.5	...	36,793	65	1,996	4.2
1911	108	2,024	...	167	3,492	17.9	...	40,770	65	1,463	4.6
1912	...	2,139[27]	...	175	3,685	17.8	...	44,556	76	...	6.0
1913	126	3,698	...	198	3,826	22.0	...	97,650	...	...	...
1914	...	3,740	27	...	3,865	26.1	...	...	...	...	...
1915	...	3,947	30	...	...	...	...	...	...	...	...
1916	...	4,378	35	...	...	...	...	...	...	...	...
1917	...	4,966	35	...	...	...	...	...	...	...	...
1918	...	5,749	35	...	...	...	...	...	...	...	...
1919	126	6,067	39	...	...	...	...	...	24	...	...

Abbreviations used:— (a) = All mail items (millions); (b) = Telegrams (thousands); (c) = Telephone calls (millions); (d) = Total unregistered mail items (millions); (e) = Telegrams (thousands); (f) = Telephone calls (millions); (g) = Total mail items (millions); (h) = Telegrams (thousands); (i) = Total unregistered mail items (millions); (j) = Telegrams (thousands); (k) = Telephone calls (millions).

See p. 698 for footnotes

G 8 Post, Telegraph, and Telephone Services

1870–1919

	Spain		Sweden			Switzerland			United Kingdom		
	(a)	(b)	(c)[4]	(d)	(e)[12]	(f)[4]	(g)	(h)	(i)	(j)	(k)
1870	...	1,050	13	590	...	47.6	1,510	...	978	[8.6][31]	...
1871	...	...	14	655	...	57.0	...	...	1,069	11.8	...
1872	...	...	16	779	...	61.6	...	...	1,184	14.9	...
1873	...	...	17	910	...	69.1	...	...	1,233	17.3	...
1874	75.3	938	18	972	...	71.0	...	...	1,399	19.1	...
1875	...	1,591	26	994	...	76.6	2,656	...	1,376	20.8	...
1876	86.5	1,561	28	983	...	70.1	2,706	...	1,411[32] / 1,478	21.6[32] / 22.2	...
1877	...	...	31[30] / 35	1,016	...	70.4	2,527	...			...
1878	85.2	2,104	37	932	...	70.9	2,179	...	1,536	24.5	...
1879	...	...	36	860	...	75.7	2,325	...	1,588	26.5	...
1880	...	2,286	41	986	...	79.6	2,505	...	1,662	29.9	...
1881	95	2,617	43	1,118	...	84.7	2,717	...	1,776	31.4	...
1882	...	2,869	47	1,175	...	88.1	2,636	0.7	1,854	32.0	...
1883	111	3,218	49	1,209	...	90.0	2,586	1.7	1,914	32.7	...
1884	118	3,204	53	1,179	...	91.3	2,560	2.1	1,984	33.3	...
1885	...	3,323	59	1,167	...	96.3	2,623	3.6	2,065	39.1	...
1886	121	3,550	61	1,172	...	99.5	2,751	6.7	2,159	50.2	...
1887	124	3,770	62	1,190	...	98.4	2,825	8.2	2,243	53.3	...
1888	133	4,085	65	1,368	...	110	3,026	8.5	2,324	57.7	...
1889	164	4,168	66	1,709	...	111	3,226	7.7	2,469	62.3	...
1890	164	4,501	72	1,755	...	120	3,185	5.8	2,578	66.5	...
1891	194	4,879	75	1,850	...	126	3,214	7.4	2,667	69.8	...
1892	169	5,400	78	1,867	...	133	3,150	8.0	2,732	69.9	...
1893	167	4,349	78	1,863	...	144	3,181	9.6	2,800	70.9	...
1894	168	5,039	82	1,807	...	145	3,120	11.7	2,851	71.5	...
1895	173	5,433	86	1,905	...	155	3,252	14.6	2,970	78.8	...
1896	175	5,507	93	1,989	58	166	3,183	16.2	3,079	79.5	...
1897	...	5,352	101	2,120	76	173	3,153	19.0	3,250	83.1	5.9
1898	264	5,452	105	2,295	97	190	3,254	19.7	3,426	87.0	7.1
1899	332	5,058	112	2,489	119	208	3,359	23.5	3,514	90.4	8.1
1900	361	5,131	121	2,506	136	224[30] / 267	3,272	25.4	3,642	89.6	9.0
1901	381	4,628	138	2,579	155	284	3,234	26.8	3,833	90.4	10.1
1902	411	4,693	163	2,556	169	298	3,274	28.5	4,056	92.5	11.6
1903	412	4,843	179	2,638	178	300	3,371	30.8	4,206	90.0	13.5
1904	...	4,948	188	2,749	193	325	3,485	33.2	4,383	89.0	15.5
1905	433	5,243	194	2,920	234	344	3,736	36.5	4,585	89.4	18.1
1906	425	5,171	205	3,195	271	365	3,949	39.3	4,759	89.5	19.9
1907	330	5,606	223	3,510	301	367	3,909	42.4	4,863	86.0	22.1
1908	292	6,025	216	3,574	314	380	2,904	44.8	4,922	84.8	23.6
1909	333	6,317	223	3,714	322	397	4,099	50.3	4,988	86.9	26.7
1910	361	6,692	237	3,900	337	419	4,396	56.4	5,161	86.7	30.2
1911	376	6,366	258	4,136	309	461	4,717	62.2	5,359	89.2	33.7
1912	393	7,008	270	4,636	313	480	4,862	68.5	5,479	88.5	36.0[33] / 833
1913	459	7,378	277	4,799	322	497	4,831	72.6	5,783	87.1	872
1914	491	7,634	276	5,504	334	373	5,282	71.0	5,520	91.2	856
1915	511	7,695	279	6,557	347	361	5,217	66.5	...	84.2	816
1916	518	8,931	287	6,967	352	395	5,076	78.7	...	79.0	740
1917	529	10,643	349	7,059	355	401	4,403	88.7	...	80.0	744
1918	551	10,996	391	6,887	494	386	5,273	103.0	...	89.0	763
1919	602	13,196	375	8,390	607	418	7,707	118.0	5,732	101.0	902

Abbreviations used:— (a) = Total mail items (millions); (b) = Telegrams (thousands); (c) = Total mail items (millions); (d) = Telegrams (thousands); (e) = Telephone calls (millions); (f) = Total mail items (millions); (g) = Telegrams (thousands); (h) = Telephone calls (millions); (i) = Total mail items (millions); (j) = Telegrams (millions); (k) = Telephone calls (millions).

See p. 698 for footnotes

G 8 Post, Telegraph, and Telephone Services

1920–1944

	Austria[1]		Belgium			Czechoslovakia			Denmark[3]		
	(a)[1]	(b)	(d)	(e)	(f)	(g)[4]	(h)	(i)	(j)[4]	(k)	(l)
1920	...	...	788	24,037	76	762	23,025	155	264	5,175	387
1921	...	5,871	849	20,394	99	785	21,821	167	242	4,555	397
1922	742	...	950	19,044	122	750	17,304	177	230	4,400	399
1923	674	6,903	1,020	20,315	145	719	14,452	189	236	4,760	416
1924	635	6,123	1,048	18,441	160	707	15,798	174	239	4,733	443
1925	773	5,481	1,084	14,660	144	798	15,736	190	253	4,721	462
1926	890	5,957	1,091	14,202	155	908	15,242	215	254	4,509	474
1927	886	5,448	1,130	12,250	158	909	15,673	211	254	4,475	486
1928	954	5,177	1,207	11,321	178	966	16,417	224	273	4,460	503
1929	968	4,883	1,390	11,921	202	1,084	17,095	237	273	4,614	546
1930	986	4,118	1,453	10,944	222	1,111	15,900	243	281	4,311	542
1931	846	3,162	1,351	9,768	229	998	14,150	251	275	3,969	563
1932	789	2,579	1,385	8,187	229	1,026	11,683	246	294	3,452	549
1933	770	2,425	1,313	7,592	239	940	9,946	241	286	3,432	515
1934	713	2,500	1,304	7,009	245	657	9,814	237	284	3,221	610
1935	770	2,540	1,292	7,089	274	661	10,508	236	289	3,160	639
1936	770	2,510	1,412	7,440	295	715	10,678	250	301	3,214	663
1937	...	...	1,430	7,725	315	710	11,337	268[36]	321	3,166	692
								18.1			
1938	...	...	1,425	7,403	320	...	12,214	17.9	333	3,169	702
1939	...	...	1,397	7,565	328	...	...	...	342	3,388	732
1940	...	...	...	...	156	...	...	...	352	1,609	729
1941	...	...	662	960	205	...	...	...	292	1,583	752
1942	...	...	660	2,093	294	...	...	...	305	1,748	823
1943	...	...	696	3,925	363	...	...	...	325	3,917	894
1944	...	...	...	2,764	294	...	...	...	350	4,156	969

Abbreviations used:— (a) = Total unregistered Mail items (millions); (b) = Telegrams (thousands); (c) = Telephone calls (millions); (d) = Total mail items (millions); (e) = Telegrams (thousands); (f) = Telephone calls (millions); (g) = Total mail items (millions); (h) = Telegrams (thousands); (i) = Internal telephone calls (millions); (j) = Total unregistered mail items (millions); (k) = Telegrams (thousands); (l) = Telephone calls (millions).

See p. 698 for footnotes

G 8 Post, Telegraph, and Telephone Services

1920–1944

	Finland			France			Germany			East Germany		
	(a)[4]	(b)[7]	(c)[20]	(d)	(e)	(f)	(g)[4]	(h)	(i)	(j)	(k)	(l)
1920	65.1	836	0.2	4,162	50,599	...	4,550	76.6	3,180	...	...	...
1921	65.5	881	0.3	4,150	48,050	...	4,594	74.7	2,971	...	...	...
1922	68.5	875	0.4	4,467	48,911[38] 56,144	...	3,682	57.1	2,068	...	...	...
1923	74.1	924	0.6	4,958	57,366	...	3,010	52.1	1,852	...	...	...
1924	78.0	948[5] 858	0.8	5,326	55,297	...	4,129	36.6	1,820	...	...	...
1925	84.7	863	1.1	5,678	54.316	788	6,219	39.9	2,039	...	...	...
1926	87.0	900	1.5	6,086	47,985	687	6,332	36.5	2,052	...	...	...
1927	95.1	883	2.0	5,920	44,684	703	7,345	30.0	2,595	...	...	...
1928	98.8	932	2.4	6,057	46,924	740	7,443	33.3	2,426	...	...	...
1929	105	848	3.7	6,146	48,391	782	7,448	30.9	2,599	...	...	...
1930	102	728	4.7	6,281	46,699	836	6,099	25.1	2,541	...	...	...
1931	94.7	597	5.6	6,308	45,280	852	5,616	19.7	2,375	...	...	...
1932	83.9	530	5.8	5,704	41,930	861	5,306	17.0	2,167	...	...	...
1933	84.4	523	6.3[20] 28.6	5,625	40,413	847	5,241	18.3	2,176	...	...	...
1934	90.2	531	64.4	5,610	37,266	877	5,334	17.4	2,289	...	...	...
1935	93.2	542	62.8	5,582	38,986	903	5,577	17.0	2,433	...	...	...
1936	101	562	65.4	5,704	38,546	940	6,401	17.5	2,562	...	...	...
1937	113	581	82.4	5,707	37,734	962	6,540	17.2	2,722	...	...	...
1938	118	597	89.5	5,664	36,444	960	7,562	21.9	2,973	...	...	...
1939	119	660	...	5,261	40,016	852	7,584	26.2	3,175	...	...	...
1940	130	589	92.3	4,354	31,943	592	...	...	...	...	...	...
1941	185	597	99.6	4,572	26,741	774	...	...	...	...	...	...
1942	191	672	95.5	3,493	32,299	1,008	...	...	...	...	...	...
1943	202	777	107	3,723	40,333	1,156	...	...	...	...	...	...
1944	202	920	111	2,342	33,383	1,099	...	...	...	...	...	...

Abbreviations used:— (a) = Total mail items (millions); (b) = Telegrams (thousands); (c) = Telephone calls (millions); (d) = Total mail items (millions); (e) = Telegrams (thousands); (f) = Telephone calls (millions); (g) = Total unregistered mail items (millions); (h) = Telegrams (millions); (i) = Telephone calls (millions); (j) = Total letter post items (millions); (k) = Telegrams (millions); (l) = Telephone calls (millions).

See p. 698 for footnotes

G 8 Post, Telegraph, and Telephone Services

1920–1944

	Greece			Hungary[8]			Southern Ireland[43]			Italy		
	(a)	(b)	(c)	(d)[4]	(e)	(f)	(g)	(h)	(i)	(j)[4]	(k)	(l)
1920	67.3	5,123	...	186	10,618	3.3	...	...	...	1,808	20.7	10.9
1921	67.5	5,042	...	216	14,702	5.0	...	...	...	1,809	19.4	11.8
1922	73.3	5,231	...	208	10,454	6.0	...	...	...	1,731	19.1	12.3
1923	68.6	5,050	...	183	4,977	5.2	...	...	...	1,801	23.5	14.9
1924	76.9	5,974	...	189[16] 202	4,698	4.4	204	3.8	16	1,829	26.7	17.3
1925	84.1	6,532	...	246	4,950	3.8	198	3.5	18	2,021	28.0	18.7
1926	86.7	5,928	...	276	5,275	3.9	201	3.3	19	2,005	28.7	22.2
1927	99.0	4,716	...	316	4,995	4.1	197	3.1	20	2,167	29.5	21.9
1928	107	4,663	...	333	5,030	4.6	203	3.0	21	2,173	31.6	25.2
1929	118	4,678	...	356	4,999	5.0	202	2.5	21	2,363	31.2	27.0
1930	122	4,578	...	353	4,456	4.7	...	2.1	22	2,406	29.6	28.7
1931	120	4,258	...	300	3,427	4.3	206	2.0	22	2,309	26.7	30.3
1932	113	4,463	...	274	2,617	3.6	...	1.8	23	2,236	25.7	31.4
1933	109	4,549	...	269	2,370	3.4	193	1.7	25	2,279	24.9	31.5
1934	115	4,650	...	339	2,342	3.6	191	1.6	26	2,445	24.5	32.0
1935	117	4,083	...	332	2,339	4.1	...	1.5	27	2,557	25.1	32.2
1936	118	5,239	...	358	2,428	4.3	197	1.5	29	2,598	25.3	35.1
1937	116	4,901	...	386[41] 471	2,625	4.7	219	1.5	31	2,767	26.4	36.6
1938	113	4,884	...	510	2,922	5.6	...	1.5	35	2,856	28.5	39.6
1939	111	5,088	...	610	3,724[34] 3,153	...	226	1.5	37	3,003	33.3	45.4
1940	...	...	...	707	4,106	...	220	1.5	39	3,389	37.0	54.2
1941	...	...	...	953	6,069	...	...	1.4	41	3,657	40.6	54.0
1942	...	...	...	1,053	7,438	...	186	1.7	44	...	...	64.4
1943	...	...	...	...	...	...	...	1.9	45	...	...	..
1944	...	...	...	...	...	...	...	2.1	48	...	...	...

Abbreviations used:— (a) = Total mail items (millions); (b) = Telegrams (thousands); (c) = Telephone calls (millions); (d) = Total unregistered mail items (millions); (e) = Telegrams (thousands); (f) Telephone calls (millions); (g) = Total unregistered letter post items (millions); (h) = Telegrams (millions); (i) = Telephone calls (millions); (j) = Total letter post items (millions); (k) = Telegrams (millions); (l) = Telephone calls (millions).

See p. 698 for footnotes

G 8 Post, Telegraph, and Telephone Services

1920–1944

	Netherlands			Norway			Poland			Portugal		
	(a)	(b)	(c)	(d)	(e)	(f)	(g)	(h)	(i)	(j)	(k)	(l)
1920	833	10,165	11.3	161	7,068	11.1	414	6,545	...	...	6,385	20
1921	804	9,804	12.1	141	5,959	11.3	507	7,417	121	113	6,435	22
1922	822	8,458	12.4	148	5,557	11.4	595	7,581	158	139	6,818	30
1923	776	7,915	13.4	144	5,277	11.9	673	7,711	475	123	4,551	28
1924	791	8,692	15.0	143	5,078	12.7	584	7,800	497	...	3,988	31[5]
1925	802	8,416	15.8	155	5,094	13.2	672	8,686	...	...	4,957	44
1926	810	8,443	17.3	145	4,836	13.4	736	7,748	...	...	5,155	46
1927	854	8,113	18.9	145	4,638	13.4	833	8,070	615	...	5,403	46
1928	915	8,030	20.9	149	4,515	13.5	934	7,739	544	135[53]	5,286[27]	53
											2,939	
1929	1,024	7,808	22.9	151	4,471	13.7	999	7,196	723	155	2,799	59
1930	1,081	7,191	26.4	154	4,448	14.1	978	6,294	792	159	...	70
1931	1,081	6,521	30.1	150	4,095	14.1	847	5,118	565	159	...	80
1932	1,016	5,529	29.6	149	3,809	13.7	691	3,617	527	166	2,091	92
1933	1,017	5,314	30.9	148	3,649	13.4	677	3,143	532	152	2,420	94
1934	1,016	4,901	31.9	155	3,555	13.7	742	3,169	526	159	2,239	129
1935	997	4,547	35.8	159	3,509	14.2	735	3,544	518	174	2,293	116
1936	990	4,715	41.1	166	3,643	15.2	885	3,721	530	182	2,722	116
1937	1,078	5,306	49.7	183	3,927	16.7	908	3,940	561	...	2,772	106
1938	1,120[45]	5,429[46]	58.1	191	3,907	17.6	1,002	4,161	619[50]	201	2,769	104
	1,227	7,380							29			
1939	...	8,004	68.5	195	3,930	18.1	...	...	...	[156][54]	2,910	108
1940	990	5,175	67.4	171	3,950	18.6	...	...	...	...	3,070	114
1941	941	2,450	70.9[12]	195	3,568	20.3	...	...	...	[160][54]	3,458	125
1942	...	6,419	84.9[12]	219	4,570	24.0	...	...	...	167	3,845	138
1943	...	10,863	98.8[12]	239	6,210	27.9	...	...	...	180	4,420	130
1944	...	9,620	...	245	7,553	29.4	...	...	...	...	4,961	113

Abbreviations used:— (a) = Total unregistered letter post items (millions); (b) = Telegrams (thousands); (c) = Telephone calls (millions); (d) = Total letter post items (millions); (e) = Telegrams (thousands); (f) = Telephone calls (millions); (g) = Total letter post items (millions); (h) = Telegrams (thousands); (i) = Telephone calls (millions); (j) = Total mail items (millions); (k) = Telegrams (thousands); (l) = Telephone calls (millions).

See p. 698 for footnotes

G 8 Post, Telegraph, and Telephone Services

1920–1944

	Romania			Spain			Sweden		
	(a)	(b)	(c)[12]	(d)	(e)	(f)	(g)[4]	(h)	(i)
1920	...[55]	5,807[55]	21.3[55]	549	14,593	...	380	8,414	603
1921	...	[6,670]	[21.8]	553	15,670	...	366	6,833	538
1922	...	5,443	57.6	656	15,111	...	353	6,329	555
1923	247	8,778	63.3	714	14,608	...	397	6,259	572
1924	322	9,224	67.4	563	16,022	...	413	6,262	609
1925	338	9,511	50.1	589	15,737	...	420	6,409	639
1926	324	9,945	70.7	605	15,674	...	443	6,427	662
1927	327	8,084	...	884	14,616	...	454	6,460	694
1928	407	8,006	81.3	709	14,012	7.4	490	6,577	718
1929	428	8,101	99.4	753	13,762	10.1	511	6,556	752
1930	376	7,619	105[5]	772	13,519	12.8	541	6,260	790
1931	379	6,400	81.6	868	13,318[46]	14.2	552	5,911	822
					24,546				
1932	311	4,938	85.1	885	21,603	16.8	571	5,171	830
1933	278	4,277	97.8	884	21,800	18.3	563	5,011	832
1934	326	4,290	112	852	25,872	19.5	586	4,984	877
1935	386	4,125	131	948	26,937	21.8	622	5,061	930
1936	375	3,946	155	...	...	18.1	626	5,143	983
1937	455	4,413	200	...	...	16.0	660	5,388	1,046
1938	422	4,553	214	...	...	23.8	704	5,348	1,117
1939	462	5,448	249	...	...	20.0	713	5,913	1,170
1940	408	4,796	...	601	27,725	27.7	731	5,391	1,193
1941	344	6,420	...	690	31,292	31.6	753	5,151	1,236
1942	214	7,806[34]	...	653	26,330	30.2	849	5,437	1,377
1943	...	...	...	622	32,601	39.1	895	5,909	1,452
1944	...	...	...	706	33,819	41.7	967	5,378	1,576

Abbreviations used:— (a) = Total unregistered mail items (millions); (b) = Telegrams (thousands); (c) = Telephone calls (millions); (d) = Total mail items (millions); (e) = Telegrams (thousands); (f) = Trunk telephone calls (millions); (g) = Total mail items (millions); (h) = Telegrams (thousands); (i) = Telephone calls (millions).

See p. 698 for footnotes

G 8 Post, Telegraph and Telephone Services

1920–1944

	Switzerland			United Kingdom			Yugoslavia		
	(a)[4]	(b)	(c)	(d)	(e)	(f)	(g)	(h)	(i)
1920	470	7,134	120	5,579	88	901	214	7,325	...
1921	456	5,423	118	5,231[59] 5,455	83[59] 80	734[59] 790	228	8,708	...
1922	429	4,625	126				245	6,143	...
1923	455	4,644	133	5,585	78	902	185	...	...
1924	473	5,093	145	5,840	79	930	202	7,347	3.2
1925	520	5,103	152	6,060	77	1,017	233	6,667	3.0
1926	526	4,866	160	5,800	75	1,101	332	5,575	3.6
1927	542	4,916	172	6,200	74	1,174	341	5,700	4.2[33] 61
1928	580	4,871	191	6,230	72	1,266	404	5,949	81
1929	593	4,756	212	6,400	71	1,323	441	6,204	67
1930	642	4,390	228	6,475	66	1,371	438	6,058	101
1931	660	4,002	248	6,540	61	1,431	490	5,551	116
1932	626	3,304	256	6,640	57	1,491	476	4,208	131
1933	631	3,168	268	6,753	58	1,581	433	3,819	144
1934	632	2,846	275	6,935	55	1,681	332	3,593	167
1935	650	2,679	278	7,345	65	1,824	316	3,700	229
1936	622	2,699	277	7,690	72	1,983	334	3,624	254
1937	649	2,814	288	7,990	71[60] 57	2,167	363	3,664	267
1938	656	2,720	302	8,150[61] 8,240	58	2,237	365	3,678	277
1939	620	3,031	322	7,460	63	2,215	392[62] 581	3,695	...
1940	540	3,168	324	6,310	61	2,092	...	...	...
1941	589	3,004	340	6,150	67	2,035	...	...	...
1942	597	2,711	374	6,390	76	2,103	...	...	...
1943	620	2,871	410	6,480	71	2,151	...	...	...
1944	626	2,956	457	6,600	71	2,228	...	...	...

Abbreviations used:— (a) = Total mail items (millions); (b) = Telegrams (thousands); (c) = Telephone calls (millions); (d) = Total mail items (millions); (e) = Telegrams (millions); (f) = Telephone calls (millions); (g) = Total letter post items (millions); (h) = Telegrams (thousands); (i) = Telephone calls (millions).

See p. 698 for footnotes

G 8 Post, Telegraph, and Telephone Services

1945–1975

	Austria[1]		Belgium			Czechoslovakia			Denmark[3]		
	(a)[1]	(b)	(c)	(d)	(e)	(f)[4]	(g)	(h)	(i)[4]	(j)	(k)
1945	...	...	...	5,586	289	...	...	...	354	3,296	1,027
1946	...	...	1,248	9,843	368	825	6,449	33.9	379	4,134	1,059
1947	478	6,069	1,492	10,333	408	...	...	42.1	430	4,260	1,044
1948	485	3,935	1,691	9,655	428	998	7,452	35.8	439	4,436	1,040
1949	484	4,355	1,825	9,212	448	927	7,801	44.5	431	4,491	1,023
1950	535	4,877	1,975	9,386	485	998	8,168	51.5	451[5]	4,577	1,082
									415		
1951	592	5,556	1,829	9,161	502	1,103	8,582	56.9	433	4,535	1,083
1952	557	4,794	1,851	8,690	505	1,149	8,742	59.4	437	4,310	1,088
1953	695	4,019	1,832	8,614	521	1,126	8,977	62.7	441	4,781	1,118
1954	734	4,251	1,942	8,551	548	1,174	9,377	68.2	459	4,864	1,187
1955	670	4,510	2,093	8,803	580	1,261	9,677	71.6	466	4,755	1,195
1956	726	4,711	2,125	8,692	622	1,311	10,032	75.5	479	4,605	1,237
1957	781	4,821	2,323	8,289	642	1,353	10,089	78.8	483	4,488	1,226
1958	817	4,606	2,609	7,758	668	1,443	10,072	84.0	497	4,270	1,267
1959	895	4,646	2,405	7,343	686	1,543	10,516	92.7	533	4,294	1,307
1960	886	4,574	2,335	7,283	735	1,681	11,650	101	547	4,364	1,381
1961	933	4,619	2,388	7,003	785	1,836	12,720	104	571	4,262	1,484
1962	962	4,841	2,387	6,966	842	1,935	12,998	107	599	4,196	1,570
1963	991	4,967	2,354	6,989	922	1,960	12,926	109	620	4,183	1,634
1964	1,027	5,091	2,452	7,039	970[35]	1,974	12,908	114	637	4,046	1,681
					945						
1965	1,061	5.186	2.574	7.066	999	2.087	13,002	122	660	4,176	1,744
1966	1,075	5,064	2,522	7,092	1,041	2,132	13,213	128	697	4,030	1,752
1967	1,031	4,655	2,428	6,625	1,073	2,092	13,474	133	716	3,839	1,773
1968	1,024	4,489	2,584	6,388	1,129	2,068	14,188	139	749	3,627	1,796
1969	1,032	4,330	2,637	6,391	1,173	1,989	15,161	143	777	3,396	1,891
1970	1.081	4.026	2,693	6,678	1,220	2,013	14,272	152	820	2,942	2,001
1971	1,122	3,819	2,818	4,772	1,241	2,045	14,366	166	870	2,623	2,078
1972	1,148	3,603	2,647	4,464	1,284	2,031	14,085	176	911	1,954[70]	2,204
1973	1,218	3,510	2,694	4,352	1,218[64]	2,062	14,179	191	928	1,838	2,195
					1,065						
1974	1,292	3,364	2,701	4,167	1,075	2,178	14,392	204	964	1,672	2,290
1975	1,393	3,075	2,317	3,705	1,075	2,184	14,334	218	953	1,481	2,329

Abbreviations used:— (a) = Total unregistered Mail items (millions); (b) = Telegrams (thousands); (c) = Total mail items (millions); (d) = Telegrams (thousands); (e) = Telephone calls (millions); (f) = Total mail items (millions), (g) = Telegrams (thousands); (h) = Internal telephone calls (millions); (i) = Total unregistered mail items (millions); (j) = Telegrams (thousands); (k) = Telephone calls (millions).

See p. 698 for footnotes

G 8 Post, Telegraph, and Telephone Services

1945–1975

	Finland			France			West Germany[40]			East Germany		
	(a)[4]	(b)[7]	(c)[20]	(d)	(e)	(f)	(g)[4]	(h)	(i)	(j)	(k)	(l)
1945	180	975	124	3,694	56,458	1,358	...	...	...	...	...	...
1946	182	1,130	129	3,989	45,697	1,457	...	...	...	...	...	...
1947	195	1,161	134	3,841	38,707	1,491	...	...	...	...	...	...
1948	200	1,095	132	3,924	33,224	1,534	...	...	...	...	...	...
1949	184	1,031	132	3,838	24,325	1,441	3,904	27	1,828	...	...	...
1950	170	1,068	138	4,050	25,156	1,537	4,181	28	2,039	1,120	9.8	717
1951	182	1,158	137	4,293	24,792	1,729	4,497	26	2,197	1,104	7.8	736
1952	190	1,155	137	4,504	24,165	1,766	4,949	27	2,363	1,097	7.3	792
1953	241	1,080	141	4,493	23,973	1,913	5,234	28	2,531	1,148	7.6	799
1954	244	1,172	141	4,710	25,368	2,108	5,551[40]	28[40]	2,674[40]	1,226	7.5	855
							5,744	29	2,904			
1955	246	1,235	155	4,996	25,701	**2,347**	6,161	29	3,147	1,249	7.6	855
1956	292	1,211	151	5,313	27,497	2,624	6,687	30	3,377	1,246	8.0	859
1957	314[5]	1,171	150	5,629	27,015	2,935[39]	7,158	32	3,531	1,306	8.6	880
						2,799						
1958	279	1,110	...	5,802	25,295	3,100	7,637	31	3,734	1,335	8.6	907
1959	304	1,164	134[37]	6,062	22,543	3,405	7,914[40]	32[40]	4,118[40]	1,309	9.3	933
			37.2									
1960	339	1,150	141	6,093	22,268	3,849	8,498	33	4,561	1,355	10.3	985
1961	372	1,174	166	6,471	22,507	4,389	9,092	32	4,880	1,136	10.7	1,007
1962	443	1,166	252	6,737	24,566	5,012	9,315	33	5,198	1,152	10.7	1,024
1963	401	1,129	389	6,954	25,335	5,703	9,056	32	5,679	1,341	11.4	1,041
1964	442	1,121	664	7,255	25,516	6,171	9,275	32	5,749	1,337	11.2	1,051
1965	471	1,121	855	7,432	24,973	6,773	9,673	31	6,331	1,353	11.8	1,074
1966	526	1,115	1,031	7,854	25,728	...	9,436	29	6,903	1,310	11.5	1,114
1967	563	1,064	1,517	8,116	25,476	...	9,358	26	7,427	1,390	11.4	1,149
1968	619	1,074	1,816	7,726	25,201	...	9,787	25	8,141	1,334	11.8	1,200
1969	640	1,061	2,357	8,094	26,965	...	10,177	25	9,107	1,380	12.1	1,246
1970	691	1,083	2,882	8,260	26,902	...	10,680	24	10,216	1,376	12.3	1,304
1971	719	1,055	3,317	8,453	26,998	...	11,526	21	11,679	1,360	11.4	1,367
1972	783	1,052	3,772	8,965	25,390[65]	...	11,102	18	13,132	1,272	10.6	1,419
					27,819							
1973	802	944	4,847	9,331	28,741	...	10,425	17	14,045	1,286	10.7	1,544
1974	738	940	6,411	8,641	26,853	...	10,490	16	13,897	1,257	10.6	1,575
1975	740	912	8,956	9,404	25,968	..	10,479	15	14,063	1,219	10.9	1,668

Abbreviations used:— (a) = Total mail items (millions); (b) = Telegrams (thousands); (c) = Telephone calls (millions); (d) = Total mail items (millions); (e) = Telegrams (thousands); (f) = Telephone calls (millions); (g) = Total unregistered mail items (millions); (h) = Telegrams (millions); (i) = Telephone calls (millions); (j) = Total letter post items (millions); (k) = Telegrams (millions); (l) = Telephone calls (millions).

See p. 698 for footnotes

G 8 Post, Telegraph, and Telephone Services

1945–1975

	Greece			Hungary[8]			Southern Ireland[43]			Italy		
	(a)	(b)	(c)	(d)[4]	(e)	(f)	(g)	(h)	(i)	(j)[4]	(k)	(l)
1945	35.7	...	...	...	...	...	228	2.2	53	...	18.8	49.1
1946	62.3	...	...	166	3,597	...	...	2.5	58	2,481	25.8	68.1
1947	80.9	5,079	...	408[41,42]	3,615	...	...	2.8	62	2,580	24.4	76.5
1948	85.8	4,942	...	339	4,702	...	...	2.9	64	2,651	26.0	81.1
1949	138	5,138	...	325	3,740	187	272	2.6	68	2,617	28.1	87.5
1950	137	5,880	...	395	3,967	231	276	2.6	74	2,797	30.2	101
1951	140	6,438	...	384	4,330	264	277	2.7	82	3,054	29.4	121
1952	146	5,934	276	440	4,946	319	287	2.4	86	3,185	29.7	143
1953	152	5,698	276	463	5,262	382	292	2.6	89	3,423	30.4	164
1954	180	5,995	285	495	5,810	419	318	2.4	93	3,565	32.2	193[24]
1955	185	6,173	308	469	5,745	442	332	2.3	96	3,876	34.4	206
1956	188	6,331	336	430	6,243	463	...	1.9	112	4,339	35.1	239
1957	202	6,098	376	404	6,185	443	314	1.4	106	4,648	34.4	307
1958	210	6,041	411	429	6,491	473	326	1.3	102	4,834	33.0	349
1959	211	5,986	460	492	6,917	504	...	1.2	123	4,867	33.5	402
1960	206	5,927	520	559	7,398	538	...	1.2	135	5,147	34.5	445
1961	221	6,392	618	566	7,642	558	352	1.1	149	5,116	36.4	517
1962	225	6,592	713	503	8,024	572	...	1.1	159	5,292	39.3	603
1963	239	7,183	794	537	8,602	596	360	1.0	170	5,664[24]	40.9[24]	716
1964	211	7,675	899	514	8,867	606	351	1.0	182	[2,869][44]	[21.6][44]	787
1965	310	7,879	1,133	522[42]	8,877	553	358	0.9	199	5,600	37.5	869
1966	281	8,159	1,480	927	9,165	570	359	0.8	221	5,850	31.8	936
1967	251	7,862	1,773	988	9,755	597	364	0.8	237	5,923	29.0	1,070
1968	262	7,480	2,011	1,010	9,975	618	372	0.8	262	5,936	26.4	1,185
1969	259	7,718	2,415	1,020	9,212	645	378	0.8	293	6,292	26.4	1,380
1970	270	7,548[5]	3,024	1,064	9,711	660	387	0.8	302	6,356	25.9	1,609
1971	273	6,507	4,181	1,127	9,832	674	382	0.7	329	6,267	25.2	1,839
1972	367	6,463	5,329	1,168	10,064	687	382	0.7	367	6,589	25.5	1,974
1973	385	6,576	6,576	1,180	10,043	709	365	0.7	405	6,473	25.7	2,128[63] 1,971
1974	[298][71]	6,869	8,097	1,912	10,719	749	382[66]	0.7[66]	490[66]	6,432	24.3	2,231
1975	386	5,721	7,973	1,956	11,257	853	387	0.7	531	5,889	23.0	2,356

Abbreviations used:— (a) = Total mail items (millions); (b) = Telegrams (thousands); (c) = Telephone calls (millions); (d) = Total unregistered mail items (millions); (e) = Telegrams (thousands); (f) = Telephone calls (millions); (g) = Total unregistered letter post items (millions); (h) = Telegrams (millions); (i) = Telephone calls (millions), (j) = Total letter post items (millions); (k) = Telegrams (millions); (l) = Telephone calls (millions).

See p. 698 for footnotes

G 8 Post, Telegraph, and Telephone Services

1945–1975

	Netherlands			Norway			Poland			Portugal	Portugal	
	(a)	(b)	(c)	(d)	(e)	(f)	(g)	(h)	(i)	(j)	(k)	(l)
1945	...	5,034	...	249	7,816	29.0[33] 462	...	...	...	[187][54]	5,517	122
1946	1,479	12,842	99.3	273	7,966	465	510	6,140	32	[195][54]	6,230	133
1947	1,569	11,172	122	271	8,256	508	769	7,576	42	[218][54]	6,124	152
1948	1,697	11,857	134	274	7,576	504	818	6,044	40	[220][54]	5,370	161
1949	1,693	11,703	144	282	7,296	506	820	6,309	39	237	3,939	162
1950	1,702	11,522	161	288	6,956	498	844	7,178	47	263	3,639	169
1951	1,711	10,532	175	288	6,912	502	912	7,885	56	263	3,644	186
1952	1,839	9,832	189[33] 848	304	6,699	527	1,025	8,700	68	286	3,502	205
1953	1,870	9,757	921	317	6,282	506	1,086	9,280	78	308	3,459	222
1954	1,974	9,612	1,000	327	6,121	508	1,177	9,931	89	325	3,417	244
1955	2,007	9,720	1,083	350	6,006	520	1,312[51] 716	10,331	97	364	3,536	273
1956	2,124	9,785	1,179	360	5,978	571	781	10,755	101	400	3,651	302
1957	2,022	9,142	1,234	382	5,912	576	829	10,890	94	425	3,661	326
1958	2,032	8,595	1,288	400	5,411	588[48]	867	10,655[69] 10,120	95	442	3,739	348
1959	2,068	8,603	1,387	413	5,140	566	919	10,075	102	461	3,886	430
1960	2,178	8,553	1,510[47] 1,505	435	5,055	598[49]	953	9,943	109	483	3,887	474
1961	2,240	8,164	1,600	458	4,904	635	972	10,280	115	486	4,008	520
1962	2,373	8,024	1,732	462	4,746	656	1,016	10,736	119	497	4,049	585
1963	2,490	7,972	1,870	467	4,348	672	1,079	11,520	123	508	4,197	671
1964	2,568[5]	8,029[34]	1,944	490	4,057	673	1,155	11,963	124	522	4,336	789
1965	2,394	3,700	2,037	515	3,868	679	1,226	12,417	132[52] 225	534	4,591	804
1966	2,462	3,527	2,155	522	3,747	722[35] 718	1,315	13,228	251	544	4,738	896
1967	2,462	3,196	2,218	546	3,707	769	1,405	14,192	273	551	4,895[34] 3,768	975
1968	2,597	3,051	2,386	554	3,520	803	1,478	15,006	347	560	3,977	1,092
1969	2,792	2,868	2,521	580	3,412	843	1,544	15,913	396	572	3,935	1,284
1970	2,941	2,771	...	601	3,169	876	1,587	16,547	434	583	3,896	1,495
1971	3,065	2,508	...	623	2,970	921	1,640	17,191	472	596	3,911	1,728
1972	3,057	2,134	...	655	2,705	954	1,665	17,040	489	656	3,783	1,969
1973	3,105	2,031	...	677	2,342	997	1,380	14,870	553	704	3,672	2,292
1974	3,260	1,989	...	703	1,958	1,026	1,437	15,516	617	674	3,331	2,410
1975	3,456	1,806	...	653	1,651	...	1,458	15,103	653	544	2,555	2,435

Abbreviations used:– (a) = Total unregistered letter post items (millions); (b) = Telegrams (thousands); (c) = Telephone calls (millions); (d) = Total letter post items (millions); (e) = Telegrams (thousands); (f) = Telephone calls (millions); (g) = Total letter post items (millions); (h) = Telegrams (thousands); (i) = Telephone calls (millions); (j) = Total mail items (millions); (k) = Telegrams (thousands); (l) Telephone calls (millions).

See p. 698 for footnotes

G 8 Post, Telegraph, and Telephone Services

1945–1975

	Romania			Spain			Sweden		
	(a)	(b)	(c)[12]	(d)	(e)	(f)	(g)[4]	(h)	(i)
1945	...	...	...	734	38,097	42.4	975	7,278	1,694
1946	...	...	...	752	42,840	43.0	1,066	[4,021] [57]	[902] [57]
1947	...	...	...[12]	808	43,305	46.0	1,010	8,340	1,871
1948	190	3,056	12.0	925	42,194	47.7	999	8,267	1,941
1949	...	...	...	995	40,311	50.9	1,021	8,210	1,989
1950	318	3,504	22.7	1,073	40,882	56.3	1,063	8,643	2,099[5]
1951	363	4,193	26.3	1,128	43,537	63.1	1,080	8,785	2,087
1952	478	3,771	30.2	1,210	45,360	67.3	1,098	8,291	2,138
1953	891	4,659	33.9	1,278	45,403	70.8	1,119	7,911	2,174
1954	900	4,670	30.3	1,377	43,786	74.4	1,184[58]	7,887	2,218
							1,082		
1955	968	4,486	34.9	1,423	41,222	80.5	1,149	7,892	2,564
1956	955	4,795	38.4	1,581	43,585	91.4	1,231	7,861	2,927
1957	958	4,847	40.5	1,784	45,112	96.3	1,272	7,780	3,256
1958	1,066	4,715	43.9	1,885	43,619	105	1,287	7,132	3,713
1959	1,124	4,523	45.3	1,987	41,624	112[56]	1,305	6,872	...
1960	1,218	4,635	47.8	2,037	39,109	104[56]	1,425	6,857	...
1961	1,349	4,972	51.7	2,055	39,812	111[56]	1,511	6,728	...
1962	1,405	5,304	56.4	2,152	42,483	120[56]	1,598	6,614	...
1963	1,461	5,724	60.9	2,261	44,519	117[56]	1,589	6,410	...
1964	1,497	5,901	63.9	2,607	46,378	133[56]	1,730	6,410	...
						164			
1965	1,539	6,186	70.0	2,992	49,776	176	1,732	6,314	...
1966	1,566	6,714	74.8	3,308	50,016	206	1,824	6,293	...
1967	1,618	6,776	76.4	3,641	46,134	242	1,829	5,935	...
1968	1,654	6,688	...	3,758	44,320	277	1,890	5,515	...
1969	1,741	6,851	...	3,891	43,919	377	1,915	5,162	...
1970	1,736	7,210	...	4,069	41,682	445	2,026	4,863	...
1971	1,917	7,299	...	4,191	40,077	540	1,979	4,438	...
1972	2,074	7,702	...	4,236	38,811	636	2,014	3,689	...
								3,465	
1973	2,168	7,720	...	4,362	37,200	734	2,153	3,329	...
1974	...	...	...	4,426	35,805	902	2,216	2,611	...
1975	...	...	...	4,535	34,796	1,077	2,295	2,298	...

Abbreviations used:— (a) = Total unregistered mail items (millions); (b) = Telegrams (thousands); (c) Telephone calls (millions); (d) = Total mail items (millions); (e) = Telegrams (thousands); (f) = Trunk telephone calls (millions); (g) = Total mail items (millions); (h) = Telegrams (thousands); (i) = Telephone calls (millions).

See p. 698 for footnotes

G 8 Post, Telegraph, and Telephone Services

1945–1975

	Switzerland			United Kingdom			Yugoslavia		
	(a)[4]	(b)	(c)	(d)	(e)	(f)	(g)	(h)	(i)
1945	689	3,545	521	6,550	74	2,368	...	...	...
1946	790	4,478	569	7,300	63	2,714	425	3,571	...
1947	859	4,961	601	7,600	58	2,898	542	4,446	...
1948	879	4,922	607	8,050	54	3,047	666	5,710	...
1949	925	4,586	626	8,350	52	3,175	775	6,848	...
1950	939	4,570	657	8,500	65	3,326	786	7,434	...
1951	960	4,723	703	8,750	62	3,492	634	6,035	...
1952	1,004	4,486	736	8,800	58	3,429	465	2,875	...
1953	1,045	4,581	775	9,100	56	3,648	467	3,337	...
1954	1,080	4,652	823	9,500	48	3,921	459	3,896	...
1955	1,179	4,873	881	9,700	43	4,198	505	4,722	...
1956	1,216	4,956	939	9,700	39	4,064	566	5,032	...
1957	1,264	5,055	994	9,600	37	3,998	652	5,883	...
1958	1,337	4,945	1,047	9,700	35	4,043	745	6,582	...
1959	1,409	5,207	1,112	10,200	35	4,287	808	7,154	...
1960	1,503	5,267	1,211	10,600	35	4,726	912	8,317	...
1961	1,596	5,491	1,299	10,500	34	4,977	939	9,142	...
1962	1,702	5,615	1,395	10,600	33	5,295	974	9,761	...
1963	1,751	5,670	1,513	11,000	31	5,724	1,008	11,649	...
1964	1,756	5,738	1,598	11,200	32	6,336	1,151	13,252	...
1965	1,813	5,721	1,689	11,300	31	6,891	1,158	10,493	...
1966	1,851	5,666	1,790	11,400	31	7,380	1,199	9,594	...
1967	1,844	5,555	1,881	11,500	31	7,944	1,244	9,800	...
1968	1,750	5,346	1,999	11,300	29	8,627	1,248	9,300	...
1969	1,799	5,331	2,139	11,400	29	9,622	1,260	10,604	...
1970	1,912	4,902	2,152[68]	10,500	26	10,747	1,290	11,496	...
1971	1,998	4,750	...	10,550	27	12,029	1,279	12,008	...
1972	2,031	4,266	...	10,790	27	13,539	1,302	12,847	...
1973	1,970	4,158	...	11,010	28	14,845	1,288	12,398	...
1974	1,972	3,912	...	10,878	26	15,836	1,280	12,714	...
1975	1,950	3,286	...	9,903	21	16,092	1,255	12,544	...

Abbreviations used:— (a) = Total mail items (millions); (b) = Telegrams (thousands), (c) = Telephone calls (millions); (d) = Total mail items (millions); (e) = Telegrams (millions); (f) = Telephone calls (millions); (g) = Total letter post items (millions); (h) = Telegrams (thousands); (i) = Telephone calls (millions).

See p. 698 for footnotes

G 8 Post, Telegraph, and Telephone Services

NOTES

1. SOURCES:– The official publications noted on p.xv with gaps filled from League of Nations and United Nations, *Statistical Yearbooks,* and the following data supplied by the respective national statistical offices: Finland mail to 1888 (1st line) and telegrams to 1917; Netherlands 1965–69; and Poland telegrams 1938–57 and telephones 1938 (2nd line) to 1969. The Romanian telephone data for 1948–67 were kindly supplied by Mr. G. Radulescu of the *Encicolpedica Romana.*

2. So far as possible, and except as indicated in footnotes, internal mail, telegrams, and telephone calls are counted once, whilst international communications are counted both on sending and receipt.

3. The nature of the postal statistics differs considerably between countries. So far as possible the classifications used here are those which give the longest comparable series within each country.

FOOTNOTES

[1] Austria-Hungary to 1848 (1st line); Cisleithania from 1848 (2nd line) to 1916, with Lombardy excluded from 1860 and Venetia from 1866; Republic of Austria from 1921.
[2] From 1 September 1850 to 31 December 1851.
[3] Mail statistics are for years ended 31 March. Telephone statistics are aggregates of figures for calendar years and figures for years ended 31 March following that indicated.
[4] Excluding newspapers.
[5] The reason for this break is not given.
[6] Previously excluding outgoing overseas mail.
[7] Figures to 1882 (1st line) are of telegrams sent, received, and in transit. Subsequently they are of telegrams sent only.
[8] Transleithania to 1917, and the territory established by the treaty of Trianon subsequently. Local telephone calls are excluded for the latter area.
[9] Previously internal mail only.
[10] Excluding local calls.
[11] Previously only paying letters or telegrams.
[12] Excluding international calls, which were very small. The statistics from 1948 are of trunk calls only.
[13] Figures to 1864 (1st line) are of internal letters only.
[14] Newspapers, packets, etc. are included for the first time in 1856.
[15] Double-counting was subsequently eliminated.
[16] Subsequently including official mail.
[17] Subsequently including official telegrams, other than those of the meterological service.
[18] Subsequently including telegrams on the railway companies' network. These numbered 134 thousand in 1900.
[19] In 1905 a revised figure was given for 1900 at 42.3 million. The series given here for years before 1905 may therefore be too low.
[20] Inland trunk calls only, in million 3-minute units. Figures to 1933 (1st line) are for the state network only.
[21] Alsace-Lorraine was included in Germany rather than France from 1871 to 1918.
[22] Previously excluding telegrams sent from railway stations.
[23] **Subsequently including *correspondences pneumatiques* (but see footnote [65]).**
[24] From 1884 to 1963 (or 1954 for telephone calls) the figures are for years beginning 1 July.
[25] Subsequent figures are for years ended 31 March. The 1900 figure for telegrams is for a 15-month period.
[26] Including service telegrams in these years. They numbered 587 thousand in 1889 and 246 thousand in 1892.
[27] Up to 1904 (1st line) and for 1913–28, internal as well as external telegrams are counted twice.
[28] Years to 31 October.
[29] Fourteen months ended 31 December.
[30] Previously excluding incoming international mail.
[31] From 5 February.
[32] Subsequent statistics are for years ended 31 March following that indicated.
[33] Previously excluding local calls.
[35] Subsequently international calls were given in minutes and cannot be aggregated with internal calls.
[36] Subsequently interurban calls only.
[37] Subsequent statistics are of millions of counting impulses at 5 pennies on the automatic system. In addition, the following 3-minute units were counted on the manual system (in millions):—

1959	83.0	1962	64.7	1965	60.9	1968	58.6
1960	59.4	1963	65.6	1966	62.0	1969	58.4
1961	62.7	1964	61.0	1867	61.0		

[38]Subsequently including official telegrams and radio telegrams.
[39]Previous statistics are the sums of metered calls (in units of basic price) and other longer-distance calls in 3-minute units. From 1957 (2nd line) the figures are simply the number of calls made.
[40]Figures are for years ended 31 March following that indicated. Saarland is excluded to July 1959, and West Berlin to 1954 (1st line). Only letter post is included in the mail statistics.
[41]From 1937 (2nd line) to 1947 the figures are of all items of mail, including newspapers.
[42]From 1948–65 the figures are of letters carried. Subsequently they are of all mail sent and received.
[43]Figures are for years ended 31 March.
[44]Second half-year only.
[45]Subsequently including registered mail.
[46]Internal telegrams are subsequently counted twice.
[47]Subsequently excluding incoming international calls.
[48]Subsequently only paying calls.
[49]Subsequent statistics are for calendar years.
[50]Subsequently long-distance calls only.
[51]The reason for this break is not clear, but is probably the previous double-counting of internal mail.
[52]Previous figures exclude calls made automatically.
[53]Previously mail received only.
[54]Internal mail only.
[55]Previous figures are for years ended 31 March following that indicated. The 1921 figures are for 9 months.
[56]Excluding calls on the automatic system.
[57]The 1946 figure is for the first half-year. Subsequent figures are for years ended 30 June.
[58]Subsequently excluding certain printed papers.
[59]Subsequently does not include Southern Ireland.
[60]Subsequently excluding telegrams sent via private cable companies.
[61]Subsequent statistics are of mail forwarded rather than delivered.
[62]Subsequently all unregistered mail items.
[63]A different method of calculation was adopted subsequently by the state system.
[64]Subsequently excluding interzonal calls.
[65]Subsequently excluding *correspondences pneumatiques,* but including international telegrams arriving and in transit, as well as sent.
[66]The 1975 figures are for the calendar year. Statistics for the period April–December 1974 are as follows:– Letters 289; telegrams 0.6; telephone calls 400.
[67]Subsequently excluding transit.
[68]Interurban and international calls are subsequently given in minutes. The following are the statistics of local calls in thousands and of other calls in million minutes for 1970–75.

	Local Calls	Interurban and International Calls
1970	988	3,497
1971	1,052	3,693
1972	1,085	3,903
1973	1,143	4,229
1974	1,072	4,471
1975	1,080	4,164

The break between 1973 and 1974 is unexplained.
[69]Subsequently excluding incoming international telegrams.
[70]Subsequently excluding giro advices and similar telegrams.
[71]Excluding foreign mail received, which came to 82 million in each of 1973 and 1975.

G 9 RADIO AND TELEVISION RECEIVING LICENCES (in thousands)

1920–1975

	Austria		Belgium		Bulgaria		Czechoslovakia		Denmark[5]		Finland	
	Radio	TV	Radio	TV	Radio	TV	Radio	TV	Radio	TV	Radio	TV
1920	...	–	...	–	...	–	–	–	...	–	–	–
1921	...	–	...	–	...	–	–	–	...	–	–	–
1922	...	–	...	–	...	–	–	–	...	–	–	–
1923	...	–	...	–	...	–	. .	–	...	–	–	–
1924	...	–	...	–	...	–	2					
1925	...	–	...	–	...	–	15	–	...	–	–	–
1926	...	–	...	–	...	–	175	–	...	–	4	–
1927	...	–	...	–	...	–	220	–	131	–	37	–
1928	...	–	...	–	...	–	238	–	212	–	74	–
1929	...	–	...	–	...	–	268	–	254	–	98	–
1930	...	–	...	–	...	–	315	–	340	–	107	–
1931	...	–	...	–	...	–	385	–	438	–	117	–
1932	...	–	...	–	...	–	472	–	472	–	120	–
1933	507	–	...	–	...	–	573	–	493	–	121	–
1934	527	–	600	–	9	–	694	–	523	–	129	–
1935	560	–	744	–	17	–	848	–	549	–	145	–
1936	594	–	891	–	21	–	928	–	586	–	177	–
1937	620	–	957[1]	–	32	–	1,044[4]	–	620	–	231	–
							1,034					
1938	682	–	1,081[1]	–	47	–	764	–	668	–	294	–
1939	...	–	1,113[1]	–	60	–	...	–	713	–	333	–
1940	...	–	...	–	83	–	...	–	761	–	348	–
1941	...	–	...	–	...	–	...	–	792	–	375	–
1942	...	–	...	–	...	–	...	–	822	–	425	–
1943	...	–	...	–	...	–	...	–	866	–	479	–
1944	...	–	...	–	...	–	...	–	895	–	497	–
1945	...	–	...	–	...	–	...	–	905	–	542	–
1946	880	–	...	–	...	–	1,662	–	906	–	561	–
1947	970	–	1,081	–	205	–	1,891	–	968	–	602	–
1948	1,106	–	1,227	–	210	–	2,108	–	1,015	–	622	–
1949	1,210	–	1,395	–	212	–	2,259	–	1,058	–	664	–
1950	1,319	–	1,548	–	226	–	2,421	–	1,087	–	722	–
1951	1,440	–	1,637	–	...	–	2,545	–	1,114	–	785	–
1952	1,550	–	1,794	–	225	–	2,638	–	1,162	–	853	–
1953	1,624	–	1,863	–	445[3]	–	2,676	–	1,205	–	905	–
1954	1,683	. .	2,000	–	350	–	2,744	4	1,240	–	968	–
1955	1,736	1	2,135	72[2]	627	–	2,839	32	1,209	4	1,021	–
1956	1,790	4	2,229	150	754	. .	2,915	76	1,218	16	1,066	–
1957	1,842	16	2,307	250	898	. .	2,971	173	1,256	62	1,112	2
1958	1,893	50	2,409	223	1,059	. .	3,055	328	1,297	137	1,140	8
1959	1,944	113	2,477	392	1,246	1	3,085	519	1,326	251	1,187	34
1960	1,988	193	2,588	618	1,431	5	3,104	795	1,350	388	1,228	93
1961	2,036	291	2,734	821	1,601	11	3,141	1,089	1,362[6]	583	1,290	190
1962	2,079	377	2,896	1,018	1,733	31	3,132	1,356	735	726	1,330	336
1963	2,110	465	2,935	1,206	1,843	66	3,112	1,630	592	860	1,397	476
1964	2,134	586	2,919	1,375	1,959	122	3,094	1,899	508	939	1,456	622
1965	2,154	711	3,026	1,543	2,055	185	3,100	2,113	383	1,031	1,541	732
1966	2,171	853	3,047	1,660	2,144	288	3,179	2,375	380	1,097	1,605	822
1967	2,146	978	3,120	1,779	2,218	420	3,185	2,600	302	1,145	1,663	899
1968	2,071	1,129	3,200	1,894	2,245	621	3,287	2,864	267	1,188	1,701	958
1969	2,044	1,277	3,313	2,000	2,271	829	3,221	2,996	236	1,228	1,744	1,015
1970	2,026	1,426	3,396	2,100	2,292	1,028	3,174	3,091	207	1,311	1,783	1,058
1971	2,160	1,586	3,497	2,203	2,305	1,181	3,140	3,187	183	1,375	1,817	1,099
1972	2,154	1,695	3,560	2,289	2,302	1,286	3,127	3,305	164	1,411	1,896	1,183
1973	2,157	1,779	3,662	2,376	2,266	1,383	3,115	3,404	151	1,442	1,944	1,224
1974	2,170	1,856	3,768	2.464	2,273	1,457	3,237	3,602	144	1,527	1,997	1,261
1975	2,170	1,910	3,891	2,549	2,271	1,508	3,245	3,689	137	1,556	2,099	1,336

Abbreviations used throughout this table:– TV: Television

See p. 704 for footnotes

G 9 Radio and Television Receiving Licences (in thousands)

1920–1975

	France		Germany[7]		East Germany		Hungary		Ireland[9]		Italy	
	Radio	TV	Radio	TV	Radio	TV	Radio	TV	Radio	TV	Radio	TV
1920	...	–	–	–	...	–	–	–	–	–	–	–
1921	...	–	–	–	...	–	–	–	–	–	–	–
1922	...	–	–	–	...	–	–	–	–	–	–	–
1923	...	–	–	–	...	–	–	–	1	–	–	–
1924	...	–	9	–	...	–	–	–	1	–	–	–
1925	...	–	1,022	–	...	–	17	–	8	–	–	–
1926	...	–	1,377	–	...	–	60	–	19	–	–	–
1927	...	–	2,010	–	...	–	83	–	24	–	–	–
1928	...	–	2,235	–	...	–	169	–	26	–	63	–
1929	...	–	2,838	–	...	–	267	–	26	–	...	–
1930	...	–	3,238	–	...	–	308	–	26	–	176	–
1931	...	–	3,732	–	...	–	325	–	29	–	239	–
1932	...	–	4,168	–	...	–	322	–	33	–	305	–
1933	1,368	–	4,533	–	...	–	328	–	51	–	373	–
1934	1,756	–	5,425[8]	–	...	–	340	–	66	–	431	–
1935	2,626	–	6,725	–	...	–	353	–	88	–	529	–
1936	3,219	–	7,584	–	...	–	365	–	105	–	697	–
1937	4,164	–	8,512	–	...	–	384	–	140	–	826	–
1938	4,706	–	9,598	–	...	–	419	–	155	–	978	–
1939	5,220	–	...	–	...	–	...	–	170	–	1,142	–
1940	5,089	–	...	–	...	–	...	–	184	–	1,321	–
1941	5,098	–	...	–	...	–	...	–	176	–	1,583	–
1942	5,180	–	...	–	...	–	...	–	171[9]	–	1,827	–
1943	5,248	–	...	–	...	–	...	–	169	–	1,784	–
1944	5,117	–	...	–	...	–	...	–	171	–	1,608	–
1945	5,346	–	...	–	...	–	...	–	173	–	1,646	–
			West Germany[8]									
1946	5,668	–	...	–	...	–	...	–	180	–	1,850	–
1947	5,750	–	...	–	...	–	386	–	187	–	1,982	–
1948	6,104	–	7,299	–	...	–	475	–	261	–	2,205	–
1949	6,421	--	...	–	...	–	539	–	280	–	2,566	–
1950	6,889	4	...	–	3,489	–	606	–	298	–	3,135	–
1951	7,407	11	9,493	–	3,813	–	701	–	327	–	3,683	–
1952	7,923	24	10,182	–	4,210	–	887	–	383	–	4,228	–
1953	8,368	60	11,108	2	4,511	–	1,080	–	406	–	4,800[6]	–
1954	8,853	125	11,730	22	4,776	2	1,236	–	428	–	5,391	88
1955	9,266	261	12,238[8]	121[8]	5,009	14	1,432	–	445	–	5,637	179
			13,160	127								
1956	9,715	442	13,672	393	5,218	71	1,587	1[10]	461	–	5,869	366
1957	10,199	683	14,531	835	5,306	159	1,774	1	477	–	6,009	673
1958	10,646	989	15,194[7]	1,513[7]	5,378	318	1,963	16	485	–	6,042	1,096
1959	10,793	1,368	15,900	3,375	5,489	594	2,102	53	486	–	6,014	1,573
1960	10,981[6]	1,902	15,892	4,635	5,574	1,035	2,224	104	494	–	5,882	2,124
1961	10,411	2,555	16,270	5,888	5,602	1,459	2,314	206	495[6]	–	5,726	2,762
1962	10,349	3,427	16,696	7,213	5,670	1,893	2,390	325	389	127	5,580	3,458
1963	10,151	4,400	17,099	8,539	5,739	2,379	2,452	471	337	201	5,279	4,285
1964	9,567	5,414	17,494	10,024	5,759	2,801	2,484	675	293	259	4,886	5,216
1965	8,937	6,489	17,878	11,379	5,743	3,216	2,484	831	259	297	4,571	6,045
1966	8,390	7,471	18,232	12,720	5,820	3,600	2,485	996	230	320	4,196	6,855
1967	6,940	8,316	18,587	13,806	5,881	3,933	2,479	1,169	210	389	3,844	7,666
1968	6,306	9,252	18,988	14,958	5,942	4,173	2,514	1,397	185	395	2,553	8,347
1969	5,675	10,121	19,368	15,909	5,983	4,337	2,531	1,596	161	433	2,197	9,016
1970	5,027	10,968	19,622	16,675	5,985	4,499	2,531	1,769	138	438	1,823	9,717
1971	4,371	11,655	19,026[12]	16,669[12]	6,016	4,649	2,543	1,943	123	474	1,506	10,344
1972	3,841	12,279	19,199	17,100	6,050	4,820	2,542	2,085	–	514	1,253	10,951
1973	3,474	12,955	19,329	17,351	6,082	4,966	2,533	2,199	–	514	1,022	11,426
1974	...	...	19,396	17,556	6,114	5,096	2,541	2,295	–	556	825	11,816
1975	...	...	19,598	17,796	6,167	5,224	2,537	2,390	–	565	715	12,103

See p. 704 for footnotes

G 9 Radio and Television Receiving Licences (in thousands)

1920–1975

	Netherlands		Norway		Poland		Portugal		Romania	
	Radio	TV	Radio	TV	Radio	TV	Radio	TV	Radio	TV
1920	...	–	–	–	–	–	...	–	...	–
1921	...	–	–	–	–	–	...	–	...	–
1922	...	–	–	–	–	–	...	–	...	–
1923	...	–	–	–	–	–	...	–	...	–
1924	..	–	–	–	–	–	...	–	...	–
1925	...	–	–	–	5	–	...	–	...	–
1926	...	–	46[1]	–	48	–	...	–	...	–
1927	...	–	63	–	120	–	...	–	...	–
1928	...	–	64	–	184	–	...	–	...	–
1929	...	–	77	–	203	–	...	–	...	–
1930	429	–	84	–	246	–	...	–	...	–
1931	524	–	102	–	310	–	...	–	...	–
1932	560	–	123	–	296	–	...	–	...	–
1933	648	–	138	–	311	–	16	–	...	–
1934	909	–	157	–	374	–	28	–	101	–
1935	947	–	189	–	492	–	40	–	132	–
1936	989	–	240	–	677	–	54	–	162	–
1937	1,072	–	305	–	922	–	69	–	218	–
1938	1,109	–	365	–	...	–	81	–	274	–
1939	1,438	–	423	–	...	–	89	–	317	–
1940	...	–	429	–	...	–	98	–	...	–
1941	...	–	468[1]	–	...	–	114	–	...	–
1942	...	–	...	–	...	–	120	–	...	–
1943	...	–	...	–	...	–	123	–	...	–
1944	...	–	...	–	...	–	129	–	...	–
1945	...	–	226	...	168	–	136	–	...	–
1946	...	–	373	...	475	–	142	–	...	–
1947	1,467	–	539	...	667	–	145	–	219	–
1948	1,615	–	654	...	974	–	179	–	258	–
1949	1,816	–	737	...	1,176	–	212	–	...	–
1950	1,957	–	786	...	1,464	–	228	–	313	–
1951	2,106	–	824	...	1,747	–	310	–	...	–
1952	2,216	1	860	...	2,001	–	354	–	...	–
1953	2,333	3	895	...	2,211	–	393	–	750	–
1954	2,487	9	925	...	2,661	–	443	–	...	–
1955	2,691	41	948	...	3,057	–	479	–	1,164	–
1956	2,878	99	968	...	3,624	5[10]	534	–	1,326	- -
1957	2,888	239	985	–	4,005	22	596	1	1,499	3
1958	2,998	391	997	- -	4,465	85	689	13	1,655	16
1959	3,095	585	1,008	6	4,931	238	791	28	1,841	30
1960	3,126	801	1,021	49	5,268	426	848	46	2,008	55
1961	3,064	1,040	1,034	107	5,487	648	902	68	2,165	88
1962	3,072	1,275	1,038	204	5,620	959	1,005	90	2,372	110[2]
1963	3,097	1,574	1,060	292	5,701	1,295	1,068	119	2,549	245
1964	3,130	1,836	1,071	407	5,788	1,698	1,127	151	2,684	357
1965	3,093	2,113	1,089	490	5,646	2,078	1,173	180	2,790	501
1966	3,134	2,370	1,110	574	5,593	2,540	1,240	214	2,925	712
1967	3,154	2,559	1,135	662	5,539	2,934	1,345	271	3,019	916
1968	3,174	2,717	1,152	739	5,598	3,389	1,391	293	3,031	1,115
1969	...	2,939	1,171	796	5,649	3,828	1,406	352	3,050	1,288
1970	...	3,086	1,191	854	5,658	4,215	1,368	387	3,075	1,484
1971	...	3,240	1,204	895	5,709	4,709	1,411	472	3,106	1,703
1972	...	3,353	1,235	951	5,795	5,200	1,449	542	3,112	1,944
1973	...	3,462	1,255	986	5,872	5,687	1,505	569	3,077	2,145
1974	...	3,545	1,277	1,021	...	6,100	1,516	572	3,066	2,405
1975	...	3,646	1,300	1,051	...	6,472	1,519	575	3,084	2,692

See p. 704 for footnotes

G 9 Radio and Television Receiving Licences (in thousands)

1920–1975

	Spain[11]		Sweden		Switzerland		United Kingdom[5]		Yugoslavia	
	Radio	TV	Radio	TV	Radio	TV	Radio	TV	Radio	TV
1920	...	–	–	–	–	–	–	–	–	–
1921	...	–	–	–	–	–	–	–	–	–
1922	...	–	–	–	–	–	–	–	–	–
1923	...	–	5	–	–	–	125	–	–	–
1924	...	–	40	–	17	–	748	–	–	–
1925	...	–	126	–	34	–	1,350	–	–	–
1926	...	–	243	–	51	–	1,960	–	–	–
1927	...	–	328	–	59	–	2,270	–	–	–
1928	...	–	381	–	70	–	2,483	–	–	–
1929	...	–	428	–	84	–	2,730	–	–	–
1930	...	–	482	–	104	–	3,091	–	45	–
1931	...	–	550	–	151	–	3,647	–	48	–
1932	...	–	609	–	231	–	4,620	–	57	–
1933	...	–	666	–	300	–	5,497	–	59	–
1934	213	–	733	–	357	–	6,260	–	67	–
1935	304	–	834	–	418	–	7,012	–	83	–
1936	...	–	944	–	464	–	7,618	–	96	–
1937	...	–	1,074	–	504	–	8,131	–	112	–
1938	...	–	1,227	–	549	–	8,589	–	135	–
1939	...	–	1,358	–	593	–	8,968	–	155	–
1940	281	–	1,470	–	634	–	8,951	–	...	–
1941	...	–	1,551	–	680	–	8,752	–	...	–
1942	...	–	1,628	–	729	–	8,683	–	...	–
1943	...	–	1,709	–	780	–	9,242	–	...	–
1944	...	–	1,784	–	820	–	9,555	–	...	–
1945	...	–	1,840	–	855	–	9,711	–	180	–
1946	...	–	...[13]	–	891	–	10,396[6]	–	198	–
1947	552	–	1,895	–	923	–	10,763	15	223	–
1948	657	–	1,959	–	970	–	11,134	46	252	–
1949	...	–	2,025	–	1,008	–	11,621	127	301	–
1950	...	–	2,095	–	1,037	–	11,876	344	336	–
1951	...	–	2,153	–	1,079	–	11,605	764	357	–
1952	...	–	2,205	–	1,120	–	11,304	1,449	387	–
1953	1,313	–	2,256	–	1,158	1	10,750	2,142	422	–
1954	1,622	–	2,317	–	1,199	4	10,188	3,249	497	–
1955	...	...	2,391	–	1,233	11	9,477	14,504	592	–
1956	1,839	3	2,462	–	1,268	20	8,522	5,740	711	4[10]
1957	2,105	3	2,548	13	1,308	31	7,559	6,966	890	4
1958	2,293	21	2,608	76	1,350	50	6,556	8,090	1,088	7
1959	2,464	140	2,651	244	1,388	79	5,481	9,255	1,342	12
1960	2,717	250	2,686	599	1,445	129	4,535	10,470	1,562	30
1961	3,174	...	2,744	1,030	1,490	194	3,909	11,268	1,826	62
1962	3,491	375	2,843	1,327	1,538	274	3,538	11,834	2,078	126
1963	4,000	850	2,938	1,626	1,583	366	3,256	12,443	2,278	212
1964	4,000	1,100	2,950	1,821	1,619	492	2,999	12,885	2,520	393
1965	4,550	1,750	2,947	1,964	1,654	621	2,794	13,253	2,783	577
1966	5,920	2,325	2,954	2,085	1,677	752	2,611	13,567	3,003	777
1967	6,475	2,685	2,925	2,160	1,725	868	2,506	14,267	3,059	1,002
1968	6,951	...	2,928	2,268	1,752	1,011	2,557	15,089	3,171	1,298
1969	7,042	...	2,927	2,345	1,800	1,144	2,464	15,496	3,320	1,546
1970	...	4,115	–	2,420	1,852	1,274	2,301	15,883	3,372	1,796
1971	7,174	4,520	–	2,513	1,900	1,403	–	16,658	3,476	2,061
1972	...	5,200	–	2,619	1,958	1,536	–	17,125	3,556	2,354
1973	8,000	5,719	–	2,701	2,003	1,627	–	17,325	3,685	2,544
1974	8,050	6,125	–	2,758	2,036	1,714	–	17,701	4,081	2,784
1975	8,075	6,525	–	2,841	2,076	1,759	–	17,729	4,181	3,076

See p. 704 for footnotes

G 9 Radio and Television Licences (in thousands)

NOTES

1. SOURCES:—The official publications noted on p.xv with gaps filled from United Nations, *Statistical Yearbooks,* and the following data supplied by the respective national statistical offices:— Finland 1926–29; 1931–33, and 1936–37; Italy 1942–46; Netherlands 1930–39; Poland 1924–36; and Portugal 1933–34.

2. So far as possible the data apply to 31 December in each year.

FOOTNOTES

[1] At 30 June.
[2] Estimates of number of receivers in October.
[3] This is a later revised figure.
[4] The figures from 1937 (2nd line) are for the post-Second World War territory.
[5] At 31 March.
[6] Television licences subsequently included radio licences.
[7] Figures to 1958 are at 1 April.
[8] Saarland is excluded up to 1934 and from 1948 to 1955 (1st line), and West Berlin is also excluded from 1948 to 1955 (1st line).
[9] Figures to 1942 are of licences issued during the year ended 31 March following that indicated.
[10] Estimates of the number of receivers.
[11] At 1 July.
[12] Subsequently only taxed receivers.
[13] Subsequently at 30 June.

H. FINANCE

Financial statistics exhibit some very great contrasts as regards availability. Some were collected and published from a very early date. Others may have been collected, but were regarded as state secrets. And yet others were not collected for a long time because they were regarded as private secrets, publication of which it was beyond the competence of the state to compel. Finally, in the period since the Second World War, the centrally-planned economies of eastern Europe have returned to the policy of treating many financial statistics as state secrets.

The first three tables in this section showing various monetary statistics, point some of these contrasts very well. The banknote issues of the Bank of England are available from before the beginning of our period, yet publication of those of other British banks was not compelled until 1833. Experience in most other countries was similar, with publication from the start by the central bank, but little or no information from other issuers for a long time. In general, however, this has been of much less importance than in the British case, because in many countries the privilege of note issue has always been confined to a single bank; and where it was not, such restriction has usually been imposed before bank notes became a really important part of the money supply.

Table H.2, showing commercial bank deposits, demonstrates both the scarcity of such data before the interwar period, outside north-western Europe, and the secretive reactions of regimes in eastern Europe since the Second World War. It also, unfortunately, displays a lack of uniformity in what was regarded as a commercial bank deposit in different countries. Savings bank data, on the other hand, are both more homogeneous and more readily available for earlier periods. Not being part of the work of high finance, there was no reluctance to compel publication of their statistics; indeed, they were more likely to be seen as something of which a government could be proud, indicating the prosperity of ordinary citizens.

Two tables are given showing the public finance statistics of central governments. Table H.4 shows total expenditure, and H.5 shows, so far as possible, total current revenue and its main tax constituents. There is, of course, a great deal of data available on the details of expenditure, but this is so heterogeneous, is often not available in any meaningful form, and changes in nature so often, that in many cases it would require considerable research effort to put the statistics of even a single country on a reasonably uniform basis. Regretfully, therefore, only the totals of expenditure are included. Tax yields, on the other hand, exhibit both less disguise and less change—at any rate until very recently.

It is noteworthy for how few countries statistics of their public finances are available much before the middle of the nineteenth century. And only for Great Britain, and in summary form for the Habsburg monarchy, are there are eighteenth century data. Both of these latter are the result of retrospective exercises in the middle of the nineteenth century, and it is fair to say that, in general, and with some exceptions, consistent and fairly full information of state finance only became available when parliamentary regimes of one sort or another had established some sort of control over taxation. Even then, accounting systems often remained archaic; there were several changes in them ; it was often still in the government's interest to hide or disguise some of their income, or, more frequently, their expenditures. Altogether, it would be unwise to assume that all the figures in tables H.4 and H.5 are fully comprehensive or that all their inconsistencies have been identified in the footnotes.

H 1 BANKNOTE CIRCULATION

1750–1799

	Sweden (a)	Sweden (b)	United Kingdom[1] (c)
1750	2.7	10,834	4,318
1751	3.0	11,933	5,195
1752	3.4	13,457	4,750
1753	3.3	13,228	4,420
1754	3.4	13,546	4,081
1755	3.4	13,798	4,115
1756	4.3	17,017	4,516
1757	6.1	24,313	5,150
1758	7.3	29,332	4,864
1759	9.2	36,887	4,800
1760	8.3	33,200	4,936
1761	10	39,616	5,247
1762	11	35,056	5,887
1763	11	44,024	5,315
1764	11	42,525	6,211[1]
1765	9.6	38,570	...
1766	9.6	38,261	5,846
1767	9.1	36,347	5,511
1768	8.2	32,633	5,779
1769	7.9	31,771	5,707
1770	8.8	35,141	5,237
1771	9.1	36,421	6,823
1772	9.4	37,535	5,962
1773	10	39,573	6,037
1774	11	42,634	...[1]
1775	11	44,482[36]	8,762
1776	12	7,833	8,626
1777	11	7,304	8,033
1778	10	6,919	7,099
1779	9.2	6,158	8,145
1780	8.5	5,655	7,376
1781	8.4	5,567	6,701
1782	8.9	5,944	7,394
1783	8.9	5,928	6,991
1784	7.9	5,295	5,898
1785	7.7	5,149	6,247
1786	7.4	4,934	7,883
1787	8.0	4,347	9,008
1788	9.1	6,067	9,782
1789	8.3	10,757	10,465
1790	5.6	12,153	10,737
1791	4.5	11,078	11,556
1792	3.8	12,813	11,157
1793	3.1	13,388	11,377
1794	2.8	14,562	10,515
1795	2.6	16,356	12,440
1796	2.2	16,921	9,988
1797	1.9	16,306	10,394
1798	1.7	16,031	12,638
1799	1.5	17,039	13,175

1800–1849

	Austria-Hungary[2] (d)	Finland[3] (e)	France[4] (f)
1800	–	–	–
1801	–	–	–
1802	–	–	–
1803	–	–	–
1804	–	–	–
1805	–	–	–
1806	–	–	–
1807	–	–	85
1808	–	–	96
1809	–	–	95
1810	–	–	101
1811	–	–	101
1812	–	–	111
1813	–	2	81
1814	–	4	28
1815	–	11	41
1816	–	15	69
1817	–	16	84
1818	26.7	15	100
1819	43.8	16	102
1820	51.9	18[3]	154
1821	34.8	23	180
1822	48.3	18	187
1823	51.0	16	189
1824	68.1	16	222
1825	82.1	15	218
1826	82.3	15	169
1827	87.4	14	191
1828	95.7	11	199
1829	108	12	201
1830	112	11	224
1831	124	10	217
1832	120	9	233
1833	125	9	212
1834	136	11	206
1835	151	12	222
1836	154	14	214
1837	146	14	205
1838	167	14	212
1839	167	15	214
1840	167	20	223
1841	167	127	227
1842	173	178	233
1843	179	172	237
1844	198	181	254
1845	215	177	267
1846	214	184	272
1847	219	204	251
1848	223	168	342
1849	250	153	422

Abbreviations used:– (a) = Bank of Sweden issue (million kronor); (b) = Total note circulation (in thousand dalers silver mynt); (c) = Bank of England issue (thousand pounds); (d) = National Bank issue (million gulden); (e) = Bank of Finland issue (thousand markkaa); (f) = Bank of France issue (million francs).

See p. 715 for footnotes

H 1 Banknote Circulation

1800–1849

	Ireland[7] (a)	Netherlands[8] (b)	Norway (c)	Sweden (d)	Sweden (e)	United Kingdom: G.B.[1] (f)	United Kingdom: G.B.[1] (g)
1800	...	...	...	1.5	19,085	15,946	...
1801	...	...	...	1.5	19,610	15,385	...
1802	...	...	...	1.5	...	16,142	...
1803	...	...	...	2.4	18,789	15,652	...
1804	...	...	...	5.3	...	17,116	...
					(h)		
1805	...	...	...	8.4		17,130	...
1806	...	...	...	10	...	19,379	...
1807	...	...	...	13	...	18,315	...
1808	...	...	...	25	...	17,650	...
1809	...	...	...	31	...	19,059	...
1810	...	...	...	32	...	22,907	...
1811	...	...	...	34	...	23,324	...
1812	...	...	...	34	...	23,218	...
1813	...	...	...	30	...	24,020	...
1814	...	...	...	29	...	26,585	...
1815	...	1.8	...	29	...	27,255	...
1816	...	3.7	...	31	...	26,886	...
1817	...	5.3	...	35	...	28,471	...
1818	...	5.0	...	37	...	26,987	...
1819	...	5.8	13	36	...	25,190	...
1820	...	8.7	13	36	...	23,892	...
1821	...	13	14	36	...	22,090	...
1822	...	11	14	35	...	18,065	...
1823	...	14	14	35	...	18,812	...
1824	...	20	15	37	...	19,935	...
1825	...	14	16	37	...	20,076	...
1826	...	12	16	37	...	23,516	...
1827	...	12	16	36	...	22,319	...
1828	...	14	17	36	...	21,669	...
1829	...	20	18	37	...	19,709	...
1830	...	26	19	37	...	20,758	...
1831	...	14	19	38	...	19,069	...
1832	...	14	19	38	...	18,016	...
1833	5,334[6]	20	20	37	...	19,500	13,047[6]
1834	5,216	23	20	36	1.3	19,046[1]	13,404
						18,820	
1835	5,186	24	21	38	1.5	18,107	13,798
1836	5,500	23	22	41	2.5	17,827	14,988
1837	5,119	21	21	43	4.1	18,288	13,683
1838	5,636	26	20	40	7.3	18,950	14,538
1839	5,848	24	22	40	9.1	17,677	14,963
1840	5,391	24	22	40	10.0	16,839	13,708
1841	5,356[7]	31	23	38	10.7	16,948[1]	12,923[9]
1842	5,114	27	23	33	9.8	18,440	11,127
1843	5,168	29	23	31	9.5	19,523	10,379
1844	5,937	34	22	30	9.8	21,216[1]	11,126
1845	6,949	37	23	36	12	20,674	11,004
1846	7,260	32	23	39	13	20,252	11,135
1847	6,009	32	22	43	16	19,123	10,911
1848	4,829	37	19	39	16	18,086	9,456
1849	4,310	44	19	34	15	18,438	9,344

Abbreviations used:– (a) = bank issues (thousand pounds); (b) = bank issues (million gulden); (c) = Bank of Norway issue (million kroner); (d) = Bank of Sweden issue (million kronor); (e) = Total note circulation (thousand rixsdalers); (f) = Bank of England issue (thousand pounds) (g) = other bank issues (thousand pounds); (h) = other bank issues (million kronor).

See p. 715 for footnotes

H 1 Banknote Circulation

1850–1899

	Austria/ Hungary[2] (a)	Belgium (b)	Bulgaria (c)	Denmark (d)	Finland[3] (e)	France (f)[4]	Germany (g)	Ireland (h)[7]	Italy (i)	Netherlands (j)[8]	Norway (k)
1850	255	–	–	–	143	486		4,512	...	49	20
1851	216	53	–	–	147	530	102	4,463	...	51	21
1852	195	67	–	–	163	621	113	4,818	...	67	21
1853	188	82	–	–	177	660	113	5,650	...	78	27
1854	383	95	–	–	184	614	119	6,296	...	94	31
1855	378	100	–	–	188	638	129	6,362	...	92	31
1856	380	99	–	–	225	620	245	6,652	...	91	29
1857	383	105[11]	–	–	222	594	288	6,822	...	81	27
1858	389	119	–	24	163	625	320	6,183	...	76	26
1859	467	114	–	24	184	716	366	6,870	...	87	24
1860	475	118	–	24	224	750	463	6,840	...	99	26
1861	467	118	–	25	292	745	533	6,266	...	104	25
1862	427	123	–	24	304	805	521	5,658	...	95	27
1863	397	117	–	25	267	796	524	5,405	...	99	27
1864	376	113	–	25	276	762	527	5,594	...	92	26
1865	351	125	–	24	261	839	579	5,987	...	105	29
1866	284	124	–	26	219	937	564	5,884	...	113	28
1867	247	138	–	27	237	1,082	637	5,811	...	109	29
1868	276	172	–	26	284	1,233	684	6,181	...	119	26
1869	284	199	–	25	329	1,355	703	6,608	...	136	27
1870	297	203	–	28	366	1,544	854	6,880	...	132	28
1871	317	229	–	33	420	2,075	1,074	7,544	1,207	143	34
1872	318	298	–	35	498	2,401	1,378	7,674	1,363	168	39
1873	359	321	–	38[12]	609	2,857	1,368	7,077	1,454	165	47
				m kroner							
1874	294	329	–	64	735	2,597	1,325	6,768	1,513	166	46
1875	286	340	–	61	575	2,461	1,054	7,064	1,561	175	37
1876	296	365	–	66	527	2,484	990[13]	7,500	1,586	184	40
							1,118				
1877	282	342	–	60	442	2,490	1,045	7,399	1,569	187	36
1878	289	314	–	65	384	2,339	988	6,968	1,612	200	31
1879	317	335	–	70	370	2,199	1,112	6,066	1,672	188	33
1880	329	340	–	70	486	2,305	1,130	5,727	1,689	191	39
1881	354	355	–	78	448	2,576	1,182	6,587	1,676	194	38
1882	369	356	–	70	451	2,732	1,167	7,297	1,672	195	41
1883	380	358	–	72	471	2,926	1,159	7,124	1,512	186	41
1884	376	358	–	71	450	2,928	1,192	6,514	1,510	186[8]	39
1885	364	367	–	71	410	2,846	1,183	6,063	1,442	186	37
1886	372	379	49	75	400	2,789	1,336	6,019	1,479	198	39
1887	391	389	1,036	77	431	2,719	1,323	5,885	1,471	195	40
1888	426	376	183	80	488	2,676	1,402	6,114	1,421	193	44
1889	435	402	402	76	553	2,876	1,461	6,663	1,461	204	49
1890	446	405	1,958	77	525	3,060	1,401	6,800	1,469	208	50
1891	455	422	1,303	77	489	3,085	1,416	6,500	1,464	195	48
1892	478	428	472	...	460	3,151	1,430	6,189	1,480	189	45
1893	487	451	1,231	81	444	3,445	1,398	6,317	1,573[14]	193	47
1894	508	470	825	78	491	3,476	1,503	6,327	1,618	200	48
1895	620	477	1,681	83	563	3,527	1,621	6,380	1,595	204	51
	m kroner[10]										
1896	1,319	493	2,397	85	640	3,607	1,553	6,287	1,572	200	53
1897	1,400	513	1,957	88	715	3,687	1,621	6,226	1,662	202	57
1898	1,475	545	3,156	91	768	3,694	1,655	6,144	1,686	203	63
1899	1,458	590	7,972	96	734	3,820	1,661	6,363	1,674	219	63

Abbreviations used:— (a) = National Bank issue (million gulden); (b) = National Bank issue (million francs); (c) = National Bank issue (thousand leva); (d) = National Bank issue (million rigsdaler); (e) = Bank of Finland issue (thousand markkaa); (f) = Bank of France issue (million francs); (g) = bank issues (million marks); (h) = bank issues (thousand pounds); (i) = bank and state issues (million lire); (j) = bank issues (million gulden); (k) = Bank of Norway issue (million kroner).

See p. 715 for footnotes

H 1 Banknote Circulation

1850–1899

	Portugal	Romania	Russia	Spain		Sweden		Switzerland	United Kingdom: G.B.	
	(a)	(b)[29]	(c)	(d)	(e)	(f)	(g)	(h)[4]	(i)[1]	(j)[9]
1850	...	...	...	...	...	34	15	...	19,448	9,555
1851	...	...	...	...	...	34	16	...	19,468	9,453
1852	...	...	...	...	...	34	17	...	21,910	9,814
1853	...	...	...	...	...	41	21	...	22,602	10,629
1854	...	...	...	...	...	50	25	...	20,688	10,885
1855	...	...	...	–	...	59	32	...	19,830	11,005
1856	...	...	...	40	...	52	27	...	19,667	10,883
1857	...	...	...	46	...	47	21	...	19,467	10,720
1858	1,885	...	...	52	...	40	25	...	20,248	9,916
1859	2,925	...	...	67	...	37	26	...	21,326	10,541
1860	2,437	...	...	63	55	39	30	...	21,252	10,678
1861	2,128	...	...	45	59	37	32	...	19,992	10,327
1862	2,640	...	...	52	48	36	30	...	20,835	10,273
1863	2,493	...	...	68	47	31	27	...	20,664	10,244
1864	2,261	...	...	72	77	32	28	...	20,605	10,242
1865	2,483	...	664	62	...	31	33	...	21,117	10,173
1866	2,319	...	662	45	...	27	32	...	23,159	9,590
1867	2,117	...	697	49	77	26	34	...	23,438	9,666
1868	2,249	...	675	55	...	26	31	...	23,932	9,658
1869	2,434	...	703	53	...	27	35	...	23,483	9,780
1870	2,599	...	694	61	...	29	40	...	23,327	9,843
1871	2,923	...	695	79	...	31	48	...	24,416	10,228
1872	3,259	...	752	68	...	45	57	24.8	25,492	10,432
1873	3,365	...	748	55	...	45	67	...	25,645	10,706
1874	4,660	...	774	72	...	...	64	...	26,264	10,880
1875	4,771	...	764	128	–	36	60	...	27,346	10,865
1876	...	...	752	158	–	30	61	77.3	27,734	10,813
1877	...	...	767	157	–	27	51	...	27,895	10,681
1878	4,652	...	1,015	174	...	27	46	...	28,058	10,203
1879	5,575	...	1,153	193	...	32	49	...	29,212	9,116
1880	6,002	–	1,130	245	...	39	51	...	26,915	8,978
1881	7,286	34	1,085	350	...	38	49	92.9	26,321	8,892
1882	6,836	73	1,028	334	...	37	53	99.4	25,985	9,090
1883	6,285	93	973	364	...	36	52	98.2	25,568	9,196
1884	6,578	89	959	383	...	38	52	102	25,358	9,010
1885	7,076	92	900	469	...	39	50	115	24,667	8,692
1886	7,829	101	907	527	...	42	48	123	24,659	8,435
1887	9,646	106	941	612	...	40	50	127	24,350	8,140
1888	11,681	113	971	720	...	44	56	135	24,283	8,196
1889	12,110	94	973	735	...	44	59	140	24,389	8,337
1890	10,504	106	928	734	...	45	59	145	24,561	8,646
1891	37,903	124	907	812	...	44	59	152	25,145	8,683
1892	53,360	114	1,055	884	...	44	58	163	25,863	8,598
1893	...	131	1,074	928	...	48	59	163	25,858	8,488
1894	...	117	1,072	910	...	52	61	167	25,300	8,386
1895	...	119	1,048	994	...	57	61	171	25,753	8,712
1896	...	133	1,055	1,031	...	63	66	179	26,470	8,793
1897	...	139	1,134	1,206	...	69	72	190	27,198	8,745
1898	...	161	1,128	1,444	...	71	79	199	27,448	8,875
1899	...	141	1,235	1,518	...	75	80	208	27,820	9,154

Abbreviations used:— (a) = bank issues (thousand milreis or escudos); (b) = National Bank issue (million lei); (c) = all note issues (million rubels); (d) = Bank of Spain issue (million pesetas); (e) = other bank issues (million pesetas); (f) = Bank of Sweden issue (million kronor), (g) = other bank issues (million kronor); (h) = bank issues (million francs); (i) Bank of England issue (thousand pounds); (j) = other bank issues (thousand pounds).

See p. 715 for footnotes

H 1 Banknote Circulation

1900–1949

	Austria-Hungary (a)	Belgium (b)	Bulgaria (c)	Czechoslovakia (d)	Denmark (e)	Finland[3] (f)	France[4] (g)	Germany (h)	East Germany (i)	Greece (j)
1900	1,494	632	22	...	97	712	4,034	1,715		...
1901	1,585	649	27	...	99	624	4,116	1,756		...
1902	1,635	676	25	...	103	703	4,162	1,777		...
1903	1,771	671	33	...	110	724	4,310	1,843		...
1904	1,751	694	40	...	111	725	4,283	1,858		...
1905	1,847	724	37	...	118	927	4,408	1,927		...
1906	1,982	770	45	...	124	924	4,659	2,023		...
1907	2,028	798	49	...	129	951	4,800	2,096		...
1908	2,113	807	72	...	133	860	4,853	2,187		...
1909	2,188	845	72	...	134	1,117	5,080	2,287		...
1910	2,376	905	82	...	137	1,239	5,198	2,291		...
1911	2,541	970	111	...	148	1,153	5,243	2,492		...
1912	2,816	1,035	164	...	155	1,175	5,323	2,778		...
1913	2,494	1,067	189	...	165[12]	1,130	5,665	2,902		245
					152					
1914	5,137	1,614	227	...	207	1,417	7,325	5,862		265
1915	7,162	1,320	370	...	220	2,316	12,280	8,360		392
1916	10,889	1,282	834	...	285	4,213	15,552	11,438		569
1917	18,440	1,268	1,493	...	338	7,645	19,845	18,246		865
						million markkaa				
1918	...	3,210	2,299	...	450	12	27,536	33,073		1,274
1919	...	4,786	2,858	4,723	489	11	34,744	50,065		1,382
	Austria (a)									
1920	30,646	6,260	3,354	11,289	557	13	38,186	81,398		1,508
1921	227,016[15]	6,415	3,615	10,323	471	14	37,679	122,500		2,161
1922	4,080,177	6,876	3,886	10,064	459	14	36,352	1,295,228[21]		3,149
1923	7,125,755	7,357	4,139	9,599	473	14	37,356	2,274		4,681
	million schilling									
1924	839	7,873	4,530	8,810	478	13	39,938	3,891		4,866
1925	890	7,814	3,655	8,408	438	13	44,071	4,627		5,339
1926	937	9,432[18][19]	3,481	8,203	386	13	53,420	5,081		4,865
1927	998	10,035	3,727	8,417	354	15	53,490	5,470		4,966
1928	1,064	11,512	4,173	8,466	360	15	60,061	5,653		5,690
1929	1,094	13,437	3,609	8,230	367	14	64,647	5,635		5,193
1930	1,090	15,818	3,296	7,824	360	13	72,119	5,409		4,803
1931	1,183	18,015	2,919	7,679	346	13	79,033	5,389		4,003
1932	914	18,053	2,635	6,816[20]	332	11	82,139	4,163		4,714
				6,267						
1933	952	16,981	2,984	5,906	375	12	83,065	4,220		5,449
1934	964	17,591	2,449	5,640	386	13	81,037	4,471		5,686
1935	976	20,637	2,497	5,761	384	14	82,163	4,865		5,988
1936	944	22,452	2,571	6,478	399	16	84,069	5,354		6,203
1937	944	21,460	2,569	6,902	417	21	88,308	5,884		6,776
1938	...	22,018	2,800	...	441	21	101,556	8,605		7,239
1939	...	27,898	4,245	...	600	40	128,514	12,756		9,453
1940	...	34,426	6,518	...	741	56	181,807	15,135		15,369
							thousand million francs			
1941	...	48,246	13,467	...	842	73	240	20,577		48,798
1942	...	67,718	18,922	...	983	96	313	25,639		335,000
1943	...	83,711	...	...	1,359	108	435	34,702		3,199,000
1944	...	38,834	...	...	1,658	157	568	51,110		...
										thousand million new drachmae[23]
1945	...	69,892	...	24,233	1,561	136	541	...		...
1946	5,657	72,162	...	43,589	1,633	182	638	West Germany		538
1947	4,326[16][17]	78,343[19]	...	58,539	1,641	252	808	million Deutsch-marks		974
		80,374								
1948	5,635	84,861	...	...	1,614	274	849	6,641	...	1,202
1949	5,721	87,890	...	...	1,627	296	1,110	7,698	3,288	1,859

Abbreviations used:— (a) = National Bank issue (million kroner); (b) = National Bank issue (million francs); (c) = National Bank issue (million leva); (d) = bank issues (million koruna); (e) = National Bank issue (million kroner); (f) = Bank of Finland issue (thousand markkaa); (g) = Bank of France issue (million francs); (h) = bank issues (million marks); (i) = national note issues (million marks); (j) = Bank of Greece issue (million drachmae)

See p. 715 for footnotes

H 1 Banknote Circulation

1900–1949

	Hungary (a)	Ireland (b)[7]	S. Ireland (c)[7]	N. Ireland (d)[26]	Italy (e)	Netherlands (f)[8]	Norway (g)	Poland (h)	Portugal (i)	Romania (j)[29]
1900	...	6,830	...	...	1,602	214	66	...	...	117
1901	...	6,763	...	...	1,606	222	63	...	...	130
1902	...	6,810	...	...	1,624	222	63	...	...	164
1903	...	7,272	...	...	1,682	234	61	...	...	175
1904	...	6,713	...	...	1,722	236	60	...	...	179
1905	...	6,401	...	...	1,849	259	66	...	...	196
1906	...	6,470	...	...	2,043	277	69	...	...	239
1907	...	6,784	...	...	2,289	260	73	...	...	273
1908	...	6,681	...	...	2,299	266	73	...	...	263
1909	...	6,882	...	...	2,365	274	78	...	...	272
1910	...	7,439	...	...	2,469	281	84	...	...	299
1911	...	7,611	...	...	2,678	283	93	...	...	382
1912	...	7,410	...	...	2,711	299	99	...	...	463
1913	...	8,293	...	...	2,783	310	108	...	87	424[29]
										437
1914	...	9,095	...	...	3,593	313	134	...	96	578
1915	...	13,585	...	...	5,050	472	162	...	115	762
1916	...	17,571	...	...	6,329	618	251	...	140	1,452
1917	...	20,880	...	...	10,265	746	326	...	193	4,110
1918	...	27,496	...	—	14,087	890	436	1	274	4,638
1919	...	30,580	...	...	18,814	1,023	454	5	370	6,364
1920	14,308	26,863	...	...	22,277	1,052	492	49	611	10,455
1921	25,175	20,602	...	...	21,754	1,052	419	230	737	13,908
1922	75,887	18,067	...	...	20,496	996	395	793	1,054	15,162
1923	931,000	17,081	...	...	19,810	966	406	125,372	1,420	17,917
								million zlotys		
1924	4,514,000	16,559	...	...	20,514	1,018	401	642	1,763	19,356
	million pengos[24]									
1925	416	15,876	...	...	21,450	915	365	663	1,821	20,126
1926	471	15,013	...	...	20,134[14]	852	337	880	1,854	20,951
1927	487	14,666	...	...	18,776	819	331	1,170	1,857	21,026
		million pounds								
1928	513	14.2	0.9	...	17,456	810	315	1,394	1,990	21,211
1929	501	10.8	6.0	...	16,854	833	318	1,404	2,046	21,144
1930	469	10.4	7.1	...	15,681	837	312	1,331	1,994	19,605
1931	423	9.5	7.1	...	14,295	860	334	1,220	2,062	23,750
1932	353	9.2	7.0	...	13,672	1,006	315	1,003	2,001	21,594
1933	369	9.3	7.5	...	13,243	990	327	1,004	1,989	21,219
1934	381	9.5	7.3	...	13,145	937	333	981	2,137	22,307
1935	417	9.7	7.8	...	16,944	889	348	1,007	2,205	23,127
1936	436	10.1	8.4	...	17,831	792	428	1,034	2,257	25,663
1937	466	10.3	9.2	...	18,818	823	449	1,059	2,224	29,391
1938	863	10.4	9.9	5	20,811	934[8]	477	1,406	2,279	34,902
		S. Ireland Bank and State[7]								
			17			992				
1939	975		18	6	26,880	1,152	575	1,928[27]	2,550	48,800
1940	1,387		21	8	34,204	1,552	...	...	2,903	64,349
1941	1,984		24	11	53,759	2,116	...	...	4,488	96,650
1942	2,958		30	14	78,778	3,034	...	...	5,481	117,351
1943	4,392[5]		34	16	180,823	3,478	...	...	6,910	160,016[5]
1944	12,424		38	16	318,985	5,078	...	...	7,642	374,000
					thousand million lire			thou m zlotys		
1945	765,446		43	16	382	1,386	...	...	8,166	1,232,000
	million pengos[25]									
1946	1,024		45	16	505	2,748	1,953	59	8,793	6,397,000
1947	2,099		49	15	788	3,010	2,111	90	8,752	...
1948	2,947		50	12	963	3,115	2,191	129[28]	8,696	...
								3,921		
1949	2,761		55	11	1,048	3,036	2,334	5,157	8,456	...

Abbreviations used:— (a) = National Bank issue (million koruna); (b) = bank issues (thousand pounds); (c) = Eire state issue (thousand pounds); (d) = bank issues (thousand pounds); (e) = bank and state issues (million lire); (f) = bank issues (million gulden); (g) = Bank of Norway issue (million kroner); (h) = Bank of Poland issue (thousand million marks); (i) = bank issues (million escudos); (j) = National Bank issue (million lei).

See p. 715 for footnotes

H 1 Banknote Circulation

1900–1949

	Russia	Spain	Sweden		Switzerland		United Kingdom: G.B.		Yugoslavia
	(a)	(b)	(c)	(d)	(e)	(f)	(g)[1]	(h)[9]	(i)
1900	491	1,592	72	82	–	217	29,366	9,189	...
1901	555	1,639	101	56	–	214	29,552	9,007	...
1902	542	1,623	137	26	–	223	29,407	8,742	...
1903	554	1,609	166	4	–	222	28,944	8,497	...
1904	578	1,599	173	3	–	228	28,313	8,147	...
1905	854	1,550	185	1	–	233	28,968	8,036	...
1906	1,208	1,525	202	–	–	235	28,926	7,925	...
1907	1,195	1,557	190	–	159	196	28,911	7,880	...
1908	1,155	1,643	201	–	204	98	28,840	7,536	...
1909	1,087	1,671	202	–	262	48	29,257	7,373	...
1910	1,174	1,715	206	–	297	–	28,300	7,271	...
1911	1,234	1,763	218	–	315	–	28,610	7,322	...
1912	1,326	1,863	228	–	339	–	28,788	7,476	...
1913	1,495	1,932	234	–	314	–	28,723	7,703	...
1914	1,665	1,974	304	–	456	–	31,605[31]	8,629	...
							60,896		
							million pounds	million pounds	
1915	2,947	2,100	328	–	466	–	90	11	...
1916	5,617	2,360	418	–	537	–	157	14	...
1917	9,104[30]	2,799	573	–	702	–	206	17	...
1918	...	3,334	814	–	976	–	311	23	...
1919	...	3,867	748	–	1,036	–	413	27	...
1920	...	4,326	760	–	1,024	–	449	29	3,344
1921	...	4,244	628	–	1,009	–	437	27	4,688
1922	...	4,137	584	–	976	–	400	24	5,040
1923	220	4,353	576	–	982	–	388	23	5,790
1924	523	4,547	537	–	914	–	391	22	6,002
1925	958	4,440	530	–	876	–	384	22	6,063
1926	1,282	4,339	525	–	874	–	376	21	5,812
1927	1,502	4,202	526	–	917	–	375	21	5,743
1928	...	4,397	546	–	953	–	372	21	5,528
1929	...	4,458	569	–	999	–	362	21	5,818
1930	...	4,767	594	–	1,062	–	359	21	5,397
1931	...	4,993	583	–	1,609	–	355	21	5,172
1932	...	4,834	598	–	1,613	–	360	21	4,773
1933	...	4,825	648	–	1,510	–	371	21	4,327
1934	...	4,696	708	–	1,440	–	379	21	4,384
1935	...	4,837	786	–	1,366	–	395	22	4,890
1936	...	...	893	–	1,482	–	431	22	5,409
1937	...	...	980	–	1,531	–	480	23	5,834
1938	...	...	1,061	–	1,751	–	486	24	6,921
1939	...	...	1,422	–	2,050	–	507	25	9,698
1940	...	...	1,482	–	2,273	–	575	29	13,834
1941	...	13,536	1,700	–	2,337	–	651	34	15,281[32]
1942	...	15,738	2,016	–	2,637	–	808	44	...
1943	...	16,381	2,266	–	3,049	–	966	54	...
1944	...	17,729	2,492	–	3,548	–	1,136	61	...
1945	...	18,951	2,782	–	3,835	–	1,284	65	17,811
1946	...	22,777	2,877	–	4,091	–	1,358	68	20,500
1947	...	26,014	2,895	–	4,383	–	1,383	72	29,493
1948	...	26,472	3,113	–	4,594	–	1,254	66	39,229
1949	....	27,645	3,287	–	4,566	–	1,269	69	45,097

Abbreviations used:— (a) = all note issues (million rubels); (b) = Bank of Spain issue (million pesetes); (c) = Bank of Sweden issue (million kronor); (d) other bank issues (million kroner); (e) = National Bank issue (million francs); (f) = other issues (million francs); (g) = Bank of England issue (thousand pounds); (h) other bank issues (thousand pounds); (i) = National Bank issue (million dinari).

See p. 715 for footnotes

H 1 Banknote Circulation

1950–1975

	Austria (a)	Belgium (b)	Denmark (c)	Finland[3] (d)	France[4] (e)	Germany (f)	East Germany (g)	Greece[22] (h)	S Ireland[7] (i)	N Ireland[26] (j)
1950	6,349	88,599	1,709	344	1,389	8,232	3,363	1,887	57	10
1951	8,032	94,967	1,817	448	1,679	9,243	3,331	2,198	62	9
1952	9,048	97,784	1,966	462	1,934	10,509	3,353	2,476	67	9
1953	10,474	101,592	2,118	450	2,133	11,547	3,564	3,503	72	8
								million new drachmae[34]		
1954	12,252	102,679	2,145	479	2,348	12,350	4,298	3,890	75	8
1955	13,026	107,556	2,217	559	2,604	13,641	4,123	4,950	77	8
1956	14,260	111,533	2,372	607	2,895	14,511	4,496	5,870	76	9
1957	15,403	112,670	2,432	606	3,135	16,133	3,479	6,813	81	10
1958	16,598	117,353	2,642	651	3,296	17,661	3,756	7,448	79	9
					million new francs[33]					
1959	17,693	118,325	2,892	694	33,516	19,040	4,161	8,601	78	9
1960	18,727	124,090	3,006	727	35,329	20,470	4,543	10,187	82	9
1961	20,878	129,078	3,318	837	40,077	22,992	4,225	11,630	87	9
1962	22,419	138,481	3,504	774	45,253	24,147	4,413	13,761	91	8
1963	23,970	150,508	3,835	944	51,049	25,427	4,512	16,121	99	7
1964	25,740	160,287	4,117	1,003	55,710	27,692	4,503	19,320	114	7
1965	27,547	170,269	4,442	1,029	64,170	29,456	5,162	22,338	112	7
1966	29,606	175,311	4,906	1,106	67,628	30,770	5,466	25,076	119	8
1967	31,240	177,482	5,084	1,052	70,508	31,574	5,844	32,327	125	9
1968	32,450	183,243	5,444	1,160	72,193	32,499	6,428	31,896	138	11
1969	34,121	183,002	5,816	1,298	72,398	34,617	7,045	34,182	144	13
1970	35,666	188,212	5,387	1,344	75,621	36,480	7,407	37,545	159	15
1971	38,998	201,766	5,382	1,479	77,430	39,494	7,684	41,553	169	22
1972	44,730	222,560	5,874	1,730	83,678	44,504	8,778	48,953	188	27
1973	48,857	238,506	6,523	1,907	88,930	46,247	9,181	62,897	221	28
1974	52,365	256,104	6,732	2,260	96,955	50,272	9,581	77,959	248	30
1975	56,036	288,381	8,206	2,617	106,743	55,143	10,139	89,077	295	34

Abbreviations used:— (a) = National Bank issue (million kroner); (b) = National Bank issue (million francs); (c) = National Bank issue (million kroner); (d) = Bank of Finland issue (million markkaa); (e) = Bank of France issue (thousand million francs); (f) = bank issues (million Deutschmarks); (g) = National note issue (million marks); (h) = Bank of Greece issue (thousand million new drachmae); (i) = Southern Ireland Bank and state issues (thousand pounds); (j) = bank issues (million pounds).

See p. 715 for footnotes

H 1 Banknote Circulation

1950–1975

	Italy	Netherlands[8]	Norway	Poland	Portugal	Spain	Sweden	Switzerland	United Kingdom Great Britain		Yugoslavia
	(a)	(b)	(c)	(d)	(e)	(f)	(g)	(h)	(i)[1]	(j)[9]	(k)
1950	1,165	2,911	2,415	4,649	8,526[37]	31,661	3,513	4,664	1,287	70	39,966
					7,747						
1951	1,292	2,991	2,667	5,595	8,400	36,239	...	4,927	1,342	74	38,346
1952	1,381	3,118	2,916	6,216	8,638	38,493	...	5,122	1,435	81	49,579
1953	1,449	3,330	3,128	8,447	8,923	38,758	...	5,229	1,532	90	67,647
1954	1,538	3,579	3,321	10,094	9,388	42,954	...	5,412	1,630	96	87,774
1955	1,671	3,955	3,305	11,573	9,876	47,045	5,319	5,516	1,760	102	87,070
1956	1,818	4,073	3,502	17,419	10,319	55,821	5,598	5,810	1,875	109	94,319
1957	1,914	4,187	3,469	19,672	10,875	66,653	5,840	5,931	1,966	117	125,444
1958	2,061	4,418	3,511	22,613	11,479	72,519	6,059	6,109	2,035	119	140,710
1959	2,237	4,513	3,675	23,175	12,154	74,116	6,266	6,344	2,105	121	173,825
1960	2,424	4,900	3,823	26,333	12,776	78,927	6,559	6,854	2,211	125	190,541
1961	2,779	5,278	4,043	30,549	14,777	88,593	6,870	7,656	2,306	128	242,779
1962	3,234	5,565	4,287	32,564	15,689	103,823	7,330	8,506	2,327	126	280,277
1963	3,699	6,019	4,517	33,231	16,501	119,853	7,869	9,035	2,398	126	355,514
1964	3,914	6,742	4,756	36,656	17,514	141,564	8,386	9,722	2,562	129	455,102
											million new dinari[35]
1965	4,282	7,479	5,118	39,382	19,681	164,847	8,746	10,043	2,727	130	5,089
1966	4,595	8,060	5,501	44,052	20,031	187,018	9,297	10,651	2,893	134	6,874
1967	5,126	8,350	5,918	48,358	20,501	209,196	9,965	11,327	2,972	136	7,822
1968	5,390	8,442	6,257	53,273	19,916	226,558	11,243	12,047	3,119	142	9,423
1969	6,100	8,865	6,644	57,425	19,603	253,191	10,962	12,518	3,244	148	11,742
1970	6,619	9,316	7,365	58,644	22,520	273,880	11,319	13,106	3,417	155	14,702
1971	7,281	9,763	8,070	67,328	24,544	308,772	12,704	14,310	3,682	164	18,038[5]
											18,349
1972	8,747	10,684	8,801	78,196	26,911	349,787	13,925	16,635	3,955	177	23,524
1973	10,029	11,244	9,536	96,312	31,109	418,168	15,229	18,296	4,430	196	28,964
1974	11,160	12,153	10,866	117,151	61,859	487,991	17,274	19,436	4,964	227	34,783
1975	12,921	13,843	12,461	141,197	103,682	580,014	20,106	19,128	5,724	266	41,887

Abbreviations used:— (a) = bank and state issues (thousand million lire); (b) = bank issues (million gulden); (c) = Bank of Norway issue (million kroner); (d) = Bank of Poland issue (thousand million zlotys); (e) = bank issues (million escudos); (f) = Bank of Spain issue (million pesetas); (g) = Bank of Sweden issue (million kronor); (h) = National Bank issue (million francs); (i) = Bank of England issue (million pounds); (j) = other bank issues (million pounds); (k) = National Bank issue (million dinari).

See p. 715 for footnotes

H 1 Banknote Circulation

NOTES

1. SOURCES:— The main sources were the official publications noted on p.xv with gaps filled from League of Nations, *Statistical Yearbooks, Memorandum on Currency and Central Banks, Money and Banking,* and *Monthly Bulletin of Statistics.* The Germany figures to 1913 are taken from W.G. Hoffman, *Das Wachstum der Deutschen Wirtschaft seit der Mitte des 19 Jahrhunderts* (Berlin, etc., 1965); the British and Irish figures to 1938 from B.R. Mitchell & Phyllis Deane, *Abstract of British Historical Statistics* (Cambridge, 1962), where the original sources are given, or the Bank of England, *Statistical Summary* (for Irish and legal tender notes); the Russian figures to 1917 from P.A. Khromov, *Economic Development of Russia in the 19th and 20th Centuries, 1800–1917* (Moscow, 1950); the Bank of Spain figures to 1873 from J-A. Galvarriato, *El Banco de España* (Madrid, 1932) and the Swedish total note circulation 1750–1803 from L. Jorberg, *A History of Prices in Sweden 1732–1914* (2 vols., Lund, 1972). In addition the following data were supplied by the respective national statistical offices:— Belgium to 1857; Finland to 1899; and Netherlands to 1864.

2. Unless otherwise indicated, the statistics are of circulation at the end of each year.

FOOTNOTES

[1] Figures to 1764 are at 31 August. For 1766–73 they are at 28/29 February. From 1775 to 1834 (1st line) they are averages of end-February and end-August figures. From 1834 (2nd line) to 1841 they are averages of 12 monthly figures. From 1842–44 they are averages of average weekly circulation in thirteen 4-week periods; and from 1845 onwards they are averages of 52 weekly figures.

[2] The circulation in the Italian provinces is not included. In 1857 it amounted to 25 million gulden.

[3] Figures to 1820 are at 31 March. The original currency units have been converted into markkaa.

[4] Averages of 52 weekly figures.

[5] Subsequently including a small amount of coin.

[6] September-December only.

[7] **Averages of 12 monthly figures to 1841, and averages of average weekly circulation in 13 4-week periods from 1842 to 1938 (1st line). Figures from 1938 (2nd line) are at 31 December. Note: *All* Irish banks are included up to 1938 (1st line), and only southern Irish banks subsequently.**

[8] Averages of 12 month-end figures for years ended 31 March up to 1884. Circulation at 31 March from 1885 to 1938 (1st line), and year-end figures subsequently.

[9] Country bank and Scottish bank issues, being averages of 12 monthly figures to 1841, and averages of average weekly circulation in 13 4-week periods subsequently.

[10] Two kroner = 1 gulden.

[11] Figures to 1857 are averages of monthly figures. The year-end figures for 1851 and 1855 are 50 and 96 respectively.

[12] Figures from 1874 to 1913 (1st line) are at 31 July. 2 kroner = 1 rigsdaler.

[13] Subsequently including state note issues, for which only isolated figures are available previously, viz:- 1850 154; 1862 98; 1863 101; 1864 104; 1865 108; and 1872 184.

[14] At 1 June or 1 July for 1894–1926.

[15] January 1922.

[16] At 7 December.

[17] The figures are subsequently averages of 12 month-end figures.

[18] At 25 October.

[19] For 1927–1947 (1st line) at 25 December.

[20] Subsequently excluding 10 and 20 koruna notes.

[21] 1 new mark = 1 million million old marks.

[22] Including the issues of the Bank of Crete and the Ionian Bank up to 1919 when they ceased.

[23] 1 new (1944) drachma = 50 thousand million old drachmae.

[24] 1 pengo = 12,500 paper koruna.

[25] 1 forint = 400,000 quadrillion pengoes.

[26] Averages of average weekly circulation in 13 4-week periods.

[27] August.

[28] The figures from 1948 (2nd line) is of total monetary circulation, and is in million new (1950) zloties, one of which equalled 100 old zloties.

[29] Averages of 12 monthly figures to 1913 (1st line), and year-end figures subsequently.

[30] On 1 October 1917 (according to P.I. Lyaschenko, *History of the National Economy of Russia*) the circulation was 17,175 million rubels.

[31] Treasury-issued currency notes are included from 1914 (2nd line) until 1928, when they were absorbed into the Bank of England issue.

[32] March.

[33] 1 new franc = 100 old francs.

[34] 1 new (1954) drachma = 1,000 old drachmae.

[35] 1 new dinar = 100 old dinari.

[36] **Subsequently in thousand Rixdalers. In 1776 6 dalers silvermynt equalled 1 Rixdaler.**

[37] **Subsequently cash in the hands of the public.**

H 2 DEPOSITS IN COMMERCIAL BANKS

1848–1899

	Belgium[1] (a)	Finland[2] (b)	France[3] (c)	Germany[4] (d)	Norway[5] (e)	Russia[6] (f)	Sweden[7] (g)	United Kingdom[8] (h)
1848	...	...	...	...	0.1	...	...	...
1849	...	...	...	...	0.3	...	...	...
1850	...	...	...	...	0.3	...	...	...
1851	...	...	...	...	...	...	...	...
1852	...	...	...	6	...	...	...	...
1853	...	...	...	19	...	...	...	...
1854	...	...	...	22	...	...	...	...
1855	...	...	...	30	1.5	...	...	...
1856	...	...	...	42	...	...	...	...
1857	...	...	...	51	...	...	...	...
1858	...	...	...	58	...	...	...	...
1859	...	...	...	52	...	...	...	...
1860	...	...	...	157	16.4	...	...	...
1861	...	...	...	180	...	...	...	...
1862	...	1,837	...	202	...	...	...	...
1863	...	5,709	...	...	...	...	...	...
1864	...	11,235	...	...	...	...	...	...
1865	...	15,210	...	...	25	...	...	...
1866	...	13,535	...	...	...	...	...	...
1867	...	15,502	...	...	...	...	...	...
1868	...	17,996	...	...	...	...	...	...
1869	...	17,553	...	220	...	...	...	...
1870	...	18,556	...	230	35	...	...	...
1871	...	19,286	...	250	...	...	...	...
1872	...	20,188	...	498	...	...	...	...
1873	...	22,429	...	716	...	275	...	...
1874	...	28,671	...	648	...	300	...	...
1875	455	30,899	...	542	55	278	201	...
1876	423	34,509	...	479	68	227	235	...
1877	430	31,848	...	385	64	275	235	555
1878	468	28,259	...	424	65	254	230	505
1879	562	27,100	...	527	70	197	242	525
1880	537	33,145	...	529	81	207	269	495
1881	653	39,004	...	678	85	227	275	535
1882	687	43,533	...	626	97	212	288	555
1883	766	46,742	...	780	99	214	306	565
1884	700	49,967	...	921	100	219	326	565
1885	701	54,096	...	1,034	100	264	333	555
1886	639	56,048	...	1,084	98	255	348	565
1887	646	55,819	...	1,058	101	235	354	575
1888	643	62,492	...	1,142	105	212	354	605
1889	694	77,143	...	1,558	117	230	354	635
		million markkaa						
1890	705	89	...	1,509	120	288	371	665
1891	690	98	...	1,548	114	320	385	685
1892	673	106	...	1,531	123	285	391	675
1893	676	118	...	1,558	127	268	405	675
1894	703	132	...	1,999	136	308	420	695
1895	736	167	...	2,242	151	305	435	765
1896	804	197	...	2,251	153	354	453	775
1897	1,044	232	...	2,547	179	448	510	785
1898	915	256	...	2,995	203	551	583	815
1899	1,033	282	...	3,449	219	548	688	835

Abbreviations used:— (a) = million francs; (b) = thousand markkaa; (c) = thousand million francs; (d) = million marks; (e) = million kronor; (f) = million rubels; (g) = million kroner; (h) = million pounds.

Other abbreviations used where space demands:— Czech: Czechoslovakia; U.K.: United Kingdom

See p. 721 for footnotes

H 2 Deposits in Commercial Banks

1900–1939

	Austria[9] (a)	Belgium[1] (b)	Bulgaria[13] (c)	Czech[15] (d)	Denmark[16] (e)	Finland[2] (f)	France[3] (g)	Germany[4] (h)	Greece[22] (i)	Hungary[23] (j)	Ireland[25] (k)	Italy[26] (l)
1900	...	1,128	...	...	...	289	4.5	3,742	...	...	...	...
1901	...	1,079	...	...	...	306	5.0	3,730	...	...	...	...
1902	...	1,085	...	...	...	301	4.7	4,141	...	...	...	...
1903	...	1,168	...	...	...	326	5.3	4,409	...	...	...	...
1904	...	1,240	...	...	...	336	6.6	5,182	...	...	...	...
1905	...	1,455	...	...	...	398	6.5	6,060	...	...	...	...
1906	...	1,707	...	...	...	394	7.1	6,876	...	...	...	...
1907	...	1,666	...	...	...	456	7.4	7,662	...	...	...	...
1908	...	1,846	...	...	...	478	8.5	8,027	...	...	...	...
1909	...	1,938	...	...	...	517	9.2	8,915	...	...	53	...
1910	...	2,150	...	...	...	544	9.7	10,025	...	...	55	...
1911	...	2,362	...	...	...	582	10.1	10,344	...	...	57	...
1912	...	2,512[1]	...	...	...	591	10.3	10,369	...	...	58	...
1913	4,181[10] 2,720	2,335	170	...	...	619	11.4	10,606[4] 9,720	207	4,739[24]	62	1,707
1914	...	...	...	...	...	640	...	...	...	...	66	...
1915	...	...	...	...	...	724	...	...	...	...	67	...
1916	...	...	...	...	...	917	...	...	...	...	75	...
1917	...	...	...	...	...	1,470[2]	...	...	...	...	91	...
1918	9,974	...	...	...	...	2,846	...	...	439	...	121	7,681
1919	16,378	...	...	...	...	3,385	25.1	...	636	...	153	12,377
1920	37,204[11] 77,908	8,271	1,578	9,207	...	3,613	25.3	...	797	...	183	16,524
1921	370,410	8,518	2,247	11,616	1,195	2,788	26.3	...	1,053	...	194	18,468
1922	7,452,300	9,506	2,461[13] 3,266	13,091	1,067	4,136	27.9	...	1,138	...	193	...
	million schillings											
1923	1,378	10,156	4,729	12,048	910	4,746	30.6	1,995[20]	1,669	...	178[25] 147	12,330
1924	1,856	9,815	5,394	10,629	612	5,402	28.0	5,086	2,104	...	141	14,533
1925	2,093	11,264	6,497	10,646	589	5,464	39.0	7,103	2,232	1,125	133	14,968
1926	2,667	14,294	7,139	10,777	515	6,102	47.0	9,678	2,617	1,502	128	15,916[26] 17,379
1927	2,947	18,159	8,635	11,675	618	6,982	54.0	11,666	2,941	2,123	128	18,321
1928	3,219	20,734	11,726	12,711	554	7,380	72.9	13,197	5,289[22] 11,287	2,703	128	19,591[26] 22,431
1929	2,714	21,290	12,678	12,566	551	7,481	74.3	13,831	11,192	2,820	124	22,411
1930	3,210	...	12,492	12,993	614	7,698	79.9	12,653	11,950	2,970	123	21,844
1931	...	20,037	12,256	11,221	545	7,378	75.2	8,902	10,610	2,413	122	19,789
1932	1,691	17,506	11,983	10,832	533[17] 514	7,155	74.4	7,575	9,778	2,164	131	19,808
1933	1,449	18,083	11,280	10,884	554	7,498	67.8	6,953	10,714	2,099	124	20,351
1934	1,372	...	11,823	11,471	559	7,635	66.9	7,297	11,877	2,100	120	20,311
1935	1,374	16,067[12]	12,306	10,857	560	7,966	54.3	7,876	12,021	2,182	118	20,614
1936	1,307	17,312[12] 24,100[1]	13,135	10,946	610	8,598	62.3	8,560[4] 6,573	12,597	2,183	119	22,613
		thou m francs										
1937	1,180[11]	23.0	14,301	11,115	674	10,030	70.4	7,263	13,737	2,352	117[25] 21.8	24,053[26] thousand million lire 19.0
1938	...	19.7	15,187	...	670	10,755	85.4[3] 80	8,298	12,381	2,403	22.4	21.1
1939	...	16.0	16,401[13] 12,070	...	833	10,365[18] 9,400	107	...	12,753[22]	2,685[23] 1,038	24.3	26.6

Abbreviation used:— (a) = million kronen; (b) = million francs; (c) = million leva; (d) = million koruna; (e) = million kroner; (f) = million markkaa; (g) = thousand million francs; (h) = million marks; (i) = million drachmas; (j) = million pengos; (k) = million pounds; (l) = million lire.

See p. 721 for footnotes

H 2 Deposits in Commercial Banks

1900–1939

	Netherlands[27] (a)	Norway[5] (b)	Poland[29] (c)	Portugal[30] (d)	Romania[31] (e)	Russia[7] (f)	Spain[32] (g)	Sweden[6] (h)	Switzerland[33] (i)	U.K.[8] (j)	Yugoslavia[35] (k)
1900	...	257	...	...	...	536	...	772	...	845	...
1901	...	284	...	...	...	545	...	838	...	845	...
1902	...	281	...	...	...	613	...	874	...	865	...
1903	...	291	...	...	...	722	...	915	...	845	...
1904	...	298	...	...	...	776	...	957	...	845	...
1905	...	302	...	...	...	671	...	1,042	...	865[8] 861	...
1906	...	339	...	...	...	761	...	1,174	1,179	877	...
1907	...	373	...	...	...	818	...	1,314	1,221	883	...
1908	...	391	...	...	...	977	...	1,395	1,295	906	...
1909	...	428	...	...	...	1,262	...	1,414	1,494	926	...
1910	...	449	...	...	...	1,675	...	1,465	1,585	957	...
1911	...	482	...	...	...	1,817	...	1,516	1,717	990	...
1912	...	520	...	...	...	2,293	...	1,602	1,844	1,024	...
1913	292	592	...	...	...	2,539	...	1,692	1,837	1,075	...
1914	...	630	...	...	...	2,873	...	1,794	1,863	1,227	...
1915	...	856	...	...	...	3,931	...	1,999	2,260	1,373	...
1916	...	1,441				6,748	...	2,497	2,797	1,579	...
1917	...	2,200	...	63	...	...	...	3,221	3,416	1,825	...
1918	1,001	2,720	...	101	...	...	...	4,502	3,906	2,112	...
1919	1,265	2,973	1,895	328	...	...	...	5,018	4,308	2,424	...
1920	1,351	3,113	6,733	...	8,068	...	...	5,095	4,440	2,560	4,461
1921	1,328	2,982	32,626	...	13,059	...	...	4,853	4,050	2,589[8] 1,812	5,353
1922	1,207	2,697	136,603	...	18,406	...	...	4,325	3,789	1,774	6,962
1923	1,235	2,261	... (l)	...	17,729	...	...	3,869	3,863	1,674	7,464
1924	1,201	2,065	183	707	20,357	...	4,124	3,675	4,117	1,671	8,713
1925	1,261	1,993	306	736	28,286	...	3,577	3,484	4,251	1,662	10,898
1926	1,293	1,993	458	815	33,519	...	3,916	3,453	4,708	1,665	10,682
1927	1,367	1,765	661	867	39,268	...	4,823	3,484	5,247	1,713	11,448
1928	1,390	1,645	716	984	46,860	...	4,591	3,431	5,738	1,766	12,226
1929	1,355	1,596	679	1,048	57,314	...	5,078	3,481	6,462	1,800	13,185
1930	1,473	1,498	642	883	53,323	...	5,552	3,631	6,781[33] 3,267	1,801	14,172
1931	1,242	1,373	486	811	30,206	...	4,067	3,554	3,035	1,760	11,733
1932	1,112	1,245	448	818	26,183	...	4,485	3,556	2,731	1,791	9,556
1933	996	1,137	456	838	22,997	...	4,605	3,629	2,544	1,953	8,682
1934	944	1,048	496	965	18,284	...	4,727	3,552	2,544	1,880	8,060
1935	776	864	487	956	21,015	...	5,508	3,632	2,094	1,999	7,713
1936	964[27] 917	840	602	1,133[30] 3,680	19,965	...	...	3,833	2,712[33] 3,198	2,142[34] 2,216	7,745
1937	1,489	939	737	3,770	21,882[31] (m) 23	...	...	3,999	3,868	2,287	7,311
1938	1,493	1,011	776	3,680	25	...	...	4,260	3,789	2,277	5,940
1939	1,189	985	...	4,170	24	...	...[32]	4,401	2,986	2,248	6,452

Abbreviations used:— (a) = million guilders; (b) = million kroner; (c) = million marks; (d) = million escudos; (e) = million lei; (f) = million rubels; (g) = million pesetas; (h) = million kronor; (i) = million francs; (j) = million pounds; (k) = million dinars; (l) = thousand million new zlotys; (m) = thousand million lei.

See p. 721 for footnotes

H 2 Deposits in Commercial Banks

1940–1975

	Austria[9] (a)	Belgium[1] (b)	Bulgaria[13] (c)	Czechoslovakia[15] (d)	Denmark[16] (e)	Finland[2] (f)	France[3] (g)	West Germany[21] (h)	Greece[22] (i)	Hungary[23] (j)	Ireland[25] (k)	Italy[26] (l)
1940	...	20.1	13,240	...	949	12.2	114	...	...	1,219	26.6	36.8
1941	...	24.0	15,700	...	1,239	13.4	...	...	...	1,637	32.1	47
1942	...	29.9	23,700	...	1,475	15.8	...	...	...	2,074	37.9	63
1943	...	41.2	34,400	...	1,823	18.6	...	...	...	2,869	44.4	88
1944	...	24.0	41,690	...	2,467	21.8	260[19]	...	...	3,664	50.7	185
				(m)						(m)		
1945	...	50.9	53,650	11.5	2,984	28.1	436	...	...	...	56.3	290
1946	...	63.6[1]	66,600	42.5	2,714	31.3	617	...	244	406	62.1	532
1947		58.5	103,290[14]	54.3	2,258	37.8	755	...	524	1,110	67.0	745
1948	...	61.6	...	53.3	2,138	44.1	1,172	5.42	720	3,740	71.9	1,044
1949	7.2	64.9	...	126.8	2,069	54.4	1,403	6.74	1,483	6,494	78.9	1,226
1950	7.3	62.9[36] / 63.8	...	...	2,041	61.0	1,530	8.11	1,974	...	79.8	1,410[18]
1951	8.9	69.4	...	...	2,058	89.5	1,795	9.79	2,643	...	87.0	1,693
1952	9.5[9]	72.5	...	...	2,139	87.8	2,035	10.49	(n)	...	88.3	2,059
1953	9.3	74.4	...	...	2,232	103	2,320	11.4	1.94	...	90.6	2,395
1954	12.0	76.9	...	...	2,136	118	2,715	13.7	2.18	...	105	2,621
1955	11.0	82.0	...	...	2,201	134	3,059	15.2	2.69	...	98.8	2,882
1956	10.9	84.5	...	...	2,341	135	3,404	16.4	2.51	...	101	3,117
1957	11.3	82.5	...	...	2,414	141	3,794	18.6	3.23	...	107	3,280
1958	12.8	89.2[1]	...	...	2,968	162	4,026[19] / 3,979	21.8	3.58	...	113	3,678
							(o)					
1959	14.5	95.0	...	...	3,184	206	48.21	25.1	4.28	...	120	4,293
1960	15.2	93.6	...	...	3,272	236	55.34	26.6	5.00	...	129	4,981
1961	15.9	105	...	...	3,706	268	65.00	31.3	5.61	...	139	5,776
1962	18.4	113	...	...	4,103	291	79.14	33.8	6.19	...	155	6,968
						(p)						
1963	20.1	124	...	...	5,062	3,156	90.76	36.5	6.81	...	174	7,859
1964	21.3	134	...	...	5,831	3,500	99.00	39.5	8.02	...	181	8,463
1965	23.5	145	...	...	6,623	3,826	109.54	42.9	9.06	...	189	10,101
1966	23.7	161	...	...	7,757	4,262	119.33	43.0	9.76	...	199	11,621
1967	25.7	170	...	...	8,545	4,731	125.38	49.7	9.97	...	217	13,610
1968	28.4	191	...	...	10,545	5,413	140.05	55.4	12.15	...	233	15,612
1969	31.5	201	...	...	11,531	6,262	136.97	58.6	13.53	...	249	18,206
1970	34.2	228	...	...	10,596	7,241	156.85	65.4	15.45	...	275	24,357
1971	41.5	256 / 216[38]	...	...	11,219	8,305	180.81	75.0	18.79	...	256	29,559
1972	53.3	259	...	...	12,255	9,947	216.89	85.6	25.50	...	302	34,863
1973	58.3	280	...	...	14,029	11,127	240.41	85.0	28.29	...	303	43,705
1974	59.1	295	...	...	14,309	13,333[18]	282.39	97.1	31.26	...	310	48,058
1975	73.9	348	...	...	...	16,115	322.60	112.9	37.24	...	379	53,553

Abbreviations used:— (a) = thousand million schilling; (b) = thousand million francs; (c) = million leva; (d) = thousand million koruna; (e) = million kroner; (f) = thousand million markkaa; (g) = thousand million francs; (h) = thousand million marks; (i) = thousand million drachmae; (j) = million pengos; (k) = million pounds; (l) = thousand million lire; (m) = million forints; (n) = thousand million new drachmae; (o) = thousand million new francs; (p) = million new markkaa.

See p. 721 for footnotes

H 2 Deposits in Commercial Banks

1940–1975

	Netherlands[27] (a)	Norway[5] (b)	Poland[29] (c)	Portugal[30] (d)	Romania[31] (e)	Spain[32] (f)	Sweden[6] (g)	Switzerland[33] (h)	U.K.[8] (i)	Yugoslavia[35] (j)
1940	1,634	1,401	...	5,020	26	...	4,321	3,649	2,506	5,819[35]
1941	2,046	1,844	...	7,420	45	15.6	4,879	3,827	2,970	...
1942	2,063	2,161	...	10,280	71	15.3	5,157[18] / 5,352	4,047	3,275	...
1943	2,922	2,555	...	11,840	87	16.2	5,958	4,206	3,677	...
1944	3,678[28]	2,782	...	14,870	138	19.0	6,377	4,196	4,153	...
1945	2,714	3,538	...	17,080	409	20.5	7,062	4,677	4,692	...
1946	3,392	3,255	41.1	18,460	1,801	26.0	7,328	5,133	5,097	...
1947	3,892	3,914	88.6	18,040	...	29.5	7,725	5,341	5,650	...
1948	4,164	3,987	150	17,760	...	29.9	7,848	5,449	5,913	...
1949	4,467	3,998	...	16,420	...	33.4	8,609	6,201	5,974	...
1950	4,148[28] / 3,842	3,923	...	17,330 / 17,358[30]	...	38.1	9,141	6,423	6,014	...
										(k)
1951	3,945	4,633	...	19,328	...	44.6	10,728[18] / 10,513	6,640	6,162	...
1952	4,526	4,807	...	20,285	...	52.4 / 48.9[32]	10,358	6,824	6,083	...
1953	4,830	4,831	...	21,050	...	55.1	11,839	7,227	6,256	88
1954	5,100	4,952	...	23,205	...	61.5	12,727	7,369	6,495	139
1955	5,482	5,146	...	24,692	...	72.7	12,609	7,690	6,454	115
1956	5,014	5,252	...	26,721	...	90.0	13,090	8,370	6,288	146
1957	4,703	5,369	...	27,988	...	103	14,263	8,620	6,432	240
1958	5,557	5,335	...	29,712	...	120	15,987	10,090	6,636	250
1959	5,913	5,629	...	32,471	...	128	18,950	10,650	6,935	301
1960	6,225	6,047	...	34,152	...	125	18,524	11,920	7,236	339
1961	6,711	6,316	...	33,992	...	145	19,415	14,020	7,395	481
1962	7,155	6,719	...	36,027	...	176	22,080	15,630	7,611	660
										(l)
1963	7,890	7,145	...	41,783	...	207	24,410	17,010	7,971	10,910
1964	8,285[37] / 8,269	7,921	...	49,566	...	252	26,649	18,010	8,550	13,850
1965	9,197	8,548	...	52,177	...	272	27,731	18,720	8,989	14,020
1966	9,784	9,297[18] / 9,969	...	57,002	...	299	30,303	19,170	9,376	13,700
1967	10,573	11,074	...	60,853	...	340	35,017	20,710	9,772	13,170
1968	12,642	12,823	...	68,935	...	387	40,442	23,850	10,431	15,830
1969	13,812	14,488	...	79,914	...	451	41,050	27,350	10,610	17,190
1970	15,279	16,857	...	79,965	...	471	43,098	31,150	10,151	19,370
1971	16,981	19,174	...	87,982	...	531	47,493	38,170	11,328	22,090 / 20,700[39]
1972	19,165	21,493	...	109,029	...	724	54,426	38,860	14,580	29,800
1973	25,284	25,042	...	141,702	...	936	63,419	37,130	19,708	45,800
1974	32,228	27,994	...	121,236	...	1,118	89,878	34,010	24,715	58,800
1975	32,446	32,674	...	142,840	...	1,303	98,573	36,640	...	83,400

Abbreviations used:— (a) = million guilders; (b) = million kroner; (c) = million zlotys; (d) = million escudos; (e) = thousand million lei; (f) = thousand million pesetas; (g) = million kronor; (h) = million francs; (i) = million pounds; (j) = million dinars; (k) = thousand million dinars; (l) = million new dinars.

See p. 721 for footnotes

H 2 Deposits in Commercial Banks

NOTES

1. SOURCES:— The main sources were the League of Nations, *Memorandum on Commercial Banks, Money and Banking,* and *Statistical Yearbooks;* United Nations, *Statistical Yearbooks;* International Monetary Fund, *International Financial Statistics;* and the official publications noted on p. xv German statistics to 1913 are taken from W.G. Hoffman, *Das Wachstum der Deutschen Wirtschaft seit der Mitte des 19 Jahrhunderts* (Berlin, etc., 1965), and data for the U.K. to 1938 are taken from B.R. Mitchell & Phyllis Deane, *Abstract of British Historical Statistics* (Cambridge, 1962). Belgian data to 1912 were supplied by the Belgian National Institute of Statistics, and Norwegian data for 1848–50, 1865, 1870, and 1875 were supplied by the Norwegian Central Office of Statistics.

2. So far as possible interbank deposits and savings account deposits are excluded.

3. Except as otherwise indicated the statistics are for the end of each year.

FOOTNOTES

[1] Figures to 1912 are of all deposits. From 1913 to 1936 (1st line)they are of deposits of less than 1 month's notice in commercial banks (including overseas branches and agencies). From 1936 (2nd line) to 1946 they are of all deposits in commercial banks, and from 1947 onwards they are of all 'bank money', but deposits of over 1 month's notice are excluded from August 1958.

[2] All deposits in commercial banks, though the coverage of some accounts is incomplete until 1917.

[3] Total bank money (excluding interbank deposits). The figures to 1938 (1st line) are estimates by the I.N.S.E.E., and the 1939 and 1940 figures are official estimates.

[4] Figures to 1913 (1st line) are of all deposits in the credit banks, as they are also from 1936 (2nd line) to 1938 (excluding interbank deposits). From 1913 (2nd line) to 1936 (1st line) they are of all deposits in commercial banks (excluding interbank deposits).

[5] All deposits in commercial banks (excluding interbank deposits).

[6] All deposits in commercial banks.

[7] All deposits by the public in commercial banks.

[8] Figures to 1905 (1st line) are estimates by *The Economist,* having a range of £5 million on either side of the figures fiven here. Initially they included all deposits in U.K. banks (including the Bank of England), but by the 1890's it seems that the estimates are of commercial bank deposits alone. (See R.P. Higonnet in *Quarterly Journal of Economics* (1957) p. 344). From 1905 (2nd line) to 1921 (1st line) the figures are estimates of all deposits (other than bankers' deposits in the Bank of England) in banks operating primarily in the U.K. From 1921 (2nd line) they are of all deposits in the London Clearing Banks.

[9] All deposits in commercial banks to 1937, and all chequeing deposits from 1949 (excluding government deposits from 1953).

[10] Previously Cisleithania, subsequently the Republic.

[11] From 1920 to 1937 (1st line) deposits in agricultural credit institutions are included.

[12] Including one bank operating mainly in the Congo, which had not been included previously.

[13] Figures to 1922 (1st line) are of all deposits in the ten main commercial banks and in the Agricultural and Cooperative Central Banks. From 1922 (2nd line) to 1939 (1st line) the Popular Banks and the smaller commercial banks are also included. Subsequently only commercial banks are covered.

[14] At 30 June.

[15] Figures to 1937are of current account deposits in commercial banks. Subsequently they are of all unblocked accounts.

[16] Sight deposits in commercial banks.

[17] Subsequently excluding foreign accounts.

[18] There was a change in the method of reckoning.

[19] Saarland is included from 1945 to 1958 (1st line).

[20] At 1 January 1924 in the new currency.

[21] All chequeing deposits (excluding interbank and government deposits).

[22] Figures to 1928 (1st line) are of all non-savings deposits in the five main commercial banks. From 1928 (2nd line) to 1939 all commercial banks are covered. From 1946 figures are of all chequeing deposits (excluding interbank and government deposits).

[23] Figures to 1938 (1st line) are of all deposits in commercial banks. Subsequently they are of demand deposits (excluding the government's).

[24] This figure is for Transleithania.

[25] Figures to 1923 (1st line) are of all deposits of joint stock banks. From 1923 (2nd line) to 1937 (1st line) they are of all deposits in financial institutions (excluding interbank deposits) in southern Ireland. From 1937 (2nd line) they are of demand deposits in commercial banks (excluding interbank and government deposits).

[26] Figures to 1926 (1st line) are of all deposits in the four main banks. From 1926 (2nd line) to 1928 (1st line) they are of all deposits in commercial banks (excluding interbank deposits, with deposits in public credit institutions added from 1928 (2nd line) to 1937 (1st line). From 1937 (2nd line) they are of all chequeing deposits (excluding interbank and government deposits).

[27] Figures to 1936 (1st line) are of all deposits in the six main banks (including agencies and branches overseas). Subsequently they are of all chequeing deposits (excluding interbank and government deposits).

[28] From 1945 to 1950 blocked accounts are included.
[29] Current account deposits in commercial banks.
[30] Figures to 1936 (1st line) are of all deposits in commercial banks operating mainly in Portugal. From 1936 (2nd line) to 1950 (1st line) they are of chequeing deposits in banks based in Portugal (excluding interbank and government deposits). Subsequently they are of sight deposits in the hands of the public.
[31] Figures to 1937 (1st line) are of all deposits in commercial banks having a capital of 40 million lei or more (excluding interbank deposits). Subsequently they are of all deposits in commercial banks (excluding interbank and government deposits).
[32] Figures to 1935 are of all deposits in commercial banks (excluding interbank deposits), though the number of banks covered varies slightly from year to year. From 1941 to 1952 (1st line) they are of chequeing deposits (excluding interbank and government deposits. Subsequently they are of the demand deposits of residents, excluding interbank deposits and deposits with the central bank.
[33] Figures to 1930 are of all deposits other than in savings accounts. From 1931 to 1936 (1st line) they are of chequeing accounts and deposit accounts in the big banks and in the cantonal banks. Subsequently they are of chequeing deposits (including deposits in the central bank).
[34] The District Bank is included subsequently.
[35] Figures to 1940 are of all deposits in commercial banks (excluding interbank deposits). Figures from 1953 are of chequeing deposits (excluding interbank and government deposits).
[36] Subsequently including Luxembourg.
[37] Subsequently excluding non-resident's balances in giro accounts.
[38] New and improved series subsequently.
[39] Subsequent statistics relate to "business banks" only.

H 3 DEPOSITS IN SAVINGS BANKS

1817–1869

	Austria[1] (a)	Belgium[3] (b)	Denmark (c)	France (d)	Germany (e)	Hungary[5] (f)	Netherlands (g)	Norway (h)	Sweden (i)	United Kingdom (j)	United Kingdom (k)
1817	...	—	...	—	...	...	—	...	...	0.2	—
1818	...	—	...	—	...	...	—	...	...	1.7	—
1819	...	—	...	—	...	...	—	...	...	2.8	—
1820	...	—	...	—	...	...	—	...	...	3.5	—
1821	...	—	...	—	...	...	—	...	...	4.7	—
1822	...	—	...	—	...	...	—	...	...	6.5	—
1823	...	—	...	—	...	...	—	...	...	8.7	—
1824	...	—	...	—	...	...	—	...	...	11.7	—
1825	...	—	...	—	...	...	—	...	...	13.3	—
1826	...	—	...	—	...	...	—	...	...	13.1	—
1827	...	—	...	—	...	...	—	...	...	14.2	—
1828	...	—	...	—	...	...	—	...	...	15.4[7]	—
1829	...	—	...	—	...	...	—	...	...	14.3	—
1830	...	—	...	—	...	...	—	...	...	14.6	—
1831	...	—	...	—	...	...	—	...	...	14.6	—
1832	...	—	...	—	...	...	—	...	...	14.4	—
1833	...	—	...	—	...	...	—	...	...	15.3	—
1834	...	—	...	—	...	...	—	...	2.3	16.3	—
1835	...	—	...	62	...	...	—	...	...	17.4	—
1836	...	—	...	97	...	...	—	...	...	18.8	—
1837	...	—	...	108	...	...	—	...	...	19.6	—
1838	...	—	...	145	85	...	—	...	...	21.4	—
1839	...	—	...	171	95	...	1.1	...	...	22.4	—
1840	...	—	...	192	108	...	1.2	...	5.2	23.5	—
1841	...	—	...	250	122	...	1.3	...	...	24.5	—
1842	40	—	...	302	134	...	1.4	...	...	25.3	—
1843	46	—	...	347	149	1.0	1.6	...	...	27.2	—
1844	51	—	...	393	159	1.7	1.8	...	...	29.5	—
1845	54	—	...	394	167	...	1.9	...	7.7	30.7	—
1846	59	—	...	396	180	...	2.1	...	...	31.7	—
1847	61	—	17	358	191	...	2.2	...	...	30.3	—
1848	48	—	16	...	179	...	2.0	...	...	28.2	—
1849	...	—	15	74	195	...	3.5	...	...	28.6	—
1850	...	—	16	135	212	...	3.8	17	13	28.9	—
1851	67	—	19	158	230	...	4.1	...	...	30.3	—
1852	...	—	21	245	247	...	3.2	...	...	31.8	—
1853	...	—	26	286	270	...	3.5	...	...	33.4	—
1854	75	—	32	272	295	...	3.7	...	...	33.7	—
1855	...	—	41	272	322	...	4.0	35	22	34.3	—
1856	...	—	47	275	354	...	...	...	...	35.0	—
1857	83	—	48	279	388	...	...	...	...	35.2	—
1858	93	—	44	311	419	...	...	...	...[6]	36.4	—
1859	96	—	50	337	441	...	...	...	25	39.2	—
1860	107	—	57	377	477	...	5.5	44	27	41.5	—
1861	107	—	64	401	529	...	...	...	30	41.7	—
1862	112	—	68	424	578	...	...	...	31	40.8	—
1863	113	—	72	448	648	...	...	...	32	41.2	1.7
1864	112	—	75	462	667	...	6.5	...	33	39.5	3.4
1865	113	0.3	83	493	714	...	8.0	68	36	39.0	5.0
1866	...	2	90	529	720	...	8.3	...	38	36.7	6.5
1867	[157][2]	7	102	571	755	64	9.0	...	40	36.8	8.1
1868	[200][2]	15	111	633	786	85[5] / 86	10.1	...	43	37.2	9.7
1869	245	17	112	711	849	110	11.1	...	47	37.9	11.7 / 13.5

Abbreviations used:— (a) = Regulated banks (million gulden); (b) = Caisse Generale d'Epargne (million francs); (c) = all savings accounts (million kroner); (d) = private savings banks (million francs); (e) = all savings banks (million marks); (f) = all savings banks (million gulden); (g) = general savings banks (million guilders); (h) = all savings banks (million kroner); (i) = private savings banks (million kronor); (j) = trustee savings banks (million pounds); (k) = Post Office savings bank (million pounds).

See p. 732 for footnotes

H 3 Deposits in Savings Banks

1870–1919

	Austria[1]		Belgium[3]		Bulgaria	Czechoslovakia		Denmark	Finland	
	(a)	(b)	(c)	(d)	(e)	(f)	(g)	(h)	(i)	(j)
1870	286	–	20	1	–	...	...	118	–	...
1871	341	–	22	2	–	...	...	133	–	...
1872	403	–	27	3	–	...	...	153	–	...
1873	483	–	34	5	–	...	...	174	–	...
1874	539	–	37	7	–	...	...	197	–	...
1875	589	–	45	9	–	...	...	214	–	...
1876	610	–	66	13	–	...	...	221	–	...
1877	625	–	79	17	–	...	...	208	–	...
1878	649	–	92	21	–	...	...	201	–	...
1879	699	–	108	24	–	...	...	218[10]	–	...
1880	745	–	125	30	–	...	...	254	–	...
1881	792	–	128	37	–	...	...	338	–	...
1882	826	–	128	45	–	...	...	350	–	...
1883	868	4	142	53	–	...	...	366	–	...
1884	926	11	159	65	–	...	...	377	–	...
1885	986	25	189	83	–	...	...	378	–	...
1886	1,054	39	217	102	–	...	...	424	–	...
1887	1,091	41	240	122	–	...	...	462	338	...
1888	1,154	43	260	142	–	...	...	481	711	...
1889	1,236	50	283	163	–	...	...	501	1,102	...
1890	1,283	55	325	192	–	...	...	510	1,310	...
1891	1,336	62	333	205	–	...	...	520	1,253	...
1892	1,407	72	351	225	–	...	...	540	1,107	...
1893	1,462	83	390	258	–	...	...	564[4] / 438	948	...
1894	1,531	91	427	289	–	...	...	465	981	...
	million kronen									
1895	3,195	198	453	318	–	...	...	487	1,129	...
1896	3,320	228	481	347	1	...	...	509	1,386	...
1897	3,435	287	532	387	2	...	...	522	2,001	...
1898	3,518	323	564	420	3	...	...	533	2,640	...
1899	3,603	338	608	459	4	...	...	519	3,056	...
1900	3,718	360	662	504	4	...	...	514	3,731	...
1901	3,900	387	735	562	6	...	...	526	4,008	...
1902	4,155	420	731	564	7	...	...	568	4,328	...
1903	4,369	451	735	575	10	...	...	593	5,084	...
1904	4,574	456	764	601	14	...	...	615[11] / 674	5,358	...
1905	4,748	516	786	629	19	...	...	703	5,205	...
1906	4,904	606	812	655	24	...	...	717	6,290	...
1907	5,077	586	844	695	27	...	...	723	7,309	...
1908	5,394	549	886	734	29	...	...	739	7,424	...
1909	5,720	584	920	771	34	...	...	768	7,107	...
1910	6,045	622	965	814	37	...	...	803	7,238	...
1911	6,360	671	1,008	862	43	...	...	844	7,932	...
1912	6,416	644	1,058	909	46	...	...	838	8,513	...
1913	6,590	590	1,099	954	51[8]	...	...	858	8,857	...
1914	6,515	1,058	1,068	...	49	...	...	894	6,952	...
1915	6,673	1,171	1,048	...	56	...	...	981	9,550	...
									million markkaa	
1916	...[1]	1,635[1]	1,052	...	92	...	...	1,109	15.68	...
1917	4,072	...	1,090	...	184	...	...	1,253	24,23	...
1918	5,192	...	1,214	...	248	...	...	1,452	28.19	...
1919	5,255	3,425	1,306	1,121	232	5,326	1,402	1,459	33.92	360

Abbreviations used:— (a) = Regulated banks (million gulden); (b) = Post Office savings bank (million gulden); (c) = Caisse Generale d'Epargne (million francs); (d) = Post Office savings bank (million francs); (e) = Post Office savings bank (million leva); (f) = Regulated banks (million koruna); (g) = Post Office savings bank (million koruna); (h) = all savings accounts (million kroner); (i) = Post Office savings bank (thousand markkaa); (j) = other savings banks (million markkaa).

See p. 732 for footnotes

H 3 Deposits in Savings Banks

1870–1919

	France		Germany	Greece	Hungary[5]	Italy		Netherlands		Norway
	(a)	(b)	(c)	(d)	(e)	(f)	(g)	(h)	(i)	(j)
1870	632[12]	–	908[14]	–	121	...	–	11.1	–	82
1871	538	–	1,031	–	147	...	–	13.2	–	...
1872	515	–	1,200	–	162	447	–	14.8	–	...
1873	545	–	1,427	–	161	450	–	16.6	–	109
1874	574	–	1,663	–	169	467	–	18.9	–	125
1875	660	–	1,878	–	185	527	–	23	–	128
1876	769	–	2,051	–	203	553	2	27	–	134
1877	863	–	2,190	–	206	574	6	30	–	137
1878	1,016	–	2,294	–	216	602	11	33	–	136
1879	1,155	–	2,434	–	243	657	26	33	–	133
1880	1,280	–	2,615	–	260	687	46	37	–	139
1881	1,409	–	2,774	–	284	715	67	40	1	144
1882	1,754	48	2,962	–	294	744	85	42	2	152
1883	1,816	77	3,179	–	314	801	117	44	3	159
1884	2,022	115	3,415	–	325	888	156	47	5	166
1885	2,211	154	3,658	–	336	954	184	49	6	168
1886	2,314	191	3,943	–	357	1,033	229	53	9	169
1887	2,365	224	4,234	–	364	1,077	249	56	11	170
1888	2,495	267	4,545	–	389	1,112	276	58	14	175
1889	2,684	332	4,863	–	423	1,139	300	60	18	187
1890	2,912	431	5,134	–	458	1,166	323	62	21	194
1891	3,053	506	5,340	–	490	1,177	348	62	24	197
1892	3,227	616	5,587	–	521	1,215	380	63	28	201
1893	3,140	611	5,925	–	534	1,258[16]	416[16]	66	32	207
1894	3,287	691	6,270	–	554	1,307	441	70	38	217
					million kronen					
1895	3,395	754	6,792	–	1,151	1,344	481	73	44	226
1896	3,382	785	7,244	–	1,185	1,347	496	76	53	235
1897	3,427	844	7,707	–	1,246	1,361	555	78	62	252
1898	3,400	875	8,162	–	1,311	1,382	586	79	70	271
1899	3,407	930	8,486	–	1,330	1,431	644	77	78	288
1900	3,264	1,010	8,824	–	1,366	1,467	696	80	85	306
1901	3,349	1,080	9,541	–	1,435	1,505	734	79	94	322
1902	3,283	1,107	10,313	88	1,496	1,572	796	82	102	334
1903	3,188	1,118	11,089	209	1,577	1,630	878	84	110	349
1904	3,246	1,187	11,895	256	1,668	1,718	992	88	120	365
1905	3,377	1,278	12,663	197	1,763	1,811	1,085	92	130	374
1906	3,434	1,339	13,414	247	1,860	1,898	1,228	93	140	403
1907	3,543	1,434	13,908	258	1,946	2,041	1,435	91	145	430
1908	3,580	1,539	14,547	306	2,054	2,165	1,524	97	152	452
1909	3,833	1,640	15,646	279	2,207[15]	2,305	1,604	107	160	478
					[3,413]					
1910	3,933	1,710	16,782	293	[3,782][15]	2,397	1,792	111	164	507
1911	3,909	1,704	17,820	305	[4,229][15]	2,463	1,890	119	171	539
1912	3,947	1,746	18,682	323	[4,146][15]	2,492	1,965	124	177	567
1913	4,011[13]	1,818	19,687	584	[4,236][15]	2,595	2,108	130	184	607
1914	3,939	1,807	20,500	719	[3,684][15]	2,546	2,021	118	185	638
1915	3,692	1,656	20,400	1,180	[4,226][15]	2,561	1,990	121	189	724
1916	3,342	1,429	21,400	1,375	[5,419][15]	2,975	2,193	136	207	952
1917	3,563	1,455	25,400[14]	1,246	...	3,430	2,708	152	223	1,244
1918	3,910[12]	1,612[12]	31,800	1,686	...[15]	4,428	3,478	176	242	1,566[17]
1919	5,144	2,087	37,000	5,012	...	5,454	5,189	205	268	1,838

Abbreviations used:— (a) = private savings banks (million francs); (b) = National Savings Bank (million francs); (c) = all savings banks (million marks); (d) = Post Office savings bank (thousand drachmae); (e) = all savings banks (million gulden); (f) = ordinary savings banks (million lire); (g) = Post Office savings bank (million lire); (h) = general savings banks (million guilders); (i) = Post Office savings bank (million guilders); (j) = all savings banks (million kroner).

See p. 732 for footnotes

H 3 Deposits in Savings Banks

1870–1919

	Romania	Russia	Spain		Sweden		Switzerland	United Kingdom	
	(a)	(b)	(c)	(d)	(e)	(f)	(g)	(h)	(i)
1870	–	5	...	–	57	–	...	38.3	15.1
1871	–	...	...	–	71	–	...	39.2	17.0
1872	–	...	...	–	87	–	...	40.3	19.3
1873	–	...	...	–	106	–	...	41.2	21.2
1874	–	...	16	–	124	–	...	42.3	23.2
1875	–	5	23	–	133	–	...	43.5	25.2
1876	–	...	28	–	143	–	...	44.6	27.0
1877	–	...	38	–	145	–	...	45.6	28.7
1878	–	...	43	–	139	–	...	45.9	30.4
1879	–	...	50	–	135	–	...	45.6	32.0
1880	–	8	57	–	146	–	...	46.0	33.7
1881	1	9	61	–	160	–	...	46.4	36.2
1882	2	11	68	–	173	–	...	47.2	39.0
1883	4	13	71	–	190	–	...	47.8	41.8
1884	5	17	74	–	204	0.8	...	48.9	44.8
1885	6	25	81	–	219	1.5	...	49.7	47.7
1886	7	42	81	–	231	2.1	...	50.4	50.9
1887	9	65	99	–	240	2.9	...	51.1	54.0
1888	10	88	82	–	253	4.7	...	50.4	58.6
1889	12	111	104	–	268	8.5	...	49.1	63.0
1890	15	139	95	–	275	13	...	48.0	67.6
1891	18	191	139	–	284	16	...	47.0	71.6
1892	18	239	128	–	291	20	...	46.7	75.9
1893	21	283	136	–	308	23	...	46.7	80.6
1894	21	330	149	–	324	30	...	48.1	89.3
1895	23	368	155	–	339	38	...	50.0	97.9
1896	24	409	161	–	360	50	...	51.4	108
1897	27	466	155	–	384	58	...	53.1	116
1898	32	537	153	–	403	64	...	54.6	123
1899	29	608	172	–	415	60	...	56.0	130
1900	29	662	179	–	437	56	...	56.0	136
1901	32	723	191	–	467	54	...	56.5	140
1902	37	784	218	–	496	54	...	57.1	145
1903	42	861	239	–	531	54	...	57.2	146
1904	45	911	260	–	568	55	...	57.2	148
1905	52	831	283	–	602	55	...	58.3	152
1906	59	1,035	299	–	645	54	1,367	59.4	156
1907	62	1,149	310	–	682	51	1,402	59.3	158
1908	61	1,208	376	–	714	46	1,490	59.9	161
1909	60	1,283	395	–	760	45	1,592	62.0	165
1910	63	1,397	420	–	809	46	1,691	63.3	169
1911	64	1,503	448	–	857	47	1,753	65.2	177
1912	54	1,595	478	–	904	48	1,763	67.2	182
1913	58	1,685	500	–	953	48	1,771	68.7	187
1914	57	1,835	479	–	987	45	1,800	69.5	191
1915	57	2,449	529	–	1,065	48	1,841	66.8	186
1916	50	3,890	574	16	1,207	54	1,935	68.5	197
1917	51	...	650	32	1,382	64	2,079	66.5	203
1918	67	...	742	47	1,624	75	2,337	75.1	235
1919	105	...	849	66	1,871	83	2,621	86.8	266

Abbreviations used:— (a) = National Savings Bank (million lei); (b) = all savings banks (million rubels); (c) = private savings banks (million pesetas); (d) = Post Office savings bank (million pesetas); (e) = private savings banks (million kronor); (f) = Post Office savings banks (million kronor); (g) = all savings accounts (million francs); (h) = trustee savings banks (million pounds); (i) = Post Office savings bank (million pounds).

See p. 732 for footnotes

H 3 Deposits in Savings Banks

1920–1969

	Austria		Belgium			Bulgaria	Czechoslovakia		Denmark
	(a)	(b)	(c)	(d)	(e)	(f)	(g)	(h)[9]	(i)
1920	6,781	7,776	1,504	1,322	...	224	5,887	2,213	1,517
1921	11,304	34,666	1,712	1,486	...	278	7,407	2,399	1,620
1922	138,343	742,238	1,845	1,609	...	279	8,706	2,343	1,785
1923	880,000	1,715,437	1,971	1,777	...	256	10,421	2,355	1,823
	million schillings								
1924	267	209	2,235	2,022	...	279	11,565	1,954	1,872
1925	529[18] / 536	246	2,571	2,339	...	299	12,489	2,057	1,931
1926	766	288	2,760	2,475	...	356	13,772	1,825	1,949
1927	987	314	3,516	3,144	...	508	15,497	2,164	1,967
1928	1,246	356	4,267	3,838	...	638	17,030	2,635	2,018
1929	1,414	381	5,549	5,011	...	684	18,033	2,275	2,097
1930	1,635	396	7,768	7,060	...	874	19,656	2,289	2,179
1931	1,479	321	9,248	8,435	...	1,268	21,742	1,953	2,169
1932	1,520	303	9,864	9,106	...	1,486	21,904	1,823	2,162
1933	1,512	290	10,054	9,252	...	1,706	20,688	1,681	2,185
1934	1,584	350	10,589	9,698	...	2,024	20,620	1,626	2,190
1935	1,677	368	10,809	9,812	...	2,252	21,350	1,768	2,181
1936	1,733	366	11,966	10,330	...	2,520	21,252	2,072	2,190
1937	...	390	13,022	11,608	...	2,858	20,922	2,256	2,198
1938	...	...	13,158	11,806	...	3,330	...	2,382	2,264
1939	...	...	12,404	11,163	...	3,613	...	...	2,180
1940	...	...	11,934	10,753	...	4,047	...	...	2,203
1941	...	...	12,255	10,831	...	5,061	...	...	2,439
1942	...	...	13,667	11,926	...	6,632	...	...	2,728
1943	...	...	17,248	14,998	...	8,400	...	...	3,158
1944	...	...	20,672	18,081	...	9,363	...	...	3,769
1945	...	2,191	19,404	16,766	...	11,169	...	...	4,272
1946	...	3,615	21,459	18,434	3,833	...	7,280	11,273	4,539
1947	1,137	2,394	25,835	21,716	4,263	...	11,931	13,934	4,718
							thousand million koruna		
1948	1,487	1,024	30,407	25,514	4,789	...	...	...	4,814
1949	1,739	1,239	33,715	28,400	5,469	...	...	...	4,983
1950	2,103	1,292	35,615	30,361	6,001	...	...	...	4,993
1951	2,389	1,552	38,457	32,291	6,780	...	...	...	4,991
1952	3,114	1,753	44,686	37,722	8,258	...	...	...	5,169
1953	4,223	2,577	49,884	42,164	9,864	...	...	...	5,408
1954	5,806	2,882	53,823	45,925	11,543	...	...	6,145	5,510
1955	7,038	3,413	56,793	48,741	13,848	...	...	7,041	5,688
1956	8,586	3,872	61,170	52,311	15,741	...	...	8,306	5,961
1957	10,482	4,456	64,931	55,963	17,558	...	...	9,000	6,299
1958	12,860	5,605	72,118	61,914	20,049	...	...	10,045	6,853
1959	16,241	6,838	78,808	68,833	23,456	...	...	11,080	7,436
1960	19,090	6,846	83,042	72,875	25,832	...	...	11,971	7,876
1961	21,131	7,567	88,745	78,014	29,451	...	...	11,329	8,461
1962	24,511	8,768	97,542	85,039	34,815	...	...	12,035	9,083
1963	28,402	9,835	103,087	89,643	41,274	...	...	12,607	9,946
1964	33,470	9,996	107,503	93,062	46,714	...	...	12,850	10,787
1965	37,778	10,979	117,664	96,820	54,510	...	...	12,525	11,722
1966	41,896	10,962	125,966	106,221	62,996	...	...	12,812	12,898
1967	46,808	11,994	138,047	113,079	69,122	...	...	13,225	13,995
1968	52,080	12,505	152,406	119,357	78,099	...	...	13,599	15,611
1969	58,745	12,563	163,913	122,188	86,295	...	...	14,069	17,026

Abbreviations used:— (a) = Regulated banks (million kronen); (b) = Post Office savings bank (million kronen); (c) = Caisse Generale d'Epargne (million francs); (d) = Post Office savings bank (million francs); (e) = private savings banks (million francs); (f) = Post Office savings bank (million leva); (g) = Regulated banks (million koruna); (h) = Post Office savings bank (million koruna); (i) = all savings banks (million kroner).

See p. 732 for footnotes

H 3 Deposits in Savings Banks

1920–1969

	Finland			France		Germany	East Germany	Greece	Hungary[5]
	(a)	(b)	(c)	(d)	(e)	(f)	(g)	(h)	(i)
1920	60.32	1,010	8.7	5,833	2,354	44,600	...	5,572	...
1921	86.52	1,190	11.6	6,993	2,697	...	...	9,989	...
1922	108	1,390	15.9	7,799	3,052	million new marks	...	15,108	...
1923	127	1,590	21.7	8,287	3,272	5	...	33,807	49,441
									million pengo
1924	147	1,820	28.1	8,577	3,419	595	...	62,756	261
								million drachmae	
1925	162	2,110	46.1	9,854	3,936	1,693	...	103	341
1926	184	2,340	82.4	11,237	4,418	3,182	...	120	330
1927	198	3,120	156	14,607	6,674	4,839	...	176	417
1928	209	3,710	274	17,962	9,085	7,205	...	260	472
1929	225	3,930	349	20,314	11,659	9,314	...	385	541
1930	242	4,180	400	23,570	15,033	10,752	...	673	561
1931	279	4,224	420	30,175	20,686	10,123	...	1,084	533
1932	299	4,223	420	33,669	23,614	10,195	...	1,256	547
1933	327	4,410	450	34,739	24,120	11,953	...	1,767	536
1934	356	4,770	520	35,337	24,696	12,814	...	2,139	364
1935	376	5,200	620	36,575	25,456	13,819	...	2,402	316
1936	402	5,870	790	34,921	23,975	14,615	...	2,871	316
1937	455	6,930	1,150	36,256	25,112	16,062	...	3,203	358
1938	502	7,580	1,380	37,563[12]	26,028[12]	18,009	...	3,624	419
1939	453	7,720	1,480	39,294	27,456	...	...	3,211	490
1940	1,170[19]	8,140	1,720	40,013	27,672	...	...	3,713[21]	606[22] / 499
1941	1,870	8,180	1,920	44,829	31,761	...	...	3,553	582
1942	2,970	9,370	2,430	53,405	39,166	...	...	...	541
1943	5,450	11,510	3,430	69,640	52,678	...	...	...	807
1944	7,990	13,700	4,500	96,554	81,713	...	...	...	...
	thousand million markkaa			thousand million francs					
1945	11.37	18.83	6.93	139	131	...	...	...	...
						West Germany million D. marks			
1946	13.65	20.78	8.39	152	140	...	...	...	...
1947	19.93	24.92	11.37	162	147	...	...	...	...
1948	21.94	29.33	14.03	206	192	1,159	...	...	...
1949	27.24	37.46	18.19	249	238	2,197	...	...	...
1950	32.30	41.90	21.61	317	301	2,898	1,093	...	...
1951	42.24	55.26	31.76	357[12]	337[12]	3,563	1,231	...	...
1952	48.86	68.96	39.25	450	389	5,314	1,729	...	...
1953	51.31	80.62	44.52	560	469	8,120	2,130	...	...
								million new drachmae	
1954	55.7	97.1	54.6	669	560	11,930	2,988	29	...
1955	58.5	114	63.9	850	664	14,791	3,852[20] / 3,861	123	...
1956	64.7	118	66.0	991	755	16,963	4,763	295	...
1957	59.1	123	70.2	1,098	823	20,487	7,080	743	...
1958	68.8	137	77.7	1,283	942	25,168	8,885	1,141	...
1959	70.9	160	89.9	1,519	1,091	31,309	11,079	1,855	...
				million new francs					
1960	77.3	189	110	17,347	12,055	36,998	13,925	2,447	...
1961	87.0	217	129	19,746	13,286	42,280	15,989	3,191	...
1962	100.5	232	138	22,925	14,900	48,611	17,158	4,229	...
1963	million new markkaa								
1963	1,117	2,448	1,503	26,376	16,794	56,517	18,902	5,682	...
1964	1,227	2,750	1,738	31,850	19,764	64,909	21,913	6,997	...
1965	1,322	3,104	2,010	36,326	22,170	75,074	25,044	8,101	...
1966	1,471	3,510	2,301	41,459	25,007	84,880	27,677	10,111	...
1967	1,595	3,810	2,493	45,741	27,122	95,985	30,885	11,156	...
1968	1,803	4,161	2,781	50,520	29,334	108,623	34,453	14,614	...
1969	2,055	4,547	3,166	60,549	33,170	120,270[32] / 120,812	38,412	17,667	...

Abbreviations used:— (a) = Post Office savings bank (million markkaa); (b) = other savings banks (million markkaa); (c) = Co-operative bank (million markkaa); (d) = private savings banks (million francs); (e) = National Savings Bank (million francs); (f) = all savings banks (million marks); (g) = all savings banks (million marks); (h) = Post Office savings bank (thousand drachmae); (i) = all savings banks (million kronen).

See p. 732 for footnotes

H 3 Deposits in Savings Banks

1920–1969

	Southern Ireland		Italy		Netherlands		Norway	Poland	Portugal
	(a)	(b)	(c)	(d)	(e)	(f)	(g)	(h)	(i)
1920	...	...	6,234	6,980	217	273	2,053	...	215
1921	...	...	7,428	8,148	240	283	2,295	...	308
1922	...	...	8,530	8,720	...	298	2,439	...	358
1923	1.6	1.1	10,211	9,078	...	305	2,528	...	463
1924	2.1	1.1	11,925	9,912	...	307	2,555	...	487[24]
1925	2.4	1.2	12,784	10,619	281	312	2,541	164	615
1926	2.6	1.2	12,954[16]	10,633[16]	306	321	2,527	307	789
1927	2.8	1.2	13,766	10,139	327	329	2,423	583	1,043
1928	3.1	1.2	15,685	10,819	354	341	2,352	889	1,447
1929	3.2	1.2	16,459	11,774	381	351	2,287	1,172	1,822
1930	3.4	1.2	17,372	13,032	430	375	2,234	1,431	1,983[25] / 1,622
1931	3.7	1.3	18,181	14,675	449	439	2,150	1,467	1,868
1932	4.2	1.3	18,743	17,016	446	511	2,114	1,568	2,208
1933	4.8	1.5	19,524	19,403	466	529	2,051	1,672	2,319
1934	5.6	1.6	19,617	20,427	485	540	1,980	1,795	2,517
1935	6.5	1.8	18,637	19,958	484	540	1,990	1,873	2,550
1936	7.5	1.9	18,803	22,309	495	546	1,863	1,896	2,611
1937	8.5	2.0	19,064	25,520	622	603	1,889	2,168	2,637
1938	9.6	2.1	17,601	29,233	628	679	1,971	2,302	2,750
1939	10.7	2.3	17,550	32,008	558	670	1,926	...	2,953
1940	11.8	2.4	19,424	37,302	481	516	1,820	...	3,215
1941	13.6	2.6	23,460	46,911	471	479	2,066	...	3,850
1942	16.7	2.9	28,255	59,465	545	543	2,424	...	5,366
1943	20.9	3.4	31,250	61,317	717	793	2,838	...	5,823
1944	26.4	4.0	43,124	65,030	848	1,008	3,325	...	7,073
								million new zlotys	
1945	32.7	4.7	76,803	91,896	1,175	1,803	4,118	...[23]	7,930
			thousand million lire						
1946	36.4	5.3	121	140	1,105	1,545	4,004	1.4	8,168
1947	36.9	5.4	176	199	1,147	1,514	4,019	4.2	8,139
1948	39.0	5.7	275	342	1,156	1,445	4,280	9.5	8,039
1949	43.9	6.6	350	522	1,238	1,440	4,488	46	7,393
1950	48.1	7.3	401	688	1,246	1,365	4,600	77	7,419
1951	53.4	8.2	451	796	1,236	1,298	4,753	190	8,330
1952	57.1	8.8	538	962	1,328	1,338	5,008	276	9,054
1953	61.8	9.5	626	1,150	1,504	1,402	5,338	436	9,587
1954	66.7	10.6	753	1,268	1,753	1,503	5,671	751	9,957
1955	71.2	11.2	887	1,363	1,996	1,697	5,961	1,274	10,508
1956	73.5	11.8	1,044	1,457	2,147	1,913	6,325	2,230	11,011
1957	76.0	12.1	1,218	1,562	2,124	1,956	6,723	5,399	11,617
1958	78.7	12.7	1,377	1,694	2,329	2,142	7,023	7,202	12,303
1959	82.5	13.9	1,622	1,869	2,654	2,369	7,414	10,987	12,998
1960	86.7	15.1	1,882	2,066	3,006	2,646	7,898	14,307	13,472
1961	91.5	16.5	2,210	2,308	3,408	2,896	8,345	16,384	13,343
1962	97.2	17.7	2,603	2,611	3,857	3,230	8,898	21,506	14,347
1963	102	18.4	2,977	2,951	4,365	3,568	9,423	28,649	15,294
1964	107	19.6	3,318	3,252	4,859	3,880	9,928	35,016	17,203
1965	110	19.8	3,904	3,627	5,426	4,209	10,769	42,256	18,500
1966	111	20.6	4,553	4,011	6,025	4,491	11,741	51,951	19,307
1967	116	21.8	5,153	4,358	6,743	4,840	12,773	63,021	20,509
1968	118	22.8	5,798	4,697	7,305	5,246	14,080	73,412	23,085
1969	121	27.5	6,344	5,018	8,059	5,594	15,282	86,890	27,203

Abbreviations used:— (a) = Post Office savings bank (million pounds); (b) = trustee savings banks (million pounds); (c) = ordinary savings banks (million lire); (d) = Post Office savings bank (million lire); (e) = general savings banks (million guilders); (f) = Post Office savings bank (million guilders); (g) = all savings banks (million krone); (h) = all savings banks (million zlotys); (i) = all savings banks (million escudos).

See p. 732 for footnotes

H 3 Deposits in Savings Banks

1920–1969

	Romania		Spain		Sweden		Switzerland	United Kingdom		Yugoslavia
	(a)	(b)	(c)	(d)	(e)	(f)	(g)	(h)	(i)	(j)
1920	137	...	939	85	2,024	84	2,731	91.3	267	...
1921	165	...	1,283	105	2,130	100	2,831	92.4	264	...
1922	175[26]	503	1,515	122	2,243	119	3,034	98.3[30]	268[30]	...
1923	167	791	1,617	138	2,359	135	3,248	103	273	...
1924	157	996	1,734	157	2,399	149	3,266	107	280	405
1925	146	1,471	1,846	177	2,489	165	3,410	110	286	447
1926	166	1,900	2,571	194	2,621	190	3,655	111	284	475
1927	183	2,172	3,012	216	2,706	206	3,873	114	285	646
1928	187	2,761	3,547	239	2,793	223	4,064	121	289	703
1929	198	4,246	4,000	252	2,884	284	4,304	124	285	1,020
							4,723[25]			
1930	255	4,553	4,672	265	2,961	338	5,339	133	290	1,188
1931	624	4,740	4,646	278	3,051	382	5,569	143	289	1,134
1932	809[27]	4,565	4,981	299	3,142	451	5,913	155	306	1,387
1933	1,539	5,061	5,380	318	3,206	440	5,877	171	327	1,722
1934	2,260	...	5,825	...	3,312	473	5,888	182	355	1,858
1935	3,091	3,667	6,500	370	3,351	497	5,766	197	390	2,030
1936	3,767	2,965	...	367	3,402	514	5,680	212	432	2,449
1937	5,301	2,712	...	391	3,523	558	5,981	224	471	3,090
1938	5,405	2,773	...	450	3,685	618	6,232	239	509	2,995
1939	5,316	...	7,020	370	3,679	628	6,138	252	551	...
1940	5,387	...	7,876[28]	318	3,596	649	5,847	276	654	...
1941	10,096	...	[5,717][29]	344	3,807	743	5,948	323	823	...
1942	18,166	...	[6,012][29]	[466][29]	4,137	908	6,274	379	1,005	...
1943	...	...	[7,063][29]	421	4,611	1,111	6,715	448	1,241	...
			6,549							
1944	...	...	8,644	475	5,106	1,269	7,166	527	1,494	...
										[31]
1945	...	...	10,940	542	5,606	1,422	7,368	603	1,777	478
1946	...	...	12,721	606	6,034	1,589	7,706	670	1,982	767
1947	...	...	15,697	698	6,357	1,722	8,104	732	1,943	1,075
1948	...	...	17,527	809	6,751	1,923	8,363	799	1,948	1,847
1949	...	...	20,409	910	7,231	2,083	8,893	857	1,948	2,268
1950	...	...	24,623	1,028	7,619	2,143	9,274	909	1,934	2,442
1951	...	...	29,393	1,185	8,060	2,325	9,700	932	1,876	2,549
1952	...	...	35,131	1,393	8,703	2,639	10,295	954	1,812	3,861
1953	...	...	40,646	1,653	9,343	2,851	11,093	969	1,747	5,797
1954	...	...	47,446	1,966	9,978	3,026	11,929	1,020	1,727	9,439
1955	...	...	55,255	2,362	10,696	3,225	12,677	1,054	1,700	14,088
1956	...	...	64,126	2,771	11,509	3,436	13,267	1,094	1,688	18,793
1957	...	...	74,374	3,402	12,459	3,723	13,810	1,140	1,677	31,651
1958	...	...	86,311	3,932	13,442	4,036	14,945	1,165	1,646	46,657
1959	...	...	95,251	4,433	14,337	4,368	16,561	1,239	1,680	67,342
1960	...	...	122,231	5,266	15,403	4,725	18,082	1,315	1,710	91,681
1961	...	...	146,179	6,480	16,391	5,016	20,153	1,501	1,737	122,750
1962	...	...	175,811	8,178	17,699	5,478	22,325	1,517	1,760	148,412
1963	...	...	209,730	10,684	18,957	5,931	24,510	1,685	1,792	213,300
1964	...	...	268,930	13,355	20,531	6,342	26,344	1,881	1,814	296,700
										million new dinari
1965	...	...	333,615	16,532	22,263	6,696	28,547	2,022	1,823	3,523
1966	...	...	463,172	19,715	24,511	7,240	30,832	2,149	1,740	5,863
1967	...	...	545,416	23,572	27,259	7,762	33,676	2,266	1,673	7,549
1968	...	...	642,342	27,298	29,685[17]	8,261	37,250	2,365	1,590[36]	9,697
1969	...	...	765,790	31,703	30,779	8,829	40,286	2,417[36]	1,757	12,927

Abbreviations used:— (a) = National Savings Bank (million lei); (b) = other savings institutions (million lei); (c) = private savings banks (million pesetas); (d) = Post Office savings bank (million pesetas); (e) = Private savings banks (million kronor), (f) = Post Office savings bank (million kronor); (g) = all savings accounts (million francs); (h) = trustee savings banks (million pounds); (i) = Post Office savings banks (million pounds); (j) = Post Office savings bank (million dinari).

See p. 732 for footnotes

H 3 Deposits in Savings Banks

1970–1975

	Austria			Belgium		Bulgaria	Czechoslovakia		Denmark
	(a)	(b)	(c)	(d)	(e)	(f)	(g)[9]	(h)	(i)*
1970	65,736	13,431	177,338	123,498	94,875	...	...	13,625	18,103
1971	74,978	16,724	208,159	132,812	114,303	...	...	14,275	19,875
1972	83,842	21,283	241,569	145,746	141,119	...	...	14,892	22,365
1973	94,287	25,946	272,539	156,510	167,014	...	...	15,481	24,835
1974	109,042	22,452	300,511	165,180	187,392	...	...	15,936	27,378
1975	132,917	...	358,479	190,485	226,603	...	...	16,103	30,304

Abbreviations used:— (a) = Regulated banks (million kronen); (b) = Post Office savings bank (million kronen); (c) = Caisse Generale d'Epargne (million francs); (d) = Post Office savings bank (million francs); (e) = private savings banks (million francs); (f) = Post Office savings bank (million leva); (g) = Regulated banks (million koruna); (h) = Post Office savings bank (million koruna); (i) = all savings banks (million kroner).

	Finland			France		West Germany	East Germany	Greece	Hungary[5]
	(a)	(b)	(c)	(d)	(e)	(f)	(g)	(h)	(i)
1970	2,296	5,058	3,641	69,912	36,648	132,346	42,041	21,699	...
1971	2,707	5,675	4,059	81,135	44,939	147,334	45,223	26,473	...
1972	3,367	6,546	4,723	83,850	50,527	164,979	49,010	30,884	...
1973	4,171	7,579[25]	5,536[25]	101,253	54,881	172,950	53,528	32,664	...
1974	5,015	8,830	6,694	117,688	64,585	190,662	58,010	39,449	...
1975	6,376	10,413	8,072	144,763	79,370	224,423	62,453	52,029	...

Abbreviations used:— (a) = Post Office savings bank (million markkaa); (b) = other savings banks (million markkaa); (c) = Co-operative bank (million markkaa), (d) = private savings banks (million francs); (e) = National Savings Bank (million francs); (f) = all savings banks (million marks), (g) = all savings banks (million marks); (h) = Post Office savings bank (thousand drachmae); (i) = all savings banks (million kronen).

	Southern Ireland		Italy		Netherlands		Norway	Poland	Portugal
	(a)	(b)	(c)	(d)	(e)	(f)	(g)	(h)	(i)
1970	139	45.5	6,110	5,186	8,769	5,999	17,423	97,226	32,736
1971	140	45.2	6,999	6,258	9,815	6,700	19,786	112,543	34,425
1972	147	55.5	8,279	7,618	10,984	7,583	22,050	139,561	38,140
1973	154	63.6	9,760	9,190	12,006	8,292	24,493	174,410	35,932
1974	165	76.9	11,596	9,787	12,901	9,026	27,290	216,213	42,655
1975	180	95.1	15,824	11,843	13,372	10,402	30,737	251,153	...

Abbreviations used:— (a) = Post Office savings bank (million pounds); (b) = trustee savings bank (million pounds); (c) = ordinary savings banks (million lire); (d) = Post Office savings bank (million lire); (e) = general savings banks (million guilders); (f) = Post Office savings bank (million guilders); (g) = all savings banks (million krone); (h) = all savings banks (million zlotys); (i) = all savings banks (million Escudos).

	Romania		Spain		Sweden		Switzerland	United Kingdom		Yugoslavia
	(a)	(b)	(c)	(d)	(e)	(f)	(g)	(h)	(i)	(j)
1970	...	...	862,326	37,302	32,128	9,566[33]	43,710	2,635	1,797	16,819
1971	...	...	1,051,894	45,784	34,986	9,989	52,306[35] 41,277	2,916	1,882	21,150
1972	...	...	1,285,603	54,312	38,008	10,418	48,624	3,270	2,047	24,971
1973	...	...	1,537,084	63,743	41,872	11,151	53,942	3,414	2,086	31,294
1974	...	...	1,737,866	74,511	45,873	11,553[34]	56,875	3,669	2,121	40,277
1975	...	...	2,183,141	88,259	50,915	...	64,768	2,982	2,181	52,539

Abbreviations used:— (a) = National Savings Bank (million lei); (b) = other savings institutions (million lei); (c) = private savings banks (million pesetas); (d) = Post Office savings bank (million pesetas); (e) = Private savings banks (million kroner); (f) = Post Office savings bank (million kroner); (g) = all savings accounts (million francs) (h) = trustee savings banks (million pounds); (i) = Post Office savings banks (million pounds); (j) = Post Office savings bank (million dinari).

See p. 732 for footnotes

H 3 Deposits in Savings Banks

NOTES

1. SOURCES:– The main sources are the official publications noted on p.xv with gaps filled from the League of Nations, *Statistical Yearbooks.* German statistics to 1913 are taken from W.G. Hoffman, *Das Wachstum der Deutschen Wirtschaft seit der Mitte des 19 Jahrhunderts* (Berlin, etc., 1965); Russian statistics to 1915 are taken from P.A. Khromov, *Economic Development of Russia in the 19th and 20th Centuries, 1800–1917* (Moscow, 1950). Spanish statistics to 1940 are taken from the *Anuario Financiero Sociedades Anonimos.* The U.K. statistics to 1938 are taken from H. Oliver Horne, *A History of Savings Banks* (Oxford, 1947). The Greek data for 1902–5 and 1954–55 were supplied by the National Statistical Service of Greece.

2. In principle, this table relates to all deposits in institutions which are described as savings banks, with government (or post office) savings banks shown separately; but there are exceptions indicated in the footnotes.

3. Except where otherwise indicated the statistics are for the end of each year.

FOOTNOTES

[1] Cisleithania (excluding the Italian provinces) to 1916, Republic of Austria subsequently.
[2] Excluding certain districts in Galicia.
[3] There are, in addition, two savings banks run by communes. In 1862 they had deposits of 5 million francs, rising to 12 million francs in 1913, 63 million francs in 1938, and 500 million francs in 1969.
[4] From 1893 (2nd line) savings banks only.
[5] Transleithania to 1918, but excluding Croatia-Slavonia up to 1868 (2nd line). Subsequent figures are for the territory established by the treaty of Trianon.
[6] Previous statistics are known to be incomplete.
[7] Previous statistics are of the amounts due by the National Debt Commissioners to trustees. In 1829 this was £0.5 million greater than the amount owing to depositors.
[8] A figure given later is 66, which may apply to the postwar territory.
[9] With the establishment of the Communist government this became the National Savings Bank.
[10] Subsequent figures are at 31 March in the year following that indicated.
[11] Statistics back to 1905 were revised upward at a later date.
[12] For 1871–1918 and 1939–51 Alsace-Lorraine is excluded.
[13] For 1914–18 includes Algeria.
[14] For 1871–1917 including Alsace-Lorraine.
[15] These figures are of all savings deposits rather than deposits in Savings Banks.
[16] From 1894 to 1926 at 1 June or 1 July.
[17] Subsequently excluding interbank deposits.
[18] Subsequently includes banks in Burgenland.
[19] Giro accounts began in 1940.
[20] The reason for this break is not given.
[21] At 31 July.
[22] Subsequently only the Post Office Bank.
[23] Subsequently deposits in the General Savings Bank.
[24] More complete coverage subsequently.
[25] There was a change in the basis of reckoning.
[26] Previous figures are at 31 March in the year following that indicated.
[27] Current accounts began in 1933.
[28] This break occurs on a change of source (see note 1)
[29] Including blocked accounts.
[30] Subsequently excluding Southern Ireland.
[31] Subsequently savings deposits in all institutions.
[32] Subsequently including Central Giro.
[33] Subsequently excluding personal accounts.
[34] At 30 June.
[35] This break is apparently caused by the exclusion of *livrets de depôts.*
[36] Subsequently at 31 March following the year shown.

H 4 TOTAL CENTRAL GOVERNMENT EXPENDITURE (in millions)

1750–1799

	Austria[1] (gulden)	U.K.[2] (pounds)
1750	...	7[3]
1751	...	6[3]
1752	...	7[3]
1753	...	6
1754	...	6
1755	...	7
1756	...	10
1757	...	11
1758	...	13
1759	...	15
1760	...	18
1761	...	21
1762	...	20
1763	...	14
1764	...	11
1765	...	11
1766	...	10
1767	...	10
1768	...	9
1769	...	10
1770	...	11
1771	...	10
1772	...	11
1773	...	10
1774	...	10
1775	...	10
1776	...	14
1777	...	15
1778	...	18
1779	...	20
1780	...	23
1781	65	26
1782	81	29
1783	71	24
1784	78	18
1785	84	16
1786	81	17
1787	82	15
1788	112	16
1789	120	16
1790	113	17
1791	112	18
1792	91	17
1793	116	20
1794	151	27
1795	136	38
1796	158	38
1797	132	46
1798	133	47
1799	154	47

1800–1849

	Austria (gulden)	Belgium (francs)	France (francs)	Greece (drachmae)	Netherlands (guilders)	Russia (paper rubels)	Switzerland (francs)	U.K. (pounds)
1800	167	...	...	...	...	...	...	[63][3]
1801	150	...	...	...	...	...	...	65[2]
1802	118	...	...	...	...	...	...	55
1803	115	...	...	...	...	109	...	53
1804	114	...	...	...	...	122	...	63
1805	146	...	...	...	...	125	...	71
1806	163	...	...	...	...	122	...	73
1807	207	...	...	...	...	159	...	73
1808	190	...	...	...	...	248	...	78
1809	262	...	...	...	...	278	...	82
1810	351	...	...	...	...	279	...	82
1811	118	...	...	...	...	272	...	87
1812	96	...	...	...	...	342	...	95
1813	111	...	...	...	...	423	...	111
1814	112	...	...	...	...	457	...	113
1815	117	...	931	...	...	391	...	99
1816	131	...	1,056	...	...	428	...	71
1817	128	...	1,189	...	...	438	...	59
1818	127	...	1,434	...	...	443	...	58
1819	160	...	896	...	...	476	...	58
1820	215	...	907	...	...	500	...	58
1821	186	...	908	...	...	482	...	58
1822	157	...	949	...	...	456	...	56
1823	189	...	1,118	...	...	479	...	54
1824	151	...	986	...	...	417	...	55
1825	146	...	982	...	...	413	...	54
1826	146	...	977	...	...	404	...	56
1827	146	...	987	...	...	422	...	56
1828	140	...	1,024	...	...	407	...	53
1829	146	...	1,015	...	...	428	...	54
1830	138	[31][4]	1,095	...	...	428	...	52
1831	187	119	1,219	...	...	447	...	51
1832	161	164	1,174	...	...	497	...	51
1833	160	97	1,134	14	...	495	...	49
1834	160	101	1,064	29	...	528	...	49
1835	164	90	1,047	16	...	587	...	48[5]
1836	156	103	1,066	16	...	583	...	50[5]
1837	153	106	1,079	18	...	573	...	51
1838	158	121	1,136	16	...	597	...	52
1839	162	124	1,179	16	...	628	...	53
						silver roubles		
1840	165	166	1,364	16	...	188	...	53
1841	163	115	1,425	16	...	196	...	54
1842	157	129	1,441	16	...	211	...	55
1843	165	120	1,445	14	...	212	...	55
1844	168	195	1,428	14	...	222	...	55
1845	171	134	1,489	14	75	224	...	54
1846	177	123	1,567	15	74	245	...	55
1847	204	128	1,630	15	76	245	...	59
1848	182	135	1,771	16	78	284	...	59
1849	255	112	1,646	16	72	270	3	55

Abbreviations used throughout this table:— U.K. United Kingdom

Other abbreviations used where space demands:— Neth'l: Netherlands; thou m: thousand million

See p. 740 for footnotes

H 4 Total Central Government Expenditure (in millions)

1850–1899

	Austria[1,8] (gulden)	Belgium (francs)	Bulgaria (leva)	Denmark[11] (kroner)	Finland (markkaa)	France (francs)	Germany (marks)	Greece (drachmae)	Hungary[14] (gulden)	Italy (lire)
1850	269	119	...	...	...	1,473	...	17	...	...
1851	296	119	...	...	...	1,461	...	16	...	...
1852	310	132	...	...	...	1,513	...	16	...	...
1853	321	135	...	...	...	1,548	...	16	...	...
1854	407	143	...	51	...	1,988	...	18	...	...
1855	441	147	...	54	...	2,309	...	19	...	...
1856	371	150	...	52	...	2,196	...	19	...	...
1857	371	146	...	57	...	1,893	...	20	...	...
1858	367[6]	145	...	57	...	1,859	...	23	...	...
1859	542	153	...	51	...	2,208	...	23	...	...
1860	524	159	...	55	...	2,084	...	24	...	...
1861	500	163	...	54	...	2,171	...	25	...	...
1862	395	177	...	57	...	2,213	...	26	...	936
1863	402	187	...	51	...	2,287	...	24	...	916
1864	411[7]	186	...	80	...	2,257	...	25	...	971
	670[8]									
1865	618	189	...	73[11]	...	2,147	...	29	...	987
1866	940	203	...	48	...	2,203	...	28	...	1,371
1867	943[1]	192	...	51	...	2,170	...	38	...	956
1868	344	192	...	49	...	1,903	...	45	169	1,129
1869	394	200	...	57	...	1,904	...	37	178	1,105
1870	422	217	...	45	...	3,173	...	36	192	1,195
1871	422	238	...	46	...	3,047	...	37	220	1,130
1872	421	252	...	43	...	2,723	1,407	33	239	1,183
1873	469	351	...	47	...	2,874	1,370	33	257	1,232
1874	471[9]	302	...	48	...	2,782	673	46	254	1,174
	730									
1875	717	292	...	65	...	2,936	634	35	234	1,210
1876	719	294	...	47	...	3,031	[679][12]	35	244	1,272
1877	881	386	...	50	...	3,027	569	35	245	1,312
1878	898	349	...	44	...	3,348	784	37	279	1,260
1879	832	344	20[10]	42	...	3,322	550	96	386	1,265
1880	674	383	27[10]	44	...	3,365	550	89	290	1,261
1881	780	402	27	48	...	3,616	612	103	505	1,303
1882	812	423	39	50	35	3,687	604	64	383	2,017
1883	770	406	33	51	37	3,715	587	68	399	1,382
1884	814	362	34	50	39	3,539	615	91	431	[679][15]
1885	764	351	45	48	44	3,467	638	123	487	[1,508][15]
1886	880	350	55[10]	50	40	3,294	694	130	348	1,467[15]
1887	967	346	48	58	43	3,261	877	107	368	1,499
1888	883	356	120	60	38	3,221	1,020	108	362	1,606
1889	782	373	74	60	37	3,247	1,111	169	814	1,768
1890	813	418	84	62	37	3,285	1,354	142	387	1,675
1891	787	402	93[10]	66	39	3,258	1,245	123	406	1,657
			93							
1892	611	406	107	65	40	3,380	1,244	108	418	1,613
1893	630	395	95	63	42	3,451	1,270	92	495	1,653
	kronen								kronen	
1894	1,384	403	107	62	47	3,480	1,337	85	2,051	1,743
1895	1,487	410	97	61	54	3,434	1,307	92	1,009	1,655
1896	1,457	438	101	74	53	3,445	1,366[13]	91	1,032	1,727
							1,629			
1897	1,525	511	99	66	54	3,524	1,746	137	1,096	1,652
1898	1,607	694	111	135	95	3,528	1,856	312	1,049	1,648
1899	1,681	570	100	76	67	3,589	1,961	105	1,027	1,650

See p. 740 for footnotes

H 4 Total Central Government Expenditure (in millions)

1850–1899

	Netherlands (guilders)	Norway (kroner)	Portugal (escudos)	Romania (lei)	Russia (paper rubels)	Serbia (dinari)	Spain (pesetas)	Sweden (kronor)	Switzerland (francs)	U.K.[2] (pounds)
1850	72	13	...	...	287	...	321	...	5	55
1851	76	15	...	...	281	...	347	...	5	54
1852	71	16	...	...	280	...	344	...	5	55
1853	71	14	...	...	313	...	353	...	5	56
1854	83	17	...	...	384	...	360	...	6	[83][3]
1855	86	17	...	...	526	...	355	...	5	93
1856	94	17	...	...	619	...	449	...	6	76
1857	95	19	...	...	348	...	485	...	6	68
1858	87	20	...	...	363	...	491	...	7	65
1859	102	21	...	...	351	...	506	...	10	70
1860	87	23	...	...	438	...	594	...	9	73
1861	98	20	...	...	414	...	630	...	9	72
1862	92	20	...	44	393	...	[975][18]	...	8	70
1863	99	21	...	44	432	...	657	...	8	68
1864	100	24	...	62	437	...	684	...	9	67
1865	99	20	...	64	428	...	694	...	10	66
1866	106	22	...	68	438	...	640	...	11	67
1867	112	22	...	61	460	...	634	...	9	72
1868	96	21	...	78	492	...	639	...	9	75[19]
1869	94	21	...	81	535	...	645	...	9	67
1870	99	20	...	72	564	...	670	...	18	68
1871	94	22	...	74	557	...	575	...	10	70
1872	109	21	...	85	583	...	501	...	11	69
1873	108	22	...	92	612	...	526	...	14	75
1874	99	31	...	90	602	...	611	...	15	73
1875	119	38	...	99	605	...	711	...	19	75
1876	113	44	...	101	704	...	641	...	20	76
1877	118	50	...	105	1,121	...	728	...	20	80
1878	116	[26][16]	35	122	1,076	...	755	...	20	83
1879	115	49[16]	37	114	812	...	791	...	20	82
1880	113	44	34	...	793	...	811	...	22	81
1881	124	44	35	[141][17]	840	...	784	80	23	83
1882	130	46	35	131	788	...	795	80	23	87
1883	138	43	35	137	804	...	843	83	24	85
1884	133	42	40	136	816	...	843	83	25	89
1885	122	41	40	130	913	...	885	85	25	92
1886	124	43	42	130	945	...	889	87	25	90
1887	122	43	45	129	931	...	828	91	28	87
1888	127	45	51	140	927	...	833	90	31	87
1889	125	44	54	161	963	...	822	93	34	91
1890	166	46	51	159	1,057	...	823	98	38	93
1891	130	53	55	162	1,116	...	821	102	43	96
1892	152	52	48	168	1,125	...	754	101	54	96
1893	135	60	46	179	1,061	...	707	105	54	98
1894	133	61	49	199	1,155	57	773	101	48	101
1895	133	62	55	210	1,521	64	802	103	47	105
1896	134	71	58	215	1,484	64	806	106	48	110
1897	139	78	58	210	1,495	69	872	118	52	112
1898	150	81	56	217	1,772	79	902	125	56	118
1899	150	91	62	225	1,785	81	[423][18]	135	59	144

See p. 740 for footnotes

H 4 Total Central Government Expenditure (in millions)

1900–1949

	Austria[1] (kronen)	Belgium (francs)	Bulgaria (leva)	Czechoslovakia (koruna)	Denmark[11] (krone)	Finland (markkaa)	France (francs)	Germany (marks)
1900	1,755	574	109	...	78	66	3,747	2,197
1901	1,877	604	103	...	79	112	3,756	2,324
1902	1,819	615	111	...	77	109	3,699	2,321
1903	1,886	628	105	...	78	103	3,597	2,357
1904	2,017	688	113	...	79	120	3,639	2,068
1905	1,999	626	149	...	99	120	3,707	2,195
1906	2,018	772	147	...	85	112	3,852	2,392
1907	2,376	768	181	...	114	130	3,880	2,810
1908	2,562	770	228	...	94	168	4,021	2,683
1909	3,081	786	191	...	108	178	4,186	3,266
1910	3,137	829	230	...	133	156	4,322	3,024
1911	3,235	811	205	...	139	160	4,548	2,897
1912	3,657	896	288	...	173[23]	166	4,743	2,893
					108			
1913	3,962	...	350	...	106	185	5,067	3,521
1914	[2,193][8]	...	291	...	111	186	10,065	9,651
1915	17,357[8]	...	314	...	156	199	20,925	26,689
1916	...	...	476	...	185	268	28,113	28,780
1917	...	...	973	...	251	488	35,320	53,261
1918	...	...	1,294	...	369	1,085	41,897	45,514
1919	...[1]	...	1,316[21]	8,615	616	1,682	39,970	54,867
1920	...	10,944	2,026	11,604	533	2,090	39,644	145,255[13]
1921	...	9,808	3,861	21,890	555	2,700	32,845	298,766
1922	(schillings)	8,749	4,518	23,076	499	2,560	45,188	...
1923	1,062	8,863	5,481	23,371	424	3,500	38,293	...
1924	1,361	9,849	8,387	19,223[22]	402	3,150	42,511	5,027
1925	1,411	13,398	7,157	17,300	417	3,950	36,275	5,683
1926	1,602	14,630	6,785	17,978	382	4,080	41,976	6,616
1927	1,835	9,286	6,696	17,374	362	3,990	45,869	7,168
1928	1,977	10,747	7,726	17,600	332	5,040	44,248	8,517
1929	1,990	12,259	10,449	17,994	323	4,510	[59,335][24]	8,187
1930	2,289	12,695	8,188	18,201	324	4,740	55,712[24]	8,392
1931	2,331	12,074	6,568	18,903	317	4,250	53,428[24]	6,995
1932	1,924[7]	11,740	5,567	18,249	333	3,000	[40,666][24]	5,965
	1,290							
1933	1,494	11,190	5,497	16,500	328	3,250	54,945	6,270
1934	1,574	11,384	[4,213][21]	14,800	393	4,100	49,883	8,221
1935	1,450	13,568	5,685	15,159	393	4,530	49,868	...
1936	1,413	13,847	6,274	15,262	405	4,860	55,789	...
1937	[1,400][7][20]	14,175	7,171	15,906	442	5,900	72,759	...
1938	...	14,482	7,202	...	497	5,430	82,345	...
1939	...	15,797	8,354	...	523	8,360	150,116	...
						(thou m markkaa)	(thou m francs)	
1940	...	...	9,873	...	611	21	204	...
1941	...	15,979	16,952	...	822	31	121	...
1942	...	17,681	...	...	892	28	133	...
1943	...	19,953	...	...	1,081	34	160[25]	...
1944	...	24,211	...	...	1,121	44	259[25]	...
1945	...	49,157	...	...	1,249	43	465	...
1946	...	77,097	...	...	1,503	100	521	...
1947	...	76,456	...	...	1,883	88	690	...
1948	5,725	141,021	...	...	1,980	105	992	...
1949	8,214	90,421	...	...	2,070	133	1,205	...

See p. 740 for footnotes

H 4 Total Central Government Expenditure (in millions)

1900–1949

	Greece (drachmae)	Hungary[14] (kronen)	S Ireland[30] (pounds)	Italy (lire)	Netherlands (guilders)	Norway (kroner)	Poland (zlotys)	Portugal (escudos)
1900	109	1,084	...	1,659	155	77	...	56
1901	114	1,102	...	1,692	153	110	...	58
1902	125	1,111	...	1,809	162	105	...	60
1903	116	2,176	...	1,793	166	105	...	...
1904	116	1,215	...	1,776	190	101	...	...
1905	116	1,192	...	1,820	176	97	...	...
1906	122	1,245	...	2,414	182	101	...	...
1907	132	1,399	...	2,079	184	111	...	...
1908	134	1,616	...	2,179	189	108	...	...
1909	137	1,722	...	2,431	193	138	...	...
1910	141	1,902	...	2,448	199	117	...	...
1911	181	1,768	...	2,650	204	121	...	...
1912	208	2,013	...	2,841	220	133	...	...
1913	261	2,319	...	3,137	232	154	...	...
1914	482	[1,444][27]	...	3,009	354	123	...	...
1915	376	6,659	...	5,795	507	165	...	...
1916	215	12,248	...	12,543	543	158	...	163
1917	317	10,911	...	21,622	704	234	...	204
1918	...	12,251[14]	...	26,502	1,074	502	...	242
1919	[1,446][26]	[11,200][28]	...	33,335	852	619	...	...
1920	1,354	[10,092][29]	...	27,827	935	648	...	...
1921	1,683	45,920	...	37,488	1,032	746	...	577
1922	2,476	54,085	...	37,206	1,123	585	...	1,045
1923	3,460	264,304	30	24,090	807	550	...	1,072
1924	5,000	8,644,649	39	24,240	737	478	1,663	1,608
		(pengos)						
1925	5,498	1,005	27	21,930	699	486	1,884	1,492
1926	6,841	1,145	26[31] / 28	22,755	689	445	1,975[32]	1,953
1927	8,687	1,250	28	24,592	645	395	2,556	1,824
1928	7,770	1,354	31	29,649	698	397	2,841	2,049[33] / 1,889
1929	9,446	1,473	29	20,841	729	387	2,993	2,043
1930	18,355	1,478	30	20,858	738	376	2,814	1,883
1931	11,176	1,628	31	25,856	865	374	2,468	1,857
1932	11,099	1,388	28	25,235	883	361	2,245	1,949
1933	9,117	1,184	37	22,855	993	309	2,231	2,069
1934	7,706	1,185	33	28,137	932	302	2,302	...[34]
1935	8,746	1,188	32	21,871	989	341	2,337	[2,886][34]
1936	10,049	1,230	33	66,923	935	384	2,213	2,734
1937	12,683	1,305	33	48,065	938	422	2,335[32]	2,070
1938	13,412	1,381	36	40,632	1,045	472	...	2,299
1939	12,652	1,723	52	42,627	1,182	567	...	2,400
				(thou m lire)				
1940	14,016	4,033	46	70	2,310	714	...	2,423
1941	...	...	39	106	3,666	1,132	...	2,820
1942	...	...	49	123	3,474	2,042	...	2,595
1943	...	...	45	160	3,686	1,896	...	3,985
1944	...	...	47	247	4,281	2,274	...	3,684
	(thou m drachmae)							
1945	...[26]	...	51	319	4,439	1,224	...	3,929
1946	314	...	56	622	4,501	2,008	...	4,630
1947	1,659	...	62	1,215	5,095	2,936	10,508	5,694
1948	3,422	...	73	1,907	5,209	2,556	20,852	5,699
1949	3,950	...	99	1,735	4,454	2,980	30,871	5,661

See p. 740 for footnotes

H 4 Total Central Government Expenditure (in millions)

1900–1949

	Romania (lei)	Russia (rubels)	Serbia (dinari)	Spain pesetas)	Sweden (kronor)	Switzerland (francs)	U.K.[2] (pounds)	Yugoslavia (dinari)
1900	235	1,883	79	856	151	60	193	...
1901	237	1,874	80	931	153	61	205	...
1902	218	2,167	79	905	167	61	194	...
1903	218	2,108	92	975	185	63	155	...
1904	230	2,738	110	949	188	66	150	...
1905	252	3,205	92	938	189	66	147	...
1906	263	3,213	89	969	196	72	144	...
1907	265	2,583	...	982	209	81	143	...
1908	269	2,661	...	1,036	216	88	145	...
1909	417	2,608	...	1,111	232	94	157	...
1910	482	2,597	112	1,138	236	91	168	...
1911	525	2,846	120	1,184	249[33]	99	174	...
1912	533	3,171	118	1,156	254	101	184	...
1913	522	3,383	131	1,532	259	106	192	...
1914	543	4,865	214	1,448	271	210[33] 224	559	...
1915	747	...	...	1,963	413	300	1,559	...
1916	...	...	...	1,691	434	346	2,198	...
1917	1,027	...	...	2,294	650	466	2,696	...
1918	787	...	...	1,858	1,718	547	2,579	...
1919	1,646	...	...	[3,087][37]	849	573	1,666	...
1920	4,331	...	...	2,700	945	616	1,188	...
1921	6,037	...	...	3,651	1,116	540	1,070	...
1922	6,818	...	...	3,414	938	426	812	...
1923	13,639	[35]	...	3,541	[389][38]	428	749	...
1924	21,403	2,318	...	[4,167][37]	775	376	751	...[39]
1925	[17,942][34]	2,970	...	3,616[37]	714	376	776	10,540
1926	28,499	4,051	...	[1,518][37]	758	383	782	11,777
1927	33,137	5,335	...	3,337	810	361	774	11,593
1928	35,224	6,465	...	3,439	740	366	761	10,983
1929	34,607	8,241	...	3,706	792	377	782	11,147
1930	31,579	12,335[35]	...	3,802	811	483	814	11,817
1931	34,702	23,146	...	3,968	819	404	819	12,470
1932	[24,891][34]	30,740[36] 34,402	...	4,430	894	432	833	11,530
1933	20,741	39,905	...	4,422	1,067	450	770	9,969
1934	19,864	52,398	...	4,289	973	497	785	9,663
1935	20,699	...	...	4,558	1,148	505	829	9,379
1936	23,060	...	...	...	1,108[33] 1,118	518	889	9,562
1937	26,762	...	...	...	1,199	537	909	10.059
1938	30,287	123,996	...	...	1,372	604	1,006	11,083
1939	...	...	...	...	1,578	964	1,401	11,814
		(new rubels)						
1940	...	17.4	...	5,594	2,880	1,807	3,954	11,920[39]
1941	...	...	...	6,383	3,878	2,142	4,876	...
1942	...	...	...	7,322	4,085	2,261	5,726	...
1943	...	...	...	8,928	4,503	2,482	5,899	...
1944	...	...	...	10,400	4,618	2,594	6,174	...
1945	...	...	...	10,625	5,232	2,323	5,592	...
1946	...	...	...	11,258	4,537	2,213	4,192	32,414
1947	...	...	...	13,533	4,108	1,947	3,354	58,071
1948	...	...	...	15,374	4,844	1,947	3,314	74,270
1949	...	...	...	16,155	5,675	1,581	3,531	113,566

See p. 740 for footnotes

H 4 Total Central Government Expenditure (in millions)

1950–1975

	Austria[1] (schillings)	Belgium (francs)	Denmark[11] (kroner)	Finland (markkaa)	France (francs)	W Germany[41] (marks)	E Germany (marks)	Greece (drachmae)	S Ireland[30] (pounds)	Italy[15] (lire)
1950	12,282	80,802	2,171	143	2,357	11,613	24,091	5,439	103	1,948
1951	17,366	89,783	2,391	207	2,914	17,837[40]	27,274	6,039	109	2,213
						17,898				
1952	21,450	100,792	2,555	204	3,656	19,762	32,282	6,612	129	2,434
								(new drachmae)		
1953	22,624	94,502	2,828	221	3,801	22,663	34,741	8,091	154	2,429
1954	24,889	96,449	3,269	214	3,702	23,657	36,143	9,845	178	2,510
1955	28,898	95,272	3,082[23]	243	3,945	22,927	38,327	11,728	180	2,759
			3,968							
1956	31,093	98,657	4,080	279	4,648	27,802	35,856	[19,636][26]	193	2,901
1957	36,279	108,422	4,496	301	5,640	31,822	36,376	15,445	213	3,069
1958	41,364	123,338	4,804	333	5,490	33,913	42,193	15,835	237	3,715
1959	42,039	134,962	5,225	355	5,946	38,072	46,530	17,514	236	3,621
					(new francs)	[41]				
1960	45,168	141,820	5,834	400	60,034	[30,820][12]	49,458	19,089	244	4,612
1961	49,993	143,865	6,246	447	66,549	47,867	50,764	21,760	299	4,634
1962	54,114	151,987	7,874	497	76,852	53,063	55,503	24,133	345	5,369
				(new markkaa)						
1963	59,075	167,090	9,186	4,875	90,805	56,069	56,085	25,386	423	6,106
1964	62,709	181,383	10,155	5,745	90,641	63,293	56,317	29,825	450	6,759
										[15]
1965	66,646	202,958	11,263	6,821	98,210	67,486	55,759	33,923	530	8,464
1966	72,259	235,610	13,146	7,167	106,464	70,697	60,831	39,039	731	9,517
1967	80,149	254,513	15,489	8,058	122,009	79,426	59,026	45,630	685	10,322
1968	86,174	285,100	18,160	9,785	133,551	82,185	59,505	52,112	744	11,841
1969	93,193	296,328	23,984	10,210	147,805	94,195	64,985	65,544	875	14,014
						81,654[43]				
1970	101,584	351,759	27,582	10,781	162,233	87,602	69,954	65,126	1,039	14,314
1971	112,567	371,876	33,402	11,944	175,550	98,388	79,125	73,875	1,036	17,588
1972	127,889	422,576	39,551	13,697	194,053	112,094	85,748	89,119	1,440	19,102
1973	141,151	495,985	44,782	16,961	220,014	122,571	93,277	105,234	1,599	23,808
1974	167,133	577,728	49,093	21,307	254,120	134,907	103,292	129,380	1,899	29,558
1975	196,697	730,281	60,379	27,546	320,322	160,032	114,160	170,507	3,440[44]	40,202

	Neth'l (guilders)	Norway[44] (kroner)	Poland (zlotys)	Portugal (escudos)	Romania (lei)	Russia (rubels)	Spain (pesetas)	Sweden (kronor)	Switz (francs)	U.K.[3] (pounds)	Yugoslavia (dinari thou m)
1950	4,968	3,042	39,586	5,118	19,073	41.3	18,694	5,834	1,637	3,417	107
1951	6,179	2,928	43,791	5,605	21,707	...	20,289	6,447	1,786	4,222	99
1952	5,955	3,543	52,597	5,854	28,988	46.0	22,628	7,831	2,162	4,531	228
1953	6,639	4,273	82,606	6,407	35,638	51.5	23,932	9,485	1,884	4,477	203
1954	7,150	4,622	100,080	6,683	38,352	...	27,218	10,077	1,959	4,517	246
1955	8,061	4,605	104,918	7,330	42,916	54.0	30,230	10,721	1,949	4,727	213
1956	8,619	4,847	110,797	7,597	41,935	56.4	37,668	11,963	1,964	5,136	203
1957	8,893	4,765	119,943	8,230	43,854	...	42,932	13,024	2,238	5,218	211
1958	8,958	5,159	127,998	8,687	44,689	64.3	55,573	14,630	2,643	5,435	289
1959	9,748	5,353	135,536	9,747	48,260	70.4	63,054	15,184	2,482	5,590	336
1960	10,428	5,761	147,412	11,338	55,423	73.1	70,193	16,373	2,601	6,157	409
1961	11,685	6,402[16 42]	175,543	13,445	63,726	76.3	78,816	17,394	3,267	6,195	539
1962	12,247	7,226	182,556	14,831	73,106	82.2	93,151	18,754	3,684	6,401	587
1963	13,171	8,078	180,408	15,705	77,715	87.0	113,494	21,483	4,083	6,776	581
											(new dinari)
1964	15,989	8,901	200,006	17,186	87,064	92.2	126,238	22,520	4,856	7,265	6,814
1965	19,505	10,023	209,606	18,308	93,057	101.6	151,364	26,777	4,920	7,967[33]	7,644
		10,138[44]								9,019	
1966	21,031	10,360	233,722	19,873	105,372	105.6	187,096	30,790	5,683		7,860
1967	23,851	11,668	235,190	23,359	124,322	115.2	215,485	35,069	5,874	10,871	8,207
1968	27,130	13,120	236,146	25,193	131,921	128.6	239,846	37,594	6,447	11,615	8,905
1969	29,796	15,340	253,070	27,435	142,805	138.5	281,439	40,188	7,081	12,822	9,399
1970	35,008	18,425	279,025	31,736	130,900	154.6	312,629	45,330	7,765	14,086	11,592
1971	41,317	21,185	280,507	36,648	134,237	164.2	382,100	49,350	8,963	15,549	15,533
1972	46,365	24,087	295,500	40,868	145,432	173.2	424,068	57,639	10,366	17,689	25,491
1973	53,824	26,670	321,171	48,894	168,100	184.0	491,063	61,942	11,625	19,965	32,878
1974	61,935	30,505	418,260	63,415	207,300	197.4	606,157	72,104	13,052	26,803	48,263
1975	78,173	38,591	544,214	86,620	242,800	214.5	704,202	84,257	13,541	36,047	59,944

See p. 740 for footnotes

H 4 Total Central Government Expenditure

NOTES

1. SOURCES:– The official publications noted on p.xv with a few gaps filled from the League of Nations, *Public Finance Statistics.* In addition statistics for Great Britain to 1965 are taken from B.R. Mitchell and Phyllis Deane, *Abstract of British Historical Statistics* (Cambridge, 1962) and B.R. Mitchell and H.G. Jones, *Second Abstract of British Historical Statistics* (Cambridge, 1971), where the original sources are given; and statistics for Russia to 1914 are taken from P.A. Khromov, *Economic Development of Russia in the 19th and 20th Centuries, 1800–1917* (Moscow, 1950).

2. So far as possible, all kinds of central government expenditure are included in this table, in contrast to H.5, showing state revenue, in which the aim has been to exclude capital receipts.

3. Except where otherwise indicated, statistics are from the closed accounts.

FOOTNOTES

[1] Austria-Hungary to 1867; Cisleithania from 1868 to 1915; and the Republic of Austria from 1920.

[2] Figures to 1800 are for Great Britain and are of net expenditure. Subsequently they are for the U.K. and are of gross expenditure. Capital items (including debt redemption) are excluded throughout.

[3] Figures for 1750 and and 1751 are for years ended 29 September. From 1752 to 1799 they are for years ended 10 October. The 1800 figure is for 15 months ended 5 January 1801. The figures for 1801–53 are for years ended 5 January following that indicated. The figure for 1854 is for the period 6 January–31 March 1855, and all subsequent figures are for years ended 31 March following that indicated.

[4] Fourth quarter-year only.

[5] Exclusive of compensation paid to West Indian slaveowners.

[6] Convention gulden to 1858 and standard gulden thereafter. The difference is negligible.

[7] Figures to 1864 (1st line) and from 1932 to 1937 do not include expenditure on tax collection.

[8] Figures to 1864 are for years ended 31 October. From 1865 to 1913 they are for calendar years (expenditure in November and December 1864 being 179 million gulden). The 1914 figure is for the first half-year only, and the 1915 figure is for the year ended 30 June.

[9] Figures to 1874 (1st line) are of cash payments from the Treasury. From 1874 (2nd line) to 1915 they include obligations undertaken and the change in the Treasury's cash balance.

[10] Revised figures were later published for each year back to 1891, but only for three years before that. The original series is given here from 1879 to 1891 (1st line). Revised figures for this period are available as follows:– 1879 21; 1880 26; 1886 36.

[11] Figures are for years ended 31 March. The Duchies of Schleswig, Holstein, and Lauenburg are included up to 1865.

[12] The figure for 1876 is for 15 months ended 31 March 1877. Subsequent figures (to 1959) are for years ended 31 March following that indicated. The figure for 1960 is for 9 months.

[13] Up to 1896 (1st line) and from 1921 onwards the expenditure of public enterprises is net of receipts.

[14] Transleithania (including Croatia-Slavonia) to 1918, and the territory established by the treaty of Trianon subsequently. Expenditure for Transleithania for the period 1 July–31 October 1918 (not shown in the table) is 6,906 million kroner.

[15] **The figure for 1884 is for 8 months ended 31 August. That for 1885 is for 10 months ended 30 June, and all subsequent figures to 1964 are for years ended 30 June. Figures from 1965 are for calendar years.**

[16] The figure for 1878 is for the first half-year only. Figures for 1879–1960 are for years ended 30 June, and subsequently they are for calendar years.

[17] The figure for 1881 is for 15 months ended 31 March. From 1882 to 1924 the figures are for years ended 31 March. The 1925 figure is for 9 months. From 1926 to 1931 the figures are for calendar years. The 1932 figure is for 15 months to 31 March 1933, and subsequent figures (to 1939) are for years ended 31 March following that indicated.

[18] The figure for 1862 is for 18 months ended 30 June 1863. Figures from 1863 to 1898 are for years beginning 1 July. The figure for 1899 is for the second half-year only.

[19] Figures to 1868 include expenditure out of the Indian Military Contribution and the Army and Navy Extra Receipts. These are subsequently excluded.

[20] Budget estimate.

[21] Figures from 1919 to 1933 are for years ended 31 March following that indicated. The 1934 figure is for 9 months.

[22] The expenditure of public enterprise is subsequently entered net of receipts.

[23] From 1912 (2nd line) to 1955 (1st line) the figures are of current account expenditure only.

[24] The figure for 1929 is for 15 months ended 31 March 1930. Those for 1930 and 1931 are for years ended 31 March following that indicated. The figure for 1932 is for 9 months.

[25] Including the budget of the Comite Francaise de Liberation Nationale in 1943, and of the provisional government in 1944.

[26] The figure for 1919 is for 15 months ended 31 March. Figures for 1920–40 are for years ended 31 March. Those for 1946–55 are for years ended 30 June, and the 1956 figure is for 18 months to 31 December.
[27] The figure for 1914 is for the first half-year only. Subsequent figures (to 1940) are for years ended 30 June.
[28] 1 November 1918 to 6 August 1919.
[29] 7 August 1919 to 30 June 1920.
[30] Figures are for years ended 31 March, except for 1975, which is for the calendar year. Expenditure in the period April-December 1974 was £1,772 million.
[31] Figures to 1926 (1st line) are of expenditure on current account only.
[32] Figures for 1926–37 are for years ended 31 March following that indicated.
[33] This break is caused by a change in methods of accounting.
[34] Figures to 1933 are for years ended 30 June following that indicated. The 1935 figure is for 18 months to 31 December.
[35] Figures from 1924 to 1930 are for years ended 30 September. Expenditure in the fourth quarter of 1930 was 4,616 million rubels.
[36] Subsequent figures include local government expenditure.
[37] The figure for 1919 is for 15 months ended 31 March 1920. The figures for 1920–23 are for years ended 31 March following that indicated. The 1924 figure is for 15 months ended 30 June 1925. That for 1925 is for the year beginning 1 July, and that for 1926 is for the second half-year only. Subsequent figures are for calendar years.
[38] The figure for 1923 is for the first half-year only. Subsequent figures are for years ended 30 June.
[39] Figures from 1925 to 1940 are for years ended 31 March.
[40] West Berlin is included from 1951 (2nd line).
[41] Saarland is excluded from West Germany until 1959.
[42] The expenditure of the second half of 1960 is omitted here.
[43] Subsequently excluding special financial transactions.
[44] Net expenditure, with debt redemption excluded until 1965 (2nd line).

H 5 GOVERNMENT REVENUE AND MAIN TAX YIELDS

1750–1799

	Austria[1 12]		U.K.[2 3]			
	Total	Direct Taxes	Total	Customs	Excise	Land and Income & Property
	(million gulden)		(thousand pounds)			
1750	...	...	7,467	1,537	3,454	2,212
1751	...	...	7,097	1,588	3,468	1,769
1752	...	...	6,992	1,635	3,402	1,685
1753	...	...	7,338	1,770	3,582	1,728
1754	...	...	6,827	1,587	3,692	1,288
1755	...	...	6,938	1,782	3,660	1,236
1756	...	...	7,006	1,699	3,649	1,375
1757	...	...	7,969	1,872	3,303	2,043
1758	...	...	7,946	1,918	3,477	2,139
1759	...	...	8,155	1,830	3,615	2,216
1760	...	...	9,207	2,113	4,218	2,407
1761	...	...	9,594	2,191	4,671	2,253
1762	...	...	9,459	1,824	4,816	2,386
1763	...	...	9,793	2,283	4,793	2,288
1764	...	...	10,221	2,282	5,027	2,316
1765	...	...	10,928	2,324	4,935	2,243
1766	...	...	10,276	2,514	4,879	2,225
1767	...	...	9,868	2,460	4,521	2,174
1768	...	...	10,131	2,453	4,746	1,895
1769	...	...	11,130	2,675	4,961	1,814
1770	...	...	11,373	2,841	5,139	1,796
1771	...	...	10,987	2,739	4,842	1,834
1772	...	...	11,033	2,457	4,995	2,092
1773	...	...	10,487	2,702	5,141	1,843
1774	...	...	10,613	2,557	4,922	1,821
1775	...	...	11,112	2,756	5,106	1,756
1776	...	...	10,576	2,684	5,383	1,875
1777	...	...	11,105	2,411	5,252	2,299
1778	...	...	11,436	2,348	5,369	2,497
1779	...	...	11,853	2,523	5,625	2,450
1780	...	...	12,524	2,774	6,081	2,523
1781	66	25	13,280	3,019	6,111	2,635
1782	75	25	13,765	2,898	6,420	2,724
1783	64	24	12,677	2,949	5,480	2,596
1784	69	25	13,214	3,026	6,139	2,460
1785	77	25	15,527	4,537	6,142	2,666
1786	74	24	15,246	3,783	6,413	2,774
1787	76	25	16,453	4,094	7,043	2,909
1788	87	27	16,779	3,996	7,257	3,013
1789	84	26	16,669	3,647	7,301	3,006
1790	86	23	17,014	3,462	7,698	2,993
1791	89	23	18,506	4,018	8,433	2,914
1792	87	23	18,607	4,100	8,741	3,020
1793	86	22	18,131	3,557	8,559	2,952
1794	93	22	18,732	4,348	8,387	3,034
1795	68	22	19,053	3,419	9,915	2,946
1796	66	20	19,391	3,645	9,096	3,021
1797	71	21	21,380	3,940	10,303	3,365
1798	73	21	26,946	4,741	11,571	4,591
1799	80	21	31,783	7,056	11,862	8,117

Abbreviations used where space demands:—Con. Taxes: Consumption Taxes; Ded. from Profits: Deductions from Profits; Direct Per. Taxes; Direct Personal Taxes; I. & P.: Income and Propety; I. & T. Taxes: Industrial and Turnover Taxes; Land and I. & P.: Land and Income & Property; P. & T. Mon.: Petrol and Tobacco Monopolies; Reg.: Registration; Salt & Tob. Monopolies; Salt and Tobacco Monopolies; Turnover & Trans.: Turnover and Transactions.

See p. 768 for footnotes

H 5 Government Revenue and Main Tax Yields

1800–1849

	Austria[1 12]					Belgium				France		
	Total	Customs	Con. Taxes	Direct Taxes	Salt & Tob. Monopolies	Total[6]	Customs	Excise	Direct Taxes	Total	Customs	Direct Taxes
	(million gulden)					(million francs)				(million francs)		
1800	86	...	...	26	...	...	...	...	...	...	...	...
1801	95	...	...	26	...	...	...	...	...	...	...	...
1802	86	...	...	30	...	...	...	...	...	...	...	...
1803	101	...	...	31	...	...	...	...	...	...	...	...
1804	108	...	...	36	...	...	...	...	...	...	...	...
1805	112	...	...	32	...	...	...	...	...	...	...	...
1806	87	...	...	27	...	...	...	...	...	...	...	...
1807	140	...	...	46	...	...	...	...	...	...	...	...
1808	162	...	...	59	...	...	...	...	...	...	...	...
1809	95	...	...	35	...	...	...	...	...	...	...	...
1810	136	...	...	30	...	...	...	...	...	...	...	...
1811	71	...	...	18	...	...	...	...	...	...	...	...
1812	87	...	...	34	...	...	...	...	...	...	...	...
1813	102	...	...	31	...	...	...	...	...	...	...	...
1814	76	...	...	21	...	...	...	...	...	...	...	...
1815	96	...	...	27	...	...	...	...	...	729	...	...
1816	125	...	...	33	...	...	...	...	...	879	...	...
1817	125	...	...	44	...	...	...	...	...	900	...	...
1818	127	...	...	53	...	...	...	...	...	938	...	...
1819	124	...	...	53	...	...	...	...	...	895	...	...
1820	121	...	...	50	...	...	...	...	...	933	...	...
1821	128	...	...	50	...	...	...	...	...	928	...	...
1822	139	...	...	50	...	...	...	...	...	933	...	...
1823	131	...	...	52	...	...	...	...	...	919	...	...
1824	128	...	...	52	...	...	...	...	...	960	...	...
1825	125	...	...	51	...	...	...	...	...	979	...	...
1826	121	...	...	47	...	...	...	...	...	983	...	...
1827	127	...	...	49	...	...	...	...	...	948	...	...
1828	121	...	...	48	...	...	...	...	...	978	...	...
1829	122	...	...	50	...	...	...	...	...	992	...	...
1830	126	...	...	48	...	[30][5]	[1][5]	[4][5]	[8][5]	971	...	...
1831	123	...	...	45	...	120	4	16	28	949	...	...
1832	133	...	...	47	...	158	7	19	27	985	...	...
1833	131	...	...	48	...	93	8	45	31	990	...	...
1834	130	...	...	47	...	101	9	21	32	1,008	...	...
1835	133	...	...	47	...	94	8	18	29	1,021	...	...
1836	140	...	...	48	...	106	8	17	29	1,053	...	...
1837	144	...	...	47	...	104	9	17	29	1,076	...	...
1838	142	...	...	47	...	125	11	19	30	1,111	...	293
1839	145	...	...	48	...	116	9	19	33	1,124	...	...
1840	147	...	...	47	...	169[6]	10	18	30	1,160	...	295
1841	144	...	...	47	...	101	10	18	30	1,198	...	...
1842	146	...	...	47	...	104	11	18	30	1,256	...	297
1843	150	...	...	48	...	105	11	19	30	1,270	...	...
1844	153	...	...	48	...	110	12	21	30	1,298	...	299
1845	154	18	22	47	38	113	12	20	31	1,330	...	...
1846	155	19	22	48	37	113	11	19	31	1,352	...	298
1847	153	20	20	48	39	113	11	17	32	1,343	139	...
1848	101	10	14	26	21	109	10	20	32	1,207	91	301
1849	101	11	15	27	24	114	12	21	31	1,257	130	...

See p. 768 for footnotes

H 5 Government Revenue and Main Tax Yields

1800–1849

	Netherlands (million guilders)				Russia[8] (million paper rubels)				United Kingdom (thousand pounds)			
	Total	Customs	Excise	Direct Taxes	Total	Customs	Excise[9]	Direct Taxes	Total	Customs	Excise	Land and I & P[3]
1800	...	...	...	...	...	...	...	...	31,585[2][3]	6,785[2][3]	10,594[2][3]	9,606[2][3]
1801	...	...	...	...	...	...	...	...	39,086	8,758	11,573	10,453
1802	...	...	...	...	...	...	...	...	41,168	7,699	15,475	8,645
1803	...	...	...	...	102	...	...	...	42,442	8,158	18,795	6,182
1804	...	...	...	...	103	...	...	...	50,206	9,425	21,451	9,710
1805	...	...	...	...	107	12	26	45	55,031	10,130	23,156	10,849
1806	...	...	...	...	106	10	35	44	60,084	10,799[3]	24,053[3]	12,552
1807	...	...	...	...	115	9	34	44	64,843	12,648	26,711	17,180
1808	...	...	...	...	123	6	36	48	68,174	12,607	27,628	19,023
1809	...	...	...	...	134	8	37	53	69,170	14,575	24,750	20,849
									(million pounds)			
1810	...	...	...	...	178	11	37	82	73	14	27	21
1811	...	...	...	...	233	16	75	81	71	13	28	21
1812	...	...	...	...	236	19	73	88	70	14	26	21
1813	...	...	...	...	270	32	75	103	75	14	27	22
1814	...	...	...	...	297	26	84	118	78	15	29	23
1815	...	...	...	...	323	26	100	133	79	14	30	24
1816	...	...	...	...	347	27	115	132	69	12	27	19
1817	...	...	...	...	357	43	110	127	58	13	23	11
1818	...	...	...	...	367	44	109	130	60	14	26	9
1819	...	...	...	...	422	44	155	133	58	13	27	8
1820	...	...	...	...	447	52	157	132	60	12	30	8
1821	...	...	...	...	410	50	152	119	62	13	30	8
1822	...	...	...	...	391	41	139	125	60	13	29	8
1823	...	...	...	...	399	41	131	134	59	14	27	7
1824	...	...	...	...	380	50	121	118	60	14	28	5
1825	...	...	...	...	397	54	117	121	58	19	23	5
1826	...	...	...	...	390	57	117	118	55	19	21	5
1827	...	...	...	...	393	63	105	126	55	20	20	5
1828	...	...	...	...	384	63	107	119	57	19	22	5
1829	...	...	...	...	404	67	112	124	55	19	21	5
1830	...	...	...	...	393	66	109	116	54	19	20	5
1831	...	...	...	...	407	68	115	118	51	18	18	5
1832	...	...	...	...	451	82	118	142	51	19	18	5
1833	...	...	...	...	429	82	117	121	50	18	18	5
1834	...	...	...	...	430	81	122	115	50	20	16	5
1835	...	...	...	...	495	78	131	157	50	22	14	4
1836	...	...	...	...	520	82	139	159	53	23	16	4
1837	...	...	...	...	527	90	140	162	50	22	15	4
1838	...	...	...	...	543	87	147	163	51	22	15	4
1839	...	...	...	...	558	89	153	162	52	23	15	4
					(million silver rubels)							
1840	...	...	...	...	155	26	44	42	52	23	15	4
1841	...	...	...	...	161	27	47	43	52	23	15	5
1842	...	...	...	...	173	30	50	45	51	23	14	5
1843	...	...	...	...	179	30	55	46	57	23	14	10
1844	...	...	...	...	186	32	57	47	58	24	14	10
1845	56	5	20	18	185	30	59	44	57	22	15	10
1846	56	5	19	18	192	30	63	45	58	22	15	10
1847	56	5	18	18	196	29	64	46	56	22	14	10
1848	55	4	19	19	195	30	64	44	58	23	15	10
1849	55	5	19	19	198	30	64	45	57	22	15	10

See p. 768 for footnotes

H 5 Government Revenue and Main Tax Yields

1850–1899

	Austria[1 12]					Belgium				Bulgaria			
	Total	Customs	Con. Taxes	Direct Taxes	S & T Mon.	Total	Customs	Excise	Direct Taxes	Total	Customs	Excise	Direct Taxes
	(million gulden)					(million francs)				(million leva)			
1850	197	21	23	63	38	117	12	21	32	...	...	...	...
1851	225	19	25	77	40	118	12	21	32	...	...	...	...
1852	230	22	28	83	43	123	14	21	32	...	...	...	...
1853	238	20	29	83	45	128	13	22	33	...	...	...	...
1854	250	19	29	87	50	132	12	22	33	...	...	...	...
1855	283	19	29	91	53	139	12	22	34	...	...	...	...
1856	290	20	32	92	57	142	12	23	34	...	...	...	...
1857	317	18	37	95	55	146	13	25	34	...	...	...	...
1858	315[1 10]	19[1 10]	41[1 10]	96[1 10]	57[1 10]	155	16	28	34	...	...	...	...
1859	261	12	43	96	48	156	16	29	35	...	...	...	...
1860	305	12	52	101	68	155	16	28	35	...	...	...	...
1861	305	12	47	98	70	156	15	25	35	...	...	...	...
1862	320	13	53	117	74	161	15	26	35	...	...	...	...
1863	329	13	59	120	65	163	14	28	35	...	...	...	...
1864	335[11]	12	53	123	[81][12]	164	13	28	36	...	...	...	...
	454[12]	[12]	[12]	[12]	[12]								
1865	447[1]	12[1]	55[1]	119[1]	64[1]	169	14	29	36	...	...	...	...
1866	472	10	50	104	67	169	13	30	37	...	...	...	...
1867	460[1]	11[1]	44[1]	112[1]	61[1]	173	14	30	37	...	...	...	...
		10	35	68	...								
1868	325	11	47	74	43	176	15	28	37	...	...	...	...
1869	323	16	45	78	44	185	16	31	37	...	...	...	...
1870	356	14	48	82	50	191	22	29	38	...	...	...	...
1871	356	18	53	88	53	208	20	25	39	...	...	...	...
1872	367	18	57	90	50	213	19	27	40	...	...	...	...
1873	386	16	59	92	50	227	18	31	41	...	...	...	...
1874	380	16	53	92	49	243	18	31	44	...	...	...	...
1875	385[11]	11	54	92	51	246	18	33	42	...	...	...	...
	510												
1876	524	6	54	91	53	255	19	33	42	...	...	...	...
1877	568	5	58	91	53	258	18	32	43	...	...	...	...
1878	623	4	59	92	53	260	18	30	43	...	...	...	...
1879	592	3	61	90	55	270	19	33	44	29[13]	5[13]		20[13]
1880	547	6	69	95	59	292	22	32	45	33[13]	6[13]		24[13]
1881	608	−1	80	93	58	297	23	34	45	24	7		14
1882	655	17	74	95	63	301	24	34	46	27	7		16
1883	653	18	76	97	64	303	23	35	47	31	8		18
1884	681	21	76	99	63	306	22	34	49	29	7		18
1885	663	5	86	100	65	313	24	39	49	27	6		16
1886	668	19	87	100	65	316	24	40	49	49[13]	10[13]		33[13]
1887	727	8	78	105	68	324	26	40	49	55	9		38
1888	696	38	46	104	67	333	28	41	50	55	11		35
1889	694	39	89	105	71	338	27	41	51	70	13		43
1890	725	39	94	108	70	341	24	42	50	70	14		43
1891	601	41	94	111	71	346	24	43	52	81[13]	16[13]		51[13]
										87	14		48
1892	618	42	101	112	70	347	24	42	51	84	15		46
	(million kronen)												
1893	1,318	96	207	223	146	352	26	43	51	78	20		39
1894	1,321	102	214	215	157	363	27	44	51	98	21		40
1895	1,397	101	224	237	160	373	30	45	52	76	26		31
1896	1,416	101	221	240	159	389	39	50	53	79	26		30
1897	1,482	117	244	243	164	431	38	69	54	78	30		32
1898	1,564	128	235	256	163	439	37	59	57	80	33		30
1899	1,598	108	252	263	170	469	41	64	57	70	29		27

See p. 768 for footnotes

H5 Government Revenue and Main Tax Yields

1850–1899

	Denmark[14]				Finland			France				
	Total	Customs	Excise	I & P	Total	Customs	Excise	Total	Customs	Excise	Reg.	Direct Taxes
	(million kroner)				(million markaa)			(million francs)				
1850	...	...	...	...	...	...	...	1,297	128	...	...	301
1851	...	...	...	...	...	...	...	1,273	120	...	...	301
1852	...	...	...	...	...	...	...	1,336	142	...	...	277
1853	49	9		8	...	...	...	1,391	143	...	...	277
1854	54	9		8	...	...	...	1,418	152	...	...	279
1855	57	11		8	...	...	...	1,536	192	...	...	282
1856	60	11		9	...	...	...	1,638	179	...	...	285
1857	54	11		9	...	...	...	1,683	185	...	...	291
1858	49	9		8	...	...	...	1,747	188	...	...	294
1859	50	9		8	...	...	...	1,728	194	...	...	297
1860	53	9		8	...	...	...	1,722	135	...	...	301
1861	60	10		8	...	...	...	1,780	128	...	...	304
1862	59	10		8	...	...	...	1,882	153	...	...	310
1863	70[14]	11		8	...	...	...	1,959	167	...	...	313
1864	78	11		10	...	...	...	1,923	134	...	...	317
1865	44	15		9	...	...	...	1,965	125	...	...	320
1866	53	15		7	...	...	...	2,018	123	...	...	325
1867	49	15		9	...	...	...	1,964	121	...	...	329
1868	58	17		10	...	...	...	1,818	124[17] / 77	306	364	336
1869	45[15] / 37	16		8	...	...	...	1,865	74	317	368	340
1870	39	18		9	...	...	...	1,662	82	276	286	343
1871	43	19		10	...	...	...	2,014	106	317	337	331
1872	42	20		8	...	...	...	2,497	110	426	433	345
1873	43	21		8	...	...	...	2,680	162	463	422	409
1874	46	22		8	...	...	...	2,518	157	516	430	403
1875	48	25		8	...	...	...	2,705	182	602	453	408
1876	46	24		8	...	...	...	2,778	200	608	471	413
1877	46	22		9	...	...	...	2,780	196	601	470	417
1878	44	22		9	...	...	...	2,853	217	612	487	421
1879	46	23		9	...	...	...	2,966	237	595	520	424
1880	49	24		9	...	...	...	2,957	262	615	550	401
1881	51	26		9	...	...	...	2,988	285	595	571	401
1882	52	27		9	36	...	...	2,980	289	590	559	414
1883	54	28		9	37	11	6	3,038	300	608	549	420
1884	55	29		9	38	11	6	3,032	291	612	524	425
1885	52	28		9	38	12	7	3,057	294	598	524	429
1886	51	27		9	40	12	7	2,940	309	590	522	434
1887	51	28		9	36	13	6	2,968	325	589	517	438
1888	54	30		9	35	13	5	3,108	362	591	514	443
1889	56	30		9	38	14	6	3,108	351	616[18]	506	446
1890	56	30		9	38	14	6	3,229	355	612	541	480
1891	56	27	4[16]	9	40	15	6	3,364	385	624	545	474
1892	55	24	7	10	45	16	6	3,370	410	601	551	469
1893	57	25	7	10	42	17	5	3,366	431	586	522	497
1894	58	25	7	10	43	17	4	3,458	446	575	529	501
1895	62	28	8	10	46	18	5	3,416	387	588	529	506
1896	64	29	8	10	49	18	6	3,436	407	596	508	512
1897	68	31	9	10	51	19	5	3,528	426	612	522	518
1898	70	33	9	10	55	22	5	3,620	470	632	533	505
1899	69	33	10	11	58	25	7	3,657	430	639	543	517

See p. 768 for footnotes

H 5 Government Revenue and Main Tax Yields

1850–1899

	Germany[19]			Greece				Hungary[21]		
	Total[7]	Customs	Excise	Total	Customs	Excise	Direct Taxes	Total[22]	Con.	Direct Taxes
	(million marks)			(million drachmae)				(million gulden)		
1850	...	...	...	...	...	...	...	...	...	...
1851	...	...	...	...	...	...	...	...	...	...
1852	...	...	...	...	...	...	...	...	...	...
1853	...	...	...	...	...	...	...	...	...	...
1854	...	...	...	...	...	...	...	...	...	...
1855	...	...	...	...	...	...	...	...	...	...
1856	...	...	...	...	...	...	...	...	...	...
1857	...	...	...	...	...	...	...	...	...	...
1858	...	...	...	...	...	...	...	...	...	...
1859	...	...	...	...	...	...	...	...	...	...
1860	...	...	...	...	...	...	...	...	...	...
1861	...	...	...	...	...	...	...	...	...	...
1862	...	...	...	...	...	...	...	...	...	...
1863	...	...	...	...	...	...	...	...	...	...
1864	...	...	...	...	...	...	...	...	...	...
1865	...	...	...	...	...	...	...	...	...	...
1866	...	...	...	...	...	...	...	...	...	...
1867	...	...	...	...	...	...	...	...	...	...
1868	...	...	...	...	...	...	...	170	13	59
1869	...	...	...	...	...	...	...	167	13	57
1870	...	...	...	...	...	...	...	176	13	63
1871	...	...	...	...	...	...	...	148	14	62
1872	182	95	74	...	...	...	...	156	13	61
1873	263	123	140	...	...	...	...	175	13	60
1874	253	104	138	...	...	...	...	183	12	68
1875	253	111	132	...	...	...	...	188	13	71
1876	[311][19]	[135][19]	[162][19]	...	...	...	...	203	12	80
1877	244	100	133	...	...	...	...	214	12	82
1878	242	101	130	...	...	...	...	218	14	82
1879	282	135	134	...	...	...	...	247	19	80
1880	294	164	117	...	...	...	...	245	20	82
1881	367	181	165	...	...	...	...	285	25	88
1882	362	187	149	...	...	...	...	280	24	90
1883	355	191	136	...	...	...	...	295	27	94
1884	375	209	137	...	...	...	...	300	28	96
1885	369	216	123	...	...	...	...	322	36	98
1886	388	232	121	...	...	...	...	312	32	94
1887	417	252	130	...	...	...	...	323	35	97
1888	507	283	183	...	...	...	...	335	35	101
1889	629	350	236	...	...	...	...	342	44	99
1890	661	368	257	...	...	...	...	373	48	101
1891	675	378	263	...	...	...	...	414	51[23]	106
1892	631	360	260	...	...	...	...	425	74	103
								(million kronen)		
1893	638	337	270	...	...	...	...	932	162	209
1894	691	363	279	...	...	...	...	951	165	215
1895	706	383	287	...	...	...	...	955	158	214
1896	790	434	298	97	27.9	34.4	18.5	1,001	167	220
1897	792	441	292	92	...	...	...	1,022	167	221
1898	847	476	306	105	...	...	...	1,018	164	221
1899	852	462	324	111	...	...	...	1,007	159	224

See p. 768 for footnotes

H 5 Government Revenue and Main Tax Yields

1850–1899

	Italy				Netherlands			
	Total	Customs	T. & B. Mon.	Direct Per.Taxes	Total	Customs	Excise	Direct Taxes
	(million lire)				(million guilders)			
1850	...	...	...	...	57	5	20	19
1851	...	...	...	...	57	5	20	19
1852	...	...	...	...	57	5	20	19
1853	...	...	...	...	58	5	20	19
1854	...	...	...	...	60	5	20	19
1855	...	...	...	...	61	5	21	19
1856	...	...	...	...	57	4	17	19
1857	...	...	...	...	58	4	18	20
1858	...	...	...	...	60	4	18	20
1859	...	...	...	...	59	4	18	20
1860	...	...	...	...	60	5	18	20
1861	...	...	...	...	61	5	18	20
1862	480	59	99	129	62	5	18	21
1863	524	60	109	131	63	5	19	21
1864	577	59	120	148	65	4	20	21
1865	647	63	128	198	65	4	19	21
1866	617	67	141	157	69	5	24	21
1867	715	66	140	227	72	4	26	21
1868	748	75	168	166	71	4	26	21
1869	871	81	140	291	74	5	28	21
1870	866	74	142	271	75	5	28	21
1871	966	81	147	320	78	5	28	22
1872	1,010	88	149	334	82	5	30	22
1873	1,047	97	148	340	85	6	32	22
1874	1,077	101	154	344	89	6	33	23
1875	1,096	104	165	347	91	6	34	23
1876	1,123	101	165	350	96	6	37	23
1877	1,243	103	172	356	95	5	38	24
1878	1,191	108	176	354	96	5	39	24
1879	1,223	134	184	361	98	4	39	24
1880	1,222	126	185	365	103	5	39	25
1881	1,278	157	189	373	106	5	40	25
1882	1,300	159	190	383	105	5	41	25
1883	1,333	179	193	385	104	5	40	26
1884	[658] [24]	[86] [24]	[124] [24]	[191] [24]	104	5	41	26
1885	[1,413] [24]	[204] [24]	[259] [24]	[392] [24]	107	5	43	27
1886	1,409	191	254	394	109	5	43	27
1887	1,453	205	249	394	110	5	44	27
1888	1,500	212	246	390	112	5	43	27
1889	1,501	206	247	461	114	5	44	28
1890	1.562	231	249	407	114	6	44	28
1891	1,540	211	252	416	118	6	44	28
1892	1,528	204	254	425	120	6	45	29
1893	1,551	204	255	427	115	6	43	32
1894	1,517	188	259	427	118	6	43	35
1895	1,570	195	261	481	121	7	43	35
1896	1,633	198	261	483	122	8	44	35
1897	1,615	202	261	483	123	9	45	33
1898	1,629	209	261	481	125	9	47	33
1899	1,658	214	270	483	131	9	47	34

See p. 768 for footnotes

H 5 Government Revenue and Main Tax Yields

1850–1899

	Norway				Portugal [26]				Romania		
	Total	Customs	Con.	I. & P.	Total [27]	Customs	Property	Business	Total	Customs	Property
	(million kroner)				(million escudos)				(million lei)		
1850	14	...	...	—	...	...	...	...	...	...	...
1851	14	9	2	—	...	...	...	...	...	...	...
1852	13	...	...	—	...	...	...	...	...	...	...
1853	14	...	...	—	...	...	...	...	...	...	...
1854	16	...	...	—	...	...	...	...	...	...	...
1855	16	9	3	—	...	...	...	...	...	...	...
1856	17	...	...	—	...	...	...	...	...	...	...
1857	18	...	...	—	...	...	...	...	...	...	...
1858	17	...	...	—	...	...	...	...	...	...	...
1859	18	...	...	—	...	...	...	...	...	...	...
1860	17	11	3	—	...	...	...	...	...	...	...
1861	18	...	...	—	...	...	...	...	...	...	...
1862	19	...	...	—	...	...	...	...	...	...	...
1863	20	...	...	—	...	...	...	...	...	3	...
1864	20	...	...	—	...	...	...	...	...	4	3
1865	20	13	3	—	...	...	...	...	...	5	3
1866	21	...	...	—	...	...	...	...	...	6	2
1867	20	...	...	—	...	...	...	...	...	5	2
1868	21	...	...	—	...	...	...	...	...	8	2
1869	20	...	...	—	...	...	...	...	...	9	...
1870	20	12	4	—	...	...	...	...	...	8	3
1871	21	...	...	—	...	...	...	...	...	7	3
1872	22	...	...	—	...	...	...	...	...	8	4
1873	25	...	...	—	...	...	...	...	...	10	6
1874	27	...	...	—	...	8	...	...	...	8	6
1875	28	18	5	—	...	10	...	...	...	9	6
1876	28	...	...	—	...	9	...	...	...	8	6
1877	31	...	...	—	...	10	...	...	...	8	5
1878	[17] [25]	...	...	—	...	10	...	...	...	10	6
1879	28	...	...	—	29	12	2.2	0.8	...	16	5
1880	34	19	6	—	24	9	2.3	0.8	...	13	5
1881	35	16	7	—	26	10	3.0	1.1	...	[16] [28]	[6] [28]
1882	39	18	6	—	29	11	3.2	1.1	...	16	8
1883	43	21	7	—	38	11	2.5	1.1	147	16	9
1884	41	19	7	—	30	12	3.0	1.1	127	20	9
1885	45	...	...	—	31	12	3.1	1.1	124	16	9
1886	44	20	6	—	32	13	3.0	1.1	137	17	9
1887	43	...	...	—	35	15	3.1	1.2	140	18	11
1888	44	21	6	—	38	14	3.1	1.2	159	21	11
1889	45	20	6	—	38	14	3.1	1.1	160	22	11
1890	50	23	7	—	39	15	3.1	1.0	170	23	11
1891	51	23	9	—	40	13	3.1	1.1	180	24	11
1892	51	22	8	—	38	10	3.1	1.2	182	29	13
1893	53	21	8	3	42	14	2.9	1.0	220	30	13
1894	54	21	8	3	46	14	3.1	1.1	200	37	13
1895	55	22	9	3	46	16	3.0	1.1	203	30	13
1896	57	23	9	4	52	15	3.1	1.9	...	31	13
1897	65	27	10	4	50	13	3.1	1.5	211	34	16
1898	74	32	11	5	49	12	3.2	1.8	237	32	16
1899	83	37	12	5	50	15	3.1	1.7	200	36	16

See p. 768 for footnotes

H 5 Government Revenue and Main Tax Yields

1850–1899

	Russia[8]				Serbia				Spain				
	Total	Customs	Excise[9]	Direct Taxes	Total	Direct Taxes	Indirect Taxes	State Taxes	Total	Customs	Con.	Tobacco Monopoly	Direct Taxes
	(million paper rubels)				(million dinari)				(million pesetas)				
1850	202	30	63	45	...	...	...	...	318	42	...	44	86
1851	212	31	75	45	...	...	...	...	314	40	...	47	90
1852	222	32	79	48	...	...	...	...	335	43	...	47	91
1853	220	28	82	48	...	...	...	...	350	40	...	48	93
1854	213	20	77	46	...	...	...	...	362	38	...	50	93
1855	209	18	81	47	...	...	...	...	371	44	...	52	93
1856	232	30	91	51	...	...	...	...	451	49	...	56	109
1857	241	36	92	55	...	...	...	...	492	53	...	62	110
1858	248	34	100	53	...	...	...	...	464	53	...	66	122
1859	279	33	123	55	...	...	...	...	497	56	...	69	124
1860	278	34	128	58	...	...	...	...	577	59	...	73	125
1861	330	33	130	58	...	...	...	...	569	66	...	78	126
1862	291	33	134	56	...	...	...	...	[791][29]	[95][29]	...	[125][29]	[188][29]
1863	344	34	135	73	...	...	...	...	577	65	...	89	126
1864	324	27	120	75	...	...	...	...	877	58	...	91	134
1865	356	26	129	79	...	...	...	...	601	57	...	90	132
1866	345	32	127	74	...	...	...	...	575	53	...	87	135
1867	402	37	143	89	...	...	...	...	767	54	...	80	148
1868	406	37	144	99	...	...	...	...	746	44	...	68	136
1869	436	42	147	104	...	...	...	...	595	51	...	56	140
1870	460	43	175	110	...	...	...	...	683	52	...	61	158
1871	488	49	187	108	...	...	...	...	522	56	...	70	170
1872	490	55	186	108	...	...	...	...	488	53	...	71	176
1873	510	56	194	108	...	...	...	...	600	62	...	65	154
1874	531	58	217	109	...	...	...	...	688	67	...	66	173
1875	558	64	212	134	...	...	...	...	636	72	...	79	184
1876	540	73	208	132	...	...	...	...	1,165	83	...	91	198
1877	526	53	210	134	...	...	...	...	885	88	...	97	206
1878	601	81	232	137	...	...	...	...	955	107	...	102	204
1879	645	93	248	136	...	...	...	...	706	111	...	107	203
1880	629	96	241	128	...	...	...	...	735	114	...	114	213
1881	652	86	242	140	...	...	...	...	1,081	121	...	120	221
1882	704	94	276	136	...	...	...	...	819	145	...	125	215
1883	699	97	282	132	...	...	...	...	821	130	...	130	220
1884	705	97	277	126	...	...	...	...	815	123	...	133	216
1885	762	95	265	131	...	...	...	...	799	126	...	132	228
1886	781	112	272	125	...	...	...	...	866	133	...	129	235
1887	830	107	305	82	...	...	...	...	787	134	...	90	242
1888	899	141	320	84	...	...	...	...	731	100	...	90	221
1889	927	138	335	88	...	...	...	...	746	127	...	90	223
1890	944	142	333	89	...	...	...	...	747	134	...	89	225
1891	892	128	312	87	...	...	...	...	745	134	...	93	220
1892	970	131	344	91	...	...	...	...	707	129	36	95	223
1893	1,046	166	346	100	56	19	9	13	736	144	35	89	237
1894	1,154	184	398	102	59	19	9	14	728	127	39	88	233
1895	1,256	179	420	106	59	19	7	16	733	113	39	90	232
1896	1,369	182	428	99	60	19	8	16	793	121	36	95	233
1897	1,416	196	453	101	62	20	9	16	775	93	30	95	229
1898	1,585	219	518	104	66	22	9	17	868	104	35	95	230
1899	1,673	219	560	121	72	24	11	19	[483][29]	[75][29]	[19][29]	[48][29]	[114][29]

See p. 768 for footnotes

H 5 Government Revenue and Main Tax Yields

1850–1899

	Sweden				Switzerland		United Kingdom[2]			
	Total	Customs (million kronor)	Excise	I. & P.	Total[31] (million francs)	Customs	Total	Customs (million pounds)	Excise	L. and I. & P.
1850	...	...	...	...	4.7	4	57	22	15	10
1851	...	...	...	...	5.6	5	56	22	15	9
1852	...	...	...	...	6.3	6	57	22	16	9
1853	...	...	...	...	6.3	6	59	23	16	9
1854	...	...	...	...	5.9	6	62[2]	22[2]	17[2]	14[2]
1855	...	...	...	...	6.2	6	70	23	17	18
1856	...	...	...	...	6.7	6	72	24	18	19
1857	...	...	...	...	7.1	6	67	23	18	15
1858	...	...	...	...	8.1	7	64	24	18	10
1859	...	...	...	...	9.4	7	70	24	20	13
1860	...	...	...	...	8.4	8	70	23	19	14
1861	...	13	8	10	8.8	8	69	24	18	14
1862	...	12	8	10	8.8	8	69	24	17	14
1863	...	13	9	10	9.2	9	68	23	18	12
1864	...	14	9	10	9.3	9	69	23	20	11
1865	...	14	10	10	9.3	9	66	21	20	10
1866	...	13	9	10	9.2	9	68	22	21	9
1867	...	13	8	10	9.0	8	68	23	20	10
1868	...	15	7	11	9.6	9	71	22	20	12
1869	...	14	8	10	9.5	9	74	22	22[32]	15
										[32]
1870	...	16	11	10	9.2	9	68	20	23	9
1871	...	19	12	10	13	11	73	20	23	11
1872	...	19	13	11	13	13	75	21	26	10
1873	...	24	14	9	15	14	75	20	27	8
1874	...	29	14	14	16	15	74	19	27	7
1875	...	24	15	10	19	17	75	20	28	7
1876	...	26	15	11	19	17	77	20	28	8
1877	...	26	13	11	19	16	78	20	27	8
1878	...	23	13	11	20	16	81	20	27	11
1879	...	25	12	12	22	17	73	19	25	12
1880	...	28	15	12	23	17	82	19	25	13
1881	87	30	17	13	23	17	84	19	27	13
1882	86	31	13	13	23	19	87	20	27	15
1883	88	34	13	11	25	20	86	20	27	14
1884	88	34	14	10	26	21	88	20	27	15
1885	88	33	16	11	27	21	90	20	25	18
1886	84	32	16[30]	9	28	22	91	20	25	19
			21							
1887	75	30	15	9	31	25	90	20	26	17
1888	91	37	22	9	33	26	90	20	26	16
1889	97	42	21	9	35	28	95	20	27	16
1890	101	42	24	10	39	31	97	20	29	16
1891	94	37	23	10	39	32	99	20	30	16
1892	95	37	24	10	43	36	98	20	30	16
1893	98	36	26	11	46	38	98	20	30	18
1894	110	38	28	14	49	41	102	20	31	18
1895	116	39	31	14	51	43	109	21	32	19
1896	121	42	34	10	55	46	112	21	32	19
1897	137	43	38	9	56	48	116	22	33	20
1898	144	51	36	9	57	49	118	21	34	20
1899	155	59	39	9	62	51	130	24	37	21

See p. 768 for footnotes

H 5 Government Revenue and Main Tax Yields

1900–1949

	Austria[1,12]					Belgium			
	Total	Customs	Con. Taxes	Direct Taxes	S. & I. Mon.	Total	Customs	Excise	Direct Taxes
			(million kronen)				(million francs)		
1900	1,654	111	275	268	176	494	44	67	58
1901	1,687	102	275	283	169	501	43	73	60
1902	1,728	105	267	279	171	504	42	72	60
1903	1,758	112	271	289	172	514	44	61	60
1904	1,798	119	304	288	177	533	46	70	61
1905	1,882	127	301	298	179	581	52	89	63
1906	2,008	135	327	310	193	597	53	81	65
1907	2,253	144	329	335	193	618	54	77	68
1908	2,388	149	338	349	198	617	54	80	68
1909	2,796	170	340	366	197	645	58	82	70
1910	2,895	171	355	370	205	682	64	78	73
1911	3,083	190	384	384	229	695	63	94	74
1912	3,173	195	370	408	247	755	71	91	76
1913	3,486	228	414	432	254	...	...	...	...
1914	[1,704][12] [12]	... [12]	... [12]	[207][12] [12]	... [12]	...	...	...	...
1915	10,039	...	488	426	286	...	...	...	...
1916	...	...	...	437	...	...	...	...	...
1917	...	...	...	...	...	...	...	...	...
1918	... [1,11,12]	... [1,11,12]	... [1,11,12]	... [1,11,12]	... [1,11,12]	...	...	...	...
1919	...	...	...	...	...	...	...	...	...
					Turnover Tax				
1920	...	...	249	1,555	35	3,766	200	115	422
1921	...	...	1,376	15,835	164	4,626	195	189	465
1922	...	260	46,018	139,605	111,230	6,720	256	205	490
1923	6,069,600	1,124,133	674,676	1,611,759	1,047,421	7,165	364	369	1,477
			(million schillings)						
1924	834	148	80	283	239	8,118	433	425	1,412
1925	901	201	85	285	226	8,304	551	435	1,899
1926	967	214	89	325	230	9,299	709	636	2,436
1927	1,024	241	86	327	241	10,763	901	802	2,737
1928	1,086	263	91	353	253	12,413	1,097	910	3,217
1929	1,164	286	102	385	257	13,714	1,319	1,001	3,668
1930	1,170	290	126	373	250	11,045	1,336	997	2,868
1931	1,142	273	185	343	220	10,767	1,303	1,036	2,678
1932	1,049	230	177	321	207	8,989	1,556	1,119	2,338
1933	970	180	160	276	252	10,357	1,496	1,280	2,883
1934	1,020	204	177	275	262	9,973	1,497	1,254	2,797
1935	1,075	211	185	298	278	10,015	1,456	1,336	2,610
1936	1,086	215	193	289	266	10,635	1,554	1,295	3,007
1937	1,134	215	194	321	281	11,102	1,587	1,429	2,828
1938	...	...	...	...	...	11,108	1,543	1,518	3,132
1939	...	...	...	...	...	11,339	1,438	1,541	3,439
1940	...	...	...	...	...	9,911	679	1,650	3,679
1941	...	...	...	...	...	13,574	583	2,007	4,872
1942	...	...	...	...	...	16,344	372	2,444	6,236
1943	...	...	...	...	...	16,802	272	2,000	7,513
1944	...	...	...	...	...	17,748	168	1,906	9,506
1945	638	6	72	476	69	20,887	188	2,383	8,392
1946	1,651	10	554	810	200	47,133	2,146	5,071	15,351
1947	3,542	17	1,150	1,722	462	46,910	3,701	6,204	12,971
1948	4,111	45	1,233	1,813	754	62,543	3,159	8,211	24,641
1949	6,520	143	1,188	3,275	1,403	66,857	3,332	8,117	27,759

See p. 768 for footnotes

H 5 Government Revenue and Main Tax Yields

1900–1949

	Bulgaria				Czechoslovakia				
	Total	Customs	Excise	Direct Taxes	Total[7]	Customs	Excise	Direct Taxes	Turnover Tax
	(million leva)				(million korunnas)				
1900	74	23		35	...	...	...	...	...
1901	92	28		31	...	...	...	...	...
1902	97	31		32	...	...	...	...	...
1903	99	33		34	...	...	...	...	...
1904	115	40		36	...	...	...	...	...
1905	128	46[33]		38	...	...	...	...	...
		15	25						
1906	134	17	22	41	...	...	...	...	...
1907	146	22	29	39	...	...	...	...	...
1908	149	22	29	40	...	...	...	...	...
1909	163	27	31	33	...	...	...	...	...
1910	172	28	31	40	...	...	...	...	...
1911	199	30	45	34	...	...	...	...	...
1912	170	31	42	18	...	...	...	...	...
1913	169	26	47	14	...	...	...	...	...
1914	224	32	52	29	...	...	...	...	...
1915	195	15	51	26	...	...	...	...	...
1916	193	14	42	33	...	...	...	...	...
1917	338	19	79	39	...	...	...	...	...
1918	567[34]	24[34]	174[34]	58[34]	...	...	...	...	...
1919	844	40	149	104	1,957	160	413	760	–
1920	2,006	423	300	288	5,453	408	1,734	1,217	500
1921	2,846	665	406	378	8,630	768	2,641	1,819	1,349
1922	4,423	1,298	653	331	8,924	947	2,106	1,853	1,631
1923	5,362	1,275	746	206	8,111	785	1,493	1,788	1,434
1924	6,858	1,470	1,006	343	8,723	871	1,368	2,187	1,553
1925	6,364	1,402	1,152	402	9,162	848	1,349	2,397	1,780
1926	6,234	1,184	1,171	465	9,939	1,010	1,420	2,494	1,934
1927	6,687	1,263	1,184	568	11,135	1,399	1,782	2,545	2,102
1928	6,282	1,374	1,338	779	11,045	1,503	1,885	1,971	2,341
1929	6,713	1,407	1,396	625	11,316	1,429	1,938	2,032	2,346
1930	5,597	853	1,323	603	10,870	1,240	1,898	1,893	2,357
1931	5,212	961	1,252	490	10,836	1,331	2,171	1,771	2,214
1932	4,751	883	1,098	392	10,651	879	2,120	2,067	2,227
1933	4,987[34]	626[34]	1,002[34]	456[34]	10,043	651	2,016	1,855	2,311
1934	[3,713]	[537]	[977]	[418]	10,077	666	1,996	1,719	2,391
1935	5,399	672	1,302	394	9,818	673	1,984	1,763	2,313
1936	6,020	823	1,445	527	10,234	743	2,106	1,868	2,365
1937	6,847	1,124	1,513	590	10,014	787	2,272	1,979	2,792
1938	7,188	1,138	1,671	608	...	...	...	...	...
1939	7,708	1,173	1,771	656	...	...	...	...	...
1940	8,994	1,178	1,969	1,012	...	...	...	...	...
1941	13,094	1,163	3,088	2,430	...	...	...	...	...
1942	...	...	...	...	...	...	...	...	...
1943	...	...	...	...	...	...	...	...	...
1944	...	...	...	...	...	...	...	...	...
1945	...	...	...	...	[12,017][35]	...	...	[7,685][35]	[1,430][35]
1946	...	...	...	...	35,211	602	5,729	15,620	6,955
1947	...	...	...	...	...	...	...	...	...
1948	...	...	...	...	...	...	...	...	...
1949	...	...	...	...	...	...	...	...	...

See p. 768 for footnotes

H 5 Government Revenue and Main Tax Yields

1900–1949

	Denmark[14]				Finland				
	Total	Customs	Excise	Income & Property	Total	Customs	Excise	Income & Property	Sales
	(million kroner)				(million markaa)				
1900	67	33	10	11	61	27	7	...	—
1901	66	32	10	11	92	30	7	...	—
1902	74	35	10	11	93	31	6	...	—
1903	79	37	10	11	100	36	6	...	—
1904	96	38	10	13	103	36	6	...	—
1905	87	37	12	14	106	38	8	...	—
1906	102	39	13	13	122	47	7	...	—
1907	96	42	13	15	133	49	8	...	—
1908	93	41	15	15	144	48	9	...	—
1909	82	29	14	16	144	49	12	...	—
1910	91	32	13	18	152	51	13	...	—
1911	102	33	15	20	158	53	10	...	—
1912	114	36	18	20	171	57	14	...	—
1913	124	35	21	24	181	58	14	...	—
1914	122	33	22	26	168	46	13	...	—
1915	142	37	23	31	194	42	4	...	—
1916	242	41	25	35	304	46	20	...	—
1917	375	30	41	74	440	34	13	...	—
1918	462	25	59	71	470	17	- -	...	—
1919	594	73	98	102	1,039	239	75	...	—
1920	499	59	116	336	1,734	334	153	...	—
1921	409	56	100	259	2,283	551	127	...	—
1922	427	72	103	138	2,669	799	141	...	—
1923	390	89	122	120	3,063	1,058	181	...	—
1924	432	80	137	132	3,158	1,042	171	...	—
1925	383	80	130	141	3,316	1,175	179	...	—
1926	369	88	120	126	3,424	1,021	184	...	—
1927	338	88[14]	117[14]	103	3,908	1,227	197	...	—
1928	312	90	113	93	4,476	1,390	215	...	—
1929	336	102	123	97	4,302	1,337	221	...	—
1930	343	108	121	104	4,275	1,405	210	...	—
1931	333	105	122	104	3,756	1,130	216	...	—
1932	335	83	128	91	2,438	1,021	217	...	—
1933	376	94	198	86	2,873	1,243	278	...	—
1934	411	104	240	100	3,367	1,490	330	580	—
1935	419	105	233	116	3,482	1,480	400	570	—
1936	469	106	248	121	3,725	1,620	400	...	—
1937	521	109	263	130	4,316	1,720	470	740	—
1938	543	114	273	193	4,862	1,830	480	1,090	—
1939	621	123	308	227	4,709	1,560	590	...	—
1940	879	105	417	348	5,182	920	940	1,440	—
1941	927	75	458	363	11,967	1,380	1,370	1,760	1,410
1942	1,125	58	541	442	17,185	1,660	1,650	3,380	3,510
1943	1,161	47	584	494	22,039	1,050	1,740	4,860	4,000
1944	1,237	49	729	562	23,640	660	1,930	4,890	4,020
1945	1,291	28	633	641	33,734	400	2,270	10,710	6,870
1946	1,901	125	966	751	66,400	2,440	4,430	17,280	13,530
1947	2,020	102	1,205	875	70,207	4,560	5,370	22,140	18,290
1948	2,170	96	1,367	1,014	99,434	9,110	7,770	28,770	27,680
1949	2,189	127	1,406	935	111,402	12,450	9,280	23,040	29,740

See p. 768 for footnotes

H 5 Government Revenue and Main Tax Yields

1900–1949

	France						Germany[19]				
	Total	Customs	Excise	Reg.	Turnover & Trans.	Direct Taxes	Total[7]	Customs	Excise	Income	Turnover
	(million francs)						(million marks)				
1900	3,815	415	668	573	–	524	887	466	341	...	...
1901	3,576	383	576	550	–	532	901	494	323	...	...
1902	3,582	365	557	567	–	533	909	498	320	...	...
1903	3,668	402	580	592	–	541	906	508	311	...	...
1904	3,739	401	614	592	–	549	928	490	345	...	...
1905	3,766	410	586[36]	626	–	555	1,055	626	326	...	...
1906	3,837	478	590	609	–	560	1,075	557	375	...	...
1907	3,968	509	603	646	–	561	1,206	645	422	...	...
1908	3,966	494	618	643	–	570	1,121	546	406	...	...
1909	4,141	526	623	686	–	577	1,360	660	464	...	...
1910	4,274	586	645	690	–	587	1,499	663	548	...	...
1911	4,689	768	680	805	–	599	1,676	734	635	...	...
1912	4,857	685	680	811	–	612	1,662	728	617	...	...
1913	5,092	778	697	834	–	634	1,665[38] 2,095	679	660	...	...
1914	4,549	603	581	611	–	611	2,399	561	776	...	...
1915	4,131	786	495	464	–	547	1,769	360	581	...	...
1916	5,259	1,422	506	525	–	608	2,045	348	679	...	...
1917	6,943	1,599	651	719	–	839	7,682	...	...	...	...
1918	7,621	1,258	780	929	–	1,460	6,830	...	...	...	...
1919	13,282	1,580	1,314	1,879	–	1,735	9,712	...	...	...	...
1920	22,502	1,916	1,888	2,724	1,757	1,910	53,046	2,163	8,994	11,195	4,988
1921	23,119	1,521	3,223	2,699	1,927	3,457	149,570	5,952	15,264	32,773	11,474
1922	23,888	2,003	2,771	2,965	2,314	3,386	...	...	...	...	...
1923	26,224	2,058	3,070	3,394	3,045	4,533	...	...	...	...	...
1924	30,568	2,153	3,567	4,614	4,120	5,838	4,650	357	1,193	2,527	1,918
1925	33,455	2,114	3,946	5,134	4,583	6,075	4,731	591	1,371	2,440	1,416
1926	41,902	2,899	5,513	6,029	7,517	8,052	5,313	940	1,520	2,636	876
1927	45,746	3,972	6,207	3,701	8,645	10,020	6,357	1,251	1,688	3,262	878
1928	48,177	4,658	6,751	4,471	9,318	9,936	6,568	1,105	1,771	3,718	1,000
1929	64,268	6,958	8,987	6,534	12,403	11,036	6,741	1,095	1,804	3,584	1,013
1930	50,794	6,139	7,041	4,879	8,744	10,531	6,634	1,083	1,980	3,211	996
1931	47,944	7,379	6,911	4,046	7,558	10,060	5,704	1,147	1,637	2,447	994
1932	36,038	5,226	4,792	2,625	5,152	8,841	4,994	1,106	1,514	1,438	1,354
1933	43,536	6,297	6,408	3,560	6,897	7,997	6,850	1,070	1,720	1,503	1,516
1934	41,070	6,575	4,970	3,245	6,387	7,841	8,220	1,149	1,945	2,040	1,873
1935	39,485	6,161	5,217	3,013	5,857	5,984	9,650	1,249	2,225	3,097	2,020
1936	38,676	6,522	5,173	2,851	6,123	5,717	11,492	1,333	2,315	4,256	2,389
1937	44,224	7,754	4,963	3,226	6,985	6,815	13,964	1,595	2,542	5,612	2,754
1938	54,606	8,823	5,120	4,094	9,848	9,245	17,712	1,818	2,828	7,769	3,357
1939	63,005	10,184	5,440	3,970	13,490	11,434	23,575	1,697	4,422	11,453	3,735
1940	71,953	8,053	5,776	2,991	18,201	13,636	27,221	1,414	5,578	14,211	3,929
1941	80,195	2,576	6,503	5,185	20,914	19,823	32,258	1,121	6,189	18,208	4,149
1942	97,320	1,610	4,731	7,450	26,005	28,548	34,700	832	6,176	19,831	4,160
1943	124,246[37]	998	4,365	8,807	37,502	40,918	...	640	5,943	20,038	4,177
1944	129,934[37]	584	4,139	7,680	35,137	44,274	...	...	...	...	...
	(thousand million francs)						West Germany[39]				
1945	222	4	9	11	66	61	...	...	...	...	...
1946	434	18	16	31	153	78	12,004	25	1,927	5,727	1,769
1947	670	37	25	40	230	163	14,377	174	2,259	6,273	2,302
1948	1,021	54	42	49	396	263	4,877[40] 8,977	72[40] 99	697[40] 1,705	2,211[40] 4,176	842[40] 2,199
1949	1,441	101	53	80	625	357	15,410	278	3,425	6,234	3,835

See p. 768 for footnotes

H 5 Government Revenue and Main Tax Yields

1900–1949

	Greece[20]				Hungary[21]				
	Total	Customs	Con.	Direct Taxes	Total[22]	Con.	Turnover	Direct Taxes	Customs
	(million drachmae)				(million kronen)				
1900	112	...	...	...	1,042	177	...	226	...
1901	115	...	...	...	1,039	175	...	228	...
1902	114	...	...	...	1,064	178	...	230	...
1903	115	34.4	45.2	19.3	1,027	185	...	187	...
1904	116	...	...	...	1,177	190	...	266	...
1905	126	...	...	...	1,015	175	...	124	...
1906	126	...	...	...	1,335	206	...	311	...
1907	126	...	...	...	1,370	219	...	295	...
1908	128	...	...	...	1,409	236	...	277	...
1909	130	...	...	...	1,452	233	...	277	...
1910	142	...	...	...	1,543	248	...	277	...
1911	136	...	62.1	23.5	1,703	268	...	310	...
1912	131	...	...	...	1,804	301	...	306	...
1913	174	...	...	...	1,839	300	...	326	...
1914	218	...	...	...	[889][21]	[153][21]	...	[133][21]	...
1915	222	...	...	...	1,829	322	...	302	...
1916	226	...	...	...	2,283	387	...	359	...
1917	234	...	...	...	2,772	312	...	495	...
1918	...[20]	...[20]	...[20]	...[20]	5,015[21]	362[21]	...	1,206[21]	...
1919	516	...	...	117	...	...	...	...	...
1920	586	...	...	...	...	...	...	...	...
1921	725	165	97	148	13,831	4,045	...	4,587	1,523
1922	978	192	...	...	33,029	3,882	...	3,223	5,629
1923	1,895	471	...	...	194,572	8,577	...	20,751	13,850
1924	3,712	1,039	...	...	4,676,719	249,361	...	365,499	263,613
					(million pengos)				
1925	5,091[20]	886	...	898	...	59	224	95	...
1926	6,045	2,151	...	...	...	83	238	159	...
1927	...	...	...	1,197	1,334	86	265	166	129
1928	9,448	2,605	1,694	1,763	1,422	97	270	191	133
1929	9,602	2,579	1,646	1,871	1,467	102	265	226	107
1930	10,322	2,709	1,654	1,755	1,372	96	232	222	78
1931	10,096	2,660	1,606	1,595	1,242	85	191	219	61
1932	9,506	3,514	1,649	1,756	1,151	78	201	252	35
1933	8,360	2,826	1,628	1,551	1,041	79	194	230	21
1934	8,476	2,739	1,763	1,656	1,102	84	198	228	24
1935	9,237	2,931	1,927	2,051	1,102	85	203	225	29
1936	10,647	3,464	2,017	2,201	1,180	93	219	230	29
1937	13,244	3,669	2,104	2,655	1,294	101	246	250	29
1938	14,131	3,893	2,524	2,988	1,352	105	251	255	50
1939	12,655	3,753	2,730	3,284	1,606	109	271	274	52
1940	12,620	...	...	...	[3,229][41]	[199][41]	[570][41]	[522][41]	[107][41]
1941	...	...	...	...	...	...	...	...	...
1942	...	...	...	...	...	...	...	...	...
1943	...	...	...	...	...	...	...	...	...
1944	...	...	...	...	...	...	...	...	...
1945	...	...	...	...	...	...	...	...	...
1946	...	...	...	...	...	...	...	...	...
1947	...	...	...	...	...	...	...	...	...
1948	...	...	...	...	...	...	...	...	...
1949	...	...	...	...	...	...	...	...	...

See p. 768 for footnotes

H 5 Government Revenue and Main Tax Yields

1900–1949

	Southern Ireland[42]				Italy				
	Total	Customs	Excise	I. & P.	Total	Customs	T. & I. Mon.	Direct Per. Taxes	Profits Tax
	(million pounds)				(million lire)				
1900	...	...	...	...	1,671	203	270	484	–
1901	...	...	...	...	1,721	187	276	485	–
1902	...	...	...	...	1,744	183	285	487	–
1903	...	...	...	...	1,795	179	285	490	–
1904	...	...	...	...	1,787	176	293	491	–
1905	...	...	...	...	1,853	170	303	494	–
1906	...	...	...	...	1,946	198	312	494	–
1907	...	...	...	...	1,954	232	319	459	–
1908	...	...	...	...	1,946	240	340	436	–
1909	...	...	...	...	2,134	256	355	452	–
1910	...	...	...	...	2,237	249	376	464	–
1911	...	...	...	...	2,403	270	388	481	–
1912	...	...	...	...	2,475	259	407	500	–
1913	...	...	...	...	2,529	271	423	519	–
1914	...	...	...	...	2,524	259	440	541	–
1915	...	...	...	...	2,560	193	462	592	–
1916	...	...	...	...	3,734	310	607	659	–
1917	...	...	...	...	5,345	470	724	695	–
1918	...	...	...	...	7,533	535	958	751	
1919	...	...	...	...	9,676	530	1,294	752	–
1920	...	...	...	...	15,207	513	1,706	986	–
1921	...	...	...	...	18,820	527	2,597	1,306	–
1922	28	2	16	5	19,701	620	2,816	1,922	–
1923	31	8	9	6	18,803	517	2,923	2,203	144
1924	27	8	8	6	20,582	523	3,006	3,217	592
1925	25	7	6	6	20,440	913	3,076	3,361	753
1926	25	7	7	6	21,043	663	3,255	4,008	873
1927	24	7	7	5	21,450	645	3,465	4,612	787
1928	24	7	7	5	20,072	1,458	3,479	4,224	644
1929	24	7	6	4	20,201	2,095	2,647	4,117	704
1930	24	7	6	5	19,838	1,848	2,786	4,147	424
1931	25	8	5	5	20,387	1,670	2,947	4,080	911
1932	30	9	5	6	19,324	1,943	2,894	4,010	1,103
1933	30	10	5	6	18,217	1,873	2,859	3,791	1,037
1934	29	9	6	6	18,057	1,836	2,816	3,705	1,052
1935	31	10	6	6	18,817	1,733	2,791	3,663	1,115
1936	31	10	6	6	20,371	1,410	2,827	3,641	1,312
1937	31	10	6	6	24,702	1,302	2,965	3,882	1,552
1938	32	10	6	6	27,468	1,365	3,245	4,278	2,241
1939	32	11	6	7	27,576	1,158	3,424	4,671	2,476
1940	35	12	7	8	32,350	1,255	3,744	4,976	3,317
1941	37	11	7	10	34,234	1,119	4,270	5,360	5,023
1942	40	11	7	13	41,224	1,159	5,808	5,737	5,988
1943	44	11	8	15	50,376	1,248	7,893	6,781	5,801
1944	46	11	9	17	47,236	499	6,993	7,655	6,272
1945	51	13	10	18	64,635	133	10,019	8,899	10,271
					(thousand million lire)				
1946	54	17	9	17	160	1	35	20	48
1947	65	22	11	18	382	4	62	40	102
1948	72	24	13	20	851	13	111	84	191
1949	74	25	13	19	1,138	7	171	112	256

See p. 768 for footnotes

H 5 Government Revenue and Main Tax Yields

1900–1949

	Netherlands (million guilders)					Norway			
	Total	Customs	Excise	Direct Taxes	Turnover	Total	Customs	Con.	Income & Property
1900	138[43] 120	10	49	35[44] 58	...	64	28	9	6
1901	119	10	51	55	...	83	35	12	6
1902	125	10	52	61	...	86	36	13	6
1903	128	11	53	64	...	84	34	13	6
1904	130	11	55	64	...	86	35	12	5
1905	132	12	55	67	...	83	33	11	5
1906	139	12	57	70	...	92	36	12	5
1907	138	12	58	71	...	99	40	11	6
1908	139	12	57	74	...	107	44	12	7
1909	145	13	59	77	...	134	53	16	7
1910	151	13	62	83	...	116	49	10	8
1911	154	14	63	88	...	123	51	10	8
1912	158	16	64	90	...	131	54	11	9
1913	166	17	67	96	...	143	51	8	13
1914	165	14	69	103	...	102	52	12	17
1915	195	15	71	123	...	112	53	13	35
1916	272	17	79	192	...	144	55	19	52
1917	503	13	89	262	...	243	65	18	390
1918	506	10	85	287	...	443	52	15	384
1919	611	33	105	370	...	488	67	19	365
1920	744	52	123	527	...	562	127	25	197
1921	666	41	132	613	...	448	69	27	196
1922	592	42	141	564	...	372	64	31	283
1923	531	39	140	492	...	317	94	41	140
1924	506	40	139	461	...	313	103	45	118
1925	540	45	149	467	...	378	126	61	120
1926	569	54	154	477	...	371	111	71	127
1927	596	58	156	483	...	363	111	67	120
1928	571	57	161	463	...	363	118	92	103
1929	606	62	156	500	...	351	106	92	83
1930	583	66	156	500	...	356	111	94	82
1931	502	70	153	460	...	330	104	92	79
1932	460	61	147	392	...	317	104	90	79
1933	455	100	156	375	...	259	99	97	71
1934	476	81	136	381	...	278	106	101	72
1935	499	89	135	383	...	293	113	108	71
1936	507	84	132	372	...	350	126	139	82
1937	582	91	138	404	...	413	140	170	90
1938	600	98	142	437	...	474	145	188	117
1939	645	123	154	448	89	533	154	201	175
1940	683	80	195	497	109	562	150	198	192
1941	1,142	22	249	856	178	940	129	480	259
1942	1,481	...	...	1,042	...	1,220	78	686	320
1943	1,460	9	161	1,083	196	1,406	61	753	394
1944	1,356	6	135	1,027	173	1,450	46	791	399
1945	645	8	85	452	116	1,353	37	760	389
1946	2,422	54	247	1,859	342	1,426	120	790	359
1947	3,328	68	316	2,331	518	2,270	218	1,114	411
1948	5,374	230	349	2,258	689	2,415	179	1,176	675
1949	4,288	258	405	2,496	746	2,769	151	1,133	1,172

See p. 768 for footnotes

H 5 Government Revenue and Main Tax Yields

1900–1949

	Poland[46]				Portugal[26]				Romania		
	Total[7]	Customs	Con.	Direct Taxes	Total[27]	Customs	Property	Business	Total	Customs	Prop.
	(million zlotys)				(million escudos)						
1900	...	...	...	...	53	16	3.1	1.7	210	18	16
1901	...	...	...	...	55	15	3.2	1.8	239	25	17
1902	...	...	...	...	53	14	3.3	1.8	250	26	17
1903	...	...	...	...	54	16	3.0	1.7	247	25	17
1904	...	...	...	...	...	17	...	...	259	23	17
1905	...	...	...	...	...	17	...	...	308	36	17
1906	...	...	...	...	...	17	...	...	292	40	19
1907	...	...	...	...	...	16	...	...	316	50	18
1908	...	...	...	...	...	17	...	...	469	49	18
1909	...	...	...	...	...	16	...	...	459	49	18
1910	...	...	...	...	...	16	...	...	583	58	18
1911	...	...	...	...	...	16	...	...	644	73	19
1912	...	...	...	...	...	17	4.8	2.7	621	66	18
1913	...	...	...	...	...	22	6.5	2.8	639	67	18
1914	...	...	...	...	...	25	6.9	3.0	755	44	...
1915	...	...	...	...	...	23	6.7	3.1	...	34	...
1916	...	...	...	...	...	17	6.8	3.2	379	90	...
1917	...	...	...	...	86	19	6.8	3.3	187	2	...
1918	...	...	...	...	100	19	6.9	...	419	8	...
1919	...	...	...	...	128	19	8.3	...	1,115	93	...
1920	...	...	...	...	...	25	...	...	3,554	1,083	...
1921	...	...	...	...	...	51	...	...	7,708	1,501	...
1922	404	31	184	150	388	50	...	...	15,114	3,816	...
1923	674	100	229	281	544	84	...	...	[18,792][28]	[5,778][28]	...
1924	1,182	238	384	291	842	114	...	...	27,744	8,085	...
1925	1,329[46]	285[46]	508[46]	363[46]	1,365	133	...	...	34,039	7,325	...
1926	1,754	213	776	513	1,369	280	109	121	31,224	8,753	...
1927	2,222	372	964	615	1,312	350	104	97	36,008	9,252	...
1928	2,628	425	1,072	766	1,642	445	109	116	32,768	6,890	...
1929	2,622	395	1,078	786	2,165[27]	633[47] / 653	179	127	36,018	5,727	...
1930	2,271	258	988	718	2,072	682	191	206	31,155	4,306	...
1931	1,859	157	849	589	1,969	664	192	176	27,643	2,518	...
1932	1,610	108	781	539	1,889	672	194	169	17,848[28]	2,019[28]	...
1933	1,595	94	800	516	1,908	658	199	162	18,364	1,869	...
1934	1,588	80	794	539	1,981	712	181	155	18,809	1,824	...
1935	1,640	83	816	522	[3,049][26]	[1,163][26]	[286][26]	[248][26]	23,096[48]	1,354	...
1936	1,851	92	821	648[45]	2,047	818	231	199	27,184	1,518	...
1937	2,049	168	856	723	2,153	806	233	204	30,345	1,511	...
1938	...	...	...	...	2,259	845	237	195	31,649	1,325	...
1939	...	...	...	...	2,177	770	230	204	35,109	...	...
1940	...	...	...	...	2,223	724	248	217	40,813	...	...
1941	...	...	...	...	2,447	819	263	223	66,763	...	...
1942	...	...	...	...	2,967	984	263	243	112,820	...	...
1943	...	...	...	...	3,269	1,011	264	257	139,960[41] [28]	...[28]	...
1944	...	...	...	...	3,340	864	266	321	...	...	...
1945	...	...	...	...	3,328	839	271	371	...	...	...
1946	...	...	...	...	3,900	1,245	275	378	...	...	...
1947	...	...	...	...	4,433	1,528	297	460	...	...	...
1948	...	...	...	...	4,433	1,436	304	525	...	...	...
1949	...	...	...	...	4,692	1,564	322	542	...	...	...

See p. 768 for footnotes

H 5 Government Revenue and Main Tax Yields

1900–1949

	Russia[8]					Spain				
	Total	Customs	Excise[9]	Direct Taxes		Total	Customs	Con.	P. & T. Mon.	Direct Taxes
	(million new rubels)					(million pesetas)				
1900	1,704	204	572	132		914	168	120	118	254[51]
1901	1,799	219	630	131		959[50] / 952	166	131	125	380
1902	1,905	225	688	133		961	140	128	132	395
1903	2,032	241	741	135		989	144	136	134	402
1904	2,018	219	743	135		990	141	138	132	404
1905	2,025	213	805	127		990	164	128	130	393
1906	2,272	241	950	163		1,051	183	133	133	405
1907	2,342	260	956	183		1,027	160	138	133	407
1908	2,418	279	956	194		1,021	156	138	136	410
1909	2,526	274	974	199		1,015	157	135	137	417
1910	2,781	301	1,059	216		1,066	169	145	143	420
1911	2,952	328	1,086	224		1,079	177	147	138	438
1912	3,106	327	1,148	243		1,111	181	143	151	447
1913	3,417	353	1,254	273		1,286	225	148	151	456
1914	2,898	304	861	281		1,227	196	137	153	445
1915	...	...	...	...		1,159	134	132	149	452
1916	...	...	...	...		1,231	150	129	164	475
1917	...[8]	...[8]	...[8]	...[8]		1,267	137	128	169	497
1918	...	...	...	...		1,303	120	140	162	531
1919	...	...	...	...		1,542[52]	206[52]	169[52]	159[52]	576[52]
		I. & T. Taxes			Ded. from from Profits					
1920	...	...	...	...	—	1,793	312	163	133	664
1921	...	...	...	...	—	2,163	402	207	186	770
1922	...	...	...	...	—	2,360	511	204	223	799
1923	...[49]	...[49]	...[49]	...[49]	—[49]	2,569	524	232	258	902
1924	2,134	113	241	296	—	2,758[52]	587[52]	225[52]	263[52]	944[52]
1925	2,872	157	508	421	—	2,816	579	239	260	951
1926	3,893	229	842	403	—	[1,396][52]	[261][52]	[128][52]	[135][52]	[475][52]
1927	5,056	349	1,210	550	—	3,096	576	244	279	1,119
1928	5,888	373	1,491	586	—	3,396	624	241	398	1,166
1929	7,497	1,056	1,803	735	—	3,568	655	258	441	1,203
1930	11,521[49]	1,941[49]	2,643[49]	1,020[49]	—[49]	3,585	568	262	480	1,246
1931	19,886	10,730	—	803	—	3,373	490	263	503	1,241
1932	27,109[49] / 33,050	17,693[49] / 17,693	—[49] / —	704[49] / 2,699	—[49] / 1,657	3,633	518	272	572	1,234
1933	43,191	23,167	—	3,310	2,072	3,701	481	280	604	1,299
1934	54,155	30,242	—	3,621	2,375	3,643	470	...	618	1,249
1935	...	...	—	...	...	3,854	472	...	662	1,350
1936	...	...	—	...	...	...	...	...	[203][53]	...
1937	...	...	—	...	...	...	...	...	[137][53]	...
1938	127,571	80,411	—	5,047	10,598	...	...	...	[270][53]	...
1939	...	...	—	...	...	...	...	...	[482][53]	...
	(million new rube s)									
1940	16.9	10.6	—	0.9	2.2	4,443	207	...	893	2,016
1941	...	...	—	...	...	6,454	249	1,260	826	2,672
1942	...	...	—	...	...	7,785	467	1,615	688	3,237
1943	...	...	—	...	...	9,674	718	2,158	865	3,471
1944	...	...	—	...	...	10,180	637	2,365	924	3,636
1945	...	...	—	...	...	9,460	423	2,292	1,164	3,927
1946	...	...	—	...	...	9,888	619	2,334	1,482	3,975
						(thousand m. pesetas)				
1947	...	...	—	...	...	11.9	805	2,717	1,533	4,957
1948	...	...	—	...	...	12.8	871	3,296	1,472	5,425
1949	...	...	—	...	...	13.7	718	3,672	2,296	5,784

See p. 768 for footnotes

H 5 Government Revenue and Main Tax Yields

1900–1949

	Sweden					Switzerland			
	Total	Customs	Excise	I. & P.	Automobile	Total[31]	Customs	Con.	I. & P
	(million kronor)					(million francs)			
1900	152	57	44	9	–	59	48	–	–
1901	140	49	45	6	–	58	46	–	–
1902	147	55	40	12	–	62	50	–	–
1903	171	56	42	27[54]	–	66	53	–	–
1904	176	59	47	21	–	66	54	–	–
1905	185	59	50	22	–	78	64	–	–
1906	187	59	44	24	–	77	62	–	–
1907	204	59	57	27	–	87	72	–	–
1908	200	57	64	25	–	85	70	–	–
1909	189	58	52	28	–	91	74	–	–
1910	221	60	63	31	–	96	81	–	–
1911	236	60	67	36	–	99	81	–	–
1912	249	64	68	37	–	103	87	–	–
1913	264	69	66	41	–	100	85	–	–
1914	261	58	68	45	–	79	65	–	–
1915	365	55	73	44	–	78	55	–	–
1916	413	61	79	67	–	150	60	–	80
1917	636	43	54	114	–	211	52	–	136
1918	766	36	56	259	–	254	44	–	202
1919	891	100	108	277	–	322	67	–	218
1920	892	145	143	307	–	265	98	–	163
1921	767	102	173	298	–	247	113	–	87
1922	672	111	172	188	–	340	159	–	23
1923	[277][55]	[62][55]	[85][55]	[9][55]	–	283	179	–	48
1924	672	149	155	143	9	308	200	–	41
1925	653	140	171	145	19	346	213	–	35
1926	653	125	169	152	22	405	222	–	160
1927	673	141	175	151	25	359	225	–	45
1928	707	142	174	150	32	399	252	–	31
1929	733	154	166	149	40	436	267	–	61
1930	779	154	181	151	44	569	289	–	182
1931	783	148	173	166	51	455	308	–	45
1932	736	138	184	163	59	442	293	–	39
1933	741	117	213	148	73	418	291	–	23
1934	783	113	231	140	79	456	299	11	43
1935	903	136	247	156	88	490	299	29	62
1936	995[56] / 831	148	268	183	97	518	280	37	59
1937	949	167	276	233	107	528	283	41	56
1938	1,069	180	308	264	117	546	291	33	60
1939	1,244	207	330	366	130	603	331	34	66
1940	1,570	223	441	513	127	795	265[61]	40	53
1941	1,730	149	619	750	30	903[31] / 877	178	55	567
1942	1,942	109	810	794	30	793	160	179	381
1943	2,330	117	1,023	930	31	788	139	255	323
1944	2,687	122	1,165	1,178	34	919	100	303	445
1945	2,875	96	1,226	1,330	32	897	104	340	373
1946	3,173	151	1,321	1,408	83	1,633	293	418	836
1947	3,237	296	1,347	1,178	203	1,516	437	519	459
1948	4,179	329	1,250	2,056	263	1,634	435	566	534
1949	4,626	243	1,471	2,077	436	1,319	388	541	296

See p. 768 for footnotes

H 5 Government Revenue and Main Tax Yields

1900–1949

	United Kingdom[12]				Serbia			
	Total	Customs	Excise	Land & I. & P.[4]	Total	Direct Taxes	Indirect Taxes	State Monopolies
	(million pounds)				(million dinari)			
1900	140	27	38	29	75	29	10	20
1901	153	31	37	37	72	26	10	20
1902	161	35	37	41	74	23	11	21
1903	151	34	37	33	78	23	12	22
1904	153	36	36	34	88	30	13	24
1905	154	35	36	34	88	28	13	25
1906	155	33	36	34	91	26	15	27
1907	157	32	36	35	...	...	...	...
1908	152	29	34	37	...	...	...	...
1909	132	30	31	14	...	...	...	...
1910	204	33	40	66	117	...	...	...
1911	185	34	38	48	120	...	...	...
1912	189	33	38	48	128	...	...	...
1913	198	33	40	50	131	...	...	...
1914	227	39	42	72	214	...	...	...
1915	337	60	61	131	...	...	...	...
1916	573	71	56	348	...	...	...	...
1917	707	71	39	462	...	...	...	...
1918	889	103	59	579	...	...	...	...
1919	1,340	149	134	652	...	...	...	...
					Yugoslavia			
1920	1,426	134	200	616	3,884	...	...	...
1921	1,125	130	194	445	6,258	...	...	...
1922	914	123	157	403	8,135	...	...	...
1923	837	120	148	356	10,344	...	...	...
1924	799	99	135	355	10,405	...	...	...
1925	812	103	135	342	10,508	1,960	3,857	2,520
1926	806	108	133	310	12,504	1,828	3,577	2,529
1927	843	112	139	314	11,319	1,754	3,594	2,388
1928	836	119	134	296	7,541	1,775	3,227	2,305
1929	815	120	128	297	9,018	2,393	3,693	2,374
1930	858	121	124	327	8,476	2,094	3,587	2,325
1931	851	136	120	367	6,758	1,785	2,802	2,133
1932	827	162	121	315	6,132	1,793	2,504	1,894
1933	809	179	107	284	6,467	2,104	2,302	1,866
1934	805	185	105	283	6,698	2,199	2,457	1,840
1935	845	197	107	291	6,950	2,196	2,551	1,911
1936	897	211	110	312	10,571	2,390	2,732	1,918
1937	949	222	114	356	11,987	2,705	3,171	2,070
1938	1,006	226	114	420	12,387	...	...	...
1939	1,132	262	138	487	12,786	...	...	...
1940	1,495	305	224	696	15,116	...	...	...
1941	2,175	378	326	1,114	...	...	...	...
1942	2,922	460	425	1,460	...	...	...	...
1943	3,149	561	482	1,760	...	...	...	...
1944	3,355	579	497	1,901	...	...	...	...
					(thousand million dinari)			
1945	3,401	570	541	1,897	9	...	...	...
1946	3,623	621	564	1,590	24	...	...	...
1947	4,011	791	630	1,570	61	...	...	...
1948	4,168	823	733	1,744	87	...	...	...
1949	4,098	813	706	1,850	119	...	...	...

See p. 768 for footnotes

H 5 Government Revenue and Main Tax Yields

1950–1975

	Austria					Belgium			
	Total	Customs	Con. Taxes	Direct Taxes	Turnover	Total	Customs	Excise	Direct Taxes
	(million schillings)					(million francs)			
1950	8,662	172	1,395	4,323	2,089	63,321	3,975	7,828	23,649
1951	12,305	305	1,934	5,644	3,454	76,866	4,353	8,131	34,259
1952	14,583	420	1,955	3,261	4,549	77,584	4,383	9,283	31,647
1953	16,355	576	2,000	7,548	4,558	76,733	4,381	8,829	32,603
1954	17,498	971	2,161	7,558	4,979	75,771	4,577	8,818	30,202
1955	18,863	1,357	2,393	7,018	5,933	82,065	4,990	10,666	32,297
1956	21,281	1,471	2,620	8,376	6,427	89,075	16,547		34,401
1957	24,989	1,730	2,972	10,623	6,957	96,290	17,499		38,579
1958	26,269	1,836	3,266	11,055	7,233	99,604	18,166		36,826
1959	27,912	2,170	3,661	11,098	7,832	102,011	19,632		38,779
1960	30,783	2,803	3,799	12,162	8,568	109,224	21,992		41,557
1961	36,275	3,297	4,557	14,829	9,472	120,412	23,766		43,495
1962	40,078	3,423	5,132	16,702	10,341	131,454	24,529		50,310
1963	43,177	3,599	5,627	17,983	11,124	140,103	25,753		52,799
1964	48,627	3,963	6,144	20,189	12,830	157,881	28,209		60,470
1965	53,179	4,266	6,772	22,531	13,700	173,558	30,080		67,638
1966	59,126	4,825	7,727	25,120	14,909	200,716	34,182		77,619
1967	61,955	4,551	8,617	26,594	15,213	222,951	37,090		87,205
1968	66,798	4,817	9,297	26,580	18,013	239,524	38,597		95,770
1969	74,486	4,811	9,939	30,568	20,290	267,529	42,792		109,698
1970	83,856	5,376	10,824	35,790	22,030	300,145	46,015		131,490
1971	95,103	6,036	12,428	40,746	25,495	325,979	46,543		151,398
1972	110,635	6,886	14,109	47,719	30,065	365,440	49,432		175,115
1973	116,352	6,938	14,430	52,432	37,210	410,621	47,247		211,609
1974	141,474	6,976	14,913	64,449	49,274	490,065	44,788		267,150
1975	149,013	5,703	14,537	65,508	56,993	581,265	57,941		336,409

	Denmark[14]				Finland				
	Total	Customs	Excise	Income & Property	Total	Customs	Excise	Income & Property	Sales
	(million kroner)				(thousand million markkaa)				
1950	2,403	145	1,499	1,091	130[58] / 121	13	11	36	34
1951	2,576	132	1,613	1,396	168	16	12	47	62
1952	2,844	145	1,713	1,599	163	21	13	52	59
1953	3,295[57] / 3,315	183	1,889	1,740	174	17	13	52	53
1954	3,455	210	1,986	1,823	180	19	14	49	57
1955	3,881	211	2,238	1,967	193	27	15	57	50
1956	4,252	251	2,376	2,427	237[58] / 220	41	17	68	62
1957	4,537	280	2,622	2,544	242	42	19	72	69
1958	5,378	285	2,891	2,652	248	39	28	63	66
1959	6,032	374	3,296	2,916	282	42	35	75	76
1960	6,498	436	3,555	3,126	314	46	39	79	89
1961	7,087	468	3,945	3,638	328	47	41	84	100
1962	8,745	531	4,792	4,595	366	43	45	104	105
					(million new markkaa)				
1963	9,829	506	5,664	4,763	3,484	307	508	990	1,036
1964	11,159	557	6,538	5,366	4,417	427	575	1,290	1,227
1965	13,082	556	7,598	6,456	4,920	522	740	1,483	1,314
1966	15,400	600	9,003	7,744 / 7,356[61]	5,465	471	912	1,712	1,425
1967	16,566	551	9,969	7,752	6,504	480	992	1,938	1,908
1968	21,725	561	12,137	9,454	7,736	914	1,061	2,349	2,107
1969	24,457	635	14,736	9,852	8,545	543	1,632	2,275	2,410
1970	34,293	684	16,703	17,733	9,432	460	1,826	2,594	2,821
1971	38,882	542	17,230	17,702	10,422	414	2,074	2,976	3,212
1972	44,928	644	21,156	20,485	12,370	459	2,321	3,903	3,760
1973	51,791	707	23,983	24,702	15,131	552	2,619	5,087	4,471
1974	55,155	786	25,069	28,375	18,451	548	3,087	6,807	5,412
1975	55,986	760	28,015	24,890	21,677	635	3,753	7,782	6,127

See p. 768 for footnotes

H 5 Government Revenue and Main Tax Yields

1950–1975

	France						West Germany[39]				
	Total	Customs	Excise	Reg	Turnover & Trans.	Direct Taxes	Total[7]	Customs	Excise	Income	Turnover
	(thousand million francs)						(million marks)				
1950	2,076	150	48	91	745	555 [61]	16,104 [59]	617 [59]	3,040 [59]	5,342 [59]	4,766 [59]
						580					
1951	2,515	204	52	107	1,008	679	21,670	829	4,460	7,373	6,821
1952	2,888	228	56	120	1,099	811	26,999	1,054	4,554	10,363	8,381
1953	3,103	248	59	123	1,091	955	29,556	1,272	4,657	11,600	8,865
1954	3,356	271	53	123	1,153	951	30,792	1,486	4,490	11,534	9,593
1955	3,450	326	54	123	1,161	975	34,175	1,793	5,178	11,864	11,118
1956	3,878	395	58	140	1,209	1,148	38,416	1,983	5,666	13,767	12,184
1957	4,985	519	79	166	1,376	1,353	40,924	2,030	6,113	15,674	12,598
1958	5,228	647	78	194	1,531	1,748	42,882	2,094	6,431	16,595	12,963
1959	6,014	677	100	234	1,754	1,938	48,047	2,482	7,283	18,296	14,239
	(million new francs)										
1960	61,965	7,232	1,054	2,486	19,559	20,617	56,253 [39]	2,775 [39]	8,223 [39]	23,289 [39]	15,871 [39]
							56,990	2,786	8,299	23,575	16,148
1961	67,764	7,939	3,419	2,718	21,635	20,185	66,234	3,130	9,455	28,743	17,866
1962	74,512	8,929	3,845	3,110	24,346	23,590	73,259	3,447	10,305	32,323	19,210
1963	85,085	10,029	4,329	3,459	28,331	26,332	77,952	3,640	11,094	34,983	20,043
1964	94,735	10,998	5,107	3,706	32,179	31,219	85,493	2,986	13,307	38,211	21,927
1965	101,807	11,685	4,983	4,101	33,937	36,628	91,397	2,898	15,010	39,706	24,219
1966	108,431	12,325	5,182	4,355	38,044	36,489	97,125	2,780	16,204	42,817	25,064
1967	117,139	13,058	5,430	4,735	40,400	39,489	99,295	2,663	18,587	42,401	24,723
1968	125,684	11,323	6,474	5,526	51,204	37,414	105,584	2,437	19,409	46,905	25,692
1969	157,224	12,666	7,388	6,348	68,544	45,385	128,099	2,980	20,648	54,941	36,753
1970	174,607	14,417	7,574	7,256	71,820	52,509	136,876	2,871	21,909	59,803	38,125
1971	187,846	15,122	7,941	7,284	82,090	54,002	153,083	3,080	23,427	68,310	42,897
1972	212,574	16,173	8,922	8,511	95,259	61,642	174,547	3,231	26,751	81,405	46,981
1973	241,809	18,055	10,448	10,068	103,183	74,136	199,202	3,172	30,569	98,594	49,825
1974	293,318	19,018	10,717	10,735	123,377	99,204	212,743	3,332	30,231	109,156	51,910
1975	316,218	19,297	11,414	13,107	137,334	100,510	214,505	3,253	31,096	109,246	54,082

	Greece[20]					Southern Ireland[42]			
	Total	Customs	Con.	Direct Taxes	Trans.	Total	Customs	Excise	I. & P.
	(million drachmae)					(million pounds)			
1950	...	...	...	...	...	77	27	13	20
1951	...	1,033	1,613	865	495	84	29	14	23
1952	...	1,222	1,921	1,295	511	96	34	16	26
1953	...	1,395	2,280	1,551	598	103	37	17	25
1954	7,729	1,792	1,539	1,677	698	107	37	17	26
1955	8,967	1,963	1,750	1,930	838	112	39	17	28
1956	[16,207] [20]	[4,207] [20]	[2,935] [20]	[3,230] [20]	[1,489] [20]	118	45	17	27
1957	15,162	4,123	2,623	2,429	1,487	123	47	17	28
1958	15,721	4,440	3,051	2,724	1,647	126	48	17	28
1959	17,449	4,258	3,272	2,502	1,696	130	45	24	27
1960	18,925	4,635	3,547	2,615	1,865	139	41	30	31
1961	21,769	5,278	3,765	3,222	2,054	152	45	34	35
1962	24,036	5,907	4,065	3,591	2,290	163	47	35	41
1963	24,823	6,481	4,683	3,606	2,650	184	50	38	48
1964	24,749	7,550	5,298	4,467	3,071	219	56	43	56
1965	28,188	9,116	6,200	4,493	3,494	241	58	49	64
1966	34,081	11,043	7,732	5,666	4,052	273	68	55	73
1967	38,941	11,814	8,858	6,729	4,882	305	70	62	82
1968	44,416	12,687	9,541	8,248	7,026	345	76	73	94
1969	57,066	14,136	10,392	9,523	8,332	411	88	88	93
1970	55,293	15,164	11,314	10,847	9,808	482	92	91	117
1971	62,860	16,230	12,249	13,222	11,144	569	101	97	153
1972	72,563	18,907	13,528	15,632	13,287	659	116	104	174
1973	87,257	23,861	16,171	18,814	16,322	793	139	116	222
1974	104,285	24,805	18,228	28,431	18,933	651 [42]	109 [42]	89 [42]	170 [42]
1975	137,143	34,639	23,645	29,604	26,585	1,091 [42]	175 [42]	157 [42]	332 [42]

See p. 768 for footnotes

H 5 Government Revenue and Main Tax Yields

1950–1975

	Italy[63]						Netherlands				
	Total	Customs	T. & S. Mon.	Direct Per Taxes	Profits Tax	Petroleum Tax	Total	Customs	Excise	Direct Taxes	Turnover
	(thousand million lire)						(million guilders)				
1950	1,419	6	202	133	252	67	4,125	355	433	2,569	870
1951	1,720	57	220	163	311	96	5,686	410	516	2,938	1,213
1952	1,737	74	244	201	337	115	6,254	362	532	3,654	1,101
1953	1,804	88	266	184	372	133	6,087	430	550	3,321	1,169
1954	2,001	109	285	212	414	170	6,303	542	562	3,223	1,315
1955	2,296	118	305	245	468	209	6,538	609	591	3,375	1,296
1956	2,527	133	328	283	518	244	7,644	721	637	4,315	1,299
1957	2,807	149	347	335	579	268	8,058	869	708	4,676	1,425
1958	3,102	157	366	365	616	298	7,691	817	733	4,396	1,393
1959	3,207	151	389	416	657	348	8,282	856	773	4,703	1,550
1960	3,585	185	420	452	749	390	9,359	956	813	5,374	1,788
1961	3,913	202	445	514	827	415	10,308	1,048	843	6,019	1,890
1962	4,496	224	479	590	909	499	10,881	1,157	872	6,342	1,987
1963	5,194	257	521	698	1,053	596	11,514	1,180	951	6,575	2,197
1964	5,952[24]	273[24]	557[24]	837[24]	1,126[24]	746[24]	13,742	1,547	974	7,806	2,643
1965	6,858	223	584	1,056	1,282	906	15,543	1,577	1,165	9,013	2,961
1966	7,418	227	627	1,152	1,408	1,022	17,563	1,914	1,208	10,197	3,400
1967	8,404	252	657	1,192	1,557	1,188	19,892	2,152	1,356	11,557	3,913
1968	9,301	199	693	1,336	1,660	1,303	21,996	2,233	1,410	12,405	4,980
1969	10,007	210	747	1,491	1,848	1,509	24,830	2,407	1,520	14,589	4,877
1970	10,990	235	793	1,532	2,045	1,717	29,020	2,680	1,592	16,076	6,657
1971	12,162	220	800	1,796	2,212	1,872	33,670	2,653	1,581	19,334	8,385
1972	13,359	233	862	2,045	2,140	1,981	39,295	3,045	1,853	22,596	9,827
1973	15,250	267	761	2,333	323	1,999	45,423	3,398	2,023	26,233	11,152
1974	19,625	334	863	4,490	699	2,517	50,753	3,621	2,191	30,310	12,064
1975	23,842	16	1,008	4,945	11	2,913	57,865	3,789	2,368	34,723	13,788

	Norway				Portugal			
	Total	Customs	Con	Income & Property	Total	Customs	Property	Business
	(million kroner)				(million escudos)			
1950	2,727	179	1,306	984	4,826	1,629	336	564
1951	3,092	174	1,471	1,151	5,527	1,943	346	574
1952	3,778	267	1,946	1,163	5,808	2,135	363	599
1953	4,368	328	2,179	1,356	6,226	1,928	378	647
1954	4,315	317	2,228	1,240	6,347	2,099	391	664
1955	4,591	383	2,392	1,228	6,731	2,301	400	676
1956	4,860	330	2,627	1,401	7,303	2,443	410	737
1957	5,264	398	2,935	1,572	7,933	2,574	421	788
1958	5,637	414	3,082	1,726	8,378	2,619	436	870
1959	5,989	395	3,210	1,785	8,835	2,788	458	881
1960	6,462[25]	438[25]	3,462[25]	1,500[25]	9,590	3,150	473	927
1961	6,943	489	4,007	1,463	10,812	3,663	497	951
1962	7,607	476	4,348	1,691	11,355	3,522	521	1,098
1963	8,317	480	4,686	1,925	12,709	3,733	554	1,142
1964	9,213	520	5,217	2,054	13,120	3,797[60]	704	1,128
1965	10,225	544	5,974	2,264	15,184	4,550	721	1,419
1966	11,321[43] 9,559	537	6,596	2,426	16,957	4,803	776	1,526
1967	10,591	501	7,377	2,713	19,896	5,154	923	1,575
1968	11,345	408	7,917	3,020	21,828	5,322	964	2,058
1969	13,064	380	9,163	3,521	...	5,994	1,029	2,504
1970	15,158	378	11,995	2,785	29,729	7,755	1,128	2,836
1971	17,932	348	14,689	2,895	32,285	7,593	1,245	2,458
1972	20,647	356	16,326	3,965	36,214	8,259	1,382	2,526
1973	22,864	358	17,633	4,872	43,387	8,623	1,547	2,860
1974	25,737	351	19,323	6,063	50,286	11,001	1,731	4,170
1975	29,234	375	22,549	6,310	54,873	11,809	1,891	4,583

See p. 768 for footnotes

H 5 Government Revenue and Main Tax Yields

1950–1975

	Romania		Russia[8]			
	Total	Transactions	Total	Industrial & Turnover Taxes	Direct Taxes	Deductions from Profits
	(million lei)		(million new rubels)			
1950	17,122	8,510	39.2	23.6	3.6	4.0
1951	20,520	11,337	...	...	...	...
1952	28,851	13,465	45.6	24.7	4.7	5.8
1953	32,746	15,104	51.0	24.4	4.6	7.0
1954	35,884	15,479	...	...	...	...
1955	38,650	17,248	52.7	24.2	4.8	10.3
1956	36,273	15,880	54.2	25.9	5.1	10.3
1957	38,636	17,087	...	...	...	...
1958	38,143	15,970	66.1	30.5	5.2	13.5
1959	41,069	15,409	72.5	31.1	5.5	16.0
1960	48,575[61]	18,015	76.2	31.3	5.6	18.6
	44,638					
1961	48,792	20,163	77.3	30.9	5.8	20.7
1962	55,456	21,733	83.1	32.9	6.0	23.9
1963	64,881	24,961	88.2	34.5	6.3	25.7
1964	72,287	26,960	94.3	36.7	6.8	28.7
1965	76,270	28,701	102.1	38.7	7.7	30.9
1966	86,380	31,397	106.1	39.3	8.4	35.7
1967	98,951	34,270	117.1	40.1	9.3	41.8
1968	100,569	36,184	130.5	40.8	10.5	48.0
1969	102,089	37,521	139.6	44.5	11.6	48.0
1970	104,513	40,543	156.7	49.4	12.7	54.2
1971	108,333	44,026	166.0	54.5	13.7	55.6
1972	116,195	45,086	175.1	55.6	14.8	60.0
1973	129,350	48,046	187.8	59.1	15.8	60.0
1974	165,500	46,000	201.3	63.5	17.1	64.4
1975	193,050	42,000	218.8	66.6	18.4	69.7

	Spain					Sweden				
	Total (thousand million pesetas)	Customs	Con.	P. & T. Mon.	Direct Taxes	Total	Customs	Excise	Income & Property	Auto-mobile
		(million pesetas)				(million kroner)				
1950	15.9	734	4,512	3,020	6,553	4,474	241	1,398	2,035	444
1951	18.4	746	5,115	3,325	7,951	5,426	367[62]	1,448[62]	2,754	472
							355	1,461		
1952	22.4	951	6,662	3,987	9,465	7,507	362	1,763	4,124	411
1953	24.9	1,155	7,378	4,444	10,827	7,808	379	1,839	4,100	520
1954	27.6	1,236	8,007	4,999	12,009	8,535	433	1,899	4,492	602
1955	30.5	1,355	9,056	5,339	13,150	8,907	505	2,007	4,600	819
1956	36.0	2,163	10,537	5,860	14,198	10,072	553	2,268	5,212	1,043
1957	42.4[61]	2,428[61]	12,551[61]	8,432	16,665	10,691	608	2,369	5,600	1,018
1958	53.2	2,675	14,458	11,009	20,917[61]	12,019	652	2,908	6,210	1,062
					22,184					
1959	57.6	2,883	16,600	11,940	23,156	12,605	654	3,284	6,401	1,086
1960	66.3	5,535	18,989	14,042	24,869	13,657	811	3,819	6,468	1,182
1961	76.7	8,373	20,296	6,802	27,465	16,641	826	5,086	8,016	1,265
1962	88.7	10,377	25,999	7,562	30,168	18,007	856	5,696	8,620	1,227
1963	101.7	12,249	25,362	8,363	33,206	19,869	867	6,679	9,025	1,587
1964	116.7	14,147	30,640	9,540	36,547	20,927	959	7,418	8,952	1,820
1965	140.1	14,459	28,395	10,656	45,406	24,257	1,058	7,926	11,088	1,962
1966	174.0	19,352	32,286	14,146	53,263	28,015	1,088	9,759	11,928	2,215
1967	196.2	18,046	38,428	17,440	60,626	30,441	984	11,119	12,669	2,384
1968	206.6	17,619	43,632	18,489	60,663	32,101	950	12,219	12,885	2,562
1969	245.7	20,982	51,691	23,444	72,313	34,836	953	12,956	14,078	2,762
1970	278.6	22,374	60,835	23,384	82,028	38,887	1,046	13,110	17,048	3,044
1971	315.9	23,922	68,822	21,791	98,647	44,378	1,036	15,875	18,441	3,223
1972	374.9	31,454	77,215	26,556	117,599	50,303	956	19,057	19,772	3,329
1973	452.5	38,789	93,173	35,246	147,503	52,647	979	20,785	18,266	3,450
1974	524.1	42,275	99,868	8,975	189,594	59,133	1,022	22,289	20,957	3,616
1975	621.5	45,862	111,670	24,856	246,418	70,022	1,250	24,282	28,091	3,685

See p. 768 for footnotes

H 5 Government Revenue and Main Tax Yields

1950–1975

	Switzerland				United Kingdom				Yugoslavia
	Total[31]	Customs	Con.	Income & Property	Total	Customs	Excise	Land & I. & P.[4]	Total
	(million francs)				(million pounds)				(million dinars)
1950	1,668	478	526	550	4,157	905	725	1,793	111
1951	1,485	493	546	324	4,629	999	753	2,114	88
1952	1,672	473	578	495	4,654	1,024	739	2,247	217
1953	1,599	514	599	318	4,606	1,042	722	2,118	189
1954	1,968	567	623	592	4,987	1,100	772	2,277	256
1955	1,842	645	659	351	5,160	1,149	865	2,293	203
1956	2,197	740	664	592	5,462	1,199	902	2,472	177
1957	2,043	770	723	350	5,679	1,208	942	2,617	227
1958	2,428	783	737	688	5,850	1,262	930	2,763	271
1959	2,302	856	719	482	6,016	1,373	909	2,686	378
1960	2,806	1,061	810	640	6,344	1,456	933	2,886	510
1961	2,978	1,281	918	452	6,645	1,616	978	3,286	547
1962	3,629	1,362	1,056	867	6,794	1,639	1,028	3,385	556
1963	3,647	1,538	1,179	581	6,890	1,723	1,043	3,313	681
									(million new dinari)
1964	4,481	1,697	1,325	1,076	7,727	2,008	1,166	3,695	7,805
1965	4,410	1,800	1,407	818	8,674	3,401		4,319	8,100
1966	5,129	1,899	1,480	1,349	9,716	3,536		4,613	8,718
1967	5,151	2,067	1,588	1,151	11,182[61]	3,721		5,336	9,979
					11,227				
1968	5,916	2,231	1,664	1,551	13,363	4,601		5,962	10,829
1969	6,349	2,436	1,831	1,508	15,267	4,953		6,965	11,554
1970	7,241	2,364	2,342	1,967	15,843	4,709		7,699	15,156
1971	7,814	2,556	2,619	2,015	16,932	5,325		8,513	18,456
1972	9,283	2,921	3,185	2,505	17,178	5,744		8,558	25,527
1973	9,807	2,987	3,552	2,594	18,226	6,220		10,030	33,012
1974	10,922	2,803	3,942	3,547	23,570	7,407		13,656	48,606
1975	11,026	2,939	3,792	3,510	29,417	9,176		17,548	59,944

See p. 768 for footnotes

H 5 Government Revenue and Main Tax Yields

NOTES

1. SOURCES:— The official publications noted on p. xv with a few gaps filled from the League of Nations, *Public Finance Statistics.* In addition, statistics for Great Britain to 1965 are taken from B.R. Mitchell & Phyllis Deane, *Abstract of British Historical Statistics* (Cambridge, 1962) and B.R. Mitchell & H.G. Jones, *Second Abstract of British Historical Statistics* (Cambridge, 1971), where the original sources are given; and statistics for Russia to 1914 are taken from P.A. Khromov, *Economic Development of Russia in the 19th and 20th Centuries, 1800–1917* (Moscow, 1950).

2. Total revenue, unless otherwise stated, means total ordinary revenue exclusive of loan receipts. Whether or not receipts from public enterprises are included (and, if so, whether net or gross) varies from country to country. Changes in composition are indicated in footnotes.

3. Except where otherwise indicated statistics are from the closed accounts.

FOOTNOTES

[1] Austria-Hungary to 1867 (1st line); Cisleithania from 1867 (2nd line) to 1916; and Republic of Austria from 1920. Lombardy is excluded from 1859 and Venetia from 1866. All yields are net.

[2] Figures for 1750 and 1751 are for years ended 29 September. From 1752 to 1799 they are for years ended 10 October. From 1800 to 1853 they are for years ended 5 January following that indicated, and subsequently they are for years ended 31 March following that indicated. Figures for the periods 11 October 1799–5 January 1800 and 6 January–31 March 1854 are not shown here.

[3] Figures to 1800 are for Great Britain, and are of net receipts. Subsequently they are for the U.K. and are of gross receipts, though Irish Customs and Excise receipts are not included under these headings until 1807. Their conbined totals were as follows (in thousands of pounds):—

1801	2,350	1803	2,801	1805	3,056
1802	3,226	1804	3,062	1806	3,482

[4] Including corporation, profits, and excess profits taxes, surtax, and capital gains tax.

[5] Fourth-quarter-year only.

[6] Total revenue to 1840 includes the proceeds of loans.

[7] Tax revenue only.

[8] Figures to 1914 relate to the Russian Empire (exclusive of Finland). Subsequent statistics are for the U.S.S.R.

[9] Including profits from the state spirit monopoly.

[10] Figures to 1858 are in convention gulden, subsequently in standard gulden (to 1892), kronen (to 1923) or schilling.

[11] The total yields to 1864 (1st line) are of fiscal receipts only. From 1864 (2nd line) to 1875 (1st line) they are of all ordinary receipts. From 1875 (2nd line) to 1915 they include certain extraordinary receipts, but not the proceeds of loans.

[12] Figures to 1864 are for years ended 31 October (though the 1864 figure for Monopolies is for 14 months to 31 December). From 1865 to 1913 the figures are for calendar years. The 1914 figure is for the first half-year only, and those for 1915 and 1916 are for years ended 30 June. Figures for the Republic are for calendar years.

[13] Revised figures were later published for each year back to 1891, but only for three years before that. The original series is given here for 1879–1891 (1st line). Revised figures are available for this period as follows:—

	Total	Customs & Excise	Direct Taxes
1879	21	6	13
1880	31	8	21
1886	41	12	22

[14] The figures relate to Denmark proper, except that total revenue to 1863 includes that of the Duchies of Schleswig, Holstein, and Lauenburg. Figures are for years ended 31 March following that indicated, except that Customs and Excise yields from 1928 are for calendar years.

[15] Total net revenue includes the proceeds of loans up to 1869 (1st line).

[16] Previously including navigation tax.

[17] Figures to 1868 (1st line) are of receipts by the customs administration. Subsequently they are of receipts from import duties.

[18] Subsequently excluding the tax on matches.

[19] The 1876 figures are for 15 months ended 31 March 1877. Subsequent figures are for years ended 31 March following that indicated.

[20] Statistics from 1919 to 1955 are for years ended 31 March. The figure for 1956 is for 21 months. Figures to 1924/5 are of budgetary receipts (excluding loans). Subsequently they are of ordinary receipts.

[21] Transleithania to 1918, and the territory established by the treaty of Trianon subsequently. The figures to 1913 are for calendar years. That for 1914 is for the first half-year only, and subsequent figures are for years ended 30 June.

[22] 'Ordinary' revenue, which includes a small amount of the proceeds from loans in some years.

[23]Subsequently including the net revenue of state monopolies.

[24]Figures for 1884 are for 9 months ended 31 August. For 1885 they are for 10 months ended 30 June. From 1886 to 1964 they are for years ended 30 June, and subsequently for calendar years.

[25]Figures for 1878 are for the first half-year only. From 1879 to 1960 they are for years ended 30 June, and subsequently for calendar years.

[26]Figures to 1934 are for years ended 30 June. The 1935 figure is for 18 months, and subsequent figures are for calendar years.

[27]All current revenue exclusive of the proceeds of loans to 1929. Ordinary revenue subsequently.

[28]Figures for 1880 are for 15 months ended 31 March 1881. From 1881 to 1922 they are for years ended 31 March following that indicated. The 1923 figures are for 9 months, and those for 1924–32 are for calendar years. Figures to 1933–43 are for years ended 31 March following that indicated.

[29]Figures to 1862 are for 18 months to 30 June 1863. For 1863–98 they are for years beginning 1 July. The 1899 figures are for the second half-year only.

[30]Subsequently including the tax on the sale of spirits.

[31]Figures are of total ordinary receipts plus extraordinary tax receipts to 1941 (1st line). Subsequently they are of tax revenue only.

[32]From 1870 most assessed taxes were replaced by licences.

[33]Figures to 1905 (1st line) include the net revenue from monopolies.

[34]Figures for 1919–33 are for years ended 31 March following that indicated. The figures for 1934 are for 9 months.

[35]May-December only.

[36]Subsequently including the tax on salt.

[37]Including the budget of the Comite Francaise de Liberation Nationale in 1943, and of the provisional government in 1944.

[38]The definition of tax revenue was enlarged in scope.

[39]Figures are for calendar years. Saarland is excluded up to 1960 (lst line).

[40]The first line for 1948 is to 20 June and is in million Reichsmarks; the second line is from 21 June and is in million Deutschmarks.

[41]Budget estimates.

[42]Figures are for years ended 31 March following that indicated, except for 1974, which is for the period April-December, and 1975, which is for the calendar year.

[43]Subsequently tax revenue only.

[44]Subsequently all income and property taxes.

[45]A new income tax system was in operation in 1937.

[46]Figures for 1926–37 are for years ended 31 March following that indicated.

[47]From 1929 (2nd line) accessory duties are excluded from customs revenue.

[48]Subsequently including arrears received during the year.

[49]Figures for 1924–30 are for years ended 30 September. Total ordinary revenue excluding loans in the fourth quarter of 1930 was 4,315 million rubels. From 1932 (2nd line) local government revenue is included.

[50]Subsequently receipts from taxes and state enterprises only.

[51]Income tax is included subsequently.

[52]Figures for 1919–23 are for years ended 31 March following that indicated. Those for 1924–25 are for years ended 30 June following that indicated. The 1926 figures are for the second half-year only. Figures for the first quarter of 1919 and the second quarter of 1924 are not shown here.

[53]Petrol monopoly only.

[54]The old property tax, which had declined to negligible proportions, is subsequently excluded.

[55]Figures for 1923 are for the first half-uear only. Subsequent figures are for years ended 30 June.

[56]Some items previously included were subsequently excluded from current ordinary revenue.

[57]Subsequent statistics are of tax revenue only. The fact that this is higher than total revenue in 1953 is due to the inclusion in the latter of losses made by public enterprises.

[58]Subsequently tax revenue only, though including the surplus of the tobacco monopoly up to 1956 (1st line).

[59]Subsequently including West Berlin.

[60]From 1965 revenue from stamps for customs purposes is included.

[61]This break is caused by a change in classification.

[62]Coffee tax was transferred from customs to excise in 1951.

[63]Value Added Tax, first imposed in 1973, had the following yields:– 1973: 2,484; 1974: 5,018; 1975: 4,975.

I. PRICES

There is a considerable array of material on prices available for most countries far back in time, before the period covered here. Most of this, however, is intractable in the extreme, and it has been decided to include none of it in this work. Instead, there are two sets of indices, based on this material but reducing it to some sort of readily comprehensible order. It was felt that annual average prices, in local currency, of (say) a kilogram of wheat were unlikely to be of use except to the specialist, and that a general indication of overall price levels would be more widely useful. Of course, there is oversimplification and distortion in the process. and, like all index numbers, those presented here require careful interpretation. In order to achieve exact comparability of an index over long periods of time, the commodities and their weightings must remain unchanged. However, in a changing economy first the weightings, and then possibly the commodities themselves will cease to be appropriate representations of the quantities and things actually used. All indices, therefore, must compromise between continuity and relevance, and the more rapid is economic change, the more frequent must be the breaks in continuity. In the period since the Second World War, the official indices in some countries have been changed very frequently indeed; whilst, at the other extreme, some of the eighteenth and nineteenth century indices remain unchanged for very long periods. Usually this does not involve much danger of lack of representativeness, since commodity consumption patterns changed very little in most countries until the second half of the nineteenth century, when increasing incomes and increasing urbanisation both began to have effects. A more serious problem in some of the early indices is lack of sufficient variety of information. Price series exist only for the most important commodities traded; and most of the series, certainly for the eighteenth century, are of prices paid by institutions, often on contracts rather than in the market place. It seems likely that these were rather rigid, for some commodities at any rate, and insulated from some of the ordinary fluctuations.

In order to facilitate comparisons between countries—though it must be understood that these are necessarily inexact owing both to the nature of indices and the variety of consumption patterns — many of the indices shown here have been converted to common base-years. Anyone wanting to use these indices for further calculations should bear in mind this shifting of the base-year, and also the fact that different indices have, where necessary, been crudely spliced together.

I1 WHOLESALE PRICE INDICES

	France	Germany	Spain[1]	G.B.: U.K.[2]
	(a)	(b)	(c)	(d)
1750	...	...	...	95
1751	...	...	111	90
1752	...	...	115	93
1753	...	...	126	90
1754	...	...	137	90
1755	...	...	131	92
1756	...	...	116	92
1757	...	...	111	109
1758	...	...	115	106
1759	...	...	109	100
1760	...	...	111	98
1761	...	...	108	94
1762	...	...	112	94
1763	...	...	121	100
1764	...	...	128	102
1765	...	...	138	106
1766	...	...	134	107
1767	...	...	130	109
1768	...	...	131	108
1769	...	...	133	99
1770	...	...	128	100
1771	...	...	129	107
1772	...	...	130	117
1773	...	...	128	119
1774	...	...	131	116
1775	...	...	128	113
1776	...	...	130	114
1777	...	...	130	108
1778	...	...	134	117
1779	...	...	136	111
1780	...	...	140	110
1781	...	...	145	115
1782	...	...	145	116
1783	...	...	144	129
1784	...	...	149	126
1785	...	...	153	120
1786	...	...	156	119
1787	...	...	153	117
1788	...	...	159	121
1789	...	...	160	117
1790	...	...	166	124
				1821–5=100[3]
				89
1791	...	...	161	90
1792	...	98	165	88
1793	...	98	171	97
1794	...	101	173	98.5
1795	...	122	187	115
1796	...	114	187	116
1797	...	108	206	106
1798	118	116	215	108
1799	117	132	205	125

1750–1849

	Belgium	France	Germany	Spain[1]	G.B.: U.K.[2]
	(b)	(a)	(b)	(c)	(e)
1800	...	118	135	194	151
1801	...	105	134	...	156
1802	...	104	131	...	122
1803	...	111	139	...	124
1804	...	104	136	...	124
1805	...	114	156	...	136
1806	...	125	157	...	134.5
1807	...	122	148	...	131
1808	...	161	176	...	144.5
1809	...	161	156	...	155
1810	...	166	132	...	153
1811	...	164	123	...	145
				1913=100	
1812	...	171	137	224	164
1813	...	160	120	180	169
1814	...	122	110	143	154
1815	...	116	112	160	130
1816	...	120	124	162	119
1817	...	129	148	173	132
1818	...	123	130	150	139
1819	...	105	103	129	128
		1901–10=100			
1820	...	153	90	111	115
1821	...	143	85	104	100
1822	...	138	84	114	88
1823	...	143	82	104	98
1824	...	133	72	108	102
1825	...	146	76	108	113
1826	...	136	72	103	100
1827	...	134	77	88	99
1828	...	129	78	86	96
1829	...	130	77	76	96
1830	...	130	78	75	94.5
1831	...	124	82	81	95
1832	79	125	80	83	91.5
1833	77	126	76	80	89
1834	77	128	76	89	86.5
1835	81	132	77	96	84.5
1836	85	135	78	96	95
1837	84	126	74	98	94
1838	87	131	78	91	98
1839	91	130	81	91	104
1840	91	135	80	81	102.5
1841	92	134	78	78	98
1842	89	131	78	82	89
1843	82	121	77.5	70	80
1844	77	118	76	76	81
1845	79	121	82	73	83
1846	87	129	88	83	86
1847	96	136	97	92	97
1848	80	112	76	89	82
1849	77	111	70	75	74

Abbreviations used:—
(a) 1820=100; (b) 1913=100; (c) 1726–50=100; (d) 1770=100; (e) 1821–5=100

See p. 777 for footnotes

I1 Wholesale Price Indices

1850–1899

	Austria-Hungary (a)	Belgium (b)	France (c)	Germany (b)	Italy (b)	Norway (d)	Spain (b)	Sweden (b)	U.K. (e)
1850	...	83	111	71	...	...	76	...	73.5
									1913=100[3]
1851	...	80	110	75	...	...	80	...	91
1852	...	75	119	82	...	...	78	...	92
1853	...	89	139	92	...	...	73	...	112
1854	...	97	148	100	...	...	79	...	120
1855	...	100	154	105	...	...	86	...	119
1856	...	101	156	105	...	...	96	...	119
1857	...	99	151	101	...	...	98	...	124
1858	...	97	137	91	...	...	83	...	107
1859	...	91	137	89	...	...	97	...	111
1860	...	94	144	94	...	...	95	99	116
1861	...	97	142	94	98	...	95	97	115
1862	...	96	142	94	91	...	102	102	119
1863	...	93	143	92	87	...	116	107	121
1864	...	96	141	91	87	...	120	108	124
1865	...	94	132	89	86	...	111	103	119
1866	...	95	134	90	90	...	120	97	120
1867	104.1	95	131	97	90	...	111	96	118
1868	97.7	93	132	97	96	...	98	95	116
1869	99.6	93	130	92	89	...	100	93	115
1870	102.4	94	133	92	88.5	...	109	92	113
1871	105.6	98	138	100	91.5	...	91	95	113[3]
									116
1872	105.1	102	144	114	99	...	90	106	125
1873	103.5	103	144	120	105	...	90	113	130
1874	99.0	102	132	112	105	...	93	107	126
1875	91.2	100	129	100	93	...	84	101	121
1876	94.5	98	130	95	90	...	91	98	118
1877	97.8	98	131	91	102	...	96	97	121
1878	89.2	92	120	83	99	...	93	88	113
1879	84.5	91	117	81	93	...	95	86	107
1880	89.3	98	120	87	93	...	90	91	111
1881	87.1	99	117	85	87	...	91	89	109
1882	86.0	98	114	81	90	...	94	88	110
1883	86.1	96	110	80	84	...	89	85	108
1884	84.5	93	101	78	80	...	81	82	98
1885	79.8	86	99	75	85	...	81	78	92
1886	76.9	81	95	72	85	...	80	75	87
1887	76.7	81	92	73	79	...	77	72	85
1888	77.1	83	96	75	81	...	78	79	87
1889	77.0	84	100	82	85	...	80	79	89
1890	77.0	86	100	86.5	88	...	84[3]	82	89
							74		
1891	78.0	86	98	86	85	53	78	82	92
1892	74.1	82	95	80	81	50	80	77	87
1893	75.2	80	94	77	76	50	78	74	85
1894	72.0	78	87	73	74	47	75	71	80
1895	72.4	74	85	72	78	47	80	70	78
1896	70.5	75	82	72	78	47	76	71	76
1897	72.1	75	83	76	77	47	82	72	77
1898	74.7	76	86	79	79	50	91	76	80
1899	76.4	82	93	83	81	50	92	81	79

Abbreviations used:–
(a) 1867/77=100; (b) 1913=100; (c) 1901–10=100; (d) 1929=100; (e) 1821–5=100

See p. 777 for footnotes

I1 Wholesale Price Indices

1900–1949

	Austria-Hungary	Belgium	Bulgaria	Czechoslovakia	Denmark	Finland	France	Germany	Greece	Hungary	S. Ireland
	(a)	(b)	(b)	(c)	(c)	(c)	(d)	(b)	(c)	(c)	(e)
1900	81.5	87	57	...	...	...	99	90	...	...	...
1901	79.8	86	57	...	...	...	95	83	...	...	...
1902	77.9	84	59	...	...	...	94	81	...	...	...
1903	80.0	83	61	...	...	...	96	82	...	...	...
1904	81.8	86	63	...	...	...	94	82	...	...	...
1905	85.3	88	69	...	...	...	98	86	...	...	...
1906	90.5	95	73	...	...	...	104	92	...	...	...
1907	94.5	96	75	...	...	...	109	97	...	...	...
1908	91.0	96	77	...	...	...	101	90	...	...	...
1909	94.4	90	80	...	...	...	101	91	...	...	...
1910	...	95	82	...	...	...	108	93	...	...	...
1911	...	96	86	...	...	...	113	94	...	...	...
1912	...	100	95	...	...	...	118	102	...	...	...
1913	...	100	100	...	70	9	116	100	...	...	...
	Austria		103				118	105			
	1929=100	1929=100	1929=100	[11][11]	94	10	1929=100	1929=100	...	...	...
1914	79	[14][7]	2.9				17	74			
1915	...	...	...	...	104	13	23	99	...	...	...
1916	...	...	...	...	144	19	31	106	...	...	...
1917	...	...	...	...	199	31	43	125	...	...	...
1918	...	...	...	...	204[13]	55	56	152	...	...	...
1919	...	...	...	...	214	69	58	291	...	...	...
1920	...	...	...	166	262	112	83	1,040	...	...	...
1921	...	[43][8]	...	156[3]	165	119	57	1,338	...	...	...
1922	78[4]	43	...	145	125	115	54	23,927	...	...	...
1923	98	58	...	106	143	104	69	11,634,000 million	...	[101][4 15]	...
1924	107	67	84	108	160	104	80	86[4]	...	116	...
					[3]						
1925	107	66	95	109	140	106	90	91[3]	...	116	...
1926	95	87	87	103	109	103	115	92	...	102	...
1927	102	100	88	106	102	104	101	96	...	109	...
1928	100	99	94	106	102	105	102	99	95	112	...
1929	100	100	100	100	100	100	100	100	100	100	...
1930	91	87	82	89	87	92	87	91	91	87	...
1931	84	74	67	81	76	86	74	81	81	82	...
1932	86	61	59	74	78	93	65	70	98	82	...
1933	83	59	53	72	83	92	62	68	110	71	...
1934	85	56	54	74	90	92	59	72	109	71	...
1935	85	63	55	77	92	93	56	74	111	78	...
1936	84	69	56	77	97	96	65	76	113	80	...
1937	87[3]	80	63	82	110	113	90	77	126	86	...
1938	86	74	65	81[3]	103	106	103	77	124	87	33
1939	87	76	66	93	109	111	108	78	123	86	35
1940	90	[98][9]	76	113	159	149	142	80	145	100	44
1941	91	...	97	121	187	182	174	82	162	123	49
1942	91	...	123	124	196	225	203	83	...	150	57
1943	92	...	156	125	197	256	236	85	...	204	63
1944	92	...	227	126	200	282	266	85	...	274	66
1945	[92][5]	...	363	140	196	406	376	...	...	...	66
										1948=100[3]	
1946	...	[246][3 10]	413	245	194	635	648	...	18,610[3]	[76][8]	66
1947	[261][6]	264	470	[263][12]	214	764	986	...	22,320	89	73
1948	275	289	...	...	234	1,009	1,699	W. Germany	31,000	100	78
	1953=100	1953=100			1953=100	1953=100	1953=100	1953=100	1953=100		
	42[3]	94	...	...	74	63	65	[90][14]	58		
1949	53	89	...	...	76	63	72	88	68	[95][16]	77

Abbreviations used:—
(a) 1867/77=100; (b) 1913=100; (c) 1929=100; (d) 1901/10=100; (e) 1953=100

See p. 777 for footnotes

I1 Wholesale Price Indices

1900–1949

	Italy (a)	Netherlands	Norway (b)	Poland (b)	Portugal (b)	Romania (b)	Spain (a)	Sweden (a)	Switzerland (b)	G.B.:U.K. (a)	Yugoslavia (b)
1900	84.5	...	56	...	...	...	97	84	...	86	...
1901	84	65	56	...	...	...	97	82	...	83	...
1902	81	65	53	...	...	...	95	81	...	83	...
1903	81	65	53	...	...	...	98	81	...	83	...
1904	77	67	53	...	...	...	100	82	...	84	...
1905	80	69	56	...	...	...	100	83	...	84	...
1906	83	69	59	...	...	...	97	88	...	87	...
1907	90	71	63	...	...	...	101	92	...	91	...
1908	87	71	63	...	...	...	99	88	...	88	...
1909	88	73	59	...	...	...	97	89	...	89	...
1910	88	71	59	...	...	...	98	91	...	93	...
1911	95	78	59	...	...	...	95	94	...	94	...
1912	103	80	66	...	...	...	99	98	...	99	...
1913	100	75	66[3]	87	...	...	100	100	...	100	...
							1929=100				
							58[3]	102[3]			
1914	96	80	69	...	...	...	59	1929=100	71	101	...
	1929=100							72		1929=100	
	20									72	
1915	26	108	100	...	...	...	71	104	...	88	...
1916	38	165	150	...	...	...	84	132	...	114	...
1917	57	186	222	...	...	...	99	174	...	148	...
1918	85	210	228	...	...	...	122	242	...	164	...
1919	93	212	216	...	...	...	122	236	...	181	...
1920	122	196	256	...	...	...	132	256	...	225[3]	...
1921	112	153	200	...	...	...	113	159	139	144	...
1922	112	120	156	...	...	...	103	124	118	116	...
1923	113	112	156[3]	...	...	...	102	116	128	116	...
1924	113	118	178	...	...	...	108	116	125	122	...
1925	126	118	172	...	...	...	110	115	116	117	...
1926	129	106	134	91	...	...	104	106	103	108	101
1927	108	102	113	103	97	...	100	104	101	104	104
1928	105	102	106	104	101	...	97	106	103	103	107
1929	100	100	100	100	100	100	100	100	100	100	100
1930	90	88	94	89	95	78	100	87	89	88[3]	86
1931	78	75	84	78	85	60	101	79	78	77	73
1932	73	65	84	68	86	54	99	78	68	75	65
1933	66	63	84	61	84	52	95	76	65	75	64
1934	65	63	84	58	90	52	97	81	64	78	63
1935	71	61	88	55	83	60	98	86	64	78	66
1936	80	63	94	56	86	69	100	87	68	83	68
1937	93	75	106	62	102	78	112	98	79	96	74
1938	100	71	103	58	99	78	126	95	76	89	78
1939	104	73	106	[57][16]	100	88	144	99	79	90	79
1940	122	92	138	...	127	133	172	96	101	120	114
1941	136	104	169	...	148	[186][17]	204	102	130	134	...
1942	152	110	175	...	171	...	224	164	149	140	...
1943	229	112	178	...	213	...	250	172	155	143	...
1944	857	114	181	...	239	...	269	172	158	146	...
1945	2,058	125	181	...	233	...	298	169	157	149	...
1946	2,881	175	175	...	228	.....	358	162	152	154	...
1947	5,154	188	178	...	239	...	420	175	159	169	...
1948	5,437	196	188	...	238	...	450	188	165	193	...
	1953=100	1953=100	1953=100		1953=100		1953=100	1953=100	1953=100	1953=100	
	104	74	67	...	93	...	57	72	102	67	...
1949	98	78[3]	68	...	97	...	61	72	97	70	...

Abbreviations used:—
(a) 1913=100; (b) 1929=100

See p. 777 for footnotes

I1 Wholesale Price Indices (1953=100)

1950–1975

	Austria	Belgium	Denmark	Finland	France	Germany	Greece	Southern Ireland	Italy
1950	82	93	86	74	78	85	71[3]	82	93
1951	103	113	109	103	100	100	86	95	106
1952	106	107	106	104	105	103	86	100	100
1953	100	100	100	100	100	100	100	100	100
1954	105	99	100	99	98	98	112	99	99
1955	108	101	103	97	98	101[3]	120	102	100
1956	110	104	106	103	102	102	131	103	102
1957	114	106	106	111	108	104	131	110	103
1958	111	102	105	120	121	103	128	114	101
1959	114	101	105	121	126	103	130	113	98
1960	113	102	105	126	130	104	132	113	99
1961	115	102	107	126	132	105[3]	134	114	99
1962	122	103	109	129	136	106	133	118	102
1963	120	106	113	133	141	106	141	120	107
1964	127	111	115	143	143	106	145	127	111
1965	131	112	120	149	145	109	148	132	113
1966	133	115	123	152	148	110	153	135	114
1967	136	113	124	157	148	109	154	138	114
1968	137	114	128	174	153	103[18]	154	147	115
1969	141	119	132	180	166	106	159	158	119
1970	147	125	143	188	177	112	165	167	128
1971	154	124[21]	149	197	188	117	172	175	132
1972	160	129	156	214	199	121	181	195[22]	137
1973	163	145	180	252	225	131	224	230	161[20]
1974	188	169	219	313	270	150	307	256	226
1975	200	172	231	355	278	161	327	321	246

	Netherlands	Norway	Portugal	Spain	Sweden	Switzerland	U.K.: G.B.	Yugoslavia
1950	87	77	99	72	76	96	80	...
1951	107	96	106	93	100	107	97	...
1952	104	101	107	93	106	104	100	...
1953	100	100	100	100	100	100	100	1958=100
1954	101	102	103	100	100	101	101	94
1955	102	104	103	104	104	101	104[19]	98
1956	104	109	107	114	110[3]	104	108	99
1957	107	113	108	133	111	105	110	99
1958	105	111	108	146	109	102	107	100
1959	106	111	107	149[3]	109	100	107	100
1960	104	112	110	152	112	101	108	102
1961	103	113	110	156	114	101	110	106
1962	104	116	111	164	117	105	111	106
1963	106	117	112	171	120	109	112	107
1964	113	121	113	176	125	111[3]	116	112
1965	116	124	117	194	131	111	119	129
1966	122	127	121	199	135	113	123	143
1967	122	129	126	200	135	113	123	146
1968	123	130	130	205	136	113	130	146
1969	124[19]	135	135	211	142	118	136	152
1970	131	144	140	214	151	124	143	167
1971	135	151	143	227	156	126	153	192
1972	139	155	151	242	165	131	160	214
1973	153	168	168	268	183	145	191	240
1974	187	198	216	315	228	168	262	312
1975	194	218	245	355	245	164	303	381

See p. 777 for footnotes

I 1 Wholesale Price Indices

NOTES

1. SOURCES:— The statistics mainly are based on the official publications noted on p. xv and on the League of Nations and United Nations, *Statistical Yearbooks.* In addition, the following have been used:— Austria–Hungary — B. Von Jankovich, in *Bulletin de l'nstitut Internationale de Statistique,* XIX, 3 (1911); Belgium to 1913 — an unweighted average of the indices of agricultural and industrial prices in P. Schöller, "La transformation économique de la Belgique de 1832 à 1844", *Bulletin de l'Institut de Recherche Economique* (Louvain, 1948), spliced on to similar indices in F. Loots, "Les mouvements fondamentaux des prix de gros en Belgique de1822 à 1913", *ibid.* (1936); France to 1819 — A. Chabert, *Essai sur les mouvements des prix et des revenus en France de 1798 à 1820* (Paris, 1945); Germany to 1913 — A. Jacobs & H. Richter, *Die Grosshandelpreise in Deutschland von 1792 bis 1934* (Sonderhefte des Instituts fur Konjunctforschung, No. 37, Berlin, 1935); Great Britain to 1938 — B.R. Mitchell & Phyllis Deane, *Abstract of British Historical Statistics* (Cambridge, 1962), quoting Schumpter, Gayer Rostow & Schwartz, Sauerbeck, and the Board of Trade; Spain to 1800 — Earl J. Hamilton, *War and Prices in Spain, 1651–1800* (Cambridge, Mass., 1947); Spain 1812–1913 (1st line) — Juan Sarda, *La Politiça Monetaria y las Fluctuacíones de la Economiá Española en el Siglo XIX* (Madrid, 1948); and Sweden to 1913 — Åmark, "En svensk prisindex för åren 1860–1913", *Kommersiella meddelanden,* III, 18 (1921).

2. Various indices have been crudely spliced together in the case of certain countries to give a rough indicator of the long-term movement of prices. The differences in the construction of these indices should be borne in mind if they are used in further calculations.

FOOTNOTES

[1] New Castile to 1800.
[2] England to 1790 (1st line).
[3] A new index has been spliced on to the old. Where this appears to be accompanied by a discontinuity a "break" line has been inserted.
[4] In prices based on gold.
[5] First two months only.
[6] Fourth-quarter year only.
[7] April.
[8] Last five months only.
[9] First four months only.
[10] Last two months only.
[11] July.
[12] Excluding December.
[13] Previous figures are for end-July rather than annual averages.
[14] Second half-year only. The figure for 1938 on the same basis is 49.
[15] At end-December.
[16] First seven months only.
[17] First half-year only.
[18] Subsequently excluding Value Added Tax.
[19] No general index was published subsequently. An unweighted average of the indices for basic materials and finished goods is given here.
[20] Value Added Tax was imposed from January, 1973.
[21] Whereas transmission tax is included previously, the subsequent Value Added Tax is excluded.
[22] Value Added Tax is included from November 1972.

I2 COST OF LIVING INDICES

1820–1869

	Belgium (a)	France[1] (b)	Germany (a)	Italy (a)	Sweden (b)
1820	...	...	44	...	...
1821	...	...	38	...	...
1822	...	...	38	...	...
1823	...	...	40	...	...
1824	...	...	30	...	...
1825	...	...	29	...	...
1826	...	...	33	...	...
1827	...	...	39	...	...
1828	...	...	40	...	...
1829	...	...	40	...	...
1830	...	...	43	...	62
1831	...	...	50	...	65
1832	...	...	47	...	65
1833	...	...	44	...	64
1834	...	...	37	...	64
1835	88	...	38	...	65
1836	95	...	37	...	65
1837	89	...	38	...	67
1838	95	...	44	...	70
1839	94	...	46	...	69
1840	96	76	45	...	68
1841	97	76	43	...	69
1842	99	78	47	...	70
1843	85	78	49	...	66
1844	85	77	44	...	62
1845	92	81	49	...	65
1846	94	82	60	...	67
1847	98	82	71	...	69
1848	91	80	47	...	67
1849	90	79	41	...	66
1850	88	76	40	...	66
1851	87	76	47	...	67
1852	88	76	55	...	69
1853	90	80	61	...	72
1854	108	83	73	...	77
1855	113	85	78	...	82
1856	113	86	76	...	91
1857	105	85	62	...	91
1858	101	83	59	...	81
1859	96	83	59	...	77
1860	100	85	63	...	80
1861	107	86	66	82	83
1862	110	86	66	82.5	86
1863	102	87	60	80	81
1864	97	87	56	78	78
1865	101	89	58	77	78
1866	106	91	63	77	80
1867	109	91	76	79	85
1868	105	91	76	82.5	88
1869	104	89	69	83	83

Abbreviations:— (a) 1913=100; (b) 1914=100

See p. 784 for footnotes

12 Cost of Living Indices

1870–1919

	Austria[2] (a)	Belgium[3] (b)	Bulgaria (a)	Czech.[5] (a)	Denmark[6] (a)	Finland (a)	France[1] (c)	Germany (b)	Greece (a)	Hungary[10] (a)	S. Ireland[11] (a)
1870	...	101	...	...	62	...	91	70	...	...	...
1871	...	103	...	...	61	...	95	76[9]	...	...	...
								69			
1872	...	107	...	...	61	...	94	72	...	...	...
1873	...	115	...	...	65	...	94	80	...	...	...
1874	...	110	...	...	66	...	94	83	...	...	...
1875	...	106	...	...	66	...	92	76	...	...	...
1876	...	112	...	...	66	...	95	70	...	...	...
1877	...	112	...	...	62	...	95	77	...	...	...
1878	...	107	...	...	59	...	93	73	...	...	...
1879	...	104	...	...	58	...	93	72	...	...	...
1880	...	99	...	...	60	...	94	76	...	...	...
1881	...	99	...	...	59	...	93	77	...	...	...
1882	...	98	...	...	58	...	93	75	...	...	...
1883	...	99	...	...	57	...	95	75	...	...	...
1884	...	92	...	...	55	...	95	72	...	...	...
1885	...	89	...	...	54	...	93	70	...	...	...
1886	...	82	...	...	53	...	93	68	...	...	...
1887	...	87	...	...	51	...	92	68	...	...	...
1888	...	85	...	...	51	...	93	70	...	...	...
1889	...	87	...	...	52	...	92	73	...	...	...
1890	...	90	...	...	53	...	92	75	...	...	...
1891	...	90	...	...	54	...	93	77	...	...	...
1892	...	87	...	...	54	...	92	76	...	...	...
1893	...	84	...	...	53	...	91	75	...	...	...
1894	...	82	...	...	51	...	92	74	...	...	...
1895	...	80	...	...	51	...	91	73	...	...	...
1896	...	77	...	...	50	...	91	72	...	...	...
1897	...	78	...	...	50	...	89	74	...	...	...
1898	...	78	...	...	50	...	90	76	...	...	...
1899	...	79	...	...	50	...	90	76	...	...	...
1900	...	89	...	...	52	...	91	77	...	...	...
1901	...	91	...	...	53	...	91	78	...	...	...
1902	...	89	...	...	53	...	91	78	...	...	...
1903	...	89	...	...	53	...	90	78	...	...	...
1904	...	78	...	...	51	...	90	79	...	...	...
1905	...	80	...	...	52	...	90	82	...	...	...
1906	...	88	...	...	54	...	91	87	...	...	...
1907	...	90	...	...	53	...	92	88	...	...	...
1908	...	91	...	...	54	...	93	88	...	...	...
1909	...	90	...	...	55	...	93	90	...	...	...
1910	...	92	...	...	55	...	94	92	...	...	...
1911	...	98	...	...	55	...	98	95	...	...	...
1912	...	105	...	...	56	...	98	100	...	...	...
1913	...	100	...	...	57	...	98	100	...	85	...
		1929=100						1929=100			
								65			
1914	90	[11][4]	3	13	59	[9][8]	100	67	5	...	57
							1929=100				
							17				
1915	142	...	4	...	67[7]	[9][8]	20	84	6	...	...
1916	303	...	...	...	78	[12][8]	23	110	8	...	...
1917	605	...	...	...	90	[22][8]	27	164	8	...	...
1918	1,047	...	...	...	103	[57][8]	35	196	19	...	...
1919	2,243	...	41	...	124	[83][8]	44	269	17	...	...

Abbreviations:– (a) 1929=100; (b) 1913=100; (c) 1914=100

See p. 784 for footnotes

12 Cost of Living Indices

1870–1919

	Italy (a)	Neth'l (b)	Norway[12] (b)	Poland[13] (b)	Portugal[14] (b)	Romania[15] (b)	Spain[16] (b)	Sweden (c)	Switzerland (b)	U.K.[19] (d)	Yugoslavia[20] (b)
1870	84	...	...	...	...	...	...	80	...	...	...
1871	87	...	...	...	...	...	...	82	...	...	...
1872	98	...	...	...	...	...	...	85	...	...	...
1873	104	...	...	...	...	...	...	92	...	...	...
1874	106.5	...	...	...	...	...	...	95	...	...	...
1875	91	...	...	...	...	...	...	94	...	...	...
1876	96.5	...	...	...	...	...	...	95	...	...	...
1877	100	...	...	...	...	...	...	94	...	...	...
1878	97	...	...	...	...	...	...	88	...	...	...
1879	95.5	...	...	...	...	...	...	83	...	...	...
1880	99	...	...	...	...	...	...	87	...	...	...
1881	93	...	...	...	...	...	...	89	...	...	...
1882	90	...	...	...	...	...	...	87	...	...	...
1883	87.5	...	...	...	...	...	...	86	...	...	...
1884	86	...	...	...	...	...	...	83	...	...	...
1885	88	...	...	...	...	...	...	79	...	...	...
1886	88	...	...	...	...	...	...	75	...	...	...
1887	87	...	...	...	...	...	...	72	...	...	...
1888	88.5	...	...	...	...	...	...	75	...	...	...
1889	90	...	...	...	...	...	...	78	...	...	...
1890	93	...	...	...	...	...	...	80	...	...	...
1891	93	...	...	...	...	...	...	83	...	...	...
1892	92	...	...	...	...	...	...	81	...	93	...
1893	90	...	...	...	...	...	...	78	...	89	...
1894	90	...	...	...	...	...	...	74	...	85	...
1895	89	...	...	...	...	...	...	75	...	83	...
1896	89	...	...	...	...	...	...	75	...	82	...
1897	89	...	...	...	...	...	...	77	...	86	...
1898	89	...	...	...	...	...	...	81	...	89	...
1899	88	...	...	...	...	...	...	84	...	85	...
1900	88	63	...	...	...	...	...	85	...	90	...
1901	88	66	51	...	...	...	...	83	...	90	...
1902	88	63	49	...	...	...	...	84	...	91	...
1903	90	63	49	...	...	...	...	85	...	92	...
1904	91	66	48	...	...	...	...	84	...	92	...
1905	91.5	66	48	...	...	...	...	86	...	92	...
1906	93	66	49	...	...	...	...	88	...	91	...
1907	98	66	51	...	...	...	...	92	...	94	...
1908	97	69	52	...	...	...	...	94	...	96	...
1909	94	69	52	...	...	...	...	93	...	96	...
1910	96.5	69	53	...	...	...	...	93	...	98	...
1911	99	71	55	...	...	...	...	92	...	98	...
1912	100	71	58	...	...	...	...	98	...	103	...
1913	100	71	60[12]	...	...	2	...	98	...	103	...
1914	100	71	60	[81][8]	[4][14]	...	55	100[7]	62	100	5
	1929=100							1929=100		1929=100	
	22							59		[61][8 7]	
1915	24	83	69	...	...	...	60	68	...	75	...
1916	30	91	83	...	...	...	64	[82][17]	...	89	...
1917	43	97	103	...	...	...	70	[98][18]	...	107	...
1918	59	117	145	...	...	...	85	133	...	124	...
1919	60	126	155	...	...	...	96	154	...	131	...

Abbreviations:— (a) 1913=100; (b) 1929=100; (c) 1914=100; (d) Jan–July 1914 = 100

See p. 784 for footnotes

12 Cost of Living Indices

1920–1969

	Austria[2] (a)	Belgium[3] (a)	Bulgaria (a)	Czech.[5] (a)	Denmark[6] (a)	Finland (a)	France[1] (a)	Germany (a)		Greece (a)	Hungary[10] (a)	S. Ireland[11] (b)
1920	4,604	52	62	...	151	80	61	661		18	...	...
1921	8,984	46	64	...	134	95	53	870		21	...	...
1922	237,568	43	87	...	116	93	51	9,766		33	...	106
1923	68[21]	49	83	[93][26]	119	93	57	10,324 billion		61	...	103
1924	77	57	94	93	125	95	65	83		64	[99][8]	105
1925	87	59	100	97	122	99	69	91		74	93	108
1926	93[7]	71	96	96	106	97	90	92		85	87	105
1927	95	90	93	100	102	98	94[7]	96		93	95	98
1928	97	94	97	101	101	101	94	99		97	100	99
1929	100	100	100	100	100	100	100	100		100	100	100
1930	100	100	92	98[7]	95	92	101	96		87	91	97
1931	95	91	80	94	90	85	97	88		87[7]	86	90
1932	97	82	74	92	90	84	88	78		92	83	88
1933	95	81	68	91	92	81	85	77		99	77	86
1934	95	76	64	90	96	80	82	79		101	76	87
1935	95	75	60	93	99	81	75	80		102	78	90
1936	95	78	57	94	101	81	80	81		105	82	91
1937	95	84	58	95	104	85	101	81		112[27]	87	98
1938	[94][22]	87	60	99	106	88	115	82		113	88	99
1939	93	88[23]	62[2]	109[7]	108	89	122	82		112	86	99
1940	95	[98][24]	69	134	135	107	145	85		124	93	118
1941	96	...	83	156	157	126	170	87		[142][24]	111	131
1942	97	...	110	169	162	149	205	89		...	129	144
1943	98	...	139	167	165	168	254	90		...	155	163
1944	98	...	209	168	166	178	311	92		[445][28]	191	170
								West 1953=100	East 1960=100	2,140		
1945	104	...	314	178	168	250	461	68	...	1953=100	...	168
										5		
1946	132	[270][25]	353	323	167	398	703	75	...	37	358	166
1947	259	285	392	309	172	517	1,049	80	...	44	402	183
1948	422	326	...	305	176	696	1,664	92	...	63	421	181
	1953=100	1953=100		1953=100	1953=100	1953=100	1953=100				1953=100	1953=100
	43[2]	95		...	80	70	63				61	79
1949	56	92	...	...	82	71	71	99	...	72	56	80
1950	70	91	...	...	85	81	78	92	202	78	59	80
1951	89[2]	100	...	...	94	95	91	100	...	87	72	89
1952	101	100	...	...	99	99	102	102	...	92	100	98
1953	100	100	...	100	100	100	100	100	...	100	100	100
1954	103	101	...	97	100	98	100	100	...	116	94	102
1955	105	101	...	94	105	95	101	102	112	122	93	104
1956	108	104	...	92	111	106	106	104	110	126	92	105
1957	112	107	...	90	115	120	109[7]	107	109	130	95	114
1958	114[2]	108	...	90	116	131	125	109	104	132[27]	95	117
1959	115	110	...	88	119	133	133	110	101	136	94	116
1960	117	110	...	81	121	138	138	112	100	139	94	117
1961	122	111	...	81	123	140	142	114	100	141	94	121
1962	127	113	...	82	128	146	149[7]	118	100	141	95	126
1963	130	115	...	82	135	153	156	121	100	145	94	127
1964	135	120	...	83	140	169	161	124	100	146	95	136
1965	142	125	...	84	147[7]	178	166	128	100	151	99	143
1966	145	130	...	84	158	184	171	133	100	158	99	147
1967	151	134	...	85	170	195	175	134	100	161	100	152
1968	155	137	...	86	184	211	182	136	100	161	100	159
1969	160	142	...	89	191	216	194	140	100	165	101	170

Abbreviations:— (a) 1929=100; (b) July 1929=100

See p. 784 for footnotes

12 Cost of Living Indices

1920–1969

	Italy (a)	Neth'l (a)	Norway[12] (a)	Poland[13] (a)	Portugal[14] (a)	Romania[15] (a)	Russia[3] (b)	Spain[16] (a)	Sweden (a)	Switzerland (a)	U.K.[19] (a)	Yugoslavia (b)
1920	79	137	180	[9,084][29]	...	...	...	105	159	...	152	...
1921	94	120	167	20,902	...	31	...	104	143	124	138	...
1922	93	106	139	42[21]	...	40	...	100	115	102	112	...
1923	93	103	131	51	...	59	...	98	105	102	106	...
1924	96	103	144	103	...	70	...	102	103	105	107	...
1925	108	103	147	119	...	77	...	104	104	104	107	...
1926	116	100	124	145	...	84	...	103	102	101	105	...
1927	106	100	112	93	...	91	...	104	101	99	102	...
1928	98	100	105	100	...	93	...	97	101	100	101	99
1929	130	100	100	100	100	100	...	100	100	100	100	100
1930	97	94	97	92	95	99	...	103	97	98	96	92
1931	87	89	92	83	84	71	...	107	94	93	90	85
1932	85	83	90	75	82	59	...	103	92	86	88	77
1933	80	83	89	67	82	55	...	100	91	81	85	66
1934	76	83	89	63	84	53	...	102	91	80	86	61
1935	77	80	91	60	84	57	...	99	92	80	87	60
1936	83	77	93	58	86	60	...	...	93	81	90	61
1937	91	80	100	62	89	65	...	...	96	85	94	65
1938	98	83	103	61	86	68	...	...	98	85	95	69
1939	100	80[7]	105	[61][30]	81	73	...	1953=100[16]	101	86	96	71
								[27][26]				
1940	119	94	122	...	85	99	72	31	114	94	112	93
1941	138	106	143	...	96	142	...	40	129	108	121	126
1942	159	114	151	...	117	209	...	43	140	120	122	...
1943	267	117	155	...	132	282	...	43	141	126	121	...
1944	1,187	120	157	...	136	423	...	45	143	129	123	...
1945	2,338	140	160	4,687	147	2,506	...	48	143	130	124	...
1946	2,759	151	164	5,620	169	15,416	...	63	144	129	124	...
1947	4,471	160	165	7,487	174	197,464	[237][31]	74	152	135	124	...
1948	4,734	166	164	7,786	164	...	197	79	154	139	134[7]	...
	1953=100	1953=100	1953=100	1953=100[13]	1953=100				1953=100	1953=100	1953=100	
	86	76	74	44	99				77[7]	96[7]	77	
1949	87	82	74	46[7]	100		168[22]	83	78	95	79	
												1953=100
1950	86	88[7]	78	56	98		135[22]	92	79	94	81	
1951	94	100	90	61	99		123[22]	100	92	98	89	124[7]
1952	98	100[7]	98	70	99		117[4]	98	99	101	97	95
1953	100	100	100	100	100		106	100	100	100	100	100
1954	103	104	104	94	101		100	101	101	101	102	98
1955	106	105	105	92	104		100	105	104	102	106	110
1956	111	108	109	91	109		100	111	109	103	110[7]	119
1957	113	114	112	97	109		100	123	114	105	114	121
1958	118	117	118	100	110		102	140	118	107	117	129
1959	118	117	120[7]	101	112		101	150	120	106	118	130
1960	121	121[7]	121	103	114		101	152	125	108	119	143
1961	125	122	124	104	114		100	156	127	110	123	154
1962	131	126	130	106	114		101	165	133	115	128	171
1963	141	132	134	107	117		102	179	137[32]	119	131	182
1964	149	139	141	108	121		102	192	141	122	135	203
1965	156	146	147	109	125		101	217	149	127	141	271
1966	159	154	152	111	131		100	230	159	133	147	336
1967	162	159	159	112	139		100	245	164	138	151	357
1968	164	165	164	114	147		100	257	168	141	159	375
1969	169	178	170	116	160		100	263	172	145	166	407

Abbreviations:– (a) 1929=100; (b) 1955=100

See p. 784 for footnotes

I2 Cost of Living Indices

1970–1975

	Austria[2]	Belgium[3]	Bulgaria	Czech.[5]	Denmark[6]	Finland	France[1]	West Germany	East Germany	Greece	Hungary[10]	S. Ireland[11]
	(a)	(a)	(a)	(a)	(a)	(a)	(a)	(a)	(b)	(a)	(a)	(a)
1970	167	148	...	91	203	222	204	145	99	170	102	185
1971	175	154	...	90	215	236	215	153	99	175	105	201
1972	186	163	...	90	229	253	229	161	99	183	107	219
1973	200	174	...	90	250	283	245	172	97	211	111	243
1974	219	196	...	90	288	332	279	184	96	268	113	285
1975	238	221	...	91	316	391	312	195	96	304	117	344

Abbreviations:– (a) 1953=100; (b) 1960=100
Abbreviations:– (a) 1929=100; (b) July 1929=100

	Italy	Neth'l	Norway[12]	Poland[13]	Portugal[14]	Romania[15]	Russia[3]	Spain[16]	Sweden	Switzerland	U.K.[19]	Yugoslavia
	(a)	(a)	(a)	(a)	(a)	(a)	(b)	(a)	(a)	(a)	(a)	(a)
1970	177	186	187	117	170	...	100	278	185	150	177	450
1971	186	200	199	117	190	....	100	301	198	160	193	521
1972	197	215	213	117	211	...	100	326	210	171	207	607
1973	217	232	229	120	238	...	100	363	224	192	226	727
1974	259	255	251	129	298	...	100	420	246	204	262	880
1975	304	281	280	133	343	...	100	491	271	218	326	1,093

Abbreviations:– (a) 1953=100; (b) 1955=100

See p. 784 for footnotes

I 2 Cost-of-living Indices

NOTES

1. SOURCES:— The statistics are mainly based on the official publications noted on p. xv and the League of Nations and United Nations, *Statistical Yearbooks.* In addition the following have been used:— Belgium to 1913 — index of retail prices in F. Michelotte, "L'évolution des prix de détail en Belgique de 1830 à 1913", *Bulletin de l'Institute de Recherche Economique* (Louvain, 1937); France to 1914 (1st line) — Jeanne Singer-Kérel, *Le Coût de la Vie à Paris de 1840 a 1954* (Paris, 1961); Germany to 1913 — J. Kuczynski, *Die Geschichte der Lage der Arbeiter unter dem Kapitalismus* (Berlin, 1961); Germany 1913 (2nd line) to 1924 — G. Bry, *Wages in Germany, 1871–1945* Princeton, 1960); Denmark to 1914 — K. Bjerke and N. Ussing, *Studier over Danmarks Nationalprodukt, 1870–1950* (Copenhagen, 1958); Sweden to 1914 — G. Myrdal, *The Cost of Living in Sweden, 1830–1930* (London, 1933); U.K. to 1914 — *18th Abstract of Labour Statistics.*

2. Where a cost-of-living index is not available, an index of retail (or consumer) prices has been given instead.

3. Various indices have been crudely spliced together in the case of certain countries to give a rough indicator of the long-term movement of the cost-of-living. The differences in the construction of these indices should be borne in mind if they are used in further calculations.

FOOTNOTES

[1] Cost-of-living in Paris to 1914 (1st line), and the retail price index subsequently.
[2] For 1939–48 this is an index of the purchasing power of money, based on retail prices, and for 1949–51 it is an index of retail prices. For 1952–58 the cost-of-living refers only to Vienna.
[3] Retail price indices.
[4] April.
[5] The cost-of-living to 1948 refers to Prague only.
[6] The index to 1914 is one devised for deflating national income estimates, but is apparently closer to a retail price index than anything else.
[7] A new index has been spliced on to the old. Where there appears to be a discontinuity a 'break' line has been inserted.
[8] July.
[9] Up to this point there is no allowance for rent in the index.
[10] The cost-of-living refers to Budapest only.
[11] Figures are for June (1922), July (1923–30), or August.
[12] The cost-of-living to 1913 refers to Oslo only.
[13] This is an index of cost-of-living in Warsaw to 1948, and of retail prices subsequently.
[14] June.
[15] The cost-of-living refers to Bucharest only.
[16] This is an index of retail prices in Madrid to 1935. From 1939 it is a national cost-of-living index.
[17] Excluding December.
[18] Excluding September.
[19] The index is of foodstuffs only to 1914 (1st line).
[20] The cost-of-living to 1941 refers to Croatia and Slovenia only.
[21] Based on prices in terms of gold.
[22] March.
[23] This is a weighted average of the old index to April and the new one from May.
[24] First four months only.
[25] Last five months only.
[26] Second half-year only.
[27] From 1938 to 1958 the cost-of-living refers to Athens only.
[28] November.
[29] December.
[30] First seven months only.
[31] Fourth quarter-year only.
[32] Subsequently the retail price index.

J. EDUCATION

Of all the subjects on which statistical material exists, probably none shows less uniformity, both over time and between countries, than education. There is no universal definition of what constitutes a primary school, or a general secondary school, and even that of a university has shown some flexibility, especially of late years. Moreover, there have been at least two major reorganisations of school systems in every country in Europe in the twentieth century; there were others earlier; and minor changes have been very frequent. Then, the statistics of pupils and teachers have not always been collected in a consistent manner, even within the same school system. The date in the school-year to which they relate has been altered on various occasions; the exact meaning of the statistics has changed, sometimes referring to all pupils on the register, sometimes to those in regular attendance, sometimes to those present on a particular day, and sometimes to those present when the inspector visited. Nevertheless, for all the onstacles in the way of precise comparisons, when used with care these statistics do provide useful comparative material, if only of a rough nature.

J 1 CHILDREN AND TEACHERS IN SCHOOLS (in thousands)

1830–1869

	Austria[1]				Belgium				France	
	Primary		Secondary		Primary		Secondary		Primary	Secondary
	P	T	P	T	P	T*	P*	T*	P	P*
1830	...	...	...	...	293	...	...	...	...	42.2
1831	...	...	...	...	355	...	...	...	...	...
1832	...	...	...	...	372	...	...	...	...	...
1833	...	...	...	...	399	...	...	...	...	...
1834	...	...	...	...	412	...	...	...	...	...
1835	...	...	...	...	408	...	...	...	...	...
1836	...	...	...	...	421	...	...	...	...	...
1837	...	...	...	...	430	...	...	...	...	...
1838	...	...	...	...	440[2]	...	...	...	...	...
1839	...	...	...	...	...	...	...	...	...	...
1840	...	...	...	...	453	...	...	...	...	41.9
1841	...	...	20.5	0.6	...	...	...	...	...	...
1842	1,365	27.3	20.4	0.6	...	...	...	...	...	...
1843	1,359	27.8	20.6	0.6	...	...	...	...	...	...
1844	1,386	28.2	...	...	...	...	...	...	...	...
1845	...	...	21.0	0.7	426	...	...	...	...	...
1846	1,426	28.4	21.5	0.7	429	...	...	...	...	...
1847	1,434	28.7	...	...	436	...	...	...	...	...
1848	...	...	20.6	0.7	451	7,965	4,438	330	...	...
1849	1,435	28.7	23.8	1.0	...	...	...	...	...	...
1850	1,426	28.4	24.3	1.3	...	...	6,989[3]	...[3]	3,322	47.9
1851	1,458	27.4	23.3	1.1	487	8,907	...	...	...	45.6
1852	1,484	26.4	23.5	1.4	492	...	9,415	733	...	45.0
1853	1,518	27.6	22.9	1.4	498	...	9,444	...	...	45.4
1854	1,513	25.8	25.1	1.5	492	8,807	9,519	919	...	46.4
1855	1,502	26.3	26.2	1.5	...	...	10,216	...	...	48.0
1856	1,530	26.3	28.3	1.6	...	...	10,586	...	...	50.6
1857	1,569	26.5	30.7	1.6	499[4] 511	9,104	11,112	...	...	52.9
1858	1,610	26.6	33.0	1.7	...	...	11,670	...	...	53.5
1859	1,644	27.2	34.4	1.7	...	...	11,879	...	...	54.1
1860	1,656	27.6	36.7	1.8	516	9,222	12,022	972	...	55.9
1861	1,651	27.6	37.6	1.9	...	...	14,021	...	...	58.3
1862	1,637	27.3	38.4	2.0	...	...	14,459	...	...	61.5
1863	1,650	27.2	41.5	2.2	545	9,633	14,510[3]	......[3]	...	63.0
1864	1,450	33.5	43.0	2.3	...	...	15,137	...	...	64.8
1865	1,669	33.8	43.6	2.3	...	...	16,062	1,142	4,437	65.7
1866	1,689	34.4	42.9	2.4	564	10,392	15,841	...	...	67.4
1867	1,682	34.6	42.7	2.4	...	...	15,939	...	...	68.6
1868	1,691	35.0	43.4	2.6	...	...	16,493	...	...	71.3
1869	...	...	43.7	2.7	593	9,528	17,124	...	...	...

Abbreviations used throughout this table: P: Pupils T: Teachers

* denotes actual number, not thousands

Abbreviations used where space demands:— U.K.: E. & W. :— United Kingdom: England and Wales

See p. 805 for footnotes

J 1 Children and Teachers in Schools (in thousands)

1830–1869

	Hungary[5]				Croatia–Slavonia		Italy			Netherlands			
	Primary		Secondary		Primary		Primary[7]		Secondary	Primary		Secondary	
	P	T	P	T	P	T	P	T	P	P	T	P	T*
1830	...	...	...	...	...	...	...	...	...	...	...	...	...
1831	...	...	...	...	...	...	...	...	...	...	...	...	...
1832	...	...	...	...	...	...	...	...	...	...	...	...	...
1833	...	...	...	...	...	...	...	...	...	...	...	...	...
1834	...	...	...	...	...	...	...	...	...	...	...	...	...
1835	...	...	...	...	...	...	...	...	...	...	...	...	...
1836	...	...	...	...	...	...	...	...	...	...	...	...	...
1837	...	...	...	...	...	...	...	...	...	...	...	...	...
1838	...	...	...	...	...	...	...	...	...	...	...	...	...
1839	...	...	...	...	...	...	...	...	...	...	...	1.4	...
1840	...	...	...	...	...	...	...	...	...	...	...	1.3	...
1841	...	...	26.6	0.8	...	...	...	...	...	...	...	1.3	...
1842	...	...	27.1	0.8	...	...	...	...	...	...	...	1.4	...
1843	...	...	...	...	...	...	...	...	...	...	...	1.5	...
1844	...	...	...	...	...	...	...	...	...	...	...	1.5	...
1845	...	...	...	...	...	...	...	...	...	...	...	1.5	...
1846	...	...	...	...	...	...	...	...	...	...	...	1.5	...
1847	...	...	...	...	...	...	...	...	...	...	...	1.5	...
1848	...	...	...	...	...	...	...	...	...	...	...	1.8	...
1849	...	...	...	...	...	...	...	...	...	...	6.2	1.8	244
1850	...	...	18.3	1.2	...	...	...	...	...	...	6.4	1.8	252
1851	...	...	19.5	1.4	...	...	...	...	...	397	6.5	1.8	251
1852	...	...	20.6	1.5	...	...	...	...	...	398	6.9	1.8	245
1853	...	...	20.1	1.5	...	...	...	...	...	392	7.0	1.8	255
1854	900[6]	20.6[6]	22.9	1.6	...	...	...	...	...	326	7.2	1.8	252
1855	...	...	24.1	1.7	...	...	...	...	...	388	7.3	1.8	252
1856	...	...	25.6	1.8	...	...	...	...	...	394	7.4	1.9	258
1857	...	...	27.3	1.8	...	...	...	...	...	406	7.4	1.8	260
1858	...	...	28.1	1.9	...	...	...	...	...	399	8.0	1.8	254
1859	935[6]	20.8[6]	...	...	...	...	...	...	...	405	7.9	1.8	255
1860	...	...	...	...	...	...	...	...	...	401	8.4	1.8	253
1861	...	...	...	...	...	...	1,009	28.2	15.8	391	9.0	1.8	254
1862	...	...	32.1	1.7	...	...	1,109	31.4	18.2	441	9.6	1.3	261
1863	...	...	...	...	...	...	1,175	34.3	17.3	453	10.2	1.8	254
1864	...	...	36.0	1.9	...	...	1,194	33.3	18.6	450	10.4	1.8	244
1865	985	17.8	37.0	2.0	99	1.6	1,214	32.4	19.6	432	10.2	1.3	243
1866	...	...	...	...	...	...	1,409	35.2	23.3	437	10.3	1.3	245
1867	...	...	...	...	...	...	1,484	38.0	22.9	434	10.4	1.3	243
1868	...	...	38.2	1.7	...	...	1,529	39.2	23.0	437	10.4	1.3	236
1869	...	...	38.1	1.7	...	...	1,573	40.3	22.8	451	10.7	1.3	231

See p. 805 for footnotes

J 1 Children and Teachers in Schools (in thousands)

1830–1869

	Norway		Portugal		Spain		Sweden	U.K.: E.& W.		U.K.: Scotland	
	Primary		Primary		Primary	Secondary	Primary	Primary		Primary	
	P	T*	P	T*	P	P	P	P	T	P	T
1830	...	...	...	...	...	...	...	...	...	...	...
1831	...	...	...	...	...	...	...	...	...	...	...
1832	...	...	...	...	...	...	...	...	...	...	...
1833	...	...	...	...	...	...	...	...	...	...	...
1834	...	...	...	...	...	...	...	...	...	...	...
1835	...	...	...	...	...	...	...	...	...	...	...
1836	...	...	...	...	...	...	...	...	...	...	...
1837	178	2,142	...	...	...	...	...	...	...	...	...
1838	...	...	...	...	...	...	...	...	...	...	...
1839	...	...	...	...	...	...	...	...	...	...	...
1840	180	2,236	...	...	...	...	...	...	...	...	...
1841	...	...	...	...	...	...	...	...	...	...	...
1842	...	...	...	...	...	...	...	...	...	...	...
1843	...	...	...	...	...	...	...	...	...	...	...
1844	...	...	...	...	...	...	...	...	...	...	...
1845	...	...	...	...	...	...	...	...	...	...	...
1846	...	...	...	...	...	...	...	...	...	...	...
1847	...	...	...	...	...	...	...	...	...	...	...
1848	...	...	37	...	...	...	...	...	...	...	...
1849	...	...	42	1,169	...	...	...	...	...	28	...
1850	...	...	...	...	...	...	...	250	...	32	...
1851	...	...	...	...	...	...	...	323	...	64	...
1852	...	...	...	...	...	...	...	...	2.0	...	...
1853	196	2,575	...	...	...	...	...	394	2.4	68	...
1854	...	...	...	...	...	...	...	447	3.0	91	...
1855	...	...	...	...	1,005	...	...	480	3.7	92	...
1856	...	...	...	...	...	...	...	531	4.4	95	...
1857	...	...	...	...	...	17.6	...	636	5.1	125	...
1858	...	...	...	...	...	19.9	...	675	6.0	127	...
1859	...	...	...	...	1,047	20.9	...	751	6.7	133	...
1860	...	...	...	...	1,252	21.5	...	774	7.6	146	...
1861	...	...	...	...	...	23.2	...	799[9]	8.0	151	...
1862	...	...	...	...	...	24.6	...	826	8.8	162	...
1863	...	...	...	...	...	27.1	...	829[10]	9.7[11]	148	...
								797	9.1		
1864	...	...	...	...	...	28.8	...	848	10.3	156	1.9
1865	...	...	...	...	...	26.4	462	863	10.9	162	2.0
1866	...	...	...	...	...	27.0	...	912	11.7	169	2.2
1867	236	3,533	...	...	1,425	28.7	...	979	12.4	182	2.3
1868	...	...	...	...	...	...	521	1,063	13.0	179	2.2
1869	...	...	...	...	...	...	...	1,152	13.7	198	2.5

See p. 805 for footnotes

J 1 Children and Teachers in Schools (in thousands)

1870–1919

	Austria[1]				Belgium				Bulgaria			
	Primary		Secondary		Primary		Secondary		Primary		Secondary	
	P	T	P	T	P	T*	P*	T*	P	T*	P	T*
1870	1,821	35.3	46.3	2.9	...	...	17,796	1,218	...	...	...	...
1871	...	...	49.8	3.3	...	...	17,731	...	...	...	...	...
1872	...	...	52.0	3.5	619	9,803	18,340	...	...	...	...	...
1873	...	...	54.1	3.8	...	...	19,312	...	...	...	...	...
1874	2,135	31.2	55.7	3.8	...	...	20,130	...	...	...	...	...
1875	...	...	57.6	4.0	669	10,751	21,006	1,319	...	...	...	...
1876	...	...	59.7	4.2	...	...	20,194	...	...	...	...	...
1877	...	...	62.0	4.2	...	...	20,594	...	...	...	...	...
1878	...	...	64.1	4.4	688[14] / 598	11,808[14] / 9,417	20,686	...	...	...	...	...
1879	2,378	52.2[12] / 48.3	65.9	4.4	...	...	22,773	...	...	...	...	...
1880	2,438	48.4	66.3	4.6	...	...	26,574	...	...	...	...	...
1881	2,591	51.2	65.9	4.6	340	8,328	25,733	...	...	...	...	...
1882	2,642	52.3	67.1	4.7	...	8,555	28,301	...	...	...	...	...
1883	2,696	53.0	68.4	4.8	346	8,669	28,153	...	...	...	...	...
1884	2,781	54.4	69.6	4.8	326	...	28,477	...	...	...	...	...
1885	2,862	55.8	71.3	4.9	589	...	29,320	...	...	...	...	...
1886	2,856	57.2	70.6	4.9	600	...	28,931	...	...	...	...	...
1887	2,899	58.8	70.2	4.8	604	...	28,865	...	...	...	...	...
1888	2,939	60.1	70.5	4.8	601	...	28,825	...	...	...	...	...
1889	3,078	61.4[12]	71.3	4.9	615	...	28,557	...	...	...	...	...
1890	3,157	63.2	72.1	4.9	616	...	28,366	...	[197][16]	[4,320][16]	...	...
1891	3,220	65.3	73.4	5.0	627	...	28,742	...	...	...	...	...
1892	3,276	67.4	75.7	5.2	641	...	28,758	...	...	...	...	...
1893	3,313	68.0	77.6	5.2	652	...	28,851	...	...	...	...	...
1894	3,379	69.8	79.8	5.3	695	...	29,370	...	...	...	...	...
1895	3,430	71.6	82.3	5.5	720	...	29,859	...	341	8,273	42	1,357
1896	3,424	72.6	84.4	5.5	752	...	29,954	...	340	7,885	44	1,428
1897	3,484	74.8	87.0	5.8	764	...	30,114	...	343	7,965	43	1,502
1898	3,542	76.6	91.0	5.9	775	...	30,320	...	340	8,008	41	1,477
1899	3,619	78.0	95.9	6.2	786	...	30,690	...	329	7,919	35	1,596
1900	3,693	79.9	100	6.4	794	...	31,333	...	318	7,761	34	1,501
1901	3,742	81.5	106	6.8	810	...	30,150	...	312	7,611	30	1,384
1902	3,822	83.1	111	7.1	827	...	32,468	...	341	7,755	29	1,408
1903	3,908	85.1	116	7.4	843	...	32,442	...	359	8,130	31	1,535
1904	4,014	87.0	120	7.8	859	...	33,122	...	378	8,403	33	1,641
1905	4,207	94.8[12] / 100	124	8.1	871	...	33,152	...	400	8,771	36	1,613
1906	4,284	102	127	8.6	884	...	32,680	...	416	8,960	39	1,691
1907	4,378	103	129	8.9	897	...	34,169	...	430	9,398	46	1,976
1908	4,454	105	134	9.2	915	...	35,027	...	436	9,945	53	2,111
1909	4,520	108	141	9.8	923	...	35,436	...	445	10,253	62	2,513
1910	4,534	110	157	11.7	929	...	35,526	...	454	10,373	71	2,917
1911	4,616	113	163	12.5	935	...	37,061	...	475	10,681	80	3,158
1912	4,634	115	165	12.8	935	...	38,236	...	241	6,254	64	2,147
1913	4,561	108	[125][13]	[10.3][13]	939	...	39,081	...	504	10,810	87	3,353
1914	4,123	100	111	9.5	[891][15]	...	25,792	...	554	11,530	92	3,710
1915	...	...	...	...	...	...	33,723	...	453	8,825	94	2,806
1916	...[1]	...[1]	...[1]	...[1]	...	...	37,783	...	534	9,594	98	2,966
1917	913	22.7	40.1	3.1	...	...	37,751	...	555	9,551	117	3,266
1918	903	26.9	40.2	3.2	...	...	36,063	...	539	11,762	134	4,249
1919	909	32.6	40.3	3.2	961	...	47,218	...	572	12,930	130	4,659

See p. 805 for footnotes

J 1 Children and Teachers in Schools (in thousands)

1870–1919

	Denmark			Finland				France		
	Primary	Secondary	All Schools	Primary		Secondary		Primary		Secondary
	P	P*	T*	P	T*	P*	T*	P	T	P
1870	...	...	...	...	...	...	...	...[20]	...	...[20]
1871	...	...	...	...	...	...	...	...	...	64.7
1872	...	...	...	...	...	...	...	...	...	69.5
1873	...	...	...	...	...	...	...	...	...	71.6
1874	...	...	...	...	...	...	...	...	...	72.3
1875	...	...	...	18	474	...	...	4,610	...	73.9
1876	...	...	...	...	...	...	...	...	...	79.2
1877	...	...	...	...	...	...	...	4,717	...	79.1
1878	...	...	...	...	...	...	...	4,870	...	80.2
1879	...	...	...	...	...	...	...	4,950	120	83.2
1880	...	...	...	29	787	...	...	5,049	123	86.8
1881	...	...	...	29	858	8,016	858	5,341	125	89.5
1882	...	...	...	33	918	8,304	911	5,442	130	90.9
1883	...	...	...	36	993	8,899	1,005	5,469	133	93.4
1884	...	...	...	38	1,069	8,938	1,020	5,531	134	92.9
1885	...	...	...	39	1,131	9,006	1,085	5,517	135	93.0
1886	...	...	...	43	1,213	9,340	1,133	5,521	137	94.6
1887	...	...	...	45	1,264	9,569	1,163	5,617	141	95.7
1888	...	...	...	47	1,332	9,708	1,192	5,623	143	93.0
1889	...	...	...	50	1,385	9,691	1,191	5,602	143[21]	91.5
1890	...	...	...	55[10] 53	1,492	10,238	1,216	5,594	146	90.8
1891	...	...	...	57	1,628	10,607	1,232	5,556	147	91.9
1892	...	...	...	61	1,736	10,677	1,231	5,554	148	94.0
1893	335	5,874	...	67	1,850	10,915	1,216	5,548	149	95.9
1894	...	...	...	74	1,967	11,665	1,278	5,540	151	95.9
1895	...	...	...	81	2,120	12,373	1,356	5,534	152	96.5
1896	...	...	...	87	2,297	12,914[19]	1,416	5,532	152	96.2
1897	357	6,838	...	94	2,503	11,546	1,418	5,535	154	96.2
1898	...	...	...	99	2,698	12,420	1,453	5,539	155	95.8
1899	...	...	...	103	2,889	13,483	1,548	5,530	157	96.8
1900	...	...	...	110	3,076	14,449	1,519	5,526	158	98.7
1901	...	...	...	117	3,263	15,483	1,609	5,550	159	102
1902	376	6,966	...	116	3,463	16,529	1,699	5,553	156	107
1903	...	...	...	124	3,596	17,149	1,767	5,555	153	112
1904	385	8,089	...	126	3,708	17,628	1,776	5,568	152	117
1905	390[17] 380	8,314[17] 17,897	10,779	132	3,987	18,819[19]	1,832	5,567	152	120
1906	389	20,181	10,923	141	4,102	19,725	1,858	5,585	152	123
1907	394	21,105	11,165	147	4,377	21,416	1,918	5,600	153	123
1908	397	23,132	11,275	158	4,679	22,263[19]	2,042[19]	5,630	155	124
1909	402	25,143	11,491	163	5,068	23,534 (thous.)	1,890	5,639	156	126
1910	406	25,621	11,519[18]	177	5,512	24.4	1,919	5,655	157	126
1911	409	26,523	14,119	183	5,738	24.8	1,953	5,682	158	128
1912	413	26,706	14,197	188	5,890	25.2	2,036	5,669	160	131
1913	418	28,659	14,298	194	6,079	25.3	2,031	...[22]	...[22]	133[22]
1914	422	28,845	14,442	197	6,199	25.2	2,131	...	...	97
1915	427	30,042	14,661	200	6,322	25.5	2,153	...	...	109
1916	431	30,849	14,697	204	6,413	26.1	2,134	...	...	118
1917	...	...	...	215	6,554	26.7	2,107	4,072	99	124
1918	435	34,489	15,091	212	7,058	27.2	2,158	3,893	99	121[22]
1919	437	36,150	15,296	248	7,556	30.0	2,340	3,836	102	140

See p. 805 for footnotes

J 1 Children and Teachers in Schools (in thousands)

1870–1919

	Germany				Greece		Hungary[5]			
	Primary[23]		Secondary		Primary		Primary		Secondary	
	P	T	P	T	P	T*	P	T	P	T
1870	...	...	...	...	...	...	1,156	18.5	33.0	2.0
1971	...	...	...	...	...	...	...	...	34.0	2.0
1872	...	...	...	...	...	...	...	...	35.6	2.3
1873	...	...	...	...	...	...	...	...	36.3[6]	2.4[6]
1874	...	...	...	...	...	...	...	...	36.5[6]	2.5[6]
1875	...	...	...	...	...	...	1,493	19.9	36.9[6]	2.7[6]
1876	...	...	...	...	...	...	1,507	20.1	37.9[6]	2.6[6]
1877	...	...	...	...	...	...	1,560	20.7	36.1	2.4
1878	...	...	...	...	...	...	1,625	21.2	37.1	2.4
1879	...	...	...	...	...	...	1,645	21.4	37.8	2.4
1880	...	...	...	...	...	...	1,620	21.7	38.6	2.5
1881	...	...	...	...	...	...	1,656	22.0	38.4	2.4
1882	...	...	...	...	...	...	1,698	22.4	38.4	2.5
1883	...	...	...	...	...	...	1,757	22.7	38.0	2.5
1884	...	...	...	...	...	...	1,801	23.1	37.5	2.7
1885	...	...	...	...	...	...	1,831	23.4	37.9	2.7
1886	...	...	...	...	...	...	1,868	24.0	38.7	2.9
1887	...	...	...	...	...	...	1,951	24.1	39.3	2.9
1888	...	...	...	...	...	...	2,016	24.4	40.0	2.9
1889	...	...	...	...	...	...	2,058	24.6	40.7	2.9
1890	...	...	...	...	...	...	2,118[24]	...	42.1	...
							2,030			
1891	...	...	...	...	...	...	2,075	25.5	43.9	...
1892	...	...	...	...	...	...	2,134	25.8	45.9	3.2
1893	...	...	...	...	...	...	2,174	26.1	48.3	3.3
1894	...	...	...	...	...	...	2,239	26.4	49.7	3.3
1895	...	...	...	...	...	...	2,224	26.7	51.7	3.4
1896	...	...	...	...	...	...	2,239	27.2	53.2	3.5
1897	...	...	...	...	...	...	2,232	27.7	54.7	3.5
1898	...	...	...	...	...	...	2,250	28.0	56.4	3.6
1899	...	...	...	...	...	...	2,278	28.6	58.0[25]	3.7[25]
									62.9	4.1
1900	8,966	147	...	...	...	...	2,315	29.1	64.2	4.2
1901	...	...	...	...	190	4,055	2,369	29.4	65.5	4.3
1902	...	...	...	...	211	4,346	2,399	30.1	66.6	4.4
1903	...	...	...	...	...	...	2,337[26]	31.4[26]	67.3	4.5
							2,281	29.2		
1904	...	...	...	...	...	...	2,294	29.9	67.7	4.6
1905	9,779	167	...	...	...	...	2,345	30.3	69.6	4.7
1906	...	...	...	...	...	...	2,376	30.8	71.1	4.6
1907	...	...	...	...	...	...	2,415	31.4	71.9	4.8
1908	...	...	...	...	241	4,346	2,441	31.9	73.7	4.9
1909	...	...	...	...	...	...	2,457	32.4	75.4	5.0
1910	10,310	187	1,016	47.4	260	4,641	2,471	33.0	77.6	5.2
1911	...	...	...	...	...	...	2,488	33.9	79.5	5.1
1912	...	...	...	...	...	...	...	...	...	...
1913	...	...	...	...	...	...	...	35.3	84.3	4.8
1914	...	...	...	...	...	...	...	...	...	...
1915	...	...	...	...	...	...	2,012	29.0	86.5	3.3
1916	...	...	...	...	...	...	2,113	29.6	89.8	3.3
1917	...	...	...	...	...	...	2,037[27]	28.9[27]	92.1[27]	3.7[27]
1918	...	...	...	...	...	...	776	14.4	56.5	2.5
1919	...	...	...	...	...	...	813	16.3	56.5	2.7

See p. 805 for footnotes

J 1 Children and Teachers in Schools (in thousands)

1870–1919

	Croatia-Slavonia				Italy				Netherlands			
	Primary		Secondary		Primary[7]		Secondary		Primary		Secondary	
	P	T	P	T	P	T	P	T	P	T	P	T*
1870	...	...	...	...	1,605	41.0	23.2	...	467	11.0	1.4[30] 4.8	230[30] 747
1871	...	...	...	...	1,723	43.4	23.8	...	474	10.9	5.1	793
1872	...	...	...	...	1,798	44.4	24.6	...	484	11.1	5.6	(841)[31]
1873	...	...	...	...	1,842	45.6	25.6	...	500	11.5	5.4	(865)[31]
1874	...	...	...	...	1,896	46.8	27.3	...	499	11.7	5.4	872
1875	...	...	...	...	1,932	47.1	28.5	...	510	12.0	5.8	913
1876	...	...	...	...	1,968	47.3	29.7	...	515	12.6	6.1	944
1877	...	...	...	...	2,003	47.6	31.6	...	523	12.3	6.4	964
1878	...	...	...	...	2,058	48.5	33.0	...	523	12.7	6.6	996
1879	...	...	...	...	2,031	48.4	33.2	...	531	13.3	6.9	1,073
1880	...	...	...	...	2,003	48.3	32.5	...	541	14.2	7.4	1,131
1881	...	...	...	...	1,976	48.2	35.4	...	545	15.1	7.8	1,189
1882	...	...	...	...	2,037	51.8	36.2	...	562	15.9	8.1	1,254
1883	...	...	...	...	2,153	54.1	38.1	...	563	16.3	8.5	1,300
1884	...	...	...	...	2,206	54.8	38.8	...	579	17.2	8.7	1,322
1885	...	...	...	...	2,253	55.3	40.5	...	594	17.3	8.9	1,311
1886	...	...	...	...	2,279	55.6	42.9	...	607	17.3	8.9	1,278
1887	150	...	3.5	...	2,308	56.9	46.8	...	617	17.6	9.0	1,291
1888	153	...	3.6	...	2,326	57.1	48.5	...	627	17.5	9.4	1,310
1889	160	...	3.6	...	2,374	58.1	57.6	...	636	17.5	9.6	1,314
1890	169	...	3.8	...	2,419	59.0	63.5[28]	...	643	18.1	9.9	1,341
1891	175	2.2	4.0	0.3	2,454	59.8	78.2	...	652	18.5	10.2	1,369
1892	180	2.2	4.4	0.3	2,488	60.4	80.1	...	659	19.0	10.6	1,375
1893	185	2.3	4.0	0.3	2,526	61.1	82.9	...	672	19.8	10.7	1,371
1894	187	2.4	4.3	0.3	2,567	61.8	84.7	...	684	20.3	11.0	1,403
1895	195	2.5	5.2	0.4	2,589	62.1	88.3	...	691	21.4	11.2	1,385
1896	199	2.5	5.6	0.4	2,564	62.2	88.0	...	702	21.8	11.4	1,393
1897	196	2.5	5.9	0.4	2,538	62.4	87.8	...	709	22.8	11.6	1,401
1898	197	2.6	6.0	0.4	2,637	62.6	87.3	...	719	23.5	12.0	1,442
1899	198	2.6	6.1	0.4	2,682	64.3	90.1	...	731	24.2	12.6	1,450
1900	199	2.6	6.3	0.4	2,708	65.0	91.6	...	740	24.7	13.1	1,481
1901	205	2.7	6.3	0.4	2,733	65.7	92.0	...	755	25.1	13.2	1,510
1902	211	2.7	6.4	0.4	2,810	66.0	98.6	...	802	25.7	13.7[32] 16.0	1,543
1903	216[26] 213	2.7[26] 2.6	6.3	0.4	2,878	66.5	101	...	820	26.1	16.1	1,651
1904	219	2.6	6.1	0.4	2,962	66.9	105	...	832	26.6	16.6	1,699
1905	230	2.7	6.1	0.4	3,032	67.0	112	...	845	26.7	17.1	1,747
1906	238	2.8	6.2	0.4	3,102	67.0	116	...	857	27.3	18.2	1,852
1907	250	2.9	6.3	0.5	3,150	66.4	127	...	867	27.5	19.0	1,889
1908	255	3.0	6.3	0.5	3,210	68.7	141	...	879	28.6	19.2	1,911
1909	260	3.0	6.6	0.5	3,250	70.5	156	...	892	29.3	19.8	1,992
1910	266	3.1	6.7	0.5	3,309	72.8	164	...	904	30.1	20.3	2,028
1911	271	3.1	6.9	0.5	3,354	75.1	...	...	917	31.2	30.7	2,038
1912	282	...	6.7	...	3,387	76.9	...[29]	...	929	32.1	21.3	2,143
1913	290	3.5	7.1	0.6	3,484	80.1	282	20.3	943	32.9	22.0	2,222
1914	...	...	...	...	3,583	83.5	294	21.4	959	33.5	23.1	2,290
1915	223	3.1	6.6	0.5	3,684	87.3	305	21.9	981	34.2	24.7	2,344
1916	...	...	...	...	3,773	90.5	322	22.5	994	34.5	26.5	2,433
1917	...	...	...	...	3,869	94.0	325	23.1	1,008	34.6	28.1	2,589
1918	...	...	...	...	3,971	97.7	354	24.1	1,019	34.7	30.6	2,738
1919	...	...	...	...	4,069	102	383	25.9	1,022	35.3	31.6	3,246

See p. 805 for footnotes

J 1 Children and Teachers in Schools (in thousands)

1870–1919

	Norway				Portugal				Romania		
	Primary		Secondary		Primary		Secondary		Primary[16]		Secondary
	P	T*	P	T*	P	T*	P	T*	P	T*	P
1870	237	3,652	...	...	...	...	...	...	...	...	...
1871	...	...	...	...	...	...	...	...	...	...	...
1872	...	...	...	...	125	...	...	...	...	...	...
1873	...	...	...	...	...	...	...	...	...	...	...
1874	...	...	...	...	...	...	...	...	...	...	...
1875	245	3,911	4.0	401	...	...	...	...	...	...	...
1876	247	4,043	4.4	450	...	...	...	...	...	...	...
1877	247	4,109	3.4	455	...	...	...	...	...	...	...
1878	249	4,221	5.4	504	...	...	...	...	...	...	...
1879	248	4,314	5.8	519	...	...	...	...	...	...	...
1880	247	4,358	6.5	576	...	...	...	...	108	3,010	...
1881	244[33] 226	4,413	6.3	556	...	...	...	...	...	...	...
1882	227	4,497	6.4	577	...	...	...	...	...	...	...
1883	239	4,557	6.7	639	236	3,649	...	...	...	...	...
1884	238	4,461	7.0	643	240	3,624	...	...	...	...	...
1885	244	4,726	7.6	692	237	3,776	...	...	135	3,627	...
1886	249	4,933	8.0[29]	759[29]	240	3,883	...	...	...	...	...
1887	255	4,916	10.0	1,043	246	3,954	2.4	...	...	...	...
1888	258	4,966	10.5	1,084	238	4,069	2.9	...	...	...	...
1889	262	5,006	10.4	1,004	...	...	3.0	...	...	...	...
1890	265[33] 287	5,128	11.0	1,113	...	...	3.5	...	191	4,356	...
1891	288	5,269	11.0	1,051	...	...	3.6	...	...	...	...
1892	301	6,090	11.2	1,085	...	...	3.6	222	...	...	...
1893	307	6,268	11.3	1,103	...	...	3.6	229	...	...	...
1894	311	6,395	11.3	1,077	...	...	3.7	222	...	...	...
1895	320[34]	6,518	12.0	1,113	...	...	4.1	234	259	5,201	...
1896	323	6,639	12.4	1,040	...	...	4.6	247	...	...	...
1897	327	6,776	9.8	1,129	...	...	5.1	264	...	...	...
1898	331	6,906	9.6	1,119	...	...	5.0	272	...	...	...
1899	333	7,115	9.9	1,114	231	...	4.8	283	...	...	...
1900	336[34]	7,283	10.4	1,088	...	...	5.2	315	352	5,950	17.8
1901	341	7,427	11.2	1,244	...	...	6.0	337	364	5,986	16.6
1902	345	7,535	11.7	1,253	...	...	6.7[35] 5.5	362	446	5,995	15.4
1903	350	7,611	12.1	1,312	...	...	5.8	364	474	6,066	14.2
1904	354	7,690	12.0	1,326	...	...	5.9	411	497	6,194	14.0
1905	359	7,750	11.0	1,319	...	...	7.1	487	505	6,375	14.8
1906	361	7,733	12.4	1,321	...	...	7.5	456	515	6,410	15.6
1907	365	7,954	11.5	1,337	...	...	8.3	484	530	6,933	15.9
1908	370	8,106	13.1	1,313	...	...	9.1	468	561	7,667	15.6
1909	374	8,279	13.9	1,357	...	...	9.7	510	585	7,784	16.4
1910	377	8,563	15.0	1,415	...	...	10.6	512	587	7,862	17.2
1911	379	8,742	16.1	1,424	...	...	11.7	531	677	8,227	...
1912	379	9,051	17.3	1,366	...	...	11.1	540	681	8,322	...
1913	382	9,251	18.1	1,519	...	...	11.0	557	683	8,247	...
1914	382	9,351	20.0	1,582	...	...	11.6	613	721	9,042	...
1915	382	9,567	18.5	1,539	...	...	12.7	607	...	...	...
1916	383	10,097	22.2	1,695	...	...	13.4	649	...	...	...
1917	379	10,484	22.6	1,697	...	...	13.7	572	...	...	...
1918	378	10,714	24.2	1,683	...	...	12.7	695	...	...	...
1919	380	10,894	25.4	1,678	...	...	...	...	778	13,123	22.7

See p. 805 for footnotes

J 1 Children and Teachers in Schools (in thousands)

1870–1919

	Serbia/Yugoslavia				Spain			Sweden			
	Primary		Secondary		Primary		Secondary	Primary		Secondary	
	P	T	P	T*	P	T	P	P	T	P	T*
1870	23.3	0.6	1.8	99	...	...	...	556	7.8	...	...
1871	25.7	0.6	2.0	116	...	...	...	...	...	...	...
1872	25.9	0.6	2.1	134	...	...	...	...	...	...	...
1873	26.6	0.6	1.8	134	...	...	...	...	...	...	...
1874	28.1	0.6	2.6	135	...	...	...	...	...	...	...
1875	28.3	0.7	2.3	149	...	...	...	613	9.3	...	...
1876	28.0	0.7	2.3	163	...	...	...	...	...	...	...
1877	...	0.7	...	156	...	...	...	...	...	...	...
1878	23.6	0.6	1.8	157	...	...	...	...	...	...	...
1879	29.7	0.7	2.2	169	...	...	...	...	...	...	...
1880	36.3	0.8	2.8	205	1,769	...	...	...	...	...	...
1881	39.7	0.9	3.3	214	...	...	...	...	...	...	...
1882	39.1	0.9	4.1	232	...	...	...	...	...	...	...
1883	39.9	0.9	4.5	267	...	...	...	...	...	...	...
1884	45.4	0.9	4.6	285	...	...	...	...	...	...	...
1885	47.8	0.9	5.0	267	1,843	...	...	...	...	...	...
1886	47.8	0.9	5.2	275	...	...	...	677	12.6	...	...
1887	57.8	1.1	6.0	306	...	...	...	...	...	...	...
1888	58.9	1.2	6.3	337	...	...	...	...	...	14	...
1889	61.9	1.3	6.6	360	...	...	...	...	...	14	...
1890	65.7	1.3	6.8	363	...	...	...	690	13.5	14	...
1891	68.0	1.4	7.3	346	...	...	...	...	...	15	...
1892	73.3	1.5	7.1	379	...	...	...	...	...	15	...
1893	76.6	1.6	7.5	402	...	...	...	...	...	15	...
1894	83.5	1.7	7.8	405	...	...	...	...	...	15	...
1895	90.0	1.8	7.8	499	...	...	...	...	...	15	...
1896	92.1	1.9	8.0	471	...	...	...	...	...	16	...
1897	93.8	1.9	7.8	473	...	...	...	...	...	16	...
1898	98.1	2.0	8.0	464	...	...	...	740	15.9	17	...
1899	101	1.9	5.3	324	...	...	...	741	16.3	17	...
1900	102	1.9	4.5	322	...	...	...	742	16.6	18	...
1901	105	2.0	4.5	333	...	...	...	743	17.2	18	...
1902	110	2.0	4.6	350	...	...	...	748	17.4	19	...
1903	112	2.1	6.2	368	...	...	...	753	17.8	20	...
1904	122	2.2	6.1	374	...	...	...	759	18.3	21	...
1905	128	2.3	6.7	392	...	...	...	762	18.8	22	...
1906	129	2.3	7.1	429	...	...	...	765	19.3	22	...
1907	132	2.4	...	...	...	...	...	772	19.9	23	...
1908	136	2.5	...	...	1,526	...	...	778	20.5	23	...
1909	138	2.6	...	...	...	...	...	785	21.0	24	1,648
1910	146	2.5	...	...	...	...	...	791	21.5	24	1,681
1911	...	...	...	...	...	...	...	795	22.0	25	1,720
1912	...	...	...	...	...	...	...	802	22.5	26	1,750
1913	...	...	...	...	...	...	...	808	23.0	26	1,798
1914	...	...	...	...	1,812	37.0	48.8	813[36]	23.5	27	1,807
1915	...	...	...	...	...	...	48.3	704	24.2	27	1,851
1916	...	...	...	...	1712	35.2	52.0	706	24.8	28	1,892
1917	...	...	...	...	...	...	52.5	708	25.3	29	1,942
	Yugoslavia										
1918	...	...	42.7	2,053	...	...	51.8	707	25.9	30	1,960
1919	801	12.5	55.5	2,656	...	...	52.4	709	26.4	32	2,048

See p. 805 for footnotes

J 1 Children and Teachers in Schools (in thousands)

1870–1919

	Switzerland				U.K.: England & Wales				U.K.: Scotland			
	Primary[16]		Secondary		Primary		Secondary[8]		Primary		Secondary[8]	
	P	T*	P	T*	P	T	P	T	P	T	P	T
1870	...	...	...	...	1,231	14.4	...	...	201	2.4	...	...
1871	...	...	...	...	1,336	16.4	...	...	206	2.6	...	...
1872	...	...	...	...	1,482	18.8	...	...	213	2.7	...	...
1873	...	...	...	...	1,679	21.2	...	...	275[9]	3.2[9]	...	...
1874	...	...	...	...	1,837	23.7	...	...	312	3.9	...	...
1875	...	...	...	...	1,985	26.8	...	...	333	4.3	...	...
1876	...	...	...	...	2,151	30.0	...	...	360	4.9	...	...
1877	...	...	...	...	2,405	34.5	...	...	377	5.2	...	...
1878	...	...	...	...	2,595	38.5	...	...	385	5.5	...	...
1879	...	...	...	...	2,751	41.4	...	...	405	5.8	...	...
1880	...	...	...	...	2,864	44.6	...	...	410	6.1	...	...
1881	434	...	25.5	...	3,015	48.1	...	...	421	6.4	...	...
1882	...	...	...	...	3,127	52.7	...	...	433	6.9	...	...
1883	...	...	...	...	3,273	57.8	...	...	448	7.2	...	...
1884	456	8,763	...	...	3,371	61.6	...	...	456	7.4	...	...
1885	...	...	...	...	3,438	64.3	...	...	477	7.9	...	...
1886	...	...	...	...	3,527	66.5	...	...	492	8.2	...	...
1887	471	9,031	33.8	...	3,615	68.7	...	...	496	8.5	...	...
1888	475	9,151	35.2	2,008	3,683	70.8	...	...	503	8.8	...	...
1889	476	9,239	35.4	2,028	3,718	73.5	...	...	513	9.1	...	...
1890	468	9,332	36.6	2,060	3,750	77.0	...	...	538	9.6	...	...
1891	470	9,418	38.3	2,085	3,871	79.3	...	...	539	9.9	...	...
1892	470	9,478	40.5	2,190	4,100	83.0	...	...	543	10.2	...	...
1893	471	9,609	41.3	2,207[37]	4,226	87.0	...	...	567	10.7	...	...
1894	469	9,550	41.5	2,018	4,325	92.6	...	...	575	10.9	...	...
1895	471	9,664	42.7	2,052	4,423	94.9	...	...	593	11.5	...	...
1896	479	9,765	43.9	2,123	4,489	101	...	...	605	11.9	...	...
1897	484	9,912	44.4	2,150	4,554	102	...	...	606	12.2	...	...
1898	473	10,116	44.4	2,181	4,637	109	...	...	612	12.7	18.3	...
1899	472	10,312	47.8	2,389	4,666	114	...	...	626	13.3	18.2	...
1900	473	10,539	49.2	2,447	4,754	119	...	...	633	13.9	17.7	0.9
1901	477	10,623	51.8	2,489	4,923	122	...	...	643	14.2	17.9	0.9
1902	485	10,797	53.9	2,531	5,057	127	...	...	665	14.8	17.9	1.0
1903	493	10,977	55.7	2,613	5,177	134	...	...	672	15.5	18.1	1.0
1904	502	11,183	59.7	2,686	5,258	141	94.7	...	682	16.3	18.2	1.0
1905	517	11,500	55.8	2,491	5,312	149	116	...	689	17.0	18.1	1.0
1906	526	11,714	59.3	2,678	5,302	153	126	...	693	17.6	18.3	1.0
1907	522	11,777	67.3	2,876	5,301	156	138	...	692	18.1	19.0	1.1
1908	530	12,023	69.3	3,103	5,355	160	151	9.3	705	19.0	20.9	1.1
1909	538	12,182	71.5	3,194	5,375	162	156	9.5	719	19.7	21.0	1.1
1910	544	12,482	73.2	3,245	5,382	164	160	9.8	732	20.0	20.5	1.1
1911	543	12,324	74.0	4,638	5,367	164	166	10.1	734	20.4	20.5	1.2
1912	...	...	...	...	5,376	165	174	10.4	729	20.6	19.6	1.2
1913	...	...	...	...	5,393	166	188	10.8	728	20.8	19.8	1.2
1914	...	...	...	...	...	...	199	...	725	21.3	19.9	1.2
1915	559	12,978	...	...	...	...	209	...	716	21.9	20.3	1.3
1916	563	13,091	76.6	4,474	...	...	219	12.0	715	22.0	21.0	1.5
1917	557	13,116	76.5	4,546	...	...	239	...	713	22.1	22.3	1.3
1918	555	13,371	76.0	4,694	...	...[38]	270	14.5	694[39]	21.7[39]	24.0[39]	1.4[39]
1919	545	13,364	80.2	4,501	5,199[38] 5,187	166	308	16.0	620	18.3	155.0	6.1

See p. 805 for footnotes

J 1 Children and Teachers in Schools (in thousands)

1920–1975

	Austria[1]				Belgium	
	Primary		Secondary		Primary	Secondary
	P	T	P	T	P	P
1920	868	31.4	38.2	3.0	968	50.8
1921	819[40]	31.0[40]	38.6	3.5	955	56.3
1922	873	31.8	39.0[40]	3.4[40]	911	57.6
1923	819	31.1	41.7	3.4	856	55.0
1924	·749	29.2[41]	44.5	3.6	805	52.1
		21.4				
1925	718	21.5	46.1	3.7	795	48.7
1926	712	21.3	47.5	3.8	800	46.9
1927	710	21.2	49.2	4.1	804	45.3
1928	723	21.5	50.3	4.2	811	43.8
1929	748	21.8	52.0	4.3	835	46.1
1930	793	22.2	55.8	4.6	871	48.4
1931	835	22.1	59.4	4.6	917	53.7
1932	875	22.1	62.6	4.7	957	61.2
1933	887	21.4	64.4	4.8	974	68.8
1934	866	20.7	65.3	4.9	974	73.7
1935	850	20.8	64.0	4.9	968	75.1
1936	823	...	...	...	965	79.2
1937	...	...	...	...	960	83.7
1938	...	...	...	...	955	86.3
1939	...	...	...	...	954	86.5
1940	...	...	...	...	939	78.5
1941	...	...	...	...	917	81.7
1942	...	...	...	...	886	81.2
1943	...	...	...	...	865	81.5
1944	...	...	...	...	...	83.5
1945	716	27.5	49.0	3.3	829	83.9
1946	...	...	...	...	...	85.8
1947	797	29.5	48.3	3.4	789	...
1948	829	34.1	47.3	3.5	771	90.7[43]
						118
1949	847	35.9	50.1	3.6	768	125
1950	867	36.4	55.2	3.4	780	129
1951	857	37.3	61.5	3.9	784	135
1952	844	37.2	67.2	...	801	139
1953	826	37.0	73.0	...	836[42]	141
					886	
1954	797	36.7	78.1	...	909	147
1955	764	35.8	79.3	4.6	933	153
1956	748	34.9	80.3	4.9	945	163
1957	735	34.0	82.6	5.1	955	175
1958	725	34.0	83.6	5.2	956	196
1959	734	34.3	82.9	5.3	960	218
1960	744	34.6	81.1	5.3	969	241
1961	742	34.7	79.1	5.4	969	252
1962	747	34.9	78.2	5.2	970	263
1963	758	35.6	79.2	6.5	980	272
1964	774	36.3	82.9	7.0	990	277
1965	794	37.1	86.4	7.3	998	283
1966	837	38.2	91.2	7.7	1,004	289
1967	862	39.9	97.3	7.8	1,016	300
1968	889	41.3	104.0	7.9	1,019	310
1969	915	41.7	112.1	8.7	1,022	314
1970	934	43.2	119.6	9.5	1,029	327
1971	944	45.0	129.9	10.3	1,022	342
1972	949	47.0	138.3	10.6	1,010	313
1973	954	49.5	143.3	11.0	992	305
1974	954	51.2	145.6	11.6	979	296
1975	945	54.2	150.2	...	959	285

See p. 805 for footnotes

J 1 Children and Teachers in Schools (in thousands)

1920–1975

	Bulgaria				Czechoslovakia			
	Primary		Secondary		Primary		Secondary	
	P	T*	P	T*	P	T	P	T*
1920	560	13,586	122	5,082	2,152	...	...	...
1921	587	14,467	137	6,051	2,186	45.8	91.9	...
1922	595	15,474	155	7,520	2,070	45.6	95.0	...
1923	541	16,007	175	8,919	1,951	45.4	100.3	...
1924	496	15,740	176	8,458	1,781	44.9	102.8	...
1925	462	14,921	166[44]	7,441[44]	1,718	42.3	100.1	...
			169	7,738				
1926	474	15,232	173	7,947	1,711	42.9	94.3	...
1927	514	15,633	181	8,282	1,729	44.0	88.4	6,356
1928	554	16,096	166	8,114	1,770	45.4	83.8	6,293
1929	609	16,641	154	7,502	1,839	47.8	81.0	6,326
1930	656	17,426	168	7,673	1,953	50.3	85.2	6,480
1931	693	18,151	207	8,626	2,086	52.8	96.3	6,768
1932	714	18,436	253	9,652	2,215	54.9	107	6,632
1933	726	18,133	281	9,063	2,271	56.5	118	6,862
1934	725	17,992	291	8,794	2,269	57.8	126	7,083
1935	710	18,038	303	9,047	2,249	58.4	133	7,406
1936	694	17,965	326	9,784	2,189	59.1	...	...
1937	662	17,534	367	10,170	1,534	60.4	...	...
1938	647	17,277	369	10,804	1,313	...	...	...
1939	639[45]	17,218[45]	371[45]	10,964[45]	1,309	...	...	...
	927	25,973	83	3,209				
1940	950	25,877	89	3,181	1,280	...	...	...
1941	1,063	28,468	102	3,519	1,261	...	...	...
1942	...	...	...	...	1,233	...	...	...
1943	...	...	...	...	1,190	...	...	...
		thousands						
1944	894	24.6	159	5,084	1,115	...	...	...
1945	...	...	...	...	1,381[46]	48.0	...[46]	5,711
					1,478		109	
1946	...	...	...	...	1,510	...	109	...
1947	...	...	...	...	1,550	...[47]	98	...
1948	876	30.2	144	5,042	1,594[46]	63.9	93[47]	...[47]
					1,523		163	
1949	...	...	...	...	1,633	66.2	141	...[47]
1950	...	...	...	...	1,686	...	145	...
1951	...	...	...	...	1,731	...	150	...
1952	871	31.7	121	4,808	1,807	70.3	157	...[47]
1953	...	...	...	...	1,787	72.4[47]	190	...[47] [48]
1954	...	...	...	...	1,802	64.2	233	11,883
1955	...	...	...	...	1,847	66.4	258	13,343
1956	961	39.2	165	7,450	1,867	69.9	285	14,308
1957	...	...	...	...	1,917	73.5	291	15,164
1958	1,008	41.1	167	8,016	1,954	74.8[47]	293	15,320
1959	...	...	...	...	2,053	96.0	297	...[47]
1960	1,054	43.0	158	8,021	2,153	103[47]	312	...[47]
1961	...	...	...	...	2,278	91.8	335	15,826
1962	1,123	46.8	158	7,957	2,273	91.9	380	16,848
1963	1,137	47.9	145	7,206	2,260	91.1	407	18,218
1964	1,155	48.8	119	6,683	2,241	93.7	422	20,070[48]
1965	1,129	49.4	125	6,969	2,221	96.0	411	20,488
1966	1,108	49.5	123	7,089	2,164	97.8	395	21,083
1967	1,096	49.5	117	6,879	2,109	97.5	384	21,299
1968	1,079	48.7	108	6,665	2,053	98.4	387	21,765
1969	1,064	48.1	103	6,242	2,002	98.6	390	22,235
1970	1,054	47.8	101	6,270	1,966	97.7	396	23,344
1971	1,028	48.5	104	6,514	1,940	97.2	400	23,336
1972	1,009	47.6	109	6,891	1,912	96.7	402	23,784
1973	993	47.7	115	7,245	1,890	96.8	405	24,121
1974	979	47.7	117	7,530	1,884	96.1	412	24,559
1975	982	48.4	117	7,637	1,881	95.6	422	24,880

See p. 805 for footnotes

J 1 Children and Teachers in Schools (in thousands).

1920–1975

	Denmark			Finland				France		
	Primary	Secondary	All Schools	Primary		Secondary		Primary		Secondary
	P	P*	T*	P	T*	P	T*	P	T	P
1920	437	38,946	15,320	264	8,014	32.5	2,380	3,697[22] 4,452	[22] 119	146[52] 243[20]
1921	464	41,233	16,037	309	8,904	35.4	2,528	4,614	120[20]	255
1922	461	42,731	16,057	327	9,616	38.1	2,629	3,995[20] 4,210	...	260
1923	453	47,316	16,080	326	10,064	40.4	2,757	3,973	121	270
1924	448	47,813	15,919	331	10,422	42.6	2,862	3,828	121	277
1925	445	47,807	16,038	330	10,722	44.6	2,926	3,754	120	281
1926	439	47,839	16,032	334	11,080	45.8	3,016	3,854	119	279
1927	444	48,043	16,081	343	11,436	46.8	3,067	3,917	119	282
1928	444	49,191	16,130	352	11,979	47.8	3,148	4,099	119	286
1929	445	50,118 (thous.)	16,214	365	12,409	48.6	3,188	4,359	120	298
1930	446	51.5	16,272	379	12,853	49.6	3,243	4,635	133	330
1931	446	53.5	16,417	395[50]	12,942[50]	49.9	3,203	4,915	137	363
1932	446	55.4	16,625	394	12,617	49.6	3,216	5,111	138	403
1933	447	58.2	16,714	400	12,855	49.7	3,238	5,200	141	425
1934	438	59.7	17,124	470	13,126	49.7	3,229	5,230	141	446
1935	429	61.6	17,172	477	13,360	50.3	3,287	5,261	142	465
1936	422	63.3	17,152	480	13,527	50.6	3,305	5,332	147	475
1937	415	64.8	17,280	492	14,027[51]	52.3	3,325	5,437	150	506
1938	408	66.1	17,350	496	18,529	53.8	3,426	5,422[53]	151	... [53]
1939	397	67.1	17,357	426	[12,364] [51]	53.9	3,119	5,032	168	432
1940	392	67.4	17,301	481	17,301	56.3	3,285	4,913	154	[53] 432
1941	390	68.9	17,491	428	[12,645] [51]	57.1	3,615	4,924	152	485[53]
1942	389	69.3	17,576	437	[13,783] [51]	61.9	3,723	4,865	152	...
1943	386	69.8	17,622	448	17,867	68.8	4,075	4,666	150	600[53]
1944	389	69.9	17,911	425	16,049	72.8	3,931	4,576[53]	154	...
1945	401	70.8	18,075	442	17,316	77.5	4,314	4,746	154	625[53]
1946	408	73.4	18,517	462	18,335	81.2	4,583	4,702	156	734
1947	412	75.4	18,707	466	18,800	84.8	4,880	4,635	155	747
1948	416	78.6	19,102	484	19,590	87.7	5,147	4,882	157	729
1949	428	83.4	19,438	484	20,103	91.7	5,398	4,669	159	746
1950	443	88.9	19,961	489	20,838	95.0	5,558	4,726	159	788
1951	442	93.6	20,617	495	21,325	99.9	5,782	4,798	160	797
1952	485	97.1	21,159	516	22,268	107	5,933	5,075	163	844
1953	509	102	21,894	541	22,688	115	6,093	5,282	167	871
1954	527	108	22,793	565	23,298	123	6,459	5,573	172	922
1955	536	118	23,526	591	24,190	134	6,863	5,873	182	969
1956	537	127	24,416	605	24,729	146	7,582	6,146	192	1,064
1957	533	140	25,257	622	25,212	162	8,168	6,355	201	1,129
1958	521	156	26,296	629	26,294	181	8,770	6,537	210	1,196
1959	547	139[49]	27,514	633	27,111	200	9,651	6,738[54] 5,720	218	1,265
1960	577	112	28,701	626	27,279	215	10,450	5,708	226	1,493
1961	578	109	30,033	612	27,278	228	11,219	5,681	225	1,608
1962	580	106	31,075	596	27,206	240	11,963	5,681	241	1,715[54]
1963	583	106	32,205	583	26,824	249	12,703	5,669	255[55]	1,560
1964	569	105	...	565	26,496	258	13,522	5,714	191	1,693
1965	573	105	...	544	26,205	268	14,072	5,650	187	1,827
1966	572	110	...	523	25,510	282	14,838	5,576	186	1,955
1967	576	116	(34,810)[84]	507[83]	24,674[83]	292	15,413	5,496	189	2,143
1968	580	121	(37,364)[84]	511	25,187	305	16,193	5,346	194	2,390
1969	583	124	45,545	522	25,951	316	16,872	5,218	196	2,619
1970	591	126	43,941	461	23,731	324	17,519	5,147	198	2,772[85]
1971	599	131	51,399	461	23,964	332	18,186	5,042	198	2,916
1972	613	139	52,662	472	25,533	319	17,888	5,038	197	2,977
1973	629	145	54,318	500	26,528	296	16,864	5,013	199	2,978
1974	633	150	58,425	546	29,957	244	15,083	4,976	190	2,968
1975	631	153	59,431	588	32,461	196	12,633	4,964	191	2,989

See p. 805 for footnotes

J 1 **Children and Teachers in Schools** (in thousands)

1920–1975

	Germany				East Germany			Greece			
	Primary[23]		Secondary		Primary	Secondary	All Schools	Primary		Secondary	
	P	T	P	T	P	P	T	P	T*	P	T*
1920	...	...	...	...	...	...	...	...	...	...	...
1921	8,894	196	1,081	49.9	...	...	...	...	...	...	...
1922	...	...	...	...	...	...	...	...	...	...	...
1923	...	...	...	...	...	...	...	...	...	...	...
1924	...	...	...	...	...	...	...	...	...	...	...
1925	6,662	187	1,080	57.3	...	...	...	...	...	...	...
1926	...	...	...	...	...	...	...	726	13,871	48.2	2,268
1927	...	...	...	...	...	...	...	738	14,556	49.4	2,214
1928	...	...	...	...	...	...	...	734[58]	15,214[58]	52.7[58]	2,236[58]
1929	...	...	...	...	...	...	...	733	14,744	72.2	3,347
1930	7,590	190	1,016	56.4	...	...	...	772	14,625	68.7	3,410
1931	...	...	...	...	...	...	...	817	14,607	67.0	3,475
1932	...	...	...	...	...	...	...	857	14,373	70.1	3,554
1933	...	...	...	...	...	...	...	889	14,478	74.0	3,734
1934	...	...	...	...	...	...	...	917	15,378	74.7	4,136
1935	7,892	185	907	53.1	...	...	...	951	16,046	78.1	4,335
1936	7,758	181	943	52.6	...	...	...	1,001	16,267	...	...
1937	...	...	944	52.6	...	...	...	985	15,573	...	4,552
1938	7,487	177	935	52.9	...	...	...	...	...	...	...
1939	7,289	171	958	53.9	...	...	...	...	...	...	...
1940	...	...	...	...	...	...	...	...	...	...	...
1941	...	...	...	...	...	...	...	...	...	...	...
1942	...	...	...	...	...	...	...	...	...	...	...
1943	...	...	...	...	...	...	...	....	...	...	...
1944	...	...	...	...	...	...	...	...	...	...	...
	West Germany[56]										
1945	...	...	...	...	...	...	...	...	...	...	...
1946	...	...	...	...	...	...	...	...	...	...	...
1947	...	...	...	...	...	...	...	...	...	...	...
1948	...	...	...	...	...	...	...	...	...	...	...
1949	...	...	...	...	...	...	...	...	...	...	...
1950	6,330	131	801	33.9	...	...	...	...	...	...	...
1951	6,142	135	879	36.7	2,374	101	75.1	936	18,932	207	6,381
1952	5,720	136	948	39.9	2,174	113	77.1	...	...	...	...
1953	5,340	137	1,018	42.1	1,981	123	77.5	982	...	219	...
1954	5,135	137	906	44.3	1,840	125	78.7	...	...	...	...
1955	4,936	136	924	46.0	1,703[57] 1,724	128[57] 107	75.6	972	21,234	...	6,716
1956	4,867	135	912	48.5	1,682	96.4	77.4	965	20,832	212	6,991
1957	4,847[27] 4,775	132[27]	1,072[27] 1,144	52.5[27]	1,687	91.3	79.5	989	21,230	...	7,004
1958	4,783[56] 4,883	144[56]	1,134[56] 1,150	54.1	1,671	89.4	78.5	923	21,810	215	7,559
1959	4,998[56] 5,138	144	1,170[56] 1,221	57.0	1,806	...	...	901	23,070	233	7,883
1960	5,291	145	1,222	58.2	1,922	82.5	86.4	896	23,251	247	8,367
1961	5,343	145	1,233	62.3	2,026	80.7	102	908	24,003	272	8,152
1962	5,445	150	1,254	65.2	2,128	76.2	105	911	24,269	284	8,571
1963	5,469	152	1,326	68.5	2,202	76.5	113	912	25,658	294	9,145
1964	5,525	158	1,388	70.5	2,248	81.1	118	953	26,639	334	10,980
1965	5,607	161	1,497	71.8	2,274	85.3	122	964	27,376	352	11,251
1966	5,711	167	1,628	76.7	2,301	92.5	125	969	27,549	365	12,111
1967	5,755	173	1,889	84.5	2,367	72.4	128	964	27,963	384	12,469
1968	5,887	177	2,032	90.1	2,437	50.5	131	948	28,192	386	12,429
1969	6,077	181	2,187	97.8	2,485	51.9	134	938	28,128	400	12,659
1970	6,347	188	2,243	104	2,534	54.7	138	907	29,336	422	12,958
1971	6,477	196	2,355	108	2,571	57.3	145	906	29,330	457	13,412
1972	6,510	210	2,548	116	2,598	55.1	147	909	28,212	470	14,935
1973	6,500	218	2,730	124	2,608	51.6	152	922	29,773	485	16,595
1974	6,481	226	2,880	131	2,602	49.2	156	928	30,458	501	17,624
1975	6,425	236	3,011	137	2,579	47.9	159	...	...	...	...

See p. 805 for footnotes

J 1 Children and Teachers in Schools (in thousands)

1920—1975

	Hungary[5]				Southern Ireland				Italy			
	Primary		Secondary		Primary		Secondary		Primary[7]		Secondary	
	P	T	P	T	P	T*	P*	T*	P	T	P	T
1920	857	17.6	56.9	3.0	...	...	...	...	4,166	105	382	26.0
1921	905	18.3	56.0	3.0	...	...	...	...	4,267	109	390	26.4
1922	821	17.5	56.8	3.0	...	...	...	...	4,167	108	383	25.6
1923	770	17.4	57.8	3.0	...	...	...	...	3,981	105	327	20.9
1924	694	16.6	60.8	3.0	493	...	22,897	2,133	3,759	100	290	18.5
1925	656	16.7	61.8	3.0	518	13,247	25,488	2,298	3,622	98	292	19.5
1926	689	17.0	61.0	3.0	518	13,310	24,766	2,256	3,635	99	372	20.9
1927	748	17.6	60.3	3.0	512	13,577	25,561	2,374	3,838	100	366	21.0
1928	833	18.4	59.5	3.0	508	13,657	26,792	2,391	4,052	102	371	22.0
1929	908	19.1	60.8	3.0	504	13,622	27,645	2,551	4,340	101	332	26.8
1930	967	19.3	64.2	3.0	502	13,652	28,995	2,643	4,595	105	312	28.0
1931	1,004	19.4	65.1	3.0	503	13,635	30,004	2,643	4,762	107	379	32.7
1932	997	19.4	65.3	3.1	505	13,615	30,966	2,675	4,799	109	441	35.4
1933	989	19.5	66.8	3.2	503	13,667	32,384	2,801	4,818	110	499	43.8
1934	969	19.6	67.8	3.2	493	13,604	33,499	2,861	4,841	111	543	41.1
1935	962	19.7	69.0	3.3	485	13,487	35,111	2,879	5,074	117	593	46.9
1936	962	19.8	69.8	3.4	478	13,426	35,890	2,948	5,187	123	675	49.8
1937	963	20.1	70.0	3.5	470	13,357	36,092	2,969	5,051	117	744	52.3
1938	...	...	...	...	463	13,260	36,676	3,019	5,095	120	809	60.7
1939	...	...	...	...	464	13,289	37,670	3,144	5,149	122	850	64.8
1940	...	...	...	...	462	13,136	38,713	3,173	5,213	127	908	76.5
1941	...	...	...	...	460	13,065	39,537	3,251	[5,110][60]	[121][60]	972	81.4
1942	...	...	...	...	460	13,084	39,787	3,357	...	...	...	...
1943	...	...	...	...	455	12,937	40,040	3,386	...	...	...	...
1944	...	...	...	...	454	12,844	41,178	3,497	...	...	...	...
1945	...	...	...	...	452	12,791	41,799	3,512	4,360	133	879	77.8
1946	...	...	...	...	444	12,772	42,927	3,584	4,703	145	894	82.7
1947	...	...	...	...	446	12,612	43,780	3,671	4,836	157	896	83.5
1948	...	...	...	...	445	12,712	45,413	3,863	4,878	165	941	89.1
1949	1,202[59]	35.0[59]	94	6.3	449	12,870	47,065	3,844	4,815	168	996	100
1950	1,230	35.2	108	6.2	451	12,792	48,559	3,929	4,640	170	1,101	106
1951	1,205	38.1	122	5.9	461	12,883	50,179	4,043	4,443	170	1,206	112
1952	1,196	39.9	139	6.1	469	13,000	52,151	4,170	4,477	173	1,317	118
1953	1,203	43.1	164	7.0	473	13,144	54,019	4,097	4,556	177	1,378	117
1954	1,207	46.0	162	7.5	479	13,231	56,411	4,417	4,614	175	1,464	126
1955	1,226	50.3	155	7.8	487	13,262	59,306	4,564	4,693[61]	175[61]	1,511[62]	129[62]
									4,741	180	906	75.7
1956	1,255	52.2	173	7.9	488	13,402	62,429	4,739	4,828	184	930	84.5
1957	1,259	53.7	159	8.1	491	13,554	66,221	4,957	4,768	190	1,020	80.8
1958	1,269	55.1	178	8.4	492	13,753	69,568	5,032	4,676	192	1,150	91.3
1959	1,314	56.4	204	8.4	492	13,866	73,431	5,178	4,498	197	1,311	105
1960	1,392	57.3	241	8.8	490	14,032	76,843	5,282	4,418	200	1,414	118
1961	1,445	58.3	284	9.2	485	14,091	80,400	5,630	4,421	201	1,539	133
1962	1,473	59.9	334	9.6	484	14,223	84,916	5,909	4,391	205	1,594	139
1963	1,469	61.5	385	10.6	487	14,297	89,205	6,161	4,420	205	1,685	147
1964	1,445	62.1	417	11.6	490	14,469	92,989	6,477	4,468	206	1,732	151
1965	1,414	62.2	407	12.0	493	14,614	98,667	6,795	4,520	207	1,795	155
1966	1,380	62.2	376	12.3	497	14,672	103,558	7,248	4,556	210	1,821	160
1967	1,331	62.3	351	...	494	14,794	118,807	8,165	4,620	213	1,891	166
1968	1,255	62.5	335	...	498	14,733	133,691	9,130	4,673[63]	216[63]	1,982	172[63]
									4,652	213		168
1969	1,178	62.8	337	...	502	14,859	144,425	9,603	4,750	217	2,064	178
1970	1,116	63.1	347	13.4	507	15,080	150,642	10,233	4,841	222	2,168	198
1971	1,078	63.4	352	...	512	15,450	157,234	10,705	4,913	229	2,287	...
1972	1,044	64.0	347	...	511	15,612	162,161	11,250	4,965	238	2,422	...
1973	1,033	64.6	349	...	515	16,137	167,309	12,076	4,963	249	2,530	...
1974	1,040	65.7	375	13.7	521	16,718	173,188	11,798	4,923	251	2,629	...
1975	1,051	66.9	382	14.1	530	17,055	182,639	12,212	4,835	253	2,762	...

... 805 for footnotes

J 1 Children and Teachers in Schools (in thousands)

1920–1975

	Netherlands				Norway				Poland			
	Primary		Secondary		Primary		Secondary		Primary		Secondary	
	P	T	P	T*	P	T*	P	T*	P	T	P	T
1920	1,032	...	32.6	3,751	386	11,091	27.0	1,815	...	...	...	...
1921	1,040	...	36.2	4,104	390	11,416	25.1	1,755	...	...	...	...
1922	1,039	35.3	40.0	4,285	394	11,558	24.3	1,773	3,132	62.0	227	...
1923	1,063	35.2	41.3	4,308	395	11,613	24.9	1,797	3,173	65.6	227	...
1924	1,089	34.5	42.7	4,399	396	11,558	23.9	1,767	3,137	66.2	220	14.7
1925	1,078	34.0	43.6	4,544	396	11,541	23.7	1,763	3,152	69.0	217	14.7
1926	1,077	33.4	42.2	4,619	394	11,448	22.7	1,686	3,245	68.4	215	14.8
1927	1,067	33.9[64] 31.1	42.4[64] 95.7	4,711	399	11,075	21.9	1,624	3,256	70.2	209	14.8
1928	1,103	31.6	97.7	4,748[65]	399	11,063	22.2	1,605	3,359	73.1	204	14.7
1929	1,161	34.9	102	...	402	11,080	22.5	1,596	3,570	76.2	203	14.3
1930	1,183	36.1	106	...	404	11,158	22.6	1,602	3,833	...	205	...
1931	1,201	36.8	114	...	403	11,106	23.4	1,584	4,113	...	203	...
1932	1,200	36.5	125	...	398	10,821	24.7	1,619	4,385	...	187	...
1933	1,176	35.5	134	...	392	10,714	25.9	1,675	4,491	...	161	...
1934	1,149	32.5	141	...	380	10,597	27.7	1,716	4,517	...	166	...
1935	1,142	31.2	146	...	370	10,531	29.1	1,798	4,539	...	181	...
1936	1,143	30.1	151	...	358	10,517	30.7	1,856	4,593	...	201	...
1937	1,144	30.0	157	...	353	11,119	32.4	1,977	4,701	76.6	221	...
1938	1,143	30.1	161	...	345	11,418	32.9	2,046	...	...	...	...
1939	1,144	30.5	162	...	338	11,458	32.9	2,074	...	...	...	...
1940	1,143	30.4	164	...	326	11,209	32.0	2,037	...	...	...	...
1941	...	...	...	...	317	11,215	30.5	2,047	...	...	...	...
1942	1,129	31.8	...	...	298	10,825	29.7	2,031	...	...	...	...
1943	1,172	34.0	185	...	294	10,506	32.2	2,071	...	...	...	...
1944	...	...	...	...	292	10,663	32.5	2,055	...	...	...	...
1945	1,172	33.8	193	...	287	10,673	35.7	2,240	3,004	58.6	224	10.6
1946	1,182	33.9	209	...	295	11,123	37.1	2,383	3,283	66.6	228	11.0
1947	1,154	34.2	213	10,686	296	11,435	35.6	2,505	3,405	74.7	202	...
1948	1,154	34.4[66]	213	...	300	11,500	33.1	2,527	3,375	76.3	219	...
1949	1,167	34.0	210	11,417	309	11,695	31.9[67]	2,560[67]	3,353	76.5	221	...
1950	1,216	34.4	211	11,640.	321	11,925	37.4	2,450	3,282	81.7	194	10.1
1951	1,240	35.0	216	11,765	337	12,159	38.3	2,482	3,177	85.8	186	9.6
1952	1,289	36.2	226	...	356	12,693	40.3	2,564	3,038	89.5	187	9.5
1953	1,357	37.6	240	...	379	13,183	43.8	2,743	3,087	93.3	188	9.6
1954	1,413	39.4	256	13,664	401	13,800	46.5	2,779	3,203	96.2	195	10.1
1955	1,452	40.7	278	15,210	421	14,321	49.1	2,941	3,386	103	201	10.4
1956	1,470	41.5	305	16,456	432	14,837	53.5	3,092	3,655	110	203	11.1
1957	1,479	41.9	332	17,204	439	15,189	60.1	3,278	3,924	120	195	11.5
1958	1,476	42.1	368	18,776	440	15,293	70.7	3,648	4,240	130	199	11.6
1959	1,448	42.0	407	...	441	15,740	80.0	4,007	4,574	140	214	11.8
1960	1,416	41.6	435	...	436	16,463	92.5	4,443	4,828	146	260	12.2
1961	1,398	41.5	453	...	...	...	...	...	4,994	151	298	12.7
1962	1,395	42.0	462	22,812	438[29]	17,316[29]	103	4,719	5,117	156	340	13.7
1963	1,395	43.1	470	...	444	18,432	106	4,918	5,182	160	379	14.9
1964	1,398	43.9	478	24,243	448	19,134	107	5,060	5,208	166	405	15.5
1965	1,409	45.0	487	25,401	458	20,125	107	5,276	5,177	172	427	15.9
1966	1,419	45.6	493	...	473	21,517	103	5,243	5,527	189	323	15.4
1967	1,428	46.0	509	..	487	23,024	98.3	5,176	5,706	201	306	15.1
1968	1,439	46.5	537	...	503	24,524	91.2	4,942	5,604	207	311	15.0
1969	1,451	47.8	562	...	519	26,202	83.8	4,562	5,443	210	310	15.4
1970	1,462	49.2	591	...	536	28,054	76.9	4,324	5,257	211	401	17.5
1971	1,464	50.1	626	...	555	30,516	72.5	4,202	5,052	211	439	...
1972	1,462	50.2	662	...	569	32,104	68.7	4,105	4,841	207	451	21.8
1973	1,455	51.0	707	...	576	31,364	66.1	...	4,634	201	471	22.8
1974	1,448	52.5	740	...	583	29,834	64.2	3,849	4,453	179	483	23.0
1975	1,453	53.5	766	...	585	29,266	66.1	3,947	4,310	191	472	23.0

See p. 805 for footnotes

J 1 Children and Teachers in Schools (in thousands)

1920–1975

	Portugal				Romania				Spain			
	Primary		Secondary		Primary[16]		Secondary		Primary		Secondary	
	P	T*	P	T*	P	T*	P	T*	P	T	P	T
1920	...	...	11.7	707	834[69]	13,676[69]	27.4[69]	...	...	...	52.3	...
					1,516	25,763						
1921	...	...	11.4	731	1,589[70]	24,562[70]	...	...	...	...	54.6	...
1922	...	...	11.5	774	1,389	24,688	...	...	...	...	57.7	...
1923	...	...	12.4	787	1,390	26,824	...	...	...	...	63.1	...
1924	...	...	12.8	756	1,460[71]	30,645[71]	...	...	...	...	68.9	...
1925	317	8,484	14.3	836	1,537	33,232	195	10,395	...[73]	...[73]	74.3	...
1926	318	8,384	16.5	935	1,599	35,199	177	11,615	1,800	...	76.3	...
1927	321	8,555	17.1	892	1,674	37,338	192	12,245	...	...	63.4	...
1928	341	9,048	15.6	768	1,787	37,773	175	12,442	1,837	...	66.4	...
1929	367	9,488	15.7	788	1,692	37,416	162	12,338	...	...	70.9	...
1930	423	9,340	18.5	877	2,111	37,800	173	13,938	...	...	76.1	...
1931	442	9,697	20.9	808	2,207	41,286	166	14,374	...	...	106	...
1932	420	9,653	24.5	869	2,330	41,705	163	16,458	2,262	49.2	115	...
1933	423	9,699	25.4	920	2,394	45,412	164	14,926	2,398	53.0	131	...
1934	429	9,752	27.0	976	2,480	47,430	178	15,808	2,500	46.8	125	...
1935	445	10,346	19.8[35]	873	2,478	46,892	185	16,147	2,502	47.9	125	...
1936	449	9,819	32.8	926	2,480	48,955	190	17,021	...	...	...	...
1937	458	10,149	33.4	958	2,491[72]	49,593[72]	201[72]	17,439[72]		...	...	...
					1,575	39.9	34.5	6,500				
1938	463	10,101	34.2	993	...	...	...	...		...	...	...
1939	468[68]	10,667[68]	34.4	1,022	...	...	...	...	2,355	50.0	156	...
1940	588	13,037	32.3	993	...	...	...	...	2,410	51.1	158	...
1941	574	13,882[68]	33.2	1,047	...	...	...	...	2,376	51.6	171	...
1942	574[68]	13,354	37.7	982	...	...	...	...	2,446	52.4	180	...
	555											
1943	542	13,422	40.5	996	...	...	...	...	2,506	52.3	178	...
1944	546	13,334	42.4	1,040	...	...	...	...	2,531	53.2	186	...
1945	556	13,880	43.6	1,123	...	...	...	...	2,600	53.2	195	...
1946	555	13,747	45.8	1,154	...	...	...	...	2,426	55.1	203	...
1947	573	14,080	45.6	1,063	...	...	...	...	2,436	55.8	212	...
1948	582	14,445	45.3	1,096	1,791	61.5	69.4	4,604	2,064	57.5	214	...
1949	606	14,758	46.5	1,112	1,790	...	...	...	2,111	58.3	215	...
1950	632	14,809	48.5	1,158	1,778	67.0	92.9	5,038	2,123	59.9	222	...
1951	666	15,685	51.6	1,199	1,766	69.5	99.1	5,216	2,119	60.6	235	...
1952	759	17,597	54.4	1,196	1,672	74.1	98.5	5,149	2,158	61.2	250	15.4
1953	795	19,032	58.7	1,293	1,664	76.4	117	5,741	2,510[74]	61.6	262	17.9
1954	813	20,001	62.7	1,315	1,614	79.2	117	5,886	2,575[74]	63.8	293	18.7
1955	829	20,930	68.9	1,408[29]	1,603	76.3	136	7,811	2,647[74]	66.2	328	18.8
1956	842	23,383	76.6	4,919	1,714	79.5	148	8,687	2,425	68.5	371	19.0
1957	852	24,383	83.0	4,484	1,819	84.2	159	6,626	2,446	73.3	405	19.6
1958	857	24,919	91.0	5,216	1,964	87.5	185	7,857	2,465[73]	...	421	19.7
									3,335			
1959	869	25,690	102	5,459	2,135	88.0	208	9,504	3,370	...	448	20.5
1960	887	26,087	112	5,702	2,346	93.1	242	10,529	3,387	...	474	21.6
1961	887	26,786	118	5,757	2,540	98.8	268	11,984	3,410	...	564	22.7
1962	...	...	...	...	2,694	106	334	13,204	3,453	...	623	23.7
1963	883	27,325	139	6,782	2,682	111	377	14,217	3,505	...	682	25.6
1964	894	27,785	145	6,965	2,992	123	330	12,563	3,763	...	745	27.0
1965	893	27,966	150	7,145	2,987	128	360	13,117	3,942	...	834	28.6
1966	891	27,666	155	7,141	2,956	130	372	13,542	4,025	...	930	31.0
1967	904	28,434	160	7,361	2,928	131	341	13,281	4,179	...	1,125	34.1
1968	962	29,266	144	7,548	2,909	132	390	15,025	4,390	...	1,207	36.0
1969	990	29,753	120	7,225	2,934	134	389	15,762	4,555	...	1,371	...
1970	992	29,554	137	7,436	2,934	136	383	15,902	4,749	...	1,522	62.3
1971	989	28,288	156	8,328	2,824	136	369	16,623	4,942	...	1,323	60.8
1972	971	31,312	179	9,138	2,720	135	350	16,107	5,262	...	1,268	60.9
1973	947	32,020	212	10,307	2,733	133	325	14,823	5,775	...	1,010	56.4
1974	933	34,596	238	13,605	2,890	137	321	13,204	6,315	...	790	49.1
1975	922	38,706	216	14,893	3,020	145	361	14,539	6,394	...	817	48.7

See p. 805 for footnotes

J 1 **Children and Teachers in Schools** (in thousands)

1920–1975

	Sweden				Switzerland				U.K.: England & Wales			
	Primary		Secondary		Primary[16]		Secondary		Primary		Secondary[8]	
	P	T	P	T*	P	T*	P	T*	P	T	P	T
1920	708	27.1	34	2,158	536	13,529	81.7	4,524	5,206	167	337	17.7
1921	705	27.7	35	2,190	531	13,546	82.9	4,503	5,181	168	355	19.0
1922	700	28.0	36	2,189	522	13,497	88.4	5,191	5,136	164	354	18.5
1923	686	28.4	36	2,202	510	13,403	85.0	5,197	5,025	163	349	18.7
1924	680	28.7	36	2,219	496	13,399	88.0	5,144	4,934	165	353	19.1
1925	665	28.9	35	2,257	491	13,612	84.4	4,892	4,950	166	361	19.6
1926	661	29.1	34	2,277	483	13,443	82.1	5,302	4,967	166	371	19.3
1927	665	29.5	34	2,341	474	13,176	81.2	4,468	4,981	...	378	20.1
1928	675	29.9	35	2,583	472	13,024	77.2	5,250	4,909	167	387	20.5
1929	673	30.3	38	2,815	472	13,224	79.5	5,212	4,941	168	394	21.2
1930	672	30.7	42	3,029	472	13,368	76.5	5,061	4,930	169	411	21.7
1931	664	31.0	46	3,191	475	13,304	82.4[80]	4,497[80]	5,006	170	432	22.3
							48.1	2,396				
1932	663	31.0	50	3,133	480	13,368	46.2	1,834	5,049	171	442	22.8
1933	642	30.8	53	3,209	480	13,600	48.5	1,850	5,066	171	448	23.0
1934	619	30.6	55	3,372	477	13,574	52.2	1,866	4,907	171	457	23.4
1935	599	30.6	56	3,536	476	13,654	51.0	1,899	4,748	170	464	24.0
1936	581	30.7	57	3,659	471	13,656	50.5	1,891	4,588	168	466	24.5
1937	568	30.7	59	3,877	464	13,620	50.2	1,884	4,527	167	470	25.0
1938	558	30.7	61	4,012	460	13,572	50.0	1,902	...	...	...	...
1939	549	30.4	61	3,947	456	13,559	49.3	1,907	...	...	...	...
1940	538	29.0	62	4,067	453	13,529	49.2	1,917	...	...	...	...
1941	530	28.6	63	4,093	448	13,487	49.3	1,923	...	...	...	...
1942	524	28.5	64	4,144	443	13,433	49.0	1,944	...	...	...	...
1943	519	28.6	66	4,260	441	13,459	49.4	1,970	...	...	...	...
1944	523	29.1	70	4,506	441	13,395	49.9	1,979	...[81]	...[81]	...[81]	...[81]
1945	528	29.6	73	4,831	431	13,539	50.4	2,045	3,736	...	1,269	...
1946	544	30.6	78	5,242	430	13,692	50.0	2,086	3,700	125	1,335	63.7
1947	556	31.2	85	5,605	431	13,932	50.0	2,065	3,812	127	1,545	69.4
1948	590	32.6	94	5,960	434	14,136	55.0	2,305	3,874	128	1,654	75.2
1949	612	33.7	95	5,883	...	...	...	...	3,955	130	1,695	78.7
1950	651	34.7[75]	101[75]	6,095[77]	...	...	...	...	4,005	134	1,733	82.1
1951	685	36.6	107	9,632	476	14,476	56.1	2,365	4,214	138	1,756	84.4
1952	726	38.1	115	10,051	...	...	...	...	4,436	142	1,770	86.1
1953	754	39.7	122	10,586	518	15,204	59.3	2,462	4,554	144	1,822	88.6
1954	785	41.3	132	11,021	...	...	...	...	4,601	148	1,914	92.4
1955	805	42.9	143	11,635	...	...	...	...	4,592	150	2,057	97.2
1956	815	44.3	157	12,542	557	16,429	77.3	2,963	4,590	151	2,187	103
1957	814	45.0	170[75]	13,129	...	...	...	...	4,508	149	2,330	110
			195									
1958	806	45.7	211	13,816	...	...	...	...	4,308	145	2,593	119
1959	794	46.5	235	14,762	572	17,243	90.0	3,423	4,201	142	2,723	127
1960	778	53.4	263	15,885	...	...	...	...	4,133	141	2,829	133
1961	746[78]	53.6	290	16,182	557	17,714	88.5	3,175	4,130	141	2,835	138
1962	714	55.4	314	17,263	...	...	...	...	4,145	139	2,781	137
1963	699	60.7	332	17,818	...	...	...	...	4,204	141	2,830	140
1964	688	61.5	339	17,129	...	...	...	...	4,273	144	2,819	142
1965	676	63.7	345	17,505	...	...	...	...	4,366	147	2,817	144
1966	661	66.1[79]	368	16,867	...	...	...	...	4,495	152	2,833	145
1967	654	84.5	386	...	...	...	...	...	4,647	156	2,895	148
1968	640	85.0	397	...	...	...	...	...	4,789	161	2,960	152
1969	644	86.4	412	...	...	...	...	...	4,905	168	3,009	156
1970	649	92.0	414[75]	...	...	...	...	...	4,987	175	3,089	162
1971	669	95.4	542	...	...	...	...	...	5,068	184	3,176	171
1972	685	99.2	540	...	...	...	...	...	5,069	189	3,239	181
1973	702	104	529	...	...	...	...	...	4,974	190	3,551	194
1974	716	106	521	...	...	...	...	...	4,899	193	3,619	202
1975	723	107	521	...	...	...	...	...	4,828	194	3,712	211

See p. 805 for footnotes

J 1 Children and Teachers in Schools (in thousands)

1920–1975

	United Kingdom: Scotland				Yugoslavia			
	Primary		Secondary[8]		Primary		Secondary	
	P	T	P	T	P	T	P	T *
1920	627	17.9	154	5.7	908	14.8	69.7	3,304
1921	615	17.8	155	5.7	989	16.2	74.9	3,543
1922	608	17.8	155	6.0	968	17.7	78.3	3,618
1923	588	17.8	153	6.1	894	17.2	85.6	3,808
1924	584	18.1	149	6.1	786	17.6	86.1	4,021
1925	587	18.4	150	6.2	768	18.2	84.0	3,949
1926	591	18.7	151	6.3	800	19.4	86.5	4,341
1927	587	18.8	153	6.4	881	20.3	82.8	4,342
1928	585	19.1	151	6.5	984	21.3	79.7	4,417
1929	591	19.5	151	6.6	1,088	22.5	73.1	4,120
1930	595	19.5	154	6.6	1,185	22.8	77.6	4,120
1931	601	19.4	160	6.7	1,245	25.1	77.9	4,475
1932	606	19.4	162	6.7	1,275	27.4	83.2	4,349
1933	607	19.4	159	6.7	1,317	29.4	88.6	4,459
1934	592	19.4	157	6.7	1,341	30.9	94.0	4,815
1935	581	19.5	154	6.8	1,342	31.1	101	4,961
1936	567	19.7	152	6.8	1,363	31.4	108	5,142
1937	557	19.6	153	6.9	1,393	32.1	117	5,403
1938	...	...	...	...	1,471	34.7	125	5,607
1939	...	...	...	...	...	...	...	...
1940	...	...	...	...	...	...	...	...
1941	...	...	...	...	...	...	...	...
1942	...	...	...	...	...	...	...	...
1943	...	...	...	...	...	...	...	...
1944	...	...	...	...	...	...	...	...
	[81]	[81]	[81]	[81]				
1945	383	...	348	...	1,442	24.3	44.2	7,059
1946	361	...	367	...	1,725	25.7	49.9	7,382
1947	364	...	403	...	1,916	27.6	48.0	7,063
1948	363	...	417	...	1,977	26.8	59.9	8,504
1949	367	...	419	...	1,988	26.9	63.8	8,577
	[82]		[82]					
1950	551	...	233	...	1,931	32.1	76.3	8,714
1951	566	18.9	236	13.8	1,815	40.0	68.5	5,783
1952	586	19.4	237	14.0	1,809	46.0	71.3	6,157
1953	595	19.9	225	14.2	1,847	51.1	77.6	6,686
1954	603	20.0	227	14.5	1,918	55.6	86.8	7,435
1955	607	19.7	232	15.1	2,036	61.3	88.3	7,117
1956	608	19.8	240	15.4	2,175	65.9	84.1	6,066
1957	610	20.2	239	15.5	2,316	71.8	80.8	5,827
1958	608	20.1	249	15.9	2,427	79.7	77.6	4,894
1959	598	20.2	272	16.8	2,590	79.5	78.8	4,873
1960	589	19.7	288	17.9	2,764	84.3	79.7	5,139
1961	587	20.1	292	18.2	2,896	89.6	94.7	5,512
1962	589	19.9	286	18.8	2,960	93.4	116	6,249
1963	595	20.2	288	19.2	2,980	96.4	142	7,404
1964	601	20.8	285	19.3	2,972	100	162	8,215
1965	608	20.8	284	19.7	2,946	102	177	8,658
1966	613	21.4	288	20.0	2,922	106	180	9,185
1967	622	21.3	296	20.0	2,894	109	181	9,666
1968	632	21.8	307	20.7	2,875	114	183	9,673
1969	642	22.0	317	20.4	2,853	117	184	10,028
1970	649	23.2	328	21.3	2,835	120	186	10,259
1971	658	24.1	338	22.3	2,835	121	189	10,318
1972	661	25.5	362	23.8	2,856	124	193	10,229
1973	663	26.4	385	25.4	2,869	126	203	10,164
1974	656	26.1	407	25.3	2,867	128	217	9,887
1975	651	27.1	412	26.5	2,856	131	212	9,827

See p. 805 for footnotes

J 1 Children and Teachers in Schools

NOTES

1. SOURCES:- The official publications noted on p. xv. Polish data on pupils for 1922–48 and on teachers for 1937, 1945, 1947, and 1948 were supplied by the Polish Central Statistical Office. Romanian data for 1938, 1948, and 1950–59 were kindly supplied by Mr. G. Radulescu, Editor in Chief of the *Enciclopedica Romana.*

2. The definition of the different sorts of schools varies from country to country and from time to time, and is not always clear. Nor is it always clear to exactly what time of year the statistics relate, and which pupils are covered by them (e.g. whether it is all registered pupils, or only those attending school regularly, or those there on a certain day). So far as possible changes in the scope of the statistics are indicated in the footnotes, but there are believed to be many which were not recorded in the sources.

FOOTNOTES

[1] Cisleithania (excluding the Italian provinces) to 1914, and the Republic of Austria subsequently.
[2] Previous figures include the part of Limburg ceded to the Netherlands, and this figure also includes the Grand Duchy of Luxembourg. Subsequent figures exclude both.
[3] Subsequent figures have a more complete coverage of private schools.
[4] *Pensionnats primaires* were previously not included.
[5] Transleithania (excluding Croatia-Slavonia) to 1917, and subsequently the territory established by the Treaty of Trianon.
[6] Including Croatia-Slavonia.
[7] The source says that exact comparisons over time are impossible owing to different meanings for the term 'elementary', but that this series is an attempt to provide as consistent a series as possible. A number of the figures is estimated – viz. 1864, 1868, 1876, 1880, 1896, 1901, 1902–6, and 1908–25.
[8] State and state-aided schools only.
[9] Children at Roman Catholic schools in Scotland are included in the English statistics to 1862, and not included in the Scottish statistics until 1875.
[10] **Previous figures include night schools.**
[11] Previous figures refer to certificated and assistant teachers employed in **all** schools.
[12] From 1879 to 1905 the number of teachers in private primary schools is not known, except in 1889 when it was 5 thousand.
[13] Excluding Galicia.
[14] Subsequent figures are for inspected schools only. There was a great fall in the number of schools covered between 1878 and 1881, which was regained in 1885 and 1886.
[15] Excluding Dixmunde canton.
[16] State schools only.
[17] Previously only lycées were classed as secondary schools, and all others were classed as primary.
[18] Previously excluding Eksamensret schools.
[19] From 1897 to 1908 certain schools were not included in the annual series published at the time, and from 1909 ancillary teachers were excluded. Statistics were given later for 1900 and 1905 as follows:–

	Pupils	Teachers
1900	14,698	1,352
1905	19,370	1,657

[20] Alsace-Lorraine is excluded from 1871 to 1922.
[21] Auxiliary teachers temporarily in charge of a class are subsequently included.
[22] From 1914 to 1918 (and 1920 for primary schools) the invaded departments are excluded.
[23] Public primary schools only to 1939. In 1910 there were 26 thousand pupils in private primary schools, and in 1921 there were 36 thousand pupils and 1.8 thousand teachers.
[24] An element of double-counting was subsequently eliminated.
[25] Subsequently including girls' high schools.
[26] Previous figures are of all Volksschulen. Subsequently only elementary schools are covered.
[27] New Organisation schools, previously wholly included in the primary category, are subsequently divided.
[28] Subsequently including teachers' training schools.
[29] Previously only state schools.
[30] Previous figures refere only to athenées, gymnasia, and Latin schools.
[31] These figures are known to be slightly defective.
[32] Previous figures do not include pupils at gymnasia who were not doing a complete course.
[33] From 1881 (2nd line) to 1890 (1st line) the figures exclude pupils in 'ambulant schools'.
[34] Revised figures, which do not, however, fit into the series, are available for 1895 and 1900. They are 331 and 339 respectively.
[35] Figures to 1902 (1st line) refer to registered pupils of state and private licees. From 1902 (2nd line) to 1935 they refer to registered pupils of state licees plus pupils of private licees taking state examinations. From 1936 onwards they refer to registered pupils at all licees plus external students taking state examinations.

[36] There was a change in the basis of collection of the statistics.
[37] There was a change in coverage in Aargau canton.
[38] Subsequently state schools only.
[39] Some schools were transferred from the primary to the secondary category.
[40] Burgenland is included subsequently.
[41] Subsequently excludes teachers of handicrafts and of religion.
[42] Subsequent figures include uninspected schools.
[43] Subsequently including private schools, but excluding preparatory departments, which had previously been included.
[44] Some special schools are subsequently included.
[45] Progymnasia are subsequently transferred from the secondary to the primary category.
[46] From 1945 (2nd line) to 1949 (1st line) pupils in the 'Eleven-year Schools' are included in the primary rather than the secondary category.
[47] From 1948 to 1953 and from 1959 to 1960 all teachers in primary and secondary schools are included.
[48] From 1953 to 1964 certain teachers of practical subjects are included who are omitted at other times.
[49] The subsequent decline was caused by the lapsing of certain classes following a new Education Act.
[50] 'People's High Schools' are subsequently excluded.
[51] Assistant teachers are excluded in these years and prior to 1938.
[52] Previous figures are for state lycees and colleges only. Subsequently pupils in private secondary schools are included.
[53] For 1939–44 (for primary school pupils) and for 1940–45 (for secondary schools) Alsace-Lorraine and Corsica (primary schools only) are excluded. Algeria is also excluded for state secondary schools in 1943–45 and for private secondary schools in 1939–41.
[54] Subsequently pupils in elementary and special classes, though such classes in lycées etc. are not transferred from the secondary category until 1963.
[55] Subsequently excludes teachers of complementary courses and of infant classes.
[56] Saarland is not included until 1958 (2nd line in the case of pupils). West Berlin teachers are included throughout, but pupils only from 1959 (2nd line). Only full-time qualified teachers are included.
[57] Middle schools were transferred from the secondary to the primary category.
[58] 'Hellenic' schools were counted as primary to 1929/30 and subsequently divided between primary and secondary.
[59] Including gygogypedagoiai schools which had 18 thousand pupils and 1.4 thousand teachers in 1950/1.
[60] Excluding Cagliari, Caltanissetta, and Messina.
[61] Certain private schools, which were not covered previously, are subsequently included.
[62] Subsequent figures are for secondary schools, properly so-called, only.
[63] **Certain private schools are excluded from 1968 (2nd line).**
[64] Higher primary schools are subsequently transferred to the secondary category.
[65] Previously excluding teachers at private gymnasia.
[66] Previously including teachers of continuation classes.
[67] Previously only schools with 'examination right' are covered. Statistics for all secondary general schools are available for earlier years as follows:—

	Pupils (thousands)	Teachers		Pupils (thousands)	Teachers		Pupils (thousands)	Teachers
1875	14.6	1,085	1900	20.1	1,478	1925	28.5	1,676
1880	16.0	1,213	1905	20.7	1,671	1930	25.3	1,457
1885	18.0	1,450	1910	22.5	1,321	1935	31.6	1,627
1890	18.7	1,572	1915	26.1	1,403	1940	36.1	1,936
1895	19.3	1,474	1920	34.0	1,643	1945	44.4	2,208

Note: In these statistics, from 1910 onwards only full-time teachers are covered.
[68] Figures to 1939 are for day courses at state schools. For 1940–42 (1st line) they are for all schools and courses, but from 1942 (2nd line) night courses are excluded.
[69] Subsequently including the newly acquired territories.
[70] Excluding Cetatea–Alba department.
[71] Excluding Ilfov and Dambovitza departments.
[72] Statistics from 1938 relate to the postwar territory. The figures for primary school teachers are in thousands. Secondary schools are differently defined.
[73] From 1948 to 1958 (1st line) the figures refer to state schools only.
[74] These statistics derive from the Central Inspectorate for Primary Education, and are not comparable with the rest of the series.
[75] There were changes in the organization of schools.
[77] This break probably results mainly from the subsequent inclusion of private secondary schools.
[78] Subsequently excluding middle school classes attached to primary schools.
[79] Subsequently all school teachers.
[80] Subsequent figures are for middle schools only. Previously they included secondary schools (so-called).
[81] Comparability across the years of the Second World War is impossible owing to the re-organisation following the 1944 Education Act. The figures of pupils, which are of average attendance prior to the War, are subsequently of numbers registered.
[82] Primary departments in secondary schools were transferred from the secondary to the primary category.
[83] Subsequently including comprehensive schools.
[84] Excluding Gymanasen, where there were 3,863 teachers in 1969.
[85] Excluding colleges of general education in Aveyron.

J 2 NUMBER OF STUDENTS IN UNIVERSITIES

1817–1869

	Austria[1]	Belgium	Finland[4]	Hungary[5]	Italy	Netherlands	Norway	Portugal[7]	Spain	Sweden
1817	...	679	...	...	...	...	...	1,426	...	...
1818	...	744	...	...	...	702	...	1,524	...	...
1819	...	773	...	...	...	735	...	1,430	...	...
1820	...	730	...	...	...	786	300	1,419	...	...
1821	...	813	...	...	...	843	...	1,288	...	...
1822	...	940	...	...	...	971	...	1,351	...	...
1823	...	996	...	...	...	1,069	...	1,204	...	...
1824	...	1,055	...	...	...	1,111	...	1,111	...	...
1825	...	1,450	...	...	...	1,223	...	1,184	...	...
1826	...	1,566	...	...	...	1,316	...	1,226	...	...
1827	...	1,627	...	...	...	1,373	...	1,262	...	...
1828	...	1,620	329	...	...	1,441	...	...	...	...
1829	...	1,612	423	...	...	1,477	...	521	...	...
1830	...	1,071	407	...	...	1,444	600	478	...	1,265
1831	...	970	—	...	...	1,624	...	...	...	...
1832	...	1,007	425	...	...	1,568	...	...	...	...
1833	...	1,139	389	...	...	1,622	...	...	...	...
1834	...	1,178	401	...	...	1,597	...	446	...	...
1835	...	1,173	438	...	...	1,527	...	665	...	...
1836	...	1,310	414	...	...	1,588	...	777	...	...
1837	...	1,312	424	...	...	1,503	...	708	...	...
1838	...	1,283	451	...	...	1,450	...	843	...	...
1839	...	1,496	444	...	...	1,397	...	782	...	...
1840	...	1,459	403	...	...	1,410	600	928	...	...
1841	[11,235] [2]	1,513	414	1,250	...	1,425	...	998	...	...
1842	8,590	1,533	429	1,134	...	1,296	...	1,086	...	...
1843	8,338	1,589	433	...	...	1,223	...	1,082	...	...
1844	...	1,604	414	...	...	1,250	...	1,102	...	...
1845	7,843	1,659	400	...	...	1,214	...	989	...	...
1846	8,508	1,660	422	...	...	1,077	...	....	...	...
1847	8,372	1,652	385	...	...	1,025	...	900	...	...
1848	12,815[3]	1,708	...	...	...	1,040	...	928	...	...
1849	12,627	1,808	476	...	...	1,037	...	1,008	...	...
1850	11,439	1,773	460	838	...	1,082	550	898	...	...
1851	11,424	1,821	492	843	...	1,226	...	884	...	...
1852	10,622	1,731	464	1,135	...	1,438	...	956	...	...
1853	10,115	1,742	410	1,104	...	1,396	...	894	...	...
1854	9,328	1,864	276	1,241	...	1,414	...	1,034	...	...
1855	9,119	2,113	338	1,063	...	1,413	605	990	...	...
1856	9,365	2,204	417	1,069	...	1,429	...	740	...	...
1857	8,168	2,221	363	1,010	...	1,327	...	796	7,528	...
1858	8,654	2,222	369	1,095	...	1,352	...	905	7,842	...
1859	8,026	2,336	402	1,133	...	1,395	...	801	7,977	...
1860	7,993	2,473	389	1,179	...	1,375	550	861	8,611	...
1861	8,043	2,440	387	1,228	6,504	1,224	...	990	7,679	...
1862	8,408	2,427	407	1,593	5,793	1,241	...	888	7,941	...
1863	8,706	2,409	411	1,831	6,316[6]	1,265	...	911	8,305	...
1864	8,798	2,466	405	1,909	...	1,283	...	789	9,704	...
1865	9,421	2,431	430	1,999	...	1,205	701	803	16,545	...
1866	9,181	2,384	471	...	9,340	1,212	...	698	12,104	...
1867	10,166	2,453	503	2,417	10,599	1,331	...	697	12,269	...
1868	10,605	2,457	528	2,538	10,765	1,217	...	779	...	...
1869	11,166	2,521	587	2,518	10,888	1,273	...	780	...	...

Abbreviations used where space demands:— U.K.: G.B.:— United Kingdom: Great Britain

See p. 813 for footnotes

J 2 Number of Students in Universities

1870–1919

	Austria[1]	Belgium	Bulgaria	Denmark	Finland[4]	France	Germany	Greece	Hungary[5]
1870	11,561	2,631	...	...	685	...	...	...	2,629
1871	12,497	2,751	...	...	508	...	...	...	2,678
1872	12,292	2,861	...	...	673	...	...	...	3,178
1873	12,434	3,025	...	...	664	...	...	...	3,295
1874	12,797	3,156	...	...	640	...	...	...	3,836
1875	12,356	3,256	...	...	627	...	...	...	3,990
1876	12,655	3,722	...	...	627	...	...	...	4,233[5]
									4,103
1877	12,497	3,863	...	...	647	...	...	...	4,120
1878	12,315	4,051	...	...	619	...	...	...	4,268
1879	12,797	4,324	...	...	662	...	...	...	4,037
1880	13,264	4,568	...	...	736	...	21,432[14]	...	4,396
1881	13,572	4,880	...	...	811	...	...	...	4,019
1882	14,252	5,182	...	...	805	...	...	...	4,183
1853	14,391	5,564	...	...	812	...	...	...	4,401
					1,477[11]				
1854	15,295	5,624	...	...	1,527	...	...	...	4,572
1885	15,909	5,768	...	...	1,662	...	...	...	4,473
1886	16,581	5,957	...	...	1,799	...	...	...	4,530
1887	17,175	5,860	...	...	1,820	...	...	...	4,690
1888	17,286	5,837	...	...	1,745	...	...	...	4,816
1889	16,919	6,203	...	...	1,816	16,587	...	...	4,723[5]
1890	17,492	5,663	...	...	1,863	19,821	28,359[14]	...	...
1891	17,562	5,226	...	...	1,868	22,336	...	...	5,218
1892	17,894	4,937	...	...	1,888	23,295	...	...	5,266
1893	18,916	4,886	...	430	1,905	24,795	...	...	5,800
1894	19,413	4,844	...	472	1,979	24,855	...	...	6,135
1895	20,206	5,031	310	456	2,037	26,941	...	...	6,651
1896	20,992	4,830	313	475	2,194	26,819	...	...	7,319
1897	21,598	4,951	354	414	2,282	28,543	...	...	7,952
1898	22,134	5,113	338	407	2,384	28,254	...	...	8,758
1899	23,204	5,265	409	452	2,606	29,377	...	...	9,298
1900	24,140	5,389	483	414	2,727	29,901	47,986	...	9,700
1901	25,548	5,459	495	383	2,795	30,370	51,042	...	10,122
1902	27,363	5,708	578	450	2,880	31,277	52,538	...	10,530
1903	28,689	5,888	796	463	2,908	32,407	53,806	...	11,018
1904	30,631	6,130	1,014	451	3,034	33,618	55,053	...	11,351
1905	31,802	6,426	1,151	521	2,285	35,670	57,375	...	11,616
1906	34,391	6,662	1,324	546	2,474	38,197	59,360	...	11,968
1907	35,095	6,998	812	585	2,724	39,890	61,946	...	12,255
1908	36,605	7,319	1,569	582	2,315	40,767	64,490	...	11,887
1909	38,817	7,661	...	745	3,099	41,044	67,877	...	12,643
1910	39,416	7,910	...	829	3,238	41,190	70,183	...	12,951
1911	40,455	8,157	2,380	839	3,468	41,194	72,194	...	13,227
1912	40,252	8,300	...	862	3,690	41,109	77,378	774	13,445
1913	42,392	8,532	2 455	918	3,849	42,037[12]	79,557	844	14,249[17]
1914	17,396	...	2,887	963	3,951	11,231	66,568	782	...
1915	13,705[1]	...	2,110	937	4,067	12,566	64,384	1,036	5,890
	6,123								
1916	[7,901][9]	...	1,304	1,022	3,811	14,121	71,809	1,274	5,504
1917	9,322	...	[1,408][10]	1,094	3,172	19,381[12]	80,100[15]	2,448	6,983[5]
1918	19,394	10,797	[5,897][10]	1,140	2,915	29,890[13]	95,986	1,795	16,984
1919	21,495	8,709	8,677	1,099	3,310	45,114	117,772	1,864	12,990

See p. 813 for footnotes

J 2 Number of Students in Universities

1870–1919

	Italy	Netherlands	Norway	Portugal	Romania	Serbia	Spain	Sweden	Switzerland
1870	12,069	1,240	1,026	801	...	224	...	...	...
1871	12,446	1,357	1,050	913	...	237	...	...	...
1872	12,013	1,354	1,010	953	...	226	...	...	...
1873	11,821	1,491	980	926	...	208	...	...	...
1874	10,666	1,556	830	903	...	207	...	...	...
1875	9,554	1,537	833	898	...	209	...	...	...
1876	9,431	1,603	880	864	...	151	...	...	...
1877	9,940	1,606	900	815	...	...	...	...	...
1878	10,601	1,564	770	794	...	146	...	...	...
1879	11,233	1,425	730	748	...	100	...	...	...
1880	11,871[18]	1,493	750	766	...	130	...	...	...
1881	12,481	1,543	810	768	...	157	...	...	...
1882	13,856	1,538	880	818	...	158	...	...	...
1883	14,675	1,852	840	948	...	192	15,732	...	...
1884	15,089	1,978	1,240	958	...	206	...	...	...
1885	16,131	2,110	1,350	1,035	...	225	...	...	...
1886	16,980	2,237	1,510	1,115	...	366	...	...	...
1887	17,191	2,418	1,720	1,097	...	233	...	...	1,966
1888	17,584	2,501	1,650	1,126	...	293	...	...	2,039
1889	17,605	2,488	1,620	1,183	...	355	...	...	2,172
1890	18,145	2,815	1,537	1,180	...	466	...	...	2,315
1891	18,685	2,915	1,460	1,157	...	565	...	...	2,532
1892	19,802	3,053	1,370	1,200[8]	...	472	...	...	2,758
				905					
1893	20,925	3,097	1,290	918	...	460	...	...	2,903
1894	22,230	3,112	1,190	948	...	480	...	...	3,119
1895	23,112	3,076	1,140	1,065	...	432	...	...	3,112
1896	24,318	3,046	1,200	1,021	...	491	...	...	3,272
1897	24,705	2,938	1,220	1,066	...	482	...	...	3,492
1898	24,632	3,021	1,330	1,084	...	466	...	...	3,589
1899	25,242	3,028	1,350	1,118	...	438	...	...	3,841
1900	26,033	3,135	1,400	1,181	5,074	415	...	...	4,208
1901	26,613	3,178	1,400	1,106	3,433[19]	405	...	...	4,315
1902	25,748	3,235	1,500	1,028	4,769	395	...	...	4,790
1903	25,436	3,294	1,600	944	5,271	465	...	...	4,942
1904	25,098	3,409	1,600	911	4,950	490	...	...	5,219
1905	25,573	3,552	1,300	953	5,075	618	...	...	5,612
1906	26,621	3,621	1,470	1,050	4,101	780	...	...	6,444
1907	26,766	3,655	1,560	1,085	4,628[20]	...	...	...	6,906
1908	27,304	3,732	1,580	1,195	3,821	...	...	...	6,752
1909	27,005	3,945	1,550	1,262	4,144	...	...	...	6,958
1910	26,850	4,128	1,540	...	3,817	...	...	7,659	6,831
1911	27,783	4,180	1,550	1,212	5,425[21]	...	...	8,092	7,134
1912	27,142	4,292	1,500	1,822	5,571[21]	...	...	8,310	7,019
1913	28,026	4,450	1,500	2,285	5,901[21]	...	...	8,373	8,110
1914	29,624	3,650	1,500	2,573	5,940[21]	...	20,497	8,123	6,814
1915	28,968	3,985	1,500	3,073	...	...	21,467	8,075[22]	6,787
								8,176	
1916	32,882	4,471	1,500	2,743	...	...	23,683	8,617	7,710
1917	38,691	4,810	1,550	2,493	...	...	23,586	9,078[22]	7,894
								8,987	
1918	46,114	5,396	1,550	2,472	...	...	23,660	8,928	7,307
1919	53,670	5,645	1,550	2,747	...	...	23,403	9,195	7,501

See p. 813 for footnotes

J 2 Numbers of Students in Universities

1920–1975

	Austria[1]	Belgium	Bulgaria	Czechoslovakia	Denmark	Finland[4]	France
1920	...[2 3]	9,329	5,487	28,155	1,094[28] 777	3,401	49,931
1921	21,967	9,036	3,351	28,303	829	3,574	50,906
1922	21,009	9,035	4,353	25,464	850	3,666	50,367
1923	18,393[23] 19,454	9,783	4,238	26,226	825	3,915	50,891
1924	18,371	9,848	4,837	27,436	894[28] 4,920	4,106	53,051
1925	17,680	8,988	5,233	27,725	5,019	4,354	58,507
1926	17,747	9,158	5,353	27,809	5,276	4,825	60,969
1927	18,579	9,371	6,500	28,899	4,956	5,217	64,531
1928	19,328	9,914	6,344	29,751	5,083	5,892	66,961
1929	20,087	11,364	6,940	31,164	4,994	6,426	73,600
1930	21,367	10,845	7,203	32,507	5,291	7,007	78,674
1931	22,479	11,407	7,906	34,112	6,076	7,444	82,655
1932	22,756	11,456	8,993	33,332	6,181	7,662	84,658
1933	19,829	11,659	9,257	32,295	6,458	8,158	87,166
1934	18,533	11,038	8,696	31,640	6,437	8,140	82,132
1935	17,837	10,727	7,926	29,327	6,686	8,161	73,778
1936	16,818[24] 18,678	10,334	8,099	23,435	6,546	8,164	72,099
1937	...	10,776	7,914	25,684	6,839	7,994	75,295
1938	...	11,566	[6,030][26]	...	6,970	8,048	78,973
1939	...	11,113	10,169	...	7,167	8,230	55,479
1940	...	12,296[25] 12,912	[9,242][26]	...	7,404	8,323	76,485
1941	...	15,701	[9,744][26]	...	7,782	6,303	89,946
1942	...	15,430	...	...	8,233	5,896	105,943
1943	...	13,514	...[27]	...	...	6,773	90,732
1944	...	15,145	26,412	...	...	10,429	97,007
1945	26,767	18,620	...	54,902	8,587	12,196	123,313
1946	...	17,473	...	60,285	8,679	12,941	129,025
1947	35,157	18,345	...	60,745	9,070	13,268	128,754
1948	31,959	19,161	39,221	57,700	9,239	13,588	129,085
1949	28,167	20,036	38,454	43,232	9,205	12,351	136,744
1950	24,793	20,698	32,969	38,884	9,104	12,113	139,593
1951	22,720	21,256	31,678	39,077	8,376	12,122	142,096
1952	20,756	21,778	31,394	42,717	8,273	12,087	147,844
1953	20,011	22,491	...	47,194	8,160	12,121	151,115
1954	19,954	23,282	...	48,613	8,390	12,519	155,803
1955	21,093	24,462	37,049	49,509	8,299	12,653	157,489
1956	22,850	25,737	37,451	52,513	8,681	13,389	170,023
1957	27,296	27,096	41,176	53,782	8,650	14,438	180,634
1958	32,608	28,275	43,085	53,993	9,388	15,872	192,128
1959	36,110	29,150	48,840	58,559	9,971	17,462	202,062[30]
1960	40,815	30,692	54,795	67,300	10,810	19,109	210,900
1961	45,110	32,726	61,424	78,053	12,746	21,592	232,610
1962	48,340	35,450	71,593	87,382	14,735	23,473	270,788
1963	50,256	38,366	78,001	94,715	16,939	25,332	308,189
1964	51,402	42,441	82,799	92,682	21,425	27,390	348,935
1965	52,169	48,800	85,021	95,023	25,351	29,205[29]	393,659
1966	52,416	53,792	83,152	96,148	28,090	40,300	433,248
1967	55,483	59,172	81,846	99,336	31,686	45,392	477,904
1968	52,471	64,779	80,345	103,595	33,163	47,752	540,010
1969	53,765	69,634	...	104,011	35,352	50,605	615,326
1970	57,297	75,106	88,609	105,634	41,443	50,424	651,368
1971	62,871	81,024	93,072	106,127	41,569	51,504	697,791
1972	70,736	78,332	100,742	106,800	45,415	51,741	735,235
1973	76,971	79,477	103,805	112,063	48,680	53,287	742,074
1974	82,372	80,980	106,343	116,953	51,016	57,854	760,590
1975	89,612	83,360	107,493	122,627	54,206	60,318	806,268

J 2 Number of Students in Universities

1920–1975

	Germany	East Germany[33]	Greece	Hungary[6]	Southern Ireland	Italy	Netherlands	Norway
1920	119,412[16]	...	1,566	12,902	3,658	53,239	5,689	1,831
1921	118,544	...	2,195	15,696	3,492	49,134	6,036	2,000
1922	121,699	...	2,663	16,691	3,446	46,561	6,815[35] / 9,524	2,300
1923	114,338	...	3,676	13,868	3,322	43,235	9,440	2,500
1924	93,510	...	3,124	12,113	3,249	43,760	9,302	2,800
1925	90,334	...	4,388	11,566	3,159	45,208	9,438	3,248[36]
1926	94,798	...	1,954	11,372	3,037	42,864	10,009	3,129
1927	100,654	...	1,331[34] / 6,550	11,916	3,171	42,450	10,428	3,562
1928	112,306	...	7,135	12,267	3,532	40,399	11,059	3,457
1929	121,183	...	6,740	12,100	3,896	44,940	11,489	3,495
1930	127,742	...	6,841	12,611	4,311	46,262	12,061	3,476
1931	126,079	...	7,781	12,408	4,639	47,614	12,739	3,615
1932	120,865	...	8,632	12,111	4,954	53,672	13,481	3,734
1933	106,673	...	8,621	12,417	4,965	57,294	13,675	3,879
1934	86,056	...	9,169	11,705	5,054	62,020	13,065	4,008
1935	76,334	...	8,248	10,843	5,011	64,944	12,628	3,905
1936	64,482	...	8,935	10,443	5,163	71,512	12,387	3,977
1937	56,395	...	7,851	9,746[27] / 11,747	5,336	74,909	12,505	4,007
1938	55,944	...	...	...	5,370	77,429	12,592	4,229
1939	[47,400][31]	...	...	...	5,425	85,535	11,251	4,118
1940	49,702	...	...	...	5,430	127,058	10,378	4,204
1941	52,344	...	...	...	5,549	145,793	10,898	3,941
1942	63,636	...	...	...	5,758	168,323	...	3,077
1943	64,783	...	...	...	5,938	157,348	...	4,243
1944	...	...	...	...	6,341	170,567	...	...
	West Germany[32]							
1945	...	...	...	...	6,620	189,665	14,551	5,991
1946	...	...	...	...	7,022	190,799	24,694	6,209
1947	...	...	...	...	6,985	180,149	25,955	6,106
1948	...	...	...	...	7,319	168,001	27,045	5,515
1949	[109,908][11]	...	...	...	7,458	146,485	28,566	5,294
1950	[116,896][11]	...	...	32,501	7,231	145,170	29,736	5,438
1951	[118,492][11]	31,512	...	40,431	7,463	142,722	29,887	4,046
1952	[119,808][11]	42,153	...	49,442	7,601	138,814	28,660	3,967
1953	116,909	55,201	...	53,330	7,729	137,789	27,987	3,656
1954	122,777	70,666	...	47,454	7,977	136,458	28,780	3,785
1955	130,496[32]	74,742	...	45,431	8,066	139,018	29,642	3,696
1956	144,874	79,979	...	42,608	8,393	145,370	30,939	4,253
1957	161,209	85,729	...	35,867	8,782	154,638	32,565	4,723
1958	180,558	82,819	...	34,037	9,399	163,945	35,131	5,813
1959	195,592	89,099	16,305	37,996	9,997	176,193	37,725	6,090
1960	212,021	99,860	17,211	44,585	10,851	191,790	40,727	6,647
1961	229,368	111,404	19,725	53,302	11,795	205,965	43,851	7,690
1962	244,421	113,166	22,863	67,324	12,711	225,796	47,787	8,854
1963	256,040	113,952	28,759	82,280	13,828	240,234	52,400	10,830
1964	263,152	113,572	35,162	91,923	14,661	259,338	58,427	12,781
1965	266,648	111,591	38,261	93,957	16,191	297,783	64,409	14,401
1966	281,339	110,523	42,003	89,544	17,215	338,516	71,260	15,489
1967	285,969	110,614	47,223	83,938	18,110	370,076	77,896	16,245
1968	304,213	115,152	50,064	78,727	19,876	425,649	84,776	17,486
1969	376,169	127,585	52,811	78,889	21,277	488,352	93,594	20,406
1970	411,520	143,163	53,692	80,536	21,664	560,605	103,382	22,975
1971	466,044	158,014	50,914	86,311	21,369	631,150	112,873	25,006 / 26,558[45]
1972	534,255	160,967	56,703	90,857	21,437	657,616	...[46]	32,553
1973	589,413	153,558	59,724	98,122	21,406	675,176	...[46]	34,036
1974	640,483	144,606	66,679	103,390	22,485	708,757	112,528	35,473
1975	675,946	136,854	...	107,555	...	736,303	120,134	36,681

J 2 Number of Students in Universities

1920–1975

	Poland	Portugal	Romania	Spain	Sweden	Switzerland	U.K.: G.B.	Yugoslavia
1920	25,904	2,990	13,683[37]	23,508	9,096	6,949	...	...
1921	35,212	3,418	14,440	23,080	8,792	6,510	...	...
1922	38,019	3,355	14,116[38]	25,690	9,125	5,974	58,952	...
1923	39,255	3,582	18,828	27,800	9,024	6,313	57,137	11,223
1924	37,984	3,899	19,513	29,650	9,398	6,623	55,922	11,005
1925	37,456	4,117	22,430	31,561	9,140	6,662	56,296	10,970
1926	40,734	4,461	27,582	39,719	9,493	6,526	57,141	12,442
1927	41,734	5,007	29,847	45,463	9,653	6,550	57,755	12,109
1928	43,607	5,013	31,143	41,229	10,237	6,615	58,548	12,534
1929	45,486	4,942	32,048	33,557	10,126	6,647	59,474	13,544
1930	48,155	5,641	28,639	35,717	10,062	6,877	62,312	14,693
1931	49,770	5,984	31,213	33,633	10,627	7,396	62,527	15,530
1932	51,770	...	30,120	31,905	11,149	7,756	64,115	14,743
1933	49,599	...	40,903	30,788	11,332	8,586	64,420	16,132
1934	47,923	...	41,307	34,490	11,400	8,771	64,050	15,913
1935	47,001	...	38,228	29,249	11,747	8,738	63,620	15,175
1936	48,024	...	34,093	...	12,527	8,706	62,492	15,308
1937	49,534	5,850	30,771[27]	...	12,545[41]	9,063	62,270	16,207
					11,682			
1938	...	6,182	26,489[39]	...	12,112	9,530	63,420	15,505
1939	...	6,596	...	54,336	12,106	8,971	49,765	...
1940	...	8,715	...	33,763	11,395	9,649	44,034	...
1941	...	6,844	...	34,669[40]	12,397[42]	10,121	46,457	...
					11,550			
1942	...	9,927	...	37,672	11,827	10,661	48,029	...
1943	...	10,110	...	41,764	12,327	11,785	48,913	...
1944	...[27]	10,787	...	39,400	13,038	12,104	49,809	...
1945	55,988	11,893	...	40,426	13,664	12,182	67,174	21,052
1946	86,461	11,976	...	42,597	13,691	12,760	86,336	31,994
1947	94,785	11,959	...	46,926	13,857	13,182	96,504	41,339
1948	103,494	12,019	48,676	49,980	14,416	13,195	101,870	39,804
1949	115,532	12,771	48,615	50,303	15,423	12,891	103,081	41,282
1950	125,096	13,489[35]	53,007	51,633	16,437	12,842	102,012	44,011
		15,780						
1951	141,706	16,198	61,123	53,434	17,771[43]	12,679	100,516	40,251
1952	131,297	16,353	71,513	58,143	18,609[43]	12,462	97,329	41,028
1953	139,985	17,043	80,593	59,580	19,942[43]	12,444	96,357	43,982
1954	155,427	17,687	78,860	53,666	21,462	11,775	97,851	50,330
1955	157,465	18,453	77,633	57,030	23,091	11,944	101,494	51,598
1956	170,331	18,812	81,206	62,215	26,277	12,147	106,074	52,311
1957	162,680	19,468	80,919	64,281	27,685	12,819	111,928	60,465
1958	156,547	20,472	67,849	62,985	30,613	13,651	116,083	66,905
1959	161,008	22,163	63,208	63,787	33,392	14,582	119,941	69,489
1960	165,687	23,877	71,989	62,105	37,405	15,658	125,530	76,462
1961	172,354	25,077	83,749	64,010	40,697	17,320	131,922	81,321
1962	190,303	...	98,929	69,377	45,006[44]	19,087	135,428	80,764
1963	212,588	29,788	112,611	80,074	49,284	20,691	142,973	76,292
1964	231,224	31,575	123,284	85,148	60,230	22,863	156,788	75,653
					59,809[47]			
1965	251,864	33,972	130,614	92,983	68,276	24,813	181,052	84,891
1966	274,471	35,933	136,948	105,370	75,500	25,831	200,724	90,675
1967	288,788	38,647	141,589	115,590	89,500	27,809	217,629	97,814
1968	305,561	41,969	147,637	134,548	100,300	29,808	232,137	117,779
1969	322,464	47,304	151.705	150,094	113,600	31,341	243,011	126,406
1970	330,789	50,362	151,885	168,612	120,100	32,264	250,494	140,282
1971	347,782	52,054	148,428	195,237	115,900	34,367	257,570	148,051
1972	364,274	54,709	143,985	210,441	113,600	36,638	261,992	157,006
1973	397,901	60,051	143,656	251,866	110,000	37,928	267,384	170,838
1974	426,701	56,982	153,000	275,300	108,522	39,769	274,710	180,498
1975	468,129	70,804	165,000	324,094	110,012	41,793	286,267	190,619

See p. 813 for footnotes

J 2 Students in Universities

NOTES

1. SOURCES:— The official publicationsnoted on p. xv. Finnish data to 1883 were compiled at the Department of Economic and Social History of the University of Helsinki, and made available through the Central Statistical Office of Finland. The Romanian figure for 1938 was kindly supplied by Mr. G. Radulescu, Editor in Chief of the *Enciclopedica Romana.*

2. Institutions of higher education other than universities are covered in some of the statistics in this table. These are indicated in footnotes.

3. Unless otherwise indicated, the statistics refer to the autumn (or winter) term or semester.

FOOTNOTES

[1] Cisleithania (excluding the Italian provinces) to 1915 (1st line), and Republic of Austria subsequently. During the period of Austrian rule the numbers at the University of Padua were as follows:—

1841	1,825	1846	1,941	1851	1,630	1856	1,348	1861	952
1842	1,905	1847	...	1852	1,751	1857	1,282	1862	1,080
1843	1,935	1848	...	1853	1,587	1858	1,568	1863	1,381
1844	...	1849	...	1854	1,388	1859	827	1864	1,433
1845	1,941	1850	1,574	1855	1,300	1860	829		

[2] Including philosophy students who were subsequently omitted.

[3] Students at Technical High Schools are subsequently included.

[4] Annual averages of the number of students in residence for five-year periods from 1861 to 1805 have been supplied by the Central Statistical Office of Finland, taken from S.E. Astrom, *Studentfrekvensen vid de svenska universiteten under 1700-talet.* They are as follows:—

1761–65	198	1776–80	189	1791-95	165
1766–70	159	1781–85	178	1796–1800	179
1771–75	161	1786–90	178	1801–05	228

[5] Transleithania to 1917, and the territory established by the treaty of Trianon subsequently. Agram (Zagreb) University is excluded from 1876 (2nd line) to 1889.

[6] Previously excluding the University of Naples.

[7] Previous figures for Portugal are as follows:—

1800	1,148	1805	850	1810	...	1815	1,068
1801	1,093	1806	871	1811	427	1816	1,215
1802	1,078	1807	748	1812	489		
1803	939	1808	576	1813	611		
1804	932	1809	517	1814	848		

[8] Figures to 1892 (1st line) are the sums of students registered in the separate facalties, and there is an element of double-counting which is subsequently eliminated.

[9] This includes students at various high schools not included in other years.

[10] Summer semester.

[11] Including those on leave of absence (from 1883 (2nd line) in the case of Finland).

[12] The University of Lille is excluded for 1914–17.

[13] Subsequently including the University of Strasbourg.

[14] Male students at universities only.

[15] Subsequently excluding the University of Strasbourg.

[16] Subsequently excluding the University of Danzig.

[17] Subsequently excluding the University of Agram (Zagreb).

[18] Subsequently excluding the School of Obstrectrics.

[19] Previously excluding students in the theological, veterinary and pharmacy faculties.

[20] Excluding students in the faculty of letters at the University of Jassy.

[21] Excluding students in the faculty of science at the University of Jassy.

[22] This break results from a change in the method of counting at the Karolin Medico-Surgical Institute.

[23] From 1920 to 1922 (1st line) Graz Technischehochschule is excluded.

[24] Subsequently including students at Arts High Schools.

[25] Subsequently including the Institut St. Louis, College Nôtre Dame de la Paix (Namur) and the Polytechnic Faculty at Mons.

[26] Excluding students at the Free University, who numbered 2,336 in 1937 and 2,775 in 1939.

[27] All higher education subsequently.

[28] Figures to 1919 (1st line) are of candidates for all examinations. From 1919 (2nd line) to 1924 (1st line) only those who passed the obligatory entrance examination are covered. Subsequently the figures are of all matriculated students.

[29] Tampere School of Social Sciences and Jyvaskyla College of Pedagogics were raised to university status in 1966. They had 6,325 students in that year.
[30] Subsequently excluding the University of Algiers.
[31] First term of 1940.
[32] Including West Berlin throughout, but only including Saarland from 1956.
[33] Including teachers' training colleges.
[34] Statistics to 1927 (1st line) are for Athens University only.
[35] Students at High Schools are subsequently included.
[36] All previous figures (except those for years ending in 0 or 5) are rounded.
[37] Subsequently including the University of Cluj.
[38] Excluding students in the faculties of medicine and pharmacy at the University of Jassy.
[39] This figure relates to the postwar territory.
[40] Excluding students in the law faculty at the University of Barcelona and in the science faculty at the University of Oviedo.
[41] This break results from a change in the method of counting at the University of Uppsala.
[42] Subsequently including the Central Gymnastic Institute and excluding the Karolin Medico-Surgical Institute.
[43] Excluding students at Music and Art High Schools, who numbered 294 in 1950.
[44] The basis of reckoning was changed from net numbers registered to numbers actually present.
[45] The State College for Teachers became the University of Trondheim.
[46] A new Act on tuition fees resulted in considerable numbers of students refraining from enrolment. Since this undermined the basis for compiling reliable statistics, no data are available for these years.
[47] Subsequently excluding the Music High School.

K. NATIONAL ACCOUNTS

Whilst it has been the general principle in most sections of this work to prefer raw data to those which have been processed, there are no such things as raw national accounts statistics, and everything in this section is "synthetic", the result of elaborate calculations by sophistacated statisticians. It is really impossible to summarise briefly all the complex operations involved, and the user who requires description of them is advised to consult the latest United Nations, *Yearbook of National Accounts Statistics,* or for more detail the United Nations , *National Accounting Practices in Sixty Countries.* Whilst interest in the nation's wealth and income can be traced in a number of countries as far back as the later middle ages, the modern national accounts concepts date from the period of the Second World War (though what is essentially one of the component concepts, the balance of payments, became operational during the interwar years). Since then a great deal of work has been done in many countries not only to improve the concepts and the collection of current statistical material with which to clothe them, but also to produce retrospective estimates going back, in some cases, a very long way into history.

Three main concepts of overall product were used for table K.1, and these differ considerably, making comparison between them extremely difficult. There are related differences in the concepts of capital formation employed. National income (or Net National Product) was the first concept to be much used, and is characteristic of most estimates made before the end of the 1940s. It relates to the disposable income of individuals, institutions, and governments, after providing for the maintenance and depreciation of capital stocks. Gross National Product (and Gross Domestic Product, which is not very different in most countries, and even in Britain was, at its maximum divergence just before 1914, more than 90 per cent of G.N.P.) is the other main concept used for western Europe, and includes depreciation and maintenance outlays. Both these concepts can be expressed in terms of either market prices or factor cost, the latter excluding the excess of indirect taxes over subsidies. In most cases market prices have been preferred here. In the centrally-planned economies of eastern Europe, the most commonly used concept is Net Material Product, which not only excludes depreciation and maintenance, but also expenditure on "unproductive" services, a category which has not been constant. So far as capital formation is concerned, it is, so far as possible, and excepting the centrally-planned economies for which net figures are preferred, given in gross terms, inclusive of the change in stocks, work in progress, etc.

It is worth remembering, in making comparisons both over time and between countries, that no national product concepts include "income in kind", amongst which are the rental value of owner-occupied buildings, and the consumption of home-produced goods (including farmers' consumption of their own products). These have tended to be proportionally more important the less developed is a country's economy, and the more dependent it is on agriculture. Another warning is in order in relation to the constant price series. Aside from technical problems associated with price index numbers, it is impossible in practice to reflect completely the changes which take place in the quality of goods having the same designation. These changes may be either improvements or deteriorations, but it seems to be generally accepted that the former predominate on balance.

Table K.2 takes Gross Domestic Product (or Gross Material Product in the centrally-planned economies) as its base, and shows estimates of the proportion contributed by each of the major sectors of the economy. Once again, it is necessary to be cautious in making comparisons between countries owing to differences in definition, though these are not usually of very great importance in this case.

Whilst the modern balance of payments concept grew out of the disruptions of international trading relations that became evident in the interwar years, concern about the balance of trade and monetary reserves (or "treasure") goes back long before that. Consequently it has been possible for latter-day analysts to reconstruct something reasonably close to a modern balance of payments for some countries for a long way back into the nineteenth century. The main components of these estimates are shown in table J.3, along with the more recent, contemporary calculations, which are generally available for most countries other than the centrally-planned economies. It must be stressed that all of these statistics are estimates, and sometimes pretty rough ones. Since the Second World War they have been mostly reliable, though significant revisions are apt to be made to the figure for any year for at least a decade afterwards. The nineteenth century figures are no doubt less reliable, because the data on which they are based were collected for totally different purposes, and much information that would be desirable is missing. Nevertheless, they are carefully made, after prolonged study of the sources. The same applies to some of the interwar statistics—those of Italy and Sweden, for example. But others from that period are probably amongst the least reliable of all. *The Banker* described those of the United Kingdom, for example, as "little more than the vaguest haphazard guessing, unworthy of this country and of the technical accomplishments of the men responsible for the task". The same might well be said of the estimates for many of the smaller countries of Europe.

K 1 NATIONAL ACCOUNTS TOTALS

1850–1899

	Denmark (in million krone at market prices)				Germany (in million marks at market prices)				Italy (in million lire at market prices)			
	Current prices		Constant prices		Current prices		Constant prices		Current prices		Constant prices	
	GNP	CF	GNP	CF[1]	NNP	CF[2]	NNP	CF[2]	GNP	CF[4]	GNP[5]	CF
							1913 prices				1938 prices	
1850	...	...	...	...	6,070	500	10,534	700	...	...	...	...
1851	...	...	...	...	6,431	570	10,568	740	...	...	...	...
1852	...	...	...	...	7,296	990	11,121	1,300	...	...	...	...
1853	...	...	...	...	7,189	470	10,630	600	...	...	...	...
1854	...	...	...	...	8,203	920	10,961	920	...	...	...	...
1855	...	...	...	...	7,882	260	10,316	370	...	...	...	...
1856	...	...	...	...	9,139	1,190	11,553	1,200	...	...	...	...
1857	...	...	...	...	8,581	560	11,845	680	...	...	...	...
1858	...	...	...	...	8,334	670	12,053	750	...	...	...	...
1859	...	...	...	...	8,134	710	12,219	880	...	...	...	...
1860	...	...	...	...	9,630	1,260	13,604	1,530	...	...	...	...
1861	...	...	...	...	9,379	720	13,002	890	8,639	572	51,398	3,017
1862	...	...	...	...	10,050	1,320	13,731	1,670	9,025	840	52,710	4,006
1863	...	...	...	...	10,372	1,500	14,639	1,970	8,470	658	51,738	3,380
1864	...	...	...	...	10,207	1,220	14,677	1,630	8,798	882	53,999	4,804
1865	...	...	...	...	10,279	1,050	14,858	1,440	9,068	994	55,712	5,455
1866	...	...	...	...	10,714	1,060	15,106	1,460	9,778	965	56,857	5,066
1867	...	...	...	...	11,558	1,850	15,108	1,070	9,417	763	52,249	3,861
1868	...	...	...	...	12,967	1,920	16,621	2,270	10,397	1,062	53,368	5,129
1869	...	...	...	...	11,750	860	15,660	1,140	10,173	1,057	55,087	5,564
			1929 prices									
1870	608	53	1,022	116	12,876	1,590	16,706	1,870	10,044	828	54,767	4,286
1871	657	56	1,106	114	14,013	1,480	17,395	1,520	10,453	828	54,973	4,210
1872	677	62	1,133	110	16,627	2,600	19,133	2,440	11,741	868	54,654	4,131
1873	732	75	1,165	118	17,950	2,370	19,768	2,120	13,290	1,378	57,269	6,035
1874	753	81	1,183	136	19,544	3,370	21,316	3,180	12,771	1,041	56,802	4,311
1875	746	81	1,164	137	18,242	2,480	21,070	2,570	11,312	1,021	58,209	4,671
1876	770	71	1,203	121	17,966	2,390	20,890	2,750	11,506	631	57,694	3,224
1877	707	55	1,172	111	17,414	1,830	20,705	2,240	12,554	873	58,440	4,023
1878	693	46	1,197	94	17,874	1,820	21,803	2,310	11,893	911	58,477	4,127
1879	702	49	1,239	108	16,678	1,210	21,193	1,820	11,889	1,059	58,894	5,282
1880	773	59	1,316	126	16,902	1,330	20,576[3] 19,874	1,860	12,599	1,504	60,894	7,246
1881	807	70	1,393	153	17,330	1,590	20,616	2,160	11,540	614	57,542	3,118
1882	816	74	1,446	154	17,489	1,530	20,444	2,110	12,343	1,552	60,583	7,542
1883	863	80	1,547	168	18,014	1,810	21,909	2,460	11,762	1,259	60,024	6,194
1884	845	76	1,573	165	18,540	1,960	22,712	2,730	11,670	1,239	61,130	6,842
1885	827	66	1,565	146	18,731	1,960	23,452	2,740	12,526	1,582	62,703	5,925
1886	773	51	1,511	116	18,935	1,980	24,142	2,830	12,984	1,915	64,555	9,279
1887	793	59	1,578	130	19,280	2,230	24,558	3,030	12,364	1,521	65,261	8,635
1888	830	63	1,664	140	20,716	2,400	25,840	2,960	11,859	1,391	63,084	7,740
1889	898	73	1,757	145	22,749	2,940	26,478	3,600	12,164	558	60,872	4,737
1890	954	81	1,828	165	23,676	3,360	27,754	4,050	13,112	1,203	65,079	6,480
1891	1,007	80	1,902	178	22,624	2,080	26,822	2,900	13,500	887	65,677	6,983
1892	1,000	77	1,906	166	24,061	3,140	28,390	3,980	12,315	1,190	62,576	4,405
1893	996	77	1,939	163	24,357	2,930	30,606	4,080	12,479	724	64,570	6,784
1894	981	76	1,967	165	24,361	2,530	30,196	3,710	11,984	707	64,059	4,883
1895	1,065	93	2,121	203	25,254	2,830	32,079	4,010	12,496	909	65,234	5,263
1896	1,086	121	2,216	251	26,979	3,590	33,377	4,860	12,529	546	66,373	5,418
1897	1,113	142	2,257	296	28,714	4,150	34,739	5,360	12,228	1,323	63.815	3,077
1898	1,230	182	2,484	356	31,028	5,330	36,813	6,650	13,801	1,204	68.667	7,299
1899	1,257	190	2,544	347	31,761	5,390	36,860	6,010	13,963	1,814	69,544	6,140

Abbreviations used throughout this table:— GDP = Gross Domestic Product; CF = Capital Formation; GNP = Gross National Product; NNP = Net National Product; NMP = Net Material Product.

See p. 838 for footnotes

K 1 National Accounts Totals

1850–1899

	Norway (in million kroner at market prices)				Sweden (in million kroner at market prices)				United Kingdom[7 8] (in million pounds at market prices)[9]			
	Current prices		Constant prices		Current prices		Constant prices		Current prices		Constant prices	
	GDP	CF[4]	GDP	CF[4]	GDP	CF[6]	GDP	CF[6]	GNP	CF[6]	GNP	CF[6]
			1910 prices				1913 prices				1900 prices	
1850	...	...	...	...	...	...	...	...	536	32.5	596	42.8
1851	...	...	...	...	...	...	...	...	561	33.0	620	43.5
1852	...	...	...	...	...	...	...	...	566	37.7	631	47.1
1853	...	...	...	...	...	...	...	...	638	41.5	655	45.6
1854	...	...	...	...	...	...	...	...	680	43.7	673	45.8
1855	...	...	...	...	...	...	...	...	703[10] 642	43.7	691[10] 714	48.8
1856	...	...	...	...	...	...	...	...	672	41.9[10] 40	742	46.5[10] 41
1857	...	...	...	...	...	...	...	...	660	35	758	37
1858	...	...	...	...	...	...	...	...	651	34	763	38
1859	...	...	...	...	...	...	...	...	677	37	779	42
1860	...	...	...	...	...	...	...	...	702	40	791	44
1861	...	...	...	...	794	50	924	88	736	46	831	53
1862	...	...	...	...	841	76	944	131	756	50	831	57
1863	...	...	...	...	826	64	984	110	787	63	839	69
1864	...	...	...	...	779	71	974	126	816	77	852	80
1865	480	62	601	76	805	54	1,006	97	846	80	877	84
1966	492	66	613	79	829	76	999	138	867	71	876	75
1867	518	67	628	79	872	63	991	115	855	61	888	66
1868	524	68	627	81	891	39	979	73	856	60	919	65
1869	537	65	651	80	830	66	966	121	885	59	947	63
1870	542	66	650	82	954	67	1,163	120	953[9] 1,155	64	1,021[9] 1,118	66
1871	562	70	661	86	1,001	72	1,192	124	1,259	81	1,190	81
1872	640	96	704	96	1,124	98	1,276	145	1,322	91	1,182	83
1873	729	123	721	109	1,294	155	1,362	205	1,365	94	1,182	79
1874	790	145	748	119	1,408	188	1,436	234	1,405	109	1,253	94
1875	771	140	769	121	1,295	178	1,335	232	1,371	115	1,271	109
1876	799	136	792	124	1,441	170	1,470	206	1,357	124	1,285	122
1877	797	136	798	128	1,396	168	1,440	208	1,335	120	1,296	120
1878	706	111	770	113	1,280	144	1,407	197	1,323	110	1,305	114
1879	662	98	777	108	1,247	123	1,467	181	1,243	90	1,281	98
1880	720	106	802	117	1,334	126	1,482	167	1,388	97	1,379	99
1881	739	108	809	120	1,415	137	1,538	187	1,362	94	1,377	98
1882	760	114	808	124	1,351	122	1,501	163	1,405	96	1,400	99
1883	750	113	805	125	1,405	133	1,579	177	1,450	102	1,461	107
1884	721	106	819	121	1,368	147	1,591	205	1,403	93	1,452	103
1885	679	97	827	117	1,370	135	1,671	189	1,364	80	1,449	91
1886	667	92	831	114	1,285	144	1,647	212	1,359	69	1,465	83
1887	659	94	842	119	1,253	103	1,670	157	1,428	68	1,536	83
1888	710	104	881	131	1,321	125	1,693	196	1,451	74	1,561	88
1889	770	126	915	148	1,456	146	1,798	208	1,501	84	1,592	97
1890	780	139	940	152	1,511	149	1,821	209	1,550	89	1,615	99
1891	802	138	949	155	1,605	122	1,888	175	1,594	94	1,670	109
1892	799	130	967	152	1,571	126	1,870	185	1,567	97	1,645	114
1893	809	132	993	157	1,558	113	1,923	172	1,550	93	1,637	113
1894	816	134	999	162	1,620	132	2,104	198	1,606	99	1,724	120
1895	832	140	1,011	173	1,595	173	2,045	260	1,637	99	1,776	121
1896	875	143	1,040	170	1,783	179	2,315	252	1,707	113	1,857	137
1897	919	162	1,095	189	1,892	226	2,365	296	1,730	132	1,862	157
1898	998	189	1,104	208	1,996	249	2,376	316	1,835	158	1,966	181
1899	1,065	220	1,138	223	2,122	288	2,439	336	1,963	183	2,069	197

See p. 838 for footnotes

K 1 **National Accounts Totals**

1910–1949

	Austria (in thousand million schillings at market prices)				Belgium (in thousand million francs at market prices)				Bulgaria (in thousand million leva at market prices)			
	Current Prices		Constant prices		Current prices		Constant prices		Current prices		Constant prices	
	GNP[11]	CF[4]	GNP	CF[4]	NNP/GDP[12] /GNP	CF	GNP	CF[13]	NNP/NMP[14]	CF[15]	NNP/NMP[14]	CF[15]
1910	...	...	...	...	...	...	1948 prices		...	...	...	...
1911	...	...	...	...	...	...	...	...	...	...	...	...
1912	...	...	...	...	...	...	...	...	...	...	...	...
			1937 prices									
1913	10.12	1.31	10.80	1.47	6.5	...	...	...	...	...	...	...
1914	...	...	...	...	...	...	...	...	...	...	...	...
1915	...	...	...	...	...	...	...	...	...	...	...	...
1916	...	...	...	...	...	...	...	...	...	...	...	...
1917	...	...	...	...	...	...	...	...	...	...	...	...
1918	...	...	...	...	...	...	...	...	...	...	...	...
1919	...	...	...	...	...	...	...	...	...	...	...	...
1920	...	...	7.17	...	...	...	...	...	...	...	...	...
1921	...	...	7.94	...	...	...	...	...	...	...	...	...
1922	...	...	8.66	...	...	...	...	...	...	...	...	...
1923	...	...	8.56	...	...	...	...	...	...	...	...	...
1924	9.26	0.63	9.57	0.63	31.3	...	176	...	44	...	47	...
1925	10.29	0.84	10.21	0.78	...	...	...	...	50	...	50	...
1926	10.28	0.96	10.38	0.89	...	...	...	...	49	...	51	...
1927	11.11	0.89	10.70	0.84	48.2	...	173	...	53	...	57	...
1928	11.68	1.14	11.19	1.03	...	...	...	...	56	...	58	...
1929	12.09	1.27	11.36	1.14	...	...	...	...	56	...	56	...
1930	11.56	1.09	11.04	1.01	66.5	...	215	...	49	...	53	...
1931	10.36	0.89	10.15	0.81	...	...	...	...	45	...	56	...
1932	9.55	0.58	9.11	0.54	...	...	...	...	39	...	53	...
1933	9.02	0.47	8.80	0.46	...	...	...	...	36	...	53	...
1934	8.98	0.51	8.88	0.50	49.4	...	209	...	35	...	55	...
1935	9.14	0.57	9.06	0.57	50.7	...	219	...	37	...	62	...
1936	9.32	0.65	9.32	0.65	59.8	...	246	...	40	...	70	...
1937	9.82	0.72	9.82	0.72	65.3	...	250	...	47	...	81	...
			1954 prices									
			63.61	6.14	65.2	...	241	...	51	...	85	...
1938	...	...	...	...	65.2	...	241	...	51	...	85	...
1939	...	...	...	...	65	...	...	...	59	...	95	...
1940	...	...	...	...	...	...	...	...	65[16] / 67	...	94[16] / 97	...
1941	...	...	...	...	46	...	...	...	89	...	107	...
1942	...	...	...	...	...	...	...	...	122	...	111	...
1943	...	...	...	...	55	...	...	...	162	...	117	...
1944	...	...	...	...	...	...	...	...	250	...	120	...
1945	...	...	...	...	...	...	....	...	286	...	91	...
1946	...	...	40.69	...	194	...	...	...	334	...	95	...
1947	...	...	44.89	...	218	...	250	...	...	...	...	...
1948	32.1	4.20	56.95	8.49	248[12] / 339	48.1	248[12] / 339	48.1	...	...	...	...
1949	41.5	6.48	67.72	11.66	347	52.5	358	54.2	...	...	...	...

See p. 838 for footnotes

K 1 National Accounts Totals

1900–1949

	Czechoslovakia (in thousand million korunas at market price)				Denmark (in million krone at market price)				Finland (in million new markkaa at market price)			
	Current Prices		Constant Prices		Current Prices		Constant Prices		Current Prices		Constant Prices	
	NMP[17]	CF[4]	GPD/NMP[17]	CF[4]	GNP	CF[1]	GNP	CF[1]	NNP[18]	CF[4]	NNP[18]	CF[4]
			1929 prices				1929 prices				1929 prices	
1900	...	...	...	...	1,342	186	2,591	340	...	...	...	...
1901	...	...	...	...	1,373	170	2,605	333	...	...	...	...
1902	...	...	...	...	1,383	189	2,638	366	...	...	...	...
1903	...	...	...	...	1,455	193	2,786	369	...	...	...	...
1904	...	...	...	...	1,485	193	2,909	369	...	...	...	...
1905	...	...	...	...	1,546	186	2,980	357	...	...	...	...
1906	...	...	...	...	1,677	239	3,161	436	...	...	...	...
1907	...	...	...	...	1,759	251	3,328	435	...	...	...	...
1908	...	...	...	...	1,723	223	3,219	395	...	...	...	...
1909	...	...	...	...	1,763	213	3,273	379	...	...	...	...
1910	...	...	...	...	1,815	213	3,351	375	...	...	...	...
1911	...	...	...	...	1,930	221	3,555	375	...	...	...	...
1912	...	...	...	...	2,128	252	3,877	408	...	...	...	...
1913	...	...	48.2	...	2,265	276	4,044	443	...	...	...	...
1914	...	...	...	...	2,276	278	3,904	428	...	...	...	...
1915	...	...	...	...	...	...	...	...	...	...	...	...
1916	...	...	...	...	...	...	...	...	...	...	...	...
1917	...	...	...	...	...	...	...	...	...	...	...	...
1918	...	...	...	...	...	...	...	...	...	...	...	...
1919	...	...	...	...	...	...	...	...	...	...	...	...
1920	...	...	43.6	4.4	...	...	...	...	...	...	...	...
1921	...	...	47.1	3.8	6,248	633	4,067	363	...	...	...	...
1922	...	...	45.8	4.2	5,351	541	4,462	431	...	...	...	...
1923	...	...	49.7	4.5	5,926	598	5,081	466	...	...	...	...
1924	...	...	54.8	5.5	6,380	675	5,054	492	...	...	...	...
1925	...	...	61.3	6.5	6.009	609	4,883	466	...	...	...	...
1926	...	...	61.0	7.1	5,308	508	5,035	486	192	...	196	...
1927	...	...	65.6	7.7	5,109	480	5,208	478	214	...	213	...
1928	...	...	71.4	9.6	5,268	506	5,402	514	226	...	219	...
1929	...	...	73.4	10.3	5,556	600	5,556	600	216	...	216	...
1930	...	...	70.9	9.9	5,565	750	5,871	746	200	...	213	...
1931	...	...	68.5	9.7	5,283	706	6,005	724	174	...	200	...
1932	...	...	65.8	8.4	4,934	510	5,737	538	173	...	202	...
1933	...	...	63.0	6.9	5,359	614	5,844	592	183	...	219	...
1934	...	...	60.6	6.8	5,889	734	6,144	718	212	...	251	...
1935	...	...	60.0	7.3	6,148	765	6,170	731	224	...	259	...
1936	...	...	64.9	8.2	6,543	780	6,431	732	250	...	278	...
1937	...	...	72.2	8.8	6,898	837	6,563	722	303	...	306	...
1938	...	...	...	...	7,273[46]	898[46]	6,592	752	296	...	294	...
1939	...	...	...	...	7,895.	1,033	7,022	854	299	...	293	...
1940	...	...	...	...	7,648	798	5,542	540	336	...	243	...
1941	...	...	...	...	8,661	908	5,016	570	408	...	264	...
1942	...	...	...	...	9,993	1,109	5,267	638	499	...	278	...
1943	...	...	...	...	10,245	1,157	5,273	621	640	...	302	...
1944	...	...	...	...	10,641	905	5,377	476	703	...	298	...
1945	...	...	...	...	12,415	921	5,899	456	989	...	254	...
1946	...	...	...	...	15,358	1,648	7,653	721	1,555	...	284	...
1947	...	...	...	...	16,375[10]	2,137[10]	7,689[10]	886[10]	2,230	...	303	...
			April 1955 prices		17,292	3,635	1955 prices					
							24,093	5,287				
1948	59.1	11.7	70.2	5.2	18,843	4,454	25,184	6,038	3,055	944	325	...
1949	74.9	16.1	77.2	...	20,201	4,674	26,181	6,105	3,212	...	330	...

See p. 838 for footnotes

K 1 **National Accounts Totals**

1900–1949

	France[19] (in million francs at market prices)				Germany (in million marks at market prices)				East Germany (in million marks at market prices)	
	Current Prices		Constant Prices		Current Prices		Constant Prices		Current Prices	
	GNP	CF[4]	NNP/GNP[20]	CF[4]	NNP	CF[2]	NNP	CF[2]	NMP	CF[1]
			1938 prices				1913 prices			
1900	...	...	...	...	32,448	5,100	36,466	5,330	...	...
1901	...	...	2,400	...	31,617	3,890	36,197	4,470	...	...
1902	...	...	2,400	...	31,928	3,520	36,918	4,060	...	...
1903	...	...	2,470	...	34,402	4,960	40,132	5,890	...	...
1904	...	...	2,670	...	36,284	5,630	42,263	6,630	...	...
1905	...	...	2,640	...	38,878	6,050	43,346	6,710	...	...
1906	...	...	2,700	...	40,643	6,680	44,299	7,040	...	...
1907	...	...	2,770	...	42,976	7,610	46,181	7,740	...	...
1908	...	...	2,790	...	42,441	5,610	46,410	6,020	...	...
1909	...	...	2,880	...	44,358	6,040	47,512	6,700	...	...
1910	...	...	2,880	...	45,785	6,100	47,457	6,610	...	...
1911	...	...	3,000	...	48,106	7,270	49,648	7,830	...	...
1912	...	...	3,280	...	51,563	8,570	51,914	8,590	...	...
1913	...	...	3,280	...	52,440	8,170	52,440	8,170	...	...
1914	...	...	...	...	...	...	...	...	...	...
1915	...	...	...	...	...	...	...	...	...	...
1916	...	...	...	...	...	...	...	...	...	...
1917	...	...	...	...	...	...	...	...	...	...
1918	...	...	...	...	...	...	...	...	...	...
1919	...	...	...	...	...	...	...	...	...	...
1920	...	...	2,700	... ...	...	...	...	...	...	...
1921	...	...	2,500	...	...	...	...	...	...	...
1922	...	...	3,040	...	...	...	...	...	...	...
1923	...	...	3,290	...	...	...	...	...	...	...
1924	...	...	3,810	...	...	...	...	...	...	...
1925	...	...	3,840	...	67,346	8,620	46,897	5,380	...	...
1926	...	...	4,010	...	65,472	4,280	46,587	3,300	...	...
1927	...	...	3,870	...	80,466	12,240	53,108	8,070	...	...
1928	...	...	4,100	...	83,964	10,980	53,950	6,880	...	...
1929	...	...	4,530	...	79,491	5,770	51,694	3,550	...	...
1930	...	...	4,470	...	71,862	2,630	49,289	2,790	...	...
1931	...	...	4,280	...	58,484	−3,150	43,913	−1,360	...	...
1932	...	...	3,980	...	50,782	−2,060	41,760	−680	...	...
1933	...	...	4,000	...	56,764	1,940	47,375	2,310	...	...
1934	...	...	3,920	...	64,604	4,730	52,102	3,250	...	...
1935	...	...	3,750	...	72,015	7,510	58,658[3] 60,352	5,790	...	...
1936	...	...	3,710	...	78,941	9,000	66,226	7,260	...	...
1937	...	...	3,840	...	87,862	13,580	73,167	11,200	...	...
1938	...[21]	...[21]	3,800[21]	...[21]	97,990	14,070	81,335	11,950	...	...
1939	...	...	4,070	...	...	...	...	...	...	...
1940	...	...	3,360	...	...	...	...	...	...	...
1941	...	...	2,660	...	...	...	...	...	...	...
1942	...	...	2,380	...	...	...	...	...	...	...
1943	...	...	2,260	...	...	...	...	...	...	...
1944	...	...	1,910	...	...	...	...	...	...	...
1945	...	...	2,070	...	...	...	...	...	...	...
1946	...	...	3,150	...	...	...	...	...	...	...
1947	...	...	3,410	...	...	...	...	...	...	...
1948	...	...	3,660	...	...	...	...	...	...	...
1949			4,140							
	in hundred thousand million francs[20]									
			1963 prices							
	88.1	21.4	206.9	49.7	...	...	...	...	22,320	2,862

See p. 838 for footnotes

K 1 National Accounts Totals

1900–1949

	Greece (in thousand million drachmae at market prices)				Hungary[23] (in million crowns/pengos)				Southern Ireland (in million pounds at market prices)
	Current Prices		Constant Prices		Current Prices		Constant Prices		Current Prices
	NNP/GDP[22]	CF[4]	NNP/GNP[22]	CF[4]	NNP/NMP[24]	CF[25]	NNP/NMP[24]	CF[25]	NNP/GNP[29]
			1929 prices				1938/9 prices	1937 prices	
1900	...	...	...	...	1,825[26]	...	2,913[26]	...	...
1901	...	...	...	...	...	...	...	...	...
1902	...	...	...	...	...	...	...	...	...
1903	...	...	...	...	...	...	...	...	...
1904	...	...	...	...	...	...	...	...	...
1905	...	...	...	...	...	...	...	...	...
1906	...	...	...	...	...	...	...	...	...
1907	...	...	...	...	...	...	...	...	...
1908	...	...	...	...	...	...	...	...	...
1909	...	...	...	...	...	...	...	...	...
1910	...	...	...	...	...	...	...	...	...
1911	...	...	...	...	...	...	million pengos		...
1912	...	...	...	...	3,328[26]	...	3,900[26]	...	...
1913	...	...	...	...	...	...	...	...	...
1914	...	...	...	...	...	...	...	...	...
1915	...	...	...	...	...	...	...	...	...
1916	...	...	...	...	...	...	...	...	...
1917	...	...	...	...	...	...	...	...	...
1918	...	...	...	...	...	...	...	...	...
1919	...	...	...	...	...	...	...	...	...
					in million pengos		in million pengos		
1920	...	...	...	...	...	...	...	...	...
1921	...	...	...	...	4,258[27]	...	3,300	...	...
1922	...	...	...	...	...	...	...	...	...
1923	...	...	...	...	...	...	...	...	...
1924	...	...	...	...	...	...	...	...	...
1925	...	...	...	...	4,966	358	3,842	311	...
1926	...	...	...	...	5,786	479	4,596	424	...
1927	44	...	47	...	5,567	624	4,402	566	...
1928	46	...	47	...	5,853	808	4,596	703	...
1929	45	...	45	...	6,435	862	4,999	740	161.4
1930	43	...	49	...	6,304	643	5,164	560	...
1931	39	...	45	...	5,649	484	5,050	438	146.9
1932	44	...	48	...	4,900	418	4,807	403	...
1933	49	...	49	...	4,512	308	4,678	324	134.5
1934	53	...	52	...	4,434	238	5,101	258	...
1935	55	...	54	...	4,577	235	5,136	255	...
1936	59	...	56	...	4,935	286	5,393	309	154.0[29]
1937	68	...	61	...	5,371	389	5,755	402	183.7
1938	67	...	59	...	5,576	455	5,626	449	...
1939	67	...	60	...	5,913	510	5,913	496	...
1940	...	...	...	...	6,782	579	6,360	546	...
1941	...	...	...	...	7,515	...	5,927	...	...
1942	...	...	...	...	9,165	...	5,961	...	...
1943	...	...	...	...	11,490	...	6,260	...	...
1944	...	...	...	...	...	...	...	...	...
						in million forints			
1945	...	...	...	...	...	...	...	...	...
1946	6,059	...	39	...	...	...	...	...	...
1947	9,821	...	52	...	14,467[28]	...	3,604	...	340.3
1948	15,273[22]	...	57[22]	...	19,855[28]	1,865[28]	4,729	351	363.8
	in million new drachmae								
	20,932	2,451	1958 prices						
			48,755	5,735					
1949	27,568	5,285	57,339	10,194	28,305[28]	4,535[28]	5,892	846	385.3

See p. 838 for footnotes

K 1 National Accounts Totals

1900–1949

	Italy (in million lire at market prices)				Netherlands (in million guilders at market prices)		
	Current Prices		Constant Prices		Current Prices		Constant Prices
	GNP	CF[4]	GNP[5]	CF[5]	NNP/GNP[30]	CF[31]	NNP/GNP[30]
			1938 prices				1963 prices
1900	14,978	2,260	73,149	9,049	1,796	...	8,980
1901	15,447	1,594	77,949	11,504	1,863	...	8,468
1902	14,891	1,856	76,307	8,282	1,901	...	9,052
1903	16,134	1,839	79,851	10,417	1,952	...	9,295
1904	16,000	1,889	79,579	9,284	1,993	...	9,059
1905	16,918	2,130	83,193	10,014	2,058	...	9,355
1906	18,372	3,668	84,637	10,790	2,156	...	9,800
1907	20,637	2,942	92,926	17,449	2,195	...	9,977
1908	19,865	3,754	90,985	13,804	2,255	...	10,250
1909	21,530	2,697	97,323	18,347	2,322	...	10,555
1910	21,580	2,697	90,407	13,048	2,408	...	10,470
1911	23,619	3,644	97,483	16,999	2,511	...	10,463
1912	24,850	3,715	99,738	16,762	2,688	...	11,200
1913	25,656	3,987	101,948	18,434	2,807	...	11,696
1914	24,044	2,568	99,238	11,905	2,730	...	11,375
1915	28,137	1,361	105,584	5,284	3,227	...	11,952
1916	40,479	556	113,498	1,443	3,692	...	12,307
1917	56,389	1,586	114,803	1,563	3,666	...	11,456
1918	68,893	2,047	109,070	2,448	4,100	...	10,789
1919	81,276	5,545	104,646	6,161	5,530	...	13,488
		thousand million lire					
1920	123.9	15.0	110.8	13.3	6,285	...	13,663
1921	116.1	10.6	106.7	9.1	5,780	327	14,821
1922	124.1	15.5	113.0	13.9	5,380	106	14,944
1923	135.5	21.0	118.3	18.3	5,304	141	15,600
1924	143.0	24.4	118.3	19.4	5,542	301	16,301
1925	179.6	32.7	125.8	23.7	5,724	317	16,835
1926	188.8	30.3	126.8	21.1	5,855	390	17,742
1927	162.2	21.8	125.5	17.9	5,965	294	18,646
1928	164.2	29.6	137.5	27.0	6,358	431	19,267
1929	163.3	27.7	139.5	26.8	6,496	543	19,685
1930	143.9	19.5	130.0	19.3	6,237	195	20,119
1931	124.4	16.4	127.2	16.9	5,490	–197	18,931
1932	117.0	16.4	132.3	19.5	4,928	–267	18,252
1933	109.5	14.4	133.2	17.7	4,779	–117	17,700
1934	108.9	15.3	132.5	19.2	4,754	–107	17,607
1935	121.2	23.3	146.1	29.2	4,682	–114	18,008
1936	126.6	21.7	142.5	25.2	4,807	–56	18,488
1937	156.7	30.3	155.1	32.2	5,310	224	19,666
1938	165.9	28.7	153.7	28.7	5,395	60	19,981
1939	181.2	34.9	162.7	34.1	5,743	6	20,511
1940	209.7	32.1	156.1	25.9	...	...	...
1941	239.6	31.2	150.5	23.5	...	...	...
1942	296.7	26.2	144.4	18.2	...	...	...
1943	398.1	18.0	129.8	11.2	...	...	...
1944	739.2	8.1	99.5	8.0	...	...	...
1945	1,402	41.3	83.2	6.1	...	...	...
1946	3,254	630	126.3	24.7	...	...	...
1947	6,995	1,617	152.5	37.1	...	...	...
1948	8,014	1,342	152.7	26.1	13,442[30]	1,867[31]	25,362[30]
					15,700	3,741	29,622
1949	8,589	1,426	162.9	27.9	17,500	4,084	30,702

See p. 838 for footnotes

K 1 National Accounts Totals

1900–1949

	Norway (in million kroner at market prices)				Poland (in thousand million zlotys at market prices)		Russia (in thousand million rubels)			
	Current Prices		Constant Prices		Constant Prices		Current Prices		Constant Prices	
	GDP	CF[4]	GDP	CF[4]	NMP	CF	GNP/NMP[32]	CF[33]	GNP/NMP[32]	CF[33]
			1910 prices							
1900	1,115	208	1,152	206	...	...	...	...	...	...
1901	1,101	194	1,181	208	...	...	...	...	...	...
1902	1,088	183	1,199	193	...	...	...	...	...	...
1903	1,081	172	1,192	185	...	...	...	...	...	...
1904	1,081	182	1,194	196	...	...	...	...	...	...
1905	1,105	174	1,203	183	...	...	...	...	...	...
1906	1,187	206	1,253	208	...	...	...	...	...	...
1907	1,265	243	1,307	238	...	...	...	...	...	...
1908	1,299	248	1,349	242	...	...	...	...	...	...
1909	1,316	228	1,378	232	...	...	...	...	...	...
1910	1,435	263	1,435	263	...	...	...	...	...	...
1911	1,530	317	1,491	305	...	...	...	...	...	...
1912	1,680	359	1,564	336	...	...	...	...	...	...
1913	1,857	384	1,649	349	...	...	...	...	...	...
1914	1,919	396	1,683	349	...	...	...	...	...	...
1915	2,594	513	1,757	372	...	...	...	...	...	...
1916	3,871	811	1,825	378	...	...	...	...	...	...
1917	4,489	1,086	1,659	335	...	...	...	...	...	...
1918	5,048	792	1,592	217	...	...	...	...	...	...
1919	6,195	2,218	1,865	606	...	...	...	...	...	...
1920	7,500	2,297	1,987	505	...	...	...	...	...	...
1921	5,448	1,290	1,795	330	...	...	...	...	...	...
1922	4,980	961	1,987	336	...	...	...	...	...	...
1923	4,997	961	2,041	371	...	...	...	...	...	...
1924	5,576	1,020	2,040	383	...	...	...	...	...	...
1925	5,633	1,052	2,166	417	...	...	...	...	...	...
1926	4,646	797	2,198	382	...	...	...	...	...	...
1927	4,218	685	2,281	387	...	...			1937 prices	
1928	4,221	793	2,382	476	...	...	14.2	4.95	123.7	10.4
1929	4,345	847	2,607	527	...	...	15.9	6.40	127.0	3.7
			1938 prices							
1930	4,377	1,005	4,746	79	...	...	18.8	9.26	134.5	14.0
1931	3,842	741	4,368	961	...	...	27.0	14.16	137.2	19.7
1932	3,862	649	4,595	840	...	...	49.4	17.79	135.7	12.8
1933	3,866	654	4,699	849	...	...	77.0	15.59	141.3	22.6
1934	4,068	771	4,870	995	...	...	99.8	20.27	155.2	29.1
1935	4,362	923	5,114	1,154	...	...	148.6	25.06	178.6	46.8
1936	4,850	1,081	5,459	1,283	...	...	189.7	34.23	192.8	35.7
1937	5,581	1,414	5,697	1,483	...	...	212.3	32.51	212.3	44.9
1938	5,827	1,473	5,827	1,473	...	...	216.1	34.34	216.1	39.9
1939	6,253	1,600	6,110	1,535	...	...	234.1	36.64	229.5	35.7
1940	...	...	...	...	...	...	315.6	39.73	250.5	30.8
1941	...	...	...	...	...	...	...	30.50	...	...
1942	...	...	...	...	...	...	...	18.26	...	...
1943	...	...	...	...	...	...	...	20.48	...	...
1944	...	...	...	...	...	...	...	34.28	...	25.6
			1955 prices		1961 prices					
1945	...	...	...	...	...	...	334.3	40.78	199.0	26.6
1946	10,778	3,347	16,533	5,814	...	15.5	470	50.20	198.4	30.0
1947	12,687	4,721	18,797	7,678	104	19.6	763	58.83	220.5	45.3
1948	13,904	5,078	20,115	7,615	136	23.9	752	74.21	250.7	46.4
1949	14,917	5,660	20,625	7,989	159	28.0	744	122.20	277.7	67.6

See p. 838 for footnotes

K 1 National Accounts Totals

1900–1949

	Spain (in million pesetas at market prices)				Sweden (in million kronor at market prices)				Switzerland (in million francs at market prices)	
	Current Prices		Constant Prices		Current Prices		Constant Prices		Current Prices	Constant Prices
	NNP[34]	CF[4]	NNP[34]	CF[4]	GDP	CF[6]	GDP	CF[6]	NNP	NNP
			1929 prices				1913 prices			1938 prices
1900	...	...	...	...	2,261	300	2,569	333	...	...
1901	...	...	...	...	2,260	262	2,628	316	...	...
1902	...	...	...	...	2,210	257	2,540	316	...	...
1903	...	...	...	...	2,474	316	2,811	376	...	...
1904	...	...	...	...	2,485	332	2,856	399	...	...
1905	...	...	...	...	2,543	329	2,890	380	...	...
1906	9,188	...	15,840	...	2,911	386	3,234	430	...	...
1907	9,689	...	16,026	...	3,077	411	3,238	426	...	...
1908	9,850	...	16,755	...	3,131	357	3,262	400	...	...
1909	9,823	...	16,935	...	3,166	324	3,333	354	...	...
1910	9,943	...	16,983	...	3,366	366	3,543	387	...	...
1911	10,486	...	18,571	...	3,464	401	3,685	420	...	...
1912	10,210	...	17,224	...	3,603	418	3,603	431	...	...
1913	10,600	...	17,776	...	4,128	509	4,128	508	3,960	5,390
1914	10,813	...	18,425	...	4,108	524	4,028	488	...	...
1915	12,163	...	17,247	...	4,891	518	4,180	411	...	...
1916	15,810	...	18,798	...	6,227	666	4,718	391	...	...
1917	19,356	...	19,607	...	7,150	878	4,307	364	...	...
1918	23,312	...	19,070	...	9,338	1,133	4,025	401	...	...
1919	24,797	...	20,358	...	11,033	1,437	4,117	449	...	...
1920	29,038	...	21,807	...	12,651	1,672	4,686	480	...	...
1921	22,975	...	20,884	...	9,539	1,177	4,129	498	...	...
1922	20,982	...	20,394	...	7,315	896	3,912	493	...	...
1923	21,892	...	21,476	...	7,372	944	4,237	504	...	...
1924	23,009	...	21,214	...	7,930	1,035	4,558	557	8,150	6,580
1925	25,013	...	22,662	...	8,840	1,152	4,995	632	...	...
1926	23,136	...	22,188	...	8,900	1,144	5,205	642	...	...
1927	23,804	...	23,781	...	9,206	1,167	5,447	682	...	...
1928	21,891	...	22,570	...	9,286	1,296	5,463	778	...	...
1929	25,213	...	25,213	...	9,945	1,403	5,920	842	10,000	8,470
1930	24,003	...	24,104	...	9,977	1,596	6,121	973	9,950	8,560
1931	24,204	...	24,028	...	8,748	1,320	5,537	837	9,170	8,310
1932	25,566	...	25,742	...	8,360	1,074	5,394	650	8,140	8,060
1933	22,011	...	23,196	...	8,249	1,014	5,463	671	8,190	8,510
1934	25,465	...	26,146	...	9,112	1,272	5,995	819	8,110	8,560
1935	24,759	...	25,289	...	9,752	1,608	6,292	1,031	8,040	8,560
1936	...	...	...	...	10,587	1,780	6,743	1,126	8,020	8,580
1937	...	...	...	...	11,579	2,026	7,192	998	8,780	8,780
1938	...	...	...	...	12,232	2,321	7,458	1,243	8,870	8,870
	thousand million pesetas									
1939	27.1	...	18.8	...	13,296	2,646	7,868	1,468	9,040	8,950
1940	36.5	...	21.2	...	14,798	2,503	7,789	1,224	9,690	8,780
1941	44.2	...	21.7	...	16,511	2,597	7,644	1,207	10,640	8,400
1942	53.6	...	23.9	...	17,795	3,277	7,670	1,399	11,490	8,170
1943	58.8	...	23.5	...	19,306	3,753	8,181	1,553	12,440	8,410
1944	66.7	...	24.8	...	20,213	3,964	8,638	1,641	12,960	8,560
1945	65.5	...	22.0	...	21,940	3,662	9,416	1,409	13,860	9,100
1946	93.9	...	26.2	...	24,328	4,841	10,396	1,945	15,450	10,210
1947	107.5	...	25.6	...	26,432	5,768	11,013	2,216	17,390	11,000
1948	114.0	...	25.3	...	29,264	5,698	11,613	2,143	18,100	11,090
1949	119.0	...	24.7	...	30,972	5,909	12,099	2,177	17,530	10,840

See p. 838 for footnotes

K 1 **National Accounts Totals**

1900–1949

	United Kingdom[8] (in million pounds at market prices)				Yugoslavia (in million dinars at market prices)			
	Current Prices		Constant Prices		Current Prices		Constant Prices	
	GNP	CF[6]	GNP	CF[6]	NMP	CF[4]	GDP/NMP[35]	CF[36]
			1900 prices				1953 prices	
1900	2,054	199	2,032	199	...	...	...	...
1901	2,125	197	2,113	207	...	...	...	...
1902	2,110	197	2,126	217	...	...	...	...
1903	2,109	198	2,127	222	...	...	...	...
1904	2,128	187	2,140	210	...	...	...	...
1905	2,182	177	2,184	202	...	...	...	...
1906	2,248	175	2,236	194	...	...	...	...
1907	2,300	150	2,243	162	...	...	...	...
1908	2,230	128	2,180	142	...	...	...	...
1909	2,301	132	2,252	146	...	...	...	...
1910	2,403	136	2,328	148	...	...	...	...
1911	2,493	132	2,389	141	...	...	...	...
1912	2,565	136	2,388	138	...	...	...	...
1913	2,717	160	2,514	157				
			1938 prices					
			4,795	270				
1914	2,743	160	4,823	274	...	...	...	...
1915	3,304	130	5,237	182	...	...	...	...
1916	3,788	115	5,219	130	...	...	...	...
1917	4,732	148	5,215	144	...	...	...	...
1918	5,418	161	5,118	143	...	...	...	...
1919	5,751	226	4,652	172	...	...	...	...
1920	6,484[8]	500[8]	4,346[8]	295[8]	...	...	595	111
	6,228	482	4,160	284				
1921	5,312	458	3,953	326	...	...	610	121
1922	4,756	381	4,094	300	...	...	628	114
1923	4,561	334	4,236	308	...	...	659	106
1924	4,615	374	4,367	359	...	...	703	123
1925	4,876	420	4,602	410	...	...	737	125
1926	4,633	401	4,413	397	...	...	785	121
1927	4,852	426	4,719	442	...	...	777	142
1928	4,899	420	4,795	438	...	...	840	141
1929	4,970	442	4,910	461	...	...	882	146
1930	4,900	435	4,905	463	...	...	868	111
1931	4,522	408	4,653	454	...	...	846	83
1932	4,403	347	4,639	396	...	...	777	79
1933	4,413	357	4,727	409	...	...	798	83
1934	4,680	427	5,043	498	...	...	825	85
1935	4,902	456	5,239	518	...	...	815	112
1936	5,100	517	5,400	565	...	...	910	130
1937	5,494	574	5,603	584	...	...	926	159
1938	5,764	592	5,764	592	...	...	995	175
1939	6,118	540	5,948	530	...	...	1,047	176[36]
1940	7,681	520	6,739	460	...	...	...	...
1941	8,971	480	7,112	370	...	...	...	...
1942	9,691	450	7,155	320	...	...	...	...
1943	10,298	360	7,274	220	...	...	...	...
1944	10,352	300	6,940	170	...	...	...	...
1945	9,911	350	6,511	190	...	...	...	...
1946	10,044	925	6,473	480	...	...	...	...
1947	10,805	1,199	6,336	560	133	75	939[35]	...
							1960 prices	
			6,521	600			1,089	620
1948	11,959	1,422	1963 prices		190	104	1,319	722
			20,309	2,205				
1949	12,605	1,577	20,880	2,497	233	129	1,429	791

See p. 838 for footnotes

K 1 National Accounts Totals

1950–1975

	Austria (in thousand million schillings at market prices)				Belgium (in thousand million francs at market prices)				Bulgaria (in million new leva at market prices)	
	Current Prices		Constant Prices		Current Prices		Constant Prices			
	GNP	CF[4]	GNP	CF[4]	GDP/GNP[12]	CF	GNP	CF	NNP/NMP[14]	CF[15]
			1954 prices				1948 prices			
1950	51.91	9.21	76.11	14.57	354	60.2	369	62.8	...	...
1951	69.08	13.66	81.31	17.63	408	63.1	388	60.0	...	...
1952	80.00	15.67	81.34	17.27	429	68.7	405	64.9	2,443	...
1953	82.52	14.91	84.94	15.06	433[12]	69.4[13]	410[12]	65.7[13]		
					411	68.4	1970 prices		2,780	200
							640	117		
1954	93.59	19.00	93.59	19.00	428	76.0	667	131	2,708	344
			1964 prices							
			130.45	24.53						
1955	107.15	23.95	144.89	30.78	457	77.8	700	131	2,820	481
1956	119.19	25.78	154.84	31.30	487	92.1	722	149	2,745	369
1957	131.95	29.79	164.32	35.42	517	97.7	736	150	3,209	380
1958	137.42	30.95	170.34	35.97	521	86.4	734	130	3,486	366
1959	146.32	34.30	175.17	39.49	537	97.1	755	148	4,220	597
1960	163.25	40.66	189.61	45.70	571	108	797	163	4,489	642
1961	180.76	47.35	200.14	51.45	606	126	835	186	4,716	687
1962	192.35	49.57	205.38	52.86	648	135	879	194	5,158	697
1963	207.32	53.91	213.91	54.68	696	144	917	195	5,676	986
1964	227.14	59.92	227.14	59.92	778	183	981	235	6,204	1,226
1965	247.43	67.59	234.94	63.82	849	190	1,019	235	6,636	983
1966	267.57	74.91	246.68	69.44	913	213	1,050	255	7,274	1,188
1967	283.16	76.24	252.56	69.64	978	224	1,092	257	7,853	1,623
1968	302.76	78.37	263.78	72.54	1,046	229	1,139	259	8,556	1,612
1969	331.73	82.60	279.22	73.05	1,160	264	1,212	285	9,350	2,041
1970	371.24	97.13	300.89	81.84	1,292	308	1,292	308	10,527	1,948
1971	412.70	115.85	316.78	92.03	1,415	326	1,345	301	10,411	1,379
1972	469.40	141.81	336.90	103.88	1,583	338	1,423	301	11,242	1,774
1973	533.27	148.65	356.41	106.82	1,798	400	1,513	337	12,148	...
1974	613.46	172.77	371.12	108.07	2,116	515	1,579	372	13,093	...
1975	654.42	174.49	363.73	101.64	2,336	497	1,553	315	14,289	...

See p. 838 for footnotes

K 1 National Accounts Totals

1950–1975

	Czechoslovakia (in thousand million koruna at market prices)				Denmark (in million kroner at market prices)				Finland (in million new markkaa at market prices)			
	Current Prices		Constant Prices		Current Prices		Constant Prices		Current Prices		Constant Prices	
	NMP	CF[4]	NMP	CF[4]	GNP	CF[1]	GNP	CF[1]	NNP/GDP[18]	CF[4]	NNP/GDP[18]	CF[4]
			April 1955 prices								1929 prices	
1950	85.4	14.0	85.0	4.9	23,132	5,885	28,343	7,316	4,130[18]	1,264	387[18]	...
									5,424		1970 prices	
											16,166	3,622
1951	103	22.5	93.1	10.9	23,403	5,828	28,281	6,214	7,901	1,867	17,672	4,699
1952	116	25.1	103	15.5	24,985	6,197	28,628	6,162	8,181	2,168	18,280	5,242
1953	129	31.6	110	18.0	26,536	7,083	30,316	7,288	8,074	1,798	18,303	4,382
1954	123	19.8	114	10.4	27,618	7,385	31,189	7,605	8,969	2,338	19,960	5,496
1955	134	25.6	125	17.6	28,706	6,971	31,269	6,971	9,922	2,685	21,467	6,111
1956	133	16.4	132	16.8	30,634	7,974	31,880	7,630	11,031	3,005	21,893	6,374
1957	141	21.3	142	21.0	32,668	8,939	33,504	8,300	12,025	3,136	22,226	6,269
1958	149	25.8	153	28.5	33,981	8,571	34,381	7,821	12,954	3,302	22,209	6,041
1959	152	26.7	163	32.2	37,435	11,012	36,592	10,066	14,079	3,750	23,819	6,767
			176	33.6								
			April 1960 prices									
1960	163	27.8	162	29.6	40,523	12,706	38,912	11,380	15,824	4,755	26,184	8,280
1961	172	34.7	173	37.3	45,375	13,815	41,200	11,592	17,625	5,513	28,292	9,120
1962	175	31.6	175	34.5	50,768	16,172	43,472	13,076	18,856	5,526	29,504	8,916
1963	173	22.3	172	25.0	53,476	15,307	43,672	11,502	20,541	5,563	30,239	8,543
1964	170	17.0	173	23.7	61,071	19,759	47,574	14,569	23,553	6,960	32,226	10,309
1965	174	15.4	179	23.7	68,291	22,406	49,857	15,532	25,828	7,579	33,884	11,036
1966	196	24.4	195	31.3	74,740	23,644	51,032	15,373	27,777	8,166	34,687	10,914
			Jan. 1967 prices									
			219	43.5								
1967	234	50.7	231	46.0	81,868	25,471	53,010	15,632	30,109	8,345	35,605	10,583
1968	258	58.6	248	50.5	89,318	27,449	55,278	16,180	34,148	9,223	36,458	9,866
1969	294	70.9	266	54.1	101,113	32,369	59,803	18,180	39,013	11,465	40,263	11,795
1970	312	80.8	281	63.1	112,591	36,578	61,450	19,289	43,592	14,375	43,592	14,375
1971	328	79.7	296	62.7	123,986	39,144	63,727	19,254	47,661	15,752	44,641	14,516
1972	346	85.0	313	67.5	139,457	43,983	66,475	19,747	54,909	16,582	47,773	13,993
1973	363	94.1	330	75.8	159,011	54,092	68,243	22,475	66,746	22,278	50,871	15,601
1974	390	109	349	86.6	182,426	61,161	69,182	21,484	84,174	32,458	53,038	17,373
1975	410	118	371	94.6	203,502	58,034	68,274	16,675	98,023	36,265	53,091	17,928

See p. 838 for footnotes

K 1 National Accounts Totals

1950–1975

	France[1 9] (in hundred thousand million francs at market prices)				West Germany[39 40] (in thousand million marks at market prices)				East Germany (in million marks at market prices)	
	Current Prices		Constant Prices		Current Prices		Constant Prices		Current Prices	
	GNP	CF[4]	GNP[20]	CF[4]	GNP	CF[4]	GNP	CF[4]	NMP	CF[1]
			1963 prices				1954 prices			
1950	101.7	23.9	221.9	51.8	97.9	21.8	112.9	25.7	29,109[41]	3,602[41]
1951	124.6	28.5	234.7	51.3	119.5	26.0	125.0	26.4	35,252	4,547
1952	146.7	32.9	242.8	50.7	136.6	30.7	135.4	29.3	40,130	5,809
1953	153.0	31.8	249.0	48.6	147.1	31.0	145.6	30.6	42,443	6,983
1954	162.0	34.9	259.4	53.8	157.9	35.6	157.9	35.6	46,063	7,138
1955	173.2	38.2	271.6	57.8	180.4	46.2	174.4	45.0	50,037[41]	8,127[41]
1956	192.6	46.0	287.8	66.3	198.8	48.8	186.4	46.3	52,288	10,219
1957	216.2	51.3	304.8	69.0	216.3	51.8	196.5	47.7	56,015	10,597
1958	248.7	60.7	313.5	74.8	231.5	54.1	206.8	48.7	62,011	12,088
	(in thousand million new francs)									
1959	272.6	61.5	323.1	71.8	250.9	62.2	221.0	55.1	67,488	14,590
1960	301.6	72.2	346.1	82.4	279.8[40]	75.0[40]	240.4[40]	64.6[40]	71,540	16,256
					303.0	81.4	254.9	68.2		
							1962 prices			
							329.2	89.7		
1961	328.3	78.5	364.7	86.9	331.4	90.7	345.0	95.8	72,670	16,454
1962	367.2	90.2	389.5	96.1	360.5	97.8	360.5	97.8	74,650	16,855
			1970 prices							
1963	412.0	102.0	552.5	132.7	382.1	101.2	370.7	98.2	77,260	17,247
1964	456.7	120.6	583.3	150.7	419.6	118.7	396.1	112.5	81,050	18,915
1965	489.8	125.6	614.5	153.2	458.2	132.2	417.5	121.8	84,760	20,707
1966	532.5	143.7	648.8	170.9	487.4	129.9	428.8	116.8	88,920	22,296
1967	574.8	153.8	680.5	178.7	493.7	113.1	429.2	102.6	93,750	24,444
1968	630.0	168.9	711.8	191.3	535.2	136.3	458.2	123.7	98,530	27,450
1969	723.5	203.8	763.9	217.6	597.7	162.2	494.2	141.0	103,650	31,802
1970	808.4	227.2	808.4	227.2	679.0	189.1	524.3	148.6	109,470	34,393
1971	898.6	243.8	851.1	233.0	756.0	203.4	541.0	147.5	114,450	34,698
1972	1,007.1	276.1	899.2	252.3	827.2	216.9	559.0	150.8	120,930	36,135
1973	1,144.0	319.4	951.5	272.9	920.1	232.6	588.1	155.5	127,650	38,886
1974	1,324.8	374.8	937.5	275.4	986.9	221.9	589.7	137.9	135,780	40,211
	1,271.8[38]	339.6[38]								
1975	1,437.1	322.2	...	...	1,030.3	211.1	569.2	127.4	142,370	42,678

See p. 838 for footnotes

K 1 National Accounts Totals

1950–1975

	Greece (in million new drachmae at market prices)				Hungary[23] (in million forints at market prices)			
	Current Prices		Constant Prices		Current Prices		Constant Prices	
	GDP	CF[4]	GDP	CF[4]	NMP	CF[25]	NMP	CF[25]
	[50]	[50]	1970 prices			[25]	1938/9 prices	1937 prices
1950	32,779	4,299	79,295	8,491	46.5[24]	5.1	45.4[24]	5.8[25]
1951	39,349	5,014	86,261	9,281	65.3	7.8	53.2	8.9
1952	41,242	1,974	86,884	4,572	73.8	9.6	52.2	10.7
1953	54,040	6,761	98,797	9,652	83.0	11.4	59.1	11.7
1954	62,412	6,935	101,879	8,989	85.6	9.5	56.7	9.5
							1959 prices	
1955	72,040	8,472	109,573	10,140	94.3	10.2	104.2	12.7
1956	83,101	11,921	118,920	14,209	82.5	8.9	83.1	8.9
1957	89,489	14,105	126,701	16,914	107.3[42]	9.2[42]	113.4[42]	10.7[42]
1958	93,792	17,162	132,572	25,506	110.0	14.2	119.6	16.3
1959	97,439	15,845	137,455	23,619	128.2	20.0	128.3	20.0
1960	105,167	19,563	143,387	28,307	142.0	24.3	139.5	25.2
							1968 prices	
							150.3	20.8
1961	118,637	23,731	159,374	34,548	148.9	21.8	157.6	19.2
1962	126,005	26,725	161,818	34,897	156.7	23.3	166.8	20.8
1963	140,714	30,026	178,220	39,350	165.1	28.5	176.1	25.8
1964	157,999	40,739	192,938	50,546	173.5	29.3	183.6	26.5
1965	179,765	47,284	211,060	57,840	170.5	26.4	184.6	26.7
1966	200,000	44,600	223,900	53,200	189.7	24.7	199.4	25.5
1967	216,097	48,240	236,207	55,342	207.5	31.9	215.6	33.2
1968	234,508	53,220	251,949	60,154	224.7	32.3	226.5	32.3
1969	266,460	69,042	276,891	75,395	253.1	37.4	244.2	36.3
1970	298,917	84,009	298,917	84,009	272.4	55.5	256.3	52.7
1971	330,300	92,248	320,198	89,273	294.3	57.7	273.2	54.0
1972	377,276	111,679	348,631	99,464	319.4	66.4	287.2	58.1
1973	484,151	166,375	374,160	121,591	354.0	72.8	308.8	60.9
1974	569,090	151,087	360,495	88,470	369.8	71.2	330.5	57.4
1975	673,430	166,833	382,799	88,020	395.9	100.0	348.8	77.8

See p. 838 for footnotes

K 1 National Accounts Totals

1950–1975

	Southern Ireland (In million pounds at market prices)				Italy (in thousand million lire at market prices)			
	Current Prices		Constant Prices		Current Prices		Constant Prices	
	GNP	CF[4]	GNP	CF[4]	GNP	CF[4]	GNP[5]	CF[4]
							1938 prices	
1950	387.9	69.5	...	...	9,475	1,650	173.3	31.9
1951	409.6	88.1	...	...	11,188	2,083	183.4[10]	35.8[10]
					11,934[10]	2,095[10]	1963 prices	
							16,511	2,537
1952	467.8	77.3	...	...	12,851	2,132	17,314	2,590
			1963 prices					
1953	513.8	88.1	663	112	14,144	2,445	18,711	2,984
1954	517.1	80.9	670	105	14,973	2,650	19,434	3,277
1955	539.7	101.6	683	126	16,484	3,184	20,745	3,883
1956	547.5	83.7	674	99	18,075	3,417	21,844	4,081
1957	568.7	73.6	678	83	19,620	3,801	23,133	4,388
1958	588.9	72.3	665	81	20,659	3,891	24,250	4,517
1959	626.2	107	692	118	21,874	4,233	25,938	4,960
1960	663	103	729	112	24,411	5,068	28,323	5,801
1961	714	119	766	125	27,113	5,760	30,763	6,443
1962	783	141	804	143	30,698	6,531	33,061	7,010
1963	838	161	838	161	35,631	7,496	35,631	7,496
1964	950	194	868	183	38,370	7,407	36,196	6,880
1965	1,020	227	893	206	42,253	7,215	38,594	6,576
1966	1,053	208	889	185	46,146	7,670	41,286	6,852
			1970 prices					
			1,376	262				
1967	1,150	216	1,446	264	50,997	8,957	44,475	7,740
1968	1,301	275	1,554	323	54,969	9,402	47,393	8,097
1969	1,494	370	1,632	399	61,431	11,152	51,191	8,987
1970	1,675	396	1,675	396	68,368	13,390	53,784	9,860
							1970 prices	
1971	1,909	449	1,751	409	74,291	13,225	69,515	12,307
1972	2,281	546	1,842	452	82,059	14,073	72,586	12,420
1973	2,744	729	1,936	539	100,603	20,151	78,047	14,875
1974	2,993	870	1,968	521	129,963	26,874	80,884	15,192
1975	3,685	804	1,954	394	142,050	22,842	77,179	11,364

See p. 838 for footnotes

K 1 National Accounts Totals

1950–1975

	Netherlands (in million guilders at market prices)				Norway (in million kroner at market prices)			
	Current Prices		Constant Prices		Current Prices		Constant Prices	
	GNP	CF[31]	GNP	CF[31]	GDP	CF[4]	GDP	CF[4]
			1963 prices				1955 prices	
1950	18,907[37]	5,003[37]	30,495[37]	...	16,425	5,815	21,646	7,806
1951	21,650	5,271	30,830	...	20,456	7,115	22,813	8,328
1952	22,688	3,910	31,511	...	22,564	7,832	23,626	8,357
1953	24,200	4,850	34,340	6,850	22,884	8,073	24,560	8,528
1954	27,000	6,678	36,000	...	24,806	9,140	25,790	9,315
1955	30,276	7,446	39,270[43]	9,250	26,376	9,675	26,376	9,675
1956	32,568	8,842	40,740	10,280	29,747	10,695	27,759	10,306
1957	35,364	9,954	41,900	10,880	31,775	11,465	28,618	10,406
1958	35,930	8,149	41,770	8,890	31,919	12,044	28,599	10,431
1959	38,443	9,181	43,820	10,080	33,946	12,084	29,831	10,304
1960	42,732	11,488	47,490	12,350	36,101	13,129	31,574	11,153
1961	45,288	12,179	49,100	12,870	39,245	14,755	33,503	12,239
							1961 prices	
1962	48,517	12,375	50,960	12,910	42,295	15,268	40,559	14,977
1963	52,858	12,862	52,860	12,860	45,661	16,538	42,669	15,980
1964	62,154	17,331	57,570	16,350	50,334	17,482	45,004	16,794
1965	69,368	18,366	60,680	16,570	55,828	20,190	47,325	18,369
1966	75,395	20,330	62,240	17,470	60,843	22,462	49,418	19,522
1967	82,997	22,068	65,840	18,610	66,902[48]	24,841[48]	52,196[48]	21,306[48]
					59,913	18,653	46,743	15,999
1968	90,404	25,587	70,180	20,400	63,903	17,094	48,216	13,877
			1970 prices				50,414	13,463
			100,970	27,970			1970 prices	
1969	103,822	27,329	109,431	29,410	69,447	17,661	76,625	19,101
1970	114,984	32,362	114,990	32,370	79,825	24,520	79,825	24,520
1971	129,850	35,200	119,860	32,120	89,098	28,513	83,434	27,265
1972	147,230	35,810	124,750	30,320	98,212	27,434	87,612	24,356
1973	169,210	41,730	132,630	33,400	111,411	33,830	91,089	27,799
1974	188,130	44,640	135,910	37,300	128,934	44,319	95,948	32,436
1975	204,270	42,160	132,950	34,810	147,934	53,167	99,113	34,685

See p. 838 for footnotes

K 1 National Accounts Totals

1950–1975

	Poland (in thousand million zlotys at market prices)				Portugal (in thousand million escudos at market prices)			
	Current Prices		Constant Prices		Current Prices		Constant Prices	
	NMP	CF	NMP	CF	GDP	CF[4]	GDP	CF[4]
			1961 prices					
1950	183.0	...	183	38.6	40.2	...	...	...
1951	196.7	...	198	43.2	...	...	...	...
1952	209.0	...	209	51.4	...	...	...	...
							1970 prices	
1953	230.7	...	231	59.4	48.9	7.9	71.9	13.6
1954	255.1	49.1	255	63.2	50.2	7.5	74.8	12.7
1955	223.1	52.6	277	65.7	53.1	7.2	77.9	9.4
1956	252.1	51.4	297	68.6	57.1	7.9	81.1	10.9
1957	301.4	74.2	328	73.5	59.7	9.9	84.6	18.0
1958	321.3	77.5	346	80.7	61.3	9.5	86.0	13.1
1959	345.4	87.4	365	94.4	65.4	10.1	90.6	11.7
1960	375.5	90.0	380	100	71.3	13.5	96.6	19.6
1961	410.7	101.8	411	108	76.7	14.1	101.9	18.0
1962	426.1	100.8	419	119	81.6	15.7	108.7	25.2
1963	460.1	113.3	449	123	88.5	15.7	115.2	18.7
1964	497.0	119.6	479	128	96.0	17.6	122.7	25.0
1965	531.3	136.9	512	141	107.2	20.1	131.9	29.1
1966	567.2	150.3	549	153	117.5	20.6	137.3	19.4
1967	605.6	152.6	580	170	131.3	26.1	147.6	26.5
1968	668.8	175.0	632	185	145.3	24.5	160.7	25.0
1969	696.1	173.9	650	201	159.4	28.0	164.1	26.6
1970	738.4[38]	143.5[38]	684[38]	148[38]	177.0	30.7	177.0	30.7
	749.2	139.5	1971 prices					
1971	855.0	184.3	855	184	197.5	37.7	187.2	35.7
1972	951.0	235.4	946	235	230.8	46.7	203.5	41.2
1973	1,064.8	300.3	1,048	299	280.5	56.5	225.8	46.0
1974	1,209.3	353.6	1,158	367	337.8	66.1	230.8	46.0
1975	1,357.0	410.7	1,261	427	373.5	38.2	222.5	15.2

See p. 838 for footnotes

K 1 National Accounts Totals

1950–1975

	Russia (in thousand million rubels at market prices)				Spain (in thousand million pesetas at market prices)			
	Current Prices		Constant Prices		Current Prices		Constant Prices	
	GNP/NMP[32]	CF[33]	GNP/NMP[32]	CF[33]	NNP/GDP[34]	CF[4]	NNP/GDP[34]	CF[4]
			1937 prices				1929 prices	
1950	676	123.82	304.3	65.6	151.8	...	25.8	...
1951	674	134.65	327.1	79.7	233.9	...	31.9	...
1952	697	140.41	351.8	80.4	250.3	...	34.1	...
1953	674	148.94	374.6	82.0	268.7	...	34.1	...
1954	687	172.24	404.1	79.3	291.9[34]	68.3	37.0[34]	...
					336.7		1970 prices	
							889	144
1955	751[32]	180.23[33]	441.6[32]	101.2[33]	375.8	78.5	935	160
			1958 prices	July 1955 prices				
	98.5	25.1	95.8	19.6				
1956	106.8	29.1	106.0	22.4	431.7	96.2	1,002	176
1957	112.8	26.4	113.7	25.3	506.1	118.3	1,045	186
1958	127.7	34.6	127.7	29.4	581.7	137.6	1,092	204
1959	136.2	35.6	137.9	33.3	603.5	114.1	1,071	169
1960	145.0	38.9	148.1	35.9	620.7	117.7	1,097	179
1961	152.9	42.9	158.3	37.5	707.0	156.2	1,226	231
1962	164.6	45.0	167.3	39.3	817.0	199.3	1,340	277
1963	168.8	42.3	173.7	41.3	964.2	235.8	1,458	308
1964	181.3	49.3	190.3	45.0	1,089	267.8	1,548	335
1965	193.5	50.2	203.0	48.7	1,288	338.4	1,660	406
1966	207.4	54.2	219.6	52.4	1,482	389.8	1,798	457
1967	225.5	59.4	238.8	56.7	1,637	380.5	1,875	439
			1960 prices	1969 prices				
			233	66.0				
1968	244.1	64.8	252	71.2	1,812	414.1	1,982	453
1969	261.9	69.4	265	73.6	2,022	482.3	2,136	507
1970	289.9	84.2	290	82.1	2,264[38]	521.3[38]	2,264[38]	521[38]
					2,575	649.8	2,575	650
1971	305.0	87.1	307	88.0	2,911	684.9	2,699	645
1972	313.6	85.3	319	94.3	3,418	844.2	2,929	745
1973	337.8	97.6	348	98.7	4,132	1,078	3,175	852
1974	354.0	98.1	365	105.7	4,941	1,378	3,336	908
1975	362.8	95.8	...	114.9	5,800	1,495	3,361	877

See p. 838 for footnotes

K 1 National Accounts Totals

1950–1975

	Sweden (in million kronor at market prices)				Switzerland (in million francs at market prices)			
	Current Prices		Constant Prices		Current Prices		Constant Prices	
	GDP	CF[49]	GDP	CF[49]	NNP/GDP[45]	CF[4]	NNP/GDP[45]	CF[4]
			1913 prices				1938 prices	
1950	33,739[44]	6,687[44]	13,027[44]	2,392[44]	18,490[45]	3,180	11,620[45]	...
	32,066	5,672	1970 prices		19,920		1958 prices	
			78,067	12,844			23,245	3,975
1951	39,593	8,883	80,408	16,124	21,615	4,605	24,845	5,250
1952	43,159	9,463	81,792	15,300	22,750	4,045	25,085	4,405
1953	44,437	8,776	84,435	14,785	23,750	3,970	26,130	4,435
1954	47,279	10,172	89,482	13,673	25,125	4,825	27,520	5,455
1955	50,827	11,468	92,171	19,113	26,865	5,860	29,040	6,465
1956	55,241	12,287	95,235	19,415	28,860	6,970	30,775	7,445
1957	58,963	13,071	97,486	19,896	30,495	7,600	31,745	7,800
1958	62,269	13,483	99,786	20,500	31,155	5,945	31,155	5,945
1959	66,245	14,473	104,989	21,969	33,395	7,500	33,325	7,495
1960	72,160	17,834	108,992	25,670	36,565	9,670	35,230	9,305
1961	78,522	19,017	115,218	26,460	40,995	12,350	37,825	11,170
1962	85,196	20,518	120,160	27,291	45,510	13,780	39,715	11,820
1963	92,109	22,048	126,422	28,301	49,815	15,120	41,560	12,075
1964	102,685	26,528	135,034	32,551	54,945	17,190	43,655	13,150
1965	113,316	30,228	140,709	35,196	59,110	17,050	45,315	12,685
1966	123,289	31,231	144,056	34,560	63,520	17,530	46,435	12,600
1967	133,368	32,624	148,934	34,907	67,660	17,935	47,195	12,665
1968	141,676	33,588	154,929	35,741	72,720[38]	19,040[38]	48,880[38]	13,240[38]
					74,895	20,690	1970 prices	
							81,455	23,570
1969	153,369	36,761	162,785	38,643	81,455	22,995	85,825	25,210
1970	170,883	42,925	170,883	42,925	90,665	29,245	90,665	29,245
1971	183,791	41,520	172,114	39,135	102,995	33,450	94,360	30,630
1972	199,426	44,301	176,521	39,712	116,710	37,095	97,380	30,765
1973	220,176	46,813	182,738	39,467	130,060	40,740	100,350	31,590
1974	249,444	60,157	190,083	44,500	141,100	44,085	101,810	32,430
1975	288,011	69,881	191,595	45,690	139,800	31,810	94,285	23,070

See p. 838 for footnotes

K 1 National Accounts Totals

1950–1975

	United Kingdom (in million pounds at market prices)				Yugoslavia (in million dinars at market prices)			
	Current Prices		Constant Prices		Current Prices		Constant Prices	
	GNP	CF[6]	GNP	CF[6]	NMP	CF[4]	NMP	CF[4]
			1963 prices				1960 prices	
1950	13,333	1,708	21,733	2,652	208	120	1,284	741
1951	14,773	1,905	22,323	2,670	231	131	1,409	799
1952	15,911	2,134	22,209	2,696	854	494	1,154	668
1953	17,102	2,395	23,226	2,992	1,022	592	1,363	789
1954	18,050	2,595	24,119	3,253	1,162	691	1,403	835
1955	19,338	2,882	24,865	3,444	1,398	805	1,609	926
1956	20,971	3,164	25,353	3,607	1,444	827	1,536	880
1957	22,182	3,451	25,861	3,805	1,829	1,053	1,933	1,113
1958	23,136	3,569	25,982	3,837	1,834	1,024	2,000	1,117
1959	24,314	3,816	26,964	4,129	2,269	1,314	2,342	1,356
1960	25,734	4,190	28,174	4,503	2,686	1,563	2,686	1,563
1961	27,491	4,704	29,146	4,945	3,110	1,799	2,616	1,607
1962	28,859	4,833	29,459	4,935	3,471	2,007	2,714	1,569
1963	30,765	5,066	30,765	5,066	4,199	2,464	3,034	1,780
1964	33,515	6,041	32,541	5,898	5,582	3,215	3,418	1,966
					thousand million new dinars			
1965	36,016	6,504	33,336	6,404	73.6	40.6	35.7	19.7
			1975 prices				1972 prices	
			83,944	16,218			149	82.1
1966	38,350	6,922	85,575	16,622	91.7	47.7	161	82.6
1967	40,467	7,523	87,768	18,024	94.4	47.5	164	82.6
1968	43,804	8,200	91,219	18,852	102	51.4	170	86.0
1969	47,056	8,591	92,830	18,924	120	60.5	186	94.2
1970	51,551	9,462	95,027	19,425	143	72.0	197	99.1
1971	57,786	10,507	97,530	19,735	186	96.9	212	115
1972	63,799	11,593	99,913	19,767	221	114	221	114
1973	74,093	14,207	108,610	21,111	276	147	282	124
1974	83,961	16,926	106,573	20,636	363	197	251	137
1975	104,711	20,545	104,711	20,545	529	246	261	121

See p. 838 for footnotes

K 1 National Accounts Totals

NOTES

1. SOURCES:— In addition to the official publications noted on p. xv the following have been used:—

Austria — 1947 to 1949 (1st line), United Nations, *Statistics of National Income and Expenditure* (1956), hereafter cited as U.N. (1956).

Belgium — 1913–38 and 1946 to 1948 (1st line), F. Baudhuin, "Prix, consommation, balance et revenus en 1957", *Bulletin des Recherches Economiques et Sociales* (1958).

— 1939–43, United Nations, *National Income Statistics* (1950), hereafter cited as U.N. (1950).

— 1948 (2nd line) to 1953 (1st line), U.N. (1956).

Conversion to constant prices up to 1953 (1st line) was by using the retail price index (see table 1.2).

Bulgaria — 1924–46, U.N. (1950).

— 1952–75, United Nations, *Yearbooks of National Accounts Statistics,* hereafter cited as U.N. *Yearbooks.*

Conversion to constant prices up to 1946 was by using the cost-of-living index (see table 1.2).

Czechoslovakia — 1913–37 — based on Frederic L. Pryor *et al,* "Czechoslovak Aggregate Production in the Interwar Period", *Review of Income and Wealth* (1971).

Denmark — 1870 to 1947 (1st line), K. Bjerke & N. Ussing, *Studier over Danmarks Nationalprodukt, 1870–1950,* (Copenhagen, 1958).

Finland — 1926–37, U.N. (1950). Conversion to constant prices was by using the implied price index derived from E.H. Luriea, "Suomen Kansantulo Vuosina", *Tilastokatsaukia* (1950).

Germany — W.G. Hoffman, *Das Wachstum der Deutschen Wirtschaft seit der Mitte des 19 Jahrhunderts* (Berlin, 1965).

Greece — 1927–39, U.N. (1950).

— 1946 to 1948 (1st line) at current prices (and the implicit price indices for later constant price figures), U.N. (1956) and U.N. *Yearbooks.*

—1948 (2nd line) to 1949, *National Accounts of Greece 1948–1970* (Athens, 1972).

— 1950 to 1975, U.N. *Yearbooks.*

Hungary — 1899–1949, Alexander Eckstein, "National Income and Capital Formation in Hungary, 1900–1950", *Income and Wealth* (series V).

— 1950–75, U.N. *Yearbooks.*

Ireland — 1929–36, U.N. (1950).

Norway — 1865–1960, Statistisk Sentralbyra, *Nasjonalregnskap 1965–1960* and *Langtidslinjer i Norsk Økonomie 1865–1960.*

Poland — U.N., *Yearbooks.*

Portugal — U.N., *Yearbooks.*

Russia — 1928–55, A. Bergson, *The Real National Income of Soviet Russia since 1928* (Cambridge, Mass., 1961) for G.N.P. at current prices, and R. Moorsteen & R.P. Powell, *The Soviet Capital Stock 1928–1962* (Homewood, Ill., 1966) for other series.

— 1956–75, U.N., *Yearbooks.*

Spain — 1906 to 1954 (1st line), *La Renta Nacional de España.*

— 1954 (2nd line) to 1975 — U.N., *Yearbooks.*

Sweden — 1861 to 1950 (1st line), O. Johansson, *The Gross Domestic Product of Sweden and its Composition 1861–1955* (Stockholm, 1967).

Switzerland — 1913 — Colin Clark, *The Conditions of Economic Progress* (3rd edition, London, 1957).

— 1950 (2nd line) to 1975, U.N., *Yearbooks.*

U.K. — 1830 to 1855 or 1856 (1st line), *Phyllis Deane,* "New Estimates of Gross National Product for the United Kingdom 1830–1914", *Review of Income and Wealth* (1968).

— 1855 or 1856 (2nd line) to 1948, C.H. Feinstein, *National Income, Expenditure and Output of the United Kingdom, 1855–1965* (Cambridge, 1972).

— 1949–75, based on Central Statistical Office, *National Income and Expenditure 1971 to 1979*

Yugoslavia — 1920 to 1947 (1st line), I. Vinski, "National Product and Fixed Assets in the Territory of Yugoslavia, 1909–1959, *Income and Wealth* (series IX).

2. For definitions of the concepts see the United Nations publications on national accounts. Not all countries use precisely the U.N. concept, and of those here, Denmark's and Italy's G.N.P. is significantly higher than on the U.N. concept.

FOOTNOTES

[1] Figures to 1950 (1st line) are of gross fixed capital formation only. Subsequently they include stocks.
[2] Net, including stocks.
[3] Estimates for the balance of payments at constant prices are incomplete to 1880 (1st line) and in 1936–38.
[4] Gross, including stocks.
[5] The constant price series differs from the current price series to 1951 (1st line) in that *net* imports are included rather than *gross* imports.
[6] Gross, excluding stocks.
[7] Earlier figures for the United Kingdom are as follows:—

	Current Prices		Constant Prices (1900 Prices)	
	GNP	CF	GNP	CF
1830	438	14.8	397	17.1
1831	438	16.5	415	19.7
1832	420	12.6	413	15.1
1833	412	12.5	415	15.0
1834	437	14.8	432	18.0
1835	462	23.2	456	26.4
1836	503	24.6	473	25.3
1837	478	27.4	466	29.9
1838	507	31.3	493	34.5
1839	535	33.3	576	35.7
1840	502	32.3	500	35.4
1841	488	23.8	490	27.2
1842	461	21.1	480	25.2
1843	452	18.6	487	23.6
1844	494	20.4	517	25.0
1845	523	31.3	545	35.7
1846	557	47.6	581	49.7
1847	598	60.3	585	61.8
1848	562	48.4	592	55.3
1849	579	41.1	602	51.7

[8] Southern Ireland is excluded from 1920 (2nd line).
[9] The G.N.P. Statistics to 1870 (1st line) are at factor cost.
[10] This break occurs on a change of source from *Sommario di Statistiche Storiche Italiane* to the latest revisions in the *Annuario Statistico Italiano*.
[12] Figures to 1948 (1st line) are of net national product; from 1948 (2nd line) to 1953 (1st line) they are of gross domestic product; and from 1953 (2nd line) they are of gross national product.
[13] Figures to 1953 (1st line) are of gross fixed capital formation only. Subsequently they include stocks.
[14] Figures to 1946 are of net national product. Subsequently they are of net material product.
[15] Net, excluding stocks.
[16] This break occurs on a change in the original source used by the United Nations.
[17] Figures to 1937 are of gross domestic product. From 1948 they are of net material product.
[18] Figures from 1950 (1st line) are of net national product. Subsequently they are of gross domestic product.
[19] Annual estimates have not been published for the nineteenth century, but the following annual averages for mainly decennial periods are available in T.J. Markovitch, *L'industrie francaise de 1789 à 1964* (Cahiers de l'I.S.E.A., 1966) (in million francs at market prices):—

	Current Prices		1905–13 Prices	
	GDP	Gross Capital Formation	GDP	Gross Capital Formation
1791–90	7,700	1,299	6,949	1,172
1803–12	9,755	2,147	7,324	1,612
1815–24	10,503	1,724	8,969	1,472
1825–34	12,503	.2,031	10,977	1,783
1835–44	14,894	2,630	12,929	2,283
1845–54	17,407	3,041	14,628	2,555
1855–64	22,824	4,675	17,972	3,681
1865–74	26,499	5,097	21,199	4,078
1875–84	27,235	5,401	23,418	4,644
1885–94	27,321	5,275	27,541	5,318
1895–1904	29,095	6,208	30,788	6,569
1905–13	38,035	7,972	38,035	7,972
1920–24	187,924	45,325	42,565	10,266
1925–34	328,527	64,388	62,529	12,255
1935–38	314,029	60,387	60,988	11,728

[20] Figures to 1949 (1st line) are of net national product. Subsequently they are of gross national product.

[21] The following estimates, comparable with figures for 1949 (2nd line) and later, have been made for 1938 (in thousand million francs):—

Current Prices		1959 Prices	
GNP	GDFCF	GNP	GDFCF
4.46	0.59	153.1	19.4

[22] Figures to 1948 (1st line) are of net national product. Subsequently they are of gross domestic product.

[23] All statistics relate to the territory established by the treaty of Trianon. For 1920—48 they are for years ended 30 June.

[24] Figures to 1949 are of net national product at factor cost. From 1950 they are of net material product.

[25] Figures to 1949 are of gross capital formation including stocks. From 1950 they are of net capital formation excluding stocks.

[26] Annual averages for three-year periods 1899—1902 and 1911—13.

[27] In 1924/5 prices.

[28] In January 1947 prices.

[29] Figures are of net national product to 1936. Subsequently they are of gross national product.

[30] Figures to 1948 (1st line) are of net national product. Subsequently they are of gross national product.

[31] Figures to 1948 (1st line) are of net capital formation including stocks, but excluding investment by public authorities. Subsequently they are of gross capital formation including stocks.

[32] Figures to 1955 (1st line) are of gross national product at factor cost. Subsequently they are of net material product at market prices. This latter series is in new (1961) rubels.

[33] Figures at current prices to 1955 (1st line) are of gross capital formation, including stocks but excluding repairs, at factor cost. The constant price series include repairs, but estimates excluding repairs are available as follows (in thousand million rubels at 1937 prices):—

1928	9.56	1935	26.26	1942	32.19	1949	45.76
1929	12.19	1936	36.08	1943	10.58	1950	55.25
1930	17.68	1937	32.51	1944	17.92	1951	60.84
1931	19.91	1938	32.97	1945	21.29	1952	64.56
1932	20.77	1939	32.95	1946	26.72	1953	71.26
1933	18.46	1940	32.19	1947	30.96	1954	81.76
1934	21.04	1941	21.57	1948	37.89	1955	94.03

From 1955 (2nd line) current price statistics are of gross capital formation, including stocks, at market prices in thousand million new (1961) rubels. The constant price series excludes stocks.

[34] Figures to 1954 (1st line) are of net national product. Subsequently they are of gross national product.

[35] Figures to 1947 (1st line) are of gross domestic product 'adjusted for international comparisons'. Subsequently they are of net material product.

[36] Figures are of gross fixed capital formation to 1939. From 1947 stocks are included.

[37] These are later revisions than the figures in the constant price series. The current price figures corresponding to the latter are 293,026 for GNP and 72,857 for CF.

[38] There was a change in the basis of calculation.

[39] The following estimates, comparable with statistics for 1938 and earlier (except for the change from Reichsmarks to Deutschmarks) have been made for 1950 (in million D. marks):—

Current Prices		1913 Prices	
NNP	Net Capital Formation	NNP	Net Capital Formation
92,063	15,820	44,904	6,970

[40] From 1950 to 1960 (1st line) Saarland and West Berlin are not included.

[41] Later revised figures have been published for these years, but not for intervening years, as follows:—
1950 N.M.P. 27,177, C.F. 3,612; 1955 N.M.P. 50,347, C.F. 8,167

[42] The definition of net material product was subsequently broadened.

[43] Previous figures (except for 1953) are based on a rounded price index, and are not accurate to the last three digits.

[44] This break occurs on a change of source (see note 1). Johansson says that his series is probably too high in its later years, but is designed to make possible comparisons over a very long period.

[45] Figures to 1950 (1st line) are of net national product. Subsequently they are of gross national product.

[46] The lates

[45] Figures to 1950 (1st line) are of net national product. Subsequently they are of gross national product.

[46] The latest official figures for 1938 are G.N.P. 7,909, C.F. 1,407 at current prices, and G.N.P. 21,300, C.F. 4,065 at 1955 prices.

[47] When subsequent revisions were later shown for the series from 1962 onwards, revised figures were also given for 1958 as follows: G.N.P. 600.9, C.F. 72.3.

[48] Subsequent statistics are based on the U.N. (1970) concept.

[49] Gross, excluding stocks in 1950 (1st line) and subsequently including them.

[50] This break occurs on a change of source (see note 1). It is negligible so far as the G.D.P. series is concerned, but the C.F. figure for 1950 in the older source is considerably larger, viz. 6,216.

K 2 PROPORTIONS OF NATIONAL PRODUCT BY SECTOR OF ORIGIN (%)

1788–1869

	France			Germany					Italy				
	A	I	Com	A	I	Con	T & C	Com	A	I	Con	T & C	Com
1788	...	...	...	...	...	...	...	...	...	...	...	...	...
1789	49	18	12	...	...	...	...	...	...	...	...	...	...
1801	...	...	...	...	...	...	...	...	...	...	...	...	...
1811	...	...	...	...	...	...	...	...	...	...	...	...	...
1815	51	22	7	...	...	...	...	...	...	...	...	...	...
1821	...	...	...	...	...	...	...	...	...	...	...	...	...
1825	48	26	7	...	...	...	...	...	...	...	...	...	...
1831	...	...	...	...	...	...	...	...	...	...	...	...	...
1835	51	25	7	...	...	...	...	...	...	...	...	...	...
1841	...	...	...	...	...	...	...	...	...	...	...	...	...
1847	45	29	7	...	...	...	...	...	...	...	...	...	...
1850	...	...	...	47	21		1	7	...	...	...	...	...
1851	...	...	...	45	21		1	7	...	...	...	...	...
1852	...	...	...	45	22		1	7	...	...	...	...	...
1853	...	...	...	44	21		1	7	...	...	...	...	...
1854	...	...	...	45	21		1	7	...	...	...	...	...
1855	...	...	...	43	22		1	7	...	...	...	...	...
1856	...	...	...	45	22		1	7	...	...	...	...	...
1857	...	...	...	45	23		1	7	...	...	...	...	...
1858	...	...	...	44	23		1	7	...	...	...	...	...
1859	45	30	7	45	23		1	7	...	...	...	...	...
1860	...	...	...	45	23		1	8	...	...	...	...	...
1861	...	...	...	43	24		1	8	57	19	3	2	15
1862	...	...	...	45	23		1	7	59	17	2	2	14
1863	...	...	...	45	24		1	7	56	18	2	2	15
1864	...	...	...	46	25		1	7	56	18	2	2	15
1865	...	...	...	44	26		1	7	56	19	2	2	15
1866	...	...	...	43	26		2	7	55	19	2	2	16
1867	...	...	...	42	27		2	8	55	18	2	2	16
1868	...	...	...	43	27		2	8	59	16	2	2	15
1869	...	...	...	41	28		2	8	58	18	2	2	14

Abbreviations used throughout this table:— A = Agriculture; I = Industry; Con = Construction; T & C: Transport and Communications; Com = Commerce

See p. 857 for footnotes

K 2 Proportions of National Product by Sector of Origin (%)

1788–1869

	Norway			Sweden					United Kingdom				
	A[1]	I	Con	A[2]	I	Con	T & C	Com	A	I	Con	T & C	Com
1788	...	...	...	...	...	...	...	...	40[3]	21[3]		12[3]	
1789	...	...	...	...	...	...	...	...	...	...		...	
1801	...	...	...	...	...	...	...	...	33	23		17	
1811	...	...	...	...	...	...	...	...	36	21		17	
1815	...	...	...	...	...	...	...	...	...	...		...	
1821	...	...	...	...	...	...	...	...	26	32		16	
1825	...	...	...	...	...	...	...	...	...	...		...	
1831	...	...	...	...	...	...	...	...	24	35		18	
1835	...	...	...	...	...	...	...	...	...	...		...	
1841	...	...	...	...	...	...	...	...	22	35		19	
1847	...	...	...	...	...	...	...	...	...	...		...	
1850	...	...	...	...	...	...	...	...	21	35		19	
1851	...	...	...	...	...	...	...	...	...	...		...	
1852	...	...	...	...	...	...	...	...	...	...		...	
1853	...	...	...	...	...	...	...	...	...	...		...	
1854	...	...	...	...	...	...	...	...	...	...		...	
1855	...	...	...	...	...	...	...	...	...	...		...	
1856	...	...	...	...	...	...	...	...	...	...		...	
1857	...	...	...	...	...	...	...	...	...	...		..	
1858	...	...	...	...	...	...	...	...	...	...		...	
1859	...	...	...	...	...	...	...	...	...	...		...	
1860	...	...	...	...	...	...	...	...	...	...		...	
1861	...	...	...	38	13	6	2	23	18	38		20	
1862	...	...	...	36	14	8	2	22	...	...		...	
1863	...	...	...	37	13	7	2	22	...	...		...	
1864	...	...	...	37	10	7	3	23	...	...		...	
1865	34	21		36	14	5	3	21	...	...		...	
1866	...	...	...	38	12	7	3	21	...	...		...	
1867	...	...	...	38	14	6	3	22	...	...		...	
1868	...	...	...	38	16	3	2	21	...	...		...	
1869	...	...	...	40	12	4	4	20	...	...		...	

See p. 857 for footnotes

K 2 Proportions of National Product by Sector of Origin (%)

1870–1919

	Austria					Czechoslovakia					Denmark[4]	France[9]		
	A	I	Con	T & C	Com	A	I	Con	T & C	Com	A	A	I	Com
1870	...	...	...	...	...	...	...	...	...	...	48	...	...	...
1871	...	...	...	...	...	...	...	...	...	...	48	...	...	...
1872	...	...	...	...	...	...	...	...	...	...	47	43	30	7
1873	...	...	...	...	...	...	...	...	...	...	47	...	...	...
1874	...	...	...	...	...	...	...	...	...	...	46	...	...	...
1875	...	...	...	...	...	...	...	...	...	...	45	...	...	...
1876	...	...	...	...	...	...	...	...	...	...	45	...	...	...
1877	...	...	...	...	...	...	...	...	...	...	41	...	...	...
1878	...	...	...	...	...	...	...	...	...	...	42	...	...	...
1879	...	...	...	...	...	...	...	...	...	...	42	...	...	...
1880	...	...	...	...	...	...	...	...	...	...	44	...	...	...
1881	...	...	...	...	...	...	...	...	...	...	41	...	...	...
1882	...	...	...	...	...	...	...	...	...	...	40	41	30	7
1883	...	...	...	...	...	...	...	...	...	...	38	...	...	...
1884	...	...	...	...	...	...	...	...	...	...	35	...	...	...
1885	...	...	...	...	...	...	...	...	...	...	34	...	...	...
1886	...	...	...	...	...	...	...	...	...	...	35	...	...	...
1887	...	...	...	...	...	...	...	...	...	...	35	...	...	...
1888	...	...	...	...	...	...	...	...	...	...	32	...	...	...
1889	...	...	...	...	...	...	...	...	...	...	33	...	...	...
1890	...	...	...	...	...	...	...	...	...	...	35	...	...	...
1891	...	...	...	...	...	...	...	...	...	...	37	...	...	...
1892	...	...	...	...	...	...	...	...	...	...	35	37	32	7
1893	...	...	...	...	...	...	...	...	...	...	33	...	...	...
1894	...	...	...	...	...	...	...	...	...	...	31	...	...	...
1895	...	...	...	...	...	...	...	...	...	...	32	...	...	...
1896	...	...	...	...	...	...	...	...	...	...	30	...	...	...
1897	...	...	...	...	...	...	...	...	...	...	28	...	...	...
1898	...	...	...	...	...	...	...	...	...	...	27	37	34	7
1899	...	...	...	...	...	...	...	...	...	...	25	...	...	...
1900	...	...	...	...	...	...	...	...	...	...	29	...	...	...
1901	...	...	...	...	...	...	...	...	...	...	30	...	...	...
1902	...	...	...	...	...	...	...	...	...	...	29	...	...	...
1903	...	...	...	...	...	...	...	...	...	...	30	...	...	...
1904	...	...	...	...	...	...	...	...	...	...	29	...	...	...
1905	...	...	...	...	...	...	...	...	...	...	30	...	...	...
1906	...	...	...	...	...	...	...	...	...	...	29	...	...	...
1907	...	...	...	...	...	...	...	...	...	...	28	...	...	...
1908	...	...	...	...	...	...	...	...	...	...	29	...	...	...
1909	...	...	...	...	...	...	...	...	...	...	29	35[5]	36[5]	7[5]
1910	...	...	...	...	...	...	...	...	...	...	30	...	...	...
1911	...	...	...	...	...	...	...	...	...	...	30	...	...	...
1912	...	...	...	...	...	...	...	...	...	...	28	...	...	...
1913	11	41	4	6	14	27	28	3	9	10	28	...	...	...
1914	...	...	...	...	...	...	...	...	...	...	30	...	...	...
1915	...	...	...	...	...	...	...	...	...	...	...	...	...	...
1916	...	...	...	...	...	...	...	...	...	...	...	...	...	...
1917	...	...	...	...	...	...	...	...	...	...	...	...	...	...
1918	...	...	...	...	...	...	...	...	...	...	...	...	...	...
1919	...	...	...	...	...	...	...	...	...	...	...	...	...	...

See p. 857 for footnotes

K 2 Proportion of National Product by Sector of Origin

1870–1919

	Germany					Hungary[6]				
	A	I	Con	T & C	Com	A	I	Con	T & C	Com
1870	40	28		2	8	...	...	...	...	...
1871	39	30		2	8	...	...	...	...	...
1872	37	33		2	8	...	...	...	...	...
1873	36	34		2	8	...	...	...	...	...
1874	38	33		2	8	...	...	...	...	...
1875	37	33		2	8	...	...	...	...	...
1876	36	33		2	8	...	...	...	...	...
1877	36	33		2	8	...	...	...	...	...
1878	38	32		2	8	...	...	...	...	...
1879	36	33		3	8	...	...	...	...	...
1880	36	32		3	8	...	...	...	...	...
1881	36	33		3	8	...	...	...	...	...
1882	36	32		3	8	...	...	...	...	...
1883	36	33		3	8	...	...	...	...	...
1884	36	33		3	8	...	...	...	...	...
1885	37	33		3	9	...	...	...	...	...
1886	37	33		3	9	...	...	...	...	...
1887	36	34		3	8	...	...	...	...	...
1888	35	34		3	8	...	...	...	...	...
1889	33	37		4	9	...	...	...	...	...
1890	33	37		4	8	...	...	...	...	...
1891	31	37		4	9	...	...	...	...	...
1892	32	37		4	9	...	...	...	...	...
1893	33	36		4	9	...	...	...	...	...
1894	32	37		4	9	...	...	...	...	...
1895	31	38		4	9	...	...	...	...	...
1896	32	38		4	9	...	...	...	...	...
1897	30	38		4	9	...	...	...	...	...
1898	30	39		4	9	...	...	...	...	...
1879	30	39		5	9	...	...	...	...	...
1900	30	40		5	9	43[5]	20[5]		8[5]	6[5]
1901	29	39		5	10	...	...	...	...	...
1902	29	39		5	9	...	...	...	...	...
1903	29	40		5	9	...	...	...	...	...
1904	29	40		5	9	...	...	...	...	...
1905	28	41		5	10	...	...	...	...	...
1906	26	41		6	10	...	...	...	...	...
1907	25	43		6	9	...	...	...	...	...
1908	26	42		6	9	...	...	...	...	...
1909	25	43		6	9	...	...	...	...	...
1910	25	43		6	9	...	...	...	...	...
1911	23	44		6	9	...	...	...	...	...
1912	22	46		6	9	44[5]	24[5]		8[5]	6[5]
1913	23	45		6	9	...	...	...	...	...
1914	...	...		...	...	...	...	...	...	...
1915	...	...		...	...	...	...	...	...	...
1916	...	...		...	...	...	...	...	...	...
1917	...	...		...	...	...	...	...	...	...
1918	...	...		...	...	...	...	...	...	...
1919	...	...		...	...	...	...	...	...	...

See p. 857 for footnotes

K 2 Proportions of National Product by Sector of Origin (%)

1870–1919

	Italy					Norway				
	A	I	Con	T & C	Com	A	I	Con	T & C	Com
1870	57	18	2	2	15	...	...	...	...	...
1871	58	16	2	2	16	...	...	...	...	...
1872	58	17	2	2	16	...	...	...	...	...
1873	60	17	2	2	15	...	...	...	...	...
1874	58	17	2	2	16	...	...	...	...	...
1875	55	18	2	3	16	33	21		...	...
1876	54	18	2	3	17	...	...	...	...	...
1877	56	18	2	3	16	...	...	...	...	...
1878	55	17	2	3	16	...	...	...	...	...
1879	55	16	2	3	17	...	...	...	...	...
1880	57	15	2	3	16	...	...	...	...	...
1881	51	18	3	3	17	...	...	...	...	...
1882	55	17	3	3	16	...	...	...	...	...
1883	52	17	3	3	17	...	...	...	...	...
1884	51	17	3	4	17	...	...	...	...	...
1885	52	17	4	4	16	...	...	...	...	...
1886	53	17	4	4	16	...	...	...	...	...
1887	49	18	4	4	17	...	...	...	...	...
1888	48	17	4	4	18	...	...	...	...	...
1889	47	18	3	4	18	...	...	...	...	...
1890	51	17	3	4	17	27	23		...	...
1891	55	15	2	4	16	...	...	...	...	...
1892	50	16	3	4	18	...	...	...	...	...
1893	50	16	3	4	17	...	...	...	...	...
1894	49	16	3	4	18	...	...	...	...	...
1895	49	17	2	4	18	...	...	...	...	...
1896	49	17	2	4	18	...	...	...	...	...
1897	47	17	2	5	18	...	...	...	...	...
1898	53	15	2	4	16	...	...	...	...	...
1899	50	17	2	4	16	...	...	...	...	...
1900	51	17	2	4	16	22	24		...	...
1901	51	17	2	4	16	...	...	...	...	...
1902	46	19	3	5	17	...	...	...	...	...
1903	50	18	3	5	16	...	...	...	...	...
1904	49	18	3	5	16	...	...	...	...	...
1905	47	19	3	5	16	...	...	...	...	...
1906	46	21	3	5	16	...	...	...	...	...
1907	47	22	3	5	15	...	...	...	...	...
1908	43	23	3	6	16	...	...	...	...	...
1909	45	21	3	6	16	...	...	...	...	...
1910	42	22	3	6	17	23	23	3	11	16
1911	46	21	2	6	15	...	...	...	...	...
1912	44	22	2	6	15	...	...	...	...	...
1913	45	21	2	6	16	...	...	...	...	...
1914	43	21	3	6	17	...	...	...	...	...
1915	41	26	2	6	16	...	...	...	...	...
1916	43	29	1	6	14	...	...	...	...	...
1917	44	30	1	4	13	...	...	...	...	...
1918	48	29	1	3	13	...	...	...	...	...
1919	47	26	2	4	16	...	...	...	...	...

K 2 Proportions of National Product by Sector of Origin (%)

1870–1919

	Sweden					United Kingdom				
	A	I	Con	T & C	Com	A	I	Con	T & C	Com
1870	39	17	3	4	20	...	...	...	...	...
1871	39	13	7	4	20	15	40		23	
1872	38	14	7	4	20	...	...	...	...	...
1873	39	11	10	4	19	...	...	...	...	...
1874	36	14	11	4	20	...	...	...	...	...
1875	36	13	10	4	20	...	...	...	...	...
1876	35	14	10	4	20	...	...	...	...	...
1877	36	12	11	5	20	...	...	...	...	...
1878	37	11	10	5	19	...	...	...	...	...
1879	36	11	10	5	20	...	...	...	...	...
1880	37	12	9	5	20	...	...	...	...	...
1881	34	16	9	5	20	11	40		24	
1882	37	13	7	6	21	...	...	...	...	...
1883	35	13	7	6	21	...	...	...	...	...
1884	35	13	6	6	21	...	...	...	...	...
1885	33	13	8	6	22	...	...	...	...	...
1886	32	12	10	6	22	...	...	...	...	...
1887	31	15	7	6	22	...	...	...	...	...
1888	33	12	8	6	22	...	...	...	...	...
1889	31	16	8	6	21	...	...	...	...	...
1890	32	15	7	6	22	...	...	...	...	...
1891	34	16	5	6	22	9	41		24	
1892	33	16	6	6	22	...	...	...	...	...
1893	32	17	6	6	22	...	...	...	...	...
1894	30	21	6	6	21	...	...	...	...	...
1895	31	14	8	6	22	...	...	...	...	...
1896	29	21	6	6	21	...	...	...	...	...
1897	28	20	8	6	21	...	...	...	...	...
1898	28	20	7	6	22	...	...	...	...	...
1899	27	20	7	6	23	...	...	...	...	...
1900	28	21	7	6	22	...	...	...	...	...
1901	27	24	6	6	22	7	43		25	
1902	26	23	6	7	22	...	...	...	...	...
1903	26	23	7	6	22	...	...	...	...	...
1904	24	24	7	7	22	...	...	...	...	...
1905	23	24	8	7	22	...	...	...	...	...
1906	23	27	7	7	22	...	...	...	...	...
1907	24	28	6	7	20	6	34	4	10	19
1908	26	27	5	7	22	...	...	...	...	...
1909	25	26	5	7	22	...	...	...	...	...
1910	25	26	5	7	22	...	...	...	...	...
1911	23	27	6	7	22	...	...	...	...	...
1912	22	27	6	8	23	...	...	...	...	...
1913	23	29	6	7	21	...	...	...	...	...
1914	23	28	6	7	22	...	...	...	...	...
1915	25	27	5	8	23	...	...	...	...	...
1916	25	32	4	9	20	...	...	...	...	...
1917	25	34	3	7	21	...	...	...	...	...
1918	28	30	4	8	21	...	...	...	...	...
1919	24	29	5	8	24	...	...	...	...	...

K 2 Proportions of National Product by Sector of Origin (%)

1920–1975

	Austria					Belgium				
	A	I	Con	T & C	Com	A	I	Con	T & C	Com
1920	...	...	...	...	...	...	...	...	...	...
1921	...	...	...	...	...	...	...	...	...	...
1922	...	...	...	...	...	...	...	...	...	...
1923	...	...	...	...	...	...	...	...	...	...
1924	15	42	3	7	15	...	...	...	...	...
1925	15	43	3	7	15	...	...	...	...	...
1926	12	43	3	8	15	...	...	...	...	...
1927	15	41	3	8	15	...	...	...	...	...
1928	13	43	3	8	15	...	...	...	...	...
1929	13	43	4	8	14	...	...	...	...	...
1930	11	41	4	9	15	...	...	...	...	...
1931	11	39	4	9	15	...	...	...	...	...
1932	14	38	3	8	13	...	...	...	...	...
1933	15	37	2	8	13	...	...	...	...	...
1934	15	38	2	8	13	...	...	...	...	...
1935	14	38	3	8	14	...	...	...	...	...
1936	14	38	3	8	14	...	...	...	...	...
1937	14	39	3	8	13	...	...	...	...	...
1938	...	...	...	...	...	...	...	...	...	...
1939	...	...	...	...	...	...	...	...	...	...
1940	...	...	...	...	...	...	...	...	...	...
1941	...	...	...	...	...	...	...	...	...	...
1942	...	...	...	...	...	...	...	...	...	...
1943	...	...	...	...	...	...	...	...	...	...
1944	...	...	...	...	...	...	...	...	...	...
1945	...	...	...	...	...	...	...	...	...	...
1946	...	...	...	...	...	...	...	...	...	...
1947	...	...	...	...	...	...	...	...	...	...
1948	16	38	8	6	12	10	40	6	8	13
1949	17	39	8	6	11	9	41	5	8	13
1950	18	40	8	6	11	9	39	5	9	13
1951	17	40	8	5	11	8	40	6	9	12
1952	16	41	8	6	11	8	38	6	9	12
1953	16	40	7	7	11	8[7]	38[7]	6[7]	10[7]	12[7]
						8	36	6	7	12
1954	16	40	7	6	12	8	36	6	7	12
1955	15	41	7	6	12	8	35	6	7	11
1956	14	41	8	6	12	7	36	6	7	11
1957	13	41	8	6	12	8	36	6	7	11
1958	13	41	8	6	12	7	34	6	7	11
1959	12	41	8	6	12	7	33	6	7	11
1960	11	41	8	6	13	7	35	6	8	11
1961	11	40	9	6	13	8	34	6	7	11
1962	10	40	9	6	14	7	35	6	7	11
1963	10	39	9	6	14	7	35	6	7	11
1964	10	39	9	6	14	6	36	7	7	11
1965	9	39	10	6	14	6	35	7	8	12
1966	8	39	10	6	14	5	35	7	8	12
1967	8	37	10	6	14	5	35	7	8	12
1968	7	38	9	6	15	5	35	7	8	12
1969	7	38	9	6	15	5	37	6	8	12
1970	7	38	9	6	14	4	37	7	8	12
1971	6	38	10	6	14	4	37	7	8	11
1972	6	38	11	6	14	4	37	7	8	11
1973	6[18]	35[18]	10[18]	6[18]	11[18]	4	37	7	8	11
1974	5	36	10	5	11	3	37	7	9	11
1975	5	34	10	5	11	4	33	7	9	11

See p. 857 for footnotes

K 2 Proportion of National Product by Sector of Origin (%)

1920–1975

	Bulgaria					Czechoslovakia				
	A	I	Con	T & C	C	A	I	Con	T & C	Com
1920	...	...	...	...	...	24	27	3	10	9
1921	...	...	...	...	...	26	27	3	10	9
1922	...	...	...	...	...	26	26	3	10	9
1923	...	...	...	...	...	26	27	3	10	9
1924	...	...	...	...	...	23	31	3	10	9
1925	...	...	...	...	...	25	31	3	9	10
1926	...	...	...	...	...	24	31	4	10	10
1927	...	...	...	...	...	24	32	4	10	10
1928	...	...	...	...	...	24	33	4	9	10
1929	...	...	...	...	...	22	34	4	10	10
1930	...	...	...	...	...	22	34	4	9	10
1931	...	...	...	...	...	23	33	4	9	10
1932	...	...	...	...	...	28	29	4	8	9
1933	...	...	...	...	...	29	28	3	7	9
1934	...	...	...	...	...	26	30	3	8	10
1935	...	...	...	...	...	24	31	3	8	10
1936	...	...	...	...	...	24	32	3	8	10
1937	...	...	...	...	...	24	32	3	9	10
1938	...	...	...	...	...	...	...	...	...	...
1939	42	17		4	15	...	...	...	...	...
1940	42	18		4	15	...	...	...	...	...
1941	40	17		5	18	...	...	...	...	...
1942	39	17		5	20	...	...	...	...	...
1943	37	18		5	23	...	...	...	...	...
1944	38	18		3	27	...	...	...	...	...
1945	37	26		5	16	...	...	...	...	...
1946	43[8]	24[8]		4[8]	12[8]	...	...	...	...	...
1947	...	...	...	...	...	...	...	...	...	...
1948	...	...	...	...	...	20	59	7	4	8
1949	...	...	...	...	...	17	63	8	4	6
1950	...	...	...	...	...	17	61	9	3	9
1951	...	...	...	...	...	14	66	9	3	6
1952	...	...	...	...	...	11	69	10	3	7
1953	30	34	7	4	22	14	67	10	3	7
1954	...	...	...	...	...	13	64	11	3	8
1955	30	34	8	5	20	16	62	10	3	8
1956	32	36	8	4	17	16	62	12	3	6
1957	34	41	7	3	12	15	62	11	3	7
1958	33	41	7	4	12	15	62	11	3	8
1959	33	43	7	4	11	14	64	10	3	7
1960	32	46	7	4	9	16	62	11	4	7
1961	32	46	7	4	9	14	64	10	4	7
1962	33	44	7	4	9	12	67	10	4	7
1963	33	45	7	4	9	14	67	8	4	6
1964	34	45	7	4	8	14	64	9	3	9
1965	34	45	7	4	8	13	65	9	3	8
1966	35	45	8	4	6	14	64	10	3	9
1967	31	46	8	5	8	13	61	12	4	9
1968	26	49	9	5	9	13	60	11	4	10
1969	25	50	8	5	10	12	59	11	4	12
1970	23	49	9	7	10	11	61	11	4	11
1971	24	51	9	7	6	12	61	12	4	11
1972	23	51	9	7	6	11	61	13	3	11
1973	22	51	9	8	7	11	62	13	3	11
1974	21	52	9	8	7	10	63	13	3	10
1975	22	51	9	8	8	9	65	13	3	9

See p. 857 for footnotes

K 2 Proportion of National Product by Sector of Origin (%)

1920–1975

	Denmark[4]					Finland[4]				
	A	I	Con	T & C	Com	A	I	Con	T & C	Com
1920	...	...	...	...	...	...	...	...	...	...
1921	23	...	...	...	...	...	...	...	...	...
1922	22	...	...	...	...	...	...	...	...	...
1923	24	...	...	...	...	...	...	...	...	...
1924	25	...	...	...	...	...	...	...	...	...
1925	22	...	...	...	...	...	...	...	...	...
1926	20	...	...	...	...	...	...	...	...	...
1927	19	...	...	...	...	...	...	...	...	...
1928	21	...	...	...	...	...	...	...	...	...
1929	22	...	...	...	...	...	...	...	...	...
1930	19	...	...	...	...	...	...	...	...	...
1931	15	...	...	...	...	...	...	...	...	...
1932	16	...	...	...	...	...	...	...	...	...
1933	17	...	...	...	...	...	...	...	...	...
1934	17	...	...	...	...	...	...	...	...	...
1935	16	...	...	...	...	...	...	...	...	...
1936	16	...	...	...	...	...	...	...	...	...
1937	16	...	...	...	...	...	...	...	...	...
1938	17	33		9	16	35	30		6	12
1939	17	...	...	...	...	34	29		7	12
1940	21	...	...	...	...	30	26		6	12
1941	20	...	...	...	...	29	27		5	11
1942	17	...	...	...	...	30	26		5	11
1943	20	...	...	...	...	31	28		5	11
1944	19	...	...	...	...	30	26		4	11
1945	18	...	...	...	...	35	34		5	12
1946	18	...	...	...	...	37	35		5	12
1947	17	35		9	15	37	35		6	11
1948	18	35		9	15	32	39		6	11
1949	19	35		9	15	26	42		7	12
1950	20[4]	36[4]		9[4]	15[4]	25[4]	41[4]		7[4]	12[4]
	21	29	7	8	16	26	30	10	7	10
1951	20	29	7	10	15	27	32	9	7	10
1952	21	28	7	9	15	29	26	10	7	11
1953	21	28	7	9	15	25	28	10	7	10
1954	19	29	8	9	15	24	30	10	7	10
1955	18	29	7	10	14	24	30	9	7	10
1956	19	29	7	10	14	22	29	9	8	11
1957	17	29	7	11	14	21	29	9	8	10
1958	16	30	7	10	15	21	28	10	7	10
1959	15	31	7	10	15	20	30	10	7	10
1960	14	31	7	10	16	20	30	9	7	10
1961	14	31	8	9	16	20	31	9	7	10
1962	13	32	8	9	16	19	30	9	7	10
1963	12	31	8	10	16	18	30	9	7	11
1964	12	31	9	9	16	19	29	9	7	11
1965	11	30	9	9	15	18	29	10	7	11
1966	10	30	9	10	15	16	29	10	7	11
1967	9	29	10	10	15	15	29	10	7	10
1968	9	29	9	10	14	15	30	9	7	10
1969	8	29	9	9	14	15	33	9	7	10
1970	7	29	9	9	14	14	34	10	7	10
1971	7	28	9	9	14	14	32	10	7	10
1972	7	28	9	9	14	13	33	10	7	10
1973	8	28	9	9	14	12	34	10	7	10
1974	8	28	9	10	14	12	36	10	7	10
1975	7	26	8	10	13	12	34	10	7	10

See p. 857 for footnotes

K 2 Proportion of National Product by Sector of Origin (%)

1920–1975

	France[9]					Germany				
	A	I	Con	T & C	Com	A	I	Con	T & C	Com
1920	...	...	...	...	...	...	...	...	...	...
1921	...	...	...	...	...	...	...	...	...	...
1922	...	...	...	...	...	...	...	...	...	...
1923	...	...	...	...	...	...	...	...	...	...
1924	...	...	...	...	...	...	...	...	...	...
1925	...	...	...	...	...	16	49	7	10	...
1926	...	...	...	...	...	16	46	7	10	...
1927	...	...	...	...	...	16	49	7	10	...
1928	...	...	...	...	...	17	48	7	10	...
1929	...	...	...	...	...	16	49	7	10	...
1930	...	...	...	...	...	18	45	7	10	...
1931	...	...	...	...	...	21	40	6	10	...
1932	...	...	...	...	...	21	38	6	11	...
1933	...	...	...	...	...	23	39	6	10	...
1934	...	...	...	...	...	19	44	6	10	...
1935	...	...	...	...	...	17	48	6	10	...
1936	...	...	...	...	...	18	49	6	9	...
1937	...	...	...	...	...	15	52	6	9	...
1938	22	36		7	14	15	52	6	9	...
1939	...	...	...	...	...	...	...	...	...	...
1940	...	...	...	...	...	...	...	...	...	...
1941	...	...	...	...	...	...	...	...	...	...
1942	...	...	...	...	...	...	...	...	...	...
1943	...	...	...	...	...	...	...	...	...	...
1944	...	...	...	...	...	...	...	...	...	...
1945	...	...	...	...	...	...	...	...	...	...
1946	21	32		9	12	...	...	...	...	...
1947	19	35		9	12	...	...	...	...	...
1948	17	38		10	12	...	...	...	...	...
1949	16	40		9	12	...	...	...	...	...
	[9]	[9]		[9]	[9]	West Germany				
1950	15	42	6	5	12	10	44	5	7	13
1951	14	44	5	5	11	10	46	5	7	12
1952	13	42	6	6	12	10	46	5	7	14
1953	12	41	6	6	12	9	46	6	7	13
1954	12	40	6	6	12	9	46	6	6	13
1955	11	40	7	6	13	8	47	6	7	13
1956	10	41	7	6	13	8	47	6	7	13
1957	10	41	7	6	12	7	46	6	7	13
1958	10	41	7	5	13	7	46	6	7	13
1959	9	40	8	5	12	7	46	7	7	13
1960	9	40	8	5	12	6	46	7	6	13
1961	9	40	8	5	12	5	46	7	6	13
1962	9	39	8	5	12	5	46	7	6	14
1963	8	39	8	5	12	5	45	8	6	13
1964	7	39	9	5	12	5	45	8	6	13
1965	7	39	10	5	11	4	45	8	6	14
1966	7	39	10	5	11	4	44	7	6	14
1967	7	38	10	5	11	4	43	7	6	14
1968	7	38	10	5	11	4	44	7	6	13
1969	6	38	10	5	11	4	46	8	6	14
	[18]	[18]	[18]	[18]	[18]	[18]	[18]	[18]	[18]	[18]
1970	6	31	8	5	14	3	46	9	6	14
1971	6	31	7	5	14	3	44	9	6	14
1972	6	31	7	5	14	3	43	10	6	14
1973	7	31	8	5	14	3	43	9	6	14
1974	6	30	7	6	15	3	43	8	6	14
1975	5	30	7	...	...	3	42	8	6	14

See p. 857 for footnotes

K 2 Proportion of National Product by Sector of Origin (%)

1920–1975

	East Germany					Greece[4]				
	A	I	Con	T & C	Com	A	I	Con	T & C	Com
1920	...	...	...	...	...	...	...	...	...	...
1921	...	...	...	...	...	...	...	...	...	...
1922	...	...	...	...	...	...	...	...	...	...
1923	...	...	...	...	...	...	...	...	...	...
1924	...	...	....	...	...	...	...	...	...	...
1925	...	...	...	...	...	...	...	...	...	...
1926	...	...	...	...	...	...	...	...	...	...
1928	...	...	...	...	...	...	...	...	...	...
1929	...	...	...	...	...	...	...	...	...	...
1930	...	...	...	...	...	...	...	...	...	...
1931	...	...	...	...	...	...	...	...	...	...
1932	...	...	...	...	...	...	...	...	...	...
1933	...	...	...	...	...	...	...	...	...	...
1934	...	...	...	...	...	...	...	...	...	...
1935	...	...	...	...	...	...	...	...	...	...
1936	...	...	...	...	...	...	...	...	...	...
1937	...	...	...	...	...	...	...	...	...	...
1938	...	...	...	...	...	40	21		6	12
1939	...	...	...	...	...	...	...	...	...	...
1940	...	...	...	...	...	...	...	...	...	...
1941	...	...	...	...	...	...	...	...	...	...
1942	...	...	...	...	...	...	...	...	...	...
1943	...	...	...	...	...	...	...	...	...	...
1944	...	...	...	...	...	...	...	...	...	...
1945	...	...	...	...	...	33	25		8	9
1946	...	...	...	...	...	41	24		6	14
1947	...	...	...	...	...	43	24		6	10
1948	...	...	...	...	...	38	20	4	7	12
1949	...	...	...	...	...	39	20	4	7	11
1950	...	...	...	...	...	35[4]	22[4]	5[4]	6[4]	12[4]
						31	17	5	7	12
1951	28	47	6	7	10	31	16	4	7	11
1952	...	...	...	...	...	29	16	4	7	10
1953	...	...	...	...	...	34	16	4	6	11
1954	...	...	...	...	...	31	17	4	6	12
1955	20	53	6	7	14	31	18	5	6	11
1956	...	...	...	...	...	30	18	5	6	11
1957	...	...	...	...	...	31	18	5	6	12
1958	...	...	...	...	...	28	19	6	6	12
1959	...	...	...	...	...	26	19	6	7	11
1960	17	58	7	6	13	25	20	6	6	11
						20[19]	17[19]			
1961	...	...	...	...	...	23	16	6	6	11
1962	...	...	...	...	...	21	16	6	7	11
1963	14	62	7	6	13	22	16	6	6	11
1964	14	62	7	6	13	21	16	6	6	11
1965	14	62	8	6	13	21	16	7	6	11
1966	14	62	8	6	13	21	17	7	6	11
1967	15	62	8	5	13	20	17	6	6	11
1968	14	62	8	5	13	17	18	8	6	10
1969	12	63	9	5	13	16	18	8	7	10
1970	12	63	9	5	13	16	19	8	7	10
1971	11	64	9	6	13	16	20	8	7	10
1972	12	63	8	5	13	16	19	9	7	11
1973	11	64	8	5	14	18	21	9	6	11
1974	11	64	8	5	14	18	21	7	6	13
1975	10	64	8	5	14	17	21	6	7	12

See p. 857 for footnotes

K 2 Proportion of National Product by Sector of Origin (%)

1920–1975

	Hungary[6 10]					Ireland[4]				
	A	I	Con	T & C	Com	A	I	Con	T & C	Com
1920	...	...	...	...	...	...	...	...	...	...
1921	...	...	...	...	...	...	...	...	...	...
1922	...	...	...	...	...	...	...	...	...	...
1923	...	...	...	...	...	...	...	...	...	...
1924	...	...	...	...	...	...	...	...	...	...
1925	33	28		10	8	...	...	...	...	...
1926	36	28		8	8	...	...	...	...	...
1927	33	32		10	8	...	...	...	...	...
1928	30	31		9	8	...	...	...	...	...
1929	32	31		8	8	...	...	...	...	...
1930	32	30		8	8	...	...	...	...	...
1931	32	29		7	7	...	...	...	...	...
1932	33	29		7	7	...	...	...	...	...
1933	33	29		6	7	...	...	...	...	...
1934	33	29		6	7	...	...	...	...	...
1935	32	30		6	7	...	...	...	...	...
1936	31	32		6	7	...	...	...	...	...
1937	32	31		7	8	...	...	...	...	...
1938	31	32		7	8	...	...	...	...	...
1939	30	33		7	8	...	...	...	...	...
1940	...	...	...	...	...	...	...	...	...	...
1941	...	...	...	...	...	...	...	...	...	...
1942	...	...	...	...	...	...	...	...	...	...
1943	...	...	...	...	...	...	...	...	...	...
1944	...	...	...	...	...	37	17		18	
1945	...	...	...	...	...	37	17		19	
1946	...	...	...	...	...	34	19		22	
1947	28	35		7	7	32	21		22	
1948	27	39		8	7	31	23		21	
1949	27	...		...	...	31	24		21	
	[10]	[10]	[10]	[10]	[10]					
1950	25	48	7	4	15	31[4]	25[4]	...	21[4]	
						29	25	...	18	
1951	34	39	7	4	17	30	26	...	17	
1952	20	61	8	4	8	31	26	...	17	
1953	25	57	7	4	7	31	28	...	16	
1954	28	55	5	4	8	29	29	...	16	
1955	33	54	6	4	3	30	28	...	16	
1956	35	50	7	4	4	27	28	...	17	
1957	36[11]	49[11]	7[11]	3[11]	3[11]	29	28	...	16	
1958	31	55	8	5	1	26	29	...	17	
1959	27	54	11	4	3	26	29	...	17	
1960	23	59	10	5	2	25	30	...	17	
1961	21	62	9	5	2	24	31	...	17	
1962	21	64	10	5	—	23	32	...	18	
1963	21	63	9	5	1	21	32	...	18	
1964	22	65	9	5	−1	22	31	...	18	
1965	21	60	9	5	4	21	32	...	18	
1966	23	58	9	6	5	19	33	...	18	
1967	21	58	9	6	5	19	34	...	18	
1968	21	44	11	6	14	20	34	...	17	
1969	21	42	12	6	15	17	35	...	18	
1970	18	43	13	6	15	17	35	...	18	
1971	18	41	13	6	16	16	35	...	18	
1972	17	42	13	6	17	18	36	...	17	
1973	19	42	12	6	17	19	36	...	18	
1974	18	44	13	6	14	16	38	...	19	
1975	17	47	13	6	15	18	35	...	17	

See p. 857 for footnotes

K 2 Proportion of National Product by Sector of Origin (%)

1920–1975

	Italy					Netherlands[4]				
	A	I	Con	T & C	Com	A	I	Con	T & C	Com
1920	48	27	2	3	14	...	...	...	...	...
1921	46	22	2	4	18	...	...	...	...	...
1922	43	26	2	4	18	...	...	...	...	...
1923	41	27	2	5	16	...	...	...	...	...
1924	38	31	3	6	17	...	...	...	...	...
1925	38	31	3	6	15	...	...	...	...	...
1926	39	29	2	6	15	...	...	...	...	...
1927	36	27	2	8	18	...	...	...	...	...
1928	37	27	2	7	17	...	...	...	...	...
1929	36	26	3	8	17	...	...	...	...	...
1930	31	26	4	8	19	...	...	...	...	...
1931	31	24	4	8	20	...	...	...	...	...
1932	33	22	3	7	19	...	...	...	...	...
1933	28	25	3	7	21	...	...	...	...	...
1934	28	24	4	8	21	...	...	...	...	...
1935	30	24	4	8	19	...	...	...	...	...
1936	27	27	4	8	19	...	...	...	...	...
1937	30	28	3	7	16	...	...	...	...	...
1938	30	29	2	8	17	7	33		11	12
1939	30	29	2	8	17	10	37		11	12
1940	30	30	2	8	18	11	38		9	12
1941	35	27	2	8	17	11	40		9	12
1942	43	22	2	8	16	11	38		10	12
1943	49	21	1	5	16	12	37		11	11
1944	61	18	1	2	13	...	...	...	...	...
1945	58	20	2	3	13	...	...	...	...	...
1946	47	29	4	3	14	13	33		12	12
1947	39	33	3	5	16	12	37		11	13
1948	36	34	3	6	15	12	38		11	13
1949	32	35	3	7	16	14	39		10	14
1950	32	36	3	7	15	13[4]	41[4]		11[4]	13[4]
						14	34	6	9	13
1951	29[1,2]	39[1,2]	4[1,2]	7[1,2]	14[1,2]	14	34	6	10	13
	22	36	4	5	12					
1952	20	35	5	5	12	15	33	6	10	13
1953	21	34	6	5	12	12	35	7	9	13
1954	19	35	6	5	12	12	36	6	9	12
1955	19	35	6	6	12	11	35	6	9	14
1956	18	35	6	6	12	11	35	7	10	14
1957	17	35	7	6	12	11	34	7	10	13
1958	17	34	7	6	12	11	34	7	9	13
1959	16	35	7	6	12	10	35	7	9	13
1960	14	36	7	6	12	9	38	7	9	13
1961	14	37	7	6	12	8	37	7	8	13
1962	14	36	7	6	12	8	37	7	8	14
1963	13	36	8	6	12	7	36	7	8	14
1964	12	35	8	6	12	8	36	7	8	13
1965	12	33	8	6	14	7	36	7	8	13
1966	11	34	7	6	14	7	36	8	8	13
1967	11	34	7	6	14	7	34	8	8	12
1968	10	35	8	6	14	6	35	9	8	12
1969	10	33	8	6	14	7	32	7	8	12
1970	9	34	9	6	15	6	32	7	8	13
1971	9	34	8	6	15	5	31	7	8	12
1972	8	34	8	6	16	5	31	7	7	12
1973	9	35	8	6	15	5	31	7	7	12
1974	8	36	8	5	14	...	...	...	...	...
1975	9	35	8	6	15	...	...	...	...	...

See p. 857 for footnotes

K 2 Proportion of National Product by Sector of Origin (%)

1920–1975

	Norway					Poland				
	A[1]	I	Con	T & C	Com	A	I	Con	T & C	Com
1920	...	...	...	...	...	...	...	...	...	...
1921	...	...	...	...	...	...	...	...	...	...
1922	...	...	...	...	...	...	...	...	...	...
1923	...	...	...	...	...	...	...	...	...	...
1924	...	...	...	...	...	...	...	...	...	...
1925	...	...	...	...	...	...	...	...	...	...
1926	...	...	...	...	...	...	...	...	...	...
1927	...	...	...	...	...	...	...	...	...	...
1928	...	...	...	...	...	...	...	...	...	...
1929	...	...	...	...	...	...	...	...	...	...
1930	17	27	4	13	14	...	...	...	...	...
1931	14	25	4	14	14	...	...	...	...	...
1932	12	28	4	13	14	...	...	...	...	...
1933	12	28	4	13	15	...	...	...	...	...
1934	13	28	4	13	15	...	...	...	...	...
1935	14	28	5	13	15	...	...	...	...	...
1936	13	28	5	13	16	...	...	...	...	...
1937	13	27	5	16	16	...	...	...	...	...
1938	14	28	5	15	16	...	...	...	...	...
1939	12	28	6	15	16	...	...	...	...	...
1940	...	...	...	...	...	...	...	...	...	...
1941	...	...	...	...	...	...	...	...	...	...
1942	...	...	...	...	...	...	...	...	...	...
1943	...	...	...	...	...	...	...	...	...	...
1944	...	...	...	...	...	...	...	...	...	...
1945	...	...	...	...	...	...	...	...	...	...
1946	15	28	7	15	14	...	...	...	...	...
1947	15	29	7	15	14	...	...	...	...	...
1948	16	31	7	15	13	...	...	...	...	...
1949	15	29	7	16	15	...	...	...	...	...
1950	14	30	7	17	15	41	38	8	...	...
1951	13	30	6	19	15	38	41	9	...	...
1952	13	28	6	19	16	35	44	10	...	...
1953	12	28	7	17	17	33	45	11	...	...
1954	13	29	7	16	18	30	44	10	...	...
						----[13]	----[13]	----[13]		
1955	12	29	7	17	17	25	52	8	3	10
1956	12	28	6	19	16	28	50	10	3	8
1957	11	27	7	19	17	29	48	9	3	9
1958	11	27	7	18	17	28	49	10	3	9
1959	10	27	7	17	17	26	50	10	2	9
1960	10	28	7	17	17	26	47	10	5	10
1961	9	28	7	17	18	27	48	9	6	9
1962	8	28	7	17	18	23	50	9	6	10
1963	8	28	8	17	18	23	49	9	6	10
1964	8	28	7	17	18	22	50	9	6	10
1965	8	28	7	17	18	23	51	9	6	9
1966	8	28	8	17	18	22	51	9	6	9
1967	7	27	8	17	18	22	49	9	6	10
1968	6	27	8	18	17	21	49	9	6	11
1969	6	28	8	16	18	17	51	10	6	11
1970	7	26	8	16	18	19	50	11	6	12
1971	6	25	8	15	19	19	51	11	7	11
1972	6	25	8	15	19	19	49	12	7	11
1973	6	25	8	15	19	19	51	13	7	9
1974	6	25	8	15	19	17	56	12	7	7
1975	5	28	8	12	19	15	59	11	7	6

See p. 857 for footnotes

K 2 Proportions of National Product by Sector of Origin (%)

1920–1975

Portugal

	A	I	Con	T & C	Com
1950	33	35		5	...
1951	...	...	...	...	...
1952	...	...	...	...	...
1953	32	27	4	5	12
1954	30	29	4	5	12
1955	30	30	4	5	12
1956	29	28	4	5	12
1957	28	29	4	5	12
1958	27	29	5	5	12
1959	26	29	5	5	12
1960	23	30	4	5	12
1961	22	31	4	5	12
1962	21	30	4	5	12
1963	21	31	5	5	12
1964	19	33	5	5	12
1965	19	34	5	5	12
1966	18	33	5	5	12
1967	18	32	5	5	12
1968	18	33	5	5	13
1969	17	33	5	6	12
1970	16	33	5	6	12
1971	15	33	6	6	13
1972	14	34	6	6	12
1973	15	35	6	6	13
1974	14	35	6	6	13
1975	16	36	7	7	14

Romania

	A	I	Con	T & C	Com
1950	28	44	6	4	12
1951	32	41	6	4	12
1952	26	48	7	4	11
1953	34	42	7	4	9
1954	37	40	5	4	10
1955	38	40	6	4	9
1956	32	43	8	5	8
1957	40	40	7	4	5
1958	35	43	8	4	7
1959	38	41	8	4	6
1960	33	44	9	4	7
1961	33	45	9	4	7
1962	29	49	9	4	6
1963	30	47	8	4	8
1964	30	48	8	4	7
1965	29	49	8	4	7
1966	31	49	8	4	6
1967	29	52	8	4	5
1968	26	54	9	4	4
1969	24[17]	57[17]	9[17]	4[17]	3[17]
1970	19	58	10	6	...
1971	22	56	10	6	...
1972	21	57	10	6	...
1973	19	58	9	6	...
1974	14	35	6	6	13
1975	16	36	7	7	14

Russia[14]

	A	I	Con	T & C	Com
1920	...	...	...	...	...
1921	...	...	...	...	...
1922	...	...	...	...	...
1923	...	...	...	...	...
1924	...	...	...	...	...
1925	...	...	...	...	...
1926	...	...	...	...	...
1927	...	...	...	...	...
1928	48	...	...	...	...
1929	43	...	...	...	...
1930	39	...	...	...	...
1931	35	...	...	...	...
1932	32	...	...	...	...
1933	33	...	...	...	...
1934	32	...	...	...	...
1935	33	...	...	...	...
1936	25	...	...	...	...
1937	31	...	...	...	...
1938	28	...	...	...	...
1939	27	...	...	...	...
1940	29	...	...	...	...
1941	...	...	...	...	...
1942	...	...	...	...	...
1943	...	...	...	...	...
1944	...	...	...	...	...
1945	25	...	...	...	...
1946	27	...	...	...	...
1947	31	...	...	...	...
1948	30	...	...	...	...
1949	27	...	...	...	...
1950	25	...	...	...	...
1951	22	...	...	...	...
1952	22	...	...	...	...
1953	22	...	...	...	...
1954	21	...	...	...	...
1955	21	...	...	...	...
1956	22	...	...	...	...
1957	21	...	...	...	...
1958	22[14] / 25	50	9	4	...
1959	21	52	10	5	...
1960	20	52	10	5	12
1961	21	52	10	6	11
1962	22	52	9	5	11
1963	21	54	9	5	11
1964	22	54	9	6	10
1965	23	52	9	6	11
1966	24	50	9	6	10
1967	22	51	9	6	11
1968	22	52	9	6	11
1969	19	54	10	6	11
1970	22	51	10	6	11
1971	21	51	11	6	11
1972	19	52	11	6	12
1973	20	51	11	6	12
1974	19	53	11	6	12
1975	17	53	11	6	13

See p. 857 for footnotes

K 2 Proportions of National Product by Sector of Origin (%)

1920–1975

	Spain[15]					Sweden				
	A	I	Con	T & C	Com	A[2]	I	Con	T & I	Com
1920	...	...	...	...	...	22	30	4	8	25
1921	...	...	...	...	...	19	30	6	8	23
1922	...	...	...	...	...	18	22	7	9	25
1923	...	...	...	...	...	19	23	6	9	24
1924	...	...	...	...	...	18	27	7	9	23
1925	...	...	...	...	...	17	31	7	8	21
1926	...	...	...	...	...	16	32	6	8	21
1927	...	...	...	...	...	15	33	6	9	21
1928	...	...	...	...	...	15	32	7	9	21
1929	...	...	...	...	...	14	34	6	9	20
1930	...	...	...	...	...	13	34	8	9	21
1931	...	...	...	...	...	13	29	8	9	22
1932	...	...	...	...	...	13	30	8	9	21
1933	...	...	...	...	...	14	28	8	9	21
1934	...	...	...	...	...	14	31	7	9	21
1935	...	...	...	...	...	14	32	7	9	21
1936	...	...	...	...	...	14	33	8	9	21
1937	...	...	...	...	...	14	35	6	9	21
1938	...	...	...	...	...	12	35	7	8	20
1939	...	...	...	...	...	12	35	7	9	20
1940	...	...	...	...	...	12	36	5	9	20
1941	...	...	...	...	...	11	37	5	9	19
1942	...	...	...	...	...	10	36	6	9	18
1943	...	...	...	...	...	11	37	6	9	18
1944	...	...	...	...	...	11	37	6	9	19
1945	...	...	...	...	...	10	38	7	8	18
1946	...	...	...	...	...	11	38	6	9	19
1947	...	...	...	...	...	10	37	7	8	21
1948	...	...	...	...	...	9	40	6	8	20
1949	...	...	...	...	...	10	40	6	8	20
1950	...	...	...	...	...	11[16]	40[16]	6[16]	7[16]	20[16]
						12	36	8	8	11
1951	41	24	3	3	9	13	40	8	9	10
1952	37	27	3	4	10	16	35	8	9	10
1953	35[15]	28[15]	3[15]	4[15]	10[15]	12	35	9	9	11
1954	22	30	5	7	12	12	36	10	9	10
1955	22	31	5	6	11	11	36	9	9	11
1956	22	31	5	7	11	11	36	9	9	11
1957	23	31	5	7	11	10	36	9	9	11
1958	23	31	5	7	11	9	36	10	9	11
1959	24	31	5	7	10	8	36	9	8	11
1960	22	29	4	6	9	7	31	9	7	9
1961	22	30	4	6	9	7	31	9	6	9
1962	22	29	4	6	9	7	31	9	6	9
1963	21	29	5	6	9	6	30	10	6	10
1964	17	30	5	6	14	6	30	10	6	10
1965	17	29	5	6	15	6	30	10	6	10
1966	16	28	5	6	16	5	29	10	6	10
1967	15	27	5	6	16	5	28	10	6	10
1968	15	27	5	6	16	4	28	10	6	10
1969	14[17]	28[17]	5[17]	6[17]	16[17]	4	29	10	6	10
1970	11	29	8	6	15	4	30	9	6	10
1971	11	29	8	6	16	4	28	8	5	9
1972	11	30	8	6	16	4	28	8	6	9
1973	11	29	8	6	15	4	30	7	6	9
1974	9	30	9	6	15	5	33	6	6	9
1975	9	30	8	6	16	4	32	6	5	9

See p. 857 for footnotes

K 2 Proportions of National Product by Sector of Origin (%)

1920–1975

	United Kingdom					Yugoslavia				
	A	I	Con	T & C	Com	A	I	Con	T & C	Com
1920	6	37	4	9	11	...	...	...	...	...
1921	6	30	5	11	11	...	...	...	...	...
1922	6	34	4	11	14	...	...	...	...	...
1923	5	35	4	10	14	...	...	...	...	...
1924	5	35	4	10	14	...	...	...	...	...
1925	4	33	4	10	14	...	...	...	...	...
1926	5	31	5	9	14	...	...	...	...	...
1927	4	33	5	10	14	...	...	...	...	...
1928	4	32	5	10	15	...	...	...	...	...
1929	4	32	5	10	14	...	...	...	...	...
1930	4	29	5	9	14	...	...	...	...	...
1931	4	28	5	10	14	...	...	...	...	...
1932	4	29	4	9	14	...	...	...	...	...
1933	4	30	5	9	15	...	...	...	...	...
1934	5	30	5	9	14	...	...	...	...	...
1935	4	31	5	9	14	...	...	...	...	...
1936	4	32	5	9	15	...	...	...	...	...
1937	4	34	5	9	14	...	...	...	...	...
1938	4	32	5	9	13	...	...	...	...	...
1939	...	...	...	...	...	...	...	...	...	...
1940	...	...	...	...	...	...	...	...	...	...
1941	...	...	...	...	...	...	...	...	...	...
1942	...	...	...	...	...	...	...	...	...	...
1943	...	...	...	...	...	...	...	...	...	...
1944	...	...	...	...	...	...	...	...	...	...
1945	...	...	...	...	...	...	...	...	...	...
1946	7	37	5	8	13	...	...	...	...	...
1947	6	39	5	9	14	...	...	...	...	...
1948	6	40	6	9	14	...	...	...	...	...
1949	6	40	6	8	14	...	...	...	...	...
1950	6	42	6	9	14	...	...	...	...	...
1951	6	43	5	9	14	...	...	...	...	...
1952	5	40	5	9	12	26	47	7	5	7
1953	5	38	6	8	12	31	42	7	5	8
1954	5	39	6	8	13	28	43	7	4	8
1955	5	40	6	8	13	32	44	6	5	8
1956	5	40	6	9	13	31	44	4	6	9
1957	4	39	6	9	12	35	40	5	6	10
1958	4	38	6	8	12	29	44	6	5	10
1959	4	39	6	8	12	30	42	6	5	11
1960	4	40	6	9	12	26	44[17] 49	7	6[17] 7	11
1961	4	38	6	8	12	25	47	8	7	12
1962	4	37	6	8	12	26	46	8	8	12
1963	4	37	6	9	12	25	45	8	8	12
1964	4	37	7	8	12	25	44	10	8	13
1965	3	37	7	9	12	25	42	10	8	15
1966	3	35	7	8	11	26	38	10	7	18
1967	3	35	7	8	11	24	37	11	8	20
1968	3	36	7	8	11	21	38	12	7	22
1969	3	37	7	8	11	21	37	11	7	21
1970	3	37	7	9	11	19	38	12	8	22
1971	3	36	7	8	11	18	38	12	8	23
1972	3	35	8	8	11	17	39	12	8	23
1973	3	34	8	9	10	19	39	11	8	22
1974	3	32	8	9	10	18	42	11	8	21
1975	3	33	7	9	10	16	40	11	8	21

See p. 857 for footnotes

K 2 Proportions of National Product by Sector of Origin

NOTES

1. SOURCES:— The following are taken from the official publications noted on p. xv Austria; Belgium 1953 (2nd line) to 1975; Czechoslovakia 1948–75; France; West Germany; Ireland; Italy 1951 (2nd line) to 1970; Norway. The following are taken from U.N. *Statistical Yearbook 1951:—* Bulgaria 1939–46; Finland 1938 to 1950 (1st line); Greece 1938–47; Netherlands 1938–47. The following are taken from U.N., *Statistics of National Income and Expenditure* (1956) and the succeeding *Yearbooks of National Accounts Statistics:—* Belgium 1948 to 1953 (1st line); Bulgaria 1953–75; Denmark 1950 (2nd line) to 1975; Finland 1950 (2nd line) to 1975; East Germany; Greece 1948–75; Hungary 1950–75; Netherlands 1948–75; Poland; Portugal 1950–75; Romania; Russia 1958 (2nd line) to 1975; Spain 1951–75; Sweden 1950 (2nd line) to 1975; Yugoslavia. The following other sources were used:— Denmark 1870 to 1950 (1st line) — K. Bjerke & N. Ussing, *Studier over Danmarks Nationalprodukt, 1870–1950* (Copenhagen, 1958); Germany — W.G. Hoffman, *Das Wachstum der Deutschen Wirtschaft seit der Mitte des 19 Jahrhunderts* (Berlin, etc., 1965); Hungary 1899–1949 — Alexander Eckstein, "National Income and Capital Formation in Hungary, 1900–1950", *Income and Wealth* (series V); Italy 1861 to 1951 (1st line) — *Annali di Statistica* (serie VIII, 9); Russia 1928 to 1958 (1st line) — based on R. Moorsteen & R.P. Powell, *The Soviet Capital Stock, 1928–1962* (Homewood, Ill, 1966); Sweden 1861 to 1950 (1st line) — based on O. Johansson, *The Gross Domestic Product of Sweden and its Composition, 1861–1955* (Stockholm, 1967); U.K. 1688–1907 — based on Phyllis Deane & W.A. Cole, *British Economic Growth, 1688–1959* (Cambridge, 1962); U.K. 1920–38 — based on C.H. Feinstein, *National Income, Expenditure and Output of the United Kingdom, 1855–1965* (Cambridge, 1972); U.K. 1946–75 — Central Statistical Office, *National Income and Expenditure* (annually).

2. Except as indicated in footnotes, the proportions shown in this table are of gross domestic product.

FOOTNOTES

[1] Including forestry, fishing and whaling.
[2] Including forestry and fishing.
[3] England and Wales only.
[4] Percentage of net domestic product to 1950 (1st line). Forestry and fishing are included with agriculture in this period (except in the case of Denmark).
[5] Averages of three-year periods centred on this year.
[6] Figures relate to the territory established by the treaty of Trianon throughout. For 1925–48 they are for years ended 30 June.
[7] Percentage of net domestic product to 1953 (1st line). Utilities are included with transport in this period.
[8] Percentage of net domestic product to 1946.
[9] Percentage of net domestic product in 1938 prices up to 1949.
[10] Percentage of net domestic product in 1939–9 prices up to 1949.
[11] Passenger transport, laundering and similar services are not included in net material product for 1950–57.
[12] This break occurs on a change of source(see note 1). It is due to the exclusion of forestry and fishing from 'agriculture', to a rearrangement of categories, and to retrospective revisions.
[13] There is a rearrangement of the categories and a change in the definition of national product in 1955.
[14] Percentage of gross national product in 1937 prices up to 1958 (1st line).
[15] Percentage of national income to 1953. Finance is included with commerce, and forestry and fishing with agriculture in this period.
[16] This break occurs on a change of source (see note 1). The major difference is the inclusion of financial and catering services with commerce in the statistics up to 1959 (1st line).
[17] This break is not explained in the source.
[18] Subsequently including Value Added Tax.
[19] Revisions in later *Yearbooks* were not carried further back than 1960.

K 3 BALANCE OF PAYMENTS

1815–1869

	Italy (in million lire)			Norway (in million kroner)			Sweden (in million kronor)			United Kingdom (in million pounds)		
	VB	IB	OCB	VB	IB	OCB	VB	IB	OCB	VB	IB	OCB
1815	...	...	...	...	...	...	...	...	...	...	...	...
1816	...	...	...	...	...	...	...	...	...	+ 4.1	+15.5	+19.6
1817	...	...	...	...	...	...	...	...	...	– 9.1	+18.3	+ 9.2
1818	...	...	...	...	...	...	...	...	...	–21.9	+22.7	+ 0.8
1819	...	...	...	...	...	...	...	...	...	–10.6	+16.5	+ 5.9
1820	...	...	...	...	...	...	...	...	...	– 7.4	+16.0	+ 8.6
1821	...	...	...	...	...	...	...	...	...	+ 0.6	+15.4	+16.0
1822	...	...	...	...	...	...	...	...	...	+ 0.2	+15.9	+16.1
1823	...	...	...	...	...	...	...	...	...	– 9.4	+17.8	+ 8.4
1824	...	...	...	...	...	...	...	...	...	– 5.3	+18.1	+12.8
1825	...	...	...	...	...	...	...	...	...	–26.5	+23.5	– 3.0
1826	...	...	...	...	...	...	...	...	...	–11.6	+18.0	+ 6.4
1827	...	...	...	...	...	...	...	...	...	–14.8	+18.4	+ 3.6
1828	...	...	...	...	...	...	...	...	...	–14.0	+17.5	+ 3.5
1829	...	...	...	...	...	...	...	...	...	–11.7	+16.7	+ 5.0
1830	...	...	...	...	...	...	...	...	...	–12.0	+16.1	+ 4.0
1831	...	...	...	...	...	...	...	...	...	–18.1	+17.0	– 1.1
1832	...	...	...	...	...	...	...	...	...	– 8.7	+16.0	+ 7.3
1833	...	...	...	...	...	...	...	...	...	–12.3	+18.3	+ 6.0
1834	...	...	...	...	...	...	...	...	...	–15.1	+19.9	+ 4.8
1835	...	...	...	...	...	...	...	...	...	–11.4	+23.3	+11.9
1836	...	...	...	...	...	...	...	...	...	–21.8	+25.8	+ 4.0
1837	...	...	...	...	...	...	...	...	...	–19.0	+23.3	+ 4.3
1838	...	...	...	...	...	...	...	...	...	–20.8	+25.6	+ 4.8
1839	...	...	...	...	...	...	...	...	...	–28.4	+27.1	– 1.3
1840	...	...	...	...	...	...	...	...	...	–29.8	+26.6	– 3.2
1841	...	...	...	...	...	...	...	...	...	–22.4	+24.5	+ 2.1
1842	...	...	...	...	...	...	...	...	...	–20.6	+22.9	+ 2.3
1843	...	...	...	...	...	...	...	...	...	–10.9	+23.8	+12.9
1844	...	...	...	...	...	...	...	...	...	–12.3	+25.7	+13.4
1845	...	...	...	...	...	...	...	...	...	–19.0	+29.3	+10.3
1846	...	...	...	...	...	...	...	...	...	–20.3	+29.7	+ 9.4
1847	...	...	...	...	...	...	...	...	...	–41.6	+35.2	– 6.4
1848	...	...	...	...	...	...	...	...	...	–26.9	+28.0	+ 1.1
1849	...	...	...	...	...	...	...	...	...	–25.7	+29.6	+ 3.9
1850	...	...	...	...	...	...	...	...	...	–19.6	+31.2	+11.6
1851	...	...	...	...	...	...	...	...	...	–22.6	+33.0	+10.4
1852	...	...	...	...	...	...	...	...	...	–18.9	+34.4	+15.5
1853	...	...	...	...	...	...	...	...	...	–32.8	+42.6	+ 9.8
1854	...	...	...	...	...	...	...	...	...	–36.6	+46.0	+ 9.4
1855	...	...	...	...	...	...	...	...	...	–25.9	+47.6	+11.7
1856	...	...	...	...	...	...	...	...	...	–32.1	+55.8	+23.7
1857	...	...	...	...	...	...	...	...	...	–40.4	+61.0	+20.6
1858	...	...	...	...	...	...	...	...	...	–23.8	+56.1	+32.3
1859	...	...	...	...	...	...	...	...	...	–22.6	+60.1	+37.5
1860	...	...	...	...	...	...	...	...	...	–45.5	+66.7	+21.2
1861	–313	–14	–325	...	...	...	–34	+5	–29	–57.6	+69.9	+12.3
1862	–223	–21	–244	...	...	...	–18	+5	–13	–58.8	+72.6	+13.7
1863	–231	–24	–255	...	...	...	–12	+5	– 7	–51.4	+81.4	+30.0
1864	–367	–43	–410	...	...	...	–10	+5	– 5	–61.5	+88.9	+27.4
1865	–367	–25	–392	...	...	– 9	– 6	+5	– 1	–51.2	+92.5	+41.3
1866	–219	–43	–262	–30	+20	–10	–15	+2	–13	–55.2	+100.9	+45.7
1867	–109	–49	–158	–23	+31	+ 8	–17	+3	–14	–48.6	+100.3	+51.7
1868	– 71	–45	–116	–32	+24	– 8	–28	+1	–27	–65.5	+106.6	+41.1
1869	–101	–12	–113	–19	+29	+10	–21	—	–21	–57.5	+108.3	+50.8

Abbreviations used throughout this table:– VB = Visible Balance; IB = Invisible Balance; OCB = Overall Current Balance

K 3 Balance of Payments

1870–1919

	Denmark (in million kroner)			France[1]			Germany (in million marks)			Italy (in million lire)		
	VB	IB	OCB	VB	IB	OCB	VB	IB	OCB	VB	IB	OCB
1870	...	...	...	...	...	...	...	...	...	– 101	+ 6	– 95
1871	...	...	...	...	...	...	...	...	...	+ 152	– 8	+ 144
1872	...	...	...	...	...	...	...	...	...	+ 35	+ 9	+ 44
1873	...	...	...	...	...	...	...	...	...	– 96	+ 59	– 37
1874	– 56	+47	– 9	...	...	...	...	...	...	– 264	+ 82	– 182
1875	– 59	+50	– 9	...	...	...	...	...	...	– 132	+112	– 20
1876	– 51	+47	– 4	...	...	...	...	...	...	– 62	+120	+ 58
1877	– 64	+49	–15	...	...	...	...	...	...	– 171	+ 99	– 72
1878	– 40	+45	+ 5	...	...	...	...	...	...	+ 6	+ 95	+ 101
1879	– 44	+44	–	...	...	...	...	...	...	– 121	+ 90	– 31
1880	– 33	+43	+10	...	...	...	+ 120	+ 168	+288	– 35	+123	+ 88
1881	– 65	+50	–15	...	...	...	+ 67	+ 290	+357	– 27	+115	+ 88
1882	– 69	+59	–10	...	...	...	+ 126	+ 329	+455	– 36	+104	+ 68
1883	– 94	+64	–30	...	...	...	+ 39	+ 224	+263	– 51	+123	+ 72
1884	–100	+65	–35	...	...	...	– 46	+ 535	+489	– 204	+127	– 77
1885	– 94	+64	–30	...	...	...	– 68	+ 575	+507	– 452	+ 94	– 358
1886	– 53	+63	+10	...	...	...	+ 101	+ 385	+486	– 373	+ 80	– 293
1887	– 72	+67	– 5	...	...	...	+ 28	+ 403	+431	– 524	+ 72	– 452
1888	– 92	+62	–30	...	...	...	– 57	+ 743	+686	– 220	+ 88	– 132
1889	–100	+65	–35	...	...	...	– 825	+1,415	+590	– 363	+168	– 195
1890	– 79	+64	–15	...	...	...	– 819	+1,249	+430	– 362	+159	– 203
1891	– 92	+72	–20	...	...	...	– 978	+1,312	+334	– 194	+220	+ 26
1892	– 79	+64	–15	...	...	...	–1,065	+1,250	+185	– 161	+219	+ 58
1893	– 91	+71	–20	...	...	...	– 870	+1,231	+361	– 172	+211	+ 39
1894	– 62	+46	–16	...	...	...	– 977	+1,618	+641	– 9	+211	+ 202
1895	–109	+88	–21	...	...	...	– 803	+1,140	+337	– 84	+252	+ 168
1896	–122	+95	–27	...	...	...	– 782	+1,372	+590	– 68	+277	+ 209
1897	– 82	+68	–14	...	...	...	–1,046	+1,712	+666	– 18	+310	+ 292
1898	–129	+68	–61	...	...	...	–1,324	+2,139	+815	– 101	+360	+ 259
1899	–130	+76	–54	...	...	...	–1,276	+1,650	+374	+ 29	+400	+ 429
1900	–134	+73	–61	...	...	...	–1,155	+1,566	+411	– 244	+436	+ 192
1901	–105	+72	–33	...	...	...	– 990	+1,408	+418	– 246	+639	+ 393
1902	–116	+77	–39	...	...	...	– 953	+1,447	+494	– 166	+613	+ 467
1903	– 92	+77	–15	...	...	...	– 988	+1,432	+444	– 240	+654	+ 414
1904	–107	+72	–35	...	...	...	–1,131	+1,770	+639	– 214	+655	+ 442
1905	– 92	+71	–21	...	...	...	–1,397	+2,702	+1,305	– 234	+976	+ 742
1906	–165	+78	–87	...	...	...	–1,663	+2,181	+518	– 494	+1,044	+ 550
1907	–184	+81	–103	...	...	...	–1,903	+2,059	+156	– 813	+942	+ 129
1908	–111	+49	–62	...	...	...	–1,268	+1,825	+557	–1,059	+956	– 103
1909	–123	+48	–75	...	...	...	–1,933	+2,350	+417	–1,098	+881	– 217
1910	– 87	+42	–45	–4,354	+11,932	+7,578	–1,459	+2,211	+752	–1,028	+1,059	+ 31
1911	– 86	+46	–40	–9,555	+12,425	+2,870	–1,601	+2,244	+643	–1,035	+1,057	+ 22
1912	–142	+60	–82	–7,213	+12,892	+5,679	–1,735	+2,188	+453	–1,155	+1,049	– 106
1913	–140	+62	–78	–7,302	+14,196	+6,894	– 673	+1,612	+939	– 991	+1,086	+ 95
1914	+ 62	+68	+130	...	...	...	...	...	...	– 459	+ 758	+ 299
1915	– 50	...	...	...	...	...	...	...	...	– 590	–323	– 913
1916	– 73	...	...	...	...	...	...	...	...	–3,140	–724	–3,863
1917	– 54	...	...	...	...	...	...	...	...	–6,883	–1,848	–8,731
1918	–200	...	...	...	...	...	...	...	...	–7,826	–2,767	–10,593
1919	–1,654	...	...	...	...	...	...	...	...	–7,774	+356	–7,418

See p. 868 for footnotes

K 3 Balance of Payments

1870–1919

	Norway (in million kroner)			Sweden (in million kronor)			United Kingdom (in million pounds)		
	VB	IB	OCB	VB	IB	OCB	VB	IB	OCB
1870	– 20	+ 35	+ 15	– 2	+ 6	+ 4	– 57.5	+112.1	+ 54.6
1871	– 19	+ 28	+ 9	– 2	+ 8	+ 6	– 46.0	+121.9	+ 75.9
1872	– 24	+ 41	+ 17	– 4	+ 11	+ 7	– 36.8	+134.1	+ 97.3
1873	– 31	+ 42	+ 11	– 38	+ 14	– 24	– 56.3	+142.3	+ 86.0
1874	– 55	+ 47	– 8	– 67	+ 18	– 49	– 69.1	+147.5	+ 78.4
1875	– 66	+ 39	– 27	– 51	+ 13	– 38	– 90.5	+147.4	+ 56.9
1876	– 44	+ 49	+ 5	– 53	+ 12	– 41	–117.8	+148.6	+ 30.8
1877	– 74	+ 44	– 30	– 78	+ 14	– 64	–141.5	+152.0	+ 10.5
1878	– 43	+ 42	– 1	– 45	+ 11	– 34	–121.8	+144.2	+ 22.4
1879	– 41	+ 44	+ 3	– 25	+ 7	– 18	–111.8	+143.9	+ 32.1
1880	– 39	+ 47	+ 8	– 31	+ 7	– 24	–121.1	+154.1	+ 33.0
1881	– 39	+ 42	+ 3	– 54	– 2	– 56	– 94.5	+154.5	+ 60.0
1882	– 29	+ 48	+ 19	– 37	– 1	– 38	–100.0	+160.3	+ 60.3
1883	– 39	+ 43	+ 4	– 66	+ 3	– 63	–116.9	+166.5	+ 49.6
1884	– 41	+ 45	+ 4	– 78	+ 2	– 76	– 91.1	+161.8	+ 70.7
1885	– 40	+ 40	–	– 87	–	– 87	– 98.5	+161.0	+ 62.5
1886	– 33	+ 41	+ 8	– 67	– 4	– 71	– 79.5	+157.8	+ 78.3
1887	– 23	+ 39	+ 16	– 45	– 5	– 50	– 78.5	+166.8	+ 88.3
1888	– 29	+ 48	+ 19	– 45	+ 2	– 43	– 85.9	+177.2	+ 91.3
1889	– 43	+ 58	+ 15	– 77	+ 13	– 64	–105.0	+187.9	+ 82.9
1890	– 58	+ 48	– 9	– 83	+ 15	– 68	– 86.3	+193.6	+107.3
1891	– 77	+ 44	– 33	– 54	+ 13	– 41	–122.1	+193.9	+ 71.8
1892	– 67	+ 49	– 18	– 46	+ 12	– 34	–128.9	+191.4	+ 62.5
1893	– 59	+ 44	– 15	– 3	+ 11	+ 8	–124.6	+180.3	+ 55.7
1894	– 66	+ 43	– 23	– 28	+ 19	– 9	–131.5	+181.0	+ 49.5
1895	– 70	+ 35	– 35	– 11	+ 16	+ 5	–126.5	+181.4	+ 54.9
1896	– 84	+ 44	– 40	+ 1	+ 24	+ 25	–137.9	+188.3	+ 50.4
1897	– 86	+ 46	– 40	– 21	+ 26	+ 5	–153.9	+191.7	+ 37.8
1898	–105	+ 43	– 62	– 86	+ 30	– 56	–168.9	+198.0	+ 29.1
1899	–133	+ 55	– 78	–129	+ 36	– 93	–153.7	+205.9	+ 52.2
1900	–125[2]	+ 57[2]	– 69	–118	+ 42	– 76	–167.0[3]	+212.7[3]	+ 45.7[3]
	–131	+ 63					–129	+163	+ 34
1901	–114	+ 34	– 80	– 93	+ 26	– 67	–136	+155	+ 19
1902	–100	+ 37	– 63	–110	+ 26	– 84	–141	+165	+ 24
1903	– 90	+ 32	– 42	– 88	+ 32	– 56	–144	+187	+ 43
1904	– 88	+ 39	– 49	–157	+ 41	–116	–140	+192	+ 52
1905	– 78	+ 42	– 45	–124	+ 45	– 79	–118	+206	+ 88
1906	– 77	+ 36	– 41	–134	+ 51	– 83	–106	+227	+121
1907	–118	+ 54	– 64	–150	+ 58	– 92	– 84	+246	+162
1908	–127	+ 57	– 70	–116	+ 49	– 67	– 93	+243	+150
1909	–115	+ 59	– 56	–142	+ 48	– 96	–111	+253	+142
1910	–106	+ 76	– 30	– 78	+ 59	– 19	– 96	+270	+174
1911	–136	+ 75	– 61	– 29	+ 62	+ 33	– 75	+279	+204
1912	–159	+106	– 53	– 39	+ 70	+ 31	– 94	+297	+203
1913	–136	+135	– 1	– 50	+ 83	+ 33	– 82	+317	+235
1914	–139	+107	– 32	+ 46	+ 64	+110	–120	+254	+134
1915	–127	+256	+129	+144	+146	+290	–340	+285	– 55
1916	–187	+579	+392	+338	+280	+618	–350	+440	+ 90
1917	–665	+579	– 86	+471	+195	+666	–420	+470	+ 50
1918	–469	+611	+142	– 13	+346	+333	–630	+355	–275
1919	–682	+613	– 69	–958	+353	–605	–470	+425	– 45

See p. 868 for footnotes

K 3 Balance of Payments

1920–1975

	Austria (in thousand million schillings)			Belgium/Luxembourg (in thousand million francs)			Bulgaria (in million leva)			Czechoslovakia (in million korunas)		
	VB	IB	OCB	VB	IB	OCB	VB	IB	OCB	VB	IB	OCB
1920	...	...	...	...	...	...	...	...	...	...	...	...
1921	...	...	...	...	...	...	...	...	...	...	...	...
1922	...	...	...	...	...	...	...	...	...	...	...	...
1923	...	...	...	...	...	...	...	...	...	...	...	...
1924	...	...	−1.2	...	...	...	+386	−618	−232	...	...	...
1925	...	...	−0.7	...	...	...	−160	−775	−935	+1,212	−644	+ 568
1926	...	...	−0.8	...	...	...	−193	−738	−931	+2,575	−714	+1,861
1927	...	...	−0.7	...	...	...	+937	−1,430	−473	+2,172	−104	+2,066
1928	...	...	−0.7	...	...	...	−236	−701	−937	+2,023	+ 33	+2,064
1929	...	...	−0.8	...	...	...	−1,774	−1,159	−2,933	+ 520	+361	+ 881
1930	...	...	−0.6	...	...	...	+1,208	−1,429	−119	+1,779	− 61	+1,718
1931	...	...	−0.4	...	...	...	+839	−1,453	−619	+1,373	−357	+1,016
1932	...	...	−0.4	...	...	...	+531	−505	− 64	− 144	−123	− 267
1933	...	...	−0.2	...	...	...	+429	−331	+ 98	+ 21	− 69	− 47
1934	...	...	−0.2	...	...	...	+273	−278	− 5	+ 898	− 62	+ 836
1935	...	...	−0.2	...	...	...	+910	−248	+662	+ 680	−502	+ 178
1936	...	...	−0.1	...	...	...	+1,134	−191	+943	+ 99	−658	− 559
1937	...	...	+0.04	...	...	...	...	...	...	+ 992	−692	+ 300
1938	...	...	...	...	...	...	...	...	...	...	...	...
1939	...	...	...	...	...	...	...	...	...	...	...	...
1940	...	...	...	...	...	...	...	...	...	...	...	...
1941	...	...	...	...	...	...	...	...	...	...	...	...
1942	...	...	...	...	...	...	...	...	...	...	...	...
1943	...	...	...	...	...	...	...	...	...	...	...	...
1944	...	...	...	...	...	...	...	...	...	...	...	...
1945	...	...	...	...	...	...	...	...	...	...	...	...
1946	...	...	...	...	...	...	...	...	...	...	...	...
1947	...	...	...	...	...	...	...	...	...	...	...	...
1948	...	...	−1.6	...	...	...	...	...	...	...	...	...
1949	...	...	−3.1 [4]	...	...	...	...	...	...	...	...	...
1950	− 3.1	+ 0.9	−2.2	...	...	...	...	...	...	...	...	...
1951	− 4.4	...	...	...	...	...	...	...	...	...	...	...
1952	− 1.1	+ 1.5	+0.4	...	...	...	...	...	...	...	...	...
1953	+ 0.1	+ 2.9	+2.9	...	...	+0.2	...	...	...	...	...	...
1954	− 1.1	+ 1.6	+0.5	...	...	−3.3	...	...	...	...	...	...
1955	− 4.6	+ 3.2	−1.4	+2.6	+ 5.7	+8.3	...	...	...	...	...	...
1956	− 1.9	+ 3.8	+1.9	+0.8	+ 8.0	+8.8	...	...	...	...	...	...
1957	− 2.8	+ 4.7	+1.9	−5.7	+11.2	+5.5	...	...	...	...	...	...
1958	− 2.9	+ 5.5	+2.6	+2.7	+13.9	+16.6	...	...	...	...	...	...
1959	− 3.7	+ 5.0	+1.3	−4.3	+ 4.4	+0.1	...	...	...	...	...	...
1960	− 6.9	+ 5.4	−1.4	−5.1	+ 6.5	+1.4	...	...	...	...	...	...
1961	− 6.8	+ 6.5	−0.2	−7.0	+ 6.7	−0.3	...	...	...	...	...	...
1962	− 7.2	+ 9.6	+2.4	−6.4	+10.6	+ 4.2	...	...	...	...	...	...
1963	− 9.3	+ 9.6	+0.3	−9.0	+ 3.8	− 5.2	...	...	...	...	...	...
1964	−11.8	+12.4	+0.6	−8.7	+ 8.6	− 0.1	...	...	...	...	...	...
1965	−13.8	+12.7	−1.1	−2.6	+10.2	+ 7.6	...	...	...	...	...	...
1966	−18.0	+12.5	−5.4	−16.6	+12.0	− 4.6	...	...	...	...	...	...
1967	−14.2	+11.3	−2.9	−3.9	+13.7	+ 9.8	...	...	...	...	...	...
1968	−14.0	+11.8	−2.2	−12.1	+13.5	+ 1.4	...	...	...	...	...	...
1969	−11.3	+13.9	+2.6	−4.6	+ 8.3	+ 3.7	...	...	...	...	...	...
1970	−18.8	+18.5	−0.2	+23.9	+11.8	+35.7	...	...	...	...	...	...
1971	−26.7	+24.5	−2.2	+20.8	+20.8	+41.3	...	...	...	...	...	...
1972	−30.3	+26.4	−3.9	+29.3	+21.9	+51.2	...	...	...	...	...	...
1973	−33.5	+26.6	−6.9	+27.4	+17.6	+45.0	...	...	...	...	...	...
1974	−32.7	+23.4	−9.3	+11.3	+24.5	+35.8	...	...	...	...	...	...
1975	−30.4	+24.9	−5.4	−15.3	+38.2	+24.9	...	...	...	...	...	...

See p. 868 for footnotes

K 3 Balance of Payments

1920–1975

	Denmark (in million kroner)			Finland (in million markkas)			France[1]		
	VB	IB	OCB	VB	IB	OCB	VB	IB	OCB
1920	−1,352	...	...	...	...	...	−35,910	+8,217	−27,693
1921	−139	+136	−3	...	...	...	−435	+9,224	+8,789
1922	−280	+129	−151	+428	−25	+403	−4,890	+10,466	+5,576
1923	−368	+168	−200	−283	+36	−247	−4,760	+9,502	+4,742
1924	−242	+199	−43	+225	+4	+229	+400	+9,794	+10,194
1925	−148	+167	+19	−15	+106	+91	−1,560	+9,988	+8,428
1926	−122	+137	+15	−116	+136	+19	−2,000[7]	+11,255[7]	+9,255[7]
1927	−131	+144	+13	−72	+105	+33	+467	+8,050	+7,746
1928	−102	+120	+18	−1,778	+175	−1,603	−4,237	+10,200	+5,720
1929	−99	+130	+31	−576	+98	−478	−9,000	+14,500	+4,489
1930	−132	+85	−47	+183	+29	+212	−11,473	+13,281	+308
1931	−150	+58	−92	+981	−23	+958	−12,762	+10,250	−3,012
1932	−18	+36	+18	+1,124	+37	+1,161	−10,015	+3,700	−6,315
1933	−62	+62	−	+1,370	−20	+1,350	−9,241	+6,050	−2,950
1934	−131	+66	−65	+1,461	+110	+1,571	−5,500	+5,600	−1,250
1935	−74	+145	+71	+913	+315	+1,228	−5,000	+5,600	−400
1936	−116	+121	+5	+1,028	+290	+1,318	−7,130	+5,520	−2,820
1937	−108	+218	+110	+238	+580	+818	−9,150	+6,055	−3,995
1938	−90	+201	+111	−72	+600	+528	−5,025	+5,980	−120
1939	−162	+250	+88	+135	+745	+880	...	...	...
1940	+140	+606	+746	−6,780	+2,750	−4,030	...	...	...
1941	−33	+836	+803	−5,910	+1,125	−4,785	...	...	...
1942	−157	+799	+642	−5,770	+765	−5,005	...	...	...
1943	+113	+1,649	+1,762	−4,185	+920	−3,265	...	...	...
1944	+193	+2,559	+2,752	−2,415	+105	−2,310	...[1]	...[1]	...[1]
1945	+208	+668	+876	...	...	...	−861	−255	−1,496
1946	−1,230	+294	−936	...	...	...	−1,527	−225	−2,049
1947	−777	+359	−418	...	...	...	−1,452	−61	−1,676
				in million new markkas					
1948	−693	+355	−338	−111	+147	+35	−1,428	−102	−1,738
1949	−652	+380	−272	−19	+149	+130	−468	−72	−707
1950	−1,298[5]	+469[5]	−829[5]	+3	+14	+17	−78	−37	−238
	−701	+328	−373						
1951	−473	+621	+148	+431	+27	+458	−770	−200	−1,058
1952	−107	+304	+197	−177	+43	−134	−79[7]	+11[7]	−68[7]
							−619	+28	−591
1953	−177	+455	+278	+81	+30	+112	−339	+222	−117
1954	−780	+262	−518	+62	+70	+132	−179	+441	+262
1955	−110	+277	+167	+40[6]	+108[6]	+148	+86	+516	+602
				+250	−102				
1956	−574	+458	−116	−7	−123	−130	−809	+125	−684
1957	−461	+754	+293	+132	−151	−19	−950	−254	−1,204
1958	+121	+746	+625	+341	−90	+251	−295	−48	−343
1959	−748	+858	+110	+219	−125	+94	+436	+275	+710
1960	−1,459	+1,062	−397	−3	−130	−133	+92	+531	+643
1961	−1,666	+911	−755	−63	−156	−219	+417	+467	+884
1962	−2,495	+838	−1,657	−134	−159	−293	+485	+287	+773
1963	−768	+933	+165	+111	−178	−67	+177	+207	+384
1964	−2,583	+1,220	−1,363	−343	−221	−563	−89[1]	+67[1]	−22[1]
							−439	+330	−109
1965	−2,495	+1,277	−1,218	−327	−280	−607	+1,917	+1,499	+3,416
1966	−2,781	+1,328	−1,453	−321	−307	−629	−189	−30	−219
1967	−3,193	+1,156	−2,037	−141	−348	−489	+1,650	−731	+919
1968	−3,407	+1,791	−1,616	+728	−458	+270	−1,512	−5,244	−6,756
1969	−4,720	+1,639	−3,081	+501	−414	+87	−6,452	−3,967	−10,419
1970	−5,702	+1,625	−4,077	−579	−425	−1,004	+3,770	−2,375	+1,395
1971	−5,314	+2,145	−3,169	−1,098	−332	−1,422	+9,608	−5,246	+4,362
1972	−3,007	+2,605	−402	−193	−287	−480	+8,261	−6,755	+1,506
1973	−7,175	+4,359	−2,816	−825	−655	−1,480	+11,475	−6,459	+5,016
1974	−11,079	+5,517	−5,562	−3,562	−1,000	−4,562	−7,115	−9,640	−16,755
1975	−7,627	+4,678	−2,949	−6,545	−1,429	−7,974	+16,649	−7,262	+9,387

See p. 868 for footnotes

K 3 **Balance of Payments**

1920–1975

	Germany (in million marks)			Greece[10]			Hungary (in million gold pengos)		
	VB	IB	OCB	VB	IB	OCB	VB	IB	OCB
1920	...	...	...	...	...	...	...	...	...
1921	...	...	...	...	...	...	...	...	...
1922	...	...	...	...	...	...	...	...	...
1923	...	...	...	– 3.5	+ 0.7	– 2.8	...	...	...
1924	...	...	...	...	...	...	...	...	...
1925	–2,444	+ 456	–1,988	...	...	...	...	...	...
1926	+ 793	+ 359	+1,152	–11.8	+ 4.5	– 7.3	– 76	– 71	–148
1927	–2,960	+ 300	–2,660	...	...	...	–377	–130	–507
1928	–1,311	+ 109	–1,202	...	...	...	–385	–141	–526
1929	– 44	– 88	– 132	–16.7	+ 7.5	– 9.2	– 44	–188	–232
1930	+1,558	– 462	+1,096	–13.2	+ 6.1	– 7.0	+ 73	–191	–119
1931	+2,778	– 750	+2,038	–12.2	+ 4.7	– 7.6	+ 27	–235	–207
1932	+1,052	– 635	+ 417	– 6.2	+ 4.8	– 2.4	– 9	– 13	– 21
1933	+ 666	– 385	+ 281	– 3.5	+ 4.1	+ 0.6	+ 66	– 32	+ 34
1934	– 373	– 161	– 534	– 3.8	+ 2.5	– 1.3	+ 48	– 39	+ 10
1935	– 9	– 99	– 108	– 3.7	+ 2.3	– 1.3	+ 50	– 23	+ 28
1936	...	...	...	– 4.6	+ 1.4	– 3.3	+ 67	– 2	+ 65
1937	...	...	...	– 7.0	+ 4.0	– 3.1	+ 95	+ 5	+100
1938	...	...	...	– 5.5[10]	+ 3.1[10]	– 2.4[10]	...	...	...
1939	...	...	...	...	...	...	...	...	...
1940	...	...	...	...	...	...	...	...	...
1941	...	...	...	...	...	...	...	...	...
1942	...	...	...	...	...	...	...	...	...
1943	...	...	...	...	...	...	...	...	...
1944	...	...	...	...	...	...	...	...	...
	West Germany in million D marks								
1945	...	...	...	...	...	...	...	...	...
1946	...	...	...	...	...	...	...	...	...
1947	...	...	...	...	...	...	...	...	...
1948	...	...	...	...	...	...	...	...	...
1949	[– 963][9]	[– 158][9]	[–1,122][9]	...	...	...	...	...	...
1950	[– 558][9]	[+ 56][9]	[– 614][9]	– 4.5	+ 0.2	– 4.7	...	...	...
1951	+1,514	+ 733	+ 781	– 3.9	+ 0.4	– 4.3	...	...	...
1952	+2,162	+ 176	+2,338	– 2.9	—	– 2.9	...	...	...
1953	+3,652	+ 477	+4,129	– 3.2	+ 1.7	– 1.5	...	...	..
1954	+3,924	+ 58	+3,982	– 3.9	+ 0.9	– 3.0	...	...	...
1955	+3,237	– 355	+2,882	– 4.5	+ 3.0	– 1.5	...	...	...
1956	+5,731	– 209	+5,522	– 6.3	+ 3.0	– 3.3	...	...	...
1957	+7,396	+ 246	+7,642	– 7.8[2]	+ 4.7[2]	– 3.1[2]	...	...	...
1958	+7,505	+ 333	+7,838	– 9.2	+ 4.3	– 4.9	...	...	...
1959	+7,752[8]	– 766[8]	+6,986[8]	–10.3	+ 4.5	– 5.8	...	...	...
1960	+8,580	– 962	+7,618	–15.4	+ 5.2	–10.2	...	...	...
1961	+9,798	–3,350	+6,448	–14.4	+ 6.2	– 8.2	...	...	...
1962	+6,228	–3,198	+3,030	–13.0	+ 7.4	– 5.6	...	...	...
1963	+9,120	–3,140	+5,980	–11.4	+ 8.1	– 3.0	...	...	...
1964	+9,544	–4,075	+5,469	–13.6	+ 5.4	– 8.2	...	...	...
1965	+5,200	–5,285	– 85	–18.8	+ 8.3	–10.5	...	...	...
1966	+11,825	–4,994	+6,831	–18.6	+ 8.6	– 8.0	...	...	...
1967	+21,009	–5,151	+15,858	–16.7	+12.0	– 4.7	...	...	...
1968	+22,703	–4,485	+18,218	–21.2	+12.7	– 8.5	...	...	...
1969	+20,089	–5,413	+14,676	–23.7	+13.0	–10.7	...	...	...
1970	+21,222	–7,878	+13,344	–25.6	+16.3	– 9.3	...	...	...
1971	+23,271	–8,693	+14,578	–29.5	+24.6	– 5.0	...	...	...
1972	+26,384	–9,902	+16,482	–34.9	+30.2	– 4.7	...	...	...
1973	+40,589	–13,251	+27,338	–57.1	+38.6	–18.5	...	...	...
1974	+57,427	–15,709	+43,718	–58.1	+39.4	–18.6	...	...	...
1975	+43,331	–16,042	+27,289	–76.2	+46.7	–29.4	...	...	...

See p. 868 for footnotes

K 3 Balance of Payments

1920–1975

	Southern Ireland (in million pounds)			Italy (in million lire)			Netherlands (in million guilder)		
	VB	IB	OCB	VB	IB	OCB	VB	IB	OCB
1920	...	...	...	–13,802	+2,932	–10,870	...	...	...
1921	...	...	...	– 8,496	+3,457	– 5,039	...	...	...
1922	...	...	...	– 6,627	+4,199	– 2,428	...	...	...
1923	...	...	...	– 5,767	+4,227	– 1,541	...	...	...
1924	...	...	...	– 5,074	+5,460	+ 386	...	...	...
1925	...	...	...	– 7,315	+6,128	– 1,187	...	...	...
1926	...	...	...	– 7,264	+6,220	– 1,034	...	...	...
1927	...	...	...	– 4,919	+4,223	– 696	...	...	...
1928	...	...	...	– 7,432	+4,180	– 3,252	...	...	...
1929	...	...	...	– 6,505	+4,103	– 2,402	...	...	...
1930	...	...	...	– 5,220	+3,700	– 1,520	– 456	+ 500	+ 44
1931	...	...	...	– 1,386	+3,154	+ 1,768	– 391	+ 382	– 9
1932	...	...	...	– 1,383	+2,155	+ 772	– 326	+ 311	– 15
1933	– 16.8	+ 15.5	– 1.3	– 2,644	+2,076	– 568	– 375	+ 254	– 121
1934	– 21.2	+ 14.9	– 6.3	– 2,378	+1,751	– 627	– 236	+ 201	– 35
1935	– 17.4	+ 13.7	– 3.7	– 2,874	+1,284	– 1,590	– 181	+ 260	+ 78
1936	– 17.4	+ 12.8	– 3.6	– 1,701	+1,962	+ 261	– 181	+ 339	+ 158
1937	– 21.3	+ 13.9	– 7.4	– 4,384	+2,392	– 1,992	– 237	+ 451	+ 214
1938	– 17.2	+ 14.5	– 2.7	– 2,281	+1,734	– 547	– 232	+ 337	+ 105
1939	– 16.5	+ 13.8	– 2.7	– 908	+ 899	– 9	– 398	+ 387	– 11
1940	– 13.8	+ 11.5	– 2.3	– 2,060	– 820	– 2,880	...	...	...
1941	+ 2.3	+ 11.7	+13.0	+ 3,409	–2,079	+ 1,330	...	...	...
1942	– 1.9	+ 14.6	+16.5	+ 2,800	–2,624	+ 176	...	...	...
1943	+ 1.4	+ 30.9	+32.3	+ 2,846	–5,333	– 2,487	...	...	...
1944	+ 1.4	+ 31.2	+32.6	–30,221	–5,358	–35,579	...	...	...
				in thousand million lire					
1945	– 5.5	+ 23.0	+28.5	– 121	– 15	– 135	...	...	...
1946	– 33.0	+ 24.1	+ 8.9	– 119	– 25	– 144	–1,330	+ 18	–1,312
1947	– 91.8	+ 53.9	–37.9	– 510	+ 155	– 355	–1,862	+ 195	–1,667
1948	– 87.0	+ 58.0	–29.0	– 208	+ 219	+ 11	–1,770	+ 323	–1,447
1949	– 67.9	+ 53.7	–14.2	– 184	+ 235	+ 51	–1,136	+ 824	– 312
1950	– 85.9	+ 50.4	–35.5	– 102	+ 216	+ 114	–1,959	+ 828	–1,131
1951	–122.4	+ 55.2	–67.2	– 171	+ 205	+ 34	–1,340	+1,071	– 269
1952	– 70.0	+ 52.7	–17.3	– 466	+ 244	– 222	+ 287	+1,468	+1,755
1953	– 68.5	+ 51.9	–16.6	– 462	+ 326	– 136	– 180	+1,539	+1,359
1954	– 64.8	+ 53.8	–11.0	– 406	+ 361	– 45	–1,136	+1,370	+ 234
1955	– 97.6	+ 52.8	–44.8	– 414	+ 386	– 28	– 967	+1,748	+ 781
1956	– 74.4	+ 55.8	–18.6	– 457	+ 403	– 54	–2,248	+1,498	– 750
1957	– 53.2	+ 49.1	+ 4.1	– 479	+ 516	+ 37	–2,125	+1,531	– 594
1958	– 68.2	+ 67.2	– 1.0	– 238	+ 587	+ 349	– 170	+1,703	+1,533
1959	– 82.2	+ 73.4	– 8.8	– 89	+ 555	+ 466	– 129	+1,912	+1,783
1960	– 73.6	+ 72.8	– 0.8	– 397	+ 606	+ 209	– 648	+1,892	+1,244
1961	– 81.8	+ 80.6	+ 1.2	– 347	+ 665	+ 318	–1,356	+1,989	+ 633
1962	–100.2	+ 86.7	–13.5	– 550	+ 724	+ 174	–1,163	+1,660	+ 497
1963	–111.2	+ 89.1	–22.1	– 1,190	+ 740	– 450	–1,735	+2,097	+ 362
1964	–127.6	+ 96.1	–31.5	– 403	+ 807	+ 404	–2,837	+2,193	– 644
1965	–151.2	+109.4	–41.8	+ 404	+1,000	+ 1,404	–2,088	+2,159	+ 71
1966	–124.5	+108.4	–16.1	+ 209	+1,143	+ 1,352	–2,607	+1,896	– 711
1967	–100.1	+115.3	+15.2	– 13	+1,049	+ 1,036	–2,269	+2,002	– 267
1968	–153.2	+136.9	–16.3	+ 645	+1,026	+ 1,671	–1,291	+1,557	+ 266
1969	–211.3	+142.2	–69.1	+ 314	+1,187	+ 1,501	–1,791	+1,937	+ 146
1970	–212.0	+146.7	–65.3	– 1,323	+2,052	+ 729	–3,425	+1,606	–1,819
1971	–216.3	+145.3	–71.0	– 964	+2,175	+ 1,211	–2,560	+1,935	– 625
1972	–190.8	+142.4	–48.4	– 1,034	+2,226	+ 1,192	+1,212	+2,925	+4,137
1973	–268.7	+186.4	–82.3	– 3,668	+2,098	– 1,570	+2,535	+3,988	+6,523
1974	–544.2	+264.0	–280.2	– 7,207	+2,096	– 5,111	+1,526	+3,892	+5,418
1975	–302.7	+285.0	–17.7	– 2,672	+2,414	– 258	+1,978	+2,191	+4,169

K 3 **Balance of Payments**

1920–1975

	Norway (in million kroner)			Poland (in million zlotys)			Portugal (in thousand million escudos)		
	VB	IB	OCB	VB	IB	OCB	VB	IB	OCB
1920	−1,445	+ 582	− 864	...	...	...	...	...	...
1921	− 570	+ 29	− 541	...	...	...	...	...	...
1922	− 461	+ 165	− 296	...	...	...	...	...	...
1923	− 491	+ 223	− 268	+ 87	+117	+204	...	...	...
1924	− 434	+ 236	− 198	−481	+ 75	−406	...	...	...
1925	− 234	+ 159	− 74	−524	− 59	−582	...	...	...
1926	− 181	+ 177	− 4	+759	−112	+647	...	...	...
1927	− 231	+ 180	− 51	−308	−174	−481	...	...	...
1928	− 256	+ 137	− 119	−872	−127	−999	...	...	...
1929	− 226	+ 186	− 40	−462	− 57	−519	...	...	...
1930	− 198	+ 130	− 68	+ 90	−238	−148	...	...	...
1931	− 246	+ 129	− 117	+314	−209	+105	...	...	...
1932	− 116	+ 171	+ 55	+124	− 99	+ 25	...	...	...
1933	− 90	+ 176	+ 86	+ 99	− 18	+ 81	...	...	...
1934	− 134	+ 173	+ 60	+176	− 10	+166	...	...	...
1935	− 172	+ 194	+ 22	+ 68	− 5	+ 62	...	...	...
1936	− 193	+ 283	+ 90	+ 21	− 11	+ 10	...	...	...
1937	− 349	+ 421	+ 72	− 62	− 22	− 84	...	...	...
1938	− 290	+ 376	+ 86	...	...	...	...	...	...
1939	− 452	+ 422	− 30	...	...	...	...	...	...
1940	...	...	...	...	...	...	...	...	...
1941	...	...	...	...	...	...	...	...	...
1942	...	...	...	...	...	...	...	...	...
1943	...	...	...	...	...	...	...	...	...
1944	...	...	...	...	...	...	...	...	...
1945	...	...	...	...	...	...	...	...	...
1946	− 782	+ 253	− 529	...	...	...	...	...	...
1947	−1,334	+ 109	−1,225	...	...	...	...	...	...
1948	− 991	+ 465	− 526	...	...	...	...	...	...
1949	−1,270	+ 690	− 580	...	...	...	...	...	...
1950	−1,310	+1,017	+ 293	...	...	...	...	...	...
1951	−1,386	+ 815	+ 571	...	...	...	...	...	...
1952	−1,817	+1,738	+ 79	...	...	...	−2.4	+0.4	−2.0
1953	−2,163	+1,324	− 839	...	...	...	−2.5	+0.7	−1.8
1954	−2,055	+ 928	−1,127	...	...	...	−2.0	+0.6	−1.4
1955	−2,021	+1,208	− 813	...	...	...	−2.3	+0.7	−1.7
1956	−1,997	+1,890	+ 107	...	...	...	−2.9	+1.2	−1.6
1957	−2,102	+1,945	+ 157	...	...	...	−4.6	+1.8	−2.8
1958	−1,895	+ 813	−1,082	...	...	...	−4.1	+2.2	−1.9
1959	−1,783	+1,292	− 491	...	...	...	−4.1	+2.0	−2.1
1960	−2,977	+2,217	− 760	...	...	...	−4.8	+1.9	−2.9
1961	−3,205	+1,890	−1,315	...	...	...	−7.9	+0.2	−7.6
1962	−3,557	+2,304	−1,253	...	...	...	−4.4	+1.5	−2.8
1963	−3,582	+2,296	−1,286	...	...	...	−5.1	+2.2	−3.0
1964	−3,597	+3,065	− 532	...	...	...	−4.7	+4.7	−
1965	−3,792	+3,062	− 730	...	...	...	−6.4	+5.9	−0.4
1966	−4,511	+3,445	−1,066	...	...	...	−8.3	+9.2	+0.9
1967	−5,190	+3,453	−1,737	...	...	...	−7.0[2]	+11.8[2]	+4.8[2]
1968	−4,955	+6,619	+ 664	...	...	...	−8.3	+10.5	+2.2
1969	−6,078	+6,989	+ 911	...	...	...	−8.8	+14.5	+5.7
1970	−8,137	+6,409	−1,728	...	...	...	−13.0	+16.4	+3.4
1971	−9,028	+5,345	−3,683	...	...	...	−18.1	+23.1	+5.0
1972	−7,526	+7,139	− 387	...	...	...	−16.7	+29.3	+12.6
1973	−9,208	+7,006	−2,002	...	...	...	−18.3	+26.9	+8.6
1974	−15,190	+8,365	−6,825	...	...	...	−50.5	+29.6	−20.9
1975	−15,203	+1,933	−13,270	...	...	...	...	...	...

See p. 868 for footnotes

K 3 Balance of Payments

1920–1975

	Spain (in thousand million pesetas)			Sweden (in million kronor)			Switzerland (in million francs)		
	VB	IB	OCB	VB	IB	OCB	VB	IB	OCB
1920	...	...	...	–1,036	+ 310	– 726	...	...	...
1921	...	...	...	– 161	+ 107	– 54	...	...	...
1922	...	...	...	+ 40	+ 78	+ 118	...	...	...
1923	...	...	...	– 137	+ 142	+ 5	...	...	...
1924	...	...	...	– 148	+ 150	+ 2	...	...	...
1925	...	...	...	– 88	+ 165	+ 77	...	...	...
1926	...	...	...	– 71	+ 191	+ 120	...	...	...
1927	...	...	...	+ 29	+ 213	+ 242	...	...	...
1928	...	...	...	– 135	+ 215	+ 80	...	...	...
1929	...	...	...	+ 37	+ 240	+ 277	...	...	...
1930	...	...	...	– 116	+ 214	+ 98	...	...	...
1931...	...	...	...	– 304	+ 176	– 128	...	...	...
1932	...	...	...	– 205	+ 294	– 89	...	...	...
1933	...	...	...	– 15	+ 227	+ 212	...	...	...
1934	...	...	...	– 4	+ 206	+ 202	...	...	...
1935	...	...	...	– 183	+ 244	+ 61	...	...	...
1936	...	...	...	– 120	+ 241	+ 121	...	...	...
1937	...	...	...	– 126	+ 311	+ 185	...	...	...
1938	...	...	...	– 243	+ 316	+ 73	...	...	...
1939	...	...	...	– 617	+ 348	– 269	...	...	...
1940	...	...	...	– 677	+ 375	– 302	...	...	...
1941	...	...	...	– 321	+ 560	+ 239	...	...	...
1942	...	...	...	– 457•	+ 710	+ 253	...	...	...
1943	...	...	...	– 667	+ 860	+ 193	...	...	...
1944	...	...	...	– 818	+ 647	– 171	...	...	...
1945	...	...	...	+ 669	+ 624	+1,293	...	...	...
1946	...	...	...	– 853	+ 747	– 106	...	...	...
1947	...	...	...	–1,984	+ 536	–1,448	...	...	...
1948	...	...	...	– 962	+ 564	– 398	...	...	...
1949	...	...	...	– 104	+ 575	+ 471	...	...	...
1950	...	...	...	– 395	+ 580	+ 185	...	...	+ 245
1951	...	...	...	+ 3	+ 900	+ 903	...	...	...
1952	...	...	...	– 832	+ 995	+ 163	...	...	...
1953	...	...	...	– 481	+ 845	+ 364	+ 35	+1,325	+1,360
1954	...	...	...	– 973	+ 830	– 143	...	...	...
1955	– 8.7	+ 6.2	– 2.5	–1,407	+ 990	– 417	– 780	+1,400	+ 620
1956	...	...	– 3.9	–1,398	+1,240	– 158	–1,470	+1,550	+ 80
1957	...	...	– 2.3	–1,544	+1,410	– 134	–1,735	+1,435	– 300
1958	– 13.4	+ 6.7	– 6.7	–1,466	+1,170	– 296	– 685	+1,580	+ 895
1959	...	...	– 2.0	–1,064	+1,030	– 34	– 995	+1,665	+ 670
1960	+ 3.9	+19.6	+23.5	–1,733	+1,140	– 593	–1,520	+1,225	+ 295
1961	– 16.3	+29.5	+13.2	– 953	+1,020	+ 67	–2,825	+1,810	–1,015
1962	– 37.6	+36.9	– 0.7	–1,025	+1,081	– 160[11]	–3,405	+1,830	–1,575
1963	– 59.8	+45.3	–14.5	– 984	+ 885	+ 213	–3,550	+1,865	–1,685
1964	– 63.0	+60.3	– 2.7	– 932	+1,100	+ 344	–4,080	+2,160	–1,920
1965	–104.4	+71.6	–32.8	–2,103	+1,176	– 927	–3,070	+2,770	– 300
1966	–117.8	+79.8	–38.0	–1,633	+ 761	– 872	–2,800	+3,330	+ 530
1967	–106.9	+70.9	–36.0	– 897	+ 713	– 184	–2,620	+3.660	+1,040
1968	–108.8	+81.6	–25.9	–1,113	+ 451	– 562	–2,075	+4,425	+2,350
1969	...	...	–38.1	–1,112	+ 93	–1,019	–2,720	+4,990	+2,270
1970	–167.4	+159.3	–8.5[2] –8.1	–1,101	– 266	–1,367	–5,730	+6,030	+ 300
1971	–106.0	+150.4	+44.4	+2,032	– 938	+1,094	–6,020	+6,360	+ 340
1972	–144.1	+158.1	+14.0	+3,131	–1,860	+1,271	–6,180	+7,020	+ 840
1973	–198.7	+201.5	+ 2.8	+6,817	–1,505	+5,312	–6,640	+7,530	+ 890
1974	–395.2	+193.4	–201.8	–2,286	–1,927	–4,213	–7,580	+8,090	+ 510
1975	...	...	...	–1,988	–4,714	–6,702	– 840	+7,520	+6,680

See p. 868 for footnotes

K 3 Balance of Payments

1920–1975

	United Kingdom (in million pounds)			Yugoslavia (in thousand million dinars)		
	VB	IB	OÇB	VB	IB	OCB
1920	−176[1,2]	+493[1,2]	+317[1,2]	...	...	...
	−148	+485	+337			
1921	−148	+341	+193	...	...	...
1922	− 63	+264	+201	...	...	...
1923	− 97	+280	+183	...	...	...
1924	−214	+292	+ 78	...	...	...
1925	−265	+317	+ 52	...	...	...
1926	−346	+328	− 18	...	...	...
1927	−270	+368	+ 98	...	...	...
1928	−237	+361	+124	...	...	...
1929	−263	+359	+ 96	...	...	...
1930	−283	+319	+ 36	...	...	...
1931	−322	+219	−103	...	...	...
1932	−216	+165	− 51	...	...	...
1933	−192	+184	− 8	...	...	...
1934	−220	+198	− 22	...	...	...
1935	−183	+206	+ 23	...	...	...
1936	−261	+234	− 27	...	...	...
1937	−336	+289	− 47	...	...	...
1938	−285	+230	− 55	...	...	...
1939	−300	+ 50	−250	...	...	...
1940	−600	−200	−800	...	...	...
1941	−700	−120	−820	...	...	...
1942	−500	−160	−660	...	...	...
1943	−560	−120	−680	...	...	...
1944	−630	− 50	−680	...	...	...
1945	−250	−620	−870	...	...	...
1946	−103	−127	−230	...	...	...
1947	−361	− 20	−381	...	...	...
1948	−151	+177	+ 26	...	...	...
1949	−137	+136	− 1	...	...	...
1950	− 51	+358	+307	...	...	...
1951	−689	+320	−369	...	...	...
1952	−279	+442	+163	− 40	+ 5	− 35
1953	−244	+389	+145	− 69	+ 3	− 66
1954	−204	+321	+117	− 36	+ 4	− 32
1955	−313	+158	−155	− 62	+ 11	− 51
1956	+ 53	+155	+208	− 50	+ 17	− 33
1957	− 29	+262	+233	− 82	+ 23	− 59
1958	+ 29	+317	+346	− 72	+ 20	− 52
1959	−115	+273	+158	− 65	+ 19	− 46
1960	−401	+157	−244	− 81	+ 23	− 58
1961	−140	+167	+ 27	−105	+ 24	− 81
1962	−100	+230	+130	− 60	+ 34	− 26
1963	− 89	+218	+129	−210	+120	− 90
1964	−510	+152	−358	−328	+149	−179
					in million new dinars	
1965	−233	+188	− 45	−2,527	+2,788	+261
1966	− 77	+186	+109	−4,442	+3,577	−865
1967	−567	+273	−294	−4,046	+2,463	−1,583
1968	−682	+396	−286	−5,739	+3,593	−2,146
1969	−172	+635	+463	−8,121	+5,099	−3,022
1970	− 42	+773	+731	−13,791	+8,025	−5,766
1971	+261	+829	+1,090	−19,696	+12,589	−7,107
1972	−722	+857	+135	−19,033	+18,671	+362
1973	−2,383	+1,384	−999	−16,890	+20,654	+3,764
1974	−5,235	+1,644	−3,591	−58,269	+27,207	−31,062
1975	−3,236	+1,381	−1,855	−54,262	+36,998	−17,264

See p. 868 for footnotes

K 3 Balance of Payments

NOTE

SOURCES:– The official publications noted on p. xv with the following additions:– Bulgaria, Czechoslovakia, Finland (to 1938), Greece (to 1938), Hungary, Poland, and Sweden (1924–35) – League of Nations, *Memorandum on Balances of Payments*. Denmark (1874–1950) – K. Bjerke & N. Ussing, *Studier over Danmarks Nationalproduct, 1870–1950* (Copenhagen, 1958). Germany – W.G. Hoffman, *Das Wachstum der Deutschen Wirtschaft seit der Mitte des 19 Jahrhunderts* (Berlin, etc., 1965). Portugal, Spain – United Nations, *Yearbooks of National Accounts Statistics.* Sweden (to 1923) – E. Lindahl *et al, National Income of Sweden, 1861–1930* (London, 1937). U.K. (to 1900) (1st line) – A.H. Imlah, *Economic Elements in the Pax Britannica* (Cambridge, Mass., 1958). U.K. (1900 (2nd line) to 1958) – C.H. Feinstein, *National Income, Expenditure and Output of the United Kingdom, 1855–1965* (Cambridge, 1972). U.K. (all others) – Central Statistical Office, *United Kingdom Balance of Payments 1977.*

FOOTNOTES

[1] In million francs to 1938 and from 1964 (2nd line). In million U.S. dollars from 1945 to 1964 (1st line). The overall current balance excludes unrequited transfers.

[2] There was a change in the system of calculation.

[3] This break occurs on a change of source (see note above). Feinstein treats all visible trade f.o.b., whereas Imlah takes imports c.i.f. Feinstein has also adjusted the trade returns to include diamonds and second-hand ships.

[4] The balance to 1949 is on goods and services, excluding some unrequited transfers.

[5] This break occurs on a change of source (see note above). Bjerke & Ussing take imports c.i.f., whereas the *Statistisk Årbog* treats all visible trade f.o.b. The former also exclude unrequited transfers, which were only significant in 1949–51, when they amounted to +484, +456, and +421 respectively.

[6] Exports are subsequently valued c.i.f.

[7] French overseas territories are included from 1927 to 1952 (1st line). The difference between columns 1 and 2 and column 3, during this period, represents the balance of current payments of the overseas territories.

[8] Saarland is included from 7 July 1959.

[9] The 1949 and 1950 figures are in millions of U.S. dollars.

[10] In million gold pounds sterling to 1938, and thousand million new drachmae subsequently.

[11] The overall balance subsequently includes adjustments to the trade returns which are not included in the visible balance.

[12] Subsequently excluding southern Ireland.

[13] Imports are subsequently valued f.o.b.